L. FRANCIS HERRESHOFF

THE FLOWERING OF GENIUS

L. FRANCIS HERRESHOFF THE FLOWERING OF GENIUS

BY ROGER C. TAYLOR

VOLUME 2 • 1931-1972

Mystic Seaport Museum®
Mystic, Connecticut

Mystic Seaport Museum
75 Greenmanville Ave.
Mystic, CT 06355
www.mysticseaport.org

First edition 2018

Project managed by Mary Anne Stets

Edited by Andrew W. German
Mystic, Connecticut

Copy edited by Connie Stein

Designed by Trish Sinsigalli LaPointe
tslapointedesign.com

Printed by GHP, West Haven, CT
www.ghpmedia.com

Taylor, Roger C.
L. Francis Herreshoff, the flowering of a genius. Volume 2 : 1931-1972 / by Roger C. Taylor -- Mystic, Connecticut : Mystic Seaport Museum, c2018.
626 p. : ill. ; cm.
Includes bibliographic references, chronology, endnotes and index.

ISBN 978-0-939511-44-0

1. Herreshoff, L. Francis (Lewis Francis), 1890-1972. 2. Naval architects--United States--Biography.
3. Yacht designers--United States--Biography.

VM 140 H4 T3.9 2018

This book is dedicated to anyone and everyone who has built or will build a yacht to a design by L. Francis Herreshoff. You enable sailors to reap the ultimate benefit of his genius.

It is also dedicated to Kathleen Elizabeth Carney, my wife, who has made many a sacrifice, large and small, in its support.

The publication of this book was made possible by the generosity of the following individuals and organizations:

Henry H. Anderson Jr.

Cruising Club of America

Michael Engelbert

Llewellyn Howland III

Kyle Endowment for Intellectual Property
Development at Mystic Seaport

Alfred Sanford

CONTENTS

PREFACE

The sentiments expressed in the preface to volume 1 hold true for this second—and concluding—volume of the biography of L. Francis Herreshoff.

The greatest satisfaction from the publication of volume 1 has been that some of Francis's closest friends have allowed that reading the book has brought them pleasant memories. I cannot claim friendship with Skipper Herreshoff, just mere acquaintanceship, yet the writing of both volumes has brought me good memories too. I subscribed to *The Rudder* as a teenager and can well remember the thrill of unrolling it—if memory of its packaging serves—each month to discover what wonderful drawings of boats L. Francis Herreshoff would share, what marine wisdom he would pound home. Every issue was almost as good as a visit to The Castle in Marblehead.

My father, Captain Conant Taylor, US Navy (Retired), also wanted to see *The Rudder*. He thought L. Francis Herreshoff designed good boats, which was important to me. Writing about Francis's difficult relationship with his father has shed light on my own paternal dealings, which shared elements with his. We both had more respect and admiration for our fathers than we had simple affection.

I have shared with Francis an affinity for the imaginary voyage. I think we could each claim hundreds of miles sailed in the mind's eye for every one actually logged. Maybe that's why writing his biography has taken me so long! But there have also been opportunities to get underway in yachts he designed. Of the boats in volume 2, I sailed in the *Ben-My-Chree*, a replica of the *Ticonderoga*, a Diddikai, an H-23, an H-28, the *Quiet Tune*, a Buzzards Bay 14, a Meadow Lark, the *Araminta*, a couple of Rozinantes, a Dancing Feather, and a Golden Ball. It was tough work, but it had to be done.

A fan of Francis's wrote to him: "It is the theory of people who know anything about literature that if you want to get to know a particular author, go to his work; forget about most of the biographies and critical works on him. Because if the author is worth your attention in the first place, his work is the most important thing in his life and you will learn more from it than anything else." This bit of common sense obviously applies to L. Francis Herreshoff's yacht designing as well as his authorship. I hope that this biography will enable you to study his yacht designs in plan and photo and will encourage you to return again and again to his writings:

The Writings of L. Francis Herreshoff, 1946, seven chapters;

The Common Sense of Yacht Design, 2 volumes, 1946, 1948, twenty chapters;

Capt. Nat Herreshoff, 1953, fifteen chapters;

The Compleat Cruiser, 1956, nine chapters;

An Introduction to Yachting, 1963, twenty-one chapters;

Sensible Cruising Designs, 1973, nine chapters;

An L. Francis Herreshoff Reader, 1978, thirty chapters.

Writing the story of L. Francis Herreshoff in the twenty-four chapters that find a resolution in this volume has been a grand labor of love.

—Roger C. Taylor

ACKNOWLEDGMENTS

As with the preface, the acknowledgments in volume 1 apply to volume 2. Llewellyn Howland III, the godfather of the book, has continued his role, encouraging, helping, even prodding at times. Arthur Brendze, the boatbuilder/psychologist, stayed on board to share his knowledge of Skipper Herreshoff and comment on my presentation of his personality. My wife, Kathleen Carney, has kept going with her auditory editing: she has listened to every word of every sentence of every paragraph and suggested excellent improvements to volume 2, as she did with volume 1.

The team at Mystic Seaport Museum—Mary Anne Stets and her assistants—have, as usual, exceeded the standards of any other publishing house. Here's a little tour behind the scenes at Mystic Seaport Museum: If you want an image out of the archives, you go to Maribeth Bielinski and get a work order (and she doesn't stop searching until she gets the right one of many, many thousands). As you will see by the illustration credits, this book kept her busy. Carol Mowrey researched the Museum's Rosenfeld Collection photographs and pulled original negatives for scanning. Mindy Matheson got out each and every Herreshoff drawing requested and turned them over to Kim Daugherty, who scanned them all! Mercy. Louisa Watrous got permission to use the illustrations from outside the Museum's collections. And through all of this intensive work, I never once heard, "why does he want so many illustrations, just for one book?"

Andy German, the editor, has tweaked my copy and responded to every last-minute change speedily and with expertise and grace. He has also mined the Rosenfeld Collection and come up with photographic gems. Connie Stein, the copy editor, having applied her eagle eye to every letter and punctuation mark in volume 1, has done the same for volume 2. Trish LaPointe, the book designer, has worked her magic again; L. Francis Herreshoff, himself, would, I am sure, approve her artistry. Marie Simon, at GHP, the printer, assured the manufacturing of books of the highest quality, as she did for volume 1. This author has, indeed, been in good hands.

I owe a great debt to Helen Bolster, Francis's secretary for forty-one years. Her method of using the backs of incoming letters for carbon copies of Francis's replies—and saving all of them—established an invaluable record of his activities and ideas. Since economy was an important consideration in Francis's household, this may have been just to save paper, but I believe that "Mrs. B." had an eye on the future. Doug Stein was keeper of manuscripts at Mystic Seaport Museum back when I was reading Francis's letters; when I showed up at the G. W. Blunt White Library every morning for months, he anticipated which folder from which box I would need next and had it ready.

The interviewees cited in the acknowledgments of volume 1 contributed their personal knowledge of Skipper Herreshoff's whole life to this story, and so have been as vital to volume 2 as they were to volume 1. I have had valuable conversations also with Howard Boardman, Guillaume Gallienne, Tom Lie-Nielsen, Frank Luke, and Allan H. Vaitses.

At a casual meeting with Dan Marcus, of Mystic, he said, "You ought to go talk to Dale Calloway, Katherine Vosburgh's daughter." I did, and Dale led me to her mother. Katherine shared with Kathleen and me the story of her friendship with L. Francis Herreshoff, a friendship that turned romantic. I will be forever grateful for her courage and candor. And thanks be to Dale Calloway and Dan Marcus.

Dan Brayton, the Marbleheader who was the only sailor to build to Francis's design No. 65 for a fine, double-ended, ketch-rigged cruiser, probably hasn't realized the importance of his encouraging words a few years back, when I was in one of those times of doubting the necessity of a biography of L. Francis Herreshoff, precisely because of the existence of his plans, letters, and published writings. Dan quickly put me back on course.

Volume 1 took a long time to write, even after "all" the research was done. Mary Anne Stets and Louie Howland managed to get it through my skull that I had to write volume 2 at a faster pace. Kathleen and I live afloat, and boats require attention, often tearing me away from my "desk." Family and friends came to the rescue, sharing their homes with us. Thanks to Kathleen's sister, Joanne, and her husband, Bob Juckiewicz, I worked not only at their dining room table in Glen Cove, New York, but also in their condo right on the beach at North Hutchinson Island, Florida. Thanks to Don and Marty Dewees, I worked beside a wood stove at their homestead in North Ferrisburgh, Vermont. And thanks to Roxy Darling, I worked overlooking Currituck Sound at Waterlily, North Carolina. Through Kathleen's cousin, Chip Carney, we were able to rent the house of French master-chef Roger Fessaguet, at the end of Long Cove Point, Maine, where, when I looked up from the computer, I could watch breakers thundering into the rocks a hundred feet away. And Janet Patterson shared her house in the woods of Damariscotta, Maine. Otherwise, I'd still be writing.

My sister, Phoebe Franklin, with her daughter, Adrienne Franklin and partner Sue Miller, and her son Christopher Franklin, continued to provide hospitality near Mystic Seaport Museum. Chris came to realize that my gift to him of all my old yachting magazines had a string: he had to look up thus and so and report.

I am grateful for the opportunity to have sailed eleven of Francis's boats that appear in volume 2. Bill Harding took me out on Buzzards Bay, Massachusetts, in the *Ben-My-Chree*, as well as in one of the Stuart Knockabouts that she spawned. Stan Bishoprick let a gang of us join his crew for a day-race off Port Townsend, Washington, in the *Radiance*, which was built to the design of the *Ticonderoga*. Robert Hefner let us share a sail on Gardiners Bay, between Long Island's eastern forks, in his H-23. I was allowed to charter an H-28 on Penobscot Bay, Maine. Maynard Bray arranged for Kathleen and me to horn in on a photo shoot of the *Quiet Tune*, as Dan Carter was donating her to Mystic Seaport Museum; we were shot on the Mystic River and Fishers Island Sound (see back flap of dust jacket). Will Howard let my son Dean and me take his Meadow Lark off for a short but stormy cruise within Cape Cod's elbow. Fred Bruenner invited Kathleen and me for a sail from Coecles Harbor to Dering Harbor on Shelter Island, tucked into the forks inside Gardiners Bay, in the *Araminta*, and then loaned us his precious boat for another sail round the island. Ted Sprague let me keep the cobwebs off his Rozinante, the *Arete*, for a whole summer on Penobscot Bay. David and Marcia Jewett gave Kathleen and me the chance to sail their *Sybil*, built to Francis's design No. 102, out of Rockland, Maine, for the day. Warren "Hasty" Miller had us on board his Diddikai, the *Moonspinner*, for a sail on Florida's Indian River. And, when we thought we would like to buy the Golden Ball *Shenandoah*, we went out of Fort Lauderdale on a sea trial with the broker's captain.

Throughout the long mission of researching and writing these two volumes, I have experienced countless random acts of kindness, for which I express my sincere thanks.

INTRODUCTION

L. Francis Herreshoff lived from 1890 to 1972. He was a New England Yankee yacht designer known for his beautiful, fast boats.

L. Francis is sometimes confused with his world-famous father, Nathanael G. Herreshoff, designer and builder at the Herreshoff Manufacturing Company, Bristol, Rhode Island, of fast steam yachts and torpedo boats, America's Cup defenders, and many one-design classes of racing yachts, large and small.

Whereas N. G. Herreshoff was a highly disciplined worker of primarily scientific mind, but also natural artistic ability, who made, himself, perhaps 600 half-hull models and produced designs that resulted in upwards of 12,000 drawings, his son, L. Francis, sought artistic and functional perfection in far fewer designs. His sense of proportion gave him the ability to produce construction plans that were equally scientific to those of his father. He completed only about 125 designs to the point where they could be built, and only about 70 of his designs resulted in finished vessels, though multiple boats were built to some 25 designs. The drawings he and his handful of draftsmen made number scarcely more than 10 percent of the drawings of his father's Herreshoff Manufacturing Company. But of L. Francis's 125 designs, 55, in my judgment, either approached aesthetic perfection, or performed nearly perfectly, or both. And these varied from dinghies to the largest of racing yachts, and from small, simple cruisers to big, elaborate pleasure craft, both sail and power. I can give no other American designer than L. Francis's father credit for so many outstanding designs. And despite Nathanael G. Herreshoff's unparalleled achievements in the design and construction of yachts, L. Francis Herreshoff brought yacht design even closer to perfection than had his more famous father.

L. Francis is the designer of the great, 72-foot ketch *Ticonderoga*, a yacht built as a daysailer and short-range cruiser in 1936. She is thought by many to be the most beautiful yacht in the world, and she has set records for the fastest time over sixteen different ocean racing courses, more than any other yacht. He designed a dozen hauntingly beautiful, double-ended racing yachts, including the successful M-boat *Istalena* (1929) and the unsuccessful J-boat *Whirlwind* (1930). He designed the best racing boat ever in the R Class, the *Yankee* (1926). He designed the H-28 (1942) for *The Rudder* magazine, a simple and pure little cruising ketch that has been built by hundreds around the world. He designed the Meadow Lark (1948), a cruising sailboat drawing 15 inches of water that was another popular *Rudder* craft. And he designed the Rozinante (1956), a slim, 28-foot, double-ended ketch whose sweet form is timeless.

Like his father, but again on a smaller scale, L. Francis is responsible for important innovations in the construction and rigging of yachts. He was the first to apply longitudinal construction to wooden yachts (1925). He was first with mast tangs and hollow, rectangular spars (1923).

L. Francis was born and raised in Bristol, Rhode Island. In his youth, he got invaluable experience for his chosen art through much sailing of diverse types of boats and yachts and through exposure to many parts of the Herreshoff Manufacturing Company. He showed an obvious ability for the designing of yachts, yet his father didn't want him in the business and decreed that he was to run a farm that belonged to Francis's mother. Francis dutifully ran the farm for seven years, until he was liberated by naval service during World War I. He never went back.

Instead, Francis became a black sheep in the Herreshoff family by going off to work for one the country's other leading yacht designers, W. Starling Burgess. He stayed with Burgess for five-and-a half years and learned a lot from this mentor. When Burgess closed his design business in Boston—the year was 1926—and moved to New York to open another, L. Francis started to design yachts on his own in Marblehead, Massachusetts. He lived in this yachting center for the rest of his life. He produced his last design in 1963 but retained a lively interest in the field until his death. L. Francis died believing that his work was misunderstood and even ridiculed, but in fact, through his designs and writings, he had great influence on the surprising revival of wooden boatbuilding and sensible yacht design in the years after his death.

L. Francis wrote 234 articles for *The Rudder,* most under the encouragement of its talented editor, Boris Lauer-Leonardi. The articles were gathered into seven published books, including what is the best book on yacht design, *The Common Sense of Yacht Design,* and an admiring and detailed biography of his father, *Capt. Nat Herreshoff: The Wizard of Bristol.* By writing for *The Rudder*, L. Francis opened his mailbox to the world. His writings exuded knowledge and experience, and any sailor with a question seemed to feel free to address him. L. Francis became per force a prodigious letter-writer, answering every correspondent promptly, courteously, and expertly.

L. Francis was a sensitive man, who, in the style of the time, sought to bury his emotions. His emotions were particularly strong around his father, whom he admired and respected greatly, but who also frustrated and angered him by failing to acknowledge his son's gifts. L. Francis was proud, shy, and judgmental; he developed lifelong friendships with some of his clients and was not on speaking terms with others.

L. Francis's much loved and revered mother died when he was fifteen. He was a bachelor all his life. He once loved a girl far younger than he, and she loved him too, but, under the guidance of her father, she broke off the romance. It was Francis's first and last. Thereafter, he nurtured the façade of a proper Edwardian gentleman, and unfounded rumors of his desire for male intimacy were heard amongst occasional speculation as to the true status of this or that lady friend.

The pain of his personal losses drove L. Francis inward. He cultivated boundaries behind which he could compensate, by creating art. He designed and drew beautiful, functional yachts, not only as a conscious vocation, but also as a subconscious spiritual practice.

He made many elegant objects out of wood and metal. His craftsmanship was of the highest order. The masterpieces he made and gave to his friends would fill a warehouse.

L. Francis was a consummate sailor and an experienced kayak paddler, who was, however, just as happy making imaginary voyages as real ones. Much as he loved the water, he loved his fireside just as much. And he loved his lathe and drawing board even more.

He lived in a small, exquisite, stone castle in Marblehead for the last twenty-eight years of his life. Never was a dwelling better suited to its occupant. The upstairs ballroom became his workshop and drafting room; the roof turrets were his lookouts over Marblehead Harbor. Every nook and cranny of the great hall was filled with some part of the superb collection he amassed over the years of all manner of antiques and art and books. There was the "Tower," a separate garage for his latest sports car. And there was a small, lower room in The Castle, a sort of "keep," where Francis lived and entertained his closest friends. Lucky were those whom he invited in.

Certain myths have grown up around L. Francis: the bad blood with his father, his irascibility, his unfailing genius. The myths are based on reality, but none is strictly true.

L. Francis Herreshoff was the consummate artist, in his values, his personality, his lifestyle, and, above all, in his creation of beautiful yacht designs. The chapters that follow, with their illustrations, presented in two volumes, will tell the story of the life and work of this remarkable artist.

CHAPTER 12

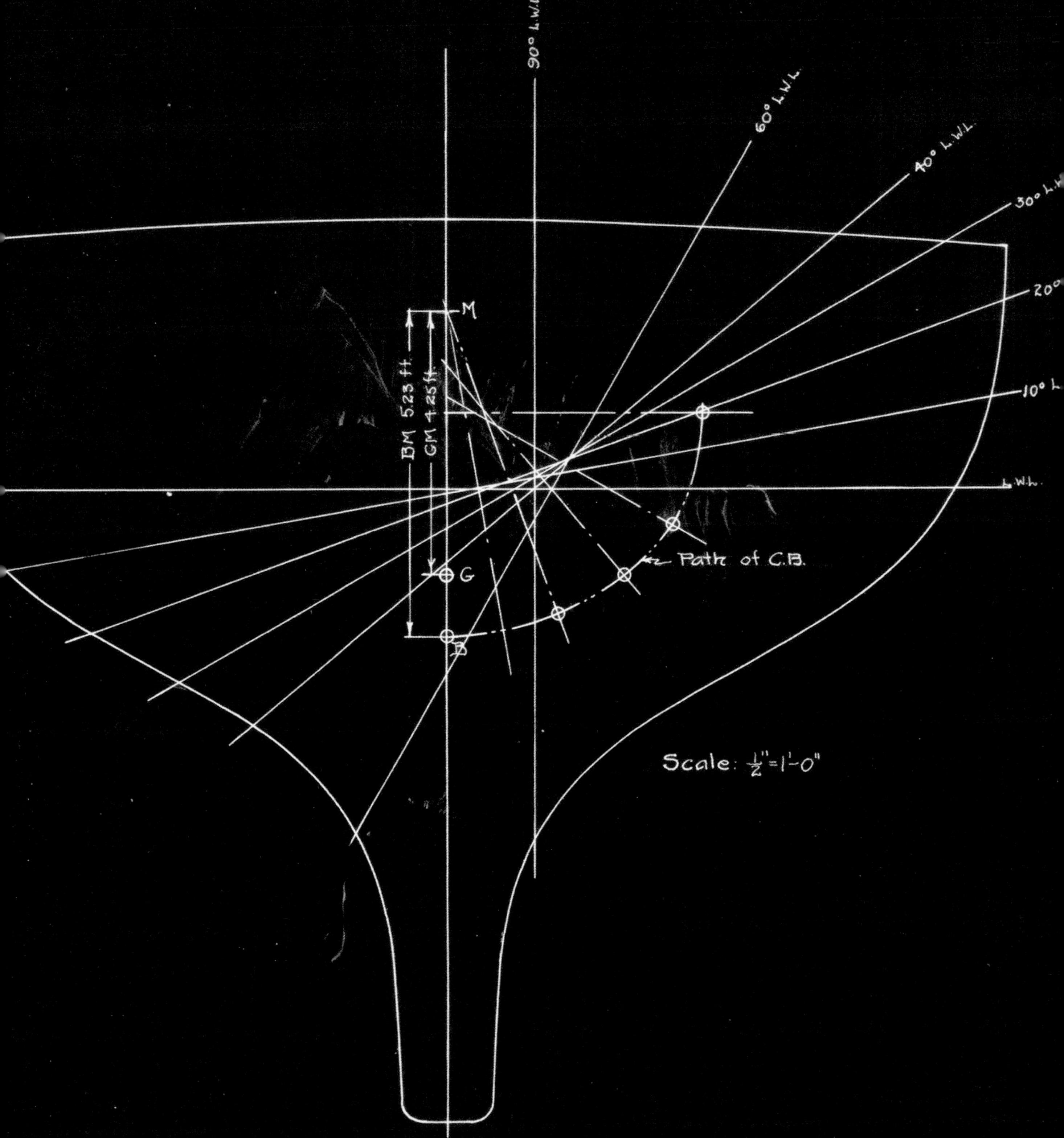

M = Metacenter
G = Center of Gravity
B = Center of Buoyancy

OCEAN RACING

"So called ocean racing is a farce..."

—L. FRANCIS HERRESHOFF, 1946

The *Whirlwind* debacle in the America's Cup trials of 1930 marked a change of course for L. Francis Herreshoff. With two exceptions, he turned away from the design of racing yachts and toward the design of cruising boats. He had invested great skill, artistry, and inventiveness in a complex and innovative design for the big J-boat, but her owners sailed her miserably. The *Whirlwind* had been the first yacht eliminated. What might have been a triumph for Francis had turned into a humiliation. He despised such incompetence in owners of racing boats and wanted never again to have to depend on them.

Despite his design of champions like the *Yankee* and the *Istalena*, L. Francis Herreshoff had operated on the fringes of racing yacht design.

Starling Burgess, Frank Paine, and Clinton Crane, the designers of the J-boats that had beaten his *Whirlwind* soundly, could attract the top racing sailors as repeat customers, but Francis had not broken into the group. As early as the summer of 1928, he had changed his advertisement in *Yachting*'s "Directory of Naval Architects" from "L. Francis Herreshoff: Racing Yachts" to "L. Francis Herreshoff: Yacht Designer and Broker." He wanted to broaden his business, but he did precious little yacht brokerage. After the *Whirlwind*, however, he did take on commissions for a greater variety of designs beyond day racers, including, with plenty of irony, the design of an important ocean racer.

Early in 1929, Edmond S. Parsons had asked Francis to design him an ocean racer. Francis accepted the commission, although he was no enthusiast of ocean racing or of its measurement rules, which he thought produced inferior designs. Under the basic form of measurement rule for ocean racers, the rating equaled .2 x Length x √ Sail Area ÷ √ Beam x Depth. So, to rate low, length and sail area were to be minimized, while beam and depth were to be maximized. The first ocean racer that Francis proposed to Parsons was thus short, fat, and deep, with a moderate ketch rig. She was certainly designed to rate low under the rule. She even took advantage of the special rig allowance given to ketches and schooners.

Francis sent Nathanael a blueprint of his outboard profile and sail plan for Parsons's ketch that showed the boat's wide midsection, explaining that he had designed her to the rule, that he didn't like her, and asking for comments. Nathanael remained tactfully silent. Parsons must have thought Francis had gone too far in search of a low rating, for he asked for a more conventional design. Francis was intrigued enough with

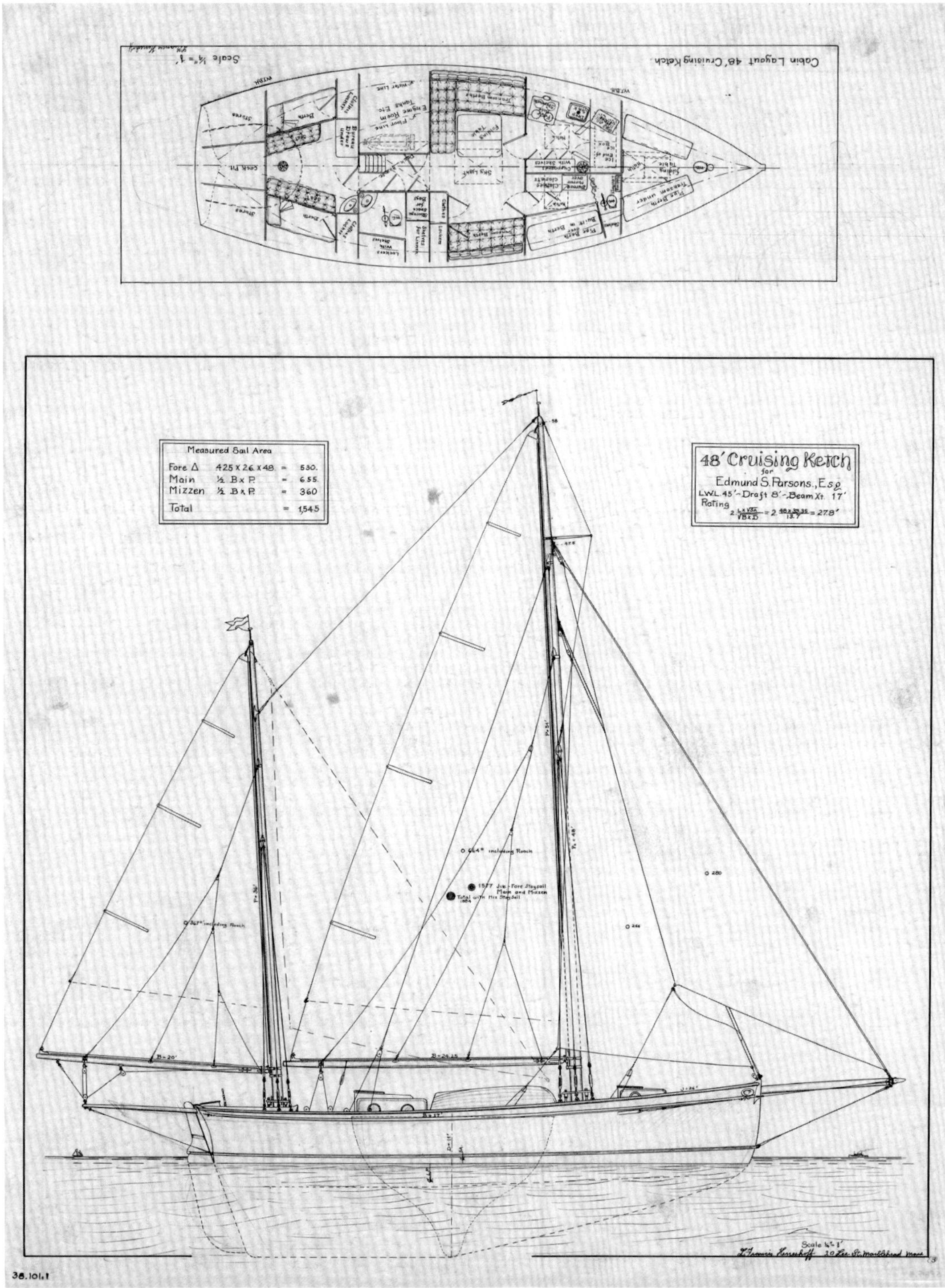
Cabin Layout 48' Cruising Ketch
Scale ¼" = 1'
Measured Sail Area
Fore Δ 425 X 26 X 48 = 530.
Main ½ B x P. = 655.
Mizzen ½ B x P. = 360
Total = 1,545
48' Cruising Ketch
for
Edmund S. Parsons, Esq.
LWL 45' - Draft 8' - Beam Xt. 17'
Rating
38.101.1

the concept of designing a wide boat to fit the ocean racing rule to make, in 1934, a preliminary drawing of a sloop with a waterline length of 35 feet and a beam of 13 feet. There was no customer for this boat, and the idea of the wide boat for the ocean racing rule was not tested until 1954, when Olin Stephens, Aage Nielsen, and Carleton Mitchell came out with the landmark design for the successful *Finisterre,* combining, in her design, wide beam with shoal draft.[1]

The 55-foot ketch that Francis next proposed for Parsons, his design No. 42, had the counter stern that Francis had penciled in on the previous design, a slightly longer bow as well, with normal, instead of wide, beam, and a little less sail area. The result is a beautifully proportioned and shaped hull with a moderate rig. It is particularly unfortunate that Parsons did not build a boat to this design; she would not, perhaps, have won many ocean racing trophies, but she would have been an outstanding cruising boat, giving consistently creditable passages and being as comfortable in heavy weather as a boat of her size can be. She may have been a victim of "Black Tuesday," the stock market crash, which came two months after Francis finished her design. Reined in from the extreme beam of her rule-beating, immediate predecessor, she is as orthodox a design as Francis ever drew. With this boat, he is not trying to invent anything or prove anything; she has no extremes. She is just perfect.

A year later, in the summer of 1930, Francis had the opportunity to design a larger version of the Parsons ketch, when Dudley Wolfe asked him to design a 50-foot-waterline ocean racer. Francis knew he had a good design in No. 42, so, for Wolfe, he merely stretched out that design by six feet on the waterline and ten feet on deck. This was his design No. 47. It was another abortive design. Wolfe decided against building her and turned to Frank Paine. He liked what he saw from Paine, Belknap, and Skene: the plans for the great cutter *Highland Light*. There is no arguing with the *Light*'s extensive, successful ocean racing career that included a long-held record of under three days for the fastest time in the Bermuda Race, but it is too bad that Francis's wonderful ketch never got to compete with her.

However, the chance for an ocean racing ketch designed by L. Francis Herreshoff to try her speed against the *Highland Light* was about to present itself. Paul L. Hammond, the New York banker with money and leisure who had been a key member of the *Whirlwind* syndicate, asked Francis to design him a fast cruiser that would rate well under the ocean racing rule and that would be the biggest boat possible allowed into the 1931 Transatlantic Race.

Francis first met Paul Hammond when Hammond returned from England at the end of World War I and would have seen him again in 1920, when he took delivery of Herreshoff S-boat number 1 to start the fleet at the Seawanhaka Corinthian Yacht Club at Oyster Bay, for Francis had conducted the trials of the new boat in Bristol Harbor. The two would have become better acquainted the following summer on the United States team during the 6-Metre racing in Cowes,

---

LEFT: **The outboard profile and sail plan of a proposed "cruising" ketch for Edmund S. Parsons. Actually, Parsons wanted to go ocean racing, and Francis designed this short-ended, wide boat, so uncharacteristic of his work, to rate well under the ocean-racing measurement rules. She was to have a length on deck of 48 feet and waterline length of 45 feet, with a beam of a whopping 17 feet, and a draft of 8 feet. Measured sail area was 1,545 square feet. Francis has penciled in a counter stern nearly as long as the boomkin, but that would have increased her rating.** (© Mystic Seaport Museum, Daniel S. Gregory Ships Plans Library, SP38.101.1)

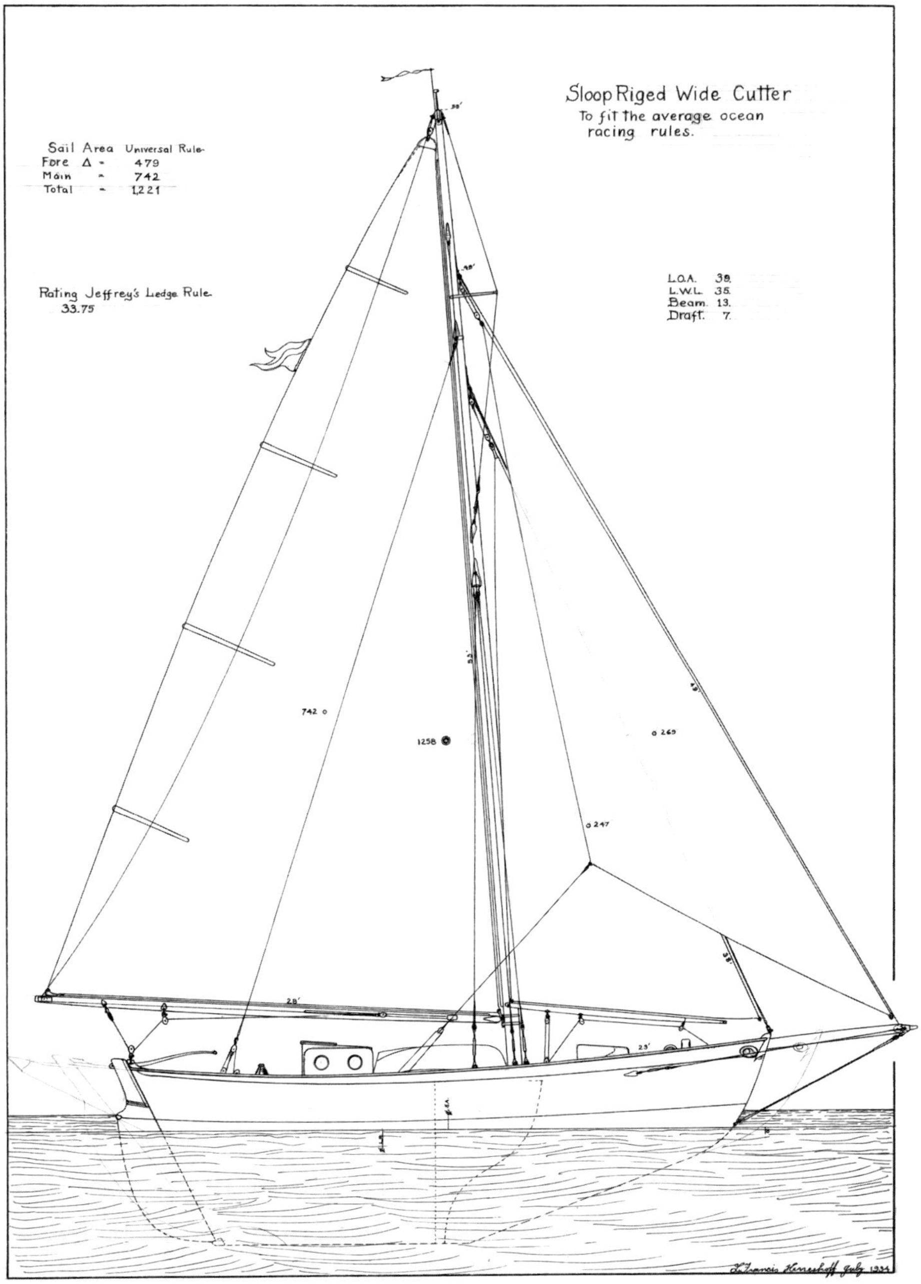

Francis's preliminary profile of a wide sloop to rate low for ocean racing. Drawn in 1934, this was a doodle that went no further. He didn't like wide boats. She is 39 feet long on deck, with a waterline length of 35 feet, a beam of 13 feet, and a draft of 7 feet. Sail area was 1,258 square feet. (© Mystic Seaport Museum, Daniel S. Gregory Ships Plans Library, SP38.155.1)

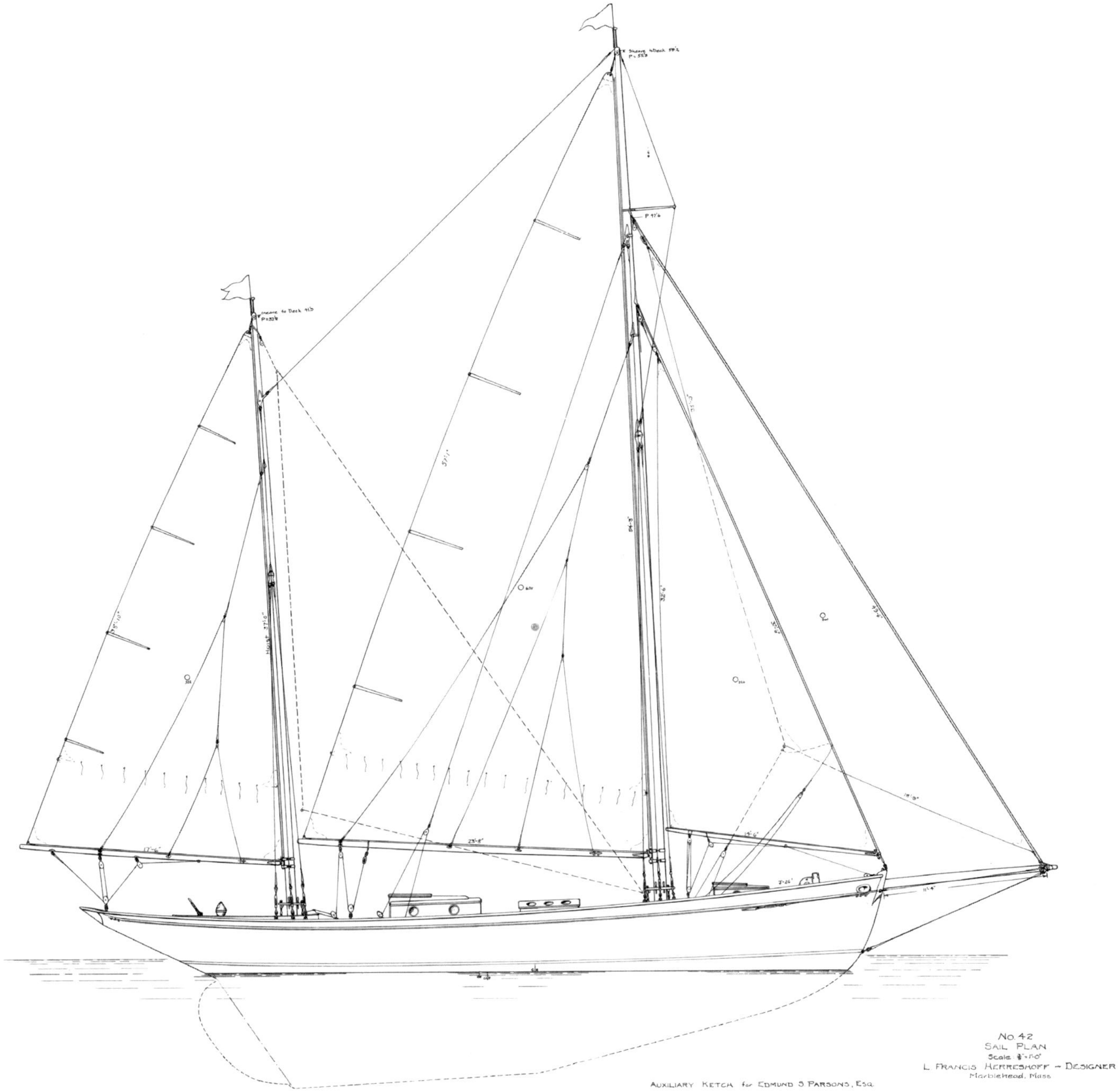

Francis's second proposal for Parsons, his design No. 42, was a much more normal vessel. Evidently, the penciled suggestion worked. He has transformed the ugly duckling into a handsome, seakindly sailing yacht. Alas, she never went racing or cruising, except in Francis's imagination, for Parsons backed off. Her sail area was to be 1,446 square feet.

(© Mystic Seaport Museum, Daniel S. Gregory Ships Plans Library, SP38.162.4)

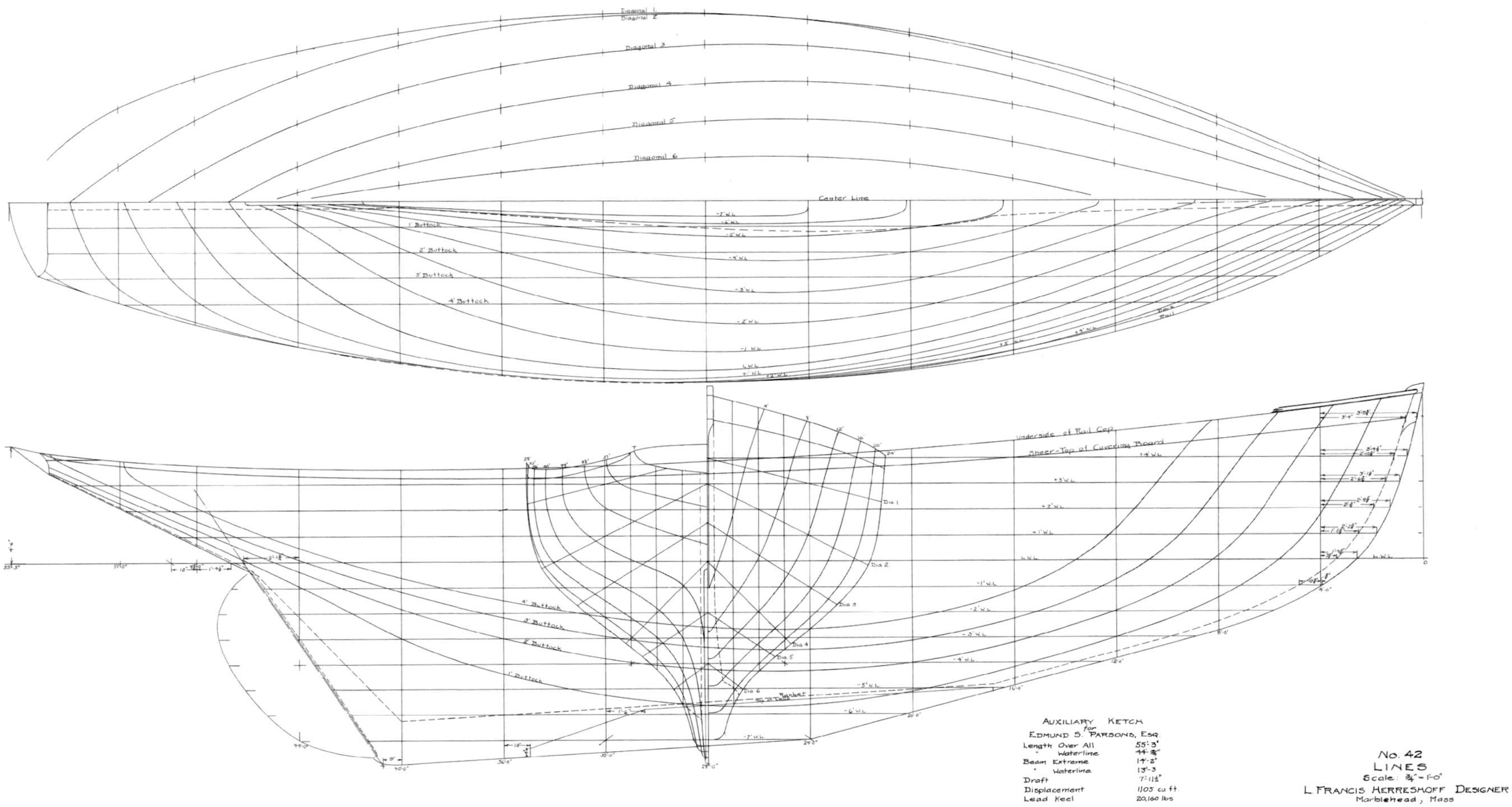

The lines of the Parsons ketch. The dimensions were to be: length on deck, 55 feet, 3 inches; length on the waterline, 44 feet, ¾ inch; beam, 14 feet, 2 inches; and draft, 7 feet, 11 ½ inches. The displacement was calculated at 70,720 pounds, of which 20,160 pounds was in the lead ballast keel, for a ballast-to-displacement ratio of 28½ percent. Her waterline length and draft are very close to those of the first proposal, but her much narrower hull shape is vastly different. The sections show her to be a deep-bodied boat; she would have an easy motion at sea. (© Mystic Seaport Museum, Daniel S. Gregory Ships Plans Library, SP38.162.1)

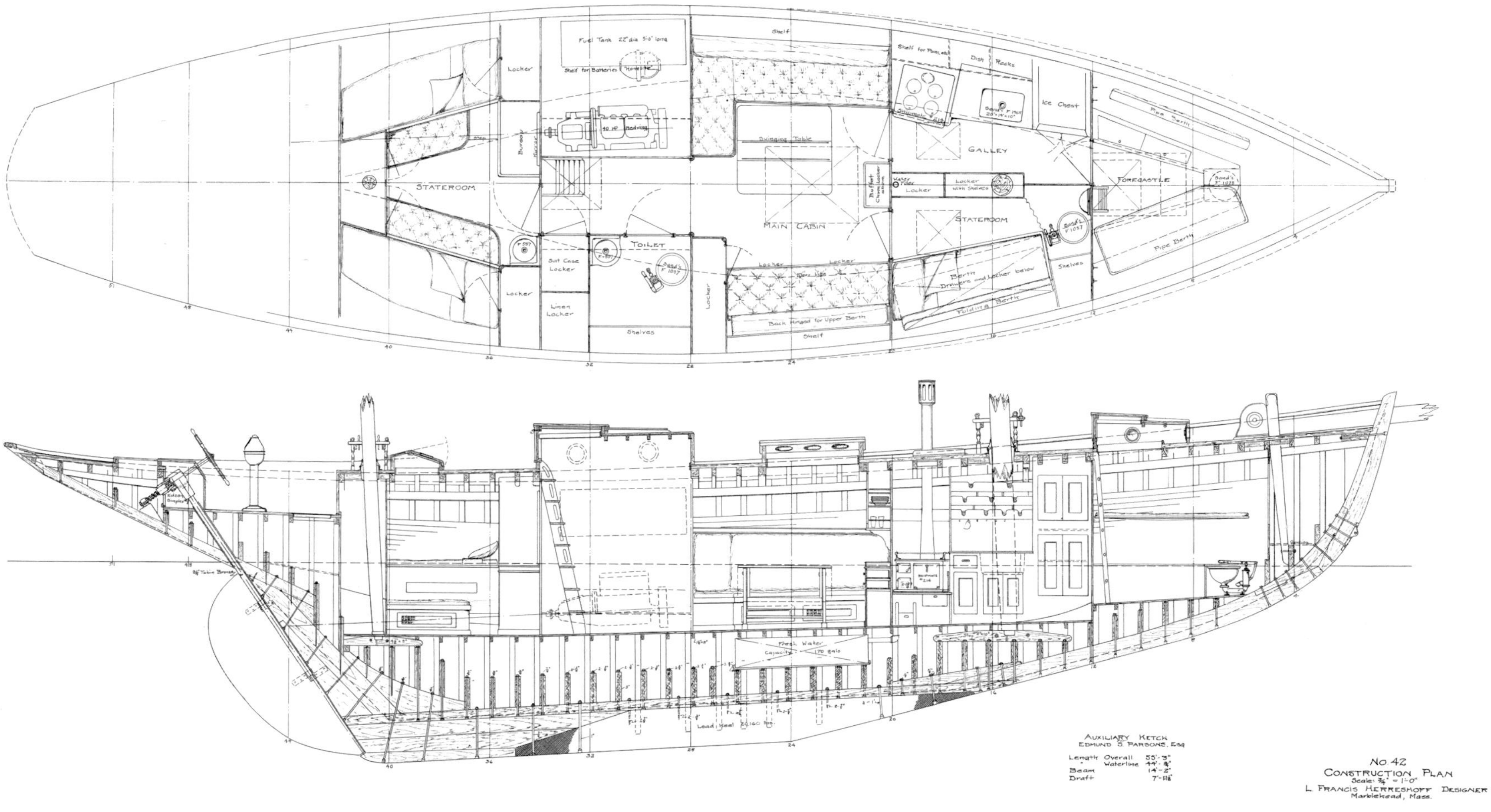

The construction and cabin plans of the Parsons ketch. For the auxiliary engine, off center to port, amidships, Francis specified a 40-horsepower Redwing.

ABOVE: **The sail plan of Francis's design No. 47, an ocean-racing ketch for Dudley F. Wolfe, designed in the summer of 1930. She is a stretched-out version of No. 42, the Parsons ketch, with proportionally more sail area at 2,348 square feet. The bowsprit is off-center to port, allowing a proud stem. The backstay from the mainmast head leads to the mizzenmast, which has running backstays. Francis has drawn two big, overlapping jibs, a flat-cut Genoa for windward work, and a full ballooner for reaching. There is also a mizzen staysail. He has given this big yacht a tiller, rather than a wheel, for he believed that the tiller allowed more sensitive steering.** (© Mystic Seaport Museum, Daniel S. Gregory Ships Plans Library, SP38.124.13)
RIGHT: **The lines of the Wolfe ketch. Her hull shape is the same as that of the Parsons ketch, with the waterline lengthened by 6 feet. Francis knew he had an easily driven, seakindly boat, so he didn't try to improve upon it. He hoped that this time his fine design would be built and sailed, but it was not to be. Length on deck was 64 feet; length on the waterline, 50 feet; beam, 15 feet; and draft, 9 feet.** (© Mystic Seaport Museum, Daniel S. Gregory Ships Plans Library, SP38.124.1)

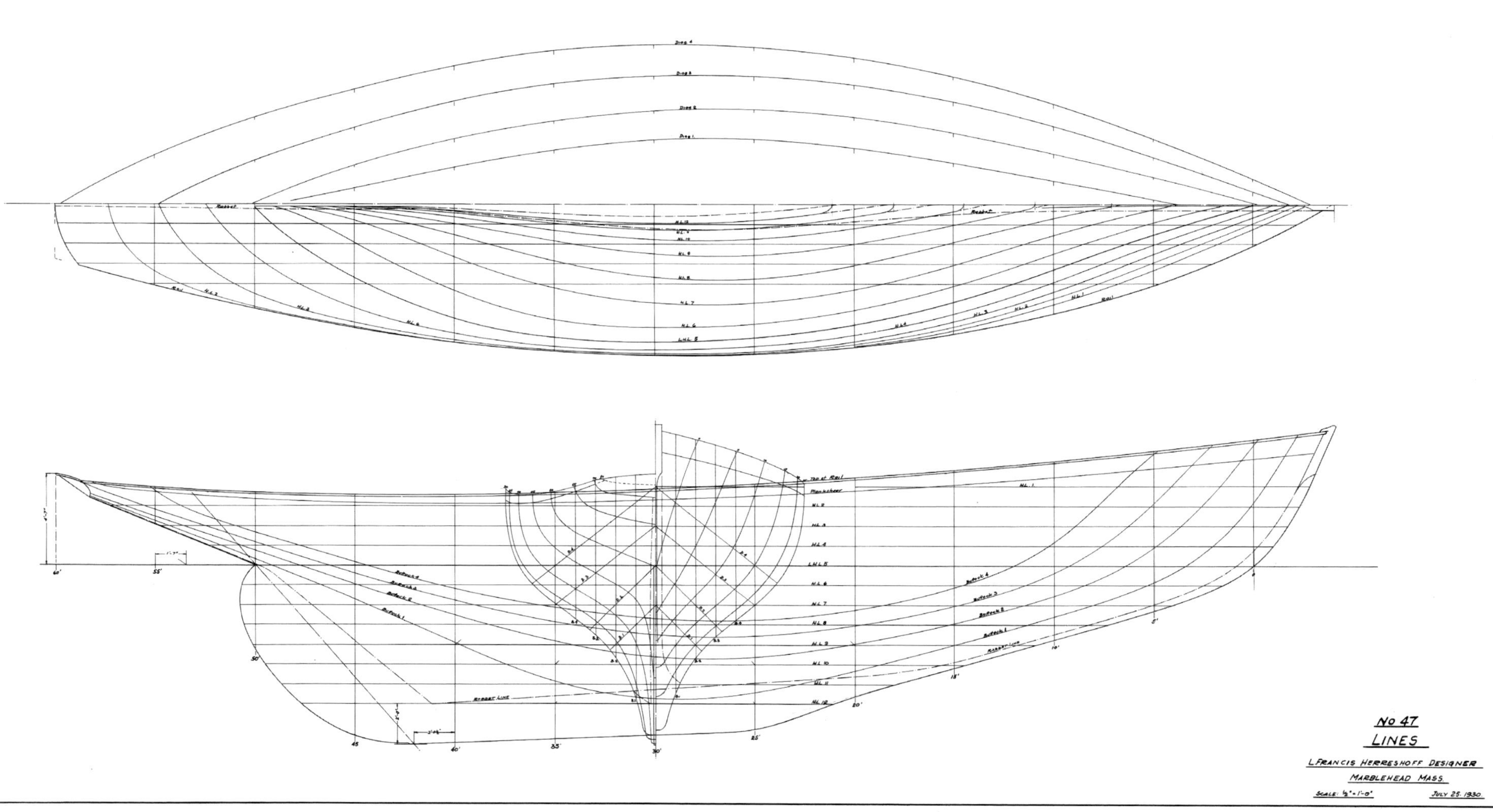
NO 47
LINES
L.FRANCIS HERRESHOFF DESIGNER
MARBLEHEAD MASS.
SCALE: ½" = 1'-0"
JULY 25. 1930

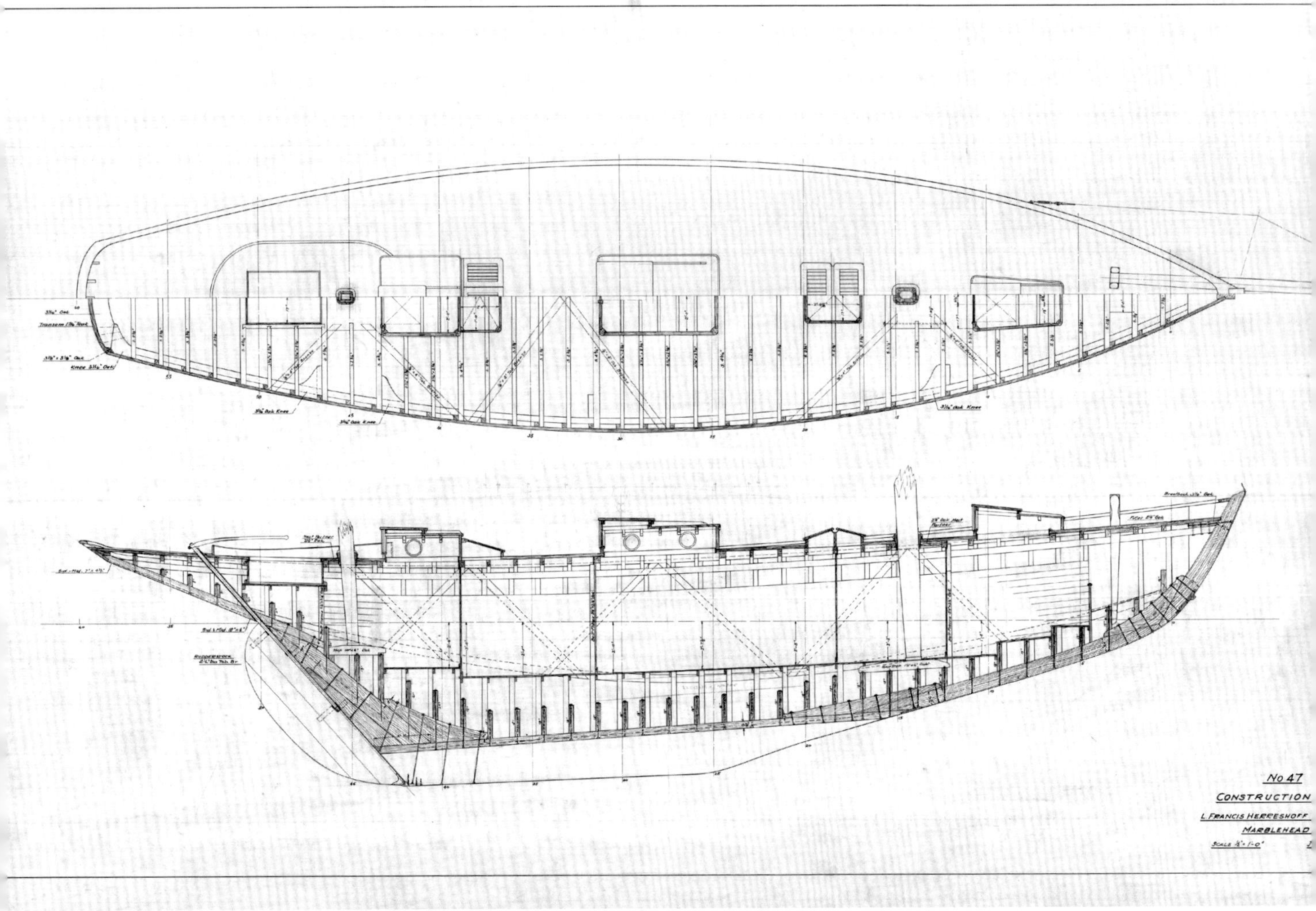

ABOVE: **The construction plan of the Wolfe ketch. She has seven diagonal bronze straps let into the planking on each side, and six per side in the deck. There were no plans for an engine in this boat.** (© Mystic Seaport Museum, Daniel S. Gregory Ships Plans Library, SP38.124.2) RIGHT: **The cabin plan of the Wolfe ketch. Two different interior arrangements were drawn up for the design; owners often had their own ideas about the accommodations they wanted. This drawing shows Francis's layout; the other plan shows a much smaller main cabin and a large owner's stateroom amidships. Dudley Wolfe was interested in Francis's design to the point of changing the cabin plan, but not to the point of building this outstanding ketch.** (© Mystic Seaport Museum, Daniel S. Gregory Ships Plans Library, SP38.124.4)

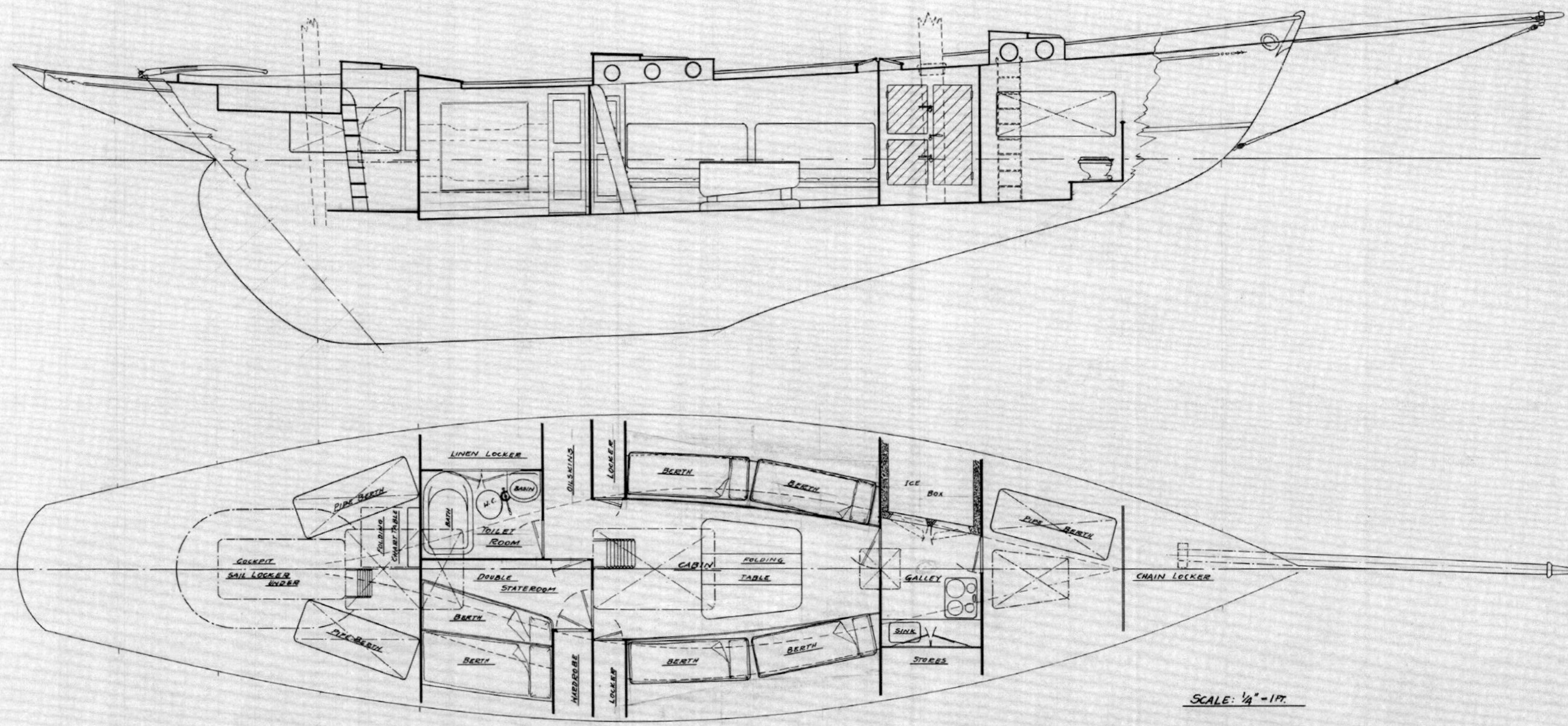
LINEN LOCKER
OILSKINS
LOCKER
BERTH
BERTH
ICE BOX
PIPE BERTH
BASIN
W.C.
BATH
TOILET ROOM
FOLDING CHART TABLE
COCKPIT SAIL LOCKER UNDER
DOUBLE STATEROOM
CABIN
FOLDING TABLE
GALLEY
CHAIN LOCKER
PIPE BERTH
BERTH
BERTH
WARDROBE
LOCKER
BERTH
BERTH
SINK
STORES
PIPE BERTH
SCALE: 1/4" = 1FT.

England, where Hammond raced his Burgess-designed, Herreshoff-built *Sheila,* and Francis crewed for Frank Paine in the *Jeanie*. And, as we have seen, Francis designed a Marconi schooner for Hammond. Soon after, Hammond went into big-boat racing: he sailed two successive New York Yacht Club 50s, and, in the second one, the *Iroquois II,* he won the King's Cup in 1924. He had acquired the famous Havre pilot cutter, *Jolie Brise*, for the 1928 Transatlantic Race from New York to Santander, Spain, but then decided to have Starling Burgess design him a new boat for the race. This was the 59-foot staysail schooner *Niña*, with which he won the Queen's (of Spain) Cup for being first to Santander in the small class, then continued on to win the 1928 Fastnet Race as well. Hammond and Francis had been involved with the *Whirlwind* debacle during the America's Cup campaign of 1930. They knew each other's foibles well. Francis must have felt at least a little vindicated that Paul Hammond came to him for his next major vessel. He would name his new yacht the *Landfall*; she was Francis's design No. 49.[2]

To enter the 1931 Transatlantic Race from the United States to England, a yacht faced the limitations of the rules of both the Cruising Club of America and the Royal Ocean Racing Club. The former limited on-deck length to a maximum of 71 feet, and the latter limited waterline length to a maximum of 60 feet. To get the biggest possible cruising boat for Europe, Hammond specified to Francis a waterline length of 60 feet, so, when Francis designed her hull, he was limited to overhangs of 11 feet.[3]

In 1931, the rule was the same as it had been in 1929, when Francis was designing to it for Edmund Parsons: .2 L x √ SA ÷ √ B x D, but the length and depth measurements had been refined. The length factor in the rule was now the length of

ABOVE: **Paul L. Hammond and his wife, Susan, in the cockpit of the *Landfall,* with her eight-foot tiller.** (Mystic Seaport Museum, 1973-3-338) RIGHT: **The *Landfall's* sail plan. Her ketch rig was better suited to her role as a comfortable cruising boat than to that of an ocean racer, particularly for the 1931 Transatlantic Race, whose rules eliminated the rig allowance for ketches over cutters. For light sails to use on the wind, Francis shows a big Genoa jib, coming back nearly to the deckhouse, and a slightly overlapping fore staysail. For reaching, he has drawn a ballooner filling the fore triangle, a big mizzen staysail tacking down just abaft the mainmast, and a huge "reaching mainsail," set loose-footed and stretching aft past the mizzenmast to sheet to the mizzen boom. For heavy weather, there is a second, deep reef in the mainsail and a mizzen trysail whose head is at the point of attachment of the main backstay and the mizzen running backstays. The bowsprit is off-center to port of the stem; its bobstay and shrouds are attached to its outer end with eye splices, not tangs! The big mainsail has an area of 1,305 square feet; total measured sail area is 3,004 square feet.** (© Mystic Seaport Museum, Daniel S. Gregory Ships Plans Library, SP38.5.6)

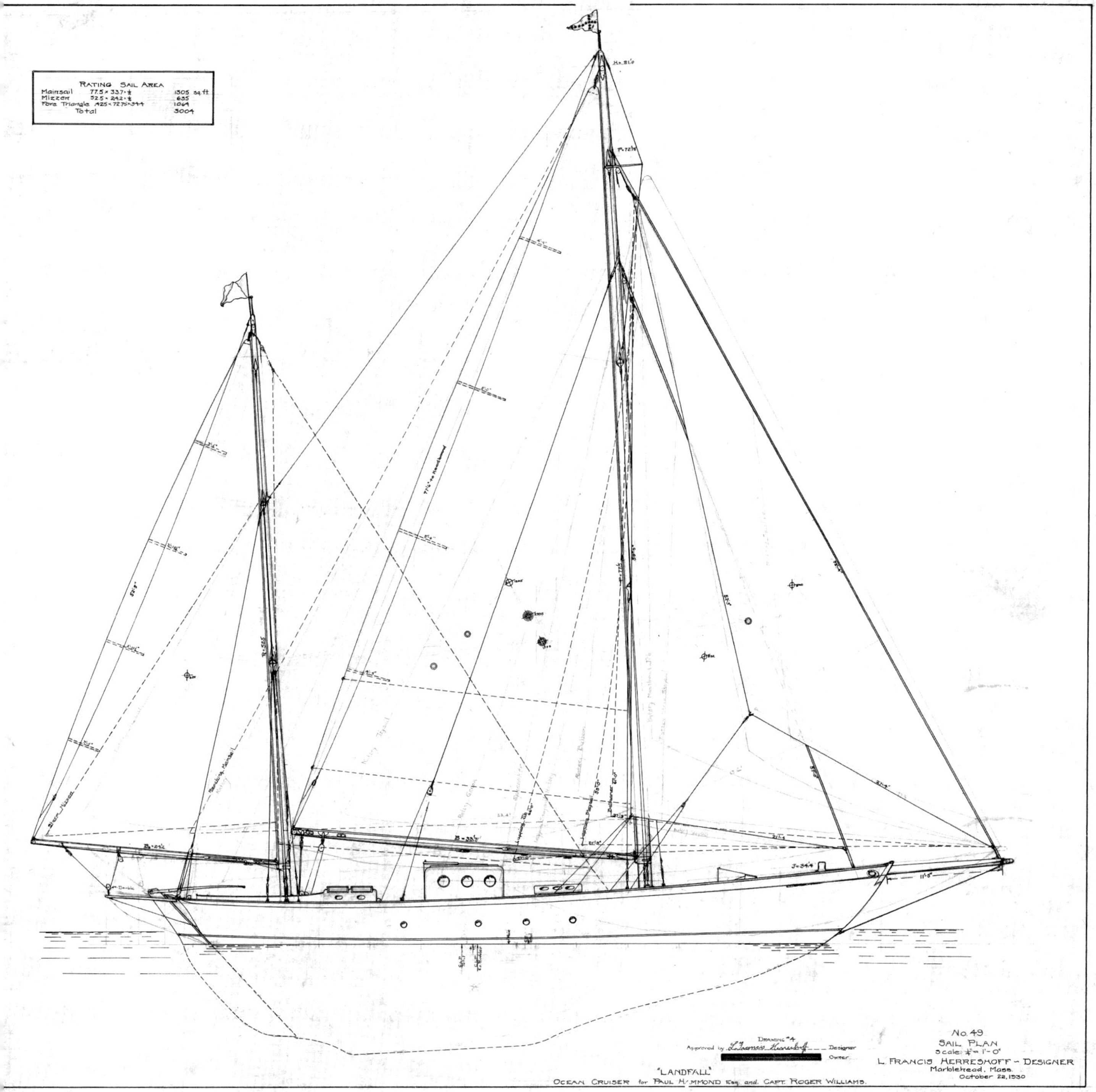
RATING SAIL AREA
Mainsail 77.5 × 33.7 ÷ ½ 1305 sq. ft.
Mizzen 52.5 × 24.2 ÷ ½ 635
Fore Triangle .425 × 72.75 × 34.4 1064
Total 3004
Drawing #4
Approved by L. Francis Herreshoff Designer
Owner
No. 49
SAIL PLAN
Scale: ¼" = 1'-0"
L. FRANCIS HERRESHOFF – DESIGNER
Marblehead, Mass.
October 22, 1930
"LANDFALL"
OCEAN CRUISER for PAUL HAMMOND Esq. and CAPT. ROGER WILLIAMS.

the hull taken at a point 4 percent of the waterline length above the waterline. For the *Landfall*, as Francis designed her hull, this number was 64.82 feet. The depth measurement was the average of depth at one-quarter of the beam out from the centerline and at three-quarters of the beam out. The constant, .2, was simply to make the rating bear some resemblance to actual length. The *Landfall*'s rating came out to 62.2.[4]

For a seaworthy hull shape, what Francis drew is a much-enlarged version of his father's 12½-foot-waterline sloop that the Herreshoff Manufacturing Company had turned out by the score and that had proved exceptionally able. The short overhangs of the 12½-footer were admirably suited to keeping the huge version of the boat within the Cruising Club's length limit—she actually exceeded the 71 feet by an inch and a half—and to keeping her rating low under the ocean racing rule. Thirteen years later, Francis wrote to an inquirer about the design: "*Landfall*, aside from her model, is mostly the owner's ideas." And, twenty years after that, he wrote to Paul Hammond: "If you remember her model was your idea and you suggested to me to make her something like the 12½-footers which I tried to do by principally leaving off the flaring sides." In any event, Francis would have preferred the long, pointed stern that he dotted in on the lines drawing, but that would have made her too long for the American ocean racing rule.[5]

Having tried the staysail-schooner rig with the *Niña*, Hammond wanted to have the experience of sailing a ketch. There was no rig allowance for a ketch in the Transatlantic Race, but the two-masted rig, with its smaller sails, would be relatively easy to handle for both racing and cruising. Hammond ordered her sails from the Ratsey loft at City Island. The first eight basic sails were mainsail, mizzen, working jib, forestaysail, Genoa jib, balloon jib, mizzen staysail, and spinnaker. The bill for these, with sail covers, came to $4,280, on which Francis would get a 10 percent commission. For auxiliary power when cruising, the *Landfall* had a Junkers three-cylinder, opposed-piston diesel. Hammond wrote to Francis, "It was so clean you could smell the boltropes on sails in same compartment and so cool you could use top for hand rail in a seaway."[6]

The *Landfall* had many of Paul Hammond's ideas. Both masts had internal tracks, and each sail "slide" that ran in them was a four-wheeled carriage, to prevent jamming. The mainmast also had a track in its forward side, with a fitting to take the inboard end of the spinnaker pole. And the bowsprit had an internal track in which the jibstay could be slid inboard, so that the jib could be set or doused in the lee of the forestaysail. The handrails on top of the deckhouse were made solid

---

RIGHT, FOLDOUT INSIDE: **The lines of the *Landfall*. She can be seen as a much larger version of Nathanael's "Buzzards Bay Boy's Boat," the 12½-foot-waterline gaff-rigged sloop of 1914 that became so popular. Francis has cut away the heel of the deadwood to reduce wetted surface and make the boat quicker to turn. She is 71 feet, 1½ inches long on deck; 59 feet, 11 inches on the waterline; with a beam of 18 feet, and a draft of 10 feet, 10 inches. Displacement is 118,000 pounds, with 49,600 pounds of outside lead, for a ballast-to-displacement ratio of 42 percent. Her stability curve shows that on the wind with full working sail set to a 30-knot breeze, she would be just rail down. Her maximum righting moment comes at a heeled angle of 80 degrees. If knocked down on her beam ends, without flooding, the centerline would be 18 inches above water. Francis shows his beloved pointed stern in dotted lines, but it was not to be, since the ocean-racing rule limited on-deck length to 71 feet, and the *Landfall* would have been a 77-footer as a double-ender. Despite the *Landfall*'s being designed specifically to enter the 1931 Transatlantic Race, her lines and construction drawings were labeled by draftsman K. Aage Nielsen, "Ocean Cruiser."** (© Mystic Seaport Museum, Daniel S. Gregory Ships Plans Library, SP38.5.1; and Construction Record for LFH Designs, SP38.5.315)

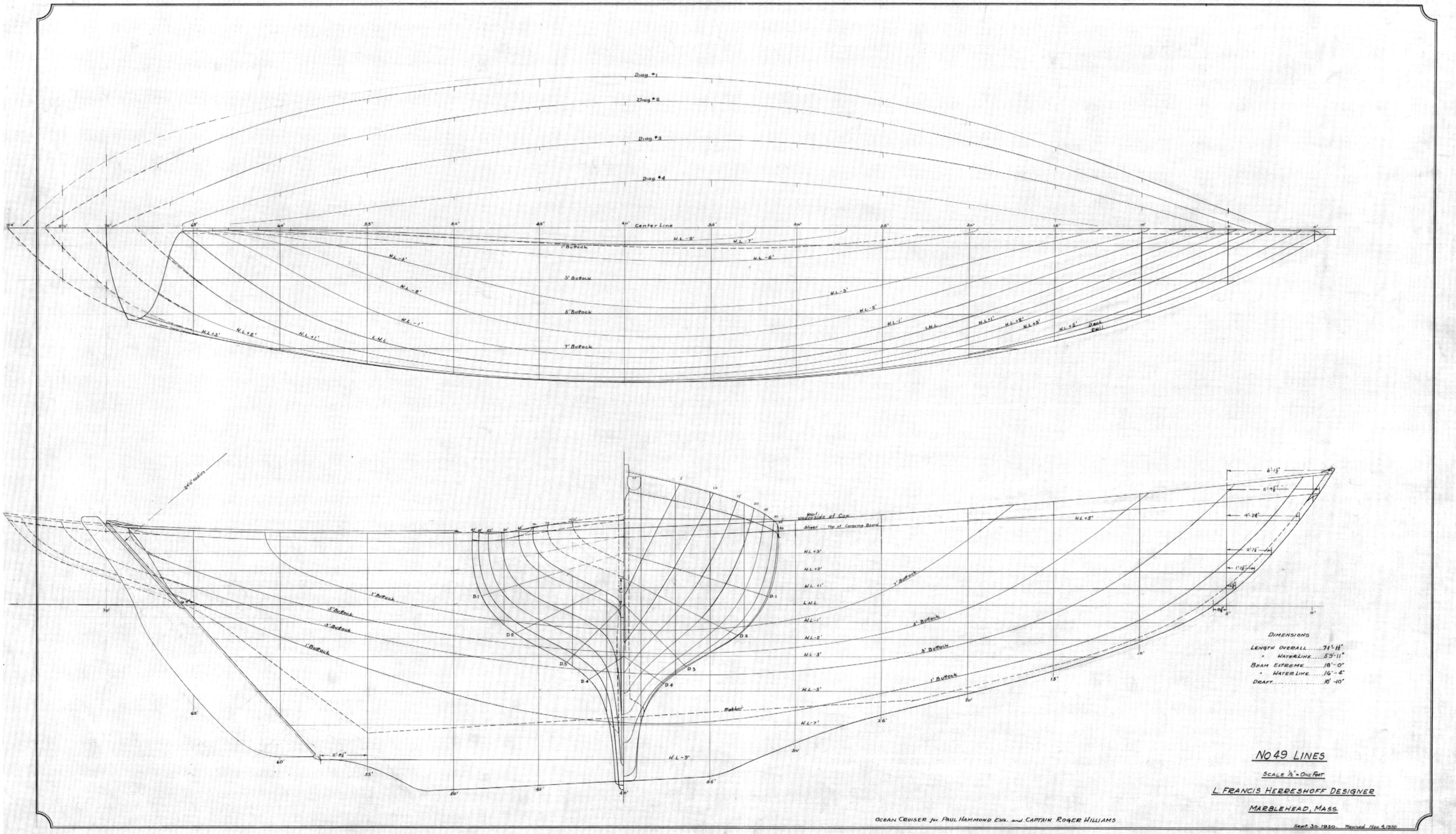

Dimensions
Length Overall.....71'-1½"
" WaterLine.....59'-11"
Beam Extreme.....18'-0"
" Water Line.....16'-4"
Draft.....10'-10"
No 49 Lines
Scale ½" = One Foot
L. Francis Herreshoff Designer
Marblehead, Mass.
Ocean Cruiser for Paul Hammond Esq. and Captain Roger Williams
Sept. 30. 1930. Revised Nov. 4. 1930

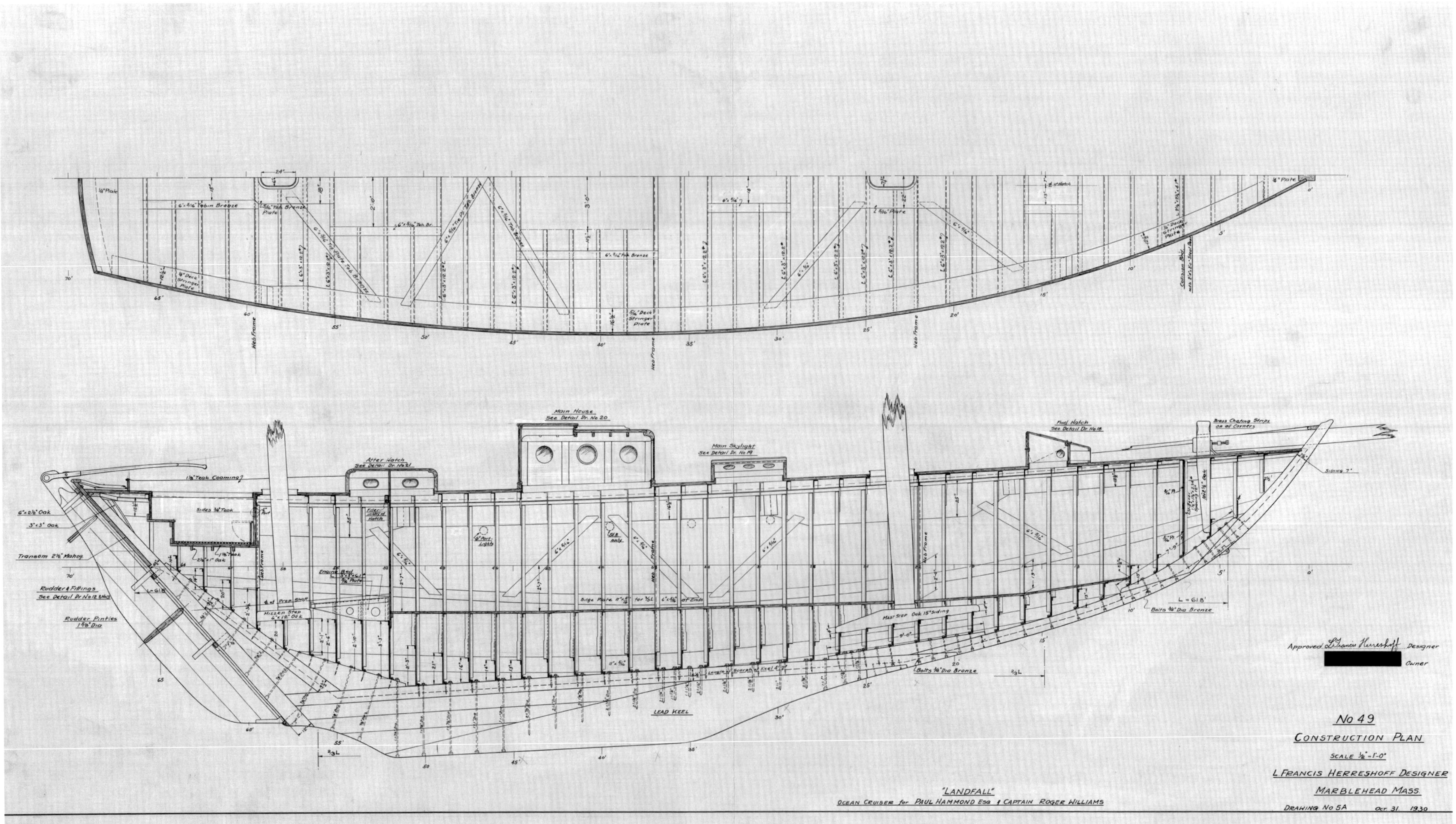
Main House
See Detail Dr. No 20
Main Skylight
See Detail Dr. No 19
After Hatch
See Detail Dr. No 21
Fwd Hatch
See Detail Dr No 18
LEAD KEEL
Approved Designer
Owner
No 49
CONSTRUCTION PLAN
SCALE ½"=1'-0"
L FRANCIS HERRESHOFF DESIGNER
MARBLEHEAD MASS.
"LANDFALL"
OCEAN CRUISER for PAUL HAMMOND Esq & CAPTAIN ROGER WILLIAMS
DRAWING No 5A
OCT 31 1930

to catch rainwater, which could be piped into a tank below. For better visibility, or in case the big tiller, back in the cockpit, was pulling too hard, there was a horizontal steering wheel on the after, starboard corner of the deckhouse, with a folding seat for the helmsman. She had two compasses in the cockpit, one on each side, set into the deck just inside the coaming. The anchor rode was a stainless steel cable hauled by a windlass below in the fo'c's'le. A wooden toilet seat clipped onto the rail at the stern for use at sea, the only item in this list of which Francis would have approved. Instead of lead weights to ballast the swinging table in her saloon, the *Landfall* had a piano built into the table. The Shipmate combination gas-and-coal range in the galley received so much praise from Hammond that he was quoted in a Stamford Foundry Company advertisement. In Francis's opinion, the *Landfall* was "complicated, expensive, and impractical." But Hammond was having fun with his concepts and his money, trying to create an ideal, early version of the racer-cruiser.[7]

Francis, the artist, did put his oar in when it came to interior decoration. Susan Hammond wrote to him, "your idea of painting the deck beams in the main cabin red with red leather cushions turned out superbly and the paneled teak makes the most lovely, warm, cozy background, especially when the stove is lit and we are seventeen for a meal!" But Francis was exasperated with all Paul's changes to the boat, and by mid-January 1931 he had obtained Paul's agreement that as far as he, Francis, was concerned, the design was finished. Any further changes would have to be worked out with the builder, Abeking and Rasmussen. A month later, Francis could report to his father, "I think everything is settled up now with Paul Hammond, much for the best of the builder who wants to design most of the parts anyway, and Mr. Hammond, who wants to change all of the parts, whoever designs them; and Mr. Hammond and I are all friendly now."[8]

The Abeking and Rasmussen yard had been founded in 1907 at Lemwerder, Germany, near Bremen. Herr Abeking provided the money until 1923, when he sold out. Henry Rasmussen ran the yard, designing, as well as building, first-class yachts. Like Francis, Rasmussen had grown up in a boatyard—his grandfather's yard in Denmark—where his father was also employed. Rasmussen traveled to the United States in both 1926 and 1927, encouraged by Starling Burgess to try to get building orders from American designers and yachtsmen. He came to Marblehead and met Francis. He met Paul Hammond. He succeeded in getting orders to build eighty of Starling's Atlantic one-designs as well as yachts in his 10-Metre Class. And Hammond, with Francis's approval, gave him the job of building the *Landfall*. Rasmussen followed Francis's basic construction plan, but

---

LEFT FOLDOUT: **The *Landfall*'s construction plan. She was built in Germany by Henry Rasmussen, who was a designer as well as a builder. The big ketch is of partial composite construction, with steel frames and deck beams, and a full-length steel bilge stringer on each side. She has a wide steel deck plate along each gunwale instead of a wooden shelf-and-clamp. The engine bed is steel, but her mast steps are of oak. Usually, with composite construction, the stem, keelson, and stern structure would be of steel, but the *Landfall*'s are all oak. Her planking is 2-inch mahogany; the transom is 2½-inch mahogany. Diagonal steel strapping is let into both planking and deck. Francis made thirty-four drawings to show the details of her hull, rig, and interior arrangement. On some, including this plan and the cabin plan, the line where Paul Hammond, as owner, signed his approval has been blacked out. As the building of the vessel proceeded, Hammond and Rasmussen added so many details that Francis felt that the owner had not really approved of his plans.** (© Mystic Seaport Museum, Daniel S. Gregory Ships Plans Library, SP38.5.3)

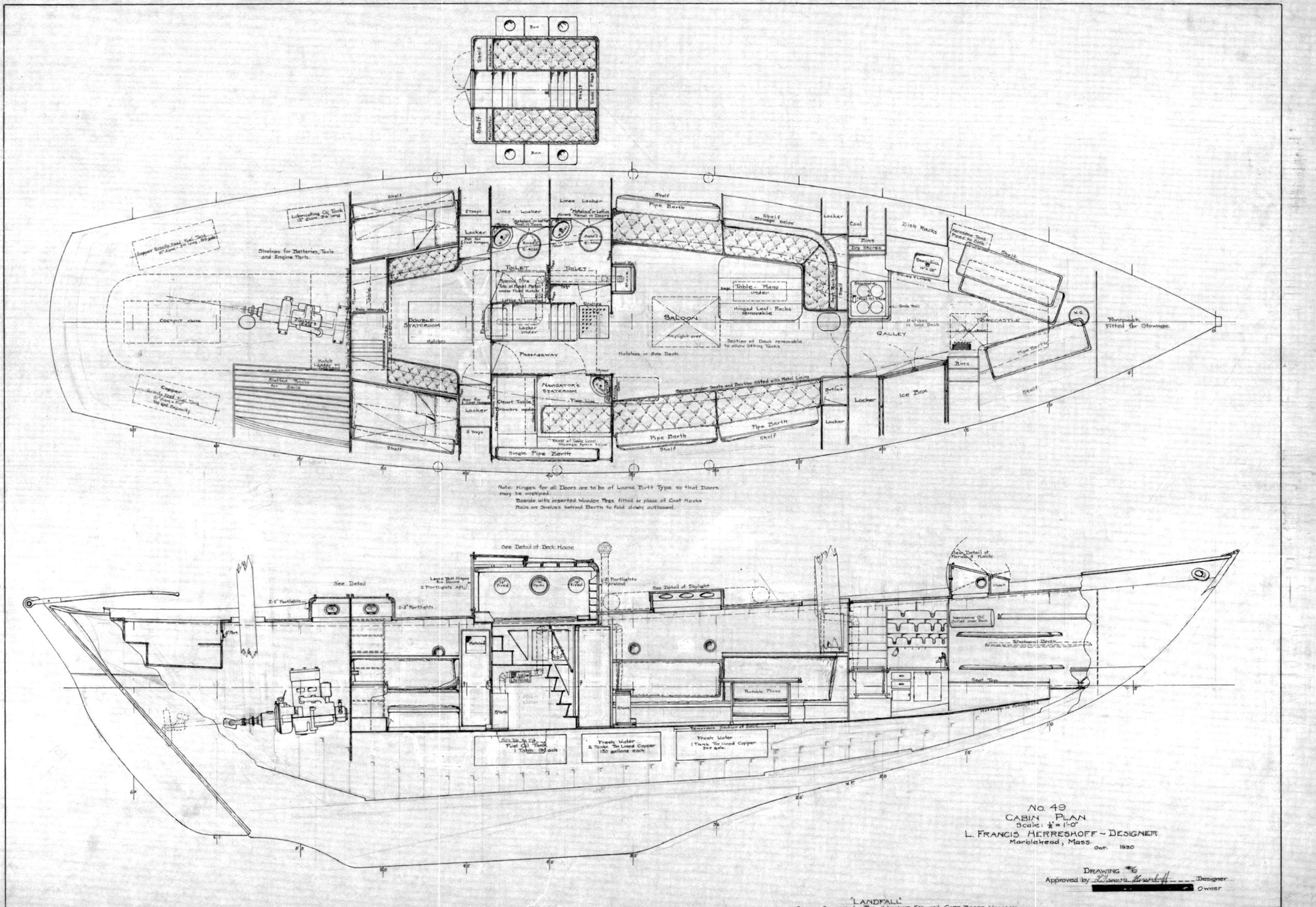

No. 49
CABIN PLAN
Scale: ½" = 1'-0"
L. FRANCIS HERRESHOFF ~ DESIGNER
Marblehead, Mass.
Oct. 1930
DRAWING #6
Approved by ______ Designer
______ Owner
'LANDFALL'
OCEAN CRUISER for PAUL HAMMOND, Esq. and CAPT. ROGER WILLIAMS
Note: Hinges for all Doors are to be of Loose Butt Type so that Doors may be unshipped.
Boards with inserted Wooden Pegs fitted in place of Coat Hooks
Rails on Shelves behind Berths to fold down outboard.
Shelves for Batteries, Tools and Engine Parts.
Lubricating Oil Tank
Slatted Racks for Sails
Cockpit above
DOUBLE STATEROOM
TOILET
TOILET
PASSAGEWAY
NAVIGATOR'S STATEROOM
Chart Table
Single Pipe Berth
SALOON
Skylight over
Section of Deck removable to allow lifting Tanks
Hinged Leaf - Racks removable
Table
Pipe Berth
Shelf
Locker
Linen Locker
Coal
Dish Racks
GALLEY
Ice Box
Buffet
FORECASTLE
Forepeak Fitted for Stowage
Space under Seats and Berths fitted with Metal Lining
Hatches in Side Deck
See Detail of Deck House
See Detail of Skylight
See Detail of Forward Hatch
See Detail
2-5" Portlights
Fuel Oil Tank
Fresh Water 2 Tanks Tin Lined Copper 150 gallons each
Fresh Water 1 Tank Tin lined Copper 300 gals.
Removable Section of Deck
Kerosene Oil Outlet over Sink
Seat Top
Shelf
Box
Coal Flap

when the inevitable questions arose he answered them himself or went to the owner, rather than going to the designer. As he looked back, twenty years later, Francis remembered that "Rasmussen did a very good job of building the ketch *Landfall*." Her construction finished, she was shipped to New York in good time to be at the transatlantic starting line by the Fourth of July 1931.[9]

The 1931 Transatlantic Race would be the sixth. In the first, in 1866, three schooners raced across in December for $90,000 in prize money. They had plenty of winter wind, averaged over nine knots, and finished within eight and a half hours of each other. The races of 1870 and 1888 were simply between two schooners, sailed in summer. The first "modern" transatlantic race was in 1905, when the 185-foot, three-masted schooner *Atlantic*, designed by William Gardner, beat ten other large yachts and set a long-standing record for a sailing vessel crossing the Atlantic of twelve days, four hours. All these races were from New York to England. They were all sailed by professional captains and crews; the owners went as pampered passengers. As we have seen, Paul Hammond won the Queen's Cup for the small class in the *Niña* in the fifth transatlantic race, the 1928 race to Spain. In that class, the boats were skippered by their owners and had amateur crews, except for the occasional cook. In the big class, professional seamen still did all the work. The 136-foot schooner *Elena*, designed by N. G. Herreshoff and launched by the Herreshoff Manufacturing Company in 1911, beat the *Atlantic* and others to win the King's Cup.[10]

Once the *Landfall* was fitted out with her sails at City Island—the inventory had grown from eight to twenty—she set off from the New York Yacht Club Station across the Sound at Glen Cove, heading for Bristol to get last-minute jobs done at the Herreshoff Manufacturing Company before the start of the race. On the way, she tried out, one after another, her different sizes of jibs, spinnakers, and mizzen staysails, as well as a huge reaching mainsail. There was even a combination square-sail-raffee that needed two poles, one aloft and one alow, to make it stand to a following breeze. When the big ketch reached Bristol, Francis drove down from Marblehead to look her over. On this occasion, he could stand on the bow looking aft at his great creation, a magnificent vessel about to go off on an exciting adventure, and he could overlook all the gadgets that Hammond and Rasmussen had added to his design. Or try to. His reason for not visiting his father at the time was that "by the time I had gotten through with Mr. Hammond I was very nearly all in."[11]

Sidney Herreshoff towed the *Landfall* from Bristol down Narragansett Bay to Newport with his launch, the *Bubble*, three days before the start, the ketch's engine having been put out of commission for the race. She anchored in Brenton Cove with

---

LEFT: **The *Landfall's* cabin plan. Francis has carefully drawn in the three-cylinder, opposed-piston Junkers engine specified, with its shaft angled off-center. The deckhouse has a transom on each side; there is a huge main saloon; and the navigator has his own cabin, with chart table, just to starboard of the main companionway. There are two heads: one for the owner's cabin aft, which has its own steps to the deck; and one for guests. With an ocean-racing crew in mind, Francis shows three extra pipe berths in the saloon and one in the navigator's cabin. Hammond fitted two extra berths in his own cabin as well, but they were not the pipe berths that Francis favored. Elihu Root had come up with a new idea for a fold-away berth: simply a piece of canvas stretched on two fore-and-aft rods that could be mounted between bulkheads in several positions to allow for different angles of heel and amounts of motion. So the racing crew assigned to upper bunks in the owner's cabin on board the *Landfall* slumbered in Root berths.** (© Mystic Seaport Museum, Daniel S. Gregory Ships Plans Library, SP38.5.7)

the nine yachts that would be her competition. The boat to beat seemed to be the big, able cutter *Highland Light*, with her designer, Frank Paine, in Dudley Wolfe's crew. There were three good schooners: George Roosevelt's *Mistress*, also with her designer, Sherman Hoyt, on board; the *Water Gypsy*, an Alden design; and the *Amberjack II*, designed at Boston Yacht Sales and built by Lawley. There was a handsome cutter with a tall gaff rig, designed by Philip L. Rhodes, the *Skal*. There was a slim, 52-foot yawl, the *Dorade*, designed by Olin J. Stephens II, age twenty-three. He was her skipper, and he had his younger brother, Rod, as mate, and his father, Roderick Stephens, the owner, in the crew. There was a big, old, gaff-rigged ketch, the *Lismore*. Two British yachts had crossed for the race: the Marconi sloop *Maitenes II* and the gaff-rigged cutter *Ilex*, sailed gamely, as ever, by her crew of Royal Engineers.[12]

Pundits foresaw different fates for the *Landfall* in the race. In a single issue of *The Rudder*, Francis could read both that she was the favorite and that tall Marconi rigs like hers should be banned from ocean racing, presumably because they might fall down and hurt somebody. She was the "scratch boat" in the fleet; that is, as the biggest boat, she had the highest rating and had to give time to all the others. Against the *Highland Light*, for example, she had to finish more than 13 hours, 7 minutes, and 39 seconds ahead to beat her on corrected time. She had to give the *Dorade* 46 hours, 28 minutes, and 44 seconds. In the *Yachting* column, "Under the Lee of the Longboat," which Alfred F. Loomis took over temporarily while its usual writer, Sam Wetherill, raced across the Atlantic in the *Water Gypsy*, Loomis predicted that the *Landfall* would finish first but would be nosed out by the *Highland Light* on corrected time. Then, with a bow to his fellow scribe, he went on to predict that both would be beaten on corrected time by the *Water Gypsy*.[13]

The *Landfall* carried a crew of twelve. Hammond, the skipper, had assembled a group of experienced sailors, each of whom had owned and skippered his own boat. They included the English yacht designer Uffa Fox—who, in his account of the race, called them "a crew of generals"—and a young Waldo Howland, early in his life in boats. For special occasions, they all were given red Basque pants, striped jerseys, and sailors' stocking caps.[14]

The race started at the Brenton Reef Lightship, outside Narragansett Bay, at noon on the Fourth of July. The *Landfall* had to work her way around a lubberly spectator schooner, so she was a little late at the line. No matter: there were 3,000 miles

to go. A gentle south-southwest breeze sent the fleet off on a close reach on the starboard tack to weather the little island of Nomans Land, off Martha's Vineyard, and then head off more for the Nantucket Lightship. After four hours, the racers had some idea of how their boats measured up, at least when reaching in mild conditions. The *Highland Light* led by half a mile. Then came the *Mistress*, with the *Dorade* not far behind. The *Landfall* was a mile astern of the leader, with the rest of the fleet strung out behind. The slippery *Dorade* was showing that she could stay with the big boys, at least until it breezed up.[15]

At Nantucket Lightship, it was decision time. Or rather, it was time to carry out the biggest strategic decision of the race, which every skipper had analyzed before the start: the most advantageous course to choose for crossing the Atlantic. It boiled down to two choices. The "southern" route would take full advantage of the easterly flow of the Gulf Stream; the "northern" route, skirting the tips of Nova Scotia and Newfoundland, would,

LEFT: **Morris Rosenfeld shot the *Landfall* as she entered Narragansett Bay via the East Passage, passing Castle Hill Light. Footing fast in a dry northeaster, she makes a fine show even without any of her fancy racing sails.** (© Mystic Seaport Museum, Rosenfeld Collection, 1984.187.46734F) ABOVE: **The *Landfall's* "crew of generals" just before the start of the 1931 Transatlantic Race off Newport. So named by Uffa Fox, seated furthest forward with his arm around a shipmate who could well be Waldo Howland, each man had been accustomed to barking orders on board his own vessel. All, that is, but Joe Fredericks, furthest forward, leaning on the deckhouse, whose responsibility was the feeding of these eleven commanders.** (© Mystic Seaport Museum, Rosenfeld Collection, 1984.187.46772F)

The *Landfall* close-hauled under working sail in a gentle breeze and flat sea. Judging by the hat, that is Paul Hammond, her fussy owner and busy skipper, on his feet at the stern, perhaps starting forward on an inspection trip. The big ketch, loaded with gadgets and gillhickies scorned by her designer, was Hammond's idea of the perfect cruiser-racer. (Edwin Levick photo 112277, The Mariners' Museum, Newport News, Virginia)

by approaching a great circle, cut 200 miles off the track and ought to provide colder, stronger winds. Hammond had decided on the southern, Gulf Stream route, so when the wind unexpectedly backed into the east at Nantucket Shoals, the *Landfall* went about onto the port tack and stood off, close-hauled, to the southeast, into the Gulf Stream, her people hoping that the breeze would soon veer into the westerly quadrant where it belonged.[16]

But it didn't. It stayed in the east or southeast for five days. The *Landfall* and all the other southern-route boats tacked back and forth trying to make their easting and trying to stay south to get the Stream's free ride. In these conditions, the *Landfall* continued a bit behind the *Highland Light,* for the ketch could not sail quite as close to the wind as could the cutter. Only the Stephens family, in the *Dorade*, decided to go north. In the winds that baffled the rest of the fleet, they could just lay the course to Newfoundland's Cape Race, and off they went. As the yachts spread out in the vastness of the ocean, there was no way their crews could tell how they were doing.[17]

At last, the wind came in from the west, and the *Landfall*'s crew could pile on her fancy light sails for running and reaching. Up went the balloon mainsail. The sail had been outlawed for the race as a mainsail, but the committee had then said it could be set forward of the mast. So the crew tacked it down to the stemhead and set it flying, sheeted to the end of the main boom. The big sail had been stowed on the main cabin sole, where it had picked up coffee stains and some jam, but Paul Hammond said that wouldn't affect its trim. Then they set the biggest spinnaker. These two huge sails gave the ketch 4,000 square feet of sail area, 1,000 more than she was measured for. That was just for running. When the wind backed a little into the southwest, giving her a broad reach, the watchstanders added the mizzen and the biggest mizzen staysail, adding a further 1,400 square feet.[18]

Meanwhile, as the *Landfall*'s navigator, Ben Ames, recorded: "Joe Fredericks of Cowes, steward extraordinary, continued to bake pies, cakes, dumplings and other delicacies, and we put in our hardest licks around the mess table. We managed to do justice to his best efforts, until one day he stopped us with about twenty pounds of English steamed pudding. Joe succeeded, to his great delight, in using up forty days' provisions in the nineteen-day passage."[19]

But as the southwest wind increased, the pace of sailing overtook the pace of eating. On July 16, it breezed up to a strong 25 knots. Reaching with mainsail, mizzen, balloon staysail, and balloon jib, the *Landfall*'s speed gradually increased until she was charging along at 11¼ knots. That speed is 1.45 times the square root of her waterline length, a high number for a short-ended boat; Francis had done well with her lines, inspired by his father's 12 ½-footer. Ben Ames described her as "remarkably steady" at that speed, and Uffa Fox said her deck stayed dry.[20]

During the evening of July 22, Larry Poole, the ship's doctor, sighted the loom of the lighthouse on Bishop's Rock at the Isles of Scilly, off the southwest tip of England. By dawn next morning, the *Landfall* was off Lizard Point, with only fifty miles to go to the finish line at Plymouth. As the light spread across the sea, somebody looked astern and made out a sail. The *Landfall* was running with her balloon mainsail and biggest spinnaker set. The sail gained until it was only a mile and half away, but then could gain no more. It belonged to the *Highland Light.* After 3,000 miles, the boats were only minutes apart. It was a fight to see which yacht would be first to finish. The *Landfall* held the *Light* off and finished 14 minutes ahead of her. It was just as Alf Loomis had predicted: the *Landfall* finished first, but the *Highland Light* nosed her out on corrected time, if you can call nearly 13 hours winning by a nose.[21]

The memorable race to the finish between the *Landfall* and the *Highland Light* was, however, an anticlimax. Ralph St. L. Peverley had come out to meet them in his Alden schooner, the *Lelanta,* with the news that the *Dorade* had been sitting in Plymouth Harbor for two days! And sure enough, here she came, relieving the boredom of her crew with a daysail. The crews exchanged hearty cheers. The *Highland Light* fell to fourth on corrected time, for both the *Skal* and the *Amberjack II* saved their time on her. The *Landfall* was sixth, behind the fifth-place *Mistress.* Loomis's predicted winner, the *Water Gypsy,* was eighth.[22]

The northern route had certainly paid off. The *Dorade* had only one day of light winds, when she made 85 miles; the *Landfall* was nearly becalmed for two days; on one of those days, she made only 26 miles. For much of the race, the *Dorade* had been able to sail at nearly her hull-speed. She had *averaged* about 175 miles a day, over 7 knots. Her hull-speed was less than 9 knots. Her best day's run was 210 miles, at 8¾ knots, very close to her hull-speed for the twenty-four hours. On board the *Landfall*, there was great excitement when she averaged 10½ knots, approaching her hull-speed, for a whole four-hour watch. The stronger winds to the north more than made up for the boost of the Gulf Stream to the south.[23]

But there was more to the *Dorade*'s victory than choosing the more advantageous route across the Atlantic. She had finished third in fleet in the 1930 Bermuda Race. The Stephens brothers were changing ocean racing. For them it was not about seeing which yacht, suitable for ocean cruising, might win an ocean race. They wanted to design and build a fast, strong yacht and then drive her to the limit, night and day, every minute of a long race at sea. They really wanted to win. Ocean racing was about to become much more competitive.

Already disenchanted with ocean racing, L. Francis Herreshoff did not welcome the change. The 1931 Transatlantic Race bore out his contention that ocean racing was no test of yacht design, but rather rewarded good judgment of weather routing. Moreover, his approach to yachting was old-fashioned, so he abhorred the derring-do of a small yacht carrying a spinnaker at night in mid-ocean in half a gale. It took him fourteen lengthy paragraphs in his treatise on yacht design to deliver himself of the emotional diatribe on ocean racing that had built up in his psyche by 1946, starting with "So called ocean racing is a farce. . . ."[24]

The *Dorade* would probably have won the race, although by a much smaller margin, even if she had stayed south with her competitors. Paul Hammond and his crew should have been worried when they couldn't pass her in the first hours of the race. Hammond was a competitive ocean racer, all right, as he had proved with Starling Burgess's *Niña*, but what he had asked Francis to design for him was a big, comfortable yacht for cruising in Europe after the Transatlantic Race. When Olin Stephens had designed the *Dorade,* he was only concerned with speed, and when he and Rod headed up their watches, day and night crossing the Atlantic, speed was also their primary concern. They left the *Landfall*'s piano and her red leather cushions far behind.

Following their wide margin of victory in the Transatlantic Race, Olin and Rod Stephens went on to win the Fastnet Race in the *Dorade*. The double feat merited a ticker-tape parade down Broadway and a painting by Tore Asplund of the *Dorade* slicing to windward in a fresh breeze on the cover of *Yachting*, along with unstinting praise from the magazine's editor, Herbert L. Stone, not to mention accolades from an enlightened Alfred F. Loomis. But L. Francis Herreshoff wasn't applauding. He pulled his Directory of Naval Architects ad out of *Yachting.*[25]

Francis detested ocean racing. In the fourteenth paragraph of his diatribe on the subject in 1946, part of his series of articles, "The Common Sense of Yacht Design" in *The Rudder*, he wrote, "I warned you that I might get overheated in some places, and that is what has happened when I thought of the type of yacht now being built under the influence of ocean racing." He said that the

ocean-racing measurement rules had produced an expensive yacht that was "a genoa jib and a parachute spinnaker attached to a washtub." His epithet, "washtub," was abusive when applied to the handsome hulls of John Alden's *Malabar* schooners that were winning their share of Bermuda Races, or to the slim hull of Olin Stephens's *Dorade* that had beaten his *Landfall* across the Atlantic by four days on corrected time. Although Francis said that he wasn't singling out any particular designers in his criticism, Alden and Stephens may be seen clearly between the lines. His derogation of going to sea with the biggest possible light sails that were not measured by the rules was common sense.

The *Landfall* just before the start of the 1931 Transatlantic Race on the Fourth of July from Newport, Rhode Island, to Plymouth, England. Her topsides are painted baby blue. On the foredeck, the crew is getting ready to add an overlapping forestaysail to her big jib, a sail combination that she would carry much of the way across the ocean. With fifty miles to go, she found herself close to her rival, Dudley Wolfe's big cutter, the *Highland Light*, designed by Paine, Belknap, and Skene. They had a memorable race to the finish, but both were beaten by the much smaller yawl *Dorade,* designed and sailed by Olin Stephens and his brother, Rod, on a different and, as it turned out, advantageous route across the Atlantic.
(© Mystic Seaport Museum, Rosenfeld Collection, 1984.187.46734F)

Of course, this was not the place to mention his claimed invention of the Genoa jib or his elimination of the headstay from masthead to stemhead that cleared the way for the parachute spinnaker. Instead, he went on to call the large crews that the big sails made necessary "gigolo yacht jockeys." Francis's father, who had not designed a yacht to compete in an ocean race, could be more objective. Nathanael wrote to Francis: "Stevens [*sic*] is a nice young fellow and so I feel rather pleased at his good luck and venture." Francis must have been disgusted. His own lack of recognition caused him to be jealous of Stephens, who was becoming famous. For his part, Olin Stephens drew part of his inspiration from N. G. Herreshoff and considered L. Francis Herreshoff to be a brilliant but erratic yacht designer.[26]

Yet Francis's dislike of ocean racing had a more fundamental basis than jealousy of another designer. Ocean racing, he pointed out, was not a test of the designs of the yachts competing, as was day racing. With sailing yachts of different lengths, and therefore different capabilities for speed, spread out over miles of ocean, one yacht might be reaching at maximum speed, while another lay becalmed. The winning yacht would not necessarily be the fastest design for her rating, but would more probably be the yacht sailed by the skipper who was either the most lucky or the most skillful at choosing a course that had the most advantageous wind patterns. The same sort of luck or skill could also play a part in an afternoon race around the buoys, but day racers were more likely to all sail in the same weather conditions than were ocean racers.

Hammond did not enter the *Landfall* in the Fastnet Race; instead, she had a leisurely sail to Cowes, where the Hammonds entertained on board for five days before leaving her in England and heading home in the liner *Homeric*. For five of the next six years, the Hammonds and their friends made summer cruises in the big ketch, first in the Baltic and then in the Mediterranean, where they explored the islands of the Aegean and visited Athens, Venice, Istanbul, Malta, Alexandria, and Naples, as well as calling at smaller ports. Paul Hammond sold the *Landfall* in 1937, sight unseen, to Richard C. Paine, who based her in Antibes, on the French Riviera. Of the many fine yachts that Hammond and his wife Susan were privileged to sail, the *Landfall* was their favorite.[27]

In the years leading up to World War II, the *Landfall* cruised in the Baltic and the Mediterranean, doubtless giving her new owner pleasure, but also serving as a base for her professional skipper, Mike Cumberlege, who was collecting port intelligence as a secret agent for Britain, an activity for which he was later captured and executed. During the war, the *Landfall* was among many vessels sunk by the Germans to block the entrances to ports on the Riviera. Soon after the war ended, Francis learned that she had been raised, that the damage of two holes blown in her hull had been repaired, but that she was in tough shape. She was restored well enough, however, both to transport wine and to appear in the movie, *The Barefoot Contessa,* with Ava Gardner's toes on her deck. By 1959, she had been given a new cabin arrangement under the ownership of Georges Gallienne of Chambourcy, France. He had reduced the size of the big saloon, added a single stateroom, and changed the arrangement of the heads. M. Gallienne enjoyed sailing the *Landfall* on the lovely Cote d'Azur at least until 1965.[28]

The *Landfall* next shows up in Florida in 1988, where she was bought, after a two-year refit, by a Mr. Zimmer and based at Fort Lauderdale. Her most recent owner is Dr. Emanuel von Kienlin, of Munich, an executive in the medical industry.[29]

Francis wasn't quite through with ocean racing when he agreed with Paul Hammond that the design of the *Landfall* was out of his hands. As we shall see, he would design a yawl to the Cruising Club of America rule for ocean racers in 1936, as a favor to a friend.

CHAPTER 13

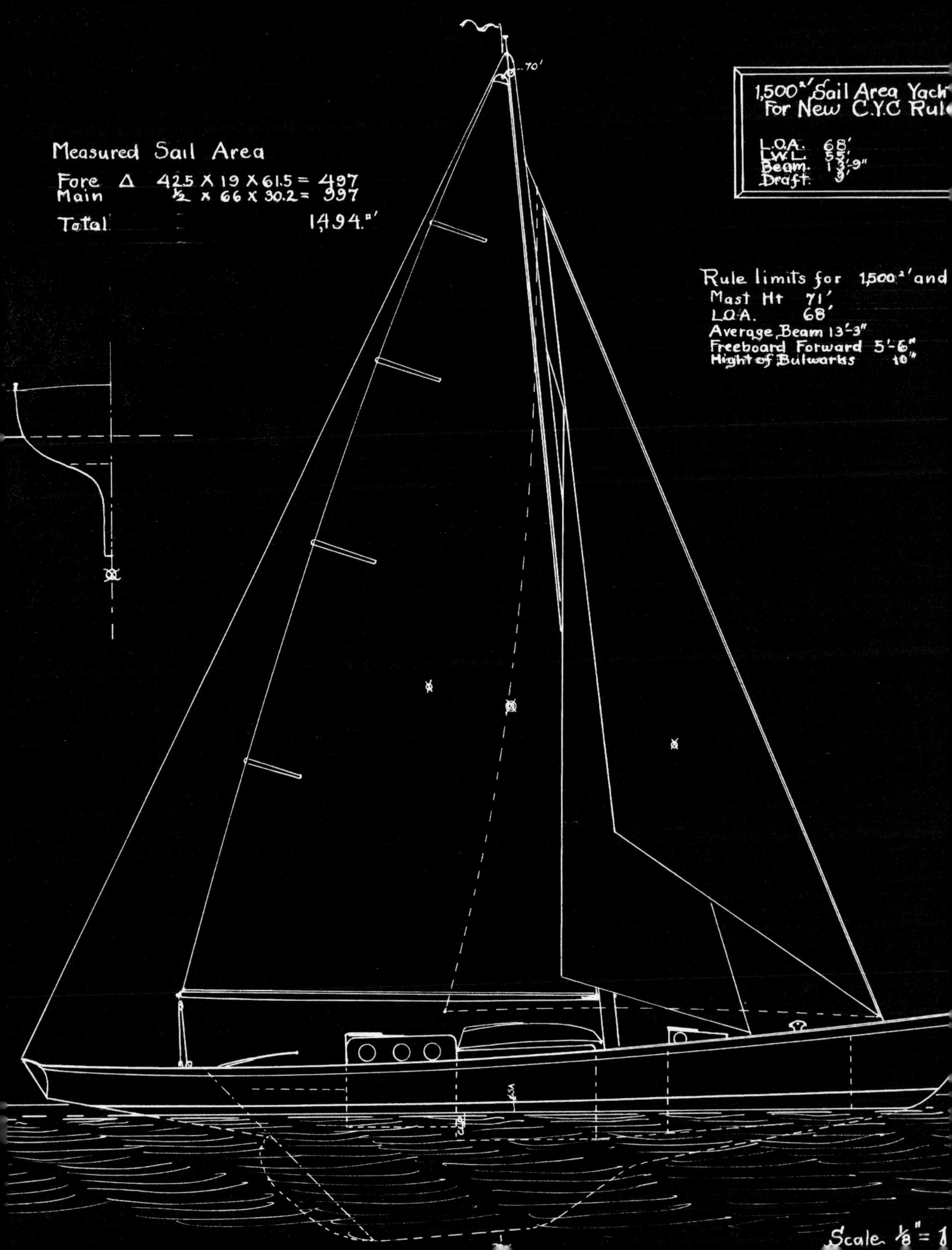
1,500²' Sail Area Yach
For New C.Y.C Rul
L.O.A. 68'
L.W.L. 55'
Beam. 13'-9"
Draft. 9'
70'
Measured Sail Area
Fore Δ 42.5 X 19 X 61.5 = 497
Main ½ x 66 x 30.2 = 997
Total 1,494.□'
Rule limits for 1,500²' and
Mast Ht 71'
L.O.A. 68'
Average Beam 13'-3"
Freeboard Forward 5'-6"
Hight of Bulwarks 10"
Scale ⅛" = 1

DEPRESSION

"It is quite important that I get some work pretty soon as I have been nearly two years without doing any really paying work."

—L. FRANCIS HERRESHOFF TO HIS FATHER, 1933

"I am as poor as almost anyone who only designs small vessels."

—L. FRANCIS HERRESHOFF TO UFFA FOX, 1935

Once the full effects of the Great Depression began to be felt, as the decade of the 1930s unfolded, economic times were hard for nearly everyone. October 29, 1929, was Black Tuesday. By 1932, the stock market had fallen by 89 percent, 40 percent of the banks had failed, and unemployment was at 25 percent. Very few people could afford luxuries, like yachts. But for L. Francis Herreshoff, yacht design was his chosen profession; there was no thought of turning to anything else. He was certainly qualified to work in a machine shop or woodworking shop, but good machinists and top carpenters outnumbered paying jobs. And for Francis, working for money with his hands, skilled though they were, would have meant stepping down a social class, which was unthinkable for him. He would keep a sharp lookout for design commissions, and he would struggle to make ends meet. His letterhead of the time, "L. Francis Herreshoff, Yacht Designer," made him appear to be a businessman, for it proclaimed: "Agent for Highest Grade Sails, Motors, Marine Hardware. Yacht Brokerage, Marine Insurance, Surveying." But, except for a few commissions on orders for sails that he got from Ratseys and a bit of boat insurance that a boarder of his was able to sell, these ancillary activities were dormant. In 1933, Francis wrote to Nathanael: "I have been staying close to home most of the time in hopes of any little job that might come up. I have made some sketches for new work and people have said that they would drop in at any time to talk them over. It is quite important that I get some work pretty soon as I have been nearly two years without doing any really paying work." Yet, as we have seen, design fees for the *Whirlwind* and *Landfall* brightened the start of the Depression for him, and there would be a half dozen more major commissions spread

through the thirties to keep L. Francis Herreshoff going, two of them resulting in the most wonderful yachts of his career.[1]

Francis's brothers were doing all right. Sidney, as chief designer at the Herreshoff Manufacturing Company, had gainful employment, even though the yard had to lay off many of its experienced boatbuilders. The struggling business would run its first-ever advertisement, a small one, in the April 1932 issue of *Yachting*. Sydney and his partner, Rebecca Chase, were finally married in June 1930. In that year, Sidney designed the Fishers Island 31 racing and cruising sloop. Francis commented to Nathanael (but not to Sidney), "The Fisher's Island boats are really very wonderful boats." And in late 1931, Sidney designed a 23-foot-waterline sloop, like a less extreme square-metre boat, for a racing class at Fishers Island. By 1936, the departures of experienced men forced him, in his father's words, into "superintending the work generally" at the yard. Griswold had been promoted to director of truck and bus construction at the Chrysler Corporation in Detroit a month before the Crash. Two years later, motorcar design also came under his direction, and, in 1934, the company came out with the streamlined Airflow model. When Nathanael wrote to Francis about Griswold's attainments, Francis replied that he was "glad that Griswold continues to be busy." Clarence had work as a draftsman in the Hull Department of the Marine Engineering Corporation in Philadelphia, then moved on, in 1931, to the drafting room of the big Newport News Shipbuilding yard in Virginia. In 1935, after some months of unemployment, he landed a job at the US Navy Bureau of Ships in Washington and worked there for the next thirty years. There was almost no contact among the brothers, although Francis and Clarence did exchange letters about canoeing, thanks to their father's gentle prompting.[2]

In August of 1935, Nathanael told Francis that Griswold and his wife Henrietta, and possibly Clarence, were to visit at Love Rocks. Sidney and Rebecca, and Francis's sister, Agnes, would be there. He hoped Francis could come down too. "It would be nice to see all the children together once more," the eighty-seven-year-old father wrote. It would also be a chance for Francis to visit with his nieces, Nathanael Jr.'s daughters, Clara, sixteen, and Natalie, twelve, as well as his little nephews, Sidney's sons, Nathanael III, five, and Halsey, two.

L. Francis Herreshoff stands ready to meet the Great Depression on his own terms. While the 1930s will bring him austerity, there will be important design commissions, not only financially, but also artistically. Yet, in a short time, Francis would not be standing with such assuredness, for he would suffer a personal catastrophe that would indeed depress him. (© Mystic Seaport Museum, 1993.120.6.24)

Francis thanked his father for the invitation and said he was too busy.[3]

In the 1930s, Francis designed three small, double-ended cruising ketches, but none of them would be built until after the Depression—so there was no payment, when he needed money the most, of ten percent commissions on construction costs. Francis would write later: "Everybody seems to forget that I started the modern craze" for double-ended cruisers. His claim could be refuted by pointing to, for perhaps the best example, John G. Hanna's design of the *Neptune* in 1923, popularized by Weston Farmer in *Mechanix Illustrated* as the Tahiti ketch in 1935. For better or for worse, there have been and are many more Tahiti ketches at sea than there are Herreshoff double-ended ketches. What Francis could have claimed is that his double-ended ketches would sail rings round a Tahiti without being any less seaworthy. And the counter-claim could be made—and would be by Hanna in *The Rudder*—that Francis's double-ended cruising ketches were not as comfortable as others, because they sailed at a greater angle of heel and had less cabin space.[4]

In the spring of 1930, Francis began work on the design of the first of his small, double-ended cruising ketches. It was slow going; he finished the construction plan on May 15 but did not ink the lines drawing until the following April 13. But during that eleven-month interval, Francis was watching the *Whirlwind* blunder her way to the bottom of the J Class; was designing Development-Class boats, designing an ocean-racing ketch rejected by Dudley Wolfe, designing the *Landfall*, and arranging for the sale of his 30-Square Metre, the *Visitor*. Also during that interval, he made, in his machine shop, through-deck leads for the backstay runners on the *Istalena*; designed a 10-foot pram for Charlie Welch; made a preliminary design for a "Special Inshore Patrol Boat" in which the Coast Guard lost interest; designed a Sonder-type boat, not built; designed an eight-oared shell for Chandler Hovey, not built; made preliminary designs for a 30-foot yawl, a 30-foot sloop, and a 38-foot, hard-chine ketch, none of which found an interested customer; and designed an anchor windlass and a sheet winch, both with innovative principles, but neither of which would be manufactured.

Also during this time, Francis had his appendix removed. The operation was performed by an old friend, such an old friend that he was privileged to use, when addressing Francis, the nickname "George." The origin of this surprising moniker is unknown, but Dr. John Cunningham was not the only longtime friend of Francis's who applied it.

The customer for the first of the double-ended cruisers, Francis's design No. 55, was Larry H. H. Johnson Jr., a Marblehead yachtsman. But, like so many others, he only dreamed over the plans. Francis thought he had designed a good boat; being a great fan of Don Quixote, he gave the name *Dulcinea* to the design.[5]

Trying to drum up interest in this boat four years after finishing her plans, Francis wrote to English yacht designer and author Uffa Fox, perhaps hoping that he would include the *Dulcinea* in his next book: "The little ketch No. 55 is my idea of the smallest sea-going ship that two or more people could cruise in comfortably. I would prefer her without a motor and use this room for storage of gear. I believe if one was sailing in this boat the land would be the only thing to fear while the grub lasted."[6]

Francis had been much impressed by the 30-Square-Metre boats, and their fine-lined hulls and small rigs influenced him as he turned to designing small cruisers. Like a 30-Square, the *Dulcinea* has a long, slim hull (though with much shorter overhangs) and small sail plan, resulting in a design that is fast for her sail area and that will come into her own when it blows hard—good

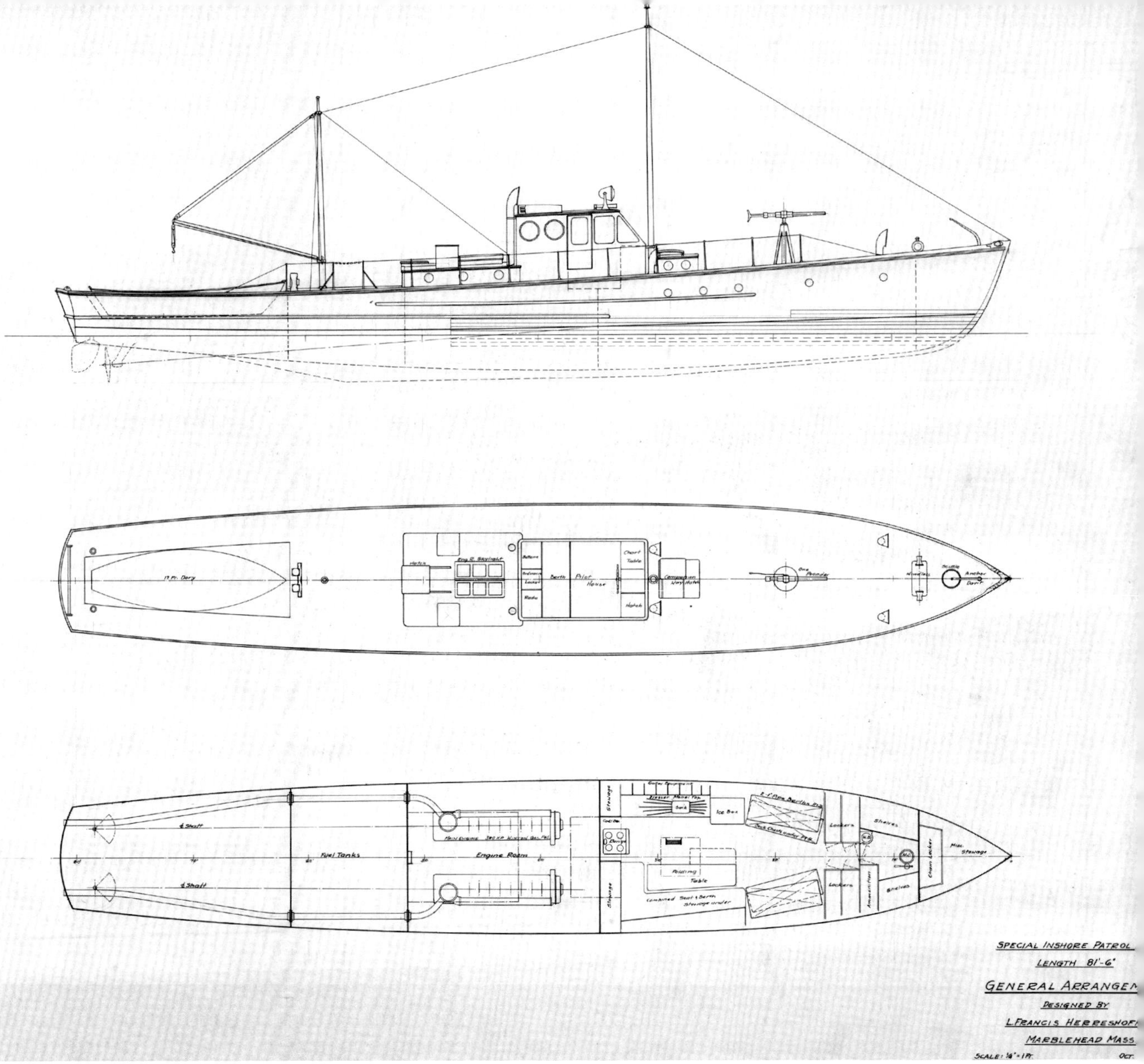

ABOVE: **The General Arrangement plan of Francis's proposed Special Inshore Patrol Boat, dated October 12, 1930. She was probably supposed to intercept rum runners, but Francis figured that her two 500-horsepower Winton gas engines would give her only a little over 18 knots of speed. Length on deck is 81 feet, 6 inches. She has a one-pounder gun on the bow and a 17-foot dory ready to be hoisted out from the stern. There are accommodations for a crew of six. Her hull form is similar to that of the 110-foot submarine chasers that A. Loring Swasey designed during World War I. This design went no further, but Francis, the former navy patrol boat skipper, probably made winter cruises around Block Island in this vessel, in his imagination.** (© Mystic Seaport Museum, Daniel S. Gregory Ships Plans Library, SP38.73.3) RIGHT: **In 1931, Francis made this preliminary design for an auxiliary cruising yawl that he hoped would be small enough to be affordable. She is 30 feet, 9 inches long on deck; 24 feet, 2 inches on the waterline; with a beam of 7 feet, 9 inches; and a draft of 4 feet, 6 inches. Sail area is 432 square feet. Power is a 12-horsepower Red Wing. There are three pipe berths in the cabin. The design was not published and drew no customer, but she would have been a fast and handy boat. At about the same time, Francis drew a preliminary plan for a similar boat with a slightly shorter, shoaler hull, and a sloop rig with a little more sail area. Nor did that design attract attention.** (© Mystic Seaport Museum, Daniel S. Gregory Ships Plans Library, SP38.104.1)

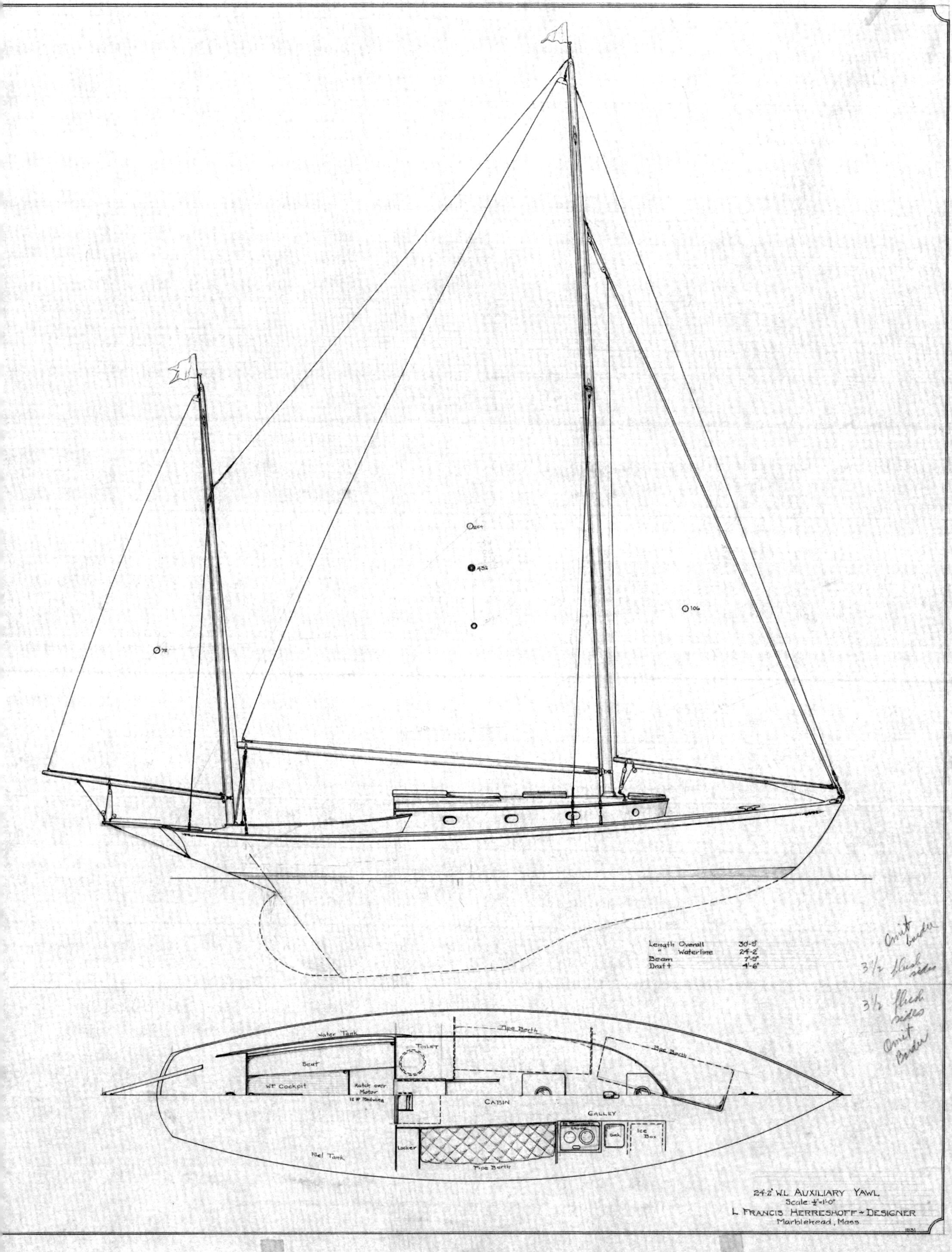

Length Overall 30'-9"
" Waterline 24'-2"
Beam 7'-9"
Draft 4'-6"
Water Tank
Pipe Berth
Toilet
Seat
W.T. Cockpit
Hatch over Motor
12 HP Redwing
Cabin
Galley
Stove
Sink
Ice Box
Locker
Fuel Tank
Pipe Berth
24'-2" W.L. Auxiliary Yawl
Scale: ½"=1'-0"
L. Francis Herreshoff ~ Designer
Marblehead, Mass.
1931

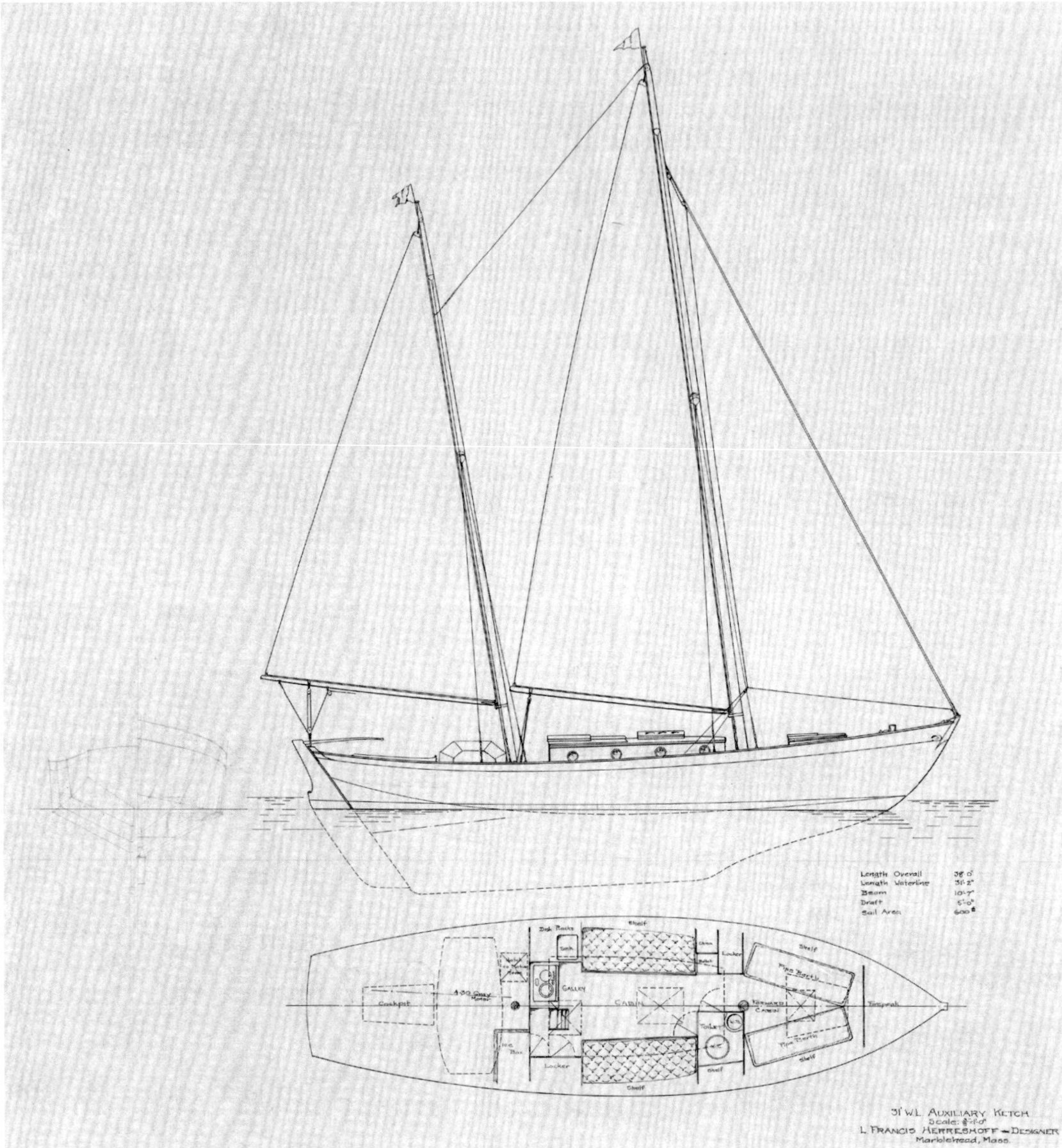

attributes for any boat, racer or cruiser. Francis wrote, "A double-ender cannot be made wide and have her steer well when she is heeled." The *Duclinea* is much narrower than other earlier, small, double-ended cruisers, such as John Hanna's Tahiti, William Atkin's *Eric* of 1925 (the design of Sir Robin Knox-Johnson's *Suhaili,* in which he was first to sail around the world, non-stop and unaided—and, incidentally winning the 1968 Golden Globe race), or Phil Rhodes's *Caribe* of 1926. Francis's design would be handier and faster than those wider boats and would be every bit as seaworthy, but, as Hanna's comment had indicated, she would suffer, in the judgment of many cruising sailors, for sailing well heeled over in a breeze and for being comparatively cramped in the cabin.[7]

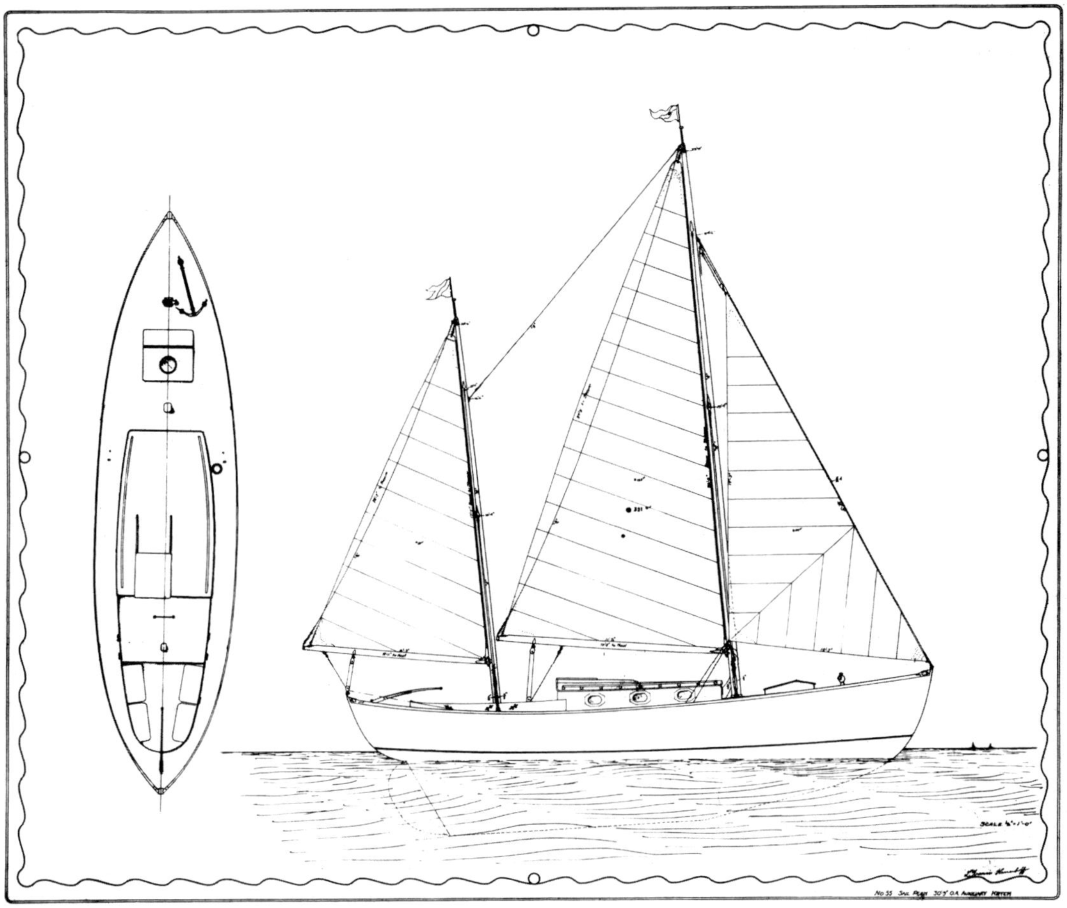

LEFT: **Another preliminary cruising design of 1931 was this 38-foot ketch. It is the only hard-chine, vee-bottom sailing boat that Francis ever drew. He must have chosen a hull type that he considered inferior in hopes that her cheaper construction would enable building with scarce Depression dollars. It was a vain hope. The line of the hard chine starts at the top of the boot top at the bow, descends to just below the waterline amidships, and then rises sharply to end halfway up the transom. Waterline length is 31 feet, 2 inches; beam, 10 feet, 7 inches; and draft, 5 feet. Sail area is 600 square feet. Power is a four-cylinder, 30-horsepower Gray. The well-raked ketch rig has a relatively small mainsail and big mizzen. The four-berth cabin arrangement is unusually normal for Francis. This is an early example of his suggesting a way of carrying a dinghy on deck by stowing it athwartships, an obstacle that, in this case, could perhaps be overcome by hanging on to the mizzen after shroud while performing the hurdle.** (© Mystic Seaport Museum, Daniel S. Gregory Ships Plans Library, SP38.106.1) ABOVE: **The sail plan and outboard profile drawing and deck plan of the *Dulcinea*, Francis's design No. 55, for Larry Johnson. Her snug rig could be easily handled by a small crew—even a singlehander. She could profit from a masthead balloon jib, set flying, in light weather. Note that her shrouds align exactly with her masts, without fore-and-aft spread and that there are no backstays. Sail area is only 321 square feet, with 143 square feet in the mainsail, 81 in the mizzen, and 97 in the jib. She would balance well under jib and mizzen and would stand some real breeze under that rig, and she would also balance well under mainsail alone. The anchor on the bow is either the 30-pounder or the 40, both of which Francis suggested she carry.** (© Mystic Seaport Museum, Daniel S. Gregory Ships Plans Library, SP38.92.14.)

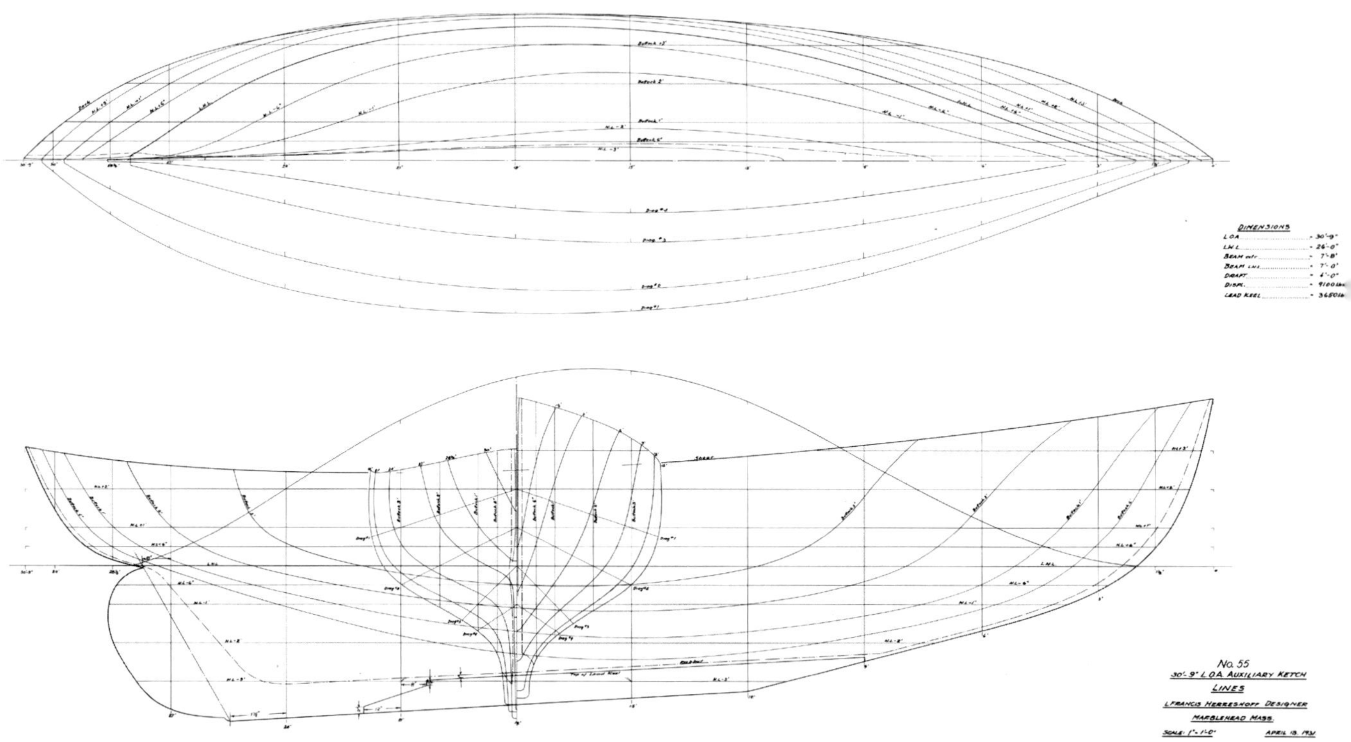

ABOVE **The *Dulcinea*'s lines. She would ship little water. Note the flair in the sections high on the bow to throw the top of a steep head sea out, rather than merely up. She would be corky, but her displacement of 9,100 pounds is enough so that her motion would be easy. She carries 3,650 pounds of lead on the keel, for a ballast-displacement ratio of 40 percent. Length on deck is 30 feet, 9 inches; length on the waterline, 26 feet; beam 7 feet, 8 inches; and draft, 4 feet. Francis dated the inked drawing April 13, 1931.** (© Mystic Seaport Museum, Daniel S. Gregory Ships Plans Library, SP38.92.1.) RIGHT: **The construction and cabin plans of the *Dulcinea*. Francis has used his numbering system to call out twenty-nine parts of the vessel; he has listed twenty-three dimensions for her scantlings. In the upper left, the builder can find the number and size of every bolt needed. Francis suggested as power plant a Gray four-cylinder engine, delivering 30 horsepower. The propeller shaft is off-center to port. Abreast the engine are a pair of 23-gallon tanks, one for gas and one for water. The versatile cockpit has four hinged seats. The head looks claustrophobic, but when its door is fully open it can shut off the whole forward half of the boat from the cabin. Though Francis shows four pipe berths, there is no doubt that, for a cruise of much length, four would be too much of a crowd on board. Headroom is 5 feet; most owners of Dulcineas modified the design to get more. Although Francis sent these three drawings off to be published in the February 1932 issue of *Yachting*, no sailor was tempted to build to them until 1946.** (© Mystic Seaport Museum, Daniel S. Gregory Ships Plans Library, SP 38.92.3)

BOLT LIST

	Floor Timber Bolts																	
Location, Dist. from St. 0	2'-2"	3'-1"	3'-0"	4'-9"	5'-7"	6'-5"	7'-3	8'-1"	8'-11"	9'-9"	10'-7	11'-5"	12'-3"	13'-1	13'-11"	14'-9"	15'-7"	16'-5"
Description	Drive	Thru	Thru	Thru	Thru	Thru	Thru	Thru	Thru	Thru	Thru	Thru	Thru	Thru	Thru	Thru	Thru	Thru
Dia	½"	½"	½"	½"	½"	9/16"	9/16"	9/16"	3/8"	3/8"	3/8"	3/8"	3/8"	3/8"	3/8"	3/8"	3/8"	3/8"
Length	18"	17"	16"	14"	13"	13"	12"	13"	14"	14"	13"	12"	12"	12"	12"	12"	12"	12"
No required	1	1	1	1	1	1	1	1	2	2	2	2	2	2	2	2	2	2
	Knees, Breasthooks, Deadwood etc.																	
Location, Dist. fr. St. 0	6"	3'-7	4'-5"	5'-1"	7'-7"	8'-5"	9'-4"	10'-4	23'-4"	22'-6	23'-8"	24'-1	24'-8"	25'-0"	25'-5"	28'-7	27'-0	27'-3
Description	Thru	W.Scr.	Thru	Thru	Thru	Thru	Thru	Thru	Thru	Thru	Thru	Thru	Drive	Thru	Drive	Thru	Thru	Thru
Dia	½"	#22	½"	½"	½"	½"	½"	½"	½"	½"	½"	½"	½"	½"	½"	½"	½"	½"
Length	14½"	4½"	6"	5"	6"	7"	6"	5"	12"	12"	6"	18"	15"	13"	12"	14"	11"	6½"
No required	1	1	1	1	1	1	1	1	1	1	1	1	1	1	1	1	1	1

	Floor Timber Bolts															Rudder		Fastenings	
Location, Dist. from St. 0	17'-0"	17'-10"	18'-8"	19'-6"	20'-4"	21'-2"	22'-0"	22'-10"	23'-8"	24'-6"	25'-4"	26'-2"	27'-0"	28'-8"	29'-6"			Plank	Deck
Description	Thru	Thru	Thru	Thru	Thru	Thru	Thru	Thru	Thru	Thru	Thru	Drive	Drive	Thru	Drive	Drive	B.Scr.	W. Scr.	W. Scr.
Dia	3/8"	3/8"	3/8"	9/16"	9/16"	9/16"	9/16"	9/16"	9/16"	9/16"	3/8"	½"	½"	½"	½"	3/8"	#26	#14	#14
Length	12"	12"	12"	16"	23"	18"	27"	27"	26"	27"	3"	21"	13"	12"	12"	17"	7½"	1¼"	1¼"
No required	2	2	2	1	1	1	1	1	1	1	2	1	1	1	1	5	7		
		Lead Keel Bolts																Mast Partner	
Location, Dist. fr. St. 0	30'-3	9'-3	10'-0	10'-9	11'-7"	12'-5	13'-3	14'-1"	14'-11"	15'-9	16'-8"	17'-7"	18'-5"	19'-3"	20'-1"	20'-11"	21'-9"	Main & Mizzen	
Description	Thru	W.Scr.	Thru	Thru	Thru	Thru	Thru	Thru	Thru	Thru	Thru	Thru	Thru	Thru	Thru	Thru	Thru	Thru	
Dia	½"	#20	½"	½"	½"	5/8"	5/8"	5/8"	5/8"	5/8"	5/8"	5/8"	5/8"	5/8"	½"	½"	½"	½"	
Length	8"	3"	9"	7½"	10"	11"	11"	11"	11"	8"	11"	11"	11"	8"	11"	8"	8"	23"	
No required	1	2	1	1	1	1	1	1	1	1	1	1	1	1	1	1	1	4"	

1	¼" Bronze Stem Band	17	Partition Builtup Panels
2	Bowchocks Cast Bronze	18	Sands Plate F-1080
3	2'-7"x 2'-4" Hatch Mahog	19	Galley with No 211 Shipmate Range
4	Piano Hinges, Canvass under		14"x18"x10" Sink (Sands Pl. 1448)
5	9" Dia Fixed Light		and Dish Racks
6	Mast collars	20	6'-3 x 24 Shaped Pipe Berth
7	4"x7" Port Lights	21	Transom Locker Lids in top
8	3'-6" Ash Tiller, Swinging Fitting	22	Fore Peak Bulkhead
9	Hatch Doors Hinged	23	Fresh Water Tank 23 gals. 15"d. 30" long
10	Stairs 12" wide. 7½" off ℄ to Port	24	15" O.D. 1.67 I.D. Copper Tubing brazed to Copper Plate
11	Gray 4-30 Engine	25	⅝" Cockpit Floor Lifting in Sections
12	2"x2"x¼" Angle Bar Engine Bearer	26	Hinged Seats ⅝" Mahogany
13	W.T. Bulkhead	27	Gasolene Tank. 23 gals. 15"d. 30" long
14	Cabin Bulkhead 17" high	28	Chainplates - Main 2⅝"x¼"x24", Mizzen 2"x¼"x21" Tobin Br.
15	4'-5"x1'-9" Settee	29	Windlass - E.J. Willis Fig B-728 #1
16	6'-3 x 24" Shaped Pipe Berth		

SCANTLINGS

Frame Spacing .... 10"
Keel W. Oak moulded .... 2¼"
Stem W. Oak sided 3⅛" moulded 4⅜"
Frames W. Oak at Head 1⅛" square, max. 1½" square
Length of Taper 4'-6"
Floor Timber W. Oak .... 1¼" and 9" high
Planking Mahog .... ⅞"
Clamps Pine .... 1⅜" square
Deck Beams moulded .... 1⅞" and 1⅜" at Ends
Sided regular .... 1⅛"
" at masts .... 1⁷⁄₁₆"
" heavy .... 1⅞"
Deck Planking Canvas Covered .... 13/16"
Planksheer Mahog. wide .... 3"
Cabin Trunk Sides Mahog .... ¾"
Coaming Mahog .... ⅝"
Cabin Floor Hatches as needed .... ⅝"
Cabin Floor Beams moulded .... 1⅝" sided ¾"
Rudder Stock Tob. Bronze .... 1½" Dia
3 Hanging Knees W. Oak .... 9"x9"x1¼"
Cabin Deck Canvassed .... ¾"
Cabin Deck Beams W. Oak .... 1½" moulded and ⅞" sided
Horn Timber W. Oak sided .... 3⅛"

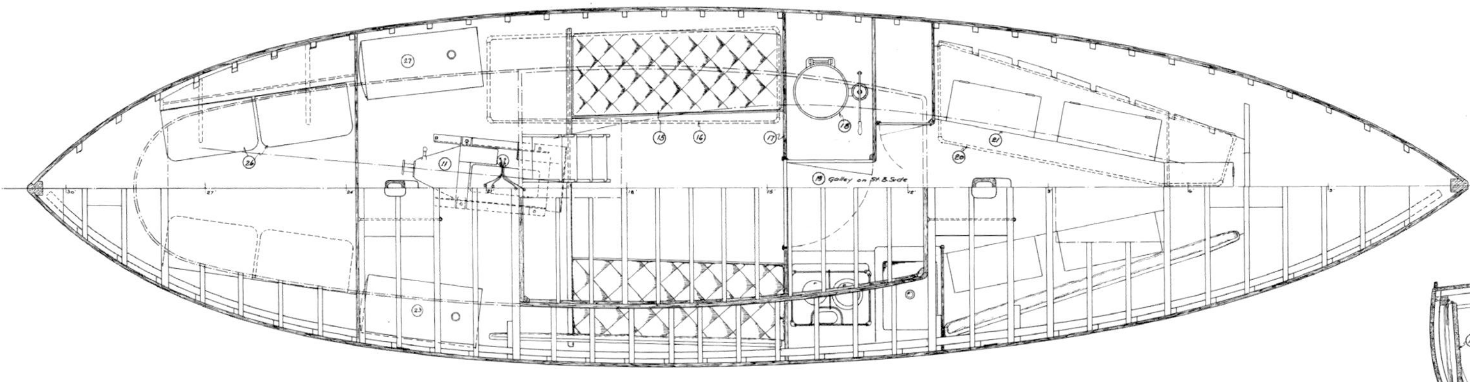

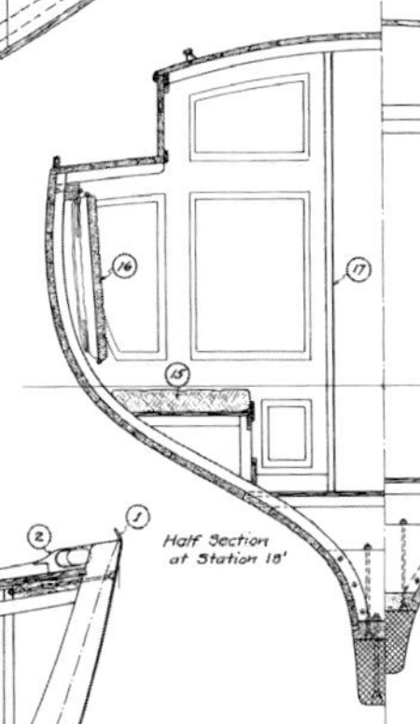

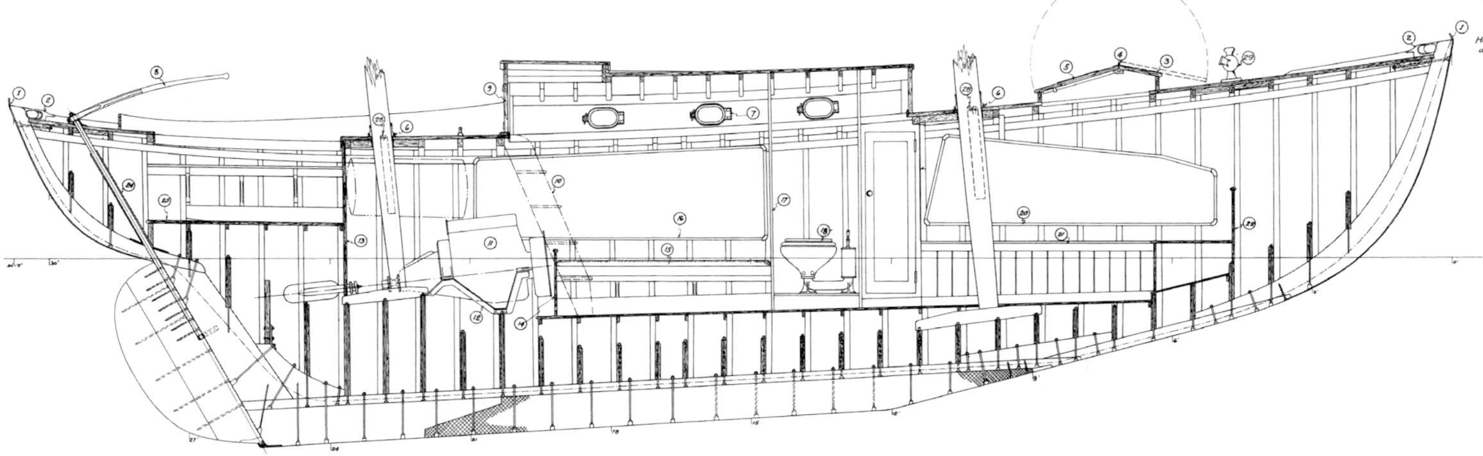

No. 55

30'-9" L.O.A. AUXILIARY KETCH

CONSTRUCTION PLAN

L. FRANCIS HERRESHOFF, DESIGNER

MARBLEHEAD, MASS.

SCALE: 1"=1'-0" MAY 15 1930

Eventually, several boats were built to design No. 55; the first, for Howard W. Ahern of Brooklyn, at Hodgdon Brothers in East Boothbay, Maine, did not go down the ways until 1946. Allan H. Vaitses, a commonsensical builder whom Francis had come to respect, built a No. 55 at his yard in Mattapoisett, on Buzzards Bay, that was launched in 1958. Her owner, "Mr. [J. M.] Hitchcock," accepted Francis's *Dulcinea* for her name. In the 1960s, two of the ketches were built on Lake Lucerne in Switzerland and one in Australia.[8]

Mr. Hitchcock made friends with Allan Vaitses to the point where he was allowed to spend time in the shop as the *Dulcinea* took shape. Vaitses did keep him out of harm's way when he poured the lead keel. "The lofting went very smoothly, very few corrections with the offset table," Vaitses was able to report to Francis. Vaitses and Hitchcock puzzled over the scantlings of horn timber, stern piece and knee, and after floors. They were tempted to beef things up at the stern, but they didn't want to lose the pretty, hollow, after waterlines. "Says I to Hitchcock," Vaitses wrote to Francis, "that's the way he drew it, so let's build it like that: says Hitchcock, he must have had his reasons, so I'm not afraid if you aren't. Well, it's a strong part of the boat anyway."[9]

Vaitses continued: "Mr. Hitchcock is busy, between helping me, with rearranging the cabin plan. . . . His present preoccupation is with how much the cabin sole can be lowered and the part of the trunk over the galley [moved aft] raised to get full headroom." Mr. Hitchcock would get his doghouse and his full headroom. Francis would write later about the design: "She does not have full headroom, but it has often been said that a sailor man prefers to sit down when he eats and very much prefers to lie down when he sleeps. Almost all of the other time at sea he is either standing in the hatchway or sitting down in the cockpit or kneeling or squatting."[10]

Soon Vaitses was reporting to Francis: "We had good bending stock and got the timbers [frames] out and bent in three working days; just Mr. Hitchcock treading them in, myself clamping and toenailing, and my son tending the [steam]

ABOVE: **The *Dulcinea* full-and-by the wind in a nice breeze. Some cruising sailors might object to so much angle of heel, but that is the price to be paid for her speed-allowing narrow hull. The owner, "Mr. Hitchcock," had builder Allan Vaitses raise her freeboard two inches and give her a doghouse, sacrificing good looks for headroom. She was launched in 1958.** (*The Rudder* (December 1959): 73) RIGHT: **Francis drew this bigger version of the *Dulcinea*, his design No. 65, also for Larry Johnson. Like the *Dulcinea*, she has a snug ketch rig. Total sail area is 546 square feet. The mainsail has but 270 square feet; jib and mizzen are each 138 square feet. This drawing is dated May 1935.** (© Mystic Seaport Museum, Daniel S. Gregory Ships Plans Library, SP38.117)

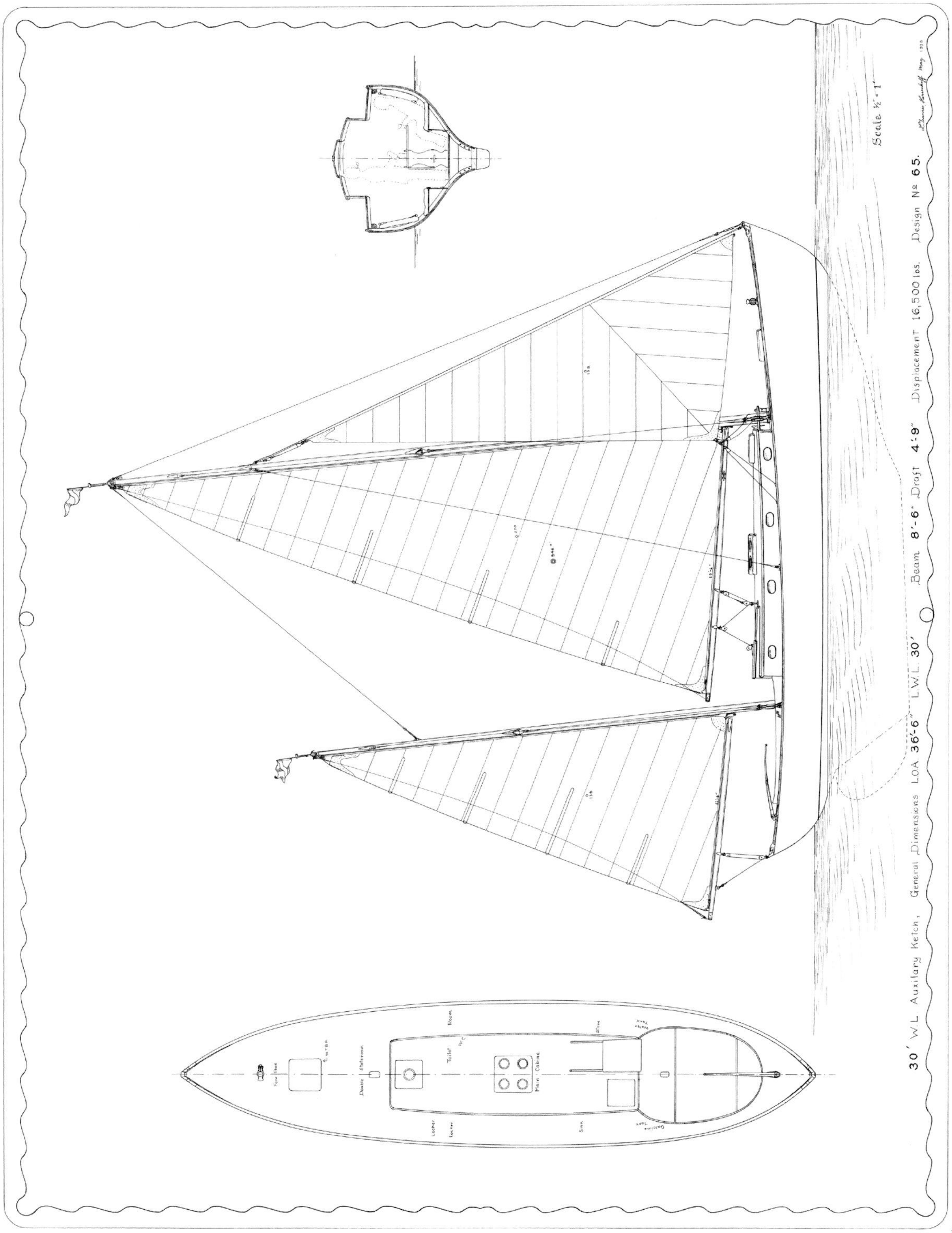
30' W L Auxiliary Ketch, General Dimensions LOA 36'-6" L.W.L. 30' Beam 8'-6" Draft 4'9" Displacement 16,500 lbs. Design № 65.
Scale ½" = 1'

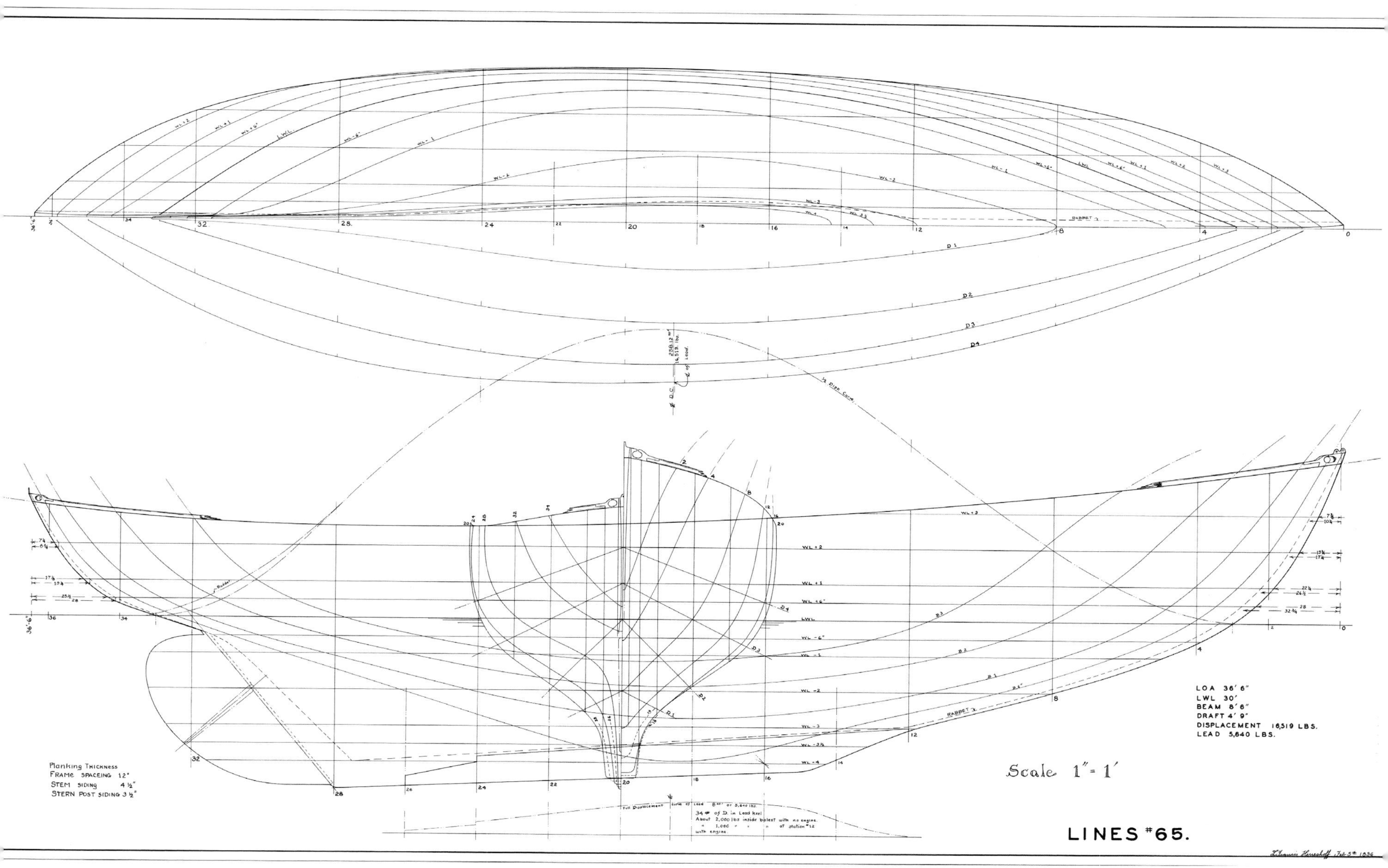
Planking Thickness
Frame spaceing 12"
Stem siding 4 ½"
Stern post siding 3 ½"
LOA 36' 6"
LWL 30'
BEAM 8' 6"
DRAFT 4' 9"
DISPLACEMENT 16,519 LBS.
LEAD 5,840 LBS.
Scale 1" = 1'
LINES #65.

tank and running them in. . . . We are very enthusiastic about her looks, set up in the shop; there is something very petite and/or dainty about her."[11]

As the *Dulcinea* was nearing completion in May 1958, Vaitses wrote Francis: "As for the ketch, I think we have an excellent hull; but I must say that after reaching the sheer we are way adrift from the plan in the size and shape of the house, layout of the cockpit, etc. . . . but Mr. H. is having a wonderful time arranging this and that. . . . The arrangement now is: galley aft, two settees with pipe berths that make seat backs when they are not upper berths amidships, and the head forward. If you are wondering what happened to the tanks, we squeezed the gas tank under the cockpit floor, which is non self bailing and has been lowered; and the water tank has gone way forward of the head, there being an ice box (loaded through the bridge deck) taking up the space where one tank was. Well, now I hope you won't be . . . dismayed: probably you gave up long ago; but Mr. H. says he is not as salty as the guy must have been for whom the boat was designed, and he wants his comfort." Vaitses needn't have worried about Francis's reaction to all this. When Mr. H. had started with his changes, Francis had written to Vaitses: "I think Mr. Hitchcock is very wise to take some time and trouble to work out a cabin to suit himself for I am rather cracked on believing that no cabin plan is best for all ages, families, and sexes."[12]

Besides "ages, families, and sexes," Francis might have included temperaments. He himself couldn't understand why anyone would want to give up for very long the comforts of the hearth for the limited quarters of a boat—he wouldn't and didn't—so he did little to make his cabins other than simple and never thought of cabin space as a factor that ought to affect design. Phil Bolger, a designer who was no creator of sumptuous boat cabins himself, wrote: "L. Francis Herreshoff was the worst designer of cabins ever to make a mark designing boats, but he was a great philosopher; his chapter on cabin arrangements [emphasizing simplicity] is one of the best in the only great book on boat design [*The Common Sense of Yacht Design*]."[13]

The *Dulcinea*, with all her changes, none of which were to the hull and rig, was turned over to her owner on August 6. Hitchcock and Vaitses tried her out that day. Her builder reported to Francis: "Your little thirty foot nine inch double ender is the sweetest sailing cruiser I have ever seen. She is easy, fast, dry, beautifully balanced, sure footed, and responsive; I am crazy about this model, and could rave on about her indefinitely. She is the kind of sailer that makes one want to tear the motor out by the roots and throw it overboard. . . . I wish you could have seen us sail this boat under mainsail up a narrow, winding creek against a South West breeze right up to a dock. . . . She is an uncanny sailer!" And, Vaitses reported, he and Mr. Hitchcock had reached across a fine sou'wester from off Wing's Neck to the mouth of the Weweantic River, a distance of two and a quarter miles, in just over 17 minutes. This run computes to a little under 8 knots, which would be about 1.5 times the square root of her sailing waterline length. Vaitses wrote, "I have always

---

LEFT: **The lines of No. 65. She and the *Dulcinea* are fine examples of the canoe yawl that had been popularized by Albert Strange and others in England, even though Francis gave his boats ketch rigs. Length on deck is 36 feet, 6 inches; waterline, 30 feet; beam, 8 feet, 6 inches; draft 4 feet, 9 inches. Displacement is 16,519 pounds, with 5,640 pounds of lead on the keel, for a ballast-displacement ratio of 34 percent. Except for a penciled construction plan, Francis did not proceed beyond these two drawings, this one being dated February 3, 1935.** (© Mystic Seaport Museum, Daniel S. Gregory Ships Plans Library, SP38.117.1)

thought that this design No. 55 was the saltiest and jauntiest craft if its size I have ever seen; and it was gratifying to find that her performance matches her looks."[14]

Francis never sailed the *Dulcinea* himself, but, on September 20, 1958, he was able to get on board and inspect her. He wrote to Vaitses: "I was much more than pleased, and surprised, at the fine job she is, and I particularly admired all of the small fittings that are carried out in just the right proportions. Below deck I am sure she is the most complete and best fitted out boat of her size that I have ever seen. I believe Mr. Hitchcock is very much pleased with her, and I shouldn't be surprised if she were one of the best sea boats of her size anywhere in the world." Tweed and Marie Josie Hunter wrote a letter published in *The Rudder*'s "Mail Buoy" for February 1962, stating that they had cruised in their Dulcinea, the *Denet Chee*, 5,000 miles between Cape Cod and Florida, "in often heavy going and can report that this boat will never be strained."[15]

The *Dulcinea* cost Mr. Hitchcock $12,000. Allan Vaitses bought the boat's plans from Francis for $25.00. Apparently, the owner paid the designer no commission. In subsequent years, Francis sold four sets of plans for No. 55 for a total of $153. It was almost as if the Great Depression carried on into the 1950s and '60s. In any event, Francis had to wait a long time to gain the satisfaction of having a builder he respected exude over his design of 1930, build a good boat to it, try her out, and exude some more.[16]

As of this writing, the *Dulcinea* is in the capable hands of Alex Brainard at his Artisan Boatshop, Rockport, Maine, awaiting a new owner willing and able to restore her.[17]

Dr. Daniel Brayton Sr.'s *Deva* on a reach, with a masthead Genoa jib adding to her modest ketch rig. She was built to Francis's design No. 65 by Bradford Story at Essex, Massachusetts, in 1985 to celebrate the design's fiftieth anniversary, and was finished by her owner and put in commission in 1987. (Alison Langley photo, courtesy *WoodenBoat*)

Francis designed his second double-ended ketch, a four-foot-longer version of the *Dulcinea,* his design No. 65 in 1935, also for Larry Johnson, but he never did get to see her built. Even before Francis could ink her construction plan, Johnson backed out. Although he commissioned Francis's creation of two outstanding cruising boat designs, Johnson never held the tiller of either one.

Another possible customer showed interest in No. 65, and Francis got a construction bid from the Quincy Adams yard. Nothing came of it. The sail plan drawing of No. 65, published in the March 1947 issue of *The Rudder* as part of Francis's chapter, "Choosing A Cruiser," in his "The Common Sense of Yacht Design" series, drew an inquiry. Francis offered to sell the sail plan, lines, and offsets to J. H. Peacock in North Hollywood, California, for $25, assuring him that any good builder could work out construction and rigging details. This offer led nowhere. By that time, Francis was too busy designing and writing for *The Rudder* to work out the details of an old design himself.[18]

In 1984, twelve years after Francis died, Dr. Daniel Brayton Sr., a Marblehead dentist and sailor, decided to build a No. 65. He and Muriel Vaughn, Francis's former secretary, made the surprising discovery that Francis had drawn a construction plan in pencil. Brayton would name his boat the *Deva,* Sanskrit for deity. For a builder, he went to Brad Story, the seventh generation in the family to run the Story Shipyard in Essex, Massachusetts. The Storys started the yard in 1813 at the head of navigation on the Essex River; Essex, in its heyday, was home to fifteen shipyards that launched 4,000 major wooden vessels.[19]

Brayton had known and admired L. Francis Herreshoff. He determined that in building Herreshoff's forgotten design No. 65, the boat would be constructed in accordance with Francis's philosophy of simplicity and economy. And as a dentist, with his quest for perfection in fine work and the dexterity to come close to perfection, he would set a high standard and would do as much work on the vessel himself as his time would permit.[20]

Story would build the hull, deck, cockpit, and cabin house, and would install bulkheads. His estimate for this was $23,250. Initially, there would be no engine and no cabin furniture. Brayton would make and install all the trim for the deck, cockpit, and house, build the spars, and make patterns for all the fittings. Francis had trained him in patternmaking; turnbuckles, chainplates, and bow chocks would come from Francis's designs.[21]

Story poured the *Deva's* lead keel on October 4, 1984. Dr. Brayton provided much of the lead, collected over years of retiring patients' protective shields from x-rays. Brayton insisted that Story fasten the yellow pine garboard planks (all the planking was recycled from a demolished building) directly to the lead keel, eliminating a wood keelson, as Francis preferred. Story completed his work in six months. By July 1987, Brayton, working part time, had the *Deva* ready to sail.[22]

After a season, Brayton installed a Westerbeke 21A diesel engine with Francis's usual off-center propeller. And he gradually built into the boat a galley, bunks, and lockers. There was no cabin plan for No. 65, but Francis had designed his third double-ended cruising ketch in 1937, the *Diddikai,* design No. 74, and Brayton based his below-deck arrangement on her four-bunk cabin plan.[23]

Brayton rigged his boat as a sloop, rather than the ketch that Francis had designed. He thought that a sloop would be handier than a ketch for short-handed sailing with wind-vane steering. But his son, Dan Jr., would write: "In 1997 the captain and crew of *Deva* decided that her designer had been right in designing her as a ketch in the first place, and that we would convert the rig back to the original sail plan. On a squally 1,500-mile sail from Norfolk to the Virgin Islands in November 1996, a greater variety of optional sail configurations than the sloop would allow, as well as shorter booms when sailing in heavy seas, had become desirable. We agreed that Skipper [as his close friends called him] had had good reasons for putting a relatively short rig on a narrow cruising boat of shallow draft, and that our having altered his design was likely to have karmic consequences that we no longer wanted to risk. We were also just plain curious about how she would perform as a ketch."[24]

Brayton observed that the ketch was not quite as close-winded as the sloop. With either rig, Brayton wrote of her: "I could not think of any boat of that size that would be more seaworthy than *Deva*.[25]

Brayton loved the boat and sailed her for many years. On the trip south with three on board, one of them, Arthur Brendze, who had been good friends with Skipper for the last four years of his life, said that it seemed as if Francis himself was with them as a fourth hand, for Brendze knew that Francis had sailed many miles in this boat in his imagination. As for Dan Brayton, he believes that Skipper Herreshoff's presence was always on board the *Deva*. The ketch is still sailing, now owned by Carl Cramer, former publisher of *WoodenBoat* magazine.[26]

The third of Francis's double-ended ketch designs during the Depression was No. 74, drawn in 1937 for a Mr. Schaeffer, in Honolulu. This customer, like Larry Johnson, retreated from having her built. But in 1942, Boris Lauer-Leonardi, who had just joined the editorial staff of *The Rudder*, began courting L. Francis Herreshoff as a contributor to the magazine. Boris already had a casual acquaintanceship with Mr. Herreshoff, and on a visit in April, Francis gave him the plans of No. 74 to publish. The design was spread over two and a half pages in the June issue, with the construction and cabin plan, turned sideways, taking up a full page, and Boris's write-up of the design, "really what you dictated," as he wrote to Mr. Herreshoff, going into detail. The headline read: "Double-Ended Deep Sea Ketch Designed by L. Francis Herreshoff for Honolulu Yachtsman."[27]

When sailors dream of getting a boat, the fantasy often includes putting to sea on a real voyage. Words like "Deep Sea Ketch" leap off magazine pages and ensnare would-be circumnavigators. Lauer-Leonardi's headline brought a number of inquiries to Francis. Over the years, Francis sold at least fourteen sets of plans for No. 74, netting him $720; at least seven boats were built to the design around the world. No. 74 was more popular than either Nos. 55 or 65. Nor was the

RIGHT: **The outboard profile and sail plan of Francis's design No. 74 of 1937. Like the two double-ended cruising ketches that Francis drew for Larry Johnson, this third one, for G. E. Schaeffer, of Honolulu, was just a dream ship, until other sailors built to her plans. Between 1946 and 1972, at least seven No. 74s were built. One of these was *Diddikai*, written up in *The Rudder*. Of fourteen recorded sales of these plans, netting Francis a total of $720, only one set was used to build a boat. Schaeffer had asked for a boat designed to sail among the Hawaiian Islands, often in boisterous ocean conditions. Accordingly, Francis gave her only 510 square feet of sail, 36 square feet less than No. 65, though her displacement, at 17,843 pounds, is 1,324 pounds more than No. 65. Besides her working sails, Francis shows a main trysail, smaller than the double-reefed mainsail; a small jib; and a masthead, overlapping jib. Surprisingly, Francis shows eyes in the upper ends of the standing rigging, rather than his tangs, perhaps aiming for simplicity of repair in remote cruising grounds.**

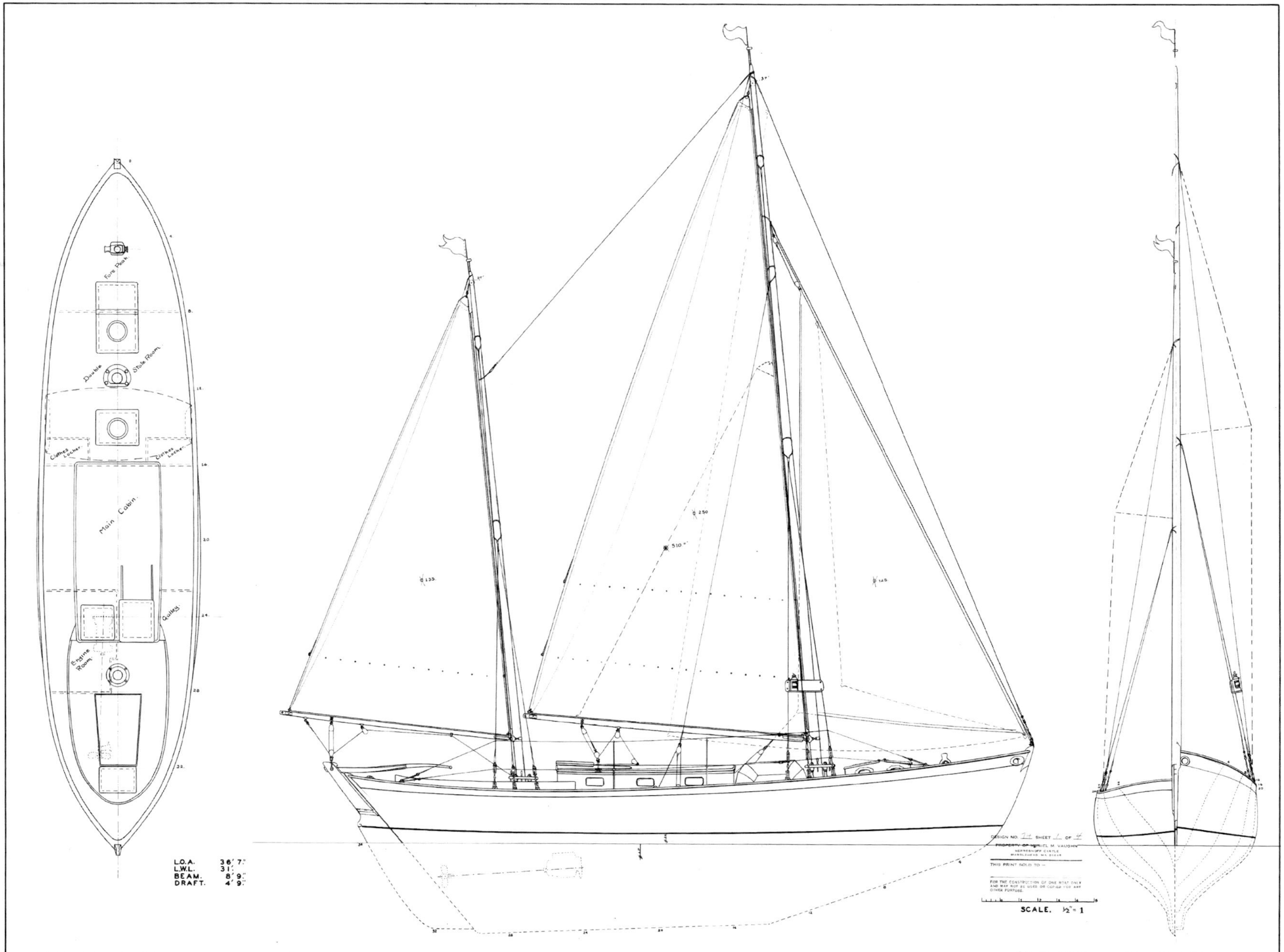
Fore Peak
Double Stale Room
Clothes Locker
Clothes Locker
Main Cabin
Galley
Engine Room
L.O.A. 36' 7"
L.W.L. 31'
BEAM. 8' 9"
DRAFT. 4' 9"
DESIGN NO. 74 SHEET 1 OF 4
PROPERTY OF MURIEL M. VAUGHN
HERRESHOFF CASTLE
MARBLEHEAD, MA. 01945
THIS PRINT SOLD TO —
FOR THE CONSTRUCTION OF ONE BOAT ONLY AND MAY NOT BE USED OR COPIED FOR ANY OTHER PURPOSE.
SCALE. ½" = 1
DESIGN NO 74.
L. Francis Herreshoff March 1938

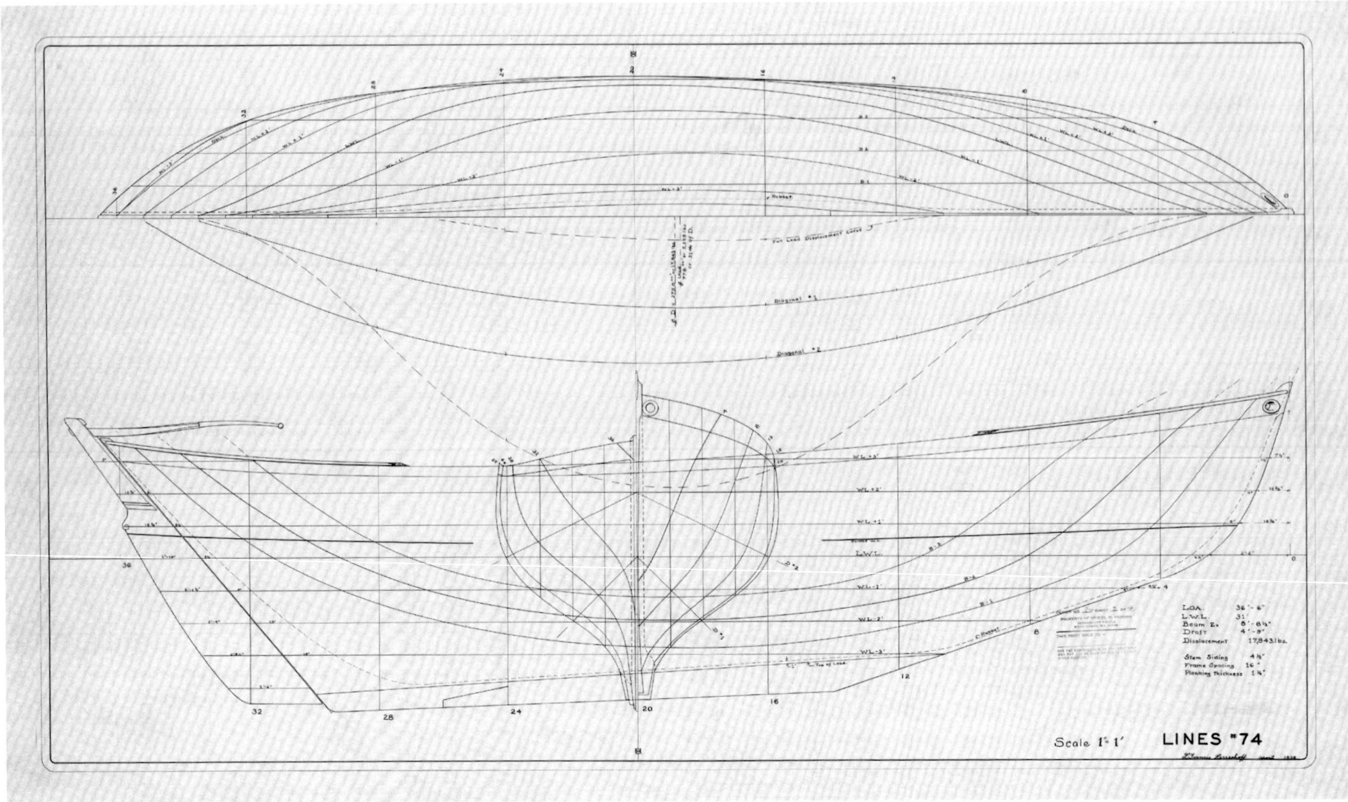

ABOVE: **The lines of No. 74. Compared to No. 65, she is an inch longer on deck, a foot longer on the waterline—mostly due to her straight sternpost for the outboard rudder—and 3 inches wider, with the same draft. A subtle difference is that her beam is carried well out into her ends, giving her a slightly wall-sided appearance. As a result, she doesn't have quite the grace of No. 65. Instead, she has a more purposeful look, the purpose being added stability in her shoulders and quarters. Freeboard is almost identical for both boats. No. 74 is 36 feet, 7 inches long on deck; 31 feet on the waterline; with a beam of 8 feet, 9 inches; and a draft of 4 feet, 9 inches. She has 5,508 pounds of outside lead ballast, for a ballast-to-displacement ratio of 31 percent, a bit lower than that of No. 65, and hence having a slightly easier motion in rough water.** (© Mystic Seaport Museum, Daniel S. Gregory Ships Plans Library, SP38.94.1) RIGHT: **No. 74's construction, cabin, and deck plans. At the left, Francis lists seventy-nine items corresponding to their numbered locations on the drawing. He specified an oak keel, 12 inches wide by 3½ inches thick, to take the garboard planks, rather than use his system of fastening the garboards directly to the lead ballast keel; planking is 1¼-inch mahogany on 1¾-by-1¾-inch white oak frames, fastened with 3½-inch, No. 18 Everdur bronze screws; shelf is 2-inch-by-2-inch fir; clamp, 1-inch-by-3-inch fir. There are two 2¼-by-2¼-inch "strong beams" to give the deck extra strength in way of the mast partners. The deck thickness is 1 inch if canvassed, 1¼ inch if not. The engine room bulkhead is ⅞-inch plywood, and the engine is a Gray Sea Scout turning a two-bladed Hyde feathering propeller. The pipe berths in the main cabin are to measure 6 feet, 4 inches by 2 feet, 3 inches. Francis wrote of the cabin arrangement: "Way forward is a forepeak for storing nautical supplies. Next a double stateroom. Then there are two clothes lockers, one opens into the double stateroom and the other into the main cabin. Then comes an enclosed engine room on one side; opposite side is the galley." When Boris Lauer-Leonardi, associate editor of *The Rudder,* wrote up the design in the June 1942 issue, he confronted a situation that Francis dodged: the boat's lack of a head. Lauer-Leonardi wrote: "Toilet has been omitted for various reasons, among which are: waste of space, hull openings below waterline, odor apt to develop in the tropics. If toilet is desired, it can be placed either in the forepeak, or portside forward of the engine."** (© Mystic Seaport Museum, Daniel S. Gregory Ships Plans Library, SP38.94.2)

①	Stem, White Oak, natural crook, Total siding full length 4½".
②	Stern post the same as ①.
③	Planking 1¼" Mahogany.
④	Floor Timbers 1½" white Oak.
⑤	All Frames 1¾" x 1¾" white Oak.
⑥	Deck Beams Oak 2¼" x 1½", Crown 3½" in 9'
⑦	Strong " " 2¼" x 2¼" " " "
⑧	Deck 1" if Canvased, 1¼" if Colked.
⑨	House Sides 1¼" thick Mahogany or Teak.
⑩	Hard wood ½" x 3"
⑪	House Beam Clamp Oak 1" x 3".
⑫	House Beams Oak 1¾" x 1⅛" Crown 2½" in 5'
⑬	House Deck ¾ Soft Pine Tong & Grove, Canvased.
⑭	Gunwale 1" or 1¼" thick.
⑮	Stanchions Oak 1¾" x 2½" x 2'-6" 5 on a side.
⑯	Knightheads Oak 1½" x 12" x 3'-6".
⑰	Rail Cap Teak 1⅝" x 2¾".
⑱	Forward Section of Keel, Oak, 4" deep.
⑲	Main Keel, Oak 3½" deep-12" wide, 20'-8" long.
⑳	Stern Post Knee, Oak sided 4½".
㉑	Shelf 2" x 2" Fir.
㉒	Clamp 1" x 3" " .
㉓	Inner Stem Band Bronze 3/16" x 4½" x 2'-6".
㉔	Outer " " " 3/16" x 1½" x 16".
㉕	Hawse Pipe like Lauflin Fig G 468 - 2½".
㉖	W. C. & Co Navy Windlas Fig 574 - No O.
㉗	" " " " Outside Port Lights 4" x 7" - 4 required.
㉘	" " " " Round Frame for glass Fig 5260 - #9.
㉙	Two strips of Brass continuous hinge 1½" wide
㉚	Hard wood Pin Rail and Stanchions
㉛	All of the moldings and Deck Trim should be of the same wood as Rail Caps.
㉜	W.C. & Co Port Lights Fig 5250 - 5x9 - 3 Required.
㉝	" " " " Marine windows Fig 5258 5x12 - 6 "
㉞	Companion Slide (no sharp corners).
㉟	Hatches Hardwood (" " ").
㊱	Steam Bent Oak Coambing ¾" thick.
㊲	Coambing Fastening over tanks Oak 1" x 1".
㊳	Tiller of Locust, Ash or Oak (See description)
㊴	Rudder Oak 2" thick. (" ")
㊵	Mizzen Sheet Attachment, (" ")
㊶	Rudder Pintles & Goodgeons, (See detail)
㊷	Shaped water tank of 64 Galons capacity.
㊸	Conical Gasoline Tanks 41 Gal's each.
㊹	Water Tight Bulkhead about ¾" thick.
㊺	Built in Bearths, (See description)
㊻	Mast Step Oak 4" x 7" x 3'.
㊼	Main Mast Round, Solid 6½" dia at deck.
㊽	" Chain Plates all 1¾" x 3/16" x 30" (See description)
㊾	Mizzen " " " 1⅝" x 3/16 x 24" (" ")
㊿	Special Cast Bronze Hoisting Eyes (See detail)
51	Hoisting Sling ⅜"-6x19 Galv Cast St. (See description)
52	Special Cast Bronze Link (See detail)
53	Clothes lockers, P. & S. (See description)
54	Folding Pipe Bearths 6'-4" x 2'-3" (" ")
55	Cabin Table Hard wood, Folding.
56	Engine Room Bulkhead ⅝ laminated (See desc.)
57	The lower Part of B.H. removable.
58	Gray-"Bobtail" Sea scout.
59	1½" Exaust Pipe (See description)
60	Special Cast Bronze Stuffing Box.
61	Bilge Pump (See detail)
62	Special Bronze "one legged" Strut.
63	Hyde Feathering Propeller, 2 Blade 14" x 10".
64	Hand Hole Plate for ⑬ with 4" opening.
65	Sheet Block attachment Merriman 416 - 3½".
66	Tobin Bz. Traveler ⅝" x 3'-6".
67	B.H.B. Blocks (See Block list)
68	Mast Step Oak 3½" x 6" x 1'-10".
69	Mizzen Mast, Round Solid 5½" Dia at Deck.
70	Scuppers 1" Copper Tube flanged (See descrip.)
71	Galley Dresser. (See description
72	¼" I.D. Copper tubes draining into cockpit.
73	Richie 5" underlit Compas and Deck Plate.
74	For Back stays - P. & S. Merriman Fig 416.
75	Mast Partners - 1¾ Thick.
76	Cabine Sole or Floor ¾" thick.
77	5,500 lbs. of Lead (See description
78	Mattress, Bedding Etc. (Furnished by Owner)
79	Planking Fastenings 2½" - #18 Everdur.

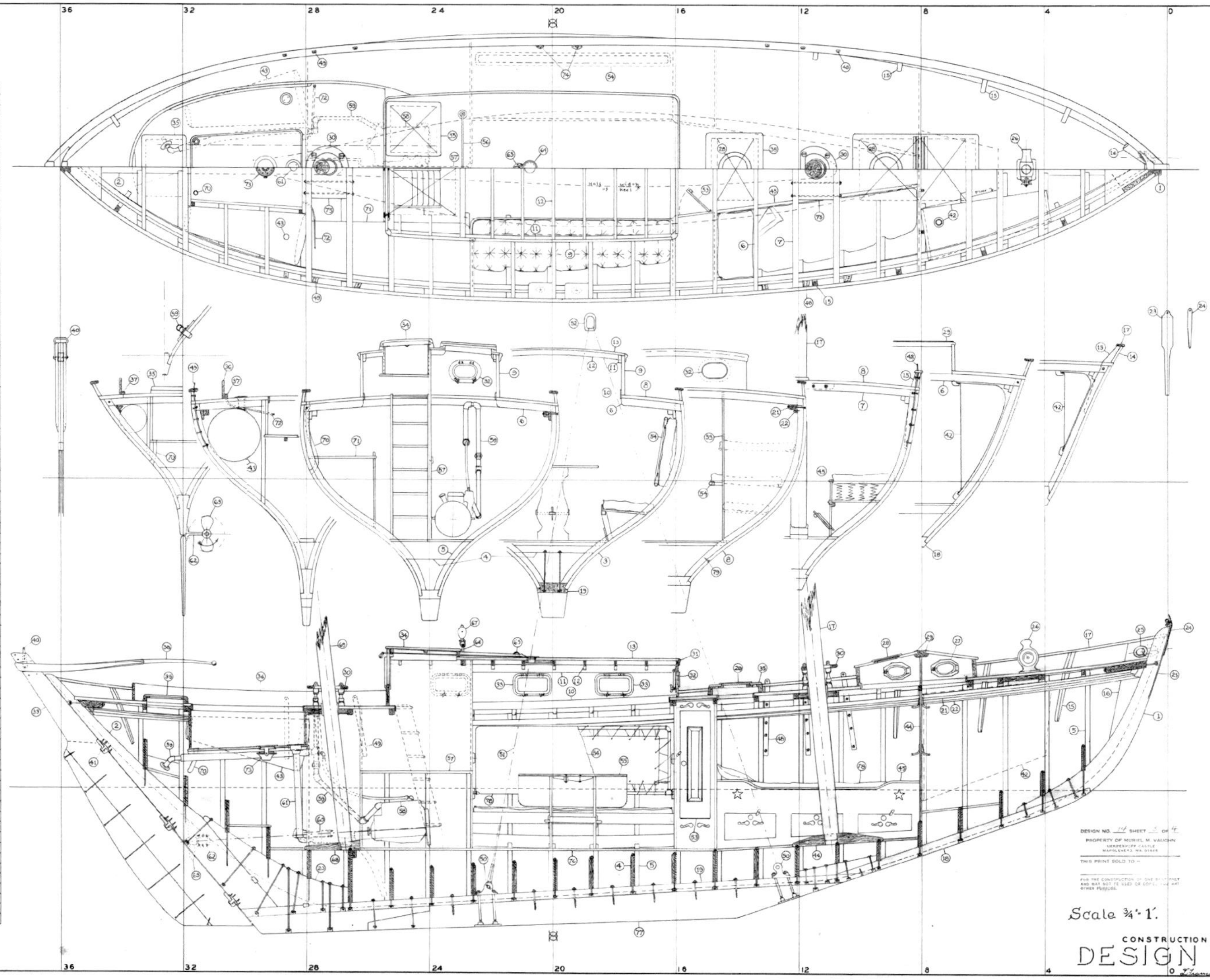

Bolt List

Station Nos.	Number Required	Diameter	Length	Type of Head
Brest Hook	1	7/16	1'-10"	N.B.E.
2'-9"	1	"	1'-8"	T
3'	1	"	9"	T
3'-9"	1	"	8"	T
4'	1	"	1'-5"	T
4'-8"	1	"	7"	T
5'-5"	1	"	1'-2"	N.B.E.
6'-9"	1	"	1'-2"	N.B.E.
8'	1	"	1'-2"	N.B.E.
9'-5"	1	"	12"	N.B.E.
9'-8"	1	"	7"	N.B.E.
10'-5"	1	"	8"	N.B.E.
10'-9"	1	"	1'-4"	N.B.E.
11'-1"	1	"	8"	N.B.E.
11'-6"	1	9/16	10"	N.B.E.
11'-9"	1	7/16	7"	N.B.E.
12'	1	"	1'-4"	N.B.E.
12'-6"	2	¾	See	㊿
13'-9"	1	7/16	1'-4"	N.B.E.
14'	1	9/16	8"	Hanger.
14'-9"	2	7/16	1'-4"	N.B.E.
15'-4"	1	9/16	8"	H.
16'	2	7/16	1'-4"	N.B.E.
16'-9"	1	9/16	8"	H.
17'-5"	2	7/16	1'-4"	N.B.E.
18'	1	9/16	8"	H.
18'-9"	2	7/16	1'-4"	N.B.E.
19'-4"	1	9/16	8"	H.
20'	2	7/16	1'-4"	N.B.E.
20'-8"	1	9/16	8"	H
21'-3"	1	7/16	1'-4"	N.B.E.
22'	2	⅝	See	㊿
22'-7"	1	7/16	1'-4"	N.B.E.
23'-9"	1	9/16	8"	H
24'	1	7/16	1'-4"	N.B.E.
24'-7"	1	9/16	1'-1"	H.
25'-4"	1	7/16	1'-4"	N.B.E.
25'-10"	1	9/16	1'	N.B.E.
26'-7"	1	7/16	2'-1"	N.B.E.
26'-10"	1	7/16	10"	N.B.E.
27'-3"	1	9/16	1'-7"	N.B.E.
27'-6"	1	7/16	1'	N.B.E.
28'	1	7/16	1'-9"	Drive
28'-3"	1	7/16	1'-5"	N.B.E.
28'-7"	1	9/16	2'-2"	N.B.E.
28'-10"	1	7/16	2'	N.B.E.
29'-3"	1	7/16	1'-9"	Drive.
29'-9"	1	7/16	1'-8"	N.B.E.
30'-8"	1	7/16	2'	Drive
31'-2"	1	"	1'-2"	N.B.E.
32'	1	"	1'-6"	Drive.
33'-4"	1	"	1'-6"	Drive.
Brest Hook	1	"	1'-2"	N.B.E.

DESIGN NO. 74 SHEET 3 OF 4

PROPERTY OF MURIEL M. VAUGHN
HERRESHOFF CASTLE
MARBLEHEAD, MA 01945

THIS PRINT SOLD TO –

FOR THE CONSTRUCTION OF ONE BOAT ONLY AND MAY NOT BE USED OR COPIED FOR ANY OTHER PURPOSE.

Scale ¾" - 1'.

CONSTRUCTION PLAN

DESIGN NO 74

L. Francis Herreshoff

headline mere hype. In No. 74, Francis made minor changes from No. 65, all of them for the purpose of increasing seaworthiness and ease of handling, for Schaeffer's fantasy was to make ocean passages, albeit short ones, among the Hawaiian Islands.

In a marginal note in his copy of Douglas Phillips-Birt's *An Eye For a Yacht*, Francis wrote: "The author does not know why a double ender is the best sea boat, but the fact is that if one end has more bulk than the other the smaller end will be shoved under in a seaway." Francis may have been remembering, as an example of this principle, Uffa Fox's description, in his first book, *Sailing, Seamanship, and Yacht Construction,* of what happened to the *Typhoon,* in which he was crewing, crossing the Atlantic from England. The ketch, designed by William Atkin—a designer Francis respected—had far more bulk in the stern than in the bow. Running before it in a gale, a big following sea lifted her stern high and she buried her bow. She corkscrewed and was rolled down so far that the coal stove landed on the cabin overhead. That the vessel and her crew survived and completed the voyage attests to her sound construction and their resilience. Francis's point was that a double-ender would be far less prone to such trouble. Francis wrote of his design No. 74, "she was designed to be an extremely good sea boat."[28]

Yet the first two boats built to No. 74 were not double-enders. In the summer of 1945, Richard S. Flaherty of Oakland, California, bought a set of plans for No. 74 from Francis for $50, plus $2.50 shipping. He inquired whether it would be all right for his friend to use the plans to build a second boat, and Francis agreed. A week later, Flaherty, realizing he was preying on Francis's generosity, said he'd get the friend to pay Francis $25, or whatever Francis "required." Again, Francis agreed and wrote, "in fact you are a real gentleman to protect me on this and not just turn the drawings over to someone else as sometimes happens."[29]

In sixteen months, a builder named Gottfriedson had finished the first No. 74, and apparently this one, named the *Genie,* went to the friend. In another sixteen months, Gottfriedson had finished a second No. 74 for Flaherty. He named her the *Natoma.* On both these boats, Flaherty made the same changes to the design: he extended the cabin house forward, giving up deck space for stowing the tender to gain headroom below, and made a number of small changes in the cabin and cockpit. And, instead of Francis's pointed stern, he gave these boats a high, narrow transom, three feet across at the rail, to gain deck space aft. He did not consult Francis about any of this, but simply sent him photographs of the finished vessels.[30]

Had he been consulted by Richard Flaherty, Francis would probably have explained the advantages of the double-ender, but, being confronted with a fait accompli, he was simply encouraging: "These boats look to me to be most excellent sea boats—in fact they both look like real little ships and I cannot tell you how pleased I am with their general looks. I also think the sterns are very nice indeed and undoubtedly easier to build than the double ender, and undoubtedly just as good in all respects." In fact, Francis had, in 1942 as we will see, designed an ocean cruiser for William A. Robinson with a high, narrow transom. Such a stern did not deviate much from the principle of equal bulk at each end of the hull. And it's possible that Flaherty may have gotten his idea for a different stern for No. 74 from the design for Robinson, because Francis had published it as an illustration for his chapter on hull shapes in "The Common Sense of Yacht Design" in the April 1944 issue of *The Rudder*. Francis did report to Flaherty that, in the summer of 1947, Hodgdon Brothers in Maine built a No. 74 according to his design. This boat went up Long Island Sound to Port Washington.[31]

Flaherty wrote to Francis about the *Natoma*'s trial sail on March 27, 1948: "I must say that there wasn't a single thing to mar a perfect sail. She is fast on all points of sailing, perfectly balanced, and a real pleasure to sail."[32]

The boat that gave her name to design No. 74 was the *Diddikai*, because she was given publicity in *The Rudder.* She was built over four and a half years of spare time by an amateur builder, Wilfred C. Wild, at Cape Town, South Africa, and launched in 1956. Wild even made his own sails for the boat. The publicity was because her builder and his wife, with an additional crewman and a cat, set off on a world cruise in the *Diddikai.* They went north to the Mediterranean, then crossed to the West Indies. They liked the Caribbean so much that the cruise ended in St. Thomas, where they ran the boat as a charter vessel for a dozen years.[33]

Before leaving Cape Town, Wild had added a small deckhouse in way of the mizzenmast to protect the cockpit at sea. One observer described the structure as "simply hideous." But with this obstruction already restricting the view from the helm, he could stow the dinghy fore-and-aft atop the cabin house rather than athwartships forward of it, as Francis suggested, without creating a further obstacle, thus clearing the side decks for going forward. Yet apparently the *Diddikai*'s watchkeepers didn't have to stand up at the tiller all the time to see ahead well. Francis wrote, "Mr. Wild says that across the ocean *Diddikai* steered herself much of the way." And he claimed: "The most remarkable thing about this design is that it is self steering in anything but hard wind and heavy weather." Francis never sailed a Diddikai, so he had to take Wild's word for the self-steering quality of the boat. And we don't know details of Wild's claim, such as whether or not he used twin poled-out jibs running in the trades or whether he sacrificed speed to achieve balance in the sail plan.

There was no mention of self-steering gear to bring the boat back on course once she yawed.[34]

What we do know is that Warren H. "Hasty" Miller Jr. designed and built an ingenious steering gear for his No. 74, the *Moonspinner.* Tweed Hunter built the hull of this Diddikai in Miami in 1964. Miller finished the construction in 1967 according to Francis's design, adding many of his own innovative details. There was a handsome cabin table whose height could be adjusted readily for dining, coffee-table level, or go all the way up against the overhead to clear the saloon. His masts were in tabernacles so they could be lowered for bridges, inspection, or maintenance.

Building on the boat's excellent balance, Hasty Miller, who was trained as an aeronautical engineer, modified her steering arrangement. Here is how he described to Francis what he had done:

The *Diddikai*, the No. 74 built by Wilfred C. Wild in Capetown, South Africa, in 1955. She is well heeled over to a fresh breeze, strapped down and slicing to windward. In this view, she is carrying two headsails. Her pram dinghy is placed athwartships, just forward of the house, as Francis showed in his outboard profile drawing. That way it doesn't obstruct the helmsman's view, but what about going forward to muzzle the jib on a dark and stormy night? (*The Rudder* (November 1956): 26)

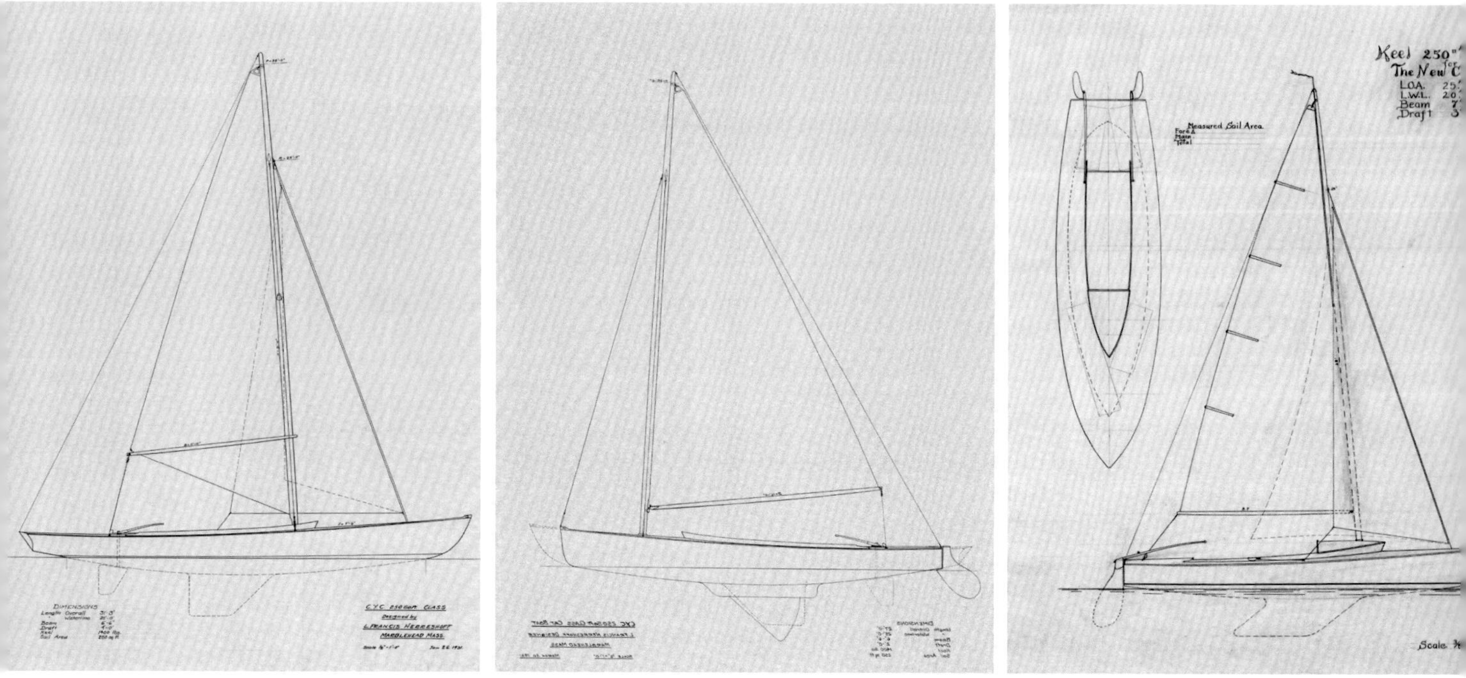

These three drawings show the diversity of hull and rig that might result from the sail-area rating rule that Francis proposed for the Corinthian Yacht Club in Marblehead in 1931. The sail area of each has been restricted to 250 square feet. The first boat is 31 feet, 3 inches long on deck; 25 feet on the waterline; with a beam of 6 feet, 6 inches; and a draft of 4 feet. Francis has made her a fin-keeler (1,400 pounds) with a separated rudder that would later be dubbed a "spade," similar to a few of his father's much earlier designs. The mainsail of her sloop rig has a high-cut foot extended by a wishbone boom, such as that being adopted by his brother, Sidney, for some of his designs at the Herreshoff Manufacturing Company. Apparently, as a nod toward those yachtsmen who liked to "cheat" a measurement rule for racing by setting unmeasured sail area, he has shown a jib whose overlapping (of the mast) area would not be included in the 250 square feet. (© Mystic Seaport Museum, Daniel S. Gregory Ships Plans Library, SP38.54.3) The second boat is a keel-centerboarder drawing only 2 feet. Although in her outboard profile and sail plan, superimposed on the hull of the first boat (dotted lines), she appears to have the same waterline length as the first boat, Francis gave her waterline as a foot longer, at 26 feet. Beam is the same, but he has shortened on-deck length to 27 feet. She has a deep, outboard rudder and the most efficient rig of all, that of the catboat. She would make a fine, fast daysailer. (© Mystic Seaport Museum, Daniel S. Gregory Ships Plans Library, SP38.55.1) The third boat is small and modern, with light displacement, a swept-back fin keel, and a small cuddy in which crew or passengers could keep out of the spray. She has twin rudders, with their tillers connected by a bar. She is only 25 feet long on deck, with a waterline of 20 feet, a beam of 7 feet, and a draft of 3 feet, 3 inches. Francis took the trouble to draw the lines and make a construction plan for the first boat, but they were of no use. The Corinthian Yacht Club wasn't buying his idea for a 250-square-foot racing class. (© Mystic Seaport Museum, Daniel S. Gregory Ships Plans Library, SP38.56.1)

[She has] that wonderful barn door of an outboard rudder. Its size is responsible largely for the maneuverability of the boat, and in tight quarters it makes a fine brake, but it forms an appreciable amount of the total lateral resistance. With the boat trimmed to sail tiller free, she makes considerably more leeway than trimmed with about three degrees of weather helm. But this three degrees, due to the rudder area, amounts to about 15 or 20 pounds at the tiller, which gets tiresome. So I struck a line from the aft face of the rudder head to the lower aft corner of the rudder, and cut off that portion of the rudder aft of the line (about six inches). I then hung a piece of ¾-inch stainless pipe in gudgeons from the rudder head down along the cut, and bolted the cut-off piece of rudder to the pipe. A six-inch lever from the top of the pipe out to port, then a turnbuckle forward to fixity on the tiller, and we have a trim tab. This has turned out in practice to be the handiest thing since paid hands were invented. You simply set the sails for optimum trim for the course, set the trim tab for neutral helm, and walk forward to enjoy the sail. With the helm free she follows wind shifts far faster than with it lashed, and with the tab set at zero, the rudder is exactly the same as before vivisection.[35]

Francis suspected that the *Moonspinner*'s heavy helm might have been caused by the big rudder trying to float up when the boat heeled, which could have been remedied by simply adding lead to the rudder, but he wrote to Miller about his trim tab, "your arrangement sounds very good, indeed."[36]

A fair number of Diddikais are still cruising. Included in this special squadron are fiberglass vessels built in the late 1980s by Parkins Marine in Fort Lauderdale, Florida. These boats were slightly modified from Francis's design No. 74, but retained all the design's superlative qualities. The Parker ketches have inches more on-deck length, beam, and draft than Francis drew, and a masthead rig. The cabin house has been extended to just forward of the mainmast, and the cabin has a double berth forward, an enclosed head, a convenient galley, and a quarter berth. The engine is under the bridge deck in way of the mizzenmast, with an on-center propeller.[37]

As he looked back on the Diddikai design late in life, Francis was pleased. He wrote, "she is a boat that could go anywhere." And, "I believe her to be the best boat I have designed for ocean cruising." Even, "I feel she is one of the best designs I ever made." Over the years, Francis gave superlative status to several of his designs in letters to sailors inquiring about them. We can take his mature judgment of his own work at face value, for he was not prone to hyperbole, unless, of course, he was disparaging the work of other designers. Francis also wrote; "It would be pretty hard for me to say which was the favorite of my designs, but sometimes I like the small boats pretty well and must tell you frankly that some of the designs by Fife, Watson, and Steers please me ever so much more than my own do."[38]

We have noted that it took Francis a long time to complete the design of the first of his double-ended cruising ketches, the *Dulcinea*, in 1930. Part of the delay was caused by Francis involving himself in an attempt to "develop a much better type of boat for cruising than we now have," as he wrote in a proposal to the Corinthian Yacht Club in Marblehead on November 6, 1930. He hoped that such development would occur if the Club adopted "a simple rule for measuring cruising boats and auxiliaries," to be used when they race and when they compare port-to-port runs. By mid-December, Francis was put on a committee of four, the others not known, to come up with such a "simple rule."[39]

After the deliberations of the committee, Francis wrote a measurement rule in which the rating was determined entirely by sail area. The rule also provided for the standard rig and propeller allowances of the day, and included penalties for excessive overhangs, low freeboard, narrow beam, lack of bulwarks, and small cabin houses. Helen Bolster needed only two pages when she typed it up on her italic typewriter. Francis proposed eight classes, with sail areas of from 250 square feet to 5,000 square feet, and he made preliminary designs for three different types of hull and rig for the 250-square-foot class, a ketch for the 1,000-square-foot class, and a cutter for the 1,500-square-foot class.[40]

Francis submitted his simple measurement rule to *Yachting* along with an expository article and

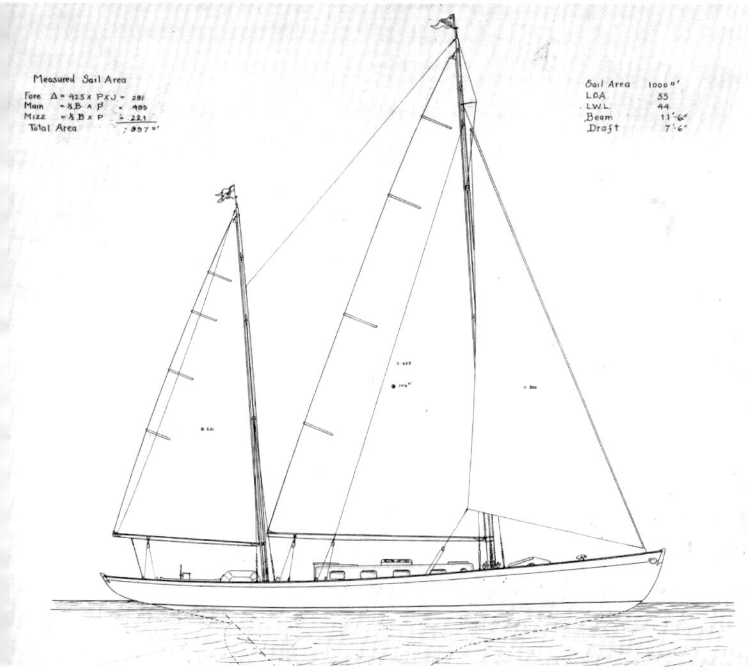

ABOVE: **The outboard profile and sail plan of Francis's design for the 1,000-square-foot class under his proposed rule for the Corinthian Yacht Club. He has given her his favorite hull form, that of the double-ender. Her stern is much more dainty than her bow, but Francis's artistry with the sheerline and curved sections results in a most harmonious hull. Her moderate ketch rig, low cabin house, and spacious deck complete the beautiful picture. The ketch's biggest sail is all inboard, where it is easiest to hand or reef. At 495 square feet, is just within the limit of 500 square feet that Uffa Fox decreed was all that could be handled by one person. This boat could make fast passages with a small crew. But it was not to be. Despite publication of her design in *Yachting*, no one wanted her built.** (© Mystic Seaport Museum, Daniel S. Gregory Ships Plans Library, SP38.154.5) RIGHT TOP: **The lines of the 1,000-square-foot-sail-area ketch. She is 55 feet long on deck; 44 feet on the waterline; with a beam of 11 feet, 6 inches; and a draft of 7 feet, 6 inches. Displacement is 30,420 pounds. With her fine, even hollow, waterlines forward and fuller ones aft, her stern would lift to a steep, following sea, but she has enough bulk and freeboard forward so that her bow would be hard to bury. She has considerable flare above the waterline, slack bilges, and deep-slung ballast; she'd have low initial stability, but it would be hard to get her rail under. And she'd have a relatively easy motion for such a deep, narrow boat.** (© Mystic Seaport Museum, Daniel S. Gregory Ships Plans Library, SP38.154.1) RIGHT BOTTOM: **The cabin and construction plan of the 1,000-square-foot-sail-area cruiser. There are three pipe berths and two fold-down berths over the transoms in the main cabin. The Scripps F-4 motor is sealed off in a separate engine room. Between the mizzenmast and the cockpit is a big sail locker with its own deck hatch. But in his critique of Francis's proposed restricted-sail-area rule in the March 1931 issue of *Yachting*, the editor, Herbert L. Stone, wrote; "For a boat 55 feet over all and 44 feet on the water, we doubt if the accommodations shown in the design are sufficient to appeal to the real cruiser who wants comfort. While more than adequate for the sail area, they are hardly what one has come to demand for the length in a real cruising boat." Perhaps for fear of being dubbed as other than a "real cruiser" by the respected editor of *Yachting*, no sailor built to this design.** (© Mystic Seaport Museum, Daniel S. Gregory Ships Plans Library, SP 38.154.3)

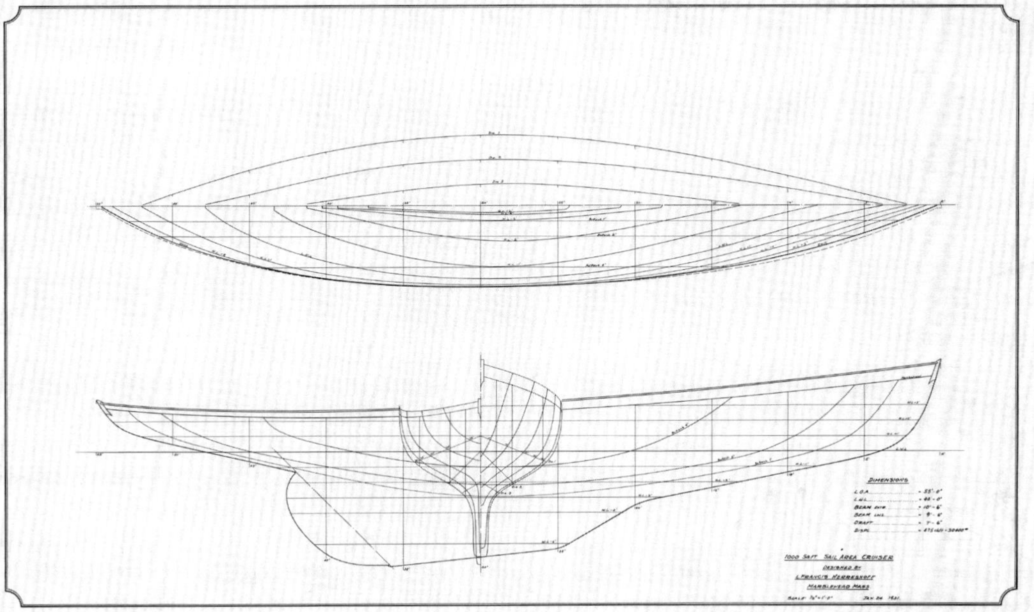
DIMENSIONS
L.O.A. = 55'-0"
L.W.L. = 44'-0"
BEAM EXT. = 10'-6"
BEAM L.W.L. = 9'-6"
DRAFT = 7'-6"
1000 SQ FT SAIL AREA CRUISER
DESIGNED BY
L FRANCIS HERRESHOFF
MARBLEHEAD MASS

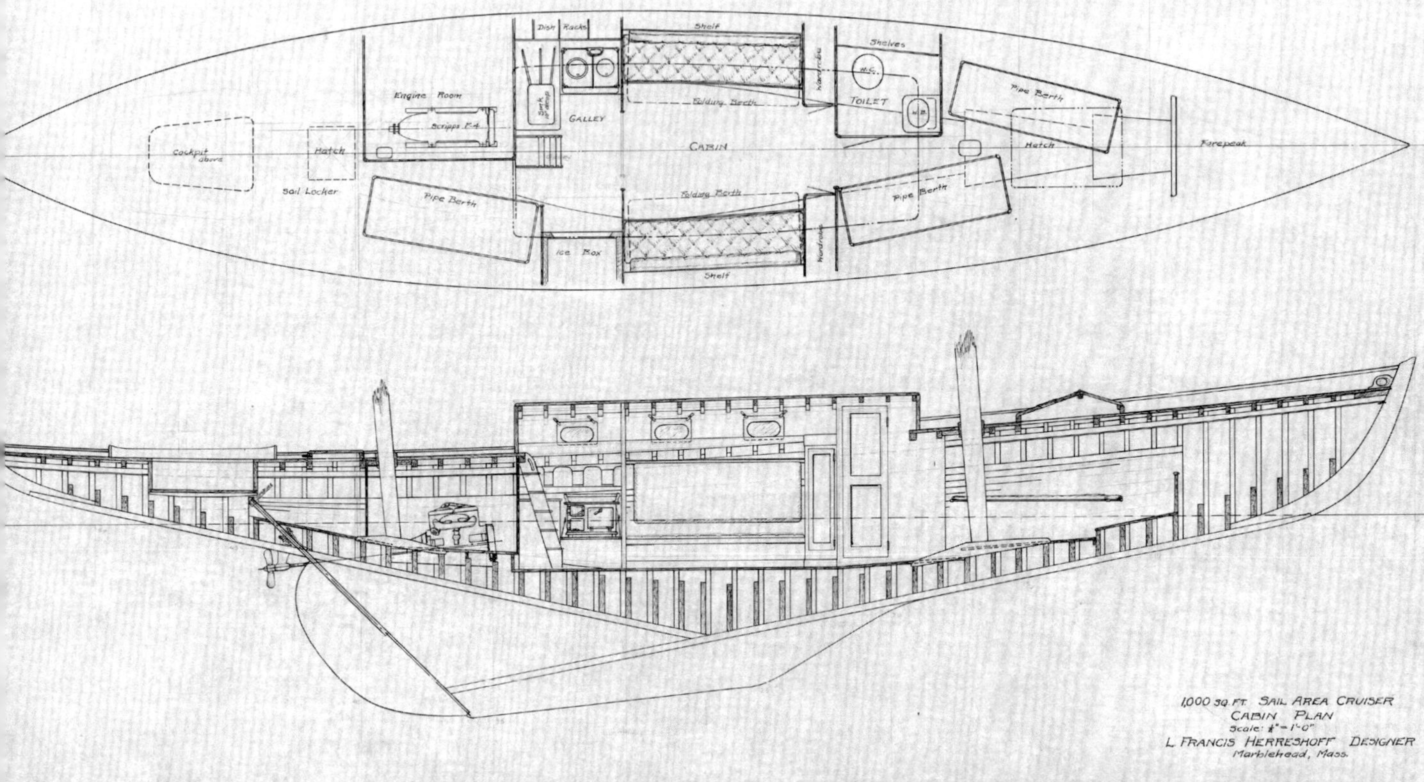
Dish Racks
Shelf
Shelves
W.C.
Engine Room
Scripps F-4
GALLEY
Folding Berth
TOILET
Pipe Berth
Cockpit above
Hatch
CABIN
Hatch
Forepeak
Sail Locker
Pipe Berth
Folding Berth
Pipe Berth
Ice Box
Shelf
1,000 SQ FT. SAIL AREA CRUISER
CABIN PLAN
Scale: ¾" = 1'-0"
L. FRANCIS HERRESHOFF DESIGNER
Marblehead, Mass.

two of his sample designs, one of the 250-square-footers and the ketch. Although the magazine's editor, Herbert L. Stone, published Francis's rule just as he wrote it, along with his two sample designs, all credited to him, he replaced most of Francis's accompanying explanation and reasoning with his own critique and ran "A Proposed Restricted Sail Area Rule" without a byline. Although Stone agreed with Francis that good boats could be developed under his proposed rule, he was afraid that the rule would fail to prevent the design of bad boats. He wrote, "Displacement is one of the factors governing speed, and its control cannot be disregarded without danger of getting unhealthy types." But Francis had exerted control over displacement by including the requirement that, to be measured under his rule, boats had to be built to the commonly accepted scantling rules, as certified by an inspector.[41]

Francis wrote to Nathanael: "This article was so much changed by Mr. Stone that it practically contained nothing that I wrote. Mr. Stone is on a committee down in New York that is developing a rule for cruising boats so that he removed all the good arguments for this simple rule which I had written up." But when Nathanael had read the article, he agreed with Stone, and he wrote to Francis that he thought his 1,000-square-foot-sail-area ketch would be too expensive and that cruising boats should have more beam.[42]

Nathanael's ideal for a cruising boat may be found in his design of the *Belisarius* of 1934. She had a yawl rig and a relatively wide, shoal, keel-and-centerboard hull. Compared to Francis's restricted-sail-area ketch, she was 1 foot, 2 inches longer on deck; 4 feet shorter on the waterline; with 2 feet, 6 inches more beam; and 1 foot, 10 inches less draft, with the centerboard up. With her yawl rig, the mainsail was all inboard, as on Francis's ketch, but had more area to handle than that of the ketch. Compared to the accommodations of the ketch, those of the *Belisarius* included a bigger cockpit, a private stateroom for her owner, Carl B. Rockwell of Bristol, and more spacious amenities in the cabin. But she would not have been able to compete with the ketch if trying to work to windward in a hard chance. Francis's ideal of the fast, extremely able, easily handled cruising boat that sacrificed cabin space and comforts in the design compromise was coming up against the reality that most cruising sailors preferred that cabin space and those comforts over optimum sailing performance. It's no wonder that L. Francis Herreshoff felt a kinship with Don Quixote.

The ketch that Francis drew as an example for his 1,000-square-foot-sail-area class is a quintessential L. Francis Herreshoff design. Harmony is the key word for this yacht, and Albert Einstein wrote that "there is no true greatness in art or science without the sense of harmony." It is probable that Francis embarked on many a vicarious voyage in this vessel. He would write of himself as "one who does most of his sailing in the sphere of imagination." In particular, he would have worked her to windward under jib and mizzen in frightful conditions of sea and wind, and he would have worked her to windward in that frustrating condition of light breeze and leftover sea. He would not have found her wanting. And, in his imagination, there would have been runs of forty miles in a four-hour watch, the ketch slicing down the seas under full sail on a broad reach, perhaps chasing sunbeams, or even flying fish.[43]

Although no 55-foot, restricted-sail-area ketch has been built, the design has had its admirers. One was M. Dale Troglin, who wrote to L. Francis Herreshoff perhaps the most effusive, heartfelt, fan letter that he ever received. Troglin wrote, "Mr. Herreshoff, I am certain you must be aware of the deep feeling of admiration and respect that many of us have for you and how much we cherish your works. . . . Have you ever considered doing an autobiography?" He added, "I can tell you sincerely that nothing gives me more pleasure than to spread out some of your drawings and let my mind become absorbed as my eyes scan the lines, unless of course, it would be to make a model from those lines." The model he chose to make was from the lines drawing of the restricted-sail-area ketch published in *Yachting,* and it "turned out to be very beautiful."[44]

On the coast of Maine, Willoughby H. Stuart Jr. had a summer place on one of Maine's many Bear Islands, this one just across the New Meadows River from Cundy's Harbor. With a good anchorage and his own marine railway, Stuart had an ideal base for the sailing he loved. He had a 36-foot Alden schooner, the *Tyehee*, but he had no particular desire to keep cruising the Maine coast, because when he picked up his home mooring he was in as pretty a spot as any. He found himself using the *Tyehee* for daysailing. By the end of the 1931 sailing season, Stuart decided to get a boat designed purely for that purpose.

Willoughby Stuart knew just what he wanted: a good-sized daysailer that would be fast, yet easily handled, with a cockpit comfortable for four people, occasionally more. And he wanted his boat to be very easy on the eyes. He took his concept to L. Francis Herreshoff.[45]

A year earlier, Francis had been working up preliminary designs for his restricted-sail-area rule, and he thought that one of his plans for a 250-square-foot boat, the one that he had given a fin keel and separated rudder with a wishbone rig, might be a good starting point. Perhaps this boat, with either a conventional keel-and-center-board or a full keel—in either case with the rudder attached to the keel—and given a normal sloop rig, would be suitable.

Francis probably approached his client warily with his suggested design. Willoughby Stuart was the only correspondent who addressed him as "Dear Herreshoff." At any rate, after considerable consultation on the details with Stuart, Francis drew the plans for a 28-foot knockabout whose hull form, aside from its appendages, was very close to that of the 250-square-foot boat. Stuart's new boat would be a little shorter and wider than the 250 and would have the slightly shorter knuckle bow that Francis favored. Her sail area would be just 250 square feet.[46]

On the plans for this design, his No. 53, Francis drew both centerboard and full-keel options, and he drew both open-cockpit and cuddy-cabin arrangements. He hoped that this design for Stuart might become popular, so he wanted to give potential owners choices. Stuart chose the center-board version with the open cockpit. He named his daysailer the *Ben-My-Chree*, darling of my heart in Gaelic, though linguists claim that a more pure form would be Be'an Mo Chroi. In any event, the boat is well named, for she was loved by the Stuart family for many years.

In 1950, Claire S. Stuart, Willoughby's widow, put the *Ben* up for sale, asking $4,750. Francis thought he might have a buyer for her, but, instead, she stayed in the family, and Stuart Pratt, a grandson, took her over. Eventually, she ended up stored in a shed at the Story Shipyard in Essex, Massachusetts.

William G. Harding was raised racing in the Herreshoff 12½-foot class out of Hospital Cove at Cataumet, on Buzzards Bay. When he grew up, he left the financial world in Boston and started a sail loft in Marion, just across the bay from Hospital Cove. He continued racing and sailing his 12½–footer. But the big fleet, nicknamed the "Doughdishes," particularly by superior skippers of the big E-Class 15-footers, was diminishing, old-age gradually eliminating boats from the starting line. In 1972, Harding decided to take action. Teaming with Edey and Duff, the boatbuilders further down the bay at Mattapoisett, he developed plans for a foam-core fiberglass sister-ship to the 12½-footers built by the Herreshoff Manufacturing Company. Thus was born the Doughdish, no longer merely a deroga-tory nickname, soon approved to race against the

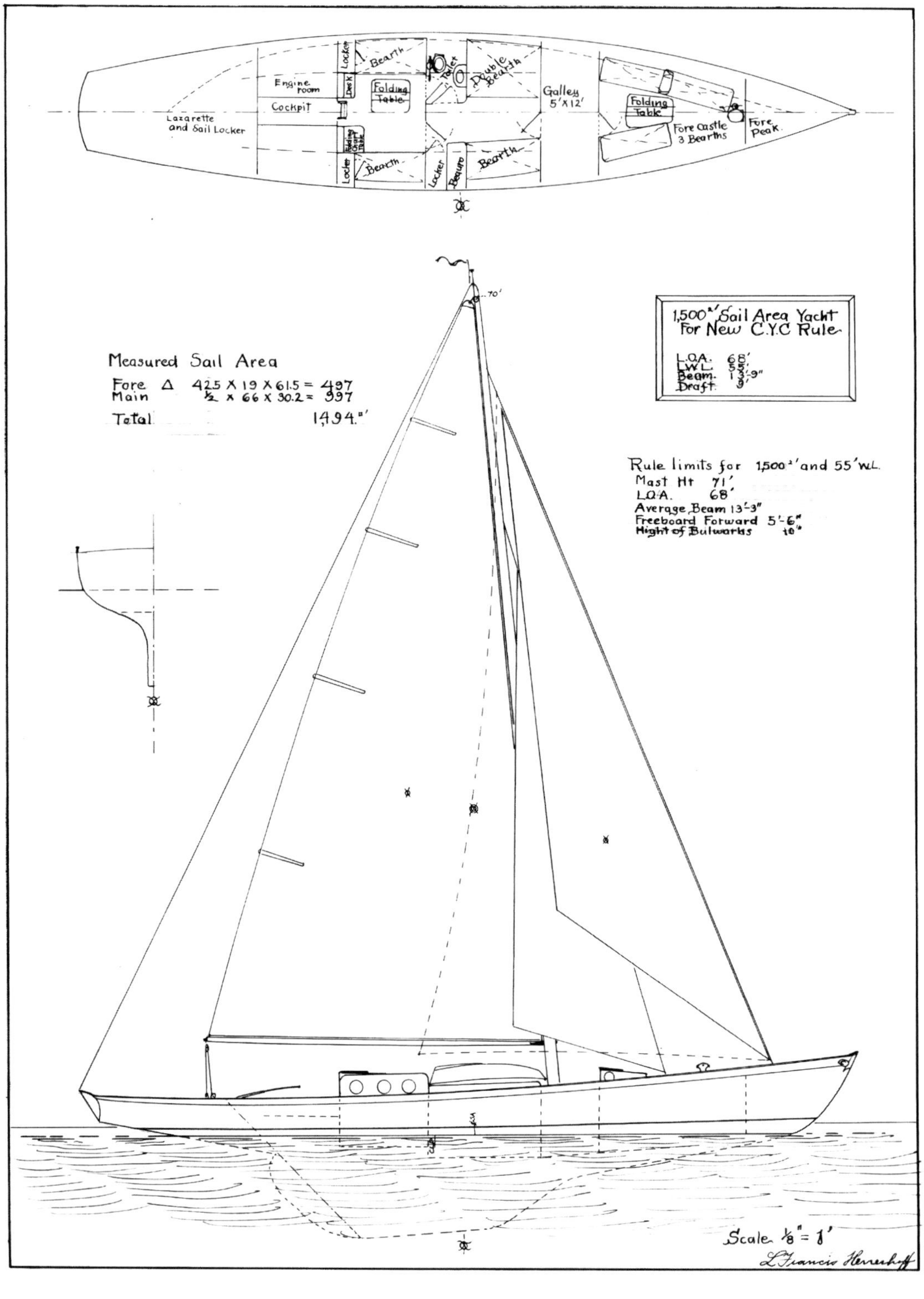
1,500□' Sail Area Yacht
For New C.Y.C Rule
L.O.A. 68'
L.W.L. 55'
Beam. 13'-9"
Draft 9'
Measured Sail Area
Fore Δ 42.5 X 19 X 61.5 = 497
Main ½ x 66 x 30.2 = 997
Total 1494.□'
Rule limits for 1,500□' and 55' W.L.
Mast Ht 71'
L.O.A. 68'
Average Beam 13'-3"
Freeboard Forward 5'-6"
Hight of Bulwarks 10"
Lazarette and Sail Locker
Engine room
Cockpit
Locker
Desk
Folding Table
Bearth
Toilet
Double Bearth
Galley 5' X 12'
Fore castle 3 Bearths
Fore Peak
Scale ⅛" = 1'
L. Francis Herreshoff

wooden boats on equal terms, and, eventually, to outnumber the entire fleet built at Bristol.

In 1984, Harding delivered one of his Doughdishes to Dana Story's yard. As he parked her trailer in a boatshed, he spied, back in the shadows, an interesting looking boat. Inspection showed him a remarkable hull that he couldn't identify, except that she looked as if she might be an L. Francis Herreshoff design. She was, of course, as Bill Harding discovered, the *Ben-My-Chree.* He thought it a shame that no one was sailing her, and got permission from Stuart Pratt to try her out. Harding wrote: "In 1986, she was commissioned and she proved, in many trials, to be exceedingly fast, comfortable, remarkably capable and fun to sail. Not being able to put aside the idea, and after discussions with Edey & Duff, we decided we wanted to reproduce the boat." Harding would call this fiberglass near-replica of the *Ben-My-Chree* the Stuart Knockabout. There are about eighty of these boats now sailing, and they are still being built, now by Stuart Knockabout LLC, Ballantine's Boatshop, at Cataumet. L. Francis Herreshoff's hope for his design No. 53 came through, but not in his lifetime. And the *Ben-My-Chree* herself is still going strong, her beauty and speed having not only saved her, but also having spawned a fleet of sisters.[47]

A friend of Francis's, Thomas Taylor, who worked in Boston and sailed from Manchester, on the North Shore, liked design No. 53 and, in 1955, wanted the full keel model with the cuddy house. In response, Francis reviewed his plans and, remembering having to add inside ballast to the *Ben*, increased the size of the lead keel slightly to bring it up to 1,950 pounds. He balked at Thomas wanting to have a toilet in the boat and informed him, through Norman Hodgdon, who was to be

LEFT: **Francis's preliminary design for a 1,500-square-foot class under his proposed Corinthian Yacht Club rule. She is 68 feet long on deck; 55 feet on the waterline; with a beam of 13 feet, 9 inches; and a draft of 9 feet. Her mainsail has an area of 997 square feet. Francis shows "bearths," as he spells the word on the drawing, for eight, including a double! This design was not submitted to Herb Stone at *Yachting*, so he had no chance to comment. This cutter would make a fine, fast cruiser.** (© Mystic Seaport Museum, Daniel S. Gregory Ships Plans Library, SP38.156.1) ABOVE: **The outboard profile and sail plan of the *Ben-My-Chree,* Francis's design No. 53, for Willoughby H. Stuart Jr. Francis shows alternate keel-and-centerboard and full-keel versions of her underbody and either an open cockpit or a cuddy cabin. Stuart chose the former in both cases. Sail area is 250 square feet. She could easily have been another example of a boat designed to Francis's proposed restricted-sail-area measurement rule. This drawing was inked by Sam Brown, who dated it January 25, 1932. The *Palmetto* was built to the full-keel design for Thomas Taylor in 1955.** (© Mystic Seaport Museum, Daniel S. Gregory Ships Plans Library, SP38.194.5)

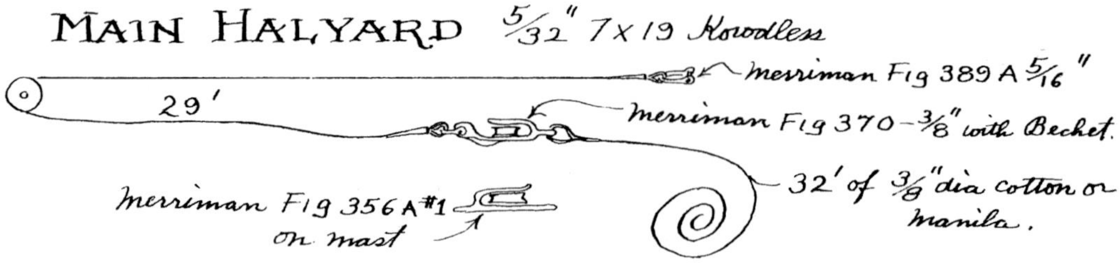

the builder at his yard in East Boothbay, Maine, of his belief that "a good cedar bucket, properly arranged, is ever so much the best in a boat of this size. It is easier to use and better all around if the person knows how to use it."[48]

The Hodgdon Brothers yard estimated that it would cost $5,200 to build the *Palmetto*, as Taylor would name his boat. She was completed in July 1956, at a cost of $6,197. For his commission, Francis rounded it off to $600 and then charged his friend only 5 percent: $300. "After you are satisfied with everything and get around to it," he wrote, "you could pay me either in installments or altogether." Francis always had a hard time taking his father's advice to be businesslike.[49]

Willoughby Stuart came back to Francis for the design of another daysailer in 1936. Stuart wanted a smaller version of the *Ben-My-Chree* for his teenage son, Harborne. The *Koala*, as the new boat was called, was Francis's design No. 70. She was 4 feet shorter than the *Ben* on the waterline; had 2 feet, 3 inches less beam, making her very narrow indeed; and had a fin keel drawing 1 foot, 1 inch more than that of the centerboarder.

Britt Brothers charged Stuart $1,413.97 for building the *Koala*. Francis's commission for designing the boat was $141.40, which Stuart paid promptly. If Francis was going to be addressed as

ABOVE: Francis's drawing of the main halyard arrangement for the *Palmetto*, taken from his Rigging List drawing, shows the ingenious, simple system for gaining purchase that he had conceived by 1955. To the bitter end of the wire, single-part halyard, he attaches an open, single block, with a long, rope tail on its becket. This bitter-end block is paired with a similar open cheek-block low down on the mast. With the sail down, the bitter-end block is far up the mast. Hoist the sail with the single part halyard, and, when it is almost up and you need more power to stretch the luff taut, the bitter-end block will be down within easy reach. Reeve the tailrope down into the cheek-block on the mast, back up into the bitter-end block, and you have a three-part tackle just where and when you need it. (Detail, © Mystic Seaport Museum, Daniel S. Gregory Ships Plans Library, SP38.194.10) RIGHT: The lines of the *Ben-My-Chree*. Underwater, she resembles a smaller Buzzards Bay E-Class boat designed by N. G. Herreshoff, but from the waterline up, she is all L. Francis Herreshoff, with her knuckle bow; short, counter stern; and delicate, curved, wineglass transom. The full-keel drawing, with the keel slightly enlarged from the original plan, was used to build the *Palmetto*. Both these boats are still sailing. Length on deck is 28 feet; waterline, 22 feet, 10 inches; and beam, 6 feet, 11 inches. The *Ben* draws 2 feet, 8 inches, board up; the *Palmetto*, 4 feet. Both boats displace 4,000 pounds. The *Ben*'s lead keel weighs 1,775 pounds; that of the *Palmetto*, 1,950.The *Ben* needed about 250 pounds of inside lead ballast to bring her down to her lines. (© Mystic Seaport Museum, Daniel S. Gregory Ships Plans Library, SP38.194.2)

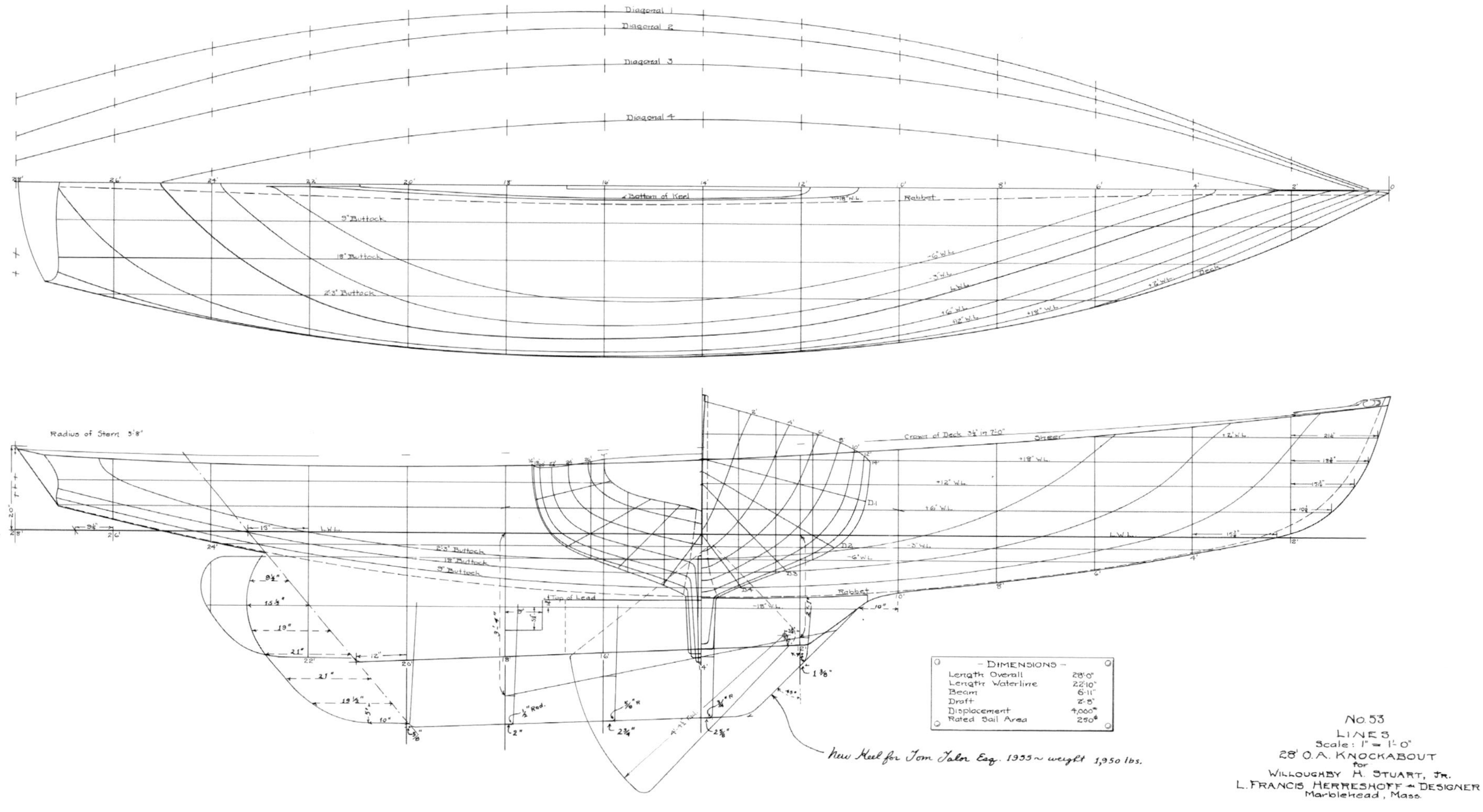
Diagonal 1
Diagonal 2
Diagonal 3
Diagonal 4
Bottom of Keel
Rabbet
9" Buttock
18" Buttock
23" Buttock
Deck
Radius of Stern 3'8"
Crown of Deck 3½" in 7'-0"
Sheer
L.W.L.
Top of Lead
- DIMENSIONS -
Length Overall 28'0"
Length Waterline 22'10"
Beam 6'11"
Draft 2'8"
Displacement 4,000#
Rated Sail Area 250#
New Keel for Tom Tolor Esq. 1955 ~ weight 1,950 lbs.
No. 53
LINES
Scale: 1" = 1'-0"
28' O.A. KNOCKABOUT
for
WILLOUGHBY H. STUART, JR.
L. FRANCIS HERRESHOFF ~ DESIGNER
Marblehead, Mass.

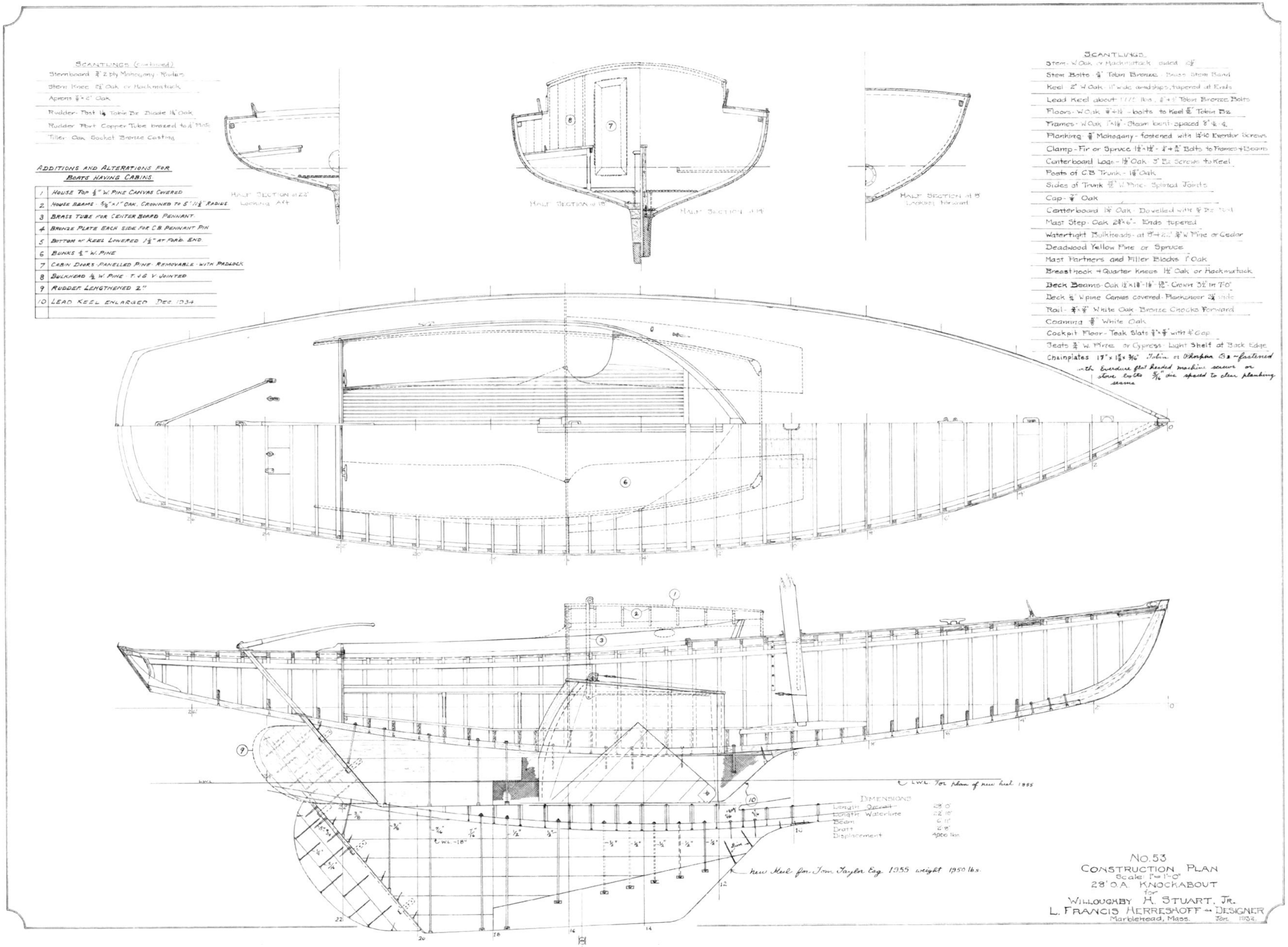
SCANTLINGS (continued)
Sternboard 3/4" 2 ply Mahogany - Radius
Stern Knee 2 1/2" Oak or Hackmatack
Aprons 7/8" x 2" Oak
Rudder - Post 1 1/4 Tobin Bz. Blade 1 1/4" Oak
Rudder Port Copper Tube brazed to 1/4" Plate
Tiller Oak Socket Bronze Casting
ADDITIONS AND ALTERATIONS FOR BOATS HAVING CABINS
1 HOUSE TOP 1/2" W. PINE CANVAS COVERED
2 HOUSE BEAMS - 5/8" x 1" OAK, CROWNED TO 5' 11 1/2" RADIUS
3 BRASS TUBE FOR CENTER BOARD PENNANT
4 BRONZE PLATE EACH SIDE FOR C.B. PENNANT PIN
5 BOTTOM OF KEEL LOWERED 1 1/2" AT FORD. END
6 BUNKS 1/2" W. PINE
7 CABIN DOORS - PANELLED PINE - REMOVABLE - WITH PADLOCK
8 BULKHEAD 1/2 W. PINE - T. & G. V. JOINTED
9 RUDDER LENGTHENED 2"
10 LEAD KEEL ENLARGED DEC. 1934
Half Section at 24' Looking Aft
Half Section at 18'
Half Section at 14'
Half Section at 8' Looking Forward
SCANTLINGS
Stem - W. Oak or Hackmatack sided 2 1/2"
Stem Bolts 3/8" Tobin Bronze - Brass Stem Band
Keel 2" W. Oak - 11" wide amidships, tapered at Ends
Lead Keel about 1775 lbs., 5/8" + 3/4" Tobin Bronze Bolts
Floors - W. Oak 7/8" + 1 1/4" - bolts to Keel 3/8" Tobin Bz.
Frames - W. Oak 1" x 1 1/8" - Steam bent - spaced 8" c. - c.
Planking 5/8" Mahogany - fastened with 1 1/4"-10 Everdur Screws
Clamp - Fir or Spruce 1 1/2" x 1 1/2" - 1/4" + 5/16" Bolts to Frames + Beams
Centerboard Logs - 1 3/4" Oak 3" Bz. Screws to Keel
Posts of C.B. Trunk - 1 3/4" Oak
Sides of Trunk 1 1/2" W. Pine - Splined Joints
Cap - 7/8" Oak
Centerboard 1 1/4" Oak - Dowelled with 3/8" Bz. Rod
Mast Step - Oak 2 3/4" x 6" - Ends tapered
Watertight Bulkheads - at 8' + 22' 3/4" W. Pine or Cedar
Deadwood Yellow Pine or Spruce
Mast Partners and Filler Blocks 1" Oak
Breasthook + Quarter Knees 1 1/2" Oak or Hackmatack
Deck Beams - Oak 1 1/4" x 1 1/8" - 1 1/8" - 1 1/2" - Crown 3 1/2" in 7'-0"
Deck 1/2" W. pine Canvas covered - Plankshear 2 3/4" wide
Rail - 7/8" x 7/8" White Oak - Bronze Chocks Forward
Coaming 5/8" White Oak
Cockpit Floor - Teak Slats 3/4" x 7/8" with 1/4" Gap
Seats 7/8" W. Pine or Cypress - Light Shelf at Back Edge
Chainplates 17" x 1 1/8" x 3/16" Tobin or Phospor Bz. - fastened with Everdure flat headed machine screws or stove bolts 5/16" dia spaced to clear planking seams
LWL For plan of new keel 1955
DIMENSIONS
Length Overall 28' 0"
Length Waterline 22' 10"
Beam 6' 11"
Draft 2' 8"
Displacement 4000 lbs.
new Keel for Tom Taylor Esq. 1955 weight 1950 lbs.
No. 53
CONSTRUCTION PLAN
Scale: 1" = 1'-0"
28' O.A. KNOCKABOUT
for
WILLOUGHBY H. STUART, JR.
L. FRANCIS HERRESHOFF - DESIGNER
Marblehead, Mass. Jan. 1932.

LEFT: The *Ben-My-Chree*'s construction plan, overlaid by a separate drawing of the *Palmetto*'s keel. The *Ben*'s rudder has been lengthened by 2 inches. On the drawing, Francis has listed all the scantlings in the upper right corner, continued upper left, and has also given the parts and scantlings for the optional cabin house at the upper left. Planking is ⅝-inch mahogany; transom, ¾-inch, two-ply mahogany. The keelson, floors, frames, stem, centerboard, centerboard trunk except the sides, mast step and partners, breasthook, deck beams, rail, coaming, aprons, rudderpost, and tiller are all white oak. The rudder is not listed, but presumably oak. The sides of the centerboard trunk, watertight bulkheads, cockpit seats, and deck are white pine, and the deck is covered with canvas. The clamp is fir or spruce, and the deadwood is yellow pine. Inked by Sam Brown in January 1932, this plan was followed carefully at Britt Brothers. The *Palmetto*'s keel was added to the drawing in 1955. (© Mystic Seaport Museum, Daniel S. Gregory Ships Plans Library, SP38.194.4) ABOVE LEFT: The *Ben-My-Chree* slicing to windward on the coast of Maine. Willoughby Stuart enjoyed many summers of such daysailing from his mooring at Bear Island, across the New Meadows River from Cundy's Harbor. On this day, he has a nice sou'wester, perfectly trimmed mainsail and jib, and two companions. (Courtesy Mrs. Charles D. Gowing, Mystic Seaport Museum, 1999-4-225) ABOVE RIGHT: William G. Harding fell in love with the *Ben-My-Chree* in 1984, and by 1986 he had arranged to use her design to reproduce, in fiberglass, a large class of daysailers that he called the Stuart Knockabout. Here he is sailing one of them past Scraggy Neck toward Buzzards Bay. A lifelong sailer, sailmaker, and the force behind the fiberglass replica class of Herreshoff 12½-footers called the Doughdish, Harding made small, intelligent changes to Francis's design in order to reduce slightly the boat's weather helm. (Author photo)

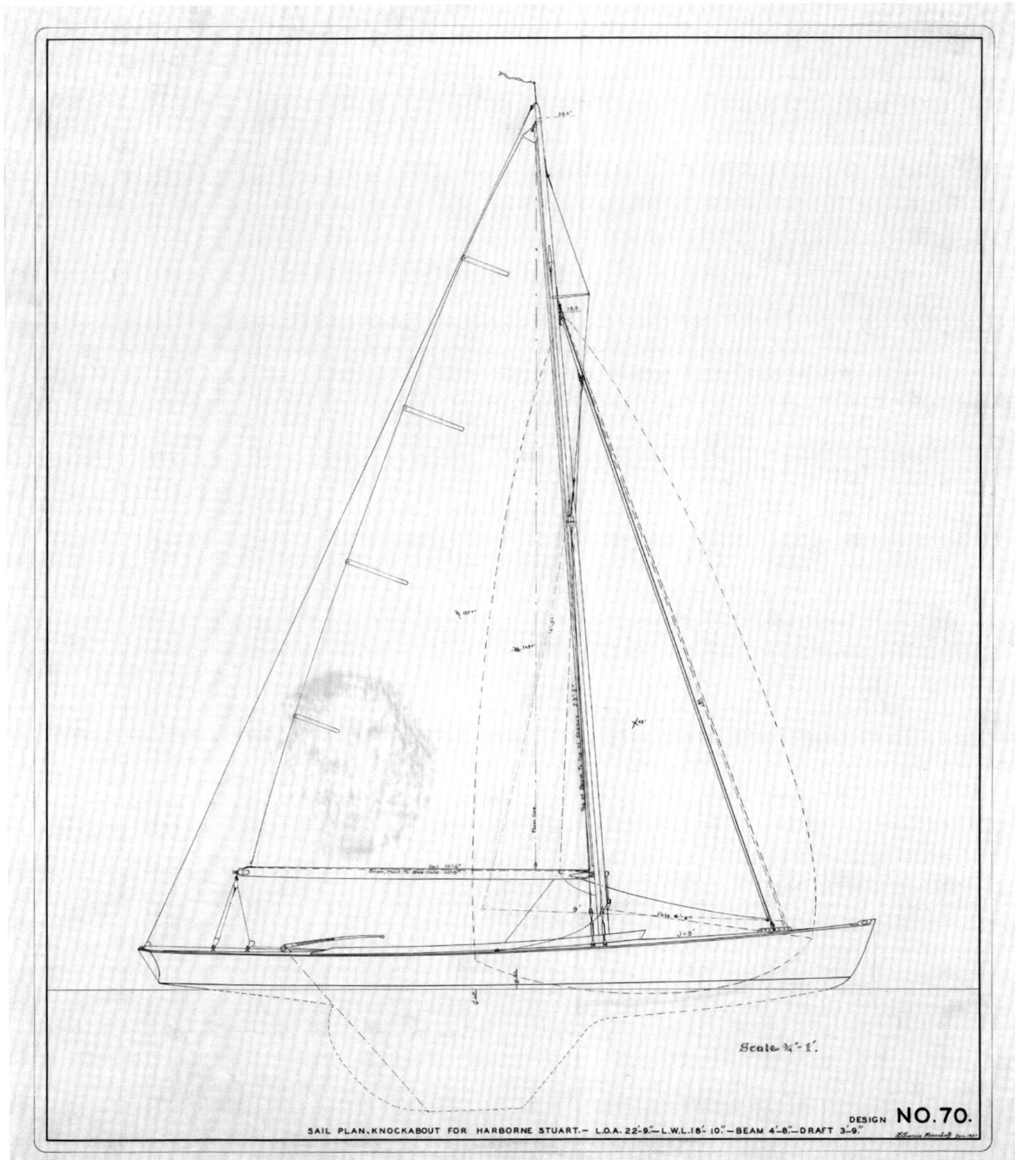

The outboard profile and sail plan of the *Koala*, a smaller, fin-keel version of the *Ben-My-Chree.* Francis designed her in 1936 for Willoughby Stuart to give to his son, Harborne, a fine present for the sixteen-year-old. Sail area is 165 square feet. Francis shows an overlapping jib and a spinnaker. Her mainsail is roller-reefing; the footrope runs in a slot in the boom, and an axle extends from the forward end of the boom through the mast to a permanently mounted crank handle, a device that must have involved a universal joint. The sails were made by the Ratsey loft at City Island. In 1956, Francis revised this plan, giving the design a taller rig with 30 square feet more sail area. (© Mystic Seaport Museum, Daniel S. Gregory Ships Plans Library, SP38.196.4)

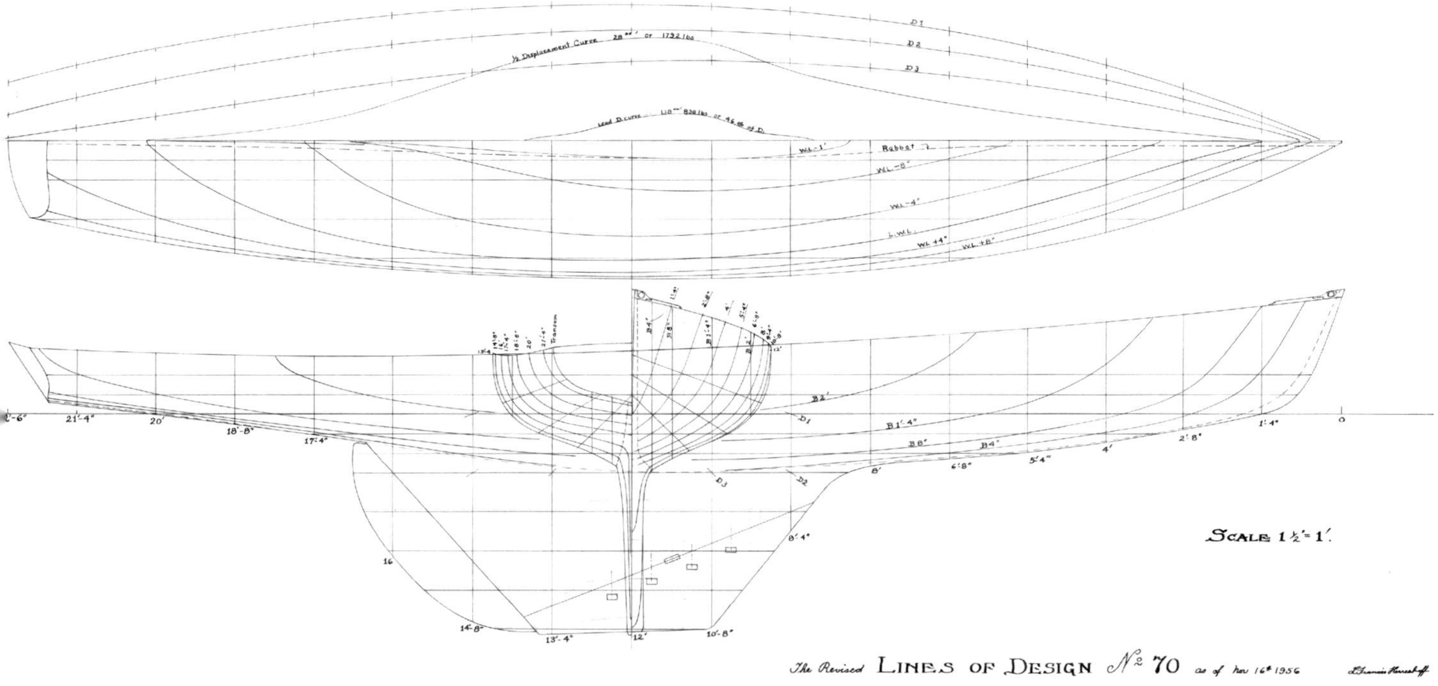

"Herreshoff," he would be businesslike. He also earned another 10 percent commission from Ratsey & Lapthorn, $5.00 or so, for giving the sail loft the order.

In the sailing season of 1937, members of the Stuart family enjoyed brushes against each other with their two Herreshoff thoroughbreds, but their designer heard nothing about how the smaller boat turned out. By June 29, he was writing to Stuart, "I should be very much interested to hear how the boat [*Koala*] floated and how she looked in general, and it would be very pleasing indeed if the little boat did have some good things about her, and it certainly would help some if I thought the special patterns that I made myself and the machine work of the fittings, etc., that I made myself and did not charge for, were appreciated a little." On July 9, Stuart replied, "I am so tired of hearing from Harborne how much better his Herreshoff hand turned bronze plates are than those on the *Ben* that I am not sure it was a good thing to do to have you make them so well."[50]

And Stuart was impressed with the *Koala*'s speed. He reported to Francis: "We have not run

---

The *Koala*'s lines. This drawing is dated November 16, 1956, twenty years after the design was made. Francis had not inked in waterlines or diagonals in his original lines drawing; his reason for revisiting the design is not known. In 1936, four years after designing the *Ben-My-Chree*, he has snubbed in the *Koala*'s knuckle bow more severely than that of the *Ben*, giving the new design a more modern look. She is 22 feet, 9 inches long on deck; 18 feet, 10 inches on the waterline; with a beam of 4 feet, 8 inches; and a draft of 3 feet, 9 inches. Displacement is 1,792 pounds, with 830 pounds of lead on the keel, for a ballast-displacement ratio of 46 percent. (© Mystic Seaport Museum, Daniel S. Gregory Ships Plans Library, SP38.196.8)

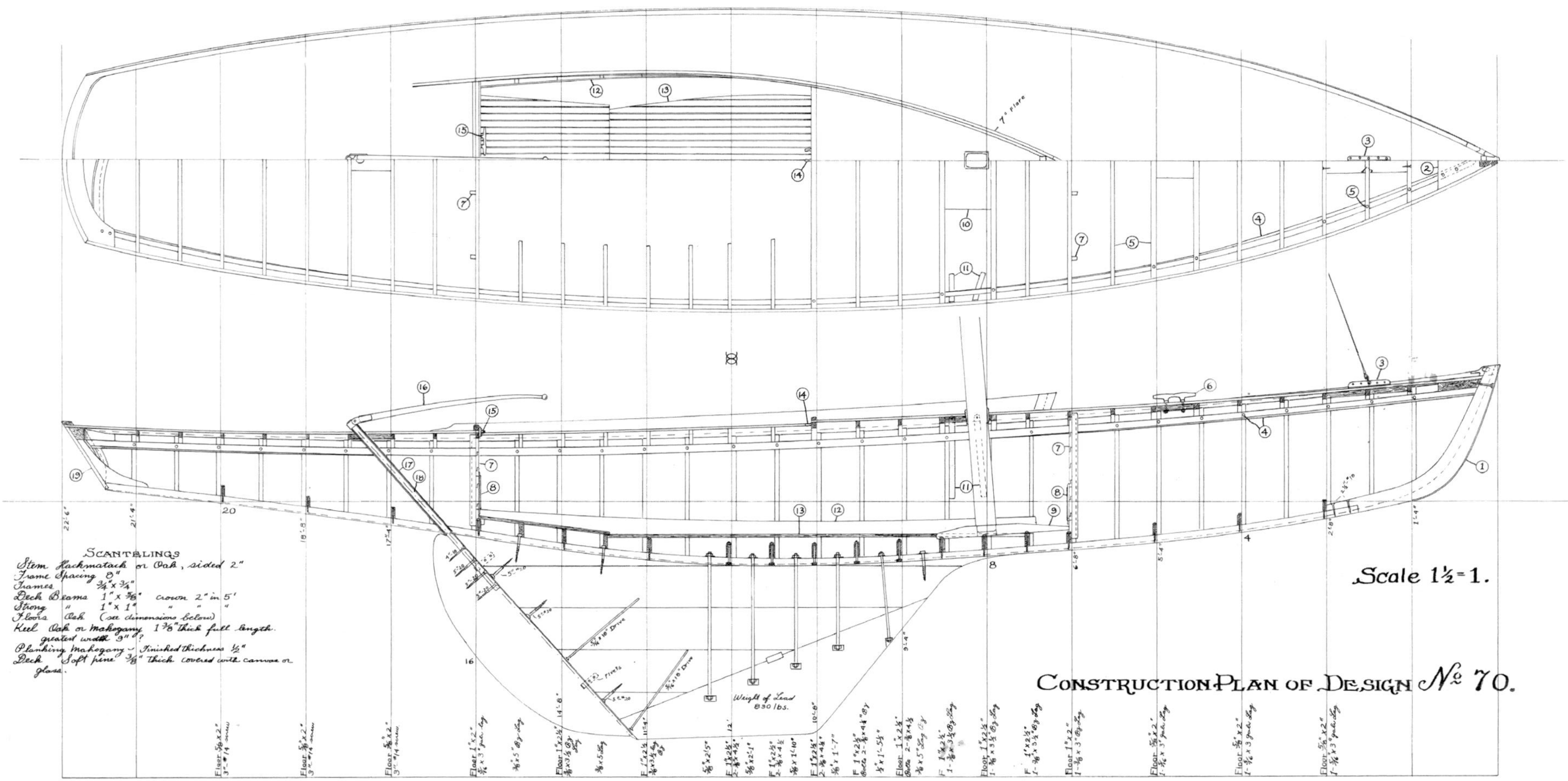
SCANTLINGS
Stem Hackmatack or Oak, sided 2"
Frame Spacing 8"
Frames 3/4" x 3/4"
Deck Beams 1" x 7/8" crown 2" in 5'
Strong " 1" x 1" " " "
Floors Oak (see dimensions below)
Keel Oak or Mahogany 1 3/8" thick full length. greatest width 9"?
Planking Mahogany ~ Finished thickness 1/2"
Deck Soft pine 3/8" thick covered with canvas or glass.
Weight of Lead 830 lbs.
7° Flare
Scale 1½=1.
CONSTRUCTION PLAN OF DESIGN № 70.

up against anything so far large or small that seems to be in the same class as *Koala*. She is fast and I have an idea she is quite as fast as *Ben-My-Chree*." But his wife pointed out that the brushes seemed to go to the sailor rather than to the boat. Stuart's last comment to Francis on the *Koala* was, "we think she is a peach."[51]

Even before hearing that the *Koala* was such a success, Francis tried to promote his design No. 70. Waldo Brown was looking for plans for a one-design racing class for Northeast Harbor. Francis sent him No. 70, without result. At the same time, he submitted the design to *The Rudder* to compete against Paine, Alden, and Crowninshield for a proposed class of 23-foot knockabouts for Marblehead. Nor did anything come of this, for any of the designers.[52]

Back in 1928, as we have seen, Francis had been associated with the Dyer Motorcraft Corporation as chief designer. Although the position hadn't worked out for the independent Francis, Bill Dyer had popularized a line of fast runabouts. Now, in 1930, Dyer turned to even smaller boats and started a new business, The Anchorage, Dyer Boat Company, at Warren, Rhode Island. He developed and manufactured a small tender for cruising boats that became popular as the "Dyer Dink." The purpose of the little boat was to tow well and row reasonably well with good carrying capacity. And each dinghy could have an optional sailing rig with centerboard and rudder. Some cruising sailors realized that they could

LEFT: The construction plan of the *Koala* that was followed by the Britt brothers and their boat carpenters. Planking is ½-inch mahogany. Across the bottom of the drawing, Francis gives the dimensions of each of her twenty floors, five keel bolts and three lags, and five deadwood lags. He has given four deck beams an extra ⅜-inch of width, one pair in way of the mast and another in way of the Herreshoff Manufacturing Company mooring cleat. The plate on the bow to take the forestay has five alternate positions. The chainplates are inside the planking. She has two watertight bulkheads, one at the forward end of the mast step and one at the after end of the cockpit; each has a 6-inch hand-hole plate for ventilation. The bulkheads provide air tanks fore and aft so she won't sink if she fills her cockpit in a knockdown. One sits on the cockpit sole in this narrow boat; Francis specified a comfortable 7-degree flare for the coaming. (© Mystic Seaport Museum, Daniel S. Gregory Ships Plans Library, SP38.196.9) ABOVE: The *Koala* slipping along close-hauled in a light breeze. Her helmsman, sitting to leeward watching his jib, is close to the water going by. (Mystic Seaport Museum, 1973-3-258)

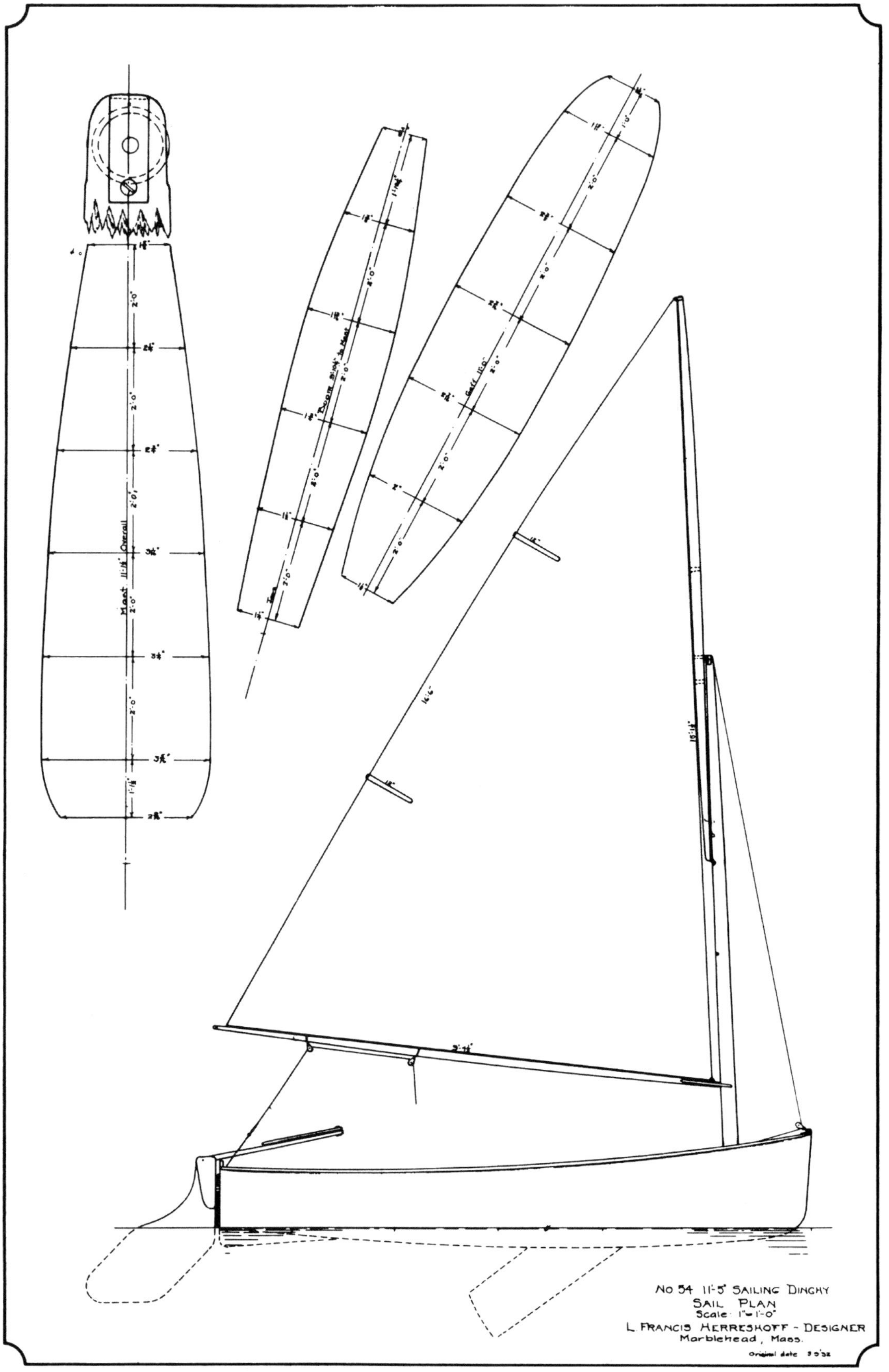

No 54 11'-5" Sailing Dinghy
Sail Plan
Scale 1" = 1'-0"
L. Francis Herreshoff - Designer
Marblehead, Mass.
Original date 3-5-32

stretch the season by sailing their Dyer Dinks after their sloops, cutters, yawls, ketches, and schooners were laid up for the winter. It would be easy to keep a small sailing dinghy in commission, ready to be trailed to the nearest harbor on a decent winter day. Why mope about, reading *Yachting* and *Rudder*, waiting for spring?[53]

And sailors *will* race. In December 1931, William H. Taylor, the yachting reporter for the *New York Herald Tribune*, invited a few sailors to his house in Port Washington, on Long Island's north shore, to discuss the idea of organizing winter racing for Dyer Dinks and other sailing dinghies. These sailors held the first event of Frostbite dinghy racing, as they dubbed the sport, nearby in Manhasset Bay on January 2, 1932.[54]

The sport took off and quickly grew beyond racing the existing dinghies and far beyond the waters of Manhasset Bay. Plenty of sailors jumped at the chance to get out on the water and compete in the "off" season. The magazine editors, grateful to have yacht races to write about in winter, gave the Frostbiters extensive coverage. Yacht designers, happy to have work involving even smallcraft during the Depression, were intrigued by the idea of drawing plans for new dinghies that might give their customers an edge in the racing. Sea lawyers raised their ugly heads. The need for measurement rules emerged; dinghy classes had to be specified. Class A would be for standard boats, Class B for specially designed development boats.

By the spring of 1932, L. Francis Herreshoff was hooked. He had designed small sailing boats for the Development classes in 1928 and 1930 in order to experiment with hull forms and rigs to see which were fastest, and the new interest in sailing dinghies presented a similar opportunity that was irresistible.

In early March, Francis designed a Frostbite dinghy, to be named *La Petite*, his design No. 54, which he intended to build himself for his own use. He drew lines showing a broad, flat stern. This boat would take advantage of planing; that is, she would be flat enough in hull form so that under ideal conditions, reaching in plenty of wind and down a following sea, she could rise up out of the trough of her own wave, cast aside the speed limit of a displacement hull, and zoom. The ability to achieve such bursts of speed, brief though they might be, would separate dinghies that were flat enough to plane from those that were too round to do so.

But when Francis came to build *La Petite*, he couldn't bring himself to follow his own lines drawing and bend the boat's frames with such a sharp turn at the bilge and with so little deadrise. He didn't want a boat with such a wide, nearly rectangular transom. *La Petite* would have a far more traditional shape, with easy bilges and more deadrise than he had drawn. She would not be nearly as likely to plane as would a boat built to her designer's original lines plan. Francis wanted his own boat to be a good all-around sailer, not a specialized racer. He wrote to his father that he liked a dinghy with good stability, "as I often sail alone off shore here." *La Petite* would qualify for Class A.[55]

Four additional dinghies were built to design No. 54, including one named the *Sinbad*, for Larry Johnson, the reluctant client for both the *Dulcinea*

LEFT: **The sail and spar plan of *La Petite*, Francis's design No. 54, the 11-foot, 5-inch, Class A Frostbite dinghy that he designed and built for his own use in 1932. The gunter rig allows a triangular sail with a luff taller than the boat is long, yet with spars that will stow inside the boat. The halyard leads down through a block on the stem so that it doubles as a forestay. Sail area is 72 square feet, and the sail was made with a shallow reef, not shown.** (© Mystic Seaport Museum, Daniel S. Gregory Ships Plans Library, SP38.172.9)

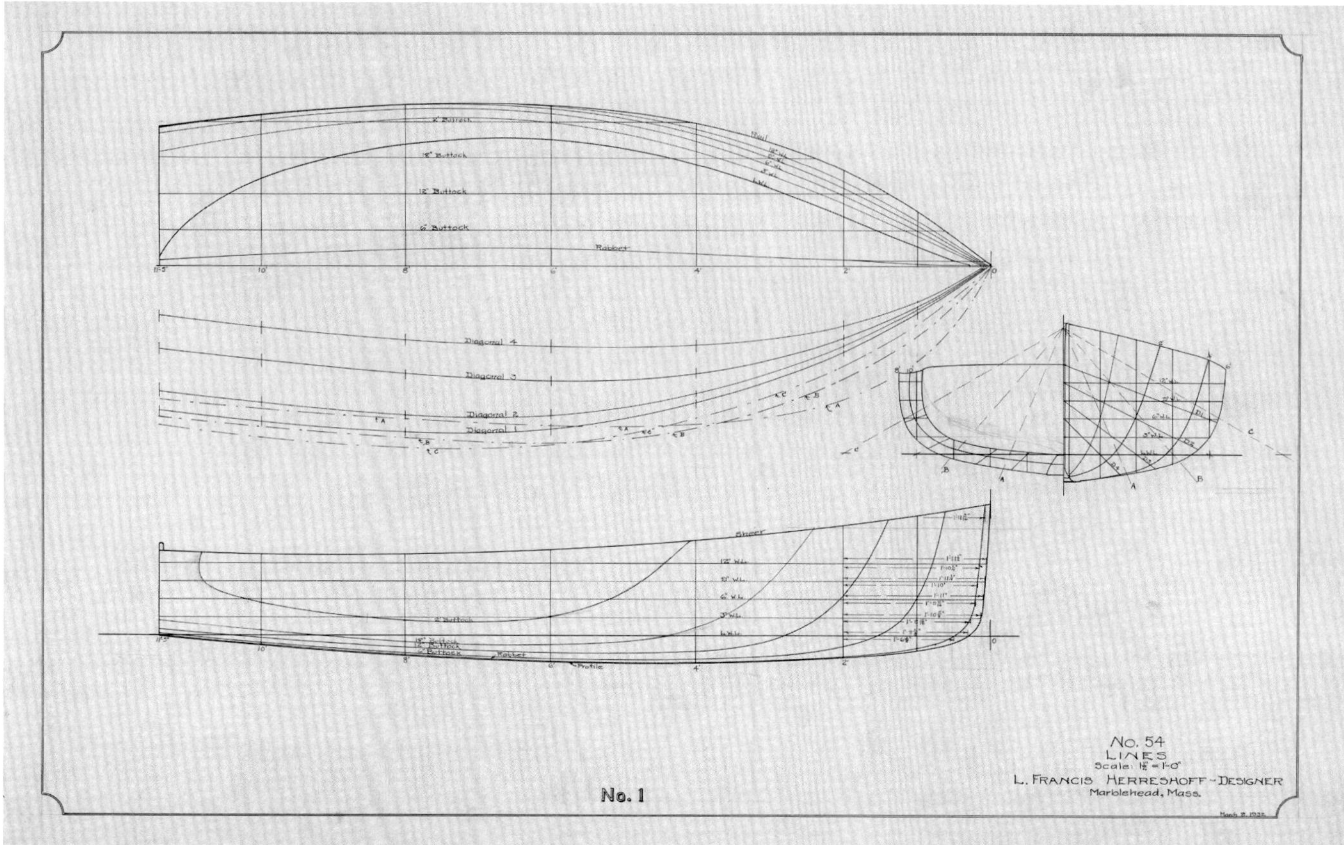
Diagonal 4
Diagonal 3
Diagonal 2
Diagonal 1
Rabbet
Sheer
No. 54
LINES
Scale: 1½" = 1'-0"
L. FRANCIS HERRESHOFF – DESIGNER
Marblehead, Mass.
No. 1

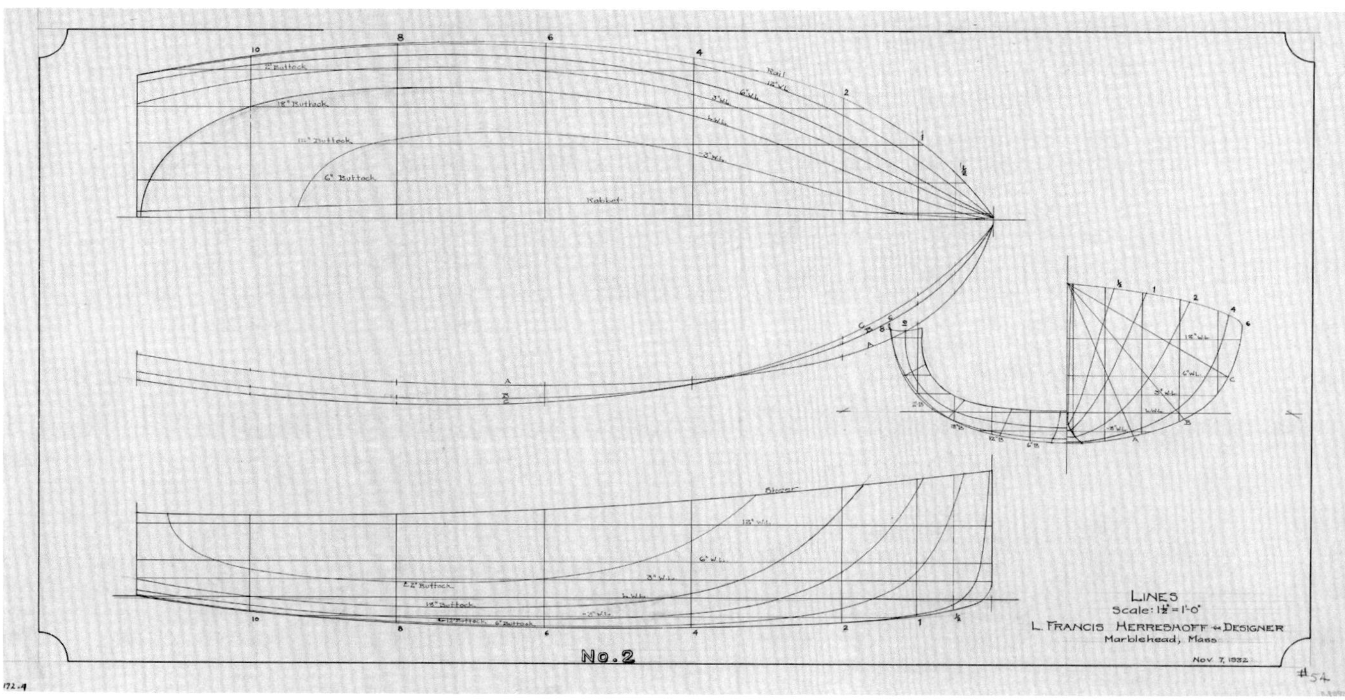
Rabbet
Sheer
LINES
Scale: 1½" = 1'-0"
L. FRANCIS HERRESHOFF – DESIGNER
Marblehead, Mass.
Nov. 7, 1932
No. 2
#54

and design No. 65. For the *Sinbad,* Francis designed a gunter rig with a curved yard, which put her into the hotshot Class B.

Francis sent Nathanael a photograph of *La Petite.* His father commented: She "looks almost exactly like one I designed for Junius Morgan built by HM Co last winter." Francis replied: "It is quite interesting that you and I designed dinghies which were so similar. I am sure that the boat you designed would have rowed and towed better than mine."[56]

By October 1932 there were already enough Frostbiters to warrant intersectional races between New York and Boston. A regatta was held at Mason's Island, at the mouth of the Mystic River on Fishers Island Sound, roughly halfway between

LEFT TOP: ***La Petite*'s lines. The wide, flat stern shown was to encourage planing when on a reach in a fresh breeze. These lines, given No. 1 and dated March 8, 1932, are the first of six variations on the theme that Francis drew. But when he built the boat, he gave her a more conventionally rounded transom and sections throughout that were more rounded, less flat. L. Francis Herreshoff was not a fan of the small, planing dinghy.** (© Mystic Seaport Museum, Daniel S. Gregory Ships Plans Library, SP 38.172.1) LEFT BOTTOM: **He drew lines No. 2, dated November 7, 1932, much closer to the way he had built *La Petite* several months earlier. Just outside the border of this second drawing, Francis has written, "#54," his design number.** (© Mystic Seaport Museum, Daniel S. Gregory Ships Plans Library, SP38.172.4) BELOW: **The construction plan that Francis didn't follow, as to hull shape, when he built *La Petite.* Lapstrake planking was 5⁄16-inch cedar, copper riveted, on oak frames 6 inches apart. Sternboard to be ¾-inch mahogany, "double in way of outboard motor," but no such device ever sullied her transom. Centerboard and rudder, ⅞-inch mahogany, the former weighted with a 4-by-8-inch piece of lead. Note the dory-type handle for raising and lowering the centerboard and the hiking stick on the tiller.** (© Mystic Seaport Museum, Daniel S. Gregory Ships Plans Library, SP38.172.3)

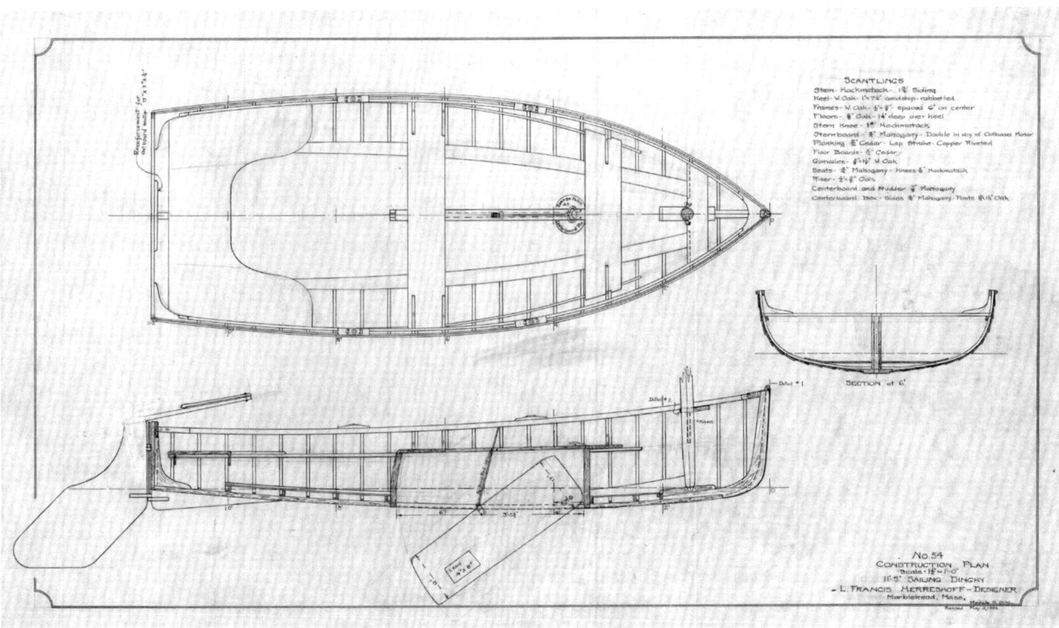

the cities. The winning boat was *La Petite*, with E. Arthur Shuman Jr. of the design firm of Belknap and Paine, who had won the skipper's position as the "Boston champion," at the tiller and Francis tending sheet.[57]

Despite *La Petite*'s big win at Mason's Island and many smaller wins, Francis didn't like her. In a long letter to Uffa Fox, who had been designing racing dinghies in England since 1923 and was the leading designer of planing dinghies, Francis stated his primary requirement of a sailing dinghy: "A boat capable of being driven in a breeze so that I can get the thrill of changing speed an exhilaration which after all is the principal sport of sailing." To Fox, Francis disparaged Frostbite dinghies, including his own *La Petite*, as being "slow, homely, wet and no good for my purposes outside of racing, i.e., too cramped for two or more grown people; poor to row, and dangerous in a sea and wind when a longer boat would lift and plane when driven hard." Yet the short dinghies, as Fox had demonstrated, could be designed to lift and plane, too.[58]

Nathanael G. Herreshoff did not approve of sailing small boats in cold weather. Francis wrote to his father, "we certainly agree almost exactly about winter dinghy sailing and I believe within a year several others will see that the most fun can be had in the dinghies in warm weather." Francis wrote a poem, published only posthumously, poking fun at Frostbiting. And he would write a prose-poem presented as a play in four acts, called

ABOVE: *La Petite* shows her well-rounded transom and bilge as she eases along on a close reach in a light breeze. Francis, with his beret, is enjoying a quiet out-of-season sail. Without having to think about it, he has placed his weight carefully just so, to give the boat a little heel, but he is braced to shift to windward for a puff. That may well be his draftsman, Sam Brown, who inked all of *La Petite*'s plans, at the tiller, for they often sailed together. (Courtesy Herreshoff Marine Museum, Bristol, Rhode Island) RIGHT TOP: Uffa Fox, the convivial English dinghy designer, sent this portrait of himself, drawn by Francis's friend Rolf Armstrong, to William. P. Stephens as a Christmas card in 1940. Fox designed and built sailing canoes as well as planing dinghies. In 1933, he came to Canada's Thousand Islands with a sailing canoe and won the International Canoe Trophy. One of the sailors he bested and befriended was the artist, Armstrong, who drew the sketch at the time. The trophy was presented to Fox by Stephens, who, besides being the dean of American yachting historians, was also the dean of American sailing canoeists. (Copy photo by Benmosche Studios, New York, courtesy Eleanor Stephens, author's collection) RIGHT BOTTOM: Uffa Fox was so impressed by Francis's 9-by-3-foot drawing board that he drew up this plan for it and had it reproduced in his *Uffa Fox's Second Book*. He wrote: "The plan and table of sizes explains itself, and any amateur carpenter could build this table from them without any great difficulty, and then he could be happy evermore, for when not actually sailing he could be drawing his dream ship." (*Uffa Fox's Second Book*, 354)

"A Midsummer Night's Sail," that was published in *The Rudder* and that used his sailing dinghy as the set for a fantastical adventure that included both fairies and a fierce thunder squall. Yet Francis did go out in the *La Petite* in winter; in 1932, he enjoyed a sail in his dinghy on Christmas Day.[59]

Francis wrote to Nathanael, "the thing that worries me most now about the future of the dinghy is the changes in the rules the New York people are making, and the start of a so-called class B which has all the same measured dimensions and into which apparently any fast dinghy is put whether she wants to or not." He found himself in the thick of it. The Boston Dinghy Club was formally organized in

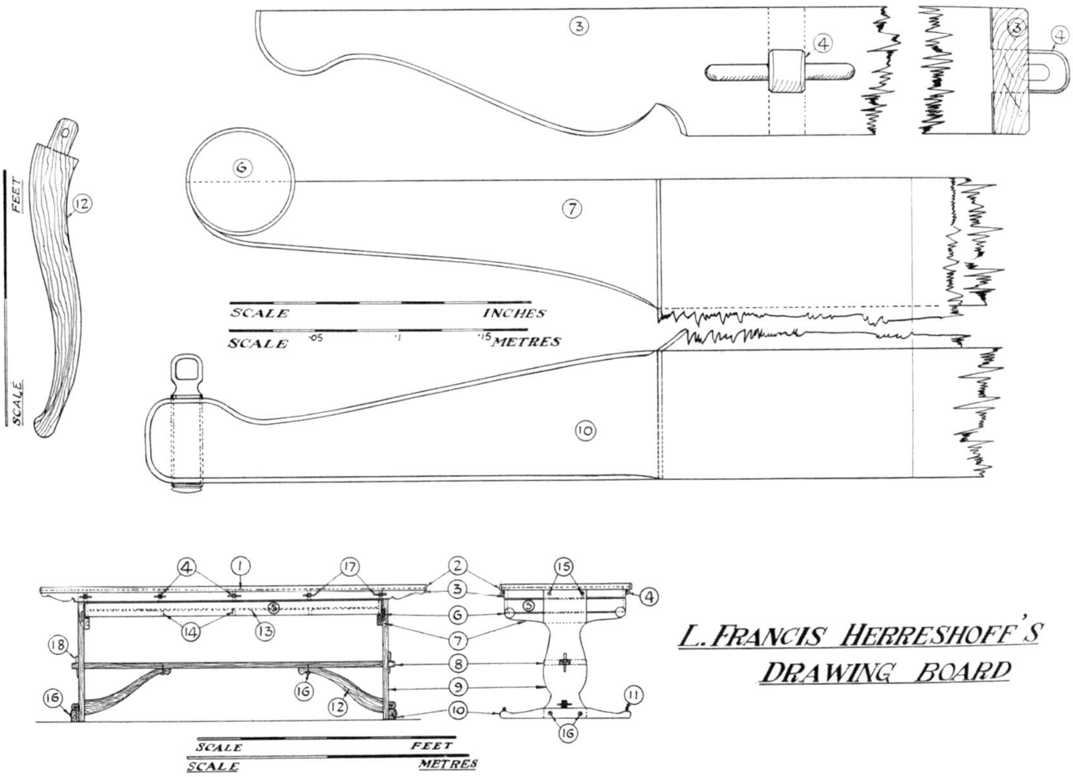

SCANTLINGS

(1) Top Clear Soft Pine, Planed, Sandpapered and Shellacked—About $\frac{7}{8}$ in. thick.
(2) Oak, $1\frac{1}{2}$ in. × $\frac{1}{2}$ in., fastened with 8-gauge screws 9 inches apart.
(3) Oak Side-Pieces, $\frac{7}{8}$ in. × 3 in. × 9 ft.
(4) Oak Cross Pieces, $\frac{7}{8}$ in. × 3 in. × 3 ft.
(5) Draw Sides and Fronts. Oak, $\frac{7}{8}$ in. × 4 in. Front, 7 ft. long, Ends, 2 ft. 10 in. wide.
(6) Guide Pieces, $2\frac{1}{2}$ in. diameter, $\frac{7}{8}$ in. thick.
(7) Cross Pieces, $1\frac{1}{2}$ in. × 3 in. × 2 ft. 10 in. Oak.
(8) Shelf Oak, $1\frac{1}{2}$ in. × 12 in. × 7 ft. 7 in.
(9) Uprights, Oak, $1\frac{1}{2}$ in. × 12 in. × 3 ft. $1\frac{1}{8}$ in.
(10) Shoes, Oak, 3 in. × 2 in. × 3 ft.
(11) Adjusting Screws.
(12) Oak Diagonals, $1\frac{1}{2}$ in. × $4\frac{1}{2}$ in. × 2 ft. 6 in.
(13) Drawer Bottom, about $\frac{1}{4}$ in. thick, Ply wood.
(14) Drawer Bottom, Supports, $\frac{7}{8}$ in. × $1\frac{1}{2}$ in.
(15) Black Iron Lag Screws, about $\frac{3}{8}$ in., with washers, $2\frac{1}{4}$ in. long.
(16) Black Iron Lag Screws, about $\frac{3}{8}$ in., with washers, 3 in. long.
(17) Oak tapered pins, $3\frac{1}{2}$ in. long × $\frac{3}{8}$ in. × $\frac{5}{8}$ in. at big ends.
(18) Oak tapered pins, $4\frac{1}{2}$ in. long × $\frac{1}{2}$ in. × $\frac{7}{8}$ in. at big ends.

February 1933, and Francis was named chairman of the measurement committee. The title was not enough; Francis was not good at selling his own ideas. "Every time the things that I have suggested have been turned down," he would report to his father. The North American Dinghy Association made new rules for the 11-foot, 6-inch, 72-square-foot-sail-area dinghies of Classes A and B. As *Yachting* reported in April, "The older and slower stock boats in Class A will continue to have keen, even racing . . . whereas Class B enthusiasts can outbuild each other to their heart's content. . . . New designs are expected soon from the boards of Francis Herreshoff, Paine-Belknap, John Alden, and others."[60]

One of the designs that the editors at *Yachting* were expecting from Francis Herreshoff turned out to be a radical dinghy indeed. Henry Bill Selden, an old friend, wanted Francis to design and build a new and different sort of boat for him, one that would show her heels to the other Frostbite dinghies. The two men, Selden four years older than Francis, were congenial. Francis believed in following one's own inclination, and Selden had run away from Princeton to become an artist and never looked back. Among other subjects, Selden painted the New England harbor scenes that Francis loved. Selden founded the art department at Connecticut College in New London in 1915 and pioneered the giving of credit for art courses. And, like Francis, he enjoyed turning metal objects of his own design on his lathe.[61]

Selden was confident of Francis's genius and was an enthusiastic client. For the new boat, they settled on Francis's Frostbite dinghy concept No. 6, by far the most unusual one. She was wide and flat, and much of her width was carried all the way forward, on deck at least, into her bow. She had a turtleback in case a wave broke over that bow. For the rig, they decided to use the curved gunter arrangement that Francis had designed for the *Sinbad,* together with his patented solution for reducing wind resistance in the rig, a double-luff sail forming an unbroken surface around, in this case, the curved club of the gunter rig, rather than the mast. Selden wrote to Francis: "I have been thinking most of the time about that new boat. I think there is very little doubt but what it will be probably the fastest dinghy yet built in the world and certainly the most interesting, and I am greatly pleased to be able to have such a thing."[62]

While the boat was taking shape under Francis's expert hands in the ground-floor shop in the old customhouse at 20 Lee Street, Selden made visits to Marblehead from New London to enjoy seeing the progress and to confer with Francis on all sorts of details. In between visits, he wrote Francis long, garrulous letters discussing every aspect of the innovative little craft. We know that Francis replied, but, atypically, none of his letters to Selden have come to light.

Selden wanted a track to hold the gunter club to the mast, and he wanted the foot of the sail to be held to the boom in a slot, rather than be laced. He sent Francis sketches of these ideas with "now don't get mad Francis, you can't expect me not to dream about that boat night and day."[63]

A week later, after a visit to Francis and the dinghy, Selden wrote, "the boat is certainly a wonder and I don't want you to feel that I don't think and know that it is undoubtedly the best dinghy yet built, because I certainly do." The two had collaborated on designs for a special masthead fitting to take the standing rigging and halyard and special drain plugs for the hull. Selden made the fittings on his lathe and sent them to 20 Lee Street, with many words of assurance that his feelings wouldn't be hurt if they didn't pass Francis's inspection. (They did.) And Selden wrote, "I know it is a big job to finish up the boat, but I am of course anxious to get it as soon as you can manage so as to get it and myself all tuned up to make the best possible showing on May 14th!"[64]

Addressing Francis with his close-friend nickname, Selden continued: "Now, George, this is *not a suggestion* merely a statement no more no less" and went on to say that he had some sheets of stainless steel of two different thicknesses that might "be *useful* and *save you trouble*." He enclosed a payment of $100, making $200 that he had paid on the boat so far. Then, on page 5 of another letter, Selden wrote: "Don't let these things or all this rambling disturb you now, George you know it is never meant to."[65]

Selden named the new Frostbiter the *Whim*. Francis finished building his friend's strange-looking dinghy in time for him to race on May 14 in a regatta at Mason's Island, but not in time for him to tune her up. The racing was a disaster. Although sailed not only by Selden, but also by other more experienced dinghy sailors, including Nick Potter—Francis's friend who as a designer and sailor was a great enthusiast of Frostbiting—no one could make the boat go. Selden's report to Francis began with a positive comment, but then quickly changed course:

> *1. The boat seemed to "ghost" along very well in the lightest of breezes.*
>
> *2. It was quite impossible for any of us to make her go to* ***windward.*** *I cannot see what caused this condition but it was very marked.*
>
> *3. She certainly showed a flash of speed once or twice in strong puffs when off the wind, but to my surprise was very wet in the very moderate chop at M. I. [Mason's Island].*
>
> *4. She took water in over the bow in serious amounts so that bailing was necessary. She seemed to push a white wave in front of her all the way.*[66]

Selden continued: "She was greatly admired by almost everyone and since the race I've had a very nice letter from Corny Shields [a prominent Long Island Sound racing sailor] hoping that with study she will get going and I certainly hope so. I

The sail plan of the *Whim*, design No. 56, an experimental Class B Frostbite dinghy that Francis designed for his friend, the Connecticut artist Henry Bill Selden. She was the sixth and last of the different ideas for Frostbite dinghies that Francis put on paper. The double-luff sail forms a sleeve around the curved gunter club. The mast can rotate on ball bearings. The sheerline is absolutely straight, with the bow slightly higher than the stern. Despite much attention to detail by both designer and owner, the experiment failed. The drawing is dated March 17, 1933. (© Mystic Seaport Museum, Daniel S. Gregory Ships Plans Library, SP38.173.2)

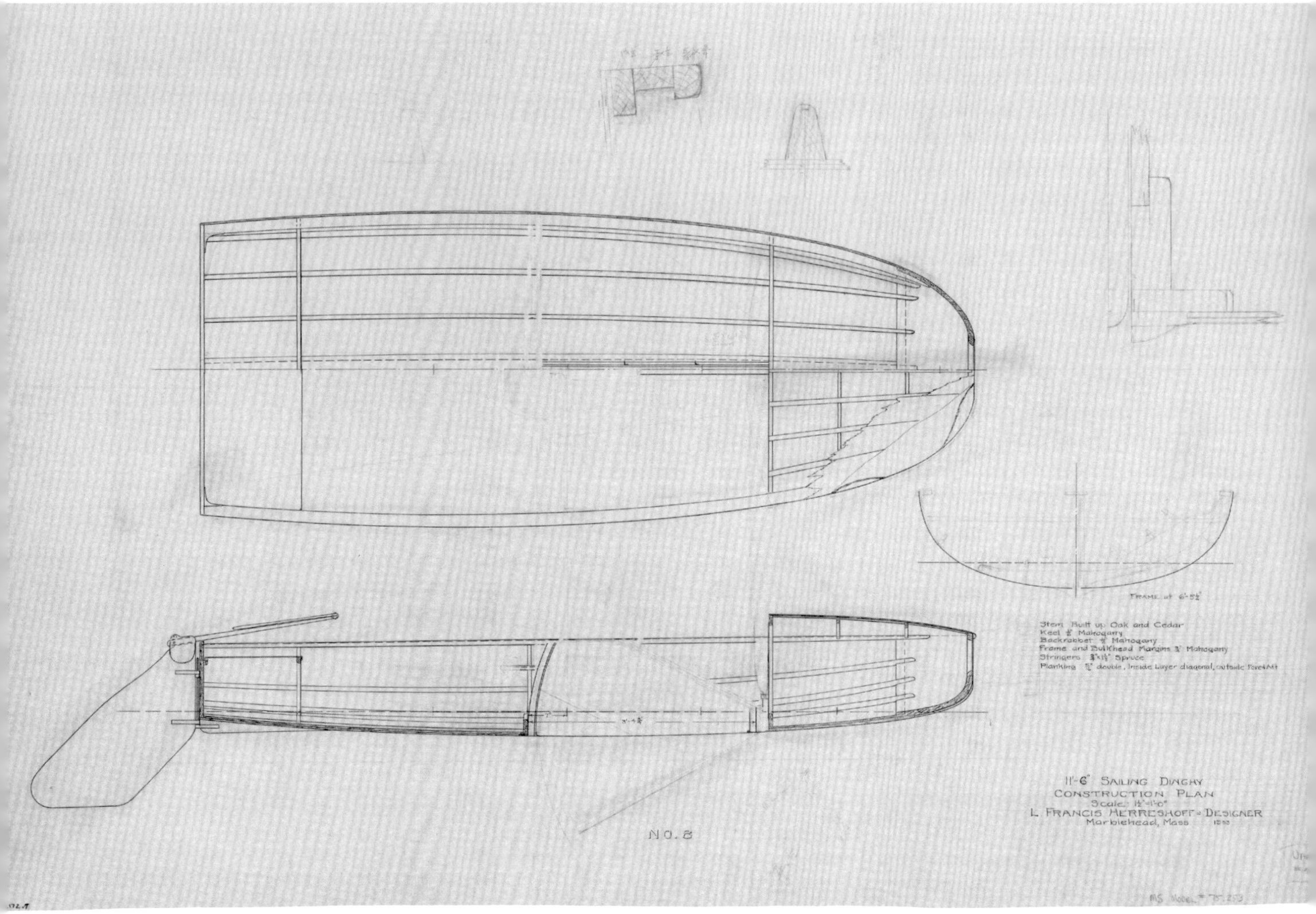

ABOVE: **Francis built the *Whim* himself, following this construction plan. To keep the boat light, yet strong, he returned to the longitudinal construction system that he had originated in the 1920s. He double-planked the boat, with the inner layer diagonal and the outer, fore-and-aft, to a total thickness of $^5/_{16}$ inch.** (© Mystic Seaport Museum, Daniel S. Gregory Ships Plans Library, SP38.173.7) RIGHT: **No lines plan for the *Whim* has come to light, but this photograph of the boat shows the shape of her troublesome bow. Although the dinghy has fine waterlines forward, the wide, blunt shape, where a sharp stem would normally be, could, and apparently did, dig into the waves when she was trying to get to windward. The mast is well supported by twin headstays and aft-leading shrouds.** (*The Common Sense of Yacht Design*, vol. 2, 60)

am very anxious to hear from you with suggestions for what to do."[67]

And Selden wrote, "I know I would have been more 'sensible' to have taken advantage of your very sporting offer to 'let me out' and have *La Petite* instead but I would always have felt that I had let you down and behaved badly and somehow I feel we can manage this difficult matter without getting into any squabbles, which after all these years would be pretty ghastly."

Alas, the friends were not to have much opportunity to "manage this difficult matter." Nine months later Henry Bill Selden's widow, Hazel, was writing to Francis looking for help, not to get the *Whim* going, but to get rid of her. She wrote: "I personally can never see it again—Henry was so grieved by it."[68]

We can glean something of Francis's reaction to the *Whim* disaster from Selden's comments on Francis's letters. Francis evidently thought the problem might be more with the rig than with the hull shape. He apparently suggested replacing the short mast and curved gunter yard with a tall, straight mast, though such a spar, unless jointed, would have been too long to fit inside the boat with the rig stowed. And it does not seem that he was overly dismayed by the boat's slow start. Selden had written: "I am very glad you do not feel sore or disappointed. I know, as you say that many of your boats after a poor start have turned out to be very remarkable and I think that is liable to be true of *Whim*. I am *not discouraged*." But both friends must have been extremely frustrated that all their innovations, care, and hopes had come to nothing. Selden's death would have been doubly sad for Francis.[69]

The *Whim*'s rounded snub bow was not a new concept for Francis. His successful R-boat *Live Yankee* had one. But her bow, snubbed off in profile, was very fine in plan view. Not so the *Whim*'s, which was very broad in plan view. Selden's statement that "she seemed to push a white wave in front of her all the way" is damning.

It is inexplicable how L. Francis Herreshoff failed to recognize that the *Whim*'s innovative bow shape was the primary cause of the boat's failure.

And the puzzle deepens. Francis sent his father a photograph of the *Whim* and wrote: "I thought she would be quite fast, but at the races on Mason's Island she turned out to be very slow. . . . However, she had a very poor sail and was very poorly sailed . . . I now hope for her to do something with a different sail and possibly a different sail plan." Moreover, Francis was building a boat to design No. 56 for himself. He sent Nathanael a model of her, saying he thought his father would find her shape "quite unusual." He suggested that "she is something like the famous *Shadow* and if so she should slip through the water quite well." And this was nearly three weeks after the debacle at Mason's Island.[70]

While it may be true that the *Whim*'s sail was not the best and that her helmsmen may not have known how to get the most out of her "quite unusual" hull shape, it was surely her bow that was the main problem. Any resemblance to the *Shadow* would have been an improvement. Francis's blindness to the situation is baffling.

It took a sail in his Development boat, the *Butterfly*, to open Francis's eyes. About two months after comparing his design No. 56 to the *Shadow*, he wrote to his father, "since sailing in her [the *Butterfly*] I am very discouraged about working on

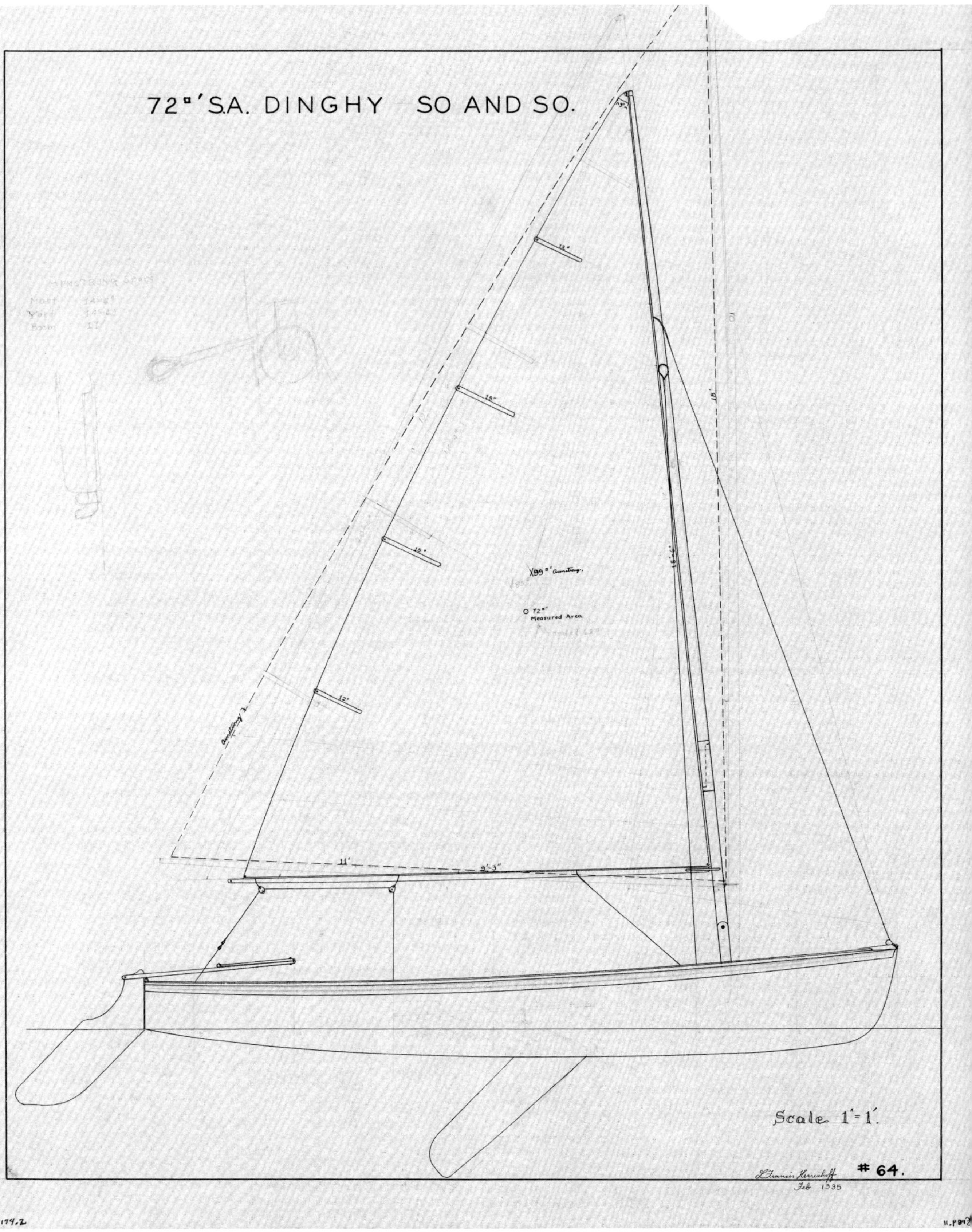

72□' S.A. DINGHY SO AND SO.
12"
15"
15"
12"
11'
9'-3"
18'
18'-6"
X 99□' armstrong.
O 72□' Measured Area.
Scale 1"=1'.
L. Francis Herreshoff
Feb 1935
64.

my Frost Bite Dinghy and may not even finish her up now." Finally, dawn breaks over Marblehead.[71]

In 1935, Francis put the *Whim* setback well astern by designing for himself a more ideal sailing dinghy than any Frostbiter, his design No. 64. He lengthened the new dinghy, from the 11½ feet of *La Petite* to 15 feet, so that he would have "a boat capable of being driven in a breeze," as he had stated his prime requirement for a sailing dinghy to Uffa Fox. Although he gave the boat the disparaging name of *So And So,* she turned out to be his favorite among the four sailing craft that he would own, the others being *La Petite,* the Development boat *Butterfly,* and the 30-Square-Metre boat *Visitor*.

The Massachusetts Institute of Technology was looking for a design for a class of sailing dinghies for its students to use on the Charles River, and Francis submitted design No. 64 for consideration. But the Tech Dinghies, as they would be called, were built to plans by MIT's Professor George Owen, Francis's design being considered too racy and tender for the purpose.

The hull of the *So And So* was built at the Herreshoff Manufacturing Company, in the shop where Francis had worked as a child. The invoice, dated May 7, 1935, was for $100, which Francis paid promptly. It took him all summer to make her spars and rigging, fit her out, and get a sail made. He wrote to Nathanael: "On Labor Day I finally succeeded in getting my dinghy *So And So* going. I like her very much as she really rows very well and is very dry when sailing. She seems fast in spite of a poor setting sail."[72]

The next summer, Francis raced the *So And So* during Marblehead Race Week "in a special open class for any kind of boats under 21 feet long," as he reported to his father. "I had very good fun because all of the boats in the class had from two to three times the sail area of *So And So* and I came in second, which I thought was very good. However, the Regatta Committee gave me first place under some arbitrary handicap which they had, but I should have been perfectly satisfied with second place as my little boat is in very good shape and should beat bigger ones in my opinion." Francis kept the *So And So* on a 20-by 12-foot float of his own design right around the corner from 20 Lee Street at Charlie Welch's house. He sailed this dinghy more than he had any of his other three boats, even the lively *Butterfly*.[73]

In 1939, Raymond Hunt, a Marblehead racing skipper, designed, and George Lawley and Sons built, a new and different sort of small racing boat, one that was supposed to give its owner the fast, exhilarating sailing that Francis loved, at low cost. The class took its name, 110, from its sail area. The boat was 24 feet long, built like a box out of plywood, and had an iron fin keel. Cost, without sails, was $350. Although Hunt's lightweight 110 couldn't have been a more different boat from Francis's heavyweight R-boat *Live Yankee*, the long, low, skinny, double-ended, flat-bottomed hull of the 110 did bear some resemblance, above the waterline, to the *Live Yankee.* Because of her strange appearance, the 110, like the *Live Yankee*, suffered the initial jeers of conservative sailors, with

LEFT: **The sail plan of the 15-foot *So And So,* Francis's design No. 64, for his own use. He shows a Frostbite-sized rig of 72 square feet in solid lines, and a 99-square-foot sail in dotted lines. The boat's mast can pivot to swing down above the rail, as if in a tabernacle, and the spar is jointed about 4 feet above the rail so that the top section of the mast, about 14 feet long, will stow on the boat without overhanging. This plan is dated February 1935.** (© Mystic Seaport Museum, Daniel S. Gregory Ships Plans Library, SP38.174.2)

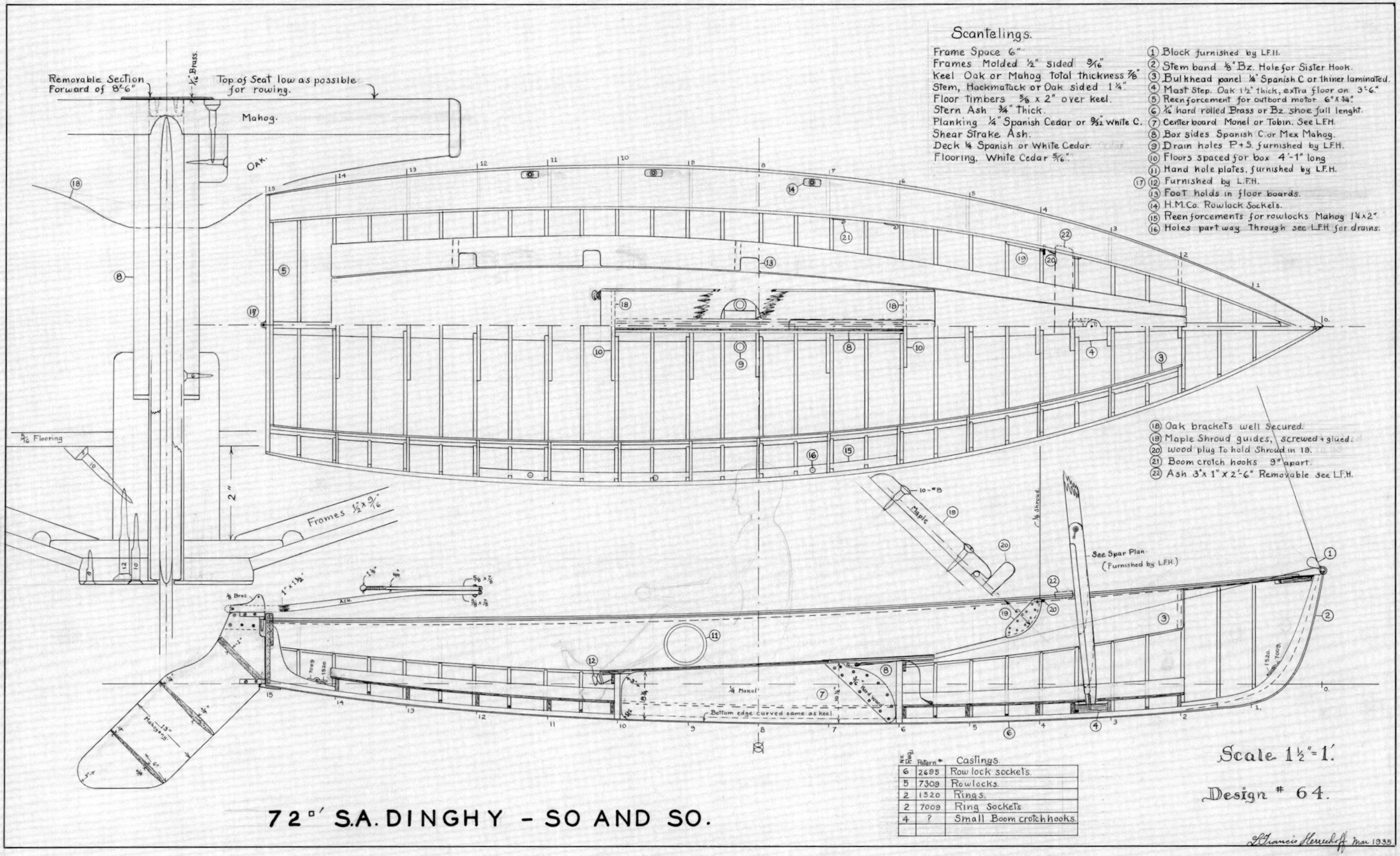
Scantelings.
Frame Space 6"
Frames Molded 1/2" sided 9/16"
Keel Oak or Mahog total thickness 7/8"
Stem, Hackmatack or Oak sided 1 1/4"
Floor timbers 3/8 x 2" over keel.
Stern Ash 3/4" Thick.
Planking 1/4" Spanish Cedar or 9/32 White C.
Shear Strake Ash.
Deck 1/4 Spanish or White Cedar.
Flooring. White Cedar 5/16".
(1) Block furnished by L.F.H.
(2) Stem band 1/8" Bz. Hole for Sister Hook.
(3) Bulkhead panel 1/8" Spanish C or thiner laminated.
(4) Mast Step. Oak 1 1/2" thick, extra floor on 3'-6".
(5) Reenforcement for outboard motor 6" x 3/4".
(6) 1/4 hard rolled Brass or Bz. shoe full lenght.
(7) Centerboard Monel or Tobin. See L.F.H.
(8) Box sides Spanish C. or Mex Mahog.
(9) Drain holes P+S. furnished by L.F.H.
(10) Floors spaced for box 4'-1" long
(11) Hand hole plates, furnished by L.F.H.
(17) (12) Furnished by L.F.H.
(13) Foot holds in floor boards.
(14) H.M.Co. Rowlock Sockets.
(15) Reenforcements for rowlocks Mahog 1 1/4 x 2"
(16) Holes part way Through see L.F.H for drains.
(18) Oak brackets well secured.
(19) Maple Shroud guides, screwed + glued.
(20) wood plug to hold Shroud in 19.
(21) Boom crotch hooks 9" apart.
(22) Ash 3" x 1" x 2'-6" Removable see L.F.H.
Removable Section Forward of 8'-6"
1/16" Brass.
Top of Seat low as possible for rowing.
Mahog.
Oak.
5/16 Flooring
Frames 1/2 x 9/16
2"
See Spar Plan. (Furnished by L.F.H.)
1/8 Shroud
Maple
1/4 Monel
Bottom edge curved same as keel
No. Req. | Pattern # | Castings.
6 | 2695 | Rowlock sockets.
5 | 7309 | Rowlocks.
2 | 1520 | Rings.
2 | 7009 | Ring Sockets
4 | ? | Small Boom crotch hooks.
72'' S.A. DINGHY - SO AND SO.
Scale 1 1/2" = 1'.
Design # 64.
L. Francis Herreshoff Mar 1935

Francis adding to the chorus. Eventually the 110s, built in hundreds, were far more popular than any L. Francis Herreshoff design. But it particularly pleased Francis that his *So And So* "could generally beat them (the 110s) quite easily."[74]

Francis kept his favorite sailing boat for seven years. In the winter of 1942 he sold her to his friend Rolf Armstrong, an artist and small-boat sailor, with the arrangement that she would be kept on her float in Marblehead and would be available most of the time to Francis. He sailed her not only for his own pleasure, but also as a training ship for youngsters.

One of his apprentices in the *So And So* was Helen Bolster's daughter, Anne. Francis became her mentor on the water, training her to be a good crew. She described Francis as a relaxed skipper until a squall came up; then he expected his crew to react quickly to his orders. Unlike with Kay Jones, whom he taught to sail, with Anne, Francis did all the sailing. Sometimes they would have a brush with Rolf Armstrong in his Curry racer. Afterwards, Armstrong would say to Anne of Francis, "he's forgotten more than I've ever learned." By 1945, Anne was looking for a job and Francis was trying to convince *Rudder* editor Boris Lauer-Leonardi to hire her. On August 11 that year, Anne crewed for Francis in a race in the *So And So*. "I asked her to ask me as many questions as she could to forward her training for *The Rudder*," Francis reported to Leonardi, "but I guess that there were so many things to see and do in the racing that she didn't ask many."[75]

The *So And So* was indeed "racy and tender." One had to be agile to sail her well. As Francis approached the age of sixty, he no longer felt he had the balance and quick reflexes to get the most out the boat, and, when he stopped sailing her, Rolf Armstrong sold her.[76]

LEFT: The *So And So*'s construction plan. She is lightly built; Francis specified planking either of ¼-inch Spanish cedar or 9/32-inch white cedar. There is a 1/16-inch brass shoe on the keel the full length of the boat, for she was to be hauled out on a float when not in use. The transom is reinforced to take a phantom outboard motor. She has a mahogany fore-and-aft seat atop the centerboard trunk for rowing, using any of the three oarlock positions, and also for the crew's toes to be hooked under when hiking out in a breeze. There are footholds in the floorboards for rowing. She has side decks to keep the water out when she heels to a gust, and they are closed in to form flotation tanks in case she heels the deck under and fills. Such heeling was opposed by a heavy centerboard of either Monel or Tobin bronze. The 15-foot dinghy's beam is 4 feet, 5 inches. (© Mystic Seaport Museum, Daniel S. Gregory Ships Plans Library, SP38.174.1) ABOVE: Francis sailing his *So And So* with an unidentified crew. The photo shows her flaring sides and the shape of the transom. The rig is apparently the bigger of the two shown in the sail plan, with a shallow reef to bring it down closer to the size of the smaller sail plan. She has the adjustable headstay leading aft through a block on the stem shown in the plans, but the shrouds have been left off. She has a colored sail, a trend started by Nantucket's Rainbow Fleet of little catboats about eight years before Francis set his. (Courtesy Anne Bondy, Mystic Seaport Museum, 1999-4-220)

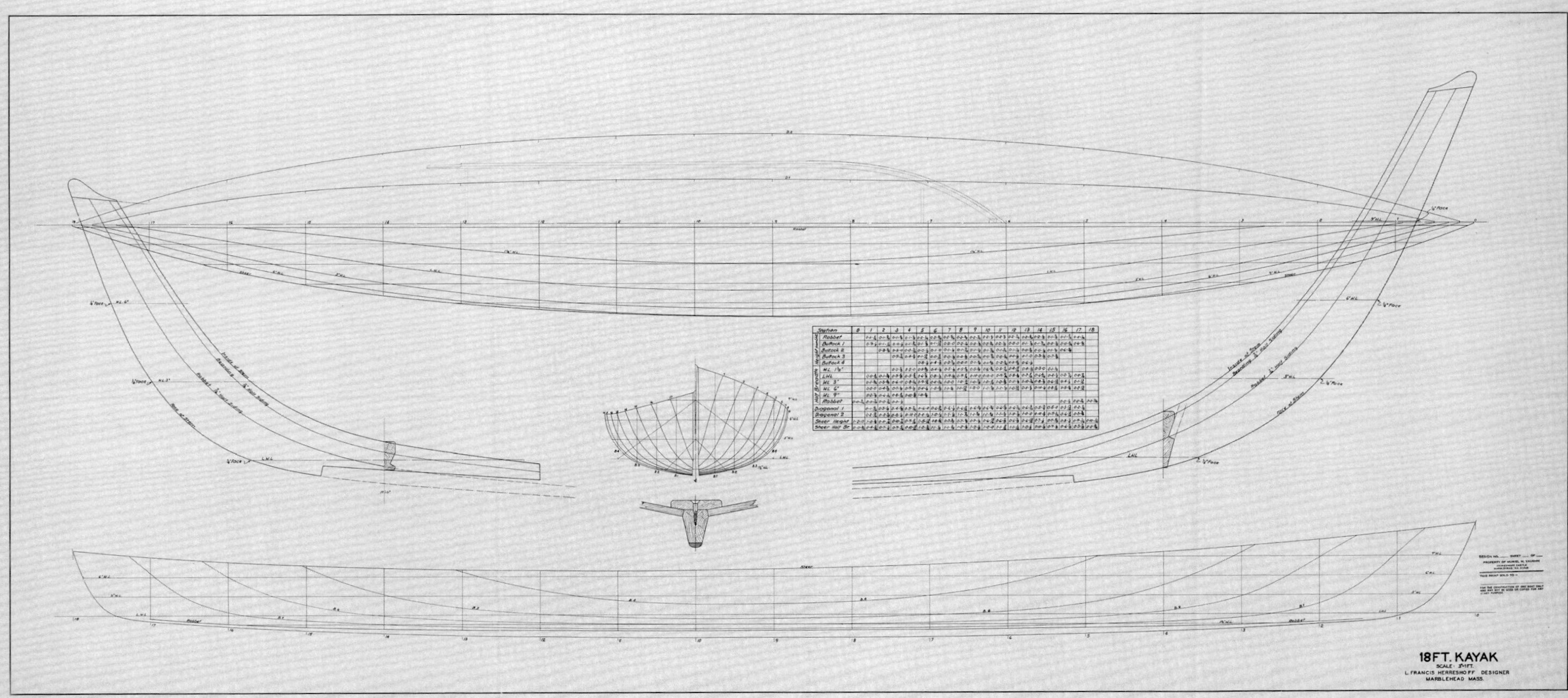

The lines and offsets of an 18-foot kayak that Francis designed and built in about 1927. Her long, open cockpit can accommodate two paddlers, or one and a passenger. The sections show that the boat picks up bearing everywhere as the weight of paddlers is added and as she heels; she is stable, and her generous length adds to her stability. Furthermore, her live ballast is dynamic and can react to heeling by leaning into the heel to lessen it. The double-bladed paddle can also be used to counter heeling. (© Mystic Seaport Museum, Daniel S. Gregory Ships Plans Library, SP38.205.1)

With paying customers few and far between during the depression years, Francis was free to mess about with smallcraft. He wrote, "the smaller the boat is the more fun you are apt to get out of it." Francis spent much time afloat not only in his sailing dinghies, but also in his very favorite sort of boat, the kayak, or double-paddle canoe, as he preferred to call the type. He particularly liked to paddle in the winter. He wrote: "I can say from experience that this form of sport [paddling a double-paddle canoe in cold weather] is so vastly superior to frostbite dinghy sailing that there is no comparison. In the frostbite dinghy you are apt to have wet backsides and sit around in most uncomfortable positions with so little exercise that you spend most of your time shivering. Not so in the double paddle canoe for after you have paddled far enough to set up a circulation of the blood, you can keep comfortably warm much easier than when walking, and this is because much of the body is shielded from the wind."[77]

Starling Burgess had introduced Francis to paddling close to the water back in 1921, when Francis worked for him in Provincetown. Francis's first kayak designs were elegant, long, low, lapstrake boats, similar to the kayaks Starling had designed and built for his own use before World War I at his yard in Marblehead.

In 1927, Francis designed and built an 18-footer. He wrote, "I have always owned and designed several double paddle canoes and think I have had the most pleasure in them of any boat." And he wrote euphorically that when paddling, "the whole body sings a happy tune and the world is a happy place to be in." Francis would often put in to Marblehead Harbor at Henry Baay's boatyard, right near 20 Lee Street, where planks between the launching ways provided an ideal ramp.[78]

In a small notebook, Francis kept a brief, penciled log of many of his kayak trips, the only

The 18-footer at rest for the photographer in Marblehead Harbor about 1934. In the background is the lighthouse on the end of Marblehead Neck. Francis's attire indicates that he is not concerned about spray on this flat calm midday. He is resting his paddle on his trousers, so he has kept it dry despite its lack of anti-drip rings. He didn't like to get wet, and he cussed powerboats for their wakes. His companion, who looks perfectly relaxed, is probably Miss P. Bolds, a Marblehead lady who often joined him for kayak outings. The photograph shows some of the details of the boat's lapstrake construction. Planking is ¼-inch Spanish cedar with six strakes per side, including the mahogany sheer strake. The mahogany coaming is 2¾ inches high forward, tapering to 1¼ inches aft. The 7/32-inch cedar deck is covered with muslin sheeting. Below the waterline, she has six longitudinal chafing battens of lancewood, "to be furnished by L.F.H.," to protect the bottom planking when Francis hauled her out on one of the islands outside the harbor for a picnic. There is also a ½-inch, half-oval brass shoe on the bottom of the keel. (Mystic Seaport Museum, 1973-3-510)

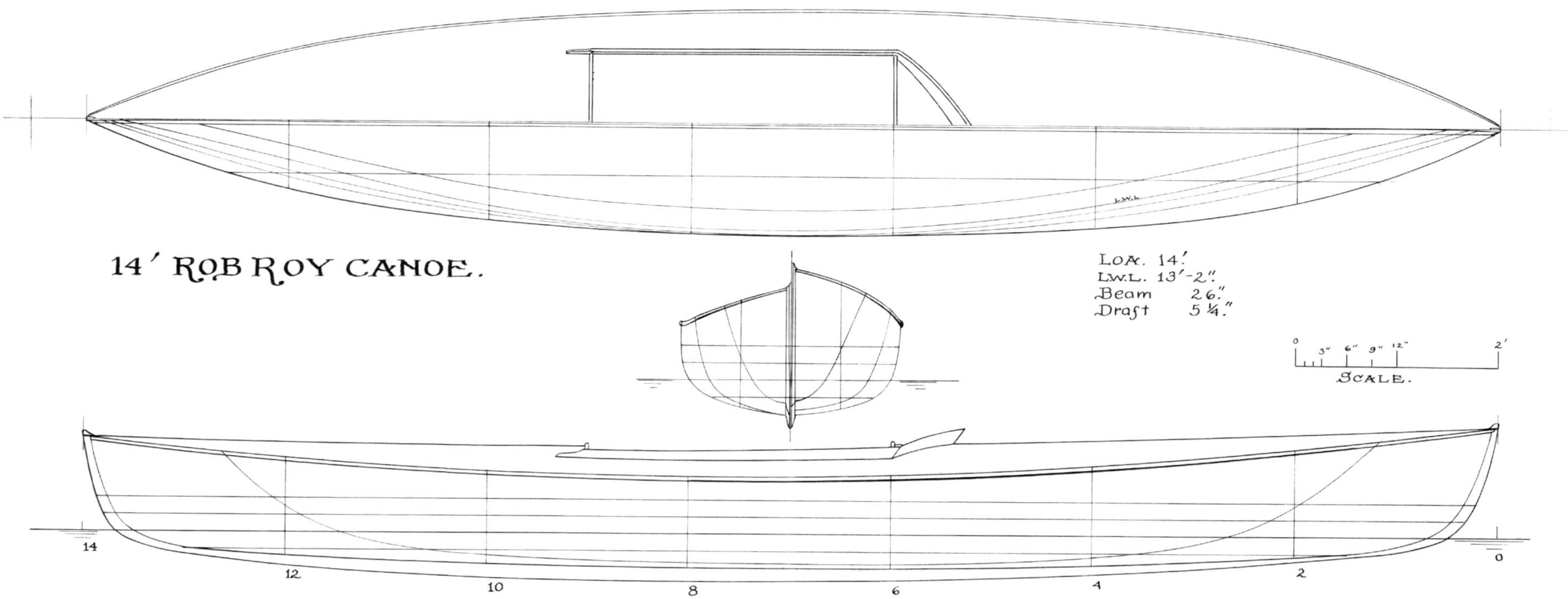

The lines of Francis's 14-foot Rob Roy canoe, named after the boat of John MacGregor, who popularized canoe cruising by writing books about his extensive voyages. Francis did not number the design, nor is there a date on the drawing, but from mention of the Rob Roy in letters, we know that more than one was built in the 1930s and that Starling Burgess and his fourth wife, Nannie Dale Biddle, had one, and possibly two. For greater seaworthiness, Francis has given her harder bilges and more freeboard than has the 18-footer. (© Mystic Seaport Museum, Daniel S. Gregory Ships Plans Library, SP38.10.1)

kind of boating he so recorded. The logs tell where he went and when, distance covered, weather details, including temperature and wind direction and force, and wildlife seen, birds and seals. There is much mention of the *Katrina*, a shortened, 16-foot version of the 18-foot lapstrake design. She was built for Francis at Warren, Rhode Island, by Henry Vincent, a former worker in the small-boat shop at the Herreshoff Manufacturing Company. From 1927 to 1934, Francis paddled her "almost every pleasant day that the thermometer was over 40 [and some when it was less pleasant and colder] during the winter."[79]

From December 27, 1932, to April 27, 1933, Francis paddled 122 miles in Marblehead Harbor and to and from its nearby islands, on 40 trips, mostly in the *Katrina*, though he brought her into the ground-floor shop at 20 Lee Street for three weeks in January for varnishing. On January 5, 1933, in a light northwest breeze with the temperature at 40 degrees, he "paddled to and landed on Orn[e] Is. climed to top and set in worm sunlight on the lea of rocks near the top." (The dyslexic Francis's kayak logs did not have the benefit of the spelling corrections that Helen Bolster applied to those of Francis's writings that she typed.) On

The lapstrake, double-paddle canoe *Katrina*, in which Francis paddled many miles, shown landed on a winter beach. He designed and built her for single-handed cruising. Similar to the 18-footer, she was shortened to 16 feet, 4 inches and had a beam of 2 feet, 6 inches. In this boat he travelled to the Dry Breakers, a rocky ledge off Marblehead, spent the night, returned ashore, and wrote an essay about the adventure for *The Rudder*. She is now in the Watercraft Collection at Mystic Seaport. After much experience in the *Katrina*, Francis noted in his kayak log that she could be improved by making her a foot longer on deck and a foot-and-a-half longer on the waterline; making her a little deeper; giving her a little more freeboard, with less crown in the deck at the ends, more amidships; raising the seat slightly; lowering the foot rest slightly; and extending the deck opening further aft to allow more room for a passenger. (Mystic Seaport Museum, 1973-3-593)

February 17 he "padeled to (Children's) Cat Island walked around and looked at all the buildings." Two days later, in a moderate northeaster with the thermometer at 35 degrees, he was on Orne again. "It was a little rough coming back," he wrote. In a northwest gale on March 5, "with very hard gusts possibly 60 M.P.H," and the temperature just at freezing, Francis ventured out to Orne Island "by keeping very close under the lea of shore, landed set in the sun at the top and in the lea." He was pushing his kayaking to the limit of safety, but he knew the local conditions and he had confidence in his boat and in his ability to handle her. But he had his limits. His entry for December 29, 1933, reads: "Last night the thermometer went down to -16 or sixteen below 0. No padeling today."[80]

Part of Francis's cold-weather confidence came from his warm-water experiments with intentional capsizing. He wrote: "Most of the double paddle canoes that I have designed and used in the last twenty-five years have had water-tight bulkheads at both ends. In such a craft if one is upset it is quite easy to get aboard again and bail her out. The procedure in getting aboard is as follows: after one has righted the canoe he swims to her stern and then, facing forward, presses the stern under water until he can sit astride on the after deck. Next he moves forward in short stages by throwing his weight on his hands, which are at the gunwale, until he has come to the cockpit. Then by throwing both legs forward he can slide into his seat. All during this operation a person is balancing the little craft with his feet in the water, which seems to keep her from capsizing again." Fortunately, Francis never had to perform "this operation" in cold water.[81]

Francis wrote to reassure his father about the safety of his double paddle canoes: They "are very safe for the following reasons:

> *The kayak is the same construction as a rowboat with 5/16ths lapstrake planking. She is nearly 2/3 watertight bulkheads [two-thirds of her volume sealed off by the bulkheads for flotation].*
>
> *Her shape makes her an exceptional seaboat and her shear makes her self-righting. [The latter part of this statement is surely an exaggeration. Her modest sheer would give her a slight tendency toward self-righting. Nathanael G. Herreshoff was probably not impressed by this statement from his knowledgeable son.]*
>
> *Her small and narrow cockpit keeps one from sliding sideways [when the boat heels]. You sit right on the bottom in this form of paddling and the weight is so low that she is nearly non-capsizable." [And, Francis could have added, the weight is dynamic, for the paddler can lean into a roll. Moreover, he could have mentioned the potential stabilizing force of the paddle.]*[82]

Knowing that his father believed that kayaking was dangerous, especially in cold weather, Francis censored his accounts when writing to Nathanael. "You have guessed right about my winter paddling," he wrote in February 1933. "It is only done in pleasant weather and we have really had many very pleasant, safe days for it this winter and you would be surprised how much more light wind we have here than at Bristol. Also I keep very close to shore and constantly keep an eye on the weather although I know from summer experiments that the kayak I am using this winter [the 16-foot *Katrina*] can weather very hard winds and surprising seas. As far as the temperature is concerned, many times I have been out this winter it has been 40 degrees and with the constant exercise of paddling this is actually pleasanter and more exhilarating than the average summer temperature."[83]

Francis's next paddling season, the winter of 1933-1934, seems to have been a closer match to his report to his father. He was more cautious

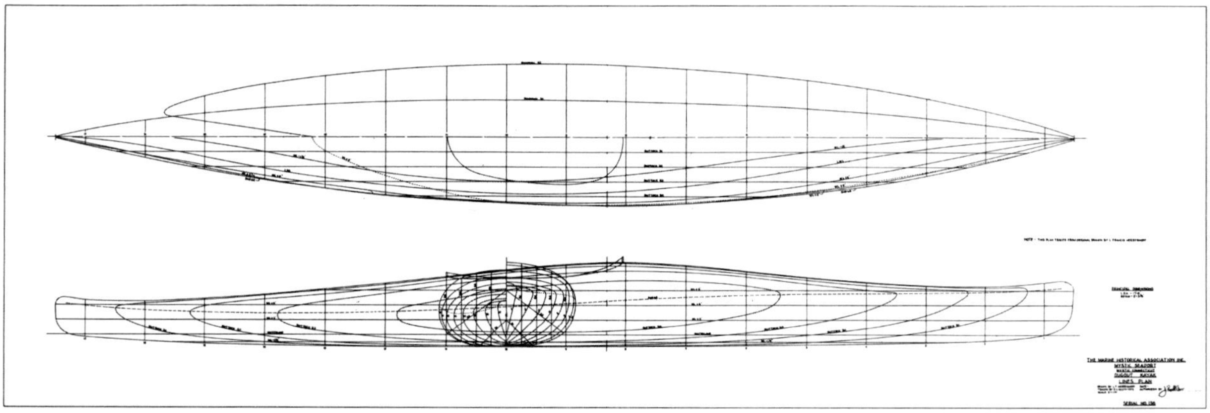

about going out in cold, windy weather, because he sometimes squeezed a passenger into the *Katrina*, most often "P. B," Miss P. Bolds, a local lady, or, sometimes, Helen Bolster's young daughter, Anne. Being small, Anne would be sent into the ends of the kayak on cleaning missions; later, she was allowed to take out one of Francis's double-paddle canoes on her own. On January 12, 1934, Francis and Miss Bolds went out in Marblehead Harbor and "watched [Frostbite] Dingeys race about." On March 4, in a flat calm and thick fog, temperature 40 degrees, Francis "padeled various corces with P. B. had amusing navigating with cumpas etc." Sometimes Francis and Lee Nielsen would lift a kayak atop the old Buick and drive to Ipswich or Newburyport to explore their labyrinths of marshy waterways. Lee remembered that on these trips Francis always found something new that fascinated him.[84]

From late November to late February of the following winter, 1934-1935, Francis lost his ideal put-in place, when Henry Baay ripped up the planking on his ways to replace it. Francis sold the *Katrina* to his kayaking mentor, Starling Burgess. She was later donated to the Mystic Seaport Museum by Starling's son, Frederic Tudor.[85]

Francis kept using his kayaks right through the next decade. In 1947, he described paddling "on an inland river [the Parker] at Byfield [Massachusetts]" to his sister Agnes: "The river goes right through country that must be just the same as it was when the Indians were here and on that day the woods and swamps were green and fresh and beautiful." And in 1968, at age seventy-seven, he would write: "I was paddling a kayak when I was seventy-five, and if I get a chance I will go again this summer."[86]

Francis enjoyed building double-paddle canoes as much as he enjoyed paddling them. In his book, *The Compleat Cruiser*, he has Goddard, an alter ego, describe his work table, 29½ inches above the floor for easy planing, and say, "I have built two or three double paddle canoes on it." And in *The Common Sense of Yacht Design*, he wrote,

The lines of Francis's 17-foot, white, dugout, double-paddle canoe of 1930. Her streamlined shape gives her minimum water and wind resistance and allows 18 inches of lying-down "headroom" just forward of the cockpit, which was enough for single-handed camp-cruising. She wasn't dug out of a log; rather, she was made up from fore-and-aft lifts, like a ship's half-hull model, but with the lifts being vertical, rather than horizontal, and made in rings, rather than being solid. She weighed more than 100 pounds. (*WoodenBoat* 14 (January/February 1977): 56)

"to stand at the bench knee deep in cedar shavings, planing up the planks for a canoe or rowboat, is one of the pleasantest things I know."[87]

Back in the 1933-1934 season, Francis noted paddling trips in a "white kayak." This was a 17-foot dugout that had been built to Francis's design in 1930 by Bror Tamm at Lawley's. Francis wanted to experiment with a boat whose construction would not limit her shape in any way, so that he could streamline her to his heart's content. And streamline her he did. Neither water nor wind can get much of a grip on her. She has an artistic, futuristic shape.

The construction of this boat is unique. The hull shape is created by vertical lifts running fore-and-aft. Starboard and port halves of the boat are built separately and then glued together. Each 1½-inch-thick, Virginia cedar lift is shaped to the lines of the hull both outside and inside, and is glued to its neighbor, like building, on its side, a hollow contour map of a gently rising hill whose summit is at the maximum beam of the boat. This procedure resulted in a hull that is ¾-inch thick at the bottom, ½-inch at the turn of the bilge, and ⅜-inch on top, when smoothed. As with building the *Whirlwind*'s giant mast in the same year, Francis imagined the general scheme and Bror Tamm worked out the details. For the dugout, these were practical tasks in the Lawley shop that took Tamm more than a thousand words to describe in writing, even with the aid of pictures. He wrote, "It was a long and expensive and interesting job and the result was spectacular and beautiful." Once Tamm had the rough hull put together, Francis did all the smoothing and finishing. Unlike their disagreement over the construction of the *Whirlwind* mast, Francis and Tammy were in accord on the unusual dugout.[88]

Francis said that the dugout was wet in much of a chop, and she has but a small coaming. Maynard Bray, *WoodenBoat* magazine's longtime technical editor, tried her out and found that she was heavy and slow to accelerate, had a fast cruising speed, was steady and slow to turn, and disturbed the water hardly at all. Tamm said that Francis preferred a heavy kayak and carried 75 to 100 pounds of ballast in sandbags when he paddled alone in his lighter boats. Francis wrote, "in paddling to windward in a good breeze and sea a little weight even seems to be a help."[89]

Francis kept the dugout kayak all his life. Soon after his eighty-first birthday, he wrote to Tammy: "I do not want to part with my kayaks for I like to look at them." Because the dugout needs neither frames nor bulkheads, and all the grain in her hull runs fore-and-aft, she can swell or shrink without opening her glued seams. After Francis's death, his secretary, Muriel Vaughn, donated the dugout to Mystic Seaport Museum. When she was

Francis's caption for this photograph in *The Common Sense of Yacht Design* was "The author's cabin cruiser with a guest [his poodle, Muffin] aboard." (*The Common Sense of Yacht Design*, vol. 1, 38)

put on display, after many years out of water, her hull was still so smooth that she required a sign saying that she was a wooden boat more than forty years old, because most viewers thought that she had been made recently of plastic. Kayaks to the dugout design were actually made of plastic by the Graves yard in Marblehead in the 1960s. Francis was paid $5.00 per boat, and he received $25.00 for the fiscal year ending in May 1966.[90]

In 1933, Francis designed a far simpler double-paddle canoe than either his lapstrake models or the dugout. His objective was to produce plans for a kayak that would be straightforward enough to build to attract the amateur. He also wanted to design a boat that would be seaworthy for her type and would move easily through the water. For inspiration, he turned to the dory.

The dory is a wonderful old hull form that was created almost accidentally when sawn planks first became available. If you set up a raking stem and sternpost, bend sawn planks between them—letting the planks flair into a natural, convex shape—and then fill the oval space created beneath the planks with a flat bottom, you have an extremely simple construction: a dory. Moreover, you have built a most useful boat. The dory, with its flaring sides, will carry a heavy load and, up to a point, will increase its ability to fend off waves as weight is added. You can modify this natural shape with more complex curves, add a high, narrow, tombstone transom or not, and so create many types of dories. For Francis's design No. 57, his simple double-paddle canoe, he drew a slightly curved stem and sternpost, kept his dory narrow, long, and low, and gave her gentle concave curves at the waterline. He created an elegant, graceful, flat-bottomed boat. The achievement of elegance and grace presents a challenge when the designer is restricted by a flat bottom. The dory-kayak is the only flat-bottomed boat that Francis designed. After he tried her out, he wrote to Starling Burgess, "it is a very good all 'round boat and particularly good sea boat."[91]

Francis's drawings of the dory-kayak were inked by Fenwick C. Williams. Williams was a yacht designer in his own right. A bachelor like Francis, and eleven years his junior, Williams lived nearby with his divorced mother at 58 Gregory Street, not far beyond Charlie Welch's house. And, like Francis, Williams had struggled in school and had no formal training in naval architecture. He was often to be found in the group of boat-talkers sipping rum and yarning around Francis's hearth of an evening. Williams would recall that Francis "was not one to suffer fools gladly, and one hesitated to pursue a difference of opinion too strongly for fear that one's rating might drop rather sharply. He once proclaimed to me: 'Crosby [the famous designer and builder of Cape Cod catboats, Williams's favorite sort of boat] never designed a decent boat; they're all a lot of flat bottomed, ram bowed, slow sailing tubs; there, what do you think of that, Capt. Williams?'" The challenge would have been delivered rapid-fire; when Francis was onto something, his mind and tongue operated at a high rate of knots. Williams perhaps tried to change the subject to the advantages of different marine engines, a topic the two friends could discuss with equanimity.[92]

Despite being terribly nearsighted, Williams had worked in the Alden office and, by 1931, was partners with Murray Peterson in Marblehead. The summer of 1933 appears to have been "one or two brief periods," in Williams's words, when he worked for Francis, probably on the side. It is not known why Francis, hardly overworked, employed a draftsman to trace his double-paddle canoe drawings. Philip Bolger once asked Fenwick Williams how much supervision Francis gave him on the drawings for design No. 57. Williams answered that Francis's supervision was absolute, that he was tracing, not creating, and he contrasted the situation with the far less strict control that he

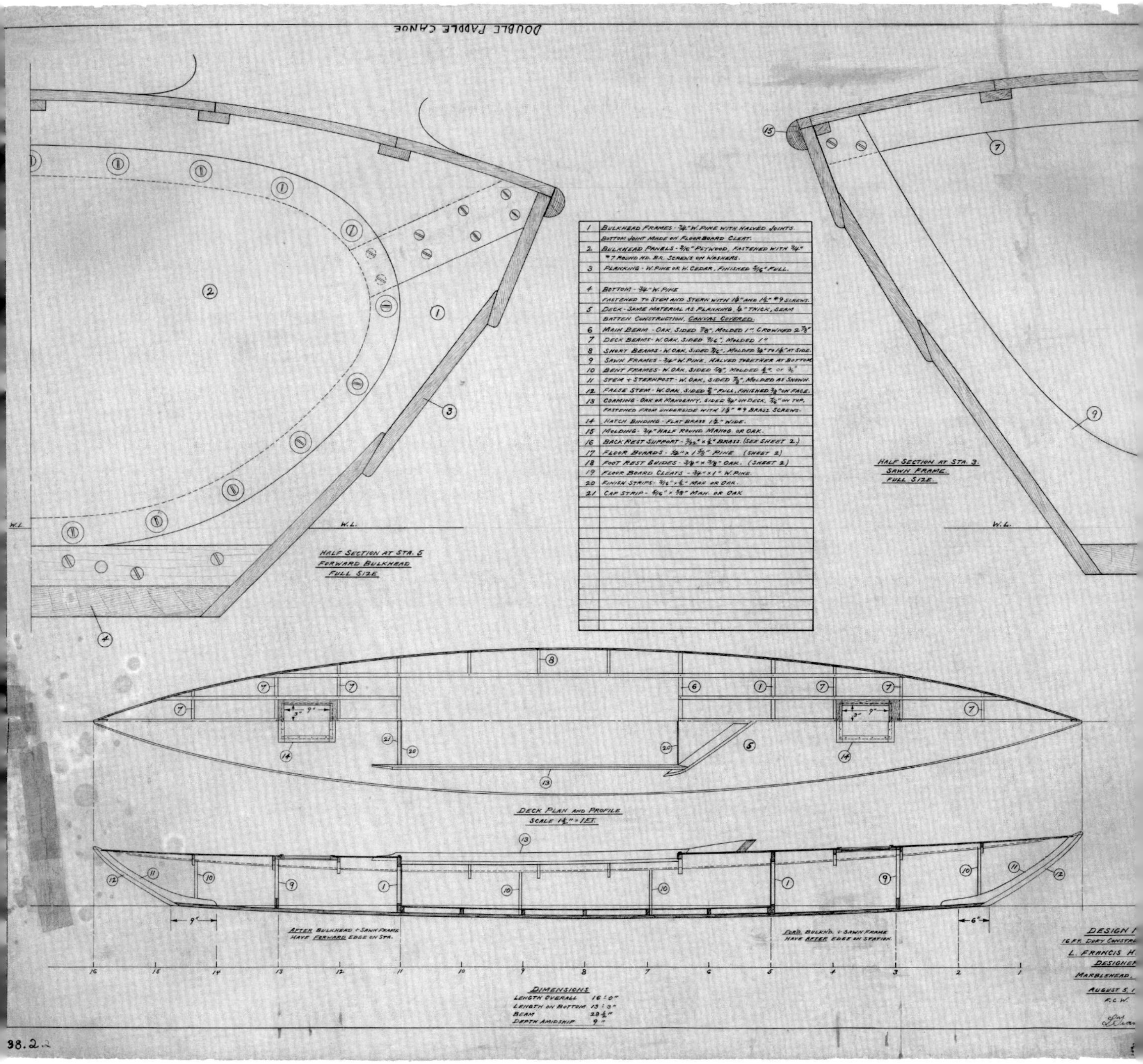
DOUBLE PADDLE CANOE
HALF SECTION AT STA. 5
FORWARD BULKHEAD
FULL SIZE
HALF SECTION AT STA. 3.
SAWN FRAME.
FULL SIZE.
W.L.
1 BULKHEAD FRAMES - 3/4" W. PINE WITH HALVED JOINTS.
BOTTOM JOINT MADE ON FLOORBOARD CLEAT.
2 BULKHEAD PANELS - 3/16" PLYWOOD, FASTENED WITH 3/4" #7 ROUND HD. BR. SCREWS ON WASHERS.
3 PLANKING - W. PINE OR W. CEDAR, FINISHED 5/16" FULL.
4 BOTTOM - 3/4" W. PINE
FASTENED TO STEM AND STERN WITH 1 1/4" AND 1 1/2" #9 SCREWS.
5 DECK - SAME MATERIAL AS PLANKING 1/4" THICK, SEAM BATTEN CONSTRUCTION, CANVAS COVERED.
6 MAIN BEAM - OAK, SIDED 7/8", MOLDED 1", CROWNED 2 7/8"
7 DECK BEAMS - W. OAK, SIDED 7/16", MOLDED 1"
8 SHORT BEAMS - W. OAK, SIDED 7/16", MOLDED 3/4" TO 1 1/4" AT SIDE.
9 SAWN FRAMES - 3/4" W. PINE, HALVED TOGETHER AT BOTTOM.
10 BENT FRAMES - W. OAK, SIDED 5/8", MOLDED 1/2" OR 3/8"
11 STEM + STERNPOST - W. OAK, SIDED 7/8", MOLDED AS SHOWN.
12 FALSE STEM - W. OAK, SIDED 7/8" FULL, FINISHED 3/8" ON FACE.
13 COAMING - OAK OR MAHOGANY, SIDED 3/4" ON DECK, 7/16" ON TOP, FASTENED FROM UNDERSIDE WITH 1 1/2" #9 BRASS SCREWS.
14 HATCH BINDING - FLAT BRASS 1 1/2" WIDE.
15 MOLDING - 3/4" HALF ROUND MAHOG. OR OAK.
16 BACK REST SUPPORT - 3/32" x 1/2" BRASS. (SEE SHEET 2.)
17 FLOOR BOARDS - 1/2" x 1 5/8" PINE (SHEET 2)
18 FOOT REST GUIDES - 3/8" x 3/8" OAK. (SHEET 2)
19 FLOOR BOARD CLEATS - 3/4" x 1" W. PINE.
20 FINISH STRIPS - 3/16" x 1/2" MAH. OR OAK.
21 CAP STRIP - 5/16" x 5/8" MAH. OR OAK
DECK PLAN AND PROFILE
SCALE 1 1/2" = 1 FT.
AFTER BULKHEAD + SAWN FRAME HAVE FORWARD EDGE ON STA.
FORD. BULKHD. + SAWN FRAME HAVE AFTER EDGE ON STATION.
DIMENSIONS
LENGTH OVERALL 16' 0"
LENGTH ON BOTTOM 13' 3"
BEAM 28 1/2"
DEPTH AMIDSHIP 9"
DESIGN
16 FT. DORY CONSTR
L. FRANCIS H
DESIGNER
MARBLEHEAD,
AUGUST 5, 1
F.C.W.
38.2.2

had experienced from John Alden. An artist, whom Francis mentored when she was young, said, "an artist like Herreshoff has to work alone, not depend on others who may not share his vision."[93]

Design No. 57 was one of Francis's most popular boats. The plans were published in the September 1947 issue of *The Rudder* to illustrate Francis's article, "The Double Paddle Canoe." Boris Lauer-Leonardi wrote Francis: "Your article on the double paddle canoe has brought in an overwhelming amount of mail. In fact more than any one article since I have been editor, and that's six years."[94]

Francis wrote, in his article, "I am sure if someone built double paddle canoes similar to this design they would sell like hot cakes." A few builders took him up on his suggestion. Boris reported that the Hopps Boat Company in his town of Port Washington, on the north shore of Long Island, built three kayaks to the design in the winter of 1948 and made a "nice job" of them. The price was $250, without paddle and seat. Two were for Boris and his wife. Thad Danielson at Redd's Pond Boatworks in Marblehead built some much more recently. He beefed up the size of the gunwale for more secure fastening of the deck. The price went up to $3,500.[95]

And design No. 57 did attract amateur builders. In 1969, Francis estimated that "perhaps a hundred" of the dory kayaks had been home-built. Welles K. Rice of Hartford, Connecticut, built one, calling it "the easiest paddling and handling canoe I ever owned." One day in May 1949 he paddled across Long Island Sound from Indiantown Harbor, Connecticut, to the north fork of Long Island at Terry Point, and back, twenty-two miles, much of the trip in thick fog. As he passed the Cornfield Point Lightship three miles off the mouth of the Connecticut River, one of her crew looked down and said, "You have an awful nerve being out here in that thing." John J. Slager built one in September 1954 for a materials cost of $80. She weighed 80 pounds. Her builder used her to explore Chesapeake Bay creeks at 2½ to 3 mph without fatigue. Stan Ellis of Anacortes, Washington, built one in the early 1960s and "added a small skeg which greatly improved her directional stability without seriously affecting her maneuverability. The plans were a joy to work

LEFT: The construction plan for the dory-kayak. She is 16 feet long on deck, 13 feet, 3 inches on the bottom, with a beam of 28½ inches. Because Francis drew the construction sections at full size, no offsets were necessary. The bottom is ¾-inch white pine; planking 5/16-inch white pine or white cedar; deck ¼-inch pine or cedar, canvas-covered. There are two bulkheads, two sawn frames, and four bent frames. The bulkheads are at each end of the cockpit, so that about half of the volume of the boat would not flood in a capsize, as long as the two deck hatches were secure and watertight. These air spaces in the ends of the boat would, of course, be diminished by any cargo. This drawing, inked on August 5, 1933, by Fenwick Williams, was published in the September 1947 issue of *The Rudder*. (© Mystic Seaport Museum, Daniel S. Gregory Ships Plans Library, SP38.2.2) ABOVE: Fenwick C. Williams steering one of his designs for a small cruising boat. His hands are sure and relaxed on sheet and tiller, but his vision was poor, so he has to squint. (Courtesy William Peterson)

from: precise, beautifully detailed and drawn." George B. Kelley of Hyannis, Massachusetts, built a No. 57 in 1965. He wrote: "Dear Mr. Herreshoff, Sir: I am very pleased with the result. As all good boats deserve a good name I propose to call this one 'L. Francis' if you do not object." Francis replied: "I shall be much pleased and flattered if you name the boat 'L. Francis.'"[96]

In 1935, Francis had another success in kayak design, at least in terms of creating a boat that became popular. It is not known how much money design No. 61 earned him, but, as we have seen, kayak design was not a lucrative business. The boat was a 17-foot racing kayak, and the client was Ludwig Hansen of Nordens Kano & Kajak Kompani, a canoe-builder in Soborg, Denmark. The company named Francis's design the Rainbow and built and sold twenty-two kayaks in the first year at Kr. 190, then worth a bit more than $41. There was talk of Francis designing a single scull for the company, but nothing came of it. Francis did make a preliminary design for Ludwig for an 18-foot inboard-motor launch, but that project went no further.[97]

Ludwig reported to Francis on the racing kayak: "She is a very fast boat, and one thing they all like, she is very easily started, in the start she goes much ahead of the other types, and she won the 1,000 meter race here in Denmark. She can stand quite a lot of rough water too, which are not the case with other German boats of her type." And he wrote to Francis that a Norwegian customer paddled his Rainbow home from Soborg on a two-week trip and then proceeded to take first prize in a Norwegian regatta in both the 10,000 meters (52 minutes, 16 seconds; 6.27 knots) and 1,000 meters (5 minutes, 5 seconds; 6.44 knots).[98]

L. Francis Herreshoff, shy with adults, particularly women, felt at home with young people, at least with young people who demonstrated curiosity and a willingness to listen and learn. Giving to a youngster of his knowledge and experience was a joy to him. Perhaps, unconsciously, he liked acting like the father he wished he'd had. But if a child didn't pay close attention to him, he couldn't be bothered. He'd be nice to such a one, but soon would say, "you'll have to excuse me now, because I have work to do."[99]

The November 1947 issue of *The Rudder* carried the first advertisement for the plans of Francis's double-paddle canoe, his design No. 57 of 1933. He described the hull shape as a "lengthened-out dory." The magazine would also advertise his plans for the spoon-bladed double paddle and the backrest shown in this drawing, at $2.00 each. Hundreds of all these plans were sold, but it is not known what was Francis's share of the receipts. (*The Rudder* (November 1947): 89)

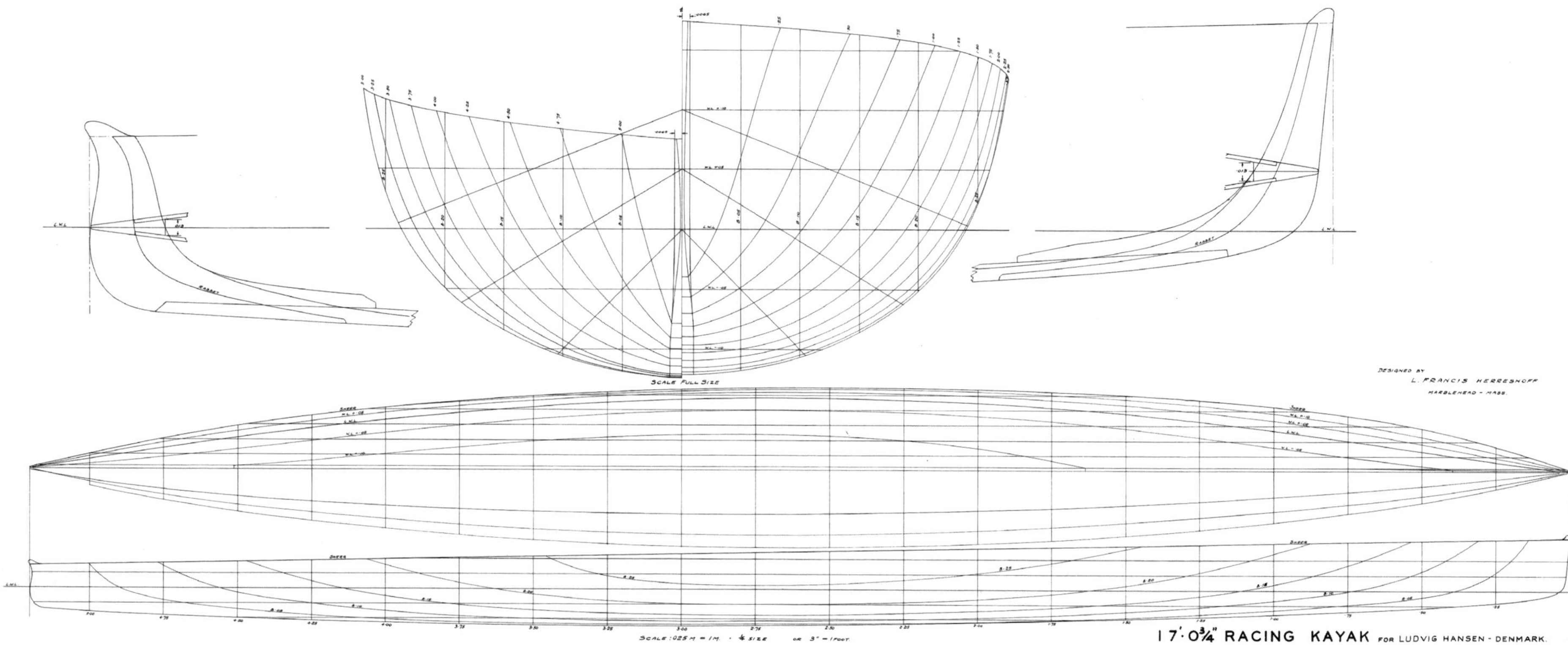

ABOVE: **The lines of Francis's 17-foot, ¾-inch racing kayak. Designed for a Danish client, the boat became popular in Denmark, Sweden, and Norway. Except for the tiniest bit of flare in the bow, all her curves are convex. Her nicely shaped sternpost extends underwater to form a small skeg. This was Francis's design No. 61, dated December 1934.** (© Mystic Seaport Museum, Daniel S. Gregory Ships Plans Library, SP38.185.1) LEFT: **Ludwig Hansen in one of the racing kayaks he built and sold in Denmark to Francis's design No. 61.** (© Mystic Seaport Museum, 1993.120.4.115)

One of the youngsters to whom Francis was particularly attracted was Katherine Jones, who, as we have seen, got tips on sailing from him and was even allowed to shoot the mooring in his 30-Square-Metre boat (see volume 1, pages 283, 313). Katherine's father was Ichabod Howland Jones, a Boston architect who loved boats and taught his only child to love boats too. Katherine had a close relationship with her father.

Katherine's parents had sailed into Marblehead, liked what they saw, and bought a colonial house at 10 Tucker Street, just up the hill from Francis's place in the old customhouse. The hill was known locally as Shittin' Hill, because in former days, after a rain, the contents of its outhouses ran down over its granite slope. The Joneses had Francis up to their house often; they played a lot of pinochle together.[100]

And Francis met their twelve-year-old, polite, open daughter. She had a naturally bohemian streak, a characteristic that enabled her to skip past his tendency to formality and that he found fascinating as a balance to his Bristol propriety. He welcomed Katherine into his workshop, where she demonstrated a keen interest in things mechanical, and he even allowed her to interrupt him at his drawing board, the only person with such a privilege. For Francis, the attraction to Katherine Jones was magical, irresistible. Francis admired Katherine's openness, but he continued to set up his own defenses and devise ways to keep out people whom he knew could hurt him. He needed no defenses with Katherine; she made him feel safe.[101]

For Katherine, Francis always had answers to satisfy her curiosity, and he never talked down to her. "He always had something interesting to show you," she remembered, "some little doo-dad he'd just gotten as an antique. He loved children, and he always made you feel that you had as much sense as he did." When Katherine graduated to a T-Class sloop, a small racer designed by Starling Burgess, "Francis would come down and see if I was treating her right, rigging her right. He didn't think much of me as a rigger. I liked to scrape and sand and paint."[102]

More than a doo-dad was the small English steam engine that Nathanael had stored at The Farm in Bristol, whence Francis had brought it to Marblehead. It was the type that Simpson, Strickland and Company, Limited, had installed in its launches in 1900. In the spring of 1933, Francis had the machine set up in his workshop on the ground floor at 20 Lee Street, where he carefully explained its operation to Katherine. By then, she was sixteen and their friendship had ripened into a quiet, subdued, happy romance: quiet in that it was private; subdued in that it was not consummated physically; and happy in that they shared interests and ways of being. Looking back, Katherine said: "It wasn't a sexual relationship really—it was, sort of—it was things like hugs and kisses and things like that, but that was it. But it could have developed."[103]

It did not develop. One day in late summer, Francis said to Lee Nielsen, his boarder and assistant, "well, we won't be seeing Katherine around here any more," and smothered his emotions. He gave no explanation of why, no expression of his tremendous hurt, no tears, not even a grimace. There were no further words about Katherine Jones. But perhaps memories arose of Christine Howe and the iceboat crackup of twenty-one years before.[104]

If the culprit with Miss Howe had been an iceboat, with Katherine, it was a kayak. The two had often paddled together. Much later, Francis wrote: "I have paddled with children seated in front of me, who enjoyed the sport immensely. I think one of the reasons is that you can talk to the child quietly and when paddling in shallow water, they take great interest in the bottom." But when Katherine was no longer a child, he wanted her to have her own kayak. He wrote, "the most fun of all, in my opinion, is to make a trip with two canoes (which are very much alike as to speed) with one person in each." By the summer of 1933,

Francis had designed a small, 14-foot version of his lapstrake double-paddle canoe and built two of them, one for himself and one for Katherine.[105]

When Katherine's parents realized that L. Francis Herreshoff had built a pair of kayaks so that he could go paddling with their daughter, she in a boat that he had created especially for her, alarm bells went off. "They asked him what was up," Katherine remembered. But then she added, "I think he just came up [to explain the situation] of his own initiative." In any event, what Francis told the Joneses was that when their daughter was older, he was going to marry her.[106]

"My parents said I shouldn't be seeing so much of him," Katherine remembered, "but I kept on seeing him anyway, being the age that would." Francis and Katherine did get to use the new double-paddle canoes. They would launch at Charlie Welch's float and go round to Peaches Point or out to the islands. "It was a wonderful little boat," Katherine said.[107]

It wasn't long, however, before Katherine reacted to her parents' distress. She asked if she could talk to her father about Francis ("you could talk any way you wanted with him"), avoiding her more emotional mother. For whatever reason, that conference took place after bedtime through the wall that separated Katherine's room from that of her father. "My father said it would be very exciting for a few years, but he didn't think it would last—

Francis and Katherine Jones at the height of their romance. In the ground-floor workshop at 20 Lee Street, the forty-one-year-old yacht designer is showing his sixteen-year-old friend just how an X-E1 Simpson-Strickland steam engine works. The two were fascinated with each other. (Courtesy Herreshoff Marine Museum, Bristol, Rhode Island)

and I don't think it would have either—I was beginning to wonder even then, by the time I was sixteen."[108]

Looking back sixty-six years, Katherine said: "Francis was very good in some ways and could be a pain in the neck, too. Very kind, thoughtful, and gentle, but also could be extremely class conscious and could be very opinionated about some things. I don't think my politics would have jibed with his in the long run either, although you don't talk much politics at the age of sixteen."[109]

Katherine's father's solution was to send his daughter off to school in Italy. He offered her the opportunity and advised her to take advantage of it. Katherine worshipped her father, and she took his advice. As she reminisced after a long life of marriage and parenting, the complications of her young romance and the emotions that had swirled round it were still fresh and powerful. She had not been convinced that her romance with Francis was hopeless, but she was ready to agree to the separation. "I didn't want to leave him hanging in the air, so to speak. I tried not to write to Francis," she recalled, "but I did write a couple of times. He knew when I left, I really meant it. It was hard to decide which way to go. The summer of 1933 was the last time I saw him, the last time to speak to or anything."[110]

Francis was blind to think that, at forty-three, he could fall in love with a sixteen-year-old and have clear sailing. Katherine's youth and the great age difference between them was of no concern to him. He must have been baffled by her departure; he was certainly hurt by it. He protected himself with his exit strategy: when Katherine returned home after two years, Francis shunned her. That hurt Katherine in her turn, but she understood. She said, "I guess I got mature under the circumstances."[111]

Katherine remembered: "When I came back from Italy, I had to steer clear of Francis. He was pretty hurt; he wouldn't speak to me; he'd scoot off somewhere if he saw me. He was a very shy person; that's one of the reasons I liked him. He was a wonderful guy, but he would have been difficult to live with, to put it mildly. It had its good parts and its bad parts, let's say. It was just as well it ended; on the other hand, it was something I'll never forget. He really was marvelous. I loved him."[112]

Katherine Jones was the one love of L. Francis Herreshoff's life. Because she was not available to him, he would have tried to forget her, as he avoided her, but she must have haunted his dreams and have taken a firm place in his subconscious. We can guess that Francis sublimated his feelings for his lady into his art form, yacht design.

L. Francis Herreshoff in June 1933. He knows by now that he must say goodbye to Katherine. His demeanor, so full of self-assurance in the earlier photograph at the beginning of this chapter, so contented in the previous photograph, has altered to an expression of anguish. It is not only his recently acquired beard that makes him look older. (Mystic Seaport Museum, 1973-3-337)

CHAPTER 14

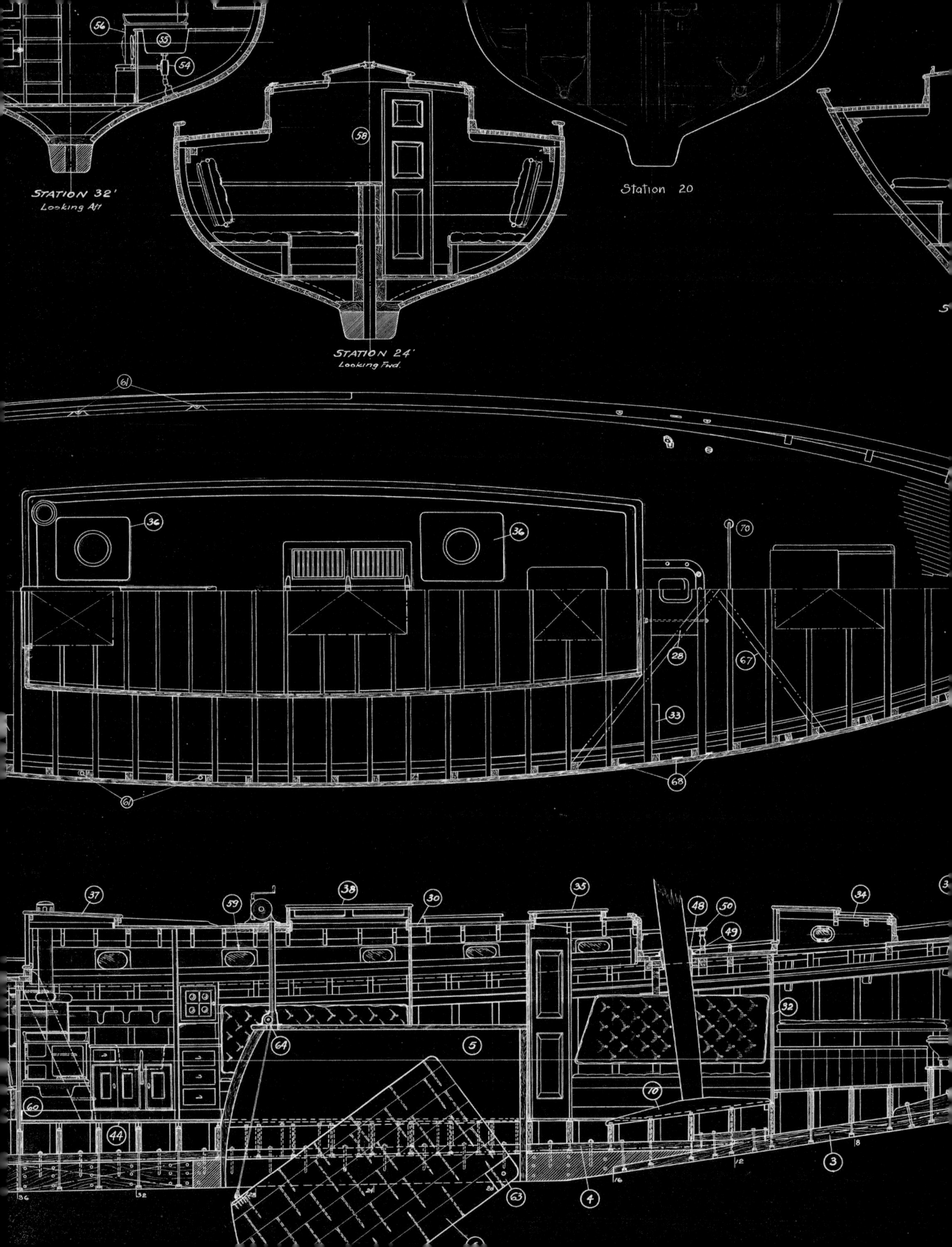
STATION 32'
Looking Aft
STATION 24'
Looking Fwd.
Station 20

THE TIOGA AND THE BOUNTY

"*Tioga* is a great favorite of the sailor men as she is not at all tiresome to look at."

L. FRANCIS HERRESHOFF TO UFFA FOX, JANUARY 14, 1935

L. Francis Herreshoff sailed through many a dark squall during the Great Depression, but at times the sky cleared and the sun shown brightly upon him, never more so than when he designed the most beautiful boat in the world.

Francis and Waldo H. Brown, for and with whom Francis had designed the *Joann* in 1923, had become good friends. They visited in Marblehead and exchanged letters starting with "Dear Francis" and "Dear Brownie." Francis made a lovely weathervane in the shape of a swordfish for Waldo's boathouse at Wychmere Harbor on Cape Cod. By the winter of 1931, Waldo decided that he wanted a new boat. Undoubtedly, his wife, Frances Gray Brown, a perfectionist who supplied most of the money in the family, contributed her thoughts to the decision. Waldo wanted to build on the success of the schooner *Joann*, and he wanted to try the ketch rig. His wife, if she had to put up with being on board a small domicile that rolled and pitched, wanted more space below, and at least a bathtub.[1]

The new design would be Francis's No. 50, and Waldo would name the vessel *Tioga,* repeating the name of a 63-foot schooner yacht that his grandfather, Joshua Brown, had modeled and built in Salem in 1881 for Henry W. Perkins. Tioga is a Native American word for beautiful wife.[2]

As friends who were fascinated with yacht design, Francis and Waldo would have discussed details of the new boat (they probably "argued like Hell" was the way Waldo's son, Paul, put it), but Waldo did not collaborate on this design the way he had on that of the *Joann*. He made no drawings for the *Tioga*. Waldo Brown had many other interests and projects.[3]

The former naval aviator flew his own planes. He became something of an expert in electronics and refrigeration. He made photographs and did his own developing and printing. He was an artist, working in oils and pen-and-ink. He learned copper-plate etching and pulled thirty-five sheets of his rendering of the Gloucester fishing schooner *Gertrude L. Thebaud*. He had a machine shop over his garage and was good with lathe and drill press. He played the piano, banjo, saxophone, and clarinet. All these activities, except the musical ones, and perhaps the refrigeration, were of interest to his friend Francis.[4]

Some people thought of Waldo as a member of the idle rich. Once when the *Tioga* was on the float at the Eastern Yacht Club, Waldo, below, overheard a member say, "Boy, that's a pretty nice boat for a man who doesn't work." Waldo was furious. Despite his yachting and his many other interests, he did work at management jobs in the aviation industry. He expanded Colonial Airlines' Ford trimotor service north to Bangor, Maine, south to Miami, and west to Chicago and Minneapolis. Later, he ran Pan American World Airways as its president. And he served on an aeronautical commission that reviewed naval aircraft. Waldo knew enough German from Andover to be able to read technical papers that hadn't been translated, another interest that he shared with Francis, who, having merely stumbled through Bristol High School, had to pick up his German as best he could. At about the time when the *Tioga*'s design was taking shape, Waldo made a trip to Germany and found that country training many glider pilots. He wrote to Franklin Roosevelt, warning him that Germany was preparing for war. He became a recruiter to help build up the US Navy's air arm. Waldo was simply too busy to become much involved with the design of the *Tioga.*[5]

As Francis began the design of Waldo's new boat, rather than go back to the *Joann,* he found inspiration in the famous George Steers schooner yacht *America.* Steers's superlative career as a modeler of pilot schooners and yachts was cut short at age thirty-six, when he was killed in a carriage accident. Francis would write, "If he had lived longer [he] might have become the greatest yacht designer of all time and eclipsed George L. Watson and N. G. Herreshoff, for there is no doubt he was a great artist." Francis undoubtedly remembered that N. G. Herreshoff had tanned him when he was a child for sailing his model of the *America.* At any rate, he would write that the *America* "has always fascinated me."[6]

"Now if you take a model like *America,*" he wrote, "cut away her deep forefoot, give her a little fuller deck line forward, put her ballast all outside, give her a smooth bottom, light spars and crosscut sails, she will leave our modern racing freaks of the same sail area hull down in a few hours. Both the mathematician and the experienced sailorman I think will agree to this. But best of all, you will have a vessel easy in a sea and cheap to build. You will have room to accommodate the crew necessary to handle the sails. She will be practical and economical to drive under power at a useful speed and will maintain that speed in a head sea. Last but not least, you will have something which is handsome, and 'handsome is as handsome does.'

FOLDOUT INSIDE: **The lines of the *Tioga*, Francis's design No. 50. The dotted lines, showing a deeper keel and rudder and a cutaway deadwood, belong to the later *Bounty*, design No. 58, built to the same lines. This drawing represents a hull of unsurpassed beauty. The almost straight rabbet line in the bow is relieved and beautified by the strong reverse curve of the billet head; the shape of the bow is a fine example of the clipper type, with a full deck-line changing gracefully to a hollow waterline. The stern, with its exquisitely shaped, well-raked, curved transom is in just the right proportion to the bow as to freeboard and buoyancy. The flair forward and the tumblehome aft are lovely. The sheerline is just perfect. Surely the design of the *Tioga* and *Bounty* is the most beautiful of L. Francis Herreshoff's clipper-bowed yachts and perhaps the most beautiful yacht design ever created. Note that, on the *Tioga*, the underwater profile is just two straight lines from 5 feet abaft the load waterline to the after end of the rudder, with a slight change of direction 17 feet abaft the load waterline. The *Tioga* is 57 feet, 6 inches long on deck; 50 feet on the waterline; with a beam of 13 feet, 4 inches; and a draft of 4 feet, 7 inches, centerboard up, and 8 feet, 9 inches, board down. Displacement is 49,460 pounds, with 14,300 pounds of lead ballast, for a ballast-displacement ratio of 29 percent. The *Bounty* draws 6 feet, 6 inches and has about 1,700 pounds more lead than the *Tioga*. This drawing is dated May 29, 1931.** (© Mystic Seaport Museum, Daniel S. Gregory Ships Plans Library, SP38.44.2)

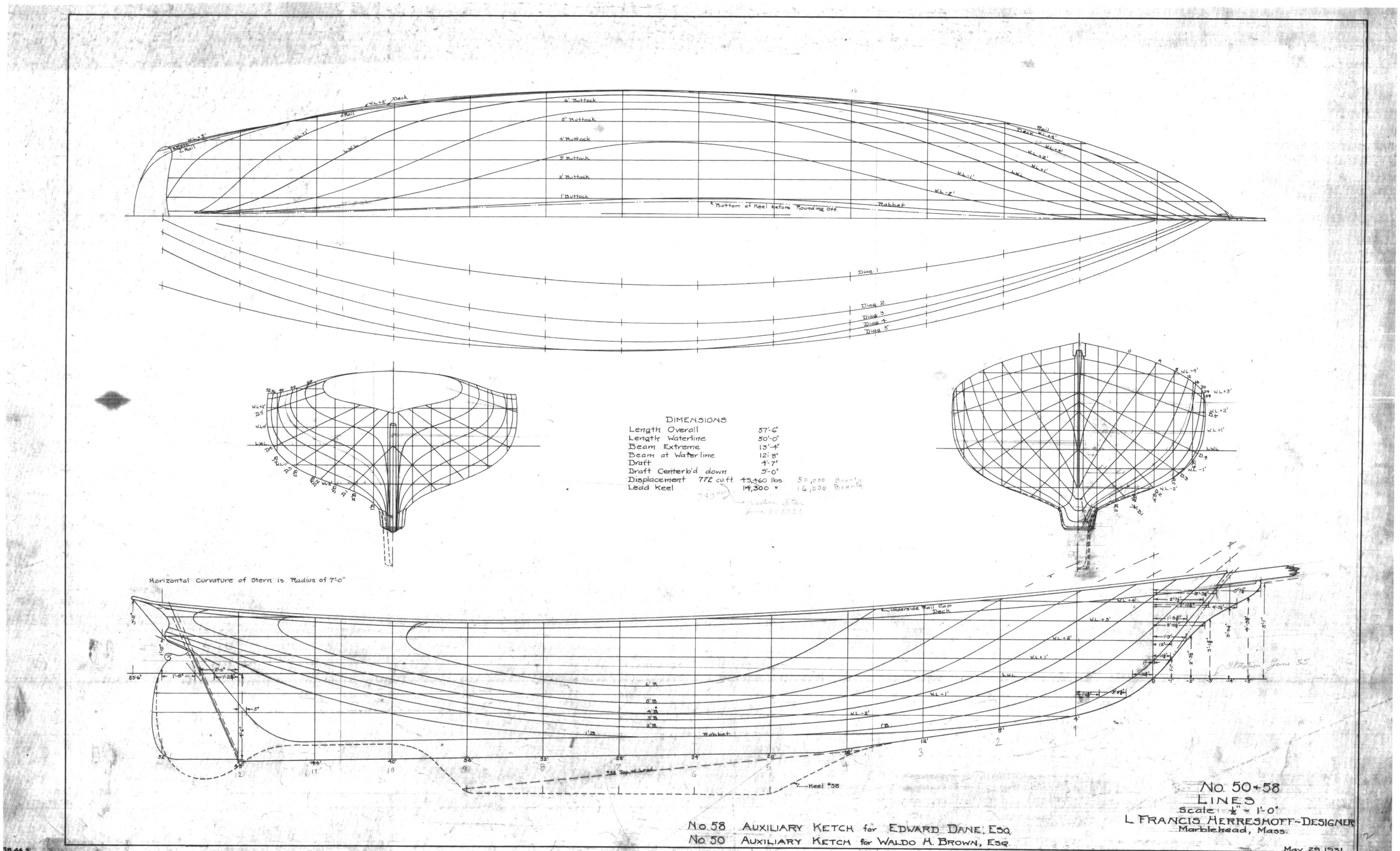

Horizontal Curvature of Stern is Radius of 7'-0"
DIMENSIONS
Length Overall 57'-6"
Length Waterline 50'-0"
Beam Extreme 13'-4"
Beam at Waterline 12'-8"
Draft 4'-7"
Draft Centerb'd down 9'-0"
Displacement 772 cu.ft. 49,460 lbs. 50,000 Bounty
Lead Keel 14,300 " 16,000 Bounty
6' Buttock
5' Buttock
4' Buttock
3' Buttock
2' Buttock
1' Buttock
Bottom of Keel before Rounding Off
Rabbet
Diag 1
Diag 2
Diag 3
Diag 4
Diag 5
Underside Rail Cap
Deck
Keel #58
No. 58 AUXILIARY KETCH for EDWARD DANE, ESQ.
No. 50 AUXILIARY KETCH for WALDO H. BROWN, ESQ.
No. 50 + 58
LINES
Scale: 1/2" = 1'-0"
L. FRANCIS HERRESHOFF ~ DESIGNER
Marblehead, Mass.
May 29 1931

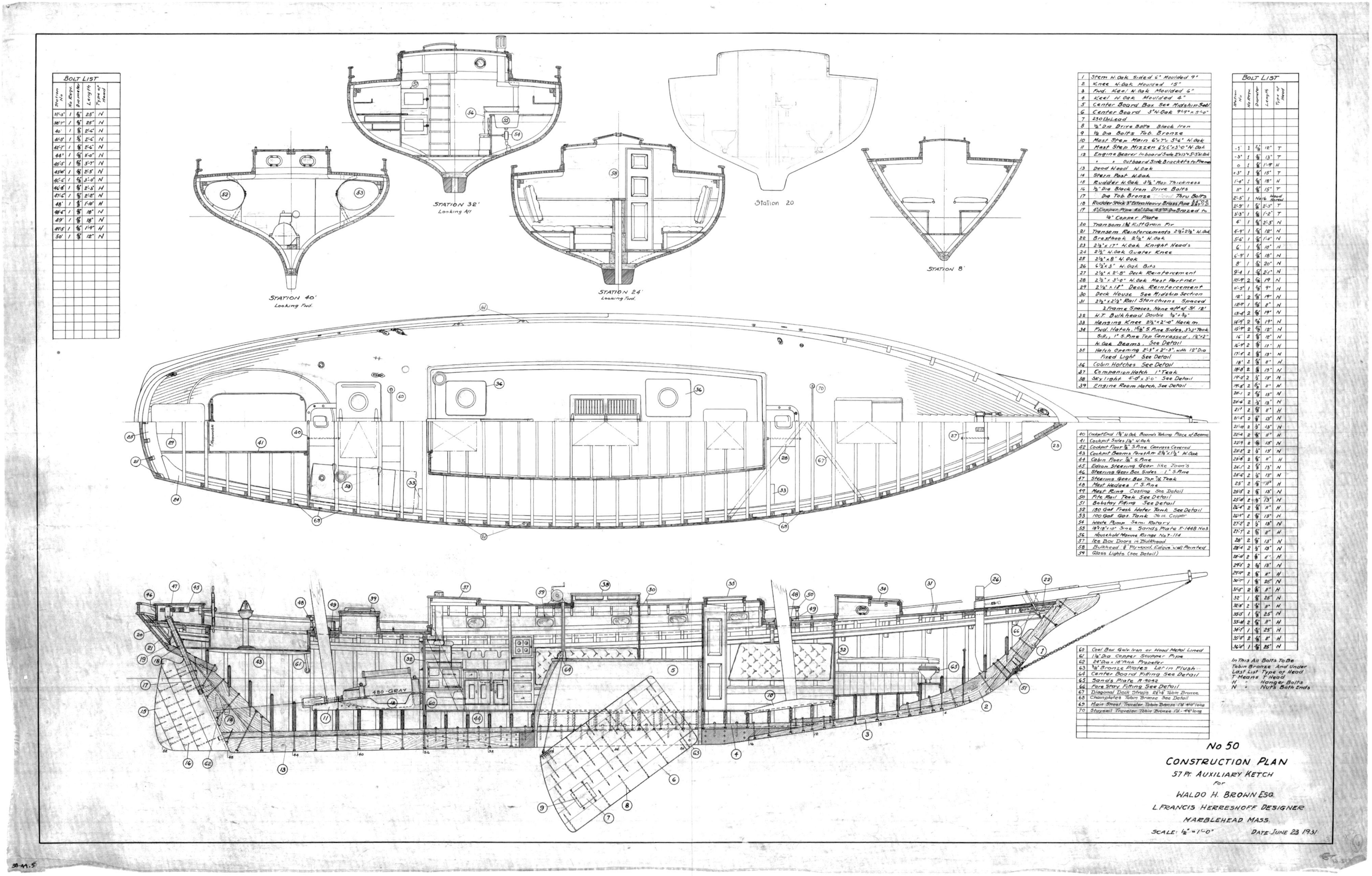
STATION 40'
Looking Fwd.
STATION 32'
Looking Aft
STATION 24'
Looking Fwd.
Station 20
STATION 8'
BOLT LIST
No 50
CONSTRUCTION PLAN
57 Ft. AUXILIARY KETCH
For
WALDO H. BROWN ESQ.
L. FRANCIS HERRESHOFF DESIGNER
MARBLEHEAD MASS.
SCALE: ½" = 1'-0"
DATE JUNE 23 1931

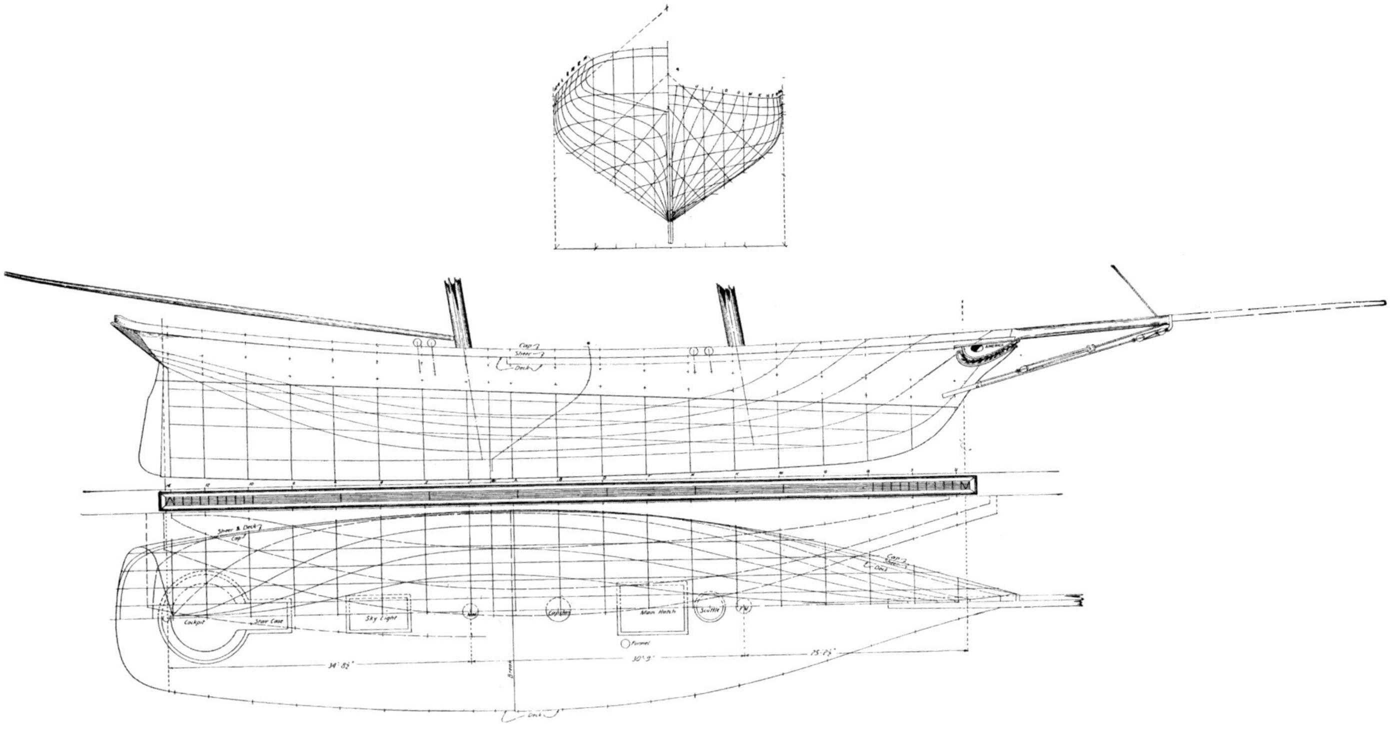

LEFT FOLDOUT: **The construction plan of the *Tioga*, showing also the deck plan, as well as the centerboard in the fully lowered position. The board carries 230 pounds of lead to ensure negative buoyancy. The narrow cabin house allows wide decks, and there is nothing to obstruct the view from the helm, well aft. Construction is conventional, with backbone and frames of white oak, though the clamp and shelf are fir. Planking is 1¾-inch fir; deck, 1½-inch California sugar pine. Rail and cabin house are trimmed out in teak. Note the diagonal, Tobin bronze deck straps in way of the mainmast. There are double-thickness, watertight bulkheads separating the forecastle and engine room from the cabin area. The chainplates to take the standing rigging are fastened inside the planking. She has an off-the-shelf steering gear made by Edson. The drawing labels the engine as a Gray, since the boat is for Waldo Brown, who had been involved with distributing Gray products, his wife's family's business, but a Lathrop was used. It turns an off-center, 24-inch-diameter, three-bladed propeller with a pitch of 18 inches. Alongside the engine are a 160-gallon water tank to port and a 125-gallon gas tank to starboard. The tanks are specially designed to take full advantage of the hull shape for more volume than a mere cylinder. On this drawing, one of twenty-nine to show the details of the design for the builders, Francis has called out seventy different parts of the yacht for explanatory notes in the column at right. At the far right and upper left he has listed the sizes of 117 bronze bolts required for fastening together the main parts of the vessel. This plan is dated June 23, 1931. The Marblehead Arts Association, of which Francis was a member, exhibited the twenty-nine Tioga drawings in April 1938 as "The Drawings of a Yacht's Design."** (© Mystic Seaport Museum, Daniel S. Gregory Ships Plans Library, SP38.44.5) ABOVE: **The best lines drawing of the schooner yacht *America* is by Howard I. Chapelle, published in the September 1934 issue of *Yachting*. The lines are based on a draft from measurements taken off the vessel on August 27, 1851, at the Royal Navy's Portsmouth Dockyard. Chapelle discovered the draft in 1933, while researching plans of American schooners in the Collection of Draughts in the British Admiralty. Francis admired a less-detailed lines drawing of the famous schooner given him by the English sailmaker Thomas Ratsey. George Steers's wonderful design for a fast, able, and beautiful yacht inspired Francis's design of the *Tioga*. The *America* was 101 feet, 3 inches long on deck; with a waterline length of 89 feet, 10 inches; a beam of 22 feet, 10 inches; and a draft of 10 feet, 11 inches. Displacement was 170 tons, and sail area was 5,296 square feet. Chapelle has used the old-fashioned baseline at the bottom of the keel, rather than at the load waterline, which to the modern eye distorts the relative heights of bow and stern in the section plan.** (*Yachting* (September 1934): 71)

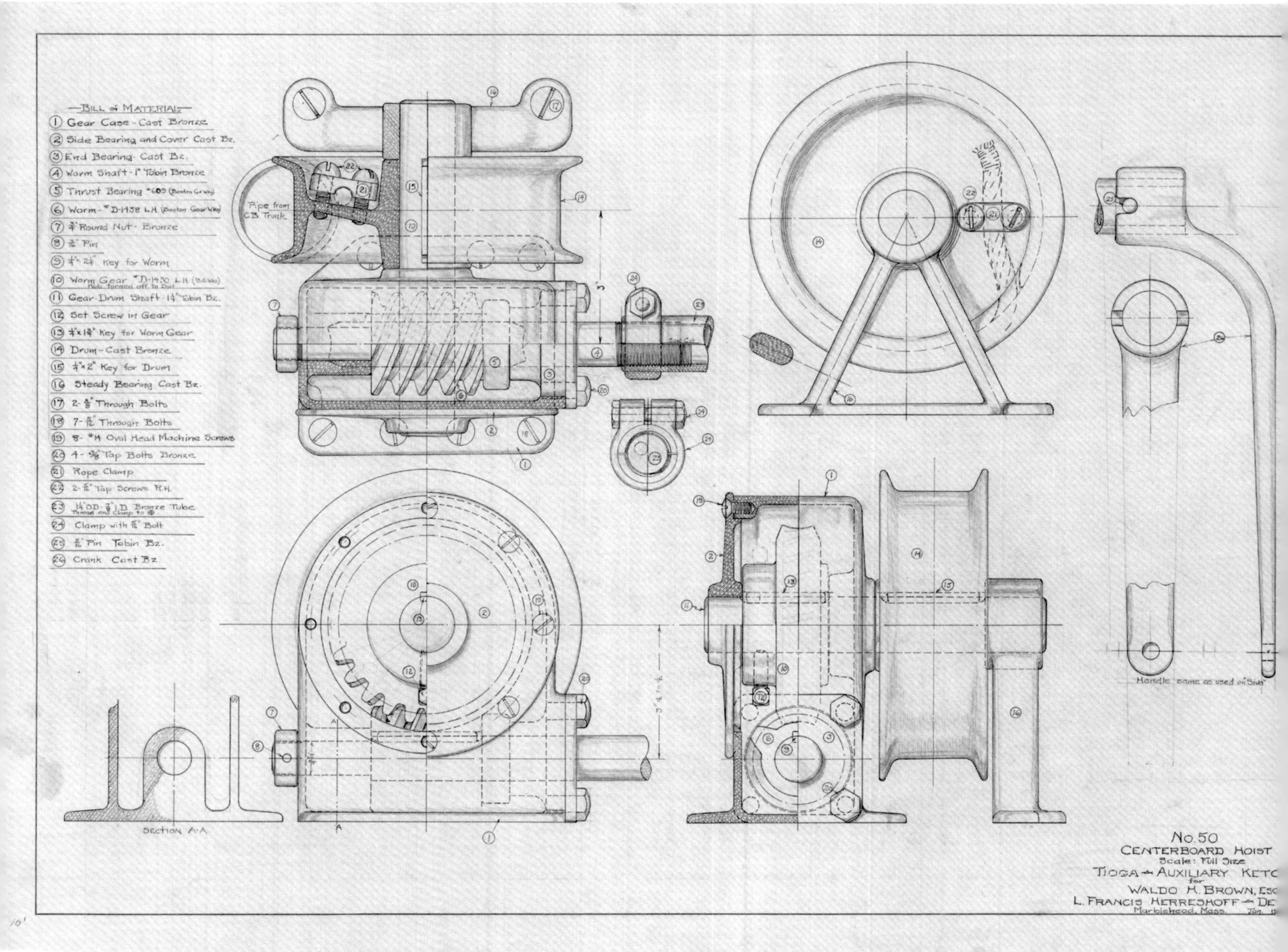

The centerboard hoist for the *Tioga*. The handle for this special worm-gear winch, seen at the far right-hand side of the drawing, may be discerned in the construction plan in its horizontal, working position atop the cabin house. Francis's Bill of Materials at the upper left lists the forty-four metal parts, including fastenings, that went to make up this superb machine. Because he designed many of the fittings for his boats, he caused extra work for the builder, making patterns for complex metal shapes, finishing them with orange shellac and black paint, and casting and smoothing the bronze parts. And he caused extra expense for the owner. Francis was as much at home designing machinery as he was at creating hull shapes and sail plans, and he could have manufactured all forty-four parts of this machine on his own lathe. This plan, drawn at full scale, is dated January 1932. (© Mystic Seaport Museum, Daniel S. Gregory Ships Plans Library, SP38.44.28)

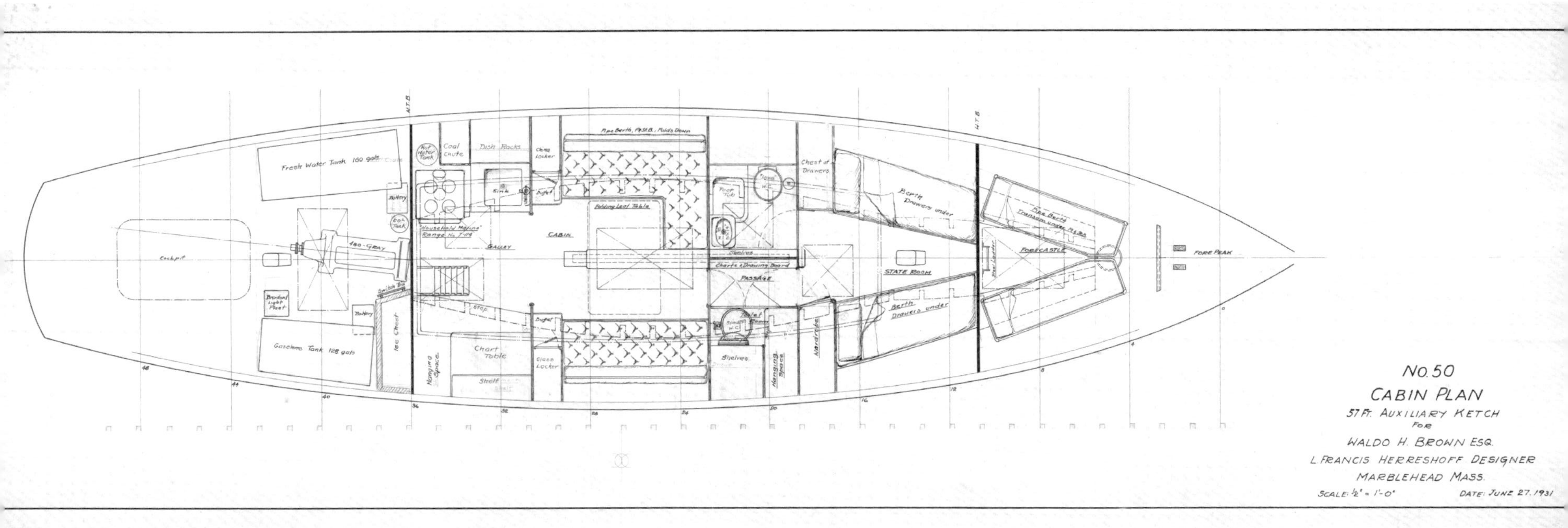

The *Tioga*'s cabin plan. Waldo's wife, Frances, wanted a bigger boat than the schooner *Joann* so that "she could have her bathtub," but, according to the note on this plan, she got only a "Foot Tub." The layout would be conventional for a smaller boat, with forward stateroom, washroom opposite hanging lockers, main cabin with fold-down berths over the transoms, and, aft, galley to port and chart table to starboard. But with a 50-foot waterline, there is not only more than the usual space in these cabins, but also room for the separate forecastle and engine room. In the saloon, the overhead, between the varnished carlings, was painted in Waldo's favorite turquoise. The galley stove was the same Household Marine model that had warmed and fed the Browns (and Francis for one winter) in the *Joann*. This plan is dated June 27, 1931. (© Mystic Seaport Museum, Daniel S. Gregory Ships Plans Library, SP38.44.9)

You will almost have a thing of beauty and a joy forever, for this model can be made to last a very long time."[7]

When we look at the *Tioga*'s lines, we can see the influence of the *America,* but Francis has not copied. As an artist, he has borrowed another artist's concept and has created something new. In his copy of Douglas Phillips-Birt's *An Eye For a Yacht,* Francis underlined the author's statement, "In the acquirement of a good eye for a boat it is, perhaps, impossible to know too much history," and noted in the margin, "This last sentence is very fine and true, but a true artist can make things beautiful by instinct otherwise no progress could be made." L. Francis Herreshoff was a great believer in the concept of progress. He used his artistic instinct to the fullest on the *Tioga,* and he advanced beyond the high standard set by the *America.* With the *Tioga*, he has designed the most beautiful yacht in the world.[8]

The clipper bow was Francis's favorite. He described it as "the natural termination of flaring sections," such sections forward helping to keep the bow dry in a head sea. For the *Tioga,* he has made the most of this "natural termination" by drawing exquisite concave curves in both sections and waterlines, as well as creating the perfect reverse curve of the stem profile, the be-all and end-all of the clipper bow.[9]

A lesser reason why Francis liked this form of bow for yachts was that it lent itself to trailboards. He loved to decorate his yachts, and one of the best opportunities was the trailboard, the nicely curved and ornamented board that "trailed" the stem of a vessel up near the rail, but a device that only worked well on a clipper bow. Francis again took inspiration from a great artist for the *Tioga*'s trailboards. He believed that those drawn by Watson for his steam yachts were the most beautiful of all. And L. Francis Herreshoff made progress, creating, by instinct, even lovelier trailboards than Watson's.[10]

As perfect as is the *Tioga*'s clipper bow, her curvaceous stern equals it. This is a key reason why the design of the *Tioga* is the most beautiful in the world. Francis's own comment on the *Tioga*'s stern, in his book on yacht design that began as articles in *The Rudder* seventeen years after he had drawn that stern, was modest enough: She has "a stern which is really quite large and deep compared to the yacht's other dimensions, but the way it is developed and decorated makes it seem not much out of proportion." This lovely piece of sculpture has plenty of ornamented curves, all melding into a structure that gives the vessel perfect balance, not only visually, but also functionally, as she heels to the wind and rolls, pitches, yaws, and scends in a seaway.[11]

And the *Tioga* has a perfect sheerline, whether seen from alongside in profile, or from on deck in plan view. Francis wrote, "sometimes if a yacht is quite full on deck at both ends I give her more sheer at the ends than is usual." The *Tioga* provides a good example of his concept. There is no yacht

---

RIGHT: **The *Tioga*'s sail plan, with the *Bounty*'s taller rig superimposed on the drawing. In this plan, we can admire the beauty of the whole vessels, with their perfectly proportioned ketch rigs and well-raked masts. The permanent backstay shown is for the *Bounty* only; both ketches have stays between the masts and running backstays on both masts. The *Tioga*'s sail area is 1,324 square feet, with 654 square feet in the mainsail, 252 in the mizzen, 207 in the forestaysail, and 211 in the jib. Francis shows a big jib topsail of 678 square feet. The *Bounty*'s sail area is almost 200 square feet more than that of the *Tioga*. Both ketches have identical mast rakes: 7 degrees for the mainmast and 8 degrees for the mizzen. Francis has raked them apart a little so that they won't appear to converge aloft.** (© Mystic Seaport Museum, Daniel S. Gregory Ships Plans Library, SP38. 44.8)

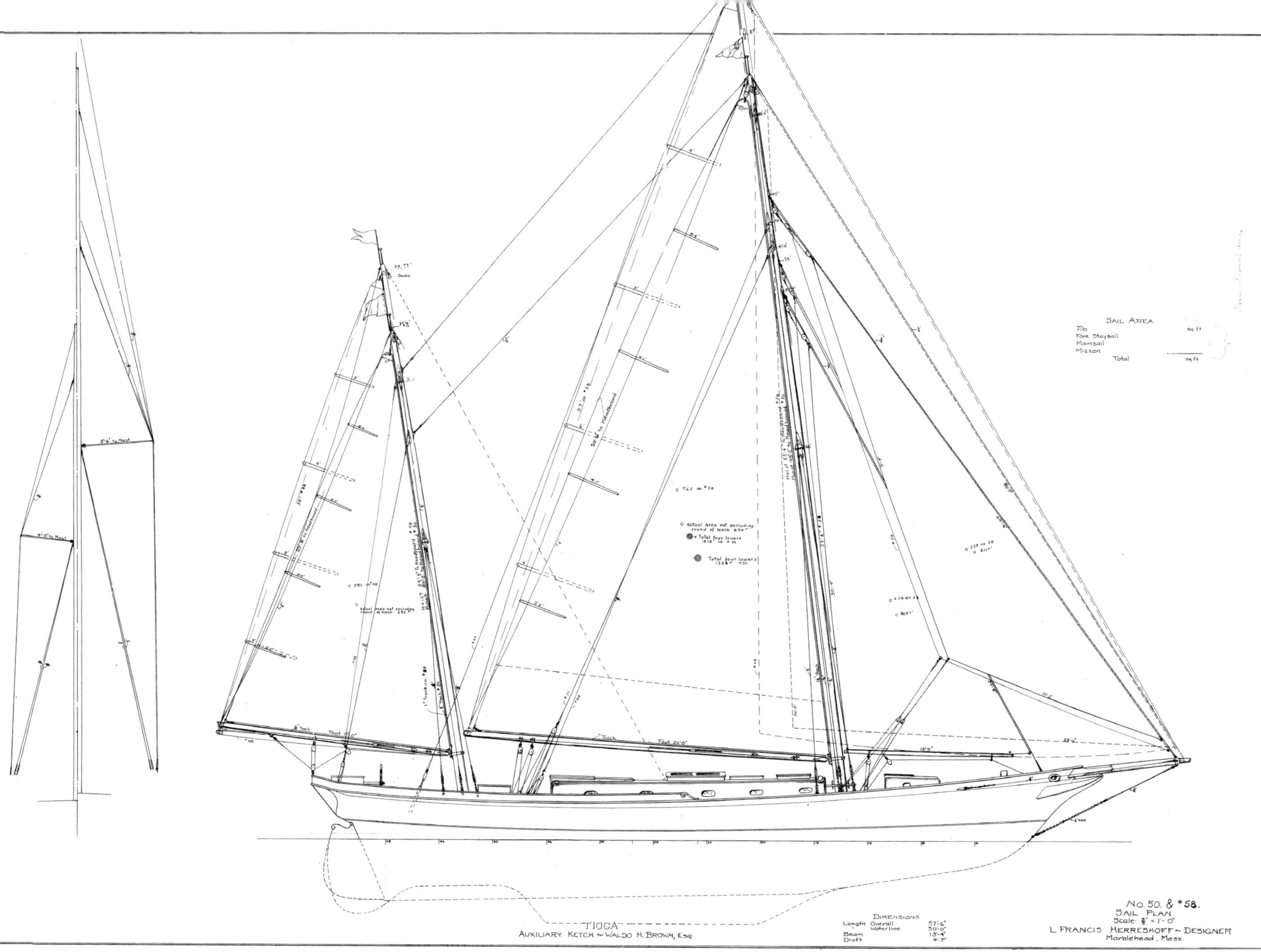
SAIL AREA
Jib
Fore Staysail
Mainsail
Mizzen
Total
sq ft
sq ft
TIOGA
AUXILIARY KETCH ~ WALDO H. BROWN, ESQ
DIMENSIONS
Length Overall 57'-6"
Waterline 50'-0"
Beam 13'-4"
Draft 4'-7"
No. 50. & #58.
SAIL PLAN
Scale: ⅜" = 1'-0"
L. FRANCIS HERRESHOFF ~ DESIGNER
Marblehead, Mass.
Actual Area not excluding round of leach 654"
Total four lowers 1324" #50
Actual Area not excluding round of leach 232
Foot 26'-0"
Foot 17'-0"
Track

that is prettier to row away from at anchor, or more delightful to watch from her wheel, as she picks her way through a sea.[12]

The underwater lines of the *Tioga,* only visible when she is on the railway, complete her perfect hull shape. Her sections are nicely hollowed, as are her well-balanced waterlines. As to her fore-and-aft curves, Francis wrote, "yes, the shape of the buttock lines is very important and it seems as if the nearer to the radius of a circle one can come with them the better it is." Again, the *Tioga*'s gentle buttock lines confirm his concept.[13]

L. Francis Herreshoff was well satisfied with his creation. Looking back thirty-five years, he wrote, "I have seen half models of *Tioga* and two or three others that I have designed and I think No. 50 makes the prettiest model of all."[14]

Waldo wanted to be able to moor his new ketch at his dock in Wychmere Harbor, so her draft had to be limited to five feet. But to improve her windward performance over that of the *Joann*, he agreed to a centerboard. Francis wrote to his father of the *Tioga*: "I really think there is some merit in this type of boat. She is quite shallow, goes well under power, surprisingly fast under sail and is quite stiff." And he wrote of the *Tioga* that she represented "the natural shape that boats would be if there were no artificial racing [measurement] rules to confine them." The time when Francis was designing the *Tioga* was the beginning of an era when numbers and quantification were becoming more and more popular in yacht design, even worshipped, but not by L. Francis Herreshoff. He was fascinated by intangibles that couldn't be measured, by beauty. That was his magic. Yet he also applied to the *Tioga* the practical lesson that he had learned in designing racing boats to measurement rules: that increasing length and displacement without increasing sail area made for a boat that was fast, stiff, and relatively easy to handle, fine qualities for a cruising boat or daysailer, as well as for a racer.[15]

Francis wrote to his father about the *Tioga* that "the ketch rig was adopted at the request of the owner and it has certainly proved to be fast, simple, and handy." Nathanael had already disagreed in an earlier letter: "I would prefer yawl rig to the ketch. The yawl gives a better balance of jib and mizzen when mainsail is off, and the mizzen mast is out of the way in the cockpit. Also main sheet in more convenient place, and with all the yawl is faster rig to windward or down the wind." This was a matter on which son and father had to agree to disagree. The key to either rig is that the mizzen must have enough area so that the vessel is able to claw off a lee shore in a hard chance under headsail and mizzen.[16]

Francis loved the looks of a rakish rig, like that of the Chesapeake pilot schooners and their descendants. He also had practical reasons for raking the *Tioga*'s masts. It made the spars easier to stay aft. The sails had more lift off the wind, and the lifted booms didn't trip in a rough sea when she rolled to leeward. True, the booms would swing more in such conditions if no preventers were rigged. On the wind, the mainsail would backwind the mizzen less. And an unfortunate standing jibe would have less force. Regardless of mast rake, Francis commented on how a ketch's sails should be trimmed: "In general, the sails on a ketch should be flatter as they go aft. The jib can have quite a little draft, the mainsail moderate draft, and the mizzen almost dead flat." This idea was to reduce the backwinding of the mainsail by the jib and of the mizzen by the mainsail.[17]

Waldo Brown wanted the *Tioga* to be fast under power as well as sail, so Francis gave her a six-cylinder Lathrop (Francis's favorite engine, rather than Waldo's proprietary Gray), rated at about 90 horsepower, in its own spacious compartment, and he placed her propeller off center. He wrote: "If I remember right, there are about four reasons why it [the off-center propeller] is best. They are something as follows: the most important thing is that it does not cut the keel bolts in that part of the boat so that the deadwood is very much stronger. The boat sails very much faster with an off-center propeller [less drag, with no aperture] and she goes faster and more economically under power [propeller working in less turbulent water]." Francis wrote that the *Tioga* made about 7 knots with the engine delivering about 45 horsepower. "She turns both ways quicker with an off-center propeller than on-center propeller. The reason is that one way the off-center propeller tries to swing her around [for the *Tioga*, to the right with her port-side propeller], and when you want to turn the other way the rudder blade [now, left] swings into the slip stream from the propeller and makes her turn fast the other way." Francis also pointed out that in order to cancel the tendency of the off-center propeller to turn the boat even with the rudder amidships, it was necessary both to get the athwartships angle of the propeller shaft just right and to make sure the propeller was turning in the proper direction. He concluded that the shaft angle from fore-and-aft, counteracting the placement of the propeller off center, should subtend 125 percent of the diameter of the propeller. And he ruled that the upper blades of the propeller swing inboard (thus, a right-hand, or clockwise-turning propeller when viewed from aft, for the *Tioga*). Her port-side propeller would tend to swing her to the right with rudder amidships, but with a right-hand turning propeller, the lower blades, working more efficiently in deeper water than the upper ones, would tend to swing her back to the left. With the proper combination of shaft angle and propeller direction of rotation, the *Tioga* went straight ahead under power with the rudder amidships. A disadvantage of the off-center propeller that Francis didn't mention is that when motor-sailing with the propeller to windward (the *Tioga* on the port tack), it may not be submerged deeply enough to be effective, though if the boat is heeling much to the breeze, presumably she would not need the help of her engine.[18]

The Britt brothers, Andrew and Chester, were the logical choice to build the *Tioga*. They had done well with her predecessor, the schooner *Joann*, as well as with Francis's complicated R-Class racers. Francis respected their boatbuilding skills, the practical way they went about achieving first-class craftsmanship with neither fuss nor pomp. He liked the Britts. Ever busy with his hands and ever generous with their products, Francis fashioned a fine bow-and-arrow for Chester's son, Andy.

Waldo Brown made time to roar off in his great Packard touring car from his winter home in Milton to the Britt yard in Lynn, where he would meet Francis and inspect progress on the *Tioga*. Client and designer would often end up spending the rest of the day talking boats.[19]

Another inspector of the *Tioga*'s construction was the young Norwegian, Oistein Lie-Nielsen. We remember that Lee had arrived in Marblehead [see volume 1, page 313] not long after Francis. He had come via his father's 8-Metre, shipped from Norway to Halifax and sailed, single-handed, alongshore to the New England yachting center. Francis respected such seamanship, and Lee became a frequenter of evening gatherings around his hearth at the old customhouse below 20 Lee Street. He also got to know and sail with Charlie Welch. Lee had sold the 8-Metre in the fall of 1927, joined the US Marine Corps for two years and fought in the Nicaragua campaign, returned to Norway for a year, but was back living in Boston, working in a Norwegian ski shop, by 1931. He was drawn to Marblehead and reconnected with his boating friends. Francis offered him an informal apprenticeship. Lee was a good seaman, knew something of mechanics, and had an eye for a boat. In the early summer of 1931, he accepted the offer from "Captain Francis," as he called him.[20]

Francis paid Lee $25 a week and added room and board. Lee wrote home to his family in Norway about his new situation:

> *I am really happy being here with Herreshoff and he is a great man and a good chief. He has a red beard, is very*

friendly, quiet and kind and is a bachelor, forty years old and a very knowledgeable man, there is nothing that he doesn't know about and, of course, particularly about boats, ships and things having to do with seagoing affairs. And I believe he is considered America's foremost yacht designer. It amazes me what he can work out regarding various details in equipment and how he is able to simplify things of that nature. I live here with him now in a 200-year old brick house close to the harbor. In the ground floor is his workshop where he makes all kind of models of boats, and where he has all kinds of different machines, as well as the central heating. In the next floor is the drafting-room which is also used as living room and it has a large old-fashioned fireplace on one wall, and it is extremely cozy and home-like. Full of model boats and old boat pictures of all sorts around on the walls. In the same

The Britt brothers, Andrew on the left and Chester on the right, perhaps looking over some specifications for the *Tioga*. One observer described the Britts' construction shed where they are standing (which would burn down later) as "a frightful old wooden building that looked like it hadn't been painted in a hundred years." But the long line of yachts that were launched from its ways made a parade of strong, handsomely finished vessels. Francis enjoyed an excellent relationship with the Britts, one based on mutual respect. (Mystic Seaport Museum, 1984-8-108)

floor there is also a little addition to the building, which is my office, large, light, and roomy. On the third floor there is a large room overlooking the harbor where we both sleep, as well as a smaller guest-room and bath and W.C. Everything is in the same old, cozy style with the exception of the latter, naturally. Mr. Herreshoff has always eaten in restaurants, so when I suggested that I would like to make breakfast and lunch at home he was very happy and he seems to like it exceptionally well. I frequently cook, for instance, fresh cod fish and potatoes for lunch which is a good meal, and probably costs less than half of what we would have to pay in the restaurant for a less tasty meal. We usually go to bed around ten o'clock and get up by seven, we are out in fresh air a great deal, sail, paddle kayaks, swim, and altogether lead an ideally healthy life.[21]

The apprenticeship was a good arrangement for both men and lasted nearly three years, until Lee married and moved into a nearby apartment. Lee's arrival gave Francis inexpensive help, and it gave him company. It also gave him someone to mentor, a situation he liked. For Lee, Francis was not just an employer, but also a teacher in the broadest sense. "He was a great guy to learn from," Lee would recall, "very patient, a wonderful person, almost like a second father to me. He was also very reserved, an extremely private person."[22]

Checking up on the *Tioga*'s construction at Britt Brothers was one task that Francis assigned to Lee in the winter of 1931. They would go over the construction plans for No. 50, and Francis would point out certain details of fastening or scantlings that he was particularly concerned be carried out exactly as he had envisioned. "When they come to this," Francis would say, "make sure they do it this way." So Lee would drive from Marblehead to the Britt yard in Francis's "old klunker Buick," as Lee called the vehicle. Francis also had a nice Buick touring car at the time, but Lee wasn't allowed to drive that one. Lee was the designer's eyes and ears, learning on the job. Britt Brothers launched the *Tioga* in the spring of 1932. She cost Waldo Brown $22,000, on which Francis would have received a 10 percent commission, good money in the Great Depression.[23]

There was a trial sail for the new ketch in Marblehead Harbor. And there was a collision. Francis would write many years later, "when I took the first *Tioga* out on her trial trip, I found she turned too slowly for modern, crowded harbors." She was tacking up the harbor, so her centerboard must have been down, giving her good lateral resistance amidships on which to pivot, but even so, she seems to have surprised Francis with her slowness in stays. Apparently, her bowsprit got tangled up with the overhanging boom of a moored yacht.[24]

In the summer of 1932, Waldo, with Lie-Nielsen in the *Tioga*'s crew, cleaned up in handicap races on Massachusetts Bay. He then took the ketch to his Wychmere haven on the south side of Cape Cod, enjoyed perhaps a dozen sails in his perfect yacht, and sold her at the end of the season. Marrying into the wealthy, entrepreneurial Gray family had its drawbacks, as well as its advantages. There was pressure on Waldo to spend less time sailing boats and more time getting on with business. Waldo was a serious, hard worker, but his many other interests, particularly boats, did interfere with his commercial career. It didn't help that when American Airlines bought Colonial in 1931, Waldo lost his job. Moreover, his wife didn't like trying to keep house on a boat. For her, the *Tioga,* bigger and better than the *Joann*, still presented privations, not perfection. For Waldo Brown, the great ketch was a bittersweet memory.[25]

The *Tioga*'s new owner, Harry E. Noyes, moored her in Marblehead, where Francis could see her from his customhouse rooftop. As a principal in his father's Buick sales organization in Boston, Noyes was able to avoid the economic

hardships of the time. As well as selling cars, he had run the Noyes Marine Sales Company from an office on Commonwealth Avenue, mostly distributing fast powerboats made by the American Car Foundry. An enthusiastic yachtsman, he had owned and raced successfully Frank Paine's 8-Metre, the *Gypsy*, and he had owned a 75-foot, 25-knot, power cruiser designed by Walter McInnis and built by Fred D. Lawley.

Francis wrote of the *Tioga* that he had designed her "for pleasure sailing and to drive efficiently under power. Strange to say, she acquired

ABOVE: **The *Tioga* on the ways. She is fully in commission, with sails bent and covered, dinghy on deck, and anchor chain adding a graceful curve to her lovely bow. Francis took pains with the design of such details as her trailboards and hawsepipes. And he specified that the waterline be painted with considerable sheer: the bottom paint would be just visible amidships, but was raised well above the waterline at the bow (perhaps an inch or two too high?), for the bobstay came to the stem just above water. There are no turnbuckles on the bobstay or bowsprit shrouds; rather, Francis designed a "bowsprit adjuster" for the *Tioga*. It consisted of threaded rods attached to the sides of the bowsprit that could be screwed aft against the heavy bitts, thus sliding the spar forward to get the desired tension on its standing rigging.** (Mystic Seaport Museum, 1996-2-91) RIGHT: **The *Tioga* on an early trial sail. Her helmsman is doing a good job of keeping her sails just asleep in the light air so that she maintains steerage way. This view shows the beauty of her stern, with its carved eagle over the ribbon that proclaims her to be the *Tioga* of Boston. The headsail set is her big, overlapping jib topsail.** (Photo from The Writings of L. Francis Herreshoff, p. 2, bottom, picture section following p. 90)

the habit of winning ocean races and particularly ones where power and sail were allowed." Noyes won the Jeffreys Ledge Race, off Marblehead, three times, and his *Tioga* was first to finish in the 104-mile New Bedford Whaler's Race in 1933.[26]

But Noyes didn't get to sail the most beautiful boat in the world any longer than had Waldo Brown. After his first season with the *Tioga*, he sold her, not to devote more time to his business, but to make way for a much bigger version of the design. This would be the *Tioga II*, which, under a series of later owners, would become world-famous as the *Ticonderoga*.

Shortly after World War II, the *Tioga* went to the West Coast, where she was renamed the *Paradise Bird*. Her owner at that time wanted protection at the wheel and had the Alden office draw up a deckhouse to go over her cockpit. Twenty years later, Francis showed that his occasional paranoia regarding other designers (we recall his accusing Sparkman and Stephens of selling the M-boat *Istalena* to the Great Lakes so she could no longer dominate her class on the East Coast) still disturbed him. He wrote of the *Paradise Bird*, "John Alden who was very jealous of this design ruined her forever by putting a deckhouse over her cockpit."[27]

Perhaps not forever. By the mid-1960s, having been renamed *Western Star* and then *Windward Star*, and having been sailed to the Caribbean, she was bought by Daniel E. Carter of San Diego. He restored her name to *Tioga*. He bought a set of plans for design No. 50 from Francis for $200. In the fall of 1966, Carter and one crewman sailed her from Martinique to San Diego. The passage from Martinique to the Panama Canal took ten days in light weather; she reached Acapulco in twenty-one days, arriving with a blown-out mizzen; and she went on to San Diego in twelve days, a total voyage of 4,400 miles. On this trip, Carter noted that she had so much gear on board that she was about a foot below her lines. Soon after selling the ketch in March 1968, Carter wrote to Francis, "part of the great thrill in owning *Tioga*, aside from the fact that she was a splendid sailing boat, was that she was exactly beautiful when viewed from any angle,

and that her details of construction were carried out to a degree of unique excellence that exactly corresponded to her standard of beauty." Perhaps we can assume that the ugly deckhouse had been removed.[28]

In 1963, at the Mallorca Yacht and Boat Construction Association, Puerto Pollensa, Baleares, Spain, Stanley Woodward Jr. built to design No. 50 the *Circe* for Thomas R. Chamberlain. According to designer Philip C. Bolger, who worked for Woodward at the time, the man laying down the lines was most particular about his work and complained that Herreshoff's offsets, especially in the curvaceous counter stern, were not accurate. But then the yard went on to build, according to Bolger, a perfect replica of the *Tioga*. The cost was $85,000. When Francis saw photographs of the *Circe*, he was well pleased, and he wrote to Woodward, "I tell you what a great kick a designer gets out of seeing a boat just as he visualized it."[29]

Chamberlain crossed to the Virgin Islands in the *Circe*, and ran her as a charter boat out of St. Thomas. Richard C. Newick, a designer who became famous for his trimarans, saw the *Circe* at St. Croix and reported on her to Francis. Newick got this answer: "While she [the *Circe,* or design No. 50] may be the natural development of the sailboat, if it were not for measurement rules, still much improvement could be made in her today. After all, I designed her 37 years ago." Here is a look ahead at L. Francis Herreshoff, aged seventy-eight, still dreaming of a better yacht design than the most beautiful yacht in the world.[30]

Sometime after designing the *Tioga*, Francis did make pencilled, preliminary drawings of a smaller version. This design, which he left unfinished, was to be ten feet shorter than the *Tioga* and had a keel rather than a centerboard. She would have been 47 feet long on deck, 41 feet, 6 inches on the waterline, with a beam of 12 feet, 6 inches, and a draft of 5 feet, 3 inches. And, as we shall see, the *Joann* and the *Tioga* spawned a series of cousins, some of smaller and some of greater stature.[31]

The carvings on the stern of the *Tioga*, simply the most beautiful yacht in the world. (© Mystic Seaport Museum, 1993.120.1.213)

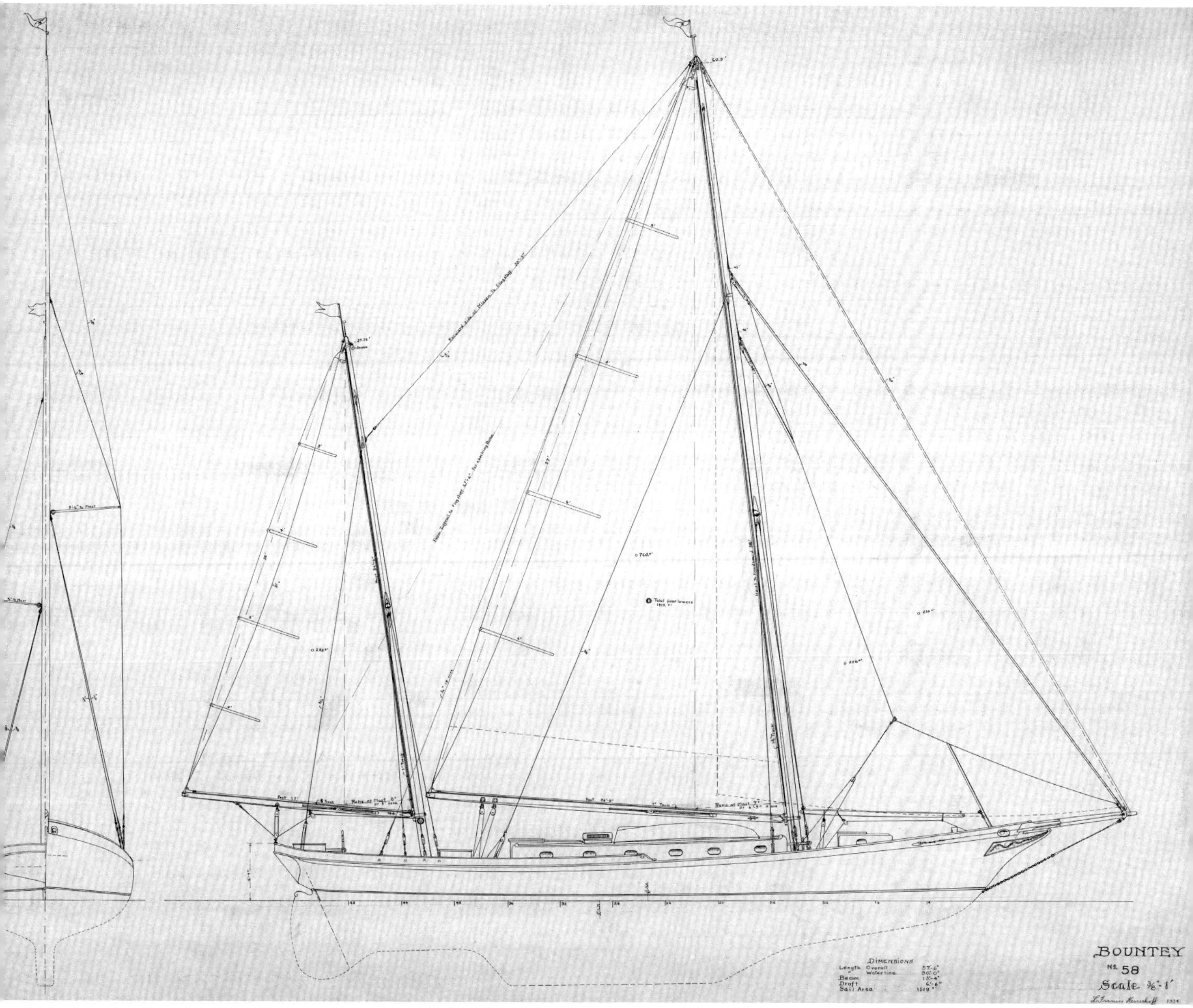

In 1934, Francis drew the *Bounty*'s sail plan by itself, as well as superimposing it on that of the *Tioga*. The later version of the design, with her deeper keel and taller rig (and her special pram stowed on the cabin house), deserved her own presentation, unshared with her near sister. Francis's drawing loses nothing from his misspelling of the vessel's name. Sail area is 1,519 square feet. For an additional light sail, Francis shows simply a masthead, overlapping jib, but the owner wanted him to order a jib topsail, a high-cut, overlapping jib, a mizzen staysail, and a spinnaker. All the sails came from the Ratsey and Lapthorn loft at City Island, at the west end of Long Island Sound, and, as was the practice, Francis would have received a 10 percent commission for bringing Ratsey the order. (© Mystic Seaport Museum, Daniel S. Gregory Ships Plans Library, SP38.1.1)

Meanwhile, the *Tioga* herself is still going strong. As of this writing, she is listed for sale in France at a number of Euros that converts to about $875,000. She is missing her trailboards and seems to have a taller rig. Over the years, she has been rebuilt to the point where there is nothing of her original structure left, but she is still the *Tioga*.

Ernest B. Dane Jr. was an independently wealthy Boston banker who had homes in Brookline, in Seal Harbor, Maine, and in the well-heeled Boston North Shore community of Magnolia, between Marblehead and Gloucester. He had raced successfully in Marblehead class boats, including 30-Square-Metres. His father owned the *Vanda*, a 240-foot diesel yacht designed at Henry J. Gielow, Inc., and built at Maine's Bath Iron Works in 1929. Dane had seen the *Tioga* sailing in and out of Marblehead Harbor in her first two seasons and was doubtless familiar with the reputation she was building for speed. He thought a boat like her would be just what he wanted for daysailing, cruising, and a bit of racing.

Dane talked to Francis about having a sister ship built. He had no need for limiting the boat's draft, so, in the winter of 1933, Francis brought out onto his drafting table the plans for No. 50, added a deeper keel on the lines drawing, and superimposed a slightly taller rig on the sail plan. This became Francis's design No. 58; Dane would name the *Tioga*'s near-sister the *Bounty*. The changes added nearly 2 feet of draft and 1,700 pounds of outside ballast, and about 200 square feet of sail area to the *Tioga*'s design, but otherwise the hulls and rigs of the two boats were identical. Perhaps remembering his trial sail in the *Tioga*, Francis cut away the deadwood and gave her a bigger, deeper rudder.

The Britt Brothers yard was the obvious builder. Francis wrote, "it is very possible that the Britts were one of the four or five best builders in the world before World War II." One of the many good artisans that the Britts attracted to their team was a caulker named Archie O'Neill. His brother was a caulker at Lawley's. These specialists knew by long practice just how much cotton to pound into a yacht's seams in hull and deck under just how much impact from the caulking iron. Archie O'Neill caulked all the boats that went down the Britt ways, so it was he who made the *Bounty* as tight as a bottle.[32]

And watertight she was, when launched on

RIGHT: **Ernest B. Dane Jr., the Boston banker for whom the *Bounty* was designed, wanted her galley forward next to the forecastle, for he was used to sailing with a paid crew; yet, no doorway is shown in the cabin plan in the bulkhead between forecastle and galley, because this was an extra heavy, watertight, collision bulkhead. In the resulting layout, the 'midships space was quite cut-up with a cramped stateroom and a wide transom in a long, narrow passageway, but the washroom has space for a shower bath, with a rotary hand pump. Francis much preferred the *Tioga*'s more spacious cabin arrangement. The construction plan for the *Tioga* was to be followed, using a detailed list of specifications for the *Bounty*. All fittings and fastenings were to be of Tobin bronze. The keelson could be white oak, teak, or mahogany. Planking was to be 1¾-inch rift-grain fir, "unless yellow pine can be had, if neither available, then mahogany." Sheer strake was white oak. The deck structures to be teak, and "no corners or sharp edges will be allowed." The deck was soft pine, covered with canvas. In the bulwarks, there would be four scuppers per side (versus three for the *Tioga*) "as it has been found No. 50 does not free her decks as rapidly as might be desired." Francis also specified, "The plumbing is to be arranged under the supervision of the architect and in accordance with some few drawings which he may make to simplify and perfect this part which was not entirely satisfactory on No. 50." Partitions were to be built up and paneled to avoid shrinking and swelling, but if laminated, the edges were to be painted very carefully.** (© Mystic Seaport Museum, Daniel S. Gregory Ships Plans Library, SP38.1.2)

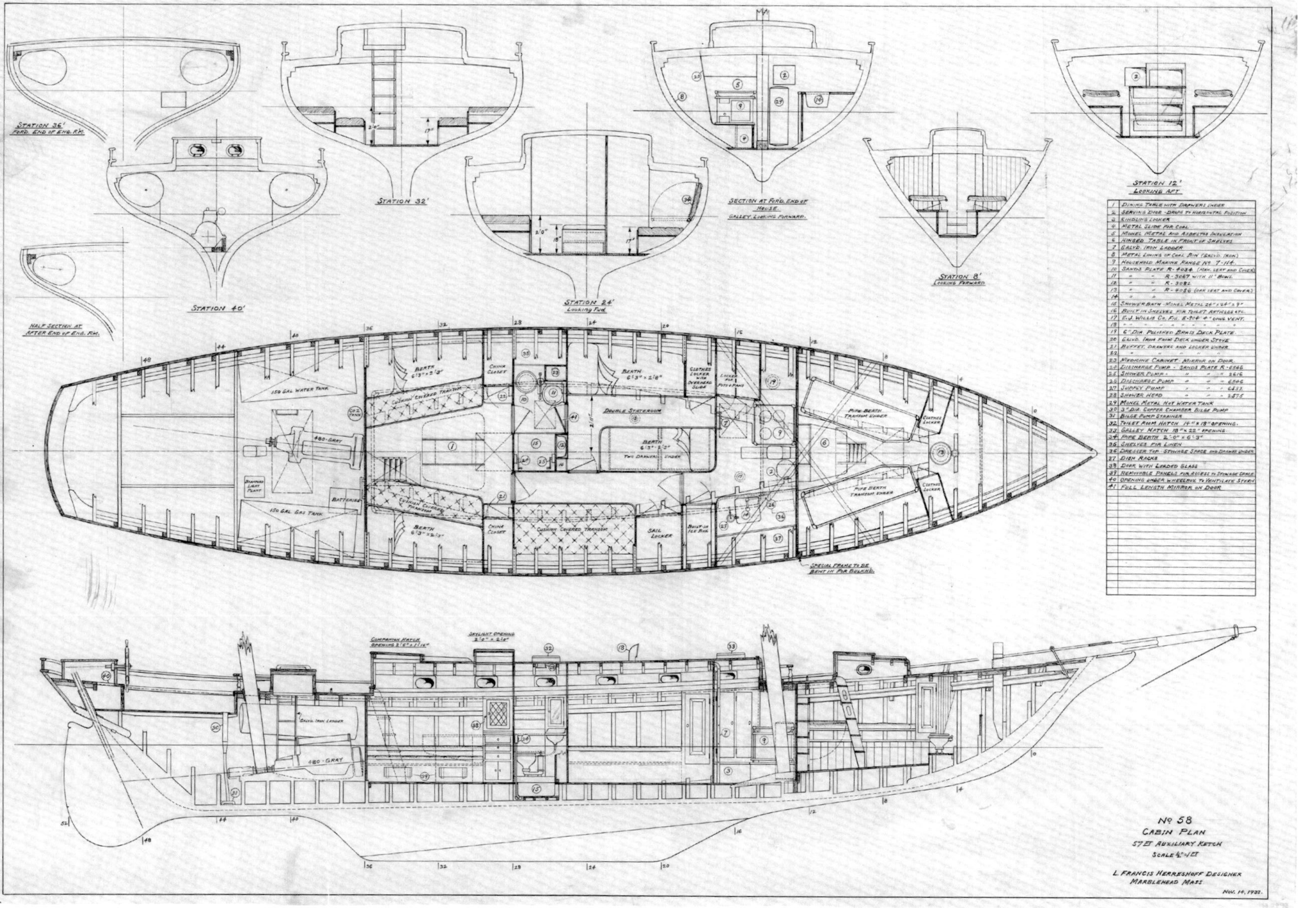
STATION 36' FORD. END OF ENG. RM.
STATION 32'
STATION 24' LOOKING FWD.
SECTION AT FORD. END OF HOUSE. GALLEY LOOKING FORWARD.
STATION 12' LOOKING AFT
STATION 8' LOOKING FORWARD
STATION 40'
HALF SECTION AT AFTER END OF ENG. RM.
1 DINING TABLE WITH DRAWERS UNDER
2 SERVING DOOR - DROPS TO HORIZONTAL POSITION
3 KINDLING LOCKER
4 METAL SLIDE FOR COAL
5 MONEL METAL AND ASBESTOS INSULATION
6 HINGED TABLE IN FRONT OF SHELVES
7 GALVD. IRON LADDER
8 METAL LINING OF COAL BIN (GALVD. IRON)
9 HOUSEHOLD MARINE RANGE Nº 7-114.
10 SANDS PLATE R-4034 (MAH. SEAT AND COVER)
11 " " R-3067 WITH 11" BOWL
12 " " R-3082
13 " " R-4056 (OAK SEAT AND COVER)
14 " "
15 SHOWER BATH - MONEL METAL 24" x 24" x 9"
16 BUILT IN SHELVES FOR TOILET ARTICLES ETC.
17 E.J. WILLIS CO. FIG. E-904 4" COWL VENT.
18 " " " " " " " " "
19 6" DIA. POLISHED BRASS DECK PLATE.
20 GALVD. IRON FALSE DECK UNDER STOVE
21 BUFFET, DRAWERS AND LOCKER UNDER.
22 " " " " "
23 MEDICINE CABINET - MIRROR ON DOOR.
24 DISCHARGE PUMP - SANDS PLATE R-6546
25 SHOWER PUMP - " " " 2616
26 DISCHARGE PUMP " " " 6546
27 SUPPLY PUMP " " " 6537.
28 SHOWER HEAD " " " 2575
29 MONEL METAL HOT WATER TANK
30 3" DIA. COPPER CHAMBER BILGE PUMP
31 BILGE PUMP STRAINER
32 TOILET ROOM HATCH 14" x 18" OPENING.
33 GALLEY HATCH 18" x 22" OPENING.
34 PIPE BERTH 2'-0" x 6'-3"
35 SHELVES FOR LINEN
36 DRESSER TOP - STOWAGE SPACE AND DRAWER UNDER
37 DISH RACKS
38 DOOR WITH LEADED GLASS
39 REMOVABLE PANELS FOR ACCESS TO STOWAGE SPACE
40 OPENING UNDER WHEELBOX TO VENTILATE STERN
41 FULL LENGTH MIRROR ON DOOR
Nº 58
CABIN PLAN
57 FT AUXILIARY KETCH
SCALE 1/2" = 1 FT
L. FRANCIS HERRESHOFF DESIGNER
MARBLEHEAD MASS
NOV. 14, 1932.

38-1.2

May 2, 1934. The Britt boatbuilders had taken just five months to cut and shape all her pieces, fasten them together, install her Gray 420 engine (rated at 75 horsepower at 1,200 rpm), make her spars and fit her rigging, fashion her cabin furniture, and complete the thousand and one details that go into an exquisite yacht. One of the details, for example, was that somebody had to make, from Francis's separate drawing, two beautifully proportioned and tapered "pig sticks" to carry the yacht's club pennant and owner's private signal at the mastheads, dainty flagstaffs of 19-1/4 inches for the mainmast and 13-1/8 inches for the mizzen. Again, Francis used Lee Nielsen's eyes and ears to help oversee the details.[33]

The *Lynn Daily Item* claimed that the *Bounty* was "one of the most expensive boats of its size built in this section of the country," putting her cost at $25,000. But her contract was for $20,000, less by $2,000 than that for the *Tioga*, since she avoided the complication of a centerboard trunk. It is not known what commission Francis earned for modifying the *Tioga*'s design.[34]

Unlike Waldo Brown, Dane was in a position to enjoy his elegant Herreshoff ketch for nineteen years. He cruised downeast on the coast of Maine to the Canadian border and up to the westward all the way to the New York Yacht Club station at Glen Cove, on Long Island Sound. This idyll was only interrupted by World War II, when she went on patrol, painted gray. After the war, apparently to counteract such drabness, Dane had her all dressed up with bright green topsides, set off with her prominent boot-top in scarlet, a hue that may also have spread across Francis's countenance when he saw the disaster from his rooftop. Fortunately, by the summer of 1950 her beautiful hull shape was again accentuated in gleaming white over a dark-blue boot-top, and Francis could write to Dane: "I want to thank you for keeping *Bounty* looking so nice. People all say she is the best looking boat in the harbor."[35]

It is hard to say which of these two equally beautiful yachts is the faster. Conventional wisdom would give the nod to the *Bounty,* with her additional sail area and the deeper ballast keel to carry it. Yet there was at least one race in which the *Tioga* beat the *Bounty,* including on the windward leg. Francis thought it was "perhaps because the centerboard went down into deeper and more solid water." With her board down, the *Tioga* drew 2 feet, 3 inches more than the *Bounty*, at least with the after corner of her centerboard. Off the wind, with the board up, one might give the nod to the *Tioga.* But we must remember that the difference in speed between two near-sister ships would have more to do with the different skills of their skippers than with any differences in their designs. This axiom was a frustration to L. Francis Herreshoff, designer of racing yachts, and was a key reason why he had turned away from them. At any rate, after the Jeffreys Ledge Race of 1934, Francis must have been glad to hear from his father, "I was very much pleased at *Tioga*'s winning

---

RIGHT: **The construction drawing for the *Bounty*'s pram tender. This boat was built to the lines of the M-boat *Istalena*'s 8-foot, 3-inch dinghy (the rules required the big racing yacht to carry a minimalist small boat) stretched out to a length of 11 feet, 1 inch. Her ends have been kept low to keep her from blowing around when she is rowed in a breeze. She has hoisting rings on the outside of her transoms, whose top edges are made concave to reduce her height when stowed bottom up on the cabin house. There is a flat deck, 1 foot, 9 inches long, across her stern to keep the water out when she is launched, stern first, from the *Bounty*'s deck. Note the D-shaped, foot-brace holes in the floorboards for her forward and 'midships rowing positions. This drawing is dated January 5, 1934.** (© Mystic Seaport Museum, Daniel S. Gregory Ships Plans Library, SP38.1A.3)

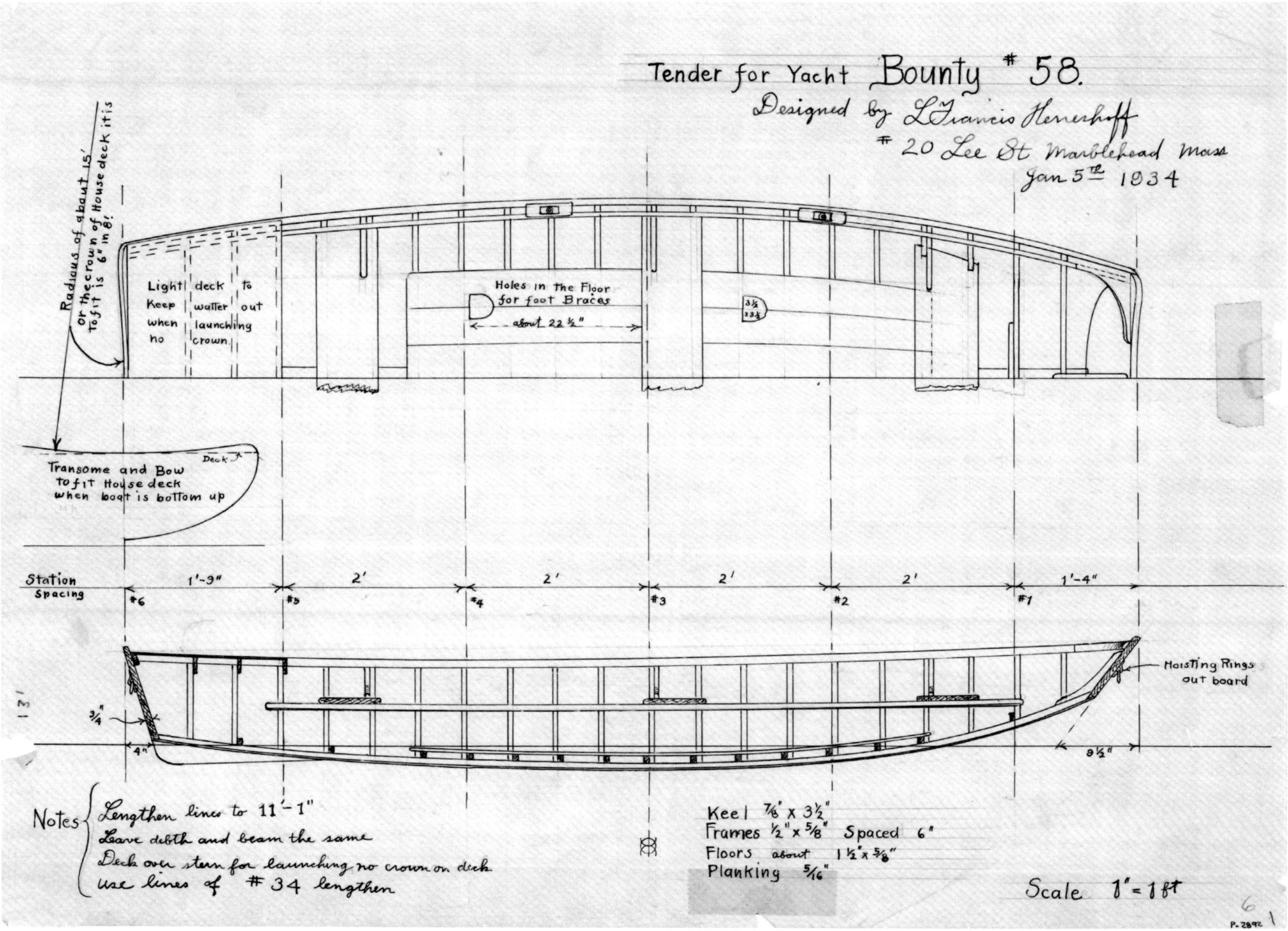

Tender for Yacht Bounty # 58.
Designed by L. Francis Herreshoff
20 Lee St Marblehead Mass
Jan 5th 1934
Radious of about 15' or the crown of House deck it is To fit is 6" in 8'
Light deck to Keep watter out when launching no crown.
Holes in the Floor for foot Braces
about 22 1/2"
3 1/2
3 3/4
Transome and Bow to fit House deck when boat is bottom up
Deck
Station Spacing
1'-9"
2'
2'
2'
2'
1'-4"
#6
#5
#4
#3
#2
#1
3/4"
4"
9 1/2"
Hoisting Rings out board
13'
Notes
Lengthen lines to 11'-1"
Leave debth and beam the same
Deck over stern for launching no crown on deck
Use lines of # 34 lengthen
Keel 7/8" x 3 1/2"
Frames 1/2" x 5/8" Spaced 6"
Floors about 1 1/2" x 5/8"
Planking 5/16"
Scale 1" = 1 ft
6
P. 2892

and *Bounty* second in that long-distance race, and I congratulate you on the result."[36]

Francis preferred the *Bounty* to the *Tioga*. "I would say for many reasons that the keel version of this design is the best," he wrote. "Some of the reasons are that it is cheaper, less apt to let worms in, and often simpler to dock [haul out]." While the *Tioga*'s centerboard gave her a versatility that the *Bounty* lacked, had Waldo Brown not required a draft limit of five feet, there would have been no centerboard version of this great design.[37]

Dane sold the *Bounty*, in "perfect condition inside and out," according to the broker, to Clarence E. Knapp of Boston in 1953. Her home port changed to the South Shore harbor of Cohasset, and she continued to cruise the coast of Maine. She also went south through the Cape Cod Canal: when Hurricane Carol struck New England in 1954, she was anchored in Woods Hole. The storm surge deposited her well ashore with considerable damage. It is not known just what this was and how well it was repaired.[38]

The *Bounty* reaching fast in a fresh breeze. Her raked masts allow her booms to lift, doing little harm to the set of the sails off the wind, and keeping them out of harm's way when offshore. The pram rests unobtrusively on the house. The ketch may have just gotten underway, for the man at the mainmast appears to be coiling down. Perhaps that is Dane standing at the weather side of the wheel, guiding the wonderful creation of L. Francis Herreshoff and the Britt brothers down the wind and watching her go. (Lucy Tulloch www.thelucy.com)

By 1957, she was in the hands of Stacy B. Lloyd, proprietor of Island Dairies in St. Croix, Virgin Islands. Perhaps without realizing that he was writing to a knowledgeable dairy farmer, Lloyd sent Francis a description of his operation, including the fact that he supplied milk to the islands of St. Thomas and St. John, as well as to customers on St. Croix, and that, when local boats failed him, he used the *Bounty* for deliveries. Francis's reaction to the *Bounty* as milk wagon is not recorded, but he must have been glad to learn that on one occasion she made the 38-mile run to St. Thomas in 3½ hours, at nearly 11 knots (over 1.5 times the square root of her waterline length). Lloyd didn't dare tell Francis that he once sailed the *Bounty* across the 40 miles of open water from St. John to St. Croix with three tranquilized donkeys draped over her cabin house.[39]

Stacy Lloyd knew that his vessel, occasional farm cart though she might be, was exquisite. She had been painted black, and Lloyd realized that both aesthetically and practically, in the tropics, she'd be better off white. He sent photographs of the *Bounty* to Francis. Francis wrote back, "several of my visitors who have looked at the splendid pictures you sent have said they think she is one of the prettiest boats they ever saw, and both they and I think she is ever so much prettier when painted white." And Lloyd wrote to Francis: "To me *Bounty*'s hull is such a thing of beauty it is like a work of art, a fine poem or a lovely picture. As I row around it, every angle is perfection. Her sail plan with her tall raked masts adds to this picture."[40]

Lloyd also enjoyed the *Bounty*'s speed. He reported to Francis on the Memorial Day race of 1964 from St. Croix to St. Thomas: "There were some 35 boats in three classes over a 38-mile course. We gave [Classes] B and C an hour's start and passed everyone nicely but for *Victoria* an old Alden schooner who went better to windward than we did and beat us in." But then he added that the "windward" work was all on the port tack and that the *Bounty* sailed much better on the starboard tack. Lloyd's son Robin, who had been on board that day as a youngster, remembered it this way: "We were beating to windward heading for the finish line in Charlotte Amalie harbor. An old Alden schooner called the *Victoria* sailed tighter to the wind and narrowly beat us by several lengths." Francis replied to Stacy Lloyd, "of course I suppose in a race of this kind there are tides and wind variations that may have favored the Malabar that you speak of; and, too, she may have been a larger vessel so far as I know."[41]

The *Bounty*, beaten to windward by an Alden schooner? Mercy. These accounts are incredulous, even if we surmise that the *Victoria* was sailed by a wizard. Was the schooner one of the yachts that had an hour's head start on the *Bounty?* In the easterly trade wind, how could most of the northerly course have been on the port tack? Why did the *Bounty* sail "much better" on the starboard tack? How could an Alden schooner sail "tighter to the wind" than the *Bounty?* At age 73, Francis didn't seem overly concerned.[42]

But, four months earlier, Francis and Lloyd had started to correspond on a more serious matter: the *Bounty* was leaking. Or, rather, she was still leaking. Back in late 1959, Lloyd had written to Francis wondering if it might be sensible, in order to make the *Bounty* "absolutely tight," to cover her hull with fiberglass! Francis did not honor this suggestion with a comment, but, in any event, the *Bounty* remained a purely wooden boat. Evidently, an over-zealous caulker, perhaps in repairing hurricane damage, or maybe in one of the island boatyards that Lloyd had used to help him maintain the *Bounty,* had ruined Archie O'Neill's good work. In 1965, Lloyd put William R. Chandler, who ran the St. Croix Marine and Development Company at Christiansted, in touch with Francis, as a consultant on the leaking problem. Chandler wrote to Francis: "It appears that the bulk of *Bounty*'s problems began when all that oakum crammed into her seams started to work loose. We have found an instance where the fore scarf [in the keel] had been caulked to the point that the port side was down ½ inch from the apron while the starboard side was snug—three through-bolts were broken in this area." Chandler could diagnose the situation, but his yard apparently didn't have the capacity for the major work needed to correct it. For that, in 1967, Lloyd took the desperate step of sailing the *Bounty* all the way to a top yard up on the coast of Maine, that of Paul Luke in East Boothbay. But when Luke inspected the *Bounty*, he recommended that it would be as economical to build a new hull as to repair the damage done to the Britt brothers' fine boat.[43]

With support from Francis, Lloyd accepted Luke's advice, and commissioned him to strip the *Bounty* of her ballast keel, rig, cabin house, steering wheel, and any other fittings that could be reused on a new *Bounty*, build a hull to Francis's design No. 58, and fit her out with the original boat's accoutrements. So the beautiful *Bounty*, fallen on hard times, was reduced to a hulk and abandoned to the weather. Yet even as a skeleton covered with a withered skin, her lovely shape was discernible. Like many another derelict vessel, it was her beauty that would save her.[44]

Paul Luke took his time making an outstanding job of building Lloyd's new *Bounty.* He profited from some on-the-spot counsel from an aging Francis, who apparently had no objection to a plywood deck covered with fiberglass and overlaid in teak. Luke launched the new boat in the spring of 1969. Lloyd took her south to the Virgin Islands and enjoyed her fine performance in the trade winds until 1981. Ten years later, she was bought in Mobile, Alabama, by the German boatbuilder Michael Schmidt, who sailed her across the Atlantic and gave her a new home port at Greifswald, Germany, on the Baltic.[45]

The waterfront grapevine works well on the Maine coast. It didn't take long for the news of the *Bounty*'s stripping and abandonment to reach the ears of O. Lie-Nielsen, by then running his own boatbuilding operation, Lee's Boatshop, in Rockland. Lee couldn't believe that the wonderful yacht whose construction at Britt's he had observed so carefully could be treated like that. He went to see for himself.

As a good friend of L. Francis Herreshoff, and because of his own experience with the *Bounty,* Lee Nielsen had sentimental reasons for refusing to accept the vessel's demise. But, never one to pass up an economic opportunity, he also saw a basically sound hull of exquisite shape, a hull that could be made watertight again and fitted out as the outstanding cruising yacht that she had been. In 1969, he bought what was left of the *Bounty* for $5,000, and hired a house-mover to truck her to his yard in Rockland. At this time, Francis, approaching eighty, used to have his then-secretary, Muriel Vaughn, drive him downeast to Rockland for an occasional visit to Lee's Boatshop, where he would reminisce with its proprietor and have a look at one or two boats of his design that Lee was building. One of these trips happened to coincide with the day the *Bounty*'s hull made the voyage to Rockland over the road. As Francis's grey Ferrari overtook the house-mover's low-slung rig, Francis, in the passenger's seat, cried out: "That's my boat! That's my boat!"

Lee and Francis had lunch while the *Bounty* was being shored up at Lee's Boatshop. When Francis had inspected her carefully, he told Lee, "you won't have any problem fixing her up." And he didn't. The *Bounty*'s planking was just spread apart too much from the over-enthusiastic caulking. Lee reamed out her seams, refastened her planking as it had been originally, recaulked her properly, poured her a new lead keel, and built her a new cabin house, following Francis's drawing. When it came to building a new interior, rather than repeating the *Bounty*'s cut-up arrangement, he gave her a more open cabin like that of the *Tioga.* He rigged her according to her original design.[46]

Francis kept up with the rebuilding process on more visits to Rockland. Sometimes his driver would be a young friend, Arthur Brendze, who had come under Francis's mentoring influence. Once, when the two were looking under her hull, Francis called Brendze's attention to the *Bounty*'s cutaway deadwood. He pointed with his long, but by now somewhat crooked, forefinger and said: "See that? They all laughed at me when I did that; now they're all doing it and they'll be doing it even more. I did it because when I took *Tioga* out for her trial and was tacking up Marblehead Harbor, I hit a boat. So I cut *Bounty* away so she'd turn quicker."[47]

Lee Nielsen relaunched the *Bounty,* which he renamed the *Poquita*, on September 19, 1972. Francis attended, looking, in perhaps the last photograph made of him, particularly pleased and relaxed. Lee quickly sold the boat to Phil Long, who took her to Newport Beach, California, and gave her another new name: the *L. Francis Herreshoff.*

Roger Riddell, a movie producer, bought the ketch in 1976 and changed her name yet again: she went back to being the *Bounty.* Riddell had a lot more work done on her, including putting in a teak interior with his own arrangement. He enjoyed the boat for twenty-four years, mostly for weekend trips to Catalina Island, but also for movie, magazine, and commercial photo-shoots.[48]

In October 2000, an electrical short caused a major fire in the *Bounty*'s cabin. Riddell figured she was finished, but Sean Fagan, who described himself as "kind of a hippie," bought the pretty ketch from the insurance company and spent the next five years replacing fire-blackened wood with new, while living on board.

Saved more than once by her beauty, the *Bounty* has recently undergone yet another round of major repair. Eric Blanc-Gavin, a French businessman, fell in love with the idea of owning a yacht of classic beauty and had the ketch trucked across country to Rockport Marine, in Maine, to get a whole new backbone, many new frames, and new planking from the garboards up four feet from the keel. Despite her unusual career at the hands of a hurricane and many boatbuilders subsequent to the Britts, two-thirds of her original structure remains. Blanc-Gavin has sailed the *Bounty* to New York, where she weathered Hurricane Sandy, to Antigua, where she participated in the classic yacht regatta, and to France, where her new home port is Marseille.

Francis and Lee Nielsen at Lee's Boatshop, Rockland, Maine, on the day when Francis happened to discover what was left of the *Bounty* being trailered there for rebuilding. (O. Lie-Nielsen photo))

In the 1960s, Francis sold to individual buyers a recorded eight sets of the thirty-four drawings making up the plans for his design Numbers 50 and 58 at $200 each. He probably sold more without the record of correspondence. It is not known how many boats were built to these plans, if any, but one enthusiastic purchaser wrote to Francis, "there should never be the slightest doubt that your contribution to *society* [emphasis added] is a standard by which all others are measured, and by it all men are evaluated."[49]

The Mallorca Yacht and Boat Construction Association, builders of the *Circe* to the Tioga design, built a Bounty in 1964, the *Denebola,* for Bernard Catu of Nogent-sur-Seine, France. Phil Bolger designed for her a different cabin arrangement, with Francis's blessing. She was painted black and had trailboards with lion's teeth, a sternboard with a lion's head, and lion's paws on the forward ends of her cap rail.

In 1966, American Marine Shipyards at Clearwater Bay, Kowloon, Hong Kong, built a Bounty named the *Charade* for a Honolulu real estate developer and building contractor, John Barkhorn. The cost was $100,000. Francis, aged 73, had made Barkhorn a new cabin plan, dated May 28, 1964. It was a standard arrangement like the one that he had drawn for the *Tioga*, but with three outboard berths squeezed into the saloon. The *Charade* had an offset propeller, as designed by Francis. Barkhorn wrote, "she will turn in her own length and with a little initial care she can be powered backwards with precise direction." On a four-day visit to Francis, by then ensconced in his Castle in Marblehead, Barkhorn got Francis to agree to a masthead rig for his Bounty. But it wasn't long before Barkhorn was writing: "I feel in all respects that Mr. Herreshoff was right in the first place. She was a better sea boat, handled better, and we were happier with her as originally designed." In 1969, William A. Robinson, of *Svaap* fame, on a visit to Honolulu in his Burgess-Herreshoff designed brigantine *Varua*, reported to Francis that the *Charade* had been stolen and had disappeared.[50]

The design of the *Bounty* continued to be popular. In 1988, a Bounty was under construction at Covey Island Boatworks at Petite Riviere, Nova Scotia. Legendary Yachts, Washougal, Washington, built one in 1997. And, in 2001, John Kendall, a great appreciator of L. Francis Herreshoff's art, added a Bounty, the *Catriona,* built at the Brooklin Boatyard in Maine, to his collection of boats built to his friend's designs.

Meanwhile, as we have seen, the original *Tioga* and the original *Bounty*, the most beautiful yachts in the world, have survived, still sailing, still turning heads, more than eighty-five years after Francis put their lines on paper. The *Tioga* and the *Bounty* mark L. Francis Herreshoff as an artistic genius at the forefront of his profession.

CHAPTER 15

Area
31= 1041
5= 1321
3= 535
2897
264
1271
2541
394
376
Nº 66
Sail Pl
Scale 1/4" = 1.
L. Francis Herresho

THE TICONDEROGA

"When *Ticonderoga* was designed I had become somewhat developed artistically so that she was put together practically without mathematics and this, together with her records, is a great source of satisfaction to me."

L. FRANCIS HERRESHOFF, 1966

Harry E. Noyes, the wealthy Buick dealer and pleased owner of the 57-foot, clipper-bowed ketch *Tioga*, went onto the spacious lawn of his estate, Tioga Towers, out near the lighthouse on Marblehead Neck, and measured and marked out an outline. He wanted to show his four children—and, we can assume, his wife—the size of a new yacht he had in mind. Noyes loved the looks and liveliness of the Herreshoff ketch he had bought from Waldo Brown in 1932; he wanted to duplicate her virtues in a new vessel large enough to accommodate his family and friends in higher style.[1]

Noyes fancied enlarging the *Tioga* as soon as he started sailing her. Francis wrote to his father as early as June 9, 1933, "I expect to make some sketches for a larger yacht similar to *Tioga*." He sent a blueprint of a preliminary outboard profile of such a vessel to Nathanael in September 1934, but it was July 16, 1935, before he penned a postscript on a letter to his father: "I now have the order to go ahead on the clipper bowed ketch like a blueprint I sent you some time ago. She is 72 feet on deck." *Yachting* informed its readers in the September issue that L. Francis Herreshoff was "working on the plans of a large clipper-bow leg-of-mutton rigged ketch of the *Tioga* type." Francis was doubtless happy to have such a wonderful commission.[2]

Without Harry E. Noyes's love of the *Tioga*—and his money—there would have been no new, big *Tioga*. The money had started accumulating in 1907, when his father, Harry K. Noyes, moved from farming in Haverhill, New Hampshire, to selling Stanley Steamers in Lowell, Massachusetts. By 1915, he had become the Buick distributor for Boston and, five years later, for all New England, with thirty-five dealerships. When he died in 1935, Harry E. took over the business.[3]

Noyes had grown up with his father's motor yachts, but when he first tried sailing a small boat, he drifted, out of control, down onto the rocks. He determined to do better, much better. By the time he bought the *Tioga*, Harry E. Noyes was the champion of the 8-Metre Class in Marblehead. Among other feats accomplished with Frank Paine's *Gypsy* of 1929, he retired the Hovey Gold Bowl by winning it for three consecutive years.[4]

While Francis was not in Noyes's social circle,

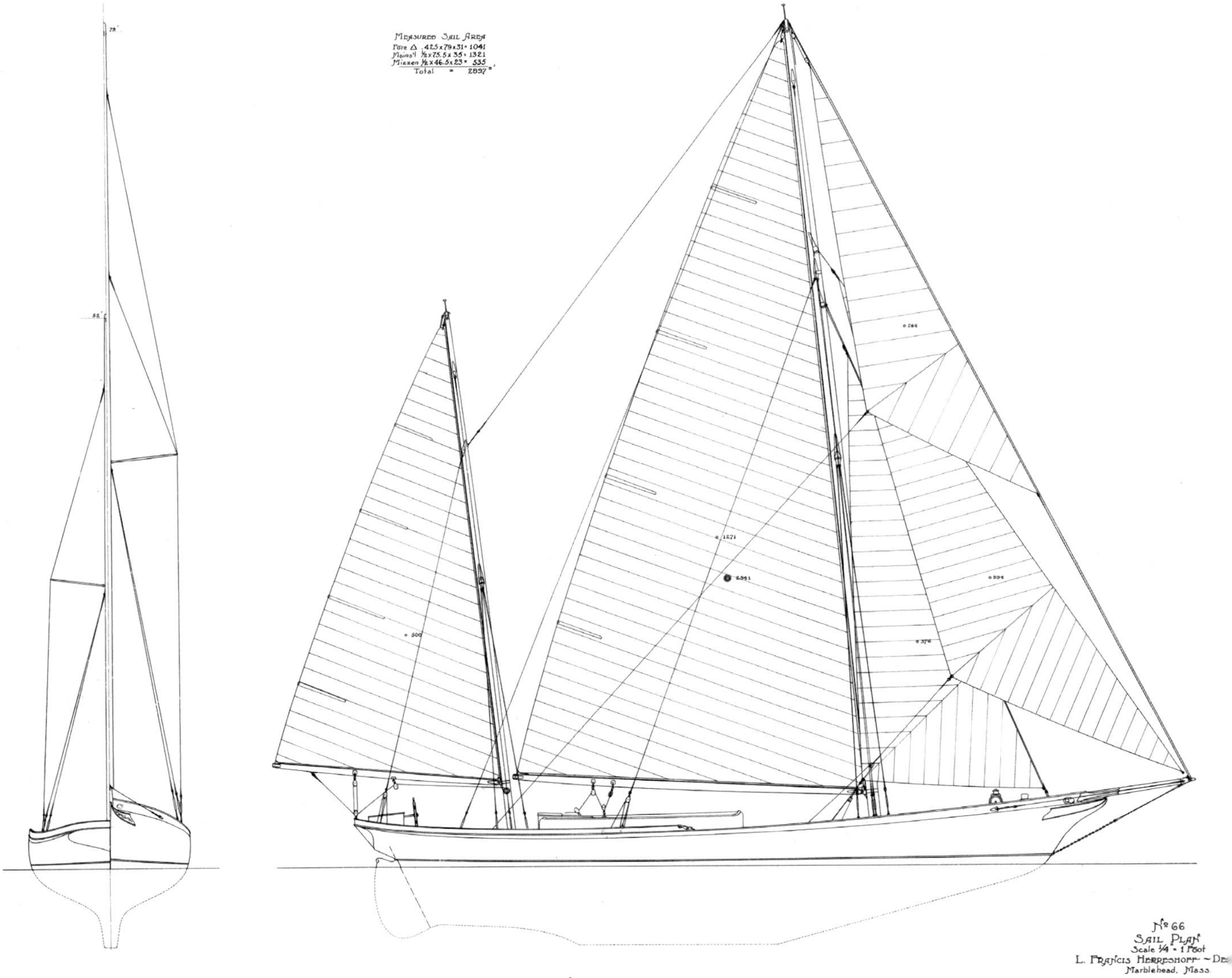

The outboard profile and sail plan of the great *Tioga II*, better known through a succession of owners and broken elapsed-time records on ocean racing courses as the *Ticonderoga*. Her working sail area is 2,897 square feet. In the family of Harry E. Noyes, the original owner, the single-spreader mainmast, standing about 80 feet above the deck, was known as "the rubber mast." The ketch did suffer a dismasting early in her career. Noyes then went to the John Alden office for the design of a new, double-spreader rig. Francis has not drawn in any reefs in mainsail or mizzen. He wrote to the Ratsey loft, "I have found that on an auxiliary with the sail plan cut up into four or five sails, it is seldom necessary to reef a sail so that all reefs can be dispensed with unless the sailmaker prefers to put them in." He envisioned that the forestaysail and mizzen would be set in heavy weather. Reefs would certainly be desirable for adjusting sail area in a race, but the yacht was supposed to be used primarily for daysailing. Fred Goeller made this tracing and dated it July 22, 1935. (© Mystic Seaport Museum, Daniel S. Gregory Ships Plans Library, SP38.15.7)

they shared a mutual friend in Waldo Brown, and all three shared an interest in cars. Moreover, at that time, Francis drove Buicks. As Francis began work on design No. 66, which he labeled *Tioga II,* he wrote cordial letters to Noyes, inviting him to "drop in" and look over the drawings.[5]

One aspect of the design that the two discussed was her cabin house. When Nathanael saw Francis's preliminary profile plan, he suggested a flush-deck with greater freeboard and no house. "I believe you could still make a fine looking vessel of it," he wrote, "besides saving labor cost of construction, getting more strength, a clearer deck and much more internal room, with less chances for overhead leakages." Francis didn't argue, but replied, "we don't think it will be possible to persuade the owner to make her a flush deck vessel for he seems very much against making many changes in looks from the *Tioga* which he now owns." With her relatively shoal hull, moderate freeboard, and low house, the *Tioga II*'s headroom below deck was a worry to Francis. It was, in fact, a problem that he never solved.[6]

It is a mystery why L. Francis Herreshoff's construction and cabin plans for the *Tioga II* show a minimum headroom under the beams in both main and forward cabins of only 5 feet, 10 inches. That is an unheard of dimension for a yacht of her size. It is a further mystery why the error went undetected until it was physically experienced during construction. Certainly Noyes would have objected had he realized that the new *Tioga* would have less headroom than the old one. Fortunately, the *Tioga II*'s hull was deep enough so that the problem could be corrected by removing and reconfiguring tanks and lowering and narrowing the soles. But the bother and expense made Noyes angry at his designer. Francis's reaction was defensive: the boat's cabin was not supposed to be a dance hall![7]

The design of the *Tioga II*, like those of her predecessors, the *Tioga* and *Bounty,* provided Francis with the chance to prove the truth of his belief that measurement rules were ruining yacht design. Their owners did not come to Francis for racing yachts, but rather for comfortable vessels that would look good and sail well. Should they be tempted to join handicap racing with their fast beauties (and, of course, they were), they would suffer high ratings, because Francis ignored the advantages and penalties provided by the rule. He wrote of the *Tioga II*: "Her model above water is similar to some of the fast yachts of seventy-five years ago with the grace and seaworthiness of this type before measurement rules showed their effects. Underwater her forefoot is cut away more like later yachts and like them she has a pronounced lead keel amidships which will give her sail-carrying ability. Aft of the lead keel the deadwood is curved upward slightly to allow her to turn quicker than some of the old timers did, but the model of the yacht in this region is [as] fine as yachts like *America*, *Magic,* and *Sappho*. It will be very interesting to see how she will go with the modern yacht of her same sail area for she can meet them on even terms as far as outside ballast, hollow spars and modern rigging are concerned." Francis would not be disappointed with the *Tioga II*.[8]

The *Tioga II* provides us with a study of engineering compared to art in yacht design. Olin J. Stephens II, the great designer of the firm of Sparkman and Stephens, wrote that "good boats result from rational thinking." He gave, as an example, that at low speeds, the important factor resisting speed is wetted surface area, while at high speeds, that factor is a high displacement-length ratio. By these criteria, Stephens would have rated the *Tioga II* as a good boat, because she has relatively low wetted surface and a low displacement-length ratio. While Francis would not have disagreed with Stephens's principles, his approach to the design of the *Tioga II* was entirely different. He wrote, "when *Ticonderoga* [as she would be renamed early in her long career] was designed I had become somewhat developed artistically so that she was put together practically without

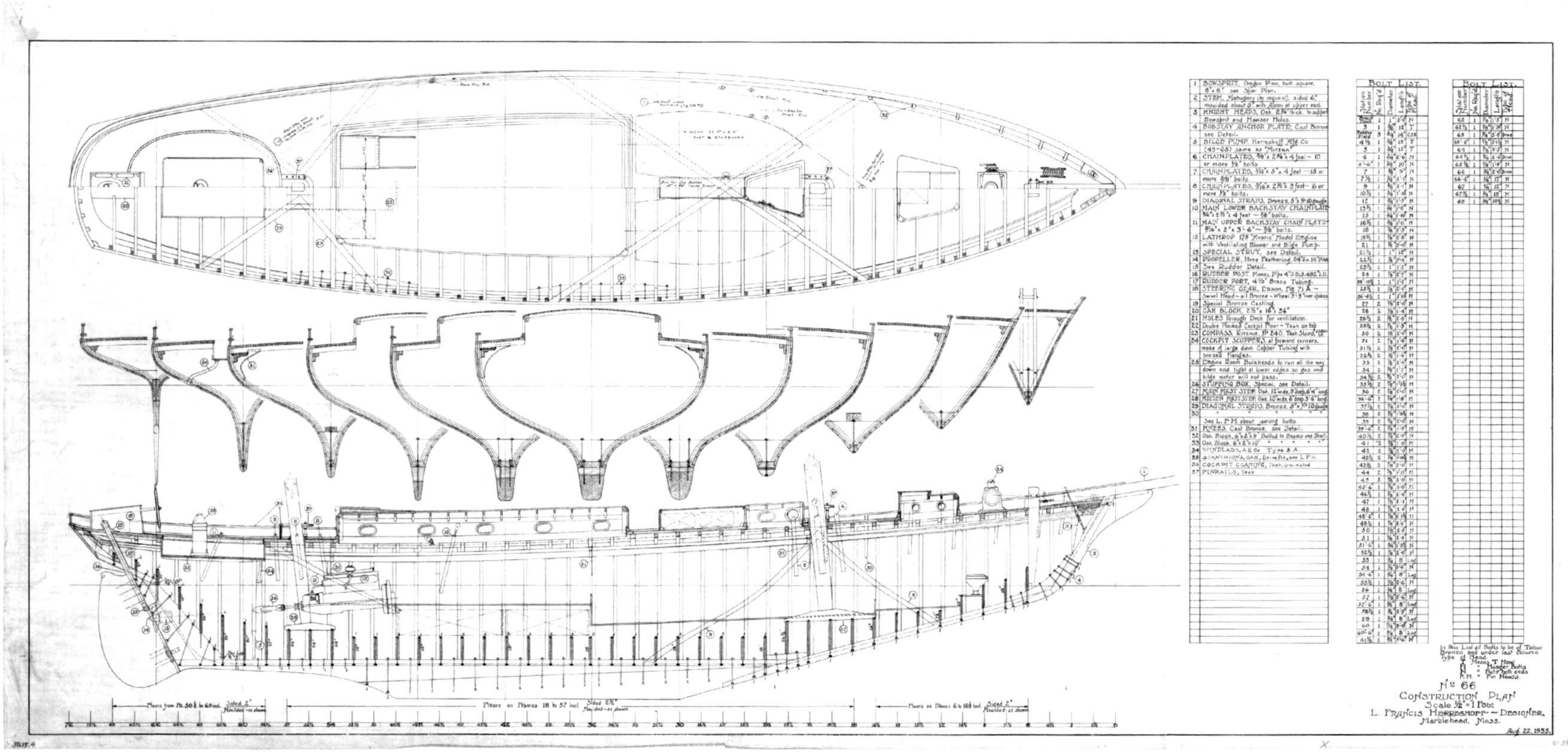

The construction plan of the *Tioga II*. The keel was to be 4¾-inch mahogany; frames laminated in two layers of white oak, total dimensions molded 3 inches and sided 2¾ inches, on 18-inch centers; garboard plank and lower planking up to the turn of the bilge, 2-inch yellow pine; upper planking, double, of mahogany to a total thickness of 2 inches. Note that Francis shows only four keel bolts, two at each end of the lead, the other thirty fastenings holding the lead being lags, or "lead hanger bolts," as Francis labeled them, arranged in fifteen pairs. Although Francis took the trouble to draw one of these lags at full size, showing its diameter as ⅞ inch and its bury in the lead as 7 inches, 6⅛ inches of which was threaded (these lengths varied slightly from forward to aft), Noyes's Quincy Adams yacht yard would not follow this scheme of securing the fifteen tons of lead, but rather followed their own practice of using bolts for all the fastenings. The engine shown is a Lathrop Mystic model of 175 horsepower. Francis went along with Lathrop's recommendation of a Hyde feathering propeller with a diameter of 24 inches and a pitch of 14 inches. At different times, he gave the boat's speed under power as 11 mph and 12 knots. (© Mystic Seaport Museum, Daniel S. Gregory Ships Plans Library, SP38.15.4)

mathematics and this, together with her records, is a great source of satisfaction to me."[9]

Francis anticipated that his design No. 66 would be a demanding project, and he let it be known that he might be looking for drafting help. Fred W. Goeller got the welcome news from Bror Tamm. He wrote to Francis, addressing him as "Dear Skipper," and received an offer to "start very soon." And since "Mr. Goeller" lived in Quincy, Francis, being between boarders, even offered him a temporary room. Fred Goeller joined the team at 20 Lee Street in time to draft some of Francis's plans for the *Tioga II,* but he didn't move in. He had been on the staff of *The Rudder* and had been editor of the short-lived *Sea Stories Magazine* in the 1920s, had worked in the design office of Lawley's in 1927, and had hung up his own shingle as a naval architect by 1929. Francis would praise Fred Goeller as the "neatest" among his draftsmen. After the *Tioga II*'s plans were completed, Francis cut back his staff sharply; Fred Goeller went on to design handsome powerboats for the John Trumpy Company in Annapolis, and to draw lovely sailboats on his own.[10]

It was K. Aage Nielsen who inked Francis's construction plan for the *Tioga II.* Like Tamm, he had crossed the Atlantic from Denmark, seeking to continue his career in boat design in America. He worked for John Alden from 1925 to 1931, then joined Murray G. Peterson in Marblehead. Nielsen lived in Marblehead, so it was easy for him to moonlight on the design of the *Tioga II.* He would become a principal in the Boston office of Sparkman and Stephens from 1936 to 1941, preceding his independent career as the designer of elegant cruising yachts, many based on boats of his Danish heritage.[11]

Francis paid Nielsen 60 cents an hour. Perhaps at that wage, even in 1935, he was not expected to do more than trace, but, in tracing, would he not have reacted to the lack of headroom in the *Tioga II*'s cabin? It is unbelievable that a man of Nielsen's ability didn't sense danger when he inked a cabin sole 5 feet, 10 inches away from a deck beam, and another the same distance from a cabin house carlin on a 72-foot yacht. Maybe Nielsen did recognize the problem, but was reluctant to raise it with his boss? Or maybe he did raise it, to no avail? We just don't know. We do know that Francis, working with Aage Nielsen in the drafting room on the second floor of the old customhouse at 20 Lee Street, did think highly of him.[12]

Another business that Harry Noyes inherited when his father died was the Quincy Adams Yacht Yard. The yard had been started by Fred Lawley under his own name, after he had a falling out with his family and left the big George Lawley yard at Neponset. Fred Lawley's design and boatbuilding business never did well financially; Harry's father, an important customer, kept pumping money into the operation, and eventually took it over and gave it the Quincy Adams name. By the time Francis's sixty-two drawings of the *Tioga II* were ready to be followed by boatbuilders, Quincy Adams was owned by the junior Noyes. Ralph E. Richmond ran the yard, but Noyes Buick met the payroll. Francis didn't get to choose Britts or Lawleys or the Herreshoff Manufacturing Company to build his majestic design; the job would go to Noyes's Quincy Adams yard.[13]

At first, it was a happy choice. After an inspection trip in February 1936, when the vessel was about one-third completed, Francis wrote to Noyes, "I think the workmanship on your boat is very good indeed and so far everything seems to be very nearly perfect." But then Noyes and Richmond began taking liberties with Francis's construction drawings (beyond correcting the headroom problem), and when Francis noticed these changes and wrote his objections, they were ignored. The headroom fiasco must have made Noyes and Richmond lose confidence in Francis. For Francis, having the yard do things like enlarge the cockpit by extending it further aft, meant that he had lost control of having the *Tioga II* built to his plans. And Noyes went to Merriman's, the marine

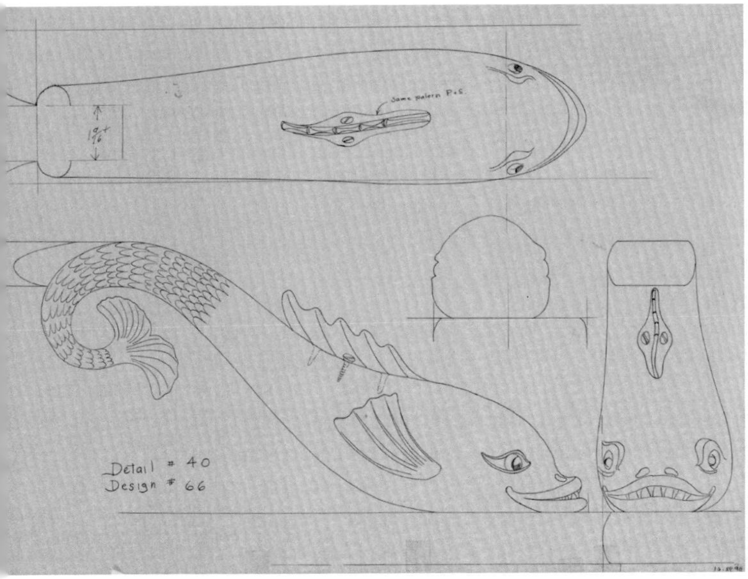

hardware company, for blocks of a different size than Francis had specified. The blocks "affected the safety, looks, and functioning of the rig," Francis wrote. "My original list [was] found necessary," he added with bitter satisfaction, when the blocks had to be replaced.[14]

And there was another troubling consequence of having the *Tioga II* built in the client's own yacht yard. Back when Francis was writing friendly letters to Noyes, he seems to have agreed to a design commission of only $2,500, which would indicate an estimated building cost of $25,000, just marginally higher that the costs of the first *Tioga* and the *Bounty*. This estimate is obviously low, since the *Tioga II* would displace more than twice as much as those yachts. And Francis told "Dear Harry" that he assumed a value of the completed yacht for insurance purposes of only $30,000. Francis was no businessman, and he appears to have allowed his initial friendship with Harry Noyes, his pleasure at receiving a fine design commission, and his relief at pulling in 2,500 Depression dollars to make him feel generous toward Noyes. If so, it was not a feeling that would last.[15]

There is no record of the actual cost of building the *Tioga II*, but Noyes's son Bradley has tried to figure it out. His number is a believable $42,000. Whatever the cost, Francis made a bad bargain for his commission. But rather than facing that reality, he saw himself as a victim of cheating. Francis harbored this grudge. He told one friend that the *Tioga II* cost $84,000; then, four years later, told the same friend she had cost $70,000. Earlier, he told an interviewer from *Popular Boating* that she cost $75,000. And he told Lee Nielsen that Noyes had paid him only a quarter of what his design fee should have been, which, at the usual 10 percent, would bump the construction cost up to $100,000.[16]

It didn't help the designer-client relationship when Noyes insisted on getting his sails (mainsail and mizzen, with covers; forestaysail; jib; jib topsail; balloon jib; Genoa jib; mizzen staysail; and spinnaker), from Ratsey England instead of Ratsey City Island, thus giving Francis the chore of getting them through customs, and at half his usual commission from the sailmaker. In later life,

---

ABOVE: **Francis's design for the bronze dolphins that adorn the forward ends of the *Ticonderoga*'s caprail. When Francis, at age eighty, went on board in Marblehead, he pointed out that one of the fishes had lost its screwed-on fin.** (© Mystic Seaport Museum, Daniel S. Gregory Ships Plans Library, SP38.15.59) RIGHT: **The almost-disastrous launching of the *Tioga II*. The poppets under her starboard side gave way, but she was hurtling down the ways so fast that she cleared the shed and got afloat with surprisingly little damage, and the man cartwheeling off her bow landed in the water unhurt. Weeks later, Art Hansen, the photographer who took the picture, was gawking at the yacht from a dock, was invited on board by Harry Noyes, and was shown his photograph—as published for $100—in the *Saturday Evening Post*.** (© Mystic Seaport Museum, 1995.84.1)

Francis referred to "Dear Harry" simply as "Noisy." For his part, Noyes, when he wanted to have a fine yacht built for his sons in 1938, steered clear of L. Francis Herreshoff and went to the Alden office for a 54-foot, clipper-bowed yawl, the *Tioga Too,* a beautiful boat that rated well under the Cruising Club of America Rule and that promptly won the Marblehead-to-Halifax Race.[17]

With relations strained, Francis did not attend the launching of the *Tioga II* on August 10, 1936. He missed a spectacular event. As the vessel started down the ways, the poppets holding up her starboard side gave way, and over she went! She just barely cleared the shed, but she did crush her starboard garboard plank. The yard crew hauled her back out, replaced the plank overnight, and re-launched her next day. When the boat tumbled over, John Rhyn, the paid captain of Noyes's 8-Metre, landed in the water. He was only upset that his new uniform might shrink.[18]

Francis sent his father Arthur Hansen's photo of the wild launching from the Boston *Herald* and reported: "Although I did not go to the launching, it is my belief that the boat was not held fore and aft on the cradle any way and none of the cradle poppets had any diagonal supports. The boat is quite long and straight on the keel and I believe that when she struck the water the resistance of the cradle was so great that the cradle stopped and she slid on before it. She is quite wide on the bottom of the keel and I am surprised that she canted over at all. However, no damage was done [*sic*] but it

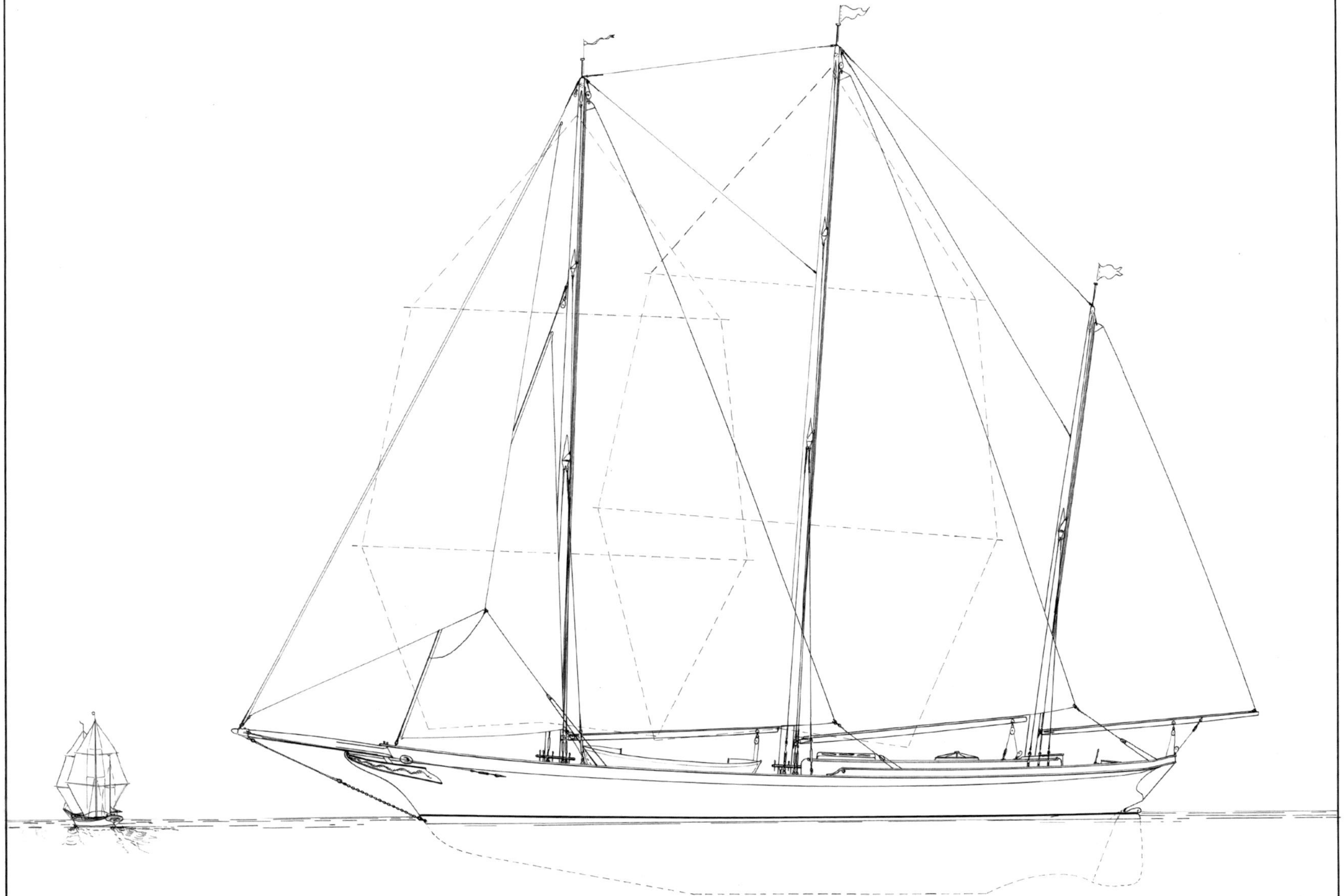

110' O.A. YACHT FOR EXTENDED CRUSING RIGGED WITH HAMMOND YARDS.

Scale 1/8" = 1'

might have been very serious." It is not only true that a yacht with a long, straight keel, with little drag, makes for a boat that is easy to haul on a cradle, but also that such a shape saved the *Tioga II*—and her people—from "very serious" injury at her launching.[19]

By August 24, Francis could report to Nathanael, "the new *Tioga* has arrived here in the harbor [Marblehead] and is making a very good impression." He also sent his father a photograph of the yacht hauled out on a railway, viewed from astern. Nathanael's reaction was: "I think the view of the stern and after form show very beautiful form and skill in design." L. Francis Herreshoff had finally won unstinting, unadulterated praise from his father. He replied, "I appreciate it very much that you like the looks of the stern of *Tioga II*."[20]

When Harry Noyes discovered how fast his big ketch was, he began to race her. For the *Tioga II*, better known as the *Ticonderoga*, it was the start of an extraordinary racing career. She once held more than thirty elapsed-time records, including both transatlantic and transpacific races. And the *Ticonderoga* still graces race courses.[21]

Noyes's first test of the *Tioga II* was the 138-mile Jeffreys Ledge Race of 1936. It blew hard, and Noyes decided to put in to Gloucester for a couple of hours to rest his green crew. She still finished first, but did not win on corrected time. It was an outcome that would be repeated often. Not designed to a measurement rule, she had a high rating for her size. Thus she would almost always be scratch boat, having to give time to every other boat. With the longest, speed-giving waterline, in any race where it blew hard enough for the boats to reach their maximum hull speed, she would be expected to finish first, but the margin was usually not enough to beat, on corrected time, yachts designed to the rule.[22]

Harry E. Noyes was hooked. To be able to sail his big, handsome boat around a racecourse and finish ahead of every other boat out there was a huge pleasure for him. And there was always a nice silver prize for the first boat to finish, no matter what she did on corrected time.

After the 1936 season, Noyes determined to improve the racing performance of the *Tioga II*. He did not go to L. Francis Herreshoff for the changes he had in mind, but rather to the office of John G. Alden. He felt that the mainmast of the ketch was too flexible. Watching it bend in the Jeffreys Ledge Race may have been a factor in his putting in to Gloucester. The Alden people beefed up the mast and added a second set of spreaders and a set of jumper struts. Noyes also thought that the boat should be steadier on her helm than she was. He had the cut-away deadwood filled in. And he bought new overlapping headsails.[23]

These changes did not improve the *Tioga II*'s performance immediately. In the 1937 Miami-

---

LEFT: **A preliminary drawing for a 110-foot version of the *Ticonderoga*. The prospective customer was Paul Hammond, so Francis drew on her sail plan Hammond's idea of setting running sails on spinnaker poles to form a sort of square rig, an arrangement that he had found worked well on the *Landfall*. The area of the five fore-and-aft sails is about 6,000 square feet, with the mainsail having about 1,600 square feet; the running sails, shown set in the small sketch at lower left, spread even more canvas to the wind. Foresail and mainsail overlap their masts; there were four sheets to tend when tacking, but the mainsail and foresail each had self-tending booms to take most of the strain. Waterline length is 93 feet, beam unknown, draft 10 feet, 7 inches. The big tender stowed on deck beneath the fore boom is reminiscent of the *Carpenter*. The round skylight that Francis drew atop the cabin house doubtless lights a majestic saloon. He dated this drawing 1937, not a good year for making dreams like this three-master come true. She never sailed except in Francis's imagination, and in Paul Hammond's.** (© Mystic Seaport Museum, Daniel S. Gregory Ships Plans Library, SP38.190.1)

Nassau Race, she finished third, behind the big Alden yawl *Mandoo II* and the much smaller *Stormy Weather*, designed by Olin Stephens. Both these boats were designed to rate well under the Cruising Club of America Ocean Racing Rule; the Noyes ketch dropped to twelfth on corrected time. The *Stormy Weather* was an easy winner with her handicap; ocean racing sailors were having a hard time catching up to the high standard set by the Stephens brothers, Olin and Rod, in driving a boat as hard as possible twenty-four hours a day, a boat well designed to the rule.[24]

But the *Tioga II* won plenty of silver in the summer of 1938, really coming into her own in the New London-Marblehead Race, a 171-mile course inside Martha's Vineyard and Nantucket and around Cape Cod. After a slow start, there was plenty of breeze, and the yachts never had to come closer to the wind than a close reach. Harry Noyes not only had the pleasure of beating the fleet, but also of breaking the course record, finishing in 18 hours, 37 minutes, for an average speed of 9.2 knots. This was the first of many course records that would fall to the *Ticonderoga*. As usual, though, she would drop down in the standings when her time was corrected.[25]

The *Tioga II* and the *Stormy Weather* met again in the 1940 Miami-Nassau Race. This time, the big ketch finished first and broke the course record, but she couldn't save her time on the Stephens yawl and fell to second on corrected time.[26]

After this race, Noyes put his pride and joy on a mooring off his house in Palm Beach, with her crew standing by to take him and his family out on day sails whenever he could take time off from selling Buicks in New England. But on April 16, the house cook came running down to the waterfront to shout the awful news to the crew: "The boss has been killed!" Harry Noyes was flying down from his business chores in Boston for a weekend of sailing. The weather was bad enough to halt commercial flights, so he chartered a Stinson Reliant with certified pilot John Hartwell from Intercity Aviation to take him to Palm Beach, via New York. The plane crashed in a freak snow squall in Connecticut. The pilot and one passenger survived, but another passenger and Noyes did not. He was forty-two.[27]

The crew delivered the *Tioga II* to Marblehead, and Ruth Noyes did use her, once having seventeen family members out for an afternoon sail, but her heart wasn't in it. Her reluctance to go out in the boat may have been increased by an accident: the jib topsail sheet had once ripped its winch out of the deck, and the missile flew close by her head.[28]

When World War II came, the *Tioga II,* along with many another seaworthy yacht, went into Coast Guard service, looking for U-boats. The Cruising Club of America proposed using private boats for naval service in 1941, and in May 1942 the Navy requested the Coast Guard to take over and organize the Coastal Picket Patrol. With mixed crews of yachtsmen and Coast Guard recruits, the yachts patrolled along the 50-fathom

---

RIGHT FOLDOUT, INSIDE: **The lines of the *Tioga II,* as Francis designated her on his hand-written list of his designs. She is long on the waterline and narrow, with moderate draft. Length on deck is 71 feet, 11 inches; length on the waterline, 63 feet 10 inches; beam, 16 feet, ¼ inch; draft, 7 feet, 9 inches; and displacement, 108,288 pounds, with 30,730 pounds of lead outside ballast, for a ballast-displacement ratio of 28 percent. She is an enlargement of the first *Tioga*, but she is not a copy. She is almost as beautiful as the most beautiful yacht in the world, but her grace is masculine rather than feminine. All the gorgeous curves of the *Tioga* have been strengthened just enough to give the *Tioga II* her own distinctive look. She is simply the handsomest yacht in the world. The lines of these two yachts are the best demonstration there is of L. Francis Herreshoff's genius as an artist.** (© Mystic Seaport Museum, Daniel S. Gregory Ships Plans Library, SP38.15.2)

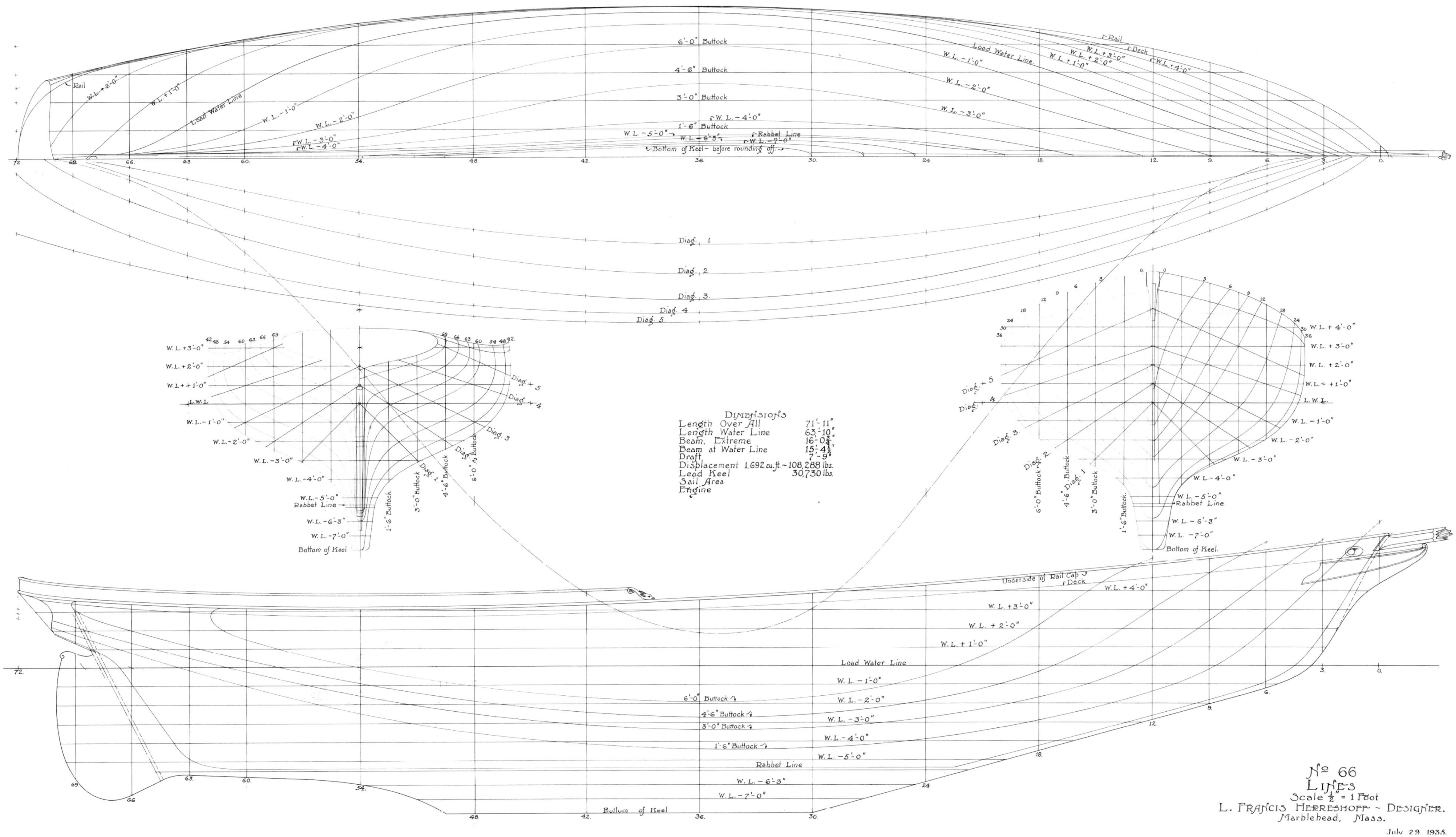
6'-0" Buttock
4'-6" Buttock
3'-0" Buttock
1'-6" Buttock
Load Water Line
Rabbet Line
Bottom of Keel - before rounding off
Rail
Deck
Diag. 1
Diag. 2
Diag. 3
Diag. 4
Diag. 5
Underside of Rail Cap
Bottom of Keel
DIMENSIONS
Length Over All 71'-11"
Length Water Line 63'-10"
Beam, Extreme 16'-0¾"
Beam at Water Line 15'-4½"
Draft 7'-9"
Displacement 1,692 cu.ft. ~ 108,288 lbs.
Lead Keel 30,730 lbs.
Sail Area
Engine
No 66
LINES
Scale ½" = 1 Foot
L. FRANCIS HERRESHOFF ~ DESIGNER.
Marblehead, Mass.
July 29. 1935.

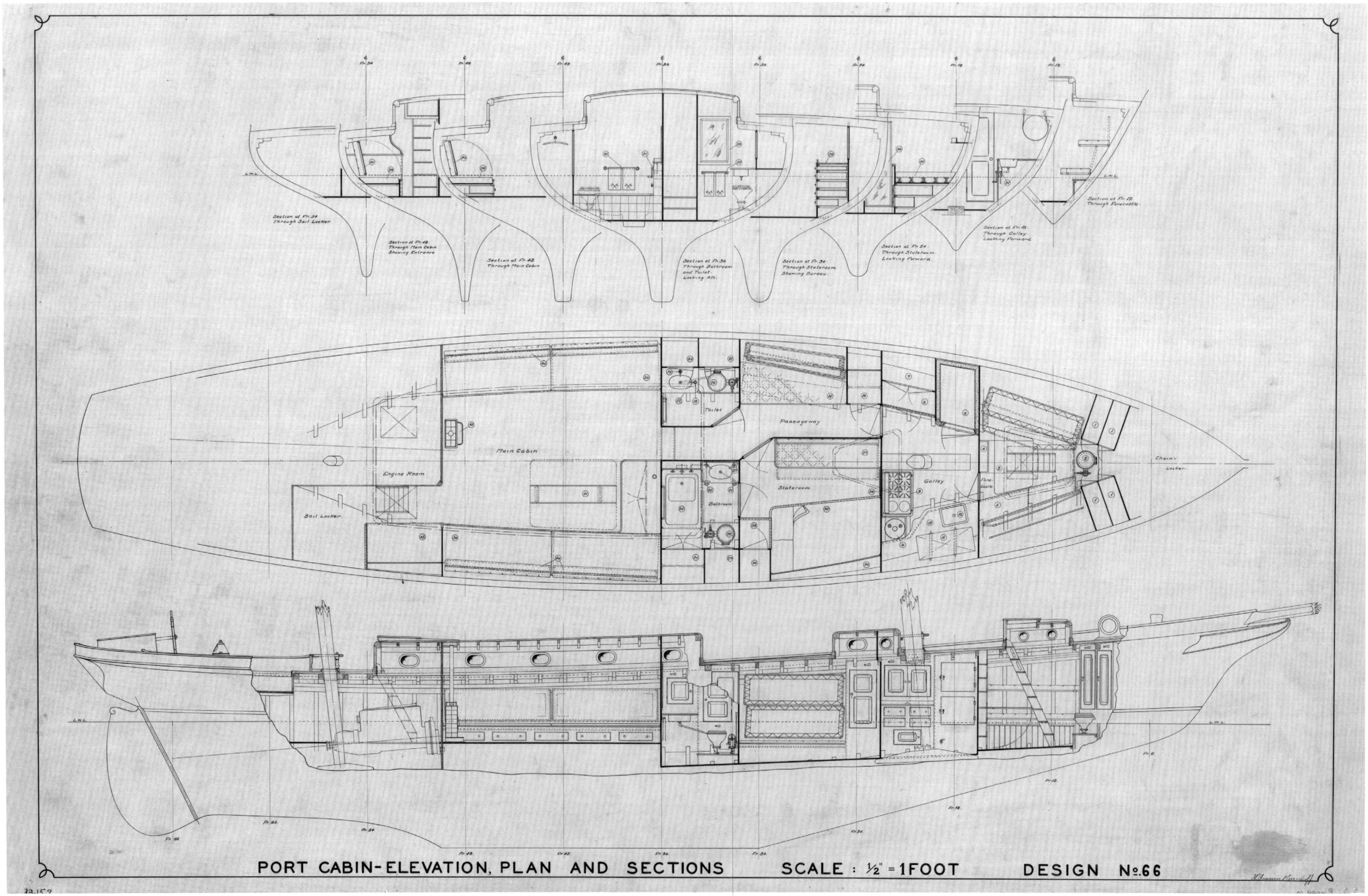

Section at Fr. 54
Through Sail Locker
Section at Fr. 48
Through Main Cabin
Showing Entrance
Section at Fr. 42
Through Main Cabin
Section at Fr. 36
Through Bathroom
and Toilet
Looking Aft
Section at Fr. 30
Through Stateroom
Showing Bureau
Section at Fr. 24
Through Stateroom
Looking Forward
Section at Fr. 18
Through Galley
Looking Forward
Section at Fr. 12
Through Forecastle
Toilet
Passageway
Main Cabin
Engine Room
Sail Locker
Bathroom
Stateroom
Galley
Chain Locker
PORT CABIN-ELEVATION, PLAN AND SECTIONS
SCALE : ½" = 1 FOOT
DESIGN No. 66

curve. Assigned to the Boston sector of the Coastal Picket Patrol on July 7, 1942, the *Tioga II* was given the number CGR-2509, two .30-caliber machine guns, and enough grey paint to cover everything, even including her stern carving. Her home port became Nantucket, and she patrolled east of the island and Cape Cod, assigned a square fifteen miles on a side as much as 150 miles offshore. This was a dangerous place to be in a winter northeast gale. Her crew of seven took her out for three to four days at a time, then came back in for two days. There is no report of her being in difficulty or sustaining damage. Nor is there any report of her ever sighting a German submarine.[29]

The Picket Patrol was disbanded in October 1943, though a few boats remained in service longer. When the Coast Guard returned the *Tioga II* to Ruth Noyes on May 31, 1944, the vessel was praised as being "very able and very fast." But she was in terrible shape; all her gear had either been stripped or so damaged as to be useless. Her owner had to spend $10,000 to restore the yacht to decent enough condition to put on the market.[30]

Allen Pinkerton Carlisle bought the *Tioga II* in 1946. He couldn't really afford her, at least not easily, but, like many another sailor, he had fallen for her charms. As his finances waned and waxed over the next thirteen years, he kept selling her

---

LEFT FOLDOUT: **The cabin plan of the *Tioga II*. She has a huge main saloon and a spacious double stateroom with its own head and shower. There are berths for four forward and eight aft. The large chart table is handy to the companionway. The separate engine room is entered from its own hatch in the after, port corner of the cabin house. As Francis designed them, the cabin soles fore and aft are so high and wide that the headroom under the beams in the cabin house is only 5 feet, 10 inches, with no more under the deck beams forward. During construction, tanks had to be pulled and reconfigured and the soles lowered and narrowed. This error is especially surprising, because Francis had recently had to make provision for headroom for a 6-foot, 4-inch son of the owner in the smaller, clipper-bowed ketch *Mobjack*.** (© Mystic Seaport Museum, Daniel S. Gregory Ships Plans Library, SP38.15.9) ABOVE: **Francis's design of the decoration of the transom of the *Tioga II*. His eagle looks to starboard over clutched arrows; the olive branch is to port. The direction of the eagle's gaze would not be traditionally correct until the vessel went to war six years after she was launched. Francis has carefully controlled the fineness and coarseness of the great bird's feathers, and he notes that the olive leaves are to be painted green. The elaborate stern decoration, including the cast-bronze border rope, cost $175. Harry Noyes simply kept the name *Tioga* for his bigger ketch, and he reserved the name when he sold her; for clarity, I have used Francis's own designation of the yacht, *Tioga II*, until she was renamed the *Ticonderoga*.** (© Mystic Seaport Museum, Daniel S. Gregory Ships Plans Library, SP38.15.105)

ABOVE: **Allan Carlisle, out for a sail in his *Ticonderoga,* recently stripped of her Coast Guard grey in 1946. He has her footing well, close-hauled under just working sail. Her lee-rail dolphin is well clear of the white water rushing past. Note the two tenders stowed under the main boom.** (Mystic Seaport Museum, 1990.37.1049) RIGHT: **The *Ticonderoga* just far enough off the wind to carry a modest balloon jib. She is lifting nicely and making knots. This is what the great ketch was designed for: the pure joy of sailing fast in a gorgeous yacht, feeling her power and speed, sensing her easy motion in a soft seaway.** (Photo 132929, The Mariners' Museum, Newport News, Virginia)

and buying her back. To help make ends meet, he would charter her out for a race, then go along as navigator or even sailing master.

The Noyes family retained the name *Tioga*. Carlisle renamed the boat *Ticonderoga*. Ticonderoga is an anglicization of the Iroquois word for the place between two waters, in this case Lake Champlain and Lake George, the location of Fort Ticonderoga. As a Scot, Carlisle perhaps was honoring the poem, "Ticonderoga," by Robert Louis Stevenson, which recounted the ghostly legend of Major Duncan Campbell with a dramatic ending at the fort. Or perhaps he just wanted a similar sounding name to Tioga and one also of Native American origin. In any case, it was as the *Ticonderoga* that the vessel would be become famous.[31]

Or, occasionally, infamous. In the Miami-Nassau Race, on February 11, 1947, a Gulf Stream norther dismasted her an hour after the start. She was carrying a big Yankee jib. Someone decided it would be a good idea to set up on a *lee* main cap shroud! She hit a sea, the headstay turnbuckle carried away, the mainmast broke 45 feet above the deck, and the triatic stay tore off the top of the mizzenmast. No one hurt. This was the beefed-up Alden rig, but there was an extenuating circumstance beyond straining the mast to leeward. Not long before the race, she had suffered rig damage when a bridge tender on the Intracoastal Waterway accidentally lowered his charge on her, and the damage had been hastily repaired.[32]

It didn't take long for the *Ticonderoga* to repair her racing record. Rerigged for the 1947 Marblehead-Halifax Race, she reached downeast in a fresh breeze to break the course record and win on both elapsed and corrected times. And in the 1948 Miami-Nassau event, with considerable windward work, she finished first and came in fifth on corrected time.[33]

O. "Lee" Lie-Nielsen, Francis's friend and former apprentice, who had helped supervise the construction of the first *Tioga,* once spotted the *Ticonderoga* tied up in Palm Beach. He asked a guy working on deck if he could tell him where the owner was. Lee was talking to Carlisle, who quickly identified himself. As did Lee. Carlisle: "Are you a sailing man, then?" Lee: "Yes." Carlisle: "How would you like to be captain of her?" Lee: "I'd love it!" Thus did Lee Nielsen get to sail what many have thought was his mentor's finest design. Carlisle chartered her out for the 1950 Lipton Cup Race with Lee as professional skipper. She won the race on both elapsed and corrected times. Nielsen described the *Ticonderoga* as "extremely well balanced." He said that "even with the wind aft,

you could leave the wheel, go below for coffee and come back—she'd be right on her course, though not with a sea running." He also said that she was a delight to sail and went very well to windward when she was sailed right.[34]

Three years later, Lee made a beautiful half model of the *Ticonderoga*, complete with trailboard, carved eagle on the nameboard, and dolphins at the quarter rail, all finished with gold leaf. Francis reacted to a photograph of the model with: "I certainly am very much pleased with the wonderful job you made of the *Ticonderoga* model." In the winter of 1965-66, this model, together with plans and photographs of the *Ticonderoga,* formed an exhibit on her design at MIT and then at the Peabody Museum in Salem, Massachusetts. Francis proposed the idea for the exhibit to his nephew, Halsey, then on the staff at MIT, and it was put together by the curator of the Hart Nautical Museum, naval architect and historian William A. Baker. Francis was pleased to view it with Margrete Stinnes, daughter of Hans, from whom he had bought the 30-Square-Metre boat *Gluckauf IV.* Miss Stinnes, known as Gretl, had moved to the United States from Germany after

ABOVE: **The gorgeous bow of Francis's design No. 66, renamed the *Ticonderoga*. The strong reverse curve of her billethead, her hollow waterline, the beautifully carved, oakleaf trailboard surmounted by a traditionally shaped hawsepipe, the entry of the bowsprit into the bulwarks, even the exact point of attachment of the bobstay chain—all blend into harmonious perfection. Francis took great care with the garnish on the ketch, not only on this trailboard on the bow, but also with much decoration on the stern, as well as a pair of dolphins on the rail amidships. He sought ideas for these sculptures from his father and also from Howard I. Chapelle, whose research into the design of traditional sailing craft had extended into such matters, but L. Francis Herreshoff alone is responsible for their beauty. It was as if he was dreaming of derring-do from this daysailer. Yet he would write later that he was never quite satisfied with the trailboards.** (Eveleth photo, *The Rudder* (June 1951): cover) RIGHT: **The *Ticonderoga*'s macho ocean racing crews (Francis called them "gigolo yacht jockeys") took pride in "drowning the dolphins," as they referred to a scene like this. In fact, they were not getting the best out of the big ketch. When working to windward in a strong breeze, driving her that hard actually slowed her down. Once, when the dolphins were well under, sails blew out, and the crew was surprised to see the boat's speed increase, when she straightened up and started sailing more on her lines. Had cooler heads prevailed more often, the *Ticonderoga* might have exceeded her own records and added more corrected-time trophies to her first-to-finish awards. A notation on the back of Francis's copy of this photograph reads: "about ten minutes before she let go," evidently referring to the bending main traveller.** (© Mystic Seaport Museum, 1990.37.263)

the war and was a friend and neighbor of Francis in Marblehead.[35]

The *Ticonderoga* didn't always need a fresh breeze to do well on the racecourse, nor did she always need the wind aft. The 1949 Fort Lauderdale to Cat Cay Race presented her with a lot of windward work in a breeze that never grew to more than 15 knots. She finished first and was second on corrected time, and this despite slowing to make a repair on her mainsail. Her moderate draft was not ideal for beating to windward, especially when it blew hard, and especially if she were not shortened down. In those conditions in the 1949 Miami-Nassau Race, she was beaten to the finish by two deep-draft Olin Stephens designs, the *Blitzen* and the *Windigo*, and the *Blitzen* was only 55 feet long. The *Ticonderoga* fell to tenth on corrected time.[36]

Bradley Noyes said that it was his father's opinion that the boat needed a centerboard. Maynard Bray, longtime technical editor of *WoodenBoat,* said that he observed cavitation from the after end of her keel, indicating abnormal leeway. A centerboard would stop the cavitation. While a centerboard would be an unnecessary complication for the *Ticonderoga* as a daysailer, it would be a boon to her as an ocean racer, working to windward in a fresh breeze or more.[37]

But again, as we've seen, the *Ticonderoga* won the 1950 Lipton Cup Race, and this in a light breeze, increasing to moderate. The course was a 28-mile triangle off Miami Beach; she didn't star on the spinnaker run, but worked out her winning lead on the beat and reach. As a Christmas present, Lee Lie-Nielsen sent "Dear Captain Francis" a photograph of the *Ticonderoga* rounding the Coast Guard cutter mark boat in her Lipton Cup victory. Captain Francis loved it.[38]

At the end of the 1951 racing season, Carlisle sold the *Ticonderoga* to John Hertz Jr., son of the car-rental mogul. The selling price was about $100,000, and Hertz spent another $90,000 on a thorough overhaul. He asked Lie-Nielsen to stay

on as skipper, but Hertz's reputation as an aggressive drinker caused Lee to decline the offer.[39]

In the 1952 St. Petersburg-Havana Race, the big ketch got her perfect conditions, mostly reaching in strong-to-gale-force winds. At one point, the Coast Guard escort vessel measured her speed as 13 knots; she averaged 9 and set a new course record. Thanks to Senors Batista and Castro, who shut down the race, the record still stands; though, with the thaw between Cuba and the United States, it may once again be challenged. The *Ticonderoga* thus became the only yacht to break every record in the Southern Ocean Racing Circuit (SORC).[40]

She did poorly in the light weather of the 1952 Bermuda Race, her first, but then, in the heavy-weather of the Monhegan Island Race in Maine that summer, with half the fleet dropping out to seek shelter, she romped home to break the 128-mile course record. Still racing on the coast of Maine, she had a meeting with one of its famous, unmarked "sunkers," a granite ledge just far enough under water to be dangerous. Here is how Francis described the accident: "The yacht *Ticonderoga* was in a race off Bar Harbor where there are several ledges. There was a good breeze, and the *Ti* was under spinnaker and all when

William L. Brittain at the wheel of his *Ticonderoga* in the thirty-mile Nassau Cup Race of 1961. She is strapped down, rail just under, going to windward in a fresh breeze with a big Yankee jib set. She finished first, as usual. Note that the stern decoration has been reversed from Francis's design, with the name ribbon beneath the eagle instead of crowning the bird, thus compromising the relationship of the design to its space. (Ray Eaton photo)

she was jumped over a ledge that was said to be three feet shallower than her draft. She was taken to Southwest Harbor, where she needed only minor repairs."[41]

The *Ticonderoga* entered thirty-seven races in the years 1936-52 and finished first on elapsed time in twenty-four of them, as she should have with her longest-in-the-fleet waterline.[42]

Rod Stephens modified *Ti*'s rig in 1953, adding a roller-furling backstaysail, nicknamed the "Mule." This sail set on the main backstay and sheeted to the mizzen masthead. With the Mule and all her other sails pulling, she broke the course record in the Cornfield Lightship Race on Long Island Sound.[43]

The 1954 Bermuda Race again produced light winds, favoring the smaller boats. The 40-foot Concordia yawl *Malay* was the overall winner. The new Olin Stephens yawl *Bolero* finished first and won Class A on corrected time, but dropped to twenty-first on corrected time in the fleet. The *Ticonderoga* finished thirty-seventh in the fleet and dropped to seventy-second (of seventy-seven) on corrected time.[44]

Ti made her first two Atlantic crossings in 1955, a round-trip that included a race from Havana to San Sebastian, Spain, in which she finished second of four yachts. In the winter of 1956, on a delivery run from St. Thomas to Miami, she made a noon-to-noon run of 264 miles and a three-day run of 667 miles. This was under working sail with a strong quartering breeze.[45]

The *Ticonderoga* had a new owner from 1960 to 1963. Hertz sold her to William T. Brittain, who put her into the charter business out of Fort Lauderdale, with the boat and business run by Baxter Still, a longtime crew-member. She broke the course record in the 400-mile St. Petersburg-Fort Lauderdale Race in 1962, and then went to the Great Lakes, where, in the 1962 Chicago-Mackinac Race, she was badly beaten by the 12-Metre *Mitena* in ghosting conditions. As we shall see, the *Mitena* was designed by L. Francis Herreshoff.[46]

When the 12-Metres *Weatherly* and *Gretel* raced for the America's Cup off Newport in 1962, the *Ticonderoga* was among the spectator fleet. Hans Stinnes had come over from Germany to visit his daughter, Gretl, in Marblehead, and Francis took his friends to Newport in his launch, the *Freelance*, to see the races. Francis thought a couple of the race days were too rough for his boat to be comfortable, but arranged for Bill Brittain to take them all aboard the *Ticonderoga*. This would be the only time Francis was underway in his design No. 66.[47]

As Gretl Stinnes remembered it: "*Ti* was fabulous. We motored out to watch the race and turned off the motor and began to sail. It was an incredible experience—the sound of it. Absolutely fantastic. Francis was very approving of the performance of the *Ticonderoga*. He didn't approve of all the things that had been added to her; he didn't approve of the people on board. He just watched from the cockpit, he didn't take part in sailing the boat." They got to witness a bit of heroism by the crew. Under power, *Ti* almost lost her propeller shaft. In reverse, the shaft backed out but didn't quite fall off. The experienced crewman, Ray Eaton, staunched the flow with a rag and then went overboard and rigged tackles on the shaft, enabling his shipmates to haul it back in! Francis admired the feat.[48]

Robert F. Johnson, an Oregon lumberman, chartered the *Ticonderoga* for the 1963 Transpacific Race from Los Angeles to Honolulu for $20,000. She finished first and was second on corrected time. Near the finish at Diamond Head, running with a big spinnaker set in 30 knots of wind, she averaged nearly 15 knots for about an hour. Johnson was hooked. After the finish, he bought the *Ti* for $85,000.[49]

Francis came to appreciate this new owner of his pride and joy. Johnson consulted with him about ways to make the boat sail better. He believed in Francis's design and realized that the *Ti* had gained weight over the years and was floating well below her lines. With her designer's hearty concurrence, he took eight tons (!) of various amenities out of her. He also restored Francis's cutaway deadwood.[50]

Moreover, Johnson was that rare owner who took the trouble to write Francis detailed descriptions of how his design sailed in varying conditions. Here is what he told Francis about the early hours of the Transpacific Race: "Shortly after the start we had lots of wind west of Catalina (probably about 30-35 knots). *Ti* went right under to the cabin roof [!] and I consulted with Ray [Eaton] suggesting we should shorten. He agreed but said, 'She always does that, and that's the way they always sail her.'" Johnson changed that habit of "drowning the dolphins," as her former macho crews called sailing her on her ear with the decorative taffrail dolphins under water. Sailing the ketch more upright with less sail not only saved her from a battering, but also increased her speed. Near the finish of the 1965 St. Petersburg-Fort Lauderdale Race, on a close reach "under short sail" in a 35-knot northeaster, "*Ti* made 60 miles in 4 hours, 15 minutes [at 14.1 knots]—the Gulf Stream helping," as Johnson wrote Francis. And this with

no damage to the vessel, whereas an earlier crew had driven her hard in similar weather on the same stretch of water—with broken ribs in the bow to show for it. Johnson wrote to Francis: "Her bow and forefoot *cut* the water instead of slamming her down *on her side* at the bow sections. And I'm sure she went faster." Putting the *Ticonderoga* under short sail was sometimes learned (and would have to be relearned) by accident. In a St. Petersburg-Venice Race, 108 miles, in which she finished first and broke the course record, she was on a close reach in a strong breeze. The crew lowered the mainsail to tie in a reef. The ketch straightened up and increased speed to 9.5 knots. They furled the mainsail.[51]

And the *Ticonderoga* continued to prove that she was more than just a "reaching fool." In a 1965 SORC event, a windward-leeward course off Fort Lauderdale, she finished first on both elapsed and corrected time and beat the 12-Metre *Anitra* to the weather mark. On that day, she needed no centerboard.[52]

L. Francis Herreshoff enjoyed following the races of the great ketch he had designed to no measurement rule, none more than her win on both elapsed and corrected time in the 1965 Miami-to-Montego Bay, Jamaica, Race, a course of 850 miles. One of her day's runs was 248 miles. The icing on the cake was that she broke the *Bolero*'s course record by more than twelve hours, and the *Bolero* was designed by Olin Stephens. Only the *Ticonderoga* could mitigate Francis's jealousy of Stephens's success and popularity.[53]

But perhaps the most thrilling race of all for the *Ticonderoga* and Bob Johnson was the 2,250-mile 1965 Transpacific Race from Los Angeles to Honolulu. Of the fifty-five yachts in the race, the boat to beat, for the *Ticonderoga,* was clearly the *Stormvogel*, a 74-foot, light-displacement flyer from The Netherlands, designed by E. G. van de Stadt and built of plywood manufactured by the owner, Cornelius Bruynzeal.

The fleet was threatened by Tropical Storm Bernice. Bob Johnson, as owner-navigator, decided to steer the *Ticonderoga* right toward the storm. The strategy worked perfectly: by the time the ketch felt the northern edge of Bernice's punch, she had been downgraded to a tropical depression, so the *Ticonderoga* got just what she loved most—a gale-force fair wind with big following seas. She was put dead before it under her full mainsail and a small, heavyweight spinnaker. It was blowing 50 knots. Here is how Johnson described what happened next in a letter to Francis: "We locked in twice on two giant waves. The speed indicator banged right up against the pin—20 knots, plus we don't know how much—and old *Ticonderoga* stayed with the wave. Finally, the 4-ounce spinnaker exploded into confetti, and the main ripped from leech to luff. Then the gooseneck ripped loose from the mast; the poles, spinnaker bells, and the cars went into orbit overboard. We put on a staysail and jib, and meanwhile, the crew strapped the boom hardware back on and made up a sort of charm bracelet of cable clamps and jib-track cars to hold the spinnaker pole. We sailed more than 250 miles during this 24-hour period, half of it with no main."[54]

Three days later, the *Ticonderoga,* approaching the finish, continued running, now with a 3,800-square-foot, 2.2-ounce spinnaker, jury rigged, set to 40 knots of wind. And who

---

LEFT TOP: **Gretl Stinnes at the 1962 America's Cup races at Newport.** (Photo by Hans Stinnes, courtesy Margrete Stinnes, author's collection) LEFT BOTTOM: **Francis, age 71, at the wheel of the *Ticonderoga* observing the America's Cup races off Newport in 1962. He is steering, closely monitored, under power; otherwise, as Gretl Stinnes remembered it, "He didn't take part in sailing the boat."** (© Mystic Seaport Museum, 1990.37.271)

should emerge from a squall, not far astern, but the *Stormvogel*! Johnson said the final jibe for the line was "not exactly child's play." He added that it was something "that a professional seaman wouldn't attempt. Good sense and the union rules wouldn't permit it." Nevertheless, the jibe was made, and the *Ticonderoga* held off the *Stormvogel* and beat her by six minutes. Both boats bettered the course record set by the 98-foot *Morning Star*. The *Ticonderoga* had a day's run of 266 miles, and she had *averaged* 10.4 knots for the 2,400 miles that she had actually sailed in the race. The fact that the race was won on corrected time by a newly designed, lightweight planer, a Cal 40, didn't bother Johnson. He was proud of his vessel, and he shared his pride in the *Ticonderoga* in a long letter to her designer, written three days after the race. But of all the accolades that Francis received for his big ketch's performance in the 1965 Transpac, perhaps his favorite was a letter from a California architect, who wrote: "Dear

ABOVE LEFT: **"Big *Ti*" strutting her stuff. She is on her way to breaking the course record in the 1965 Montego Bay Race, roaring along on a broad reach, her helmsman steering small, her crew tending carefully to the trim of her huge racing sails.** (© Mystic Seaport Museum, 1990.37.1081) ABOVE RIGHT: **The *Ticonderoga*'s knotmeter registering 19 during the 1965 Transpacific Race. It certainly paid to drive her when off the wind. There are stories of this instrument being pegged at 20 for seconds when she was surfing down a big sea. With her longest-in-the-fleet waterline, the *Ticonderoga* always stretched out ahead when the wind came aft and blew.** (Courtesy Muriel Vaughn, author's collection)

Mr. Herreshoff, Congratulations on *Ticonderoga's* performance to Diamond Head. It is a vindication of Yankee judgment and skill over computers, test tanks, and rule beaters. Sincerely, Bolton C. Moise, Jr." The *Ticonderoga* was almost forcing L. Francis Herreshoff to embrace ocean racing.[55]

Back in San Francisco for the 1965 Big Boat Series, the *Ticonderoga* was third in a fleet of fourteen, and fell to ninth on corrected time. The winner on corrected time was a handsome sloop, the *Vixen,* originally the yawl *Persephone,* designed by Francis to the Cruising Club of America's ocean racing measurement rule a year after he designed the *Ticonderoga.*[56]

Although the *Ticonderoga* had proved she could compete successfully against a light displacement fin-keeler of her own size like the *Stormvogel,* at least boat-for-boat disregarding time allowance, she had no hope of saving her time against smaller versions of the new lightweight flyers like William Lapworth's breakthrough Cal 40 design, especially when working to windward. In the 1966 Bermuda Race, with a lot of windward work, she was 113 in a fleet of 156. But she was back in her old form in the Transatlantic Race of that year with plenty of wind from aft, sailing 3,572 miles from Bermuda to Copenhagen at an average speed of 9.1 knots, enough to finish first.[57]

And then the *Ticonderoga* entered Denmark's 1966 Skaw Race, on its hundredth anniversary. The 360-mile course started off Elsinore Castle at Copenhagen, headed north the length of the Kattegat and round the Skaw, the northern tip of Denmark, then west across the Skagerrak to a mark off Kristiansand, Norway, back east across the Oslo Fjord to a mark on the coast of Sweden, and back to the finish at Skagen, the port at the Skaw. This course proved to be a 220-mile beat, a 90-mile run, and a close reach of 50 miles, in extra-rough conditions, even for these Scandinavian waters. *Ti's* anemometer carried away at 55 knots. Of the fleet of 179 starters, 97 retired and sought shelter.[58]

Bob Johnson was learning how to sail the *Ticonderoga* to windward in heavy weather: he had her under a main trysail, forestaysail, and a small jib, and he concentrated on keeping her going through the head seas, rather than on pointing high. The lee dolphin stayed reasonably dry. And, once round the Skaw, he stood off on a long port tack to gain something of a lee under the Norwegian shore. His competitors let him go and made far shorter tacks to stay closer to the rhumb line direct to Kristiansand, but they were sailing in rougher water. This time, a Herreshoff boat, sailing in different conditions from the rest of the fleet—Francis's bête noir of ocean racing—gained an advantage. She led the second boat by an hour and a half at the windward mark and increased her lead to 3 hours, 40 minutes on the run and close reach, winning the race on both elapsed and corrected time. Johnson wrote to Francis: "She'll do things that no other boat we know of will do, and she has to be sailed differently than other boats. We think we're just finding out how to sail her!"[59]

In the three years since Johnson bought the *Ticonderoga* in the summer of 1963, she had sailed 50,000 miles, traveling to and participating in ocean races, something of a record in itself. Her last big win on the racecourse was a first-to-finish in the 1967 Miami-to-Montego Bay Race. She was then "retired," for it was found that her fastenings were shot, apparently through the vessel having been struck by lightning, though neither Johnson nor any of his crew members could remember such an event.[60]

In 1967, Johnson donated the *Ticonderoga* to Nova University in Fort Lauderdale for use as a research vessel in the school's oceanography program. Nova quickly woke up to the fact that keeping a thirty-year-old wooden vessel in good shape costs money and sold her to the Robador Corporation, a privately owned company (by Robert S. Robe, of Oyster Bay, Long Island) that operated charter yachts in the Caribbean. Nova got $30,000 for *Ti,* and Robador spent over $100,000 to overhaul her and modify the cabin plan for charter guests. As the only air-conditioned boat in the Caribbean charter fleet, the *Ticonderoga* brought in from $2,500 to $3,000 a week twenty-six times a year, although her beauty and her reputation probably had more to do with her success than the AC.[61]

Brian and Angela Coen, who ran *Ti* for Robador for three years, bought her in 1970 for $70,000 and continued to delight charterers with her aura. The Coens were the first of a series of lucky owners in the 1970s and '80s who saw the *Ticonderoga*'s market value rise by leaps and bounds, like a poker hand under the cup being passed from player to player in a game of Liar's Dice. The next year, they sold her to Gerard McAllister, of the New York tugboat family, for $150,000. She continued in the charter game, run by Ken and Fran Mackenzie, who had a 25 percent nominal interest in the vessel.[62]

The new team took the *Ticonderoga* north in the summer of 1971, looking for charter business, and they called at Marblehead. Francis, at age eighty, spotted her at a dock and had Muriel Vaughn, his secretary, drive him down in his grey Ferrari. A crewman on deck found himself addressed by a gentleman in tweed knickers, coat, tie, and matching cap, and with a walking stick: "Young man, my name is L. Francis Herreshoff, and I designed this boat. May I come aboard?" Francis was welcomed aboard indeed. He spent several hours going over the *Ticonderoga*, commenting on changes he approved and those he didn't. The experience of being recognized for who he was by the Mackenzies and their crew meant a lot to Francis. He signed the guest log on board his most famous yacht design on August 6, 1971, the first signature in Ken and Fran Mackenzie's new book.[63]

The Mackenzies pushed hard for seasonal charters in New England, the Chesapeake Bay, and the Caribbean. In the fall of 1973, on the way south to the Caribbean via Bermuda, they met the edge of Hurricane Gilda. They ran *Ti* off under bare poles towing warps. A big breaker pooped her. Ken, at the wheel, was thrown against it. The wheel splintered and Fran, next to him, had her leg gashed.[64]

In charter boat races, the *Ticonderoga* could still finish first and break course records if she got her ideal weather, wind aft and plenty of it. And in the Op Sail 1976 run from Bermuda to New York, she went well west of the rhumb line, found her own breeze, and was first in fleet.[65]

In 1979, the Mackenzies bought out McAllister, but after nine years of hard charter work, they were exhausted. In 1981, they sold the *Ticonderoga* to David Edwards, a Colorado doctor and real estate developer for $325,000. After five years of ownership that didn't provide him with much sailing or much charter income, Edwards sold the *Ticonderoga* to Robert Voit, an entrepreneur in California, for $440,000.[66]

Voit didn't need to charter *Ti* to make ends meet; he could afford to spend money on the boat. In 1988, the *Ticonderoga* sailed across the Atlantic and cruised in the Baltic before winding up at Southampton Yacht Services in England, where it was found she needed a major rebuild. Eleven months and $920,000 later, she had sister frames; new planking above the waterline; new deck beams, deck, and bulwarks; and a new engine. Her Formica, charter-proof interior was changed to mahogany and white-painted wood.[67]

Robert Voit took seriously the responsibility of ownership of a vessel that ranked high in importance among the world's fleet of classic yachts. His dedication to the *Ticonderoga*, and his money, gave her a new lease on life. And he enjoyed sailing her all that his busy schedule allowed. There were cruises in the Mediterranean (she lost her mizzenmast to a faulty fitting in Greek waters), the Black Sea, and the Caribbean. In 1991, he brought her home to Newport Beach, California. Two years later, with the boat back in the Caribbean, in Belize, he sold the *Ticonderoga* for $875,000 to L. Scott Frantz, a thirty-two-year-old venture capitalist who lived in Greenwich, Connecticut.[68]

And under that caring, appreciative ownership, L. Francis Herreshoff's wonderful clipper-bowed ketch, the handsomest boat in the world, has stayed. Scott and his wife, Icy, have cruised in the *Ticonderoga* in New England, the Caribbean, and the Mediterranean. They have raced her in classic-yacht regattas and twice in the Bermuda Race. *Ti* has again distinguished herself on the race course and has also finished in the middle of the fleet, but, for the Frantzes, competition and winning seem to be no more important than sharing a treasure with their friends.[69]

On August 10, 1996, the Frantzs threw a party on board and at the dock in Nantucket for 300 sailors to celebrate the *Ticonderoga*'s sixtieth birthday. In 2001, she crossed the Atlantic to participate in the gigantic America's Cup Jubilee at Cowes; in the racing, she finished second in the Vintage Class. In 2011, she was given another Nantucket birthday party, to celebrate her seventy-fifth year. She was also celebrating the fact that she had just broken her own record of 1947 in the Marblehead-Halifax Race: she got a 30-knot southwester and romped to the finish, hitting 13 knots at times.[70]

The best possible news about the *Ticonderoga* is that Scott Frantz's only plan for her is to keep her racing and cruising. He writes: "She has meant a tremendous amount to our family and myself personally. She has delivered way beyond the expected amount of joy to ourselves, friends and strangers all of whom became friends. She is a magnet at the same time the glue that keeps outstanding sailors and friends coming back after two decades of sailing and racing together. She makes you smile and she makes some people cry. It seems that no one can have a bad day on this beautiful ship who was born not only to win but to inspire and bring joy to all who appreciate grace, character, and wood."[71]

At least two other vessels have been built to Francis's design for the *Tioga II*. In 1974, P. Voss Ltd., a shipyard in Auckland, New Zealand, launched the *Victoria*, a No. 66 of cold-molded wood. She had modifications: her 210-horsepower Caterpillar diesel was forward, with the engine

Francis dusting off his framed copy of another aerial photograph taken sequentially with the strutting-her-stuff picture, this one from above her starboard quarter. Francis scorned carrying so much sail at sea, but he still loved these glorious photos of his ketch. (Gilbert E. Friedberg photo, Mystic Seaport Museum, 1999-8.220)

room space aft given over to a double stateroom. There was a doghouse over the companionway. In 1992, she was listed for sale at $575,000.[72]

Stanley Bishoprick, an Oregon lumberman, was a great admirer of L. Francis Herreshoff. He established Legendary Yachts across the Columbia River in Washougal, Washington, primarily to build boats to Francis's designs. The most important would be a No. 66, which he wanted as a family cruiser, as did Harry Noyes, but also to demonstrate his company's ability to build a first-class yacht. He chose composite construction, with 2-inch mahogany planking, sheathed with Dynel below the waterline, over a skeleton of galvanized steel. Displacement came out 18,000 pounds lighter than that of the *Ticonderoga.* The sail plan was unchanged, but the masts would be of carbon fiber with rod rigging and setting fully battened sails. The *Radiance* was launched on August 8, 1994, two days before *Ti's* fifty-eighth birthday.[73]

Her builder was a cruising man, though he did some low-key racing with the *Radiance.* With his family, he sailed her around the world. In contrast to reports of drowning the dolphins racing in a gale, Bishoprick can give us reports of how she behaved when comfortably hove to in such conditions. He used Francis's suggested method of lying-to in a ketch: set the mizzen only (Bishoprick reefed it) and let the rudder go where it seems to want to. He said she lies 45 degrees off the wind or closer, wandering a bit, with the helm hard alee drifting to leeward at less than a knot.[74]

Bruce King took inspiration from Francis's designs for both *Tiogas* when he drew, in August 1975, the lines for the *Whitehawk*, a 92-foot ketch. Proportionally, King made his design a bit narrower forward with a little less flare in the bow and a slightly higher stern, gave her less deadrise, but more hollow in the garboards, and less draft (than No. 66). The rig was proportionally taller, possible with the increased stability of the bigger boat. The *Whitehawk* has been a superb vessel.[75]

Although he made a bad bargain with Harry Noyes for the design of the *Tioga II,* Francis was able to make a little money from later sales of the drawings. When anyone expressed interest in the plans for No. 66, Francis offered them a set of 35 of the drawings (out of 62) for $1,000. William A. Robinson, the owner of the brigantine-rigged *Varua* inquired from Tahiti, but backed away from the price. Francis backed away from a correspondent in California who wanted to build a ferro-cement *Ticonderoga*, advising him to try a rowboat or model yacht first. But Vicomte R. de Dampierre, the Consulat General de France, in Florence, Italy, did send in his thousand dollars promptly; it is not known what use he made of the lovely drawings.[76]

Lee Nielsen, who knew Francis well, who had been a professional skipper aboard the *Ticonderoga,* and who had made the half model of her that Francis heartily approved, believed from Francis's comments that the *Ti* was his favorite among his designs. Ten years after designing her, Francis wrote: "I would say that I have not designed many boats but think perhaps the most outstanding ones have been R-boat *Yankee,* M-boat *Istalena;* 72-foot ketch *Tioga.*" For sailors on the fringe of the sport, all they may know about L. Francis Herreshoff is that he designed the *Ticonderoga*.[77]

The big, fast, gorgeous ketch brought Francis great satisfaction. Her design, more than anything else in his life, brought him the recognition he craved. The *Ticonderoga* showed the world who L. Francis Herreshoff was.

And she performed him one last service: she conveyed his ashes to sea. But that is getting ahead of our story.

CHAPTER 16

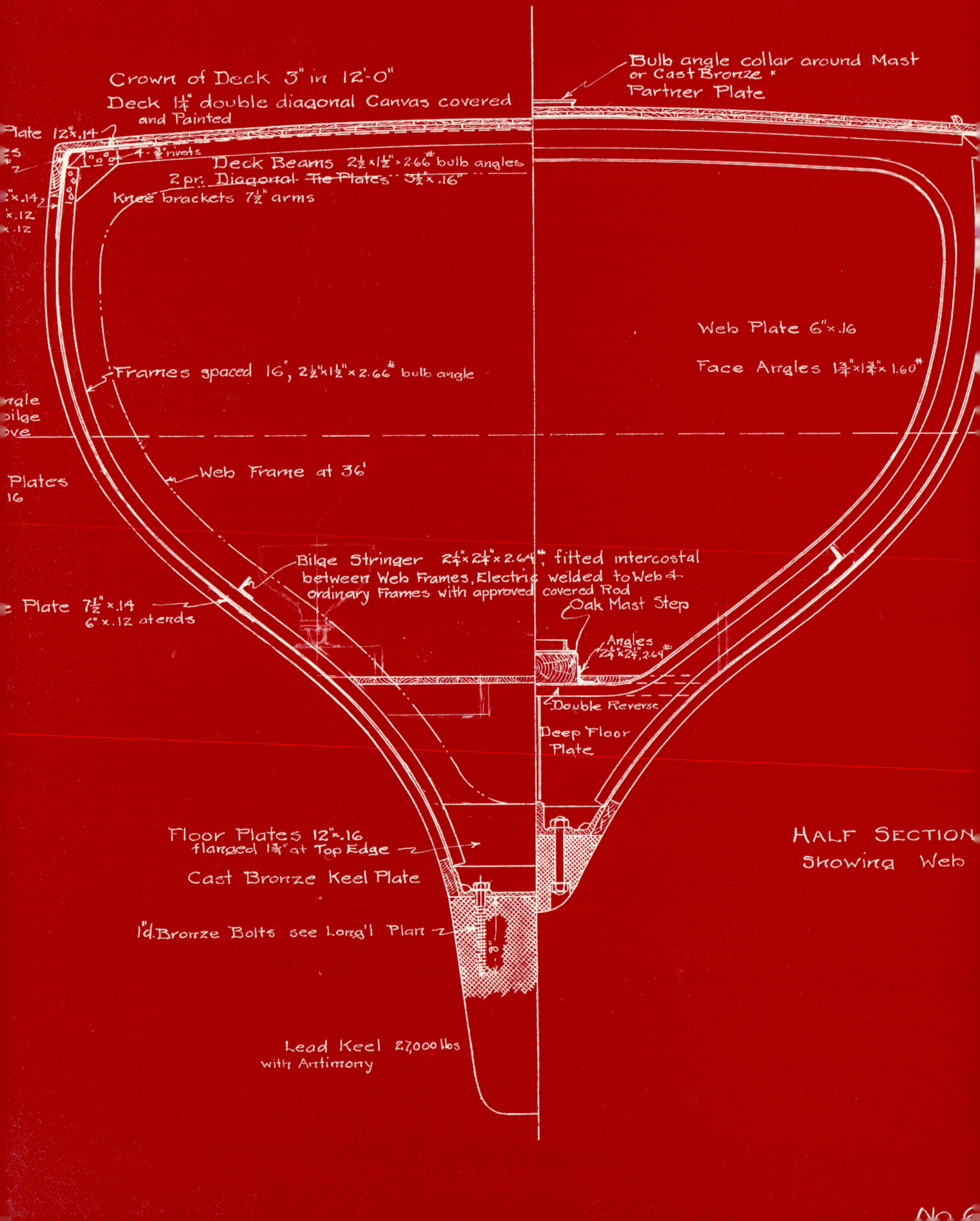

HALF SECTION
Showing Web

THE LAST TWO RACERS

Now are you happy Francis?

—LLOYDS INSPECTOR JOHN S. HECK, 1935

As the Great Depression deepened, L. Francis Herreshoff was lucky. Not only did he have a commission to design a 72-foot ketch, but also, just when his friend and patron Charlie Welch was lured away from sailboat racing and cruising by the attractions of a lovely farm on Chappaquiddick Island, Martha's Vineyard, another man of means came over the horizon to take his place. William J. Strawbridge, heir to profits turned by Strawbridge and Clothier, the Philadelphia department store, bought the *Istalena* in 1934 and became a devotee of Francis Herreshoff. Billy Strawbridge was lucky too: the construction of S & C's huge limestone store, put up at the corner of Market and 8th and opened in 1931 at a cost of ten million dollars, didn't quite bankrupt the company. He was able to indulge his love of sailing and persuade Francis to design him a 12-Metre boat and an ocean racer, as well as six other boats, only three of which would be built. Like Charlie Welch, Billy Strawbridge would try Francis's patience at times, asking him to design boats that would never sail. But, again like Welch, Strawbridge would become a good friend to Francis.

At about the same time Francis's patrons were changing, so were his boarders. Lee Nielsen moved out to get married in early 1934, and his place at 20 Lee Street was soon taken by Captain John Albert Chambers, a Marbleheader newly retired from the US Navy. Al Chambers was far more social than L. Francis Herreshoff. He was an active member of the Cruising Club of America, serving on race committees, and he had connections in New York, including a close friendship with Alfred F. Loomis, writer of a monthly column in *Yachting,* "Under the Lee of the Longboat." Chambers quickly became a convivial talker at Francis's evening fireside discussions of yachting, where he proved adept at encouraging the flow of both conversation and rum. Chambers wrote to Alf Loomis that he belonged to "a nice little drinking organization called the Saturday Night Club," a short-lived operation that Francis would surely have scorned. Chambers explained to Loomis that the drinkers met only three times. The first Saturday, there was a car crash; the second, a tippler started home for Marblehead Neck and ended up in Bridgeport, Connecticut; and the third, everybody passed out and all the pipes froze. During the week, Chambers had a role in Francis's business, handling yacht brokerage and boat insurance, but, in the depths

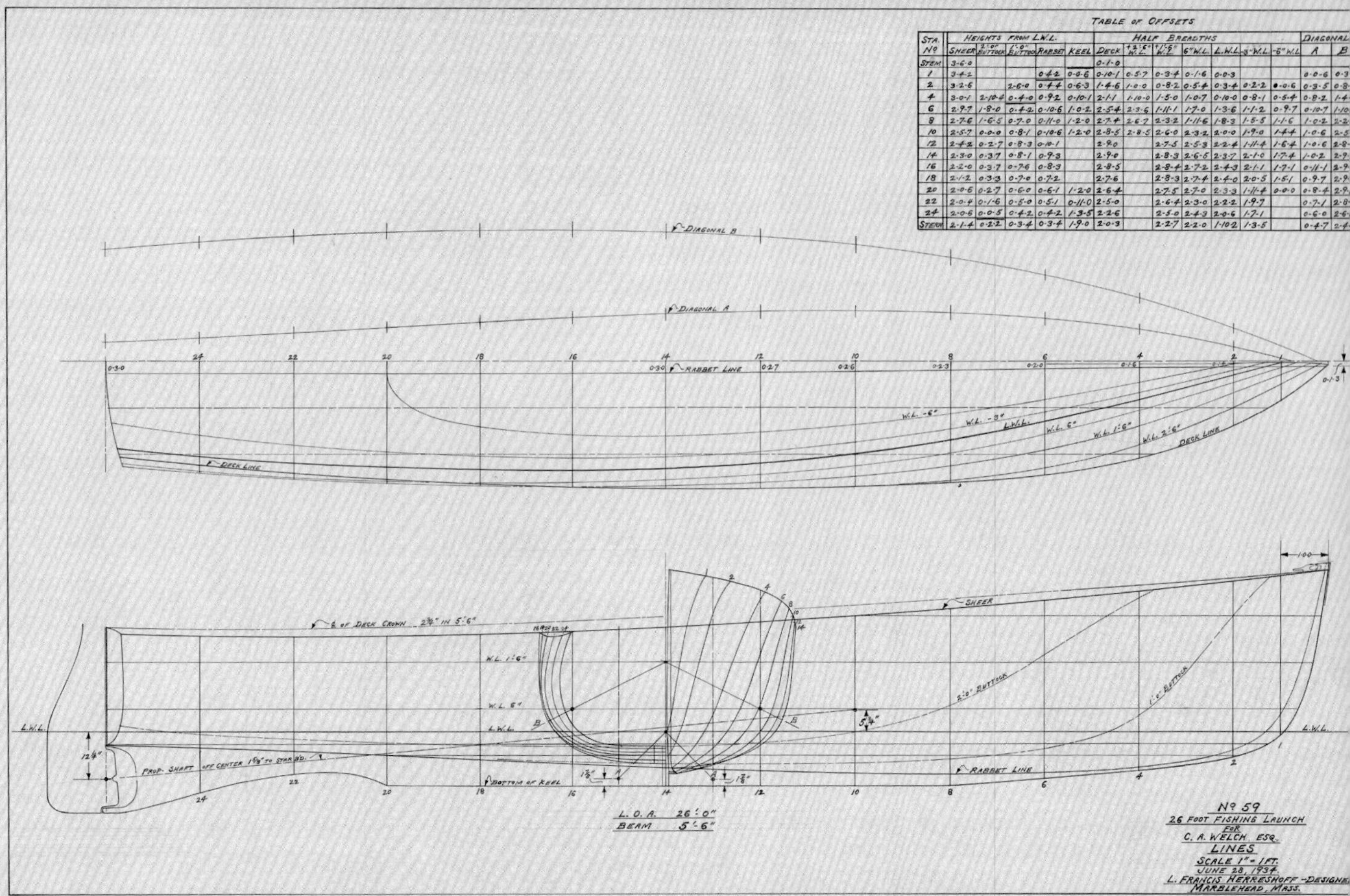

of the Depression, his abilities as salesman were largely wasted. It was Al Chambers's good humor and genuine interest in yacht design that enabled the two very different personalities to coexist under one roof. With a break to stay with another friend in Boston for a year, Chambers would board with Francis until 1943.[1]

Francis had other work before he returned to designing racing yachts at the behest of his new patron, Billy Strawbridge. There were more small craft to draw; there was another clipper-bowed ketch to create. And Charlie Welch, as he turned gentleman farmer, needed one more design from Francis: a fishing launch to enable him to add to his Martha's Vineyard harvest.

ABOVE: **The lines of the *Gadget*, a 26-foot fast fishing launch, the last boat that Francis designed for Charlie Welch that was built. Her beam is a narrow 5 feet, 6 inches, and the draft is a shoal 1 foot, 11 inches. The propeller shaft is submerged just over a foot. Fenwick Williams inked Francis's drawing and dated it June 28, 1934.** (© Mystic Seaport Museum, Daniel S. Gregory Ships Plans Library, SP38.86.1 RIGHT: **The *Gadget's* construction plan. At this slow time, Francis had the luxury of being able to make the detailed, inked drawing himself, with its twenty-four call-outs of specifications and its list of sixty-four bolts, with their location, sizes, and head types. The boom, goose-necked at the forward end of the coaming, serves as a ridgepole for a canvas cockpit shelter. The engine is a six-cylinder Lathrop. The two fuel tanks forward hold 17½ gallons each. She has a fixed thwart amidships and removable thwarts aft. The towing bitts at the quarters are also removable. In the bow is an enclosed forepeak. The nicely curved tiller is of oak.** (© Mystic Seaport Museum, Daniel S. Gregory Ships Plans Library, SP38.86.2)

1	Cast Bronze Stem Band	15	Removable box over shaft
2	Special Bronze Bow Chocks – see L.F.H.	16	Engine controlles arranged later by owner and architect.
3	Merriman Fig 400 – 10½" long	17	Strong Thwart, (not removable.) 1" or more thick.
4	Light Flooring	18	Strong Knees.
5	Hinged Door to Fore Peak 2'×18" water tight below Threshold	19	Stringer for removable thwarts.
6	Oak Block for Back Bone Gooseneck	20	Teak Toe board about ⅜"×3"
7	Vent Outboard	21	High grade Bronze Stuffing Box.
8	Tin lined Copper 1'×3'–17½ Gal.	22	Removable Towing Bitts, Oak block at bottom Brass Strap top.
9	Brass strap 2"×3/16"	23	Oak Tiller
10	Teak slat floor, Center Sections removable	24	See full size detail.
11	Large feed line with strainer.		
12	Oak engine beds, Cutaway to reach base hand hole. Bed logs spaced 1'7¾" ℄ to ℄ Logs 1⅜" thick with special		
13	metal brakets to engine		
14	Lathrop L.H.6 – costs $665. approximately.		

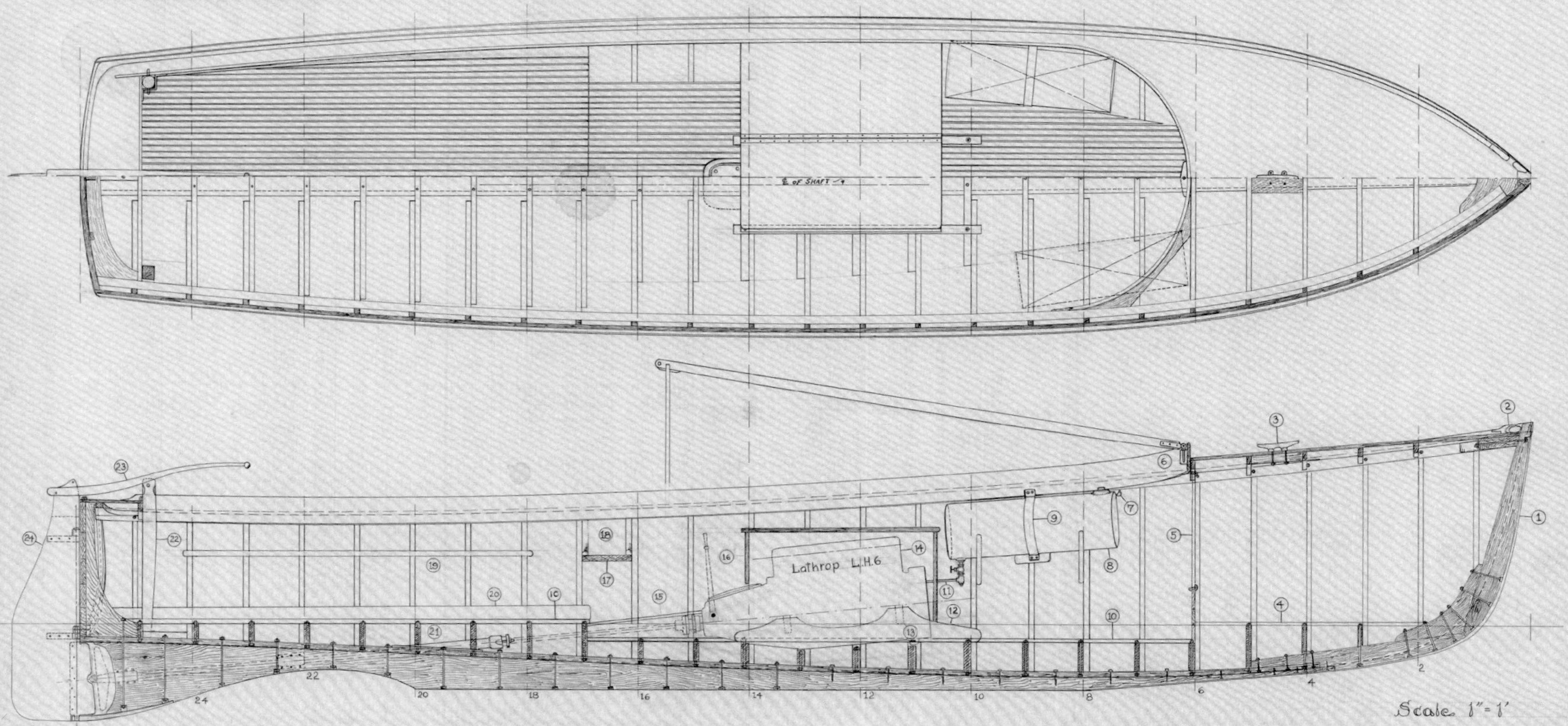

Scale 1" = 1'

Bolt List. all bolts and fastenings bronze.

Location	25'-3"	Floor 25	24'-6"	Floor 24	23'-6"	Floor 23	22'-6"	Floor 22	21'-6"	Floor 21	20'-6"	Floor 20	19'-6"	Floor 19	18'-6"	Floor 18
No Required	1	2	1	2	1	2	1	2	1	2	1	2	1	2	1	2
Length	1'-8"	4½"	1'-3"	5"	10½"	5½"	7"	6"	5½	6½	7"	7"	9"	7½"	8½"	8"
Diameter	⅜"	5/16"	⅜"	5/16"	⅜"	5/16"	⅜"	5/16	⅜	5/16	⅜"	5/16"	⅜"	5/16"	⅜"	5/16"
Head Type	Nut	Both	Ends	to	Station	13	—	—	—	—	—	—	—	—	—	—

Location	17'-6"	Floor 17	16'-6"	Floor 16	15'-6"	Floor 15	14'-6"	Floor 14	13'-6"	Floor 13	12'-6"	Floor 12	11'-6"	Floor 11	10'-6"
No Required	1	2	1	2	1	2	1	2	1	2	1	2	1	2	1
Length	8"	8½"	7½"	5½"	7"	6"	6"	6½"	6"	4"	3"	6"	3"	7½"	3"
Diameter	⅜"	5/16"	⅜"	5/16"	⅜"	5/16"	⅜"	⅜"	⅜"	⅜"	⅜"	⅜"	⅜"	⅜"	⅜"
Head Type	—	—	—	—	—	—	—	—	—	—	Lag	N.B.E.	Lag	N.B.E.	Lag

Location	Floor 10	9'-6"	Floor 9	8'-6"	Floor 8	7'-6"	Floor 7	6'-6"	Floor 6'	Floor 5'	Scalf	Floor 4'	Floor 3'	Stem Knee
No Required	2	1	2	1	1	1	1	1	1	1	3	1	1	4
Length	8"	3"	8"	3"	8"	3"	7½"	2"	8"	11"	3½"	10"	9½"	7"
Diameter	⅜"	⅜"	5/16"	⅜"	⅜"	⅜"	⅜"	⅜"	⅜"	⅜"	⅜"	⅜"	⅜"	⅜"
Head Type	N.B.E.	Lag	N.B.E.	Lag	N.B.E.	Lag	N.B.E.	Lag	N.B.E.	NBE	N.B.E.	N.B.E.	N.B.E.	T. head

DESIGN NO. 59 – 26 FOOT FISHING LAUNCH FOR C. A. WELCH

Designed by L. Francis Herreshoff 26 Lee St. Marblehead
July 1934

Charlie wanted to be able to get to the best fishing spots quickly; he wanted his launch to be fast. He named her the *Gadget*. We may recall an accident in this fast boat (see volume 1, pages 329, 334). Francis and Waldo Brown were bringing the *Gadget* in to the Beverly Yacht Club after a sail on Buzzards Bay in Waldo's 30-Square-Metre *Gem*. There had been a heated argument over the trim of the jib. Francis, at the controls, had come in fast, had rammed a granite wall, and had sunk the *Gadget*. The damage was repairable.

The *Gadget* was one of the few boats to survive the 1938 hurricane in Edgartown Harbor. She dragged her mooring but stayed afloat and was undamaged. Next day, the Lathrop "started like a kitten purring." During World War II, Charlie used her to patrol the entrance to the harbor, controlling traffic. The Concordia Company, in Padanaram on Buzzards Bay, bought her in 1950 for a boatyard launch. There were complaints that though she went fine (and fast) in a straight line, she was hard to maneuver. And there seemed to be an unusual amount of disturbance in the propeller wash instead of the boat's signature, clean, rooster tail. A young Llewellyn Howland III accompanied his father to Marblehead to deliver the bad news to

ABOVE: **Charlie Welch, in shirtsleeves, supervising an early trial run of the *Gadget*. She appears to be steering herself. Even at slow speed, there is the start of the rooster tail for which she became famous, a running characteristic produced by Francis's contra-propeller.** (Mystic Seaport Museum, 1996-2-93) RIGHT: **Francis's graph of the *Gadget's* speed-for-horsepower was used by Norman Skene, his former draftsman, as an illustration for a revised edition of his book, *Elements of Yacht Design*. It shows that with the Lathrop wide open at 2,300 rpm, delivering 90 horsepower, she could make 23½ knots, or 26 miles per hour. At half throttle, delivering 45 horsepower, she would still go 20 knots, and it took only 6 horsepower to give her 10 knots, a lesson in the economics of speed under power.** (Mystic Seaport Museum, G. W. Blunt White Library, 138:16/9)

the boat's designer. Francis suggested that maybe somebody had removed the contra propeller and reinstalled it upside down, so that instead of directing the prop wash straight aft, it sent it even more to the side than if the device were left off. This proved to be the case. The *Gadget*'s agility, her rooster tail, and her reputation were restored.[2]

Eighteen months after designing the *Gadget*, Francis drew a preliminary plan for another fast day-launch, this one big enough to house a crew of three. Louise N. Grace, of the Gracefield estate at Great Neck on the north shore of Long Island, was heiress to the Grace shipping line fortune. She wanted a bigger, better vessel than her Consolidated motorboat, the *Veado*, so she could commute to New York City by water, and also so she would have a tender for her sailboats. Francis drew a preliminary plan, and he thought through the design in detail, as evidenced by his written description to present to prospective builders.

For ventilation in the wheelhouse, the after windows were to drop down into pockets. The wheelhouse "divans" were to be covered in red leather. No engine instruments would defile the wheelhouse, for the vessel would always have her

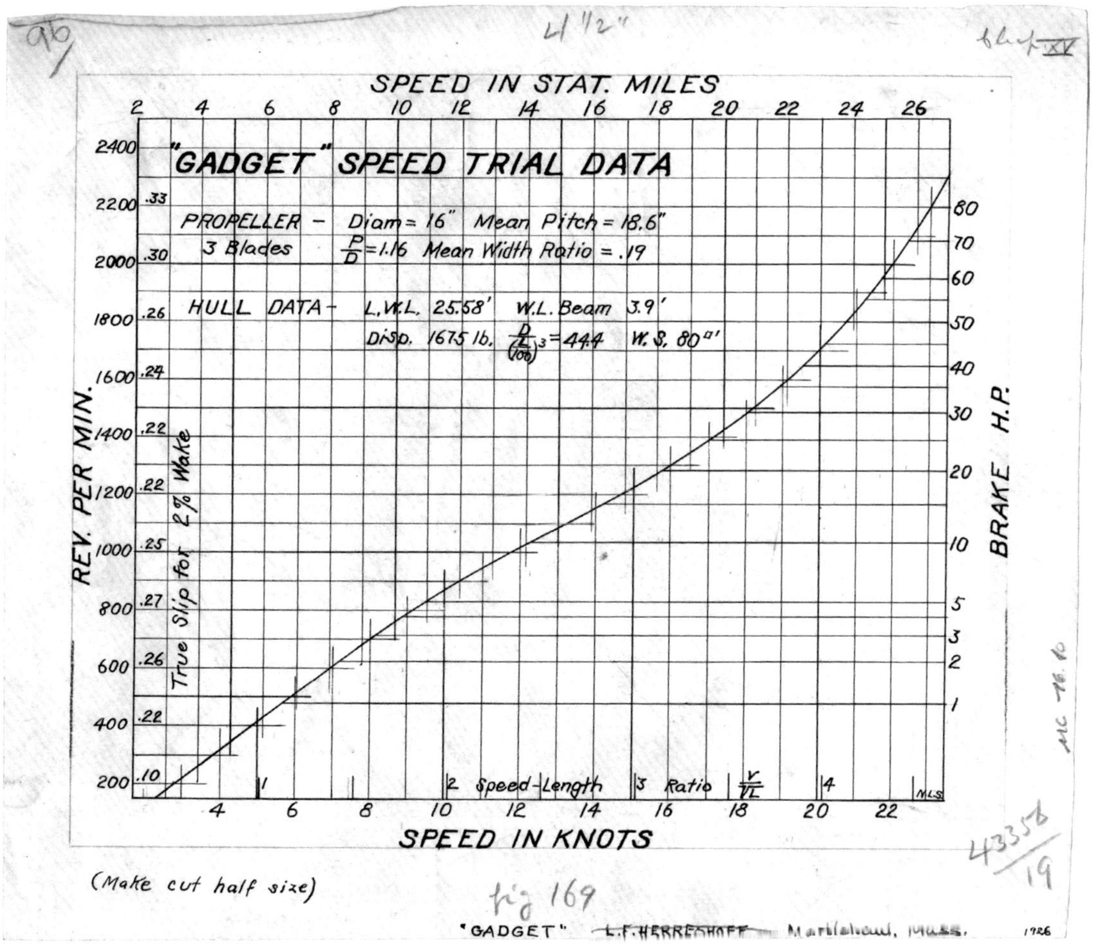

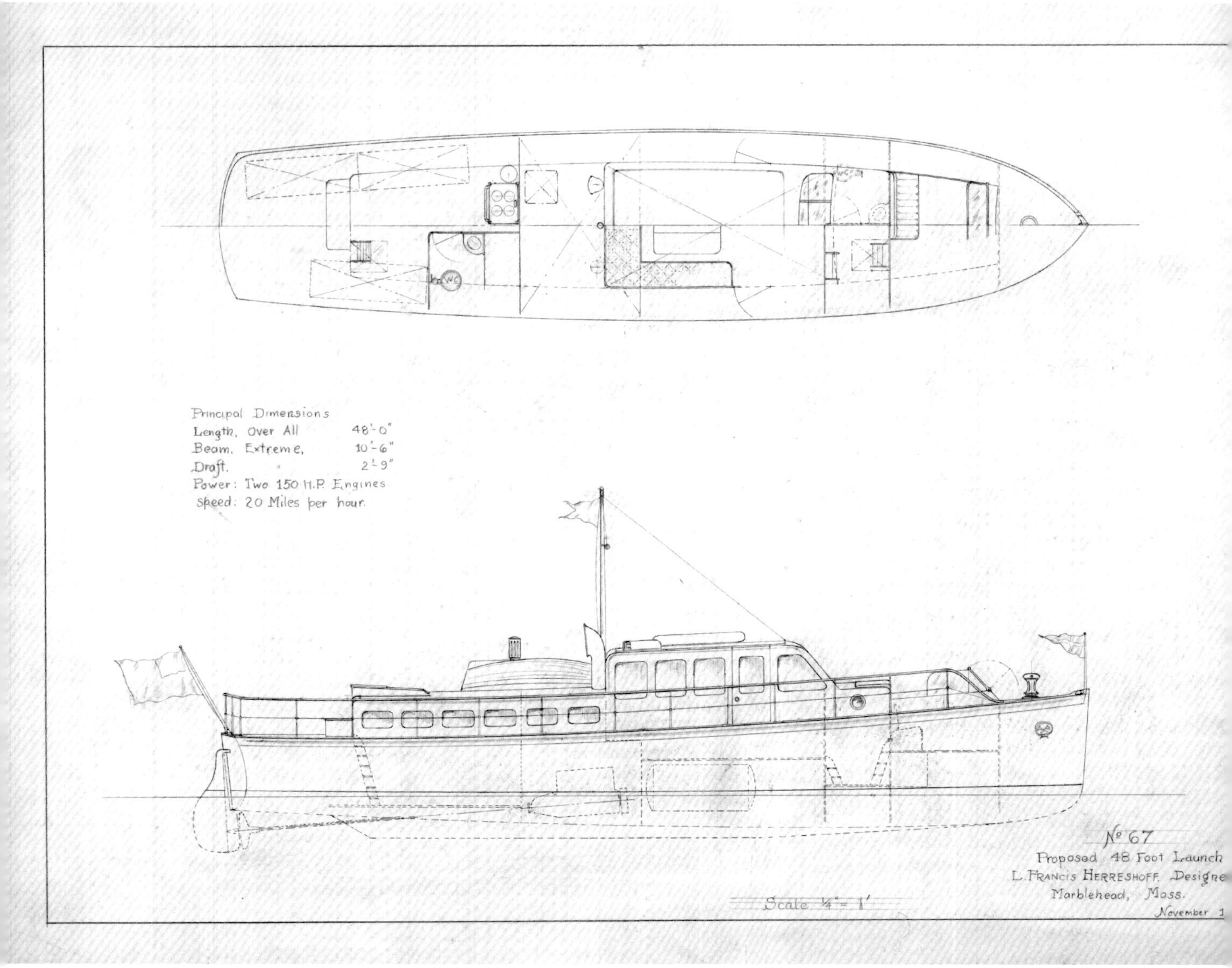

A proposed commuter that Francis drew for "Miss Grace." She was to be 48 feet long on deck; 47 feet, 3 inches on the waterline; with a beam of 10 feet, 3 inches; and a draft of 2 feet, 9 inches. Twin engines would deliver 230-380 horsepower, depending on make, and speed would be 20 knots or more. The accommodations were arranged for a crew of three to live on board, back aft. The owner and her guests could ride either in the spacious deckhouse, sharing it with the captain at the wheel, or in the forward cockpit. Despite Francis's writing of detailed specifications for the vessel, his securing bids from three top builders, and his corresponding at length with Louise N. Grace and her captain about his design No. 67—even how the wealthy Miss Grace might help pay to build to it—nothing came of the project. The drawing is dated November 1935. (© Mystic Seaport Museum, Daniel S. Gregory Ships Plans Library, SP38.195.2)

engineer on duty in the engine room. There would be a separate generator to charge batteries on board the sailboats. The crew would have a hand-pump shower-bath with 10 gallons of water heated by a 215 Shipmate stove. Atop the wheelhouse would be "an oval balsa-wood life raft about 5 feet by 2½ feet which will cost $75," supplementing the 8-foot, 6-inch dinghy in case of disaster. Francis added a page of scantlings, dimensioning the vessel's main construction members. He wrote, "this launch must be built of the highest grade materials and will be subject to the usual careful inspection of this designer."[3]

The bids from three yacht yards to build Miss Grace's proposed commuter were close: with each yard to provide two 190-horsepower Speedways. Quincy Adams (this was before Francis's falling out with its owner, Harry E. Noyes) bid $23,030; Lawley's, $24,500; and the Herreshoff Manufacturing Company, $25,400. Francis wrote his careful evaluations of each builder to both Miss Grace and her captain, William Stanley, admitting that he naturally favored the Herreshoff yard. Miss Grace, apparently worried about any leakage from her large bank account, wanted to sell the *Veado* before committing to build the new boat, and Francis uncharacteristically took the initiative to get the builders to accept her old boat as part payment. He advised Miss Grace to go ahead quickly, before prices went up and less skilled workers were hired. But Miss Louise N. Grace was not to be pressured. She decided not to commute to the City by water after all. Francis filed away his drawing for No. 67.[4]

Perhaps under the influence of designing these nice launches for Charlie Welch and "Miss Grace," Francis chartered a launch for his own use in the summer of 1934 and took on consignment another launch that he could run from 1935 to 1938. He liked to watch from close aboard the many racing boats of Marblehead to see just how they performed in various wind and sea conditions. The first launch was the *Mary Ann*, ex-*Polly Thomas*, owned by George A. Brown of Swampscott. The charter fee was the $194.45 it cost to fit her out for the season at J. H. Frazier's boatyard, right in front of Francis's old customhouse dwelling. The second was the *Echo II*, ex-*Lang Syne*, a 46-footer, Herreshoff Manufacturing Company hull No. 251, designed by his father and built under his supervision in 1905. Perhaps, as a teenager, Francis saw her go together, and he may even have given her a trial run. For the *Lang Syne*, as he always referred to her, Francis entered into a complicated agreement with her owner, boatbuilder George A. Gulliford of Saugus, Massachusetts. Francis would broker the boat without commission but, for a fee, would have the use of her until she sold. For three summers, he paid a total of about $500 for the privilege. Then he sold the *Lang Syne* at a price of $3,500 to his brother Sidney. During this time, Francis could get afloat at his whim, and he must have particularly enjoyed running a Herreshoff launch.[5]

As a young man, Francis had been sent off to agricultural school by a father who, at the time, didn't believe that his son had the ability for designing yachts. While learning to be a farmer, Francis had to find ways of coping with his great disappointment. One of the ways was to leave behind the Rhode Island State College Short Course in Agriculture and go to a nearby lake to race sailing canoes. We may recall his description of the intense pleasure he got from hiking out on such an exciting craft, watching her hull slice through the water with "sensations of speed more pronounced even than in flying" (see volume 1, pages 151, 152).[6]

The sailing canoe, as developed for racing in the last decades of the nineteenth century, was so

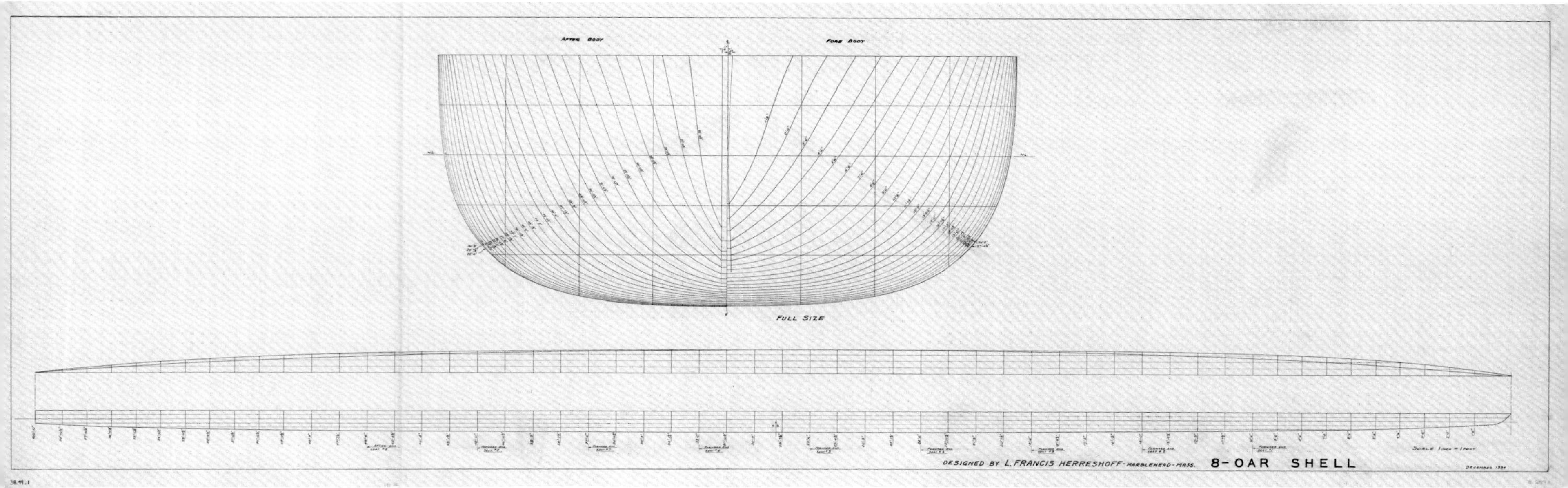

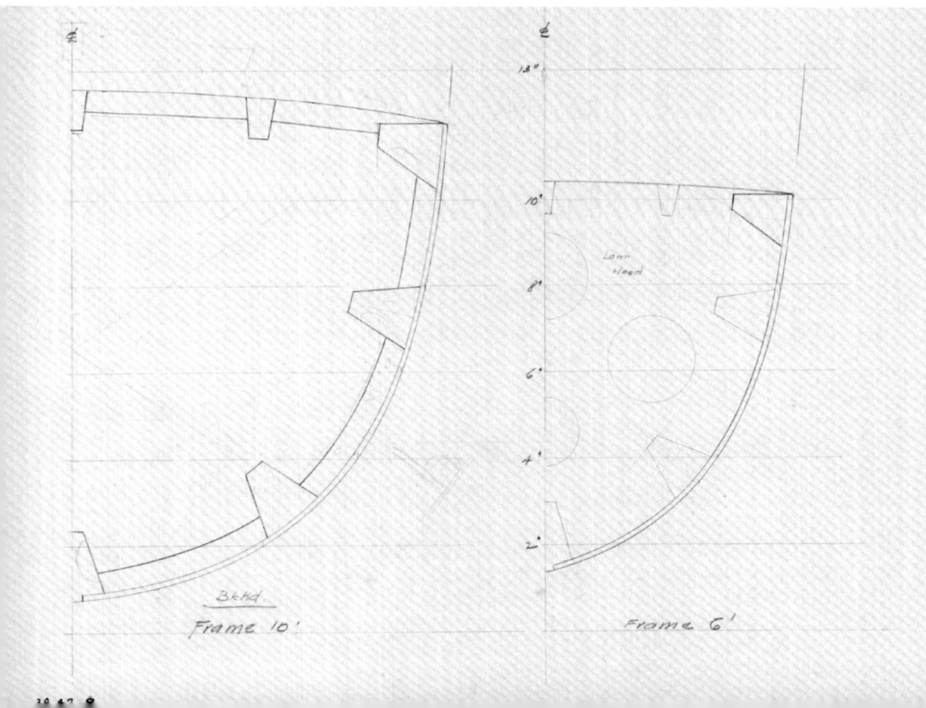

ABOVE: **The lines of an eight-oared racing shell that Francis drew in December 1934. It is not known who the customer was, if any. Francis had designed a similar shell for Chandler Hovey four years earlier, a design that proved abortive. For this shell, despite Francis's working out the details of his longitudinal construction, no boat was built to the plans, so neither of his shells would be tested on a racecourse. The boat is 60 feet long, with a beam of 2 feet, 6 inches.** (© Mystic Seaport Museum, Daniel S. Gregory Ships Plans Library, SP38.49.1) LEFT: **The shell's construction sections, showing the sizes and shapes of her ten longitudinal stringers and one of her bulkheads, with circular cut-outs for lightness. Francis figured the weight of the shell's hull at 195 pounds, 47 of which was her ⅛-inch cedar planking. Seats, footrests, outriggers, oarlocks, oars, rudder, and pump added another 114 pounds, for a total of 309 pounds, ready to race. Francis estimated that eight beefy oarsmen (he wouldn't have imagined females in the boat) and one small coxswain would weigh 1,615 pounds, for a (live) ballast-to-displacement ratio of 84 percent.** (© Mystic Seaport Museum, Daniel S. Gregory Ships Plans Library, SP38.47.8)

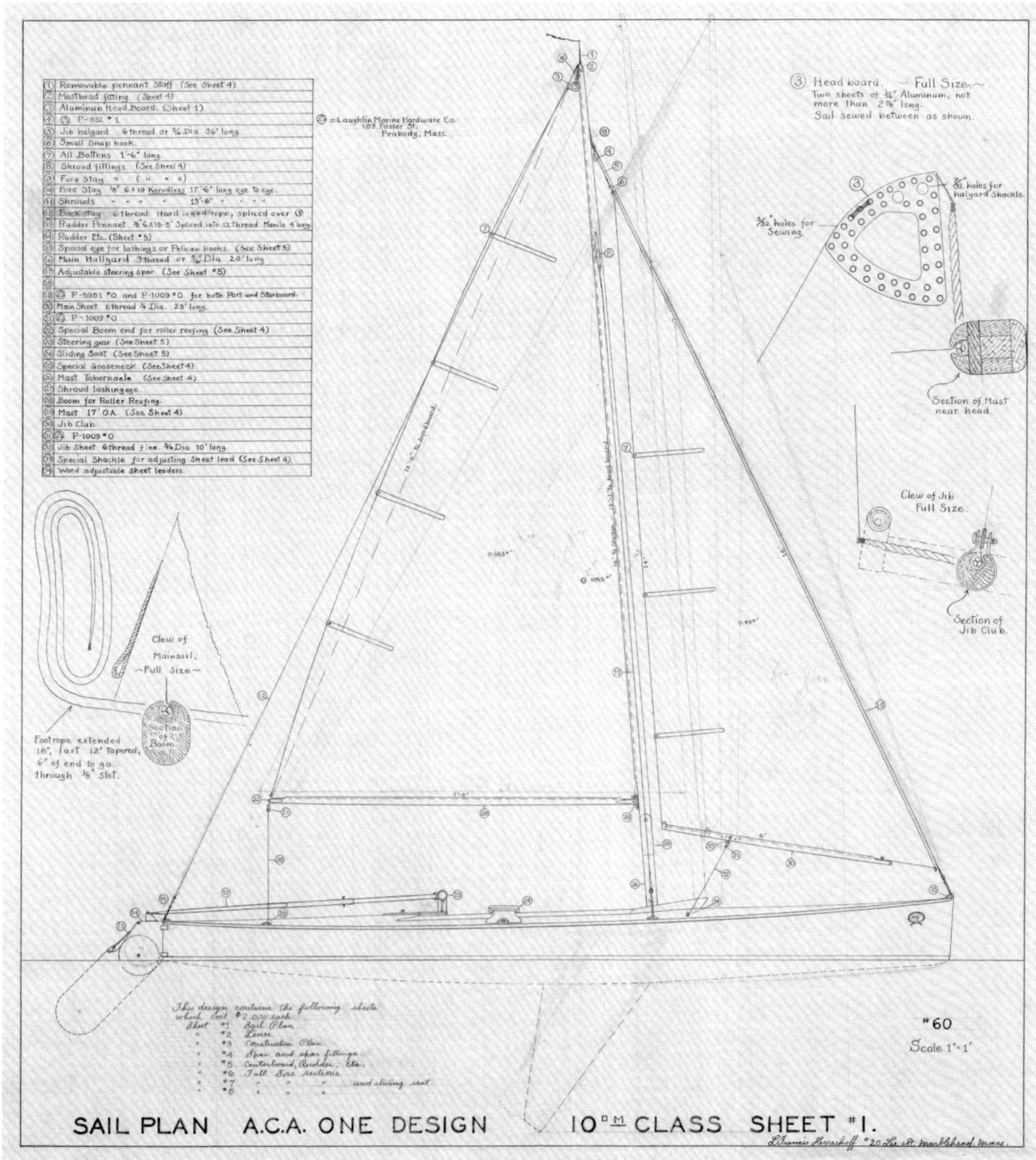

The sail plan of the American Canoe Association sailing canoe. The one-design class was based on a sail area of 10 square metres, or about 110 square feet. The different mast positions, in pencil, show that Francis moved the center of effort aft as he developed the design. He drew the special headboard for the mainsail, upper right, at full size, as he did the arrangement of the clews of the jib and mainsail. The weight of the canoe's metal centerboard helped her skipper keep her upright. The long tiller has a crossbar reachable from any position on the sliding seat. (© Mystic Seaport Museum, Daniel S. Gregory Ships Plans Library, SP38.96.3)

slim and had so much sail area that she could only be kept upright by live ballast, the skipper's weight, shifting as necessary, on a 'thwartships sliding seat. To regulate the natural excesses to which daring sailors would go, the American Canoe Association was formed in 1880. On these skinny canoes, the ACA reduced sail area from 200 square feet to 90. In 1922, the organization began commissioning one-design classes to lower the high cost of building the delicate boats. The standard size became 16 feet by 30 inches.[7]

Francis kept track of these doings by subscribing to *The American Canoeist*, the journal of the ACA, published from Park Avenue, New York City. And he could write to his father in the late summer of 1934, "At present I am designing a 17-foot canoe for the American Canoe Association." This would be Francis's design No. 60.[8]

The ACA put restrictions on Francis: the canoe had to be a double-ender and she had to have a sloop rig. The requirement of a pointed stern would seem no hardship to L. Francis Herreshoff; yet, years later, when advising a correspondent about starting a new class of sailing canoe in California, he

The sailing canoe's lines, showing her chine at the waterline and her arc bottom. She is 17 feet long, with a beam of 3 feet, 4 inches. Freeboard at the bow is 8 inches; least freeboard is 4 inches. Surrounding the lines, Francis shows construction details of stem, sternpost, floor timbers, and frames. (© Mystic Seaport Museum, Daniel S. Gregory Ships Plans Library, SP38.96.1)

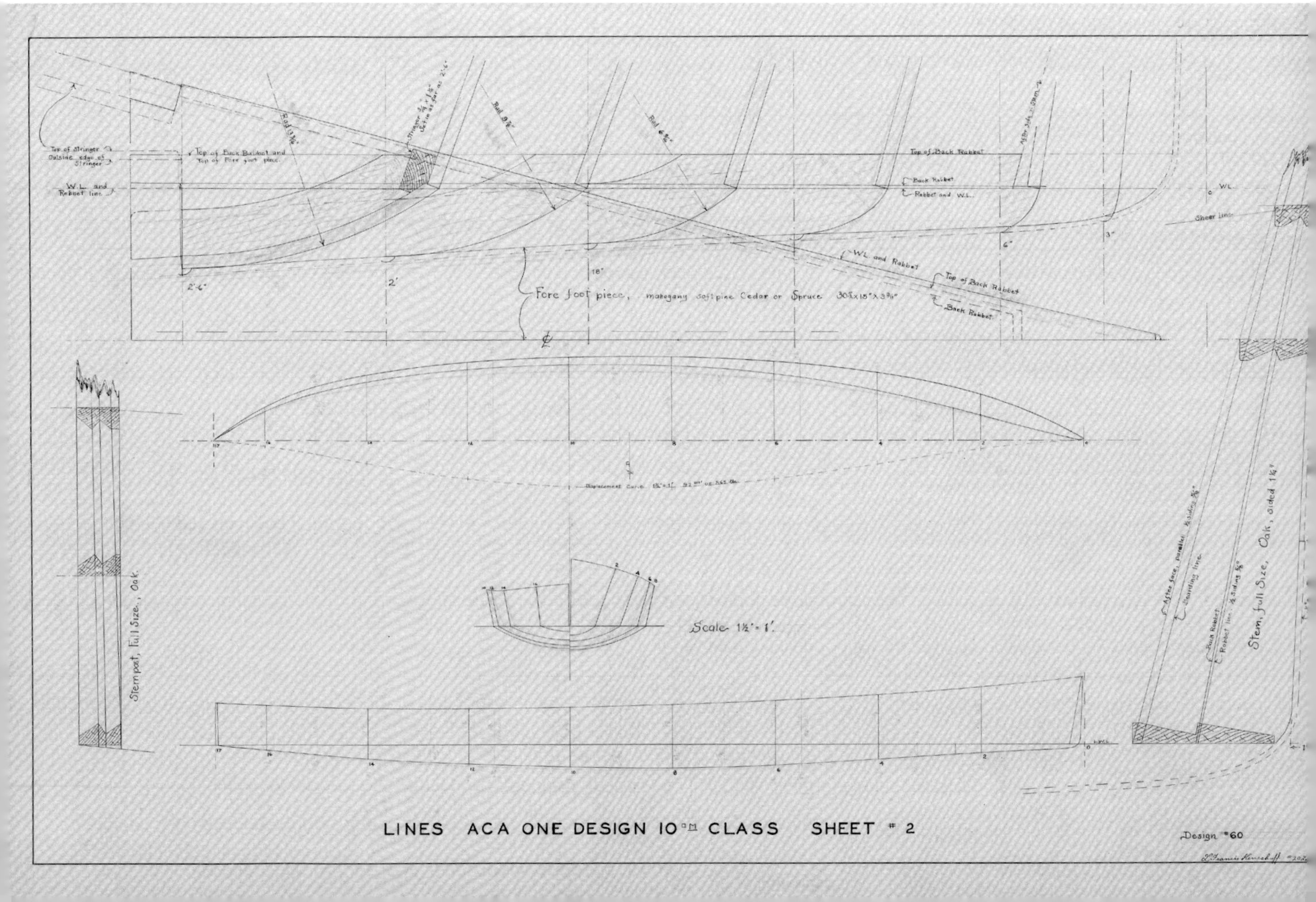

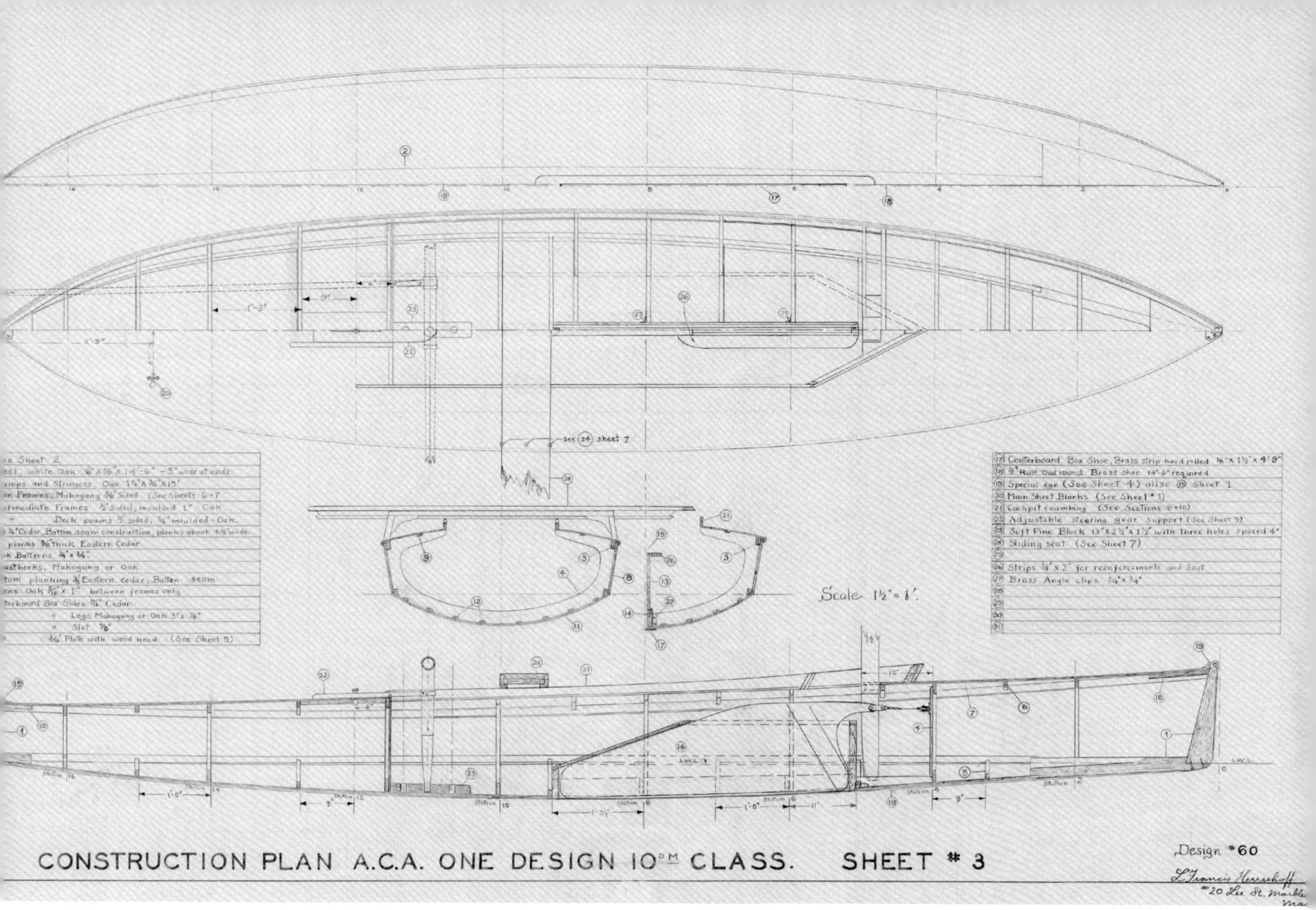

wrote that if the ACA allowed the canoes "to have a square stern, they would be very much cheaper to build, just as light, and quite a little faster." He did chafe at the sloop requirement, for he believed that a fine rig for the canoe would be the cat ketch that he liked so much on his Development boat, the *Dragon Fly* of 1928 (see volume 1, pages 268-70).[9]

The ACA canoe project provided a rare point of contact between Francis and one of his brothers. With Nathanael and Ann not going to Florida for the winter, the family convened for Christmas at Love Rocks in 1934. Clarence, an enthusiastic canoeist, wanted to know all about Francis's design for a sailing canoe. When he got back to Marblehead, Francis sent Clarence the eight sheets of plans for his design No. 60.[10]

It is not known how many canoes were built to Francis's design, but we do know that Allan Vaitses, at Mattapoisett, built one in 1957 for Bobby Gibbs, a Buzzards Bay sailor who, as we shall see, also sailed happily in two of Francis's designs for shoal-draft cruisers.[11]

The construction plan of the ACA canoe. She has wide side decks to keep the water out if she is well heeled over in a gust. Her fifteen deep frames, doubled at the mast, are widely spaced. Can it be that the sliding seat, as indicated on the drawing, was made with a width of only four inches? (© Mystic Seaport Museum, Daniel S. Gregory Ships Plans Library, SP38.96.2)

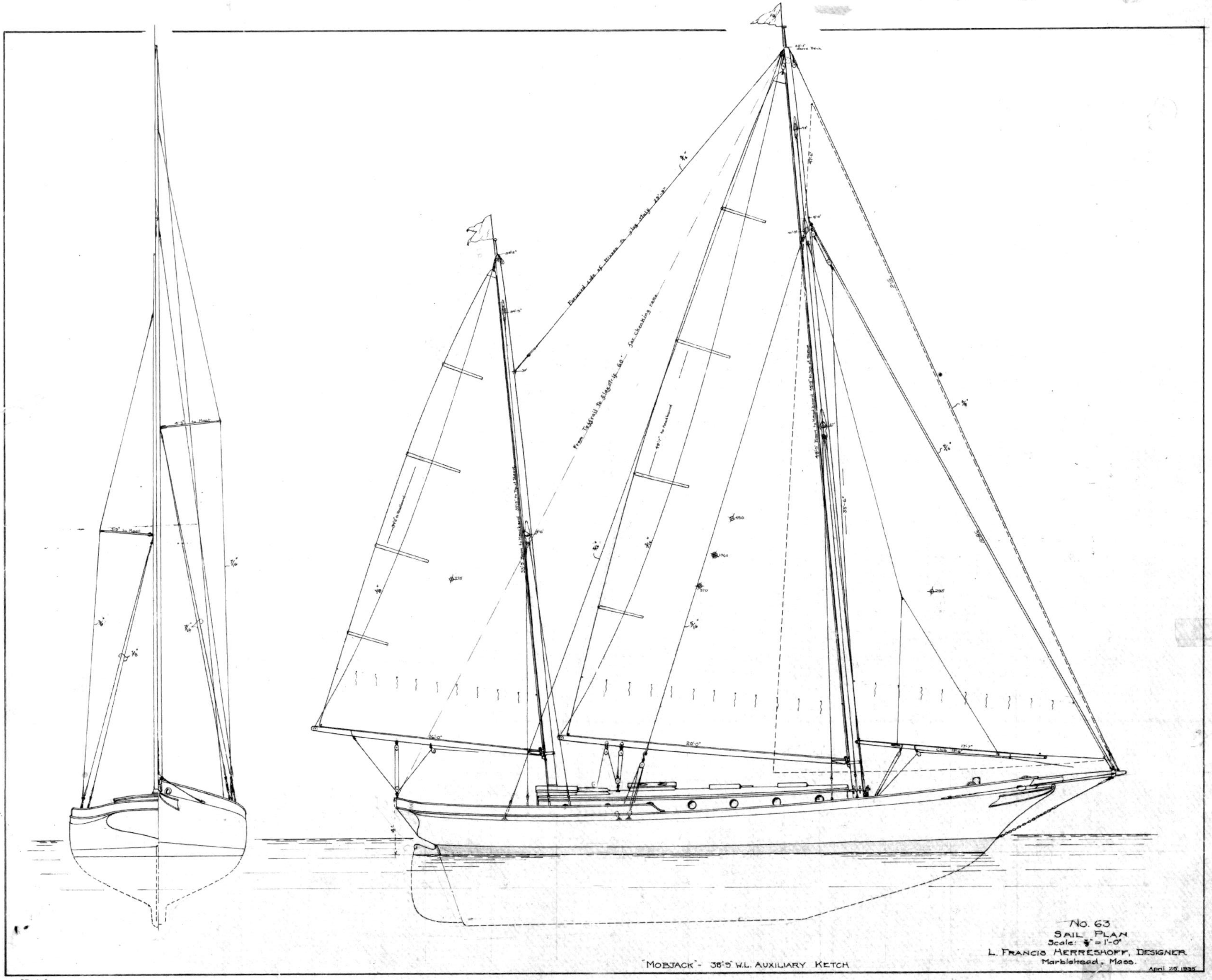
No. 63
Sail Plan
Scale: ⅜" = 1'-0"
L. Francis Herreshoff, Designer
Marblehead, Mass.
April 25 1935
"Mobjack" - 38'-5" W.L. Auxiliary Ketch

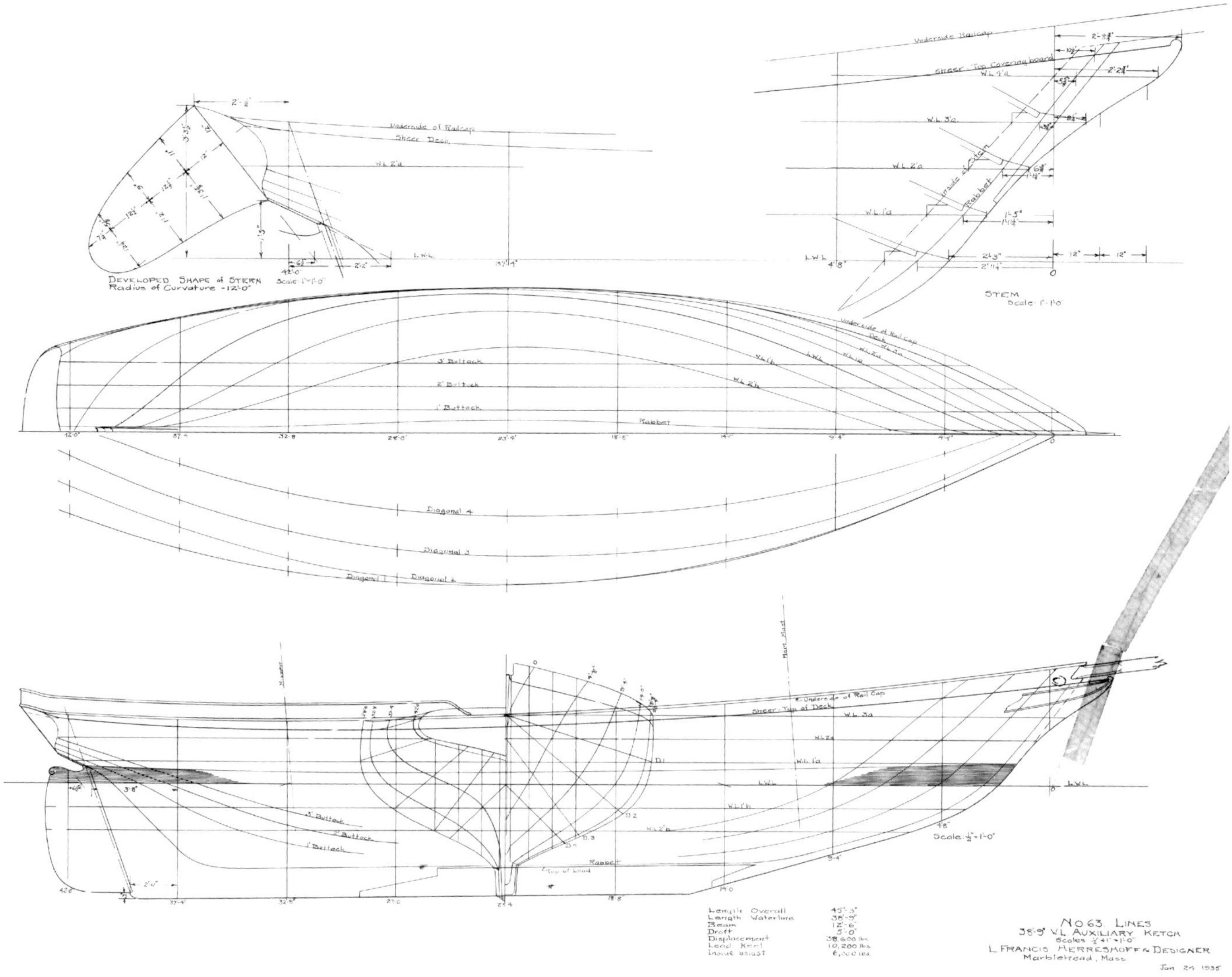

LEFT: **The sail plan of the *Mobjack,* Francis's design No. 63, dated April 25, 1935. She is not a diminutive *Ticonderoga*, but rather, with her full sections and ample beam, a slightly smaller version of the *Joann*. Total sail area is 1,060 square feet, with 490 square feet in the mainsail, 275 in the mizzen, and 295 in the jib. The big, self-tending jib, with its partial boom, is easier to handle than the *Tioga*'s double-head rig, with jib sheets to tend when tacking. Moreover, in a strong breeze, the *Mobjack* would balance better under her single, self-tending jib and mizzen than she would under a self-tending, smaller fore staysail and mizzen. Francis has drawn an overlapping, masthead balloon jib for light weather.** (© Mystic Seaport Museum, Daniel S. Gregory Ships Plans Library, SP38.18.6) ABOVE: **The lines of the *Mobjack*. Francis's experience of drawing the lines of the *Tioga* and *Ticonderoga* shows in this drawing: although the *Mobjack* is a husky cruising boat like the *Joann*, she has inherited grace from her immediate ancestors in his family of clipper-bowed yachts. She is 45 feet, 3 inches long on deck; with a waterline length of 38 feet, 9 inches; a beam of 12 feet, 6 inches; and a draft of 5 feet. Displacement is 38,600 pounds, with 16,200 pounds of ballast, 6,000 pounds of which is inside lead, for a ballast-to-displacement ratio of 42 percent. As with the *Joann*, the *Mobjack* could profit from a centerboard for best windward performance. One owner of a vessel built to the design reported cavitation from the heel of her keel when sailing close-hauled, indicating abnormal leeway.** (© Mystic Seaport Museum, Daniel S. Gregory Ships Plans Library, SP38.18.1)

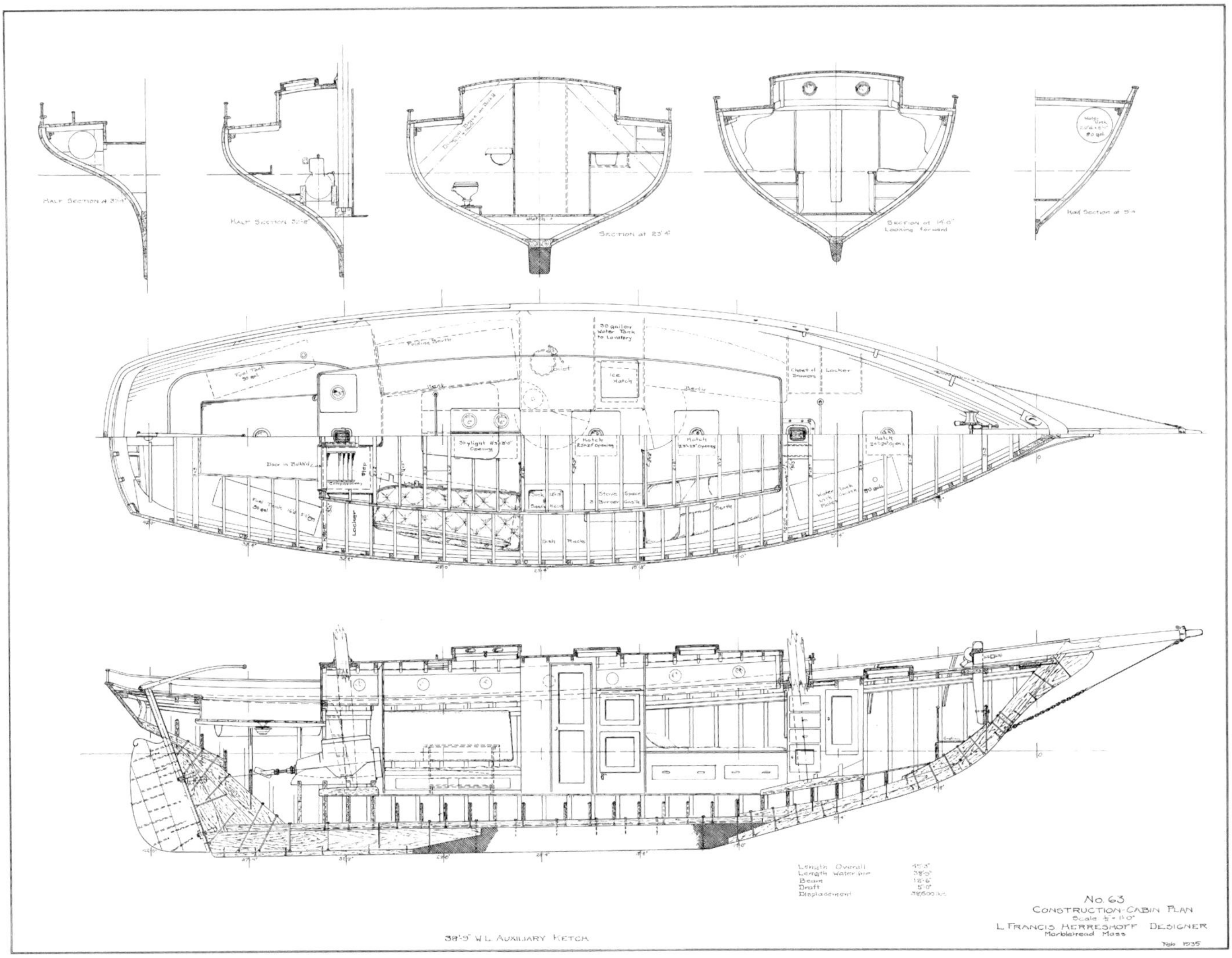

George Upton, for whom Francis had designed the graceless schooner *Mañana* in 1924 (see volume 1, pages 118-21), admired both the *Tioga* and the *Bounty* coming and going in Marblehead Harbor, and he was also familiar with Waldo Brown's schooner *Joann.* Upton wanted a moderate-draft ketch like the *Tioga,* but he wanted the fuller hull form of the *Joann.* He intended to make passages between his summer place, next door to Charlie Welch's house in Marblehead, and his winter home on Mobjack Bay in Chesapeake country. He was more interested in an easy motion offshore than in speed.

And so, in late 1934, Francis started to draw the plans for his fourth clipper-bowed yacht, the 45-foot ketch *Mobjack.* As we have seen, he would begin actual design work on the fifth, the *Tioga II,* shortly, and those two projects would overlap.

In terms of beauty, the *Mobjack* falls between the gorgeous *Tiogas* and the merely winsome *Joann.* As to performance, Francis wrote that "she sails along at a good clip and is very easy in a seaway." The second part of this comment was not from first-hand experience, for Francis only sailed his design No. 63 in smooth water. He was making a summary of reports from Mobjack owners. The design became one of his most popular, and sailors wrote to Francis of their pleasure in handling their boats in rough water. But Francis did sail a Mobjack in his imagination. He wrote, "I have cruised quite a little on Long Island Sound and all along our New England coast and cannot think of any boat that I would have more fun on than Mobjack."[12]

Upton had sons who were six feet, four inches, and six feet, three inches tall, so Francis had to deal with the question of headroom that would plague the *Tioga II.* For the *Mobjack,* he solved the problem by drawing a low cabin sole in the first place, a solution that, as we have seen, initially escaped him for the *Tioga II.* Despite this, a later builder of a Mobjack installed a doghouse to get even more headroom, which, surprisingly, Francis said, "does not seem to spoil her appearance." (The wife of this builder had sent a telegram to Francis: "This is a plea from a lady in dire distress. As days progress without plan of Mobjack arriving husband is becoming increasingly difficult to live with. Beseech your aid to see if plans are lost in mail.")[13]

The original *Mobjack* was a Depression boat, on which owner and builder cut costs, rather than following Francis's detailed specifications. He wrote, "although the *Mobjack* has stood up well, she was what I would consider a rather cheap job." She cost only $12,000 at George Gulliford's yard, perhaps $3,000 less than she would have cost at Britt Brothers for a better job. Thus, Francis earned merely a $1,200 commission, although the popular design would earn him more later through the sale of plans.[14]

LEFT: **The *Mobjack*'s construction drawing, including the cabin arrangement. Helen Bolster typed six closely spaced pages of specifications for builder George Gulliford of Saugus, Massachusetts, to follow. The frames, 2¼ inches square, were to be sawn in her ends, but steam-bent for 15 feet of her length amidships. All fastenings, including keel bolts, were of Everdur bronze or Monel. "Planking—selected rift grain Fir of fine grain kiln dried after seasoning so that all has the same percentage of moisture. Planks all to be narrow above the garboard and to have a thickness after planing of from 1½" to 1⅝"." But cypress could be used below the waterline, and the garboards could be of oak, cypress, yellow pine, or mahogany, as well as fir. Francis gave Gulliford wide choices of wood in other structural parts of the vessel as well. The decking could be "Clear white pine, Port Orford Cedar, or extra selected rift grain Fir of unusually close grain, or California Sugar Pine." L. Francis Herreshoff knew his woods. Whatever the wood, the deck was to be crowned 6 inches in 14 feet. Note the diagonal braces on the bulkhead amidships. "Scuppers—The main deck and cockpit are to have copper tube scuppers of at least 1" I.D. draining to below the painted water line, all to be flanged on the outside as shown on the detailed drawing of same. There will be 6 main deck scuppers and 2 cockpit scuppers. No sharp bends." Francis wanted an engine developing about 50 horsepower at 2,000 rpm, a machine whose cost he thought would be $700. "Lathrop L H-G will do." He specified, "The shrouds are to be secured [to the masts] with special phosphor bronze plates, according to the latest practice, on the highest grade yachts." He could have added, "as invented by the designer." Francis specified two "Merriman Herreshoff-type" anchors, one of 75 pounds and one of 65; the total cost of these would be $71.00. The *Mobjack*'s main cabin and forward stateroom were separated by the galley and head amidships, an arrangement that the owner, George Upton, wanted and of which Francis disapproved. There was a fo'c's'le forward; the separate engine room was entered through a hatch in the after, port corner of the cabin house; the engine and propeller shaft were off-center to port. In the cockpit, Francis's nicely curved tiller would be replaced by Upton's wheel.** (© Mystic Seaport Museum, Daniel S. Gregory Ships Plans Library, SP38.18.3)

Like the *Tiogas,* the *Mobjack's* clipper bow was to be garnished with carved trailboards. Francis worked hard on the design of those for the *Tioga II*, struggling to make oak leaves and acorns, symbols of naval architecture, look just right, but he was apparently never quite satisfied with them. For the *Mobjack*, he quickly worked up a trailing vine that he thought looked perfect.[15]

Francis's design No. 63 struck a chord with many sailors. Who wouldn't want an affordable *Ticonderoga?* Of course they weren't getting a small *Ticonderoga*, but rather a slightly smaller, ketch-rigged *Joann*, but still. Francis sometimes claimed that the Mobjack was his most popular design, though his later little H-28 ketch would be built in greater numbers. Correspondence provides evidence of 43 sets of Mobjack plans sold, and there were certainly more. At various times, Francis gave different estimates of plans sold and boats built to them; his latest and highest guess in 1970 was 200 sets of plans sold and 100 Mobjacks built. At any rate, the design did give him a small, but steady, flow of cash. Initially he got $50 for a set of her plans, and then, by 1965, had raised the price to $75. A priest in French Guiana had to pay $150 for his.[16]

The *Mobjack* with her big overlapping jib pulling her along nicely in a gentle breeze. The lump amidships is, of course, her dinghy. (Phillips Library, Peabody Essex Museum, Salem, Massachusetts)

The Mobjack design was popular Down Under. A Melbourne ship pilot, J. R. Dingle, reported to Francis that he was building one for his retirement. Philip Weate sailed his Mobjack, the *Windsong IV*, from Hobart to Sydney, via San Francisco and the Caribbean. While on the West Coast, he flew to Marblehead to tell Francis how pleased he was with the boat. Another Mobjack merely won the Sydney-Hobart Race. The Australian government used a Mobjack for recording oceanographic conditions along the Great Barrier Reef. Two interested sailors, one from Australia and one from Honolulu, wanted to know if it was all right to put a schooner rig on the Mobjack? Francis's reply was that "possibly she will be an even better looking boat" as a schooner, but that "you will find that the ketch is faster and easier to handle and better in every way."[17]

John P. Kendall, Boston investor and experienced cruising man homeported in Marion, Massachusetts, is a great fan of L. Francis Herreshoff. He has acquired and sailed yachts built to four different clipper-bowed designs by Francis, including the Mobjack *Quark.* He chose the Mobjack design after careful comparison with the Bounty (which he also had built for a different purpose), and chose the Mobjack as the better boat for cruising with a three-generation family, not all of whom were necessarily able sailors. The choice was successful. The *Quark,* renamed *Heritage*, is now the flagship at the Apalachicola Maritime Museum in Florida.[18]

George Upton used the original *Mobjack* as intended for several years and was well satisfied with her. After World War II, he sold her to Dr. Peer P. Johnson, who changed her summer mooring from Marblehead to nearby Manchester. Johnson loved cruising in the boat, took her south to the West Indies one winter, and kept her for the rest of his life. In 1965, she went to a new home in Florida.[19]

In 1937, Upton came to Francis for another powerboat design. She was to be a far bigger cruiser than the cabin launch that Francis had drawn for Upton in 1926 (see volume 1, pages 155-57), but, like her, she would be abortive. Francis produced design No. 72, a 58-footer with forecastle, galley, and main cabin forward; wheelhouse and engine room amidships; and double stateroom, toilet room, and cockpit aft. She was to have a contra-propeller to drive a hull of 67,000 pounds displacement. But Upton backed away from building this major vessel, and the project died on Mylar.[20]

By 1935, Nathanael G. Herreshoff's health was failing. He was eighty-seven years old, had long suffered from rheumatism, and now his heart was weakening. Francis visited him at Love Rocks in April. The visit was typically brief: Helen Bolster—"Mrs." to Francis—packed a picnic and drove him down to Bristol and back the same day in his Buick touring car. In July, Nathanael was writing to Francis, asking him to return: "There is always a room and a place at the table for you." In September, Nathanael wrote: "For some time I have been confined to our room by weak heart action. Am feeling a little stronger and hope to get out again. Ann [his wife and former nurse] gives me the very best care. Hope you will get time to run down soon." Francis's reply didn't address his father's hope, but, instead, listed all the yachts of his father's design and build that had recently visited Marblehead Harbor. "The principal peculiarities of all these boats is that they have retained a fair, true shear line and there are no other boats of their sizes and ages which have done so. Some time I want to talk to you about this." We don't know whether or not this conversation took place, but it is evident that Francis was unable or unwilling to respond to his frail father reaching out to him.[21]

Nathanael issued a specific invitation to Francis for Thanksgiving dinner, but he responded, "I have already accepted an invitation for

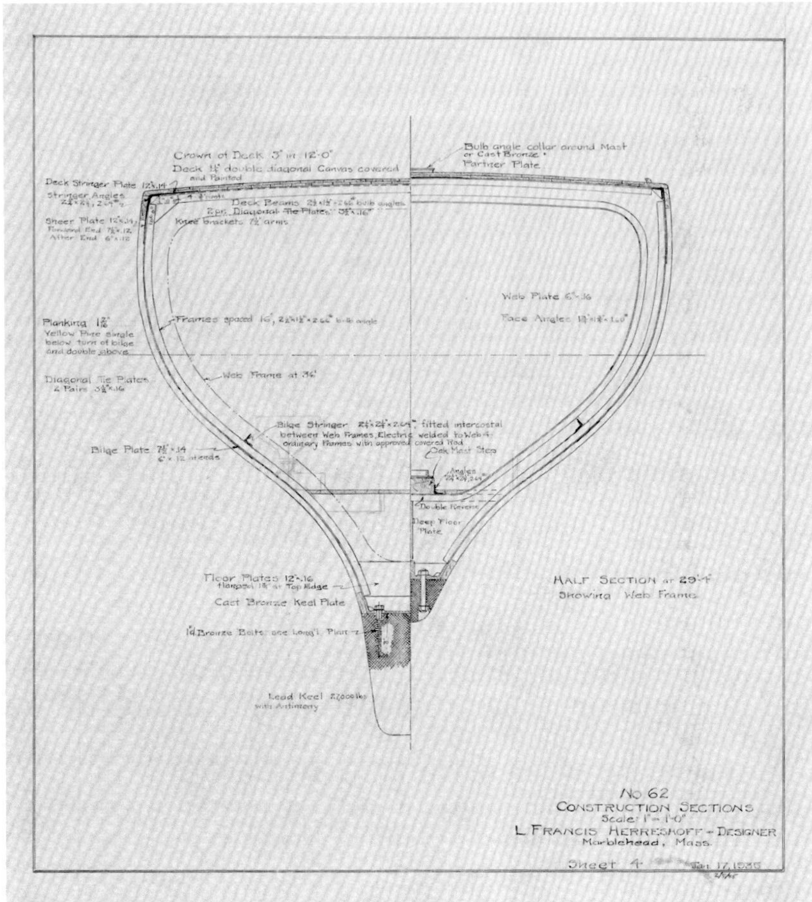

ABOVE AND RIGHT FOLDOUT, INSIDE: **The construction drawings for the composite *Mitena,* showing the details of her metal skeleton and wood planking. The lead keel was to have antimony. The keel plate was bronze, and the twenty-six keel bolts were 1-inch-diameter bronze. The floors were to be bronze in the deepest part of the bilge, otherwise steel, which was used in the rest of the metal structure. There was just one element of Francis's longitudinal construction method: four web frames, 6 inches deep, one pair just fore and aft of the mast, one amidships, and one aft, near the top of the deadwood. Although this drawing shows a pair of bilge stringers, well below the waterline, as required by the Lloyds inspectors, Francis, after a battle in which Strawbridge took a strong part, got permission to leave them out. Still, he would complain that "*Mitena*'s hull structure was compelled by Lloyds to be so heavy that very little lead could be used on the keel and she cannot carry her sail properly." The long sheer plates and deck plates reinforcing the hull-deck joint were 12 inches wide amidships, tapering to 7½ inches at the bow and stern. Two pairs of diagonal tie plates in the planking, one pair in way of the mast, the other amidships, kept her from wringing. The deck was braced by two further pairs of diagonals. The stem and deadwood were mahogany. Planking was 1 7/16-inch yellow pine, single below the turn of the bilge and double above. The mast step was a piece of oak, 12 inches wide, spanning four floors. The drawing refers the Herreshoff Manufacturing Company builders to seven additional ones that amplified details. The construction plan was inked by Francis himself; the construction section drawing was inked by Sam Brown.** (© Mystic Seaport Museum, Daniel S. Gregory Ships Plans Library, SP38.43.8 and SP38.43.4)

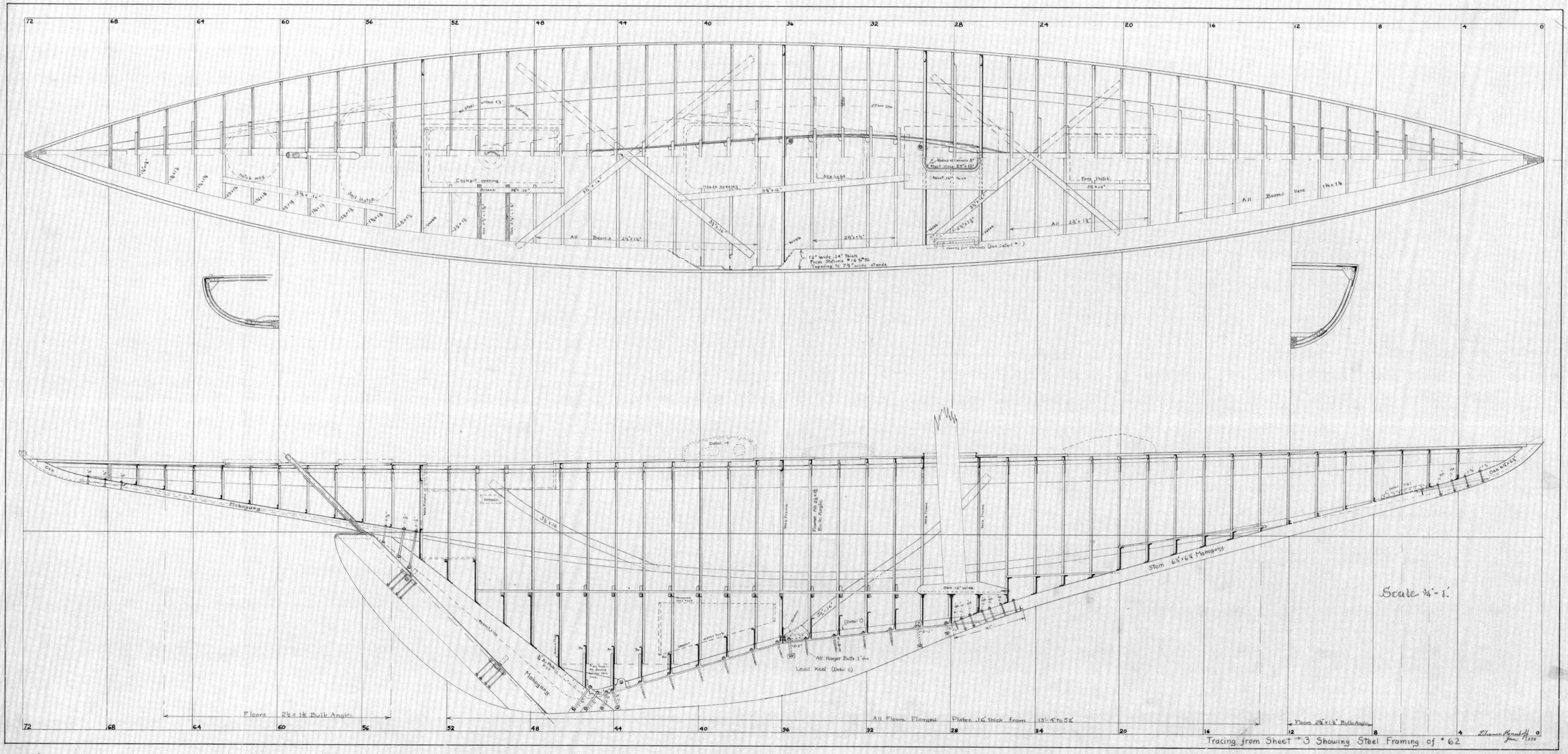

Scale 3/4" = 1'
Floors 2½" x 1½" Bulb Angles
All Floors Flanged Plates 3/16" thick from 13' 4" to 32'
Floors 2½" x 1½" Bulb Angles
Stem 6½" x 6½" Mahogany
Lead Keel (Detail 5)
All Hanger Bolts 1" dia.
Mahogany
Tracing from Sheet #3 Showing Steel Framing of #62
L. Francis Herreshoff
Jan 1935

38.43.8

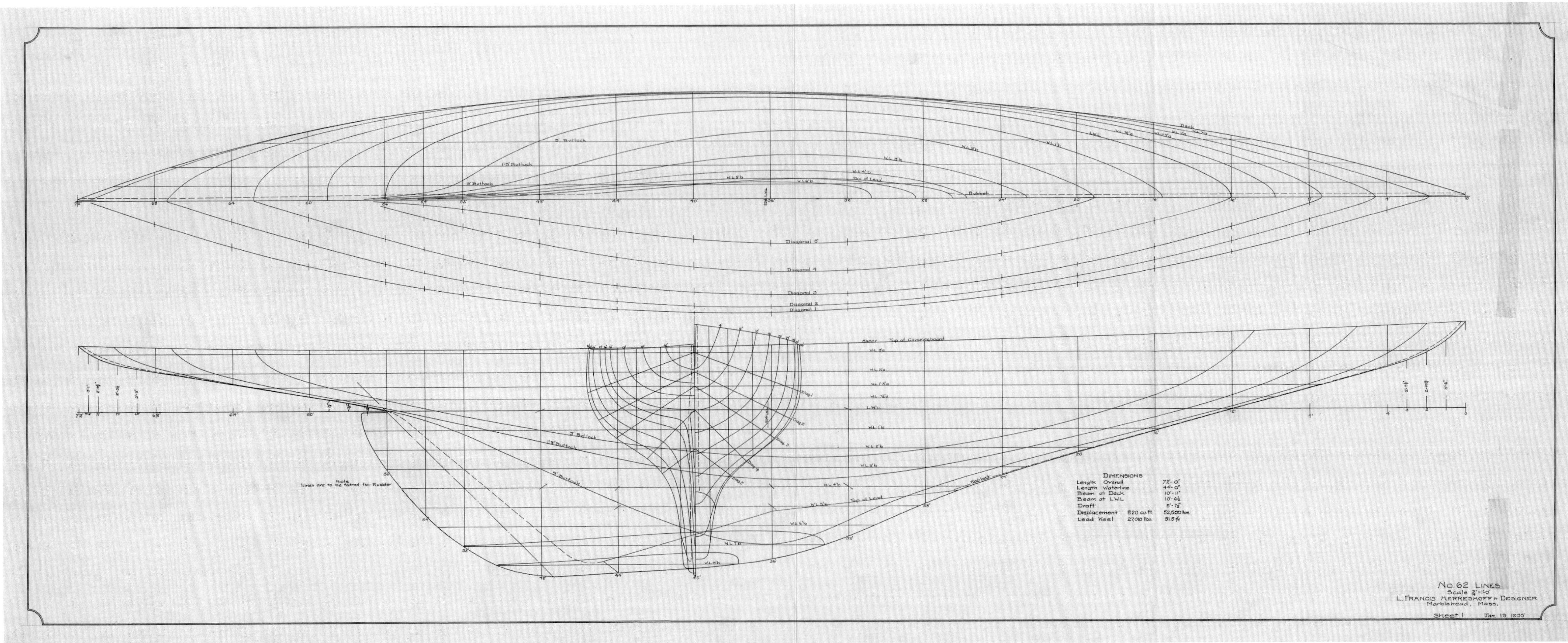

The lines of the *Mitena*. She is 72 feet long on deck; 44 feet on the waterline; with a beam of 10 feet, 11 inches; and a draft of 8 feet, 7½ inches. Displacement is 52,500 pounds, of which 27,000 pounds is in the lead keel, for a ballast-displacement ratio of 51 percent. Francis wrote to Nathanael, "I think this boat will have quite a little stability from her full ends." But later he wrote in *The Common Sense of Yacht Design* that he believed her forefoot and leading edge of the keel were too rounded off, so that her bow would blow off to the extent that she did not have enough weather helm. Gone is the *Whirlwind*'s raking mid-section (see volume 1, page 366). The diagonals are unusually straight and fair, indicating low resistance when sailing heeled. This drawing is dated January 19, 1935. (© Mystic Seaport Museum, Daniel S. Gregory Ships Plans Library, SP38.43.1)

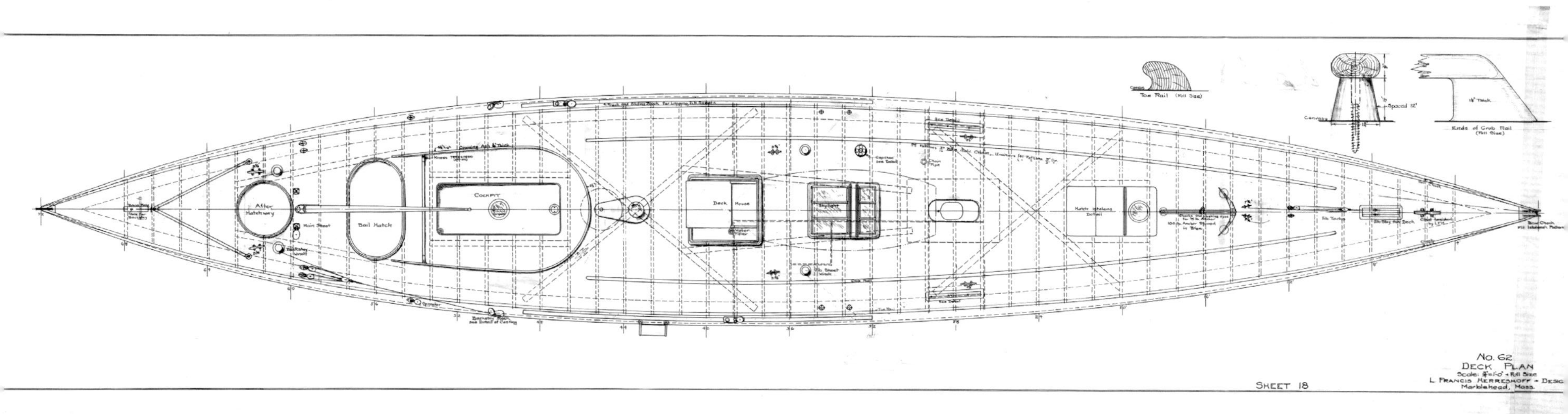

The *Mitena*'s deck plan. "Spinnaker Liz" reported in *Yachting* that "her designer has given her deck the minimum number of winches and cleats and has produced a streamline effect on her deck erections not unlike some of our modern automobiles, even having non-breakable glass in the skylight." The designs for the bow chock and forward hatch were borrowed from the *Istalena*. Francis made the big mooring cleat on the bow himself. A 75-pound Herreshoff anchor was stowed on deck forward; a 100-pounder, taken apart, was to be stowed in the bilge, to keep its weight low; 55 fathoms of 2-inch chain went below through a pipe in way of the mast. Francis shows, in dotted lines, that an 8-foot pram was to be carried, upside down, over the skylight just abaft the mast. An ash coaming, 4½ inches high, kept deck run-off from entering the cockpit. The compass was set into the cockpit sole, and Francis specified that there was to be no steel within 2½ feet of it. There is a large, oval sail hatch beneath the 8-foot tiller and a small, round hatch further aft. Francis shows his standard, folding boom crutch, out of the way, yet always ready. (© Mystic Seaport Museum, Daniel S. Gregory Ships Plans Library, SP38.43.3)

Thanksgiving dinner with Commodore Lawrence Percival here at Marblehead which I think will be a good thing for me to accept." Francis evidently hoped for a design commission from this prominent Corinthian Yacht Club figure who had been involved with his Development Class boats in 1928 and for whom he had designed a motor launch in 1929, a boat that was not built (see volume 1, pages 268, 269, and 276). The following Thanksgiving, both Nathanael's invitation and Francis's reason for not accepting it were repeated, yet Francis designed no more boats for Percival. That year, though, Francis did go to Bristol for Christmas. Or, at least, for Christmas Eve. He returned to Marblehead on the twenty-fifth "because there is so much for me to do here, taking care of my house, and so on."[22]

The relationship between father and son was still complicated. When Francis spoke of his father to a friend in later life, "He talked of his father not in very loving terms, but in very respectful terms. He knew his father's accomplishments, who he was, and what he had done. He respected his father a great deal, but he didn't sound as if he loved his father very much."[23]

In 1934, Uffa Fox, the English yacht designer, began writing a series of outstanding books on yacht design, construction, racing, and cruising. He asked Francis to contribute plans for some of his designs, and Francis responded with drawings of the *Istalena, Whirlwind*, and *Landfall.* Francis also sent Fox a glowing account of the career of Nathanael Greene Herreshoff, an account that he shared with his father. Nathanael wrote: "I was quite surprised as well as pleased at your long letter to Uffer [*sic*] and of what you said of my active life and perhaps more than I deserve. But certainly it was pleasant coming from one that at times had condemned me so ungraciously." This reprimand from Nathanael seems harsh. Francis had argued with his father about details of yacht design and had complained that his father was against improvements that he himself hadn't originated, but such disagreements and criticisms were private. In public, no one praised Nathanael G. Herreshoff more ardently than L. Francis Herreshoff. But Francis didn't argue the point. He simply replied, "I want to thank you very much indeed for your two nice letters." Nathanael still needed to rebuke his son; in this case, Francis deflected the barb and tried to smooth over his sometimes prickly relationship with his father.[24]

Fox published Francis's letter praising his father's career, somewhat edited but without attribution, in his third book in his series, *Sail and Power,* that Scribner's brought out in New York in 1937. Francis loaned the book to his father when he went to Bristol for Christmas. Nathanael's wife, Ann, read it to him aloud. Nathanael recognized Francis's hand in the section on himself and perhaps, by then, could simply enjoy his son's praise. Fox's plagiarism aside, Francis was so impressed by the book that he wrote "a little description" of it and sent the positive review to several of his friends, including Starling Burgess and Waldo Brown.[25]

And, about this time, Paul Hammond visited Nathanael in Bristol and reported to Francis that his father was full of praise for him. Would that it had come directly. But Francis wrote his father a letter of appreciation anyway.[26]

In his April 1935 issue, editor Herb Stone told the readers of *Yachting* that the International Rule's 12-Metre Class was getting an injection of new energy for the coming racing season. It was needed. There had been only five Twelves actively racing in the class, and none of these were designed and built in the United States. Stone's news was that two new 12-Metres, the first purely US boats, were building, so that seven yachts would soon be at the starting line.[27]

One, the *Seven Seas,* was going together in the Nevins Yard at City Island, to a design by Clinton

H. Crane for Van S. Merle-Smith. The other was taking shape at the Herreshoff Manufacturing Company as hull No. 1275, to drawings by L. Francis Herreshoff. The owner was William J. Strawbridge. This Twelve would be named the *Mitena,* Francis's design No. 62.[28]

"Billy" Strawbridge, as Francis would come to address him, gave Francis the order to draw the plans for a 12-Metre in early January, so the yacht had to be designed and built in five months. At first, the relationship between designer and client was cool. A man accustomed to wealth and a man of interests beyond yachting, Strawbridge could be demanding, once he had made up his mind what he wanted. Twenty-two years Francis's junior, this young man was in the habit of doing as he pleased, even if his actions rankled his elders or those in authority. When Strawbridge had bought the *Istalena*, Francis had written his father, "I never knew or took to Mr. Strawbridge very much." What saved Billy Strawbridge for Francis and fostered their friendship was Strawbridge's obvious, genuine interest in boats. After all, he had been kicked out of Harvard for building sailing dinghies in his room, boats whose launching required removing and rebuilding a wall, forgiven the first time, but not the second.[29]

Strawbridge, like Francis, was dyslexic. He was more of a listener than a talker. One of his sons would put it this way: "My father never put three words together in his life." Francis had found someone to mentor; for him, there was no clearer path to friendship. Later, during the times when Billy's attention was focused on yacht design, he would stay overnight with Francis so that the two could talk boats without interruption. Billy wrote to Francis: "I certainly enjoyed myself staying with you as usual. You are very kind to have me and always give me a very happy time." Or, they could talk boats almost without interruption. After meeting Billy's wife, Francis wrote him, "I think you are lucky to win such a sensible girl, and such a good sport." But later, when "Mrs. Billy," as Francis always referred to her, not wanting to sound too familiar, would call Billy away from a discussion of yacht design, Francis would perhaps think that he was the lucky one to be a bachelor. Strawbridge had lost both his parents by the time

Mr. and Mrs. William J. Strawbridge pose at the bow of the 12-Metre *Mitena* on launching day at the Herreshoff Manufacturing Company, June 7, 1935. (*The Rudder* (July 1935): 33)

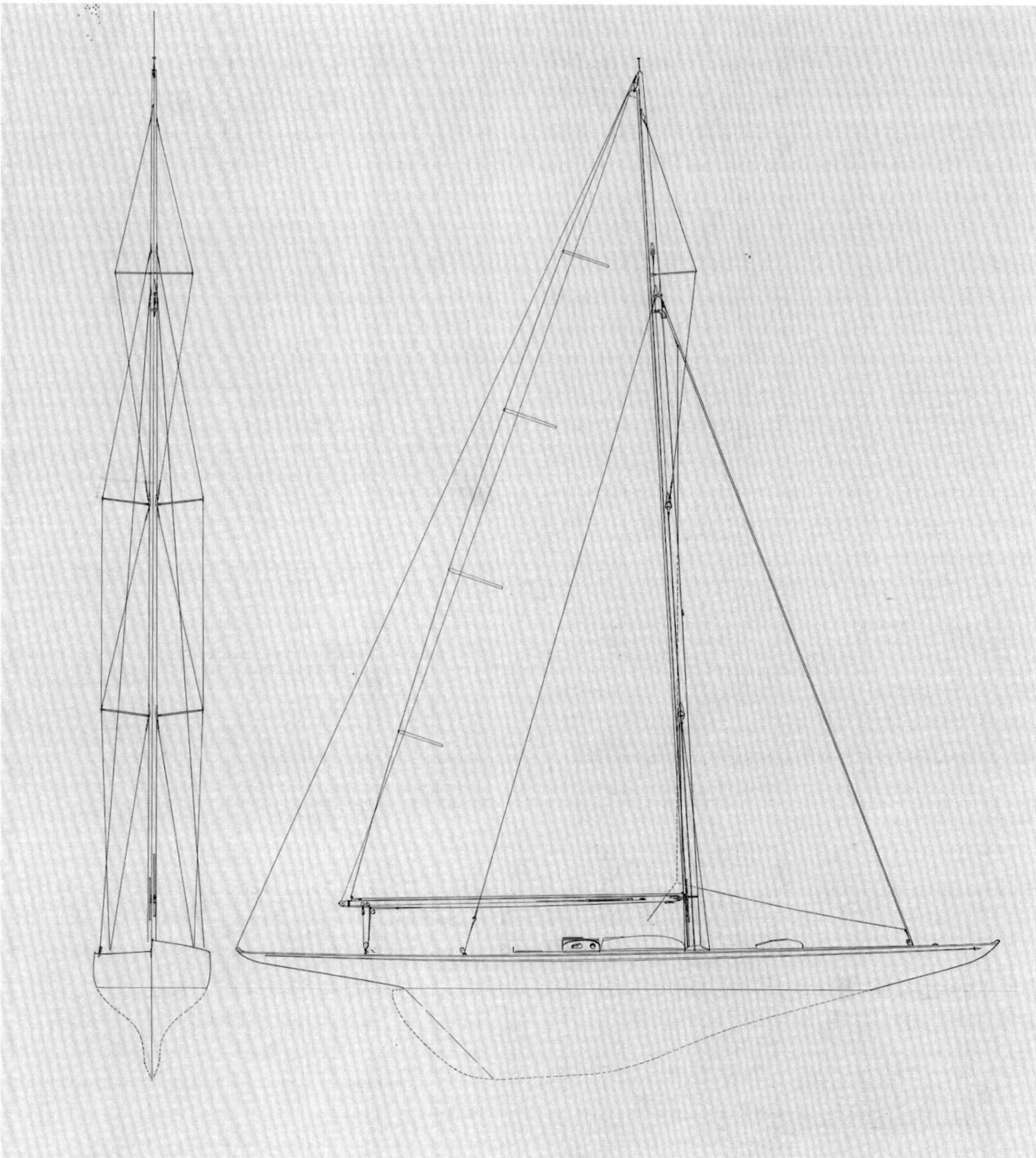

The *Mitena*'s sail plan. Sail area is 1,771 square feet, over 200 square feet less than spread by 12-Metres being designed by Clinton Crane, Johan Anker, William Fife, and Henry Gruber. Francis worried about the difference, but not enough, evidently, to stop him from trading, under the International Rule, sail area for low freeboard. L. Francis Herreshoff hated to detract from the beauty of a yacht design by increasing freeboard, and, after all, the low topsides would decrease her wind resistance when beating. Note the shrouds set inboard 12 inches to allow close trimming of an overlapping jib. Strawbridge tried a loose-footed, miter-cut mainsail to gain curvature in the foot of the sail, but the rules prevented him from rigging the wishbone boom he wanted. (© Mystic Seaport Museum, Daniel S. Gregory Ships Plans Library, SP38.43.5)

he was fourteen; at twenty-three, he found a surrogate father in L. Francis Herreshoff.[30]

As well as racing the *Istalena,* Strawbridge had competed in the 30-Square-Metre Class. His *Teana* had won the 1930 Northeast Harbor (Maine) Fleet race. But Billy lacked the total concentration on boats of, say, the up and coming C. Raymond Hunt, to become a top racing sailor. The *Mitena* would be in good hands, but there would be times when Billy Strawbridge was not quite up to his competition.

Francis must have approached the design of the *Mitena* with misgivings. Just as he began thinking about creating a 12-Metre, he learned that the *Whirlwind* was to be broken up. Thoughts of the debacle of his failed try for the America's Cup came flooding back (see volume 1, chapter 11). He didn't want to go through *that* again. But a healthy commission was not to be turned away in 1935, and Francis decided to take on the job of designing a 12-Metre racing boat for a man with whom, at first, he seemed to have little in common. As it turned out, his decision led to another life-long friendship, and the racing record of the new Twelve became secondary.

Francis was familiar with the International Rule through designing the 6-Metre *Wasp* in 1928 (see volume 1, pages 251-58). But it was his artistic side, rather than his scientific side, that was evident in the finished design for a 12-Metre. Francis was determined to draw another beautiful double-ender, and he was unwilling to take full advantage of the rule's formula, because he thought the rule produced bad-looking boats. The resulting *Mitena* was gorgeous, but she evidently suffered when sailed against the other Twelves.

It took some forty drawings to show and explain to the builders in Bristol all of Francis's ideas for the *Mitena.* Most of the plans were inked by Sam Brown, although Francis drew a few finished plans himself, for details like his special high-speed jib sheet winches, his main tack adjuster, and the particulars of the masthead.

When he learned that his son was designing a 12-Metre boat, Nathanael, perhaps with the *Whirlwind* in mind and despite his declining health, wrote to Francis, "I suppose it is none of my business, although I am intensely interested in your success with this yacht." And, when Francis sent him plans of the boat, Nathanael wrote, "I am very much pleased with the lines." Francis responded, "I am pleased that you take so much interest in the new 12."[31]

When Clinton Crane had offered to share his knowledge of 6-Metre design with Francis when he was drawing the plans for the *Wasp,* Francis had rebuffed him (see volume 1, page 251). But now, knowing that Crane was also designing a 12-Metre, Francis took the initiative and offered to have Strawbridge show Crane the plans of the *Mitena.* Crane "would be delighted to have Mr. Strawbridge call and show me what you are doing for him." In this spirit of cooperation, Crane reciprocated by sending Francis the lines of Merle-Smith's Twelve. Francis expressed his gratitude and sent Crane his detailed comparison of the two designs. He pointed out that the Crane boat would have the three advantages of a higher ballast-displacement ratio, a little more sail area, and a little less wetted surface, but that the *Mitena* would benefit from straighter diagonals, the fore-and-aft hull lines on which a heeled-over boat actually sails. The *Seven Seas* gained her three-to-one advantage over the *Mitena* because Francis failed to minimize his Twelve's length measurements under the rule and took a penalty for low freeboard, one of the keys to her beauty. The two great designers enjoyed this interchange; they were comparing finished designs, so there was no question of copying.[32]

As the builders in Bristol started work on the *Mitena*, the readers of *Yachting* could follow their progress. In her "Narragansett Bay Gossip" column in the April issue, Spinnaker Liz reported that the *Mitena*'s lead keel had been poured and her frames set up. Francis was also keeping up

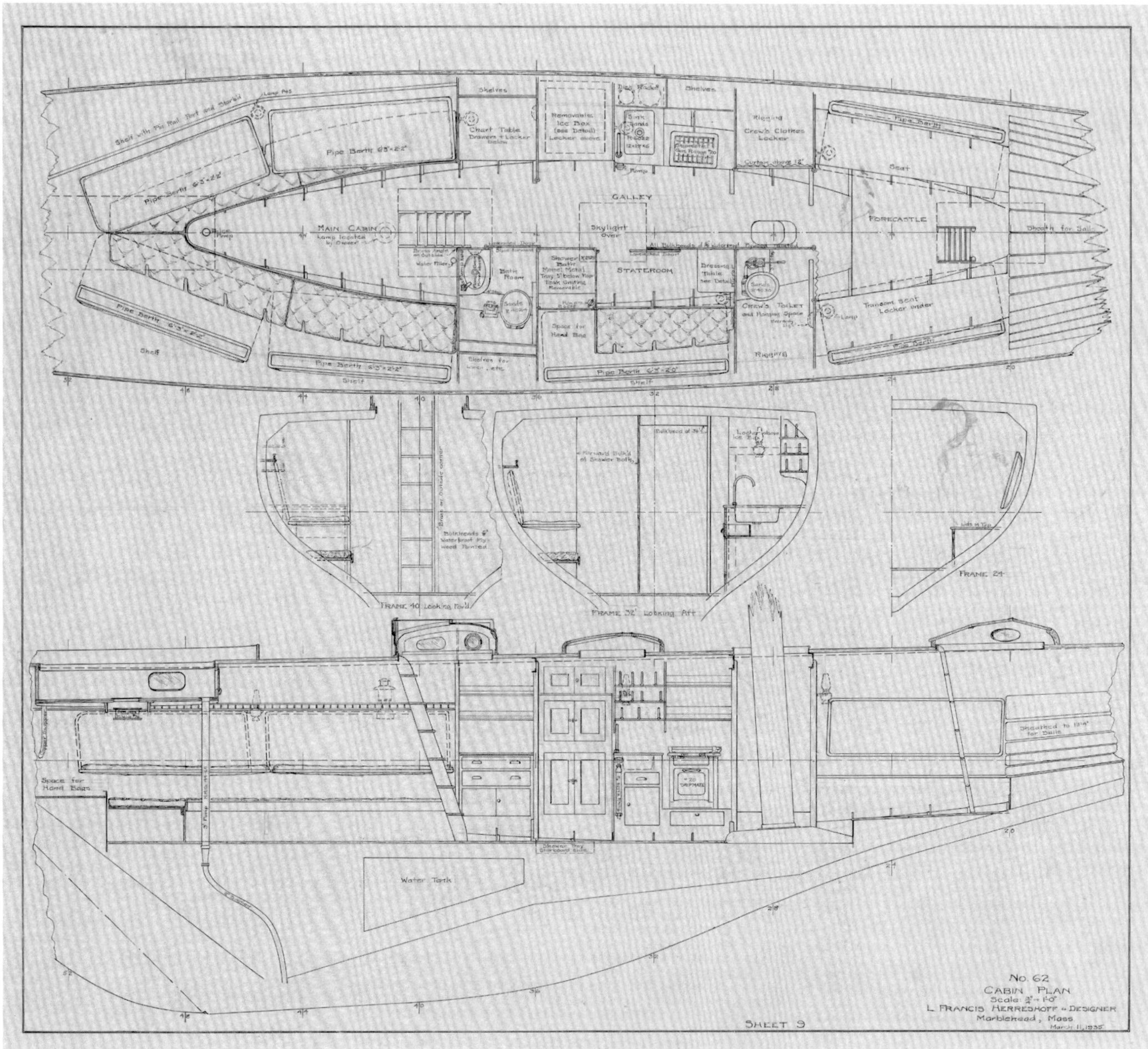

The cabin plan of the 12-Metre. In the bow is a big, sheathed sail locker. There is a forecastle for two crew, and they have a toilet room and a large clothes locker (to be shared with "rigging"). The galley is amidships, to port, with a single stateroom to starboard. At the foot of the companion ladder is a chart table to port and a bathroom, with separate shower, to starboard. The big saloon, with four pipe berths behind the transoms, is all the way aft. It has a utilitarian decoration: the discharge pipe for the bilge pump comes right up through the cabin to the cockpit, whence it drains overboard, a good opportunity for coxcombing knotwork. (© Mystic Seaport Museum, Daniel S. Gregory Ships Plans Library, SP38.43.9)

with her construction. He went to Bristol almost every Wednesday. He had praise for loftsman John Brecken, writing to Nathanael, "he laid her all down himself and never asked any foolish questions." Francis was particularly pleased that her sheer came out just as designed.[33]

The Herreshoff Manufacturing Company contract to build the *Mitena* was signed by Rudolph Haffenreffer, L. Francis Herreshoff, and William J. Strawbridge, and was witnessed by Francis's boarder, John Albert Chambers. It was a cost-plus contract, the cost being for materials, yard overhead, and labor, at $1.00 per hour, and the plus being profit, fixed at $3,000. Delivery of the vessel was to be no later than June 1, 1935. In the event, the total building cost, including the yard's profit, came in at $28,000, or $500 under the estimate, and to that sum were added $3,000 for sails, and a $2,000 design fee, for a grand total of $33,000. It is not known how Francis's design fee was negotiated, but Billy Strawbridge got a bargain. Without the design fee, the total cost of the yacht would have been $31,000, so Francis's normal fee would have been $3,100.[34]

Spinnaker Liz told her readers that the *Mitena* was launched on June 7, a week late, and that she was painted white with a green waterline and a green stripe just below the deck line. Francis didn't get down to Bristol until the tenth, so he missed the launching. He did stay overnight, so he had time to inspect his creation. A month later, he wrote to his father to explain that he had asked Tom Brightman, the yard superintendent, to gather the

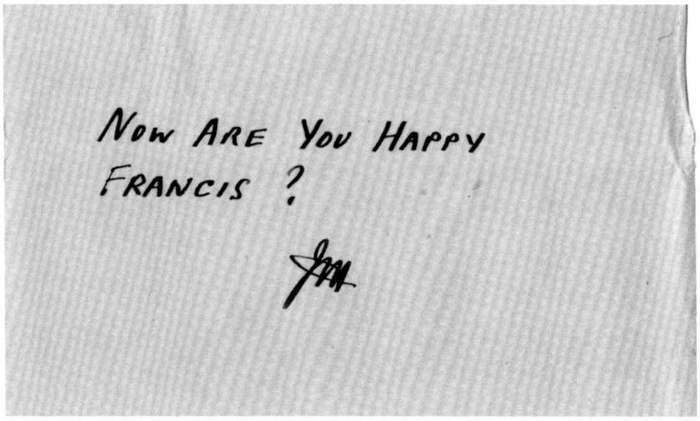

Mitena's plans and deliver them to Captain Nat. Francis who wanted his drawings kept safe, until he could pick them up. Francis wrote, "I thought this was a diplomatic way to collect the various prints of the boat so that they will not eventually get to John Alden's office, which has happened in some other cases." What these "other cases" were is unknown, but it would appear that Francis was showing his paranoid side.[35]

After the racing season of 1935, Francis wrote to Uffa Fox that "*Mitena* has not done very well although she has had good sails and been well handled." Francis had joined Strawbridge and sailed "Up Sound" in the *Mitena*, perhaps even including some racing. He had used poor sails and bad handling to excuse the lackluster performance of some of his racing boats, but, having sailed with Strawbridge, he couldn't do that with the *Mitena*. At Larchmont Race Week, only four Twelves raced: the *Mitena* came in last.[36]

The question of whether or not the bilge stringers could be left out of the *Mitena*'s construction had to go all the way up to the secretary of Lloyds, in London. He allowed it. Knowing how anxious Francis was to have the decision, the Lloyds inspector in New York, John S. Heck, sent Francis a telegram, and he ended it with "Hooray." In the follow-up letter confirming the telegram, he eliminated the un-Lloyds-like word, but added this note. It shows that Francis must have hidden his often scornful disparagement of Lloyds' standards of yacht construction well enough so that at least one inspector could joke a little with him. When Helen Bolster typed Francis's grateful reply, she uncharacteristically added a postscript of her own: "(Yes, Francis is *very* happy)." (Mystic Seaport Museum, G. W. Blunt White Library, 138:8/3)

12
US10

LEFT: The *Mitena* hard on the wind and footing fast. (© Mystic Seaport Museum, Rosenfeld Collection, 1984.187.71971F) ABOVE: The *Mitena*, slicing along close-hauled in smooth water. Her helmsman, probably Billy Strawbridge, sits on the cockpit floor to leeward, watching the set of his Genoa jib. Some successful racing sailors, including Ray Hunt, said that you should keep the upper part of the Genoa's luff just lifting, which is what's happening here. Note the slack line leading from the center of the sail forward through a block on the headstay and down to the deck and aft, used, when tacking, to help the sail around the mast. (Mystic Seaport Museum, 1997-1-31)

On July 29, Francis received a telegram from Strawbridge: "*Mitena* lost mast yesterday due to faulty construction. Please forward mast blueprints to H. B. Nevins immediately. Billy." By mid-August, on the New York Yacht Club cruise, the *Mitena* was racing with a new mast. But her performance did not improve; she won no races and, on the run from Montauk to Newport, she had to be towed off Shagwong Reef.[37]

Francis didn't sail in the *Mitena* during the summer of 1936. He knew she was racing, but he heard nothing from his friend, Billy Strawbridge. He was frustrated, and he wanted money. He wrote to Strawbridge on July 10:

> *Dear Billy,*
>
> *I hear that Mitena has gone down the Sound and so am writing to you at your last summer's address [Greenwich, Connecticut]. If you ever get a chance to write, even if it is a very short note scribbled any way in pencil, I should appreciate very much hearing about the new mast;—if it seems to stand all right, or if it makes any perceptible difference to the stability and speed. Did they get the intermediate shrouds in the right place? Did the new arrangement on the spinnaker boom work?*
>
> *Anything else that you can tell me about the boat will be greatly appreciated. For instance, is the new captain and crew as good as last year? Has the Seven Seas had alterations made? Is there much interest in the 12s, and do you think there will be another one built next winter?*
>
> *Enclosed I am sending you a bill. I am only doing this because I am very hard up and the bill only represents actual expenses to me.*
>
> *Very sincerely,*[38]

Presumably the expenses were related to the new mast. One of Francis's frustrations with Billy Strawbridge was that this client often forgot that he owed money to his friend and designer.

Although Strawbridge certainly enjoyed sailing the *Mitena*, he was becoming frustrated too, since she was outclassed on the racecourse. After the 1936 season, "Davy Jones," in his *Rudder* column, "Long Island Soundings," wrote: "Word comes that Bill Strawbridge has given up the one-sided struggle to make *Mitena* a contender in the 12-meter class and is building a cruising yawl. Billy is a game guy, and nobody could have asked for a better try than he gave the Herreshoff double-ender, but the boat just didn't have it in her."[39]

A top sailor who was interested in trying to make the *Mitena* into a winner was Frank Paine. He asked Francis to get a price on her from Billy Strawbridge. Francis wrote to Billy: "Now I really do wish you could give me your really lowest price for Frank Paine only buys boats when they are cheap. I do think that if he purchases her for his own use he will try to fix her up and make whatever small changes that are necessary and try to make her do well." We don't know what selling price for the *Mitena*, if any, Billy gave Francis, but Frank Paine was not to sail her.[40]

Strawbridge didn't sell his Twelve until 1939, continuing to take great pleasure in her beauty and speed, even though she wasn't bringing home silver. And, despite their respective frustrations, designer and client continued to build their friendship.

George E. Ratsey and Aemilius Jarvis bought the *Mitena*, and she stayed Up Sound. Eventually, she went to the Great Lakes, where John and June Van Voorhis sailed her out of Rochester in the 1950s; Louis and Charles Whitney became her owners in 1963; and Paul Brown was at her helm by 1965. Then she fell into disrepair. She is now owned by James Henley and his son Pat and is hauled out for major work at Port Huron, Michigan. Her beauty has saved her.

Thanks to Billy Strawbridge's friendship, and despite the *Mitena*'s poor showing on the

Billy Strawbridge sailing his *Mitena* to windward, rail down. In this view, he is sitting to windward, where he can not only watch the luff of his mainsail, but also inspect the approaching ripples in order to predict with accuracy just what the breeze is about to give him. Judging by the angle of the tiller, the boat is carrying a normal and healthy amount of weather helm. Note the curvature in the foot of the mainsail; Strawbridge has set her loose-footed sail. (© Mystic Seaport Museum, Rosenfeld Collection, 1984.187.72533F)

ABOVE: **Billy Strawbridge and his wife enjoying their yacht. Morris Rosenfeld's camera caught them on July 18, 1935, during Larchmont Race Week, obviously between races.** (© Mystic Seaport Museum, Rosenfeld Collection, 1984.187.72158F) RIGHT: **In the spring of 1936, Francis moved a short distance from 20 Lee Street to this house at 25 Front Street in Marblehead. The move itself seemed almost to overwhelm him, but he was glad to be in his own place with no rent to pay.** (© Mystic Seaport Museum, 1993.120.6.109)

racecourse, the experience of designing the *Mitena* was positive for Francis. The project reawakened his interest in the challenge of designing a boat to a racing rating rule. He disagreed with much of the International Rule because of what he considered to be the unnecessarily ugly and clumsy boats it produced. Yet, despite his aversion to the effect of measurement rules on yacht design, the *Mitena* drew him back into the intriguing problem of balancing the speed-producing elements of a yacht design against their effects on increasing the rating. The designing of a racing boat whose owner he liked overcame the boat's lack of success. Strangely enough, the creation of the unsuccessful *Mitena* may have softened the blow administered by the disastrous *Whirlwind*.

And Francis wanted to design another 12-Metre for the 1936 season. In reply to a letter from Philip J. Roosevelt, who was trying to promote the class, Francis wrote, "I should be very glad to communicate with any one interested in a new 12 and can answer questions about cost, etc., more definitely than before *Mitena* was built." But no yachtsman beat a path to the door of the designer of another also-ran.[41]

In early May 1936, Francis moved house. The old customhouse at 20 Lee Street had been satisfactory, but, after ten years, Francis was tired of paying rent. It had cost him nearly $9,000 to live there. He also wanted "a warm place of my own to sit in winter nights with my things around me. For nearly twenty years now I have lived in boats, boarding houses, hired buildings and what-not and hope for better health in a regular house." Francis's health was fine; in those days there was undue emphasis on minor problems of digestion.[42]

As the Depression got a good grip, Francis had no work that whole summer, and so no income. But he had the money from the *Mitena* and the *Tioga II*. In June, he received a bonus of $833 from the Navy Department for his service in World War I under the World War Adjusted Compensation Act. He was able to buy an old three-story house from Walter K. Shaw Jr., 25 Front Street, only a couple of hundred yards easterly from the old customhouse. The new house cost $3,000 and, for $500 more, he added the small, 110-foot-by-70-foot lot on its west side. Francis took over a $1,200 mortgage on the property, paying 6 percent interest. He paid $800 of the remaining $1,800 with part of his extra money and agreed to pay off the other $1,000 in four payments of $250 over two years, in effect an interest-free loan. To help out, Nathanael offered Francis another interest-free loan. Francis's response was: "It is certainly extremely kind of you to offer to help me with a loan of some money, and I may have to take advantage of it, but I am going to try awfully hard to carry on without help as I believe if every young man did this the country would be better off. However, it is very consoling to know that in case of sickness, if I don't get new work, there is something I can fall back on." His answer reflects Francis's pride in being determined to be financially independent.[43]

Francis had to move out of the customhouse quickly, for he was subletting the place to finish out his lease, and the new renters "wanted it at once." But he had the help of Al Chambers, who, after a year in Boston, had moved back to boarding with him. Despite that help and his father's offer of financial aid, he wrote to Nathanael:"I am having a hard time moving. Pretty soon I expect to be physically, mentally, and financially very low." Rather than being excited about his move, Francis seemed to be overwhelmed by it and was perhaps becoming more depressed than the situation called for.[44]

Nathanael, still frail but feeling stronger, sought to dispel his son's gloom with practical advice: "a) get a title search b) get your tools into a room at 25 Front c) put up a ready made garage on your lot for your kayaks." But Francis had already spent "about $50" to get a clear title back as far as 1715 (the original part of the house had been built in about 1695). And he had provided for his tools, his kayaks, and the sailing dinghy *So And So* by renting back the ground floor at the customhouse for $5.00 per month. While there was only room for a small workshop at 25 Front Street, Francis hoped to build a proper one on his lot.[45]

His new house was squeezed in between Front Street and the hill on the harbor that was now Crocker Park. The side lot had been the site of the Snow Crest Inn; fortunately, all that was left of that ungainly five-story building was its foundation. At the back of the house, snuggled up against the hill, was a complete, separate apartment. That is where Al Chambers would stay, paying rent to Francis.[46]

Here is how Francis described 25 Front Street to his father:

> *The front of the house is right on the street but this part of Front Street is very quaint, being one of those less frequented byways not far from the main thoroughfare, as often found in New England towns—a sort of back water from the main channel only used by the natives.*
>
> *On the SE side of the house is a narrow public park which borders on the harbor and has a public landing stage. This park is on a steep little knoll which shuts off all my view of the harbor and this was fortunate for me for had the house a good view I could not have bought it as all such locations in Marblehead are quite expensive. Also I have found that the view of the harbor only distracts me from my work during the day time, and after all in the long winter nights the view isn't very essential. In pleasant summer weather I shall often be on the water as in a few steps out the back door I can get the very best view of the harbor.*
>
> *The house is built on quite a sloping land and the street floor is very small consisting of only a hallway, a room about 11 x 10 with a fireplace (probably originally a kitchen and now to be used by Mr. Chambers for yacht brokerage) and a room about 9 x 7 in which I am installing a gas burning hotwater heating furnace. The next floor up is quite interesting and is entered by a quaint curved [outside, stone] stairway. It contains a sitting room with fireplace and built-in corner china cupboard; a small bedroom and a very good modern kitchen, a bath room and a small glass enclosed room about 7 x 10.*
>
> *The third floor is what I bought the house for. It is mostly one room with lots of windows and here the drafting room will be. This was all built new inside about 1930. There is also a bedroom on this floor where I will sleep and a bathroom. The house in general has been quite completely rebuilt about 1930 by a wealthy woman who liked its looks and spent about $8,000 on it. The chimney was rebuilt to the ground; the roof mostly new; all new window sashes and*

frames; all new modern plumbing, and most completely wired.[47]

Nathanael wanted to come up and see for himself, but, in November, he wrote: "I think the trip to see you and your house will have to be given up. I get out for short afternoon rides when pleasant, only."[48]

A neighbor, who had been allowed into the house as a youngster, remembered "how Spartan, almost Shaker in appearance, the interior finish of the living quarters seemed to be." Another neighbor recalled, "he lived so simply." Yet Francis would make 25 Front Street homey and comfortable, as he had 20 Lee Street, with his pictures, books, and models, and with his dolphin andirons on the hearth.[49]

An advantage to Francis's short move was that he could still easily drop in at the boatyard in front of the customhouse, where he liked to spend time yarning with the new owner of Frazier's Yacht Yard and Railway, Edwin H. Oxner, the longtime Lawley's superintendent, as well as with the usual group of yacht captains, boatbuilders, and machinists to be found in "The Office," as they called it, expounding about boats. The windows overlooked the harbor, huge photos of J-boats racing were tacked up, and the big pot-bellied stove seemed to encourage the flow of the latest waterfront gossip, whether or not the weather called for its glow. Francis felt almost as much at home over at Oxner's as he did at his own hearth.[50]

He was less comfortable at the few meetings of the Marblehead Art Association and of the

Francis moving rocks with a crowbar on his lot beside the house at 25 Front Street. The foundation belongs to the former Snow Crest Inn, which was torn down in about 1929. In the background is the southwest corner of his new house. The three-story dwelling is built against the steep hill of Crocker Park. Front Street is out of sight to the far left. The multi-windowed room, added to the old house in about 1930, is on the third floor and is Francis's drafting room, "what I bought the house for." But by the time Francis moved in, lack of new work forced him to lay off his draftsmen. (Courtesy Anne Lawrence Bondy, Mystic Seaport Museum, 1994-4-222)

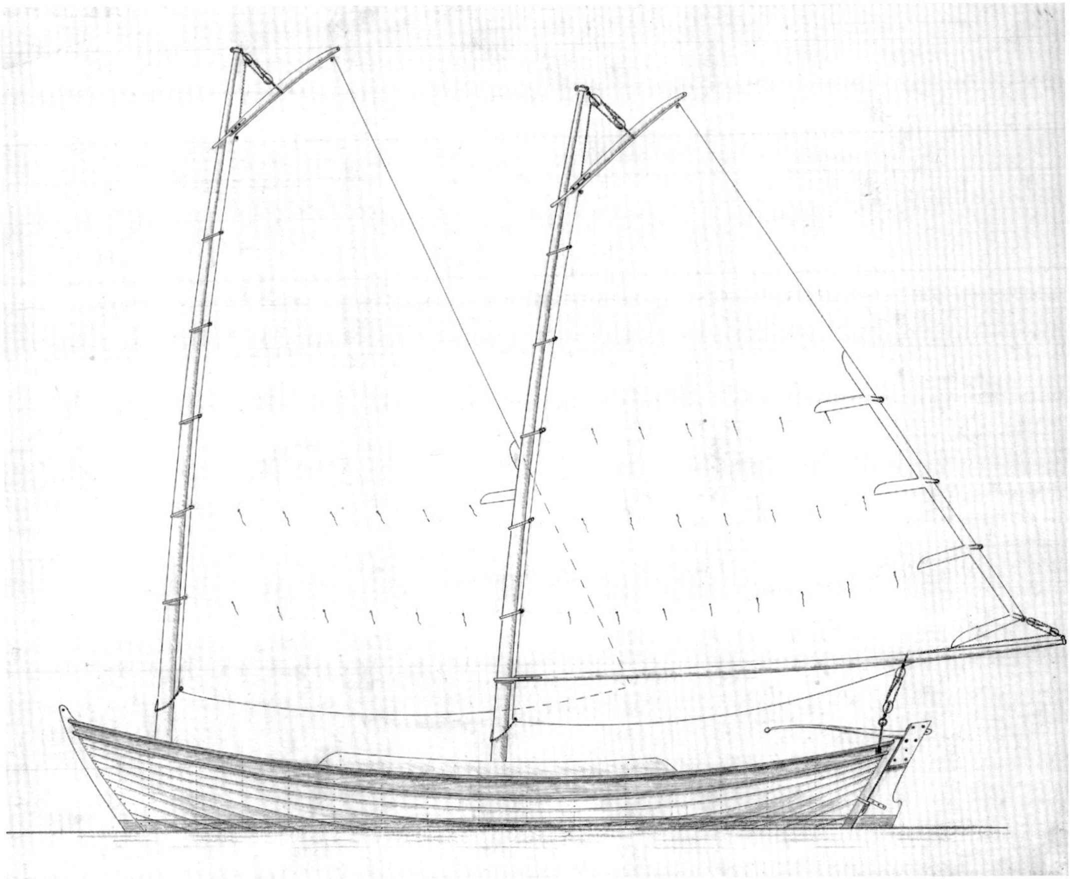

ABOVE: **Francis made this drawing of a Block Island boat back in 1920, based on a wreck he had examined when his naval duties during World War I took him to the island. When Billy Strawbridge decided he wanted a cruising boat like the type, Francis sent him a print of this drawing to enhance their discussions of the design.** (© Mystic Seaport Museum, Daniel S. Gregory Ships Plans Library, SP38.284.1) RIGHT: **Francis's "Study of a Elongated Norwegian Pilot Boat" is, as his title implies, a stretched-out version of Colin Archer's designs. Her hull is finer than the similar Archer vessels, and she has a more generous rig, so she would be faster than they were. Yet, with her long waterline and ability to shorten down to jib and jigger, she would be relatively safe in a hard chance. She is 43 feet long on deck; 35 feet on the waterline; with a beam of 11 feet, 8 inches; and a draft of 5 feet, 9 inches. Sail area is 810 square feet. This is a pedestrian design for Francis. Her cabin arrangement is standard for her size. The cabin house extends further forward than he would normally draw it in order to give her crew what he considered to be extra, unnecessary headroom. The only idiosyncrasy he has allowed himself is the off-center propeller. This design has an artistic refinement that would be rare coming out of the Alden office, but there it would probably have been finished and built to. For Francis it remained a study.** (© Mystic Seaport Museum, Daniel S. Gregory Ships Plans Library, SP38.112.2)

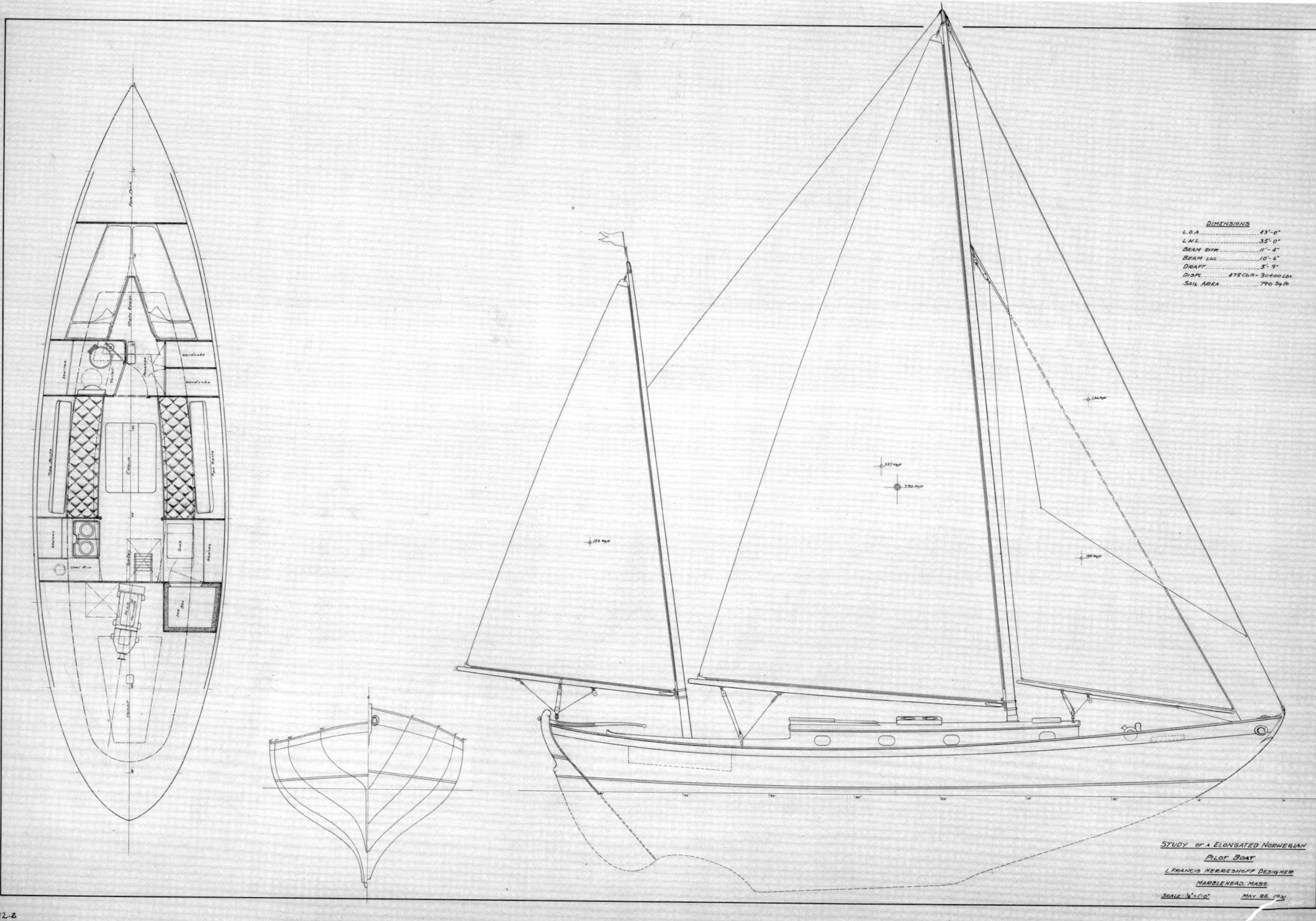

DIMENSIONS
L.O.A. .... 43'-0"
L.W.L. .... 35'-0"
BEAM EXTR. .... 11'-4"
BEAM LWL .... 10'-6"
DRAFT .... 5'-9"
DISPL. .... 475 Cu.Ft. = 30400 Lbs.
SAIL AREA .... 790 Sq.Ft.
STUDY OF A ELONGATED NORWEGIAN
PILOT BOAT
L. FRANCIS HERRESHOFF DESIGNER
MARBLEHEAD, MASS.
SCALE: ½" = 1'-0"
MAY 26. 1931

historical society that his great interest in art and history bid him attend. Of the former, he wrote, "the town had its art club, but about the only art that they practiced was the art of handling the knife and fork, and the members' sole accomplishment seemed to be in pretending they were someone other than themselves." Of the latter, he complained that, "while our historical society was in a fine old building, the dear old ladies who dominated it believed contradiction was the general object of conversation."[51]

Less than two years after Francis's move to 25 Front Street, his father was urging him to get on with building his shop next door. But Francis was more ambitious: he wanted to have built a two-story dwelling on the old hotel foundation, a building that he would design himself. Nathanael, ailing though he was, joined in to help. "Excuse me," he wrote, "I don't want to meddle with your affairs but I certainly do take interest, so I have formulated what might be done (only one way of a hundred)." Then he wrote a detailed description of his son's new house as he had worked it out in his head. "My sight is so poor," he added, "I cannot make scale drawings. I do hope you will not lose your patience and explode." Far from exploding, Francis welcomed his father's help. He made his own design, incorporating some of his father's ideas and rejecting others. He also consulted with one of his customers, R. P. Jenks, partner in the Providence architectural firm of Jenks and Ballou. And he told his father that he had showed his plans to "an instructor in architectural drawing at the Massachusetts Institute of Technology. He specializes in the outside looks and proportions of buildings and is a severe critic. I showed him the sketches that I sent you and his opinion is that it was a finely balanced and nearly perfectly proportioned building."[52]

The new house was put up by a local contracter, Herbert J. Haskell. The ground floor was given over to a garage; the second floor was living quarters and included a much smaller drafting room than in the old house, now that Francis was working on his own. He moved in and rented out 25 Front Street. The new house took over that street number; the old 25 Front Street became 25½. Francis's renters were the Coe family, whose children, Chris, Peter, and Suzy, soon became the recipients of their landlord's mentoring, as well as the products of his lathe. Francis would live at the new 25 Front Street through World War II. He gave over his garage to the activities of the Marblehead Chapter of the British War Relief Society, whose ladies packaged Bundles for Britain and sold dusty ceramics bearing the portraits of King George, Queen Elizabeth, and the princesses.[53]

Many a yachtsman's wife was reluctant to go afloat because the boat was too tippy or her cabin was too cramped and lacked a bathtub. Among Francis's best friends and customers, both Waldo Brown and William Strawbridge faced this problem. (Charlie Welch didn't; Ruth liked boats as much as he did.)

As he began to race the *Mitena* with less enthusiasm, Billy Strawbridge began thinking about also getting a cruising boat that would entice "Mrs. Billy," to sail with him with more enthusiasm. When he discussed the idea with Francis, he pushed for the Block Island boat as a type on which to base a comfortable cruiser. This was preaching to the choir. As a child, Francis had heard his father praise this beamy double-ender with a Dutch-style schooner rig as a seaworthy vessel with an easy motion if the water got rough. Sailing out of Bristol as a young man, Francis could have seen the occasional Block Island boat still going about her business from and to the island, particularly at Newport. And later, during World War I, when Francis's naval patrol duty took him often to Block Island, he had the chance to study the beached wreck of one of the boats in the southwest corner of Great Salt Pond. Francis would

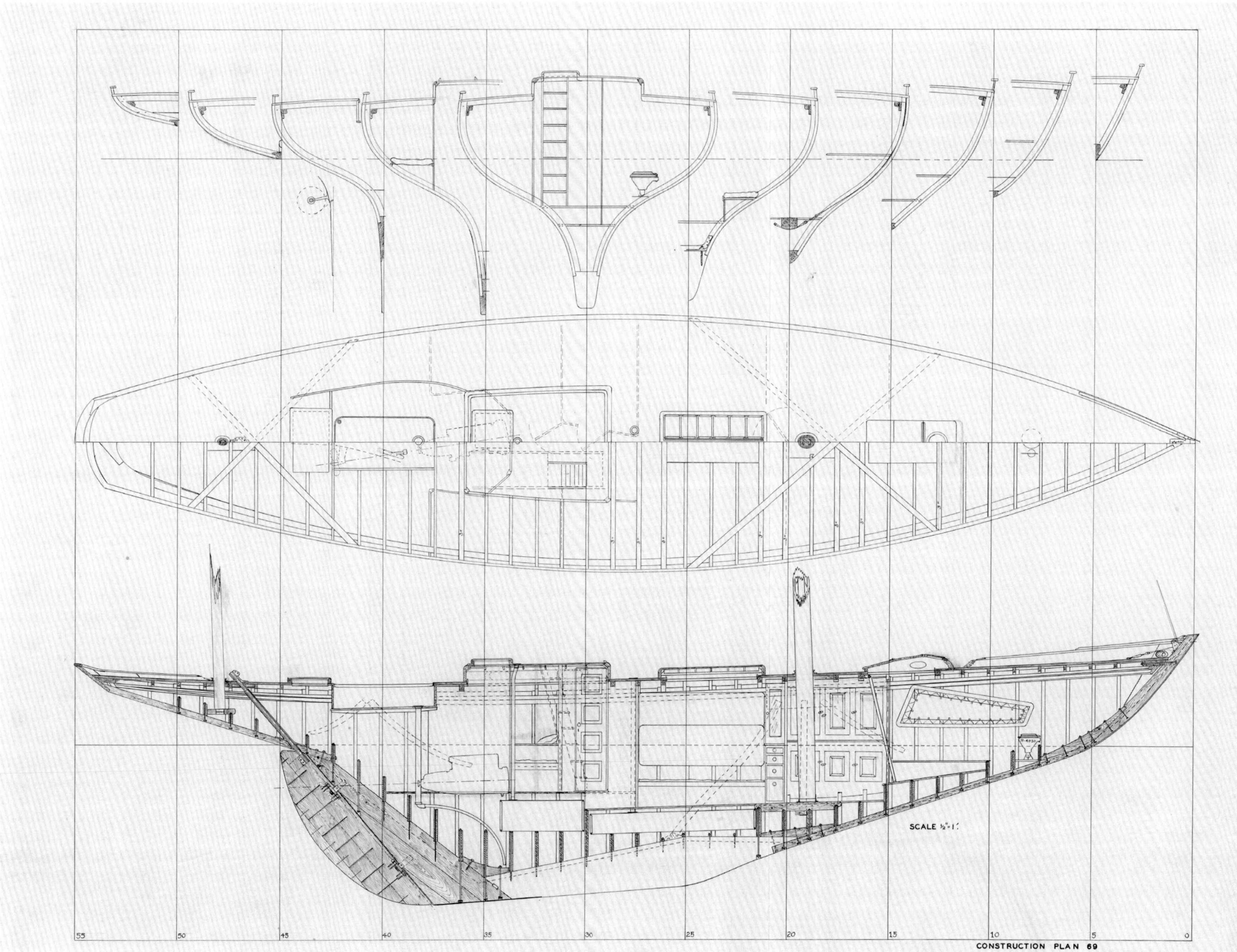

The *Persephone*'s construction drawing. This plan shows diagonal metal strapping in the deck; Francis made a separate drawing, after discussion with Billy Strawbridge, that showed diagonal strapping in the hull as well. Frames were sided 2 inches and molded 2½ inches, on 15-inch centers. Planking was to be 1½-inch yellow pine or mahogany below the waterline, and double, ¾-inch mahogany and ¾-inch cedar above. Note the hatch in the after, port corner of the short, low cabin house, Francis's favorite way to get good headroom and ventilation in the engine room. The bilge pump discharges into the watertight cockpit, and hence overboard through scuppers.

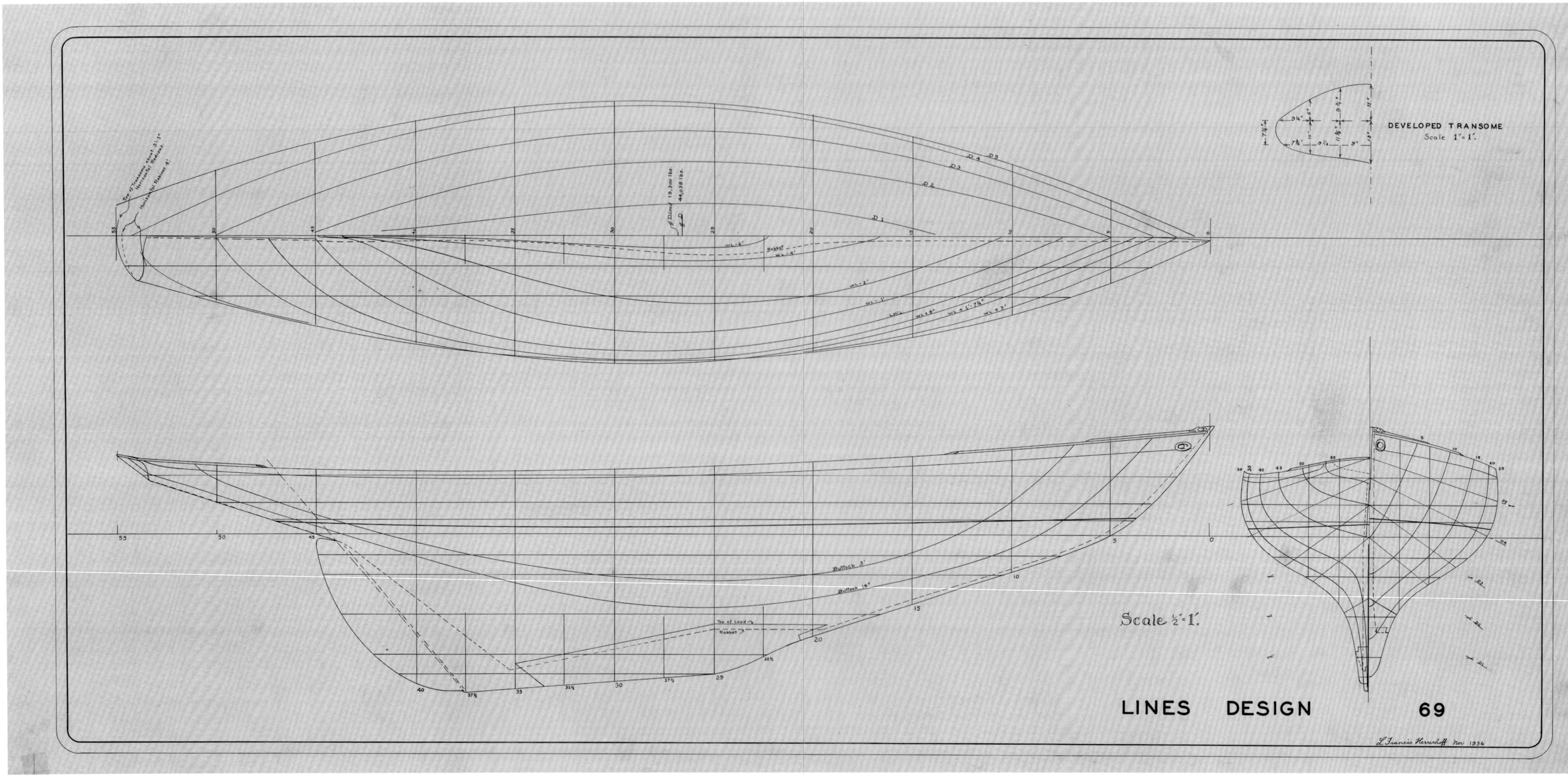

The lines of the *Persephone.* Her hull shape excited admiration wherever she went. The constantly changing curve of the bow profile is subtle; the wineglass section of her dainty transom at the end of her long counter stern is equally subtle. Nathanael thought her overhangs should be balanced, the bow longer, the stern shorter; fortunately, Francis ignored this advice from his famous father. Her length on deck is 55 feet, 10 inches; length on the waterline, 40 feet, 10 inches; beam, 12 feet, 6 inches; and draft 8 feet. On November 16, 1936, Francis figured her displacement at 44,038 pounds. By this time, Francis had no draftsmen; he was on his own. (© Mystic Seaport Museum, Daniel S. Gregory Ships Plans Library, SP38.51.1)

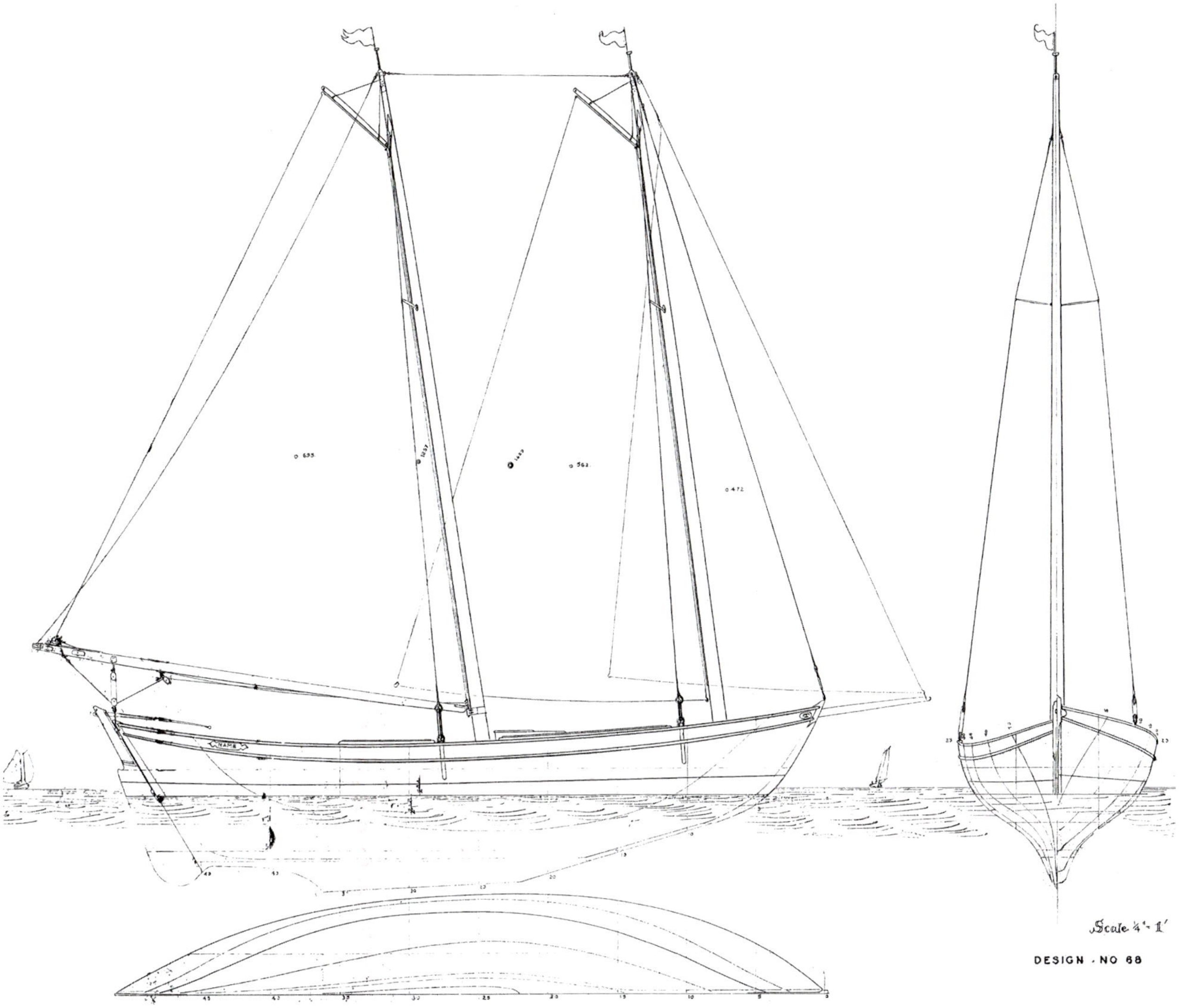

The sail plan of the Strawbridge Block Island boat, Francis's design No. 68. Total area is 1,729 square feet, with 695 square feet in the mainsail, 562 in the foresail, and 472 in a light-weather reaching jib that set flying on an off-center, reefing bowsprit for which Francis designed a removable rod bobstay. The original type had no jib, but Francis thought the substantial sail area of the boat should be broken into three sails for ease of handling. She was supposed to balance in a fresh breeze under just the mainsail and foresail, as did her ancestors. The old boats had no standing rigging, but Francis added a headstay and single shrouds over short spreaders, writing that he "would not like to see the masts waving round as they did in old times." Because of the spreaders, the luffs of mainsail and foresail would be held to the masts by tracks, rather than the mast hoops of the original boats. Billy Strawbridge, being used to trimming the *Mitena*'s big Genoa jib, planned to trim his overlapping foresail in similar fashion with single-part sheets to winches. This boat would have had the two or three reefs in mainsail and foresail of the originals. Since the mainsail was loose-footed like the originals, Francis worried about handling the clew earings on the mainsail. "Reefing the clew of a loose-footed sail over the stern of a double-ender might be quite dangerous," he wrote. Yet the old Block Island sailors had obviously managed. Note how her foot-high bulwarks almost hide her cabin houses. (© Mystic Seaport Museum, Daniel S. Gregory Ships Plans Library, SP38.19.6)

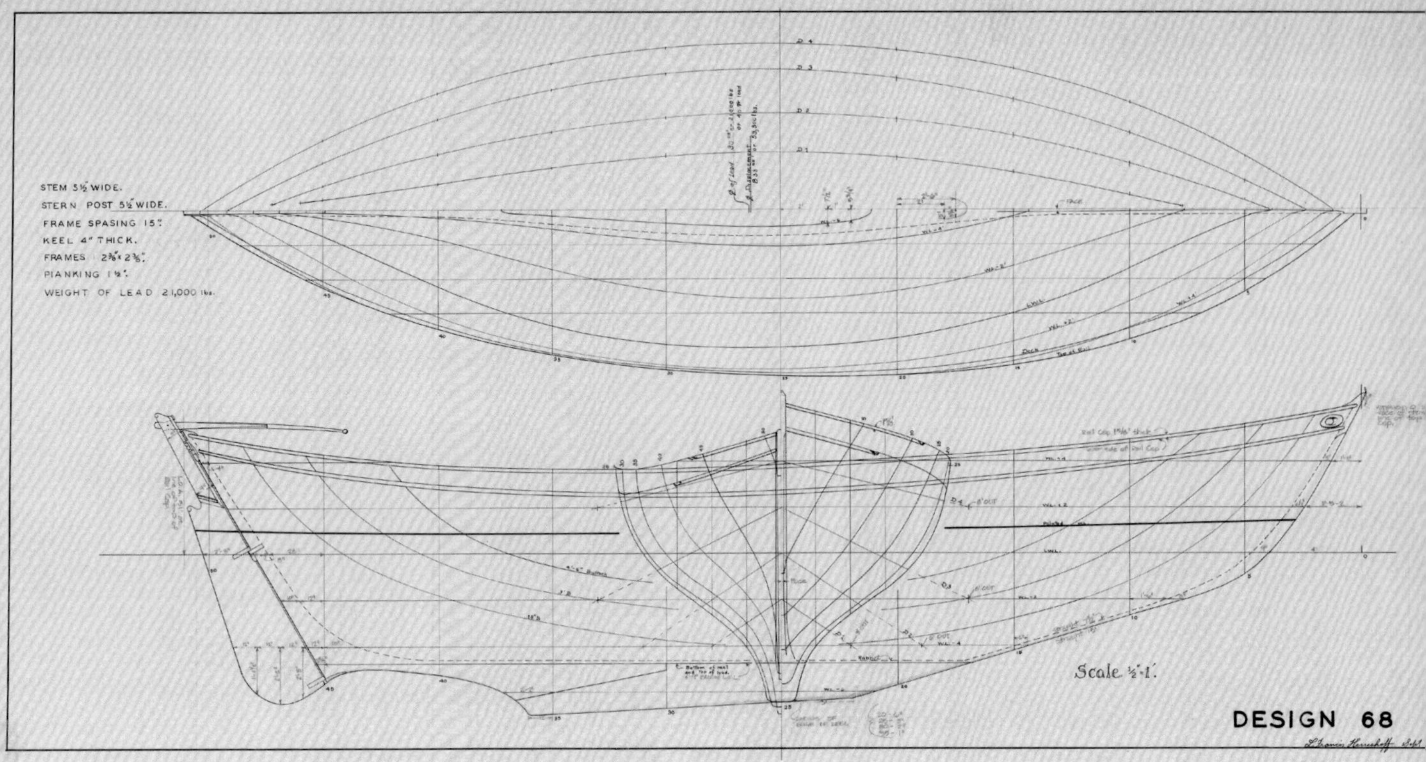

demonstrate his familiarity with and admiration for the type by having the skipper of the *Rozinante* describe and illustrate the Block Island boat to his young crew members in his work of fiction, *The Compleat Cruiser*.[54]

And so, in the late summer of 1936, Francis threw himself into the design of a Block Island yacht. He wrote to Nathanael, "it is very nice to be working on some different types of boats from the standardized crafts being designed by Stephens, Alden, and Paine." "I like the opportunity of designing boats of very varying types," he continued. "I always admired your ability at designing, most of all because you could design anything from a high-speed launch to a house boat, whereas almost all designers today and even in your time, generally could design only one line of boats. I think to be versatile and able to design well any sort of a craft that a customer might desire requires much more skill and I welcome this opportunity to design this unusual boat. I am still really a very young man [45] and hope to have an opportunity to explore many other types, as you did so successfully during your time."[55]

This was all very well, but Nathanael didn't think much of the idea of basing a cruising boat on

The Block Island yacht's lines. Francis has cut away the profile of the forefoot compared to that of the original boats in order to move the center of lateral resistance aft. This was to achieve balance, because without the jib the center of effort of her two working sails would be further aft than on the original type. The cutaway deadwood is to improve maneuverability. He has made the yacht narrower than the workboat so she would sail faster, and he has regained stability with depth of keel and outside lead ballast. The old boats carried beach stones inside. To increase cabin space, Francis has raised the freeboard amidships and carried the width of the boat down toward the keel. She is 51 feet long on deck; with a waterline length of 44 feet; a beam of 14 feet, 6 inches; and a draft of 7 feet. Displacement is 53,280 pounds, with 20,400 pounds of lead, for a ballast-displacement ratio of 38 percent. This plan is dated September 1936. (© Mystic Seaport Museum, Daniel S. Gregory Ships Plans Library, SP38.19.5)

Strawbridge was in a hurry to see the cabin plan, so Francis sent him this penciled drawing. At the bow, she has a forepeak, with a collision bulkhead just abaft the foremast. Next comes the galley, with its own hatch and entry ladder. The saloon is under the aft end of the forward cabin house. It has two pipe berths above the settees and an unusually wide table. Strawbridge intended to sail the boat with a paid hand; he would share his pipe berth and head with a Lathrop Engineer's Model power plant on the port side, amidships, with his own entry through a hatch in the after, port corner of the forward cabin house. To starboard of the engine room are large storage lockers. There is a full-width head with shower under the after cabin house, with a two-berth sleeping cabin further aft. Francis put a great deal of time and effort into this cabin arrangement; he has used the available space in the boat with ingenuity. And he couldn't resist decorating the pipe berths he liked so much with sketches of a Block Island boat, a brigantine, and a swordfish. This is one of the best cabin plans he drew, but he would not ink it, and no builder would use it. Billy Strawbridge changed his mind. (© Mystic Seaport Museum, Daniel S. Gregory Ships Plans Library, SP38.19.3

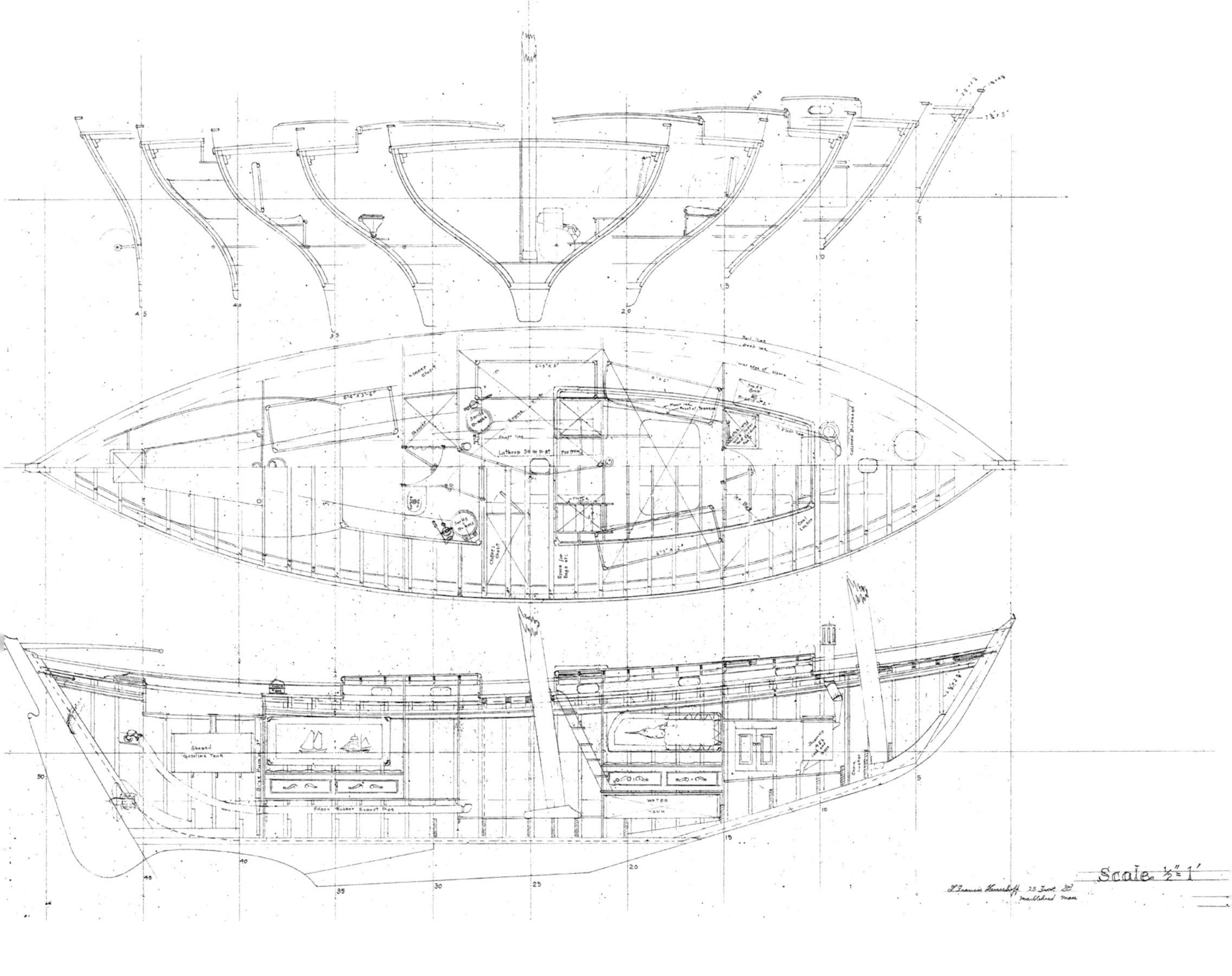

a Block Island boat. After all, he and his son had made great advances in yacht design; why didn't Strawbridge get a *Tioga* with an inboard sloop rig and a raised deck, he wanted to know.[56]

Francis had already suggested to Billy that he have for a cruising boat an adaptation of the *Bounty*, but "he did not seem to respond to it at all, and I still do believe that for his use, where he probably will have a racing sailboat of some kind, and a high speed motor boat, that if he does want a comfortable, able, roomy boat and does not care for shallow draft, that the Block Island boat really will be the safe, comfortable boat for him to take his wife out on. And I believe one of the things he is trying to do is to have a boat which his wife will not be uncomfortable on, so that she will get to like sailing more." For his part, Francis hoped that a yacht like a Block Island boat would compare favorably with the "foreign boats" that were becoming so popular, "the double ended Norwegian type boats that were designed by Colin Archer." Francis's patriotism was coming to the fore: he wanted to show that an American boat type was just as good as anything from Norway. Yet, five years before, he had made a "Study of a Elongated Norwegian Pilot Boat," a design inspired by the work of Archer. Building on Archer's handsome double-enders, Francis had created a more graceful vessel without sacrificing seaworthiness.[57]

As he worked on the plans of Billy Strawbridge's Block Island boat yacht, Francis wrote to him: "I am going ahead with the lines and cabin layout, so if you decide on any changes please let me know soon. I appreciate very much having this opportunity to make the prospective plans, even if the boat is not built, for they represent such an interesting craft." And before long, Francis was writing to his father, "it now appears that after [my] doing quite a little on this boat, Mr. Strawbridge may not stick to the type which may cause me a lot of extra work if he does change to some other design." Nathanael's derogation of the design appeared to be vindicated. He replied to Francis: "Perhaps Mr. Strawbridge is beginning to realize a Block Island boat type would not be best for a family cruiser. I hope he will appreciate your studies for him and compensate you for the extra time you have spent." Francis's apprehension proved to be all too valid. Billy Strawbridge lost his enthusiasm for the project, and the "interesting craft" that Francis had created on paper remained a dream-ship for the two friends. It is not known if Francis received compensation other than the satisfaction of making the design. Nor is it known how much, if anything, "Mrs. Billy" knew about the Block Island yacht being planned for her, or what she may have thought of the vessel.[58]

When *Yachting* had reported that William Strawbridge was giving up racing seriously in the 12-Metre *Mitena*, the news was that his next boat would be a "cruising yawl." As we have seen, Billy wanted a cruising boat, but it was a Block Island yacht that intrigued him. When he discarded that idea, he did, indeed, turn to a yawl, but she would be no out-and-out cruiser: he asked Francis to design him an ocean racer to the Cruising Club of America (CCA) Rule. This would be Francis's design No. 69, the graceful *Persephone*, named after Zeus's daughter, the queen of Greek mythology's Underworld, the place where souls went after death. Persephone was also the goddess of fertility. Billy's mother had urged him to make the change from racing to cruising, reminding him, "you have a family now," for Mrs. Billy would soon give birth to William Strawbridge III. Francis, who had advertised himself as a designer of "Racing Yachts," agreed with such a shift. He would write to a young Naval Academy midshipman: "I agree with you that short cruising is by far the pleasantest, and the long ocean races, or even the long cruises, become tiring work. Yes, a good thrash to windward for three or four hours and then coming to anchor in a sheltered place is very good fun."[59]

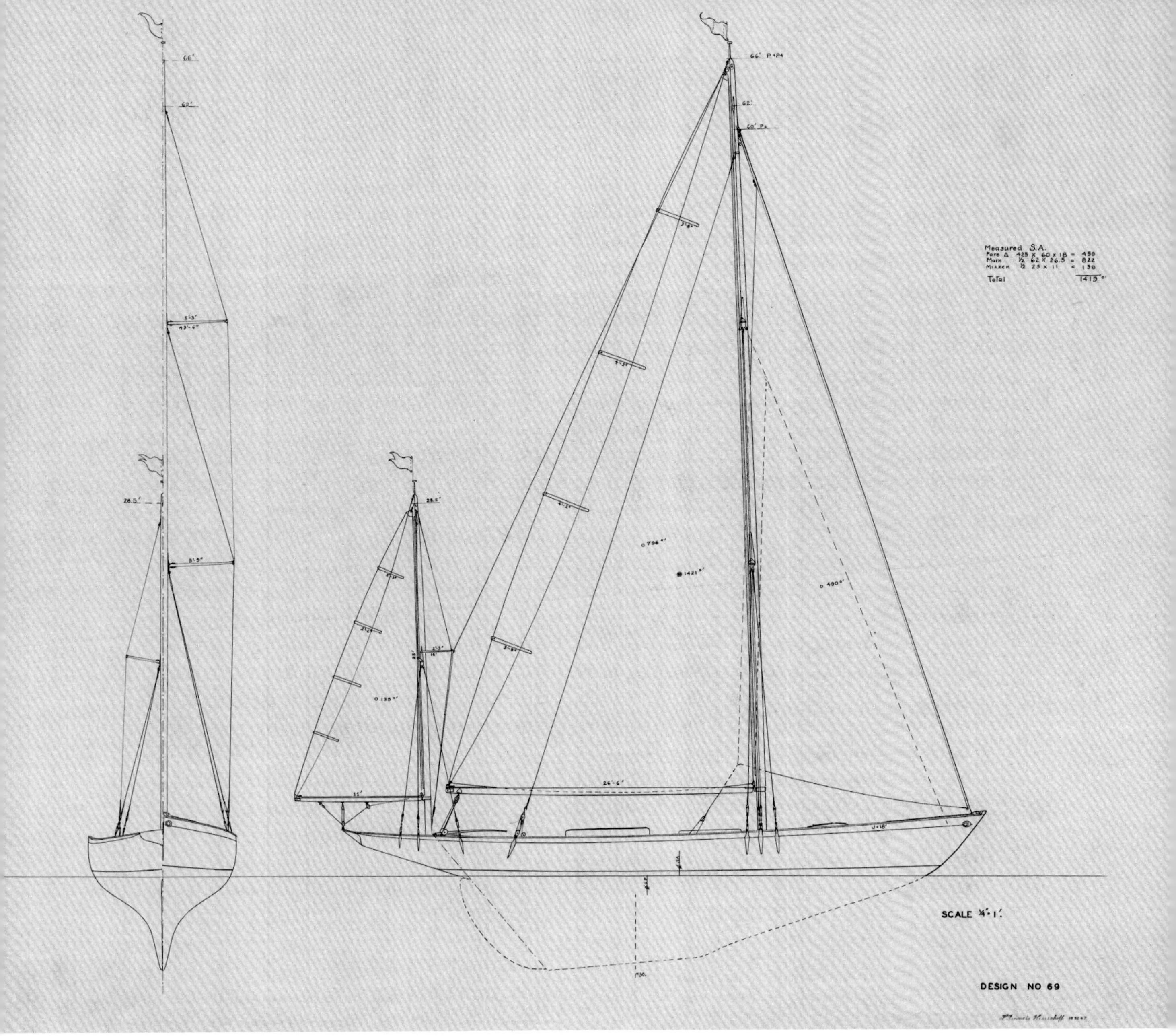

Billy Strawbridge's ocean racer, the *Persephone*, designed by Francis to the Cruising Club of America Rule, was the last racing boat that he created. She carried the yawl rig that the rule favored in its Rig Allowance (by counting 97 percent of the measured sail area instead of 100 percent). But the rule required that a yawl's mizzen had to have an area of at least 10 percent of the total sail area, and the *Persephone*'s didn't, so she must have taken a penalty, perhaps being denied the 97 percent rig allowance. The *Persephone*'s measured sail area under the rule, counting 100 percent of the fore triangle, was 1,419 square feet, so the mizzen had to have at least 141.9 square feet to meet the rule's requirement. Instead, it was only 135 square feet, which seems strange. Making the mizzenmast taller would not only have agreed with the rule, but also would have allowed a bigger mizzen staysail, which the rule did not measure. Her booms are parallel to the waterline, but the mizzen boom looks droopy because of the boat's lovely, gentle sheerline at the stern. Note the permanent backstay on the mainmast, led to the mizzen jumper strut so the main boom can't hit the stay in a jibe. (© Mystic Seaport Museum, Daniel S. Gregory Ships Plans Library, SP38.51.5)

Starting in the fall of 1936, Francis and Billy put their heads together on their latest boat idea. Billy made some drawings that Francis shared with his father. Nathanael wrote, "I notice his sketches are following the type of extreme racing yachts that have been developed by Stephens, Paine, etc., which certainly cannot make the most comfortable and satisfactory cruiser." And again the world-famous designer recommended that Strawbridge consider his son's Tioga design, albeit with the raised deck that he liked for cruising boats. But Billy, despite family pressures and his designer's dislike of ocean racing, wanted a boat for racing under the CCA Rule. The idea behind the rule was to produce yachts that would make good cruising boats as well as ocean racers. How well the rule succeeded in this secondary objective is a matter of opinion (we see what N. G. Herreshoff thought). The major problem with the rule for producing good cruising boats was that the boats were designed with relatively small working sail areas, in the knowledge that they would be raced with big, largely unmeasured Genoas, spinnakers, and mizzen staysails. Without their big racing sails, CCA boats were not much fun to sail in a gentle breeze. With them, they needed strong, trained, and big crews, rather than just families out for a cruise.[60]

In any event, Francis immersed himself in the fourth rating rule that he would learn (the others being the Universal, International, and Square-Metre Rules) and went ahead on the design. The Depression had forced him to lay off all his draftsmen. The *Persephone* was the first yacht that he had to design all by himself. In the midst of the project, he wrote to his father, "it seems as if I were busy every minute doing the housework, making drawings, tracing them in, going to Boston to have blueprints made, and inspecting the work."[61]

As usual, Francis designed all the *Persephone*'s fittings, down to her three halyard winches. By December 10, he was writing to Billy Strawbridge: "I have been drawing pictures for you for two or three months now. I know I have worked slowly but all the drawings are accurate. I am pretty hard up and any time that it is convenient for you I should appreciate it if you could make me a payment toward the design." Francis may have been afraid that his friend would change his mind again, but Billy, not realizing what it was like to live hand-to-mouth, was in the habit of letting his bills pile up and then paying them all at once. In this case, responding to Francis's request, he promptly sent a check.[62]

The Cruising Club of America was started in 1921 to promote offshore cruising. But almost every cruising sailor likes to try his boat's speed against others; there is no way to discourage racing. Thomas Fleming Day, the first and longtime editor of *The Rudder*, had organized five races from New York to Bermuda in the years from 1906 through 1910, really with the prime objective of proving that offshore *cruising* was safe. The CCA picked up the Bermuda Race ball in 1923, when twenty-two boats crossed starting and finish lines. And if there is a natural law that cruising boats *will* race, there is also a law that boat racing, as it continues, *will* get more complicated. A fairer way to measure different designs and level the playing field is always just around the corner, and that new measurement rule always takes more pages to explain than the one before it. Thus was the relatively simple ocean racing measurement rule under which Francis had designed the *Landfall* in 1931 replaced by a far more complex rule in 1933, the CCA Rule. (And the juggernaut would continue. The CCA Rule was "improved" over the years, making it ever more complicated, until it was largely superseded by the *really* complicated International Offshore Rule (IOR) in 1970. The playing field was leveled; the boats encouraged by the new IOR had less displacement and thus slightly higher average speeds. They also became far less seaworthy and thus more dangerous, as was discovered in the disastrous 1979 Fastnet Race. Fortunately for Francis, his life overlapped that of the IOR by only a couple of years.)

We have seen that Francis was intrigued enough by the 1933 CCA Rule to try a design to it that was the widest boat for her length that he ever designed. But that boat had no customer. Now, he had an important customer, and a friend, clamoring for a CCA boat that might try her luck at sea.

Here is the way the CCA committee members that formulated the new measurement rule in the winter of 1933 approached their task: they based the rule on existing cruising boats that seemed to be fast and seaworthy. They didn't want new boats built to the rule to have an advantage over these good, existing boats. In formulating a new rule on this principle, the committee had the advice of Clinton Crane, John Alden, Olin Stephens, Philip Rhodes, B. K. Sharpe, and Gordon Munroe. The rule expressed "normal" ratios of length, beam, draft, freeboard, displacement, etc. for these good

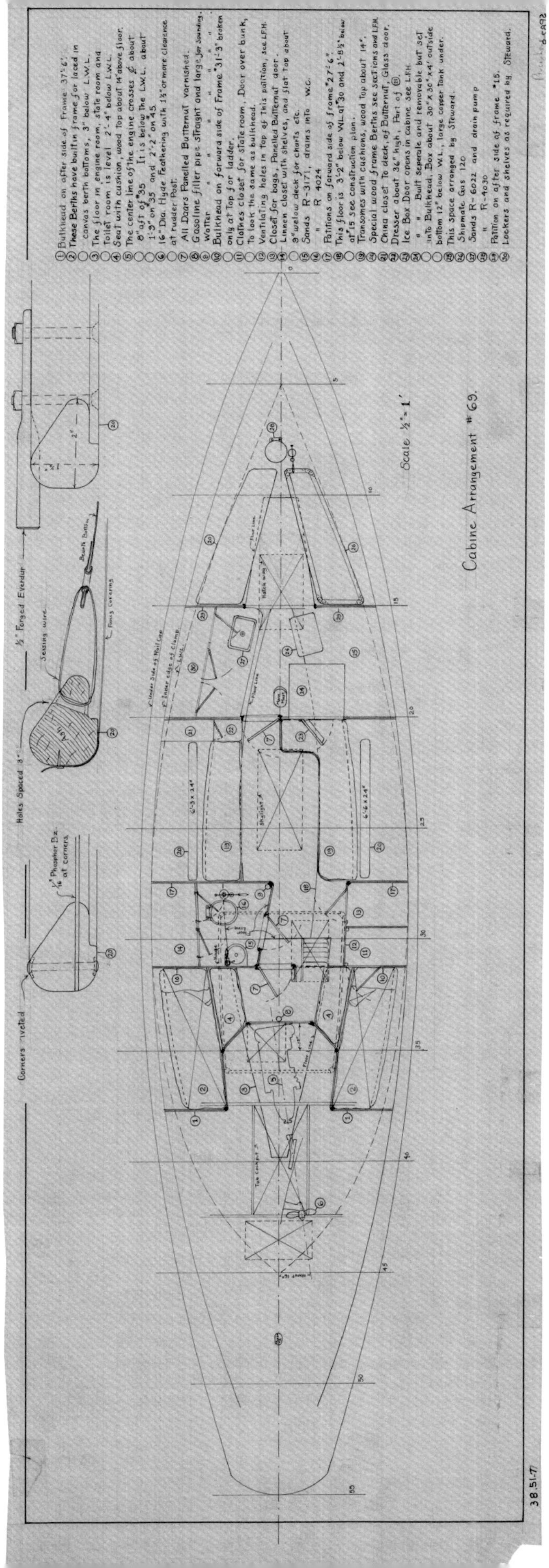

The cabin plan for the *Persephone*. This is the standard layout that most designers used for this type of vessel. The engine room intrudes a bit more than normal into the after stateroom, and the engine itself is canted to drive an off-center propeller, which, as we have seen, Francis preferred to the more usual placement of the propeller in an aperture on the center line. Francis specified a 16-inch diameter Hyde feathering propeller with a minimum of 1½ inches of clearance at the rudderpost. The main companionway is in the forward, starboard corner of the house. The three drawings at the top of the plan show details of the berths; they had folding wood frames, to which canvas was laced. All doors were to be paneled, varnished butternut. Because the icebox was right beside the mast, its door opened into the cabin, instead of into the galley. Francis's detailed "Description of Painting on #69" called for "Wardroom green" in the galley; "Blood red" on the clamp in the saloon, to set it off from the white of the planking and frames, with the partitions to be covered with "tapestry, red and white color;" the aft stateroom to be "Very light green," with a carpet allowed on the sole. The whole engine room was to be in the "Blood red." (© Mystic Seaport Museum, Daniel S. Gregory Ships Plans Library, SP38.51.7)

boats. The rule allowed variations from the norms, but taxed them. An unusual amount of length or draft, for example, would result in an unusual increase in the boat's rating.[63]

The formula for a boat's rating was: .6 √ SA x Rig Allowance + .4L + or – B + or – D + P + F + A + C. SA is sail area, with the spinnaker pole to be no longer than the base of the fore triangle without penalty. The 97 percent rig allowance for yawls is explained in the caption for the *Persephone*'s sail plan. L is the length of a plane 4 percent of the length on the waterline (LWL) above the LWL. B is beam, to decrease rating if more than the norm and increase it if less, with the norm being set at .23L + 2 feet. D is draft, to decrease rating if less than the norm and increase it if more, the norm being set at .14L + 1.5 feet. P is displacement in cubic feet, with less displacement than either of two norms adding to the rating but no advantage given for heavier displacement than the norm. The difference between the boat's displacement and the applicable norm was taken as its cube root and multiplied by 3. The norm was either 1.1 (.2LWL + 5) cubed or (.18L + .52) cubed, whichever was greater. F is freeboard, measured as the average of the freeboard at the forward and after ends of the waterline plus half the average of the height of the rail or bulwarks at these points, with a maximum rail height for credit of 8 inches. Freeboard would increase rating if less than the norm, but no advan-

Billy Strawbridge steering his new yawl. The companionway hatch is open, as is the engine room hatch. Note the set-up on the running backstay: the stay runs through a lead block at the rail and to a tackle on deck, which leads to a winch. The two-part main sheet must also have a tackle on deck to gain purchase when there is more wind than in this photo. (Mystic Seaport Museum, 1973-3-259)

tage was given for higher than normal freeboard. The norm was .06L + 1 foot. If the freeboard was less than the norm, the difference was multiplied by 3 and added to the rating. A is the horizontal distance from the forward end of L to the forward end of the waterline, this waterline length to be measured at twice the height of L above the actual waterline. The rating was increased if A exceeded 8 percent of LWL, and the difference was multiplied by three. This was to discourage an excessively long overhang at the bow. And, finally, C was similar to A, but at the stern, under a different formula. The maximum ballast-to-displacement ratio allowed under the rule was 46 percent. A special CCA committee would enforce the rule; if the committee members decided that the rule was unfair to a particular design, they could adjust that yacht's rating as they saw fit.[64]

As Francis developed the lines of the *Persphone*, he knew that her hull shape could not vary greatly from those of previously designed boats that had raced successfully under the CCA Rule. The *Persephone* is not all that different, for example, from the *Stormy Weather*, designed by Olin Stephens in 1934. In 1935, *Stormy* won both the transatlantic and Fastnet races and went on winning races in a long career that continues to this day. But Francis certainly wasn't copying Olin Stephens. It's just that the CCA Rule naturally encouraged boats of a certain type, boats whose hulls were "normal" and so would rate well under the rule. Yet the *Persephone* is immediately recognizable as an L. Francis Herreshoff design. Her gently curved bow profile, the curve ever changing to nearly straight at the top; her perfect, moderate sheerline; her beautifully rounded topsides; her extremely fair, easy diagonals; all these mark her design as art of the first order.

In July 1936, a major fire destroyed the Britt brothers' 106-foot-long boatbuilding shed on the Saugus River in West Lynn. The fire was started by accident after dark, by young boys sneaking smokes behind the building. Varnish and gasoline exploded, making fireworks that were seen in Salem. Along with the shed went three cabin cruisers under construction. Everything that the Britts used to build yachts was destroyed: machinery, tools, lumber, and office equipment. Records went up in smoke. Among the very little that could be salvaged were two Herreshoff anchors. The loss of more than $100,000 was covered by insurance. A decade after the fire, Francis, who admired the Britts as "real genuine down east Yankees" and excellent, practical boatbuilders, would write, "the Britts were not geniuses at cleaning up and it is surprising that they did not have a fire before."[65]

Andrew and Chester Britt bounced back quickly from the disaster. Before the month of July was out, they wrote to Francis (as well as to other yacht designers): "We want to announce that on and after October 1st we will again be in business at 3 Ballard St., Saugus, Mass. [downstream and across the Saugus from the original yard]. We expect to be able to build larger boats than before as we will have better water facilities than before. Any business that you may send our way at that time will be greatly appreciated."[66]

Francis replied, "no one is more pleased than I am that you have rebuilt and I intend to come to call on you some day soon and find out what your maximum length, beam and draft will be." By late November, he could report to Billy Strawbridge that the Britts were "figuring on the boat." They got the job of building the *Persephone,* and in mid-December were "progressing rapidly and are now laying the boat down [lofting her lines]. On January 7, 1937, Francis wrote to Billy, "at Britts' the deck beams are all [cut] out; the stem and wooden keel; the molds [for the frames] are mostly made and yesterday they were finishing off the wooden pattern to pour the lead into." And on March 12: "The work on the boat is now progressing pretty well—the boat is three-quarters planked up. The single planking is a very good job and very fair." The total bill from Britt Brothers was $16,527.59. Ratsey and Lapthorn at City Island made the

sails, "of the best quality material and completed with first-class workmanship in every respect": mainsail, mizzen, working jib, storm jib, "Genoa-balloon" jib, spinnaker, and mizzen staysail, with three sail covers "dressed waterproof with our own special composition." The estimated cost was $2,060, the bill, $2,095. In a rare piece of self-promotion, Francis wrote to Ernest Ratsey saying that he liked the *Persephone*'s sails and suggesting that Ratsey get a good photo of the boat and use it in an ad. The Herreshoff Manufacturing Company supplied one of their tenders for the *Persephone,* and she would have a pair of Herreshoff anchors—presumably not the ones salvaged from the fire.[67]

Francis expected the yawl to be launched on June 12, 1937, but she was "about a month late at delivery, and the last two weeks of finishing her off were very disappointing, but the owner was very helpful and patient," as Francis reported to Nathanael. As soon as the *Persephone* was in commission at Marblehead, Billy Strawbridge sailed her to Nantucket, where he had a cottage at the village of Siasconset. Francis went along on this first trip in the boat. The sail toward the

---

ABOVE: **Billy's unobstructed view forward. The cabin house is low and small, the wide decks are clear, the low bulwarks show all around. The person at the tiller can really see the nice shape of the boat, as she picks her way through the water. And, on this day at least, there is no dangerous Genoa jib to frustrate looking out. With the companionway forward, the binnacle can be placed perfectly on the centerline. What a pleasure to steer her!** (Mystic Seaport Museum, 1973-3-600) RIGHT: **The *Persephone* on the 1939 New York Yacht Club cruise. Her yawl rig may help her racing rating, and the sail area of much of her spinnaker and all of her mizzen staysail comes for free. Francis objected strenuously to such measurement-rule shenanigans, but he must have appreciated the graceful beauty of a nicely set parachute spinnaker, a sail he spawned (see volume 1, pages 126, 128).** (© Mystic Seaport Museum, Rosenfeld Collection, 1984.187.93855F)

Cape Cod Canal was made in a northeaster under just the small jib and mizzen. After a night in the Cowyard in Duxbury Bay, they went through the canal to Buzzards Bay, where they found the usual chop, pushed up by a moderate sou'wester. Now, with the boat under full working sail, Francis found her "slow, dead, and logy." She needed her big Genoa jib to bring her to life. They motored through Woods Hole and sailed on to Edgartown on Martha's Vineyard. Francis was impressed by the meals served on board. "If the *Persephone* has no other good qualities," he wrote to his father, "she does have a good galley, a good steward, and plenty of food." Then it was on to Nantucket where, at the Siasconset cottage, Francis "made a pleasant visit and saw the baby (about six months old) which Mrs. Strawbridge thinks is just about the most wonderful thing in the world, and I think maybe she is right." Francis was able to return to Marblehead with Joe Santry on board the NYYC 50 *Pleione*, (see volume 1, pages 162-65) which vessel, designed by his father, but not to any rating rule, he liked a lot better than the *Persephone*.[68]

As an antidote to his dislike of a yacht he had created to the CCA Rule, Francis quickly got praise for her. Waldo Brown wrote to him: "I saw Bill Strawbridge's new yawl at Edgartown last week. Charlie [Welch] and I agreed that she was the prettiest boat at the Regatta." A month later, Sherman Hoyt told Francis that he thought the *Persephone* "is the finest thing of her kind so far produced." And she did well on the racecourse. She brought home silver during Marblehead Race Week and won more on the New York Yacht Club cruise, where, in three races, she got two firsts and a second. The first win was in very light going off Newport; she finished forty-five minutes ahead of the second boat. The second was winning the cruising sloops and yawls division in the fresh, southwest breeze of the Buzzards Bay regatta. Next day, though, on the run from Mattapoisett to Edgartown, under the same conditions, she lost her mast.[69]

Francis heard about the dismasting via the grapevine, but he had to wait for a letter dated October 20 before he got the details from Billy Strawbridge. A spreader tip had broken, releasing the tension on a weather shroud, and that was that. All the spreaders were broken in the fall, but there was no further damage and no injuries. Billy was thrilled to win in a boat that he hadn't had time to tune up for racing. Despite the loss of the mast, he wrote to Francis, "I consider the boat a great success." Francis, "a little short of money," had written Billy asking for the final settlement of the design commission for the *Persephone*. It arrived with the letter of October 20, and Francis responded, "thank you sincerely for your check, which is very much appreciated and makes it possible for me to make the last payment on my little house [$250 on 25 Front Street]." Then, he added, "I would appreciate it very much if I could have some of your help and criticism once in a while." Francis, the surrogate father, is reversing roles with Strawbridge; he may have realized that he would not always have help and criticism from his father. He wrote to Starling Burgess: "I fear he cannot live much longer."[70]

Billy Strawbridge was restless; his interest in

LEFT: **The *Persephone* close-hauled in a moderate breeze under working jib. It's 1945, and she is under charter to Cornelius Shields, a top racing sailor; he has quite a gang aboard. Francis specified that her topsides be painted white to show off her shape. The boot top, "about 5 inches wide," was to be in "Marblehead green," the anti-fouling paint on the bottom, "Light Gray." The canvas-covered deck was "Light green." Francis knew he had drawn a pretty boat, and he didn't want somebody painting her black or worse. Actually, he didn't have to worry about the paint job on the *Persephone*: these were simply the colors Billy Strawbridge used on his boats.** (Rosenfeld photo, *The Rudder* (October 1945): 47)

yachting and yacht design fueled a need to keep trying another boat. In the summer of 1939, he chartered the *Persephone* to Philip Roosevelt, a New York banker and cousin of Theodore Roosevelt. This would-be promoter of the 12-Metre Class bought the boat at the end of his charter. He based her at the Seawanhaka Yacht Club at Oyster Bay, Long Island. Roosevelt used the CCA yawl more for cruising than racing, but he did win the Handicap Division, Class I at Larchmont Race Week in 1941. Billy Strawbridge would keep coming back to Francis for designs of yet another boat, both sail and power, but not all of them would be built.

Philip Roosevelt died at age forty-nine a month before the attack on Pearl Harbor. The *Persephone* was laid up and neglected during the war. But in the spring of 1946, she was bought by Frederick S. Ford Jr., the yacht broker in Detroit, and he had her put back in good condition. Ford wrote to Francis: "*Persephone* has proved herself an excellent sailing boat out here [on the Great Lakes]. We are more than pleased with the boat and can't say enough about her ability. She is a beautiful sea boat, dry and comfortable and we have great confidence in her." But Ford was in the business of selling boats, so she was advertised by his associated company, Yacht Sales and Service of Philadelphia, in November 1947 as "Outstanding Herreshoff designed auxiliary yawl, at a very reasonable price." She was bought by Clayton Ewing, an experienced sailor; he evidently modified her rig for Great Lakes racing.[71]

The *Persephone* was apparently sold back to the East Coast, because, in the fall of 1956, she was lying on a mooring off the Nevins Yard at City Island, mastless and for sale again. Gordon M. Curtis Jr., visiting from Los Angeles, spotted her and thought she was "the prettiest hull we had ever seen." She had been renamed the *Vixen*. Curtis bought her the day after his discovery, through Drake Sparkman of Sparkman and Stephens. He rigged her and sailed south to St. Simon's Island, Georgia, for the winter. In March 1957, Curtis, with his wife, three young children, and a hand, sailed the *Vixen* home to Los Angeles through the Panama Canal.[72]

Curtis kept the *Vixen* until 1964. He was commodore of the Los Angeles Yacht Club in 1960, so the *Vixen* became the club's flagship. Under Curtis's command, the "Outstanding Herreshoff designed auxiliary yawl" won thirty-two racing trophies, including Class A in the 1961 Ensenada Race. She finished first in her class in the 1961 Transpacific Race to Honolulu, but dropped to fifth in class and tenth in fleet on corrected time. After that race, Curtis got rid of her mizzen, and, as a sloop, she won five straight races in 1962. Curtis wrote: "*Vixen* will always be a part of our family. The kids who made the trip from Georgia to California now have college-age children of their own, but when the family gathers, the *Vixen* stories are retold! That makes me a pretty happy fellow."[73]

Curtis sold the yawl to Grant Hoag, who took her to San Francisco. In the fall of 1964, she won the Big Boat series on the Bay. Later Hoag headed south on a cruise through the Panama Canal into the Caribbean. At Roatan Island, thirty-five miles off the north coast of Honduras, she was lost in a hurricane. Later on, Francis sold two sets of her plans for $70 each. One of the sets included a requested picture of himself, presented as a gift.[74]

CHAPTER 17

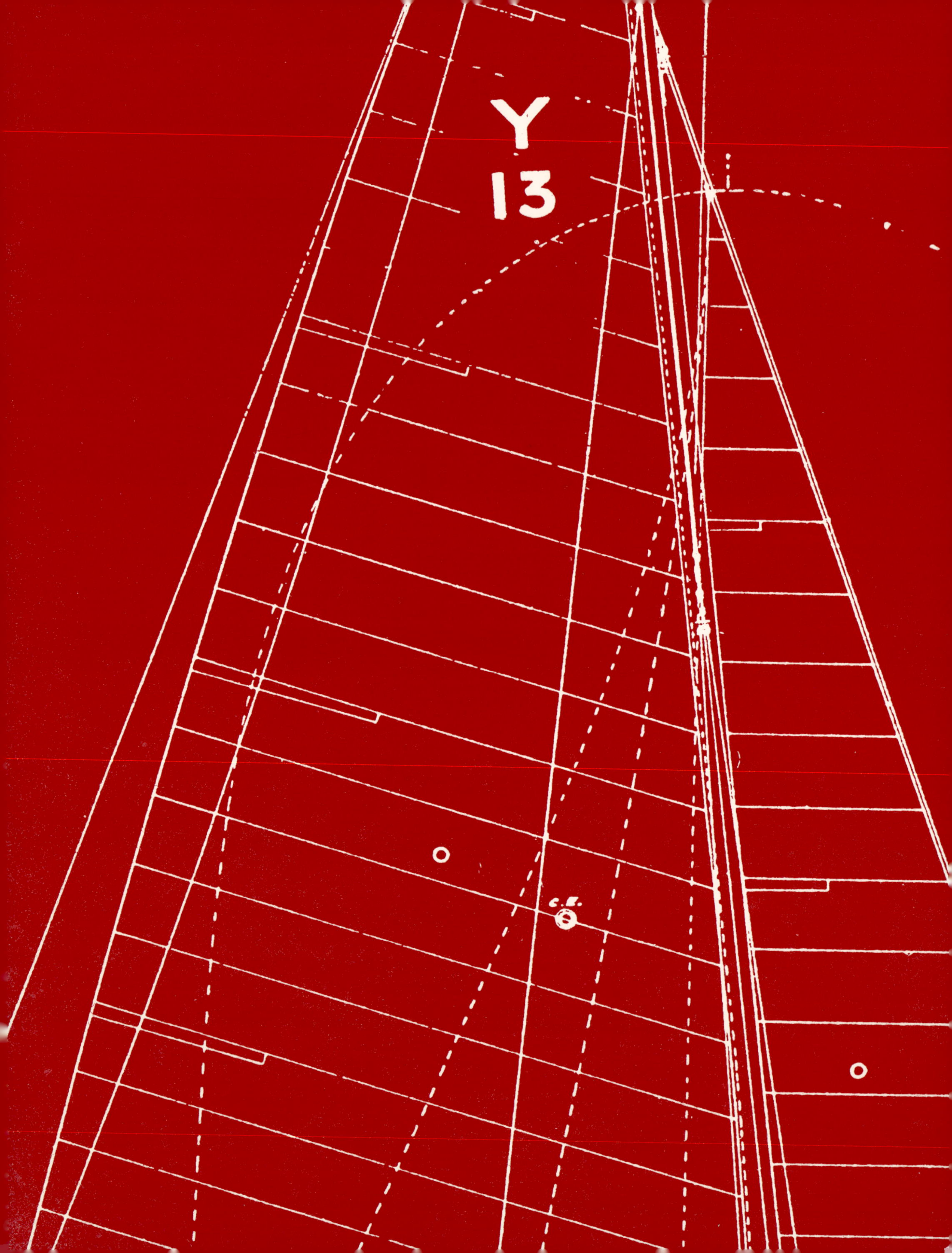
Y
13
C.E.

FRANCIS AND STARLING

"It would take an awful long time to make another man like you and it is doubtful if another one could be made as good."

—FRANCIS HERRESHOFF TO STARLING BURGESS, 1936

"Your friendship is one of the few in all the world which has meant a Hell of a lot to me."

—STARLING BURGESS TO FRANCIS HERRESHOFF, 1936

In 1936, Francis's friend and mentor, Starling Burgess, moved from New York to Maine to work at the Bath Iron Works. The town of Bath had long been a center of wooden shipbuilding, with all its attendant trades, including the making of iron fittings. In 1884, the Hyde Windlass Company expanded into the relatively new field of building whole ships of iron and became BIW. From the beginning, BIW's main customer was the United Sates Navy. In 1904, the yard launched its only battleship into the confines of the Kennebec River, the USS *Georgia*, the Navy's first 20-knot battle wagon. During World War II, a new destroyer would go down the ways every seventeen days. Burgess came to BIW before the war to do experimental design work on his concept for a lighter-displacement, and hence faster, destroyer, to be made of aluminum. His move from Manhattan to the coast of Maine, though it brought him only a bit closer to Marblehead, meant that he and Francis would again spend time together. Francis was more attuned to Maine than he was to New York. He began to drive downeast in his Buick touring car on a regular basis to visit his friend and continue those "talks more like poetry than plain conversation." Francis and Starling resumed a friendship that had started with a teenage Starling bouncing Francis on his knee and had continued with Starling rescuing Francis from the limitations of Bristol and introducing him to a new life in Provincetown and a mentorship in yacht design.

At the Bath Iron Works, Starling began by trying out his ideas for an aluminum destroyer hull on a small scale with the fast launch *Tinavette*, a boat that Francis thought was so fast as to be dangerous. With 230 horsepower, she made 40 knots. Francis was afraid that, in a sharp turn, she might capsize and break up. He wrote to Starling,

"you know it might not take a long time to build another launch like the *Tinavere* [*Tinavette*], and undoubtedly you could build another one just as good, but on the other hand it would take an awful long time to make another man like you and it is doubtful if another one could be made as good."[1]

Francis's concern and esteem touched Starling. The man of many wives and many acquaintances could still be lonely at times. His fourth wife, Nannie Dale Biddle, had a massive temper that could explode, sometimes alienating Starling's associates. She was, however, glad of her husband's friendship with Francis. Starling replied: "Your letter of July 25 is one of the finest ones I have ever received and Nannie and I have read it over and over again. Your friendship is one of the few in all the world which has meant a Hell of a lot to me."[2]

To Francis, Starling Burgess was "Skipper," just as Francis was Skipper to his own friends. The word was then a commonly used form of affection and respect among sailors, especially for the young addressing their seniors. Starling's reply to Francis's letter of July 25 was typed by his secretary, as usual, with "W. Starling Burgess" for him to sign. Instead, he crossed it out and wrote "Affectionately, Skipper."[3]

As they settled into Maine, Starling and Nannie decided to build a house. They bought thirty acres on the Sheepscot River, next east of the Kennebec, within walking distance of "the Prettiest Village in Maine," Wiscasset. Starling designed the Cape Cod cottage himself and sited it with a fine view down across his field to the river. By the winter of 1937, Starling's household expanded: he hired a new secretary just out of school, Marjorie Young. The hiring was done over the phone: "Do you like mathematics?" "Yes," with crossed fingers. Starling, as usual, wanted to pass on his knowledge. Marjorie Young was "right there, anxious to learn anything I could." She checked Starling's calculations, earning a dime for every mistake she found. "He planted a few to check me out," she recalled. Then she began doing the calculations herself and moved into drafting. Starling would show her off to visiting designers as a budding naval architect. He urged them to look at her drawings and write their comments on the corners. He himself wrote, "let every line have a beauty of its own." His brother, Charles, wrote, "always follow the fashion or be damned." Francis wrote, "study the history of the past." After working with Starling for seven years, Marjorie, by then the country's only female yacht designer, became his fifth, and final, wife.[4]

ABOVE: **W. Starling Burgess.** (© Mystic Seaport Museum, 1990.37.613) RIGHT: **Marjorie Young at her drawing board. Trained by Starling Burgess, she became America's first female yacht designer—and his fifth and final wife. Starling warned her that his friend Francis Herreshoff was a woman-hater, but she found him merely shy.** (© Mystic Seaport Museum, Rosenfeld Collection, 1984.187.96027F)

Starling spoke of Francis to Marjorie as a woman-hater. As she got to know Francis, she disagreed. She did find him shy, however, and thus sometimes abrupt. And she recalled: "I didn't feel at home with him at all. It wasn't easy for me to converse with him."[5]

Marjorie Young remembered a visit from Francis that turned sour. He found Starling, Nannie, and Marjorie working on a shed down by the river. Starling's playful side came out. "Starling had this joke going," Marjorie remembered, "that I would stay as his secretary until somebody with a red beard came along. He said 'Francis Herreshoff has a red beard, but someone gave him an electric razor and he may have shaved it off. If he's got it back and comes to see us today, then there's no hope: Marge is gone.' Sure enough, Francis arrived and walked toward us across the field. Starling said, 'I believe he has his red beard. He does! He does!' We all just burst out laughing. Francis was so upset he walked off, got in his car, and drove away." On his six-hour drive back to Marblehead, did Francis realize he had over-reacted or, more likely, did he harbor his hurt? His habit of running away from real slights to who he was, as on that disastrous day on board the *Whirlwind,* could extend to imagined ones. Francis interpreted a joke on Marjorie as ridicule aimed at him. Most people, dealing with friends, could join in the laughter, but not Francis.[6]

Francis aborted another visit when he arrived to find a car with New York license plates in Starling's driveway. He knew that its driver must be Olin Stephens, for Stephens was working with Starling on the design for Harold Vanderbilt's next America's Cup contender, the *Ranger.* The huge J-boat would be built of steel at BIW and would beat the *Endeavour II* in the 1937 Cup races.[7]

Vanderbilt's hiring of Burgess and Stephens, the successful veteran paired with the young up-and-comer, caught the public's attention. Vanderbilt made it clear that they were to be a team and that the details of their collaboration would be kept secret. Yachtsmen wondered how

the two would get along, how the work would be divided between them. How much of the final design should be credited to each? And they wondered why Vanderbilt thought that Burgess, designer of the America's Cup winners *Enterprise* and *Rainbow,* needed help.

Llewellyn Howland III, Burgess's biographer, believes Vanderbilt was worried about Starling's reliability. When the *Rainbow* had been campaigned in 1934, Starling was struggling with his drug habit. He became addicted to pain killers prescribed for his ulcers. Vanderbilt wanted access to the Burgess genius, but he added Stephens so that he would have not only a steady man always on the job, but also one with fresh ideas. Then there was the matter of Nannie Burgess's having blown up at Harold Vanderbilt on board his big motor yacht, the *Vara,* to the extent that she had to be forcibly ferried ashore. When Vanderbilt next came to Wiscasset to see Starling, Nannie turned him away, saying, "I don't care if you're

God Himself, you're not coming in." The incident must have reinforced Vanderbilt's decision to have a backup for Starling.[8]

L. Francis Herreshoff had his own strong views on the subject. He felt that his hero was being insulted. He believed that Starling Burgess needed no help, and though he certainly knew better, Francis would always maintain publicly that the design of the *Ranger* was 100 percent the work of Starling Burgess. After Starling's death, when an editor added Stephens to Francis's published account of the designing of the *Ranger,* he objected strenuously: "I am very sorry indeed that you connected Stephens' name with the designing of *Ranger*, and think it breaks up the six [America's Cup] boats designed by the Burgess family, and has no truth in it. So far as I know Mr. Vanderbilt requested Burgess, when he was designing his

The Stephens brothers, Olin and Rod, with Harold "Mike" Vanderbilt and Starling Burgess on the deck of the *Ranger*, the winner of the America's Cup in 1937. Olin Stephens worked with Starling on her design, but Francis always insisted that the young New Yorker contributed nothing. (© Mystic Seaport, Rosenfeld Collection, acquired in honor of Franz Schneider, 1984.187.79980F)

third cup defender for him, to let Olin Stephens sit in and observe the process of designing a boat, and I am quite sure that each drawing of every piece and part that was made on the boat was made in Burgess' drafting room at Bath. If she had not turned out a success certainly the Stephens's would never have been mentioned, but as she has done well they have tried to take the credit away from my dead friend."[9]

In fact, Burgess welcomed Stephens's help and, as was his habit, shared his experience with the younger designer. Stephens recalled, "we worked in the same room and discussed our ideas as we did the work." Each drew three sets of lines for the J-boat. Models were built to the six hull shapes and were tank-tested. The "winner" was one of Starling's designs, and that was the one to which the *Ranger* was built. Olin Stephens later wrote: "I think my greatest contribution to *Ranger* was persuading Starling to accept the Stevens tank. We had numbers to replace guesswork." Francis would not have agreed that this was a positive contribution. His idea of using a model as a tool for yacht designing was to "tow" one on a fishing rod in a trout stream and carefully observe its wave formation, looking for a clean run with no rolling wake and a slightly lifted forefoot at speed. When he learned of what he called the "very complicated tank tests," for the J-boat models, he wrote to his father denigrating them. Francis claimed that data from models didn't translate accurately to full-sized vessels. This is a mystery, for Francis kept up with technical developments through his reading, and he must have realized that tank-testing was being used successfully on both sides of the Atlantic. But he would rather rely on his own sense of what was right in a set of lines than depend on some mechanical device to tell him whether or not he was right. And he looked down on yacht designers who did so.[10]

Francis was not objective when it came to Olin Stephens; he was jealous. The young designer was phenomenally successful with smaller racing boats and ocean racers. Well, we know what L. Francis Herreshoff thought of ocean racing. Francis believed that it was somehow unfair that the world should beat a path to the door of Sparkman and Stephens, instead of to his own. On his part, Stephens recalled meeting Francis and trying to congratulate him on the success of the *Istalena*, but "he had no time to listen." Stephens was hurt by Francis's snub. He recognized Francis Herreshoff's genius, as he had that of N. G. Herreshoff, and he respected Francis's boldness for experimentation, though he did not always admire its results.[11]

In subsequent invitations to Francis, Starling assured him that "no one else will be present." Francis did return. He and Starling and Nannie would go kayak paddling on the Sheepscot River. Francis spent New Year's with them. And the two men had a practical reason for getting together: BIW engaged them to design marine hardware. In its August 1937 issue, *The Rudder* noted that a complete line of fittings, including blocks, turnbuckles, winches, shackles, fairleads, and cleats, would be available from BIW, "designed by W. Starling Burgess the famous America's Cup yacht designer." There was no mention of L. Francis Herreshoff. And when Francis wrote about the endeavor in "The Common Sense of Yacht Design" in *The Rudder* ten years later, describing the only fittings produced under the arrangement—blocks with ash shells—he made no mention of W. Starling Burgess. Their agreement with BIW specified that all fittings to be advertised in the "Burgess-Herreshoff-Bath catalogue" would be described as being "designed by W. Starling Burgess and L. Francis Herreshoff," with each getting credit for the specific fittings he designed. Francis would have to share with Starling half the royalty on his work, but Starling was not to share his royalty. Such was the clout of fame. And Starling, short of cash as usual, urged Francis to turn in his designs quickly.[12]

The only result of this arrangement, in fact, was one line of blocks, designed by Francis. His ash blocks were smaller and lighter for their sheave sizes than others then available. They had shackles that Francis had developed to attach at 90 degrees in either direction for ease of meeting different rigging situations. They were "easily taken apart and reassembled, which is often an advantage when a block must be put on a piece of rigging which has end fittings that will not reeve through the block," Francis wrote. Beyond these blocks, the project fizzled. Francis blamed BIW's war work. Starling was "very busy working on the plans of a high speed destroyer," as Francis reported to his father.[13]

Starling Burgess was indeed busy in 1937, far busier than was L. Francis Herreshoff. As well as his work on the destroyer, Burgess was, of course, a key player in the America's Cup campaign with the *Ranger.* Yet he had the energy to become involved in a joint project for a day-racing sailboat, a one-design that would, hopefully, appeal to many New England yacht clubs. This was the Yankee One-Design, whose creation would involve Waldo Brown, Starling Burgess, who dragged in a reluctant Francis Herreshoff, Charlie Welch, Frank Paine, and even George Owen in perhaps the most bizarre episode in the history of American yacht design.

On January 5, 1937, Francis wrote to Starling: "Dear Skipper, I believe Waldo Brown is coming down to see you in a few days about a new one-design class that he is trying to agitate. It seems that he has discovered the scheme of going to all the yacht designers to get their ideas for a one-design class and wants them to make sketches for a competition from which he and young Woods at Tech, or somebody else, is to design up the boat especially arranged so that no designer will get either the credit or the money for the design." He went on to ask Starling to use his "pleasant" way of speaking and his influence to persuade "Brownie" to forget about a one-design, but rather adopt a simple, sensible measurement rule, and then he went on to rant, "let everybody design some of the boats and not try to drive the designers out of business by producing a class of boats not designed by a designer."[14]

If Burgess tried to so persuade Waldo Brown, he failed. A week later Brown addressed "Yacht Designers of New England" with a detailed proposal for the creation of the Yankee One-Design Class. The three-page document was the work of the newly formed association's design committee, consisting of Brown, Charlie Welch, and Philip H. Benson, a yacht designer from Cohasset. The proposal called for designs to be submitted anonymously to Brown, as the association's secretary, for a racing boat about 30 feet long on deck, 20 feet on the waterline, with a draft of 4 feet, displacement of 4,000 pounds, and sail area of 300 square feet, and not to cost more than $2,000. Despite the substantial overhangs indicated by these rough length dimensions, "short ends" were recommended. A small trunk cabin was required, more for storage than for cruising accommodations. Owners could choose an open or a self-bailing cockpit; submitted designs could show either. Each designer was assigned a number to be used in lieu of his name, his identity to be known only by Brown. The deadline was February 15, just over a month away. According to the proposed timetable, by June a committee would be appointed "to determine a compromise design which will be secretly drafted." In July, a trial boat would be built to the compromise design and, if satisfactory, scantling rules would be drawn up and the design offered for sale to builders. Money from the sale of plans would be divided (proportion not specified) between the association and all the designers who participated, and their names would be publicized. A follow-up announcement identified the sponsors of the association and their yacht clubs as Brown of the Stone Horse Yacht Club, Harwich Port; Welch of the Corinthian Yacht Club, Marblehead; and Benson of the Cohasset Yacht Club; as well as A. Loring Swasey of the Edgartown Yacht Club; Homer Clark of the Sandy Bay Yacht Club, Rockport; J. Amory Jeffries of the Eastern

Yacht Club, Marblehead; Richard V. Wakeman of the Beverly Yacht Club, Marion; and Walter C. Wood of the Rhode Island Yacht Club, Cranston.[15]

The proposal went out to twenty-four design firms or individual designers. Nothing was sent to the Herreshoff Manufacturing Company, because Carl Haffenreffer was against the project, thinking it was an attempt to scuttle Herreshoff one-design classes, such as the S-boats. Nor does W. Starling Burgess's name appear on the list. Eighteen of the twenty-four designers contributed drawings. Among them were: John G. Alden, Samuel H. Brown, Belknap and Paine, Concordia Company, Samuel S. Crocker, B. B. Crowninshield, Spaulding Dunbar, Eldridge-McGinnis, Furnans Yacht Agency (Gordon Munro), Fred W. Goeller, Fred D. Lawley, Charles G. MacGregor, and Sparkman and Stephens.[16]

L. Francis Herreshoff received the proposal. His response was formal and negative. He addressed his good friend Brownie as "Dear Mr. Brown," and signed his letter, "Yours very truly." He wrote: "Your circular letter of the eleventh received with reference to the Yankee One-Design Class, and I thank you for inviting me to send in my ideas. I want you to understand that I will do what I can to help you, but feel that I cannot enter this competition for the following reasons:

"1. The arrangement for the designing fee is not in accordance with the rules of the Naval Architects' and Brokers' Association.

"2. I feel that I do not want to submit a design that might not be understood and therefore spoiled when re-designed by non-professional designers.

"3. At this particular time I am too busy with my regular work."[17]

Of these three reasons, No. 3 is spurious and No. 1 is sea-lawyerish, but No. 2 strikes at the heart of L. Francis Herreshoff's being as a yacht designer. Starting with his father and continuing throughout his career, he felt that he and his work were not understood. Moreover, Francis was a loner in his work; he suffered no tampering help with the creation of his designs.

Brown had not sent his proposal to Starling Burgess, but he clearly wanted his participation. Seizing on Francis's offer to "do what I can to help you," Waldo asked him to put in a good word for the project with Starling, knowing that the two were close. Francis did write to Starling, on January 28, but not to put in a good word: "Dear Skipper, Waldo Brown and Charlie Welch are coming to call on you tomorrow. Brownie has asked me to drop you a note and I do not know exactly why, but they want your advice about this one-design class business which they are working up, and I hope that you can help them because they might listen to you with your wonderful prestige." He went on to repeat his position, hoping that Starling would persuade Brown and Welch to give up the one-design idea and start a class of boats designed to a simple measurement rule "which all the designers can get something out of instead of adopting a class which no designer can get anything out of."[18]

It is not known exactly what transpired at the meeting of Brown, Welch, and Burgess on January 29, but the two Yankee One-Design promoters succeeded in bringing Starling into the fold. Reporting on the meeting to Francis, he wrote: "I think their idea of a light displacement, thirty foot overall boat with very moderate overhangs is really an excellent one and I am all for it." Brown may have been intending a special role for Burgess from the beginning. He was, after all, the country's leading designer of racing boats. Brown had not sent him the original proposal, but now, in a private arrangement, he asked Burgess to submit his own design, and, despite the talk of an anonymous competition, it is very possible that he guaranteed Burgess that his design would be the one selected, paid for, and built to.[19]

Waldo Brown had started the process of creating the Yankee One-Design with a wide-reaching, democratic organization. He wanted many designers to contribute in order that the resulting design might be seen as exhaustive and the boat might become popular. But he was now realizing the complications of designing a boat by committee. It was too late to turn back. His solution was to enlist one trusted designer, but he couldn't bring himself to shut down his contest publicly, for that would have spoiled the whole concept. So he pretended that the contest was real. Charlie Welch's role is obscure, but it is certain that Starling Burgess was drawn into the deception as a conspirator.

Despite knowing that the competition was a sham, Starling convinced Francis to submit a design. Their relationship of teacher and mentor was still playing out. And Francis was actually persuaded to join the committee of "Consulting Engineers," with Starling and Frank Paine, that would "determine a compromise design which would be secretly drafted," even though each would have his own design in the pot, clearly a case of conflict of interest. What in the world did Francis think of all this? Even without the chicanery, of which he was probably unaware at this point, the idea of "a compromise design" must have appalled him. He certainly didn't want his own design "spoiled when redesigned." But why did this proud, judgmental man agree to act under a conflict of interest? It was a rare case of his abandoning his principles. His often-used strategy of walking away from a situation he didn't like and couldn't control wouldn't work for him, because he was dealing with his three best friends, Burgess, Brown, and Welch. And Starling Burgess was Francis Herreshoff's great hero. Three years before, he had written to his father, "yes, I certainly feel very loyal toward Starling." Francis had to be very sure of someone before letting that person into his life, but once a friend, always a friend. Nowhere is this trait proven more strongly than in the Yankee One-Design affair, where Francis ended up winking at "Brownie" and "Skipper's" dishonest treatment of designers and the public. In any event, the competition for the Yankee One-Design, though now illusory, continued.[20]

After the February 15 deadline, Waldo Brown wrote to the designers to inform them that their work had been hung on the walls of Apartment C at 925 Boylston Street, Boston, next door to, and provided by, the Tennis & Racquet Club. (And 925 Boylston Street was also the address of "Waldo H. Brown, Naval Architect, Marine Engineer.") He invited the designers and anyone else who was interested to view the plans and write their comments, finding "paper and pencils available." A sign on the door read, "Please Leave Brass Knuckles and Blackjacks Outside." According to Brown, more than 500 yachtsmen inspected and commented on the plans. Consulting Engineers Burgess, Herreshoff, and Paine would judge the drawings and comments, Brown wrote. Each of these three would write an article showing some of the designs "to provoke discussion," Burgess for *Yachting,* Herreshoff for *The Rudder,* and Paine for *The Sportsman.* These articles were to appear in the April issues. Brown closed his letter to the designers with irony, thanking each for "your unselfish spirit of cooperation."[21]

Starling Burgess's article is a fine exposition of the design of modest-sized racing boats. He

RIGHT: **The sail plan of the Yankee One-Design. This is design No. XXII in the anonymous "contest" to see which designer could come closest to the Yankee One-Design Association's objective of a racing boat suitable for both the Buzzards Bay chop and Marblehead's light winds. No. XXII turned out to be the work of Starling Burgess, and it sailed right through to final selection, the only modification being a slight extension aft of the cabin house, as shown in this drawing. Sail area is 310 square feet.** (Editors of *Yachting, Your New Boat*, 72)

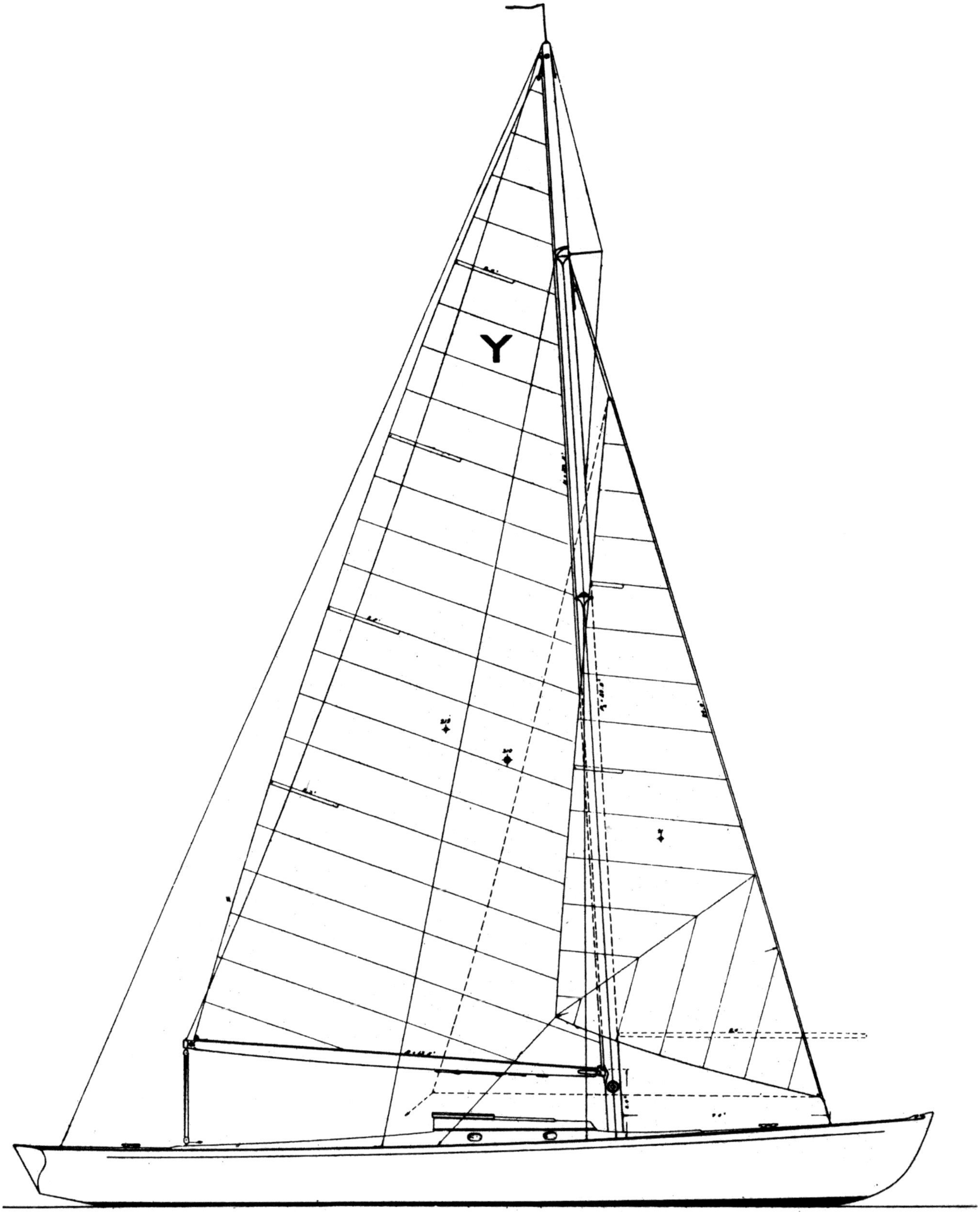
Y

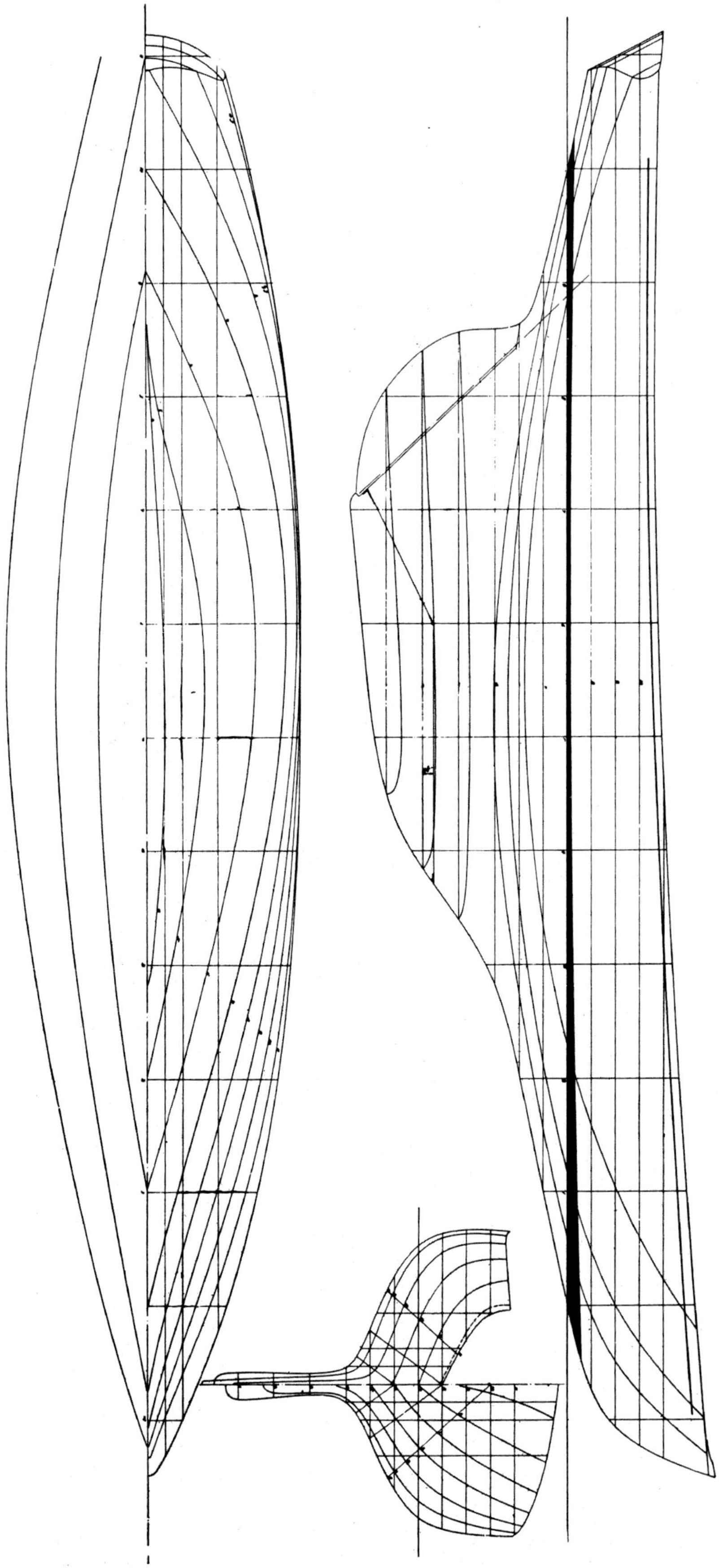

pointed out that boats built to the open class rules, whether Universal, International, or Square Metre, were relatively expensive, and had not resulted in sizable fleets that produced satisfactory intersectional racing among the various yacht clubs. Nor had the one-design classes that had been tailored to local conditions. Gloucester had its Triangles; Marblehead its Marblehead-Buzzards Bay Class M-Bs (which never caught on in Buzzards Bay); Cohasset its 17s; the Beverly Yacht Club its Herreshoff 15s (not to mention a class of seventy-five Herreshoff 12½-footers); Buzzards Bay its Herreshoff S-boats; Edgartown its Interclubs; and Wianno its Seniors. But, as Burgess reminded his readers, none of these boats was suitable enough for racing beyond its home waters to become popular throughout New England. The challenge for the Yankee One-Design Association was to produce a boat that would be able enough for the famous Buzzards Bay chop while also slippery enough for Marblehead's light airs. Burgess thought that the designs that had been submitted to meet this challenge rightly tended toward "small sail area, light displacement, moderate draft, long, easy waterlines, and unusually sweet diagonals."[22]

Starling showed plans for five of the designs. He chose two of them to praise. He said that No. XIII, which he certainly must have recognized as Francis's submission, was "the most interesting." "The designer of this boat has shown real genius as an originator," he wrote. The lines of her double-ended hull he described as "most daring. . . . I should like very much to see her tried out."[23]

Then Starling Burgess wrote a paragraph about his own design. "No. XXII is, to my eye, the most promising of the lot. Handsome is as handsome does, and this boat combines the indicated requisite of hull form and displacement with a grace and shapeliness that could have been conceived only by a designer of wide experience. If her draft is not too great, and her curved transom not too expensive to build, the committee could not go far astray with her." Burgess had a roguish sense of humor, and he may have thought that he was simply playing a joke on everybody, but this situation had the potential for an explosion.[24]

Starling's article must have amazed Francis. He would have known that Starling had recognized No. XIII as his work and been pleased that Starling included it, though the words "interesting" and "daring" did not express approval. And Francis certainly recognized No. XXII as Starling's work and must have wondered at his friend's unstinting praise of his own design. There is no evidence that Francis ever called Starling on this want of principle. Nor did anyone else. Burgess had given his submission for the Yankee One-Design the same beautifully sculpted wineglass transom that he had used on the famous racing schooner *Niña*. Certainly all the contributing designers, and also many readers of *Yachting*, recognized No. XXII as the work of Starling Burgess. Yet nobody blew the whistle when Burgess seemed to be selecting his own design as the winner of the anonymous competition. The designer of the last two America's Cup winners and the primary designer of the next Cup defender apparently could do no wrong. There was no explosion.

Francis, participating in the process, nevertheless was critical, in his article, of the Yankee

---

LEFT: **The Yankee's lines. She is 30 feet, 6 inches long on deck; with a waterline length of 24 feet; a beam of 6 feet, 6 inches; and a draft of 4 feet, 6 inches. Displacement is 4,775 pounds. The committee that set up the requirements for the contestants asked for short ends in order to break away from the long overhangs of the day. Accordingly, Burgess went for a knuckle bow, and he shaped the necessarily large stern transom like a well-rounded wine glass. He had used the same technique in 1928 on the ocean-racing schooner *Niña*, giving her a distinctive look.** (Editors of *Yachting, Your New Boat,* 72)

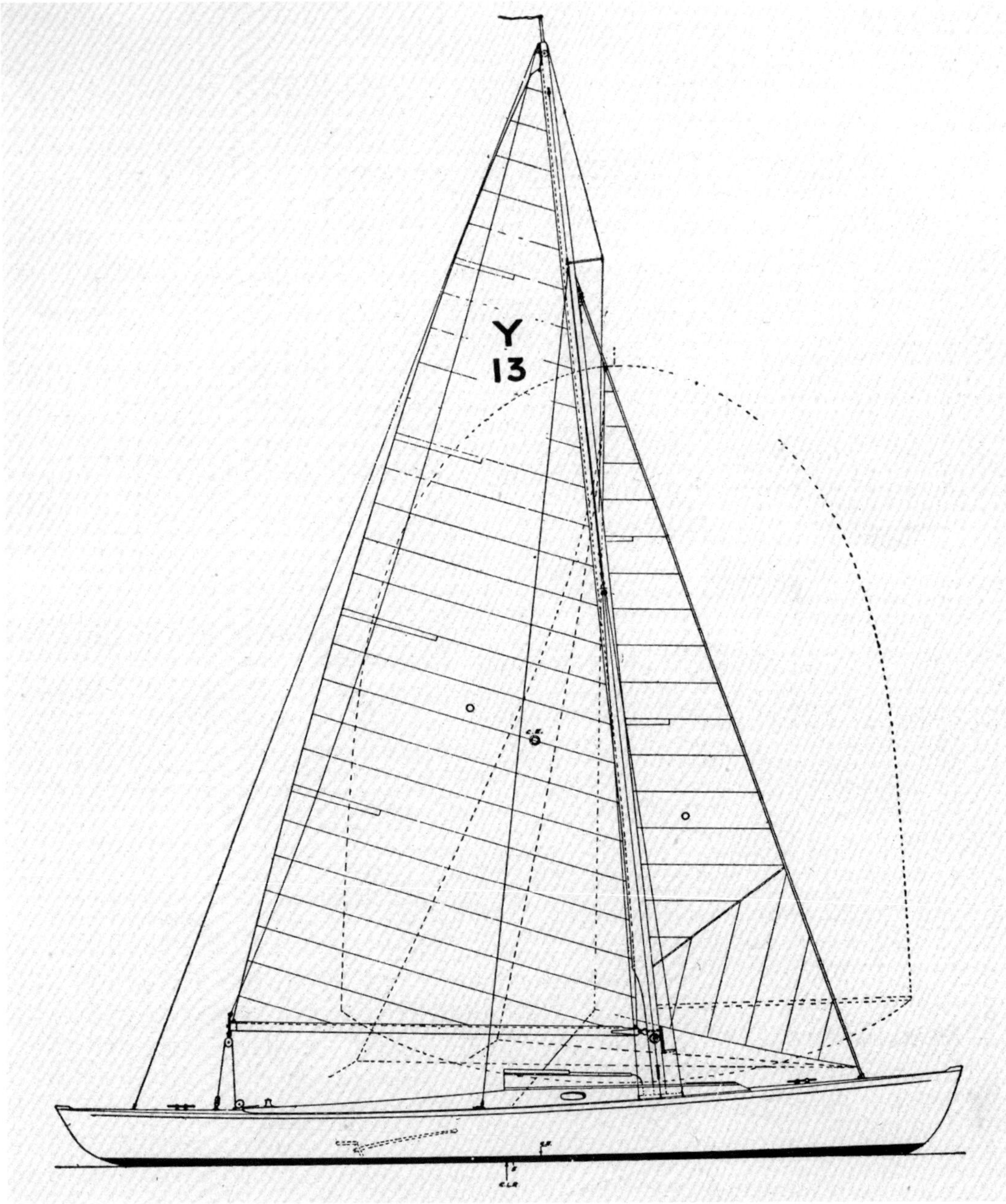

No. XIII was a double-ender turned in by L. Francis Herreshoff. The sail plans of all the submissions were similar, although there was one with a very small fore triangle. Both Francis and Starling gave their masts more rake than the others. The sail area of No. XIII was 316 square feet. Francis has shown a large Genoa jib with a concave leech, and a parachute spinnaker. (*Yachting* (April 1937): 63)

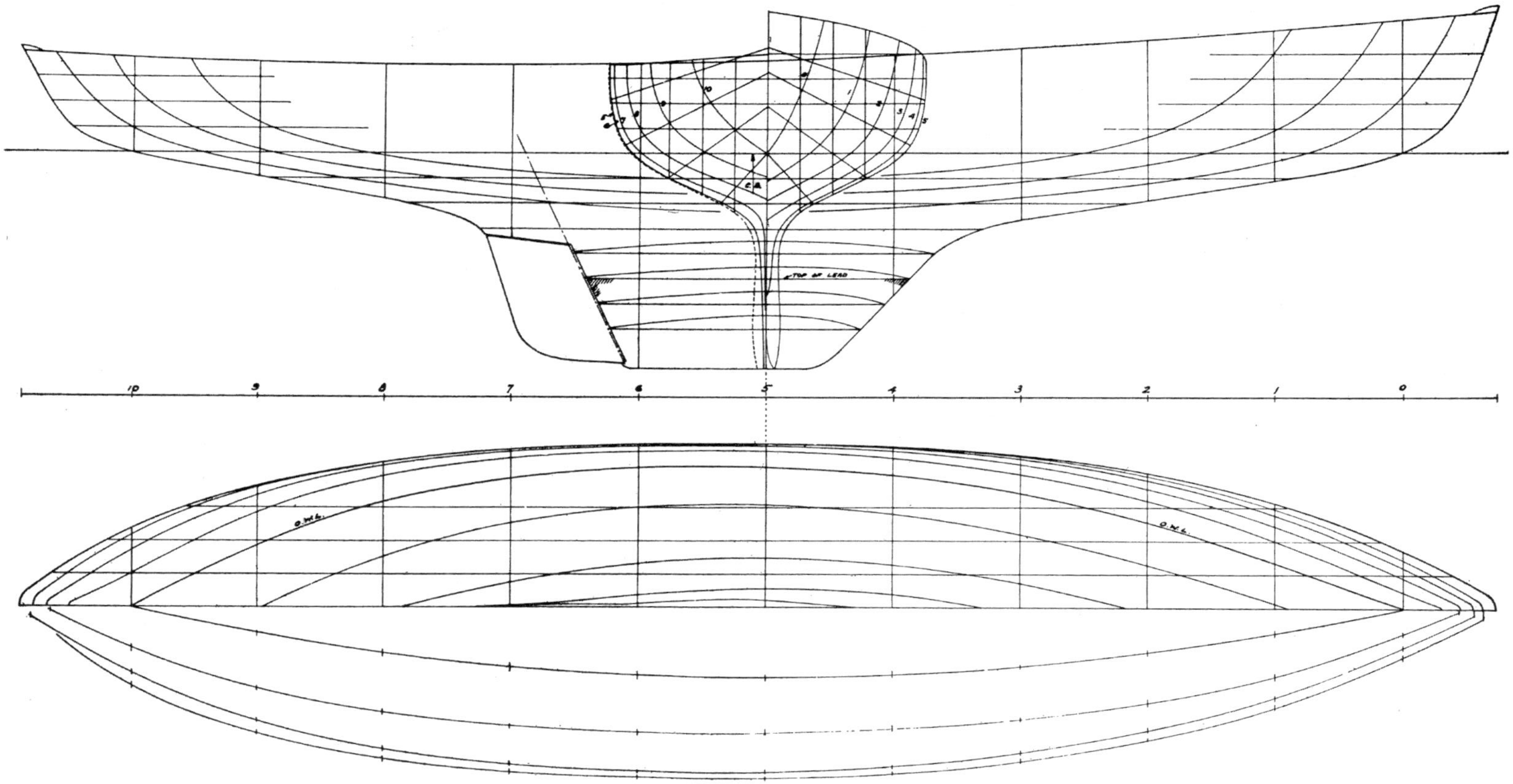

The lines of No. XIII were described by Starling as "most daring." Compared to his design, Francis's boat sits a little higher in the water. She also has a much shorter keel, with less wetted surface for those Marblehead light winds. The short keel brings the rudder far forward, which might have been a disadvantage broad reaching in a busting Buzzards Bay sou'wester. Francis has used his knuckle profiles at both bow and stern. This design not only wouldn't be built, but also would have no influence on the design of the Yankee. She is 30 feet, 3 inches long on deck; with a waterline length of 26 feet; a beam of 6 feet, 6 inches; and a draft of 4 feet, 3 inches. Displacement is 4,525 pounds, with 2,400 pounds of outside lead, for a ballast-displacement ratio of 53 percent. (*Yachting* (April 1937): 63)

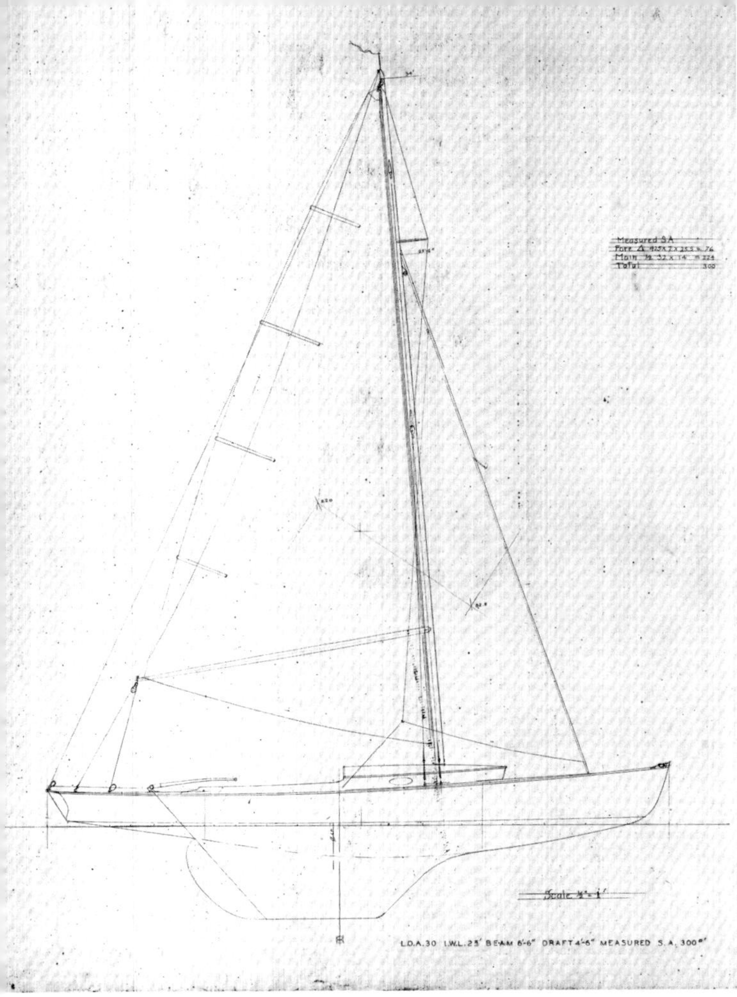

Association's approach. He gave his criteria for the concept of one-design racing, criteria that were missing from the Yankee One-Design proposal. He believed that in order for a one-design class to be successful, the boats had to be truly identical, otherwise the whole point would be lost, and racers who thought they were beaten by better boats, not better sailors, would be dissatisfied and leave the class. To Francis, that meant that all the boats had to be constructed by one builder, but the Yankee Association contemplated many builders. An advantage of a one-design class was supposed to be economy of building, but Francis explained that only after at least six boats were built at the same yard could savings of up to 20 percent be realized. And for the boats to be alike, Francis told his readers, there had to be "class rules which forbid any noticeable change in hull, rig, fittings, or equipment," whereas the Yankee Association contemplated "some latitude in deck plan and lay-out," and Waldo Brown would write, "we will not insist on uniform design of spars, rig [he must mean rigging; the sail plans had to be identical], cockpit, cabin, or fittings." For Francis, this meant that the Yankee One-Design was misnamed, but he did not say that in his article. Instead, he went on to practical considerations: the keel should be designed for easy haul-out; chocks should be extra strong for towing the boats in a row; fittings should be of strong bronze; there should be no sharp corners on deck or below; if the cockpits were to be open, watertight bulkheads or flotation tanks should be installed. "Before closing," he wrote, "I should like to say that all the designs sent in show

---

ABOVE: **Despite his misgivings about the Yankee One-Design Association's approach to one-design class racing, Francis allowed himself to be persuaded into the process and became interested to the point of making this drawing for possible submission. Except for the loose-footed mainsail set on a high-peaked boom, the design is more conventional than No. XIII. She is 30 feet long on deck; with a waterline length of 25 feet; a beam of 6 feet, 6 inches; and a draft of 4 feet, 6 inches. Sail area is 300 square feet.** (© Mystic Seaport Museum, Daniel S. Gregory Ships Plans Library, SP38.225.1) RIGHT: **And Francis even made this fanciful drawing of a possible Yankee One-Design for his own amusement. The humor involved shows his ability at times to descend to the fourth-grade level. He dubbed his interesting, modernistic creation a "4-Place Zumar" to be "Built of Tantalite on the Fibrovascular System." She has his patented double-luff sail with revolving mast, a Genoa jib overlapping the entire mainsail, a steering station up front like an automobile, and a sail-trimmer's cockpit aft. The centerboard houses in the bottom of the keel. In the bottom right-hand corner of the drawing, Francis gives the designer as "Nude Ass Reamus," his childish jibe at the racing-boat designers Knud Reimers, a Dane working in Sweden, and Bjarne Aas of Norway.** (© Mystic Seaport Museum, Daniel S. Gregory Ships Plans Library, SP38.226.1 verso)

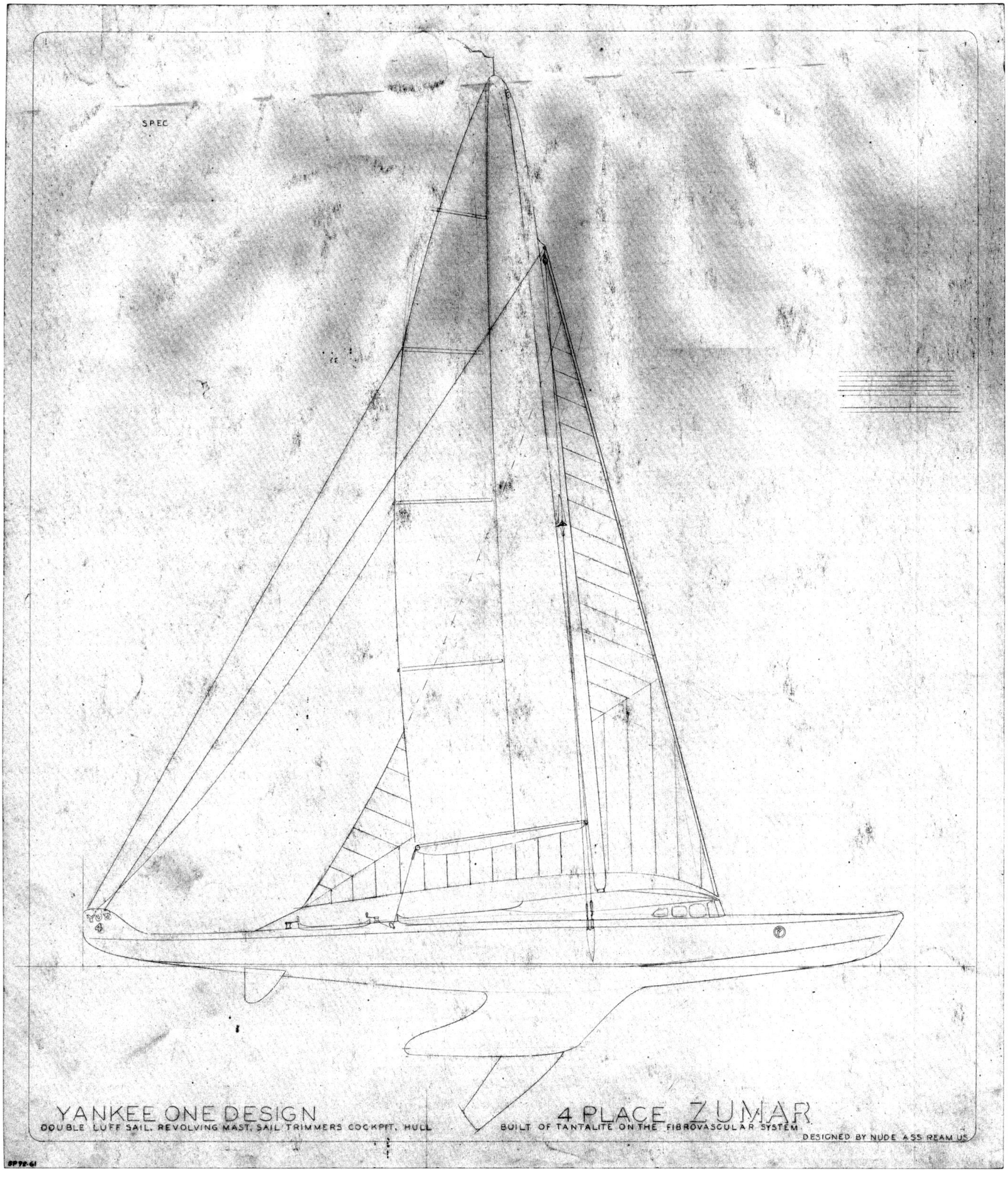
SPEC
YANKEE ONE DESIGN
DOUBLE LUFF SAIL, REVOLVING MAST, SAIL TRIMMERS COCKPIT, HULL
4 PLACE ZUMAR
BUILT OF TANTALITE ON THE FIBROVASCULAR SYSTEM
DESIGNED BY NUDE ASS REAM US

a lot of thought and careful drafting, and the total represents several hundred hours' work of our best designers." How much did Francis know at this point? Perhaps, by now, he realized that the contest was not as advertised and felt a need to show appreciation to the designers, who were being duped. He showed plans for six of the designs without commenting on them. He included his own plans, but not those of Burgess.[25]

Though there was no explosion, one naval architect did make noise. Enough noise so that on June 1, Burgess wrote to Brown: "I am terribly distressed at all this pother. If it will make it easier for you and Charlie (who have been kindness itself to me), and for your Committee, I am ready to tear up my lines and calculations and withdraw. I suppose I shall have to look to you for some remuneration for myself for actual time spent and for Mr. [Geerd] Hendel's [drafting] time. Needless to say I shall be very sorry, for it has all been a labor of love." Then Burgess went on for eight paragraphs detailing for Brown thirty years of "bad blood" between himself and George Owen, who taught naval architecture at MIT. Owen saw what was happening and let Brown know it. The executive committee met with Owen and somehow persuaded him to carry his objection no further.[26]

It is clear that Burgess did not expect Brown to accept his offer to tear up his design. Brown had raised a dozen concerns about the design and, in the same letter in which he offered to quit, Burgess wrote detailed answers to those concerns, in some cases agreeing to make modifications. The only change that Burgess made to No. XXII was a slight lengthening of the cabin house at its after end, and that was his own idea, not one of Brown's suggestions.

When Waldo Brown described in October how the Yankee One-Design had been chosen, he wrote that the committee of Burgess, Herreshoff, and Paine had selected the two designs that best met the Yankee Association's objectives and then, under their "frequent consultation," had their creators make changes toward each other's lines. "These developments were made with the aid of full models made by the Model Department of the School of Naval Architecture, M. I. T." But anyone could see, when the plans of the Yankee One-Design were published in the November *Yachting*, that the drawing was exactly the same as No. XXII, in the April *Yachting*, except for the lengthened cabin house.[27]

Brown wrote: "On or about June 15, a set of lines were decided upon—for the 'First Experimental Boat.' It was found expedient to make use of the excellent drafting facilities established in Bath, Maine for the recently completed *Ranger*, and hull plans were drawn there and lines laid down in the new mold loft of the Bath Iron Works, where, after very careful fairing on a true floor, wood patterns were made of every section, profile (full size) keel, transom, etc." Some readers must have understood the significance of the expediency for using BIW facilities that were right under Starling Burgess's nose.[28]

Whatever deliberations the committee of Burgess, Herreshoff, and Paine may or may not have made, it was Waldo Brown, as the instigator of the Yankee One-Design, who chose the design to be used. After all the plans had been returned to

RIGHT: **Andrew Britt and Waldo Brown admiring the Yankee's bow. Starling Burgess has widened and rounded it at the top, much as he had done recently on the J-boat *Ranger*. She is planked with ¾-inch mahogany over 1-inch-by-1-inch oak frames, spaced on 8-inch centers. With her open cockpit, she did have ⅜-inch-plywood watertight bulkheads fore and aft, as Francis had recommended. The boat looks about ready for her launching on September 18, 1937.** (*New England Yachtsman* (October 1937): 9)

ONE DESIGN CLASSES

Class	*L.O.A.*	*L.W.L.*	*Beam*	*Draft*	*Displ.*	*Sail Area*	*Ballast*	*Cost*
30 Sq. M.	42′	28′	7′	5′	5800	320	Sq. M Rule	$4700
Herr'ff "S"	27′6″	20′6″	7′2″	4′9″	6750	425	Univ. Rule 3350 lb. lead	3290
Aas 5 M.	33′2″	21′5″	6′9″	5′2″	6800	426	Inter. Rule 4100 lb. lead	3200
Y. O. D.	30′6″	24′	6′6″	4′6″	4775	310	2760 lb. lead	2000–3000
M–B	29′4″	17′6″	6′7″	4′4″	4585	360	2700 lb.	2650
Atlantic	30′	21′6″	6′6″	4′9″	3800	378	2000 lb.	1800
Man. 17′	27′6″	17′6″	6′	4′6″		350		
Vineyard Sd. I.	28′3″	18′	7′4″	4′6″	4500	391	2300 lb.	2500
Star	22′6″	16′	5′	3′6″	1500	285		1000
Wianno	25″	17′6″	8′	2′6″	Unk.	Approx. 450	600 lb. iron outside 600 lb. lead inside	2200

their designers, Brown drove his Chrysler Airflow from Milton, Massachusetts, to Wiscasset and asked Starling Burgess to get out his own Yankee One-Design plans. The tube was produced, the plans unrolled, and the two men looked them over and discussed the design for about an hour. Then the plans were rolled back up, put in the tube, the tube went into the Airflow, and the Airflow went back to Milton. It was a copy of these plans that was lofted at BIW where the molds were made to be used by Britt Brothers to build the prototype Yankee One-Design.[29]

The boat was christened by Waldo Brown's wife Frances on September 18, 1937, and sent down the ways at Britt Brothers' Saugus yard. Brown and Amory Jeffries, the Eastern Yacht Club's representative in the association, immediately rigged her, got a tow to Marblehead, and, that same day,

ABOVE: **A table of characteristics of ten one-design classes, including the Yankee One-Design. Only the 30-Square-Metre has a longer waterline, and only the Star has less sail area.** (*New England Yachtsman* (October 1937): 13) RIGHT: **The prototype Yankee underway off Marblehead. She is footing fast with little fuss. Over her short bow may be seen an M-B, with the long bow the Yankee's was supposed to supersede. The Yankee proved faster than both the M-Bs and the Herreshoff S-boats, as she should have, with her longer waterline, yet she has less sail area than either.** (Richard H. Anthony photo, *New England Yachtsman* (October 1937): 6)

entered her in a race of M-Bs and S-boats. She beat the winning M-B by six minutes and the leading S-boat by three.[30]

Francis raised a practical concern about the boat. He wrote to his friend Billy Strawbridge, "the new Yankee one-design boat has been sailing in the harbor lately and has not proved particularly popular because she seems to be high priced." The Cape Cod Shipbuilding Company quoted $1,995 per boat, but the Herreshoff Manufacturing Company wanted $3,275, and only if the order was for at least twelve boats. Waldo Brown gave her cost as from $1,500 to $3,000 "depending on where and how she's built, how many winches you

think you want, etc., etc." Then he went on to say, "Certain extravagances—good sails in particular—are essential to top performance, but why not let the fellow who is tough or smart enough to handle halliards without winches or who can't afford teak slat floors, or folding seats, or New York sails, or trick spreaders, to try to win if he can without them." Waldo Brown's views on one-design class racing were far different from those of L. Francis Herreshoff.[31]

Some forty Yankee One-Designs were built. A builder paid $50 for the plans, the proceeds going half to the association and half "to contributing designer"—which was as close as Waldo Brown would come to revealing his choice of Starling Burgess, who netted about $600 for his work on the Yankee One-Design. So much for all the designers sharing in the income from the project.[32]

The Yankee One-Design is a fine boat, good for both the Buzzards Bay chop and a Marblehead light air, but Starling Burgess's design was perhaps too much of a thoroughbred to achieve the objective of the Yankee Association: to create a boat that would become popular for all of New England's yacht clubs for inter-club racing. And perhaps the looseness of the association's rules for making the boats sister-ships had an adverse effect. Although it has generally become known over the years that the Yankee One-Design is the work of Starling Burgess, it is amazing that, at the time, strong objections were not raised against a contest that had been so obviously rigged. The bizarre Yankee One-Design affair testifies to the strong friendships among the major participants; apparently, only the already-sour relationship between Burgess and Owen suffered. Francis and Starling went on as if nothing had happened. For each, the most important friendship of his life continued.

In this deck view, we see the double headstays and jib halyards so that one jib can be set on top of the other when changing sails; the teardrop-section mast; the shrouds set inboard to accommodate the Genoa jib; four winches atop the cabin house and two more on the inside of the cockpit coaming; the round boom for roller reefing; and the double-ended main sheet, with only two parts; hence the cockpit winches. Four winch handles are stowed on the cabin bulkhead. The possibility of getting all this fancy gear, or not, depending on the size of the owner's pocketbook, resulted in boats that were somewhat different. This may have contributed to the limited popularity of the class, as Francis had gently warned in his *Yachting* article. (*New England Yachtsman* (October 1937): cover)

CHAPTER 18

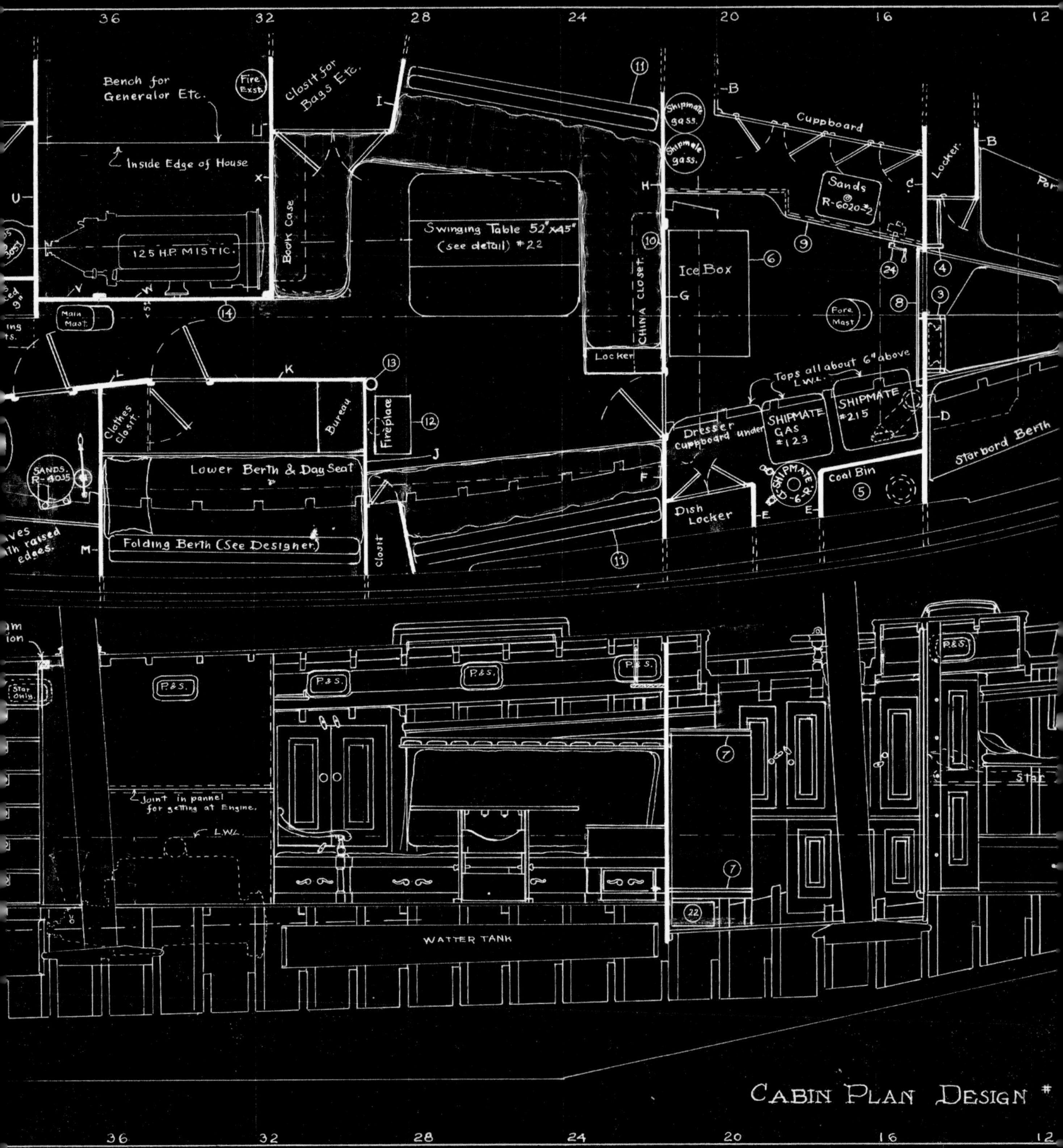

CABIN PLAN DESIGN #

EXIT NATHANAEL; ENTER BORIS

"He Designed Yachts Which Defended the America's Cup Six Times, Several U.S.N. Torpedo Boats, and in All About 2,000 Craft."

—L. FRANCIS HERRESHOFF'S PROPOSED EPITAPH FOR HIS FATHER, 1938

"Your style certainly is refreshing and original. No wonder you are getting to be more and more famous as a writer all the time."

—BORIS LAUER-LEONARDI TO L. FRANCIS HERRESHOFF, 1945

In October 1937, Francis wrote to his friend and customer, Billy Strawbridge: "I am very glad to say I have some work now. It is a schooner, a little larger than *Bounty*—wider, but very much the same shape." This was the *Mistral,* Francis's design No. 73, for Theodore Walworth Little, who had once owned the schooner *Joann.* Little was a member of the Cohasset Yacht Club and was an executive at the Walworth Company, a manufacturer of industrial valves with which his family had been connected since 1842 and which is still going strong, now headquartered in Texas oil country.[1]

After she had started building, Francis sent blueprint copies of his plans of the *Mistral* to Nathanael. This would be the last design of Francis's that the great designer would be able to judge. His father wrote: "The lines of #73 are very fine and sweet indeed!—and may have to go deeper in water than l.w.l. shown to obtain stability for sailing well. However, this is only first impression, and I may be entirely wrong." The father is giving his chosen son unstinting praise, tempered by his usual caveat, but he has softened his warning with tact. Francis replied: "I thank you sincerely for the nice criticism of #73's lines and would say in regard to the stability: 1. #73 has a light but strong hull with weights low and 30% of D [displacement] in outside lead. 2. Hollow spars and light rig. 3. These wide-stern models seem to carry sail well in a breeze." And he added, "some of the forward and after sections of #73 are not so dis-similar to your darling centerboarder 'Alerian,' [*sic*] which certainly could be driven hard on a reach."[2]

Nathanael was wrong in his surmise. The *Mistral* floated high when launched and, presum-

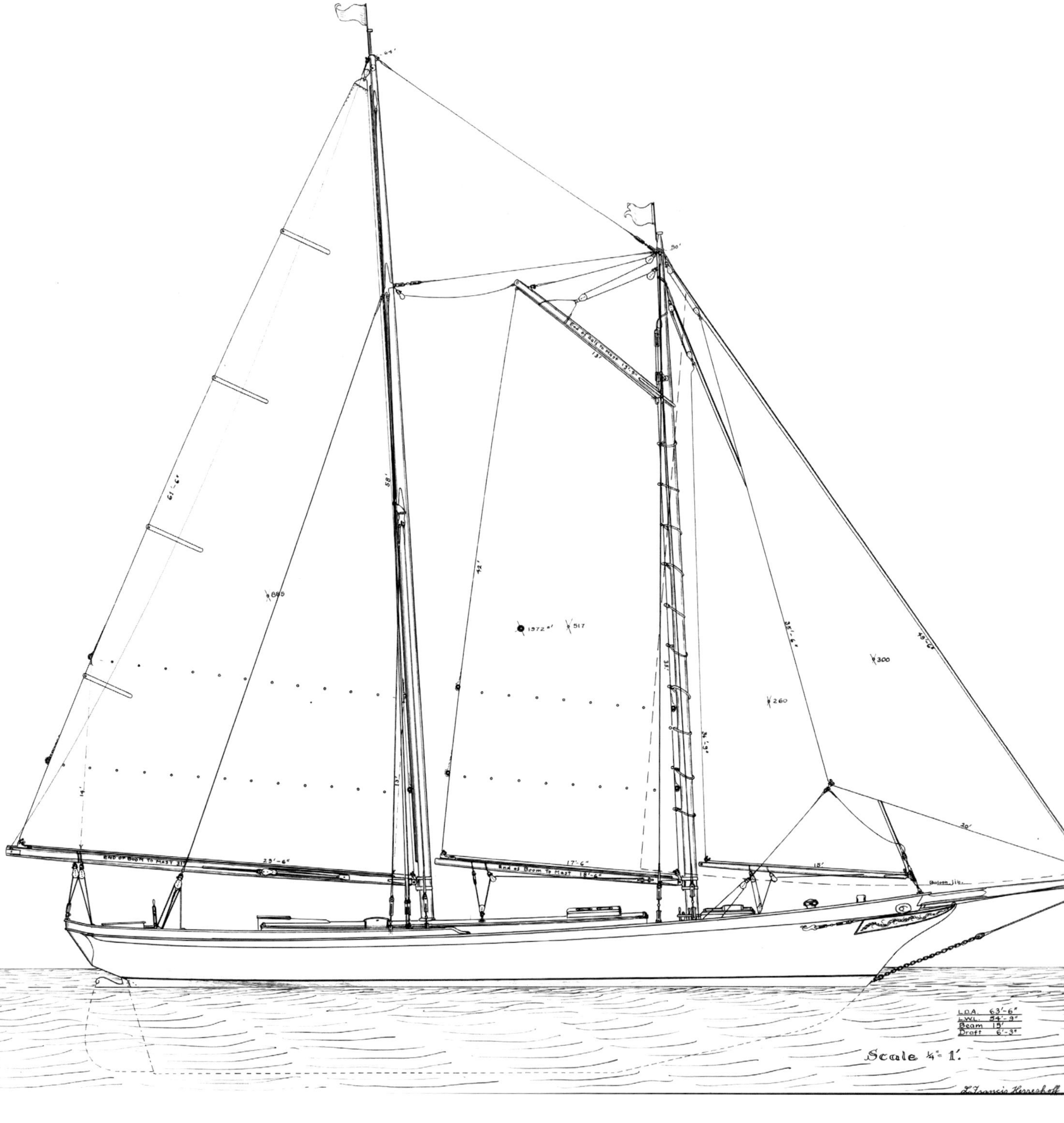
L.O.A. 63'-6"
L.W.L. 54'-9"
Beam 15'
Draft 6'-3"
Scale ¼" = 1'.
L. Francis Herreshoff

DESIGN No. 73 TABLE OF OFFSETS.

Stations	HEIGHTS above and below L.W.L. — RAIL underside of Cap.	Sheer at Deck	6' Buttock	4' Buttock	2' Buttock	Rabbet	Profile	HALF BREADTHS. — Rail	Deck	WL+3'	WL+2'	WL+1'	L.W.L.	WL.-1	WL-2'	WL-4'	Rabbet	Face of stem of keel	DIAGONALS. — 1.	2.	3.	Stations
0	6-8-4	5-8-1				5-8-1	3-9-0	1-0-4	0-3-2									0-1-0				0
4	6-1-6	5-2-2			4-2-0	0-11-6	0-0-0	3-9-0	2-9-4	1-3-2	0-9-0	0-4-0	0-0-4				0-3-4	0-0-4	0-0-6	1-7-3		4
8	5-7-7	4-9-1		4-0-0	1-2-0	-2-1-0	-2-8-2	5-3-4	4-6-2	3-3-0	2-6-4	1-9-5	1-3-4	0-8-7	0-4-0		0-3-4	0-1-2	1-2-0	3-3-2		8
12	5-2-7	4-4-6	4-10-4	1-6-7	-1-0-6	-3-4-6	-3-7-7	6-2-6	5-8-6	4-10-4	4-3-2	3-7-0	2-10-3	2-0-0	1-3-1		0-3-4	0-1-4	2-2-7	4-8-4		12
16	4-10-1	4-0-6	2-11-0	-0-4-4	-2-3-3	-4-2-0	-4-6-2	6-9-6	6-6-0	6-0-2	5-6-5	5-0-4	4-3-7	3-4-2	2-3-2	0-6-2	0-4-6	0-1-7	3-0-3	5-10-4		16
20	4-6-0	3-9-4	0-10-0	-1-6-2	-3-1-7	-4-6-2	5-4-6	7-2-0	6-8-5	6-9-0	6-5-5	6-1-0	5-5-7	4-6-7	3-4-3	0-11-4	0-6-4	0-2-5	3-8-2	6-9-3		20
24	4-2-6	3-6-4	-0-3-6	-2-2-0	-3-6-2	-4-7-6	6-3-0	7-4-5	7-3-2	7-2-0	7-0-4	6-9-0	6-3-0	5-4-1	4-2-3	1-4-0	0-7-4	0-3-4	4-1-3	7-4-7		24
28	3-11-7	3-4-1	-0-10-4	-2-6-2	-3-8-5			7-6-0	7-5-2	7-4-6	7-4-0	7-1-7	6-8-4	5-10-3	4-8-6	1-6-4	0-8-0	0-4-6	4-4-2	7-9-5		28
32	3-9-3	3-2-1	-1-1-2	-2-7-0	-3-9-3			7-6-0	7-6-0	7-6-0	7-5-6	7-3-4	6-10-4	6-0-6	4-10-6	1-7-6	0-8-1	0-5-0	4-4-4	7-11-2		32
36	3-7-4	3-0-5	-1-0-6	-2-4-6	-3-3-0	Straight.	Straight.	7-4-2	7-4-6	7-4-6	7-5-2	7-3-4	6-10-7	6-0-2	4-7-4	1-5-4	0-7-4	0-5-0	4-2-3	7-11-6		36
40	3-5-5	2-11-2	-0-9-0	-2-0-0	-2-6-4			7-2-1	7-2-7	7-2-6	7-3-4	7-2-2	6-8-6	5-8-0	4-0-0	1-2-4	0-6-4	0-4-4	3-10-1	7-10-2		40
44	3-4-5	2-10-4	-0-1-6	-1-4-4	-1-8-3			6-10-5	6-11-6	6-11-4	7-0-6	6-4-4	6-1-6	4-8-2	2-9-6	0-10-0	0-5-5	0-4-0	3-3-3	7-6-0	7-6-0	44
48	3-3-2	2-10-2	0-6-4	-0-7-0	-0-6-3	-5-1-6		6-6-0	6-7-4	6-7-3	6-8-1	5-5-4	5-2-0	3-1-5	1-7-3	0-7-0	0-4-4	0-3-1	2-7-0	7-0-4	7-1-4	48
52	3-4-3	2-10-6	1-6-4	0-3-4	0-6-3	-5-3-0		6-0-0	6-2-0	6-1-3	6-1-7	3-5-3	3-1-0	1-5-0	0-10-0	0-4-5	0-3-5	0-2-3	1-9-2	6-4-0	6-7-2	52
56	3-5-3	3-0-4		1-2-4	1-7-2	-3-3-0	6-3-0	5-4-6	5-7-1	5-7-1	5-3-2	0-1-7	1-0-3	0-5-7	0-4-2	0-3-1	0-3-4	0-1-6	0-10-4	5-4-2	6-0-0	56
60	3-7-4	3-3-7		2-1-6	2-6-2	1-0-6	0-11-3	4-7-2	4-11-1	4-11-2	3-6-4		0-0-0	0-1-4	0-1-6	0-1-6	0-3-4	0-0-0		4-3-2	5-3-4	60
63'-6"	3-11-0	3-8-0		3-0-0		2-3-5	2-3-4	4-0-0	4-4-1	3-11-0							0-3-4			3-0-0	4-7-0	63'-6"

L. Francis Herreshoff

SHEET 3 #73

LEFT: The *Mistral* was the sixth of the ten clipper-bowed yachts that Francis designed. She shares the schooner rig with the first one, the *Joann*; all the rest were ketches, except one sloop, not built. The *Mistral* was design No. 73, for Theodore W. Little of Boston and Cohasset. Her rig could not be more straightforward, other than making her the leg-o'-mutton ketch that Francis favored, but Little, a former owner of the *Joann*, had to have a schooner. He asked Francis to draw up a staysail schooner rig, too, but chose instead the traditional gaff foresail. Note the vang to keep the twist out of the tall, narrow sail. Francis shows just one light sail, a jib filling a bit more than the fore triangle. Sail area is 1,972 square feet, with 895 in the mainsail, 517 in the foresail, 260 in the forestaysail, and 300 in the jib. Francis advised Ratsey sails, as usual, but Little used the Boston firm of Cousens and Pratt, where he had a friend. (© Mystic Seaport Museum, Daniel S. Gregory Ships Plans Library, SP38.182.3) ABOVE: The table of offsets that Francis drew up for the *Mistral*. Working alone, Francis measured 299 points on his lines drawing, being heights of the buttock lines above and below the load waterline, half breadths of the waterlines out from the centerline, and locations of the diagonals, at seventeen stations along the length of the hull. His lines drawing, at a scale of ½ inch to the foot, was just under 32 inches long, one-twenty-fourth of the length of the vessel. So Francis multiplied the location of each point on his drawing by 24 to give, in feet, inches, and eighths, the dimensions to be used by the Britt Brothers loftsman to create, on a white-painted floor, his lines drawing at full scale. The enlargement of 24 times made the lofted lines 63½ feet long. Builders judged designers by the accuracy of their offset tables. Errors could creep in, and Francis had to be extra careful because of his dyslexia. He could easily measure, multiply, and think, "1' 2⅜"," but write "1-3-2" instead of "1-2-3." A loftsman sometimes had to use his own judgment. He, too, could make errors, and then blame the designer for the resulting unfairness in the lines. Two different builders, working from the same set of offsets, might have very different opinions of their accuracy. No designer was perfect. L. Francis Herreshoff, despite his handicap, seems to have been above average. (© Mystic Seaport Museum, Daniel S. Gregory Ships Plans Library, SP38.182.4)

ably, was ballasted down to her designed waterline, but surely not more. In any event, her sailing qualities elicited no complaints. Nathanael was used to judging hull shapes and waterlines by model, not by a two-dimensional drawing.

By December, Francis could write to his father: "They [Britt Brothers] are progressing quite rapidly with the boat [*Mistral*] and she is half planked up. Her planking below the floor is very nice yellow pine and above that it is fir. So far all of the framing, floors and everything is as good as I have ever seen, and because there are so few boats being built it seems possible to get very good materials." She was launched in late May 1938. When she was rigged, she sported Francis's special ash-cheeked blocks, made at the Bath Iron Works. Her cost was $45,000.[3]

The *Mistral* has had a long career under a series of owners. Marblehead was her home port for years. In 1976, she was donated to the US Naval

ABOVE: **The *Mistral* under construction at the new Britt Brothers yard at Saugus. The frames have been set up, ribbands sprung round them, and planking has started. At this point, the designer can begin to see what the shape of the vessel he has drawn on paper will actually look like.** (Mystic Seaport Museum, 1973-3-247) RIGHT: **The schooner, with her masts laid out on deck, ready to launch.** (© Mystic Seaport Museum, 1993.120.3.151)

Academy by Robert Scarborough of Wilmington, Delaware. Midshipmen, under professional skipper Louise K. Burke, sailed her hard for three years, including a crossing to Ireland and participation in the Silver Jubilee of Queen Elizabeth II. Back in private ownership, there was a major rebuild, from 1997 to 1999. She had more restoration work done in Germany in 2007 and 2008. She is currently listed for sale in Germany for a million dollars. And the *Mistral* has been duplicated, as was the *Ticonderoga*, by Legendary Yachts of Washougal, Washington.

The designing and building of the *Mistral* was a straightforward project for Francis. There was no annoyance with the owner and none of the drama surrounding the creation of some of his racing boats or of, say, the *Ticonderoga*. The *Mistral* is simply a fine schooner still sailing after seventy-five years. She is a good example of the ability of a beautiful yacht to generate love and money to achieve happy owners and long life. L. Francis Herreshoff would be proud to know that she has outlasted him by many years.

Francis had a rare visit from members of his family at 25 Front Street on Sunday, May 1, 1938. His brother Sidney and his wife Becky, with their sons Nathanael III and Halsey, and also his sister Agnes, arrived from Bristol and "only stayed a short time," as Francis reported to his father. Francis didn't remember his nephews' names; he thought one of them must be another Sidney. There wasn't a lot of socializing in the Herreshoff family. The best times had been the holiday gatherings in past years at Love Rocks. Francis "enjoyed hearing about old times" on those occasions and even

sometimes allowed himself to be the center of attention when he spun a yarn. In 1937, Nathanael's wife Ann wrote to Francis that his younger brother Clarence was coming for Christmas and hoped Francis would too. He answered that he would "and will be very glad to see Clarence again." Yet Francis didn't have much good to say about the older brothers who had bullied him as a child. Nathanael Jr. had died and Griswold was pursuing his own career in Detroit, but "Mr. Sidney" was designing yachts at the Herreshoff Manufacturing Company. Francis respected Sidney's ability as a yacht designer—a Herreshoff yacht designer—but there was for Francis a painful gap between

The *Mistral* close-hauled under plain sail in a gentle breeze. Francis did not approve of painting her black, but he would have liked the white bulwarks and taffrail. (© Mystic Seaport Museum, 1990.37.133)

that respect and his distant relationship with his brother, a gap that was particularly painful because of the potential for sharing their life work had it not existed. Francis largely felt himself an outsider and was embarrassed to talk about his insular family.[4]

His connection with his nephew, Halsey, would be a little better. Here was a younger Herreshoff yacht designer on whom Francis could practice a bit of the mentoring he enjoyed. On visits to his uncle, Halsey recalled, "He talked, and I listened." Francis wrote to his friend Bror Tamm, "my nephew was here and varnished a pair of rowing oars and I had a nice time talking with him." Francis always had his drink of rum and never offered Halsey any. Francis explained to his nephew, "Any man who drinks rum before he's forty is a fool, and any man who doesn't drink rum after he's forty is a fool." Halsey had great respect for his uncle and was always puzzled by the tension between Francis and the rest of the family[5]

Despite Francis's tensions with his father, it was Nathanael with whom Francis was closest in the family. He could, on rare occasions, share emotions with his father. He wrote to Nathanael, "you can rest assured that I am about as happy as it would be possible for a man of my nature to be." It was Nathanael, not Sidney, who received copies of Francis's drawings of yachts and commented on them. Despite Nathanael's initial denial of Francis's talent—a denial for which he never apologized and about which Francis never reproached his father—and despite Nathanael's display at times of needing to compete with his son, his criticism was important to Francis. But in early 1938, Nathanael's health was failing.[6]

The great yacht designer's body was winding down. He retained his interest in his work to the end. In the same letter in which he praised his son's lines drawing of the *Mistral,* he wrote: "The last two years, I have been much interested in design for a yacht or scientific research vessel and when you come again—soon I hope, I will be pleased to show and explain to you what I have done—if I can remember. But memory is going fast. I don't grow any stronger, and at present cannot stand alone—lost sense of balancing myself."[7]

Francis did not respond quickly to this moving message. It would be two months before he made another trip from Marblehead to Bristol. He visited his father on his ninetieth birthday, March 18, 1938. "He was propped up in bed and seemed very happy. We had a nice chat that day," Francis recorded later. He would remark on how "short-spoken" his father generally was, "but in the very last of his life he became quite a good deal more talkative." Nathanael Greene Herreshoff died on June 2, 1938.[8]

Francis proposed a lengthy epitaph for his father's headstone: "He Designed Yachts Which Defended The America's Cup Six Times, Several U.S.N. Torpedo Boats, and in All About 2,000 Craft." But it was Griswold's simpler "Yacht Designer and Marine Engineer of International Fame" that was carved.[9]

Over the years, the testy relationship between Francis and Nathanael had grown into an amiable one. Francis would send kind greetings to Nathanael on Father's Day, and they would be reciprocated on Francis's birthday. Yet, Nathanael's narcissism and Francis's resentment had proved to be insurmountable barriers to intimacy. That resentment over being sent to The Farm festered, because Francis had never had it out with his father; that kind of confrontation was not the fashion. Nathanael's genius had been an inspiration, but Francis had been his own man. Nathanael had been a valuable sounding board, but his criticism had no censorial effect. Francis had perhaps never drawn a line at his drafting table without wondering what his father might think of it, but such wondering had never caused him to change a line. Francis had shown that he shared the Herreshoff genius; his regret was that his father had never acknowledged it.[10]

And now there was no chance for such recognition. His father was gone. There would be no

ABOVE: Fortunately, the *Mistral* did not keep her black paint long. Her white topsides show off her hull shape to advantage. Her crew is experimenting with a balloon main topmast staysail, or "golliwobbler," used as a spinnaker, hoisted to both mastheads, tacked down to the bowsprit, and sheeted to the main boom, which has been eased off to trim it properly. The big sail, set all by itself, seems to be pulling her along nicely. (© Mystic Seaport Museum, 1990.37.601) RIGHT: Nathanael Greene Herreshoff at about eighty-five. (Mystic Seaport Museum, 1990.37.601)

more "affectionately" signed letters, no more praise, no more of his father's self-promoting criticisms. Francis would miss all these things. His father's death began a melancholy period in Francis's life. The work he did at his drawing board, or at his lathe for that matter, would not suffer, but there would be less of it. It would be four years before Francis produced another significant yacht design. And it would be eleven years before Francis could manage a catharsis of his troubling relationship with his father: he would then begin to write an admiring biography of the man he considered to be the highest-achieving yacht designer the world had known.

Six years before his death, Nathanael had made an extensive will. His wife Ann and his daughter Agnes were to have lifetime use of Love Rocks. Ownership of The Farm, where Francis had lived and worked in exile, was to be shared equally among the five surviving children, but, perhaps in recognition of the inappropriate assignment of Francis to that farm, Nathanael gave him all of his one-eighth interest in Point Pleasant Farm on Poppasquash Neck. Nathanael itemized sixteen of his personal possessions to go to his children, matching them to their interests. Francis was given bound volumes of the journal of the Society of Naval Architects and Marine Engineers, along with three antique guns. Sidney received his father's instruments for taking the offsets from hull models, including the pantograph and planimeter. Clarence, who worked on plans for ships instead of yachts, got "the three great volumes of Naval Architecture by John Scott-Russell, these volumes being now rare and valuable."[11]

Nathanael's estate, valued at nearly $500,000, would be held in trust, the principal to be maintained, with its income to be divided among his wife, children, and the two daughters of his deceased son, Nathanael Jr. Francis's share was just under 12 percent. He could expect a modest addition to his annual income. And when Ann Roebuck would pass away in 1954, Francis would

inherit money that would give him an annual income of about $6,000. He was never on easy street, but he was then assured that he could live as he wished, making a modest living from his design work and his writing for *The Rudder*. As we shall see, Francis could even indulge his fascination with European sports cars, his only financial extravagance.[12]

Less than a year after his father's death, Francis lost another important figure in his life. On April 4, 1939, the US Navy's newest aircraft carrier, the USS *Wasp* (CV-7), was launched at the Fore River Shipyard at Quincy, Massachusetts. As part of the ceremony, witnessed by many thousands, six SBU-2 biplanes, from the training squadron at nearby Squantum, flew over the ship in formation at 3,000 feet. One was piloted by flight instructor Waldo Brown, back on active duty.

As the planes turned back over the launching, one of Brown's wingtips struck a wingtip of the plane next to him. Brown's biplane went out of control into a dive. By the time he bailed out, he was too low. His chute hardly opened. He hit the ground and was killed. Lieutenant-Commander Brown was forty-two. His plane crashed, killing his observer, Aviation Chief Carpenter's Mate Walter Kirk. Cadet Pilot Ellsworth Benson, flying the other biplane, struggled in vain to regain control. The plane crashed, killing Benson and his observer, Aviation Chief Machinist's Mate John Aussiello. Both crashes were in a residential neighborhood. One resident had a near miss and suffered a fatal heart attack. Another met the same fate as he ran toward a burning airplane to try to help.[13]

The navy's investigation of the accident assigned no blame. But the families of Brown and Benson each blamed the other pilot. It took years for them to realize that, like most such accidents, this one could have been prevented by either party.[14]

Francis had lost his friend Brownie, with whom he had sailed in the schooner *Joann*, which they had designed together (without admitting it); for whom he had designed the fabulous *Tioga*; with whom he had argued about jib trim in the 30-Square-Metre *Gem*; and with whom he had survived the strange experience of the creation of the Yankee One-Design. Waldo Brown had been important: without Waldo, there would perhaps never have been a clipper-bowed yacht designed by L. Francis Herreshoff.

The Browns had a family legend that Francis proposed unsuccessfully to Waldo's widow, Frances. Waldo's son John remembered that "my father hadn't been dead a month before Francis Herreshoff came around at Milton to see what was what." All that we know about Francis's relationship to Frances is that he admired her for being "a brave little soul," when a squall scattered her four-course meal all over the schooner *Joann*'s galley floor (see volume 1, page 111). While it is possible that there was more than simple admiration involved, and even that her Ford Motor Company fortune may have lurked in the background, it is hard to ascribe truth to the legend, given the degree of Francis's shyness with women and his affinity for his independent life. In any event, Frances Gray Brown returned home to Detroit and married a doctor.[15]

Francis's inheritance from his father, though modest, helped him through an especially lean period. It was 1940, two years after his father's death, before any yacht design work came his way, in the form of a one-design racing class for Northeast Harbor, Maine. The boat was Billy Strawbridge's idea. He had a summer place at Northeast Harbor, and he wanted his friend Francis to make the design. Francis obliged with one of his most conventional creations, a small version of an R-boat or Q-boat, but with none of the exceptional features of his R-boat *Live Yankee* or his Q-boat *Nor'easter V*. She was simply a lovely, long-ended, narrow sloop, like a lighter version of a Universal Rule boat, but with an inboard rig, akin to that of a Square-Metre boat.[16]

Henry R. Hinckley's nearby Manset Boat Yard was the logical choice as builder. The yard turned out two boats to Francis's plans, backed up by his detailed construction notes. Hinckley's designer was Cyrus Hamlin, so it was he who had the unenviable task of relaying to L. Francis Herreshoff an owner's suggestion of adding a Genoa jib to the boat's simple sail plan. Francis complied, but he wrote Hamlin a whole page of reasons why a big, overlapping jib wasn't a good idea for the class. He explained that Strawbridge wanted to keep the boats "simple and practical" and that "a lapping jib is a nuisance and of course should not be used if the others do not have them."[17]

The class never went beyond the two boats. By the time they were launched for the 1941 season, yachtsmen were already being recruited for far more serious work than racing their sailboats around the buoys of a summer afternoon. Strawbridge himself had been pestering the Navy Department for a commission. Francis thought

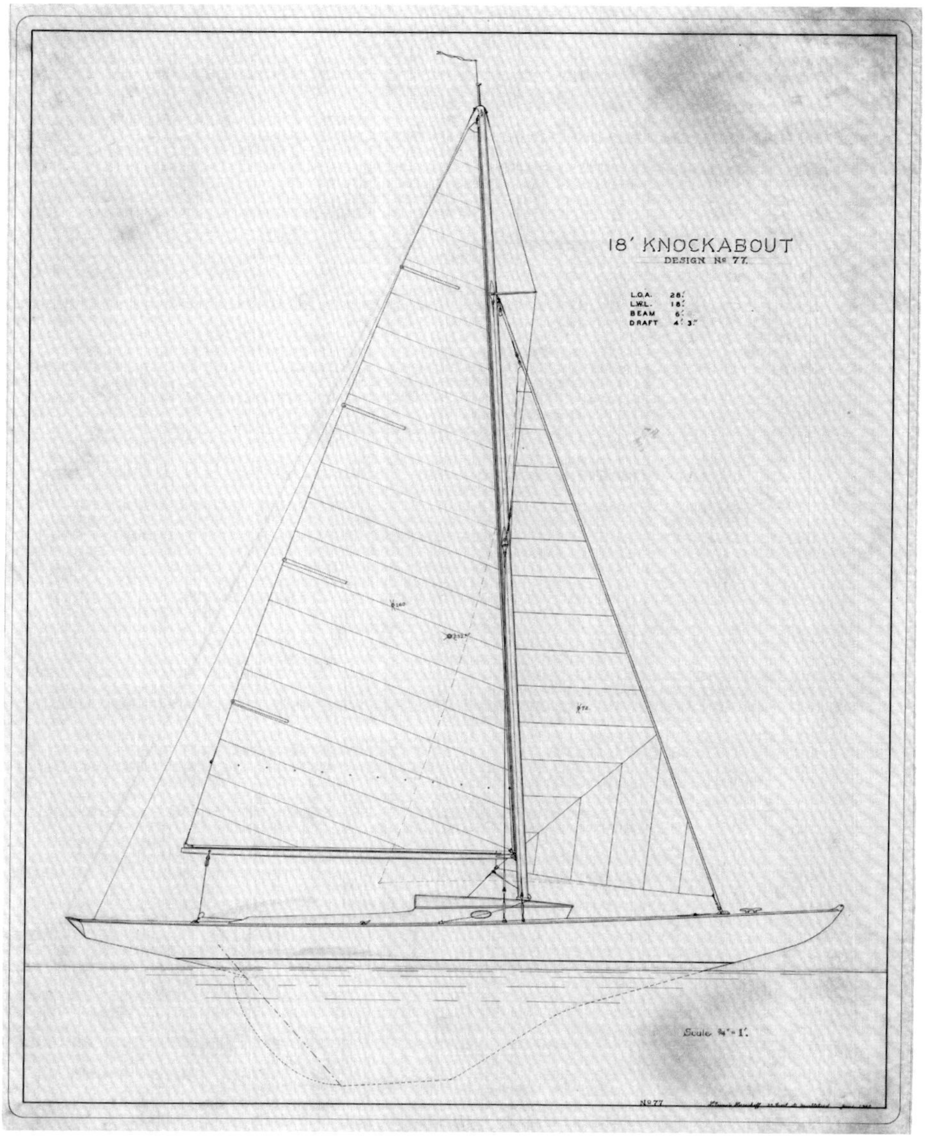

A small project that Francis had in 1939 was to design a Marconi yawl rig for the new owners of the *Cricket*, one of the thirteen Bar Harbor 31-foot-class, gaff-rigged sloops that his father had designed and built in 1903. Total sail area is 1,047 square feet, with 535 square feet in the mainsail, 165 in the mizzen, 162 in the forestaysail, and 185 in the jib. Francis called the class Bar Harbor 30s; waterline length was 30 feet, 9 inches. Frederic and Frances Day couldn't resist buying the *Cricket* with dollars they couldn't spare. They renamed her the *Desperate Lark*. Taking the risk was a good decision: they found Francis's rig handy and safe and enjoyed their boat's speed and beauty for many years. The *Desperate Lark* is still sailing. Francis sold these plans to another Bar Harbor 31 owner in 1947 for $10. (© Mystic Seaport Museum, Daniel S. Gregory Ships Plans Library, SP38.241.1)

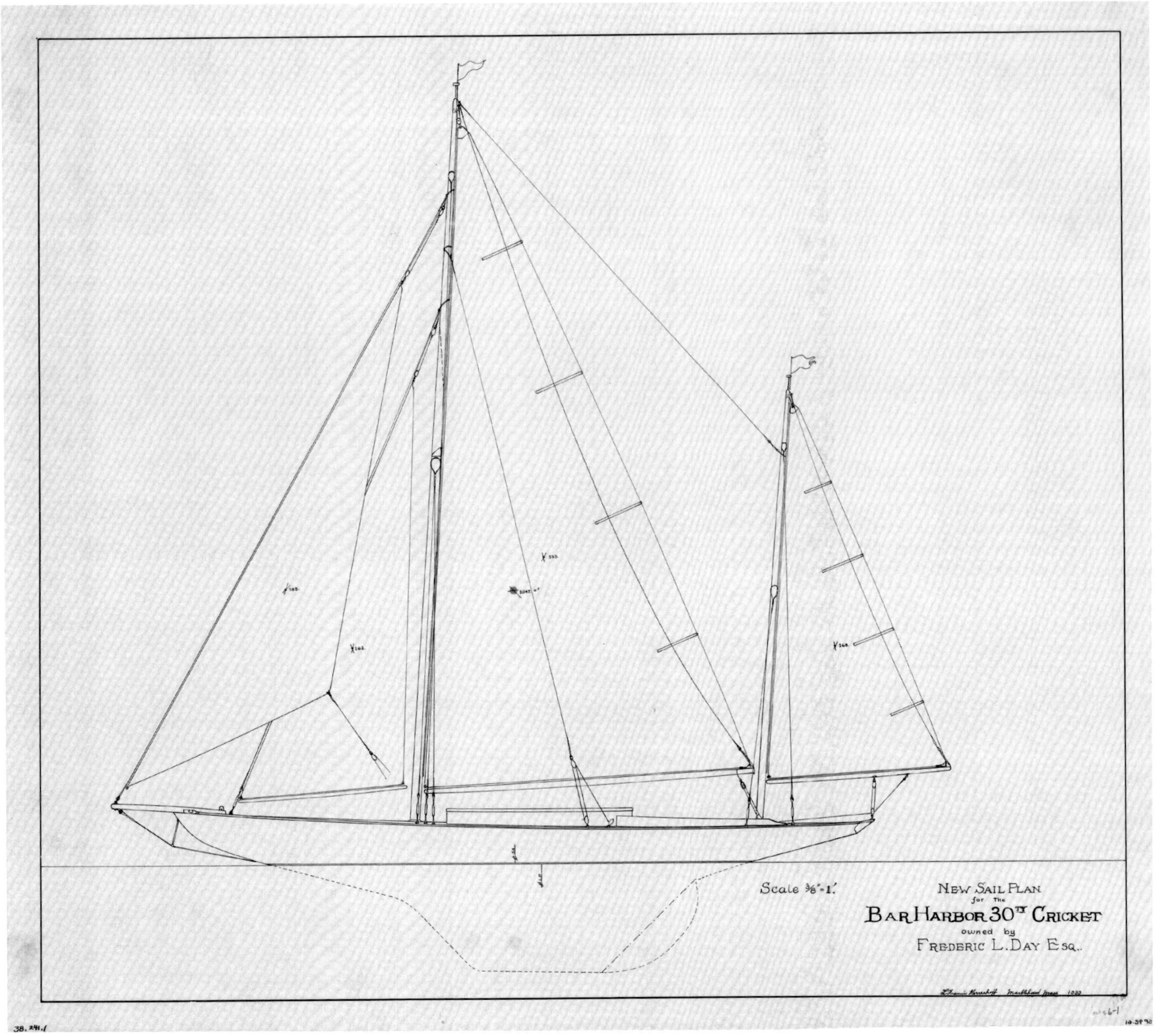

Francis's design No. 77 of 1940 was a 28-foot sloop made at the behest of Billy Strawbridge for a one-design class for Maine's Northeast Harbor Yacht Club. Sail area is 232 square feet, with 160 in the mainsail and 72 in the jib. On this small rig, the jumper stays eliminate the need for both a masthead forestay and running backstays. The permanent backstay leads through the deck and forward into the cockpit for adjustment. One owner wanted a Genoa jib, so, on this plan, Francis has drawn in the sail in merely dotted lines, perhaps demonstrating his disapproval of using overlapping jibs, particularly on one-design racers. She has an elegant, long-ended profile, and Francis has drawn a low cuddy house, coming to a point at its forward end. This was the shape that his father favored for fast, low-sided boats that, when beating in a windy chop, would have water running aft on the foredeck. (© Mystic Seaport Museum, Daniel S. Gregory Ships Plans Library, SP38.198.4)

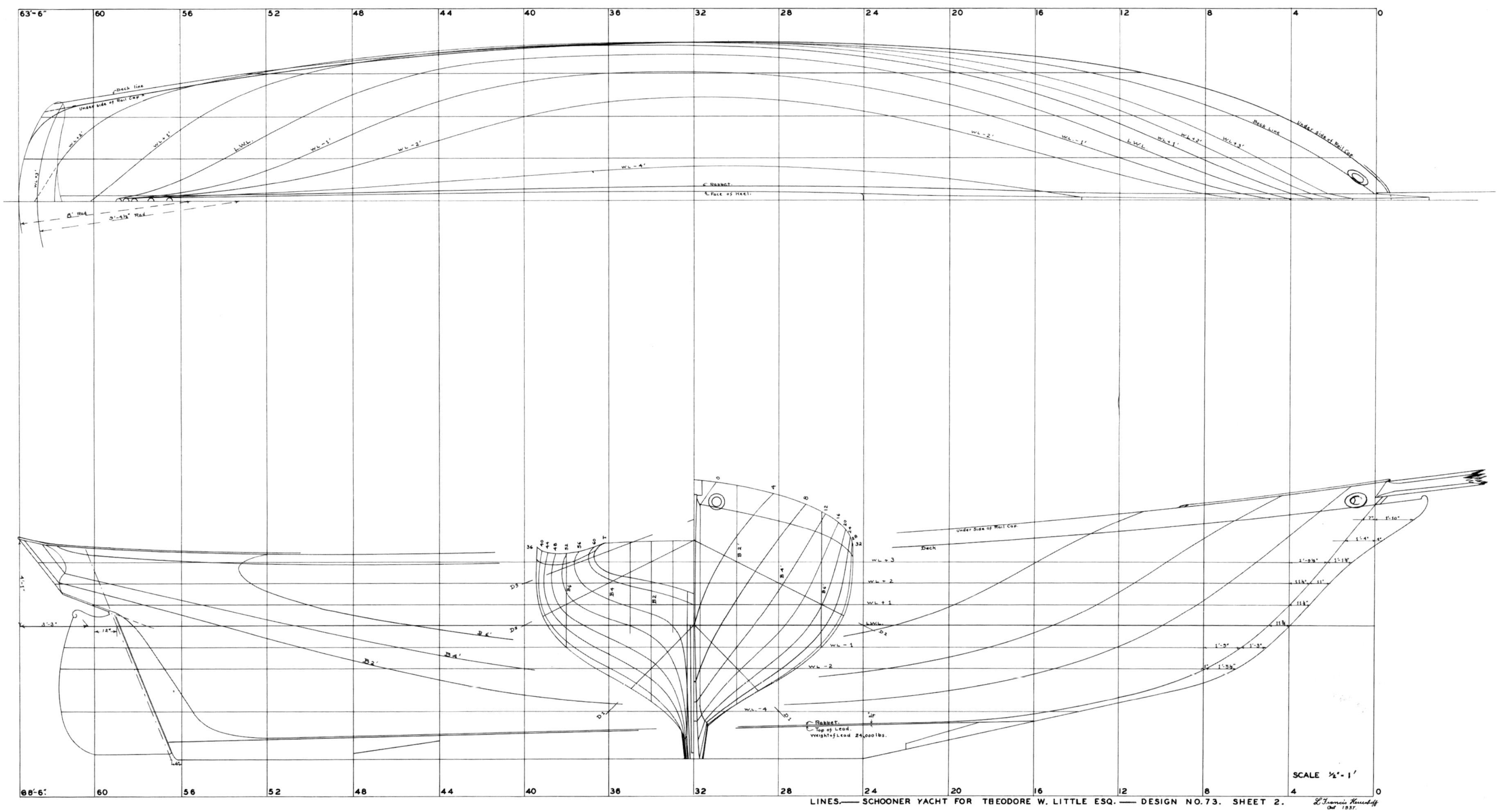

The lines of the *Mistral*. She is deeper-bodied than any of her L. Francis Herreshoff ancestors, and is closer to her original inspiration, the *America*, than any of them. Give her finer shoulders forward, a bigger transom, and a vertical rudderpost, and she would be a little *America*. The *Mistral* is 63 feet, 6 inches long on deck; with a waterline length of 54 feet, 9 inches; a beam of 15 feet; and a draft of 6 feet, 3 inches. Like her ancestors, she is long and narrow, with moderate draft. Displacement is 79,936 pounds, with 24,000 pounds of outside lead, for a ballast-displacement ratio of 30 percent. When launched, the schooner floated 3 inches high, a displacement difference of 7,885 pounds, or nearly 10 percent. Francis may have been missing Norman Skene's calculations, but at least it was far better that the vessel was too light than too heavy. This drawing is dated October 1937. (© Mystic Seaport Museum, Daniel S. Gregory Ships Plans Library, SP38.182.1)

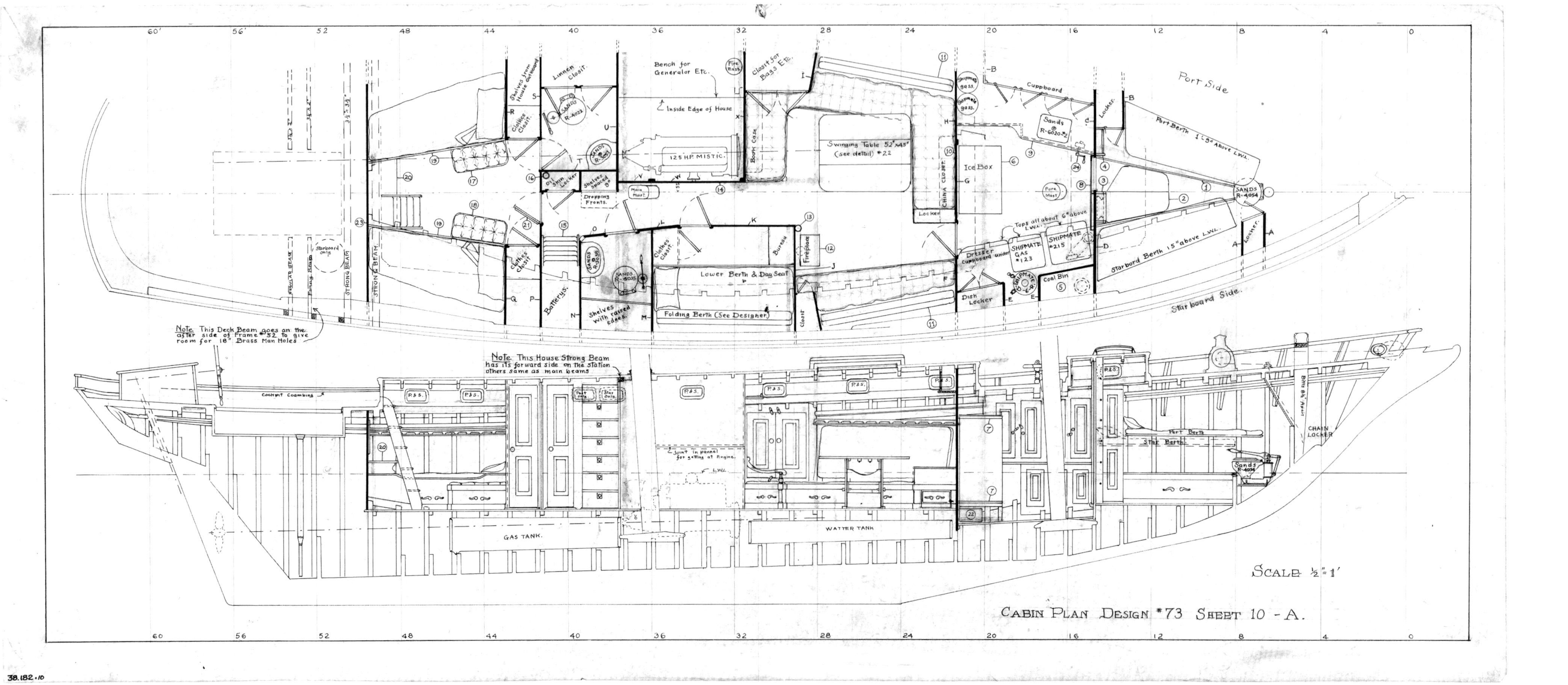

The *Mistral*'s cabin plan. Her arrangement is conventional, with, from forward to aft, fo'c's'le, galley, saloon, staterooms, and heads. But Francis has placed the off-center engine amidships, with full headroom in its compartment, and has installed a second companionway in the starboard side of her long cabin house, with an oilskin locker at its foot. He labeled the engine "125 h.p. Mistic," one of his favorite Lathrops. Big tanks are in the bilge, one for water between the mast steps and one for gasoline abaft the mainmast. The galley boasts two Shipmate stoves, one gas and the other for solid fuel. There is also a fireplace in the after starboard corner of the saloon, a Simpson-Lawrence tile stove that Francis ordered from Glasgow. (© Mystic Seaport Museum, Daniel S. Gregory Ships Plans Library, SP38.182.10)

that fifteen more boats would be built to his design after the war, but it was not to be. Norman Hodgdon did build at least one at his East Boothbay, Maine, yard in about 1950. Francis got a detailed report about how that boat sailed from John Sewall of Buffalo, a Lake Erie sailor who became a devotee of L. Francis Herreshoff.[18]

While visiting Maine, Sewall took the Hodgdon Northeast Harbor One-Design out for an afternoon sail:

> *Breeze SW, about all she could handle without a reef; maybe 18 mph most of the time with stronger puffs. Tide going out, or about opposite to the breeze. Smart chop.*
>
> *The little boat was stiffer than any other of similar size I have sailed. She put her rail right down most of the time; but developed some real power while she did it. Mrs. Sewall, who was with me, remarked that the craft made you feel it didn't matter if it blew twice as hard. On speed, she was definitely slower than either the Boothbay one designs (Hendel) or the Christmas Cove 20 footers (Charles Hodgdon); but she was much more comfortable and lively enough to suit anybody.*
>
> *Balance perfect. Nice positive weather helm, with pleasant springy feeling in the tiller (as contrasted to a "pull").*
>
> *Handling perfect. The little boat would tack, jibe, turn all the way around, or anything you wanted, and no matter how carelessly you performed the maneuver. Chop didn't seem to stop her at all.*
>
> *The helmsman didn't get hit at all by the spray; but the rest of the cockpit was of course saturated.*[19]

Francis had designed another boat that was fast for her sail area and thus easy and fun to sail. The Northeast Harbor One-Design was very different from the *Ben-My-Chree* and the *Koala*, but she shared their handling characteristics. Actually, when Billy Strawbridge returned to the idea of a one-design class for Northeast Harbor in 1956, he suggested using the design of the *Koala*, with modifications. What changes he and Francis discussed and Francis apparently worked on at his drawing board are unknown, but several months later, Francis wrote his friend asking for $46.76 in expenses on the project. "I am temporarily a little hard up," he said. No modified *Koala* design was completed.[20]

By the summer of 1940, World War II was well underway. British cruisers had forced the destruction of the German "pocket battleship" *Admiral Graf Spee* at Montevideo. Germany had conquered Czechoslovakia, Poland, Denmark, and Norway, and had invaded the Low Countries and France. In June, France fell. Every sort of vessel, including yachts, brought the surviving British army home from the beach at Dunkirk. FDR asked Congress for two and a half billion dollars to expand the army and navy. The American yachting world increasingly realized the inevitability of its being drawn into the fighting.

Since 1938 the navy had been seeking designs for a new generation of small patrol craft, which would result in the 77-81-foot wooden PT (patrol torpedo), the 110-foot wooden SC (submarine chaser), and the 173-foot steel PC (patrol craft). Using his experience in World War I commanding patrol vessels year-round in Block Island's sometimes rough waters, as well as his involvement in the design and building of antisubmarine devices at New London near the end of the war, Francis produced, in July 1940, a well-thought-out design for a 145-foot submarine chaser. This was his design No. 78, which he labeled "Submarine Destroyer."

"The principal object of the design," he wrote, "is to produce a vessel that is too small to be an

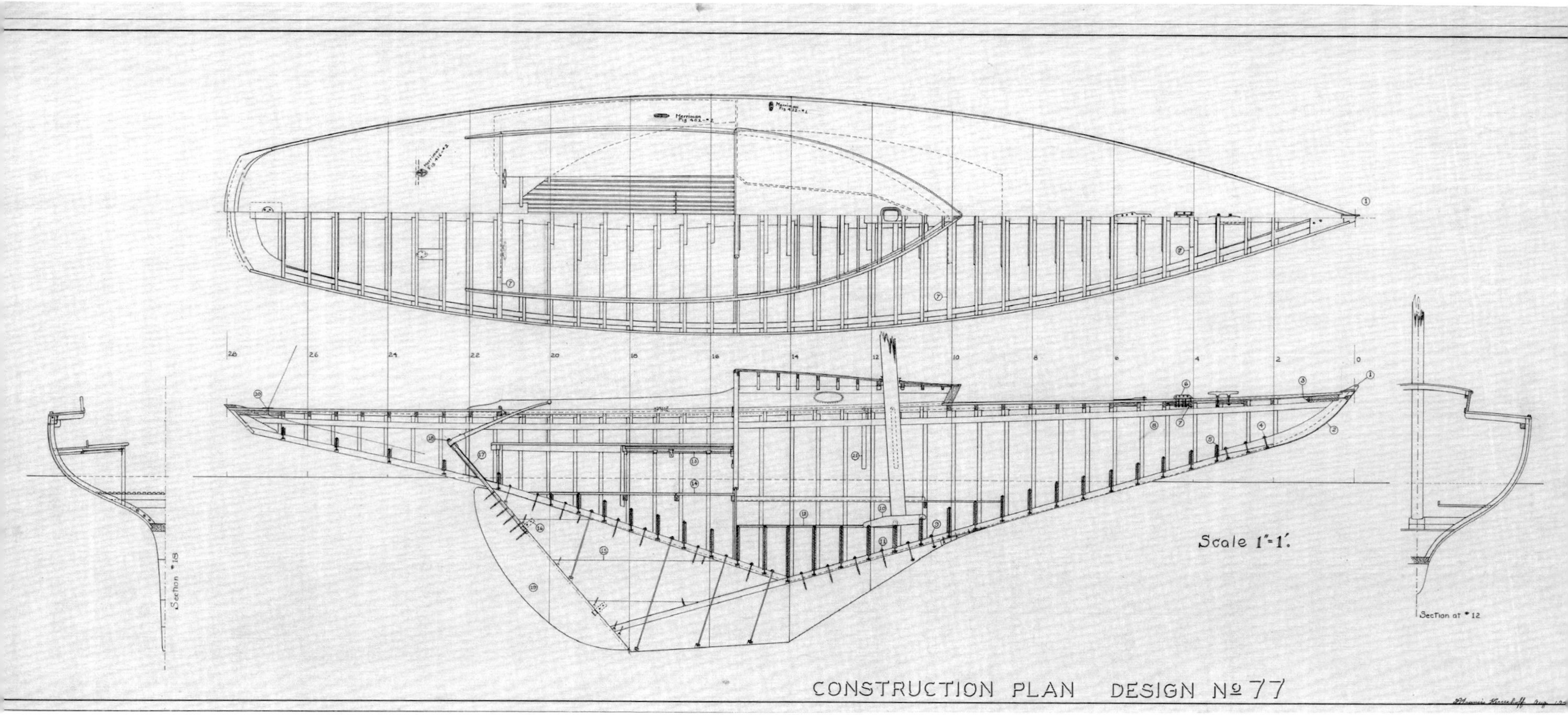

The Northeast Harbor One-Design's conventional construction plan. Francis has numbered twenty-one details for which Helen Bolster typed two pages of notes. He also wrote out a page of nineteen scantlings for Hinckley's builders to follow. Francis made a separate drawing for a bronze bow chock. "The clamp can be spruce or fir, about 1¾ inches square and tapered or beveled as required at ends." Keel bolts to be of ⅜-inch Tobin bronze. "Hanger bolts [lags] are used in the widest part of the lead and deadwood because they can be staggered more than through bolts." (Maybe Francis should have used this argument to persuade the Quincy Adams builders to put lags into the keel of the *Ticonderoga,* instead of the through-bolts they insisted on.) "The rudder of this yacht is so narrow that it can probably be made of one board and will not require drive [drift] bolts to keep it straight if it is made of rift-grain mahogany or white oak, but if it is not rift-grain it surely will warp." Frames to be steam-bent white oak, 1 inch square. Planking either ¾-inch cedar or ⅝-inch mahogany. Deck ⅝-inch tongue-and-groove soft pine. Cockpit floor teak slats ⅝ inch thick, ⅞ inch wide, and spaced ½ inch apart. (© Mystic Seaport Museum, Daniel S. Gregory Ships Plans Library, SP38.198.3)

easy target for bombs or torpedoes, but still has the fire power generally associated with much larger and more expensive craft which require a crew of approximately three or four times the number that would be required on this vessel." And, he noted, "she was designed from the keel up to locate and destroy submarines and stay at sea in winter weather."[21]

Paul Hammond was already back on active duty in the navy and was working in antisubmarine warfare. Francis sent him his preliminary outboard profile drawing of the Submarine Destroyer with a five-page description of her objectives and design details. Hammond and at least one other officer were impressed with the "beautiful little sub-chaser," but the Navy Department expressed no further interest in the design. Francis also offered to send design No. 78 to a member of the British delegation to the US in Washington, hoping to find interest for it in the Royal Navy, but his offer was ignored. "The time may come," Francis wrote, "when some craft like these will be urgently needed, and the small wooden ones now being built will be of no possible use." Francis was right; the steel 173-footers designed by the navy's Bureau of Construction and Repair—closer to his steel 145-footer—were far more effective than the smaller wooden vessels. But the navy did well to choose the proven design principles of the 173-foot PCs, rather than spend precious time evaluating his innovations. The PC-461 class vessels acted as convoy escorts, and their depth-charge attacks on U-boats reduced merchant ship losses. They even sank a few submarines.[22]

But Francis's design for a submarine chaser was still a remarkable achievement. The designs of her crow's nest, conning tower, rotating gun turret, protected antiaircraft guns, listening gear, depth charge deployment, and bomb protection for the depth charge stowage all represent original thinking and could have presented to the navy ideas that might have been developed to improve the fleet's effectiveness in the war at sea.

Making the crow's nest and conning tower of aluminum to save weight aloft was questionable, given the material's propensity for catching fire and burning intensely when struck by projectiles, but that propensity would not be fully realized until the British-Argentinian action off the Falkland Islands in 1982. And, after all, Starling Burgess had proposed an entire destroyer made of aluminum.

The gun turret was to be revolved by electric motors, controlled by the gun sight. Elevation of the balanced guns was by hand. Here is how Francis described his unique design for the guns, and their operation: "The guns are not mounted on trunions, but at their axes is a cylinder six feet in diameter, open at the turret or inboard side, where the loading is done as follows. After unlocking the breach the after barrel is slid aft and loaded with a light spool-shaped water retainer made of plastic material. Then the water is turned on, filling this chamber. After the cartridge is placed in the forward barrel, the after barrel is brought forward and the two locked together, as in the Davis gun. This motion actuates a piston valve closing the water chamber (seen on top of the barrel in the drawing). Because these guns have practically no recoil, the whole turret and gun mounts can be very light." It is not known how far Francis took his ideas for this gun, or how practical it might have been. He was using his lifelong interest in firearms.[23]

Francis thought that his big hatches over the antiaircraft guns could be slid out of the way more quickly than gun covers could be removed, and he knew from experience that their crews would be more effective, particularly in winter, if they had protection from the weather. Similarly, having the depth charges below deck rather than topside, where the navy carried them throughout the war, allowed the crew to make last-second adjustments from inside the vessel before releasing the weapons. That location also gave these highly explosive devices whatever protection his

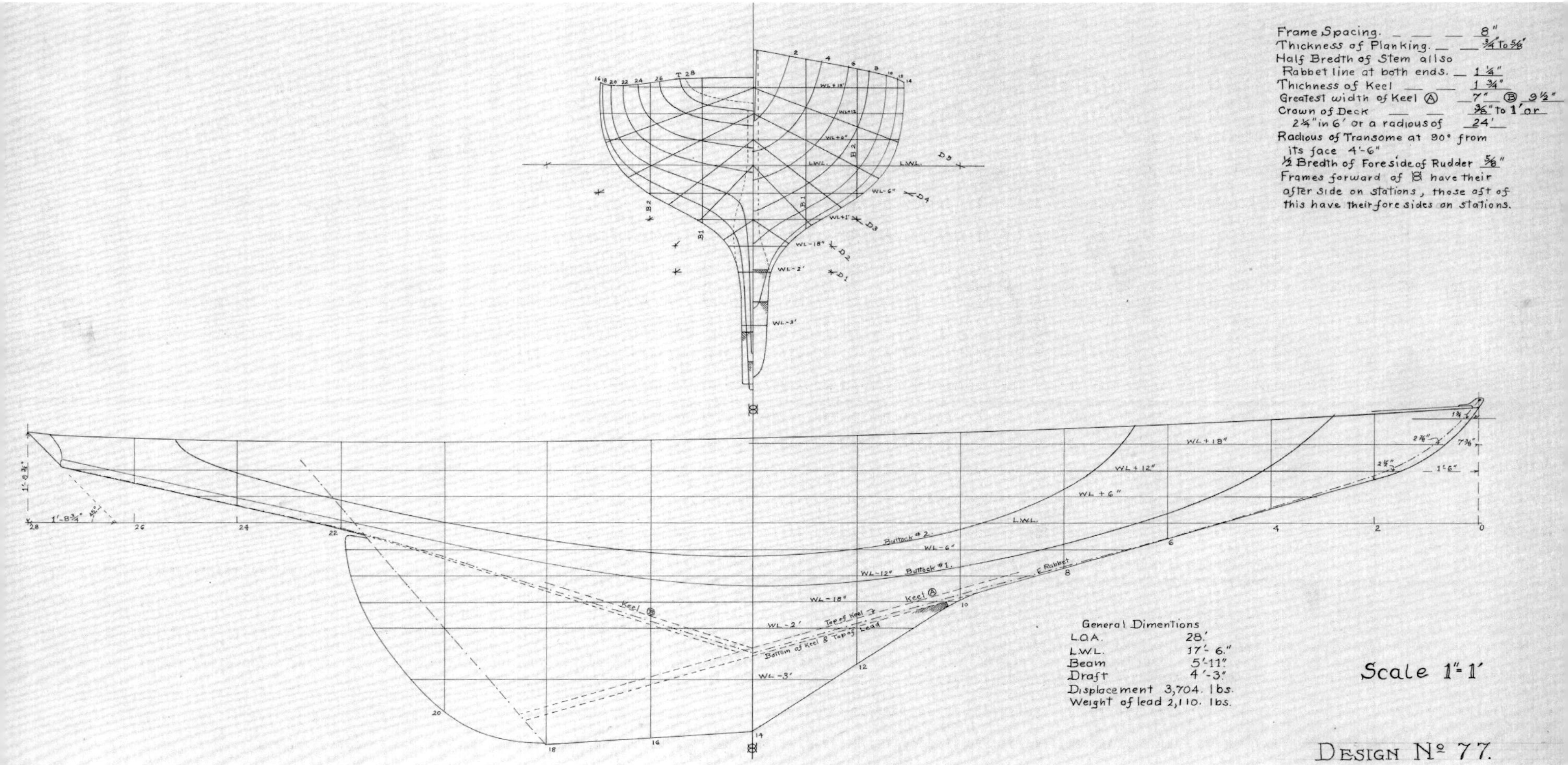

The lines of the Northeast Harbor One-Design. There must have been a separate half-breadth drawing showing the shape of the waterlines so that a table of offsets could be produced and the builders at Henry Hinckley's Manset Boat Yard in Maine could loft the shape of her hull. Length on the waterline is 17 feet, 6 inches; beam is 5 feet, 11 inches; and draft is 4 feet, 3 inches. Displacement is 3,704 pounds, with 2,110 pounds of lead on the keel, for a ballast-displacement ratio of 57 percent. For the hull of this day-sailer, Francis has not repeated the long waterline and short ends of his No. 70, the *Koala*, but instead has returned to a small version of a Universal Rule boat. (© Mystic Seaport Museum, Daniel S. Gregory Ships Plans Library, SP38.198.1)

"Bomb-Proof Pneumatic Mattress" might have afforded. And Francis knew, also from experience, how important it was to protect listening gear from water disturbance.[24]

Francis's design for a submarine-chaser shows his versatility and originality as a naval architect (a term he never used for himself). His Submarine Destroyer might have been an effective man-of-war had she been tried.

Francis must have enjoyed using his practical, imaginative, engineering mind, and also his naval experience, as he worked out the details of his design No. 78. The would-be sub-chaser was his single contribution to the war effort. Francis was forty-nine, not far above draft age. He had no pressing obligations, yet he did not get a naval commission, as did many men with valuable maritime experience. Paul Hammond was serving. A year before, Waldo Brown's naval commission had cost him his life. Francis, in correspondence with a naval officer about yacht design, did write, "referring to your question as to whether I have joined the service, I would say that, after my experience in the Naval Experimental Station, and seeing how civilian professors there could accomplish very much more than the enrolled officers because they were free of drill duties, etc. if or when an experimental station is opened up, I should be glad to join their forces as a civilian and continue the work [on anti-submarine warfare devices] which I left off in 1919." But he did not pursue this idea. Francis would really prefer to work by himself, putting his experience and imagination to work, unfettered, on a complete warship.[25]

Fifteen years later, Francis's talent for designing boats for combat would be called on again, after the Korean War. It was the army, rather than the navy, that made the request; the army had more bottoms than the navy, even though the army fleet contained no battleships or aircraft carriers. In 1955, Francis received a letter from Lieutenant Colonel Ned W. Glenn, commanding the Eighth Army Liaison Detachment in San Francisco. Glenn was in charge of army intelligence for the Japan and Korea sector, and he had been an observer of French actions in Vietnam. It appears that he wanted a fast boat for surveillance along the Korean coast, which has a large tidal range, and perhaps elsewhere in unstable Asia. As a reader of *The Rudder,* he was familiar with and impressed by Francis's powerboat designs of 1950, the *Barracuda* and *Piquant.* He asked for the design of a 60-to-75-foot vessel, able to take the ground and drawing no more than four feet, with a cruising speed of 20 knots for 750 miles, and space for sixteen people and eight berths. He wrote: "I would appreciate it if no publicity be given to the location where this vessel is to be used or to the persons desiring it." Francis replied quickly that he could and would design such a vessel.[26]

Glenn wrote back with more detailed suggestions for the craft and included a rough profile sketch of what he had in mind. A requirement was that the boat had to carry a substantial tender that could be launched readily. Glenn drew a small boat, stowed upside down on the stern with davits. He wrote: "Cedar bucket toilets would simplify everything." He asked what a finished design would cost.[27]

Francis answered: "I am convinced that the proper way to launch a small boat is to shoot her out of the stern of the mother craft while the latter is traveling slowly to windward. Although there have been no vessels especially designed for this I see no reason why it cannot be arranged easily, and am making a drawing of such a craft which I believe could launch or haul an eighteen foot high speed outboard motor boat in a matter of seconds, without damaging herself or the mother craft."[28]

As to cost, Francis quoted $100 per sheet of drawings, but $500 for the more complicated construction plan. He estimated that there would be nine sheets, plus the construction drawing, for a total cost of $1,400. "It will take me a few days to work out the drawing and the general problem, then I will send you some prints together with the

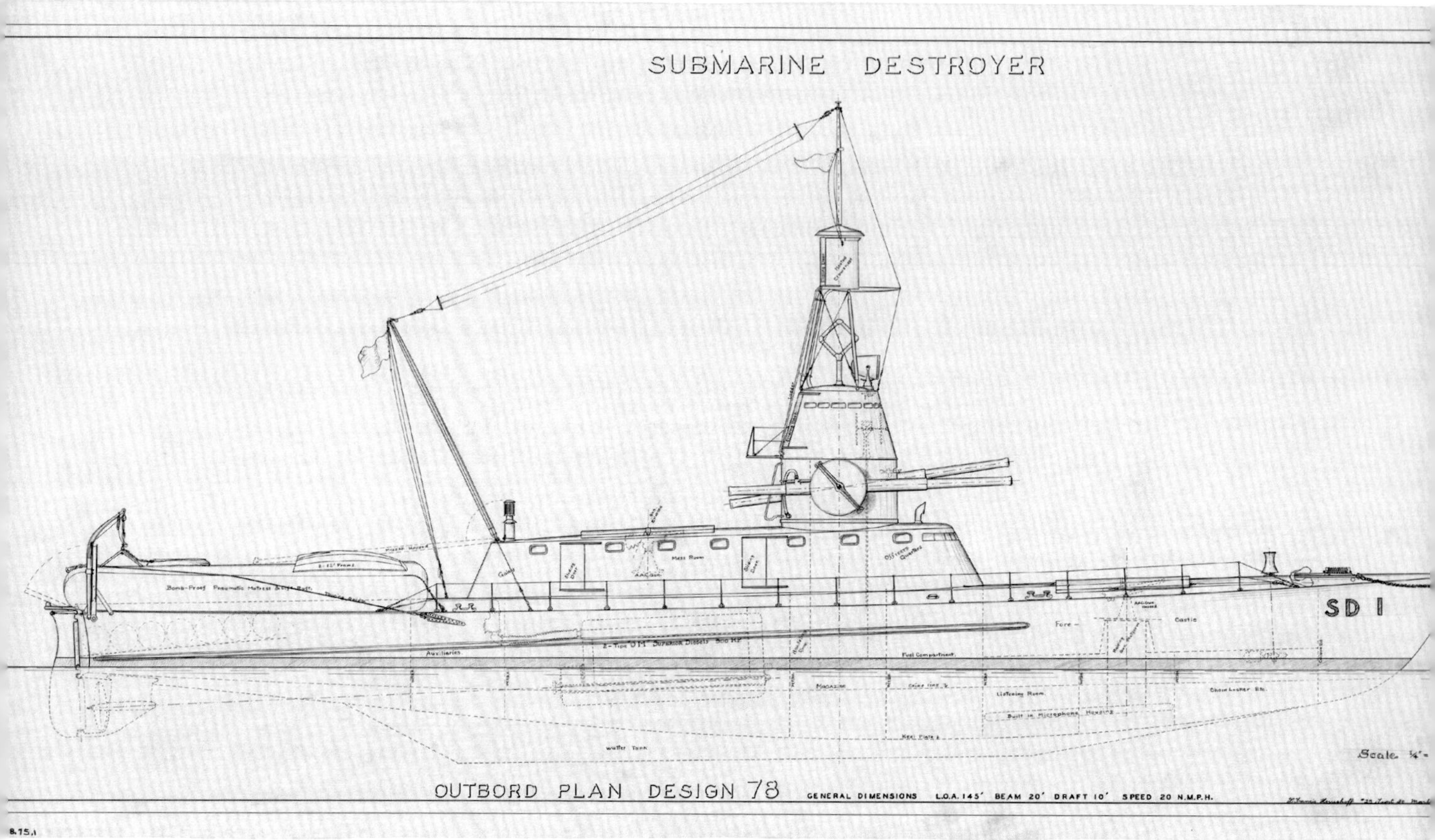

Francis's preliminary design for a 145-foot, steel sub-chaser, or "Submarine Destroyer," as he called his design No. 78, of July 10, 1940. Her beam is 20 feet, and she draws 10 feet. Suggested power was twin Superior diesels of 900 horsepower each, giving 20 knots. Armament is a pair of 5-inch recoilless guns firing shrapnel shells, and two smaller anti-aircraft guns, mounted below for weather protection and firing through quick-opening hatches. The forward anti-aircraft gun could be raised to deck level for firing at small surface craft. The main armament against submarines was depth charges that rolled overboard through the transom between her twin rudders from their compartment in the stern. These were controlled from the conical, aluminum conning tower atop the pilothouse. Note the double steering-wheel arrangement in the conning tower. One wheel is abaft the binnacle for steering by compass, and the other is far forward so the helmsman's eyes will be close to the small windows for best observation during close-quarters action, especially valuable at night. The after deck covering the depth-charge compartment is protected by a 4-foot-thick, rubber-and-wire-mesh pneumatic mattress, inflated to 40 pounds, for bomb protection. This device could also serve as a 35-foot life raft. There is a heated, aluminum crow's nest on the mast, 40 feet above the water. Francis designed the shape of the bow and keel forward to create the least possible disturbance in the water for best reception on the listening microphones. These were set flush with the hull in a 20-foot row on each side of the vessel, starting 25 feet abaft the forward end of the load waterline. The noise-proof listening room was just inboard of the microphones. The sub-chaser has ten watertight bulkheads and was designed for Francis's (and his father's, since this was a steel vessel) longitudinal construction. (© Mystic Seaport Museum, Daniel S. Gregory Ships Plans Library, SP38.75.1)

numbered description." Just a week after he wrote these words, Francis had his drawing finished and inked for blueprinting and his detailed description written and typed by Mrs. Bolster in seven single-spaced pages. It took Glenn more than three months to get army approval to purchase design No. 97. This was good news to Francis, but he was cautious enough to write: "Before the design progresses very far I should like to have an opportunity to go over all of the features that are numbered on the drawing [43] to be sure that they are wanted."[29]

Alas, none of Francis's design features of the patrol boat were wanted, or, perhaps, could be afforded. The project died aborning, most likely the victim of Congressional cutting of the army's budget. Francis hung his quick but thorough drawing, showing many novel ideas, in Pocket 3, Folder 1 of his plans file near his long drafting table. His only reward was the enjoyment he took from accommodating the requirements of a "60-foot Vedette Boat, for special service."

The Rudder magazine was born in the same year as L. Francis Herreshoff, 1890. From the beginning it was more practical and less elitist than *Yachting* magazine, which followed in 1907, as their names suggest. Thomas Fleming Day, *The Rudder*'s founding editor, represented everyman, because he believed that a yachtsman could get as much pleasure from a small boat as from a large yacht. As we have seen, Day had shown that small boats could be safe at sea when he organized a race from New York to Bermuda, and he further proved his point when he crossed the Atlantic in the little yawl *Sea Bird,* and then in the motorboat *Detroit*.

Day started a "How To Build" series of articles in which a naval architect would design a boat that was practical for amateur builders, present her plans, and write a description of her construction process. The series proved popular and was continued by later *Rudder* editors. One of them, William F. Crosby, even designed a few of the boats and wrote about them himself, including, in 1931, the 15-foot, centerboard sloop, Snipe, of which perhaps 30,000 were built around the world.[30]

In 1942, a thirty-six-year-old travel agent with a great interest in boats, Boris Lauer-Leonardi, joined *The Rudder*'s staff as associate editor, to replace Edward A. Hine, who had gone off to war. Lauer-Leonardi was exempt because one leg was shorter than the other. The new man was promoted to editor within four months, when Crosby went to Washington to help design warships. Boris Lauer-Leonardi turned out to be the perfect man for the job.

Boris had grown up in Russia, from which he and his mother fled on foot to France to escape yet another of the mid-1930s purges of bourgeois not deemed absolutely loyal to Stalin. The two continued on to America, and Boris eventually established his own travel agency in Harvard Square, Cambridge, Massachusetts.[31]

In the summer of 1941, before Boris joined the *Rudder* staff, Lee Nielsen happened into his place of business, and the two fell to yarning about boats. Boris said he was looking for a boat to charter for a short cruise he was organizing for about twenty people. Lee knew of a big, black schooner. Boris would charter her if Lee would go as skipper. On the cruise, the *Duchess* called at Marblehead, and Lee introduced Boris to his friend L. Francis Herreshoff, the yacht designer.

This was an introduction that Boris valued. He wanted to soak up all the knowledge he could about boats, and he saw in Mr. Herreshoff a wonderful source. Francis was happy to support this affable younger man's quest. Francis could see that, relative greenhorn though Boris was, he shared Francis's traditional views on yachting, even if he was less elitist than Francis. The fact that Boris had owned a Block Island boat replica, the *Roaring Bessie*, doubtless helped him break through Francis's reserve.[32]

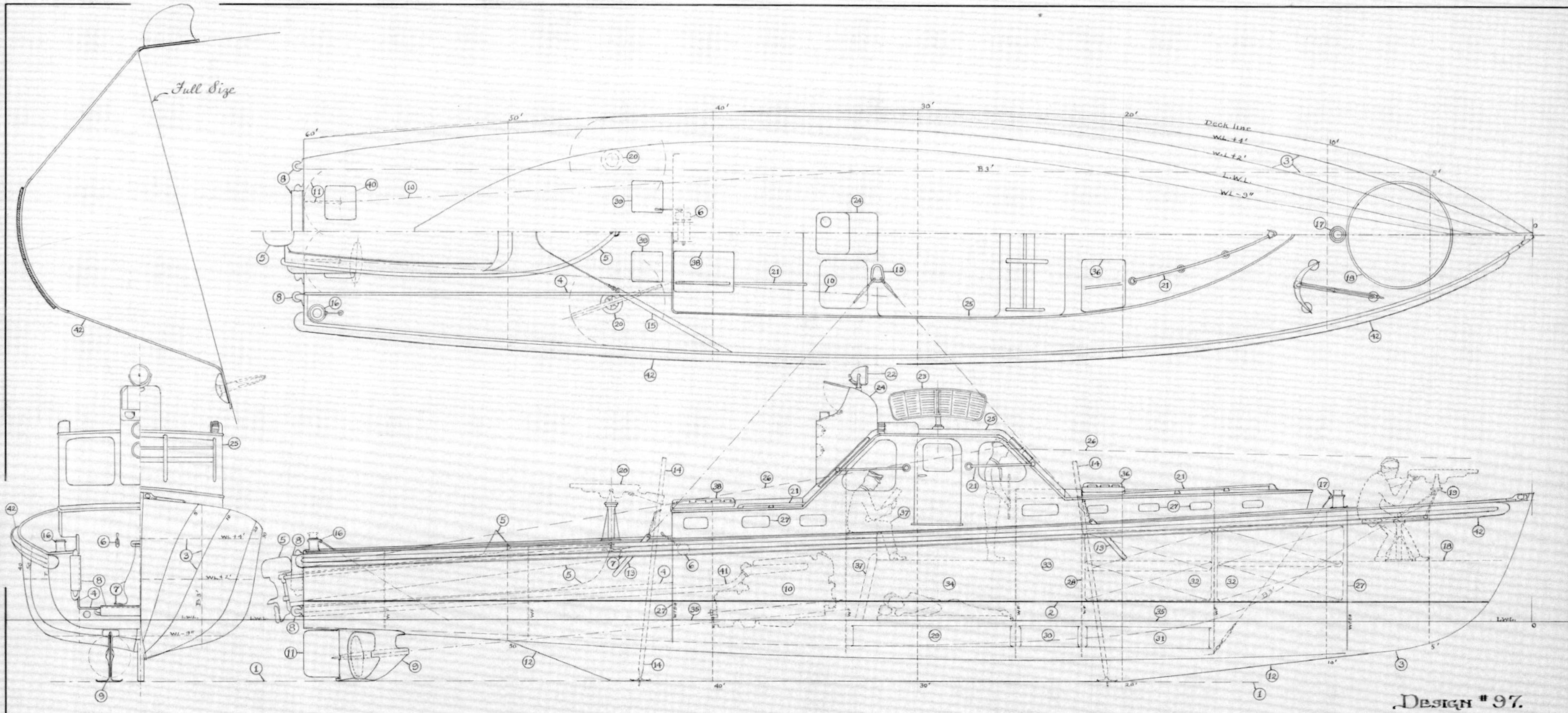

Diagramatical Plan of a 60ft VEDETTE BOAT For special service ~ SCALE ½" 1' ~ L. Francis Herreshoff The Castle, Marblehead, Mass. Dec 15 1955.

B.74.1

When Boris went to work for *The Rudder* in May 1942, he realized that Mr. Herreshoff would also be a wonderful source of material for the magazine, and, as we have seen, quickly published the plans of the *Diddikai* as "Deep Sea Ketch" in the June issue. Boris commuted to the *Rudder* office at 9 Murray Street in downtown Manhattan from Port Washington, Long Island. In his harbor, he spotted a good-looking little cruising sloop and got to know her owner, Russell Genner. The boat proved to be the *Button*, designed by Francis Herreshoff. Genner told Boris that "she is a fine sea boat and faster than anything else of her type." Boris lost no time in writing "Dear Mr. Herreshoff," asking for her plans for his magazine. The *Button* was built in 1940 by George Gulliford at Saugus, Massachusetts, to Francis's design No. 71. Francis made this design in 1937 for Richard Jenks, who called his boat the *Hard Tack*. Boris published the plans for No. 71 in his September 1942 issue, the same issue in which his name first appeared as editor.[33]

Francis knew that the *Button* had a new home in Port Washington because he chanced to have been the broker on the sale to Russ and Jane Genner. His duties had included getting the *Button*'s gear from the prior owner and storing it for the Genners over the winter. He wrote to Jane Genner, "you can be quite sure that the broker expects to do quite a lot for his commission, and don't be apologetic about requests for service that you think of."[34]

Rudder readers responded to the plans of No. 71 with requests for building information. They had to wait three years until the October 1945 issue for Francis to get around to writing a "How-To-Build" article on the design, by then named the Prudence H-23, but, by that time, readers had been able to enjoy more than fifty other articles by Mr. Herreshoff, including a long series on her larger successor, the H-28. Boris wrote to Francis: "The article on the Prudence is wonderful—I enjoyed every word of it and I know all your readers will be pleased. Your style certainly is refreshing and original. No wonder you are getting to be more and more famous as a writer all the time." Miss

---

LEFT: **Francis designed this 60-foot vedette, or scouting, boat for the US Army for patrol and surveillance duty late in 1955, as the country's military maintained peace in Korea and prepared for an expanding role in Asia. Believing that the army was in a hurry, and being between *Rudder* assignments, Francis finished this drawing in a week. The project fizzled; the army, facing budget cuts, shelved the project. But Francis had designed another intriguing small warship, his design No. 97. Draft is 3 feet; she is designed to take the ground every low tide on a level keel, with four 11-foot legs to keep her upright, as well as protection for the propellers and rudders. Francis thought she would make 20 knots with two 225-horsepower engines. She could carry sixteen men, including a boarding party. A principal feature of the boat is a launching platform for a 16-foot, fast outboard boat. Francis believed that this boat could be launched with the mother ship at full speed. The rudder support is Francis's contra-propeller. Francis worked out many details for this design: note the "backstay" to give the forward Samson post extra support in case the boat had to be towed; he shows Herreshoff anchors, probably unavailable to the army at the time, lashed down on either side of the foredeck; the forward gunner sits on a bicycle seat arranged so that his weight balances that of the gun, helping him to swing the weapon rapidly around the 5-foot-diameter cockpit; the dotted lines from the helmsman show his line of vision fore and aft. To save weight, the boat would be built with Francis's longitudinal construction system. There are bunks everywhere: in the fo'c's'le, in the pilothouse, under the pilothouse, and in the engine room. In the upper left-hand corner of the drawing, Francis shows, at full size, a special guardrail to be "made up of sponge rubber covered with strong rubberized fabric, and capped on the outside with a 1/16-inch layer of spring bronze rolled into a 3-inch-wide section." It was designed to save 1,500 pounds of weight over a conventional guardrail.** (© Mystic Seaport Museum, Daniel S. Gregory Ships Plans Library, SP38.74.1)

Cora Hill, Francis's unsmiling teacher of English in Bristol, would have been amazed (see volume 1, page 36).[35]

In his article, Francis explained his thinking behind the design of the Prudence via an imaginary conversation between himself and "the Editor," in which he lambasted "lapping jibs, winches or a lot of advertised claptrap" seen on many boats and extolled the lack of same on the H-23. He recommended advertising the H-23 to the readers of *The Rudder* this way:

> *I wouldn't tell them she was the biggest boat in the world, but rather that she was small enough so when they got through taking care of her they would have some time left over for sailing. I wouldn't tell them she was the fastest boat in the world but that she would sail with her original two sails and those who want to can keep the sails bent ready for hoisting. You might tell them that if they wanted to get away from the telephone, the radio and all the other strains of modern civilization, that perhaps they can do it in the Prudence as cheaply as any way that you know of. Tell them that if they build her without a motor they can sail thousands of miles with little expense and without using any fuel. But I would warn them that a boat like the Prudence had two disadvantages, for people will constantly want to borrow her, and she is apt to be stolen.*[36]

ABOVE: **Boris Lauer-Leonardi, editor of *The Rudder*, alongside Francis's sailing dinghy, the *So And So* at Marblehead Harbor. He brought L. Francis Herreshoff out of the doldrums with a second career, writing.** (*The Rudder* (August 1944): 28) RIGHT: **In the September 1942 issue of *The Rudder,* Boris Lauer-Leonardi published Francis's design No. 71, the 23-foot cruising sloop *Hard Tack,* drawn in 1937 for Richard P. Jenks. Three years later, Francis would name this design Prudence, after her forerunner, design No. 43 of 1929, also for Jenks, and Boris would present her to his readers as the H-23 in a "How-To-Build" article by L. Francis Herreshoff. The sail area in her nicely raked, low-aspect-ratio rig is 293 square feet.** (© Mystic Seaport Museum, Daniel S. Gregory Ships Plans Library, SP38.95.3.)

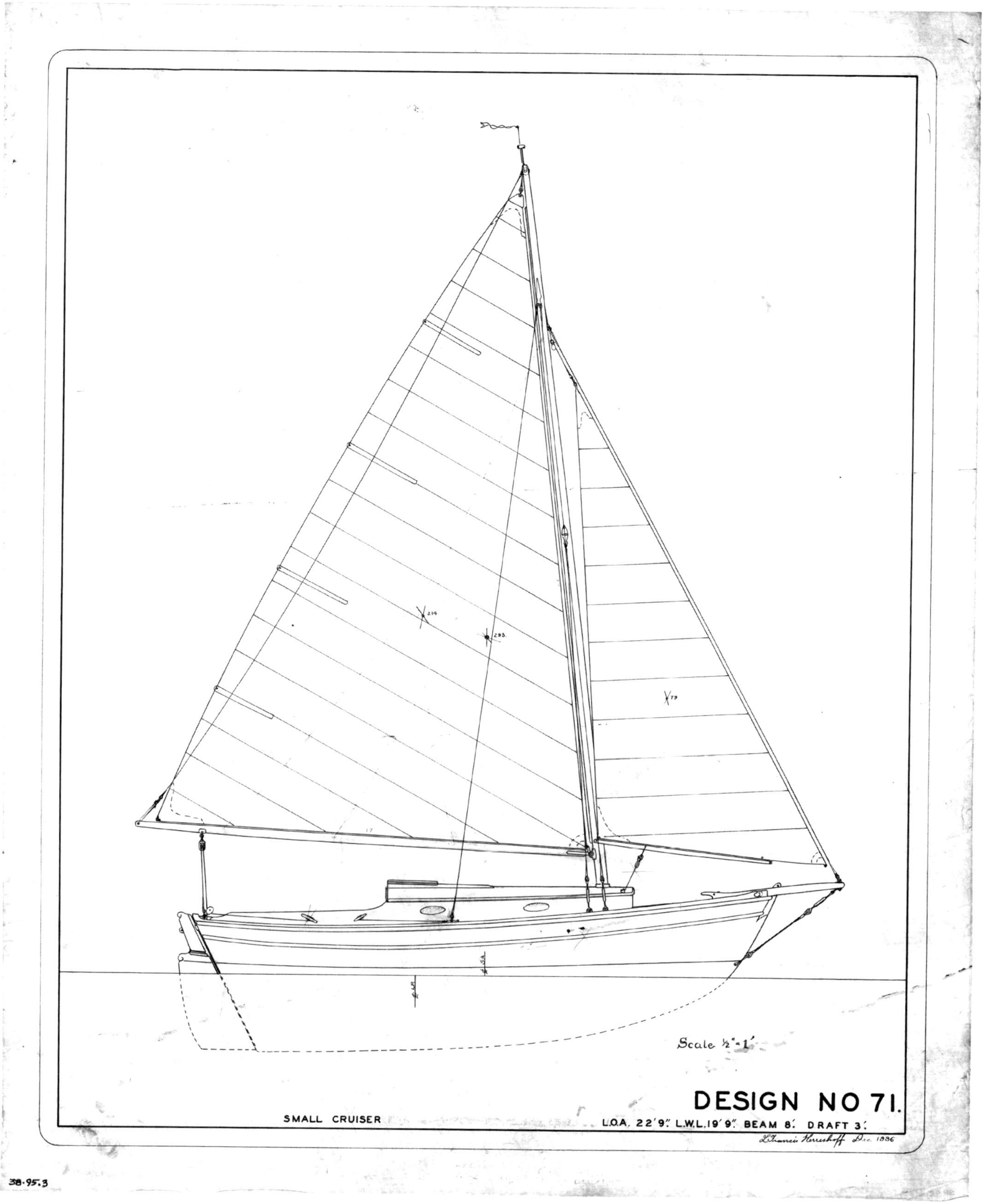
Scale ½" = 1'
DESIGN NO 71.
SMALL CRUISER
L.O.A. 22'9". L.W.L. 19'9". BEAM 8'. DRAFT 3'.
L. Francis Herreshoff Dec 1936
38-95.3

Station Numbers	Hights above and below L.W.L.: Top of Deck at Side	Buttock #1	Buttock #2	Buttock #3	Rabbet	Profile	Half Breadths: At Deck	WL+2'	WL+1'	WL+6"	L.W.L.	WL-6"	WL-1'	WL-18"	WL-2'	WL-2'6"	Rabbet	Face	Diagonals: 1.	2.	3.	Station Numbers
0	3-2-6					3-2-6	0-1-0										0-1-4	0-1-4				0
2	2-11-2	1-10-6			0-2-4	-0-0-6	1-7-0	1-0-6	0-6-4	0-3-0	0-0-4						0-1-4	0-0-2	1-4-7	0-11-3	0-0-3	2
4	2-8-2	0-1-6	1-7-4		-1-1-1	-1-2-6	2-7-0	2-3-0	1-7-4	1-3-2	0-10-4	0-5-3	0-2-0				0-1-4	0-0-6	2-5-4	1-11-3	0-8-1	4
6	2-5-4	-0-8-6	0-2-6	1-10-4	-1-6-0	-1-11-0	3-3-0	3-0-6	2-6-5	2-2-4	1-9-3	1-2-7	0-8-6	0-3-0			0-2-6	0-1-4	3-2-4	2-8-3	1-2-4	6
8	2-3-1	-1-2-6	-0-6-0	0-7-2	-1-7-6	-2-4-2	3-7-7	3-7-2	3-2-4	2-11-3	2-6-5	2-0-0	1-3-6	0-7-6	0-3-3		0-4-2	0-2-3	3-9-1	3-3-1	1-7-2	8
10	2-1-1	-1-6-1	-0-10-5	-0-1-2	-1-9-3	-2-7-2	3-10-6	3-2-4	3-7-2	3-5-2	3-0-7	2-6-3	1-9-1	1-0-0	0-4-6	0-3-4	0-5-2	0-3-0	4-1-5	3-7-6	1-10-1	10
12	1-11-4	-1-7-0	-1-0-0	-0-4-4	-1-11-2	-2-9-2	4-0-0	3-7-2	3-9-6	3-10-0	3-4-3	2-9-5	2-0-0	1-1-3	0-5-0	0-4-0	0-5-0	0-3-2	4-3-6	3-10-5	1-11-1	12
14	1-10-3	-1-5-5	-0-11-6	-0-4-4	-2-0-7	-2-10-3	4-0-0		3-10-6	3-8-5	3-5-1	2-10-2	1-10-7	0-11-3	0-5-3	0-3-7	0-4-2	0-3-0	4-4-4	3-10-7	1-10-1	14
16	1-9-6	-1-2-3	-0-9-2	-0-2-4	-2-2-4	-2-11-1	3-11-0		3-9-7	3-7-2	3-3-2	2-6-5	1-4-1	0-7-5	0-4-0	0-2-7	0-2-7	0-2-2	4-3-3	3-9-2	1-7-0	16
18	1-9-5	-0-3-0	-0-4-3	+0-2-1	-2-4-2	-2-11-6	3-8-4		3-7-0	3-3-6	2-8-7	1-8-1	0-7-2	0-3-5	0-2-4	0-1-7	0-2-0	0-1-3	4-1-0	3-5-2	1-2-2	18
20	1-10-1	-0-2-0	+0-2-4	+0-9-6	-1-0-0	-3-0-0	3-4-4		3-1-6	2-7-1	1-4-7	0-5-2	0-2-6	0-1-1	0-1-5	0-1-1	0-2-0	0-0-6	3-8-2	2-10-4	0-8-0	20
22	1-11-4	0-7-2	0-10-6				2-11-0			0-7-0							0-2-0		3-2-6	2-1-2	0-0-6	22
22'-9"	2-0-2						2-8-4															22'-9"

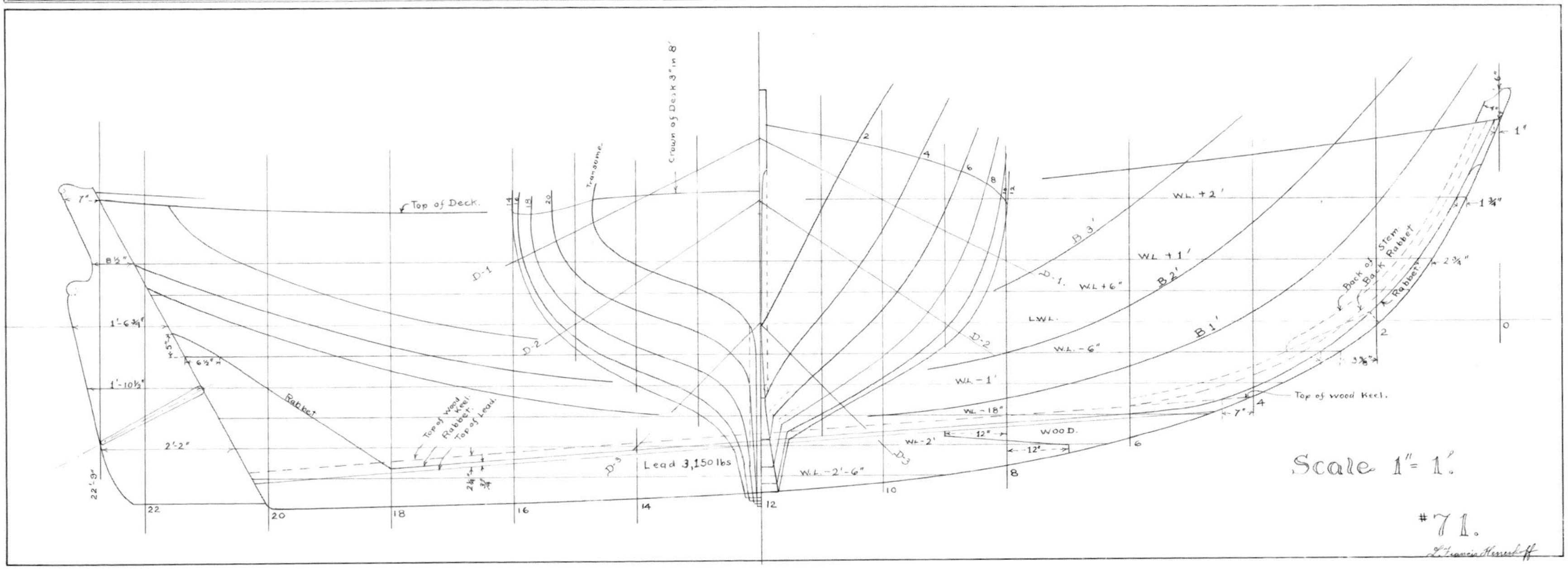

Scale 1" = 1'.

#71.

L. Francis Herreshoff

An appreciative amateur, building his H-23 from Francis's plans, wrote to him, "as I have progressed with the construction and studied the plans in detail, I am very favorably impressed with the simplicity and all-around utility of the design," but then he wanted more detail on the spars. The publication of his plans in *The Rudder* brought Francis plenty of chores.[37]

It is not known how many No. 71s were built. The Quincy Adams yard built two on speculation, backed up by a four-page flyer, "The Last Word in Small Cruising Yachts," that claimed, "for its price, this small cruiser has more usable room in the cabin, lead on the keel, strength, seaworthiness, durability, and speed than any other stock or semi-stock boat we have yet seen." Malcolm Seavey in Thomaston, Maine, advertised that he would build Prudences "priced at less than $100 a foot!" but the ad failed to draw. *The Rudder* sold about forty sets of plans over the years.[38]

And Gulliford built an enlarged version based on Francis's simple outboard profile and sail plan drawing that he labeled "No. 71½." There was no new lines drawing; Francis and his customer relied on Gulliford to lengthen the design by four feet and meet Francis's expanded dimensions of 26 feet, 9 inches length on deck; 23 feet, 3 inches on the waterline; identical beam of 8 feet; and draft of 3 feet, 3 inches. The new sail plan showed a slightly higher-aspect-ratio rig of 344 square feet, with 252 square feet in the mainsail and 92 square feet in the jib.[39]

One owner of a No. 71 was the noted dealer in second-hand nautical books, Alfred W. Paine, for whom Francis modified his design by adding a little more lateral plane aft. His and his wife Carola's enjoyment of the boat was interrupted by the war. Alfred did not survive his naval service, but Carola carried on the book business and also kept sailing the little Herreshoff cruiser.[40]

Francis sold plans to amateur builders for $20. One asked Mr. Herreshoff about raising the cockpit floor and making the cockpit watertight. Francis replied: "The cockpit could be made self-bailing, but I believe it is entirely unnecessary in such a seaworthy type of hull, and the cockpit would be much less comfortable."[41]

The sale of H-23 plans continued. In 1969, Francis sold a set to a young college teacher, Craig R. Humphrey, for $35. Humphrey promised Mr. Herreshoff that he would install a cedar bucket, not a Sands marine toilet.[42]

In 1981, Maureen Kane, despite having "sailed once in my life," determined to buy a small sailboat, live aboard, and go cruising. She looked at a lot of boats, but fell in love with a Prudence. She sailed from Key West to Nantucket with side trips to the Bahamas and Florida's west coast. "I thrived aboard my boat," she wrote. "In my readings of L. Francis, I discerned a man who relegated women to the galley and the shopping chores. I hope he would have been pleased to know he designed a boat a woman, who had never sailed before, could sail, single-handed, for thousands of miles." He would, indeed, have been pleased; Kane could have been the role model for one of Francis's characters in his book, *The Compleat Cruiser,* exemplifying how to cruise well in a small, simple boat.[43]

LEFT: **The lines and offsets of the *Hard Tack*. Again, the half-breadth plan, with waterlines and diagonals, was a separate drawing that has not come to light, though the table of offsets enables her to be built without it. She is a wholesome little vessel with enough lateral plane without a centerboard, and with just enough curve in the stem and rake in the wineglass transom to avoid looking plain. Length on deck is 22 feet, 9 inches; length on the waterline, 19 feet, 9 inches; beam, 8 feet; and draft, 3 feet. Displacement is 6,888 pounds, with 3,150 pounds of lead on the keel for a ballast-displacement ratio of 46 percent.** (© Mystic Seaport Museum, Daniel S. Gregory Ships Plans Library, SP38.95.1.)

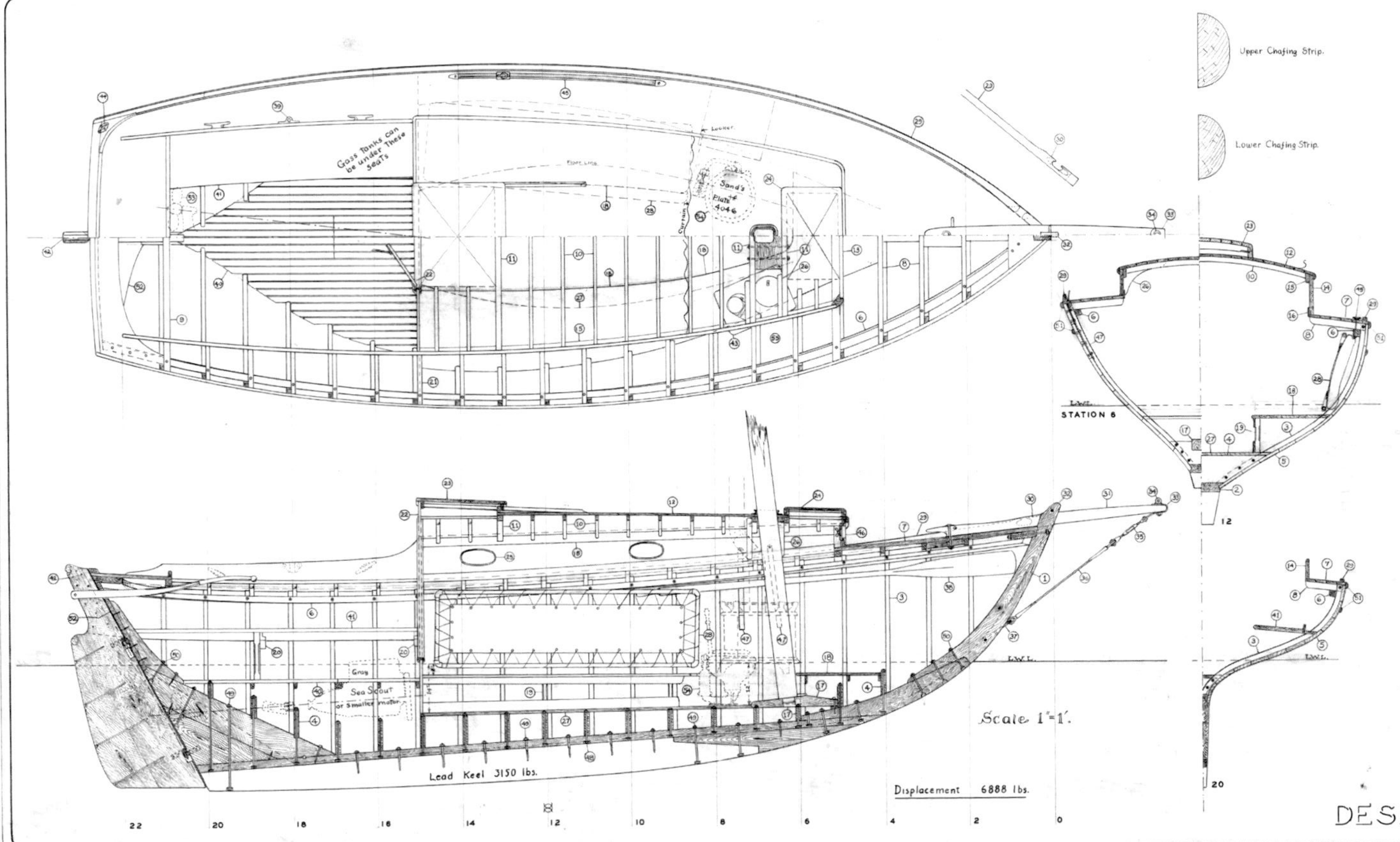

1. Stem, Oak Sided 4".
2. Keel " width 12" Depth 2¼".
3. Frames " 1¼" x 1¼" Spaced 12".
4. Floor Timbers Oak sided 1¼".
5. Planking ⅞" Cedar or ¾" Fir.
6. Clamp Hard Pine 2" x 1¾".
7. Deck, Pine ⅝ Tong' & Groove Canvased.
8. Deck Beams Oak 1" x 1¾" Crown 3" in 8'.
9. Strong " " 1¾"x1¾" " " " ".
10. House " " ¾"x 1¼" " 7" " 6'.
11. " Strong Beams 1½ x 1¼" " " " ".
12. " Deck Pine ⅝" Tong' & Groove Canvased.
13. " Front 1" Oak.
14. " Sides & coambing ¾" Oak.
15. Carline Oak ⅞"x 2½".
16. Finish Strip ⅜"x 2".
17. Mast Step Oak 5" wide 3" deep, Set into Floor #6-2".
18. Transom ¾" Pine, Top 3" below W.L.
19. " Supports
20. Rack for Cabin doors when unshipped
21. Cabin partition ½ Pine tong' & groove
22. " Doors Paneled pine, with Hook hinges- and Brass Hasp – See Designer.
23. Companion slide Oak or Mexican Mahogany.
24. Hatch " " " "
25. Fixed lights set in putty.
26. Two knees each side abreast Mast.
27. Cabin floor ⅝ Pine, Painted,
28. Showing position of Pipe Berths 6'-3" x 22".
29. Tapered Toe Rail 1" at top 1½" at Bottom – debth on stations as follows #2-2¼" – #4-2" #6-1¾" – #8-1½" – #10-1¼" - to 1" aft.
30. Bow Chocks Fashioned out of the Rail- and 2¾" high.
31. Hard Pine Bowsprit, Shaped for Mooring Bitt, about 5½" x 3" at Stem head.
32. Stem head about 1¼" thick.
33. Brass or Bronze Band 3" x ⅜".
34. Special Eyebolt of strong Bronze, Forged with shoulder drilled eye, ½" S.A.E. Nut.
35. Merriman Fig-377 - 7⁄16"
36. ⅜"-6x7 KORODLESS.
37. Special forged Everdur ⅜" Shackle ½" pin.
38. 9' Ash Oar. if no motor.
39. Rowlocks and Sockets from Herreshoff Mfg Co.
40. Hard wood slat floor, Center section lifting
41. Seats slanting back as shown. ⅞ Thick.
42. Rudder center piece 1½" Thick.
43. Household Marine Range No. 6-92-3" legs. front legs only used. (or smaller Stove).
44. Merriman - Fig 416 #3. P.+S.
45. " " 448 with after bolts through clamp.
46. Oval Brass Port Wilcox, C. & Co. Fig 527 - 4"x7".
47. Tobin Bronze 5⁄16" x 1¼" x 24".
48. All Floor Timber Bolts ⅜" Tobin Bronze.
49. " Bolts Through or into the Lead ½" Tobin.
50. " " Beyond #4 and #20 ⅜" T. Head.
51. Oak Chafing Strips as shown Above.
52. Stern Transome 1¼" Oak.
53. Hyde 12" dia -3 Blade for big-2 Blade for small Engines.
54. Sand's (Winsted) Plate 4046 - Left Hand Pump. there can be a locker back of same if desired.
55. There can be shelves back of stove, depending on tipe of stove used.

DESIGN NO 71

LEFT: **The *Hard Tack*'s construction and cabin plan. The oak keelson is a foot wide, with a depth of 2¼ inches. Oak frames are 1¼ by 1¼, spaced 12 inches. Planking to be ⅞-inch cedar or ¾-inch fir. The transom, with its slight curve, is 1¼-inch oak. Francis designed no fittings for this boat, instead specifying hardware that could be purchased off the shelf, including oarlocks and sockets, in the coaming, from the Herreshoff Manufacturing Company. (In dotted lines, he shows a Gray Sea Scout engine protruding above the cockpit floor.) Note the mooring bitt, shaped on the inboard end of the bowsprit. Just to starboard of the mast, Francis has drawn in a Household Marine stove, plenty of heat for this little cabin, but he added "(or smaller stove)" in his list of specifications on the right-hand side of the drawing. To port, mounted permanently and taking up more space than the cedar bucket that he preferred, he shows a Sands No. 4046 toilet with left-hand pump, since a handle on the right would foul the mast. Mercy.** (© Mystic Seaport Museum, Daniel S. Gregory Ships Plans Library, SP38.95.2) ABOVE: **The sail plan of the original *Prudence,* Francis's design No. 43, also for Richard Jenks, drawn in 1929. As shown, she was to be built lapstrake for light displacement. Her rig would be very easy to handle, with a four-part main sheet and two parts on the jib, together with lazy jacks on each sail. As designed, she may have had a little too much weather helm: the additional lateral plane aft, shown in a second set of dotted lines beneath the deadwood and rudder, was "Suggested for A. W. Paine in 1939," as Francis noted later on the drawing. Since this was a cruising boat, Francis showed eye splices, rather than his tangs, for attaching the standing rigging to the mast. "It was a big mess—never again," he wrote. Sail area is 325 square feet, with 236 square feet in the mainsail and 89 in the jib.** (© Mystic Seaport Museum, Daniel S. Gregory Ships Plans Library, SP38.126.3)

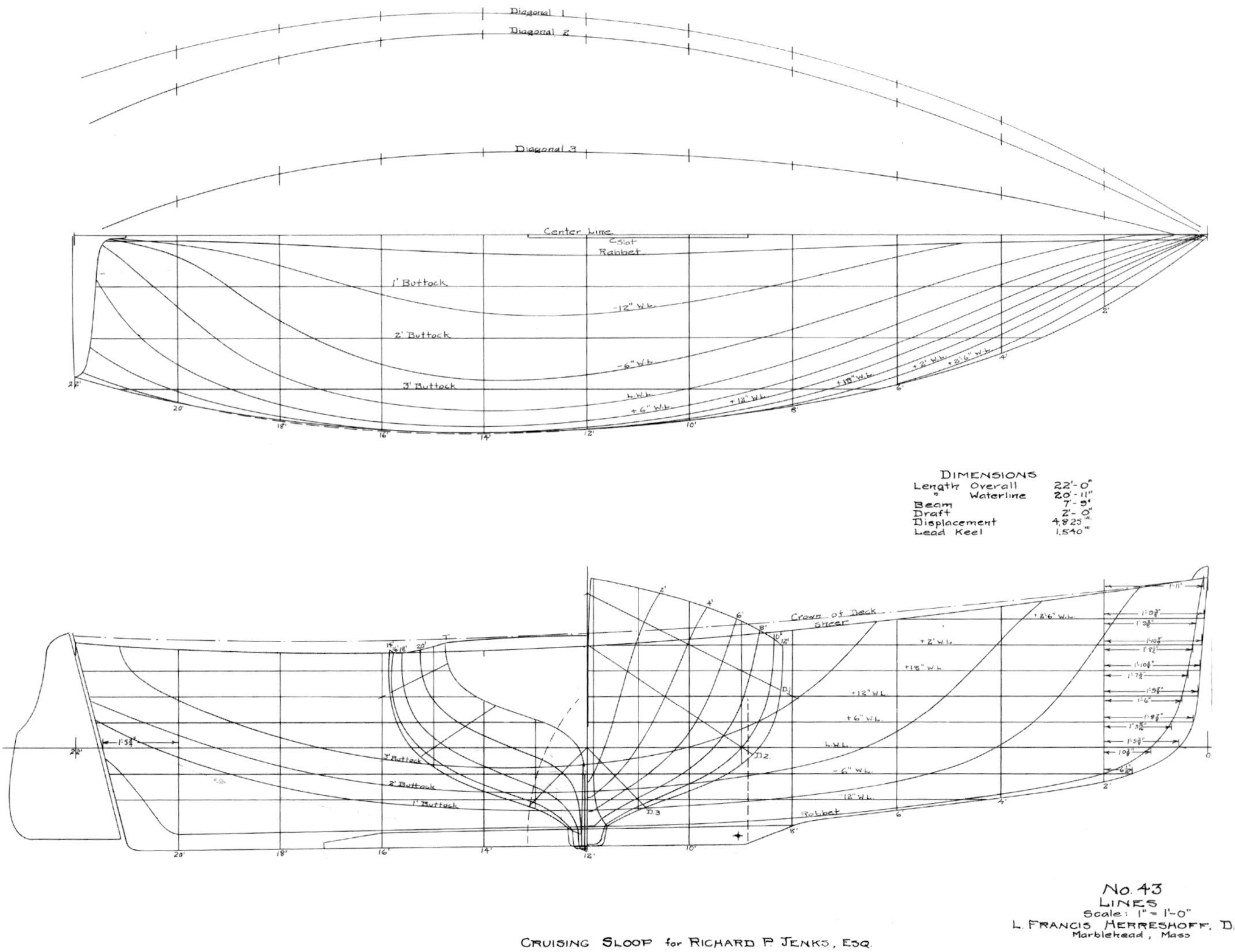

ABOVE: **The *Prudence*'s lines. She is relatively narrow for a shoal-draft centerboarder; there is little to hold her back. Length on deck is 22 feet; length on the waterline, 20 feet, 11 inches; beam 7 feet, 9 inches; and draft, board up, is 2 feet. Displacement is 4,825 pounds. The dimension that Francis gives on this drawing shows a lead keel of 1,540 pounds, but on his construction drawing, Francis notes a keel weight of 1,030 pounds. The former figure, still giving a ballast-displacement ratio of only 32 percent, seems more reasonable.** (© Mystic Seaport Museum, Daniel S. Gregory Ships Plans Library, SP38.126.1 RIGHT: **The construction and cabin plan of the *Prudence*. Frames are 1¼ inches square, on 12-inch centers; lapstrake planking ⅝-inch white cedar, copper riveted. Francis wrote on the plan, "Note. Builder is to line off planking using at least twelve strakes." The centerboard trunk, 1-inch white pine or cypress; board to be 1½-inch, wood not specified, but oak probably used. The board was weighted with 25 pounds of lead. The flat transom is ⅞-inch oak; the rudder, 1¼-inch oak. Headroom is 4 feet up by the mast, gaining a little as you go aft. There is room to crouch round either end of the centerboard trunk, and it can serve as the base for a folding-leaf table. Francis shows a Shipmate No. 211 stove and a Sands No. 1075 toilet. And he has penciled in a big engine taking up a lot of space in the cockpit, doubtless at the wish of the owner. These three drawings of the *Prudence* were traced by Sam Brown in August 1929.** (© Mystic Seaport Museum, Daniel S. Gregory Ships Plans Library, SP38.126.2))

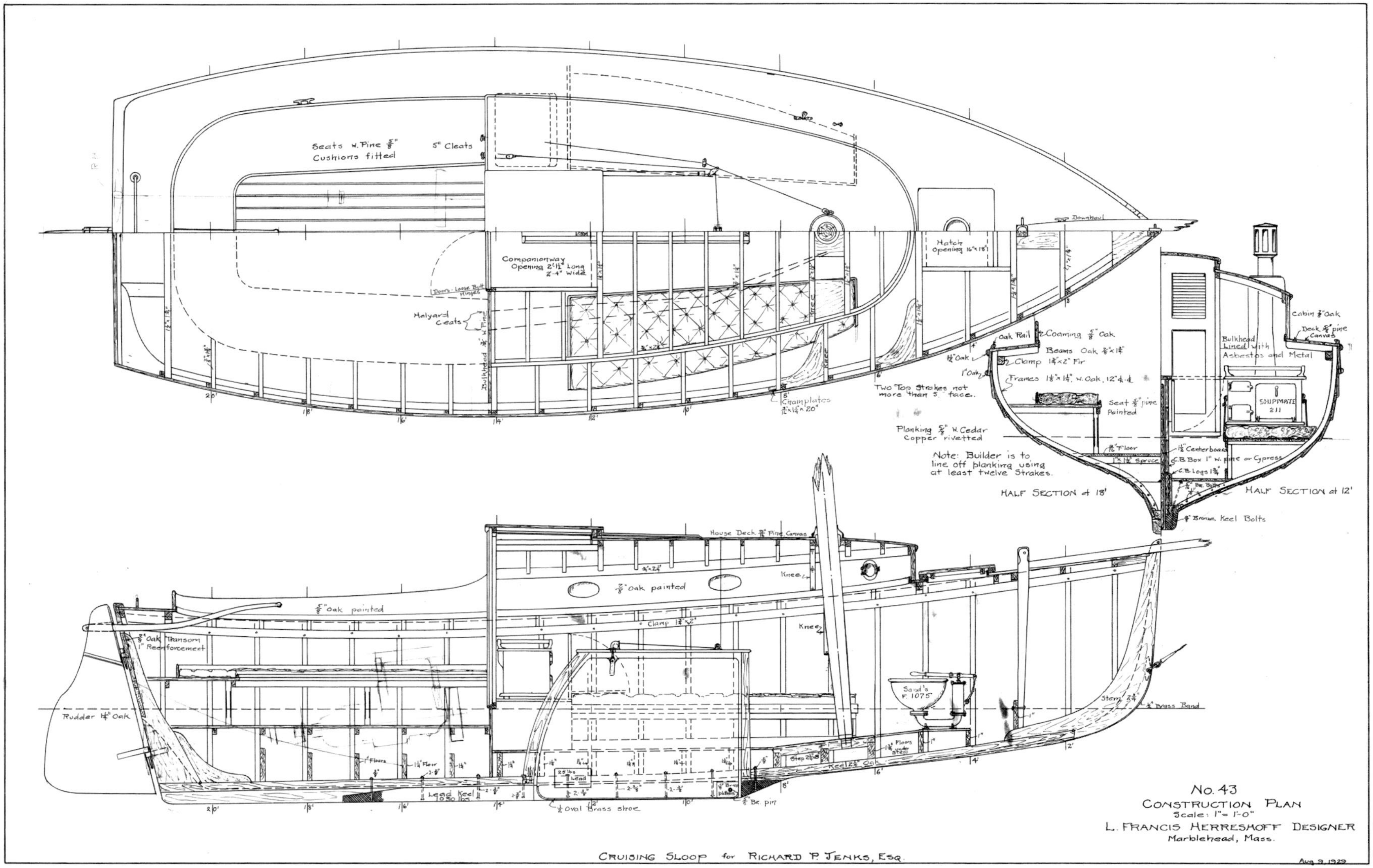

Seats W. Pine
Cushions fitted
5" Cleats
Companionway
Opening 2'-1½" Long
2'-4" Wide
Halyard Cleats
Bulkhead
Hatch Opening 16"x 18"
Downhaul
Chainplates
Two Top Strakes not more than 5" face.
Planking W. Cedar copper rivetted
Note: Builder is to line off planking using at least twelve Strakes.
Oak Rail
Coaming Oak
Beams Oak
Clamp Fir
Frames W. Oak
Seat pine Painted
Floor
Centerboard
Cabin Oak
Deck pine Canvas
Bulkhead Lined with Asbestos and Metal
SHIPMATE 211
Bronze Keel Bolts
HALF SECTION at 18'
HALF SECTION at 12'
House Deck Pine Canvas
Knee
Oak painted
Clamp
Oak Transom
1" Reenforcement
Rudder Oak
Sand's F. 1075
Stem
Brass Band
Floors
Step
Keel Oak
Lead
Lead Keel
Oval Brass shoe
No. 43
CONSTRUCTION PLAN
Scale: 1" = 1'-0"
L. FRANCIS HERRESHOFF DESIGNER
Marblehead, Mass.
CRUISING SLOOP for RICHARD P. JENKS, ESQ.
Aug 9 1929

The H-23 was one of Francis's designs that he sailed on the water, as well as in his imagination. He wrote: "It is surprising that the little Prudence boats, called H-23, sail so well because with their shallow draft I did not expect them to do well and was agreeably surprised when I sailed in one myself." Finding her "fast and able," he didn't have to depend on the reports of others to back up his vicarious voyages, but still he must have been very happy to hear from a sailor who told him, "I have found her one of the best little boats I have ever handled at sea" after covering the whole south coast of Australia, all of the Great Barrier Reef, and even the rough crossing to Tasmania in his H-23. Francis had never intended that the H-23 would put to sea, and he would have considered crossing the 150-mile-wide Bass Strait in her foolhardy and unpleasant, but he could still enjoy hearing about such a feat by the little boat.[44]

Robert J. Hefner, a historic preservation consultant of East Hampton, Long Island, has a Prudence named the *Lively.* She was built in 1956 by the Clark Boatyard in Atlantic Highlands, New Jersey. In the spring of 2002, Hefner took Kathleen and me for a fine sail across Gardiners Bay. The waters around Gardiners Island and Shelter Island, between the forks at the east end of Long Island, are ideal for the 23-foot sloop. The *Lively* lived up to her name in the gentle breeze. She was fun to sail, and the word "comfortable" kept cropping up in our conversation. This design of L. Francis Herreshoff is a quintessential small, simple cruising boat.

The name Prudence for the H-23 had come from a predecessor that Francis had designed, also for Jenks, in 1929. The earlier *Prudence* was a 22-foot, plumb-bow centerboarder, design No. 43. She was built in Warren, Rhode Island, by Henry Vincent, the ex-Herreshoff Row Boat Shop man who had built Francis's kayak, the *Katrina*. Francis wrote to the son of Lyman H. Smith, one of her later owners, who was singing her praises: "I think it is only natural that a boat like *Prudence*, built to no rule at all, makes a better boat than the average type of so-called cruiser which has been affected by the various rating boats [rules] for the last fifty years."[45]

We have seen Richard Jenks's ideas for a small cruiser progress from the radical to the conservative as he gained sailing experience. Back in 1923, he had asked Francis to design him a cruising R-boat, an abortive attempt to develop a cruiser from an out-and-out racer (see volume 1, page 227). In 1929, he returned to Francis for the design of an out-and-out small cruiser, and, in the *Prudence,* he got a relatively light displacement, relatively narrow centerboarder with a relatively generous rig. She was no racer, but she was a lively, smart sailor. Then, in 1937, as we have seen, Jenks asked Francis to design him another boat, the *Hard Tack,* similar to the *Prudence,* but with a full keel instead of a centerboard, and hence a heavier boat. Even with a little less sail than the *Prudence*, the *Hard Tack* had a decent turn of speed, and she could carry full sail appreciably longer as it breezed up than could the *Prudence*. For coastwise cruising in ordinary weather, No. 43, the *Prudence*, neither radical nor conservative, would be the

---

LEFT: **L. Francis Herreshoff was super-critical of any paintings made of his designs. One that passed was of the H-23 *Prudence* by Victor Weidner, a Port Washington neighbor of Boris's. Weidner's oil painting, showing the little vessel heading home for land, an easy sea lifting her along on a broad reach, was used on the cover of *The Rudder* (and also on the dust jacket of Francis's posthumous book, *Sensible Cruising Designs*). Francis wrote to Boris: "Not only is the drawing all perfectly correct but the water and sky are beautifully done and the coloring most pleasing." Boris arranged for Weidner to make a gift of the painting to Francis.** (Victor Weidner painting, courtesy of author)

most fun, because she has enough sail area for her displacement to have that wonderful feeling of a Herreshoff boat: a beautifully shaped hull dancing over the waves.

Maynard Bray, technical editor of *WoodenBoat* magazine, has recently acquired a No. 43, the *Lily*. He writes, "she blew me away with her sailing ability." We can assume that the pun is unintentional, but we can take stock of the superlative statement, coming from a sailor who has tried a wide variety of designs under sail. Bray has found that his boat "sailed so well in light air and moved so easily with a sculling oar" that he eschewed auxiliary power. "She needs early reefing," he has learned. And he writes: "*Lily* under mainsail alone is remarkable in that, sheeted in with either a full main or a single reef, and the tiller free, she'll slowly—very slowly—make her way to windward, first on one tack, then on the other. Then, if you want to start sailing, she'll do that consistently. Just pull on the tiller and give her a bit of sheet and she's off." Bray has also learned that with the partial boom on the jib, you can make her sail herself on the wind by trimming in the weather sheet just enough to counterbalance her weather helm, without losing speed appreciably. The jib sheet arrangement also lets you turn her quickly when maneuvering under sail by trimming the weather sheet in hard to spin the bow round. Bray has added a bit of height to the after ends of the cockpit seats for better visibility over the cabin house from the tiller. He threatens to add small wedges under the laps in the *Lily*'s planking at the waterline forward, because the waves chuckling along the lapstrakes can hinder sleeping in a choppy anchorage. Maynard Bray feels lucky to have a boat built to this unheralded design by L. Francis Herreshoff.[46]

Francis did little work at his drafting table from the time of his father's death in mid-1938 until mid-1942, when Boris Lauer-Leonardi recognized him as a sage for *The Rudder*. Those four years were the doldrums of Francis's life. He was depressed over the loss of his father. Between the effects of the Depression and the effects of the war, there was little demand for his talent as a yacht designer. Except for the creation of the Northeast Harbor One-Design, there was no satisfying work. Instead, there was the isolation and frugality of unemployment.

As well as his father, Francis had lost his good friend, Waldo Brown. Charlie Welch's attention was focused on his Martha's Vineyard farm. Francis was not in touch with Frank Paine. His continued friendships with Starling Burgess and Billy Strawbridge were vital, but they both would be busy with war work. At age fifty, Francis was becalmed.

Then, into these doldrums blew a trade wind. L. Francis Herreshoff truly picked up the trades on his voyage when Boris Lauer-Leonardi came into his life. Here was someone who not only saw Francis for who he was, but also had the means to provide Francis a way to show the yachting world who he was. Boris opened the pages of *The Rudder* to L. Francis Herreshoff to gain readers for his magazine and, in the process, provided Francis with an audience. Francis, too shy to speak in

RIGHT: **A boat built to design No. 43 smoking to windward off Lopez Island, in Washington's San Juans. She was built in about 1980 by professional builder David C. King for his own use. Writing that "she'd be a hellish boat to plank lapstrake," he used the cold-molded method that he was accustomed to. He added roach, and hence battens, to the mainsail and made the jib self-tending. He apologized for "an unfortunate decision about the appearance of the foredeck hatch"—apparently increased height above the deck.** (Courtesy David C. King, author's collection)

public, was not at all shy about speaking his mind in writing. He loved to mentor, and writing for *The Rudder* gave him the chance to mentor the multitude. He found a style that was direct, informal, opinionated. Thousands of readers got to know L. Francis Herreshoff personally through his writing. They found him to be a marine sage, all right, and a sage who could get on his high horse at times, but also one who could dismount and be friendly, open, even funny. Francis loved to talk around his fireside the way he wrote, seeking to enlighten his friends with the common sense of yacht design; Boris Lauer-Leonardi's *Rudder* gave him the opportunity to start a crusade. The doldrums would soon be far astern.

CHAPTER 19

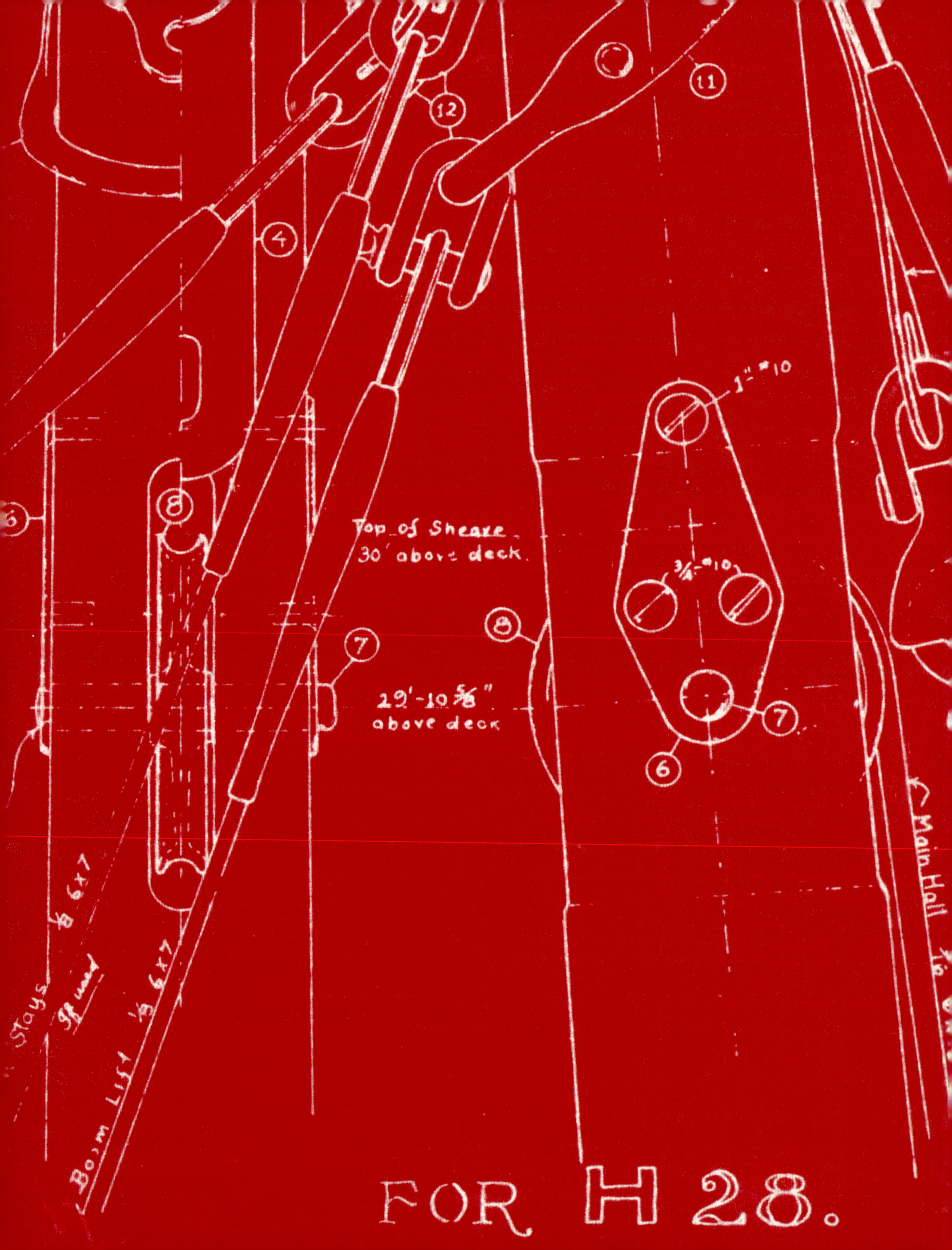
Top of Sheave
30' above deck
29'-10 5/8"
above deck
1"-#10
3/4"-#10
11
12
4
8
7
6
Stays 5/8 6x7
Boom Lift 1/2 6x7
FOR H 28.

THE H-28 AND THE COMMON SENSE OF YACHT DESIGN

"I am rather surprised that I have brought myself to do some writing during the last few years but it is only because I have felt so strongly that someone should do something to help straighten out yachting and to bring forward more commonsense thought on the matter."

—L. FRANCIS HERRESHOFF, 1947

When L. Francis Herreshoff began writing regularly for *The Rudder* in late 1942, the experience changed his life. Now his "customer" was Everyman, not just the yachtsman of means. Francis had not been comfortable with the yachting clique; he had enjoyed the company both afloat and ashore of Charlie Welch, Waldo Brown, and Billy Strawbridge, but he had kept his distance from most of the men for whom he designed yachts. In writing for *The Rudder,* Francis stepped outside this circle of the privileged. How would his words and ideas be accepted by ordinary sailors?

Having "made a complete failure of English in school," he did not think of himself as a writer. But he had strong ideas about yacht design and yachting, and he loved to enlighten others to his point of view, as long as they showed interest and would listen. He was not a natural writer, but he was a natural teacher, and so he had no trouble finding the words to preach his lesson. He would lay out his text as best he could and see if anyone cared. And he knew how to spin a yarn. In a way, it was as if Francis had spent the first fifty years of his life preparing to be the perfect contributor to *The Rudder.* Francis would write: "I am rather surprised that I have brought myself to do some writing during the last few years but it is only because I have felt so strongly that someone should do something to help straighten out yachting and to bring forward more commonsense thought on the matter."[1]

Francis's life-change would not have happened but for Boris Lauer-Leonardi. One yacht designer and builder wrote to another as follows: "As for Boris, I think he was one of the most decent

people I ever met and I cannot think of a single person who came in contact with him that was not helped in some way by knowing him." Francis was certainly helped by knowing Boris; perhaps even saved by him.[2]

Boris was friendly and lively. He was also tactful and respectful. He recognized in Mr. Herreshoff someone who could help him immensely as he took over *The Rudder* and worked hard to make its contents the best that he could and thus, hopefully, increase the magazine's circulation. He cultivated his friendship with Francis through frequent correspondence and during many visits to Marblehead. He sought Francis's guidance for the magazine, and encouraged his writing. He recognized Francis's wisdom and knowledge about yachting; he also recognized that Francis was proud and could be easily offended. He was able to draw Francis out of the doldrums and stimulate him to show his genius to the world. On Francis's side, he felt seen and heard by Boris. The editor gave him exactly what had been missing in his life. Francis shunned the limelight socially, but he knew the high value of his artistic and technical abilities, and he craved professional recognition. Boris and *The Rudder* gave him the opportunity to fill that need.

And Francis became Boris's mentor. He could see that Boris had a lot to learn about boats, and he could see that Boris was aware that the editor of *The Rudder* ought to know a lot more than he did know, and so he was eager to learn. Francis, the teacher, had gained the perfect student.

Writing for *The Rudder* brought Francis a steady, if modest, flow of cash. It gave him the opportunity to work at his drawing board creating boats for *Rudder* readers when he had little other

L. Francis Herreshoff on one end of a sailing rig behind his house at 25 Front Street at about the time he designed the H-28. (Katherine H. DeWolf photo, Mystic Seaport Museum, 1997-1-54)

work. As he drew a design for *The Rudder*, then rolled up the plans on a stick and shipped them off, Francis knew that his drawings would be published and used by builders; there would be no more creating yacht designs that would be filed in the bottom desk drawers of yachtsmen who decided they didn't want that sort of boat after all. It must have been a huge relief for Francis, as he worked at his board, to know that the drawing in front of him would not be rejected. And also a huge relief to know that there would be no rating rule to bow down to, no scantling rule or bothersome inspectors to enforce it, and no inept racing skipper to cause his design to fail. Instead, he could hold his vision of a lovely boat dancing through the waves.[3]

Francis considered himself to be part of Boris's team, trying to keep the magazine going and improve it. He influenced Boris to use the work of top marine artists, like Warren Sheppard, on the cover. He evaluated technical articles for Boris. Both editor and writer would have the satisfaction, during the war, of receiving evidence from servicemen that getting *The Rudder* was important to their morale.[4]

Boris came to consider his dealings with Skipper Herreshoff to be a private and personal interchange between friends, as well as *Rudder* business. It wasn't long before "Dear Mr. Herreshoff" became "Dear Skipper," and the letters were signed, "Your Boris." And his letters, at first written at the office on *Rudder* letterhead, soon arrived in Francis's mailbox on plain copy paper and were written from home during evenings and weekends. Francis would reply to Boris at 21 Mackey Avenue, Port Washington, New York.[5]

Francis's writing career began in the midst of war. The American victory at the Battle of Midway, in June 1942, was a turning point in the Pacific. For the first time since Pearl Harbor, Americans could dare to imagine a time "after the war," even though that time would not be soon. Boris suggested to Francis that he design for *The Rudder* a cruising boat that would be simple enough for amateur builders to tackle and small enough to be affordable for a G. I. or Bluejacket returning home. He was asking Francis to design a boat, not for a rich client, but for Everyman. Francis, an elitist who nevertheless liked to yarn with the ordinary man on the waterfront, would need to make the most of his Populist proclivities. In mid-September 1942, he wrote to Boris, "I have just started on a design of a boat for *The Rudder*." The profile drawing and sail plan appeared in the December 1942 issue as the H-28, presented as the first article in a new How-To-Build series. The designation as a Herreshoff 28-footer was Boris's idea, to take advantage of Francis's name and reputation. He had already told Francis: "You have no idea how happy I am that you agreed to design a boat for us. I am saving some money, after the war will have one built for myself by some good builder. Then at last I will have a boat designed by you."[6]

Francis would bring the same degree of excellence to the H-28 that he brought to a design for a wealthy yachtsman. He based the design on both his own experience of cruising in small, simple boats and his view—common sense—of what sort of boat would be good for the ordinary sailor. Because he thought, "Why anyone should want to make yachting democratic I don't know," he had to idealize his view of Everyman. His H-28 owner wanted to leave the problems and cares of life behind to go off cruising—enjoying nature, being quiet, even contemplating the universe. The H-28 was to be the simple, reliable, inspirational conveyance for such a quest.[7]

There was a certain independence to designing for an imagined Everyman that at least one Francis Herreshoff fan recognized: "I am happy that you are now in a position to design your yachts with complete freedom; that is without an owner looking over your shoulder, so to speak." In any event, the key to Everyman's boat was

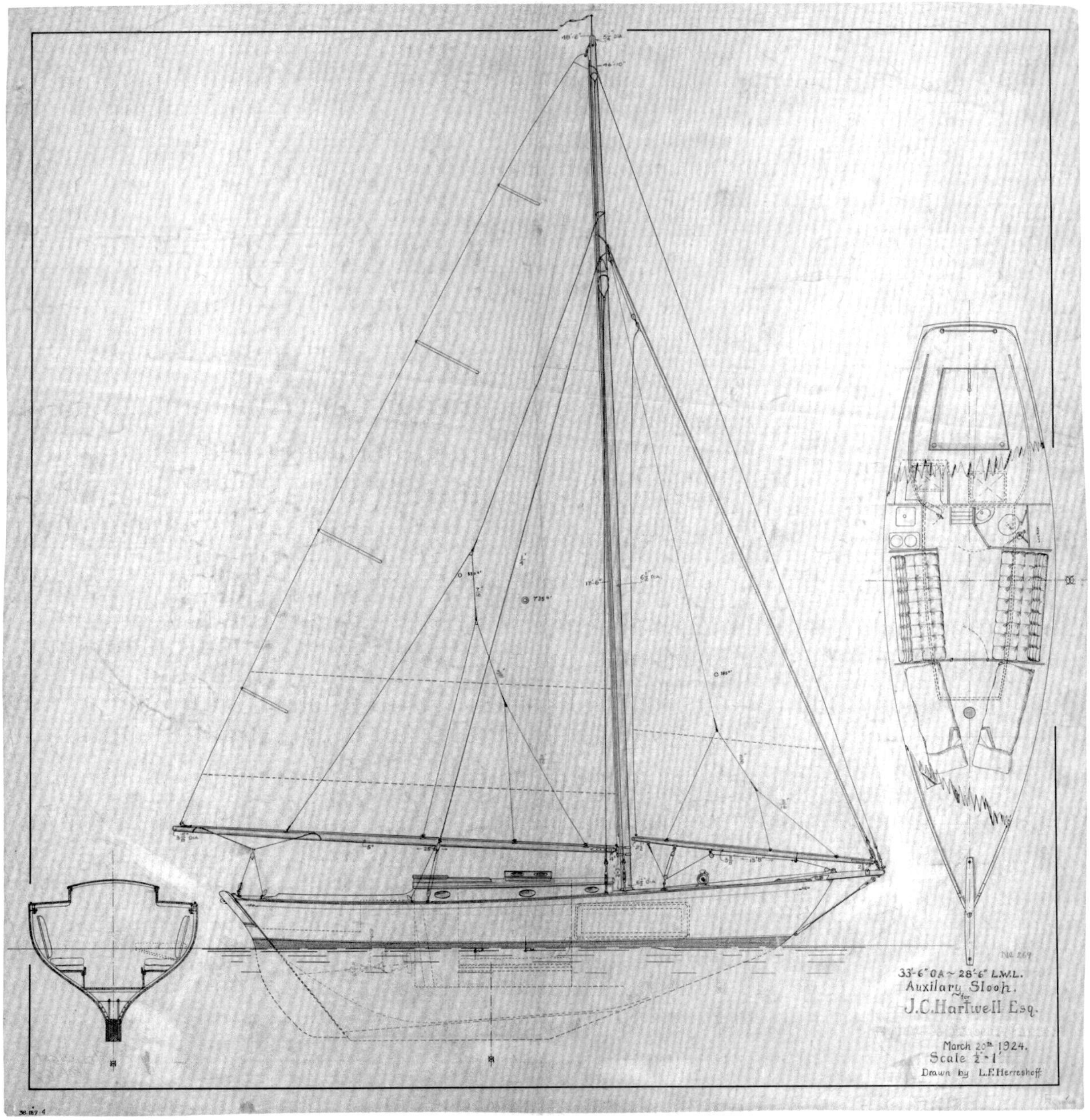

A forerunner of the H-28 was the sloop *Santee* that Francis drew in 1924 while working at Burgess, Swasey, and Paine. She was BSP No. 269, for J. C. Hartwell. Sail area is 735 square feet, of which 550 square feet is in her big mainsail. She is a larger boat than the H-28, designed for cruising with four people instead of two. (© Mystic Seaport Museum, Daniel S. Gregory Ships Plans Library, SP38.187.4)

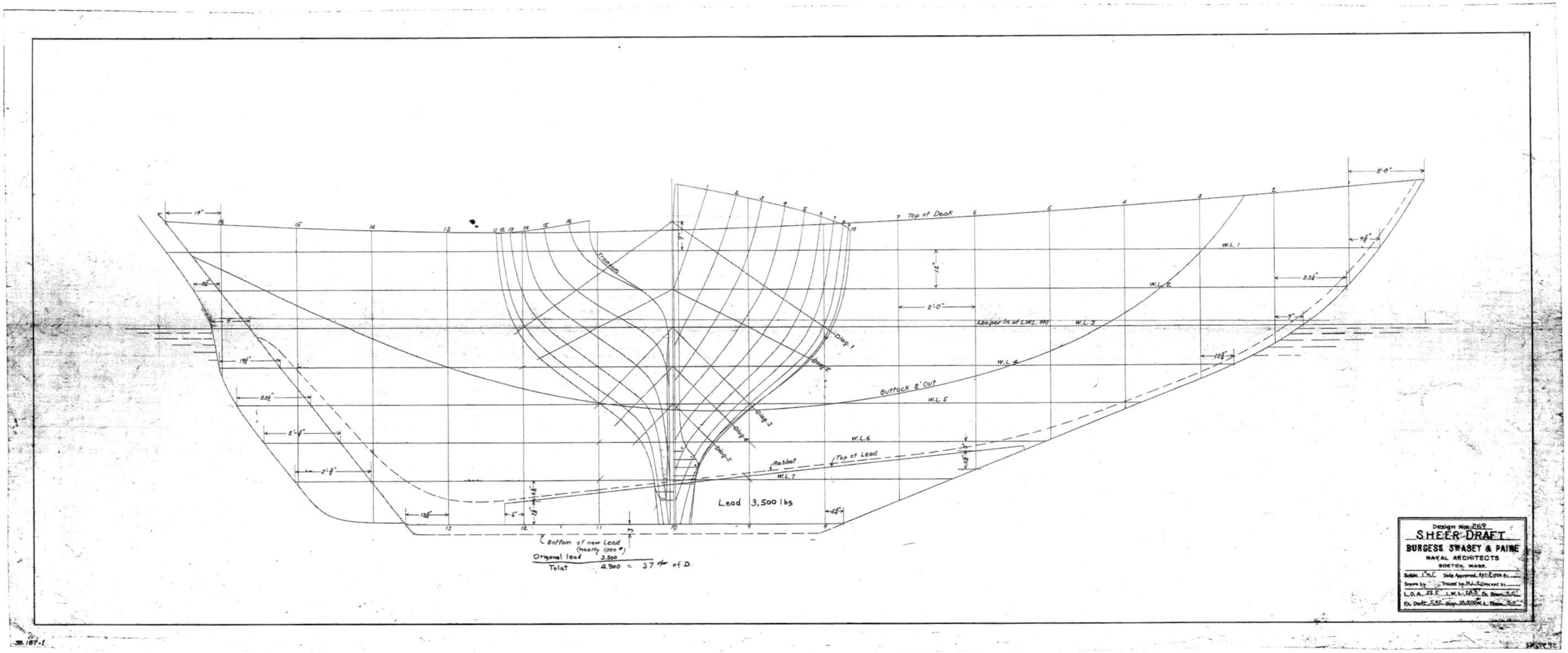

The *Santee*'s lines. Length on deck is 33 feet, 6 inches; length on the waterline, 28 feet, 6 inches; beam 8 feet, 6 inches; and draft, 5 feet, 5 inches. She is deeper and heavier in proportion than the H-28, yet the hull has a similar shape, though with a narrower transom. On the copy of this drawing that Francis saved, he rubbed out the initials "FCP," (Frank Cabot Paine) after "Drawn By," reason unknown. Perhaps Francis's friend, who was a partner in the firm whereas he was a mere draftsman, was stealing his thunder? (© Mystic Seaport Museum, Daniel S. Gregory Ships Plans Library, SP38.187.1)

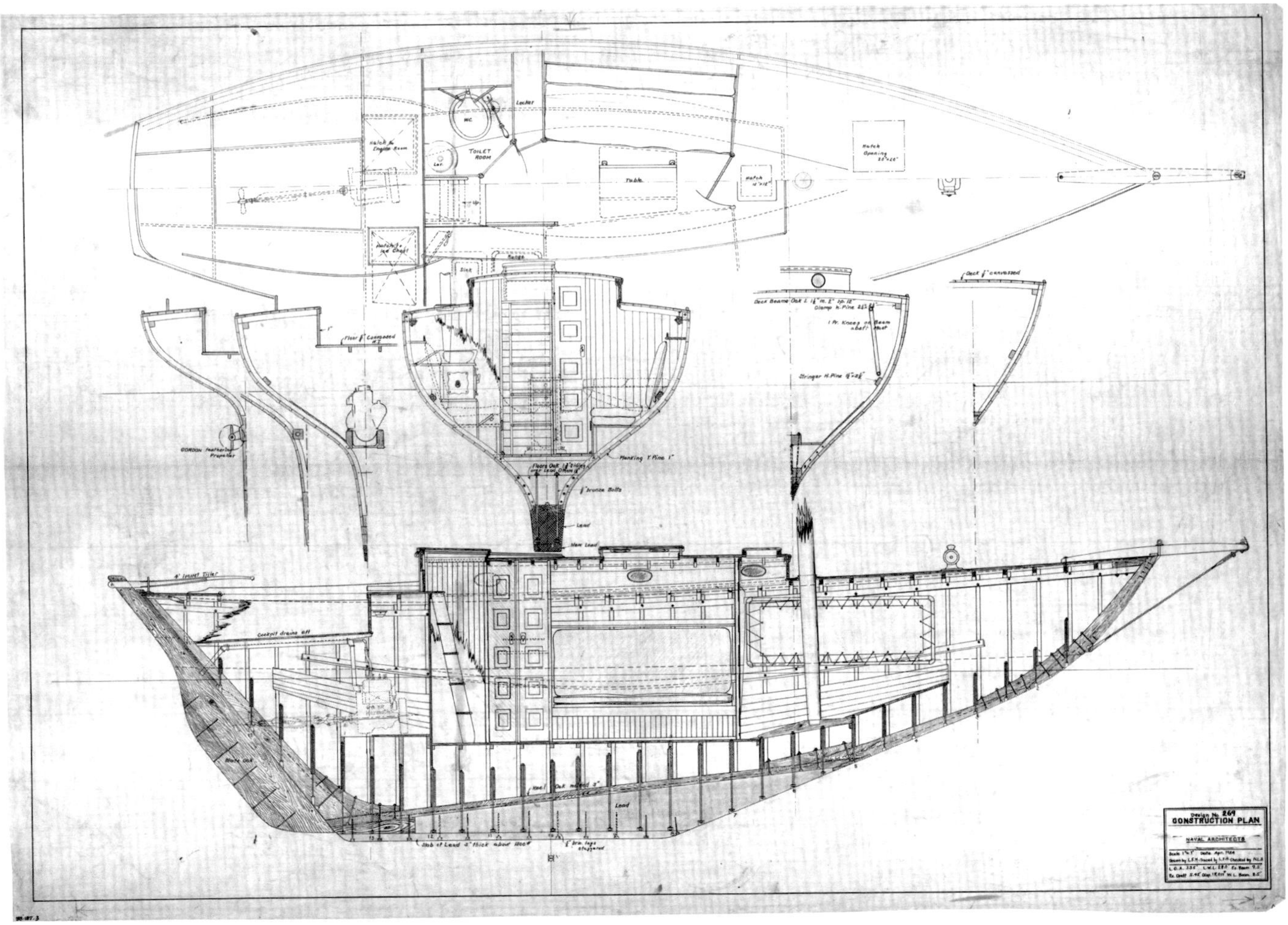

ABOVE: **The construction and cabin plans of the *Santee*. This is a conventional design, but notice the off-center propeller and the lovely reverse curves in the tiller. Francis both drew and traced in ink the detailed construction drawing; it was checked by his colleague, Norman Skene.** (© Mystic Seaport Museum, Daniel S. Gregory Ships Plans Library, SP38.187.3) RIGHT: **In 1946, Francis drew a taller, narrower rig for the *Santee*, by then having been renamed *News Boy* and finally *Blessed Event*, and then owned by Alexander A. Cameron of Concord, Massachusetts. The addition of a second running backstay to the masthead suggests that Cameron intended to set a masthead Genoa.** (© Mystic Seaport Museum, Daniel S. Gregory Ships Plans Library, SP38.187)

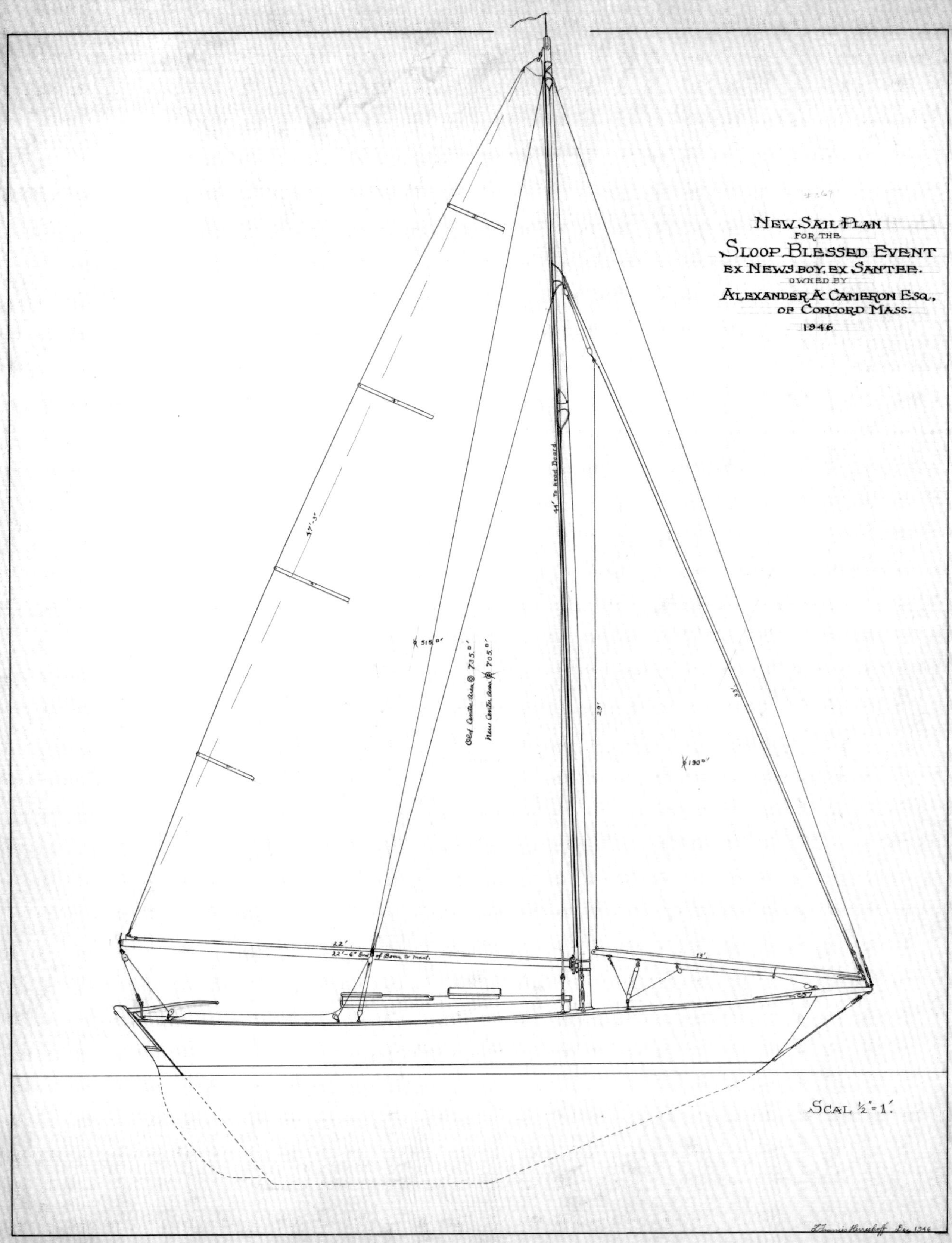
New Sail Plan
for the
Sloop Blessed Event
ex News boy, ex Santee.
owned by
Alexander A Cameron Esq.,
of Concord Mass.
1946
47'-3"
41' To head Board
515.0'
Old Center Area ⊕ 735.0'
New Center Area ⊕ 705.0'
29'
33'
190.0'
22'
22'-6" End of Boom to mast.
13'
Scal ½" = 1'.
L. Francis Herreshoff Dec 1946

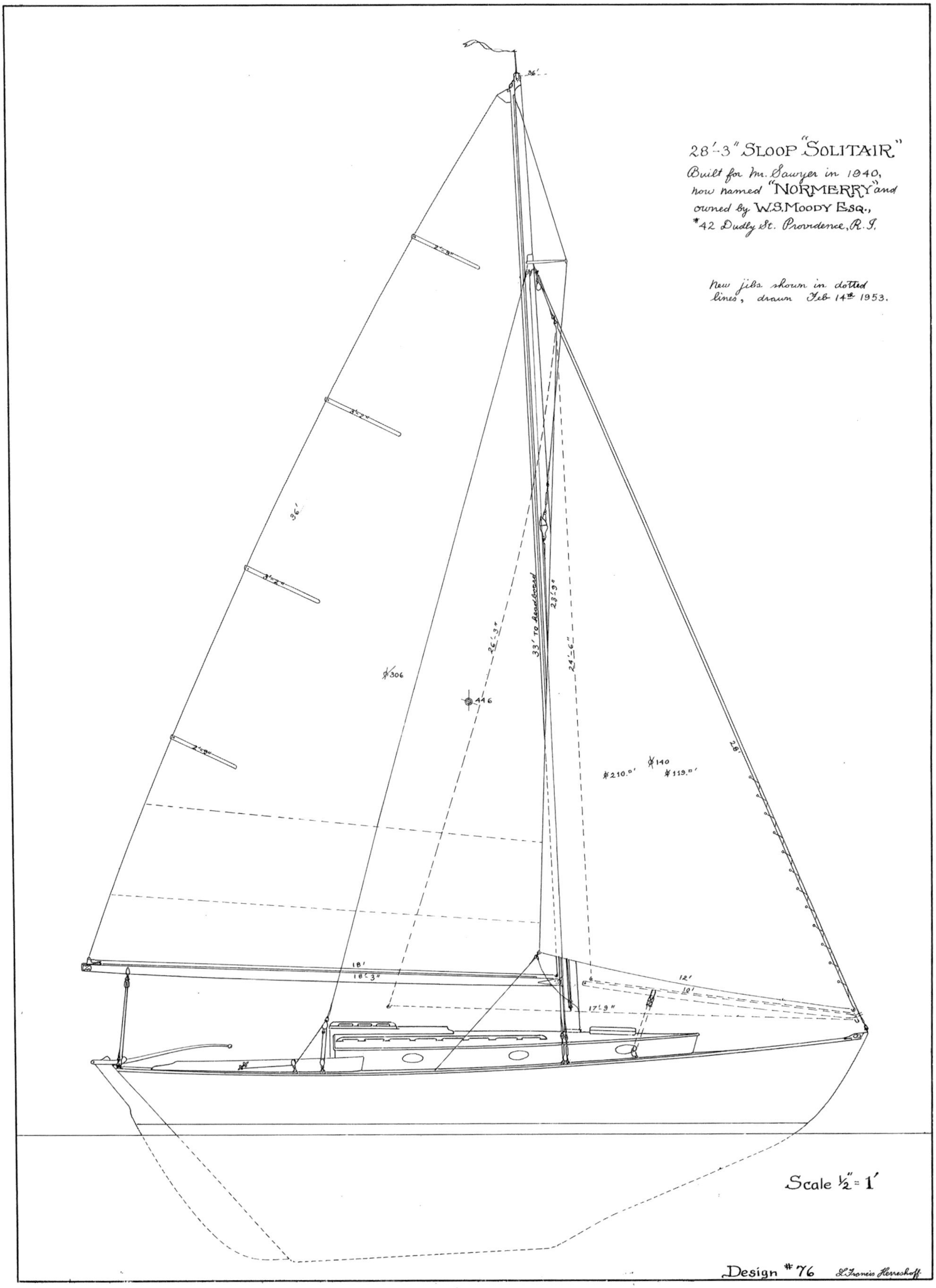
28'-3" Sloop "Solitair"
Built for Mr. Sawyer in 1940, now named "NORMERRY" and owned by W.S. Moody Esq., #42 Dudly St. Providence, R.I.
New jibs shown in dotted lines, drawn Feb 14th 1953.
Scale 1/2" = 1'
Design #76
L. Francis Herreshoff

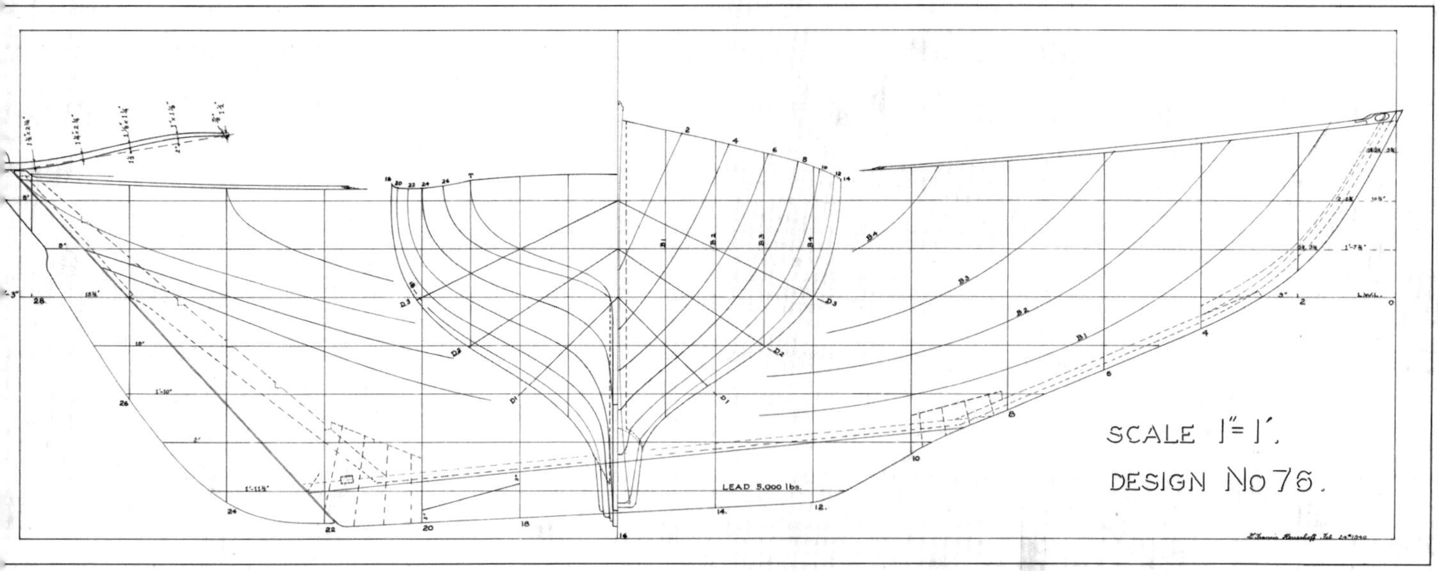

simplicity. Francis wrote: "The H-28 was designed to accommodate two people in cruising, and they would have the most Spartan accommodations including a bucket toilet, and most simple galley arrangements. In my opinion the whole secret of a pleasant cruise in a boat of this size is to have a cabin plan that can be very quickly and easily taken care of and where none of its space is used up by cupboards, partitions, etc."[8]

After producing five articles, illustrated with plans, describing the boat and her construction details, Francis wrote a fanciful story called "H 28—Or the Building of the Snarke." He said that the editor had asked him to write "something more," perhaps "'incidences' that might come up during construction," something to take people's minds off the war. For the piece, Francis imagined God creating man and woman, and he imagined the man building an H-28 and the woman getting involved with the project after awakening from a transformative dream. They named the boat the *Snarke* after Jack London's *Snark*, but with the *e*

LEFT: **Closer in size and proportion to the H-28 was another forerunner, the 28-foot sloop *Solitaire* that Francis designed in 1940. Sail area is 446 square feet, with 306 square feet in the mainsail and 140 square feet in a loose-footed working jib. He also shows a club jib of 119 square feet and a seven-eighths, lapping jib of 210 square feet. Rather than the *Santee*'s long, masthead forestay, Francis has used the jumper stays he invented. This boat also had an off-center propeller. Her cabin was laid out with two quarter-berths, a third berth forward, and the galley and head amidships. The forward end of the cabin house is vee-shaped, a functional solution to shipping water over the bow favored by Nathanael.** (© Mystic Seaport Museum, Daniel S. Gregory Ships Plans Library, SP38.141.4) ABOVE: **The *Solitaire*'s lines. Length on deck is 28 feet, 3 inches; length on the waterline, 23 feet, 3 inches; beam, 9 feet, 3 inches; and draft, 4 feet, 10 inches. Outside lead ballast is 5,000 pounds. Her displacement and draft are less proportionally than those of the *Santee*, and the H-28 will continue that trend. The *Solitaire*'s transom, compared to that of the H-28, has a little more of the wineglass curvature and comes up to the deck-edge vertically instead of with the H-28's distinctive flare.** (© Mystic Seaport Museum, Daniel S. Gregory Ships Plans Library, SP38.141.1)

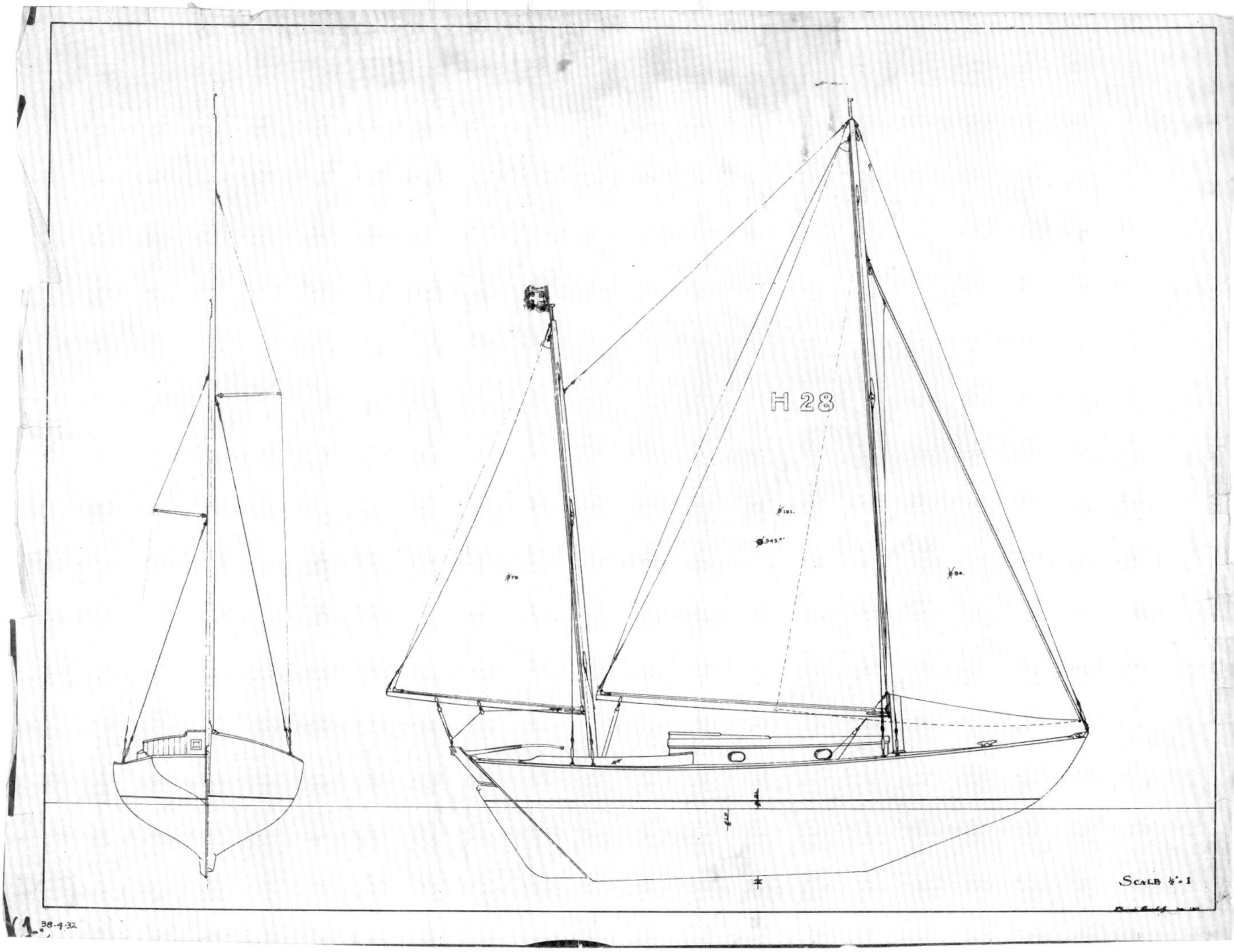

ABOVE **When readers of the December 1942 issue of *The Rudder* got to page 14, they were greeted by this sail plan opposite the title, "How To Build H 28: Twenty-Eight Foot Auxiliary Cruising Ketch: Designed by L. Francis Herreshoff." This drawing of a perfectly proportioned, small cruising boat and the plans that followed in the magazine stirred the hearts and minds of many a sailor and led to the design being built by the hundreds on the world's waterfronts. Francis has kept the rig as simple as possible: there is a single, long headstay to the masthead instead of jumper struts and stays. And he has left off running backstays to keep the jibstay taut, at the specific request of Boris Lauer-Leonardi; the *Rudder* editor believed that his readers might be put off by the necessity of handling runners when tacking in so small a boat. Sail area is 343 square feet, with 181 square feet in the mainsail, 78 in the mizzen, and 84 in the jib.** (© Mystic Seaport Museum, Daniel S. Gregory Ships Plans Library, SP38.4.32) RIGHT: **To simplify the amateur builder's job, Francis specified as much store-bought marine hardware as possible, but he couldn't bring himself to use off-the-shelf spar hardware. He championed science (as well as art) in yacht design, so he worked up plans of his own fittings that would be lighter and more streamlined than those available from vendors. This made more work for builders, though Francis wrote that his fittings "will only require three quick simple patterns and little machine work"; over the years, he helped many a customer, working from his plans, by making his special fittings himself and selling them at very low prices. This drawing shows the fittings necessary to rig the mastheads of the H-28. Note at the top of the drawing the trucks and flagstaffs, carefully proportioned to the different mast sizes.** (© Mystic Seaport Museum, Daniel S. Gregory Ships Plans Library, SP38.4)

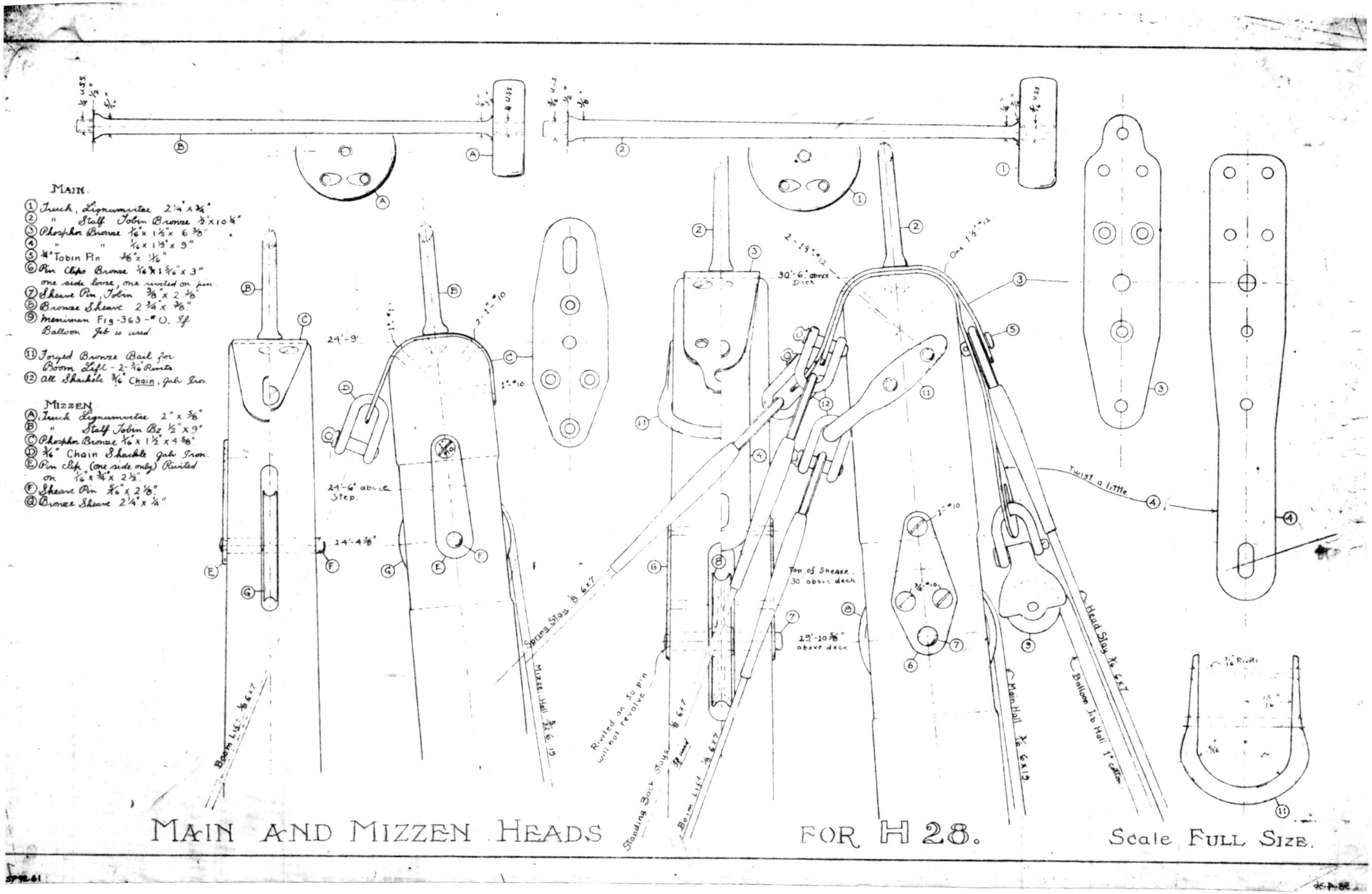
MAIN AND MIZZEN HEADS FOR H 28.
Scale Full Size.
Main.
① Truck, Lignumvitae 2¼" x ¾"
② " Staff Tobin Bronze ½" x 10⅛"
③ Phosphor Bronze 3⁄16" x 1½" x 6⅜"
④ " " 3⁄16" x 1½" x 9"
⑤ ¼" Tobin Pin 3⁄16" x 1⁄16"
⑥ Pin Clips Bronze 1⁄16" x 1 5⁄16" x 3" one side loose, one riveted on pin
⑦ Sheave Pin, Tobin ⅜" x 2⅛"
⑧ Bronze Sheave 2¾" x ⅜"
⑨ Merriman Fig-363-#0. If Balloon Jib is used.
⑪ Forged Bronze Bail for Boom Lift - 2-3⁄16" Rivets
⑫ All Shackles 3⁄16" Chain, Galv. Iron
Mizzen
Ⓐ Truck Lignumvitae 2" x ⅜"
Ⓑ " Staff Tobin Bz ½" x 9"
Ⓒ Phosphor Bronze 3⁄16" x 1½" x 4⅜"
Ⓓ 3⁄16" Chain Shackle Galv. Iron
Ⓔ Pin Clip (one side only) Riveted on 1⁄16" x ¾" x 2½"
Ⓕ Sheave Pin 3⁄16" x 2⅛"
Ⓖ Bronze Sheave 2¼" x ¼"
24'-9"
24'-6" above Step.
24'-4⅜"
30'-6" above Deck
Top of Sheave 30' above deck
29'-10⅜" above deck
Twist a little
Spring Stay ⅛ 6x7
Mizzen Hall 3⁄32 6 19
Boom Lift ⅛ 6x7
Riveted on 50 pin will not revolve
Standing Back Stays ⅛ 6x7
Boom Lift ⅛ 6x7
Main Hall ⅛ 6x19
Balloon Jib Hall 1" cotton
Head Stay 3⁄16 6x7
3⁄16 Rivets

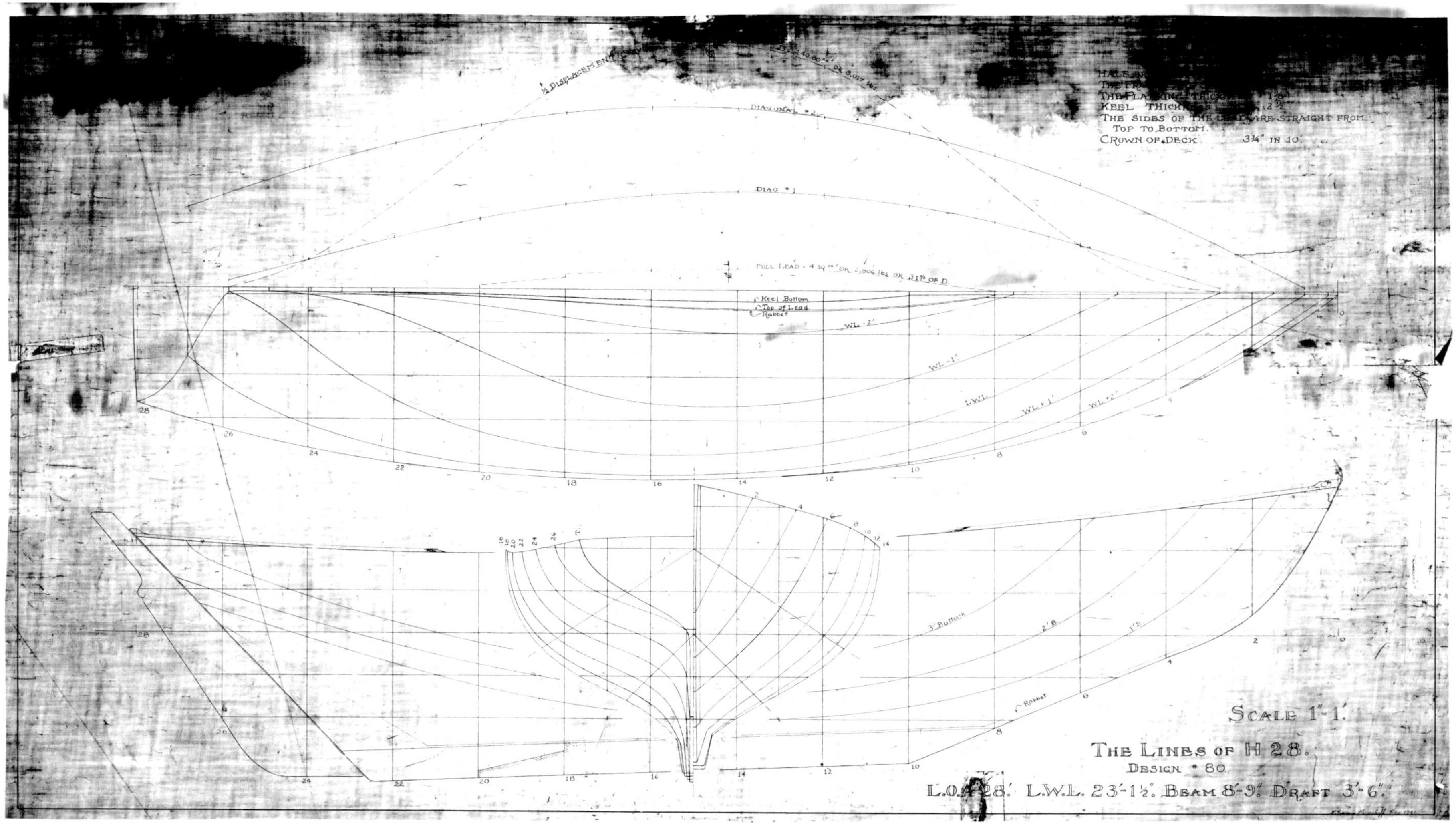

Keel Bottom
Top of Lead
Rabbet
Diag #1
3' Buttock
2' B
1' B
Rabbet
L.W.L.
WL -1'
WL -2'
WL +1'
WL +2'
Crown of Deck 3¼" in 10'
Top to Bottom.
Scale 1"-1'.
The Lines of H 28.
Design # 80
L.O.A. 28'. L.W.L. 23'-1½". Beam 8'-9½". Draft 3'-6".

added so that there would be the same number of letters either side of the outboard rudder. And the man and the woman had two children, and they all went off happily cruising together in the *Snarke* (even though she was designed just for two).

Francis called "The Building of the Snarke" a "queer story," but Boris loved it. He wrote: "Dear Skipper, I have just finished reading your manuscript for the third time and, frankly, I don't remember when I have been so amused. You are turning into a top notch writer, and I would say offhand that you have a real gift for it. You understand, Skipper, that as far as I am concerned, I would just as soon the articles on the H 28 went on forever." Such unstinting praise, even for mere writing, which for L. Francis Herreshoff fell below lathe work, yacht designing, and boat handling on the ranking of his art forms, must have been welcome music.[9]

Boris had offered, and Francis had accepted, $150 for the right to publish the design of the H-28. Francis would also receive a percentage of the income from the sales of plans. With Boris's praise ringing in his ears, he wrote, "I do think that this article [The Building of the Snarke] and some others that I may write, I should be paid for as they are really separate from the H-28 design." His letter crossed with Boris's offer to pay for the article and his saying, "Naturally, you will be paid for everything you write for me."[10]

As usual, the construction plan was the most time-consuming and difficult of the drawings of the H-28. Francis was proud of his work on it. He wrote to Boris: "I think it will be one of the most complete construction plans of a boat of this size ever made, and I congratulate myself on the draftsmanship. Besides it being a useful drawing for those building the boats, I think probably it is the most correctly drawn construction plan of modern construction that has so far been published." Boris agreed, writing, "there is more dope on it than on anything I have ever seen." Both men are lavishing praise on what for Francis was a normal construction drawing, but this was the first one of them that would be published, and that was why he was so excited about it. And as the series of articles went on and Boris received the drawings for mast fittings, spreaders, and rudder hangings, he wrote to Francis: "We have never had anything in *The Rudder* even approaching this in detail."[11]

As Francis worked up the design of the H-28, he was reminded of a much earlier *Rudder* How-To-Build series, on the *Sea Bird*, a little, vee-bottomed cruising yawl designed by Charles D. Mower at the instigation of editor Thomas Fleming Day. Francis wrote: "The present editor of *The Rudder* has taken a great interest in the development of H 28, perhaps as great an interest as the Old Man [Day] did [in the *Sea Bird*] in 1901, and it has been a great pleasure to develop the drawings for him. It is hoped that the H 28 will give as much pleasure as the *Sea Bird* did in its day." And Francis compared the dimensions of the two boats, showing that his H-28 had a little

---

LEFT: **The lines of the H-28, Francis's design No. 80. He has achieved a fast, weatherly hull of moderate draft, by giving her a gently curved vee-shape to reduce wetted surface and a long keel and big rudder for lateral resistance. Her flaring sides give her good hull-form stability, aiding her rather shallow ballast keel. Gentle is perhaps the best word to describe the shape of the H-28: every curve changes direction slowly. And she is indeed a work of art: the subtle wineglass shape of the well-raked transom, with its quietly ornamented rudder, goes perfectly with the moderately knuckled, slightly flaring bow. Builders could hardly wait to get started on this boat. She is 28 feet long on deck; 23 feet, 1½ inches on the waterline; with a beam of 8 feet, 9 inches; and a draft of 3 feet, 6 inches. Displacement is 9,017 pounds, with 2,806 pounds of lead outside ballast, for a ballast-displacement ratio of 31 percent.** (© Mystic Seaport Museum, Daniel S. Gregory Ships Plans Library, SP38.4)

TABLE OF OFFSETS FOR H-28

GIVEN IN FEET ~ INCHES ~ AND EIGHTS OF INCHES.

Station Numbers	Elevations above and below L.W.L.							Half Breadths										Diagonals		Station Numbers
	Top of Deck at Side	Buttock 3'	Buttock 2'	Buttock 1'	Rabbet	Top of Lead	Profile	At Deck	WL+3'	WL+2'	WL+1'	LWL	WL-1'	WL-2'	WL-3'	Rabbet	Top of Lead	Face	#1	#2	
0	3-6-0				3-8-2		3-6-0	0-1-0								0-1-6		0-1-0			0
2	3-2-5			2-6-0	0-9-0		0-5-6	1-4-3	1-3-0	0-9-2	0-3-3					0-1-6		0-0-4		0-8-4	2
4	2-11-4		2-2-6	0-6-7	-0-5-3		-0-6-3	2-4-4		1-10-4	1-3-4	0-6-6				0-1-6		0-0-4	0-5-0	1-7-4	4
6	2-8-6	2-5-6	0-6-7	-0-6-1	-1-3-1		-1-4-2	3-1-2		2-9-5	2-3-2	1-6-1	0-5-3			0-1-6		0-0-5	1-0-6	2-5-3	6
8	2-6-2	0-10-0	-0-4-6	-1-2-7	-2-0-5	-2-2-2	-2-2-1	3-7-5		3-5-7	3-1-1	2-4-7	1-3-3	0-2-2		0-1-6	0-0-6	0-0-6	1-7-1	3-1-7	8
10	2-4-0	-0-0-6	-0-11-7	-1-8-2	2-2-4	2-3-1	-3-0-0	3-11-7		3-11-3	3-7-7	3-0-6	1-11-1	0-7-4		0-4-3	0-3-6	0-1-0	1-11-5	3-7-7	10
12	2-2-1	-0-6-4	-1-3-7	-1-11-2	2-3-4	2-4-0	-3-1-0	4-2-5		4-2-4	4-0-1	3-6-1	2-5-4	0-10-7		0-6-0	0-5-1	0-2-7	2-2-6	4-0-1	12
14	2-0-1	-0-9-1	-1-4-7	-2-0-0	2-4-4	2-5-0	-3-2-0	4-4-0		4-4-0	4-2-2	3-9-2	2-8-1	0-11-6		0-5-7	0-5-1	0-3-1	2-3-4	4-2-4	14
16	1-11-5	-0-9-3	-1-4-2	-1-10-7	2-5-4	2-6-0	-3-2-7	4-4-3			4-3-3	3-9-6	2-7-7	0-10-5		0-4-6	0-4-4	0-2-6	2-2-4	4-2-6	16
18	1-10-7	-0-6-7	-1-1-1	-1-7-5	2-6-3	2-6-7	-3-3-7	4-4-0			4-2-4	3-8-0	2-2-4	0-7-5		0-3-5	0-3-3	0-2-2	1-11-5	4-0-7	18
20	1-10-4	-0-2-6	-0-8-7	-1-3-0	2-7-3	2-7-7	-3-4-6	4-2-6			4-0-5	3-3-5	1-5-0	0-4-5		0-2-3	0-2-2	0-1-4	1-7-4	3-9-4	20
22	1-10-7	+0-3-0	-0-3-0	-0-8-4	2-2-4	2-8-7	-3-5-6	4-4-0			3-8-4	2-6-5	1-7-2	0-2-0		0-1-6	0-1-2	0-1-2	1-1-7	3-4-2	22
24	1-11-5	0-10-2	+0-3-3	-0-1-2	-1-0-1		-1-11-3 -3-4-4	3-8-1			3-2-0	1-3-1	0-1-7			0-1-6		0-1-0	0-8-0	2-9-6	24
26	2-0-6	1-6-6	+0-10-7	+0-6-0	+0-1-4		+0-1-5 -2-0-4	3-2-5		3-2-3	2-3-0					0-1-6		0-2-6		2-1-6	26
28	2-2-3		+1-7-2	+1-1-5			+2-2-3 +1-5-2	2-8-0													28
Transom			+1-3-2	+0-8-0				2-8-0		2-7-1	1-6-7	0-1-2	0-1-0	0-1-0				0-2-6	0-1-6	1-10-0	Transom

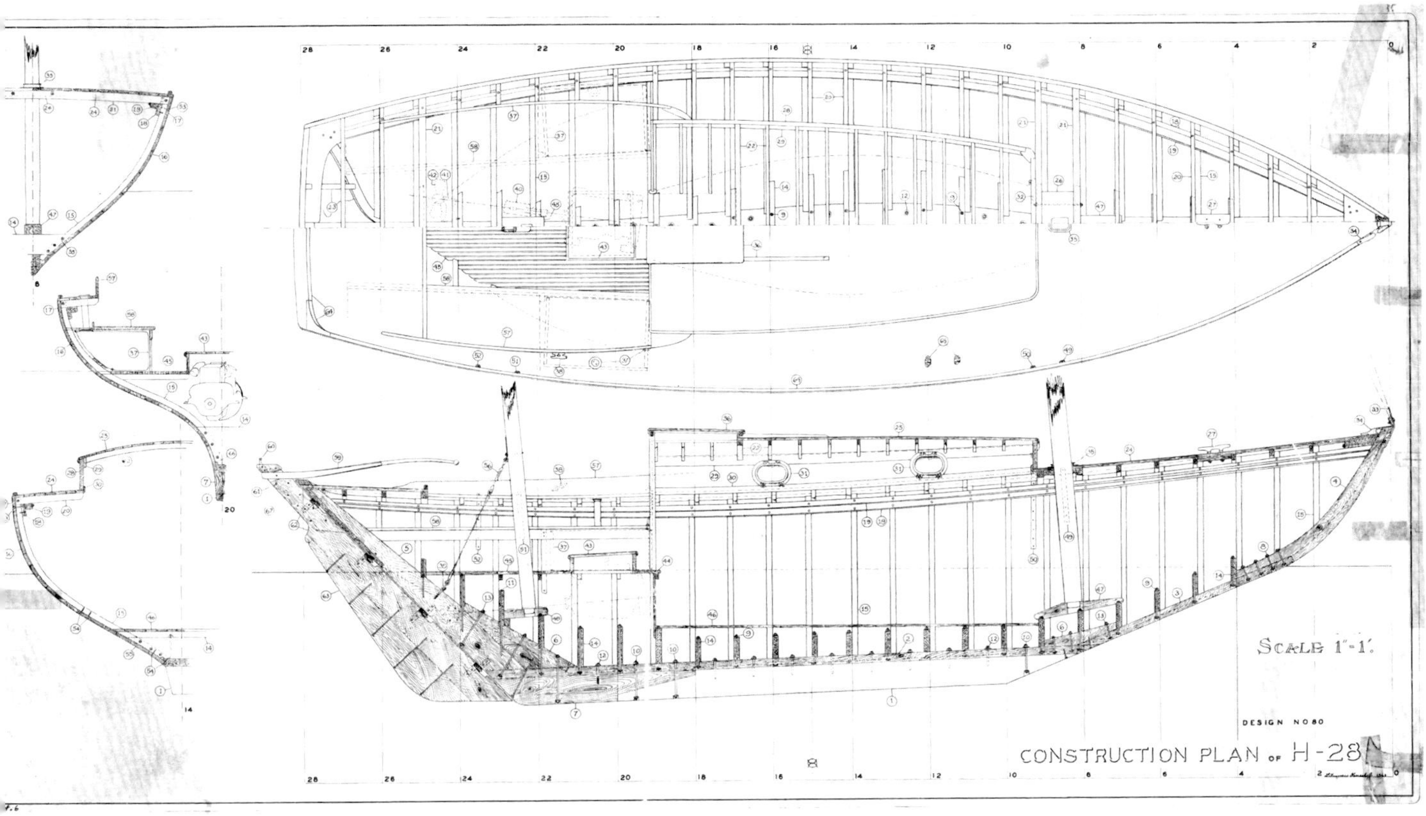

LEFT: **Francis was hesitant about publishing the table of offsets for the H-28, which would be a new experience for him, because he feared builders would use it to build boats without buying the plans. But he did allow Boris to publish the offsets—without apparent detriment, because the price of the H-28 plans from *The Rudder* was so reasonable.** (© Mystic Seaport Museum, Daniel S. Gregory Ships Plans Library, SP38.4) ABOVE: **The construction plan for the H-28, the first of Francis's detailed construction drawings to be published. Francis has numbered sixty-seven parts of the vessel for which he wrote detailed descriptions in his How-To-Build articles. For example, the keel was to be 2½ inches by 13 inches, 16 feet long, of oak; keel bolts to be of 1½-inch Tobin bronze; floors 1½-inch oak; frames 1⅝ inches square on 12-inch centers; planking 1-inch rift-grain fir, fastened with No. 14, 2½-inch Everdur bronze screws; and transom of 1-inch oak. The cockpit was not watertight; Francis recommended a floor of teak, elm, or oak slats, 1 inch wide by ¾ inch thick, spaced ¼ inch apart. Note the short after stay to steady the mizzenmast. Francis wrote that it could be replaced by a thwart across the cockpit if desired. He shows an engine in dotted lines under the cockpit floor, with an access hatch. It's a "bobtailed" Gray Marine Sea Scout, with magneto ignition and an impulse starter. With a Hyde, 12-inch-diameter propeller, he figured she would go 6 knots burning 1¼ gallons of gas an hour, or 4 knots burning ¾ gallon. He wrote that any such simple motor would do, but he also suggested leaving out the motor to eliminate expense and complication, writing: "I, myself, enjoy the interesting game of pitting my wits against the weather gods."** (© Mystic Seaport Museum, Daniel S. Gregory Ships Plans Library, SP38.4)

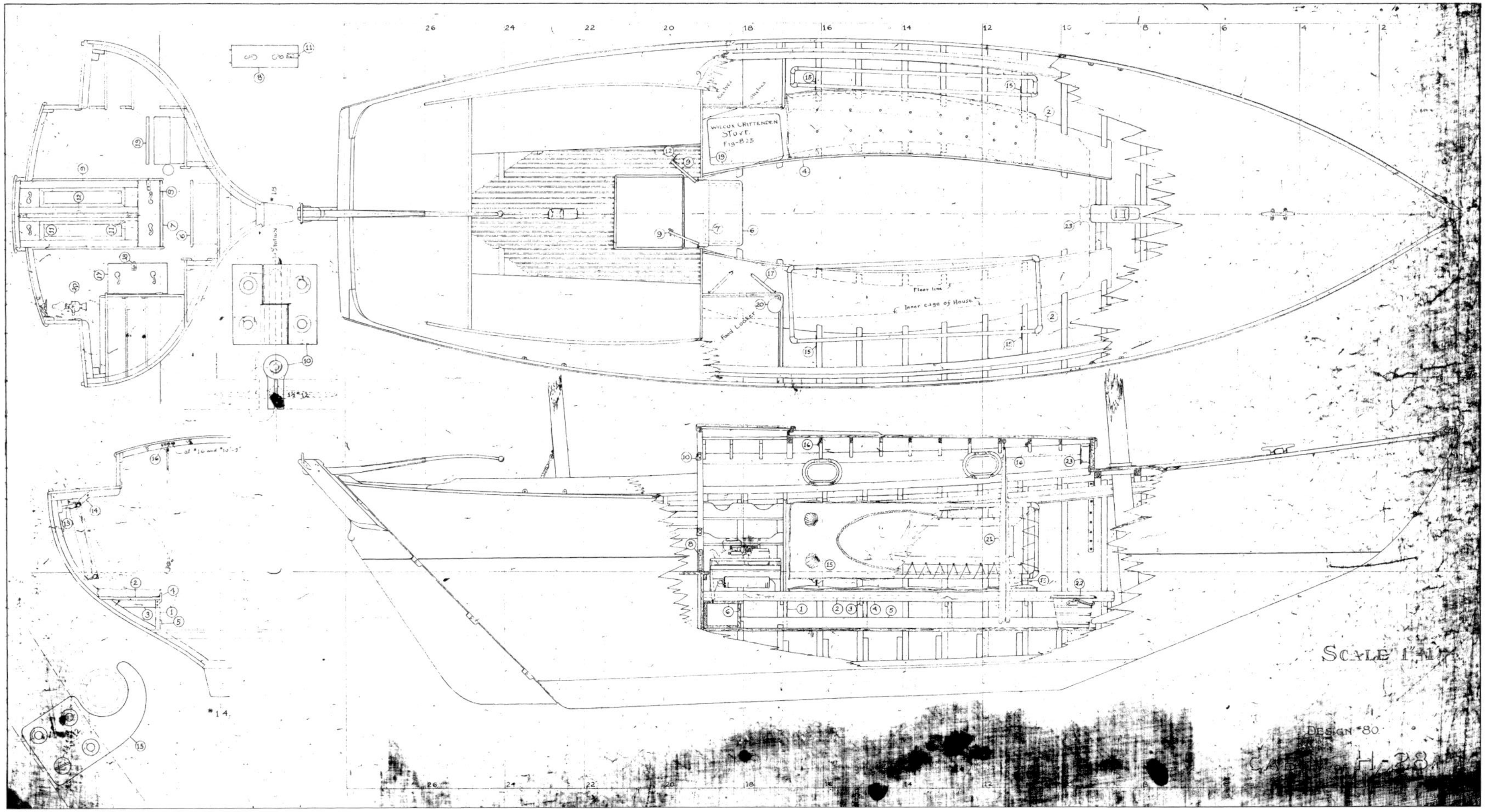
Wilcox Crittenden Stove Fig-B25
Floor line
Inner edge of House
Food Locker
Scale 1" = 1'
Design #80
H-28
58-4-48

more length, beam, and draft, with more ballast and displacement than Mower's centerboarder, but with an almost identical sail area. Primarily because of her greater stability, the H-28 would be a better performer under sail than the *Sea Bird.* Francis wrote, "the H-28 would be ever so much more seaworthy than the *Sea Bird* and dryer and if properly handled would be perfectly all right to go to Bermuda or Nassau [presumably with a water-tight cockpit]." Day produced the *Sea Bird* to show that small boats can be safe at sea; although Francis designed his little ketch for coastwise cruising, she also showed, as we will soon witness, that small boats can be safe at sea.[12]

The writer had the temerity, at age sixteen, to send Mr. Herreshoff a letter critical of the stern of the H-28, as lacking enough curvature in the wineglass shape. To my utter amazement, Mr. Herreshoff replied: "You are quite right, the stern of the H-28 is too V-shaped, and I don't know just why I did this excepting possibly I increased the weight on deck when I was making the lines to give a little more cockpit room aft. If she had been a bit fuller halfway between the waterline and the deck line she would have been a very much handsomer boat, but possibly no better sea boat for the larger stern would have had a tendency to depress the bow when the bow and stern were each in a wave." There is no evidence, however, of any H-28 owner being less than happy with the stern of his or her boat. In a reminiscence on her H-28, published in *WoodenBoat* magazine, one owner wrote: "Her graceful wineglass transom has always been beautiful to me."[13]

After the appearance of only the first article, Boris wrote to Francis that "the H-28 has pulled in more mail than *any* design we have ever published." The editor was being overwhelmed by the stacks of letters and, realizing that his readers wanted to have their responses from Mr. Herreshoff, not from him, he shifted that burden to Francis.[14]

Francis responded to every letter promptly, courteously, and, of course, expertly. As he sifted through his newly increased deliveries from the postman, he told Boris, "it almost seems as if some people take more interest in the writing than in the design of the H 28." Indeed, his story, "The Building of the Snarke," brought many congratulations, none more cherished than that from the poet, Starling Burgess.[15]

Francis anticipated that some builders would want to change his design. "Someone might want a narrower cockpit, or a self-bailing cockpit," he wrote, "and all such things would be an improvement for certain uses." But after the letters asking about changes came piling in, he wrote to Boris,

LEFT: **The H-28's cabin plan. Francis has designed his little cruiser with relatively low freeboard and a low cabin house that is narrow enough to allow fairly spacious side decks. Sitting at the tiller, the builder-owner can see ahead over the house, can walk forward comfortably, and can enjoy fully the never-ending spectacle of the nearby water being cleaved by a handsomely shaped hull. But it is true that the dimensions of this design that permit such wonderful pleasures restrict the headroom in the cabin to 4 feet, 8 inches and do not allow sitting back under the deck. Many an H-28 builder proved willing to trade the above fundamental joys of sailing for mere standing headroom, by raising the freeboard, raising the cabin house roof, erecting a doghouse, or some combination thereof. Francis was wont to explain that the sailor spends but little time standing up below, which is fair enough, but in the H-28 even sitting comfortably is a problem. One owner has solved the situation nicely by making a simple wooden backrest so that he has support while seated far enough toward the centerline for headroom under the cabin house. Again, Francis uses his numbering system for twenty-three items that he wants to call to the attention of the prospective builder. No. 23 is his suggested position for his favorite clock, a Chelsea, at the forward end of the cabin house, with its steady ticking bringing to the boat a measure of peace.** (© Mystic Seaport Museum, Daniel S. Gregory Ships Plans Library, SP38.4.48)

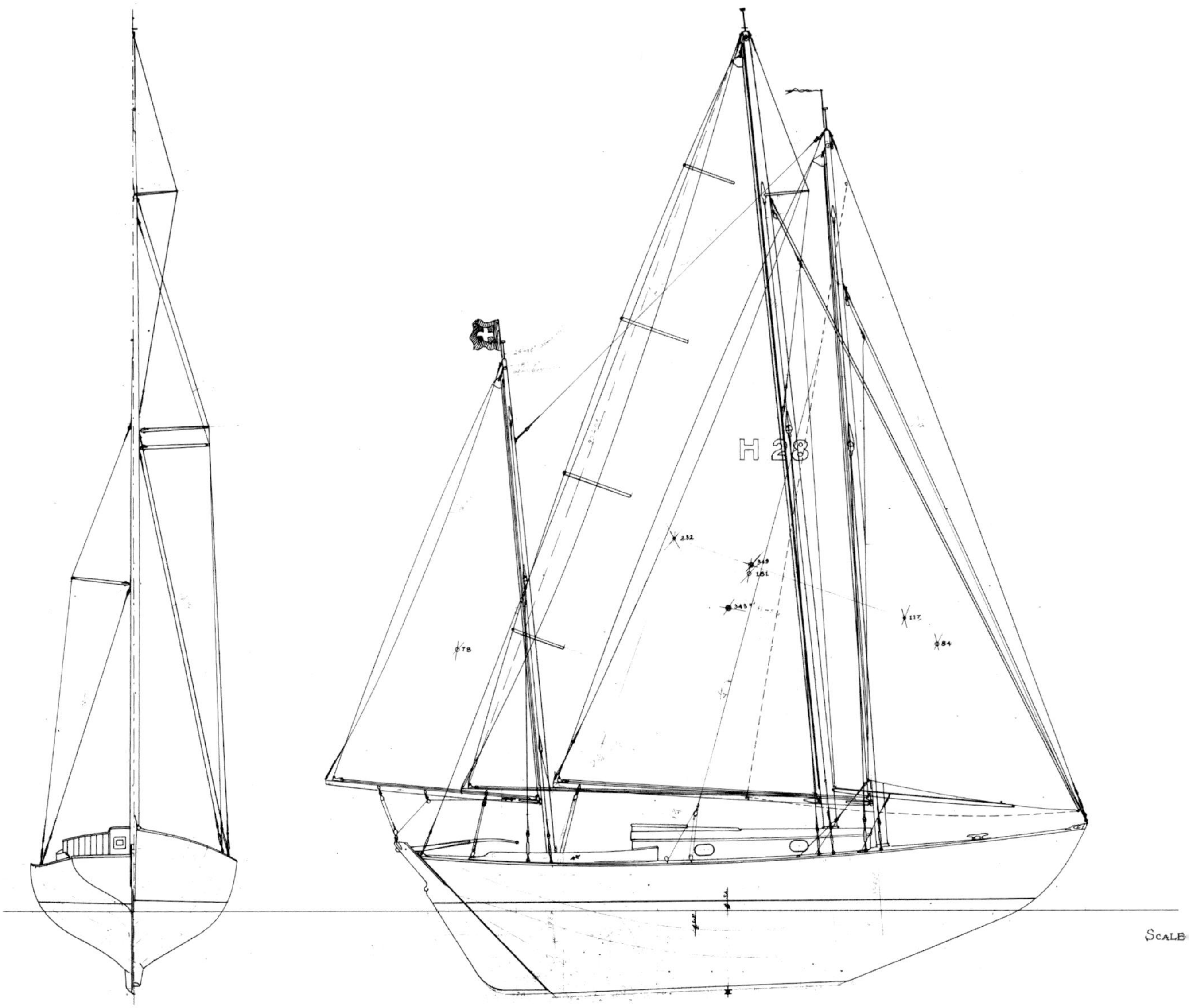

So many admirers of the H-28 wanted the simplicity of a one-masted rig that Francis had to draw her as a sloop. Here, he has superimposed the sloop rig on the sail plan of the ketch, allowing an easy comparison of the two. The sloop has a total sail area of 349 square feet, 6 square feet more than the ketch, with 232 in the mainsail and 117 in the jib. This drawing shows clearly how much more total mast length a ketch needs compared to a sloop in order to achieve her more easily handled divided rig. (© Mystic Seaport Museum, Daniel S. Gregory Ships Plans Library, SP38.4.24)

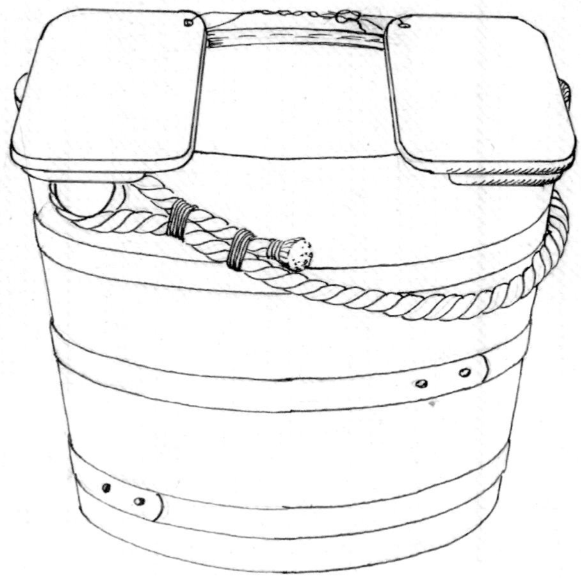

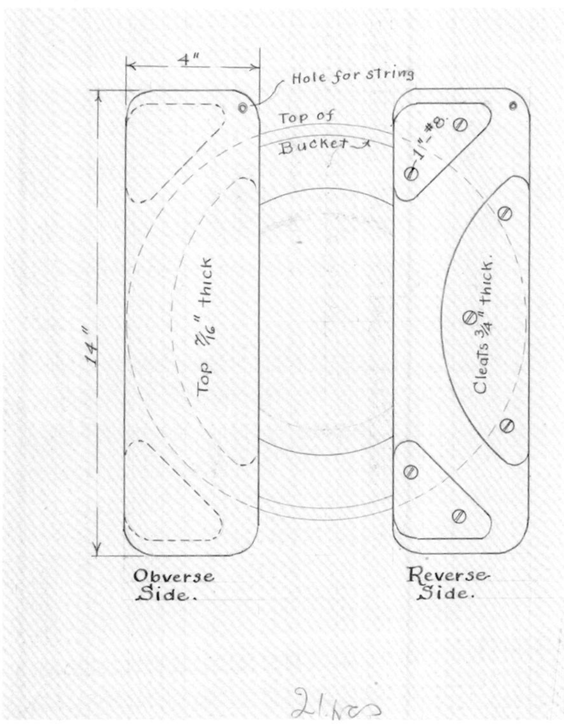

Francis's drawings of his famed cedar bucket, complete with adjustable seat, which he recommended for the toilet in the H-28. No. 22 on the Cabin plan shows his suggested position for the device, just abaft the mainmast. Of course one of the advantages of the bucket as toilet is that it can be used anywhere in the boat, on deck or below, depending on circumstances. When not in use it can go under the stern deck, Francis suggested. He claimed that Noah had in his Ark a whole battery of cedar buckets, with widely adjustable seats. (© Mystic Seaport Museum, Daniel S. Gregory Ships Plans Library, SP38.326.1 and 38.326.2)

"almost all these people who do make changes write me letters that ask for some additional work and I know that, when later on the things do not turn out well, they will bother you and me quite a little." To one prospective builder who wanted a longer stern with an inboard rudder, he advised: "I believe anyone who makes changes in the detail drawings of the H-28 will run into complications and to have the changes in perfect proportion they will have to have these things done by a naval architect and the cost of them will be more than the whole set of plans for the boat. I certainly am too busy at present time to attempt any alterations in design." Many H-28 dreamers wanted more headroom. Francis tried to dissuade them: "I think that any increase in the H-28's headroom by raising the topsides or raising the deck house would take away from her looks and general performance."[16]

Quite a few sailors were put off by the complication of a two-masted rig in so small a boat. Requests for a sloop rig for the H-28 were so numerous that Boris implored Francis to draw one. Francis gave in. On one H-28 sloop, the builder, to compensate for the higher center of effort of the sail plan, lowered the lead ballast 1 inch and added 2 inches of lead, increasing the draft by 3 inches. The boat proved to be so stiff that the added and lowered ballast wasn't necessary. The sloop rig seemed to improve her speed in light weather, and "her owner liked her very much."[17]

Francis hoped that *The Rudder* would sell sets of H-28 plans for as much as $30, but he agreed when Boris proposed setting the price at only $10, with $5 coming to him as royalty. After several months, Boris raised the price to $15, but Francis still got just the $5. The price raise had no adverse effect on sales; the plans moved. Boris reported: "The H-28 is sweeping to success day by day. The sale of plans are exceeding anything in our previous experience." In the third year of selling the plans, *Rudder* paid Francis $430 on 86 sets. And sales continued for decades, with a further price increase to $20.[18]

After the war, Boris Lauer-Leonardi's dream

ABOVE: **Boris used Victor Weidner's painting of an H-28 working to windward on a fine summer afternoon as the cover illustration for his September 1945 issue of *The Rudder*.** (*The Rudder* (September 1945): cover) RIGHT: **Booms lifting, bow wave curling, William Healy's H-28 is giving him an exhilarating sail.** (© Mystic Seaport Museum, Rosenfeld Collection, 1984.187.134053FA)

10Y1815

of having a boat designed by L. Francis Herreshoff came true. At first there was a concern about the cost of getting the boat built; Hodgdon Brothers, in East Boothbay, Maine, wanted $3,250 for a completed H-28 hull, without engine, rig, or sails. Boris figured the boat ready to go would run him about $6,000, "much too much for me. I guess boats are going out of sight." Francis advised him to forego the engine, and thought he could get out of it for $3,700. But Boris somehow came up with the money and went ahead, engine (a Universal Fisherman), Shipmate range, and all. He told Francis that the Hodgdon builders "like your blueprints immensely and said they are the easiest to understand and to follow. They had the construction plan on the bench and were referring to it."[19]

Boris had great fun with the details of his boat. He wanted Francis to make sketches for the "embroideries" on the backs of the pipe berths, as shown in his drawing, "Cabin of H-28." He was going to use candles instead of kerosene lamps. His private signal would feature the three scallop shells of *The Rudder*'s insignia. He would name his boat the *Nebula*, because "that I should own the boat of my dreams built for me was as distant as a nebula."[20]

Boris took delivery of the *Nebula* on April 15, 1947. He gave Francis a preliminary report on his trip home to Port Washington from Down East. The sail was mostly the typical windward work of getting up to the westward and included a beat through Block Island Sound in a southwester of nearly gale force. She went well under jib and mizzen, Boris said, though he couldn't get her to lie to under just the mizzen, as Francis always advised for a ketch. He also reported that the engine he had chosen was "too feeble." Under power in a calm, the *Nebula* could make only a little more than four knots, and "a small sea and headwind will stop it dead." When he read this, Francis must have worried that his friend would be disappointed in his boat, and that the editor's disappointment would be reflected in poor sales of plans through *The Rudder*.[21]

Francis needn't have worried. Later, when Boris gave a full account of what he thought of his H-28, he wrote: "A finer cruising sailboat I have never handled, and never will, at least in that size. She is really a sailing witch. She is remarkably fast for her short rig. She is steady, so you have time to do what needs to be done and she keeps her course. Her balance is perfect. She has easy motion always, so the crew doesn't wear out holding on all the time." And then Boris gave a positive account of her speed under power, writing, "with the small 5 h.p. motor she'll do five and a half miles in still water." He concluded: "I am extremely pleased with *Nebula* and feel a deep affection for her, and she certainly can take a lot more than I." Francis must have been relieved.[22]

By the time Boris was having Hodgdon Brothers build his H-28, the Truscott Boat and Dock Company of St. Joseph, on the southeastern shore of Lake Michigan, was offering the H-28 as a stock boat. The company was still building military vessels in November 1944 when it advertised "The Truscott H-28" under the headline, "When Victory is Won." The expected price was $3,300 with sails and rigging, with an engine as an optional extra. In early February 1946, Francis went to the Sportsman's Show in Boston to see the first Truscott H-28. His impression is unrecorded, but something made Boris shy away and spend extra money to have his H-28 built by a yard that he and Francis knew and trusted. In any event, Truscott went ahead and built H-28s according to Francis's design. It is not known how much, if any, money Francis was paid by Truscott for the rights; he was not prone to press such matters.[23]

And Francis heard from Kendall S. Jones, proprietor of the Oceanside Boat Builders Shop at Baldwin Harbor, on the South Shore of Long Island, that he was intending to build H-28s as modified by Elwood Sprague, "who has considerable experience in building and designing small auxiliary

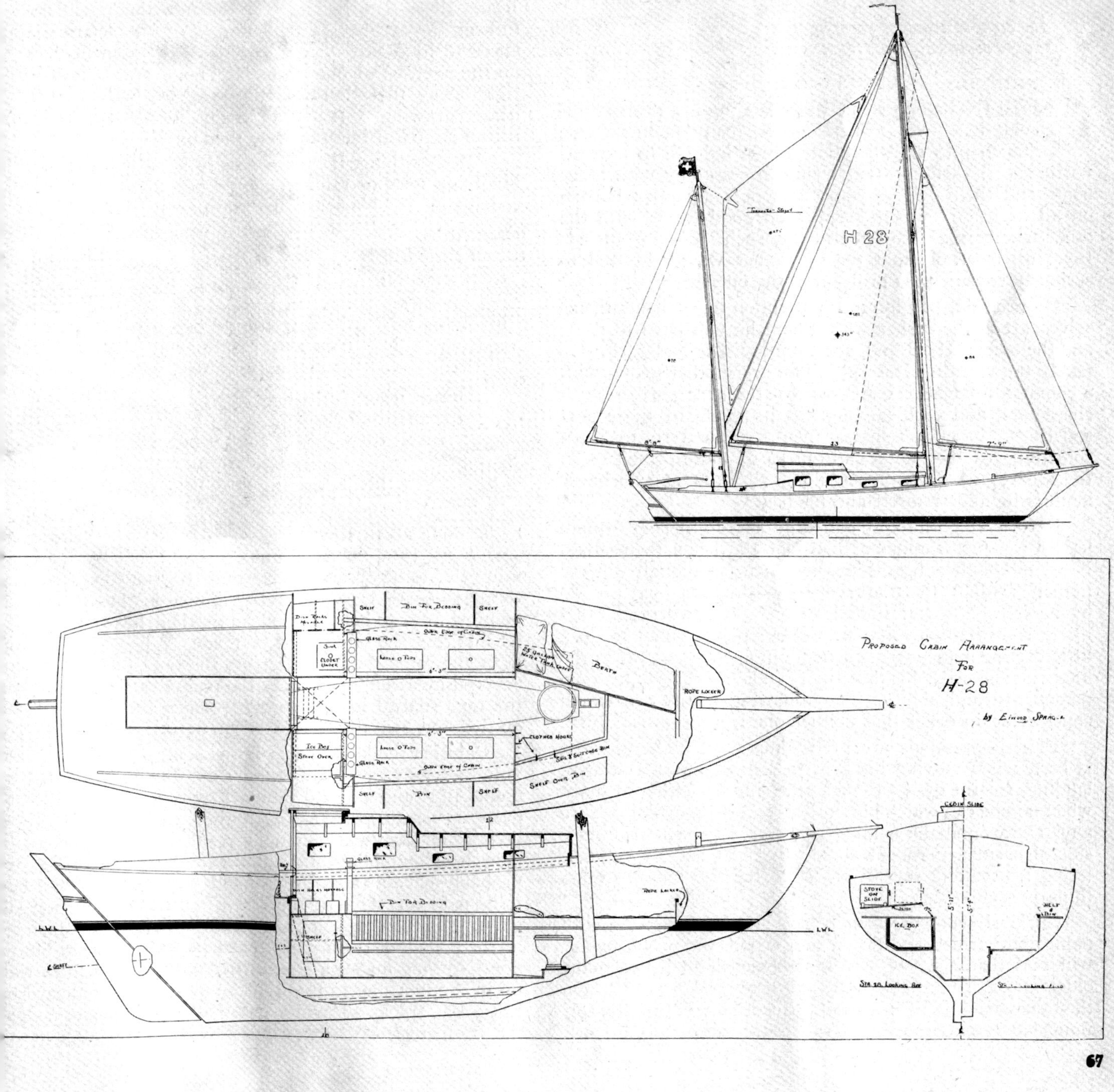

The H-28 as modified by designer Elwood Sprague. He has added sail area, a watertight cockpit, headroom in the cabin, another bunk, and a permanent toilet. The bowsprit allows for a big overlapping jib, balanced by a backstaysail sheeted to the mizzen masthead. The cabin sole has been lowered and narrowed to allow headroom in the main cabin of 5 feet, 3 inches, and a doghouse gives headroom aft of 5 feet, 10 inches. But the doghouse obstructs the view from the tiller of the great little boat sailing, which not only diminishes pleasure, but also hinders the function of a proper lookout. (*The Rudder* (June 1946): 67)

sailing craft." Francis replied to Jones's cordial and flattering letter by warning him that "different people will want various changes," and that "the principal changes that you have made will simply increase the cost of the boat." But Francis was encouraging, writing, "You are very lucky to have such an experienced man as Mr. Sprague to work for you and this in itself may make your enterprise a success." There was no talk of money from either side. Oceanside Boat Builders Shop advertised its H-28 "Designed by L. Francis Herreshoff," price, "subject to change without notice," $6,650.[24]

The Camden Shipbuilding and Marine Railway Company of Camden, Maine, offered a stock boat based on the H-28 as modified by Brampton Parker. She was given a clipper bow; she was a double-head-rigged sloop with a bowsprit; her cabin house was extended forward and raised aft; she had four built-in berths, an enclosed head, and a full galley. Her wooden construction was what the company called Fabribond, described as "prefabricated and glued planking for a stiffer hull." It is not known (but can be guessed) what L. Francis Herreshoff thought of this vessel when he saw her described on page 54 in the November 1944 issue of *The Rudder.*

A more sensible way to gain cabin space and headroom was to enlarge the whole boat, rather than try to cram more into the 28-foot design. H. W. Janson, of Braintree, Massachusetts, did just that, reporting in *The Rudder* that he had proportionally increased the design to 32 feet and produced a successful boat with accommodations for four and good headroom without the need of a doghouse.[25]

Francis was generally tolerant of changes to

the design of the H-28. He wrote to Boris: "I think it will not be good policy to discourage people who want to make changes. The design, to quite an extant, is gotten up so variations could be made and I have mentioned that in past articles and there is allowance in inside ballast enough to make up for any reasonable variations. You will find that there are always a lot of cranks who have queer ideas and I think it is just as well to let them go. It will not spoil my name."[26]

One H-28 that was built exactly to Francis's drawings was a sailing model made by Charles Hakanson, an experienced pattern-maker. He wrote to Francis to "compliment you on turning out such excellent drawings and details that require no explanation." The model-maker brought his little vessel to Marblehead to show it to the designer. Francis was impressed and described the model to Boris as "a very nice model of the H-28. He has made it exactly like the drawings all the way through, including all of the fittings, bow chocks, cabin arrangement and everything else. It is a sailing model and good and strong so she can be handled and looked at."[27]

By 1946, three years after the How-To-Build series started, a Club H 28 had been formed, and "Club H 28 News" became a regular column in *The Rudder*. Owners thus had a forum in which to share experiences building and sailing their H-28s. The design had caught on. Ten years later, there were about 350 boats. The H-28 is the most popular boat designed by L. Francis Herreshoff.[28]

The very first H-28 to be launched (January 1945) and get underway (March 1945) seems to have been the boat of John R. Dingle of Melbourne, Australia. Francis was glad to get long letters from Dingle, describing his H-28's performance. Like many an Australian sailor, Dingle was prone to driving his boat. He gave her a watertight cockpit, 6 inches above the waterline forward and 7 inches aft. He reported to Francis that his "*Marloo* carries her sail well in strong winds and I have raced her with full working sails in winds

LEFT: **The H-28 *Helena* about to round the buoy off the Ruins, the remains of Fort Tyler near Gardiners Island, in an Off Soundings Race in 1953. Her backstaysail was probably inspired by Elwood Sprague's addition of the sail to his H-28 modification. The sail may have to come as the sou'wester freshens for the beat across Gardiners Bay to the finish. The *Helena* was built at Bridgeport, Connecticut, in 1947.** (© Mystic Seaport Museum, Rosenfeld Collection, 1984.187.136200F) ABOVE: **A gang enjoying a quiet sail in the H-28 *Lorelei* on Kentucky Lake. This view shows well the flaring wineglass shape of the transom.** (*The Rudder* (January 1954): 56)

of 35 miles per hour with the decks still clear of the water. She appears to become extremely stiff as the lee rail gets down, and providing it is not too rough, the natural wave formation keeps the deck clear of water. I have noticed, however, particularly when reaching and she is at her maximum speed, although the deck amidships is clear of water the wave formation runs across the deck for about two feet on the lee side right at the transom. This has proved no disability; there is no tendency to spill into the cockpit."[29]

Because of his sail-carrying, Dingle not only added the main running backstays that Francis had omitted at Boris's insistence, but also added two permanent backstays to the mainmast head and an extra main shroud on each side. And he reported on various mast failures and subsequent beefing up of standing rigging by H-28 competitors on the racecourse due to their carrying masthead Genoa jibs in heavy winds. Having read in *The Rudder* what L. Francis Herreshoff thought of such shenanigans, he was quick to point out that he was relaying information about added standing rigging merely out of interest and not in any form of complaint.[30]

In summary of the sailing scene in Melbourne in 1948, Dingle wrote to Francis: "The H-28 still carries pride of place and there are now so many of them that I personally have not been able to keep track of them all. However, I do know of at least thirty that are sailing and quite a number also in the boat builders' hands."[31]

And the H-28 could sail. The little coastwise cruiser began to get a reputation for making ocean passages and for surviving heavy weather. Bill Quodling reported in Club H 28 News leaving Sydney, Australia, in his *Cimba,* heading twenty miles up the coast to Broken Bay with a fair wind blowing fifty knots.

> *We left under mizzen and jib and making about six and a half knots, the seas about twenty feet and breaking. On getting well outside we hove-to, where she lay very comfortably, shipping a little spray. After about ten minutes we dropped the jib and she still lay quietly about six points off the wind. We then put the helm up and she ranged ahead and went off with the wind again. Not many ketches would handle like this under mizzen only. We reached Broken Bay in two and a half hours, averaging a good six knots under mizzen only. It was still blowing hard when we hoisted all sail and beat into the bay. These H-28s are remarkable little boats—they carry all sail in winds up to nearly fifty and yet ghost along in the lightest of airs. We tried to sail her back [to windward] in a southwest gale, but the winds and seas were too much for such a little boat so we returned to the bay.*[32]

Even Australian sailors sometimes use common sense.

On the 600-mile passage from Sydney to Brisbane, the sloop-rigged H-28 *Gypsy Queen* encountered a cyclone measured ashore at seventy knots. "In the mountainous breaking seas her sea anchor carried away and she ran under bare pole. She was pooped several times but came through unscathed even though her cockpit is not self bailing." Mercy.[33]

In 1948, John W. Fisk Jr. sailed his H-28 *Patience* from Newfoundland to New York, and William Shirley made a passage in his *Trade Winds* from Panama to Los Angeles. In 1965, Francis learned that an H-28 had completed two-thirds of a circumnavigation and was in Greece.[34]

In the summer of 1964, Ray Wilkinson and his wife Julia crossed the Atlantic in their H-28, the *Odette.* They had built the boat themselves in Nassau. They made their passage from Fort Lauderdale to Bantry Bay, Ireland, with a stop at Bermuda, where Robert Wingate joined the crew. A third of the trip was made under jib and mizzen in heavy weather. "With a little care self-steering could be achieved for points of sailing between a reach and a beat by adjustment of sail settings and shock cord restricting the movement of the tiller." They used Francis's method of lying-to under mizzen alone, but found that when she headed up, the sail flogged and put excessive strain on the boom slides.

The *Odette* was thirty-one days from Bermuda to Bantry Bay. In a gale that built up to forty-some knots on the quarter, she self-steered under jib alone and then lay beam-to under bare poles, "comfortably absorbing the blows from the occasional wave that broke over her. It appeared that her shallow draft allowed more give than a normal deeper draft vessel would under the circumstances." A second gale reached sixty knots, and they ran off before it towing 600 feet of line in a bight with a canvas bundle attached for extra drag, steering to keep the stern square to the following, breaking seas. Still, the little ketch was pooped many times, and one person was kept busy with a bucket, helping to clear the shallow, "self-bailing" cockpit before the next one came aboard. The gale subsided, and the H-28 came through. The *Odette* brought her crew safely into harbor, as had Francis's fanciful *Snarke* before her. Ray Wilkinson wrote an account of the voyage for the English magazine, *Yachting Monthly,* a copy of which a reader sent to Francis four years after it was published. It was the first he had heard of the boat's feat. Although he much preferred the exploits of the *Snarke* to those of the *Odette*, he must have been pleased that his design had stood up to such a beating.[35]

It was perhaps inevitable that entrepreneurs would be attracted to the popular H-28 design for the building and marketing of plastic boats. Or, at least builders of fiberglass boats were attracted to the H-28 as modified to provide greater accommodations. The operations were widespread: three companies built modified H-28s in the US, two in Japan, and one each in China, Australia, and New Zealand. Staysail Yachts, in Huntington, Long Island, came closest to Francis's original design, simply squeezing berthing for four and an enclosed head into the existing cabin space. Parkins Marine, in Fort Lauderdale, enlarged the cabin house and used a sloop rig. Middleton Marine, in La Crosse, Florida, offered a doghouse and sloop rig as options. International Marine Japan had Eldridge-McGinnis work up modifications including a big cabin trunk with doghouse and a sloop rig. They called the boat the Samurai class. Far East Yachts in Japan made similar modifications to their Far East 29. Cheoy Lee in China produced the Bermuda 30 and Offshore 31 loosely based on the H-28. The Walker Boat Company, in Geelong, Australia, gave rig options and full headroom in the doghouse to its version. Mercifully, most of these boats were launched when L. Francis Herreshoff was no longer around to comment.[36]

But Francis gave "tacit approval" of "subtle design changes" for by far the most successful of these operations, the one in New Zealand. Compass Yachts, in Auckland, chose the sloop rig, and John Lidgard made small increases in all the dimensions of the boat, arriving at: length on deck, 29 feet, 7 inches; length on the waterline, 23 feet, 9 inches; beam, 9 feet; draft, 4 feet; and sail area, 360 square feet. Because of fiberglass construction, displacement was reduced to 7,783 pounds with 4,000 pounds of outside ballast, thus increasing the ballast-displacement ratio from 31 percent to 51 percent. Many of the Compass H-28s were sold as bare hulls to be completed by their owners. These boats have been fast and able; they were certainly popular, amassing a fleet of about 350, thus perhaps tripling the number of H-28s worldwide to more than a thousand.[37]

But when the Pre-Stressed Concrete Company of Auckland reported to Francis that they had built H-28s of ferro-cement, that was too much. Francis denigrated the concept and expressed no curiosity as to how the boats had turned out.[38]

L. Francis Herreshoff's design of the H-28 met *The Rudder*'s objective of being a simple, affordable boat for servicemen returning from war, and for anyone else who might want a boat for realizing the dream of exploring coastlines and harbors under sail. H-28s have satisfied many a sailor with their speed and easy handling. And the boats have fulfilled the desire of many to own a handsome object expertly designed to function perfectly. There are thousands upon thousands of memories of sails in H-28s, from the peaceful, to the pleasant, to the exciting. That a few of the boats have made successful offshore passages and survived heavy weather is an unintentional bonus. Francis applied to the design of the H-28 both his common sense of yacht design and his great artistry. He produced the quintessential small, cruising, sailing boat.

Edwin M. Hill, of Damariscotta, Maine, was attracted to L. Francis Herreshoff's work by the *Rudder* articles of 1943 on the H-28. He wanted Mr. Herreshoff to draw him a boat like the H-28, but with the design changed for daysailing instead of cruising. Hill didn't intend having the boat built until after the war; Francis could take his time. So he interspersed designing and writing about the H-28 for *The Rudder* with working leisurely on the plans for Hill's boat. Hill paid him for each drawing as it was finished, these amounts to be deducted from his commission of 10 percent of the construction cost.[39]

In his H-28 article in the January 1943 issue, Francis quoted a few lines from Samuel Taylor Coleridge's *The Rhyme of the Ancient Mariner*:

> *It ceased; yet still the sails made on*
> *A pleasant noise till noon,*
> *A noise like of a hidden brook*
> *In the leafy month of June,*
> *That to the sleeping woods all right*
> *Singeth a quiet tune.*

These lines inspired Hill to name his daysailer the *Quiet Tune.*

Once he had finished inking the drawings for design No. 82 in 1944, Francis took them in to Boston to B. L. Makepeace, Inc., the print shop he used to make blueprints from his linen sheets. The blueprints would be used by the boatbuilders at Hodgdon Brothers to build the *Quiet Tune* in 1945. Copies would not be sent to any other builders, however, because Hill asked Francis not to sell the plans of his boat in New England. Although Francis sold sets later to three customers outside New England (one just barely outside, in Flushing, New York, the other two in California) no other boat has been built to design No. 82.[40]

Edwin Hill kept the *Quiet Tune* for eight years and enjoyed many a sail among the islands of the Maine coast from his mooring in Pemaquid Harbor. The next owner, Archie T. Morrison, also sailed the boat from Pemaquid, for eight years. In 1961, she went to George M. "Jay" Jenkins of Wings Neck on Cape Cod, who sailed her with great joy for many years on Buzzards Bay.[41]

It is unfortunate that sailors have not so far enjoyed sisterships of this wonderful boat. They can, however, sail the *Quiet Tune* herself, for her last private owner, Daniel Carter, donated her to Mystic Seaport Museum, where she is in the livery fleet. Her design is very special: she represents L. Francis Herreshoff at his best. He, himself, wrote: "I consider this one of my favorite designs."[42]

Captain Albert Chambers, who had started boarding with Francis in 1934 at 20 Lee Street, moved out of the back apartment at 25 Front Street in 1943. The rooms then became a summer rental for Rolf Armstrong, one of the most popular artists in America. Eighteen months older than Francis, Armstrong was a racer of sailing canoes, and he had sought the acquaintance of L. Francis Herreshoff as the designer of the ACA canoe. He revered Skipper Herreshoff as both a top-notch small-boat sailor and as an artist.

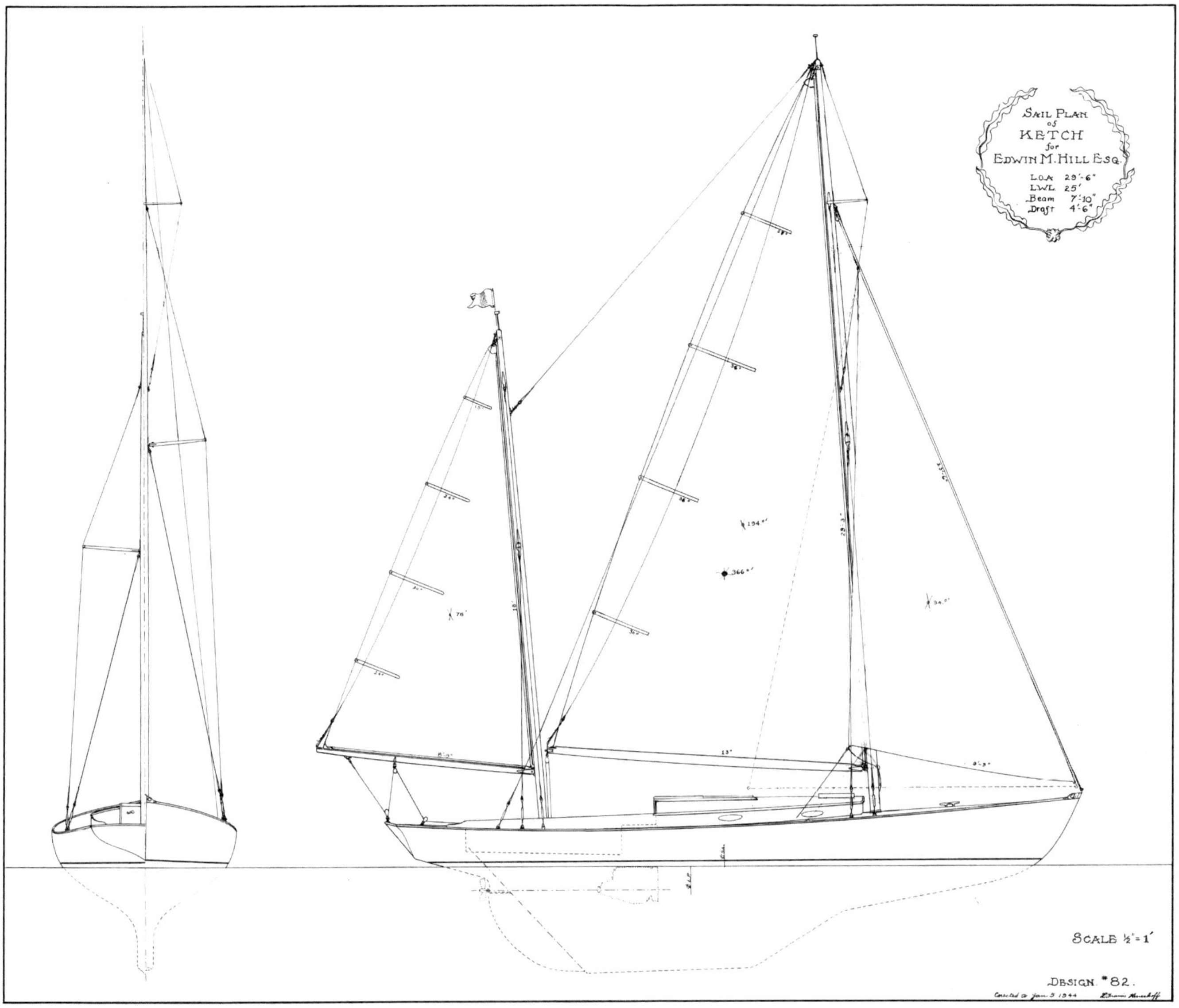

ABOVE: **The outboard profile and sail plan of the *Quiet Tune*, Francis's design No. 82, a day-sailer drawn for Edwin M. Hill during 1943 and 1944, and thus overlapping his work on the H-28. The sail plan is exactly the same as that for the H-28, but Francis has replaced the masthead headstay with his jumper stays and has added a pair of permanent backstays leading to the quarters either side of the mizzenmast. He used the same roller reefing gear on the mainsail that he had designed for the Beverly Yacht Club 30-Square-Metre boats (see volume 1, pages 332 and 333). This drawing was published in the June 1943 issue of *The Rudder*.** (© Mystic Seaport Museum, Daniel S. Gregory Ships Plans Library, SP38.93.4)

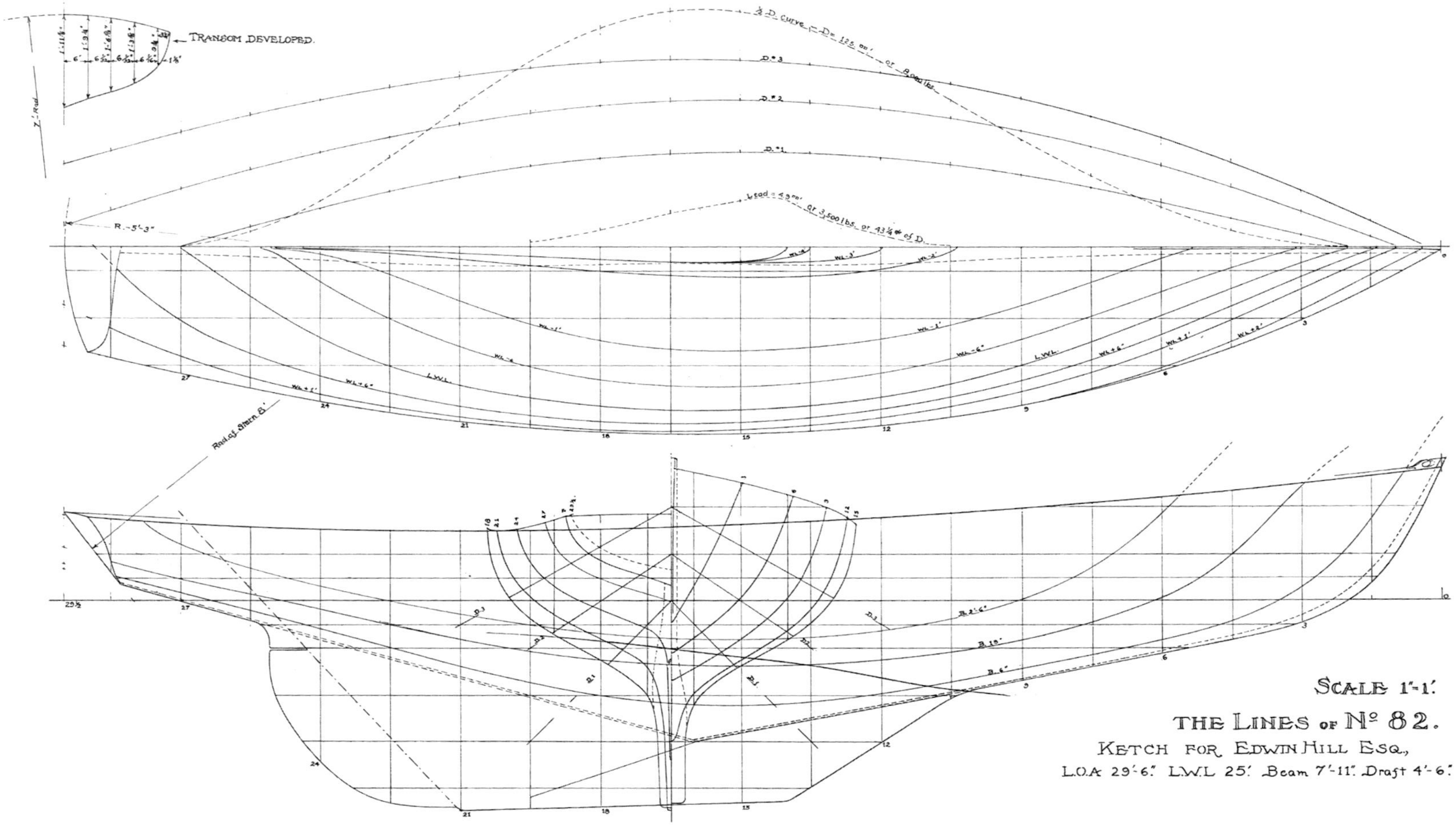

The lines of the *Quiet Tune*. She is much finer than the H-28 and is a little longer, narrower, and deeper. Compared to her huskier sister, she has a flatter sheer and less freeboard, with much more hollow in the waterlines forward and a narrower transom. Like the H-28, she has lots of flare all around, so that she looks light on her feet and picks up bearing as she heels for good hull-form stability. Dimensions are: length on deck, 29 feet, 6 inches; length on the waterline, 25 feet; beam, 7 feet, 11 inches; and draft, 4 feet, 6 inches. Displacement is 8,000 pounds, with 3,500 pounds of outside ballast, for a ballast-displacement ratio of 44 percent. When she was launched, it was found that the *Quiet Tune* needed 500 pounds of inside ballast to bring her down to her lines, a normal and healthy requirement. One inquirer, Percy Brewer in San Francisco, asked Mr. Herreshoff the usual question about more headroom. He replied that it would be all right to raise the freeboard and cabin house 2 inches each, but no more, and added that the change "might even improve her looks." Mr. Brewer took the matter no further. (© Mystic Seaport Museum, Daniel S. Gregory Ships Plans Library, SP38.93.1)

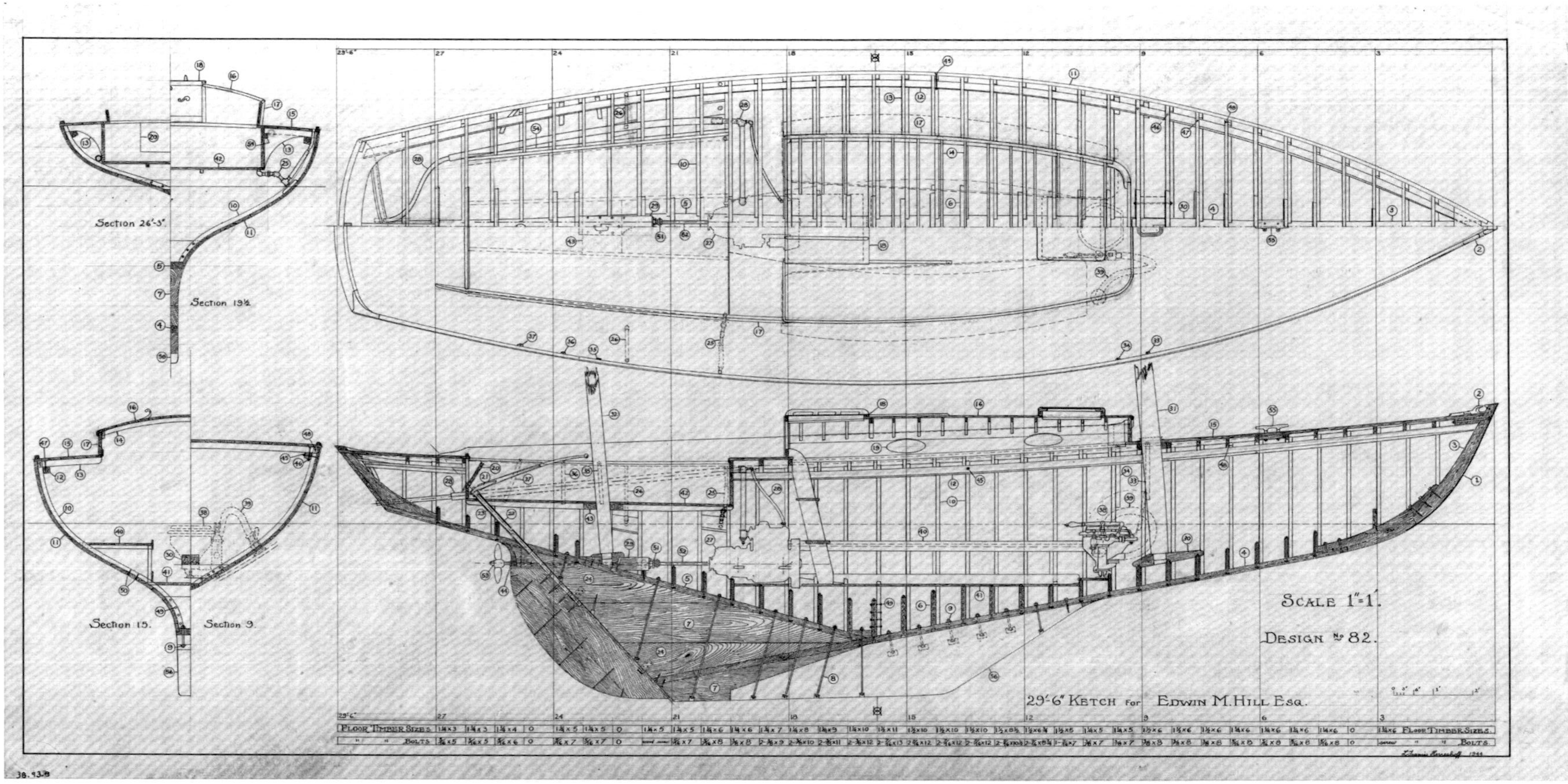

The *Quiet Tune*'s construction plan shows that her scantlings are a little lighter than those of the H-28. Her cabin space is limited; there is room for two pipe berths, but no galley. Hill asked for a permanent toilet up forward where Francis would have placed his cedar bucket. The short bridge deck allows more space for the engine. The level propeller shaft is angled just enough to clear the rudder on the port side. Hill specified a watertight cockpit, more to keep out rainwater at the mooring than to minimize the effects of a knockdown or boarding sea, for he did not intend taking this boat in harm's way. The table at the bottom of the drawing lists the sizes of floor timbers and bolts. (© Mystic Seaport Museum, Daniel S. Gregory Ships Plans Library, SP38.93.8)

ABOVE: The *Quiet Tune* being sailed by the author on Fishers Island Sound on a brisk April day. On a fast, close reach, she shows that beautiful wave that the hollow bow produces. The breeze was moderate to fresh at times; when close-hauled, she put her rail just down, but not under. With plenty of wind for her modest rig, she felt amazingly like a Buzzards Bay 25-footer, which was Nathanael G. Herreshoff's absolute favorite among the many, many models he carved. (Maynard Bray photo, author's collection) LEFT: The *Quiet Tune*'s self-bailing cockpit is shallow and has no seats. As in a Beetle Cat, you can get comfortable, with a little practice, sitting on its floor and leaning against its coaming. (Author photo)

Francis outside his house at 25 Front Street with his French poodles, Hector and Lady. Hector had the reputation for being "an idiot," while Lady was "a great dog." Lady was replaced by another poodle, Princess, and Princess soon had two puppies, Aurora and Aphrodite, posing in the second photo. Previous to all these dogs was a black poodle, Muffin, beloved by Marbleheaders as well as by his owner. Muffin was struck down by a taxi in the summer of 1942. The purchase of his replacements, Hector and Lady, was funded by Francis's grieving neighbors. Helen Bolster loved Francis's poodles, but he was not a dog groomer. One neighbor remembered: "God, they used to stink." And there is the story of Francis serving a young visitor lunch, letting the dogs lick the empty plates, and then just putting the plates back on the shelf. At any rate, Francis, the bachelor, enjoyed the company of his dogs, once writing, "as I sit here writing at this moment [about the H-28] my two dogs sit looking at me with beseeching brown eyes." (Courtesy of Anne Lawrence Bondy, Mystic Seaport Museum, 1999-4-221 and 1999-4-223)

Rolf Armstrong's forte was painting beautiful women. He made spectacular, glamorous portraits of Mary Pickford, Greta Garbo, Marlene Dietrich, and Katherine Hepburn. He painted Boris Karloff. He counted among his Hollywood friends James Cagney, another sailor. His paintings appeared on magazine covers and in advertisements. His pin-up calendars, with paintings made from models, sold in the millions. He had built a mansion on Little Neck Bay in Bayside, Long Island, on the north shore, with a private cove for his small sailing craft. Now, he was living in the Hotel des Artistes, just off Central Park in Manhattan, and keeping his little fleet at City Island, until he moved the boats to Marblehead for the summer.[43]

Francis wrote, "Rolf Armstrong, the great portrayer of feminine beauty, keeps a seraglio of five or six beautiful sailing canoes with which he satiates his artistic cravings without fear of jealousies." Armstrong cut a dramatic figure, posing in his billowy shirt, sash, and beret. Well, so did Francis, in his own way, sporting his beard and *his* beret, and whistling a flute-like tune, as he walked his poodles down a quiet Front Street on a spring morning. The two artists didn't talk art, though; they yarned about small craft and sailing, for it was messing around in boats that brought these two men together from their very different worlds.[44]

Armstrong was generous with Skipper Herreshoff. Francis had sold both the *Butterfly* and the *So And So* when he was hard up for cash. Armstrong later bought both boats and kept them in Marblehead, where he shared them with Francis, who then could continue mentoring Helen Bolster's daughter, Anne, in the *So And So*. Armstrong would often come out in one of his small craft for a brush with them. Anne also got to sail in Armstrong's boats. As a Christmas present, Armstrong once sent Francis a pile-lined overcoat from Brooks Brothers, a coat he wore for many years. Rolf Armstrong would spend several more summers with Francis, and the two stayed in touch until Armstrong moved to Hawaii in 1956 to pursue a new interest in catamarans.[45]

ABOVE: **Anne Lawrence sailing one of Rolf Armstrong's canoes. Francis would use this photo as an illustration in his "The Common Sense of Yacht Design."** (*The Rudder* (November 1945): 39) RIGHT: **Francis found the time away from his *Rudder* work to respond to a call for designs for a one-design class from the Southern Yacht Club in New Orleans with this proposal for a 33-foot sloop. She is handsome and wholesome, quite beamy, and with the wide, flaring transom of the H-28. Waterline length is 28 feet; beam, 10 feet; and draft, 4 feet, 9 inches. Sail area is 582 square feet, with 387 in the mainsail and 195 in the jib. The toasting gentlemen in the sectional drawing show that there is just standing headroom under the cabin house and just sitting headroom under the deck. Francis has succumbed to a pump toilet installed well forward. The open cockpit is 8 feet long and has seats that pivot to stretch canvas berths between their inboard sides and the hull under the deck, for warm-weather sleeping under a boom tent. Francis's design did not make the Southern Yacht Club's short list. It is somewhat reminiscent of his father's design of thirty years earlier of the Newport 29.** (© Mystic Seaport Museum, Daniel S. Gregory Ships Plans Library, SP38.53.2)

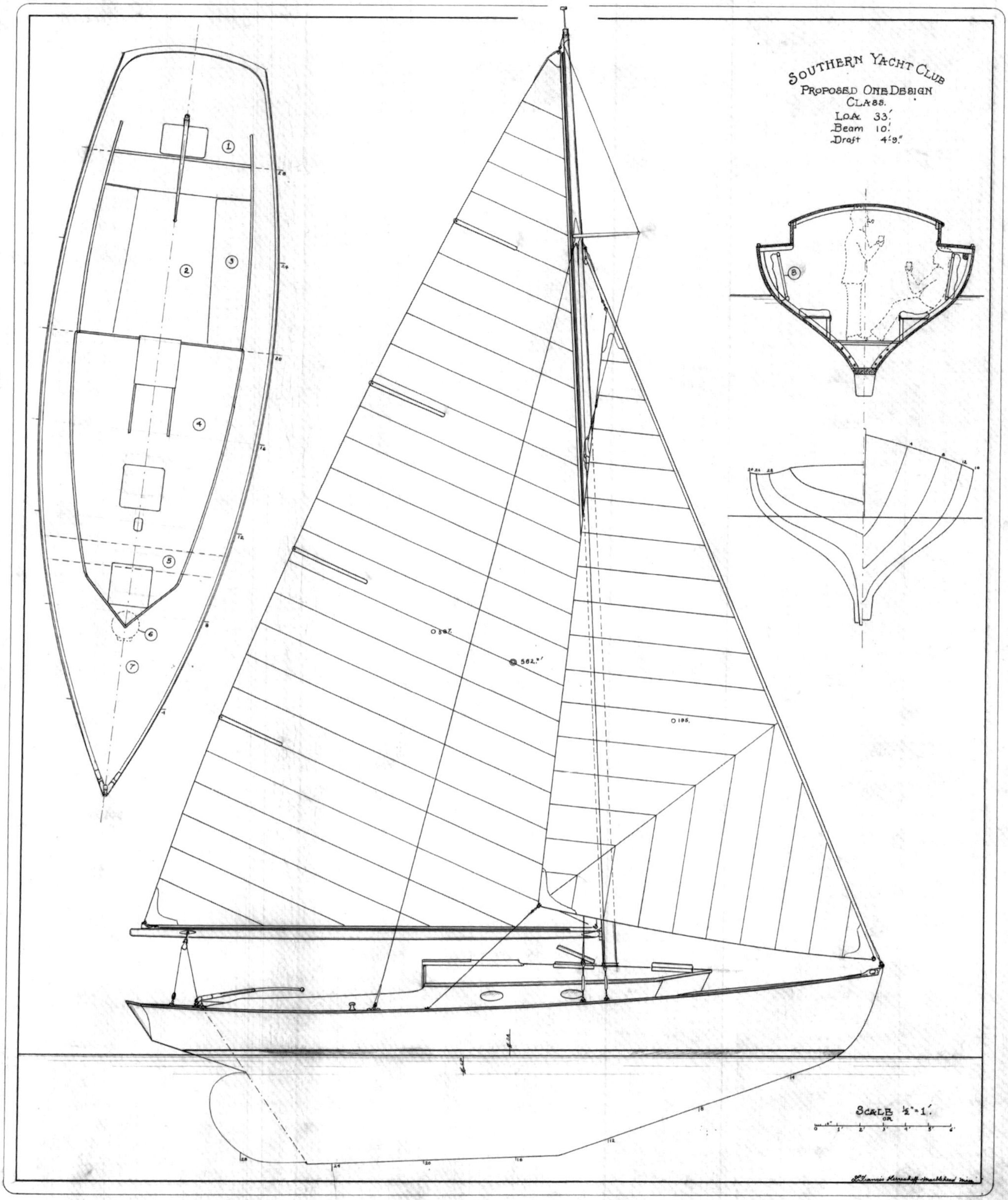
SOUTHERN YACHT CLUB
PROPOSED ONE DESIGN
CLASS.
L.O.A. 33'
Beam 10'
Draft 4'9"
SCALE ½" = 1'

As he designed and wrote about the H-28, Francis also embarked on his crusade to "straighten out yachting." Between the June 1943 and February 1944 issues of *The Rudder*, readers were treated to half a dozen articles from the Sage of Marblehead, as some were starting to call L. Francis Herreshoff. He wrote on subjects from the foolishness of unmeasured light sails on racing boats in "Lapping Jibs and Double Spinnakers," to calling a sloop a cutter just because it had two headsails, in "Cutters, Laying To, Etc." He wrote a most favorable review of *The Ashley Book of Knots.* Boris was delighted to get anything from Francis's pen, knowing that he was becoming a drawing card in the subscription department, and he continued to encourage Francis's writing.[46]

But as well as preaching his sermons on rating rules and traditional yachting nomenclature (and behavior), Francis had fun with his writing. His "A Sail in the *Alerion,*" was a reminiscence of one of his favorite delivery trips, sailing single-handed in his father's wonderful 26-foot daysailer from New York to Bristol (see volume 1, pages 50 and 60). In "A Midsummer Night's Sail," he waxed poetic in a description of being caught out in a thunder squall in a sailing dinghy. That drama may well have been based on an experience sailing his *So And So* with Anne Lawrence. Francis was becoming quite a collector of marine art, and he wrote a piece called "Marine Pictures" that showcased some of his paintings and extolled such artists as E. W. Cooke and Frederick S. Cozzens. Francis always emphasized the importance of studying the past in yacht design; he taught that lesson in "Some Reasons for the Peculiarities of Vessels of the Past." L. Francis Herreshoff was indeed becoming as well known for his writing as for his yacht designing. He was lucky to have Boris Lauer-Leonardi in his corner, helping him fight what he saw as the glitz of yachting with his sense of tradition.

In October 1943, Boris suggested to Francis that he follow the H-28 design with a plywood sailing skiff that would be a good learning boat, a craft similar to the popular Penguin-class dinghy that Phil Rhodes had drawn the year before. Francis replied: "In a great many ways I do not think very much of the Penguin for beginners, although probably she is a very good boat for poor grownups who can carry rather more sail than is right for beginners." Two weeks later, he was planning to design the sailing skiff. Boris wanted her both for *The Rudder* and for himself.[47]

By early 1944, Francis had received a $50 "first payment" for the design and by February 3 he could write to Boris: "I think 14 feet is much

RIGHT: **The sail plan of the H-14 dinghy, Francis's design No. 84, drawn in 1944 for Boris to publish in the July issue of *The Rudder* as a new How-To-Build series. She was a fine, little boat but never became popular like the Penguin or Snipe. Sail area is 75 square feet. The upper end of the halyard was secured in a slot in the yard so that the yard would fit snugly against the mast when the sail was set; Francis specified two additional slots for shifting the halyard up the yard when the sail was reefed. The halyard doubles as forestay. The three-part sheet has plenty of power and leads well clear of the crew. Seeking simplicity, Francis advised sewing the sail to yard and boom, writing, "tracks grooves, etc. are an expense and a nuisance: they are only trick things that soon get out of order." On the other hand, he designed a half dozen special fittings for the boat and wrote, "if there had been any suitable stock patterns I would have recommended them," and to an amateur builder who baulked at making them, "it will be fun for you to whittle out these patterns."** (© Mystic Seaport Museum, Daniel S. Gregory Ships Plans Library, SP38.3)

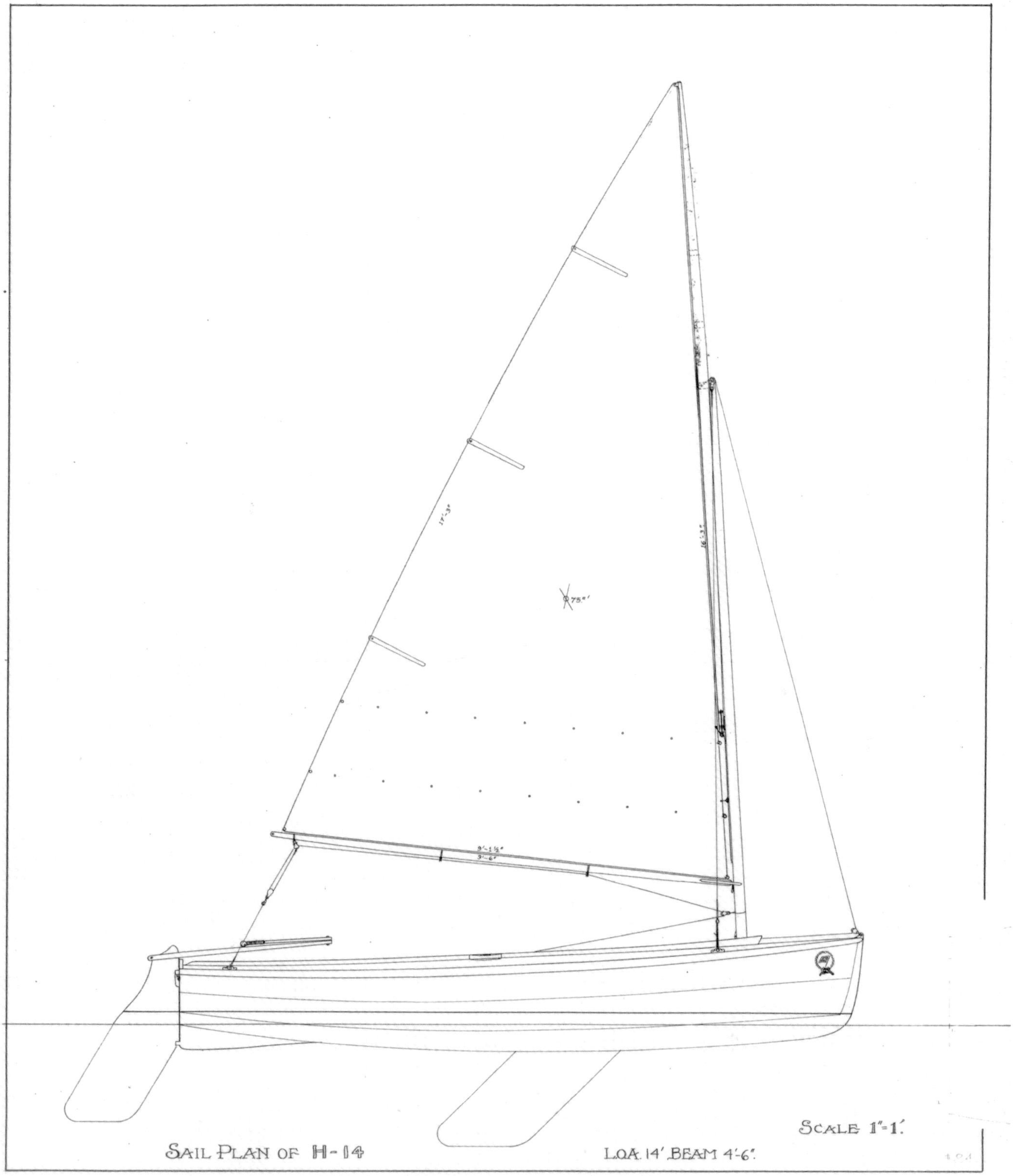
SAIL PLAN OF H-14
LOA 14' BEAM 4'-6"
SCALE 1"=1'

the best [length] for the dinghy because that brings her out of the Frostbite class and in a slightly different field. In other words, she will be a boat to keep on a float and big enough for two people and not spoiled by trying to be small for a tender to hoist on deck." Ten days later, Francis sent in the sail plan for what Boris would call the H-14.[48]

While Francis was developing the design, Boris was promoting it. He stimulated his friends, the Genners, owners of the H-23 *Button*, with the news that Skipper Herreshoff was drawing the plans for a 14-foot sailing dinghy. Jane Genner was so stirred up that she wrote to the designer himself: "Every time Boris receives something new on the dinghy, there is a buzz of excitement. The telephone wires on this end of Long Island get busy, and the question of the day is, 'Have you heard that the sail plan for the dinghy has come through?'" Francis got caught up in it all: "It is quite thrilling that there are so many people who plan to build the little dinghy."[49]

And Boris went beyond talking up the boat with his friends. He persuaded Ensign J. Oakley, faculty advisor for the Cadet Midshipman's Sailing Club at the United States Merchant Marine Academy at King's Point to adopt the H-14 as their training boat. At King's Point, she was to be called the Mariner. Boris even lined up a builder for the four initial Mariners: The Little Shipyard at Sea Cliff, run by Herman Otterstedt. The spars were to be made by the Pigeon Hollow Spar Company, East Boston. Oakley wrote Francis that he was anxious to get the four boats for spring and summer sailing. Francis replied: "I will try to push the drawings of the H-14 as much as I can but I am a very slow draftsman and the tracing takes some time."[50]

The design wasn't ready to be published in *The Rudder* until the July and August issues. In his brief introduction to "How To Build H 14," Boris wrote optimistically,

"The dammed up interest in this design is assurance that many will be built throughout the country."[51]

In Francis's accompanying text, he wrote that he was attempting to design something uncommon, a good, yet inexpensive, boat.

> *We have adopted dory construction for the framing, which means there are a few sawn frames (which will act as molds when the boat is being built), and a few bent frames between, which can be put in after the planking has been fastened, as in dory construction. The side planking (only two strakes) is also like dory construction. The bottom, which is quite flat, is batten seam construction, and at the bow, where there is often trouble bending and twisting the planks, we have adopted a shoe piece or built up forefoot made of layers of boards glued together and shaped out as model yachts are generally built. This piece is only about three feet long.*
>
> *We have adopted the dagger type of centerboard because of its cheapness and because it gives more room in the boat. It also will save much trouble, for the usual long centerboard slot often opens and closes if a boat is kept on a float. The little boat is decked over at the sides and forward, perhaps enclosing more than one-third of her deck area, and this, besides keeping out a surprising amount of water, has a tendency to prevent the dinghy from twisting when driven hard.*
>
> *As for the rig, we believe it is most important to have a sail plan that can be lowered away instantly, so have adopted an improved sliding gunter rig. With this rig the dinghy can be rigged or unrigged very rapidly, and when reefed there will not be a long masthead above the sail which is often detrimental in a sailing dinghy.*
>
> *In short, the dinghy is intended to be easy and quick to get under way, robust*

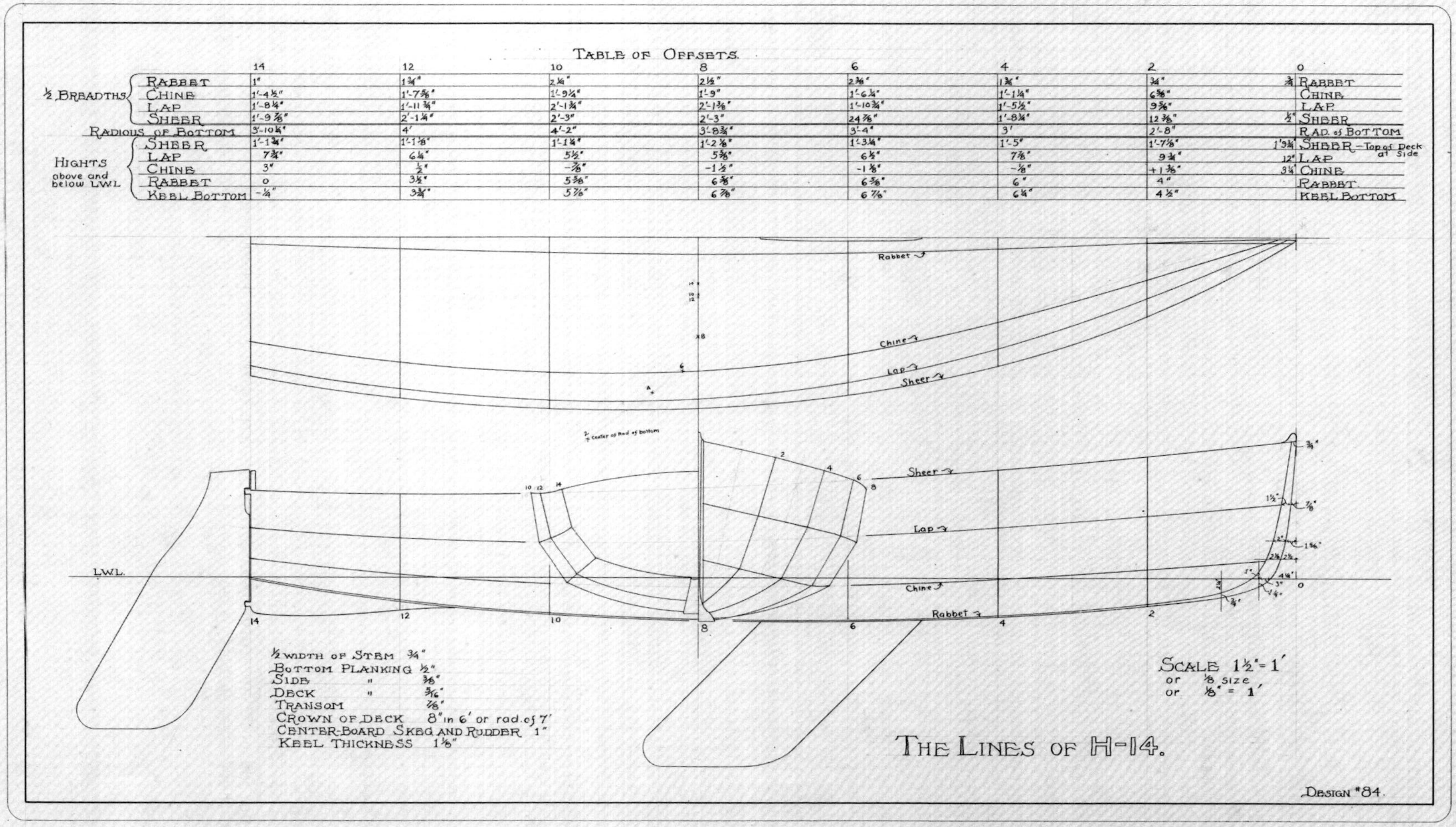

The H-14's lines. Francis has achieved essentially a round-bottom shape, with his "quite flat" arc-bottom and double chines. The H-14 is not designed for really shoal-water work, for her non-swinging daggerboard draws about 2½ feet and the rigid rudder nearly as much. Francis shows the offsets at each frame location in the table at the top of his drawing. (Mystic Seaport Museum, Daniel S. Gregory Ships Plans Library, SP38.3)

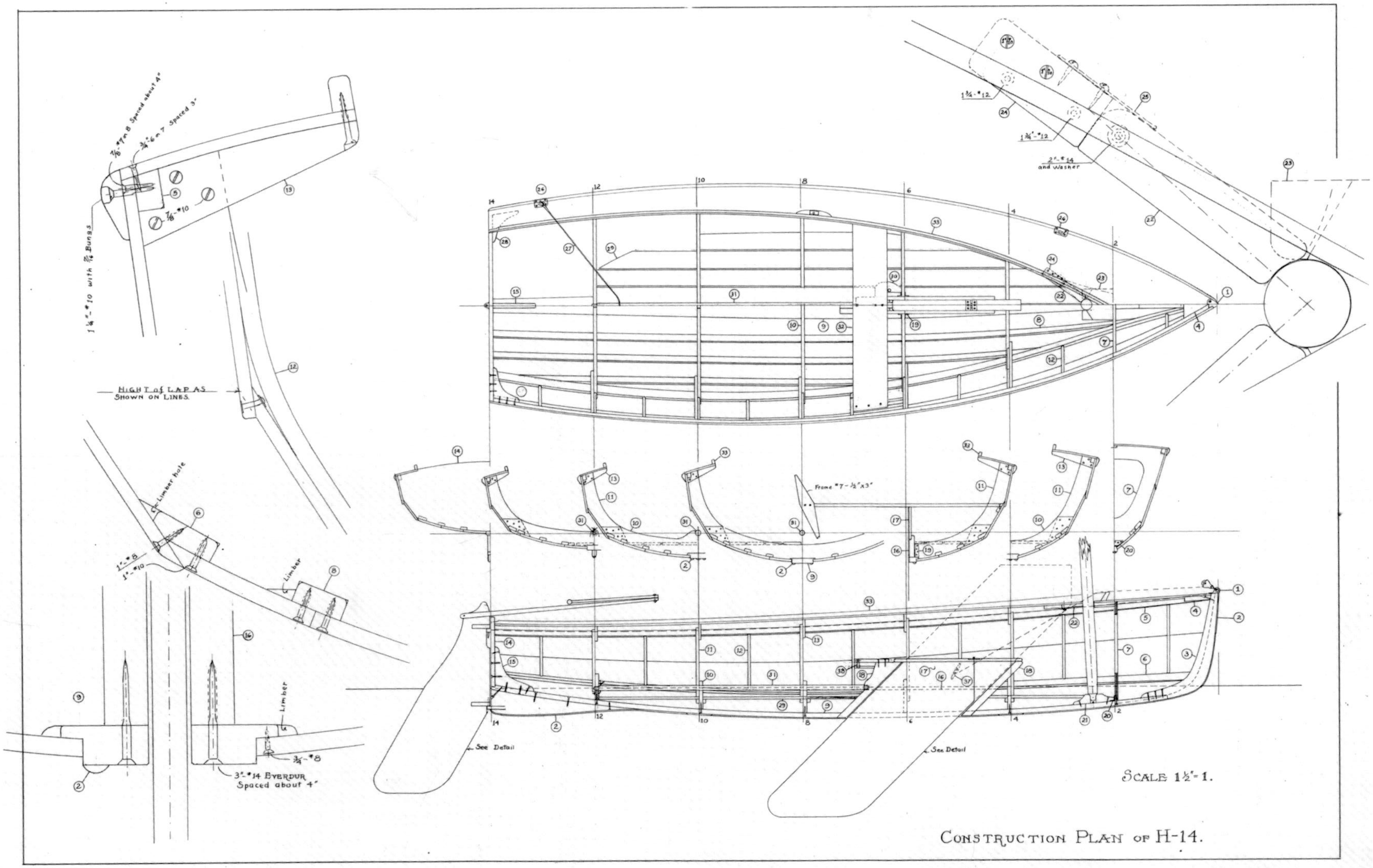

CONSTRUCTION PLAN OF H-14.

enough to leave in the sun and rain on a float, and lively enough for real sport in racing.[52]

As well as building four H-14s for King's Point, Otterstedt's Little Shipyard was producing a boat each for Boris (but Boris baulked and decided to put his H-14 money into his H-28) and the Genners, and one for himself and another for his son. He was building these last three exactly to the design but was making "quite a few changes" to the construction on the King's Point boats. The Merchant Marine Academy changed the deck, the mast step, and "several other things," including eliminating a handy foot brace on the centerline. One of the academy's officers wrote Francis of the H-14 that he was "very pleased with her performance." King's Point ordered ten more H-14s to be built by the Minneford yard at City Island.[53]

Despite a promising start, however, the H-14 never caught on. Sales of the 11-foot, 5-inch, Rhodes Penguin, with its single chine and nearly flat, arc bottom, took off after its plans were published in the May 1940 issue of *Yachting*. Thousands of Penguins were built of plywood around the world. As we have seen, the 15-foot, 6-inch Snipe, a single-chine, vee-bottomed sloop, designed in 1931 as a *Rudder* How-To-Build boat by the magazine's then editor, William F. Crosby, was well on its way to becoming one of the world's most popular one-design racing classes. In 1963, Phil Bolger was involved with building a few H-14s at Stanley Woodward's Mallorca Yacht and Boat Construction Association at Puerto Pollensa. He wrote to Francis that the boat was "plainly a thoroughbred and delightful to sail." The problem

LEFT: **Boris had in mind a plywood sailing skiff, presumably a single-chine boat, but what Francis gave him, as seen in this construction plan, is a more complex, double-chine structure, with fore-and-aft, inside battens covering the seams. Francis did specify plywood for the boat's deck and, as an alternative, for the sides of the centerboard trunk. Note the web frame just forward of the mast. *The Rudder* sold the H-14's sail plan, lines, and offsets, construction plan, and two detailed drawings for spars and fittings, and rudder, tiller, and centerboard as a set for $5.00. Francis got a dollar a set as royalty, earning $28.00 for *The Rudder*'s fiscal year ending April 1, 1947.** (© Mystic Seaport Museum, Daniel S. Gregory Ships Plans Library, SP38.3) ABOVE: **Here is L. Francis Herreshoff in June 1944, after finishing his series on the H-14 and designing and writing about the H-28. Francis said of this photograph: "I think it is the best picture of myself I have seen." Its publication in *The Rudder* was perhaps responsible for Francis earning, among his admirers, the affectionate nickname, "The Beard." One H-28 owner actually named his boat *The Beard*, with Francis's approval.** (Mrs. Russell Genner photo, Mystic Seaport Museum, 1997-1-46)

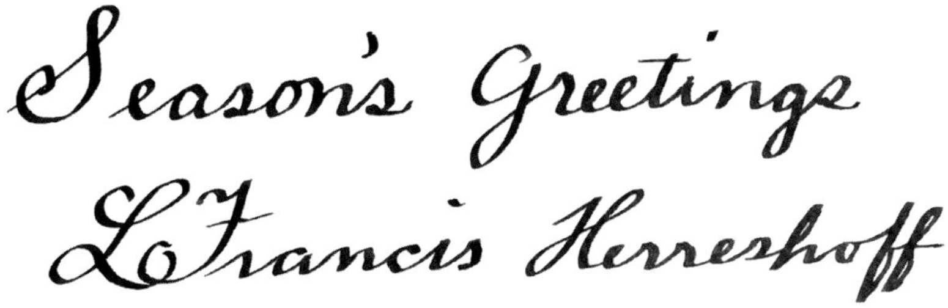

was that the H-14 had just enough complication and refinement to lift the design out of the ordinariness—and bar it from the great popularity—of the Penguin and Snipe. Francis must have seen Penguins and Snipes in Marblehead Harbor, but he never actually saw an H-14 dinghy. Yet, as usual, he had created a boat that would give great pleasure to a modest number of sailors.[54]

Soon after Boris Lauer-Leonardi recruited L. Francis Herreshoff to submit a design for *The Rudder*'s How-To-Build series, he wrote: "You know skipper what would be a great idea? You write for me informal articles on yacht design and construction, and I'll run them as a serial, and later you can revise them and we'll slap it into book form." Boris hurried to Marblehead to press his "great idea" in person. The trip was successful; on his return home, Boris wrote: "It was swell to see you, and I am tickled pink that you have consented to give us a series of articles on yacht designing. I consider it a scoop for *The Rudder,* and I know that it will help hundreds of young fellows along the right road. It might even get me so that I can draw a straight line."[55]

Two weeks later, Francis wrote to Boris: "About the series of articles on yacht designing to make up a book:—these may come along quite slowly but I have started a little on the first one and they will be quite informal chats and I hope easy to read." In another ten days, Francis wrote, "I will soon get started on the articles about yacht design. It will be more or less of a conversational piece and free from mathematics and other professional stuff that confuses the reader." All this was even before his first H-28 plans were published, but the seeds of Francis's yacht design articles "to make up a book" took time to germinate. Boris would publish sixteen more monthly issues before the first of Francis "conversational pieces" would appear in the March 1944, issue, under the series title, "The Common Sense of Yacht Design." Looking ahead to book publication, Francis had suggested this title to Boris as "a little different title then the previous several books" (such as Skene's *Elements of Yacht Design*). Boris wrote: "Your suggested title is a masterpiece. I could not think of a better one no matter how hard I tried."[56]

ABOVE: **Francis's carefully written signature.** (Mystic Seaport Museum, 1996-10-16) LEFT: **In August 1944, with his articles on the H-14 concluded, Francis had only to meet the deadline for the September installment of "The Common Sense of Yacht Design," so he had time to go sailing in his Development boat, the *Butterfly,* to observe Marblehead Race Week. Francis is having a relaxed gam alongside a visiting yacht with Tore Franzen, a colleague of his brother Griswold at the Chrysler Corporation.** (Tore Franzen photo, Herrshoff Marine Museum, 91.79)

Francis thought a lot about common sense. When a correspondent in his middle fifties wrote to him about getting his cruising boat "before it's too late," Francis reassured him by saying that the fifties—his own age—"is the beginning of the age of common sense." Francis linked common sense with experience. As he wrote in his yacht-design articles, "there is only one great teacher, and that teacher is experience." He advocated learning by doing over learning by studying. For Francis, a vital element of common sense was a sense of proportion, which he defined, in addition to being a talent for aesthetics, as knowing whether or not a construction element or fitting looks strong enough without mathematics or formulas. He believed that this sense of proportion could come only from experience. He, himself, was lightning fast when looking over boat construction, quickly noticing anything amiss." Yes, the best material to use in building a boat is common sense," he wrote, adding that "she should be well fastened with sincerity." When it came time for Boris to put the articles into a book, he wrote to Francis, "Let me know if you want to dedicate the book to anyone." Francis replied: "I think it should be something like dedicating the book to Common Sense." And so it was.[57]

Equally important to the words "common sense" in his title were the words "yacht design." Francis always considered his field of endeavor to be yacht designing, not naval architecture. He insisted on a literal meaning for the term "naval architect," namely a naval officer, who, different from a line officer, was in the engineering and design specialty. Of course, many a yacht designer who had formal education in marine design (and some who didn't) referred to himself as a naval architect. Francis wrote: "If you know of anyone who calls himself a naval architect who can design a better shape [than a Viking ship] today—well, if so, he is entitled to the next higher rank and should call himself a yacht designer." Francis wrote of yacht design as "the most interesting occupation that past or present ages have seen, or future can hope to see."[58]

"The Common Sense of Yacht Design" articles were half instruction manual on the subject and half critical screed, aimed at turning the sport of

---

In his chapter on measurement rules in "The Common Sense of Yacht Design," Francis used this photograph of his father's design of 1891, the *Gloriana*, to illustrate a breakthrough design under the Seawanhaka Rule. He wrote: "She had a pram, or spoon-shape bow, and while most people think this the secret of her success it is more probable that her great stability was a more important factor. She had larger sail area and could carry it." (*The Rudder* (August 1946): 44)

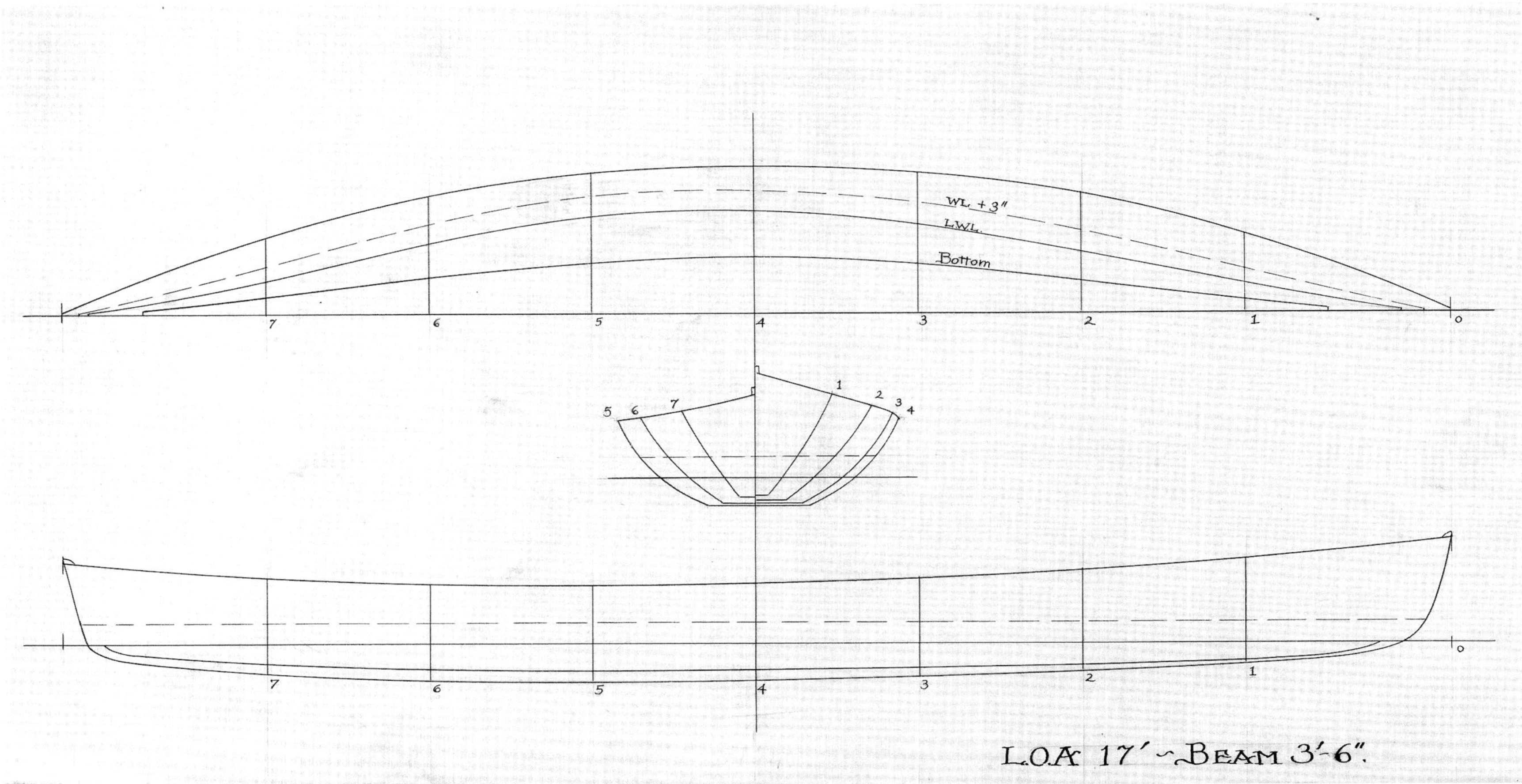

The lines of a 17-foot, double-ended rowing boat that Francis drew for "The Common Sense of Yacht Design" as an example of a small craft that would be fast and seaworthy. Allan Vaitses built two boats to these lines in 1955. One went to Hastings Harcourt, who rowed her with a sliding seat out of Southport, Connecticut. Vaitses built the other for himself to commute across Mattapoisett Harbor between his house and his boatyard. Francis wrote to Vaitses: "I wish I had had one just like her when I was young." (© Mystic Seaport Museum, Daniel S. Gregory Ships Plans Library, SP38.152.1)

yachting away from show and braggadocio and back toward the refined values of the past. Francis applied his ideas of common sense to both halves. His instructions were detailed and "scientific," as he would have said, but they did not venture very far into mathematics and complicated formulas. He shared his experience in a straightforward, informal way. He did, indeed, converse with the "Gentle Reader." He even mixed whimsy in with his common sense. He would occasionally go off on long digressive yarns to make some such point as the great advantage of simplicity in cabin arrangements, or make long, overheated arguments against, for instance, the bad influence on yacht design of measurement rules for rating racing yachts. All great teachers use such devices so that their students will remember the lesson.

As to applying common sense to the sport in general, he wrote: "The reader may think I am sort of a Don Quixote trying single handed to bring chivalry back into yachting, and am conceited enough to think that single handed I can slay all these dragons, hobgoblins and fakers who are besetting the helpless damsel—the sailboat. But that is hardly the case because you will find that I am far from being single handed in my wish to bring common sense back into yachting, for although at present I may appear to be the only one who has come out in the open (or burst forth in print), still there are thousands of others who are with me in this matter." Francis was using "The Common Sense of Yacht Design" to start what he hoped would be a crusade. And as he got into his new career, Francis must have wondered what his father would have thought about his application of common sense to their great profession. But there was actually a measure of relief for Francis: Nathanael wasn't there to criticize.[59]

Francis's comparing himself to Don Quixote was not surprising, since he had long felt an affinity with the fictional knight. As we have seen, back in 1931 he had named his design for a wonderful little cruising ketch for two the *Dulcinea*, after Quixote's lady; many years later, he would name a notable design the *Rozinante*, after the knight's horse. Francis was intrigued by Cervantes's story, and there were strong similarities between its hero and himself. We see this when we substitute Francis's ideal of yachting for the Don's ideal of knighthood. Both men were imperious and quick to anger when they suspected their ideal to be questioned. Each blamed his world for not laboring to revive the happy times when either knighthood or yachting was in its full glory. Don Quixote developed as a tragic hero in a world of fools (the Knight of the Woeful Countenance). L. Francis Herreshoff, saw himself in the same role, referring to himself as "Old Fussbudget."

Part of Francis's inspiration for writing came from the books of Uffa Fox, a series of five beautifully illustrated, readable critiques of yacht designs published in England between 1934 and 1938. Francis had written to Fox, "I am most pleased that your book [*Uffa Fox's Second Book*] went off so well and no wonder it did for it deals directly with things and tells the truth, also the wit, which was lacking in other nautical books, is a great help." Francis didn't copy Fox; he had his own style. But the two did share an ability to go straight to the heart of things and then yarn with the reader.[60]

Francis, the dyslexic who had never gotten A in English, could be apologetic to his readers. He cautioned the reader to be patient, adding, "I have a very small vocabulary." And he warned, "when I sit down to write in the evening, after having some good New England rum, my thoughts are apt to wander." Francis could, in fact, be casual. He wrote: "In all this writing about [measurement] rules I am not sticking to a chronological order or going into any great detail about the rules themselves, for I would far rather give the reader a feeling or general understanding of the thing than to be too exact in details since, as a matter of fact, I am writing almost all of this out of my head without stopping to look up exact dates and dimensions."[61]

Francis wrote, "out of his head," in pencil

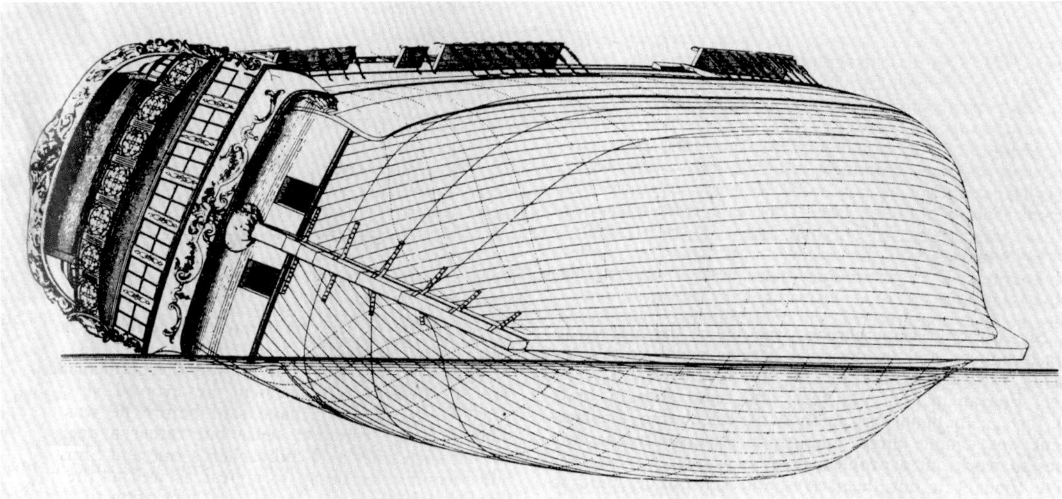

on unlined paper, filling the sheets with his fine, almost cramped hand. When writing letters, he would usually dictate to Mrs. Bolster, and then slowly sign the typed letter with handsome calligraphy. But if his words were to be published, he was more comfortable writing them out than dictating. Occasionally he would add an insert on the back of a page, but there were no cross-outs or revisions. Francis was just as reluctant to revisit his writing as he was to revisit one of his designs. He would rather say to thc reader, "I forgot to mention..." than go back and change things. Mrs. B converted the manuscript into an italic typescript on her machine, correcting Francis's spelling as she went. She also did a little minor editing, probably surreptitious, for Francis, though he made no claim to writing ability, was as fussy about his words as about his drawings. Neither Helen Bolster nor Boris Lauer-Leonardi dared try to "improve" the writings of L. Francis Herreshoff. What was printed in *The Rudder* was essentially Francis's first and only draft.[62]

Francis paid great attention to the illustrations for "The Common Sense of Yacht Design." By the time the series was concluded in the January 1948 issue, he had selected 437 plans, drawings, photographs, and art reproductions from his collections to illustrate his forty-six articles. In some instances, the "art" he sent in with his typescripts consisted of pages carefully sliced out of his books, to be carefully replaced when they had served their purpose. One attribute of "Common Sense" was to give readers a glimpse into the huge store of marine art, including his own yacht design plans, that L. Francis Herreshoff was amassing.[63]

Francis's articles on design were published in book form by The Rudder Publishing Company once they had appeared in the magazine, volume 1 in December 1946, and volume 2 in September

Francis loved to examine the exquisite drawings of Fredrik Henrik af Chapman of Sweden, often called the first naval architect, in his reprint copy of Chapman's *Architectura Navalis Mercatoria*, originally published in 1768. Francis used this example of Chapman's work, a well-decorated ship hove down, as the opening illustration for his chapter, "Figuring Displacement." As wonderful as was the writing in *The Common Sense of Yacht Design*, the illustrations were just as remarkable. (*The Rudder* (May 1946): 39)

1948. The author applied his knowledge and experience to every aspect of yacht design. He covered hull shapes, rigs and sail plans, cabin arrangement, power plants and propellers, construction, materials, spars, rigging, sails, laying off a set of lines, drafting, figuring displacement, measurement rules, power boat models, choosing a cruiser, marine hardware and fittings, ground tackle, sailing boats designed purely for speed, small craft, and, finally, the aesthetics of yacht design.

Francis described the practical, scientific aspects of all these subjects. Of course, his favorite material for building yachts was wood. He made up this table of twenty-one different woods, giving their weight per cubic foot, their strength relative to white oak, and remarks on their characteristics for boatbuilding:

	Wt. per cu. ft.	Relative Strength*	Notes
Northern white spruce	25	66	Light and stiff
Sitka spruce	26	66	Light and tough
White cedar	21	48	Light, soft; swells quickly but not fa
Spanish cedar	24	60	Hard and strong fo weight
Port Orford cedar	28	65	Clear, straight grai
Butternut	25	60	Light; does not shr and swell much
Northern soft pine	27	60	The finest working v
Douglas fir	37	86	Straight grain
Cypress	34	79	Resists rot
White ash	42	110	Strong for its size weight
White elm	37	89	Resists splitting and bends well
Yellow pine (long leaf)	40 to 45	95	Water and rot resi
Hackmatack	38	83	Tough for its weig
Mahogany (African)	38	85	Procurable in large p
Mahogany (Mexican)	35	80	Stays in shape well
Mahogany (Cuban)	40	90	Hard for its weight
Mahogany (Philippine)	39	80	Very variable
White oak	48	100	Cheap and holds fa ings well; bends w
Teak	45	85	Does not shrink an swell, or rot
Locust	51	135	Hard, strong and not rot
Lignum vitae	78	120	Hard and brittle

*Relative strength compared to oak (oak = 100)

English marine painter Edward William Cooke, who worked roughly from 1830 to 1880, was perhaps Francis's favorite. He would claim that Cooke was the only one who could be counted on to show boats that weren't misshapen when drawn in perspective. Certainly this wherry, awaiting the tide, a Cooke etching with which Francis illustrated his chapter on "Small Craft," has no twists or humps. (*The Rudder* (October 1947): 29)

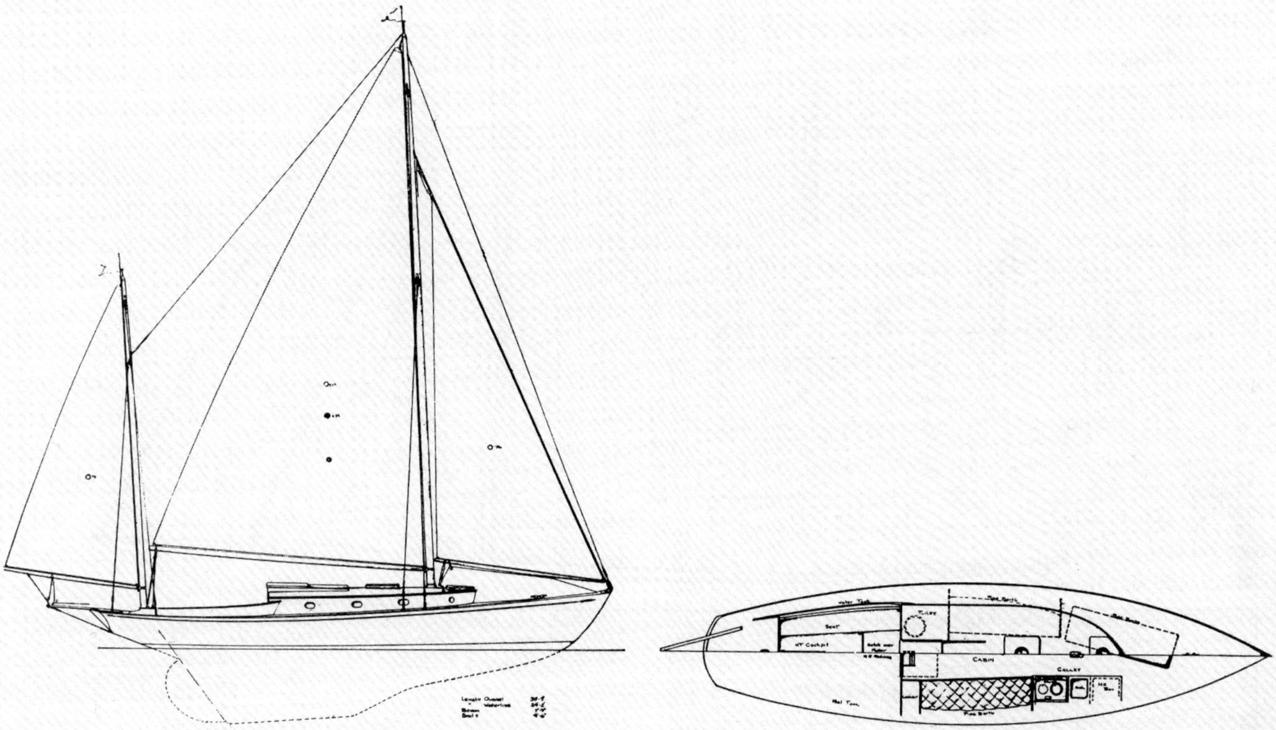

		+ Score		— Score
1.	+1 *for each person accommodated.*	3	—1 *for each thousand dollars of cost.*	7
2.	+1 *for each estimated knot of average speed under sail.*	5	—1 *for each* 100 *sq. ft. of sail area.*	4.3
3.	+1 *for each knot of speed under power.*	5	—1 *for each* 10 *cents of cost of fuel per hour.*	1.5
4.	+5 *if very seaworthy.* +2 *if moderately seaworthy.* +0 *if poor sea boat.*	2	—1 *for each foot of draft.*	4.5
5.	+5 *if self righting when hove down.* +2 *if stability is questionable.* +0 *if not self righting.*	5	—1 *for each* 10° *of heel when beached.*	4
		+20		—21.3

In a chapter called "Choosing a Cruiser," Francis devised a scoring system whereby different types of boats would be given plus points for such characteristics as number of people accommodated, speed, seaworthiness, and stability; and minus points for cost, sail area (to be handled), fuel burned, draft, and amount of heel when beached. This Marconi schooner, with overlapping, or lug, foresail, was one of the examples that Francis drew. It is too bad that no reader demanded that the design be finished and built to. (Her well-rounded, wineglass stern is what the writer had hoped for on the H-28.) (*The Rudder* (April 1947): 40)

He showed his male-chauvinist side when he jested that "the ladies" say that there are two kinds of wood: mahogany and not-mahogany.

When he got to plywood for boats, Francis pulled no punches. "It is about twenty-five years now since I started experimenting with and using laminated wood," he wrote, "and like many who have had long experience with it I have very little use for it." And he invented a conversation with an old boatbuilder to list plywood's problems: half of it is cross-grained, so it is weak for its weight; wood swells mostly crossways, so the layers with their grains in opposition are trying to separate; when working the edges, the cutting tool must go across grain for half the thickness, and the result "looks like hell"; laminated wood is difficult and expensive to mold to a desired curve.

Nor was Francis kind to the use of plastics for boatbuilding, a choice of materials that was rapidly gaining popularity after World War II. He wrote: "These plastics do not begin to have the shock resistance of natural wood—one crack with a hammer and they will shatter. As for elasticity, well, if you try to drive a screw into the stuff it will either split or crumble out. I suppose some day it will be made of an all-around strength of, say, one-half that of wood of the same weight." Francis loved wood; he was not one to keep up with the latest improvements in plastic, at least not for boats. As he waved his arm across Marblehead Harbor, Francis would exclaim: "Look at that God damn plastic cesspool!" One reader, at least, was in full agreement, writing to Francis: "I got a great 'bang' out of the 'work' on plastics and plywoods vs. natural wood. It sure showed fine courage on your part, but then, you're our champion and we look for your 'say' on stuff like that."[64]

With an eye on his advertisers, Boris wrote a disclaimer to go with Francis's text on plywood and plastic: "L. Francis Herreshoff is stating his own opinions which do not represent *The Rudder* editorial stand, but in all business, and for the sake of journalistic integrity, we have to give expression to both sides, especially where the present interest in laminated wood and plastics for boats has reached an unprecedented high among builders and the boating public." When he started the next chapter after "Materials," in which he had lambasted plywood and plastics, Francis wrote: "Even the Editor was a little abashed at some passages in the last chapter and I must admit he was a good sport to have printed all these railings and resentments and, while I have promised to tone down some in the future, still I will try not to make it all wishy-washy." Actually, L. Francis Herreshoff was not capable of "wishy-washy" writing.[65]

In fact, Francis was capable, in his writing, of singling out groups or even individuals, who remained nameless but were easy for knowledgeable readers to spot, for his obloquy. From his broadside, fired at plywood and plastics, Boris had had to "delete some minor passages, especially those which refer to some people as being socially undesirable." And in his diatribe about the harmful effects of measurement rules on yacht design, Francis took pot shots at Olin Stephens, John Alden, and the Cruising Club of America, without naming them. Of the latter, Francis wrote, "their whole idea of a rendezvous is the singing of ribald ballads and the telling of bawdy stories and there is no discourse of the art of cruising." A reader who concurred with Mr. Herreshoff's criticism of the CCA wrote, "because you have written in words of two syllables my own sentiments concerning the degeneration of the principal present purposes of the Cruising Club of America, I can only express my entire approbation of your remarks with a hearty AMEN."[66]

But Boris told Francis:

> *I have read and re-read the material, and it sounds too strong, too bitter, too personal. I don't care about Sparkman [short for Sparkman and Stephens] and Alden, but why give them the satisfaction of singling them out? What you say about*

the Cruising Club is true, but I wouldn't condemn them all. Within the group of about five hundred members there are many who are followers and admirers of yours, men who believe and heed your teachings and who would be appalled were their hero to dump them all helter skelter with the rest of the bad apples into one bag. For instance, Clinton H. Crane is a member. I hope with this in view you'll read the installment again. However return it anyway you want, changed or not.[67]

Not one to edit his work, Francis did not back down. He wrote to Boris: "In the later articles I shall make it a point to be less sarcastic and so make up for this last month's offering which I should like to go in just as it is."[68]

"Abashed" or not, Boris not only gave Francis free rein to press his arguments in his own way, but also allowed *him* to rein in those who wished to argue with him in print! Two and a half years after Francis denigrated plywood and plastic, Boris wrote him from home: "You have for several years fearlessly expounded your views on yachts and yachting. Numerous persons have taken exception to some of your opinions and have submitted articles of rebuttal. As you know, none of them have been published. You will recall numerous articles submitted to you none of which you approved." Boris was so afraid of ruffling Francis's feathers that he handed over to Francis his own responsibility for making sure that *The Rudder* was a fair forum. Francis was presented with a conflict of interest, and he seems to have made the most of it. Author and editor evidently discussed the situation in a visit at Marblehead a week later; would that we knew what they said.[69]

We do know that Boris was protective of his star writer. Back in 1943, he had shut down the combative John Hanna after Hanna chided Francis over the H-28 in his *Rudder* column, "The Watch Below" and then "sent in reams of written matter repudiating practically every word you said," as Boris reported to Francis. And, in late 1945, Boris decided, at Francis's suggestion, not to publish any more of the planing powerboat designs of Lindsay Lord. Boris Lauer-Leonardi did well to recruit and retain L. Francis Herreshoff as a designer and writer for *The Rudder*, but limiting the discussion to Francis's side, even though it may have been necessary to keep him in the fold, was paying a heavy price.[70]

Francis had taken Mrs. Bolster's daughter, Anne, under his wing. As well as teaching her to sail, he had often driven her to school in winter. To him she was "Miss Anne." To tease her, he would call her "Mizzen," and pretend that he was Robinson Crusoe. That's how he addressed and signed the letters he wrote her when she went off to college. Francis got the idea that Anne would make a good assistant for Boris at *The Rudder* after college and tried to broaden her marine education to prepare her for the job. He thought highly of Anne's intelligence and boating ability, despite his habitual putting-down of women. Francis urged Boris to hire Anne, but he baulked. After much backing and filling, Boris told Francis why: "As assistant I need a man. For some reason or other men do not like to be given information on boating matters by a girl, no matter how efficient she is." Boris told Anne that his "board refused to approve a woman in a man's job." So Francis's attempt to help his protégée came to nothing. He told Boris that he was "very disappointed for perhaps nothing would have make me take more interest in *The Rudder* than to have had some young acquaintance of mine working there. But I can understand why a girl would not be suitable for giving information or answering questions by old salts." Boris's attempt to pass off his responsibility to a "board" did not fool Anne Lawrence. Boris asked her to write an article about what women should wear in boats. Anne declined. Despite Boris's reluctance to give her editorial responsibility, Anne remembered that on any occasion when she and Boris had been together

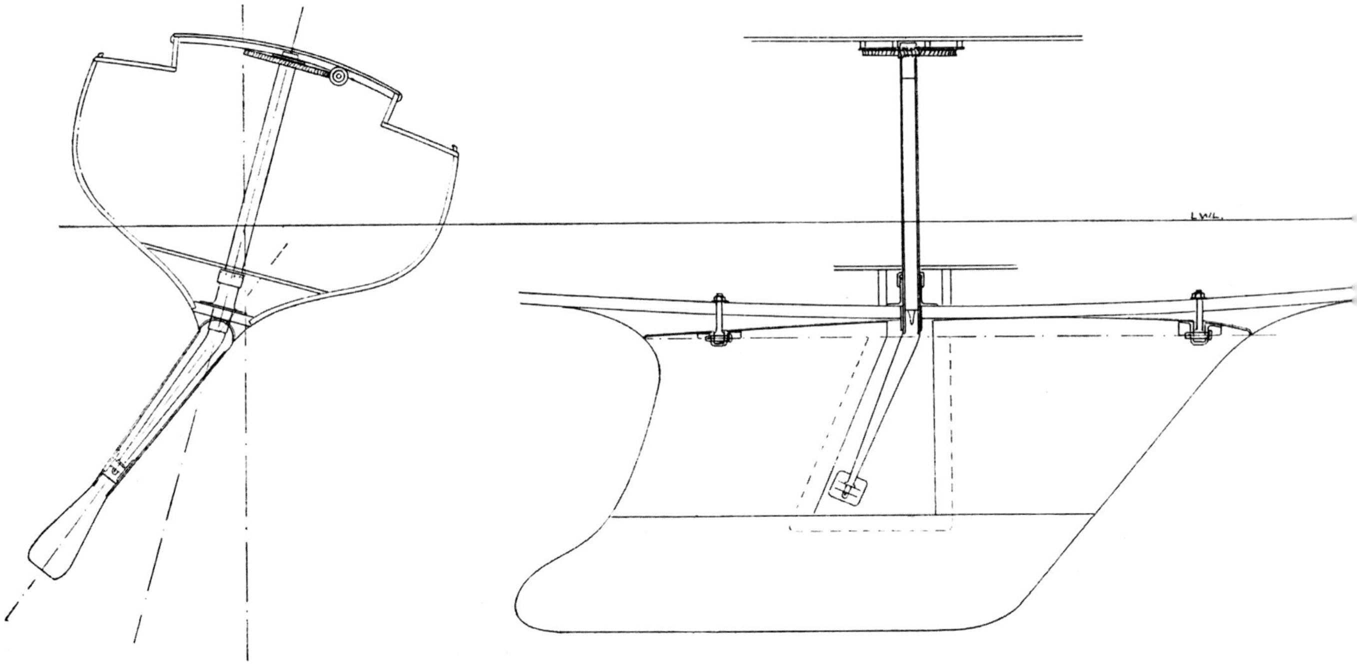

in the *So And So,* he had always deferred to her as skipper.[71]

In "The Common Sense of Yacht Design," Francis preached the importance of art. "Yacht designing at its best is one of the fine arts," he wrote. And he went into detail on curves: "A curve to be interesting must be continually changing. In the case of a sheerline or taper of spar the change, of course, is hardly perceptible, but it must be there nonetheless. Of shorter lines, like the profile of stem, the changes must be more perceptible or the line will become tiring. If the curve of varying radii is more interesting than the one of fixed center, certainly the reverse curve is vastly more interesting than either." Hence Francis's predilection for the clipper bow.[72]

Francis did not pretend that applying common sense to yacht design was going to simplify things.

Francis presented ideas for pure sailing speed in his chapter in "Common Sense" on "The Sailing Machine." Here is his drawing of a swinging keel, to shift the outside ballast 10 degrees to windward, which he estimated would reduce heeling by 6 or 7 degrees, thereby increasing the driving power of the sails. The keel is swung by a "cast bronze crank arm which passes up through a stuffing box on the keel and is revolved or oscillated by a worm and sector gear near the house top." In a slop of sea with light air, the keel could be swung a little to leeward to heel the boat enough to keep the sails asleep. Francis never tried the concept of a swinging keel on an actual boat. (*The Rudder* (July 1947): 36)

For instance, he told the budding yacht designer that he (Marjory Young was still the only female in the field) would have to keep eighteen elements in mind as he drew a set of lines: surface resistance, eddy making, wave resistance, stability, head seas, lateral resistance, changes in shape when heeling, seaworthiness, cabin space, shapes adapted to construction, keels for docking, shapes for strength, length, fairness, draft, looks, cost, and balance of centers of effort and lateral resistance. Francis leavened his discussion of all these scientific subjects with flights of fancy. When he got to the business of choosing a cruiser, he spent an entire month's installment yarning about his fireside chats with designers, sailors, and builders, each of whom defended his own favorite sort of boat so that no agreement could be reached on the best type. Francis had fun explaining how he came by the idea of objective scoring for a variety of cruising boats. And he divulged that he dreamt of many wonderful hull shapes that would never be built, because life was too short to design them.[73]

When Boris received Francis's first article for "The Common Sense of Yacht Design," he must have opened the envelope with trepidation. What if the proud Mr. Herreshoff had gone off on a tangent, or written confusingly? He read Francis's typescript not just with relief, but with wonder. "I cannot tell you," he wrote to Francis, "how much I think of this marvelous piece of work, and you are making a lasting contribution to your profession which will survive for many generations." The contents of the second envelope brought the response, "you are doing a superb job and the gratitude of the American boating public will be yours for many years to come." And Boris's praise and encouragement kept coming. He soon wrote: "The mail is flooded with letters from readers who are extremely enthusiastic about your series on yacht design. They are exuberant in their praise for you and me. I don't know why me but I am basking in the reflected glory just the same. I want you to be conscious of the fact that you are doing a real service for American yachtsmen. Everyone who gets *The Rudder* reads your articles and even if they are not studying yacht design they benefit by the great deal of correct information contained therein." And, "also there is a never ending line of compliments about your style which is refreshing and different." Two years later Boris wrote, "a friend of mine told me that at the New York Yacht Club the members rarely discuss any magazines except *Rudder*, and when they do the topic is 'Herreshoff articles.'" Boris also heard from Starling Burgess: "Has it occurred to you that he writes as Thoreau would have written had he been a sailor?" Starling, working in the Navy Department, told Boris that a great many naval officers were interested in Francis's articles. And Boris wrote to Francis that "your work is greatly appreciated by the Naval Academy, where most of the students follow your writings very closely." It must have delighted Francis especially to hear from one of the midshipmen, a lad from Oklahoma: "From your writings I have been able to see a bit of this magic that calls men to the sea." Years later, Francis would hear from a builder who specialized in fine, classic pulling boats, Dick Shew of South Bristol, Maine: "I have read much of your writing, and it has influenced me to the extent that I have been making my way building wooden craft now for some years, and I have not regretted it."[74]

Perhaps the most important praise that Francis received for his writing referred to his father. One reader wrote, "I enjoy your *Rudder* articles very much and am thoroughly convinced that your illustrious Father had little that you don't have." And Boris, himself, wrote, "in my modest opinion you have inherited your great father's genius." Francis had confidence and pride in his ability as a yacht designer, but he didn't believe himself to be on a level with his father. He would have had trouble taking these flattering statements literally, but they would have given him a lift just the same.[75]

All this early success of Francis's work for *The*

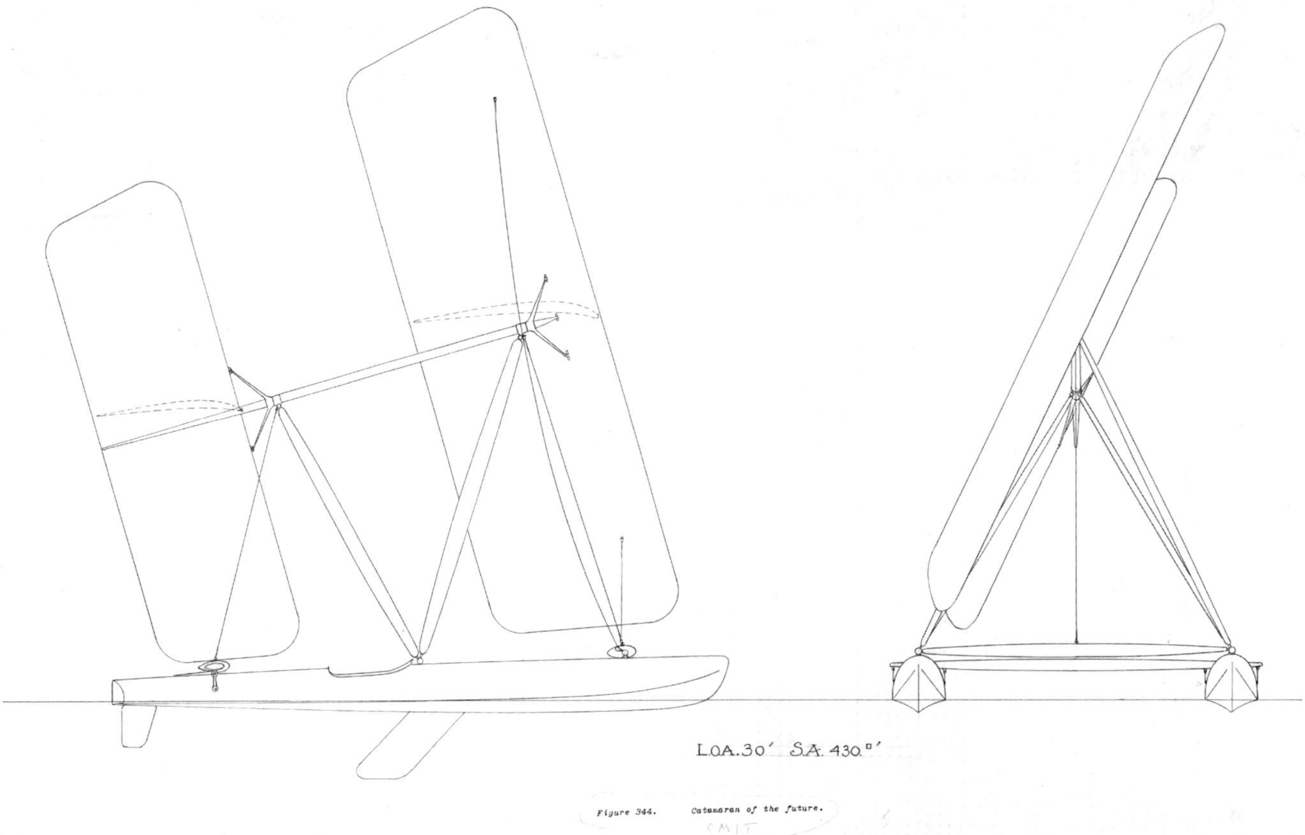

Rudder, and Boris's appreciation and encouragement, nurtured and cemented their friendship. Boris visited Francis in Marblehead all he could. Francis wrote his editor: "I am glad you enjoyed your visit for I certainly enjoy having you visit me more than I can tell you. I do hope that Mrs. Leonardi is feeling better." Boris was married to Jane Pike—"Piky"—who was often ill with a heart ailment. Francis made her a "pretty hand-carved box," and she thanked him with: "Many people have been good to me while I bide my time in bed. They bring me flowers, candy, fruit, vegeta-

---

On the various fanciful catamarans that Francis drew over the years, some, like his first of 1920 (see volume 1, pages 65 and 66), had a separate rig for each hull, and some had a single rig on an A-frame mast. In the latter group was his wingsail catamaran, with a cat-ketch arrangement, a 30-footer with an area of 430 square feet. In "The Common Sense of Yacht Design," he labeled the drawing, "Catamaran of the Future." Perhaps the future arrived in 1988, when the wingsail catamaran *Stars and Stripes* won the America's Cup. Francis wrote; "I hope I never live to see such a mechanical contraption." He got his wish. (© Mystic Seaport Museum, Daniel S. Gregory Ships Plans Library, SP38.302.1)

bles, cake and ice cream, but no one, except you, thought of giving me something I can enjoy permanently." And, she went on, "Boris, as always, enjoyed his visit with you. I wish he could spend more time there and not always have to rush off. It does him good to see you, he gains much in being with you, always comes back feeling happy and right about everything. You give him a lot that he needs, encouragement, re-assurance, and a sound and wholesome perspective on many subjects." Well, Boris was giving Francis a lot that he needed too: an appreciative audience to whom he could teach and preach, an audience that recognized the genius of L. Francis Herreshoff.[76]

As he submitted his final installment, Francis wrote to Boris, "thank God this is the last part of the Common Sense." Francis's workload from early 1944 through the end of 1947 was heavy. Besides the monthly deadline to meet on the demanding articles for "The Common Sense of Yacht Design," he was committed concurrently, as we shall see, to two new How-To-Build series, with their own monthly deadlines, and these involved major yacht designs with detailed drawings for amateur builders. All this time, *Rudder* readers could look forward to and enjoy two major articles in each issue from the pen (or pencil, actually) and drawing board of L. Francis Herreshoff. And even after "Common Sense" was finished, Francis wrote more articles, so that in every issue of *The Rudder* through 1948, his How-To-Build pieces were accompanied by another offering of his wisdom on some aspect of yachting. Beginning with the January 1947 issue, L. Francis Herreshoff was listed on the masthead as Contributing Editor.[77]

All this effort and accomplishment brought Francis but a small income. When Francis started writing "The Common Sense of Yacht Design" in 1944, Boris paid him $15 per *Rudder* page of text and illustrations. With the wartime paper shortage, *The Rudder*'s typographical design was so economical that one full page of text could accommodate 2,000 words. His first five-page article, containing 6,000 words and eight quarter-page illustrations, five of them his own drawings, brought him $75. Beginning with the October 1945 issue, with the war over and paper more plentiful, Boris increased the type size so that it took only 1,300 words to fill a page. Francis warned the reader that he might "take him round the barn," because the editor was "a funny fellow" who paid him more for a long article than for a short one. At the end of 1946, Boris doubled Francis's pay to $30 per page. For such generosity, he had to gain approval from *The Rudder*'s longtime managing editor, Andrew Patterson, "my boss, and one grand old gentleman," as Boris described him. In 1946, *Rudder* paid Francis $1,886; in 1947, $3,327; for 1949, $2,924. When Boris offered to pay Francis for answering so many letters from readers, Francis thanked him, but wrote: "I think Mrs. Bolster and I can stand the strain of answering the various letters without any expense to *The Rudder.* As a matter of fact I am glad to do this for yachting (not the magazine)." Later, Francis was glad to receive an occasional $100 for answering all the letters Boris forwarded to him.[78]

One correspondent wrote to Mr. Herreshoff, "you simply cannot write such utterly stimulating articles as those currently running in *Rudder* and then expect such serious, though amateur, students as myself not to pester you with questions and requests." And pester him they did. A young army officer sent in a whole list of silly questions, like do big boats sail faster than small boats, and Francis gave him a whole list of complete, courteous answers. The amateur builder of a 60-foot yacht designed by Arthur Wycoff asked for advice on what woods to use where and many other things, and Francis answered him as if he himself was the designer. A repeat correspondent sent Mr. Herreshoff $1.00 with the request that he "continue to be my advisor." Francis returned the dollar and sent him to J. Murray Watts, an experienced boat and ship designer in Philadelphia. The seekers of advice, or perhaps merely acquaintance, arrived at Francis's door, as well as in his mailbox. Struggling to meet his monthly writing deadline of August 10, 1945, he wrote to Boris, "the last few days before the tenth I had visitors most every day from morning until ten o'clock at night."[79]

Designing and writing for *The Rudder* left Francis little time for other design work. He was hard up. Boris was sympathetic. In January 1944, he sent Francis $50 and wrote, "if there is any other time that you find yourself requiring some ready cash, please draw on us." Francis did. He used *The Rudder* as a bank and, particularly at tax time, drew interest-free loans in the form of advances against his future earnings, and then would catch up as article payments, royalties on the sale of plans, and, later, book royalties came due.[80]

When volume 1 of *The Common Sense of Yacht Design,* including the first ten chapters, was published in 1946, it contained a perceptive foreword by Clinton H. Crane. "*The Common Sense of Yacht Design,*" Crane wrote, "is written by a man who knows his subject, who realizes that yacht designing is one of the fine arts, and at its best must be practiced by a man who has an eye for form and a love of the sea. Mr. Herreshoff combines these qualities. I know no living designer who has a better eye for form. Mr. Herreshoff is an individualist and has produced a very readable book. There will be plenty who will not agree with all he has said, but he will probably be the last one to expect, or welcome, agreement from all his readers."

When volume 2 came out, it was reviewed by W. H. de Fontaine in the November 1948 issue of *Yachting.* Ham de Fontaine saw the book's value, but took exception to Francis's attitude. He wrote: "Although the author's style is pleasing and sometimes provocative, one can wish that he was less intolerant of the work, opinions and motives of others, also that he took a more modern view of such recent developments as waterproof plywood, which he roundly condemns regardless of the fact that it is in very general use and has given satisfaction for years. In spite of the strong personal prejudices expressed (and with which many readers will disagree), there is a good deal of solid worth in this book." Francis did not think this review was "very bad," coming from *The Rudder*'s competitor.[81]

Each volume was published at $12.00. In 1947, Francis received $385.20 in royalty, 10 percent of the list price on the sale of 321 copies for the previous year. By 1950, the price of each volume had been reduced to $8.50 and you could get both for $15.00. By 1966, the books had been out of print, and Anne Klein at Caravan Maritime Books, in Jamaica, New York, reprinted them together in one volume, priced at $25.00. All these books are available today in the secondhand market, a "very musty smelling" copy of the Caravan edition at $50, for example, and a bright, clean set of the original two volumes published by Rudder, being uncommon, fetching $250.[82]

When the Caravan one-volume reprint edition came out, John Gardner, technical editor of *National Fisherman,* reviewed it in that paper. When Gardner had worked as a boatbuilder at the Graves yard in Marblehead, he had met L. Francis Herreshoff, describing him as "cutting an odd figure about town in those days with his beard and his dogs." Gardner had high praise for *The Common Sense of Yacht Design*: "Anyone purporting to be a yachtsman who has not read Herreshoff must be accounted an illiterate. But worse than that, he has missed out on something that cannot be duplicated elsewhere, an experience that is as rewarding as it is unique. For the book is unique, and nothing approaching the scope and quality of its content is to be found elsewhere in the whole range of yachting literature."[83]

Francis was happy, in June 1946, when he got his six free copies of volume 1, hot off the press. He wrote to Boris: "The books arrived yesterday afternoon and I want to tell you how much pleased I am with their looks. I have read practically the whole book through myself and must say that I like it better than when the stories appeared in the

magazine. Thank you very much for all that you have done." And when volume 2 arrived, in August 1948, he told Boris, "I have been rather fascinated myself in reading it over."[84]

Philip C. Bolger was fourteen years old when "Common Sense" came out in *The Rudder*. He soaked it up. "I've read every line he wrote over and over," he said, "but anything he wrote on boat design I thought was wonderful, and I still reread it." But he added, "I advise people to read *The Common Sense of Yacht Design* with great caution—it's full of things I don't agree with any more." Bolger went off in his own direction as a yacht designer, and his boats were very different from those of the man he admired so much.[85]

Francis received plaudits from men whose opinion he valued. Howard I. Chapelle, the maritime historian, draftsman of plans of many a historic vessel, and designer of yachts based on traditional types, was "very complimentary" about "Common Sense." Llewellyn Howland, who was writing his own charming stories of watery adventures southwest and by west of Cape Cod in *The Rudder*, wrote that he liked the final chapter, "Looks in Relation to Design," best of all. Frederic A. Fenger, "Naval Architect and Engineer" of Cohasset, author of a wonderful account of sailing a canoe through the Caribbean, wrote to Francis: "You might tell Leonardi, from me, that I think your series of articles are the best that have ever been written not only for the benefit of the younger designers who assume that they know it all. Some of the older fuddy-duddies who have been curled over their boards till their minds as well as their bodies are warped into 'S' curves, can learn a bit by reading your stuff." Uffa Fox, the English yacht designer who specialized in planing dinghies, wrote "to thank you for your lovely book and for all the trouble you took in writing it and giving the world so much of your brain and knowledge.

Francis used his sketch of a mermaid and merman displaying a Herreshoff sailing dinghy as the illustration for a "Season's Greetings" card. He was not a fan of the December 25 holiday, for he literally hated to see good small-craft spar material wasted as Christmas trees. (Author's collection)

The book has brought a great deal of pleasure to me and I still read it and it has always taught me something." And from Charles Rasmussen, the Danish yacht designer and builder working after the war in Germany, and Bevil Warington-Smyth, the English marine artist and yacht designer, came "the best letters I have received since I have been getting fan mail," as Francis reported to Boris. "Both these letters were extremely flattering and of course are from people who know what they are talking about." There was even a female fan, to whom Francis replied, "I cannot tell you how pleased I am that you like the writings in *The Rudder*, for most of it, as you can guess, was intended for male consumption." But perhaps the most satisfying letter of all that Francis got about *The Common Sense of Yacht Design* came from a draftsman at the Higgins yard, building PT boats for the navy in New Orleans: "I have had a thirty-three foot ketch on my board at home for a long time. Finally, I was stumped, but as I pored over and pondered your articles I was able to complete the sail plan and lines drawings."[86]

L. Francis Herreshoff wrote and illustrated what is still the most informative book on yacht design, whether its readers like or dislike his style of writing and whether they agree with or disagree with his opinions. *The Common Sense of Yacht Design* is the classic book in the field. The dyslexic Francis is at the head of his writing class.

CHAPTER 20

RE-TIRED

YACHT DESIGNE

L. Francis Herreshoff
Marblehead, Mass.
U.S.A.

EPHONE. No CA

THE CASTLE

"Drawing these curves of endless variation calls for special skills, and it is these curves that to a great extent put naval architecture and yacht design more in the realm of art than cold science."

—L. FRANCIS HERRESHOFF AT HIS DRAWING BOARD IN THE CASTLE, 1946

"The children are so eager to meet 'Mr. Herring.' They are sure you live in a real castle and believe you capable of magic at the very least."

—TASHA TUDOR TO L. FRANCIS HERRESHOFF, 1953

The mid-1940s were a time of transition for L. Francis Herreshoff. In his "Common Sense" article in the November 1944 *Rudder*, Francis wrote, "I have nothing to sell, am partly retired, and do not care a ---- if I never get another order for a yacht." He was fifty-four years old. He had already dropped his calling-card advertisement from *The Rudder*. He wrote: "I only design boats now occasionally for friends and acquaintances. However because several people want to write to me I am going to have a card in *The Rudder* later giving my address for, while I do not care about designing many more boats, I should like to help yachting as much as I can by answering questions which might help the sport." His calling card advertisement reappeared in the January 1945 issue, announcing that he was "RE-**TIRED**." Francis was *not* retired, or even particularly tired; Boris Lauer-Leonardi kept him hard at work designing boats and writing for his magazine, but the notice allowed him to turn away unwanted demands on his time. Francis still had twenty yacht designs ahead of him, half of them for *The Rudder*, including several that would be among his best. He turned away from welcoming design clients and devoted his energies toward trying to return yachting to its genteel roots through *The Rudder*.[1]

But Francis thought that not only yachting and yacht design were in trouble, but also the Republic, with, as he saw it, the country's politics turning populist and its citizens willing to base their culture on shaky morality. He was energized to extend his jeremiads beyond boats. He sent out printed, signed postcards saying:

Let's call it the Republic again.
Let's have law and order again.
Let's have God-fearing judges again.
Let's say the Lord's prayer again.

In "The Common Sense of Yacht Design," he wrote: "The Editor of *The Rudder* has asked me to keep clear of personalities in this writing. Perhaps he fears I may describe some of their internal arrangements as well as their sail plans, and some of the latter are not too hot. Take that Harvard cut of the jib, for instance, which seems planned for no other purpose than backwinding and whose principal results are to retard the natural progress of its owner and to keep the working man voting Democratic." Later, he ranted: "At the present time there isn't one designer in the whole world that's any Goddamned good. No one knows how to draw. No one has any *decency*."[2]

As World War II drew to a close, Francis suffered three great losses. The Herreshoff Manufacturing Company, limping along on relatively small government contracts, shut its doors forever when these ended. His family's great institution, so closely allied with the fame of his father, so vital to his own training for yacht design and construction, so important to his Herreshoff pride, was gone. It must have been difficult for Francis to think of his beloved Bristol with the great building sheds of the Herreshoff Manufacturing Company standing empty and silent. Once, when Francis was reminiscing with a young boatbuilder about the yard's long-gone, abundant stores of top-grade yacht lumber, he got so choked up that he could not continue.[3]

A deep personal loss occurred in 1945, when Charlie Welch died suddenly, at age forty-four. Among his clients, Charlie had been his closest friend. They had spent many hundreds of hours over the years yarning about boats. They had been shipmates. They had shared racing success. They had been neighbors in Marblehead, their doors always open to each other. Without Charlie's commissions in the early years of his yacht design business, Francis would have been hard pressed to survive financially. True, Charlie had turned

Francis started advertising himself as a retired yacht designer in the January 1945 issue of *The Rudder*. Like the news of Mark Twain's early death, the rumor was exaggerated. He would eventually have a telephone, though its number would be unlisted. This ad ran through July 1948, by which time it was more realistic. (Mystic Seaport Museum, 1985-5-47)

to farming on Martha's Vineyard of late, but his unexpected passing left a gap in Francis's life.

And in 1947, Francis would lose his great mentor and friend, Starling Burgess. Starling's chronic ulcers and their concomitant pain-killing drugs caught up with him at age sixty-eight. Francis had had a rough and slow start to his career as a yacht designer, but his road would have been even more difficult without Starling's rescuing him from his father's shadow in Bristol. Francis had blossomed under Starling's tutelage. The two were very different personalities: Francis shy, Starling gregarious; Francis proper, Starling free-thinking; but their mutual respect and friendship overcame their differences. Each man advanced yacht design in a practical, scientific, innovative way, Francis basing his science on his uncanny sense of proportion, Starling emphasizing mathematics. Francis volunteered to Boris to write Starling's obituary for *The Rudder*: "Starling Burgess certainly deserves a place in Valhalla, and his name should be entered in the book of fame in letters nearly as large as those of his illustrious father." (Perhaps it crossed Francis's mind that a similar comment about himself might someday be appropriate? Francis rated Starling's father, Edward Burgess, up with George Steers, designer of thc *America,* and George L. Watson, designer of the *Britannia.*) Francis would miss, above all, those "talks more like poetry than plain conversation" that he had enjoyed with W. Starling Burgess.[4]

To balance these losses came a great gain in Francis's life. Early in the new year of 1946, he was able to move just around the corner, from his house at 25 Front Street into the most perfect residence imaginable for him, a small, stone castle nestled into the ledge that formed Crocker Park on Marblehead Harbor. The romantic eyrie was built in the 1920s by stonemason John D. Regan for Waldo and Joanne Ballard. It was Mrs. Ballard who dreamed of living in a house resembling, insofar as the couple's research could reveal it, Brattahlid, the Greenland stronghold of Eric the Red almost a thousand years before. For their new home, the Ballards used the name "Brattahlid," anglicized Old Norse for "steep slope," or perhaps, "hewn out of rock." Although these terms were accurate for the situation of the Ballard's little castle, later research showed that the building itself bears no resemblance to the sod longhouse where Eric and his colony lived. In any case, Francis, and everyone else in Marblehead, simply called the place "The Castle."[5]

In mid-November 1945, Francis wrote to Boris, "I think the place that I hope to move into will be a great improvement for me." The day after Christmas, he reported "having great difficulty in moving." Two weeks later, he was living in The Castle: "It is cold and damp here and I have been working hard but I think I am going to come through all right. It has been a big undertaking." Yet, the big undertaking was not finished, for the contents of his workshop and drafting room still had to be moved. He was living in his cold, damp castle, but working at 25 Front Street. A functioning drafting space and workshop were Francis's lifeblood; a prompt changeover was vital. After six months of living in one place and working in another, he wrote to Boris, "I am having a very hard time as the movers were one whole month late in moving my things over and I am very much upset." Even after another four months, he complained, "I am working very hard here and haven't by any means got my workshop and drafting room straightened out." Nonetheless, through this difficult year of 1946, Francis wrote and illustrated two articles a month for *The Rudder*, missing only three of his twenty-four deadlines. Helen Bolster's help was vital.[6]

The struggle of moving was worth it. L. Francis Herreshoff, yacht designer, master craftsman, artist, bachelor, collector, had landed in a perfect nest. He would live in The Castle for the rest of his life. Francis had a mystical feeling about living in The Castle. It was as if he was playing out a fantasy, living a rich inner life there, as well as his outer

life. And The Castle embellished his reputation not only in Marblehead, but also among his readers, as a romantic eccentric.[7]

The three-story structure, built on the steep, rocky slope of Crocker Park, had less than 3,000 square feet of living space, for the ledge intruded into most of the ground floor. The lot was only twice the size of the building, but the adjacent Crocker Park gave access to harborside land on the southeast side. The main entrance, in terms of use, was into the ground floor, which consisted of a room where Francis ate and slept, and a small kitchen, shared with the ledge. The kitchen was dark, with one tiny window. This living space, heated in winter by an elaborately fashioned, white-enameled, cylindrical coal stove, was where Francis entertained his close friends. Most of the second floor was taken up by the great hall, 36 feet by 34 feet, with a 12½–foot ceiling. This grand room, decorated like a museum gallery with Francis's collections of antiques, paintings, *objets d'art*, clocks, and books, was where more formal visiting took place; it had a large fireplace. Off it was a spare bedroom and a second room that Francis made into an office for Mrs. Bolster. Between these two rooms was a hallway and the bathroom. An open stairway led from the great hall up to a long, narrow ballroom, the only room on the third story. This magnificent space, 38 feet by 18 feet, also with a fireplace, would be Francis's workshop and drafting room. From there, a short stairway led up to a door that opened onto the turreted roof with its sweeping view of the harbor whose boat population would grow to 2,000 in Francis's time. A separate single-car garage, built of the same stone as the castle, had an upper story with yet another fireplace and storage space above that. Francis called this "the Tower Building." A stonewall bounded the property on the northeast side, separating it from the short, narrow, dead-end Crocker Park Lane. In the wall was an arched gate, and beside the gate Francis installed a bronze sign

LEFT: **Photographer Gilbert E. Friedberg of the *Boston Globe* must have posed this picture on May 9, 1967, because the front door of The Castle, which led directly into the two-story great hall, was hardly ever used. Skipper Herreshoff used a different door, on the ground floor, down the slope to the right, out of the picture. On this day, Francis, with his cap, glasses, and beard, has been living in The Castle for more than twenty years, since 1946. The stone for the building was quarried right on site.** (Gilbert E. Friedberg photo, courtesy Paul Glynn, Mystic Seaport Museum, 1999-8-204) ABOVE: **Photographer John P. Callahan of the *Providence Journal* stood on the high rocks of Crocker Park with his back to Marblehead Harbor when he shot this picture of The Castle. The three windows are in the great hall. The crenellated roof afforded Francis a fine view of the harbor.** (John P. Callahan photo, author's collection)

reading, "L. Francis Herreshoff: Yachts."[8]

Francis's castle was stout and strong. The walls were four feet thick at the base, tapering to two feet at the top. Built into the ledge, it seemed immovable. Yet Francis kept a number of Herreshoff anchors of various sizes around the place, both inside and out. One lady visitor "'inquired why I had the old iron things on the floor.' When I answered, 'Ma'am, if it comes up to blow of a night I gets up and lets one fall out the window. After that I goes back to bed and sleeps as sound as if I had been on deck in a rainstorm.' 'I don't believe a word of it,' she said. So I continued, 'Ma'am, if you doubt my word just take a look out the window where you will see the one I let fall last week in the nor'easter.' And when she looked out the window, sure enough there lay another anchor." Anchored or not, The Castle was snug in a gale. Francis would claim that in Hurricane Carol in 1954, "When the wind was southeast [at its strongest] you would hardly know it was blowing in my downstairs room."[9]

The Castle had a coal-fired heating system that Francis changed to gas in the fall of 1954, but he also used his fireplaces and, particularly, the white enameled stove in the lower room. A visitor to that sanctuary recalled being nearly roasted and asking Skipper why he kept the stove so hot. He replied, "I'm heating the house with it." Francis would sit in his padded rocker beside the stove. In front of his chair, he had a little folding sewing table. A friend would sit on the other side of the table, perhaps in a chair or maybe on a stack of newspapers. A knowledgeable visitor could ask

ABOVE: **Francis about to give Muffin a treat. They are in the room on the ground floor of The Castle where Francis ate and slept, and where he would yarn with one or two friends by the white enameled coal stove.** (John P. Callahan photo, author's collection) RIGHT: **In the same room, Francis, age seventy-six, surveys his inherited collection of Chinese porcelain displayed in a hutch he built. The drawer-pulls, one just visible at the lower right, are his carvings of upside-down, hollowed-out half-models of peapods, the double-ended rowing boats that Maine lobster fishermen once used for hauling their traps. Silver spoons from the family home at Love Rocks stand at attention on high. A Burnside breech-loading carbine hangs on a ceiling beam. Francis was proud of this gun. It came to him from his mother. The weapon was given to her by an unsuccessful suitor before Nathanael: Civil War general Ambrose Everett Burnside, who invented the gun (and gave his name, sideburns, to his distinctive whiskers). The clocks strike every quarter hour. There is just space at the end of the cluttered trestle table, also made by Francis, for him to take his breakfast and supper, meals that he prepared in a tiny, adjoining kitchen. Behind him, against the far wall, is the narrow pallet-bed where he slept.** (Gilbert E. Freidberg photo, courtesy Paul Glynn, Mystic Seaport Museum, 1999-8-217)

to see N. G. Herreshoff's notebook with penciled calculations for a Cup defender. There might be tea laced with a little rum, always from S. S. Pierce. Francis found rum to be "one of the most compact of all foods and one that never spoils. However, I always measure it out most carefully, believing it to be as dangerous as gunpowder if two charges are taken when only one is called for." Or, there might be sherry, port, or Madeira, with Vermont common crackers. This was Francis's "place for conversation and unhurried thought." The lucky ones admitted to this sanctuary never forgot the experience.[10]

Francis's writings and designs in *The Rudder* were bringing him a measure of fame. He informed would-be callers not to show up before 9:00 a.m. or after 9:00 p.m., and to respect his hour-and-a-half meal times at noon and 5:00 p.m. But the

Coe children, Christopher, Peter, and Suzy, whose parents would buy 25 Front Street from Francis, lived close by and had *carte blanche* to knock on The Castle door, walk in with "Hi, Skipper," and stay for a chat, brief if he was busy. When young Llewellyn Howland III would visit The Castle, he'd be greeted with, "Come in and tell us a story." Peter Coe's remembrance of Skipper Herreshoff is: "He didn't wrap his arms around anybody, but he certainly wrapped his warmth around them."[11]

A later young visitor was Lucille Bonner, a twelve-year-old whose family moved to 12 Mariner's Lane, the next dead-end sideroad parallel to Crocker Park Lane to the east, in the early 1950s. She would go to play in Crocker Park, and met Francis walking his poodles. Lucille thought him to be "a nice old man, a sort of grandfather." But this grandfather figure seemed to have come out of one of her storybooks. He had a vivid imagination and could appreciate her own made-up stories. Of a summer day, when she had no school, Lucille would be awakened by a rain of pebbles on her window. That would be her signal to hurry over to The Castle to join Francis in his downstairs room for a breakfast of hot shredded wheat with milk, always finished off with pieces from a huge Hershey's chocolate bar. Francis sent enough of the shredded wheat packaging off to Battle Creek, Michigan, to earn a little Brownie camera that he gave to Lucille to start a lasting hobby. Lucille must have been well-behaved, for after breakfast she was allowed to accompany Francis up to the drafting room for half an hour. As he started work on one drafting table, she would sail imaginary ships across another. He'd say, "Now where are we sailing today?" and Lucille would make up names of fabulous places. He would ask questions about the voyage, and she would tell him what dangers lay ahead and what the islands looked like. Lucille Bonner remembered sadly, "He wrote to me in later years, but I let the friendship go."[12]

The Castle lured some of the Herreshoff family to visit. Clarence arrived in the summer of 1946 from Washington, DC, where he was working on ship design for the navy. Sidney and Becky, with their sons Nathanael III and Halsey, stopped in during the next summer. Soon after

Francis examining May buds outside the door leading into his Spartan living quarters in the ground floor of The Castle.
(Gilbert E. Friedberg photo, courtesy Paul Glynn, Mystic Seaport Museum, 1999-8-210)

their visit, Francis complimented his brother in a letter about a couple of his recent yacht designs, one of which was a fast catamaran, the *Spider,* and he also praised an article Sidney wrote about catamarans for *Yachting.* These two Herreshoff brothers had lowered their defenses somewhat after their father's death. But, still, they seldom communicated directly; Francis got his news of Sidney and his family from his sister, Agnes. Francis had great respect for Sidney's technical ability, but there was no warmth between them. One observer noted that Francis and Sidney were "almost like strangers." Much later, Halsey himself would say that his father and Francis "just quietly respected each other." Griswold, working for Chrysler in Detroit, never visited The Castle. News of him came from Lee Nielsen, who happened to meet Griswold cruising on Lake St. Clair. Francis's friend Lee wrote, "I think your brother is a very fine person and there certainly is a great deal of family resemblance." He reported that Griswold's boat was "a small raised-deck motor-sailer, rather homely but extremely roomy and comfortable." Clarence, working for the US Navy Bureau of Ships in Washington, where he specialized in the design of ventilation and air-conditioning systems, did not often visit Francis at The Castle, but spent his two-week vacations with Agnes in Bristol and went sailing in his "home" waters. Agnes's last visit to Francis in Marblehead was before he moved to the Castle. Francis got on well with his sister and he would call on her perhaps once a year in Bristol. Agnes died in 1965.[13]

A telephone would eventually be installed in The Castle's downstairs room, but initially Francis took messages from Mrs. Bolster's phone at 11 Hooper Street, close by. Like many a newcomer to the device, when Francis used his own phone he would shout into it. He did often play a radio for background company, but there would never be a television in The Castle. Francis knew of Walter Cronkite as a yachtsman, but he didn't realize why everybody else knew of him.[14]

The entrance door to the downstairs room was double, with a few feet of space between the two doors to form an air-lock to keep out the cold. Along the wall to the right of the entry was a long trestle table made by Francis, with a fine, soft, oil finish. This was the dining table, but that function had to be shared with magazines and miscellaneous paperwork. Francis eventually gave this beautiful table to Suzy Coe Fernberger as a wedding present. He replaced it with a cruder one that had originally been his building bench for a double-paddle canoe, rounding the bench's ends to give it an elliptical shape. This rougher table had the great advantage of not needing a cutting board; by the end of Francis's life, it had hundreds of precise, parallel knife marks where Francis had sliced his bread every morning.[15]

The adjacent kitchen was rough-hewn, with a two-burner gas stove and a boat-size sink. Before he got a refrigerator, Francis had a wooden bucket full of cold water to keep his quart of milk cool. This bucket was also where the dogs drank. In terms of eating and sleeping, Francis lived simply, the way he advised cruising sailors to live. This was one of the joys of his bachelorhood.[16]

Once when Francis's nieces, his deceased brother Nathanael Jr.'s daughters Clara and Natalie, came up from Bristol, he invited them to stay for dinner, saying, "you'll have to take what you get—nothing fancy." Knowing there was roast beef at their hotel, they prudently passed up their uncle's fare. They might well have missed shredded wheat with runny liederkranz cheese and strawberries, or scrambled eggs with mushrooms or sardines, and strawberry jam on pilot crackers for dessert.[17]

Over the years, Francis went out for lunch, his main meal, almost every day. He would go to Mrs. Foster's Ferry Lane House, just a little way along Front Street, or maybe to Mattie's Sail Loft, where fishermen drank beer with their lunch. Mrs. Bolster frowned on the latter, because people would see Francis's poodles outside Mattie's and know he was in there, maybe having a beer at noon

Francis stands amid his *objets d'art* in the great hall. He was a collector of beautiful antiques and, as a master craftsman, he was as intrigued by how they were made as he was by their beauty. Through his study of his collections themselves and his deep reading about them in his books and magazines, he became an expert on many artifacts, from English furniture to Chinese porcelain. We see chairs used as easels to display large marine paintings. Tables and other horizontal surfaces, such as the deep ledges formed in the Gothic windows by The Castle's thick walls, are covered with vases, small sculptures, bowls, stacks of framed photographs, and decorative boxes. The table at the lower right may be the one that Francis designed with differently turned pairs of legs, in order that it could be rotated to show whichever shape was desired. In the far southeast corner of the room, at the upper right, is a tall corner cupboard with a huge porcelain bowl, on edge. Beyond Francis, we see the dark shape of the front door, not used, blocked by shelves of further handsome pieces. At the far left, beneath the window, is a shelf of books of marine art and yachting photographs. The big fireplace, with its sitting area, is out of the picture to the left. The tall candles at the center are purely ornamental, never lighted. (Gilbert E. Friedberg photo, courtesy Paul Glynn, Mystic Seaport Museum, 1999-8-215)

(unlikely), spoiling his reputation. Later, Skipper Herreshoff's favorite lunch emporium was "The Chinaman's" or "The Chink's Place," as he variously called China Sails, Dave Wong's restaurant in nearby Swampscott. There was good Chinese art on the walls, and Francis traded Chinese antiques with Wong. Dave Wong may well have been the only non white person Francis knew.[18]

Francis always looked well, whether out in public or in his own castle. When he had worked in the office of Burgess, Swasey, and Paine, the unofficial dress code had mandated wearing a necktie, a practice that Francis continued when he started his own business. He claimed he wasn't interested in clothes, but he habitually dressed carefully, in grey flannel trousers with a herringbone tweed jacket, perhaps with leather patches on the elbows, and usually in a wool shirt instead of a white one, and always with a tie. He made his clothes hold out and never changed his style. Every few years, there would be a big day when he would go in to Boston to buy a new pair of trousers and a new jacket at Brooks Brothers. Mrs. Bolster ordered his socks and underwear.[19]

A stairway led up from Francis's living quarters into the great hall. Here were space, furniture, and trappings worthy of a castle. There was a big secretary, housing, among many books, photographs, and pamphlets, Francis's precious letters from his father, kept separate from his other correspondence in Mrs. Bolster's office. The room's many clocks included an imposing eighteenth-century Dutch tall-case clock, along with a pair of Francis's favorite Chelseas on the high mantle above the huge fireplace. Chairs and a sofa stood in front of the fire, separated from the rest of the room by an elaborately carved, multi-panel Chinese wooden screen, making a comfortable retreat. The light from the fire would glow up through the onyx top of a nearby table and reflect from the silver Chinese tea service that it held. Everything in The Castle, whether decorative or practical, represented Francis's artistic taste and some particular interest.[20]

Of course, Francis's primary interest was nautical. He had a half a dozen old sextants. He once tried to buy antique running lights from Fred L. Woods, Jr. Nautical Supplies, 36 Pleasant Street, Marblehead. Woods said slyly, "the red one is $34 and the green one is $34, so together they come to $68." Francis stalked out, livid. He threw over his shoulder, "they should be sold as a pair! "[21]

But L. Francis Herreshoff had many particular interests, each with its sphere of expert knowledge. He knew a great deal about Asian art. One collector with whom he traded objects from China was "the Irishman," as he always referred to Errol Flynn. Francis often took Gretl Stinnes with him to Boston, hunting antiques. She was with him when he bought "a huge, incredibly beautiful Chinese samovar, all dragons and fangs." He didn't use it for making tea; it sat on a table in the great hall, where he could admire it. When Tasha Tudor, the writer and illustrator of children's stories, who was Starling Burgess's daughter, happened to visit him on his sixty-eighth birthday, she admired the samovar with such fervor that he gave it to her. Francis had a big collection of decanters, some from Venetian glass. He was generous with these as well, often persuading a visitor to pick one out and carry it off. He loved plates with special designs, like paintings of clipper ships. And he had a great fondness for statues of elephants. He collected Chinese silks and Persian shawls.[22]

Francis loved to show off his treasures to those who responded to his passion for them. One of the youngsters attracted to The Castle by its romantic resident and his collections was a neighbor, Dale Vosburgh. She described the experience of entering The Castle as an adventure every time. When Francis would hand her some lovely piece, extol its beauty, and explain exactly how it had been made, her world expanded. One such object, she remembered, was "an intricate Chinese carving of a sea goddess made from an ancient tusk which had a hidden compartment in the bottom that still had a ball of opium in it."[23]

Dale Vosburgh was more than another young neighbor seeking to explore Mr. Herreshoff's magic castle. She was the daughter of Katherine Jones. Kay Jones had become Mrs. Vosburgh and lived with her family in Marblehead. Not only were the Vosburghs Francis's neighbors, but they had bought the ketch *Albacore*, the design for which had been brought to Francis by his draftsman, Sam Brown (see volume 1, pages 222-230). Kay loved the *Albacore*; in her mind, the boat had been designed by Francis. When Dale started telling Skipper Herreshoff *Albacore* stories, he would grunt and quickly change the subject. Any mention of her mother was taboo. Kay did not discourage her daughter's friendship with Francis. She seemed curious about it, but she wanted no details and gave her young daughter no hint of her own history with him. Francis and Kay were asunder, but the fascination of The Castle brought Francis together with Kay's daughter. Inspired by Francis, Dale Vosburgh Calloway found her life's work as an artist and creator of beautiful objects herself.[24]

But another important benefit besides educating the young accrued from L. Francis Herreshoff's collection of art. The elegant forms and images with which he surrounded himself inspired the shapes of the yachts he designed. He lived with the painted, curved sails of a square-rigger, the wings of a bird in a Japanese print, the contour of an ancient Chinese bowl, the etched, asymmetrical form of a Venetian gondola. Through his immense interest and patient study, Francis made himself competent in general art history and an expert in the history of marine art. As he began to draw the curves of the hull of a yacht emerging from his imagination, he had the guidance of a huge, mental catalog of humanity's best visions.

Francis had a large collection of paintings, etchings, drawings, and photographs, with the emphasis on marine art. They hung on every wall of The Castle, and they were stuffed into many a drawer. He wrote: "Now a few words in defense of pictures in general. Boats, automobiles, and liquor all have their thrills, but they either don't last long or they cost a lot to keep up. Well-selected pictures, on the contrary increase in value while constantly giving pleasure. Some of my pictures were acquired for a tenth of their present value so that they are by far the best investment their owner has ever made, and the satisfaction of acquiring them one by one is an almost continuous joy."[25]

His most valuable paintings were the two large portraits of George and Martha Washington that hung over the fireplace in the great hall. Washington had given the pictures to Francis's great-great-grandfather John Brown, the Providence merchant, for his services—profitable services to be sure—during the American Revolution, and they had come to Francis from Nathanael's estate. At one point, Francis tried, unsuccessfully, to sell them for $15,000, but then he changed his mind and held on to them. He would have invested their proceeds in marine art.[26]

Francis was devoted to the work of the yachting artist Frederic S. Cozzens of New York. Among others of his works, he owned a complete set of Cozzens's twenty-five lithographs of American yachts published in about 1918. He hung these over his long workbench up in the ballroom, where he could admire the audacious curve of a big spinnaker as he shaped a wooden bowl. Not long before his death, Francis gave to Anita Jacobsen valuable information about Cozzens for her book on the artist, a book he would have loved had he lived to study it. Francis also particularly admired the work of the nineteenth--century English artist Thomas Goldsworthy Dutton, as demonstrated by a dozen full-page illustrations in the book, *Yachting*. Francis called Dutton "the best marine lithographer of the time, or perhaps all time." And he wrote: "To me at least, the study of past art in yacht design seems the most fascinating part of the whole profession. In the study of old prints, pictures, and models you can train the eye to recognize the beautiful."[27]

Francis loved etchings. By 1953, he estimated that he owned at least "a couple of hundred." He was particularly enthusiastic about the marine etchings of the Dutch artists, partly because the vessels they depicted, even though they were workaday craft, were full of curves, and partly because he believed that Dutch craft made wonderful cruising boats. Although Francis never designed a cruiser based on a schokker, botter, hoogars, boier, or lemmeraak, he collected plans of them, and he adopted the Dutch leeboard for some of his shoal-draft cruisers. He wrote to a detractor of Dutch designs, "I must say that I thought about as you do of the Dutch boats until I had seen some of them sailing to windward in the rough waters of the Solent but now am of the opinion that they are about the best boats in the world for cruising."[28]

Uffa Fox, in one of his books, introduced Francis to the marine etchings of Edward William Cooke, another nineteenth-century English artist, and Francis began collecting everything he could by Cooke. He bought multiple copies of two editions of Cooke's *Shipping and Craft*, one with fifty and the other with sixty-five plates, and was able to acquire a dozen of his original pencil sketches. He liked Cooke's ability to depict the hulls of vessels with none of the distortions often seen, and he respected Cooke's knowledge of rigging, without relinquishing the privilege of seeking out a fouled topping lift with his magnifying glass. For Francis studied his marine pictures from the viewpoint of a practical sailor as well as from the viewpoint of an artist. The chief value he placed on his prize, three-view painting of the *America* by Fitz Henry Lane was that it showed clearly the superior sails that he thought were the main reason why she had won her famous cup.[29]

Photographs formed an important part of Francis's collections in The Castle. He treasured many prints of yachting photos by Morris Rosenfeld. Francis had great respect for Rosenfeld, not only as a recorder of yachting, but also as a fearless boat handler. "We were always afraid we would run him down," Francis remembered. Once, showing Rosenfeld photos to his young friend Arthur Brendze, who is Jewish, he said, "these are not bad for a little Jew boy with a box camera." Brendze describes what happened next:

> *Hurt by his own rudeness, he asked me to follow him, and he came to rest looking up at his two life-size portraits of George and Martha Washington. "Do you know why I have these, Brendze? They were given to my great-great-grandfather, John Brown, as a thank you gift for his help to Washington during the siege of Boston. The Americans desperately lacked powder and ball. John Brown had a foundry and was able to make the necessary cannon balls for Washington. He also had connections with the Jews of Newport. He arranged for the Jews, who had close merchant connections with the West Indies, to smuggle in the gunpowder so desperately needed by Washington's colonial troops. These portraits were Washington's way of thanking my great-great-grandfather for the valuable part he played in kicking the British out of Boston. I'm sorry that I was just so thoughtless. I meant no offense. It's just a turn of speech. But I'm telling you this story so that you never let anyone tell you that the Jews have no place here."*[30]

The fact that Brendze was a Jew had no effect on Francis's friendship for the young man, but L. Francis Herreshoff, like many in his generation, was a bigot and, occasionally, it showed.

As well as Rosenfeld images, Francis collected yachting photos by the great English firm Beken of Cowes. And he gathered in all he could from the lens of the local marine photographer, Willard B. Jackson, who shot working craft as well as yachts. Nineteen years older than Francis, Jackson worked out of Marblehead Harbor in his launch, the *Alison,* until 1937, and Francis was pleased to find Jackson images of a good many of his own designs. He was also glad to acquire Jackson's shots of Gloucester fishing schooners. As we have seen, Francis scorned basing yacht designs on fishermen and disparaged the construction and maintenance of the Gloucester vessels (see volume 1, pages 75, 76). But he still thought them beautiful, and he collected pictures of them all his life.[31]

In times of financial depression, the Gloucester fishermen had gone to "sloop boats," being smaller and cheaper than their schooners. Though the simple sloops were less grand than their big sisters, their hulls and rigs were still handsome. Howard Chapelle had published the lines of the sloop boat *Vesta* in his book, *American Sailing Craft,* and Francis was happy to get a Jackson photo of her to compare with the drawing in his copy of Chapelle's book, an example of his "almost continuous joy" as a collector.[32]

Eric Hofman of Mallorca visited Francis at The Castle looking for photographs of three steam yachts for his book, *The Steam Yachts: An Era of Elegance*. Francis was able to loan him those three, and twenty-one more. Many of these were photographic prints; others he sliced out of giant tomes like *British Yachts and Yachtsmen,* with its 600 halftone plates, or Henry Peabody's *Representative American Yachts,* or Nathaniel Stebbins's *Yacht Portraits* and *American and English Yachts*, or Henry A. Mott's *Yachts and Yachtsmen of America*. Francis had them all.[33]

Francis's copy of *British Yachts and Yachtsmen* was *The Rudder*'s office copy, loaned (permanently) to him by Boris Lauer-Leonardi. The two-volume book's subtitle was *A Complete History of British Yachting from the Middle of the Sixteenth Century to the Present Day.* It was issued in 1907 by the publisher of the magazine, *The Yachtsman*, bound copies of which Francis's father had received for years, copies that now resided in The Castle and were augmented by Francis's own subscription. In his thank-you letter to Boris, Francis wrote: "Every single page interests me. There are a great many photographs of boats that my father has designed, and a great many dates and stories of incidents that I have wanted to know about. There will be much material in this book that I can use in my writing." Not every book that Boris sent Francis received such approbation. *Naval Architecture of Planing Hulls*, by Lindsay Lord, published in New York by Cornell Maritime Press in 1946, went back to Boris with: "I have gone all through it and do not want it at all."[34]

But Francis's library was strong on the technical side of naval architecture, and he studied, slowly and carefully, his engineering books and journals. In 1936, Nathanael had given him for Christmas *The Speed and Power of Ships: A Manual of Marine Propulsion*, by Rear Admiral David W. Taylor, US Navy, a then-recent book that Francis found "of much value," as he reported to his father. Twenty years later, he was plowing through a huge text on diesel engines. Nathanael had been a member of the Society of Naval Architects and Marine Engineers all his adult life, so Francis had all the SNAME journals up to 1938. A magazine called *Light Steam Power*, published on the Isle of Man, reprinted a piece on steam launches that Francis wrote, and, when Boris sent him a copy of that issue, he liked it so much that he took out a subscription. He also took an English magazine called *The Model Engineer* because it had articles about fine lathe work. And, because of the variety of sports cars that rolled into his garage, he subscribed to *Road and Track.*[35]

The Contributing Editor of *The Rudder* had, of course, "most of the copies from 1893 onwards." Many of these were bound volumes, kept in the second story of Francis's stone garage. *Yachting* magazine was notably missing from The Castle. Francis kept up with commercial fishing news by reading the *Maine Coast Fisherman* and the *Atlantic Fisherman,* and, later, when they merged, the *National Fisherman.* Francis loved ship models, and so he read the journal of the Nautical Research

Guild. And he wanted to stay abreast of naval affairs, so he had joined the US Naval Institute in 1927 and read its monthly *Proceedings.* "During the hard times" of the Depression, he had let his membership lapse, but in 1947, Dr. Harrison J. Hunt of Bangor, Maine, whom Francis advised about the design of a cruising whaleboat, renewed it for him.[36]

Francis had been a longtime subscriber to the German yachting magazine, *Die Yacht.* And Rudder Publishing Company took several foreign yachting magazines, which Boris passed along to Francis, so that he could follow developments in France, Holland, Italy, Brazil, Australia, and New Zealand.[37]

Whenever Francis wanted the particulars on a given yacht, he could turn to his collection of *Lloyd's Register of Yachts.* His older volumes, from 1880 to 1938, came from his father's library. Seeking a run from 1938 through 1955, he queried his primary book dealer at the time, Carola Paine, in New York. She relayed his request to Marguerite Crichton at *Yachting* magazine, which was selling books at the time. Crichton wrote to Francis: "As booksellers, we don't approve of the offer we are about to make, but our boss, William H. Taylor [*Yachting*'s longtime editor], says that if you will pay the freight there will be no further charges." The day he got that letter, Francis snapped up the free *Lloyd's,* even though they did come from *Yachting.*[38]

Francis bought so many books from the Charles E. Lauriat Company, in Boston, that he had an account and paid his bill monthly, rather than book-by-book. He was also given many books, signed by their authors, including Uffa Fox, Bevil Warington-Smyth, William Avery Baker, Howard I. Chapelle, Frederick A. Fenger, and Norman Skene. When *MoToR BoaTing* magazine brought out William P. Stephens's long series of articles, "Traditions and Memories of American Yachting," in book form, Rolf Armstrong got a copy, had the author sign it, and inscribed it to "L. Francis Herreshoff, with best regards," dated September 1, 1942. Under that inscription, Francis wrote in his best draftsman's lettering, "Presented to Frank C. Paine, March, 1951, L. Francis Herreshoff."[39]

John Ives Sewall, a sailor who taught art history at Buffalo State University, sent Francis a copy of his book, *A History of Western Art.* Francis wrote him, "I read the book a little at a time so that my memory would be less confused and now feel that I have learned as much about the history of art as if I had taken a six months' course in that subject." In thanking Mr. Herreshoff for his praise, Sewall replied, "your comments come from a man whom I can respect as an artist of the first rank."[40]

The books in The Castle were vital to L. Francis Herreshoff. His dyslexia made reading difficult, but he overcame the trouble by an enormous concentration born of an intense desire to learn. His nephew, Nathanael Greene Herreshoff III, said, "he knew stuff no one else in the family knew." He read slowly, but he had plenty of time. "I had been in the habit of spending my evenings reading," he wrote. A friend said, "he recalled every word he read." And he could read aloud well, following the words with his finger.[41]

Off the great hall in The Castle was the office, presided over by Mrs. Helen Bolster. Without her, L. Francis Herreshoff would have been lost. As his secretary, Mrs. Bolster knew every detail of his business, his relationships with friends and family, and his finances. The two knew each other very well; they liked each other; they kept their relations formal. He called her "Mrs. B" or simply "Mrs." She called him "Skipper." When guests, other than close friends, arrived, she acted as his hostess. She was good at getting rid of those who exhausted his patience (sometimes quickly). She would usher them out politely, while he escaped upstairs to his workshop.[42]

The open stairway in a corner of the great hall led up to the ballroom, spacious and well lighted by windows on all four sides. Here was Francis's long drafting table along the northwest wall, a

large workbench that he made from a bowling alley lane supporting one of his lathes in the center, and, along the southeast wall, more lathes, a grinder, and the fireplace. And stored here were his many, many tools. Although, when he moved into The Castle in 1946, and for the next fifteen years, Francis would be drawing boat designs for *The Rudder* as well as for the occasional client who beat a path to his drawbridge, he would spend more time at his lathes than at his drafting board. He usually referred to The Castle's third-floor ballroom as the "workshop," rather than as "the drafting room."[43]

Near the entrance to the workshop was a case in which Francis hung the large drawings representing his life's work. He had made up a four-page list of all his designs, organized by design number and giving the type of yacht, name of yacht, name of owner, and the location in his vertical file by pocket and folder numbers. For a visitor, he would lift out the desired plans of a yacht design and spread them out on his extra-long drawing board for examination. Fascinating as this would be, a first-time visitor might have a hard time concentrating on the drawings, because there was so much else in the former ballroom to look at. Hanging overhead as a sculpture, there might be an 18-foot, double-paddle canoe, or even the famous white dugout canoe. There was the fireplace, all the lathes, an elaborate chandelier, the long workbench, the many drawers holding who knew what exotic tools, and plenty of half models, including a large one of the *Whirlwind* that Nathanael had made for his son.[44]

In cold weather, Francis heated the workshop with a coal fire. For a few years, he had a soapstone stove hooked up to the fireplace for burning wood scraps, until he gave it away to his friend Bror Tamm.[45]

Goddard, a fictional, yet autobiographical, character in Francis's book, *The Compleat Cruiser*, says, "I am quite sure that lathe has given me more enjoyment than anything I ever had including my various boats and canoes." In the book, "that lathe" was a Hjorth, just like Francis's. And he wrote: "It always seems to me to be one of the greatest satisfactions to see some beautiful object emerge from

The open stairway leading from the great hall up to the ballroom, which Francis used as drafting room and workshop. Evidence of missing plaster shows at the top of the picture. The Castle was leaky. Francis thought the walls should have had a slight outward pitch so that water seeping through would run back out. Without that feature, it seemed a hopeless task to keep plaster on, so he gave up on it. (John P. Callahan photo, author's collection)

one's own hands." When working at a lathe, Francis would lose himself, not only in the artistry of what he was fashioning, but also in the adventure of the tool cutting smoothly and precisely into the metal or wood. It was a process that he loved to experience time after time after time. Each time, it was a little different. He had written to his father while he was designing the America's Cup boat *Whirlwind* about something of equal, or perhaps even greater, importance to him: "I have gotten into the habit of judging metals somewhat by turning them in the lathe. If they machine the same all over and the shavings have the same characteristics, I consider the metal reliable." He was speaking of bronze, and he rated Tobin bronze, phosphor bronze, and Everdur good, but manganese bronze poor, perhaps, he thought, because of the iron in it for strength.[46]

Four of Francis's precision bench lathes were made by the Hjorth Lathe and Tool Company, of Woburn, Massachusetts. Francis loved these machines and had great respect for Henrick J. Hjorth. He wrote, "I have always considered Mr. Hjorth a great man and never thought that all his many inventions were entirely appreciated." Francis appreciated them, all right; in a mahogany cabinet, he had many of Hjorth's patented lathe attachments, and even the gift of a unique tool-holder whose parts were specially made at the Hjorth Company for him to assemble. Francis reported that the new holder "works very well indeed and I appreciate anything with parts made so accurately." In a corner of the workshop, Francis had a small watchmakers' lathe that had belonged to his father, made by the Rivett Lathe and Grinder Company in Boston. Sidney had inherited this lathe but had agreed to pass it along to Francis. As a Yankee, Francis was proud that his lathes were made in Massachusetts. Above the Rivett lathe, Francis hung a large photograph of the big Corliss steam engine, made in Providence, that his father had set up and run at the Centennial Exposition of 1876 in Philadelphia (see volume 1, pages 18, 19).[47]

Francis's knowledge and skill as a master mechanic may be seen in his page of "Notes on making Reversible Dynamometer Blades," technical writing of the first order on exactly how to carry out the steps required to make a part for a machine to measure the power output of an engine. At the time, as we shall see, Francis and Frank Paine were attempting to design an improved type of internal combustion engine. When Francis decided he wanted a nice, big, eight-day clock, he made one from scratch. He designed and made candlesticks with the large, horizontal drip plate mounted on hidden hinges, so that the candle could be hung on a wall with the plate, now turned to vertical, forming a heat shield. He turned beautiful, standard candlesticks on his lathes. And, as we shall see, Francis designed and made brass saluting cannons for yachts and yacht clubs. He made a two-inch working model of a cannon and gave it to Peter Coe as a toy.[48]

In the drawers of tools in Francis's workshop were many curved-blade gouges; he seldom used a square-blade chisel. In a drawer of planes, Francis kept his adjustable-throat, infill, smoothing plane, with rosewood handle, made by Norris in London. Francis modified the handle to fit his hand. This was a high-grade, valuable tool. Thomas Norris and Son started making planes in 1860. They went out of business in about 1950, and, today, Francis's plane would be worth upwards of $1,000. Woodworkers might agree that a good place to buy a comparable, newlymade plane as good as the Norris, is Lie-Nielsen's Toolworks in Warren, Maine. Tom Lie-Nielsen, Francis's friend Lee's son, went to Francis as a young man, saying he was very interested in woodworking tools and asking about suitable education for his career. As usual, Skipper Herreshoff, drawing on his own experience, said forget about formal training; just go to work doing what you want to do. Tom Lie-Nielsen followed that advice, started his tool-making company in 1981, and has never looked back. His mentor would be proud of him.[49]

When Francis sharpened a tool, he not only exhibited extraordinary control in his hands and knew the different types of edges required, but also he understood the characteristics of the different metals in each cutting tool and in the work. He pointed out that furniture makers did fine work before the invention of sandpaper. He used only planes, and claimed he could tell when sandpaper had been used by feeling the wood of a finished piece. His autobiographical character, Goddard, said, "A sandpapered surface or even a scraped surface is very inferior to that left by a very sharp plane."[50]

Francis had made handsome wooden dishes for his aged father, and reaped praise: "Since inspecting thoroughly your present [a wooden bowl], I have wondered how you held it in the lathe to do so nice a job—and it took fine mechanical skill as well as a firm lathe!" He made wooden cereal bowls for the Coe children with their initials carved in. If Anne Lawrence asked him how he made something, he would go up to the workshop, turn on a lathe and make it for her. Starling and Nannie Burgess had been the recipients of his handiwork. "You certainly are a master worker with wood," Nannie had written. "My but the salad fork and spoon are lovely pieces of workmanship." And, of course, Francis made Boris Lauer-Leonardi a cedar bucket, complete with his carved initials. When Francis heard that *Rudder* contributor Captain Charlton Smith was making Boris a sea chest for

$25, he offered to take over the job with "I believe a good sea chest needs some artistic feeling." Smith was deposed, and—more than seven years later—Boris got his "very handsome" chest as a gift.[51]

Francis stored most of his lumber in the second story of the garage, but he kept small, select pieces of wood in a corner of his workshop. When he wanted to make a picture frame, he could choose a fine stick of apple, pear, teak, cherry, locust, or mahogany. And Francis went to this treasure trove of wood when he made doll's furniture. Rosamund

LEFT: **Francis practicing his primary art form—even above yacht designing—at one of the five lathes in his ballroom workshop. He believed in spending time and money to have the best tools possible; here he could be taking hours to make a special tool that would enable him to do a tricky job tomorrow in two minutes. He had so many lathes in order to accomplish different tasks without having to change settings. Those who were privileged to watch L. Francis Herreshoff work with his hands describe the experience as entrancing, because his every delicate motion was so full of grace. But the observer was wise to stay alert for Skipper's rapid puffing on his pipe, the signal that the visitor was annoying him.** (Gilbert E. Friedberg photo, courtesy Paul Glynn, Mystic Seaport Museum, 1999-8-221) ABOVE: **This is a wobble-proof stool that Francis designed and made for his neighbor, Suzy Coe. Tightening the turnbuckle pulls all four legs in snug against the rungs.** (Author photo)

Tudor, Starling Burgess's second wife, had made a doll's house for their daughter, Starling, called Tasha, and Francis had made furniture for it. Years later, Tasha Tudor created stories around her dolls. She gained fame as an author and illustrator of children's books. Her one-fifth-size dolls and a new Victorian house for them became famous. When the grownup Tasha Tudor wrote to Francis to ask him to make furniture for her story-book dolls, she addressed him with the childhood name she had used, "Dear Mr. 'Herring,'" and signed her letters, "Love from Tasha." She wrote: "The children are so eager to meet 'Mr. Herring.' They are sure you live in a real castle and believe you capable of magic at the very least." Francis made a chiffonier; a dresser; a four-poster bed; a grandfather's clock; and a corner cupboard complete with dishes, including "very fine" pewter plates. He charged $45 for the dresser, $10 for the bed, and $4 each for the pewter plates.[52]

Most visitors to L. Francis Herreshoff's workshop were primarily interested in what happened on his 27-foot drawing board. Yet a lot happened in his designing of yachts before he sat down at the board. It is safe to say that he had a prodigious imagination for the vicarious voyage. Although he was not the lifelong habitual sailor that his father was, he had been afloat in many kinds of boats. He could visualize the behavior of a boat whose shape was taking form in his head in actual sea conditions that he had experienced, from calm to rough. He could realize that the emerging hull shape needed a little more ballast, or that the stern had a little too much buoyancy. And he would sit in front of the fire of an evening with a little pad in his lap sketching some detail of a coming design. By

ABOVE: **The famous 27-foot drawing board in the ballroom. Francis made his board this long so that it could hold several large plans of a yacht design as he worked on them simultaneously. In this view, his drafting equipment sits idle; Francis has reached his seventies, and the combination of shaky hands and poor eyesight, caused by glaucoma, has halted his drawing. He could work through these ailments in the workshop part of the wonderful space, however, for the weight of his tools steadied his hands, and he used fingertips rather than keen eyesight to make sure his joints were perfect.** (Courtesy Anne Bondy, Mystic Seaport Museum, 1999-4-226) RIGHT: **Francis enjoyed his view of Marblehead Harbor from the roof of The Castle. With binoculars or a telescope, he could keep track of visiting yachts and check on the appearance of vessels of his own and his father's designs. At the lower right is the curved mast of one of Nathanael's S-boats. At the far left stands the lighthouse on the end of Marblehead Neck. In this prewar view, all the boats are wooden, as are their masts. After the war, Francis would lament the change to fiberglass ("frozen snot") for hulls and to aluminum for masts (he hated the rhythmic ping of slack halyards in a breeze). Even so, he wrote to a friend in July 1966, "at the present time Race Week is here and the whole harbor is filled up with small boats so the view from the roof is very interesting."** (© Mystic Seaport Museum, 1990.37.145)

the time Francis laid out drawing paper and took up a very sharp, hard pencil, not only was the shape of the new design's hull firmly within his grasp, but also many details of construction, rig, engine arrangement, and steering had been worked out.[53]

Now Francis was ready to make, in pencil, careful, neat, mechanical drawings of lines (see caption for lines of the *Nor'easter V*, volume 1, page 240), outboard profile and sail plan, construction plan, cabin plan, and, usually, separate sheets of details that the builder would need clarified. He followed the customary practice of placing the bow always to the right, to be "less confusing to the workman in the shop." Next would come the calculation of displacement (see volume 1, page 192). Then Francis would ink the drawings on big sheets of linen. And finally, he would drive into Boston with the finished product to have blueprints made for the builder by the B. L. Makepeace Company at 387 Washington Street. "A well laid out drawing is a handsome thing," Francis wrote, "and when it combines useful information, neat draftsmanship and good lettering it really represents painstaking work—work that can only be done by one who has the patience of Job and the skill of an engraver." As an artist, Francis developed a distinctive form of lettering for his drawings. He turned away from his earlier open lettering and settled on solid caps and small caps, some with nicely curved tails. His lettering was certainly inspired by that of Fred Goeller, the designer who had worked for Francis during the Depression as a draftsman and who had inked some of the drawings for the *Ticonderoga*.[54]

Francis wrote, "as mechanical drawing is one of the most exact of all arts, its instruments must possess a high degree of perfection." His erasers didn't see much use, but he had good ones: 2⅞-inch Ruby Reds or Emerald Greens. In "The Common Sense of Yacht Design," he listed the ten drawing instruments that he thought were the "most convenient for yacht designing." All were made by Alteneder. Five were compasses; there were no dividers. Francis wrote, "I do not use a divider much, preferring to use the pencil compass in its place, for in transferring dimensions the pencil will mark a line rather than a dot." When he needed to get into mathematics, Francis worked with an adjustable, 20-inch slide rule made by Keuffel and Esser of New York, but he turned to it less and less as he developed his sense of proportion. A planimeter came in handy for measuring the areas of sections, when figuring

Francis on the roof of his castle. (© Mystic Seaport Museum, 1990.37.605)

displacement. He devised graduated disks of different scales, on handles, so that they could be rolled along a curved line of a drawing to measure its length. Francis recommended leaving drawing instruments out on the drawing board "night and day ready for use." What were stowed away were his antique drawing instruments. As a mark of his early ambition to be a yacht designer, he could write, "I have been collecting them ever since I was a kid." For drawing the fair curves of a hull, Francis preferred flexible, rather than stiff, battens. He made them himself of soft pine. "Drawing these curves of endless variation calls for special skills not required in dry architecture or machine drafting," he wrote, "and it is these curves that to a great extent put naval architecture and yacht design more in the realm of art than cold science, or at least allowed it to be called a combination of art and science."[55]

Whether seated at his long drawing board in the ballroom workshop of his castle, or at one of his earlier drawing boards, L. Francis Herreshoff labored with skill and patience to produce plans for some of the most original, beautiful, and high-performing yachts in the world. His drafting table was "the sole silent witness of his real life."[56]

The stairs leading from the workshop up to the roof were made from a wooden ladder decorated with carved eagles that Francis had acquired from the USS *Constitution* in 1928, when much of her gear was sold as souvenirs to raise money for a major overhaul. A visitor climbing the short steps could notice, after taking in the harbor view, a hefty, somewhat battered block of wood, set up against a corner of the crenellated wall. The battering was done by bullets, for this was Francis's shooting range, where he could try out a new gun he had added to his collection, or a gun he had made himself. He wrote to one visitor: "I am glad you enjoyed looking at some of the smaller guns I have made. The small ones are not for sale. I only make them for my own enjoyment." The occasional sounds of gunfire emanating from the roof of The Castle further enhanced Francis's reputation as an odd character. Boatbuilder and designer Edmund A. Cutts recalled helping Skipper Herreshoff in the workshop: "One night we were making a pistol and the slide would stick. All night long we blued and lapped the slide mechanism until we got it working nicely. He had small wash basins around the place and he constantly made me wash my hands so the salt was off and the steel was safe from rust. He was not strong enough to keep cocking the brute spring in that thing so I got the job."[57]

Nathanael had offered Francis a pair of antique revolvers that had been in the de Wolf family. Their grateful recipient wrote, "they will be something nice for me to work on evenings and overhaul, etc." Francis preferred the challenge of steadying a pistol more than that of a rifle (see photograph in volume 1, page 59), yet he owned, as part of his gun collection, several heavy old German muzzle-loading rifles, specially designed for the *Schuetzen* competition, firing single shots from a standing position at a target 200 yards away. And Francis wrote: "I must say that the most useful gun I ever had was a Charles Daly [importer of European guns] three barrel gun on which the two upper barrels were 12 gauge [shotgun] and the lower barrel was a 30.30 [rifle], and which also could use a supplemental chamber which took 32 caliber revolver cartridges." L. Francis Herreshoff had expert knowledge of guns, and, as a young man, he had earned medals that showed he was a good shot.[58]

When Francis moved into The Castle, he had no automobile to park in his stone garage. He had sold his 1936 Buick Limited touring car when the war brought on gas rationing. Three years after the war was over, he would start driving a series of nine autos, all but one of them sports cars, and none of them made in the USA. He once told a friend, "American cars are just like riding in a wheelbarrow." Francis was particularly scornful of the Ford and all that it stood for. He had once written to his father: "Besides disliking the Ford automobile and everything that has to do with the Ford organization, I think they are very difficult cars to drive slowly and quietly, also comfortably, and the class of people generally found in Fords are bootleggers and racketeers, etc. and always make a nuisance of themselves on the road." Well, Francis would make a nuisance of himself on the road, too, as he held up traffic, tooling along in his high-performance sports cars, proudly showing off how slowly and quietly they could go in a high gear.[59]

Francis didn't keep his cars long. He was fascinated with the machines and wanted to try out each different make that interested him. There would be a red MG TC, the classic little British roadster, followed, in 1954, by a more modern-looking British roadster from the new Austin-Healey combination, probably a 100 BN1. Interspersed between these small beauties was a Mercedes-Benz diesel sedan, perhaps a 1953 180 D. Because it was good for the engine, Francis would run the diesel in his driveway all day. He believed that the metal used by Mercedes was the best in any car.[60]

In 1955, Francis splurged on a Jaguar XK140 roadster. It was powder blue. A 190-horsepower motor (at 5,500 rpm) gave the car a top speed of 120 mph and acceleration of 0-60 in nine seconds, highway performances that Francis actually explored on rare occasions. Perhaps the Jag's best feature was more road clearance than most sports cars had, which was advantageous for Marblehead's winter streets.[61]

In 1956, Francis traded the Jaguar for a Mercedes 300 SL, the famous gull-wing coupe. Some dubbed the car the "Silver Arrow," which was the press name for Mercedes-Benz racers in the thirties, for this was the world's fastest production car. It could hit 160 mph, but not in Francis's hands. One time, Marbleheader Rodney Bowden was driving Francis north on the Maine Turnpike at high speed. They were pulled over by an enlightened state trooper, who offered to race them to the next bridge overpass in his Ford. Skipper Herreshoff said, "I think you should show him German cars are better than all the American cars put together." The Mercedes beat the Ford to the bridge. Francis wrote, "on the whole, I like the 300 SL very much indeed, and of course I use it mostly for a plaything and enjoy polishing it up and cleaning all the engine parts, and it certainly is a very interesting toy." A neighbor recalled: "He took great pride in the car and was forever cleaning it and tinkering with things that he thought weren't quite right. One time as we chatted, he put a rag onto the end of a stick and spent several minutes removing some dirt (which I didn't see) from a portion of the cast aluminum overhead valve cover. Eventually he took me for a ride around the back roads of Marblehead. He was interested in the fact that the fuel injection (this was one of the first cars to come so equipped) allowed for smooth acceleration from a slow speed. We spent most of the time in high gear (4th, as I remember) slowing down to about 15 mph and then smoothly accelerating to about 50. He repeated the demonstration four or five times." In 1958, Francis traded the gull-wing Mercedes to Billy Strawbridge for the *Piquant,* a long, narrow launch that Francis had designed for him.[62]

Francis then continued his courtship of top sports cars with a DB series Aston Martin. James Bond seemed to like the DB5 he drove in *Goldfinger*, but Francis was less than satisfied for some reason. In 1960, he tried a black Lancia Flaminia Gran Turismo with an aluminum body, a Super Legato

RIGHT: **Francis's finest car, his 1964 silver Ferrari 250 GT/E. He liked to make the short drive out to Marblehead Neck, where he could sit and contemplate Massachusetts Bay.** (Courtesy Paul Glynn, Mystic Seaport Museum, 1999-8-205) BOTTOM RIGHT: **Francis at the wheel of the Ferrari.** (Gilbert E. Friedberg photo, courtesy Paul Glynn, Mystic Seaport Museum, 1999-8-206)

made by Tourin of Milano. He was probably drawn by Lancia's reputation for mechanical innovation (his car was first with the transaxle, which moved the gearbox to the middle of the main drive shaft). Nor was the Lancia entirely satisfactory. Francis wrote, "I think it is a very fine design car, but I have had quite a lot of difficulty with minor things on it, and I do not think I would advise many people in this country to get one unless they live near where there is an expert who could work on it."[63]

Francis was lucky enough to have found such an expert mechanic, Paul Glynn, in nearby Georgetown. Glynn became Skipper Herreshoff's friend, as well as his mechanic, for Glynn was fascinated not only by Francis's knowledge of cars, but also by the multiple skills he exhibited in his workshop.[64]

The first of Francis's cars that Glynn worked on was his 1964 silver Ferrari 250 GT/E. This automobile was worth $12,900 when he bought it in the fall of 1963, trading in the Lancia for $3,000. The Ferrari was the only car that Francis bought new. This was the first production Ferrari with a rear seat, cramped to be sure. Pininfarina made a thousand of them. And Francis was driving another movie car: Peter Sellers was at the wheel of a Ferrari 250 GT/E in *The Wrong Arm of the Law.*[65]

Perhaps encouraged by having Paul Glynn in his corner, Francis bought another Lancia. At the end of 1968, he purchased, for $3,500, a red 1967 Flavia, a coupe also designed by Pininfarina. This was billed as an "Executive Car" by Lancia, but it was really another sports car. He now had a Lancia for rides in the country or trips to Mattapoisett or Maine, and the Ferrari for a jaunt to the causeway to Marblehead Neck and a look at the ocean. Francis's neighbor Bette Hunt remembered the red Lancia Flavia: "On the wonderful clear days of early autumn, when the air is so very still, I could hear him coming minutes before he sedately passed my kitchen window—doing maybe 15 miles per hour—that lovely car backfiring every foot of the way due to carbon build-up!"[66]

L. Francis Herreshoff lived in his castle for his last twenty-seven years. It was the perfect place for his simple, quiet lifestyle, for his great collections of art and books, for his entertainment of either close friends or inquiring sailors, for his designing of yachts, and for his manufacture of hundreds of beautiful objects to give to his friends. The Castle's roof even gave him a place to fire his guns. He didn't shoot at fiberglass boats; against them, he merely launched tirades.

CHAPTER 21

OCEAN CRUISING

"An awfully good boat that never took ahold right."

—L. FRANCIS HERRESHOFF ON THE MARCO POLO, 1966

L. Francis Herreshoff had no desire to put to sea in a yacht himself, but he was intrigued by the challenge of designing a good boat for ocean cruising. As we shall soon see, a couple of the first designs he drew, just as studies, were ocean cruisers. While he never wanted to emulate Joshua Slocum or Harry Pigeon, he had a certain admiration for their feats. He was ready to try to make better boats for those who did want to follow such intrepid voyagers. And designing an ocean cruiser was delightfully free of the measurement rules of ocean racers. Although Francis never sailed a yacht on a sea voyage, he had seen rough seas from a naval patrol boat in open, coastal waters in winter. Moreover, he was a great sea dreamer; he had imagined boats of every description offshore in a gale.

William Albert Robinson was one such intrepid voyager. He gained national prominence in November 1931 when he completed a voyage around the world in the 32-foot Alden ketch *Svaap*, then the smallest boat to have circumnavigated. He was honored with a hero's welcome in New York City, resulting in an invitation from Cornelius Crane, the plumbing baron, to visit his estate, Castle Hill, in Ipswich, Massachusetts. Robinson thus met and married the young, beautiful heiress, Florence Crane. Together they sailed the *Svaap* to the Pacific in 1933 and 1934, but the honeymoon voyage ended abruptly at the Galapagos Islands when Robinson had to be evacuated for an emergency appendectomy. The *Svaap* was confiscated by the Ecuadorean government and later was wrecked. The couple continued by steamer to Tahiti, where they established a home.[1]

In 1937, they returned to Ipswich, and Robinson started a shipyard under his own name on Crane riverfront land. He wanted to build handsome and able cruising vessels of traditional type. He went to Howard I. Chapelle for designs based on a fast brigantine of 1778, a Virginia pilot boat, and a Baltimore clipper. By 1940, he had launched the 70-foot topsail schooner *Swift*, the 52-foot ketch *Santa Cruz*, and the 95-foot Baltimore clipper *Carribee*.

As absorbed as he was with his shipyard, Robinson longed to return to the South Seas. As he and Florence realized that that was his first priority, their marriage came apart. He spent a lot of time visualizing and sketching the ideal vessel in which he could make his dream come true. He called on his long experience with the *Svaap*. He tutored himself in square rig by sailing a brigantine home from India. He sought lighter, stronger

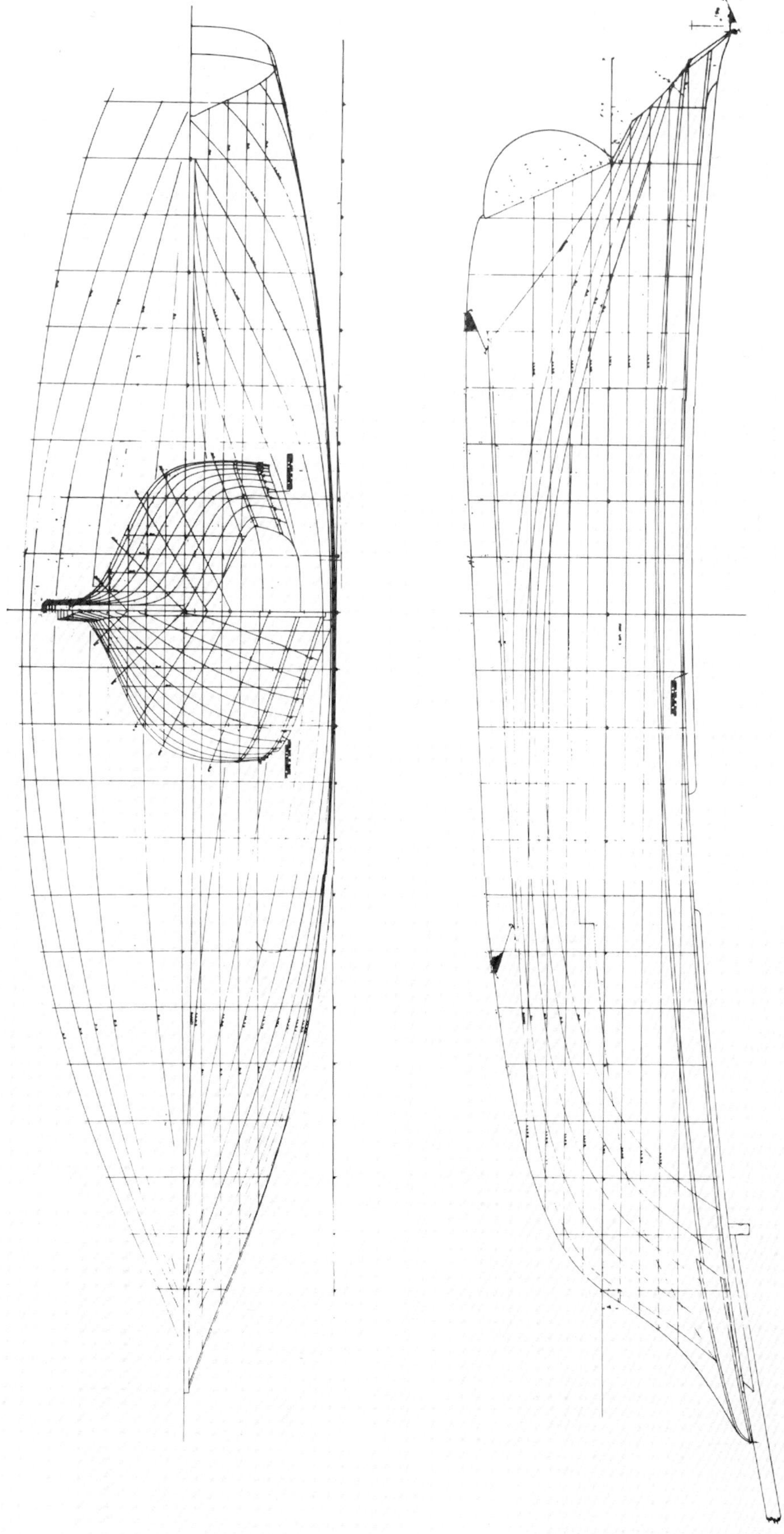

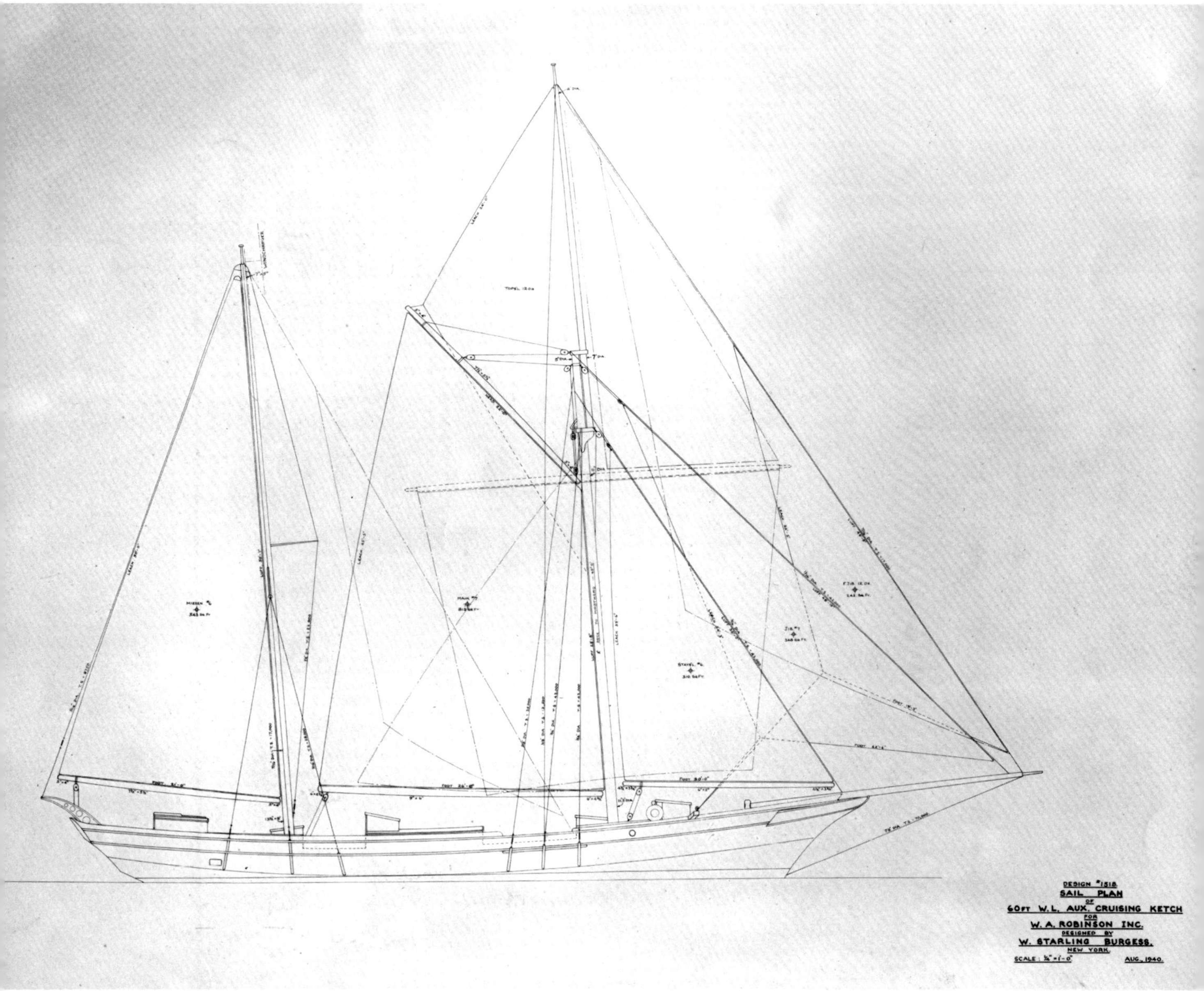

LEFT: **The *Varua*'s lines, by Starling Burgess. Robinson required a comfortable sea-boat and, particularly, a boat that would be safe running off in a big seaway. Burgess paid great attention to the shape of the run and stern; tank testing with waves led to the heart-shaped, slightly hollowed-out transom, nicknamed her double-chin. She is long and narrow, with moderate draft and rather full hull sections for easy motion and good carrying capacity. Dimensions are: 70 feet long on deck; 60 feet on the waterline; with a beam of 16 feet, 3 inches; and a draft of 7 feet, 6 inches. Displacement is 43 tons, with 15 tons of outside lead ballast, for a ballast-displacement ratio of 35 percent.** (Taylor, *More Good Boats*, 155.) ABOVE: **The original ketch rig of the *Varua*, drawn by Starling Burgess for William A. Robinson of *Svaap* fame, in August 1940. She has a generous rig of 2,886 square feet, with the big jib topsail of 619 square feet set. There is also a small jib topsail of 241 square feet. Other areas are: mainsail, 814; mizzen, 543; forestaysail, 310; jib, 348, and main topsail, 252. Note the strange little mizzen staysail, set flying. Robinson got his squaresail and triangular raffee for running in the trades; as intended from the start, he would add more square sails to his vessel later.** (Courtesy William A. Robinson, author's collection)

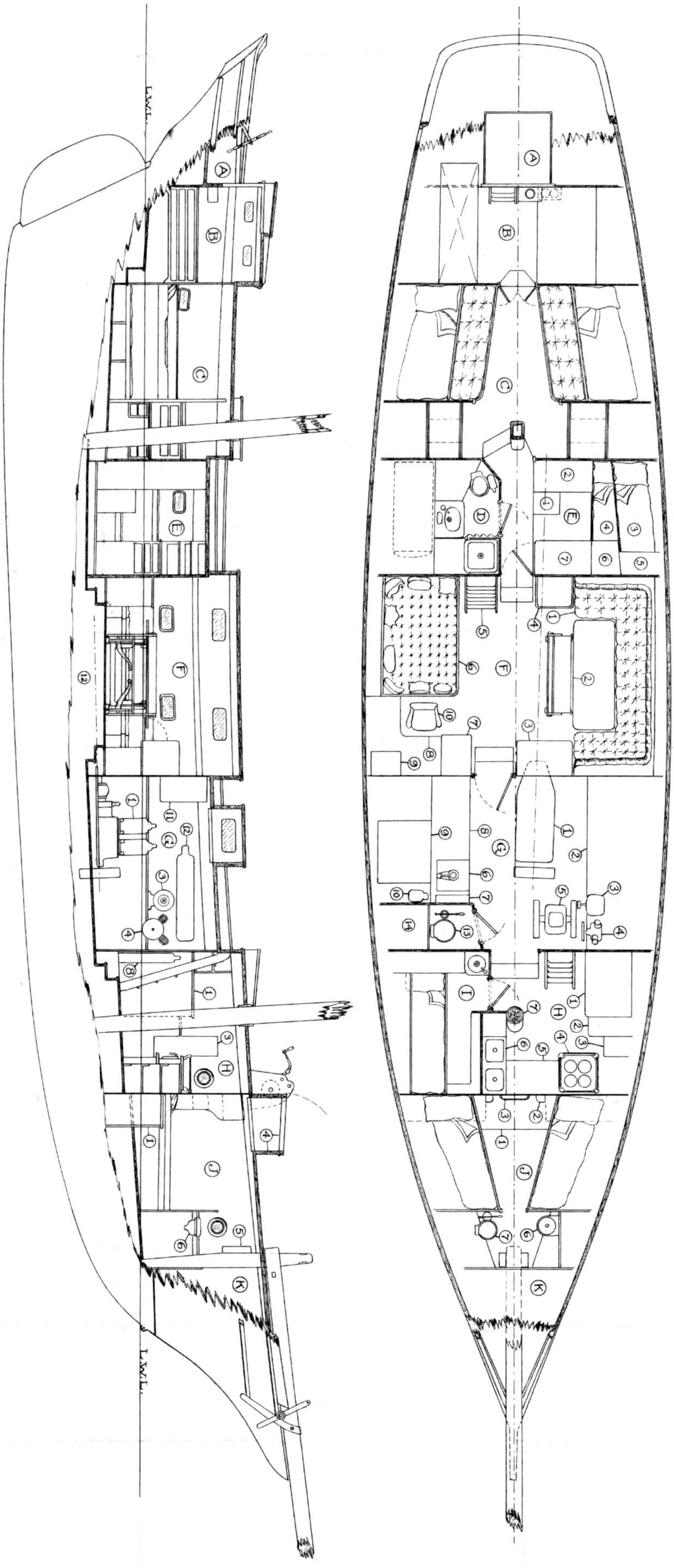

construction than traditional wood shipbuilding could provide and went to Holland to learn about using steel.[2]

In 1940, Robinson was ready to have his vessel designed. He took his ideas to Starling Burgess, whose work he admired. He wanted a fast and handsome ketch. He thought he might even try her in the Bermuda Race, but he wanted to be able to convert her readily to square rig for extensive cruising in the South Seas. He wanted to use composite construction, with a steel skeleton skinned with wood. He had to have spacious accommodations for four, a big engine room, even a workshop and photographic lab. Burgess incorporated all of Robinson's requirements into a handsome vessel, whose length grew to 70 feet. Her hull was tank-tested at the Stevens Institute in Hoboken, New Jersey, to make sure she could run safely in a heavy, following sea.

Robinson was demanding and could be irritating. When the vessel's lines were lofted, Robinson complained about the accuracy of the offsets. Burgess suggested that the reason for any inaccuracy might be that Robinson had antagonized his chief draftsman. Nonetheless, the vessel was built, was launched on March 12, 1942, and was christened the *Varua*. Now Robinson wanted the square rig conversion designed, but Burgess was too busy with war work to do it. Robinson turned to L. Francis Herreshoff, who was not busy at all.[3]

Robinson used to come the fifteen miles from his shipyard to 25 Front Street to talk boat design with Francis. The two prickly men seemed to get on well together; Francis always had time to answer Robbie's questions. In a letter, Robinson wrote, "he is one of the wisest designers living today." The fact that Robinson's correspondent relayed the compliment to Francis certainly did no harm to their friendship. Friendship aside, Francis must

---

LEFT: **The *Varua*'s cabin plan was worked out by Francis to Robinson's detailed requirements. This is Francis's drawing of it for *To the Great Southern Sea*. One of Robinson's requirements must have been the two breaks in the deck, for Francis believed that these "very much weaken the deck panel and the deck panel is one of the most important structural parts of the boat." He has borrowed his own system from construction plans, identifying items on the drawing with letters and numbers instead of labels. "A" is the cockpit, kept small in case of a boarding sea (despite the special, anti-pooping stern). "B" is the charthouse, with a large navigation table to port and the navigator's berth, handy to the steering, to starboard. The compass mounts on its after bulkhead, well protected and in view of the helm, the same way Joshua Slocum had his on the *Spray*. "C" is a large double stateroom. Notice the rectangular porthole right beside the skipper's pillow, so that he (Robinson) can keep an eye on the sea state. "D" is a toilet room, with shower. The head, far from being a cedar bucket, is electric. A large water tank is outboard. "E" is a small, double stateroom, with its own porthole above the upper bunk. "F" is the sumptuous main cabin, slightly raised under a low house, to give both more floor space and more light and air. There are portholes in the hull and a companionway to the deck. As well as seating for seven or eight at the dining table to port, there is a huge day bed to starboard, along with author Robinson's L-desk and filing cabinet. The table is gimbaled, and Francis pointed out that, with the vessel heeled over and rolling, the best seats were at its ends, with no danger of the table hitting knees or chins. He drew up a special design for the settee on the inboard side of the table, making its back reversible, so that those seated could face either way. "G" is the engine room. The main engine's shaft is offset to port. Just forward is a small Lister diesel for running a generator and an air compressor for starting the big engine. On the port side is a workbench over a fuel tank. To starboard are an enclosed head, batteries and the electrical panel, and a photo lab. "H," to port of the foremast, is the galley. It has its own companionway for good ventilation in fair weather, and there is a round porthole just by the diesel stove. "I," the cook's stateroom, is to starboard of the galley. "J" is the fo'c's'le, with two berths and a toilet room. The fo'c's'le is separated from the galley by a watertight bulkhead.** (© Mystic Seaport Museum, Daniel S. Gregory Ships Plans Library, SP38.177.8)

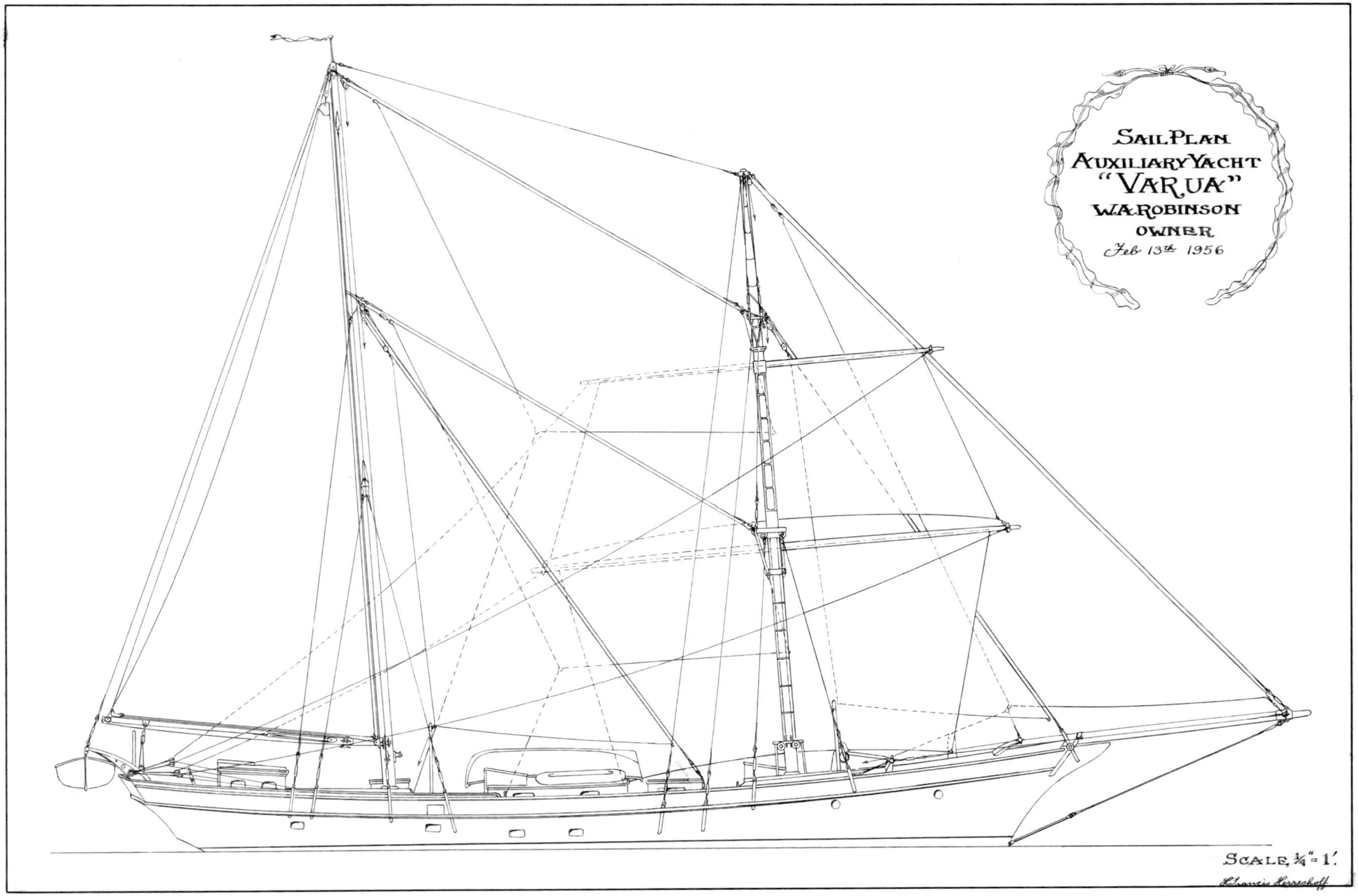
SAIL PLAN
AUXILIARY YACHT
"VARUA"
W.A. ROBINSON
OWNER
Feb 13th 1956
SCALE, ¼" = 1'
L. Francis Herreshoff

have accepted the unusual assignment of drawing up a rig that had to be based on that of another designer at least in part because that designer was his mentor and friend, Starling Burgess.[4]

The *Varua*'s cruising rig gave Francis little opportunity for creativity. He had to start with the Burgess ketch and incorporate Robinson's requirements. If he could have, he would have given the *Varua* more sail. He wrote that she "is very deficient in sail area and I think she must be very slow in light weather." Robinson's concept for this unusual rig worked very well, however, for the way he used her. He powered through calm belts and made fast passages in the trades. He sailed the *Varua* many thousands of miles short-handed, including taking her, undamaged, through an exceptionally severe storm in the far South Pacific in 1952. After thirty years of sailing her, Robinson wrote, "if it came to reconstructing *Varua*, I would make absolutely no changes whatsoever in her rig."[5]

Robinson also talked to Francis in 1942 about designing an ocean cruising boat that his shipyard could build after the war. He had in mind an enlarged version of the *Svaap*. Francis drew three preliminary profiles in pencil for a ketch about half again as long as the *Svaap*. Number 1 had a clipper bow and transom stern; number 2, a gently curved stem and a short canoe stern; and number 3, the gently curved stem and transom stern combination that was ultimately selected.[6]

This was Francis's design No. 81. She was

LEFT: **Francis completed this drawing of the *Varua*'s brigantine sail plan on February 13, 1956, for Robinson to publish in his book about the vessel and one of her cruises, *To the Great Southern Sea*. When he designed the rig in 1942, Francis had a lot of "givens:" Robinson wanted low, wide squaresails for running in strong trade winds, but also plenty of fore-and-aft sail area for reaching and windward work. He would often voyage short-handed, so no sail could have an area greater than 500 square feet. Moreover, Robinson wanted to be able to alter his vessel from ketch to brigantine with a minimum of complication. The brigantine's mainsail, set on the ketch's mizzenmast, is slightly shortened from what was the ketch's mizzen to reduce its area from 543 square feet to the required 500. The brigantine's foremast is the ketch's lower mast for her big gaff mainsail. The ketch's tall main topmast has been discarded. The mast positions are identical in both rigs, and the bowsprit is the same. The first version of the brigantine sail plan showed a very small lower mainstaysail and a big (650-square-foot) upper mainstaysail set flying, but these two sails were changed for three mainstaysails more nearly equal in size. On a broad reach in moderate weather, with everything set but her forestaysail (which would be blanketed by the foresail), she would spread 2,495 square feet of sail—391 square feet, or about 15 percent, less than the ketch had. Running, her sail area would be more limited, with only the squaresails and mainsail drawing.** (© Mystic Seaport Museum, Daniel S. Gregory Ships Plans Library, SP38.177.1) ABOVE: **The *Varua* spreads her tan-barked sails against the backdrop of the mountains of Tahiti.** (Courtesy William A. Robinson, author's collection)

ABOVE: **This is Francis's design No. 81, for William A. Robinson, dated November 1942. Francis wrote: "She has up and down cut sails for they can be carried safely in storms which would split a cross-cut sail. Her bowsprit houses entirely and when the bobstay is detached, she can be used for winter sailing and this [the housing bowsprit] is a great convenience when laying in port. The design's best point is that it has a yard running on a track at the foreside of the mainmast and the yard can be easily detached when lowered away which makes it unusually convenient for the yard lays on deck when there is much closehauled work." Her sail area is 1,112 square feet, with 381 in the mainsail, 276 in the mizzen, 202 in the forestaysail, and 253 in the jib. The squaresail has 513 square feet. It seems unusually wide; the "unusual convenience" of shifting the 31-foot yard from mast to deck, or deck to mast, would depend on the balance and muscle of the crew.** (© Mystic Seaport Museum, Daniel S. Gregory Ships Plans Library, SP38.184.11) RIGHT: **The Robinson ocean cruiser is much bigger than the *Svaap*, and is proportionately narrower and less deep, and so is more easily driven for her size. She is 49 feet long on deck; with a waterline length of 42 feet; a beam of 12 feet, 5 inches; and a draft of 6 feet, 3 inches. Her displacement is 53,760 pounds; lead ballast is 19,900 pounds, or about 37 percent of displacement.** (© Mystic Seaport Museum, Daniel S. Gregory Ships Plans Library, SP38.184.1)

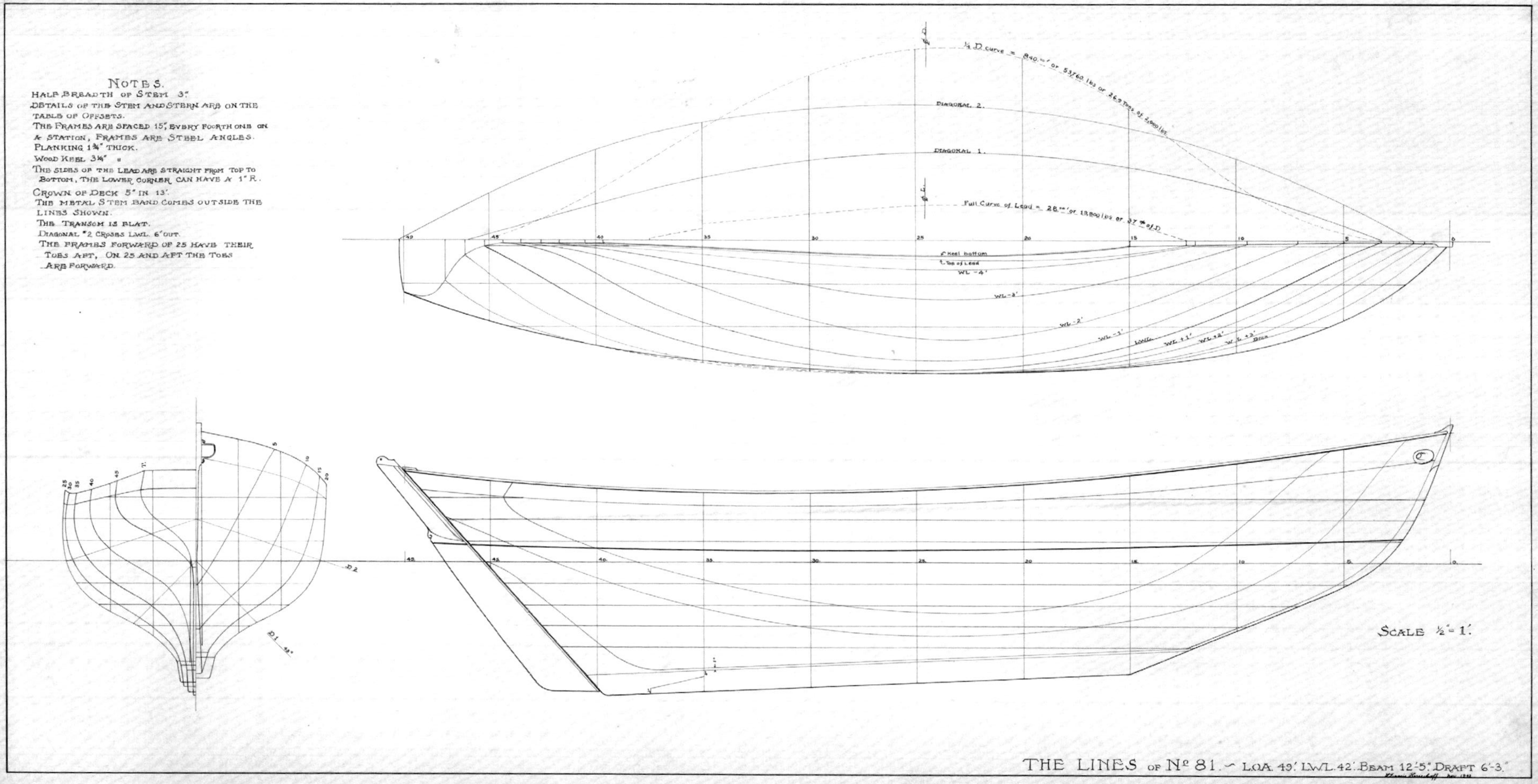
NOTES.
HALF BREADTH OF STEM 3".
DETAILS OF THE STEM AND STERN ARE ON THE TABLE OF OFFSETS.
THE FRAMES ARE SPACED 15", EVERY FOURTH ONE ON A STATION, FRAMES ARE STEEL ANGLES.
PLANKING 1¾" THICK.
WOOD KEEL 3¼" "
THE SIDES OF THE LEAD ARE STRAIGHT FROM TOP TO BOTTOM, THE LOWER CORNER CAN HAVE A 1" R.
CROWN OF DECK 5" IN 13'.
THE METAL STEM BAND COMES OUTSIDE THE LINES SHOWN.
THE TRANSOM IS FLAT.
DIAGONAL #2 CROSSES LWL. 6' OUT.
THE FRAMES FORWARD OF 25 HAVE THEIR TOES AFT, ON 25 AND AFT THE TOES ARE FORWARD.
DIAGONAL 2.
DIAGONAL 1.
WL-4'
WL-3'
WL-2'
WL-1'
LWL
WL+1'
WL+2'
WL+3'
D2
D1
SCALE ½" = 1'.
THE LINES OF Nº 81. – LOA. 49'. LWL. 42'. BEAM 12'-5". DRAFT 6'-3".

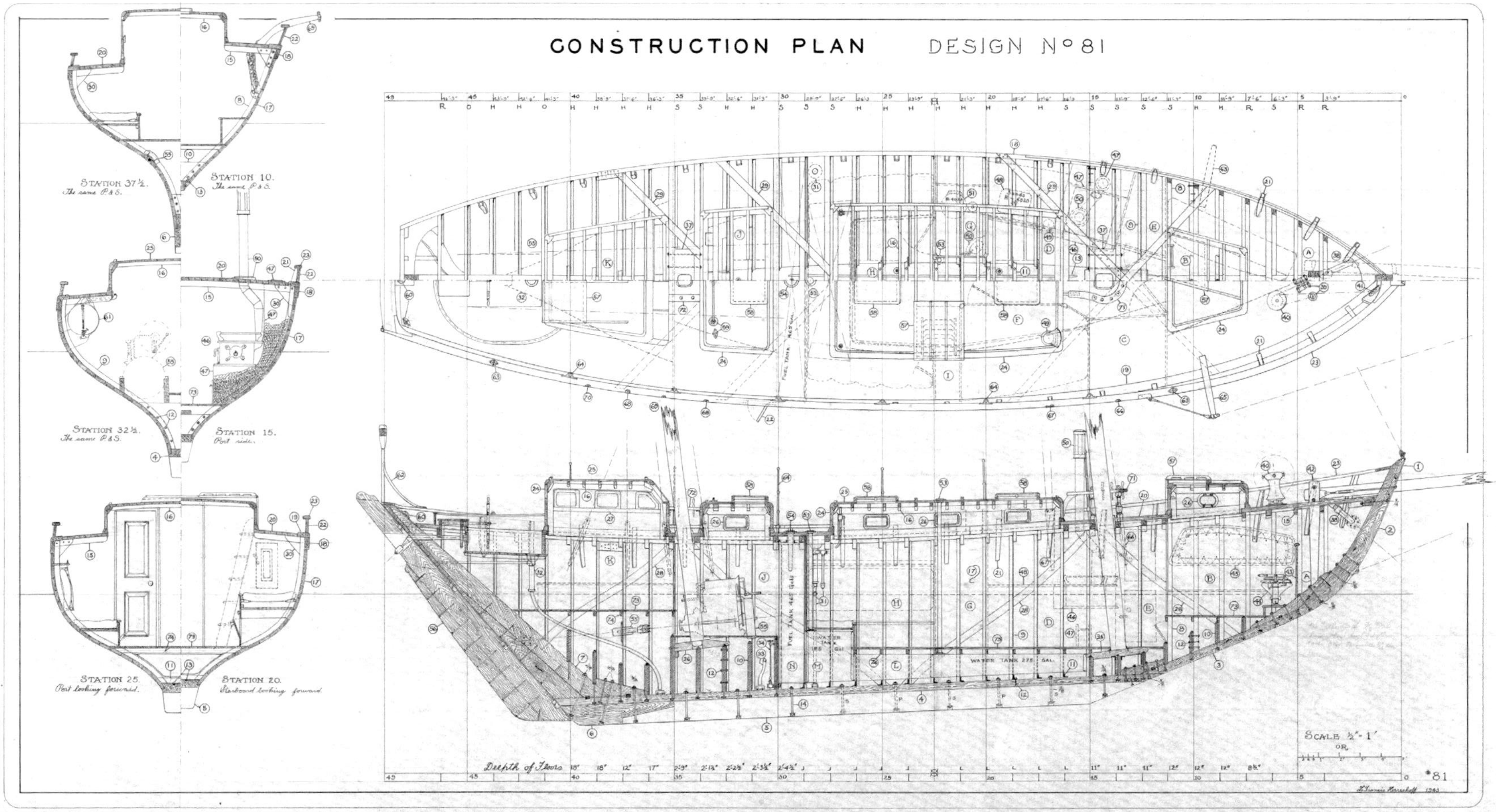

The dotted lines on No. 81's construction plan show her cabin layout. The deckhouse abaft the mizzenmast is a chart house with a bunk for the navigator. The engine room is just forward of the mizzenmast. The companionway to the main living quarters is on the starboard side of the house, and this arrangement allows for a big U-shaped settee extending right across the after end of the saloon. The head and galley are forward to port, with a stateroom opposite. Way forward is a fo'c's'le. An unusual feature of this design's construction was that Francis dispensed with a sheer clamp and shelf, replacing their lost strength by beefing up the sheer strake and covering board, each to 2¼ inches thick, and adding a knee at each frame. Frames were to be spaced 15 inches apart, every fourth one of steel angle, fastened to steel floors. Thickness of planking, 1¾ inches. He wrote: "I believe this particular design throughout to be much the strongest yacht for her size that I have ever seen." (© Mystic Seaport Museum, Daniel S. Gregory Ships Plans Library, SP38.184.10)

a 49-foot ketch that bore some resemblance to John Alden's *Svaap* but was pure Herreshoff. She had a long waterline, narrow beam, moderate draft, and a low rig. Her bow was concave at the waterline and greatly flared at the rail. She would be comfortable and dry at sea and would make fast passages without hard driving. The design was very handsome, thanks to her springy sheer, well-balanced ends, and nicely raked masts.

Robinson was busy building vessels for the navy and Francis was busy writing for *The Rudder*, so he worked only sporadically on No. 81 during the war. He completed the construction details during 1943, inking the construction plan on the back of the sheet with the three penciled preliminary profiles. At the end of the war, Robinson sold off the shipyard and sailed over the horizon in the *Varua* to make his home in Tahiti. Apparently, he had paid Francis something for design No. 81, because whenever Francis got inquiries about it (the sail plan and construction plan had been published in "Common Sense"), he checked with Robinson, and Robinson always asked him not to release the design. On a visit to Francis in late 1969, however, Robinson expressed surprise that no one had ever built No. 81, so Francis finally felt free to sell the plans. He sold a few sets at $150; the design was not complete by his standards, lacking spar plans and full-size drawings of fittings. No one has ever built a boat to design No. 81.[7]

Not an ocean sailor, Francis still could be moved to dream by No. 81. He wrote to one inquirer about the joys of lying in her bowsprit netting, being cooled by the air rising up off the water. To another, he wrote, "Frankly, if I were younger [he was seventy-eight at the time] and had more money, I would like a vessel just like her." But this was Francis's effort at salesmanship; at no age did he really want to put to sea in a yacht.[8]

Boris Lauer-Leonardi was talking shop with Francis at 25 Front Street in early November 1943, planning the series of articles that would start in four months as "The Common Sense of Yacht Design." *Rudder* readers were responding enthusiastically to the drawings and articles describing the H-28. Boris wanted to keep the pot boiling with more Herreshoff designs, and he had a gleam in his eye for something bigger.

The tide was turning in the war, so sailors could think about going sailing again. Boris was receiving letters from servicemen urging *The Rudder* to publish designs that they could build when they came home. Some were seeing the South Pacific from gray, steel decks and were looking forward to returning to islands of their own choice, on their own schedules, and in their own boats. Boris wanted a How-To-Build design from L. Francis Herreshoff that would be far more ambitious than the H-28. He thought there might be considerable interest in a design for a world cruiser.[9]

Beyond working on designs for William A. Robinson, Francis had been thinking about and drawing ocean cruisers for a long time. In 1920, he had designed a 60-foot ketch; in 1922, a 100-foot three-master; and in 1931, a 130-foot three-master; for each, "extreme seaworthiness" was the first requirement. These designs, especially the last two, would be too ambitious for *The Rudder*'s amateur builders, but their drawings would be interesting for Francis and Boris to spread out on the drafting tables in Francis's second-floor workroom at 25 Front Street. The two big three-masters would provide the basis for a smaller one that Boris could publish in *The Rudder*.

Francis, with his experience in navy patrol boats in the rough, winter waters around Block Island and the imagination to take his designs to sea, must have put these three craft through many a stormy test in his mind. In fact, the two designs for offshore cruisers that he made in the early

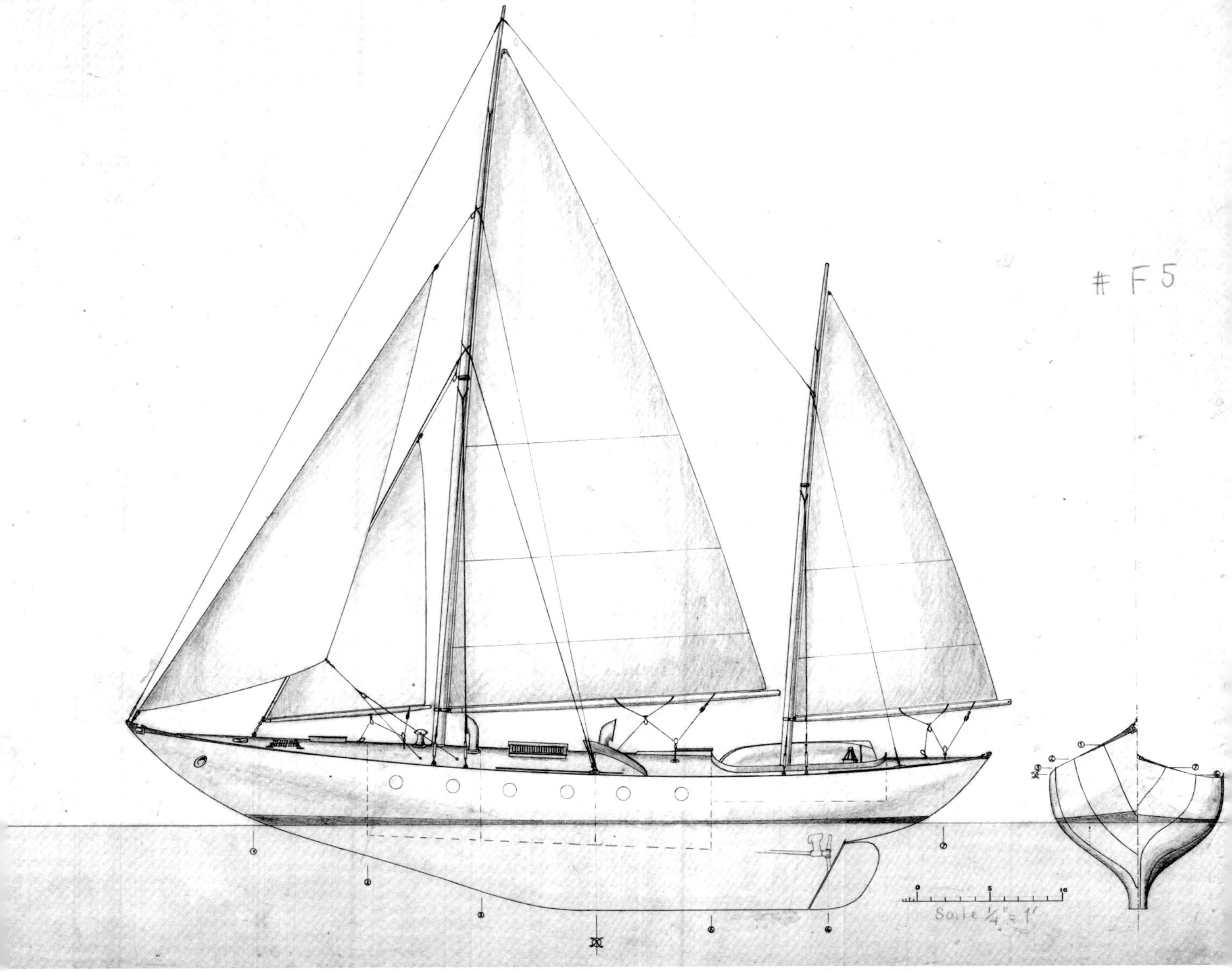

Design No. F-5, Francis's first double-ender, 1920. She is 60 feet long on deck, 45 feet on the waterline, with a beam of 12 feet, and a draft of 6 feet. Some details to note are: the closed bow chock (for a sea-anchor rode) with an open chock atop it; the carefully shaped hawespipe; the spring for the anchor rode on the foredeck; the breakwater just forward of the companionway; the big ventilators; the running backstays made down to slides along the rail; and the off-center, folding propeller. It is not clear how the dinghy could stow in the position shown without obstructing the cockpit and wheel, for her gunwale would come within about 18 inches of the centerline of the vessel.

twenties may well have taken shape in his head as he watched over the antics of SP-578 and SP-56 in the winter of 1917-18 (see volume 1, pages 55-57). However, all Francis's offshore voyages under sail were vicarious. He did put to sea with Charlie Welch in the *Stormy Petrel* and heave to overnight, but those trips were hardly voyages. He thought of a long voyage as "tiring work"; he readily admitted to a dislike for night sailing; and, most important, he hated to be away from his lathe and drawing board. Yet, he had a large collection of charts from all over the world, saved from the navy's trash bins. (On the backs of some of these, he made preliminary pencil drawings of designs that he wanted to transfer from his mind to paper.) Francis actually got afloat in fewer than one-third of the boats built to his designs; seventy-three were built, and he sailed, motored, or paddled in twenty-two. He must have sailed every one in his mind, however, whether built or not, and perhaps none more so than these three seagoing vessels. He had enough early cruising experience and enough imagination to be able to estimate the performance of a design by sailing it vicariously.[10]

Francis had drawn these vessels for his own amusement; none was for a client. The first, the one of 1920, he numbered F-5. He wrote that her hull shape combined the "Cape Cod dory, Eskimo kayak, Block Island boat, and New Bedford whaleboat. The lines of sheer, profile, deck plan, and sections were worked out by drawing the shapes of the aforementioned shapes, one over each other and then taking the mean average." Francis added a ballast keel for stability. Taking his inspiration from these seaworthy double-enders, L. Francis Herreshoff produced his own first design for a double-ender.[11]

The F-5 has the rather long overhangs of many of his early designs and enough sheer to give her high, buoyant ends. Her deck is well-crowned, and there is no deckhouse or cabinhouse, which eliminates a source of weakness and leaks. Her rig is snug, and Francis shows deep reefs in mainsail and mizzen to shorten it much further. He wrote that the rig gave sixteen different balanced sail combinations for varying wind strengths. And she has five watertight compartments.[12]

The second "Ocean Cruiser" that Francis drew was his F-16, a 101-foot, three-masted schooner, in 1922. His written description for the F-16 shows that he thought out the design in considerable detail.

His objectives were:
"1. Extreme seaworthiness
2. Safety
3. Comfort at sea
4. Long life
5. Economy."[13]

He achieved his first two objectives by shaping his vessel like a huge lifeboat, giving bow and stern extra buoyancy with turtlebacks, to make her "non-capsizable." The reserve buoyancy forward is primarily to keep her safe when running in a big sea. She is not a true double-ender, but has a dory stern. She is cut away aft to help her lie to a sea anchor and cut away forward to keep her from yawing when running in a seaway.

The "centers of weight are kept quite high for an easy motion at sea," in order to achieve objective No. 3. For example, there is a good-sized fuel tank on deck just forward of the mainmast, and the engine for the anchor windlass is also up on deck. The high center of gravity reduced stability but worked because of the vessel's short, low rig.

Francis meant to achieve long life and economy in this design by using composite construction, with an inner layer of wooden planking, fastened to metal frames with galvanized bolts, and an outer layer fastened to the inner with brass screws. There would be six watertight iron bulkheads in the vessel. She wasn't built, so the long life of these disparate metals would not be tested.

In describing the F-16's rig, Francis wrote that her helmsman could reef the mizzen as needed to

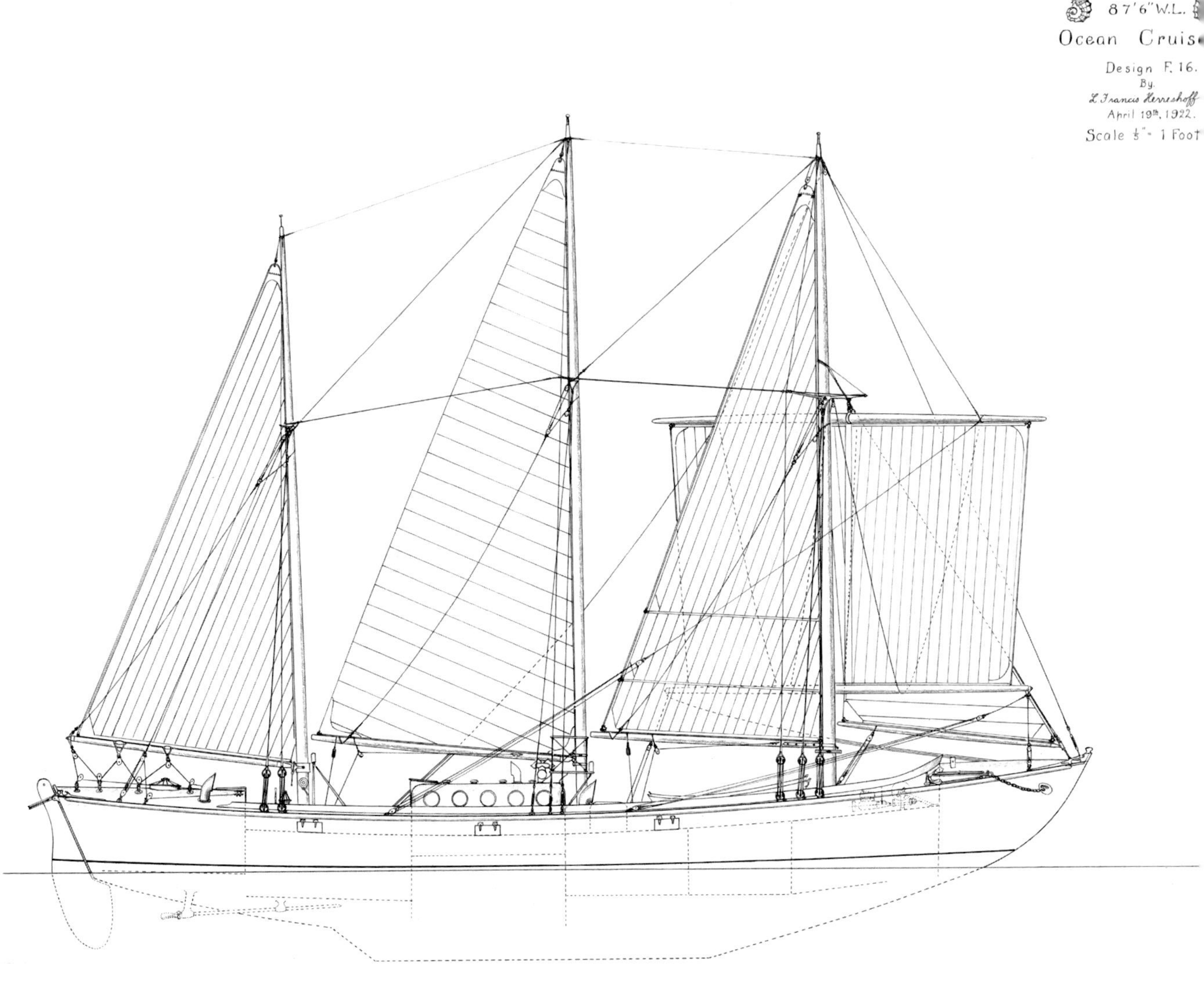

Design No. F-16, "Ocean Cruiser," drawn in 1922. She is 101 feet long on deck; 87 feet, 6 inches on the waterline; no beam given; draft, 8 feet, 9 inches. Her outboard, balanced rudder looks vulnerable. Among her interesting features are: a full-width open bridge up off the deck in way of the mainmast "for taking observations, bearings, etc."; a breakwater at the after end of the forward turtleback, extending all the way back to the after turtleback as a 2-foot, 9-inch coaming; deadeyes and lanyards on fore and mizzen shrouds, with turnbuckles on the main shrouds; and a pair of 16-foot "Cape Ann dories" nested on deck abaft the foremast, to be hoisted out fisherman-style by Spanish burtons from the masts. The lower spring stays appear to run in pairs from the ends of the foremast spreaders to the mainmast, and from the ends of the mainmast spreaders to the mizzenmast. Francis made no mention of them in his description of the design. Their purpose is not clear. Could the fore and main spreaders have been long enough for the foresail and mainsail to clear these spring stays when the sails were eased for running? The sea horses decorating the drawing's title are the first used by Francis. (© Mystic Seaport Museum, Daniel S. Gregory Ships Plans Library, SP38.122.1)

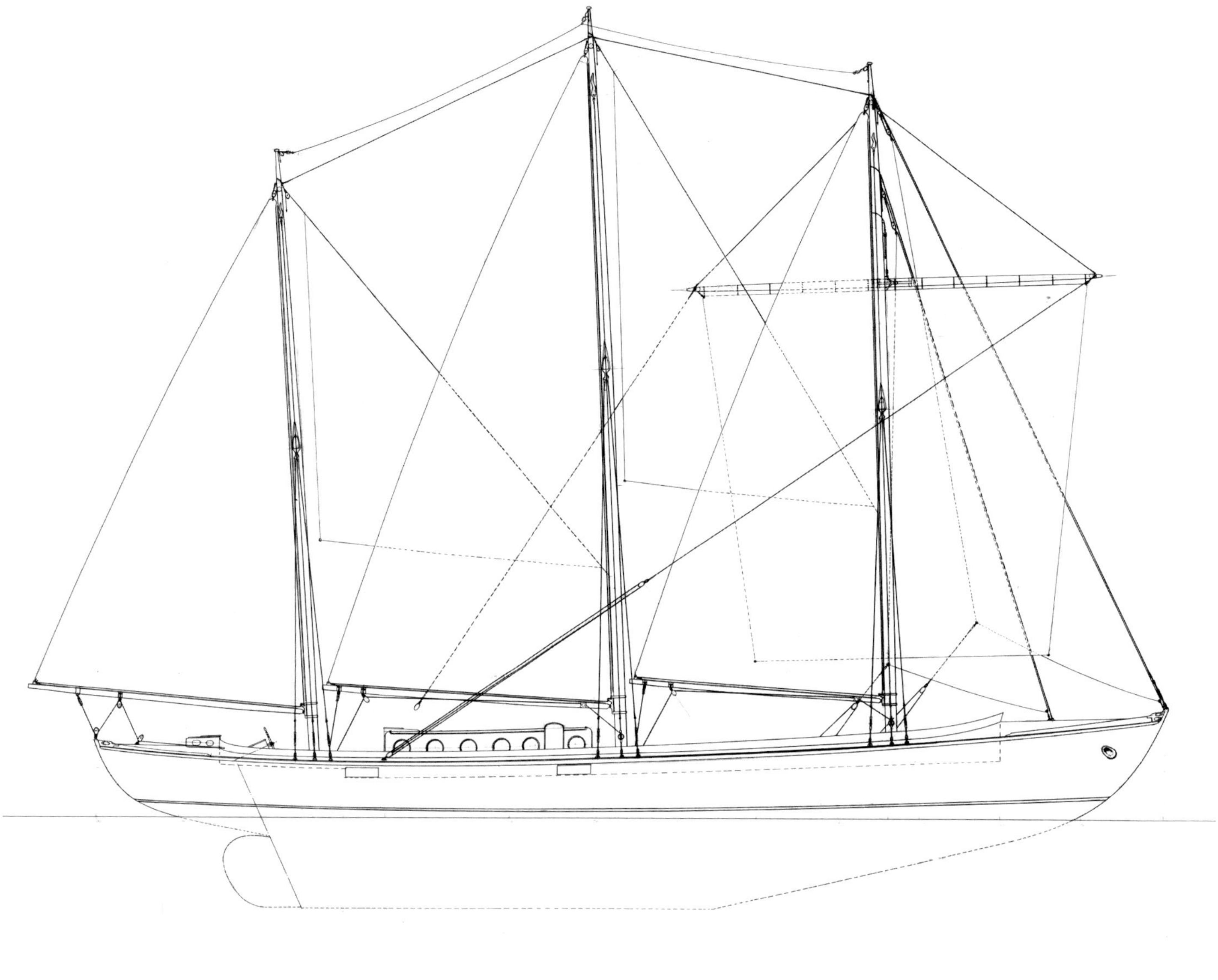

Francis's three-masted ocean cruiser of 1931 is 130 feet long on deck, 109 feet on the waterline, no beam given, and draws 11 feet. This is a big vessel; the freeboard forward is 13 feet, 4 inches. She has many of the features of her predecessor of 1922, but is more of a sailing vessel, with proportionally more sail area, draft, and ballast. Francis has eliminated those strange lower spring stays and has drawn in main- and mizzen-topmast staysails. On a preliminary drawing for this design, he penciled in a nice, 28-foot motor launch stowed on deck between the fore- and mainmast. This design and the F-16 provide an indication of how Francis matured as a designer between 1922 and 1931. (© Mystic Seaport Museum, Daniel S. Gregory Ships Plans Library, SP38.188.1)

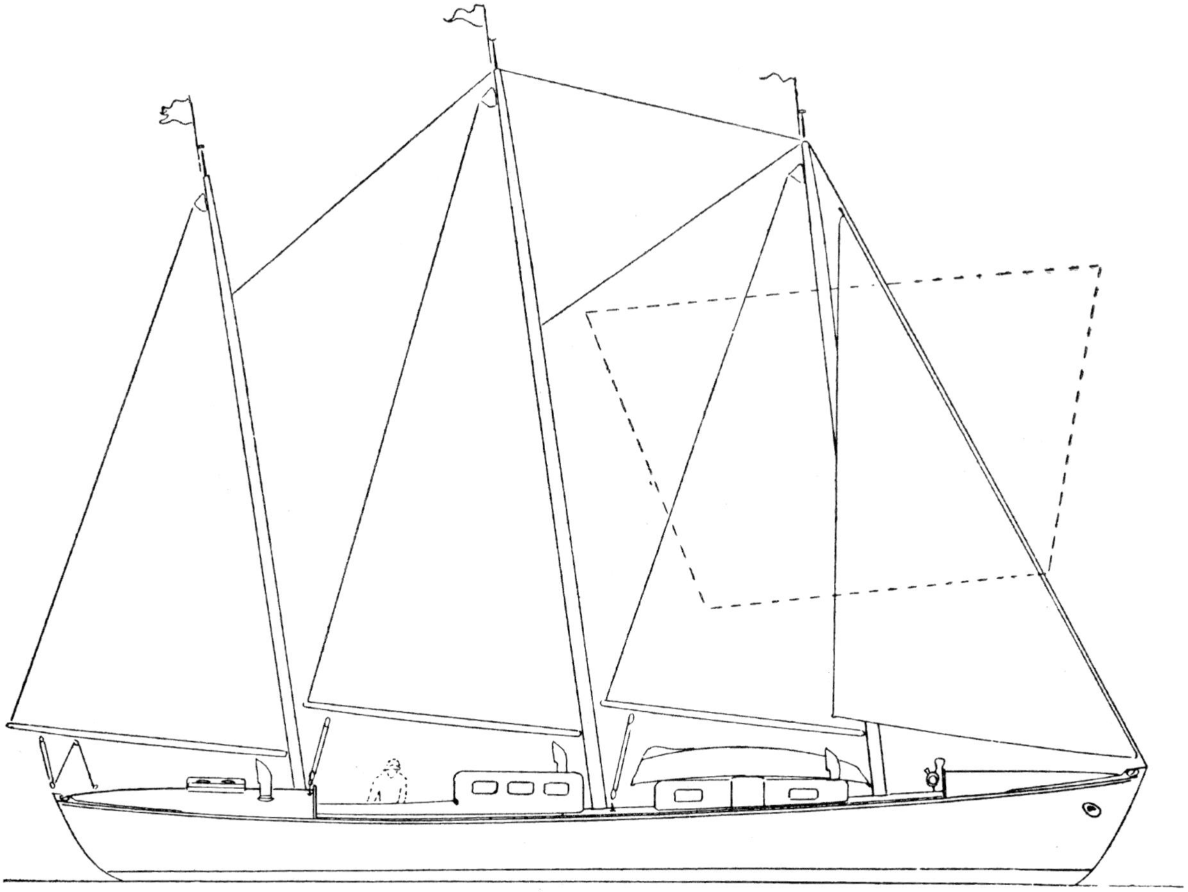

keep her balanced using roller-reefing gear, though the way he has drawn the mizzen sheet doesn't appear to make provision for the roller reefing. In further shortening sail, the crosscut mainsail and then jib were to be taken in, leaving the vertically cut, and thus stronger, mizzen and foresail. The boom on the squaresail could be rotated by the buntlines to reef and furl the sail from the deck, according to Francis's description. This seems too good to be true. Francis probably thought he could figure out such a system. Perhaps he could have, but he didn't.[14]

Francis began his description of the F-16's accommodations by stating that her deckhouse was to be of steel and contain the wardroom and galley. Elsewhere he wrote, "it would be a rough day if the steward on this ship could not serve a hot meal." There would be a forepeak and a

Tillicum II? was Francis's caption for this drawing of a three-masted ocean cruiser used as an illustration for "The Common Sense of Yacht Design," in _The Rudder_. Her name is his spelling of John C. Voss's _Tilikum_, a 35-foot Siwash war canoe that Voss built up, decked over, ballasted, rigged with three masts, and sailed three-quarters of the way around the world from 1901 to 1904. Published six months before the Marco Polo, the _Tillicum II?_ is clearly that vessel's forerunner. She is about five feet shorter than the Marco Polo, and her masts have more rake. (*The Rudder* (June 1944): 30)

fo'c's'le for four. The description ends there. The drawing shows that the engine room would be under the deckhouse, and that there were four additional living compartments, two forward of the deckhouse and two abaft it.[15]

About four years after drawing the plan of the F-16, he sent it to his father, with whom he had recently reconnected. Nathanael found "the ocean cruiser interesting but would be much better at sea with the keel carried aft and rudder hung to it in the good old way."[16]

Francis took his father's advice nine years later, when in 1931 he designed a second three-masted ocean cruiser 130 feet long, for he did indeed draw the vessel "with the keel carried aft and the rudder hung to it in the good old way." He may have drawn this big craft in reaction to the constraints placed on his design of the *Landfall* several months earlier, constraints imposed by the Cruising Club of America's rating rule for ocean racers. It is possible to see the 130-footer as an extension of the dotted lines that show what a wonderful double-ender the *Landfall* could have been. It is as if Francis is saying: "Look what a handsome, seagoing vessel I can design if I am not limited by foolish rating rules." Nor was he influenced by an opinionated, demanding client, as he had been on the *Landfall*, for this design, like the F-5 and F-16, was done for his own edification.

The meeting with Boris in November 1943 peaked Francis's interest in working up a version of his three-masted ocean cruisers that would be small enough for a *Rudder* How-To-Build design. By March 21, 1944, Francis could respond to V. R. Bruce in Wellsville, New York, a dreamer who wanted a cheap, small, seagoing cruiser, by sending him a preliminary drawing of a three-masted, double-ended, lifeboat-type craft. Her beam of 9 feet, 9 inches, and draft of 5 feet (the only known dimensions) suggest a length of about 50 feet. And by May 10, the deadline for his submission of an article on "Rigs and Sail Plans," in "The Common Sense of Yacht Design" for the June issue of *The Rudder*, Francis included, as figure 45, a small outboard profile and sail plan of a lifeboat-like hull about 50 feet long, with a three-masted rig, labeled "Tilikum II?". This drawing may well show the same design he sent to V. R. Bruce. The boat actually bore little resemblance to John C. Voss's famous *Tilikum*, a built-up dugout canoe, except that she was a long, narrow double-ender with a modest, three-masted rig. She is based on the two earlier designs, the F-16 and the 130-footer, and shows the evolution of Francis's thinking on a safe boat in which to go offshore. And she is very close to the How-To-Build world cruiser that Boris would present to the readers of *The Rudder* six months later.[17]

Francis named the design of this *Rudder* How-To-Build world cruiser after that far-reaching traveler, Marco Polo, writing that "Comfort and show were not the main objects of his life, but to get onward and visit strange places was more to be desired." This linking of the design with the explorer proved prophetic, for, as we'll see, the first published account of a passage in a Marco Polo praised the vessel's ability to get onward, but called into question her comfort.[18]

Francis must have done the basic design work for the Marco Polo, including the outboard profile and sail plan, the lines and offsets, and the essential arrangement on deck and below, in the fall of 1944. In October, Boris wrote an announcement to alert readers that the design was coming and sent it to Francis for approval. Because of the growing popularity of the H-28, Boris added "H 55" to the name, so the length of the design had been determined by then. Francis rewrote the announcement as follows: "The Marco Polo is not an adaptation of a coastwise cruiser. She is planned principally to drive economically under power and this will make her rather different from the usual conception of a long distance cruiser. She will be an exceptionally good sea boat, simplified in construction and cabin layout as much as possible. The sail area and draft will be small, she should be easily handled by

one person on watch, and is planned for watches of four hours on and eight hours off. The designer is making particular effort to make the Marco Polo a versatile design, or one which will accommodate a great variety of power plants, both single and twin screw." The announcement, published in December, went on to say that the design would appear in installments, beginning with the January 1945 issue.[19]

Francis submitted the first installment for "How To Build the Marco Polo H 55" on December 8, two days before his deadline for the January issue. His text listed his objectives and gave his rationale for the vessel's unusual features:

The principal objects tried for in the design are:

1. A very long cruising radius under power.

2. A sail plan that can be handled by one man on watch.

3. Extreme seaworthiness (the whale boat model).

4. Shallow draft which not only will allow her to visit out of the ordinary places but often will avert serious disasters.

5. She is cut away aft so that she will lay-to a sea anchor with her head well into the wind, and a balanced rudder designed to swing all the way around.

Francis's drawing of mermaids admiring an unharmed Marco Polo amidst the wreckage of other vessels was used as the opening illustration for the first two installments of the design in *The Rudder,* then dropped. The drawing of life on the beach after the great gale shows not only Francis's whimsy and artistry, but also his disdain for what he considered lesser vessels. (*The Rudder* (January 1945): 54)

Name of Engine	Number of Engines	Number of Cylinders Total	Bore & Stroke	Piston Displacement Total	R.P.M. of Engine	R.P.M. of Propeller	Horse Power Total	Piston Speed in feet P.M.	First Cost of Power Plant	Estimated Fuel Consumption in gals. P.H.	Estimated Cost of Fuel Per Hour *	Estimated Speed of Yacht ½ Loaded	Estimated Cost of Power Plant and Fuel for 10,000 N.M.	Cruising Radius with 1,000 Gal Tanks	Cost of Power Plant and Fuel for 10,000 N.M. ÷ by Speed of Yacht †	Name of Engine
Caterpillar D-4400	1	4	4¼x5½	312	1,500	750	43	1,375	$2,500	2.3	.23¢	N.M.P.H. 9.2	$2,750	4,000	299	Caterpillar D-4400
Fairbanks Morse Model 36-A	1	4	4¼x6	340	1,200	600	40	1,200	$2,200	2.3	.23¢	9.1	$2,453	3,960	269	Fairbanks Morse Model 36-A.
Gray Four-40	2	8	3 7/16x4⅜	280	1,400	700	54	954	$1,200	5.5	.82¢	10.	$2,020	1,818	202	Gray Four-40
Gray Six 77	1	6	3 5/16x4⅜						$750							Gray Six 77
Kermath Sea Chief Four	2	8	3⅛x4⅜	268	1,600	800	58	1,166	$1,200	5.5	.82¢	10.	$2,020	1,818	202	Kermath Sea Chief Four
Kermath Sea Chief Six.	1	6	3 9/16x4	239	1,600	800	52	1,066	$880	5.2	.78¢	9.6	$1,690	1,850	176	Kermath Sea Chief Six.
Kermath 35 H.P. Heavy Duty	1	4	4⅜x5½	330	1,000	1,000	35	915	$1,185	4.1	.61¢	8	$1,935	1,950	240	Kermath 35 H.P. Heavy Duty
Kermath 2-127	2	4		254	1,600	800	50		$2,550	2.5	.25¢	9.5	$2,812	3,800	295	Kermath 2-127
Kermath 4-226	1	4	4x4½	226	1,600	800	46	1,200	$2,075	2.5	.25¢	9.5	$2,335	3,800	246	Kermath 4-226
Lathrop LH-4.	2	8	3¼x4	266	1,400	700	48	933	$1,250	5.25	.79¢	9.5	$2,070	1,810	218	Lathrop LH-4.
Lathrop LH-OC4.	1	4	4x4½	226	1,800	900	47	1,350	$740	5.	.75¢	9.5	$1,530	1,900	161	Lathrop LH-OC4.
Lathrop LH-D6	1	6	4x4¼	320	1,600	800	56	1,133	$1,005	5.7	.85¢	10.25	$1,835	1,800	179	Lathrop LH-D6
Lathrop Engineers Model 60	1	4	5½x7	665	705	705	50+	825	$1,700	5.8	.87¢	10.25	$2,550	1,760	249	Lathrop Engineers Model 60
Lathrop D 50 Diesel	1	4	5½x7	665	800	800	50+	933	$3,350	3.2	.32¢	11.	$3,641	3,440	330	Lathrop D 50 Diesel
Lister Diesel Type C.E.M.-16	2	4	4½x4¾	278	1,200	600	32	875	$? 2,600	1.75	.18¢	8.	$2,825	4,575	353	Lister Diesel Type C.E.M.-16
Red Wing BB-4	1	4	4½x6	382	1,000	1,000	42	1,000	$1,020	5	.75¢	9.	$1,855	1,800	203	Red Wing BB-4.
Red Wing Hiawatha Special	1	6	4x4¼	320	1,600	800	56	1,133	$990	5.7	.85¢	10.25	$1,820	1,780	175	Red Wing Hiawatha Special
Red Wing Spark Diesel 55-60	1	4	4⅝x5¼	353	1,000	1,000	44	1,050	$1,760	2.7	.27¢	9.5	$2,044	3,520	215	Red Wing Spark Diesel.
Scripps Model F-4	1	4	3¾x5	220	1,800	900	50	1,500	$1,035	5.	.75¢	9.5	$1,825	1,900	192	Scripps Model F-4
Scripps 7000 Series	1	4	4¼x4½	255	1,500	750	50	1,125	$2,337	2.6	.26¢	9.75	$2,603	3,750	266	Scripps 7000 Series
Universal Superfour	2	8	3¼x4½	299	1,400	600	48	1,050	$1,450	5.3	80¢	9.75	$2,270	1,840	233	Universal Superfour
Universal Sea Lion	1	6	3½x4½	260	1,600	712	53	1,200	$1,090	5.5	78	10.	$1,870	1,820	187	Universal Sea Lion
Name of Engine	Number of Engines	Number of Cylinders Total	Bore & Stroke	Piston Displacement Total	R.P.M. of Engine	R.P.M. of Propeller	Horse Power Total	Piston Speed in feet P.M.	First Cost of Power Plant	Estimated Fuel Consumption in gals P.H.	Estimated Cost of Fuel Per Hour *	Estimated Speed of Yacht ½ Loaded	Estimated Cost of Power Plant and Fuel for 10,000 N.M.	Cruising Radius with 1,000 Gal Tanks	Cost of Power Plant and Fuel for 10,000 N.M. ÷ by Speed of Yacht †	Name of Engine

* Fuel is figured at .10¢ a gallon for Oil and .15¢ a gallon for Gasoline as bought in lots of 1,000 gallons.

† In the last column the lowest numbers represent the cheapest power plant for speed of yacht for 10,000 N.M. You will see that a single screw four cylinder gasoline engine at high R.P.M. is much the cheapest but does not have the longest cruising radius.

The table that Francis made up of the characteristics, performance, and cost of twenty-two engines to accompany his discussion of power plants for the Marco Polo. The table shows that the Marco Polo was, indeed, fast and economical under power. It also presents a look at medium-sized marine engines in 1945. (*The Rudder* (April 1945): 35)

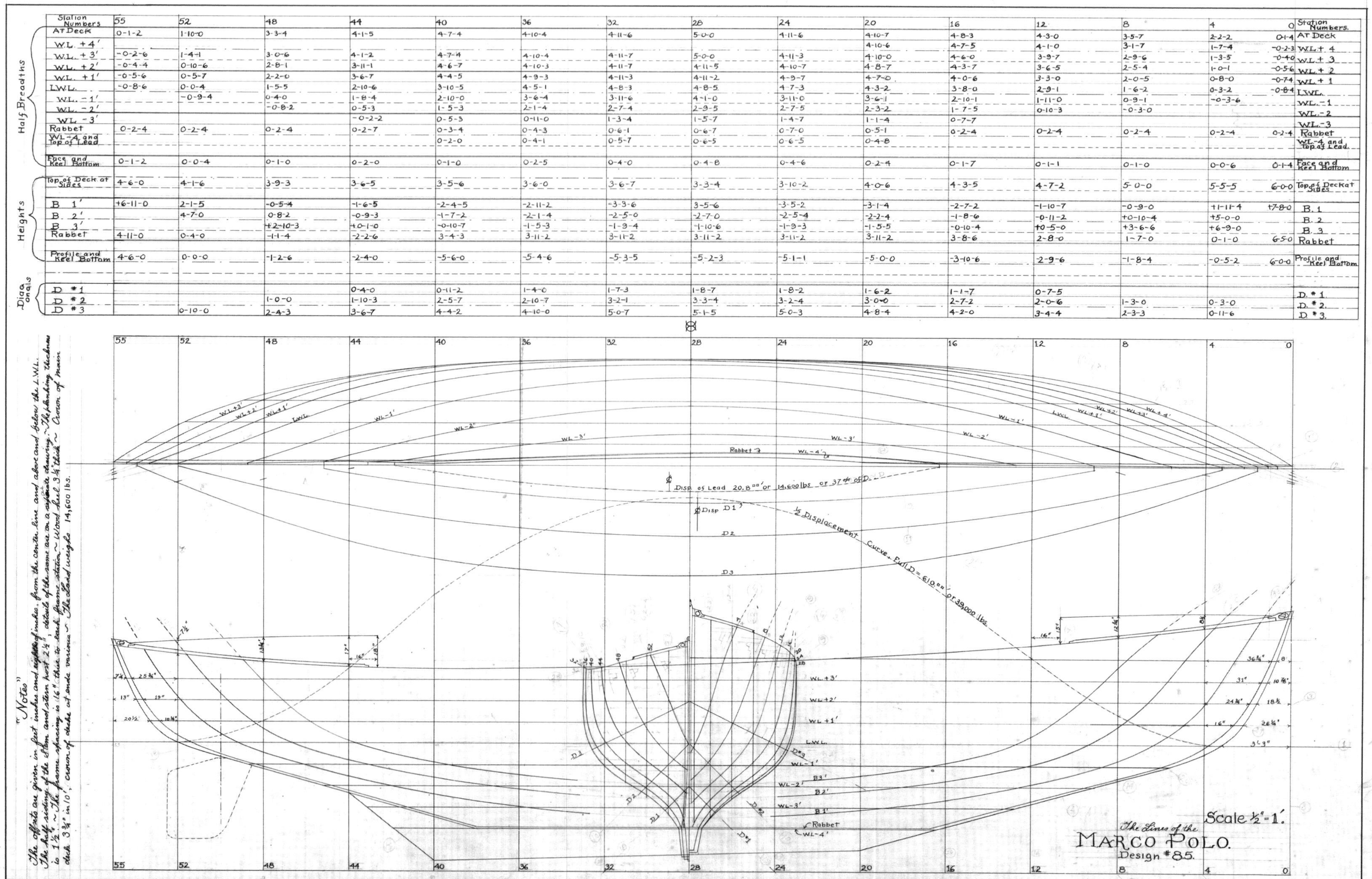

The Marco Polo's lines. At the waterline shown, she displaces 39,000 pounds, of which 14,600 pounds is in the lead outside ballast, for a ballast-displacement ratio of 37.4 percent. This is her light displacement, without fuel, water, or stores, but does include 1,000 pounds of inside, trimming ballast. Filling her tanks and putting on board, say, a ton of stores would add 12,000 pounds to her weight. Francis figured that loading her would bring her down in the water as much as nine or ten inches. (© Mystic Seaport Museum, Daniel S. Gregory Ships Plans Library, SP38.181.26)

6. Her wind resistance is cut to the minimum for laying at anchor in strong winds and to drive economically under power.

7. Her construction is simplified for economy in building as much as is compatible with strength.

8. She is arranged to sleep either four or five people, and planned to be run with one man on watch so that the watches can be four hours on and eight off. This allows a cruise to be a pleasure, but when one is not sure of eight hours' unbroken sleep the cruise is only hard work and drudgery. Few yachts have large enough hulls and small enough sails to allow this combination.

Three masts are adopted so great shifts in center of sail plan can be made. In running in heavy weather the sail can be way forward and prevent broaching-to; in laying-to the storm mizzen can be well aft (where it should be). The foremast and mizzen are very strong for heavy weather and set up-and-down-cut sails, while the mainsail is a crosscut sail on a lighter spar and easily and quickly taken in. Her spars and rigging are according to the latest scientific racing practice, but much heavier and stronger. All unnecessary top hamper is done away with to reduce chafe and wind resistance. The booms are rigged with strong forward guys to prevent them from slatting around or gybing. On this long narrow hull three masts are almost necessary if each sail is to be a high narrow airfoil. Three masts also almost entirely do away with the necessity of reefing, for one or more of her several sails can be taken in to accomplish the desired reduction of area, so that, although reefs are shown on the sail plan, they seldom would be used.

An admirer of Francis's got into a discussion of three masts with Havilah Hawkins, who was having a Maine passenger schooner, the *Mary Day*, built with two masts. "Why didn't you make her a three-master?" he asked Hawkins. Captain Hawkins wanted to know if his inquisitor had ever seen a three-master that was any good. The reply was: "I certainly liked that one Uncle Francis designed." "Is he your uncle?" asked Captain Hawkins. "Mr. Herreshoff, sir, is the uncle of us all!"[20]

Francis continued:

> *One of the features of the design is to have a place to carry a really serviceable tender, which few vessels of this displacement can do, but my experience is that an easily rowed, light tender adds to the pleasure of a cruise very greatly, for some of the most interesting places are in very shallow water. A tender that can sail, row or go with an outboard motor is almost invaluable. On this design the tender will cut off some of the forward vision, but she is in a place where she will be out of the way and can be lashed down for the very worst weather.*
>
> *The deck at both ends has a high crown like a lifeboat, and this is done to make the forward and after peaks useful for storage. The after deck too will protect the man at the wheel from a pooping sea, which is a matter of great importance, for it is believed this model of vessel can be driven very hard in a following sea as she has a small midship section, an easy run, and a cutaway forefoot—all of great importance in running.*[21]

Francis told his readers to expect about twelve drawings for the Marco Polo in future issues. In fact, when the series ended more than two years later, twenty-one drawings showing details of the design had been published. Francis designed the

Marco Polo as carefully and in as much detail as he had his racing yachts before the war.

When Boris saw the outboard profile drawing of the Marco Polo and read Francis's description of her and rationale for the design, he was enthusiastic. He wrote Francis, "the ship is perfection itself and you have again given the boating public of the world not only a fine boat, but the best of its type and as you say in your article it is the first one designed for that particular purpose."[22]

Strapped for cash, Francis asked Boris for an advance for the Marco Polo design. On the eve of publication of the first installment, December 28, 1944, Boris sent a check for $250, "representing payment in full for the plans and articles of the Marco Polo." By the time of the appearance of the second installment in the February 1945 issue, Francis wrote Boris asking for the same deal he had for the H-28: not only payment for *Rudder*'s use of the design, but also payment for the material published about the design, at the regular rate. As we have seen, *The Rudder*'s rate was $15 per page of drawings and text. This was low, for sailors reading the magazine in 1945 needed keen eyesight to decipher its tiny type and persistence to maintain headway through its long columns. Boris's response to Francis's request is not among his letters, but since Boris was always as generous as he could be to Francis under the policies of Managing Editor Andrew Patterson, it is probable that he agreed. The plans and articles for the Marco Polo took a total of 44¼ pages in the magazine, so, presumably, Boris eventually paid Francis about $665 in addition to the $250. Francis also expected royalties from the sale of plans for the design through the magazine, probably one-third of the $50 charged, or about $17 per set of plans.[23]

The second installment on the Marco Polo, in the February 1945 issue of *The Rudder*, showed her lines and offsets. In a much later letter, Francis wrote that she "is shaped like a lifeboat with a keel." In his text accompanying the lines drawing in *The Rudder*, he described her as being "rather slab-sided like many cargo vessels." As a long-distance cruiser, her loading could vary considerably; for the sake of steering balance, he wanted her beam-length ratio to change as little as possible with variations of loading. In this regard, the Marco Polo is a somewhat more extreme form of the shape of the *Diddikai*, the 37-foot ketch that Francis had designed for rough-water sailing in 1937.[24]

He also wrote, "this model has the advantages of hard bilges which makes for slow motion in a seaway." Anticipating criticism, he wrote: "Some people will say the Marco Polo has too much weight of lead for driving under power, but it is believed most people like the feeling of a boat which is absolutely non-capsizable, and some weight under a yacht of this size makes her much more comfortable. The weight is not down too low so if a little sail is carried she will not be uncomfortable." We will need to return to these statements about the Marco Polo's comfort at sea, but for now, let's simply note that the Marco Polo's bilges are not hard and that hard bilges contribute to a quick roll in rough water.[25]

Part 4 of the Marco Polo series was devoted entirely to a discussion of twenty-two different engines that Francis considered suitable for the vessel. He wrote, "Yes, the power plant of the Marco Polo is the most important part of the whole design." He was favorably impressed with the American marine engines of the day and wrote that they "are so highly perfected that they in themselves allow a long distance cruiser to be practical." No enthusiast of offshore passage-making himself, his idea was to give the Marco Polo a very long range under power to shorten her passages.[26]

His favorite engine for the design was the Lathrop Engineer's Model. He praised this engine's "agreeableness," and wrote that "to sit beside the Engineer's Model while it is running would be a pleasure." The mental picture of a Marco Polo with a Lathrop Engineer's Model in her spacious engine

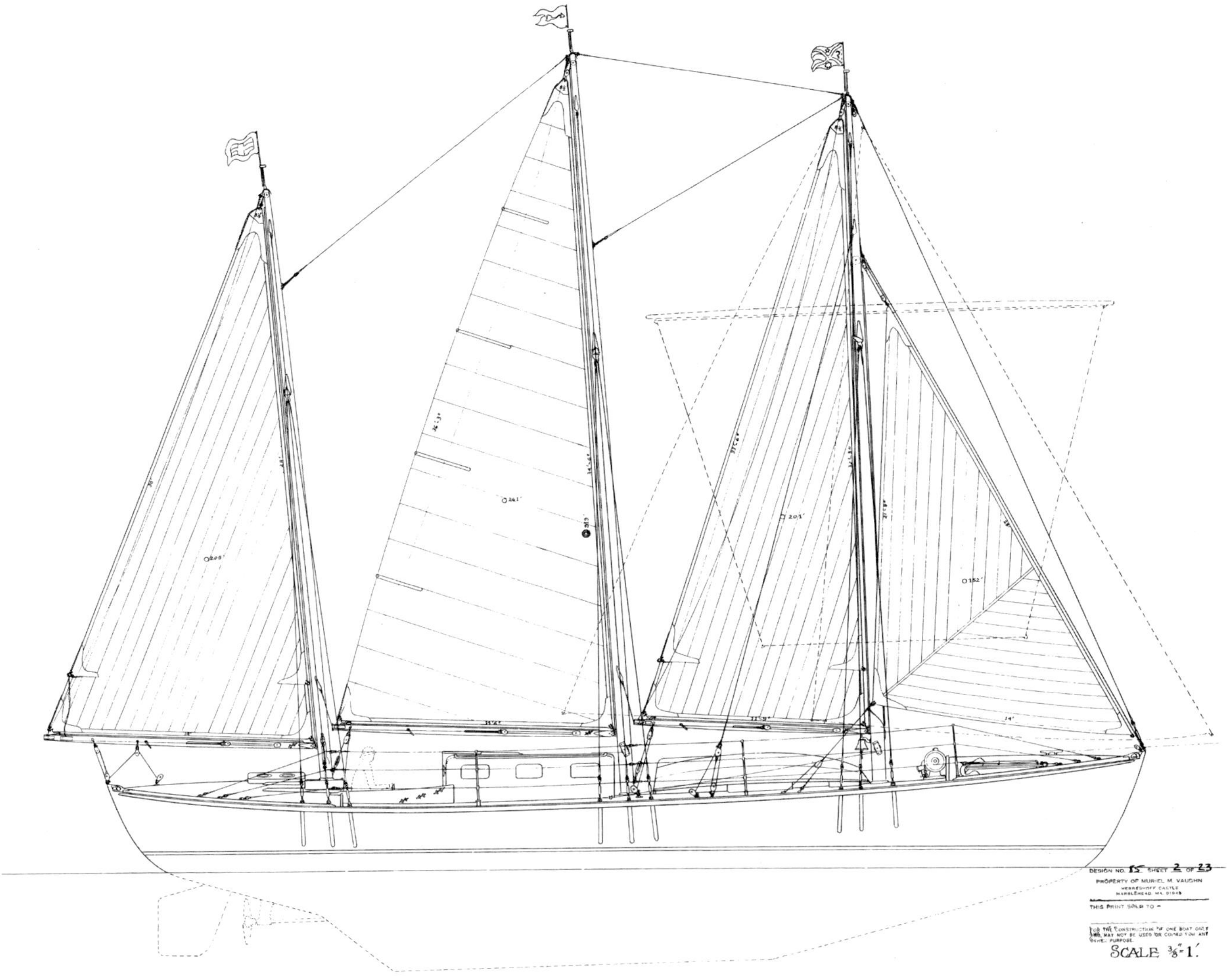

The Marco Polo's outboard profile and sail plan. For *The Rudder*, Francis added sea and sky and dimensions to this drawing, and, to make it fit, deleted the burgee at the main truck. He labeled the Marco Polo: "LOA 55' LWL 48'-9" Beam 10' Draft 5'-6" Design No. 85." On the drawing, he gives the working sail area as 919 square feet, a slip of arithmetic or the pen; it is 819 square feet. The mainsail has 261 square feet; the foresail, 201; mizzen, 205; and jib, 152. Francis wrote, "in light weather with a beam wind she sets a large balloon jib forward on a removable boom or nose pole, which is shown in dotted lines together with a light weather overlapping foresail which goes on the fore boom and has a club sheet." For running, there is the squaresail and "a bifurcated trysail [not shown] hoisted on a track on the fore side of the foremast and set like small heavy twin spinnakers, and it is believed she will be partly self steering with this rig in heavy weather."

(© Mystic Seaport Museum, Daniel S. Gregory Ships Plans Library, SP38.181.2)

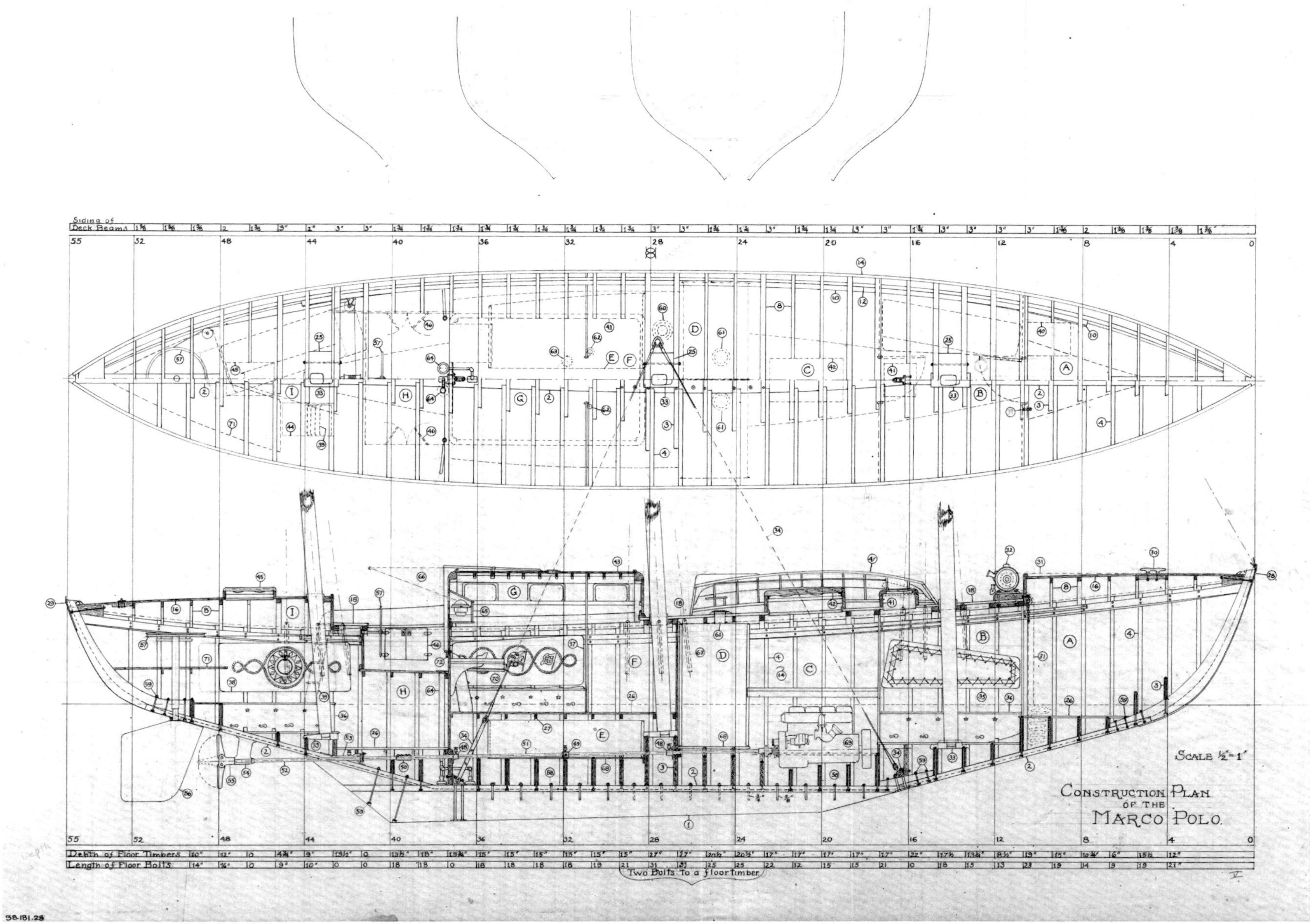
Siding of Deck Beams
Depth of Floor Timbers
Length of Floor Bolts
Two Bolts to a floor timber
Scale 1/2"=1'
Construction Plan of the Marco Polo.
58.181.28

room quite carried Francis away. "If I had a Marco Polo I would have a six foot long work bench on one side of the engine room, not for working on the engine however, but for doing scrimshaw work or any other things which might be required on a long voyage," he wrote. "On the other side of the engine room there would be a six foot cushioned transom seat and here you could sit and read when off watch. If you took it into your head to have a nap beside the Engineer's Model she would not disturb you. When you woke up she would sound just as she did when you dozed off. Yes, if you even took one of those Rip Van Winkle naps she would sound just the same when you woke up." Lathrop reprinted Francis's *Rudder* article on the Marco Polo's power plant as a promotional pamphlet.[27]

The third and fifth installments on the Marco Polo, published in the March and May issues, dealt with the vessel's construction, presenting drawings of construction sections and stem and sternpost and the construction plan. Francis knew that his hull shape would be relatively easy to build, for the frames took no hard bends and the long, narrow boat would be straightforward to plank. He wrote, "her construction is simplified for economy in building." Yet he knew that a 55-foot boat, no matter how simplified her construction, would be a daunting project for most amateur builders. In his first article about the Marco Polo, he gave his readers a dose of reality: "in general she is a vessel that could be built by any small boatyard."[28]

Though the hull of the Marco Polo might be as "simple" to build as that of any round-bilged, plank-on-frame, ballasted vessel, Francis's innovative nature, questing for perfection, brought complications to the design. Builders were not supposed to go to Merriman or Wilcox, Crittenden, except for a few of the fittings that would be required; instead, they were to make about forty-five patterns, get about ninety rough castings from a foundry, and smooth them up. There would also be much sheet metal work to do on Francis's layered chain plates, mast tangs, and masthead fittings. Francis put the builders to this trouble partly because he knew he could design fittings superior to any that could be bought off the shelf, but especially because he wanted to save wind resistance in the rig to help achieve the design's primary objective, efficient driving under power.[29]

The large and high fuel tanks would have to be very carefully supported. He explained: "The tanks of the Marco Polo are designed to be supported underneath and at their outboard sides by setting directly on sheathing. In the case of the fuel tanks, the frames will have to be shimmed up to make the sheathing fit the tanks and templates

---

LEFT: **Francis has drawn the Lathrop Engineer's Model for a power plant on his construction plan for the Marco Polo. The drawing also shows her two high fuel tanks, holding 507 gallons each (D); her two water tanks, 172 gallons each (E); the big storage area under the cockpit (H); the folding propeller; the free-standing, balanced rudder; the headroom gained by the turtlebacks at bow and stern; the dinghy stowed over the hatches between the fore- and mainmast; and even the line of sight of a seated helmsman looking over the deckhouse or at the compass. The only surprising specification in the construction plan is that for the sides and ends of the deckhouse: ¾-inch plywood! (On one Marco Polo, three of the cornerposts of the deckhouse rotted out after eight years. The owner wrote Francis, "You will be interested perhaps to know that the carpenters at the yard were amazed at the ease with which one could dismantle and reach any part.") Although Francis believed in the seaworthiness of the Marco Polo, he designed—by eye—a rig for hoisting her out onto the deck of a steamer. When a correspondent worried that this rig looked too light, Francis advised him to have an engineer check it and predicted the gear would support 2½ times the Marco Polo's weight. Note the decorations on the bottoms of the berths, folded up for backrests, the ship's flags in the deckhouse and the compass rose for the navigator.**
(© Mystic Seaport Museum, Daniel S. Gregory Ships Plans Library, SP38.181.28)

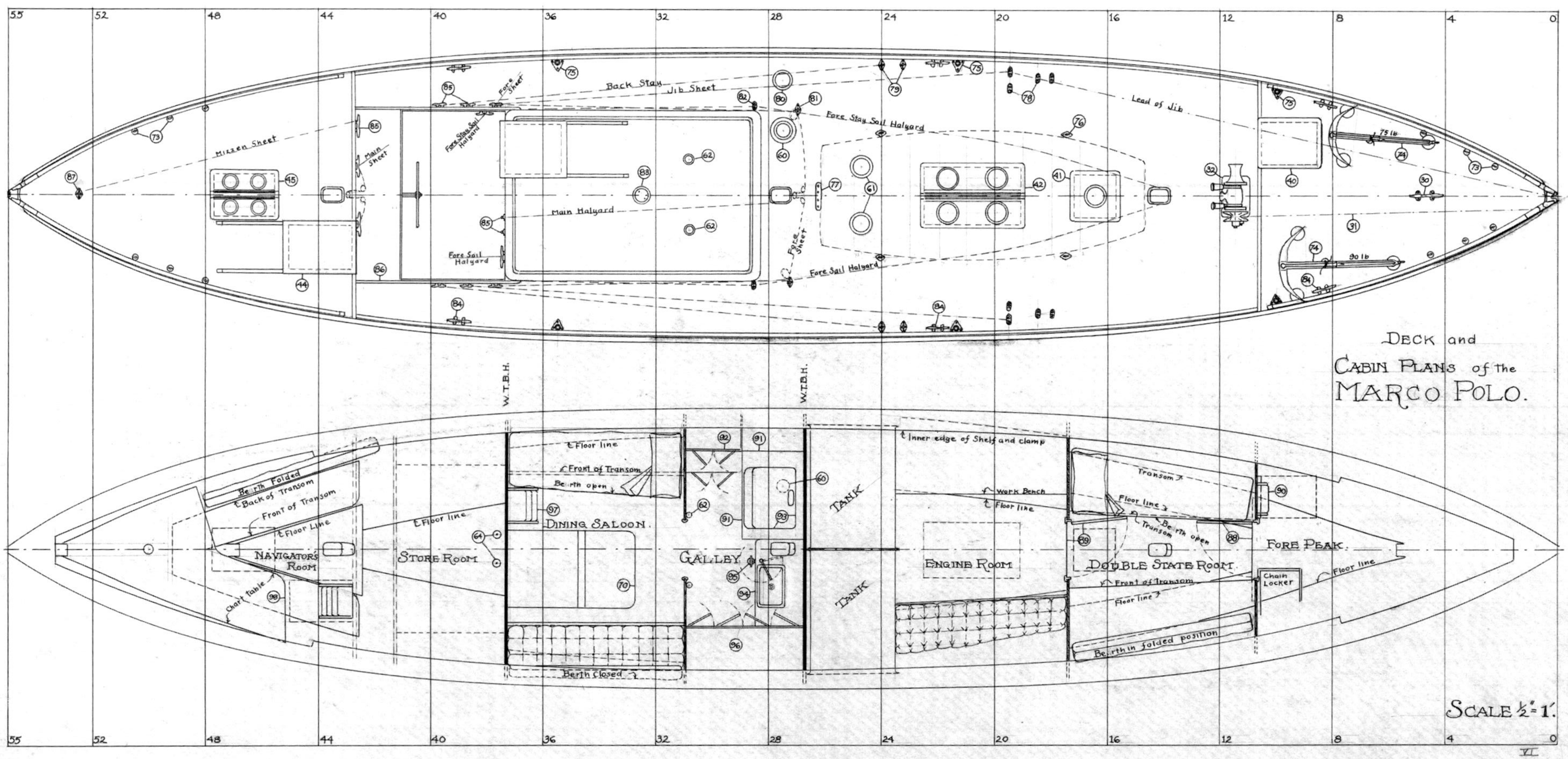
DECK and
CABIN PLANS of the
MARCO POLO.
SCALE 1/2" = 1'.
Mizzen Sheet
Main Sheet
Back Stay
Jib Sheet
Fore Sheet
Fore Stay Sail Halyard
Fore Sail Halyard
Main Halyard
Lead of Jib
75 lb
90 lb
W.T.B.H.
Berth Folded
Back of Transom
Front of Transom
Floor Line
Chart Table
NAVIGATORS ROOM
STORE ROOM
Floor line
DINING SALOON
Berth open
Berth Closed
GALLEY
TANK
Inner edge of Shelf and clamp
Work Bench
ENGINE ROOM
Transom
DOUBLE STATE ROOM
Berth in folded position
FORE PEAK
Chain Locker

must be taken from the finished sheathing for making the tanks. The tanks must be jammed in place so that they will not move in a seaway or shift if she gets knocked down." Francis seems to be presenting the builder with a chicken-and-egg situation as to whether the sheathing has to fit the tanks or the tanks fit the sheathing. At any rate, he wants the tanks rock solid athwartships. Not so, fore and aft: "In the case of the fuel tanks it is best if they can shift slightly, or slide a little way, in case of a collision or if running aground violently, for this may save them from rupturing." So, he wants the fuel tanks wedged in tightly athwartships but slightly movable fore-and-aft. This is Francis as the practical, seamanlike, engineer. He has designed the Marco Polo's fuel tanks to be able to survive a major accident.[30]

Fourteen months before the Marco Polo's cabin plan appeared in *The Rudder*, Francis had described it, in effect, in a discussion of what the crew of an ocean cruiser would need for accommodations—and what they would not need—in his chapter on "Cabin Arrangements" in "The Common Sense of Yacht Design." "The engine room on a long distance cruiser should not be cramped; there should be space, air and light all around the engines," he had written. "Perhaps here is the most important place for full headroom. The water tanks should be large so you will have some water to wash with. The ends of the little vessel should be arranged for the storage of spare sails, coal and wood for the galley, food and other stores. Now if you take out space for a good sized galley you will find there is little room left over for fancy cabins, and maybe that is fortunate for at sea you will have no use for them. If there is some room for sleeping, a little for eating, reading and working out the navigation, it should be enough, for most of the time will be spent at the helm, taking care of the vessel and sleeping." One factor in ocean cruising that Francis is ignoring here is that most world-girdlers actually spend more time in port than at sea, where perhaps not "fancy," but at least roomy, cabins have their place.[31]

Francis drew the Marco Polo's cabin plan for up to five people for offshore cruising. The big engine room, fuel tanks, and water tanks are all amidships; the power plant, "the most important part of the whole design," gets priority. Francis pointed out that for shorter-range cruising, where a big engine and big tanks would not be necessary, one of the water tanks under the deckhouse could be used for fuel and a smaller engine could go under the cockpit, so that the engine room and fuel tank space could become a double stateroom and toilet room connecting to the deckhouse.[32]

He wrote: "Perhaps you have noticed that I have not shown a toilet or an ice box on the plans, but for coastal cruising both would be very useful and there are several places where they could be located with slight changes in cabin plan. However, for ocean cruising the cedar bucket has many advantages, principally in saving space and holes through the hull. On a long cruise nature needs every encouragement and if one can retire to the place of his choosing—bucket in hand—the whole business is simplified. And if by coincidence nature should call all of the crew at the same instant, then

---

LEFT: **The Marco Polo's deck and cabin plans show her unusual arrangement. All her halyards lead to the cockpit. Each of the three living compartments must be entered by its own hatch from the deck. The bunks are well separated from each other. The galley has light, air, and a view. The table in the dining saloon folds back against the after bulkhead, allowing lots of floor space. The navigator's room is in a position of considerable motion. Francis wrote that "a large engine room makes a good workshop and a safe retreat away from the ladies."** (© Mystic Seaport Museum, Daniel S. Gregory Ships Plans Library, SP38.181.27 verso)

if there is a whole nest of buckets all can be accommodated [!].”[33]

In part 11 of the series, Francis showed and described details of the Marco Polo's rudder and steering gear. He rejected his father's advice of twenty-five years before about carrying the keel aft and hanging the rudder to it “in the good old way” and returned to a cutaway deadwood and separate, balanced rudder, such as he had drawn for the F-16 in 1922. But instead of mounting the rudder on the transom, as he had with the F-16, he designed it freestanding and all underwater. About 20 percent of the Marco Polo's rudder area is forward of its turning axis. The advantage of such a balanced rudder is that its leading edge helps it to turn, making for a light and easy helm; the drawback is that when the helm is left unattended, the rudder will quickly try to turn itself, as the water flowing by hits one side or the other of the leading edge. Because the Marco Polo's rudder was very easy to turn, the steering wheel was geared high; one revolution would swing the rudder about 45 degrees. So the Marco Polo steered very easily and could be maneuvered quickly, but she had to be steered constantly, like an automobile. Such a steering system, requiring little power, is well suited to wind-vane or electric self-steering gear, but these were not readily available in 1945.

Francis designed the rudder so that it could swing all the way around to within 30 degrees of facing forward on each side; he provided stops on the steering circle whose cable turned the rudder, so the rudder couldn't hit the propeller. For normal steering, only small rudder angles would be used; angles approaching or exceeding 90 degrees would only be used when hove to, in order to reduce the strain on the rudder when a sea threw the stern sideways or the whole boat backwards.

The freestanding rudder had to be made very strong to resist sideways forces that could become large, as when a quartering sea slewed the boat's stern to leeward and the rudder was turned against that motion to bring her back on course. It might also have to resist strong upward forces should it ever hit bottom, an unlikely event, since the rudder drew nearly a foot less than the keel, but not an impossible one. Francis specified oak for the well-tapered rudder, with a maximum thickness of 3¾ inches at the top. The oak rudder was to be encased in ⅛-inch bronze sheets, “carefully fastened to the rudder stock.” The bronze casing would give the rudder its “principal strength.” He claimed his rudder would “stand as much abuse as a deadwood.” Francis was aiming for simplicity of construction, but the Marco Polo's rudder was not simple. Edmund A. Cutts, of Cutts and Case in Oxford, Maryland, an experienced builder who admired Francis's designs (and he who helped Francis make a gun), singled out the Marco Polo's rudder as an example of his work that would be hard to build.[34]

Francis designed a pram especially as a tender for the Marco Polo. His objectives for the design were to produce a boat that would row well, including handling in rough water; sail well; be suitable for an outboard motor; tow well; and stow upside down on the Marco Polo's deck over the hatches between the fore- and mainmast with minimum obstruction of the view from the helm. To achieve these objectives, he kept her freeboard low so she would handle well in a strong breeze, and he shaped her hull rather like a spoon so she would be dry in a chop. He drew the tops of her transoms with a concave curve to fit the crown of the Marco Polo's deck to reduce her height when she was stowed on board upside down, as he had with the required tenders on his big racing boats. The forward thwart and mast partners were removable so they wouldn't interfere with the deck hatches when she was stowed. A centerboard trunk also would have interfered with the hatches, so he gave the dinghy leeboards, with the added advantage of gaining unobstructed space for her crew when sailing. The leeboards were secured very simply with lanyards. Similar to the Cape Ann dories on the F-16, the dinghy was to be hoisted

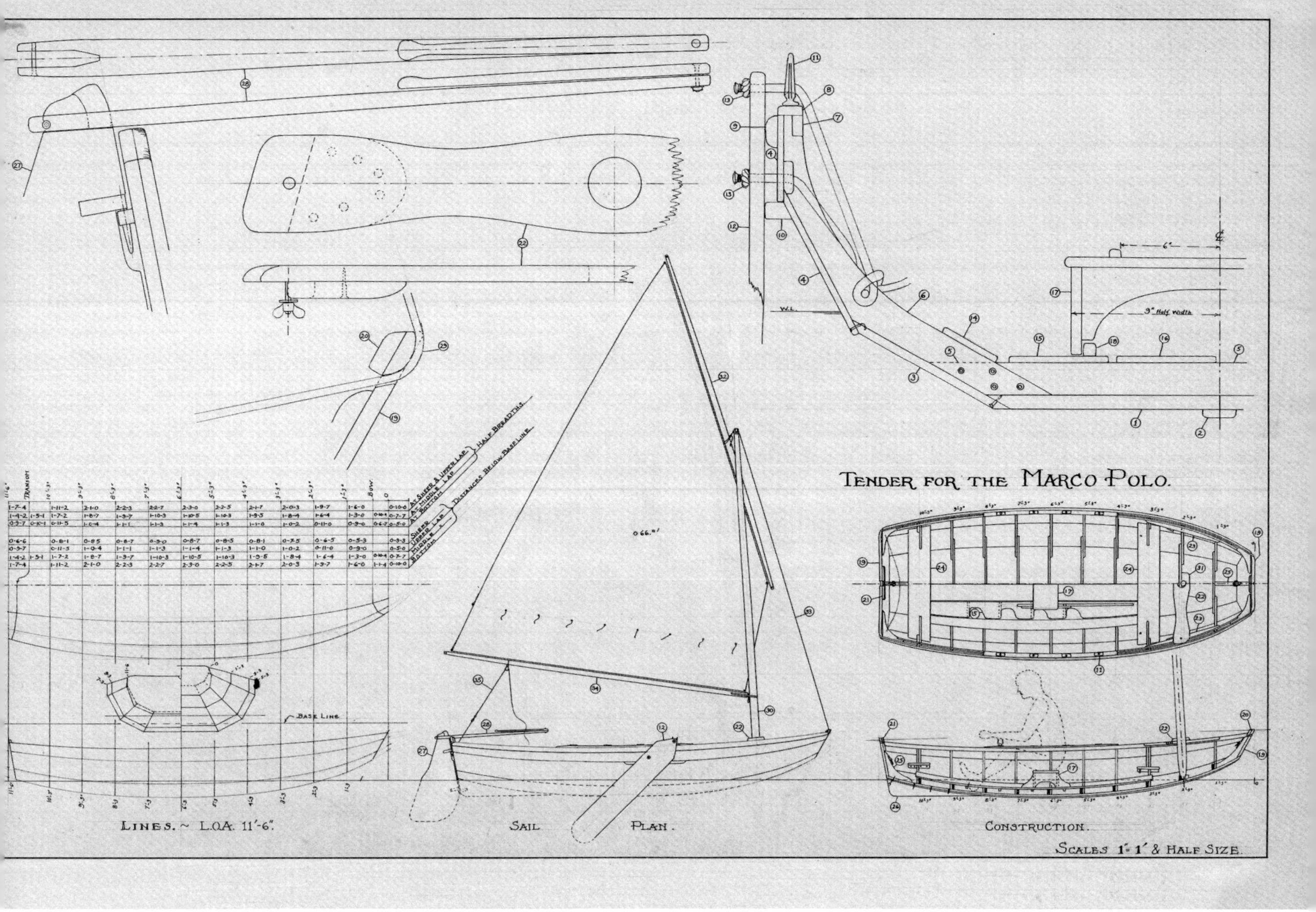

out by tackles from the fore and main spreaders.[35]

As designed, the dinghy had lee helm. Calvin T. Howell of Milwaukee built one, and he wrote to Francis about the problem. Francis advised him that it appeared that the leeboards were not wide enough and that the rudder was too big. Howell increased the width of his leeboards from 9 inches to 14 inches, and also their depth from 4 feet, 3 inches to 4 feet, 9 inches, but he left the rudder alone. Barry Thomas of Mystic, Connecticut, reported solving the same problem by relocating the leeboards further forward. Francis never bothered to change the design, and he never sailed a Marco Polo dinghy himself. Barry Thomas, John Kendall of Marion, Massachusetts, and Robert T. Todd of London, Ontario, all report that their

Francis designed the Marco Polo's 11-foot, 6-inch dinghy for simple, dory-type construction. He cautioned that to be kept tight when stowed on deck for a long passage, she ought to have a loosely woven canvas cover that would be wet down once a watch on dry days. She has a movable box seat with four oarlock sockets and corresponding foot braces, so that the rower can be positioned to trim the boat at her best. An advantage of her lug rig is that all the spars can be short enough to stow inside the boat. The halyard doubles as forestay. The tiller has a hiking stick. As designed, she had lee helm, but it was easily correctible by repositioning the leeboards further forward. (© Mystic Seaport Museum, Daniel S. Gregory Ships Plans Library, SP38.181.39 verso)

Marco Polo dinghies have performed superbly in all conditions. Thomas A. Fletcher wrote that in informal dinghy races in Coral Gables, Florida, a Marco Polo dinghy nearly always won: "she is very fast for her size off the wind." George Davis of Roslyn, New York, praised the boat's performance under oars, sail, and outboard motor, and was particularly impressed with her stability and carrying capacity. But boatbuilder John Gardner, the great historian of small craft, thought the Marco Polo dinghy to be "clunky" and wrote that she was "nothing I would want for a dinghy."[36]

Part 22, "Squaresail Gear," was the concluding installment of "How To Build the Marco Polo H 55," published in the February 1947 issue of *The Rudder*. Francis wrote: "This drawing, I am glad to say, completes the design of the Marco Polo. The entire set of plans includes twenty-one drawings, which in many cases show parts at full size. We believe it is the most complete set of plans of a vessel of this size ever offered to the public."[37]

The design of the Marco Polo was the culmination of years of thinking by L. Francis Herreshoff about the best characteristics and compromises for an offshore cruiser. Though he didn't list speed as a specific objective for the Marco Polo, it is evident that he wanted to create a vessel that could "get onward." He built the design around the fine marine engines that were developed in the United States at the time of World War II, giving her a large, workable engine room and big fuel tanks. With a Caterpillar diesel, she could power for 4,000 miles at more than nine knots. Her hull, with its small midsection and long waterline, was capable of being driven very hard on any point of sailing, especially by a rig that combined a low overall center of effort with relatively high-aspect-ratio sails. Whether the wind blew hard or not all, the Marco Polo could always turn in a good day's run, if her crew were willing to drive her. While the typical motor sailer of the time was known as a 50-50 boat, Francis called his Marco Polo a "90-90 boat." What she did not have, as Francis wrote, was "sail area enough for ordinary afternoon sailing," but if she had to heave to in a storm, she had enough ballast and reserve buoyancy to be safer than most any other 20-ton vessel.[38]

The reserve buoyancy came from the relatively high freeboard and was augmented by the turtlebacks at the bow and stern. It was these turtlebacks that gave the Marco Polo the look of a lifeboat, a look that Francis liked. In the turtlebacks, the practicalities and the aesthetics of this design meet; they help make the Marco Polo seaworthy, and they help her look seaworthy. They also made for a fault in the design: because the Marco Polo's high lifelines ended short of her bow and stern, the turtlebacks would be dangerous places to work, handling the jib or mizzen. The danger could be readily reduced by extending the lifelines to pulpits fore and aft.[39]

In achieving a 90-90 boat that was seaworthy, Francis traveled far from the norm. There had been seagoing powerboats and certainly seagoing sailing cruisers with auxiliary power, but Francis was the first designer to give the crew of a medium-sized ocean cruiser the choice of going fast and far under either power or sail. In 1938, Philip L. Rhodes had designed the *Tamaris*, the first of his handsome, full-powered, deckhoused ketches that could achieve high speed under power or sail, but the Rhodes designs gained 90-90 status through their size. The *Tamaris* was 81 feet long on deck, with a waterline length of 65 feet, a beam of 20 feet, 3 inches, and a draft, centerboard up, of 6 feet; her mainsail had nearly 1,000 square feet more area than that of the Marco Polo.[40]

Because the Marco Polo was novel and different, Francis laid himself open to criticism and his design open to rejection, and he knew it. His *Rudder* articles describing the Marco Polo are laced with expressions like "Her length may scare some people"; "Some people may say she rises too vertically from the water all around"; or "Many people will not like the balanced rudder." He knew that, for most sailors, a seagoing cruiser meant an

Alden schooner or a Tahiti ketch, and that his long, narrow, three-masted lifeboat would look strange to them. He believed that he had created a remarkably good boat for ocean passage-making. "In my opinion she would be the very best boat that has ever been contemplated to go around the Horn from east to west, or west to east," he wrote, calling her "the most important one that *The Rudder* has ever sponsored," but he had doubts as to whether or not his "complete set of plans, offered to the public" would be well received, or even really understood, by that public. He realized that he was out of step with the world, but that did not deter him from designing "a revolutionary long distance cruiser."[41]

One sailor who appreciated the design of the Marco Polo was Kenneth O'Meara of Fort Lauderdale. By the summer of 1945, the basic plans had been published, and O'Meara was hooked. Just as the war was ending, he wrote an article called "Let's Get Together and Build the Marco Polo," which was published in the September issue of *The Rudder*. Francis wasn't halfway through the series yet, and O'Meara was proposing a well-thought-out organization to obtain bids from boatyards to build a fleet of Marco Polos. The idea was to reduce the cost to each owner through building a number of boats to the design. He wrote: "Mr. Herreshoff has consented to supervise the construction of a number of Marco Polos if and when all the interested parties succeed in forming a common pool of their orders." By the December issue, *The Rudder* could report that O'Meara had "at least ten persons seriously interested in placing a building contract" for the Marco Polo and invited boatbuilders to submit estimates to him. In the end, however, nothing came of O'Meara's effort.[42]

In March 1947, a month after the Marco Polo series ended, Francis wrote to Boris of his disappointment that the design wasn't taking off as had the H-28. Perhaps trying to shield Francis from the readers' lack of response, Boris blamed it on the builders, writing, "many of our customers cancelled their orders [for Marco Polo plans] since they were unable to obtain quotations on the boats from boat builders." By June, though, Francis was thoroughly discouraged about the acceptance of the design. He wrote to Boris, "it looks now as if the Marco Polo would be a complete failure, or in other words represents something like a $2,000 loss to me." Francis may have been thinking that if he had designed the Marco Polo for a client, she might have cost $20,000 to build, so his design commission would have been $2,000, although he had given one Marco Polo dreamer an estimate of $15,000 to make his dream reality. Still, Francis

Francis's sketch of the Marco Polo shows one way he envisioned her: under full sail in a fresh breeze making knots through the seas. He drew this impression for his own amusement, not for publication in *The Rudder*. (Courtesy Muriel Vaughn)

did make money on the design, so his loss wasn't as bad as it looked; and, besides, he had no client for the Marco Polo. In June 1946, Boris decided to sell plans for the Marco Polo dinghy separately for $5.00. Francis's royalty was to be $1.00. He may well have made more royalty from the dinghy than from the mother ship.[43]

In November 1947, nine months after the last Marco Polo plan had been published, Francis received a sympathetic letter from John E. Cherubini of Bristol, Pennsylvania,, saying, "I think it is a damn shame you spent so many hours racking your brain to produce a boat [the Marco Polo] so easy to build and cheap to pay for (comparatively), because as near as I can figure, no one has started to build one yet."[44]

But someone had. In 1946, while the Marco Polo plans were still coming out every month, Delavan P. Smith, an attorney in New York City, decided he had to have this vessel and set to work. He gradually made the patterns for all the fittings Francis designed and had them cast, right through to the squaresail gear of the final installment. He tackled the construction of the rudder. He couldn't get sheets of bronze wide and thick enough for its side plates, so he used Monel, which he found hard to work. He planned to have his vessel built by a yard once he had made all the parts he could. That work took him into 1955, and by then he was reporting on the project to Francis.[45]

And Boris Lauer-Leonardi, who never saw one of Francis's designs that he didn't want to have built for himself, wrote Francis in the summer of 1949 that he was going to go partners with Josiah T. Newcomb, a friend in Port Washington, and have a Marco Polo built in Man-O-War Cay, in the Bahamas, where he and Newcomb had winter places. Boris soon dropped out of the partnership, but Newcomb, like Smith, went to work on the Marco Polo's fitting patterns. Francis introduced Smith and Newcomb through Boris.[46]

Smith selected the Morse Shipyard in Thomaston, Maine, to build his Marco Polo, and Newcomb followed suit. Roger Morse and his crew started on the two boats in the summer of 1955. They found the Marco Polo easy to frame and plank, as her designer had predicted. Francis traveled to Thomaston twice to see what his lines drawing of the Marco Polo was producing in three dimensions. He wrote, "Morse is doing a very good job indeed." These Marco Polos cost about $30,000 each, twice Francis's estimate; and their owners saved a good deal of money by making their own fitting patterns and other parts. Smith's vessel was launched in 1956 and christened *Crusican.*

Allen Beechel's wash drawing of the Marco Polo in the trades, published as the frontispiece in the October 1948 *Rudder*. Francis wrote Boris, "this drawing really shows the shape of Marco Polo to great advantage." (*The Rudder* (October 1948): 10)

She was built to the Marco Polo design with only minor modifications. Smith had to sell her, due to his divorce, before she was commissioned. Charles H. Doersam Jr. of Old Lyme, Connecticut, bought her and kept her for many years, but she has never made an ocean passage. Newcomb's boat was also launched in 1956; he named her *Talaria*, after Mercury's winged sandals. These were the first Marco Polos built in the United States. Smith's pattern-making for the *Crusican* was probably the first Marco Polo construction project started anywhere, but in September 1948, Francis heard from a correspondent in Australia that a Marco Polo was nearing completion at Geelong.[47]

Newcomb planned to make a round trip from New York to the Bahamas every year in the *Talaria,* but he had no more ambitious passages in mind, so he made the modifications to the design that Francis had suggested for coastal cruising. He replaced the big engine room and fuel tanks with living accommodations, put the engine under the cockpit, and used one of the water tanks for fuel. He also enlarged the deckhouse in both length and height.[48]

In July 1956, Newcomb sailed the *Talaria* home from Maine to Port Washington, Long Island, well up the Sound. Boris and his second wife, Julie, were in the crew. They had a typical New England summer coastal passage; there was no opportunity to try her in heavy weather. Newcomb didn't have much time to sail her the rest of that summer or the next, but he planned to make his first offshore passage to the Bahamas as soon as the hurricane season was over in 1957. When the *Talaria* put to sea from New York in a rising, cold northwest gale on November 9, her crew of four had sailed very little in the *Talaria,* or even together in any boat, and were short on offshore sailing experience. One of them had injured his knee just before departure and was in a leg cast.[49]

The *Talaria*'s navigator was Robert P. Beebe, a naval officer who was also an amateur yacht designer. He was a *Rudder* reader and a Herreshoff fan. While fighting the war in the Pacific he had become enamored with the design of the Marco Polo and had made his own vicarious voyages in her. "Ever since the lines were published I have matched the new islands and harbors we visited to what they would be like in Marco Polo." Now he had a chance to go to sea in a Marco Polo and was most interested to see how she would perform. He wrote a detailed account of the trip, which was published in the February 1958 issue of *The Rudder* under the title, "Passage to the Bahamas."[50]

On the first leg, when the boat was beam-reaching across building seas in a cold gale of 40 knots under jib, foresail, and mizzen, her motion was "very quick." All hands were seasick. She must also have been going very fast at times, yet Beebe writes, "we are gradually realizing that the boat is by no means being pressed and is ready to handle much bigger things than this." The next morning, with the wind easing to 30 to 35 knots, they kept it on the beam and gave her full sail. "We hoisted the main and made her jump. She registered twenty miles in two hours on the log once [a speed of over 1.4 times the square root of the waterline length] and was not far from it the rest of the day. Glorious sailing, though life below was far from comfortable unless one was in a bunk." Handholds had not yet been installed below.

The second night they shortened down to foresail and mizzen and headed to the southeast, across the Gulf Stream, experiencing high, steep seas in heavy, shifting squalls, generally from aft. The combination of difficult steering conditions and the *Talaria*'s high-geared steering system, with a rudder that could be turned to 90 degrees and beyond, led to a few accidental jibes. In one of these, the mizzen tore and had to be taken in and furled. Not having made any provision beyond what Francis designed for staying on the turtlebacks at sea, and not having rigged the mizzen preventer he did design, Newcomb and his crew had a long, dangerous tussle with the sail in the dark.

Now they were on a broad reach under just the foresail. Beebe described: "Black squalls bearing down, sea confused from the shifting of the wind, and building up towering crests against the current. Motion below quite violent. On deck it is a different story. *Talaria* can be seen by the light of the moon to be making her way through the seas in tremendous fashion. We are learning to love the hull and the way she rides over the biggest breaking combers with no apparent effort. The ones we think will come aboard, great towering giants with breaking crests, never do so. There has been no solid water on deck throughout the voyage. The lee rail has never been under."

By the fourth day out, with the vessel across the Gulf Stream and south of Cape Hatteras, the

The *Talaria* full and by in a moderate breeze. This view shows well the appearance of her deckhouse, slightly higher and longer than Francis drew it. The lower spring stay between the foremast and mainmast has been left off. Her high, but not-full-length lifelines have not yet been rigged, though they were for her passage to the Bahamas. All her sails are crosscut. In sailing her to the Bahamas from New York, her crew used seven different sail combinations, but they never had to reef. (Peter Barlow photo, *The Rudder* (February 1958): 8)

weather warmed up, and the breeze gave the *Talaria* an easy run. Newcomb and his crew decided to try out the squaresail. The gear all worked well; setting and taking in the sail went smoothly, which says a lot for Francis's ability to envision and design a satisfactory rig with which he had no experience. The *Talaria* liked her squaresail; having it set eased both her motion and her steering. "The [weight of the] yard [aloft] made a perceptible difference in the roll, causing it to be slower and deeper. However this was not objectionable."

A day later, the *Talaria* was again on a beam reach under jib, foresail, and mainsail in a breeze gusting over 25 knots. "The ship is going faster and faster until finally the shocks and rolls become excessive as she leaps over the swells like a live thing. Loud complaints from the watch below holding an after dinner kaffeklatsch in the cabin." So, they took the mainsail off her, feeling grateful that it was inboard and that its area was only 261 square feet.

On the next-to-last day of the passage, with the breeze going light and coming more ahead, they tried the overlapping foresail. They found it could be "rigged with ease and sets well. Adds about a knot to our speed."

On this passage, the *Talaria* carried her people just over 1,000 miles at an average speed of six knots, nearly all under sail, in weather that included the initial gale and the steep seas of northerly Gulf Stream squalls. Aside from seasickness and the lesser discomforts of the excessive motion of a boat being driven hard at times in a rough sea, the crew fared well. They never had a moment's concern about the safety of their vessel. The only damage to the boat was the torn mizzen, caused by the accidental jibe.

In summing up the *Talaria*'s performance at the end of his *Rudder* article, Beebe wrote, "The motion was described in the log several times as violent. However I am sure it was no worse than other types would have displayed in the seas and on the courses we followed. There is no doubt in my mind that the *Talaria* can be driven much harder than more conventional vessels of the same weight. It is the crew that will cry for mercy, not the hull." And he continued: "She rolls deeply and easily. Our thoughts were inconclusive as to whether more stability with the risk of a sharper snap-back would be worthwhile. Personally, I would say no, for the really vicious rolls that caused havoc below were the result of climbing over big waves that came in on the beam. It did seem that the idea that a narrow beam will reduce the 'pitch-out' at the top of one of these mountains was demonstrated." Beebe concluded: "The Marco Polo, as represented by *Talaria*, can do everything claimed for her. She is a tremendous sea boat, easy to work, quite suited to a one man watch."[51]

Boris visited Francis two weeks before Beebe's article appeared and gave him an advance look at it. Francis lost no time in writing comments to Beebe. On the violent rolling, he wrote, "Of course if *Talaria*'s center of weight were higher she would have a slower period of roll, and this would have been the case if she had had a heavy motor near the waterline, and large fuel tanks whose centers were above the LWL." In other words, the modifications to the *Talaria* for coastal cruising gave her a quicker roll. Actually, though, inspection of the Marco Polo's profile construction drawing shows that the position of the *Talaria*'s engine under the cockpit would be, if anything, a little higher in the boat than an engine in the large, forward engine room. The lack of large fuel tanks centered above the waterline was the big factor. If filled with diesel fuel, the Marco Polo's tanks would give her 7,200 pounds of weight—half the weight of her ballast—centered about a foot above the waterline. Such loading on the *Talaria* certainly would have slowed her roll, though the effect would decrease as fuel was burned.[52]

Francis and Beebe continued their discussion of the *Talaria*'s rolling in two more letters. Their analysis becomes confusing, because they intermingle reasons for rolling that is objectionably quick with rolling that is objectionably pendulum-like. Francis commented that two reasons for her quick roll were that her rig was low and that it had been carefully designed to save weight aloft. More weight aloft, however, would have made the roll more pendulum-like. This factor was demonstrated when the hoisting of the *Talaria*'s yard for the squaresail slowed and deepened her roll.[53]

The slack bilges of the design also contributed to the pendulum roll. Beebe was mystified at Francis's description of the Marco Polo's bilges as "hard" in the text accompanying her lines drawing in *The Rudder*. Beebe wrote: "I am absolutely astonished at his describing her as having hard bilges. She has about the slackest bilge of any yacht designed in this country in years and I think it shows in her motion."[54]

Years later, Beebe warned a prospective Marco Polo builder, Harmon Hunt, about her rolling: "She seemed to have no stability but the keel weight. No matter what amount of sail we carried she would roll equally each side of the vertical. In effect she was rolling like a motorboat in a rough sea, than which nothing is worse. It was a 'pendulum roll.'" He recommended "some sort of roll reduction for making her suitable as a passage-maker." As Beebe looked back on his experience in the *Talaria* from the perspective of sixteen years, and with Francis no longer alive to be offended, he wrote, "In deference to Francis I played this down in the [*Rudder*] article, but the motion below decks was so bad it was hardly possible to do anything." Beebe came to believe that, "in spite of my admiration for Francis Herreshoff's abilities, I am afraid that in this case he goofed."[55]

It is revealing, however, that Newcomb and his crew preferred to drive the *Talaria* at high speed in heavy weather and put up with her resulting violent motion, rather than heave to and get some relief from it. On one occasion, they did slow her down to ease her motion. Her design gave them the choice, for she was designed specifically for heaving to as well as for driving hard. And it is worth remembering that Beebe's experience of the *Talaria*'s most violent motion was born in a Gulf Stream northeast gale, with wind against current. Richard Henry Dana, in *Two Years Before the Mast*, wrote that the square-rigged ship *Alert*, in which he was returning from California to Boston around Cape Horn in winter, never gave her crew such a seasick-inducing motion as when she crossed the Gulf Stream in a gale. "She was pitched and jerked about in all manner of ways; the sails seeming to have no steadying power over her," wrote Dana.[56]

With regard to the *Talaria*'s steering, both in his *Rudder* article and in a letter to Francis, Beebe suggested taming the far-turning rudder with removable stops that would limit its swing for normal steering but could be taken off when heaving to, in order to let the rudder turn forward, if necessary, to relieve the strain on it. Beebe mentioned that Newcomb had intended to install such stops before the trip to the Bahamas. Francis made no comment on this idea. A later owner of the *Talaria* had no difficulty with the rudder and steering system. He wrote to Francis: "In spite of the article in *Rudder*, I find *Talaria* can be made to steer herself for short periods from close hauled through wind just abaft the beam, even without lashing the wheel."[57]

Robert Beebe's report of the *Talaria*'s performance was important to anyone seriously contemplating building a Marco Polo, because it was the first and only detailed account of how the vessel behaved at sea. While Beebe had plenty of praise for the seaworthiness and speed of the Marco Polo, his comments about the discomfort of her violent motion were a red flag to prospective owners. The naming of the design after the explorer who wanted to "get onward" without the object of "comfort," as Francis had described him, had come home to roost.

If Beebe had pulled his punches regarding the *Talaria*'s motion in his *Rudder* article, Francis certainly pulled his with Beebe. He did appreciate Beebe's careful report on the performance of his

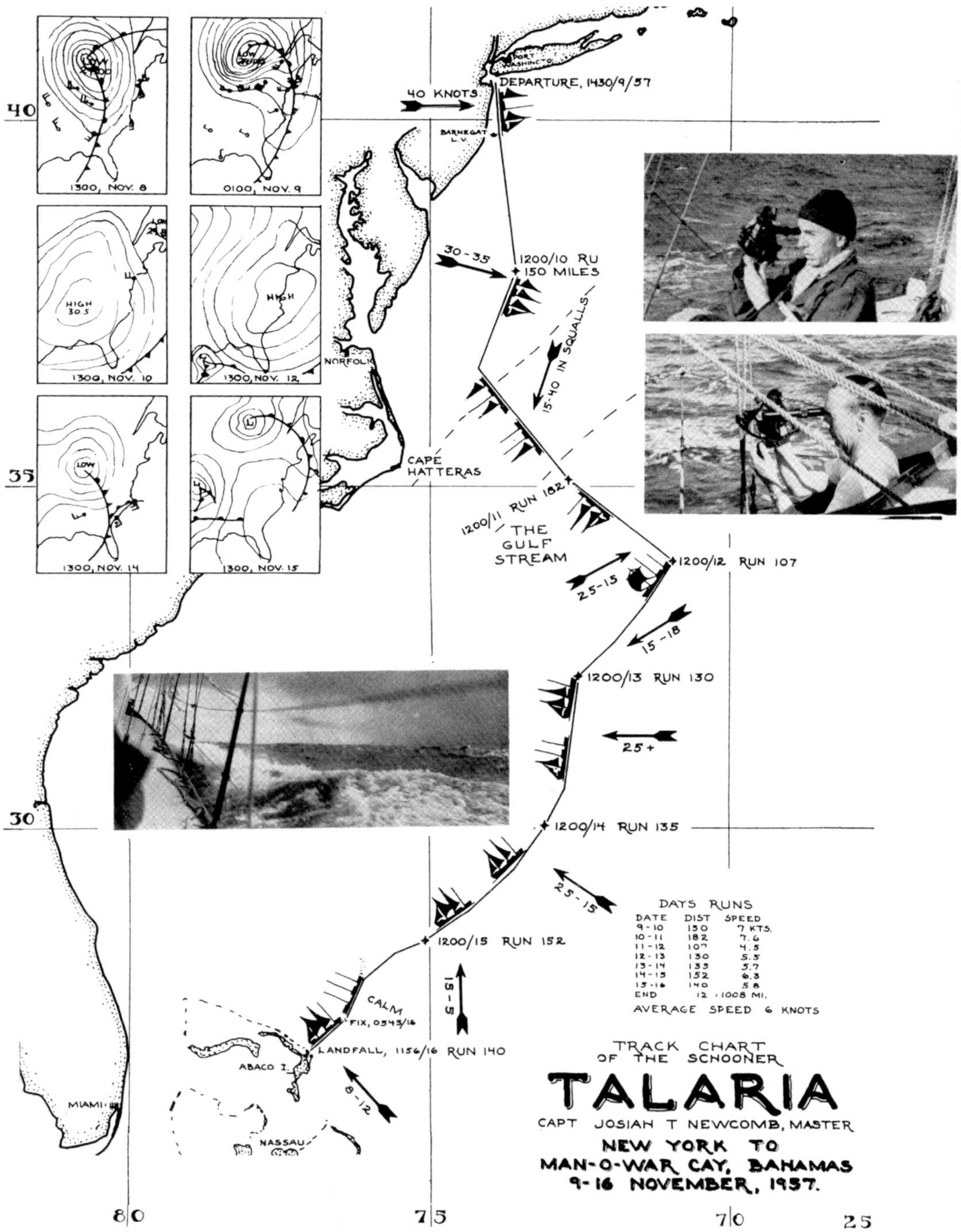

Navigator Robert Beebe's track chart of the *Talaria*'s passage. Francis was particularly pleased to see this drawing, for, with the supporting text of Beebe's article, it furnished him with a detailed report of the performance of one of his designs. This was the kind of information he could rarely get from owners and that he was not often inclined to seek by sailing with them. (*The Rudder* (February 1958): 6)

design and engaged in objective discussion of that performance in his correspondence with Beebe, but in later years, his comments about Beebe's article and about the conduct of the *Talaria*'s voyage were scathing. To one correspondent, he wrote, "as for Marco Polo, I would not pay much attention to what Captain Beebe wrote for I have talked with one of the men who went on that trip and, although Captain Beebe does not realize it, he made an awful mess of things." Francis criticized the time of day and the time of year when the *Talaria* started her voyage and the fact that she was taken to sea in a gale. "You will notice that they always seemed to use the wrong combination of sails." Francis was off base with this comment, for Newcomb generally went along with Francis's own published advice about how the boat should be shortened down. Francis went on to criticize the *Talaria*'s offshore route to the Bahamas, saying that, given the weather conditions, she should have hugged the coast. "A sailing yacht is a different proposition than an aircraft carrier [in which Beebe had served]." In commenting on Beebe's article to another correspondent, Francis wrote: "Unfortunately, it was a quite ridiculous article. It certainly tested the boat for being fool-proof."[58]

Francis did not want to hear that his long, narrow, slab-sided "lifeboat with a keel" rolled like a destroyer. It was clear that the Marco Polo was an exceptionally fast and able passage-maker; what was not clear was whether or not the crew could survive the motion that accompanied her speed and whether or not modifications could be made to the design to help them. Francis laid the *Talaria*'s occasional violent motion to the inexperience of her crew and did not take Beebe's comments seriously enough to make further analysis of the Marco Polo's hull shape, rig, and weight distribution. And, as we have seen, it was not in his nature to revisit a completed design to improve it or remove any shortcomings. Unlike some designers he scorned, like John Alden or Olin Stephens, he had no desire for and would have taken no pleasure in testing a design at sea. Far from experiencing the motion of a Marco Polo in rough weather, L. Francis Herreshoff never saw a Marco Polo afloat.[59]

The Marco Polo design did not prove popular. Critical as he was of the *Talaria*'s voyage and of Beebe's report of it, Francis did not blame Beebe for lack of sales of Marco Polo plans. While a timid sailor or one prone to seasickness might well have been put off by Beebe's article, a bolder would-be voyager with a cast-iron stomach might well have been attracted to the Marco Polo by his description of steering her through rough seas at high speed. Perhaps an all-too-typical reaction to the three-masted lifeboat was that of Charles Darcy, who delivered the *Talaria* to New York from Man-O-War Cay after Josiah Newcomb's untimely death. Darcy, who made the passage at an average of seven knots, called her "an oddball boat that no one would want."[60]

Not everyone agreed with Darcy. Harmon Hunt, of Hamilton, Massachusetts, who, in 1977, built a Marco Polo despite Beebe's warning about her rolling, said that Beebe was "too critical" of the boat in his article, but though he took her twice to Bermuda, he never had his *Huntress* in a gale at sea. Hunt had previously survived the fringes of two hurricanes on voyages from Gloucester to the Virgin Islands in his Tahiti ketch, a vessel that he praised (fortunately not to L. Francis Herreshoff) as "one hell of a boat" in heavy weather. He did comment that his Marco Polo was not close-winded, but Francis designed her specifically to be efficient when going to windward under power. A later owner, Harold Boardman, of Charlestown, Rhode Island, gave his Marco Polo perhaps the perfect name: *Roll and Go*. His comment was, "If you don't have enough sail up, she'll give you something to think about."[61]

Gretchen Snyder, an experienced captain who delivered a Marco Polo from St. Thomas to Bermuda, with some heavy-weather motor-sailing, said, "she was a very comfortable, easily handled boat." An Australian sailor wrote of a friend's Marco Polo: "Her motion in a seaway was delightful with none of the gut snatching roll one sometimes experiences in the ocean racing craft but above and beyond this she gives a great feeling of competence and ability. We took her into Port Phillip on the last of the ebb and I don't think we even got the decks wet going through the rip." Another experienced captain, Steve Macek, who regularly makes passages with his wife, Irene, in his Marco Polo, the *Star*, between Woods Hole, Massachusetts, and the Caribbean, said that her only uncomfortable rolling is in a seaway with the wind aft (like many another vessel), and he can tame the rolling by hoisting the square yard, with or without its sail.[62]

Newcomb's widow sought help from Francis in trying to sell the *Talaria* in 1959. He wrote her, "I wish I had a little more money [she was asking $25,000] and I would purchase her myself, but I am afraid I should not have the time to use her." In fact, Francis then had the money and the time for a Marco Polo, though at age sixty-eight, or at any age, he had no inclination to invest either in a cruising boat. The *Talaria* was eventually bought by a Frenchman who was a paraplegic. He sailed her across the Atlantic with the help of two crew, one of whom had no sailing experience. The Frenchman operated the *Talaria* all by himself as a charter boat in Portugal.[63]

Eight years after the *Talaria*'s voyage south, Francis called the Marco Polo "an awfully good boat that somehow or other never took ahold right." Francis made different estimates of the number of Marco Polos built, from "very few" to "about twenty." Even the latter estimate is probably conservative, but if twenty Marco Polos have been built, that is perhaps as much acceptance as could be expected for a vessel designed to "get onward" with minimum regard for "comfort." Problems of rolling aside, not many voyagers would want a 55-foot boat with the cramped accommodations of the Marco Polo. Francis, knowing the great value of simplicity in a boat, designed the Marco Polo to suit his own Spartan tastes and was disappointed when only a score or so of sailors showed that they shared and appreciated his concepts for an ocean cruiser. Just as some sailors could win races with L. Francis Herreshoff designs, while others couldn't, some sailors could live comfortably in the simple cabins of a Marco Polo, while others couldn't.[64]

And Francis chafed at the design changes that owners made to their Marco Polos. "There have been ones with no rigging, some with sloop rigs, and some with staysail schooner rigs. Only God knows why." He approved the suggestions of two early enthusiasts that they build in steel and ferro-cement respectively, but he discouraged the prospective builder of a steam-powered Marco Polo. Late in his life, Francis had the satisfaction of learning of two Marco Polos being built exactly to the design, with big engine room, big fuel tanks amidships, and all. And there was little doubt that the boats could be good performers. With a strong breeze on the quarter, a Marco Polo was driven to win an ocean race across Bass Strait to Tasmania in 1965. Another, powered with a 26-horsepower, air-cooled Deutz 2-cylinder diesel, and with tanks for only 350 gallons of fuel instead of the specified 1,000 gallons, still could motor more than 4,000 miles at 5 knots.[65]

Arthur Rowe, a NASA engineer, built a Marco Polo at Cohasset, Massachusetts, in 1975, primarily as a fall-out shelter. Her deck structure included aluminum for protection against gamma rays. The hull was wood-core fiberglass to a thickness of 1½ inches. With a Maxi folding propeller, an 80-horsepower Ford Lehman diesel, and 600 gallons of fuel, she had a range of 5,400 miles at seven knots. And she could sail. In a race from Darwin to Bali, she finished a day ahead of Swan sloops. "The Indian Ocean was a washing machine," Rowe said. "We were fine." In more moderate conditions, off the wind, Rowe used to set a Wianno Jr. spinnaker from the mainmast, dumping into the squaresail on the foremast. He also had a huge reaching jib and big main and mizzen staysails. Rowe's vessel was later the Maceks' *Star*.[66]

Inevitably, prospective owners wanted Marco Polos both smaller and bigger than Francis's design for a 55-footer. He, himself, was interested in the concept of a smaller version and drew a preliminary pencil sketch of a 46-footer. Unfortunately, the undated drawing is not reproducible. It shows a whaleboat-type hull with well-rounded sections, a short and shoal ballast keel, and a separate, freestanding rudder. She has a turtleback forward, but not aft. She is 41 feet, 6 inches long on the waterline, with a beam of 8 feet and a draft of 4 feet. Sail area is 558 square feet. She carries 650 gallons of fuel and 225 gallons of water.[67]

This smaller version is more extreme than the Marco Polo, in that she has less displacement for her length, would be even more easily driven under power and even faster under sail for her length, would have an even livelier motion, and has even less accommodation space for her length. She is not everyman's boat, but, like her big sister, would be very seaworthy and capable of remarkable passages under power or sail.

As we have seen, the Marco Polo was based on two much larger vessels that Francis had previously designed. He did not draw any further bigger versions. In 1966, however, his old friend from Bristol days, Nicholas Potter, had a client who wanted a big Marco Polo designed around his 150-horsepower diesel engine. Potter wrote Francis about the project, saying he had figured that proper dimensions would be: length on deck, 73 feet; waterline length, 65 feet; and beam, 13 feet. Francis, at age seventy-five, offered to help "in any way except making drawings." Seven months later, Potter had not progressed very far with "the blown-up version of the Marco Polo." The project died.[68]

The Marco Polo design elicits strong emotional reactions, both positive and negative. True art begets controversy. The writer is on the positive side: the Marco Polo is one of my favorite boats for a vicarious voyage. The best way to experience a Herreshoff boat, of course, is to be on board and underway, and the more days and nights the better. But, until that is possible, if you can learn to read boat plans, then you can imagine the experience of sailing the boat from the lines and sail plan that Francis drew, just as one who can read music can imagine the experience of hearing a symphony by looking at the symbols inked by Beethoven.

Of the eight objectives for the design of the Marco Polo that Francis shared with the readers of *The Rudder* in the January 1945 issue, he fully achieved six: long range under power, a sail plan that could be handled by one person on watch, extreme seaworthiness, moderate draft, a hull shape well suited to heaving to or lying to a sea anchor, and relatively low wind resistance. He partially achieved the other two, simplicity of construction and accommodations for up to five. The Marco Polo's rig and rudder were less simple to build than might be desired. She had five bunks, to be sure, but while Francis would not have minded her lack of amenities, many owners would have.

Achieving this set of objectives made the Marco Polo a revolutionary design in 1945. Francis did not develop further the concept of such a boat, nor did any other designer copy the type. To this day, the Marco Polo remains unique.

CHAPTER 22

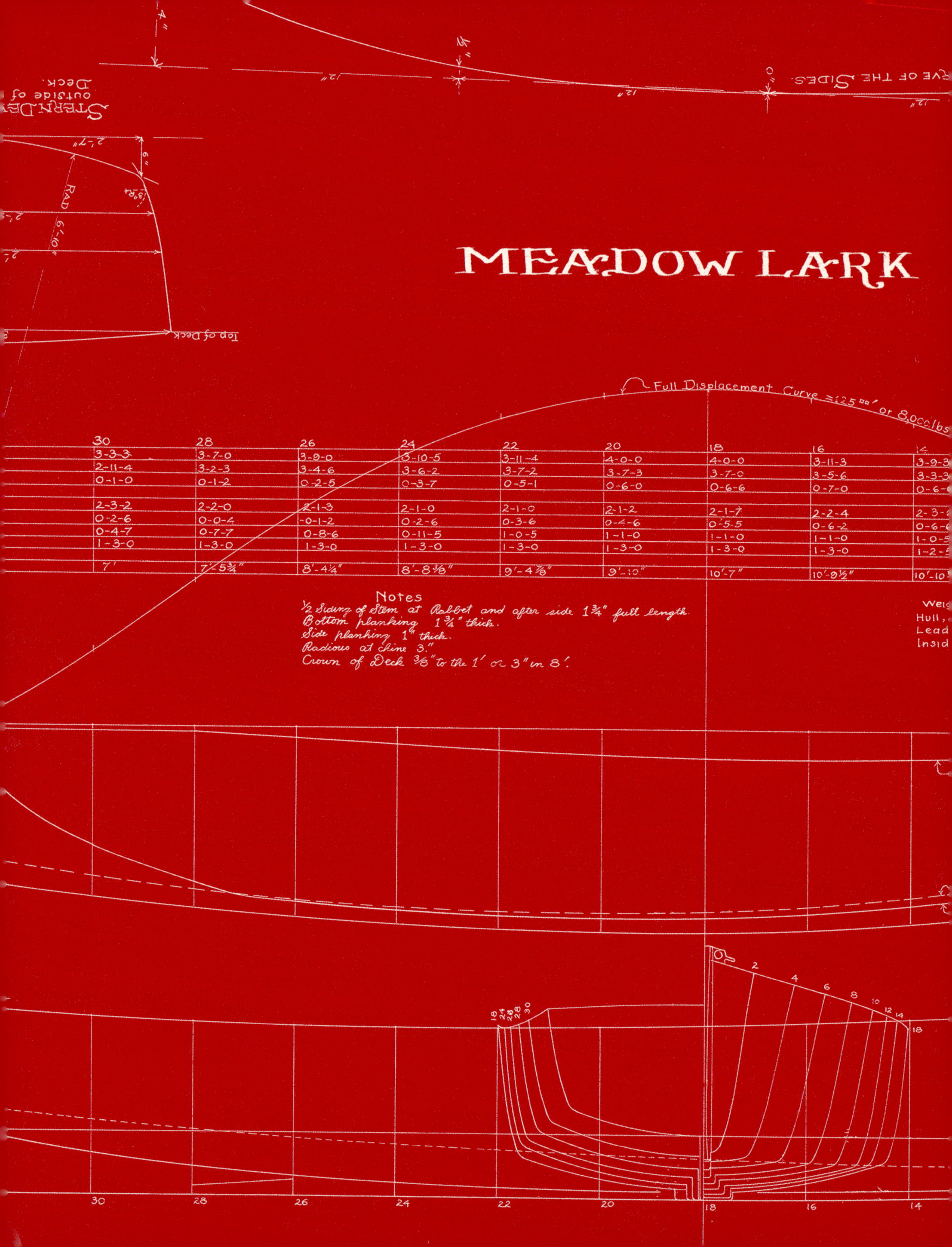

MEADOW LARK
Full Displacement Curve =125 lbs' or 8,000 lbs
Notes
½ Siding of Stem at Rabbet and after side 1¾" full length.
Bottom planking 1¾" thick.
Side planking 1" thick.
Radious at chine 3."
Crown of Deck ⅜" to the 1' or 3" in 8'.
Top of Deck

CATHARSIS

"After this next article, I am going to start the book, N. G. Herreshoff and Some of His Yachts."

—L. FRANCIS HERRESHOFF TO BORIS LAUER-LEONARDI, 1948

Boris Lauer-Leonardi, the excellent editor of *The Rudder*, was on the lookout for a first-class writer for his magazine, someone who could back up his star, L. Francis Herreshoff. During the war, Llewellyn Howland was being published in the *Atlantic Monthly*, and Boris knew that Howland was an experienced cruising man who had inspired the design, at his son Waldo's Concordia Company, of an outstanding yawl. In April 1944, Boris went to Hope's Garden, Howland's big terra-cotta house in Padanaram (South Dartmouth), near New Bedford, to recruit him. Boris reported to Francis of his visit with Howland and added: "He is a great admirer of yours." Francis knew Howland and encouraged Boris to pursue him as an author for *The Rudder.* Boris was successful; thus began a wonderful series in *The Rudder* of Howland's colorful stories about his boyhood adventures "Southwest and by West of Cape Cod," the area of Buzzards Bay and beyond used as a title when the pieces were published as a book by Harvard University Press. And thus began, also, a mutual-admiration friendship between Francis and Llewellyn Howland. Francis wrote to Boris: "I think these two [Howland's first articles] will be the best contributions to *The Rudder* during the whole year."[1]

Skipper Howland was thirteen years Francis's senior. He stayed with Francis at The Castle, and Francis journeyed to Padanaram for one or two overnight visits, rare travels for him. When Francis later had his book of imaginary cruising yarns published as *The Compleat Cruiser,* he mimicked not only Isaak Walton's title, but also his ornate, two-page dedication, beginning: "To the Right Worshipful Llewellyn Howland, My Most Honored Friend." In January 1945, Boris engineered a meeting at Hope's Garden of himself; Francis; Howland; Warren Sheppard, the fine marine artist whose work was appearing in *The Rudder;* and Clifford Ashley, another outstanding marine artist and author of *The Yankee Whaler* and the recently published *Ashley Book of Knots.* The only tangible result that we know of from this formidable gathering is Francis's praiseful review in *The Rudder* of Ashley's superb knot book; would that we had even an agenda for the meeting.[2]

Waldo Howland wanted to settle on the design of a good small boat that he could build at the Concordia Company to keep his crew busy in slow times. He considered the Herreshoff 12½-footer, since this outstanding little vessel was no longer being produced in Bristol. But E. Leslie Goodwin,

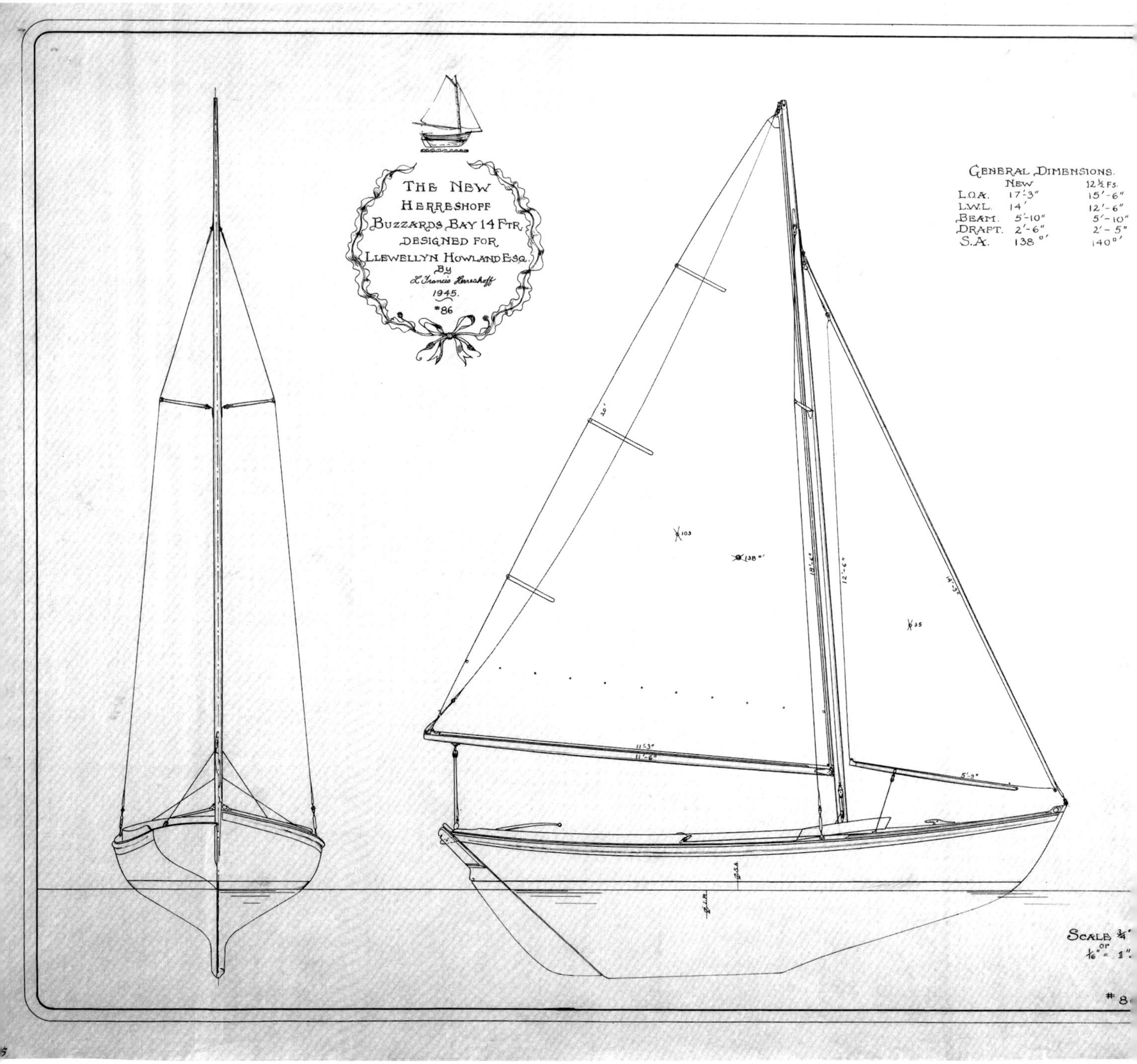
THE NEW
HERRESHOFF
BUZZARDS BAY 14 FTR.
DESIGNED FOR
LLEWELLYN HOWLAND ESQ.
By
L. Francis Herreshoff
1945.
#86
GENERAL DIMENSIONS.
NEW 12½ FS.
L.O.A. 17'-3" 15'-6"
L.W.L. 14' 12'-6"
BEAM. 5'-10" 5'-10"
DRAFT. 2'-6" 2'-5"
S.A. 138 □' 140 □'
SCALE ¾"
or
1/16" = 1".
#8

at Cape Cod Shipbuilding in Wareham, had bought the rights to Nathanael's designs for smaller yachts, so Concordia would have to pay him a royalty. The solution was for Llewellyn Howland to commission a design from his friend L. Francis Herreshoff for a slightly larger version of the 12½-footer. Concordia could build a prototype for Skipper Howland and could then go on building boats to the new design as time and the market permitted.[3]

Francis obliged with his design No. 86. He drew an outboard profile and a lines plan with a table of offsets for a Herreshoff 12½-footer stretched out to a waterline length of 14 feet, putting the design in between the 12½ and the similar 16-foot-waterline Fish Class. The design came along slowly—too slowly, as things turned out—because Francis was busy with his *Rudder* work and his move to The Castle. In January 1946, Francis wrote, "sometime this winter I expect to finish the drawings [for No. 86]." But there was no need for him to make up a construction plan; later that year Waldo Howland was able to work out an arrangement with Carl Beetle for Concordia to build Beetle cats, the little Cape Cod catboat that has proved to be even more popular than the Herreshoff 12½-footer. For Francis, the Buzzards Bay 14-footer was no more than a pleasant exercise. The design would actually be a success for him, but only posthumously.[4]

In later years, quite a few Buzzards Bay 14s would be built, perhaps stimulated by the publication of her plans in Francis's *Sensible Cruising Designs* in 1973. In 1976, Rob Pittaway, a staff member at Mystic Seaport Museum, drew up a construction plan for the design. The Boat School at Eastport, Maine, used the design as a project for second-year students in its boatbuilding program. Hodgdon Brothers built a Buzzards Bay 14 in the traditional way of wood; at least two were built of cold-molded wood, one in New Zealand; and MacDougall's Cape Cod Marine Service in Falmouth offered a fiberglass version. Today, Artisan Boatworks, in Rockport, Maine, will build you a wooden one with a taller mast and 20 square feet more sail area, which is logical, given the nearly equal sail areas of Nathanael's 12½ and Francis's 14. If, in 1946, anyone had predicted all this interest in the Buzzards Bay 14 to L. Francis Herreshoff, he would have scoffed.[5]

Back in 1943, Russ and Jane Genner, friends of Boris Lauer-Leonardi in Port Washington and great fans of Francis, asked him to design them a boat bigger than their beloved Prudence H-23, the *Button.* They didn't think that the H-28, whose plans were then running in *The Rudder*, would satisfy them. What they wanted was a 30-foot sloop, and could she have a bow like those of the *Tiogas*?

Well, yes they could, but design No. 83 became a frustrating experience for both the Genners and for Francis. Drawing an outboard profile and sail plan for the Genners' approval posed no problem; Francis had the plan blueprinted and sent it off in late October.[6]

The drawing did indeed show a beautiful clipper bow, the seventh he had designed, and

LEFT: **Francis's design No. 86 was a 14-foot-waterline version of his father's popular 12½-footer. By 1945, when Francis drew the Buzzards Bay 14, many of the 12½s had Marconi rig instead of the original gaff rig; it was the newer rig that he adopted for the larger version of the design. At 138 square feet, the sail area of the 14-footer is only a foot more than that of the 12½; the mainboom of both boats was the same length, so on the 14-footer it overhung the stern less. The customer was, ostensibly, Francis's friend and fellow *Rudder* author, Llewellyn Howland of Padanaram, Massachusetts.** (© Mystic Seaport Museum, Daniel S. Gregory Ships Plans Library, SP38.20.4)

	18'	16'6"	15'	13'6"	12'	10'6"	9'	7'6"	6'	4'6"	3'	1'6"	0	
HIGHTS.														
Top of Deck at Sides	1-9-1	1-6-5	1-4-6	1-3-5	1-3-1	1-3-1	1-3-4	1-4-4	1-5-6	1-7-4	1-9-4	2-0-0	2-3-0	Top of Deck.
Buttock 24"		1-3-0	0-7-1	+0-2-3	-0-0-7	-0-2-7	-0-3-2	-0-2-1	0-1-2	0-9-3	2-2-4			B 24"
" 18"	+1-6-4	+0-10-1	+0-3-7	-0-0-6	-0-4-1	-0-5-7	-0-6-7	-0-6-1	-0-3-5	0-1-6	1-1-2	2-10-2		B 18"
" 12"	+1-3-1	+0-7-5	+0-1-5	-0-3-2	-0-6-7	-0-9-1	-0-10-2	-0-9-5	-0-7-4	-0-3-4	+0-4-4	1-10-3		B 12"
" 6"	+1-1-2	+0-6-0	-0-0-1	-0-6-1	-0-10-6	-1-1-7	+1-3-2	-1-2-3	-0-11-7	-0-8-3	-0-2-2	0-11-1	2-11-7	B 6"
Rabbet			-0-3-0	-1-4-0	-2-0-0	-1-10-4	-1-9-0	-1-7-4	-1-6-0	-1-1-1	-0-7-4	0-1-3	2-4-0	Rabbet
Face		+1-0-0	-0-6-0	-2-0-0	-2-5-5	-2-5-0+	-2-4-4	-2-1-4	-1-7-0	-1-1-5	-0-8-2	0-0-0	2-3-0	Face
½ BREADTHS.														
At Deck	1-9-0	2-2-0	2-5-5	2-8-2	2-10-1	2-11-0	2-11-0	2-10-2	2-8-2	2-4-2	1-10-0	1-1-0	0-0-5	Deck
WL + 18"										2-3-7	1-8-4	0-9-6		WL+18"
" " + 12"	0-1-4	1-8-7	2-4-0	2-7-5	2-9-6	2-10-6	2-10-5	2-9-4	2-6-5	2-1-4	1-5-2	0-6-4		WL+12"
" " + 6"		0-6-4	1-10-3	2-4-5	2-7-6	2-9-2	2-8-6	2-7-2	2-3-6	1-9-5	1-1-2	0-3-4		WL+6"
L.W.L.		0-1-1	0-6-4	1-1-4	2-1-6	2-4-0	2-4-2	2-2-6	1-10-6	1-4-0	0-8-2	0-0-2		L.W.L.
WL - 6"			0-0-6	0-6-2	1-1-7	1-5-7	1-7-2	1-6-2	1-2-2	0-8-6	0-2-2			W.L.-6"
" " - 12"			0-0-3	0-1-7	0-4-5	0-7-6	0-9-4	0-8-4	0-6-0	0-1-7				W.L.-12"
" " - 18"			0-0-2	0-1-1	0-2-6	0-3-4	0-4-4	0-3-5	0-1-0					W.L.-18"
" " - 24"				0-0-6	0-1-5	0-2-5	0-2-7	0-1-5	0-1-5					W.L.-24"
Face		1-9-2	0-0-6	0-0-6	?	?	?	?	0-0-3	0-0-2	0-0-2	0-0-2	0-0-5	Face
Diagonal 1.				0-2-0	0-3-7	0-5-6	0-6-7	0-6-2	0-4-4	0-1-4				D 1
" 2.			0-3-3	0-8-6	1-0-3	1-2-4	1-3-4	1-3-0	1-1-2	0-8-3	0-6-0	0-0-2		D 2
" 3.	0-0-4	0-9-2	1-4-4	1-9-4	2-1-1	2-2-3	2-3-4	2-2-7	2-0-3	1-8-0	1-2-1	0-6-0		D 3
" 4.	1-4-6	2-0-5	2-6-2	2-10-0	3-0-3	3-1-4	3-1-9	3-0-0	2-9-1	2-4-1	1-9-0	0-11-3		D 4

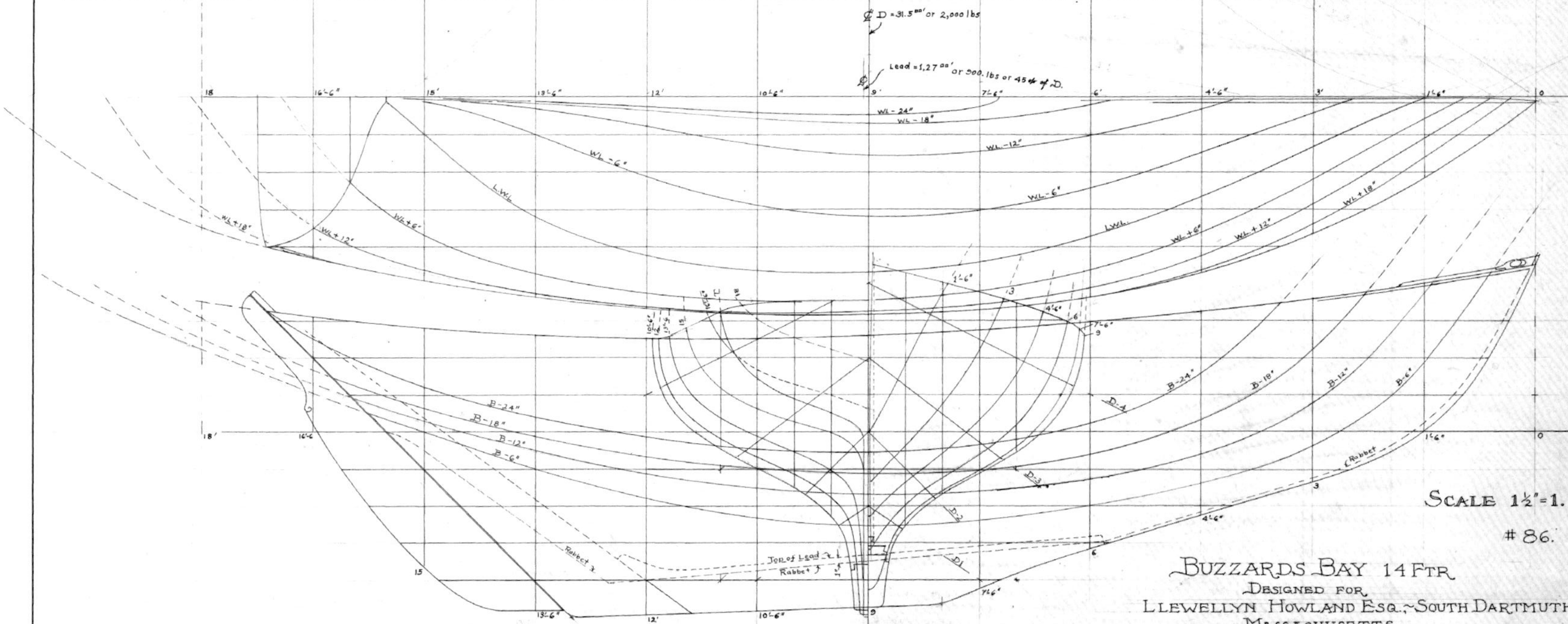

Scale 1½"=1.

 # 86.

Buzzards Bay 14 Ftr

Designed for

Llewellyn Howland Esq. ~ South Dartmouth, Massachusetts.

by then, L. Francis Herreshoff's most recognizable trademark. To keep the construction cost down, he gave the sloop a flat, transom stern, well-raked to be handsome, and an outboard rudder. Unaccountably, he curved her underwater profile between the forefoot and the ballast keel, a line that he had drawn dead straight on each of his preceding clipper-bowed designs. He gave her a generous, but not tall, double-head rig.

Russ Genner's initial response to the drawing was a complaint that it didn't show the roller reefing gear that he had specified for the mainsail. Francis wrote back not to worry, it was just a detail he forgot to draw in. Nine days after his first response, Genner was more positive: "Her pleasing sheer and character have made me fall in love with her already and she grows on me more every day."[7]

But Francis was busy with his writing for *The Rudder*. He was finishing his series on the H-28 and was also producing an essay nearly every month on some facet of marine lore, pieces that would later be published in a small book by the Rudder Publishing Company, *The Writings of L. Francis Herreshoff*. And he was starting the most demanding writing he had yet attempted, "The Common Sense of Yacht Design." More than three months went by, and in March 1944, Francis wrote to Jane Genner, "it may be some little time now before I do much more on the design." At this point, the Genners were in no hurry. They were starting their own marine business and were short on cash. Jane responded quickly to Francis with, "it will be some time before she can be built."[8]

Boris, ever the enthusiast, had encouraged Francis to take on the design project for the Genners, and he published the drawing for No. 83 in his March issue. Francis got a quick reaction from a reader who wanted the design converted to a ketch. Francis turned him aside, writing, "I am so much behindhand in my work that I cannot take on any more orders for at present I am working all alone."[9]

No. 83 lay dormant for over a year, which was all right with the clients. By June 1945, however, Jane Genner was writing Francis asking for more plans so they could build. Yet there was an unrealistic ring to her letter, for she wrote that they were thinking of selling the *Button* because they didn't have time to maintain her properly. And besides, three months before this, Francis had heard from Boris that he thought the Genners were in over their heads with their boat business and he doubted they would be able to build the bigger sloop. Francis replied to Jane Genner, "I have been so busy that I have not had time to do anything on No. 83 and doubt if I shall for some little time."[10]

As we have seen, he had been busy, but not with designing yachts for clients. He had moved from 25 Front Street to the Castle. And he now was producing two demanding articles per month for his growing number of *Rudder* fans, one for "The Common Sense of Yacht Design" and one for "How To Build the Marco Polo H 55," the latter of which required design and drawing work.

In January 1946, the Genners were again saying they would have to put off building No. 83. Francis soon wrote an inquirer about the design that he had dropped the project, but he didn't tell

---

LEFT: **The lines and offsets of the Buzzards Bay 14. She is 17 feet, 3 inches long on deck; with a beam of 5 feet, 10 inches; and a draft of 2 feet, 6 inches. Compared to the 12½-footer, she is 1 foot, 9 inches longer on deck; 1 foot, 6 inches longer on the waterline; with the same beam; and 1 inch more draft. The only change in hull shape is that Francis has straightened the curvature of the stem a little. He kept the plane curve sheerline of the 12½ that his father had given her, such that if she were turned upside down on a flat surface and then heeled over, the whole length of her deck-edge would be in contact with that surface.** (© Mystic Seaport Museum, Daniel S. Gregory Ships Plans Library, SP38.20.1)

the Genners that until another nine months had gone by, when they visited him at The Castle in early October. Following that visit, Jane wrote Francis of their disappointment and asked for the return of the $100 they had paid for the profile drawing three years earlier. Francis's reply was that he would try to get out a set of lines and a "rough construction plan." Still, there was no progress.[11]

Meanwhile, he was proceeding apace with "The Common Sense of Yacht Design"; finished the Marco Polo series; designed the Double Paddle Canoe for *The Rudder*; designed new rigs for three yachts (a sixth new rig for the Q boat *Nor'easter IV*, now *Taygeta*; made a fifth modification to the staysail-schooner rig he had designed for the New York 50 *Pleione*; drafted a new rig for his Burgess, Swasey, and Paine design, the *Santee;* and finished the design of the Buzzards Bay 14 for Llewellyn Howland. Moreover, he was starting another How-To-Build series for *The Rudder*.

The new *Rudder* How-To-Build design from L. Francis Herreshoff appeared in the March 1947 issue. The Genners must have been startled. Apparently, there was their No. 83, stretched out from 32 feet to 36 feet and given a ketch rig. The only difference was that Francis had returned to his straight line in the forward part of the underwater profile. Francis called the new design the Nereia. By August, all the basic plans for the Nereia had been published. In September, Russ Genner wrote Francis that he wanted design No. 83 finished. Francis replied that he would try to do the lines at no extra charge, but that he could do no more than that on No. 83. He never did draw the lines. And the Genners could peruse in ten more issues of *The Rudder* further detailed plans of the Nereia, right down to a special pram Francis designed as her tender.[12]

The Genners no doubt frustrated Francis with their on-again, off-again dithering over building No. 83, and he certainly must have frustrated them, when, after four years of stalling, he turned away from their sloop and instead designed the Nereia for *The Rudder*. No further letters between the Genners and Francis have come to light, so it is not known if or how the unsatisfactory situation surrounding design No. 83 may have been resolved.

Less than a year after the last installment of the H-28 series, Francis wrote to a correspondent: "People are asking for a bigger boat than the H-28. Maybe I can design one for *The Rudder*." And, long before he was finished with the Marco Polo series, Boris was asking him to follow that design with a 35-foot *Tioga* for *The Rudder.* Boris wanted an enlarged H-28 with a clipper bow. Even with this early consideration of a small *Tioga*, and probably discussion with Boris of what she should be like, it seems amazing that Francis could present her design to his *Rudder* fans the month after his last installment on the Marco Polo, without skipping a beat. Especially so, since the new design was neither simply an enlarged H-28 nor a reduced *Tioga*; she was her own unique self. But L. Francis Herreshoff had many yacht designs swirling around in his mind, and even, we can suppose, in his subconscious, so he could pull one out readily and put it on paper. Moreover, he had started on the design of a 32-foot *Tioga* for the Genners.[13]

Rudder readers who opened their March 1947

RIGHT: **The 32-foot sloop that Francis started to design for Russell and Jane Genner but never finished. Her waterline length is 27 feet, 9 inches; beam, 10 feet, 3 inches; draft, 4 feet, 6 inches; and sail area 563 square feet. Note the unusual curve in the forward part of her underwater profile (unusual for Francis, when combined with the clipper bow).** (© Mystic Seaport Museum, Daniel S. Gregory Ships Plans Library, SP38.204.1)

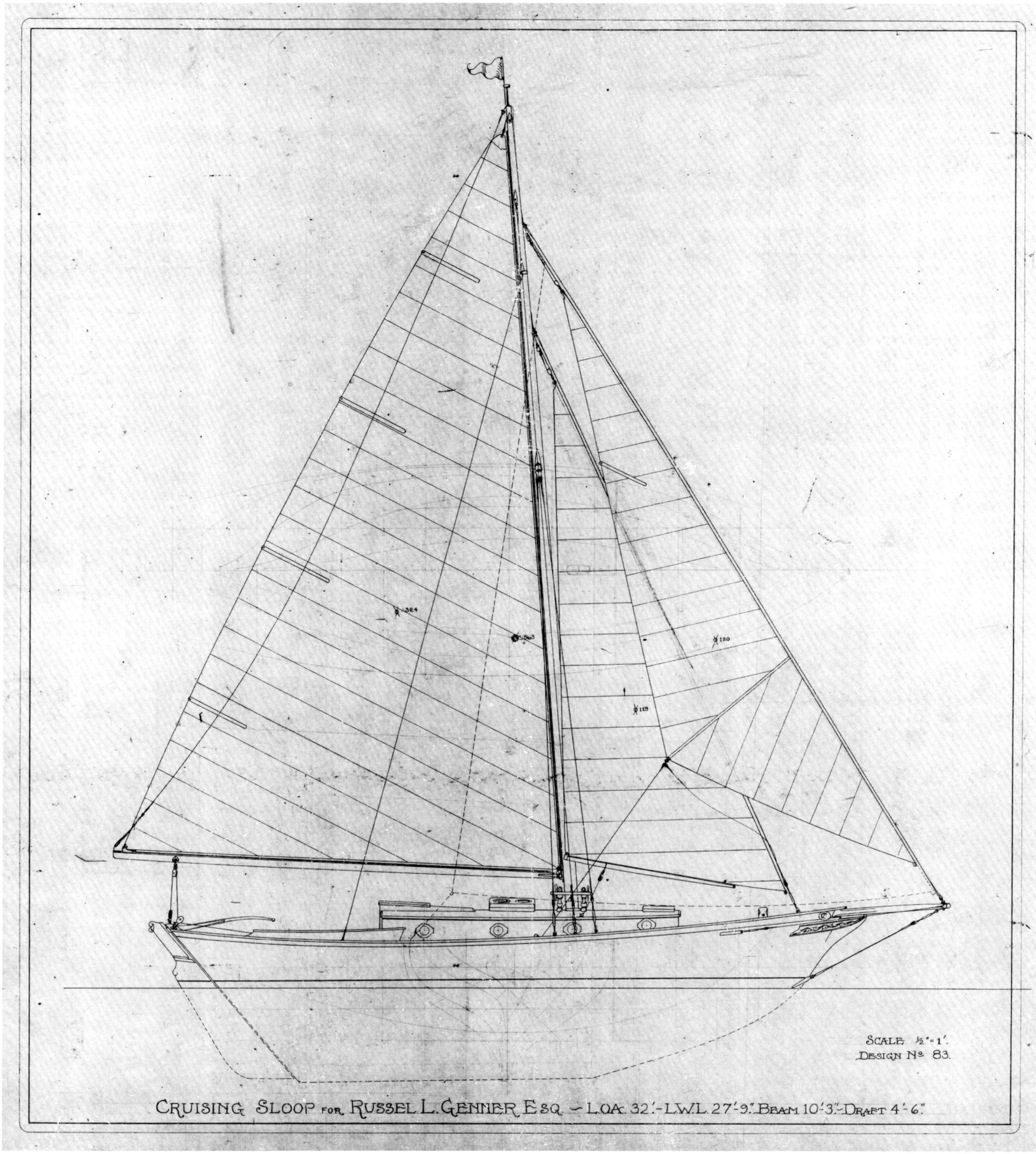
SCALE ½"=1'.
DESIGN No 83.
CRUISING SLOOP FOR RUSSEL L. GENNER ESQ. — L.O.A. 32'.-L.W.L. 27'-9". BEAM 10'-3".-DRAFT 4'-6".

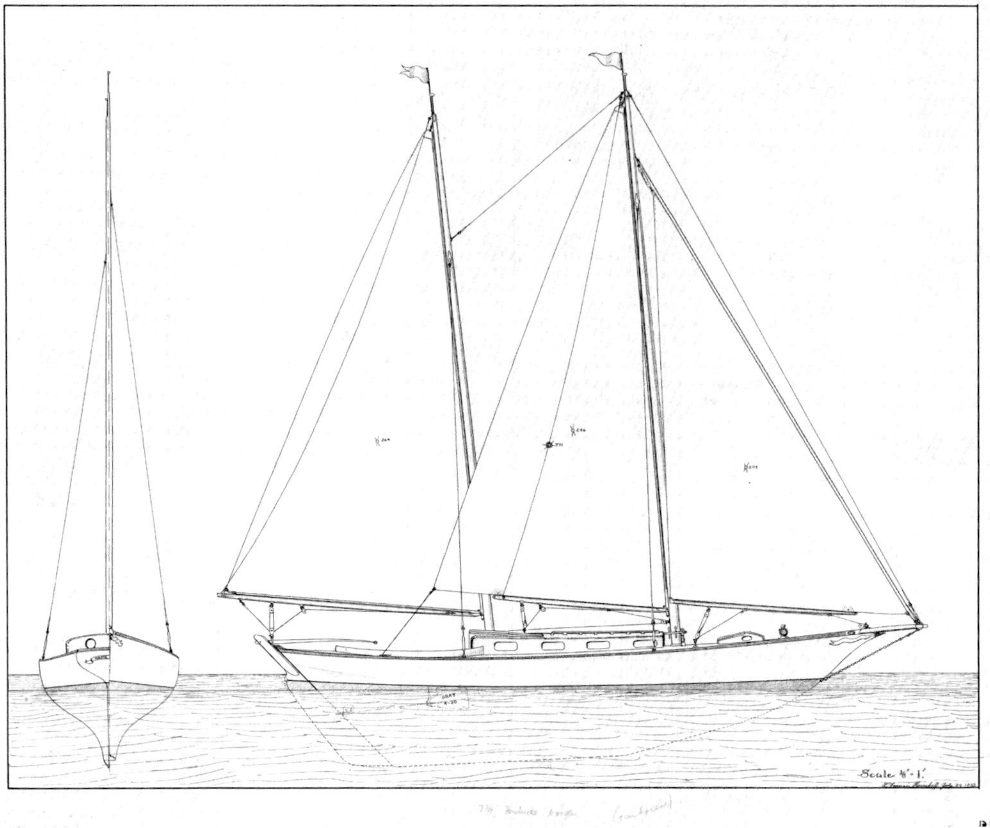

ABOVE: **A forerunner of the Nereia was this Marconi schooner whose preliminary plan Francis dated July 24, 1933, so she was drawn between the two *Tiogas*. There was evidently no customer, and Francis took the design no further. He gave no hull dimensions; she appears to be about 40 feet long on deck. Sail area is 711 square feet, with 264 in the mainsail, 246 in the overlapping foresail, and 201 in the jib. When Nathanael saw this drawing, he warned Francis, sensibly, about the difficulty of handling the foresail, with it's double-sheet arrangement, one for the partial boom and another for the clew, yet, as we have seen, Francis showed a similar foresail on the Marco Polo as an alternative light sail. Beebe thought the big foresail added as much as a knot to the speed of the Marco Polo *Talaria* when they tried it.** (© Mystic Seaport Museum, Daniel S. Gregory Ships Plans Library, SP38.291.1) RIGHT: **The outboard profile and sail plan of the Nereia, Francis's design No. 87, for his fifth How-To-Build series in *The Rudder*. She is a much smaller version of the *Tiogas,* with a flat transom instead of their gorgeously sculpted sterns. After all, this was supposed to be a design that a skilled amateur builder could tackle. Sail area is 673 square feet, with 340 in the mainsail, 170 in the mizzen, and 163 in the jib. Francis shows a masthead, overlapping jib for light weather. He drew no reefs in the mainsail or mizzen, for he believed that the ketch rig provided enough combinations of reduced sail area so that they were not needed. Note the raised taffrail. Francis indicates the pram stowed athwartships between the mizzenmast and the cabin house; some sailors might prefer her atop the cabin house, trading optimum visibility ahead from the helm for unobstructed access to the deck from the companionway.** (© Mystic Seaport Museum, Daniel S. Gregory Ships Plans Library, SP38.7)

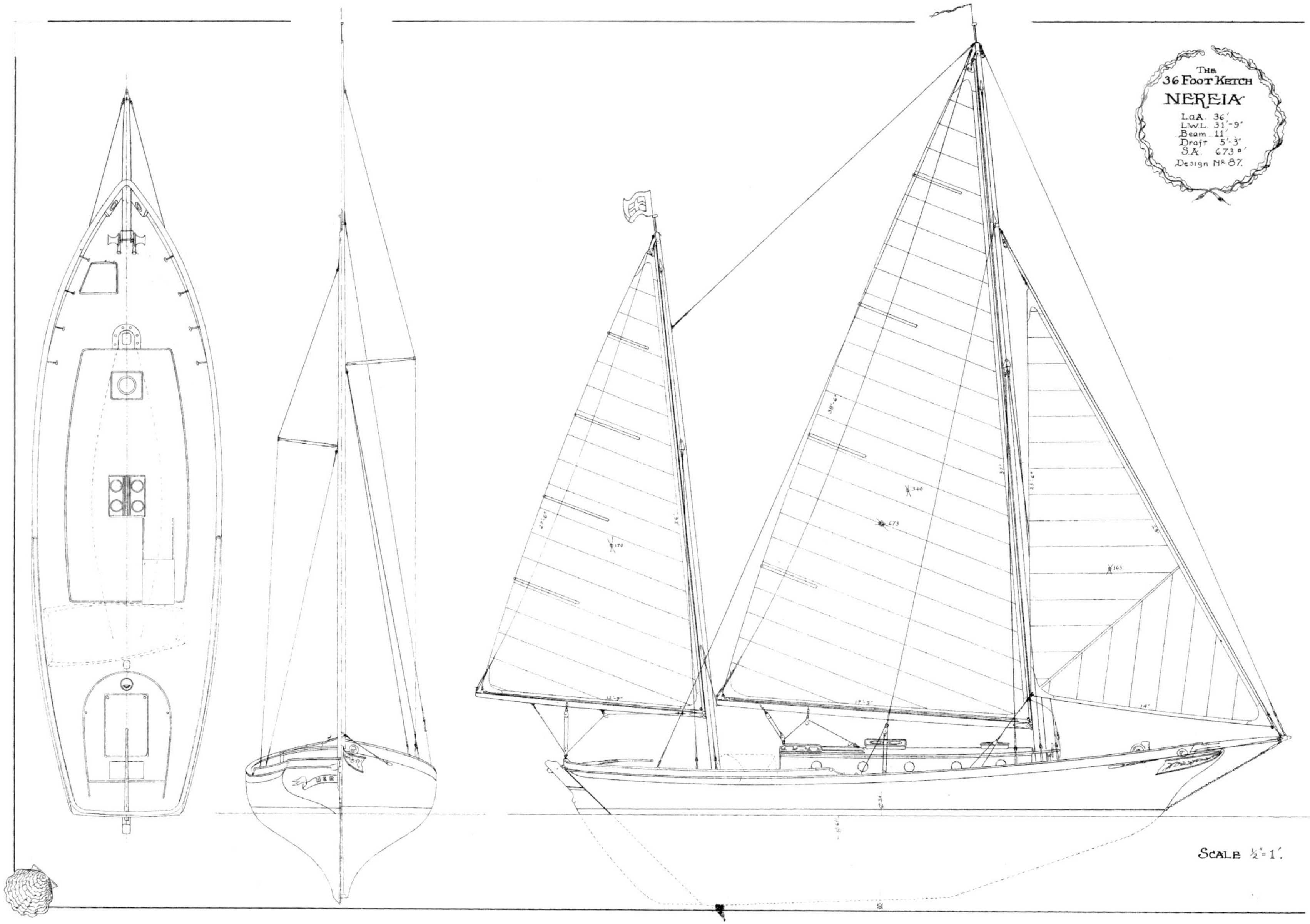
The 36 Foot Ketch
NEREIA
L.o.A. 36'
L.W.L. 31'-9"
Beam 11'
Draft 5'-3"
S.A. 673 □'
Design Nº 87.
Scale ½" = 1'.

HEIGHTS above and below L.W.L.							DIAGONALS				
STATION NOS.	UNDER SIDE OF RAIL CAP	TOP OF DECK AT SIDE	4' BUTTOCK	2' BUTTOCK	RABBET	PROFILE		D1	D2	D3	STATION NOS
0	4-1-4	3-7-5			3-9-2	3-7-5					0
2	3-10-2	3-4-2		3-11-4	0-5-7	0-0-0		0-0-6	0-4-0	0-8-5	2
4	3-7-0	3-1-1		2-0-5	-1-0-4	-1-3-0		0-7-4	1-1-1	1-8-5	4
6	3-4-1	2-10-1	3-6-4	0-6-5	-1-9-7	-1-11-4		1-2-3	1-10-4	2-7-4	6
8	3-1-4	2-7-6	2-1-4	-0-6-3	-2-6-2	-2-7-7		1-8-7	2-7-3	3-5-3	8
10	2-10-7	2-5-4	0-9-5	-1-3-0	-3-2-6	-3-4-2		2-3-0	3-3-1	4-2-0	10
12	2-8-6	2-3-3	-0-1-0	-1-9-0	-3-5-2	-4-0-5		2-8-2	3-9-4	4-8-1	12
14	2-6-6	2-1-5	-0-8-2	-2-1-4	-3-7-0	-4-9-0		2-11-2	4-2-4	5-1-0	14
16	2-5-1	2-0-0	-0-11-2	-2-4-0	-3-8-6	-4-9-6+		3-1-1	4-4-7	5-4-0	16
18	2-3-7	1-10-7	-1-0-7	-2-4-4	-3-10-4	-4-10-5		3-1-3	4-6-1	5-5-7	18
20	2-2-7	1-10-0	-1-0-2	-2-3-3	-4-0-0	-4-11-4		3-0-5	4-5-6	5-6-4	20
22	2-2-1	1-9-4	-0-11-0	-2-1-0	-4-1-5	-5-0-2		2-10-6	4-4-4	5-5-7	22
24	2-1-5	1-9-2	-0-8-2	-1-9-2	-4-3-0	5-1-1		2-7-3	4-1-1	5-4-4	24
26	2-1-3	1-9-1	-0-4-6	-1-3-6	-4-5-0	5-2-0		2-2-4	3-9-0	5-1-4	26
28	2-1-4	1-9-4	+0-0-3	-0-10-1	-4-0-0	5-2-6		1-9-2	3-2-5	4-9-4	28
30	2-2-0	1-10-1	0-6-6	-0-3-5	-2-7-0	5-6-7 5-3-0		1-2-4	2-7-4	4-4-5	30
32	2-3-0	1-11-1	1-2-1	+0-2-4	-1-1-6	1-6-2 4-3-0		0-8-1	1-11-0	3-10-1	32
34	2-4-5	2-0-6		+0-9-0		+0-6-3 -1-11-4		0-3-6	1-1-2	3-2-4	34
36	2-6-6	2-2-6		+1-2-4		2-6-6					36

DIMENSIONS IN FEET, INCHES AND EIGHTS OF INCHES.

HALF BREADTHS.													
STATION NOS.	UNDER SIDE OF RAIL CAP	DECK AT SIDE	W.L.+3'	W.L.+2'	W.L.+1'	L.W.L.	W.L.-1'	W.L.-2'	W.L.-3'	W.L.-4'	RABBET	½ WIDTH PROFILE	STATION NOS
0	0-5-0	0-1-2									0-2-2	0-1-3 0-0-6	0
2	1-11-2	1-6-7	1-4-0	0-9-2	0-4-2	0-0-5					0-2-2	0-0-6	2
4	3-0-7	2-8-6	2-7-5	1-11-3	1-3-4	0-8-2	0-2-0				0-2-2	0-1-0	4
6	3-10-7	3-7-1	3-8-3	3-0-5	2-4-0	1-6-5	0-8-4				0-2-2	0-1-2	6
8	4-5-6	4-3-2	4-5-0	3-11-0	3-3-4	2-6-2	1-5-4	0-6-2			0-2-3	0-1-4	8
10	4-10-7	4-9-0		4-7-0	4-1-0	3-4-4	2-3-4	1-1-6	0-4-7		0-2-4	0-1-6	10
12	5-2-2	5-0-6		4-11-6	4-7-6	4-0-4	3-0-2	1-8-7	0-9-4	0-2-2	0-5-7	0-1-7	12
14	5-4-1	5-3-4		5-3-4	5-0-4	4-6-7	3-7-4	2-1-5	1-1-4	0-5-2	0-8-1	0-2-0	14
16	5-5-2	5-5-2		5-5-2	5-3-3	4-10-4	3-11-0	2-4-7	1-2-6	0-7-4	0-9-1	0-4-2	16
18	5-5-4	5-5-7		5-5-7	5-5-0	5-0-4	4-0-5	2-5-6	1-3-3	0-8-2	0-9-0	0-5-2	18
20	5-5-1	5-5-4			5-5-4	5-1-1	4-0-1	2-5-4	1-2-0	0-8-0	0-8-0	0-5-2	20
22	5-4-0	5-4-5			5-5-0	5-0-3	3-10-1	2-0-7	1-0-4	0-7-0	0-6-7	0-4-5	22
24	5-2-2	5-3-0			5-3-3	4-10-5	3-4-0	1-7-1	0-9-4	0-5-2	0-5-0	0-3-4	24
26	5-0-0	5-0-6			5-0-5	4-6-5	2-7-0	1-1-1	0-6-6	0-4-0	0-3-2	0-2-3	26
28	4-9-1	4-9-6			4-9-1	3-11-2	1-7-6	0-6-5	0-3-6	0-2-6	0-2-6	0-1-0	28
30	4-5-4	4-6-3			4-4-5	2-11-0	0-8-4	0-3-0	0-1-6		0-2-2	0-1-0	30
32	4-1-1	4-1-6			3-9-3	1-4-0	0-2-4				0-2-2	0-1-0	32
34	3-8-0	3-8-6			2-9-3							1-2-0	34
36	3-1-4											3-1-4	36

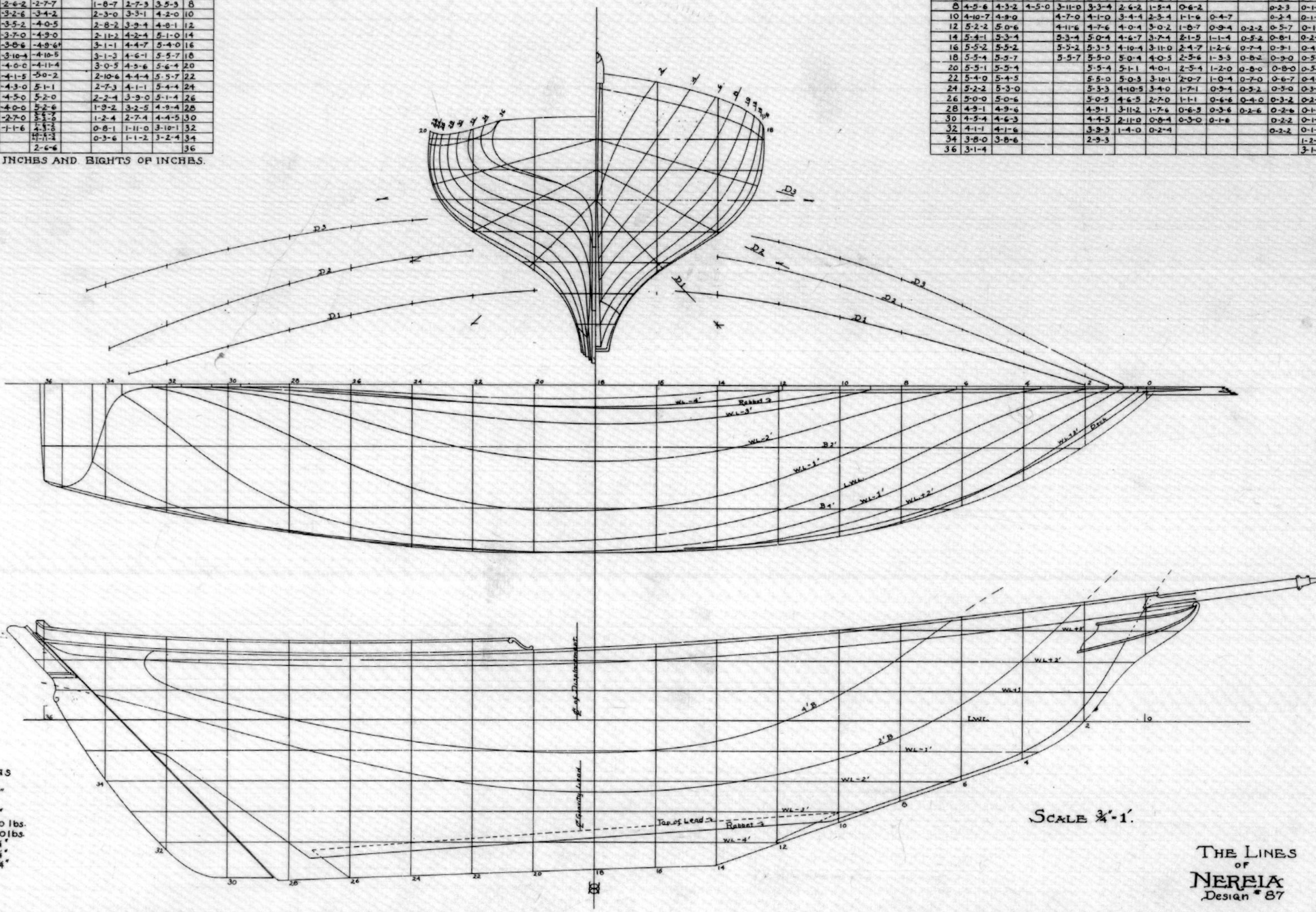

GENERAL DIMENSIONS

L.O.A.	36'
L.W.L.	31'-6"
Beam	11'
Draft	5'-3"
Displacement	24,000 lbs.
Weight of Lead	12,000 lbs.
Thicknes of Planking	1¼"
" " Deck	1¼"
½ Siding of Stem	2¼"

SCALE ¾"-1'.

THE LINES
OF
NEREIA
Design # 87

SHEET 2

issues found "How To Build Nereia," by L. Francis Herreshoff. She was a clipper-bowed ketch, 36 feet long, with a flat, transom stern for relatively easy construction, though the transom had much more curvature in section than did that of the H-28. There was no designation of H-36 for this design, because after the H-28, H-14, and H-55, "there appeared a whole flock of H-numbers ranging from motor boats to racing freaks," Francis claimed. He named the design for Nereia, daughter of the sea god Nereus, because she had sisters, which was his hope for the new boat.[14]

In his description of the new design, Francis managed, in one sentence, to let fly poison arrows at three of his perceived enemies: Norwegian double-enders, John G. Alden, and rating rules for racing yachts. "The Nereia is no chichi imitation of foreign yachts," Francis wrote, "or a copy of those vessels which were developed to carry dead fish to market, but is a descendant of the purely American type of yacht that was developed for ladies and gentlemen to sail on before racing measurements spoiled the cruising yacht." It was also true that the Nereia's design (and that of the earlier clipper-bowed yachts from his board) owed more to the work of Edward Burgess, Starling's father, than to that of his own father.[15]

In a total about-face with regard to measurement rules, when a correspondent complained about the Nereia's high displacement and great amount of lead ballast, Francis defended himself not only by blaming *The Rudder*'s editor for demanding a roomy cruising boat, but also by stating: "If she had less displacement for her water line length, she would rate considerably more under Cruising Club Rule. This design has the normal displacement for water line length that the International Rule, old Universal Rule and Royal Cruising Club Rule require." To another inquirer, he explained that "these boats were built to fit the present Cruising Club rules and rate quite low for their size." Francis is being disingenuous. He did not design the Nereia to the Cruising Club rule, but rather is selling his soul in the name of marketing.[16]

Francis planned to design an alternate sloop rig for the Nereia, because many wanted the H-28 with only one mast, but the Nereia dodged sloop-mania, so he drew no such rig for her. It is tempting to think of Russ and Jane Genner sailing happily away in a Nereia sloop, but, as far as is known, that didn't happen.[17]

A popular feature of the Nereia design was her shippy-looking bulwarks. Francis added a taffrail, so that the boat's rail aft was nearly a foot off the deck. Many sailors like the feeling of security given by a built-up rail. While big vessels with substantial bulwarks, say at least waist high, gain real security, on a 36-foot boat with low bulwarks, the security is deceptive. As we have seen, some of Francis's fans in Australia liked to drive his boats at sea; one of them wrote to him with an objection to the Nereia's bulwarks, saying that they would trap too much water in rough going. Francis replied: "I quite agree with you that she would be better with the freeboard raised three or four inches, and the bulwark almost entirely done away with. It is certainly true that about all bulwarks do is to hold water on deck, and I personally do not like them, but strange to say the average person likes them very much."[18]

Francis was amenable to such changes to his

LEFT: **The Nereia's lines and offsets. She is 36 feet long on deck; 31 feet, 6 inches on the waterline; 11 feet beam; and 5 feet, 3 inches draft. Displacement is 24,000 pounds, with 12,000 pounds of lead ballast, for a ballast-displacement ratio of 50 percent, giving her unusually great stability for a cruising boat. Though her handsome, wineglass transom cannot rival the sterns of the *Tiogas* for beauty, her bow is in their class.** (© Mystic Seaport Museum, Daniel S. Gregory Ships Plans Library, SP38.7)

design. He wrote: "There are a great many individuals who want to express their own ideas or show some of their own individuality in the design so there are bound to be changes in any design that is put out. I have no doubt there will be all kinds of changes made in the various Nereias and, as a matter of fact, it does not bother me in the least."[19]

A sympathetic correspondent, having seen ugly doghouses put on H-28s, suggested to Francis that he design one for the Nereia before somebody else did. Francis demurred: "For my part I do not approve of doghouses or even like the name (much prefer to call them deck shelters) but those who want them probably know just exactly how much room they want. I do not like to have anything at all in the way of the helmsman's vision and do like to have a ship-shape boat, particularly among the smaller yachts."[20]

Francis did not design trailboards for the Nereia as he had for his larger clipper-bowed yachts, leaving that exacting task to the builder. Anticipating that amateur builders would have fun putting ornamentation on a clipper bow, perhaps even a figurehead, he wrote, "however the looks of the yacht as a whole can be very much affected by the decorations, which must be most carefully carried out and never overdone or made too large."[21]

Francis's monthly "How To Build Nereia" series contained sixteen articles, each with a drawing and explanatory text. He ended the series by writing: "If any questions come up on the construction, the designer will be glad to try to answer them. (The End (thank God!)" Building plans could be purchased from *The Rudder* for $30. The plans for the yacht's tender were sold separately for $5. One grateful correspondent wrote: "The detail on the construction drawings and directions are unbelievable. They are a joy to read even if I had no idea of building the boat." A customer who was going ahead with building wrote to Francis, "now that I'm starting to frame the vessel, I can really appreciate the simplicity and ease of construction called for in these designs." An army officer stationed in Japan had a Nereia built professionally and relayed the builder's admiration for the plans to Francis: "It seems that he had never used blueprints prepared by an American designer before building Nereia, and he found your instructions very easy to follow. He therefore assumed all American designers prepared equally straight forward designs. Recently he has been building a boat prepared by Mr. [William] Garden of Seattle and he has found many confusing and unclear points, making him doubly appreciative of your clarity." Francis replied, "it is very pleasing to hear that the builder of Nereia liked the drawings he worked from, and I am not surprised that he has been confused with Garden's drawings for the ones that I have looked at have also puzzled me." Yet Bill Garden, an accomplished boatbuilder himself, certainly reaped his share of praise for his complete construction drawings.[22]

RIGHT: **The cabin plan of the Nereia. Francis has chosen the orthodox arrangement for this size cruising boat: from forward to aft, stateroom, toilet room, main cabin, and galley. The head is full-width, with its doors shut. The off-center engine protrudes into the galley and perhaps would be boxed in to protect the dishwasher's left ankle from getting tangled up in the flywheel. Francis would not have agreed; he has even suggested an open, raised, metal engine bed "because the engine can be gotten at and wiped off all over." The awkward engine placement does allow for a water tank abaft the companionway, along with considerable stowage space. There is room outboard of the narrow cockpit for a fuel tank each side. She has a generous forepeak with its own deck hatch. Francis's suggested decoration for the underside of the folded berths in the main cabin is three views of the vessel under sail.** (© Mystic Seaport Museum, Daniel S. Gregory Ships Plans Library, SP38.7)

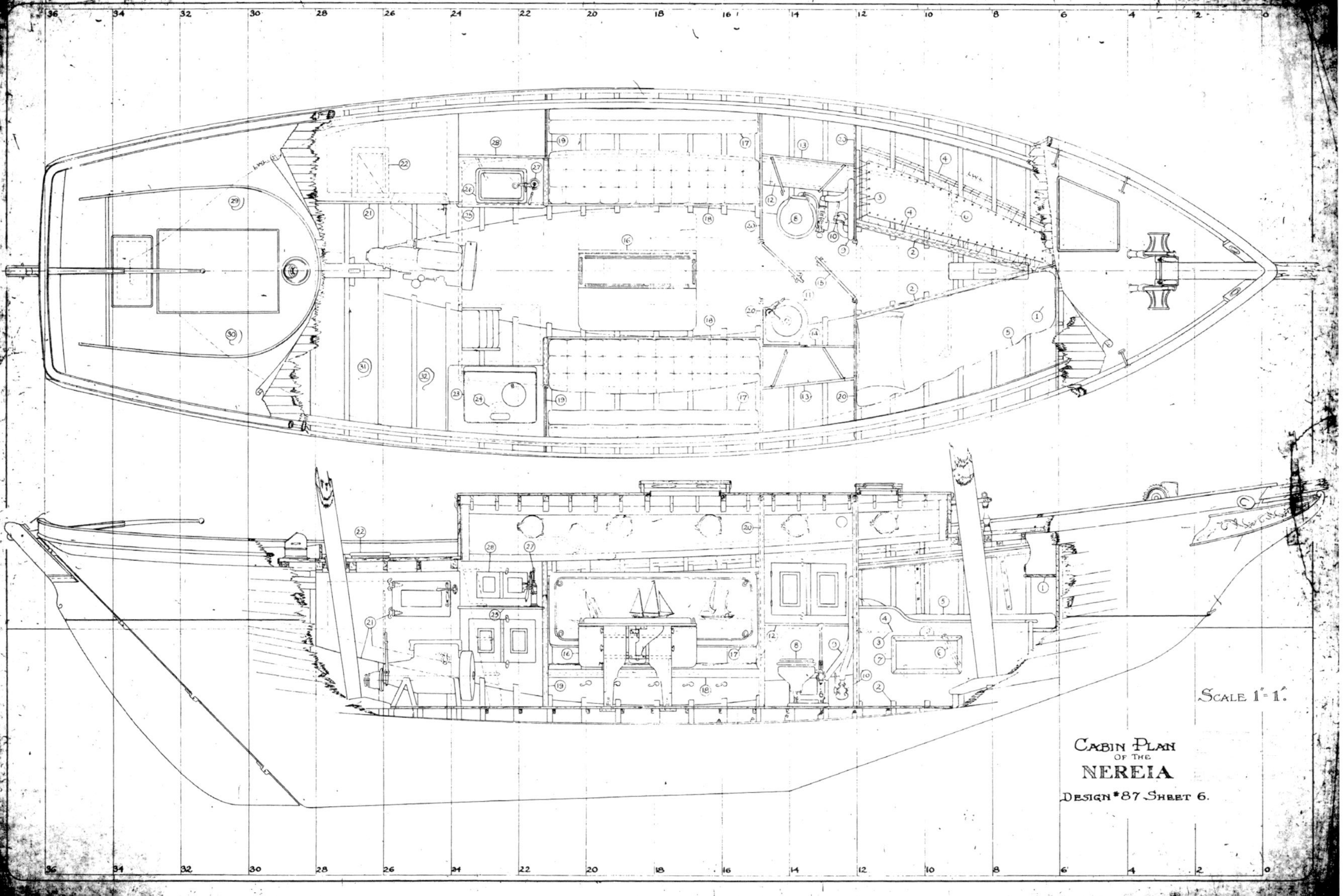
Scale 1"=1'.
Cabin Plan
of the
NEREIA
Design #87 Sheet 6.

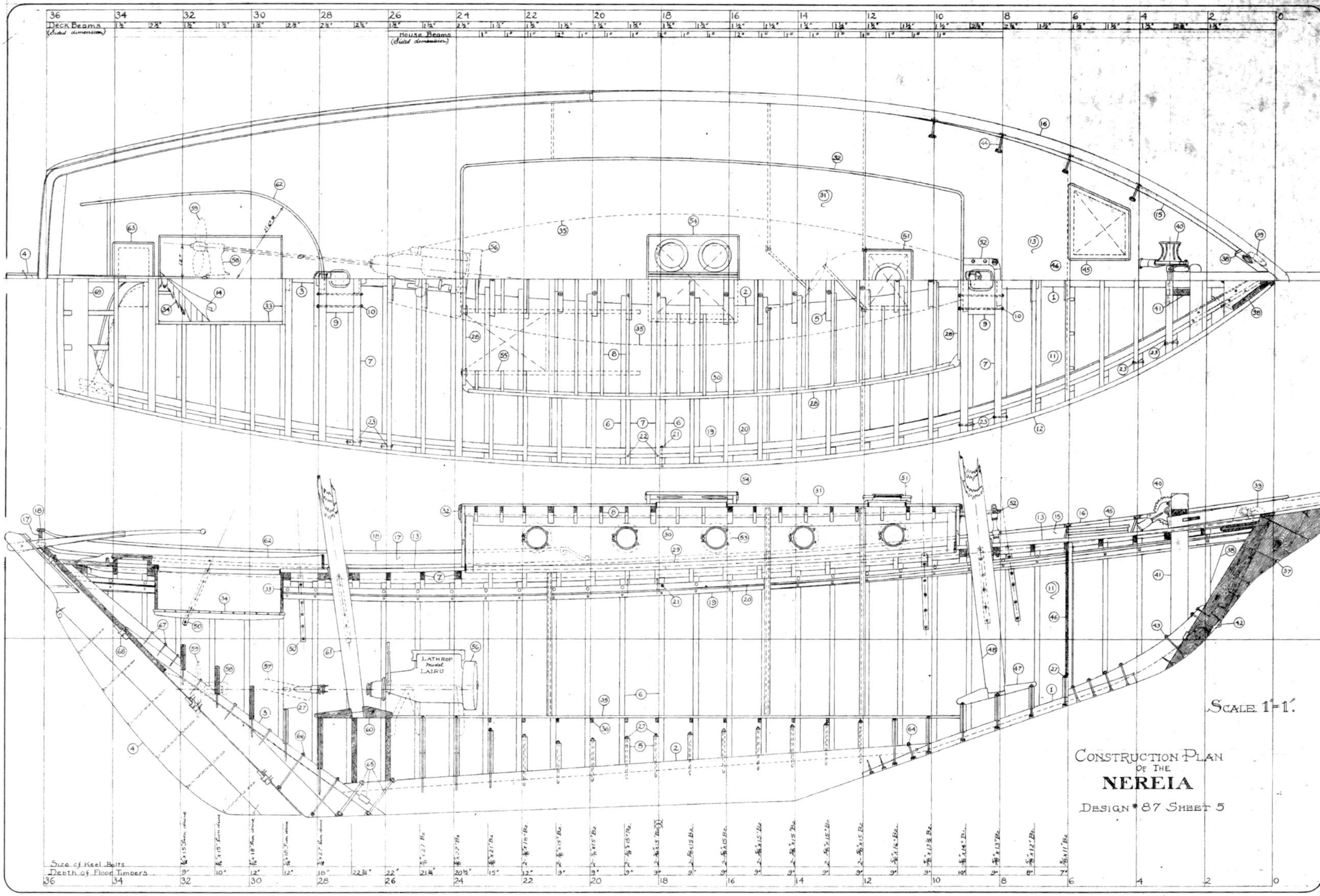

Deck Beams (Sided dimension)
House Beams (Sided dimension)
LATHROP Model LAIRU
Scale 1"=1'
Construction Plan of the NEREIA
Design # 87 Sheet 5
Size of Keel Bolts
Depth of Floor Timbers

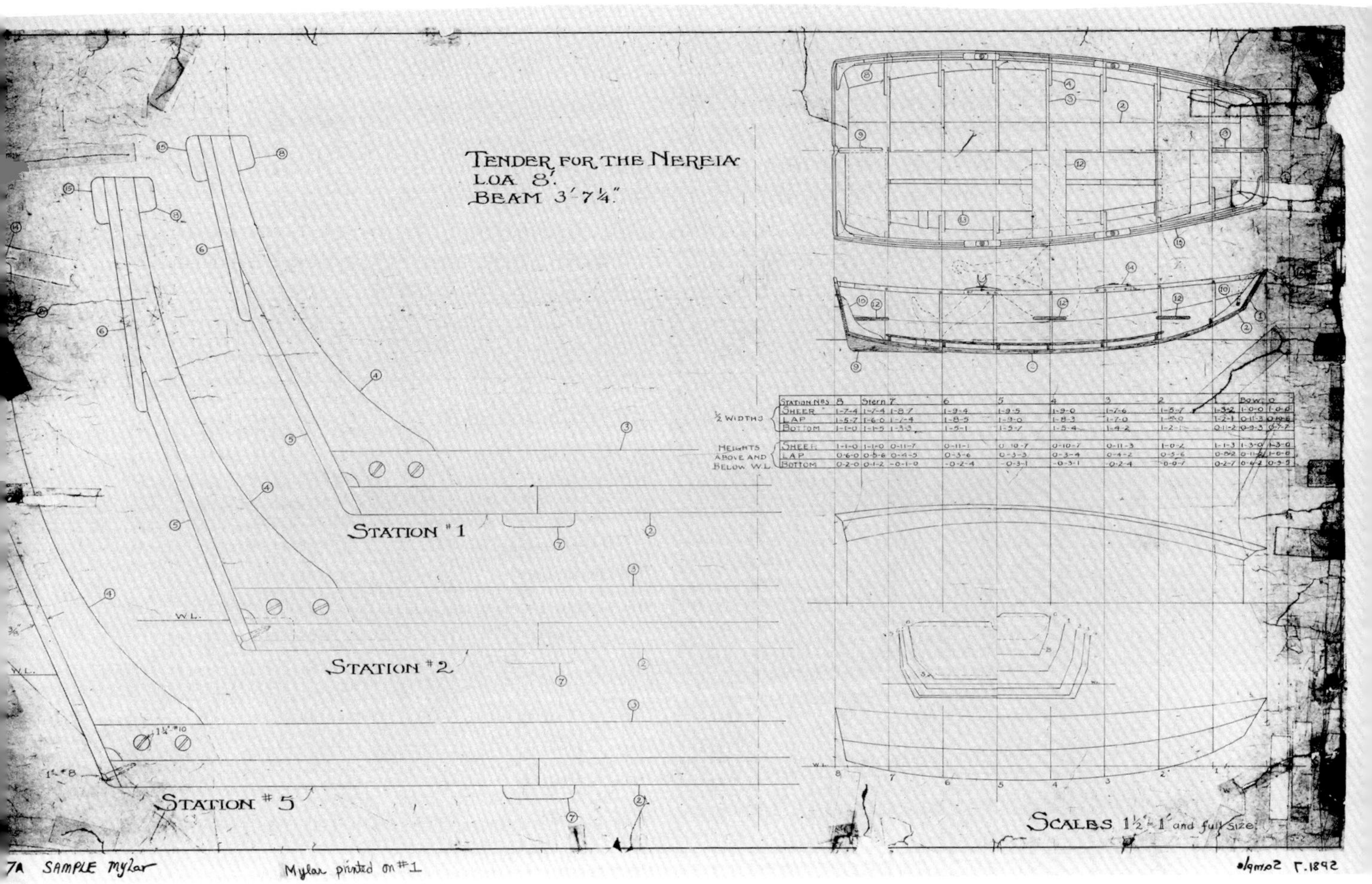

LEFT: **The Nereia's construction plan. Francis has used his numbering system for all the different parts, corresponding to dimensions and detailed instructions given in the text of his article. Note that there is no wood keelson; he has used his method of fastening the garboard plank directly to the lead keel. One builder-owner emphasized that this worked very well. Yet building a Nereia was no easy project. To pick out one small example, the builder had to make a pattern and have eight bronze castings made for braces on the inboard sides of the forward bulwarks, where they were higher and might take more of a beating in a head sea. Each casting had to be smoothed and its foot shaped to the correct angle with the deck. Of course a builder might decide to skirt this complication by beefing up the scantling of the forward bulwarks. Francis did not object to such changes to his design, as long as they made sense. For an engine, Francis shows a Lathrop Model LH-4, which would deliver 27 horsepower at 1,600 rpm.** (© Mystic Seaport Museum, Daniel S. Gregory Ships Plans Library, SP38.7) ABOVE: **The lines and offsets of the Nereia's tender. Francis has kept her low-sided for ease in rowing to windward and to make the boat less obstructive when stowed on deck. He drew the stern broad for carrying capacity in so small a boat. She is 8 feet long, with a beam of 3 feet, 7¼ inches.** (© Mystic Seaport Museum, Daniel S. Gregory Ships Plans Library, SP38.7A)

We do not know how many Nereias have been built, but perhaps a fair estimate would be one hundred, a number similar to that for the larger Mobjack design. Francis's fans in Australia built Nereias. The Dair Shipbuilding Corporation of Port Washington built a Nereia on Grand Cayman Island in the Bahamas; we can suspect the influence of Boris Lauer-Leonardi, for he lived in Port Washington and had a place on Grand Cayman. Francis had the opportunity to examine a Nereia, the *Carastee*, built by Dr. Maxwell Y. Simkin of Great Neck, Long Island, a dentist. "She is entirely an amateur job and beautifully done," Francis wrote.[23]

A Nereia called the *Galatea* was the center of a family success story. A. W. and Joyce McLoughlin and their two children built the boat at Burlington, Vermont, on Lake Champlain; they launched her in 1960. Joyce McLoughlin reported on progress in *The Rudder*: "The lofting took about two months and was a fascinating project. We tried to be as accurate as possible and found that the wonderfully detailed and carefully executed plans of the architect were quite easily understood by an amateur." They used local white oak for stem, floors, and frames and had longleaf yellow pine shipped in for the sternpost, and African mahogany for planking. Steaming and setting the frames was an all-hands operation. "It took us about twenty minutes to get a two by two inch steamed frame bent into place, my husband bending inside the boat, with the aid of a block and tackle on the pulling end of which was our twelve year old son. As the frame was bent into place, it was immediately clamped to the ribbands by my daughter and myself," Joyce wrote. She continued: "Yes, my husband learned how to spile a plank! Yes, he learned how to pry and wheedle it into place by clamps and wedges of every shape and form! Yes, they had to be fitted many times, shaped, hollowed out and fitted again! But after smoothing off with a plane, we were able to see at long last the sweet lines of the hull, and we could even say we had a boat in our back yard!" After sailing the

The *Galatea* underway on Lake Champlain. She was built to the Nereia design from 1956 to 1960 by A. W. and Joyce McLaughlin with help from their young son and daughter, and advice from Francis and from Allan Vaitses, who built Nereias professionally. The way the *Galatea* project was carried out by the McLaughlins, with common sense, persistence, and satisfaction, was precisely what L. Francis Herreshoff and Boris Lauer-Leonardi were hoping for with their How-To-Build series in *The Rudder*. (*The Rudder* (May 1961): "The Mail Barrel")

Galatea on the lake, A. W. McLoughlin could report to *Rudder* readers: "She is a splendid cruising boat with sufficient room to live aboard comfortably and is very easy to sail and handle. We are well pleased with her in every way and feel amply rewarded for the four years of work her building required." The McLoughlin's Nereia dream was fulfilled when they took the *Galatea* to the Caribbean. She even appeared on the cover of *WoodenBoat* magazine.[24]

The *Alaria* was a Nereia built by a professional in 1970. She had a discerning owner in John Kendall of Boston and Marion, on Buzzards Bay. Her builder was Allan Vaitses, who built several Nereias at his yard in Mattapoisett, not far from Marion. Both Kendall and Vaitses recognized L. Francis Herreshoff as a guru who could teach them much about the art and science of creating a beautiful yacht. The three formed a powerful team. Francis suggested the name; alaria is a genus of kelp, and the word sounds well, he thought.[25]

Francis, in his late seventies, undertook a number of trips to Mattapoisett to confer with Vaitses and inspect the work. He made patterns for castings and finished them for all the fittings in the rig. Kendall did the same for the hull fittings. For this boat, Francis designed trailboards. He also made unique pig-sticks for the masthead flags. As an active part of the team, Francis enjoyed working with the much younger men. He even attended the launching ceremony.[26]

John Kendall kept the *Alaria* for ten years. In 1974, he took his Nereia to Prince Edward Island to view a solar eclipse. He thought to cross the Atlantic the following March in order to cruise in Europe during the summer, but realized the timing was dangerous. And Francis reminded Kendall that he had designed his boat for coastwise cruising. Kendall shipped her across the ocean and enjoyed five summers of sailing the coasts of Denmark, Finland, and Sweden, laying up for the winters in Germany.

Kendall wanted to try a Marco Polo-style squaresail on his Nereia, but he wanted to leave the yard and sail aloft when not in use, rather than have it cluttering the deck. He couldn't get Francis interested in working out a solution for furling the sail without going aloft, so he fussed with various ideas for two seasons without much success, and finally got Bill Harding, the local sailmaker in Marion, to come up with roller-furling gear that could be worked from the deck. Kendall liked the sail; running with it, the *Alaria* didn't roll too much, and in a gentle breeze with sloppy sea, the squaresail didn't slat the way the mainsail would in such conditions. Sometimes, he even combined the new sail with the mizzen and a mizzen staysail, wung out. His Nereia was a good self-steerer with the squaresail set.[27]

Brian O'Donoghue raced his Nereia, the *Tarua,* as well as cruising in her from her home port of Bay of Islands, New Zealand. In 1964, he won a 1,000-mile race to Noumea, finishing fourth out of thirty-six starters, with an elapsed time of 5 days, 13 hours, a remarkable average speed of 7.5 knots (thus *averaging* 1.33 times the square root of her waterline length). Ironically, because the Nereia rated well, she moved up to first in fleet on corrected time. In the 1969 race to Suva, Fiji Islands, the *Tarua* came in twelfth, losing five hours with a bad landfall, and moved up to fifth on corrected time. O'Donoghue reported on that race to Francis: "The next day and night the trades freshened to 25 knots and shifted more on our beam. *Tarua* really surfed at times, our speed at times going over 14 knots. It was exhilarating to see such a heavy boat perform like a dinghy. We covered over 400 miles in two days on fixes, and our log read 212 and 215 miles." This was a two-day speed of just under 9 knots.[28]

Nereias were built of steel in Brisbane, Australia, and of ferro-cement in New Zealand. Nereia Yachts, Wilmington, North Carolina, built to the design in fiberglass in 1987. Middleton Marine, La Crosse, Florida, offered a fiberglass version with a taller rig and 169 square feet more sail area in 1994.[29]

The Nereia design was a most "normal" boat for Francis. She fit the standard for cruising boats in terms of her dimensions, though she had a beauty that few cruising boats of the day could match. Boris Lauer-Leonardi's influence can be felt here; he had asked Francis for a roomy design, trying, successfully, to nudge him away from his predilection for a long, narrow, moderate-draft boat. Boris didn't want another Marco Polo, capable of being driven hard, but cramped for her length. What Francis gave him was a lovely, conventional cruising boat, but one that because of her displacement and ballast could, as Brian Donoghue discovered with his *Tarua*, be driven extremely hard. A Nereia gave her owner the choice in heavy weather of high speed, or an excess of safety when slowed down. The Nereia's seaworthiness does not equal that of the Marco Polo, but she isn't just another pretty face.

When Nathanael G. Herreshoff and his wife Ann began spending winters in Coconut Grove, Florida, with Commodore Ralph Middleton Munroe, Nathanael was exposed both to Munroe's shallow-draft sharpies and to his enthusiasm for the boat type. Munroe believed that a sharpie, as he modified the design by adding depth and ballast, was as fast and able as any other boat type, and faster and more able than most. One of the Commodore's early sharpies was called the *Presto*, and his distinctive designs would become known as Presto boats. Nathanael became a believer. In 1936, he wrote to Francis extolling Presto boats and urged him to try one on William Strawbridge, instead of the Block Island boat Strawbridge thought he wanted. Francis did make pencil sketches of a Presto type, but, despite Munroe's claims, he believed that the boats lacked stability because of their narrow bottoms and that they depended too much on their flaring topsides to keep them upright. He did try, unsuccessfully, two years later, to interest Strawbridge in a shallow cruiser of his own devising, one that drew no more water than a Presto boat. It would be ten more years before Francis drew the plans of a shoal-draft cruising boat that would be built, and this one would have so shallow a hull that she would be beachable.[30]

No one needed to convince L. Francis Herreshoff of the advantages of shoal draft in a cruising boat. He had cruised enough in his youth and in his adult imagination to realize how wonderful it would be to sail or motor in the shallow water of all sorts of protected bays and unfrequented estuaries, and to find secluded berths, even right on the shore, for picnics and overnight sojourns. He was hardly alone. In 1945, a correspondent asked what it would cost to have "Dear Mr. Herreshoff" design him an H-28 that drew no more than 18 inches. Francis replied that he was too busy, but that he planned at some point to design a "very shallow draft" cruiser for *The Rudder.* Three months later, there came another request, this from an admirer of Francis's designs who lived in tidewater South Freeport, Maine, asking if he might deign to design a sharpie. Francis's reply showed that details of a sharpie design were already in his mind, for he pointed out the advantages of an arc bottom for such a boat.[31]

And *Rudder* readers asked both Francis and Boris for a shoal-draft design from the board of L. Francis Herreshoff. In March 1948, Boris wrote to Francis: "Now that the Nereia is drawing towards completion [in four months], it is perhaps not out of place to talk about the next designs, or at least to think about it. For instance, what would you think of a cruising sharpie? It occurred to me that a sharpie with leeboards might possibly offer some advantages. No centerboard trunk, more space, sturdier construction, etc. But that is just a thought." Boris need not have been so politic with his suggestion; the day before Boris made it, Francis had written to Vincent Gilpin, a disciple of Commodore Munroe, "I think the ideal shallow draft boat would be somewhat after the style of a

Connecticut River Sharpie, with possibly a slight round to the bottom instead of being straight across, and I think if she were equipped with properly arranged lee boards, (such as the Dutch use), she would be a far better cruiser than any that we have at present in this country."[32]

Boris and Francis were both excited. Boris was effusive:

The more I think about the sharpie the more I like the idea. I am planning to feature this boat as a new design development, which it is. You see people have been so used to all kinds of rehashed old tripe that they will be interested in a new development by an outstanding designer like you. The name Meadow Lark [suggested

Francis liked this wash drawing of the *Nereia* by Allen Beechel that appeared in the November 1948 *Rudder*. She is doing what every sailor loves: footing fast on a beam reach in a fresh breeze. (*The Rudder* (November 1948): frontispiece)

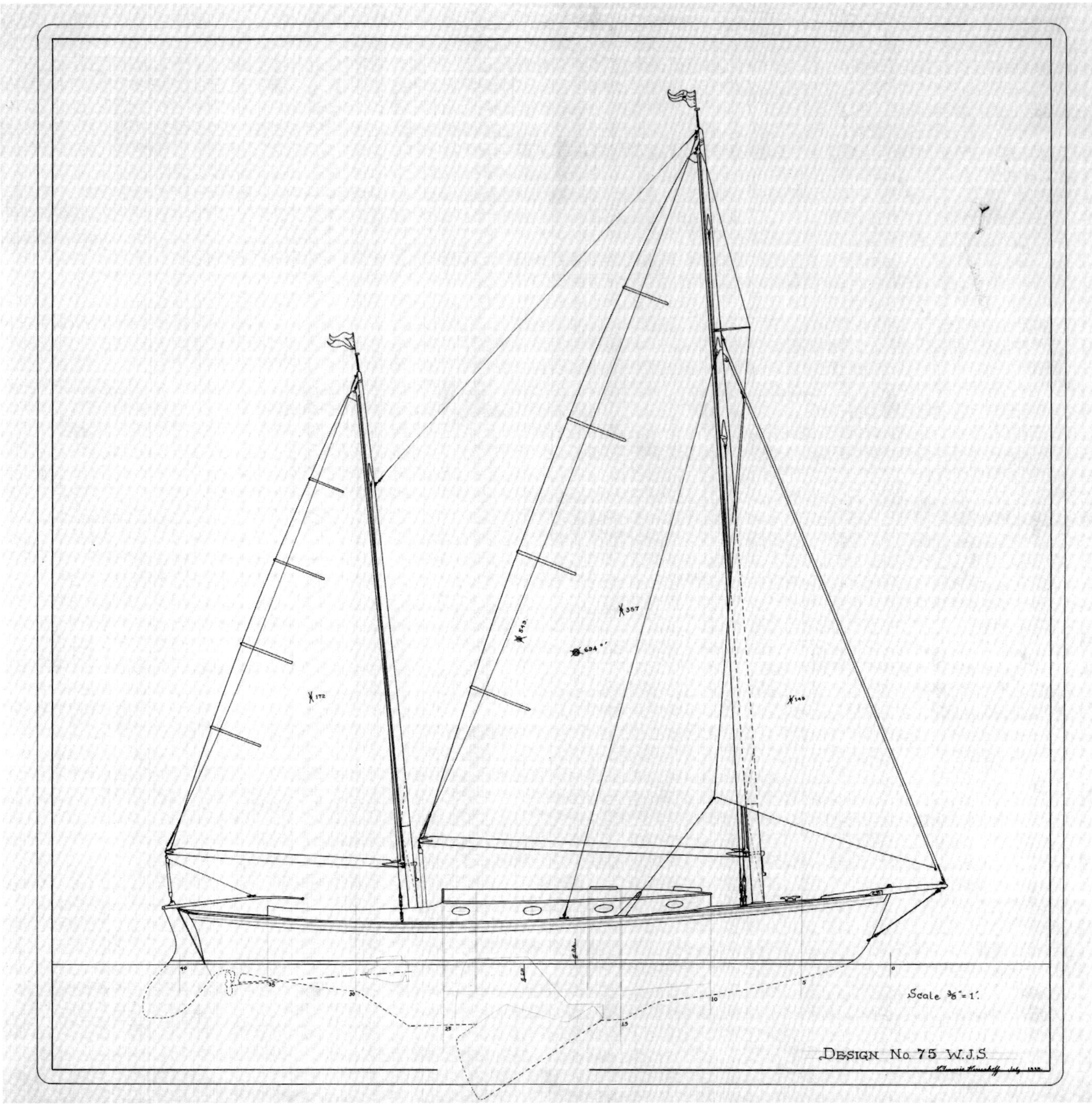

Francis's design No. 75, of July 1938, was a 38-foot, shoal-draft ketch for William Strawbridge. She is 35 feet, 4 inches long on the waterline; beam unknown, but perhaps close to 9 feet; and draft 3 feet, 3 inches, with the centerboard up. Sail area is 674 square feet (though labeled as 694), with 357 in the mainsail, 172 in the mizzen, and 145 in the jib. Since Francis assigned a number to this design, he must have had hopes that his friend would see the advantages of shallow draft in a cruising boat and have him complete the design, but it was not to be. She would, indeed, make an admirable fast cruiser for thin waters, even though she was not beachable. (© Mystic Seaport Museum, Daniel S. Gregory Ships Plans Library, SP38.45.5)

by Francis] is good, but gets away from the water somewhat. Perhaps Mermaid or similar would get back into the swim. It will open up a new era in small boat cruising. In fact a new type of cruising. A skipper will be able to enter a sheltered cove, and an hour after high tide beach his boat and remain there till next morning without even to bother to anchor. In southern waters, new cruising grounds will open up that are beautiful, unspoiled and untouched.[33]

Francis replied: "I really think the sharpie will be a remarkable boat. I think the name Meadow Lark will be all right. I do think that there is a reaction against this ocean racing fad and feel it will be an advantage to exaggerate the features of a shoal draft boat that can make so much of our best cruising ground available."[34]

The Meadow Lark wasn't actually a "new design development," as Boris claimed. There were Commodore Munroe's Presto boats, based on earlier sharpies. And, in the depths of the Depression, Howard Chapelle had advocated basing inexpensive cruising boats on the New Haven sharpie and had provided sample designs. His boats were much closer to the original type than either the Presto boats or the Meadow Lark. He changed the flat-bottomed hull but little, doing most of his modification on rigs and with thc addition of cabins to the open, workboat designs. But neither Presto boats nor Chapelle sharpies caught on, so in that sense, Boris and Francis had a new opportunity to develop.[35]

As we have seen, Francis's Nereia series ended in July 1948. Francis had the design of the 33-foot sharpie Meadow Lark ready to go, so that it could be published in the next issue of *The Rudder*. And then, as usual, he found himself having to make finished inked drawings, with written comments, against monthly deadlines. The Meadow Lark took eight installments, and he did miss one deadline so they skipped a month. As for the name (and the exaggeration of the boat's features), he wrote: "The Editor of *The Rudder* and I have thought that Meadow Lark would be a suitable name for this craft as she could venture inland and, you might say, skim over the marshes and meadows as the joyful bird of that name does over many of our fields which border the Atlantic." Now it was Francis's turn to be effusive.[36]

A main objective of the Meadow Lark design was economy. Francis designed her to be cheap to build and cheap to maintain. A particular saving was in her leeboards, eliminating the centerboard trunk. Yet his perfectionist approach to yacht design introduced subtleties to the simple, flat-bottomed sharpie that inevitably increased cost. The arc bottom and slightly curved sides, as well as his usual scientific rigging details requiring special spars and fittings, made the Meadow Lark costly in building time, compared to a Chapelle sharpie. His curves in the hull made the Meadow Lark a more seakindly sharpie, and his light rig added vital stability to the narrow, shallow boat. She was still cheaper to build and maintain than an H-28. A Meadow Lark owner who could find a suitable spot on the shore could simply haul her out on planks for the winter.

The Meadow Lark's leeboards could be viewed as a new development in American yacht design. The Dutch had been using them for centuries, but there weren't many to be seen on the west side of the Atlantic. Two years before he designed the Meadow Lark, Francis wrote: "Personally I think the lee boards are the best arrangement if one is to land on the beach very often as the center board slot generally gets jammed with sand and gravel and the centerboard is expensive to build and the box always gives trouble." In his description of the Meadow Lark for readers of *The Rudder*, Francis gave three "good reasons" for leeboards: "1. They are cheaper and no great disadvantage on a boat which will do little quick tacking. 2. They take up no room in the cabin, whereas a large centerboard

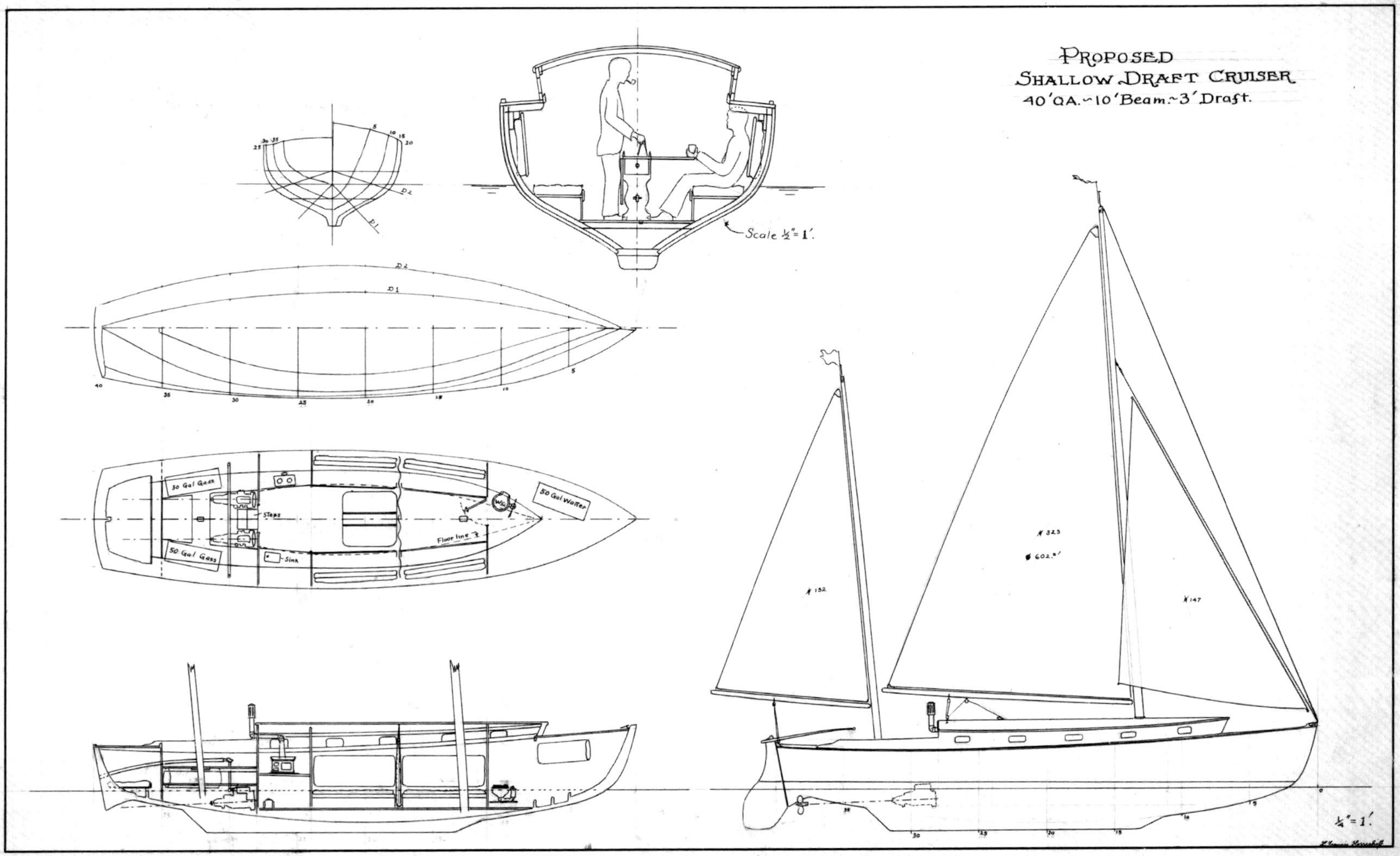

38.110.1

t.4892

box sometimes quite spoils a cabin. 3. (And most important). Having no centerboard box allows the frames to pass from side to side so the bottom can be strong enough for most any sort of stranding." And he pointed out that if there was any short tacking, there was no need to raise and lower the leeboards with each tack, so that only the leeward one would be down; both could be left down, and his two-way fittings would allow the windward board to swing away from the boat, relieving an awkward strain on it. He admitted that a boat with leeboards makes more leeway just after tacking than does a boat with a centerboard, though he saw no reason why this should be so, assuming the windward board was lowered before tacking.[37]

Philip C. Bolger, a yacht designer from Gloucester, thirty years younger than Francis, was a great admirer of his genius. On a visit to The Castle, he was allowed up into Francis's workshop, where, on the long drawing board, he saw the unfinished plans of the Meadow Lark. The drawings made a lasting impression. The fact that a designer of L. Francis Herreshoff's standing would design a leeboard sharpie encouraged Bolger to go ahead with his own ideas about the type. He went on to design a number of shallow, flat-bottomed sailing craft with leeboards, some handsome and low-sided for sheltered water, others, ugly and high sided, depending on their freeboard for ultimate stability, to be more seaworthy. All were of relatively lighter displacement than the Meadow Lark, and thus suffered a quicker motion in a chop, but all were far simpler to build, with much use of plywood. Francis's Meadow Lark led Phil Bolger into boat designs that eventually propelled him to the head of his own cult, for many of his designs were particularly attractive to amateur builders, and, like Francis, he wrote well about his boats.[38]

Robert P. Gibbs, of Cataumet on Buzzards Bay, was a devotee of L. Francis Herreshoff. He built and owned a Herreshoff double-paddle canoe, a Herreshoff ACA sailing canoe, and a Marco Polo dinghy. He was the first amateur builder to complete a Meadow Lark, the *Loon*. He reported in *The Rudder* that since her launching, in June 1950: "We have sailed her a great many miles, which included a cruise to Port Washington, Long Island. The boat has been an exceptional performer. She has been out in several strong blows and proved comparatively dry and extremely comfortable. She is a far better sea boat than her plans would indicate and we have not as yet found it necessary to reef [but see photograph, page 435]. The cabin is far roomier than one would expect." Francis had a sail in the *Loon* and said she was "quite a lot stiffer than necessary, and she certainly sails on a very even keel. She surprised me in her speed in sailing on a reach." When he peeked into the *Loon*'s cabin, "It nearly knocked me over;" every surface was covered in aluminum paint. Is it any wonder that Francis was reluctant to go on board boats that he had designed?[39]

Francis had planned the Meadow Lark for twin engines, avoiding a single, large-diameter propeller that would either extend below the deadwood or be too close to the surface. Gibbs put into the *Loon*

LEFT: **A variation on No. 75 was this "Proposed Shallow-Draft Cruiser," the lateral plane of the shallow draft being achieved by a longer keel, instead of a centerboard. She was 40 feet long on deck, with a waterline length of 37 feet, a beam of 10 feet, and a draft of 3 feet. The sectional drawing shows that she had just standing headroom under the cabin house and just sitting headroom under the deck, at least between the beams. She has twin engines; perhaps her skipper would keep the leeward one ticking over to help her to windward? Her shallow draft would never be tested on a beat, for there was no customer, and she exists only on paper. Nor was this predecessor of the Meadow Lark beachable.** (© Mystic Seaport Museum, Daniel S. Gregory Ships Plans Library, SP38.110.1)

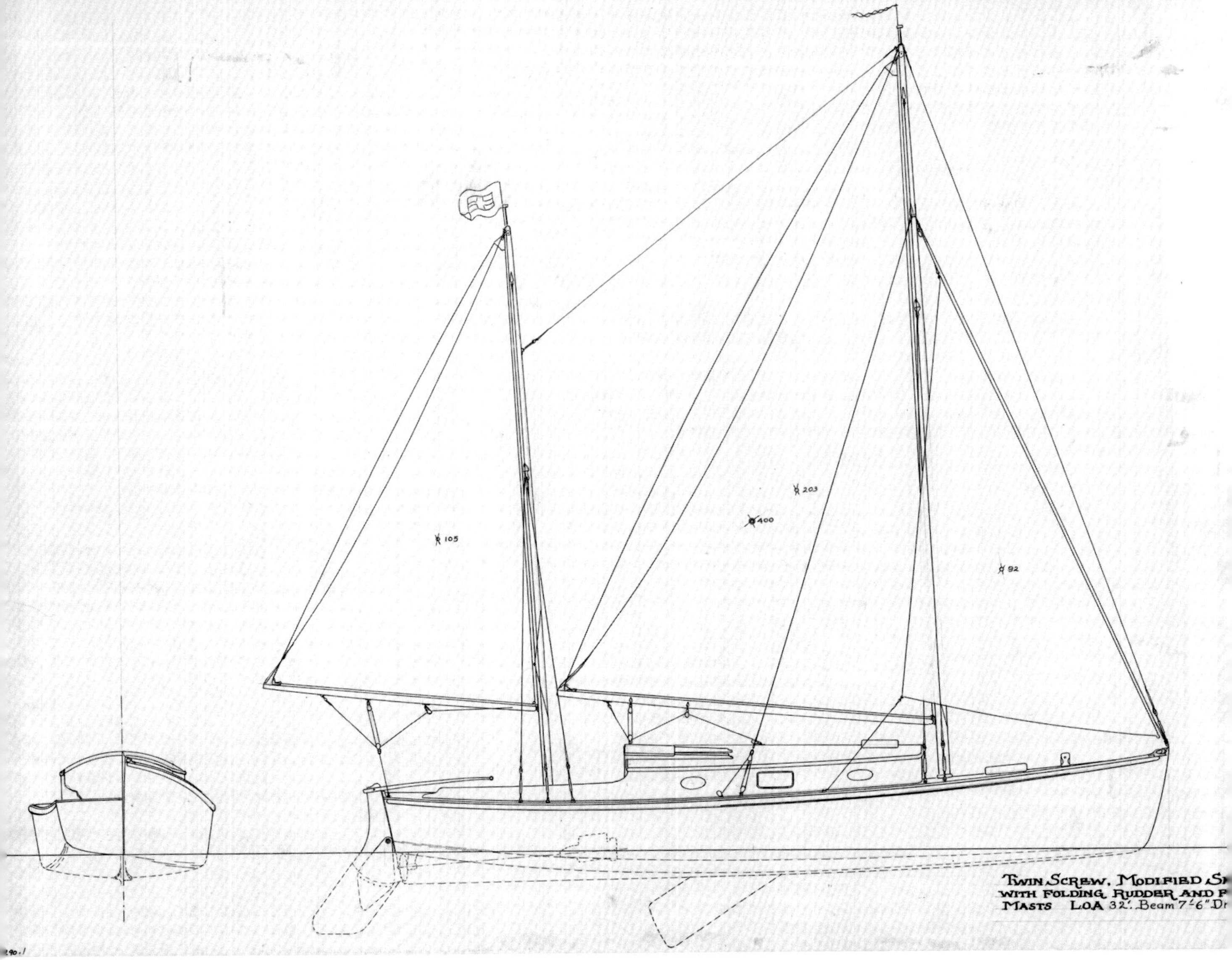

This 32-foot, arc-bottom sharpie is the true forerunner of the Meadow Lark. Francis made the drawing to illustrate a distinct type of cruising boat for his chapter, "Choosing a Cruiser," in "The Common Sense of Yacht Design." He simplified a scoring system that he had published in *Yachting* (December 1931), and gave more advantage to the sharpie type. Francis awarded plus points for number of people accommodated, speed under sail or power, seaworthiness, and stability; he gave minus points for cost of boat and fuel, sail area, draft, and amount of heel when beached. The latter two factors slanted his evaluation toward the sharpie, and it was no surprise that this design scored better under his system than the keel boats he used for other examples. Her beam was 7 feet, 6 inches; and draft 1 foot, 3 inches, centerboard up. Sail area was 400 square feet, with 203 in the mainsail, 105 in the mizzen, and 92 in the jib. She has twin engines and a swing-up rudder. No boat was built to this design, but the very similar Meadow Lark was soon to come. (© Mystic Seaport Museum, Daniel S. Gregory Ships Plans Library, SP38.290.1)

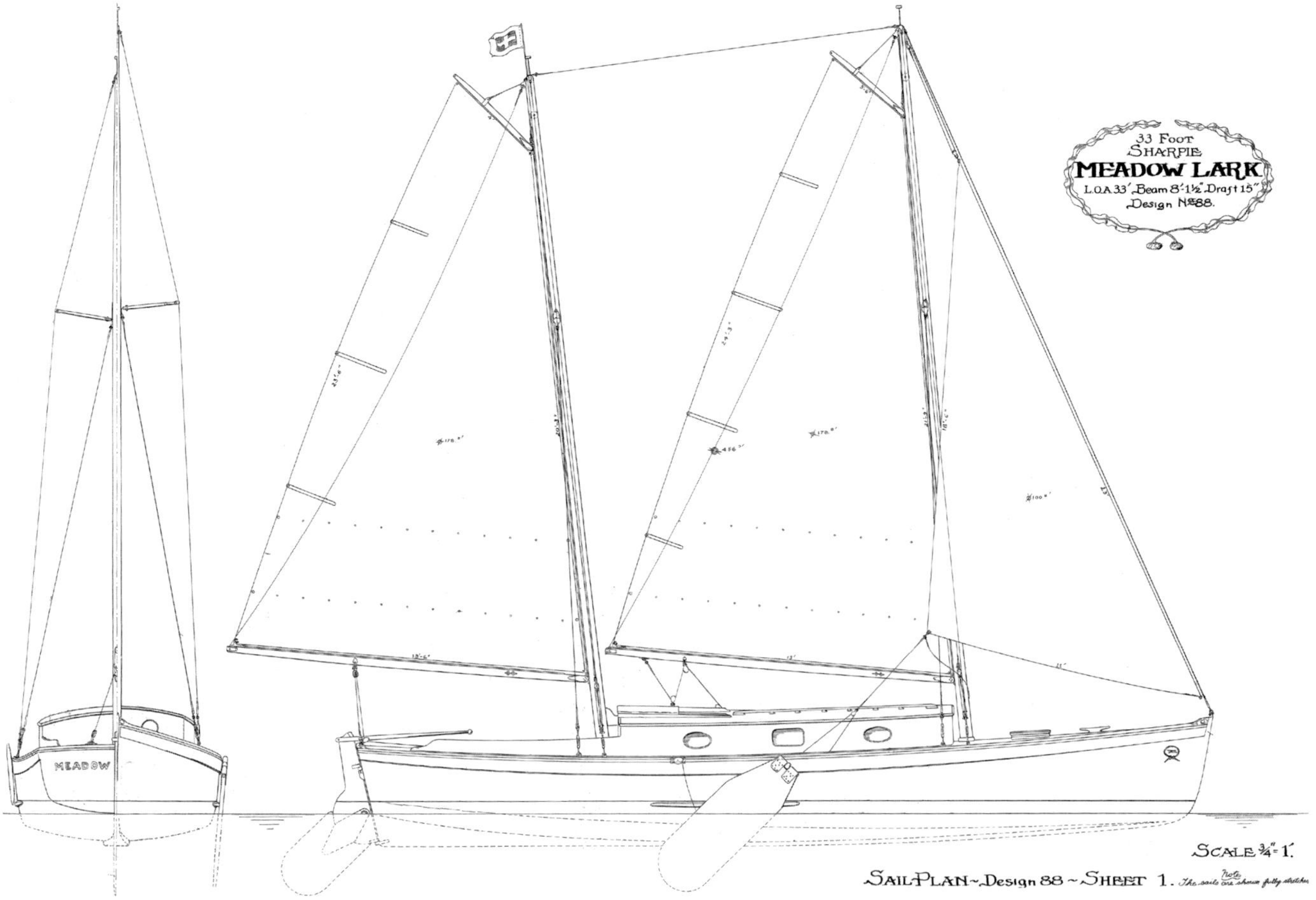

The outboard profile and sail plan of the Meadow Lark, Francis's design No. 88. Her plans were published in a How-To-Build series in *The Rudder* from August 1948 through March 1949. Sail area is 456 square feet; the mainsail and mizzen each have 178 square feet; and the jib has 100. The mainsail and mizzen are not quite identical: the mizzen is 18 inches shorter than the mainsail on the hoist, and 6 inches longer on the foot. The short gaffs reduce the height of the masts; some builders made the masts in tabernacles so that they could be lowered on board. The gaff rig also allows the skipper to change the shape of the sails by adjusting the peak halyard; easing it a little is the equivalent of a temporary reef. Francis shows two reefs in each of the gaff sails, and he believed that the sharpie would stand some real breeze with both sails double-reefed and no jib set. He drew a loose-footed jib but recognized that a self-tending jib on a club would make sense on a boat with leeboards to handle when tacking. One owner added a Marco Polo-type squaresail to the simple sail plan. The rudder will swing up if it grounds and can be raised by a lanyard for beaching. The leeboards had to be moved aft a foot to reduce weather helm; they were also made a foot longer, with their lower ends squared off to a horizontal angle when lowered. An advantage of leeboards over the centerboard is that they can be relocated easily to achieve good steering balance. (© Mystic Seaport Museum, Daniel S. Gregory Ships Plans Library, SP38.192.1)

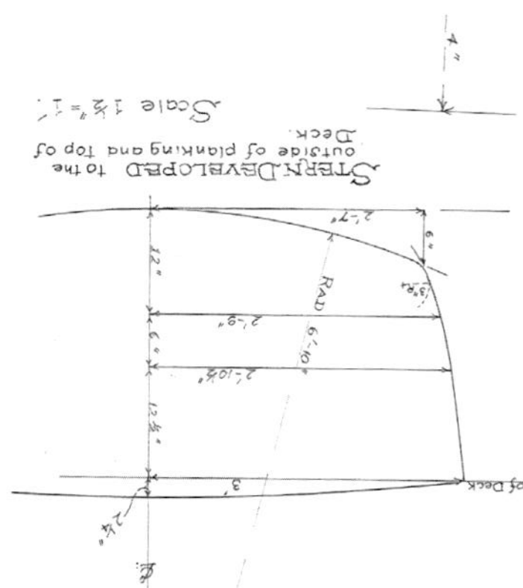

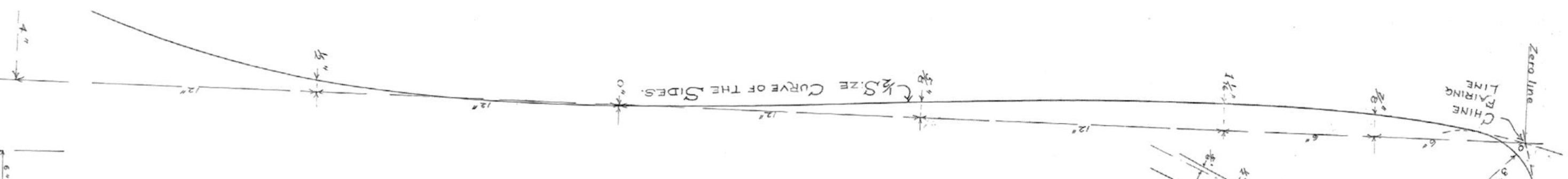

MEADOW LARK

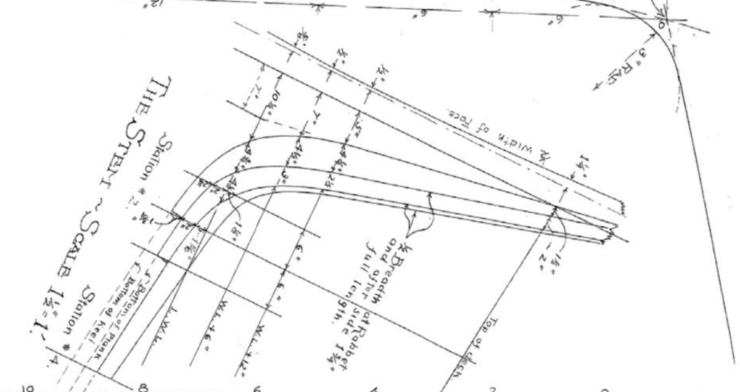

Full Displacement Curve = 125 □' or 8,000 lbs.

		33	30	28	26	24	22	20	18	16	14	12	10	8	6	4	2	0
½ Breadths	At Deck	3-0-0	3-3-3	3-7-0	3-9-0	3-10-5	3-11-4	4-0-0	4-0-0	3-11-3	3-9-3	3-7-2	3-3-6	2-11-0	2-4-7	1-9-2	0-11-7	0-1-2
	At Chine fairing line	2-6-1	2-11-4	3-2-3	3-4-6	3-6-2	3-7-2	3-7-3	3-7-0	3-5-6	3-3-3	3-0-0	2-7-2	2-1-3	1-6-3	0-10-5	0-3-0	
	Of Keel	0-0-7	0-1-0	0-1-2	0-2-5	0-3-7	0-5-1	0-6-0	0-6-6	0-7-0	0-6-6	0-6-0	0-4-7	0-3-5	0-2-6	0-1-6	0-0-7	
Heights	At Deck	2-5-6	2-3-2	2-2-0	2-1-3	2-1-0	2-1-0	2-1-2	2-1-7	2-2-4	2-3-6	2-5-0	2-6-4	2-8-1	2-10-1	3-0-3	3-3-0	3-6-0
	At Chine fairing line	0-6-6	0-2-6	0-0-4	-0-1-2	0-2-6	0-3-6	0-4-6	0-5-5	0-6-2	0-6-6	0-5-7	0-6-6	0-6-2	0-5-5	0-4-6	0-4-0	
	Of Bottom at Center line	0-1-4	0-4-7	0-7-7	0-8-6	0-11-5	1-0-5	1-1-0	1-1-0	1-1-0	1-0-5	0-11-6	0-10-6	0-9-3	0-7-7	0-6-1	0-4-0	
	Bottom of Keel	1-3-0	1-3-0	1-3-0	1-3-0	1-3-0	1-3-0	1-3-0	1-3-0	1-3-0	1-2-5	1-1-6	1-0-6	0-11-3	0-9-7	0-8-1	0-5-6	
Radius of Bottom			7'	7'-5¾"	8'-4¼"	8'-8⅜"	9'-4⅝"	9'-10"	10'-7"	10'-0½"	10'-10¼"	11'-0½"	10'-9½"	9'-2⅞"	7'-4¾"	4'-1½"		

Notes

½ Siding of Stem at Rabbet and after side 1¾" full length.
Bottom planking 1¾" thick.
Side planking 1" thick.
Radious at Chine 3."
Crown of Deck ⅜" to the 1' or 3" in 8'.

Weights.

Hull, Spars, Engines, Tanks	4,500 lbs.	– 56%
Lead Keel	2,500 "	– 31%
Inside Balast	1,000 "	– 13%

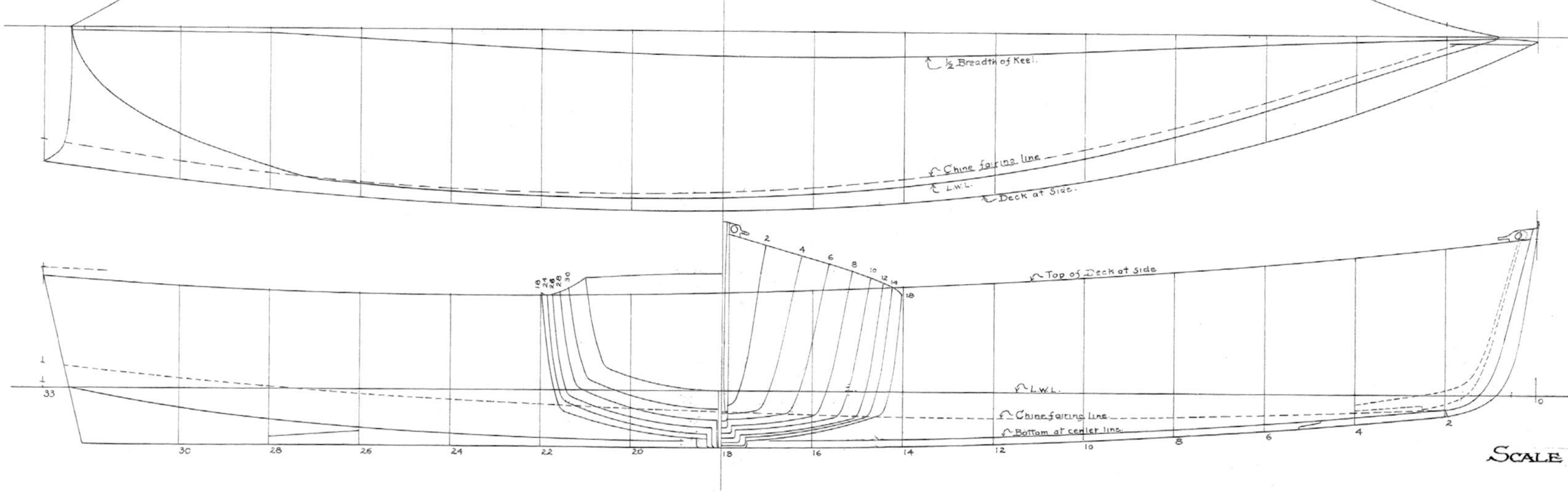

Scale 1"=1'.

Lines ~ Design 88 ~ Sheet 2.

38.112.2.

a single Universal Motor Company Atomic Four (a popular gas engine), with a 12-inch wheel. "It has worked out all right," said Francis. With Francis's permission, Universal ran an advertisement in *The Rudder* with a picture of the Atomic Four, the sail plan of the Meadow Lark, and a photograph of the designer over his signature, and quoted him as saying of the engine, "it has proved extraordinarily economical and quiet."[40]

It may well be that the total number of Meadow Larks built never reached one hundred. This was an L. Francis Herreshoff design that did not catch on Down Under. Australian and New Zealand sailors apparently wanted more of a keel under them if they were going to put to sea and drive their Herreshoff boats hard. And it took time for the odd-looking, leeboard sharpie to become even somewhat popular in American coastal waters. Eventually, though, Buzzards Bay sailors grew weary of seeing Bobby Gibbs's *Loon* beat them in rough races, then head off to spend lazy days and nights in secluded shallows that were closed to their "deep sea" boats.

Allan Vaitses, the professional boatbuilder at Mattapoisett, sailed in the *Loon* and came to realize that the Meadow Lark could "revolutionize one's thinking about cruising." First, he put the question of the sharpie's stability to rest: "On Meadow Lark, one notices a steadiness underfoot called good initial stability. Well, she has good ultimate stability too. Knocked down by a strong gust with turnbuckles dragging and water pouring over the coaming, it is most reassuring the way she struggles free. A ton and a half of lead and three-quarters of a ton of heavy bottom planking assert noticeable authority. Bobby Gibbs sailed an entire race in a forty-knot breeze under full canvas to finish second after many boats dropped out." And Vaitses discovered that the Meadow Lark could be fast: "Over four beams long with negligible draft but plenty of power to carry sail, the Meadow Lark has great potential speed. Reaching or running in a strong breeze, you know it. Running in a big sea, she surfboards beautifully." And he realized the revolutionary spirit embodied in her 15-inch draft, which opened much new cruising, even in a sailor's home waters. The boat also turned out to be a good self-steerer: "Meadow Lark's long narrow hull, long sail plan, and long (if shallow) keel and skeg work to make her self steering; not for a moment or two, but for as long as the wind holds steady. This she can do on almost all points, once the sails are set for that course with the mizzen eased the proper amount." Allan H. Vaitses became the primary promoter and builder of Meadow Larks. He would say, "the Meadow Lark is just the boat the people want but they don't know it yet." Vaitses put together "three dozen" finished boats and sold a good many more in various stages of completion. One of his customers, Dr. Lee Hill, wrote a fine

---

LEFT: **The Meadow Lark's lines and offsets. She is a hard-chine boat (with a curved radius of 3 inches at the chine), but with an arc-bottom instead of a flat bottom, for strength. Her slightly curved forward sections, just below the waterline, mitigate pounding underway in a head sea and slapping at anchor in harbor waves. The high, wide stern is to minimize swinging at anchor and to provide a roomy cockpit. She has a shallow, but substantial, lead keel for stability. Her sides have a slight curvature, a gentle S-curve with a little convexity just above the chine, and a little concavity just below the rail, as shown in the half scale representation at the top of the drawing. (To view the shape of the starboard side as seen upright, turn the drawing so that its right-hand end is at the bottom.) The Meadow Lark is 33 feet long on deck; nearly the same length on the waterline; with a beam of 8 feet, 1½ inches; and a draft of 1 foot, 3 inches, with leeboards and rudder raised. Displacement is 8,000 pounds, with 2,500 pounds of outside lead ballast and 1,000 pounds of inside ballast, for a ballast-displacement ratio of 44 percent, a huge help to stability for a sharpie. Francis dated this drawing July 1948.** (© Mystic Seaport Museum, Daniel S. Gregory Ships Plans Library, SP38.192.2

book about cruising in his Meadow Lark called *The Sharpie Sanderling*.[41]

Vaitses consulted with Francis about modifications to the design. Francis recommended both moving the leeboards aft a foot and extending the bow a foot (making the boat a 34-footer) to move the headstay, and hence the center of effort of the sail plan, forward. Both these changes were to reduce weather helm, for the first Meadow Larks were found to be hard-mouthed—they wanted to round up into the wind.[42]

And Vaitses consulted Francis on construction details. For bottom planking, he had some wonderful resin-filled yellow pine from the torn-down Gillette Building in Boston, and he asked Francis just what fastenings to use with it. On Francis's recommendation, he had 3-inch bronze spikes cast. One important construction element that the two apparently did not discuss was the chine log; or, rather, the absence of this normally vital member in a hard-chine boat. There is usually a heavy, longitudinal timber at the corner where the side meets the bottom, giving substantial wood into which to fasten both bottom planking and side planking. But with the arc-bottom planking on the Meadow Lark running fore-and-aft instead of the normal cross planking of a flat-bottomed boat, Francis thought he could get away without a chine log. He did warn the builder that the outside plank on the bottom (at the all-important corner) "must be very securely fastened, for when the planking swells it will have a tendency to start this plank, so this plank should be fastened at each main frame with two 3- or 3½-inch No. 18 Everdur screws, somewhat staggered so that one screw comes on the bottom frame and one into the side frame." There were no known complaints from builders or owners about the construction of their Meadow Larks' chines, although one restorer of a Meadow Lark did beef them up.[43]

Many customers wanted the sharpie bigger, so Vaitses added two feet more length amidships and turned out 36-footers. One of these, the *Hawk,* had a raised deck and doghouse; it was inevitable that some sharpie sailors would want more headroom. Once when Francis was at Vaitses's yard checking up on John Kendall's Nereia, he asked the builder, "what are you doing in that big shed down there?" Vaitses replied, "I hate to tell you this, but we are building Meadow Larks out of fiberglass." "Oh, I'd like to see that," said Francis. "With fiberglass maybe people will use that boat the way I wanted

---

RIGHT: **The cabin and construction plan of the Meadow Lark. She was to be heavily built for stability and to take the ground. The bottom planking, best made of longleaf yellow pine, is especially heavy at 1¾ inches thick. This planking runs fore-and-aft, whereas traditional sharpies were cross-planked, so the Meadow Lark has no chine log. Side planking is 1 inch thick, except for a sheer strake of 1¾ inches. Bottom and side frames, also of generous scantling, are bolted together and spaced on 24-inch centers. (Francis heartily approved of one amateur builder's use of angle-iron frames.) The 24-foot lead keel is 12 inches wide and 2 inches deep. Francis recommended building the boat upside down, for ease of working on the bottom; the lead keel could be bolted on after the narrow boat was turned over. The cabin has headroom of 4 feet, 5 inches. There is a generous forepeak for storage, a forward, two-berth sleeping cabin, which can be separated from the two-berth saloon by a curtain, with the galley and its coal stove aft to port, and the companionway to starboard. The cook can perform his wonders standing in the hatchway. Francis shows the cedar bucket just abaft the mainmast; the forward cabin can be used as a toilet room by day. The middle portlights are rectangular, for opening. A big feature of the cabin of this sharpie is its lack of an obstructive centerboard trunk. The floor of the 7-foot-long, watertight cockpit has a small raised section to accommodate two one-cylinder, 5-horsepower Kermath Model Sixteen 5s. When Francis heard that an amateur builder had put in a pair of 5-horsepower outboards in a well, he said that he had "made a mistake in not designing these boats for an outboard motor."** (© Mystic Seaport Museum, Daniel S. Gregory Ships Plans Library, SP38.192.3)

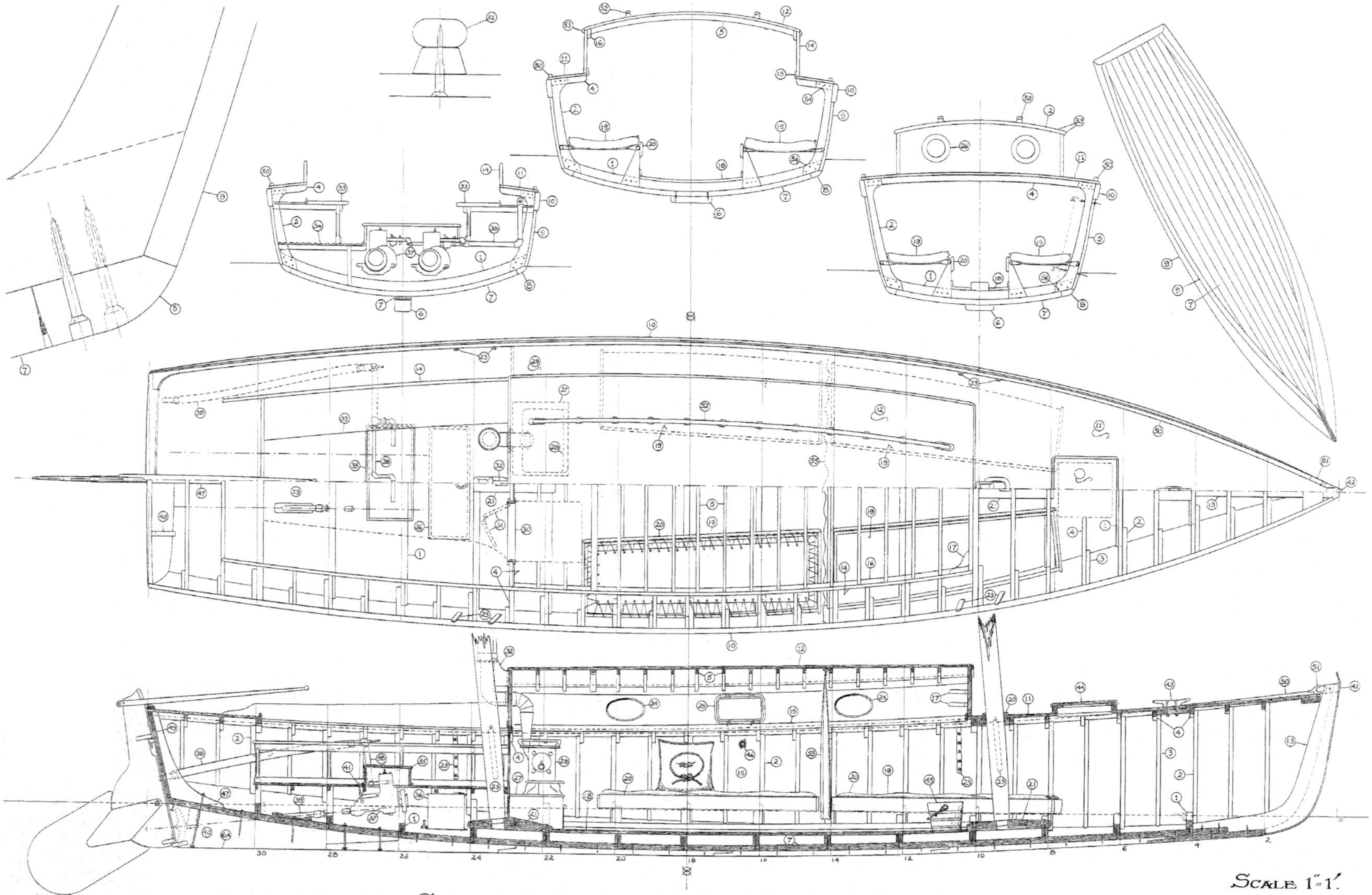

Cabin and Construction Plan of MEDOW LARK ~ Design 88 ~ Sheet 3.

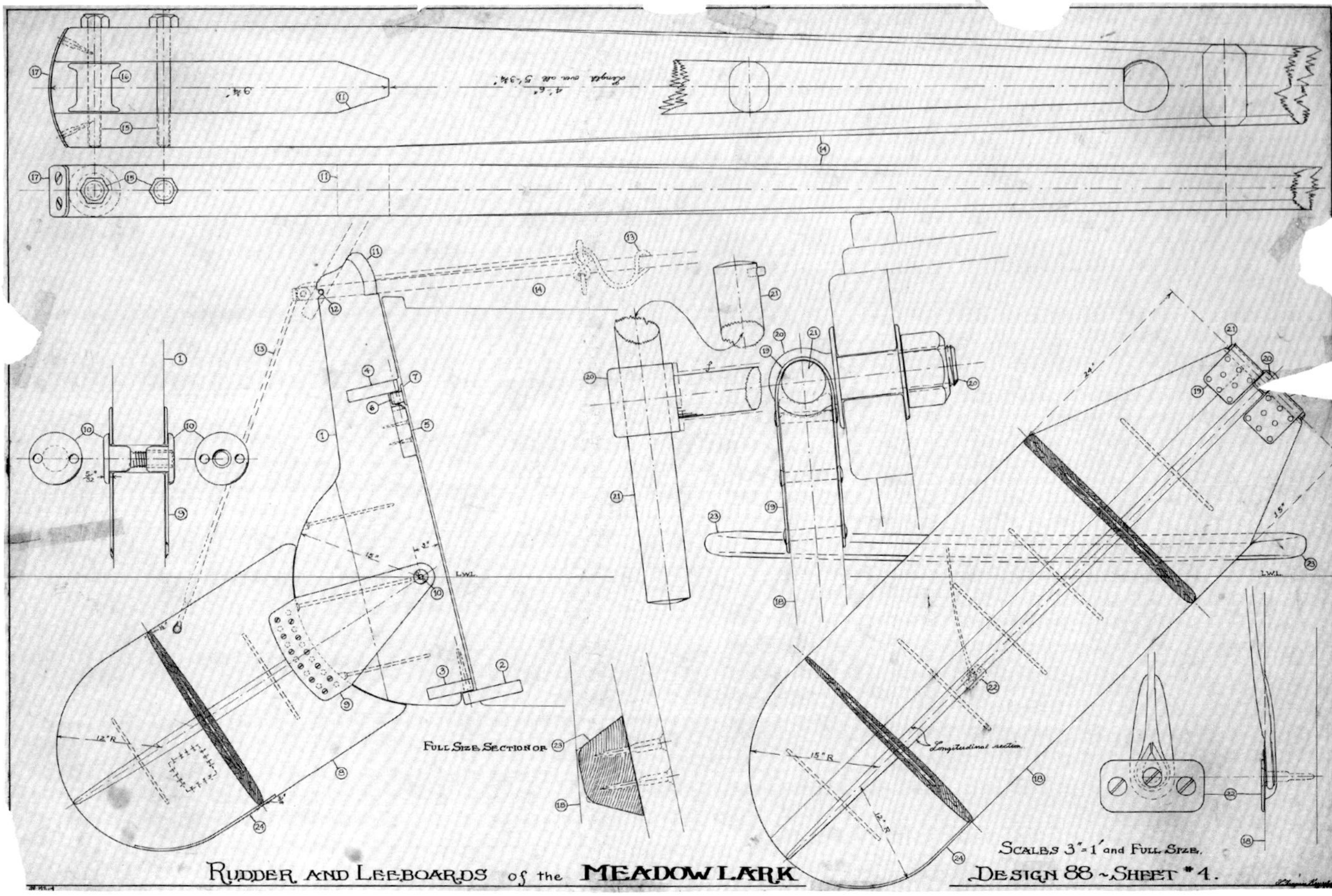

ABOVE: **Francis's detailed drawing for making the leeboards and rudder of the Meadow Lark. This gear had to function perfectly in order for the boat to be able to sail well and also beach for a picnic or the night. As shown in the rendering of the leeboard's attachment fitting in the center of the drawing, Francis designed them to swing not only up and down in the fore-and-aft plane, but also out away from the boat when she rolled, to reduce strain. The leading edge of each leeboard was shaped so that water flow would shove it back into place as the rolling force eased. The cost of reducing the strain on the leeboards was a little more leeway.** (© Mystic Seaport Museum, Daniel S. Gregory Ships Plans Library, SP38.192.4) RIGHT: **The *Loon* was the first Meadow Lark built. Her builder-owner, Robert P. Gibbs of Cataumet, Massachusetts, launched her on June 13, 1950. With a double-reefed mizzen and both gaff sails luffing to ease her, she smashes her way to windward through the Buzzards Bay chop.** (Norman Fortier photo, courtesy of the New Bedford Whaling Museum)

them to. It really disturbs me. I ask people if they take their Meadow Larks ashore and put them on the beach. They say no, they don't want to scrape the paint off. Now, maybe with fiberglass they'll use the boat the way I designed her to be used."[44]

Vaitses got out of that one. And he stretched out the stern of the fiberglass Meadow Larks by another foot, allowing space under a bridge deck for the bigger engines that owners wanted, so they were 37-footers. Vaitses did not increase the sail area on these bigger versions, but he did increase the ballast proportionately to the hull size. With longer waterlines, the boats seemed fast enough just with the original rig, and they were even stiffer than the smaller Meadow Larks. Vaitses sent Francis a photo of one of the fiberglass 37-footers under sail. Francis actually got on the phone to express his delight. He told Vaitses his Meadow Lark was a "hell of a boat." But he wanted to know why a line was hanging over the stern. Why wasn't that pulled in? Vaitses said, "wait a minute, that's the lanyard to pull up the blade of the rudder." "Oh," said Francis. Vaitses was tickled: "That was one of the big days of my boatbuilding career."[45]

A significant part of Allan Vaitses career

LEFT TOP: **The photograph of himself that Francis furnished to the Universal Motor Company for its advertisement of the Atomic Four motor as used in the Meadow Lark *Loon*.** (*The Rudder* (May 1952): 4) LEFT BOTTOM: **Allen Beechel's wash drawing of the Meadow Lark humming along on the wind in inland waters was published as a frontispiece in *The Rudder* as Francis's How-To-Build series was unfolding. The artist has minimized the boat's big stern.** (The Rudder (December 1948): frontispiece) ABOVE: **The Meadow Lark *Loon* close-hauled and rail down. She was stiffer and faster than she looked at first glance. The *Loon* has a self-tending jib on a club. Her mizzen sheet has been eased a mite; perhaps she is steering herself.** (*The Rudder* (December 1961): 30)

was building boats to the designs of L. Francis Herreshoff. "His were the most fun to build," he said, "and the ones that I feel the customers got the most satisfaction out of. Everything he did was so neat and worked so well. His drawings separated the parts of the boat and were easy to follow. He was very painstaking about keeping the drawings clear and yet detailed. The only other person who did as good a construction drawing as Francis Herreshoff was Walter McGinnis [of Eldridge-McGinnis, Boston]."[46]

Francis wrote, "shallow draft boats are very practical and seaworthy, but they require great skill in handling them and they are not non-capsizable but because they can slide off sideways when a sea strikes them they are easier in a sea than some of the deeper boats." He added, "I believe Meadow Lark would be perfectly safe to make the crossing from Cuba to Florida in certain seasons of the year if a person were accustomed to the choppy weather of the Gulf Stream, and if she had an auxiliary engine to keep up her average speed if becalmed. " Vaitses reported that one owner sailed his Meadow Lark outside from Long Island to Florida and back, negotiating some stormy weather.[47]

Francis and Boris hoped that the Meadow Lark would become popular in southern waters. It seemed that the Chesapeake Bay, Tidewater Virginia, Carolina sounds like Albemarle and Currituck, and Florida's Biscayne Bay would be ideal places for a 15-inch draft. These shallows did embrace their Meadow Larks, but by the handful,

A Meadow Lark showing off her 15-inch draft. No crowding at this anchorage; there is plenty of room for a stern anchor to hold her steady. Her dark-painted wale is duplicated on the leeboard. (*The Rudder* (December 1961): 31)

rather than the hundreds. At any rate, southern owners were enthusiastic. One Marbleheader, who retired to Coral Gables, Florida, reported to Francis: "We have had several sails lately aboard our Meadow Lark and are enjoying her more each time. There are many places where you can't approach the shore nearer than a half mile if you draw more than two feet. We regularly sail over sand flats so shallow that our rudder leaves a 'track.' It's very exciting and yet quite safe." He commented that he had removed one of the sharpie's 5-horsepower engines, reducing her speed under power to three knots, but "She has a noticeable increase in speed [under sail]—also she comes about much faster."[48]

The Meadow Lark demonstrates the versatility of L. Francis Herreshoff. His version of the sharpie is a very different boat from any other that he designed. By a careful distribution of her weights, he was able, with no increase of the draft of her New Haven ancestor, to produce a boat with enough stability to carry sail for speed and to be relatively seaworthy. The Meadow Lark's performance would equal that of a Presto boat with only half the draft. Perhaps Francis's best summary of his design No. 88 is, "all things considered, Meadow Lark may be the most fun for the money of any boat I have designed."[49]

Edwin M. Hill, who sailed the ketch *Quiet Tune* out of Pemaquid Harbor on the coast of Maine, was, in a sense, a professional boatman. He was the Maine sales representative for a dozen companies, offering everything needed to build a wooden yacht, from "selected Philippine mahogany" and "foreign and domestic hardwoods," to fastenings and bungs (the United States Bung Manufacturing Company); and from marine fittings, including propellers, to caulking cotton, paint, and turned spars. When Hill wanted to get a new boat built for himself, he would supply all the materials and manufactured gear.[50]

In 1948, Hill did want a new boat. He loved the *Quiet Tune,* but dreamed of a similar, bigger boat designed for him by L. Francis Herreshoff, and why not with that designer's signature clipper bow? Francis drew Hill's new boat in the winter of 1948-49, while he was in the middle of the "How To Build the Meadow Lark" series. Norman H. Hodgdon Jr., in Boothbay, Maine, built her, but not until 1954, when she replaced the *Quiet Tune.* Francis suggested that Hill call his new vessel the Lively Tune, but Hill chose instead the fairy-tale character Araminta.[51]

The *Araminta*, like the *Tioga* and *Ticonderoga* before her, has gorgeous reverse curves in the profile of her clipper bow and in her wineglass sections, carried all the way aft to her curved transom. To accent her bow, Francis drew trailboards that were carefully small. He loved the subtle shading produced by a trailboard's ornamental vine and raised border. The boat's flare all around the waterline and her curved sides make her look like a lovely seabird, just alighted. The *Araminta* shares fully the elegant grace of her big sisters. She is one of those L. Francis Herreshoff designs that speak even to landlubbers.

Hill enjoyed many a day-sail in his beautiful ketch until his fifth season with her, but in the summer of 1958, he found he had been out only a dozen times, and as he was considering retiring to Florida's thin waters, he put the *Araminta* on the market. The buyer, after a year, was John Kendall, who, as we have seen, would later bring into his stable a Nereia, a Mobjack, and a Bounty. It was the *Araminta* that got Kendall hooked on clipper-bowed yachts designed by L. Francis Herreshoff. And, when all was said and done, it was the *Araminta* who was his favorite of the four.[52]

Kendall first saw the *Araminta* in the back of a boatyard shed on a dark day in November 1959. Even under those circumstances, she was spectacularly beautiful to him, and he bought her on the spot and brought her to his homeport of Marion. Hill had not raced the boat, but when Kendall saw

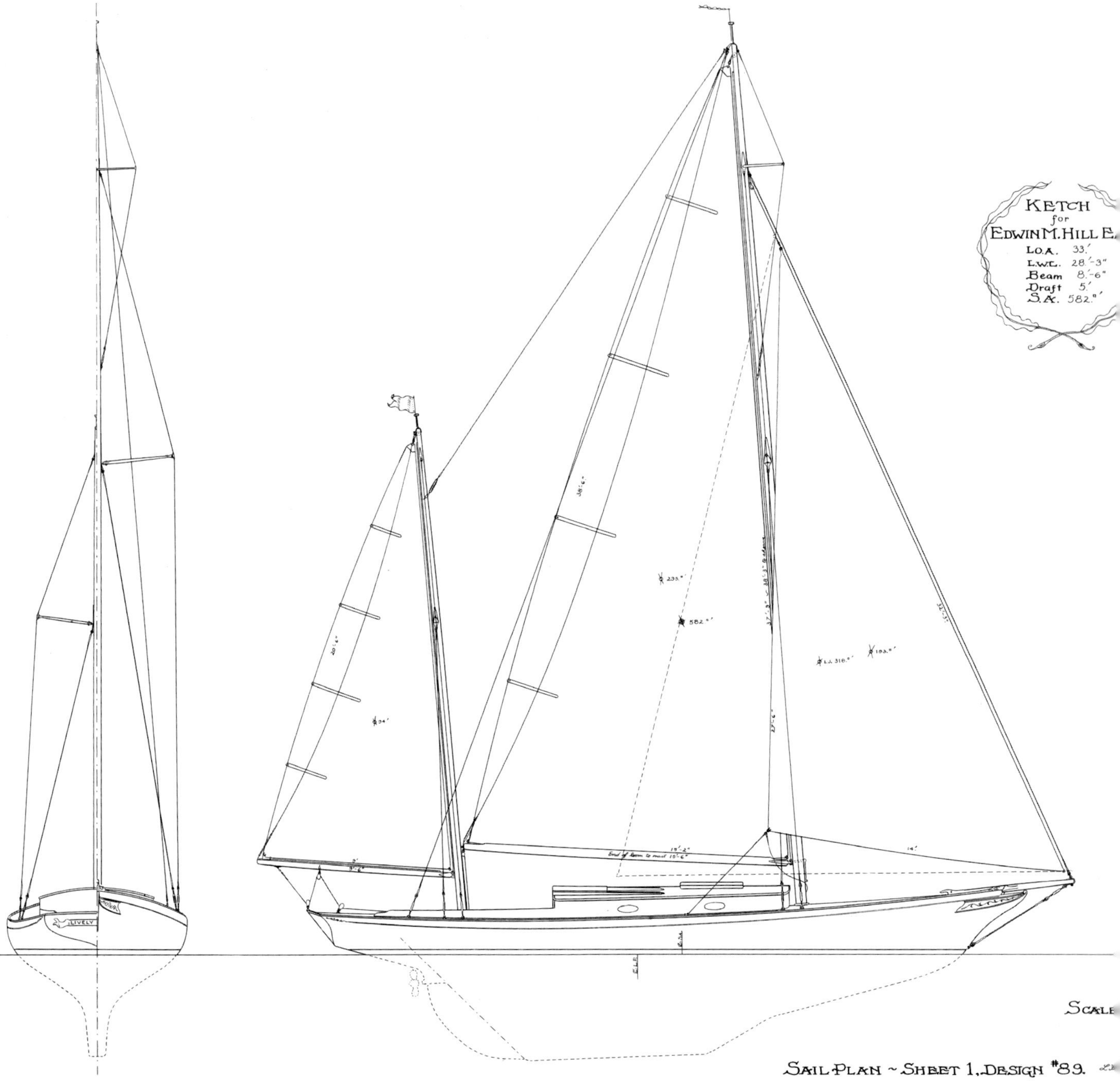
KETCH
for
EDWIN M. HILL E.
L.O.A. 33.'
L.W.L. 28'-3"
Beam 8'-6"
Draft 5'
LIVELY
SAIL PLAN ~ SHEET 1, DESIGN #89.

how fast she was, he, like the owners of the *Tioga*, *Bounty*, and, especially *Ticonderoga*, couldn't resist.

The *Araminta* was often first to finish against bigger boats in the cruising class of the Hospital Race, sailed outside Cataumet's Hospital Cove on Buzzards Bay. Francis had a chance to watch her sail in one of these races on August 14, 1960, when he brought a long, narrow, fast launch of his design down to Buzzards Bay from Marblehead. The course was a ten-mile triangle; the breeze was the bay's normal summer afternoon offering: strong southwest, with a steep chop. "They set a moderate sized jib which was snapped onto the forestay," Francis reported. "She went very well indeed and looked very well and did not appear to me to carry any more than the normal weather helm although the wind was blowing about 22 mph. The only boat that beat her was an out-and-out ocean racing boat of approximately twice the sail area, and on one of the legs of the course that was close hauled *Araminta* almost caught this boat. But on the last leg, this larger yacht set a very large parachute spinnaker and *Araminta* did not set any spinnaker so she did not overhaul the large boat but did finish close behind her." After the race, Francis rafted up his launch to the *Araminta* for a yarn, and John Kendall had the experience of Francis showing no interest in coming on board a sailing yacht of his design to look her over, much less joining Kendall for a sail. The situation was repeated for Kendall when he took his Nereia, the *Alaria*, to Marblehead. Francis's behavior puzzled Kendall. The two got on well, and Francis recognized that Kendall was a good sailor, but he had been so hurt by owners' whims in fitting out and handling his designs that he was leery of risking further pain.[53]

Kendall kept the *Araminta* for ten years. By 1968, he and his wife, Nancy, were sailing with three children on board. That summer, they introduced the youngsters to the splendors of a raft of Cruising Club yachts, joining the CCA cruise at Bristol, their home port of Marion, and Hadley's Harbor, opposite Woods Hole on Cape Cod. Designed as a daysailer with overnight accommodations for two, the *Araminta* was a bit tight with five on board. Kendall asked Francis to design him a bigger boat, but Francis was seventy-seven and had stopped designing. Kendall had to choose an existing Herreshoff design. As we have seen, he chose the Nereia.[54]

When Kendall paid Allan Vaitses for building the Nereia *Alaria*, part of the payment consisted of the *Araminta*. Vaitses wrote to Francis: "Perhaps the greatest joy that one who has always liked small sail boats could expect is to own *Araminta*. WHAT A BOAT! Just looking out at her from my house is a pleasure. One just waltzes by everything under forty to forty five feet. This I do not do to show off or be mean, but only to test the fabulousness of her again and again. It's unbelievable."[55]

LEFT: **The 33-foot ketch *Araminta* was Francis's design No. 89 of 1948. She was for Edwin M. Hill of Damariscotta, Maine, for whom Francis had designed the smaller ketch-rigged day-sailer *Quiet Tune* in 1943. The *Araminta* has 582 square feet of sail, with 295 square feet in the mainsail, 94 square feet in the mizzen, and 193 in the working jib. Francis also shows a Genoa jib of 318 square feet. At Hill's request, Francis gave her twin permanent backstays instead of running backstays, because he often went sailing single-handed. This boat has plenty of stability, so she sports a tall rig. The mainsail has roller-reefing gear. Francis envisioned her shortened down for a strong breeze under a reefed mainsail and a storm jib. She would also shorten down well under working jib and mizzen (as Kathleen and I found on a glorious circumnavigation of Shelter Island, between Long Island's eastern forks). Francis dated this plan November 5, 1948.** (© Mystic Seaport Museum, Daniel S. Gregory Ships Plans Library, SP38.143.2)

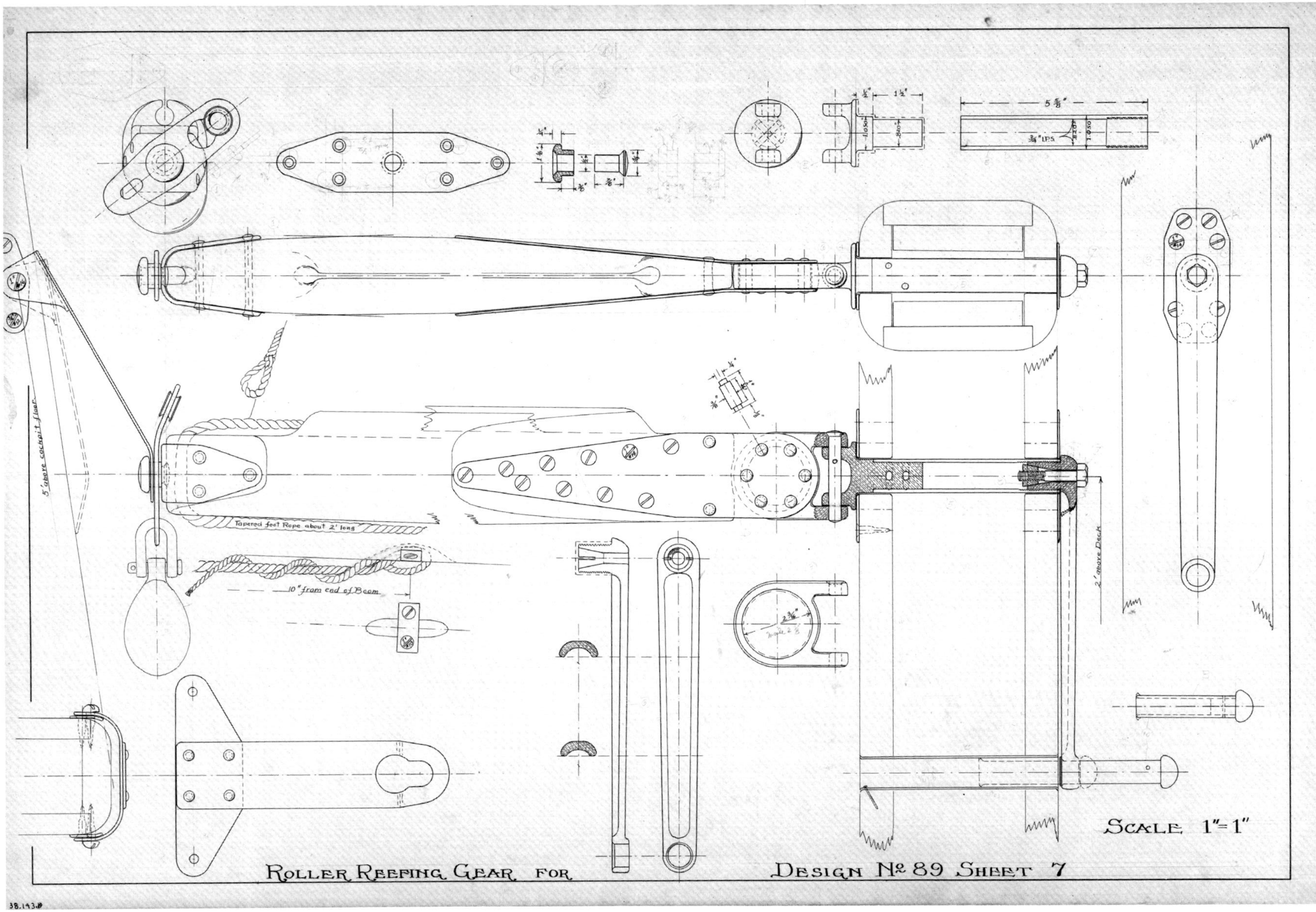

Roller Reefing Gear for Design No 89 Sheet 7

L Francis Herreshoff, like his father Nathanael, was intrigued by the concept of lightweight, multihull craft, boats that gained their stability from widely spaced hulls or pontoons instead of from deep, heavy, ballast keels. Such a boat could have a very high sail-area-to-displacement ratio, and thus could sail much faster than conventional craft. Francis had sailed in a proa, and he recognized the potential of the trimaran.

He was friends with Victor Tchetchet, a Russian artist who had emigrated to the United States, in 1924, had become interested in multihull sailboats, had coined the word "trimaran," and had been first "to make the modern trimaran really work," according to trimaran designer Jim Brown. Francis and Tchetchet traded ideas about multihulls in a lengthy correspondence that also included Tchetchet's envious comments about how wonderful it would be to live the life of a bachelor, an assumption that Francis never denied to his friend.[56]

But it was to the catamaran that Francis turned for a sailing machine, as had his father, and as had his older brother, Sidney. We have seen how Nathanael's catamaran, the *Amaryllis,* beat the fleet

LEFT: Francis's full-scale drawing of (from left to right) the *Araminta*'s boom crotch (holding the end of the main boom up to the mizzenmast when the mainsail is lowered), end-of-main-boom fittings, gooseneck, and roller-reefing gear. The latter was the same sort of gear he had designed for the Buzzards Bay 30-Square-Metre One Designs (see volume 1, pages 332, 333). The rotating shaft goes through the mast. The crank is on the forward side of the mast, and its handle slides into a hole in the mast to secure the gear in place. Francis's rectangular boom allows the foot of the sail to be closer to the boom's centerline when reefed, compared to a round boom. This reduces the torque on the boom from the foot of the reefed sail, although a later owner of the ketch reported that in a squall the strain twisted the shaft by 10 degrees. Francis copied the outhaul arrangement he shows from "the latest German and Swedish roller reefing booms" to allow the leech of the sail to be rolled down without lumps. The boom crotch allows the boom to be rotated in place when reefing before getting underway. Francis was proud of the neatness (and cleverness) of his roller-reefing arrangements. He made all these fittings for Hill on the lathes in his castle workshop. (© Mystic Seaport Museum, Daniel S. Gregory Ships Plans Library, SP38.143.19) ABOVE: The *Araminta* close-hauled in a gentle breeze, her beautiful, clipper bow forming her habitual, lovely, bow wave. (Mystic Seaport Museum, 1975-9-94)

The *Araminta* reaching fast under an overlapping jib in the Buzzards Bay chop. She is traveling at hull speed, and this photograph demonstrates clearly why she can go no faster (unless propelled by a big following sea): she has dug a wave the length of her waterline and cannot climb up out of its trough. (© Mystic Seaport Museum, 1990.37.131)

in a regatta (volume 1, page 21). In 1932, Nathanael and Sidney teamed up on a catamaran design, and, in 1942, Sidney designed the catamaran Sea Spider. Francis continued the Herreshoff tradition in 1949, when he designed the catamaran Sailski for a *Rudder* How-To-Build series.[57]

All three Herreshoffs werc ahead of their times with catamaran designs. When *The Rudder* published Francis's plans for the Sailski, from May 1949 through February 1950, most sailors thought that a multi-hull was a freak that disavowed valuable tradition (ignoring that multi-hulls celebrated the extraordinary tradition of early Pacific voyaging) and somehow cheated to gain speed. It would not be until 1961 that Arthur Javes brought out his Aqua Cat, and 1965, when Hobart Alter started

---

To accompany his thought-provoking discourse on sailing machines in "The Common Sense of Yacht Design," Francis made this drawing of a proposed catamaran with a separate sail plan for each hull. After discussions with Starling Burgess, this design evolved from Francis's far more complex catamaran of 1920, drawn when he was still in Bristol, which had its masts tipped inboard and its sails with double sheets and wishbone booms (see volume 1, pages 65, 66). (*The Rudder* (August 1947): 38)

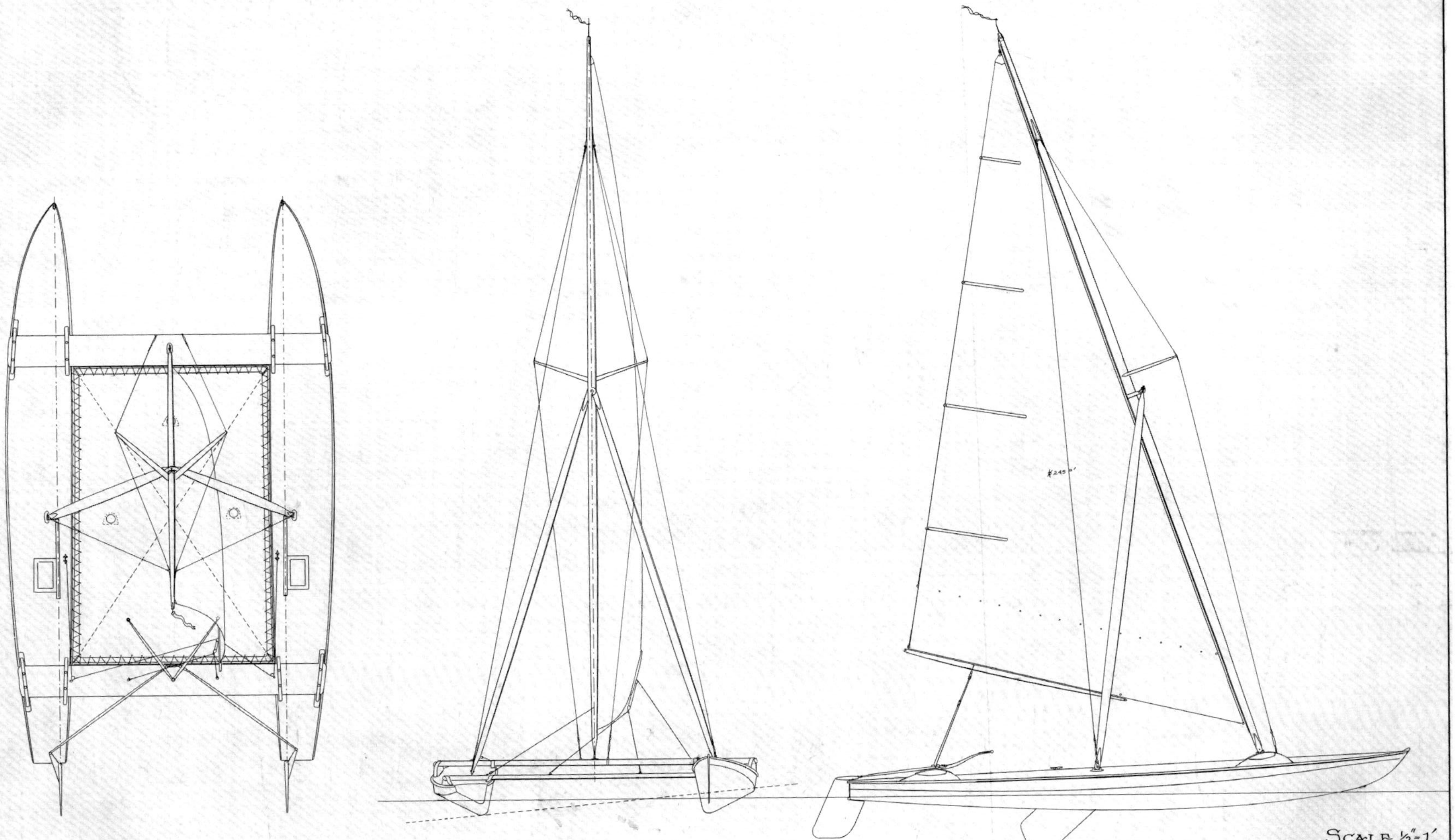

SCALE ½" = 1'.

THE SAILING MACHINE "SAILSKI" – DESIGN Nº 90, SHEET 1.

L. Francis Herreshoff March 1949.

38-168-1

building Hobie Cats. The company that Alter started has sold more than 200,000 boats. There have been probably no more than a dozen Sailskis in the world. Instead of Francis's intricate design for lightweight wooden construction for the hulls, the Aqua Cats and Hobies were mass-produced in fiberglass and so could be purchased complete for about the cost of materials for a Sailski. And the Aqua Cats and Hobies were much smaller than the 27-foot Sailski; all they needed for a base of operations was a beach. Francis had not believed that such small catamarans, 12 or 16 feet long, or really any multi-hulls, would catch on. Shortly before designing the Sailski, he wrote, "I doubt that the multi-hull sail boat will ever be popular or practical for general use." He believed that such craft were too complicated, expensive, hard to handle, and dangerous.[58]

Francis thought that the Aqua Cat had copied his Sailski's rig, with apparent justification. And both the Aqua Cat and Hobie Cat have a Sailski feature, the "trampoline" deck. The trampoline is perhaps too obvious a feature for any small catamaran to be a copy, but Francis pointed out that the Sailski was first with it. He once wrote to Francis E. Fredette, an experienced seaman and boatbuilder who was starting to design able cruising boats in British Columbia, "as far as having the designs copyrighted, you will find that if you keep thinking about your work and improving with each design you can always keep ahead of the copiers."[59]

Francis was ready with the first plan of the Sailski two months after the last installment on the Meadow Lark. He had started working on the design before the Meadow Lark articles were finished, and both projects overlapped with another major series for *The Rudder*. His Sailski plans, as usual, were extremely detailed, and his instructions, guiding the amateur builder through the drawings and warning him which joints and fastenings to be especially careful about, and not to get mixed up as to which asymmetrical hull was which, were clear, showing his development as an excellent technical writer. The various elements of the catamaran took eight articles to describe, each with an elaborate drawing. And the Sailski's light, plywood, longitudinal construction was new to Francis; he could not simply modify the scantlings of previous designs. He left nothing to chance for the builders. "Most every part has been shown," he wrote, "but if any questions come up in the

---

LEFT: **The sail and rigging plan of the Sailski, another *Rudder* How-To-Build design and Francis's own response to his consideration of the catamaran sailing machine in "Common Sense." This catamaran has a single well-raked mast stepped on her forward cross member, with the mast held by sheerlegs, as well as by a pair of shrouds and jumper stays. She sets but one sail. The hulls are 27 feet long; beam is 13 feet, 9 inches. Sail area is 245 square feet. The cross members are light enough to twist slightly, allowing the hulls to pitch independently a bit. The dotted line in the ends-on drawing in the center shows the slight angle of heel when sailing in a fresh breeze. Because of the raked mast and partial boom, the sail acts like a jib, with lift as well as drive. When heading to leeward, a catamaran goes faster jibing from reach to reach, rather than running dead before it, so a full-length boom, good for running, is not necessary, and the partial boom allows a better set of the sail. The mast is a tapered box-section; the sheerlegs are streamlined; and the boom is solid, round. The sheerlegs are attached to the mast with, in effect, a universal joint, to avoid straining the heads of these spars. There are strong reinforcements at the ends of the cross members and for the mast and sheerlegs. Note the double tillers, angled so that the person at the helm can sit to windward. One owner stowed a 5-horsepower outboard in the port hull. Mounted on a bracket on the after cross member, it "pushed her right along." The canvas "deck" between the hulls is supported by diagonal wires with a sag of 6 inches. Francis admitted that "the waves will certainly slap the underside of this canvas frequently."** (© Mystic Seaport Museum, Daniel S. Gregory Ships Plans Library, SP38.168.1)

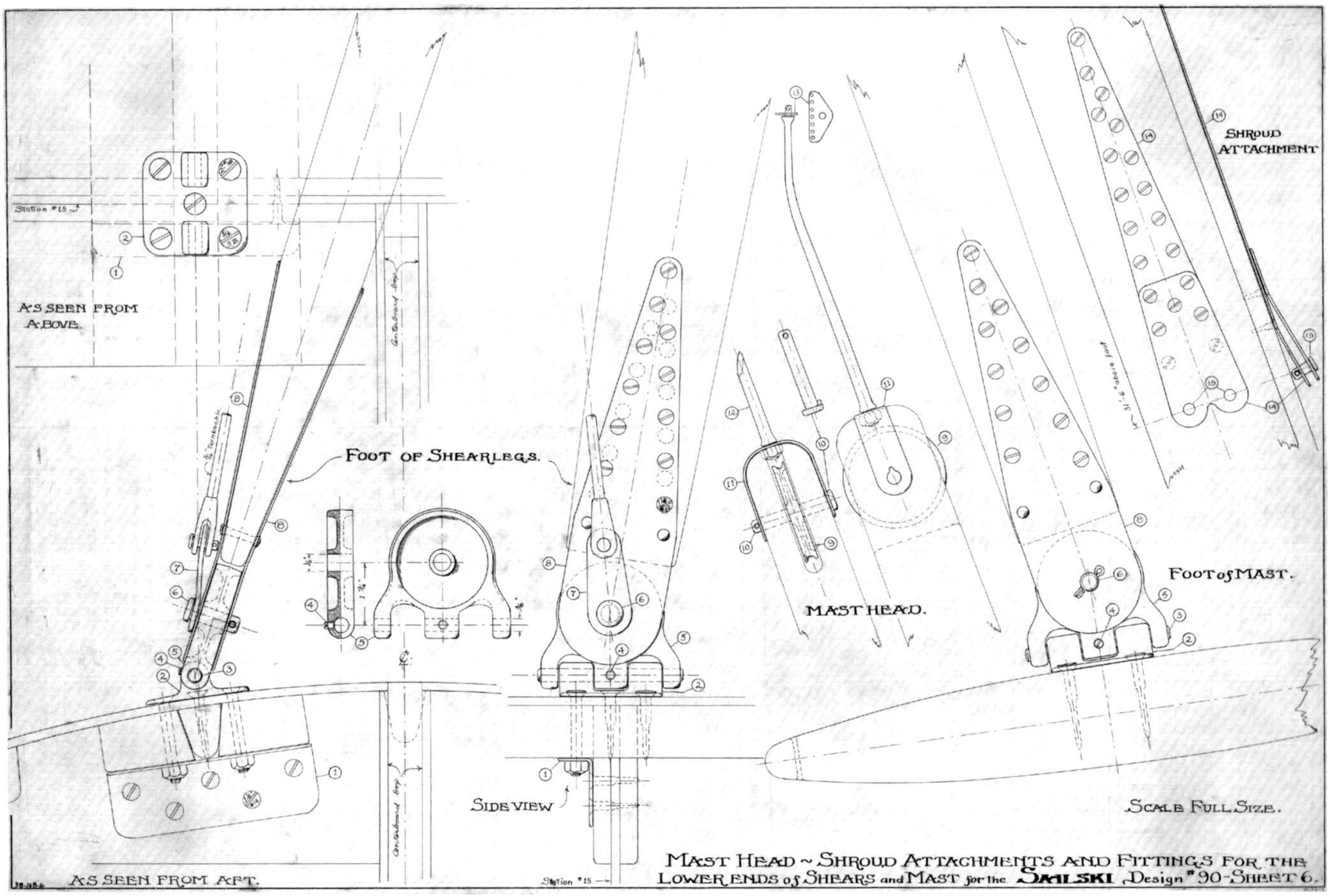

ABOVE: **Francis's drawing showing his universal-joint fittings for the feet of the mast and sheerlegs, as well as the halyard sheave at the masthead. Note the staff for a wind pennant, angled at its top to bring it to vertical from the rake of the mast.** (© Mystic Seaport Museum, Daniel S. Gregory Ships Plans Library, SP38.168.6) RIGHT, INSIDE FOLDOUT: **The lines and offsets of the *Araminta,* Francis's ninth clipper-bowed yacht. He designed her to be more like a racer than her big sister, the *Ticonderoga*. She has a deep, narrow ballast keel and a cutaway underwater profile forward and so, relatively speaking, more power to carry sail than *Ti* without an undue increase in wetted surface, and more lateral plane against leeway. She has lots of flare for dryness on deck. Waterline length is 28 feet, 3 inches; beam, 8 feet, 6 inches; and draft 5 feet. Displacement is 12,288 pounds, with 5,950 pounds of lead outside ballast, for a ballast-displacement ratio of 49 percent.** (© Mystic Seaport Museum, Daniel S. Gregory Ships Plans Library, SP38.143.1)

	33	32	30	28	26	24	22	20	18	16	14	12	10	8	6	4	2	0		
Sheer.		1-10-2	1-8-6	1-7-7	1-7-2	1-7-0	1-6-7	1-7-1	1-7-6	1-8-5	1-9-5	1-11-0	2-0-6	2-2-5	2-4-7	2-7-2	2-10-0	3-0-7	Deck at Sides	Heights.
B 3′			1-8-6	0-9-6	0-3-4	-0-0-7	0-4-4	0-7-0	0-8-4	0-8-5	0-6-6	0-3-0	0-2-5	1-2-0	2-6-5				Buttock #3	
B 2′	1-3-6	1-1-4	0-7-7	0-2-5	-0-2-3	0-7-1	0-11-0	1-1-7	1-3-5	1-4-3	1-3-1	1-0-4	0-8-4	0-1-5	+0-8-6	2-0-6			" #2	
B 1′	1-0-3	0-9-6	0-3-4	-0-2-0	0-7-6	1-1-4	1-6-4	1-10-6	2-1-7	2-3-2	2-2-2	1-10-7	1-6-5	1-0-6	0-5-3	+0-6-0	2-1-[illegible]		" #1	
Rabbet +	0-9-6	0-6-4	-0-0-2	0-6-5	1-4-0	2-9-2	4-2-4	4-0-0	3-9-6	3-6-4	3-5-1	3-2-4	2-7-2	2-0-7	1-5-6	0-10-2	+0-4-0	2-11-3	Rabbet	
Profile +	0-9-2	0-6-0	-0-0-6	0-7-2	3-9-7	4-10-3	4-11-7	4-11-2	4-10-4	4-9-6	4-9-0 and 4-8-4	3-6-7	2-8-6	2-2-1	1-7-3	1-0-4	0-0-0	2-0-0	Profile	
½ W. Deck	2-4-4	2-7-1	3-0-0	3-4-2	3-8-1	3-10-7	4-0-7	4-2-3	4-3-0	4-2-7	4-2-1	4-0-1	3-9-0	3-4-7	2-11-3	2-3-5	1-5-1	0-2-7	Deck at Side	Half Breadths.
W.L. + 2′													3-8-7	3-4-0	2-9-3	1-11-5	0-11-3		W.L. +2′	
W.L. + 1′	0-10-5	1-8-2	2-7-3	3-1-4	3-6-5	3-10-1	4-0-6	4-2-3	4-2-5	4-2-2	4-0-6	3-10-1	3-5-4	2-10-6	2-2-2	1-3-6	0-4-6		W.L. + 1′	
W.L. + 6″		0-0-5	1-7-0	2-7-2	3-2-7	3-7-4	3-10-6	4-0-5	4-1-1	4-0-5	3-11-1	3-7-6	3-2-4	2-6-6	1-9-6	0-11-6	0-2-1		W.L + 6″	
L.W.L.			0-2-4	1-5-2	2-5-6	3-1-4	3-6-3	3-8-6	3-9-6	3-9-4	3-7-3	3-3-1	2-9-4	2-1-6	1-4-6	0-7-7	0-0-6		L.W.L.	
W.L. − 6″				0-3-0	1-3-5	2-2-0	2-9-1	3-1-2	3-3-1	3-3-2	3-8-7	2-8-1	2-2-6	1-7-2	0-11-2	0-4-0			W.L. − 6″	
W.L. − 1′					0-5-0	1-2-0	1-10-0	2-3-4	2-6-0	2-6-4	2-4-6	2-0-6	1-7-5	1-0-5	0-6-2	0-0-7			W.L. − 1′	
W.L. − 2′					0-1-0	0-3-7	0-7-4	0-10-6	1-1-3	1-2-2	1-1-6	0-11-0	0-7-3	0-2-2					W.L. − 2′	
W.L. − 3′						0-1-2	0-3-2	0-5-4	0-7-0	0-7-6	0-6-7	0-4-1							W.L. − 3′	
W.L. − 4′							0-2-0	0-4-0	0-5-5	0-6-0	0-4-0								W.L. − 4′	
Rabbet		0-1-4	0-1-6	0-2-0	0-2-2	0-2-1	0-2-0	0-3-2	0-5-6	0-6-2	0-5-2	0-3-0	0-1-6	0-1-6	0-1-6	0-1-6	0-1-6	0-1-6	Rabbet	
Profile		0-0-4	0-0-5	0-0-6	0-0-3	0-0-6	0-1-0	0-2-0 and 0-3-0	0-3-0 and 0-4-6	0-3-2 and 0-5-0	0-0-0	0-0-0	0-0-4	0-0-4	0-0-4	0-0-4	0-0-4	0-1-2	Profile	
Diagonal 1					0-3-4	0-9-0	1-1-0	1-4-2	1-6-2	1-7-0	1-6-3	1-4-2	1-1-2	0-9-2	0-4-6	0-0-6			Diagonal 1	
D 2			0-1-2	0-7-2	1-1-2	1-6-0	1-10-2	2-1-1	2-2-6	2-3-6	2-2-7	2-0-6	1-10-0	1-5-5	1-0-4	0-6-7	0-0-0		" 2	
D 3		2-1-0	2-7-4	3-1-0	3-6-1	3-10-0	4-1-0	4-3-0	4-3-4	4-3-4	4-2-0	3-11-0	3-6-4	3-0-2	2-4-7	1-8-0	0-10-1		" 3	

Offsets in feet, inches and eights of inches.
Heights above and below L.W.L.

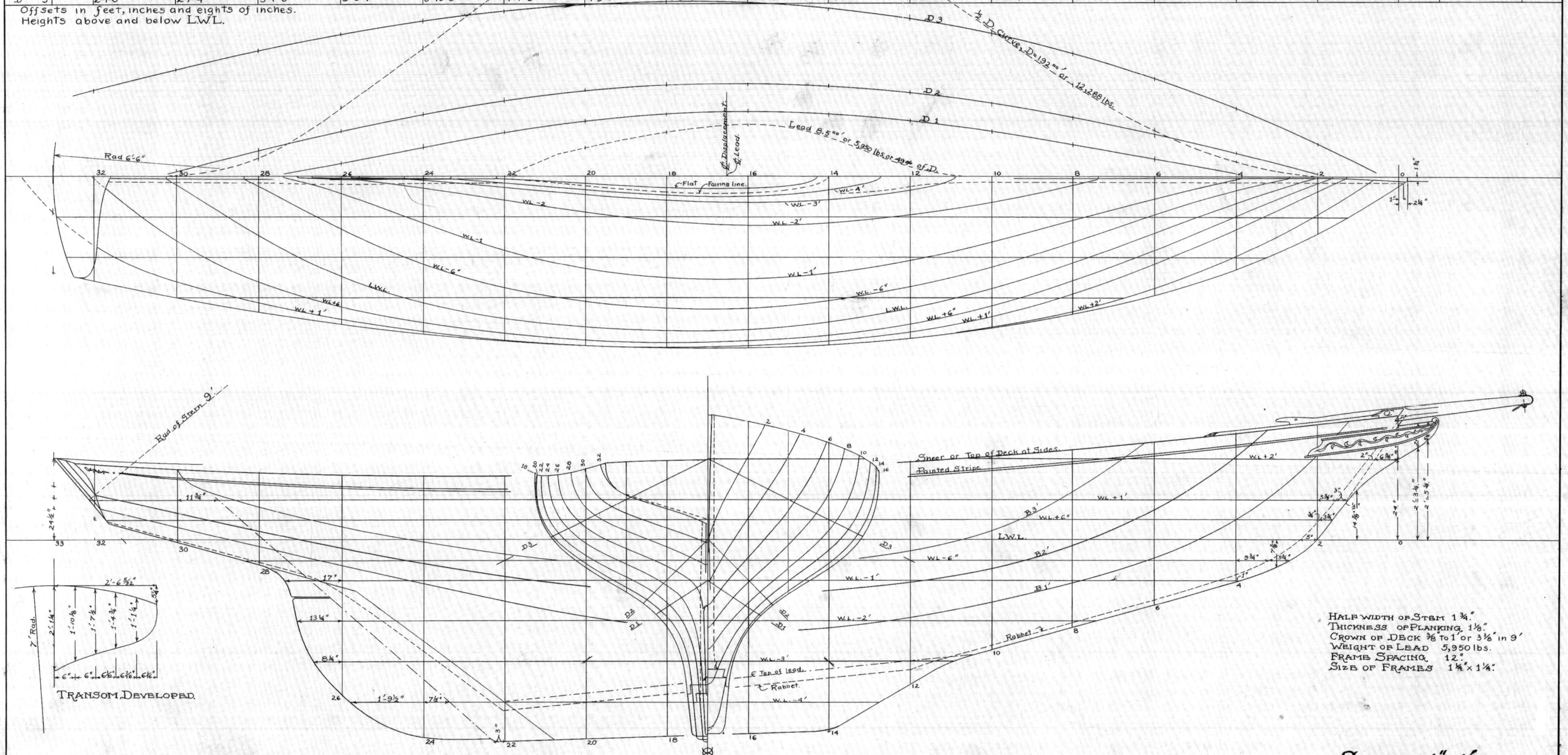

HALF WIDTH OF STEM 1¾″.
THICKNESS OF PLANKING 1⅛″.
CROWN OF DECK ⅜″ TO 1′ OR 3⅜″ IN 9′
WEIGHT OF LEAD 5,950 lbs.
FRAME SPACING 12″.
SIZE OF FRAMES 1⅛″ x 1¼″.

SCALE 1″ = 1′.

THE LINES of No. 89 ~ KETCH for EDWIN M. HILL ESQ. ~ SHEET 2.

RIGHT: The *Araminta*'s construction and arrangement plan. Her narrow, low cabin house, giving 5-foot headroom, allows wide decks for moving about and for watching her shapely hull dance through the waves. She has the same shallow, watertight cockpit without seats that Hill liked and had specified for the *Quiet Tune*. Francis shows a "Grey" Sea Scout engine driving a folding propeller with its horizontal shaft above the rudder. He also has drawn a "Krockabout" flushing toilet at the foot of the mainmast, instead of a cedar bucket. The interior of the day-sailer has been kept very simple. She was double planked with mahogany over cedar to a total thickness of 1⅛ inches on 1¼-inch-square frames spaced 12 inches apart. (© Mystic Seaport Museum, Daniel S. Gregory Ships Plans Library, SP38.143.7) RIGHT: The lines and offsets of the Sailski. The hulls are asymmetrical. Francis wrote; "When the catamaran raises her weather hull and depresses the leeward hull she tries to head off which is very alarming. I made the hulls curved to try to counterbalance this action and I have been told by people who sail them that they steer almost perfectly." He also shaped the hulls so that the windward one would throw spray out, rather than up. The catamaran was to be built of plywood, at the request of Boris Lauer-Leonardi. The reluctant designer wrote, "the model of the hulls is a developed shape on which a laminated wood panel will lie without difficulty, and that is one of the reasons the bow has so much overhang." The overhang was also to discourage pitch-poling. Each hull would weigh 400 pounds; total displacement was 1,200 pounds. (© Mystic Seaport Museum, Daniel S. Gregory Ships Plans Library, SP38.168.2)

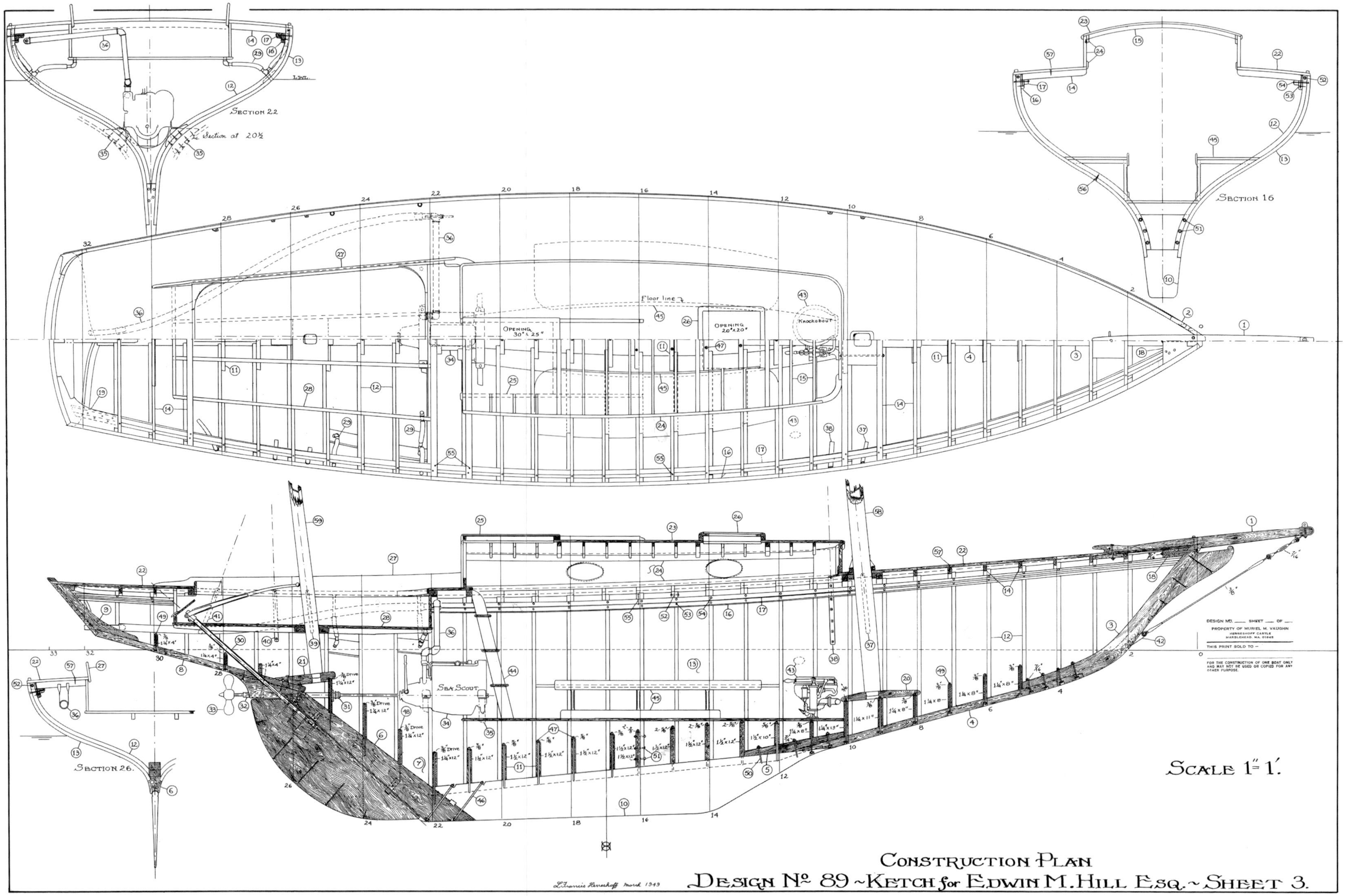

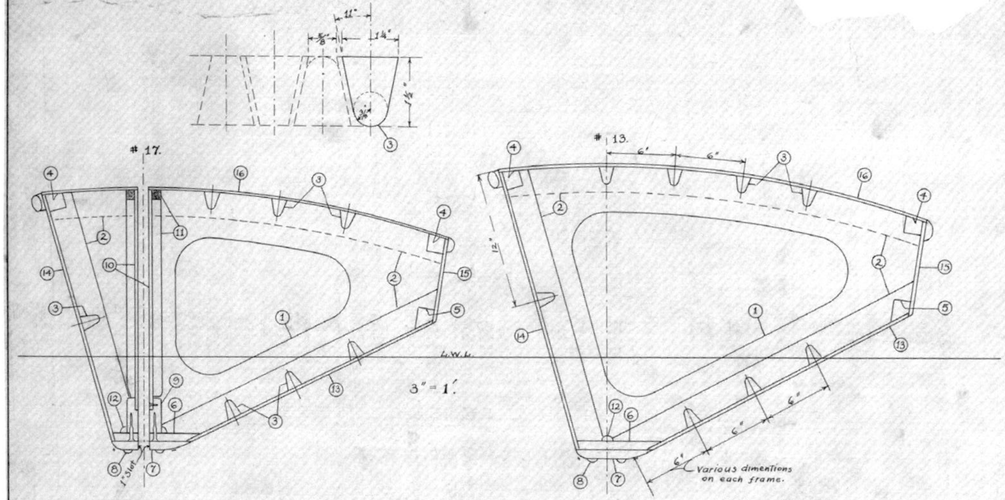

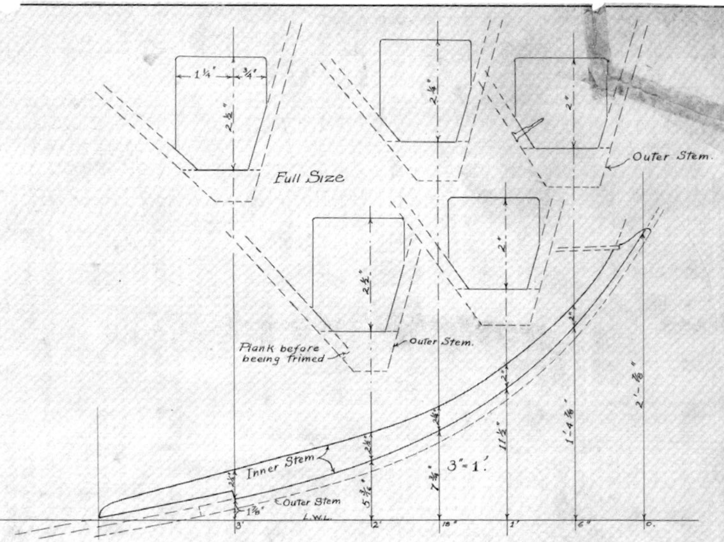

		27	25	23	21	19	17	15	13	11	9	7	5	3	2	1	0
Heights	Center of Deck	0'-9"	0-10⅛"	0-11¼"	1-0⅜"	1-1½"	1-2⅝"	1-3¾"	1-4⅞"	1-6"	1-7⅛"	1-8¼"	1-9⅜"	1-10½"	1'-11 1/16"	1'-11⅝"	Center of deck.
	Shear on inboard Side	0'-8⅞"	0-9 15/16"	0-11"	12"	1-1⅛"	1-2"	1-3⅛"	1-4⅛"	1-5⅜"	1-6½"	1-7⅞"	1-9"	1-10¼"	1-10⅞"	1-11½"	Shear inboard
	" " Outboard Side	0'-7⅞"	0-8⅛"	0-8⅝"	0-9⅛"	0-9-⅝"	0-10⅛"	0-10⅞"	12"	1-1¼"	1-2½"	1-4⅛"	1-6"	1-8¼"	1-9½"	1-10½"	" Outboard.
	Chine line	0'-2¾"	0-2⅞"	0-3"	0'-3"	0-3"	0-3"	0-3⅛"	0-3¾"	0-4¾"	0-6¼"	0-8⅝"	0-11⅝"	1-3⅛"	1-5⅛"	1'-6¾"	Chine line.
	Keel bottom	-0-2"	-0-3⅝"	-0-5"	-0-6¼"	-0-7⅛"	-0-8⅛"	-0-8¾"	-0-8¾"	-0-8½"	-0-7½"	-0-6"	-0-3⅞"	+0-1"	0-5 3/16"	+0-10½"	Keel bottom.
½ Widths	Of deck inboard Side	0-4¼"	0-5⅜"	0-6½"	0-7½"	0-8⅜"	0-9"	0-9⅜"	0-9⅝"	0-9⅝"	0-9⅛"	0-8⅜"	0-7⅝"	0-6⅛"	0-5⅛"	0-3¾"	Deck inboard
	" " Outboard Side	1'-3⅞"	1'-6¾"	1'-7⅞"	1'-11¾"	2'-1⅝"	2'-3"	2'-3⅝"	2'-4¼"	2'-4½"	2'-3⅛"	2'-1½"	1'-10⅞"	1'-6⅛"	1-2⅜"	0-9"	" Outboard.
	Of Chine line	1'-1¾"	1'-5⅛"	1'-8¼"	1'-10½"	2'-0⅜"	2'-1¾"	2'-2¾"	2'-3"	2'-2⅝"	2'-1⅝"	2'-0"	1'-9¼"	1'-4⅞"	1-0½"	0-6⅞"	Chine line.
	" Keel bottom	0-1⅛"	0-1⅝"	0-2"	0-2⅜"	0-2⅝"	0'-2¾"	0'-2¾"	0'-2½"	0-2"	0-1½"	0-1 1/16"	0-0⅝"	0-0⅜"	0-0⅞"	0-0½"	Keel bottom.

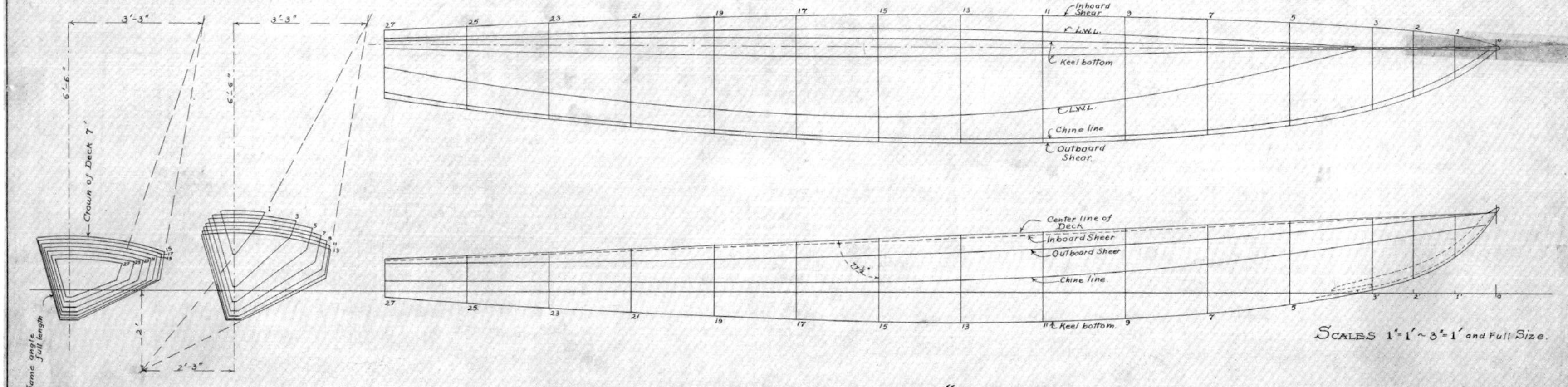

Scales 1" = 1' ~ 3" = 1' and Full Size.

The Lines of the "SAILSKI" And some Construction.

Design # 90 ~ Sheet 2.

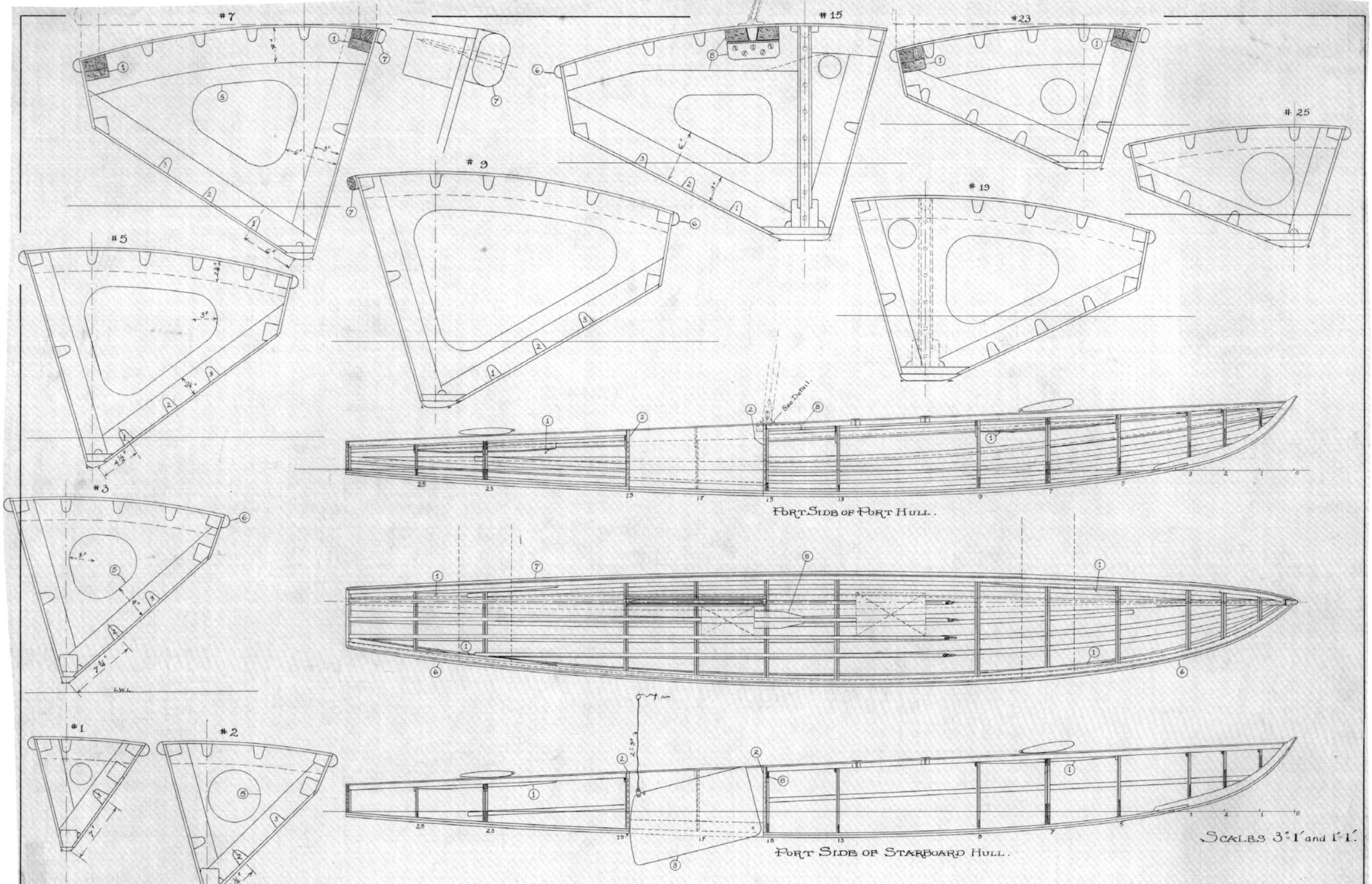

Construction Plan of "Sailski" Design 90 ~ Sheet 3.

building the designer will be glad to try to answer them." Francis was right to expect questions. He admitted that the Sailski was a "tricky contraption," and that building her was a "difficult task."[60]

The Rudder sold many sets of Sailski plans at $20, but not many boats were built. The few owners that Francis heard from "were much disappointed with them" because they were slow in light weather. Francis wrote, "these boats were designed with a very small sail area because I knew that when a catamaran capsizes it is a serious matter." And he commented that, at any rate, "she will not sink under any circumstances."[61]

But two amateur builders who did launch Sailskis were very happy with their boats: William A. Berry Jr., who sailed on Buzzards Bay, and Raymond C. Ingersoll, based at Duck Island in Northport Bay on the north shore of Long Island. Berry teamed up with his father to build the *Scat Cat*. Berry wrote: "No son ever enjoyed working with his father more than I did. We were real pals together and shared so many problems that the 'groaning chair' often needed a twin."[62]

One of the problems was just how to comply with Francis's requirement that joints must be both glued and fastened with screws. Here is the Berrys' solution: "A pistol grip automatic screwdriver proved the best and fastest way of setting the screws in the panels which were prefitted and drilled before assembly. After the screws were caught in the panel it was turned upside down and all contact surfaces with the hull were brushed with glue. The panel was then set in place and two men working at top speed could sink all the screws in twenty or thirty minutes." Berry added: "The bow called for very careful fitting as well as the proper amount of strong language to hold the panels in place while clamping and glueing."[63]

LEFT: The Sailski's construction plan. To achieve the lightness vital for a catamaran to sail well, Francis has used his longitudinal system. When building, the web frames could serve as molds, and the stringers as ribbands. The frames are of ¼-inch plywood with large cutouts to save weight. They have 2¼-inch-by-½-inch border pieces to support the longitudinal stringers. The tapered keelson has a maximum width of 8 inches; it is made of mahogany or oak, in two ¾-inch layers. Stringers are 1¼ inches wide and 1½ inches deep, rounded off on the inboard side; clamps are 1½ inches square; chine logs, 1½ inches by 2 inches; all these longitudinal members to be of spruce or Douglas fir. Planking of ¼-inch highest-grade plywood, with the outer layer of mahogany or Spanish cedar for a good finish. The deck, which is supported by stringers, of 3/16- or ¼-inch plywood. The cross members are spruce, 18 inches wide, the forward one 3 inches thick, the after one, 2 inches, both streamlined in section. Note that the forward cross member is angled upward slightly to give lift if struck by a sea. Francis wrote: "The ends of the cross members must be very strongly secured to the hulls, for when the two hulls pitch independently, there will be strong torsional strains developed, but as a plank twists easily for a few degrees it is believed the hulls will be allowed to pitch as much as is desirable." Francis designed the strong attachments of the cross members to the hull so that they could be detached for the transport or storage of the catamaran. This was done by removing four brass holding strips, each fastened by four ⅝-inch lag screws, from 5 inches to 7 inches long. The centerboard box, piercing only one frame, is of ¼-inch plywood. Francis recommended installing ¾-inch oval brass shoes running on either side of the centerboard slot. All seams and joints were to be glued, as well as fastened with screws. Centerboard to be of ¾-inch oak; the balanced rudders of 1¼-inch oak or mahogany. Francis commented that a Sailski builder could choose natural wood over plywood and achieve about the same weight and cost. In that case, he recommended ⅜-inch planking and 5/16-inch decks, canvas covered, with the seams coming on stringers. Note the two deck hatches in each hull. The larger, forward one measures 2 feet by 1 foot, 3 inches. Francis thought a sailor could "pass below deck here into a compartment 4 feet long, 3 feet wide and 2 feet high. There may be times when it would be convenient to use the cedar bucket here, and perfectly possible to sleep here with one's feet through the opening in frame 13 [!]." (© Mystic Seaport Museum, Daniel S. Gregory Ships Plans Library, SP38.168.3)

Alas, father and son would not be together at the *Scat Cat*'s launching in the summer of 1952. William Berry Sr. passed away before the boat was finished. He would never sail on the boat he had grown to love. But his son gave *Rudder* readers a detailed and glowing report of life with a Sailski:

> *Nearly perfect balance enables her to sail a considerable distance with only an occasional slight correcting touch on the tiller. At no time has there been any pronounced weather or lee helm even in the hardest blow, yet she has a beautiful feel and sensitivity. She comes about and gybes smoothly without trimming the sheet. However she will get in stays in a light breeze if an attempt is made to force her about too quickly. Let her pick her own rate of turning and she swings like a lady, coming about even with both centerboards fully up. One of her most interesting traits is her ability to sail backwards and under control. This is most helpful in taking out sailing parties and leaving crowded docks or moorings. She has taken out over a hundred children by sailing up to the marsh for a load and then backing away.*
>
> *Although the canvas deck between her hulls is like a huge bed it is comfortably firm to walk upon and perfect for taking in or setting sail. Our two year old Suki runs around on it like mad, jumping and tumbling or playing baseball by sticking her feet in the drain holes as she scoots from base to base. She never leaves the canvas unless we take her to the side of the hull to dangle her feet in the water. Quite often she drags a blanket out of the hatch, wraps herself up and goes to sleep for an hour or two. Truly no boat can touch a Sailski for relaxing, sleeping, or sunbathing. As many as a dozen young people can be carried without bothering the skipper. In light airs she could well stand more sail area, for even in a real squall she refused to lift the waterline of*

William A. Berry Jr.'s Sailski, *Scat Cat*, sailing fast, close-hauled. Even when living up to her name, she heels but little.
(Mystic Seaport Museum, 1985-5-48)

her windward hull more than a couple of inches. When planing, she takes off like the proverbial scalded cat. Many a friend has made a wild grab for the nearest handhold when she seemed to slide right out from under his feet as she picked up speed from a standstill. In rough going she has no tendency to bury her nose, but will lift over the waves, throwing spray as in a conventional boat. It is most interesting to feel the hulls move independently in a gentle fashion with no sign of strain and no creaking or groaning.

People chase us all over the bay to get a closer look while many and varied are the comments. Power boaters often forget that we can hear their remarks at a distance. Comments range from calling us a damned marine tennis court to "What the hell is that thing?" Many insist that the mast is broken or that we have her rigged wrong, but we bear our calluses with pride at the steady flow of compliments and exclamations at her grace and beauty. As we rush by a trim little catboat and a shout comes across the sparkling water, the words, "L. Francis sure did himself proud!" are music to our ears.[64]

Ray Ingersoll, as he signed a four-page letter to Francis, was a construction engineer who spent "quite a few years" building his *Magnificat*. He launched her in 1966. "A tremendous crowd was there," he wrote, "and we had sixteen on board for the first sail many of whom were youngsters who had helped in one way or another to build her. I have been sailing her ever since [for three seasons at his time of writing] around Northport, Eatons Neck and the Sound to Norwalk [Connecticut] and back and she is one of the true joys of my life." Ingersoll reported that his Sailski was slow in light airs but came into her own as it breezed up. "When the small craft warnings are out I can pass anything. I like wild weather sailing and *this is the boat* for it. I got a citation from my club for sailing across the Sound to Norwalk from Northport when the wind was too strong for anyone else to go out in the sound. The great boat could do it." He marveled at her stability. He had trouble with the balanced rudders at high speed. He had made them of mahogany, as Francis specified, but with the grain vertical. The forward, balanced part broke off, so he built new ones of mahogany plywood. He concluded his letter with, "I want you to know how much we love and appreciate our *Magnificat*." Francis replied, "I am very pleased to know that someone is able to sail this boat and am overjoyed that he and his friends have had some pleasure with her."[65]

Despite her lack of popularity, the Sailski was a great achievement for L. Francis Herreshoff. If she was built according to his instructions in *The Rudder*, she was not only light and fast, but also strong and safe. She needed—and could take—more sail area for light weather, but there were no complaints of the structure of a Sailski coming apart under the strain of sailing fast in rough water. Francis's exquisite sense of proportion enabled him to design a novel vessel that would perform brilliantly. The Sailski is a fine demonstration of his versatility.

Now that sailors have finally come to accept the catamaran as normal, rather than freakish, perhaps it is time for a builder to produce a fiberglass Sailski? It is entirely possible that the ghost of L. Francis Herreshoff would approve.

As we have seen, Francis had a conflicted relationship with his father. On the one hand, he was intensely proud of Nathanael G. Herreshoff for his many accomplishments in the designing and building of yachts, but, on the other hand, he resented Nathanael's inability—or unwillingness—to recognize his son's own genius

"SAILSKI"

4 PASSENGER HIGH SPEED LAUNCH

SUGGESTED by CHARLES NELSON STRATTON
JULY 7, 1968

WITH 1960-67 FALCON-COMET
ECONOPOWER LEHMAN MARINE
6 CYL. O.H.V. 101 H.P. AT 4400
170 CU IN BORE 3.5 STROKE 2.94
COMP. RATIO 9.1:1 TORQUE 190@2400
WEIGHT: DIR DRIVE 468 lbs

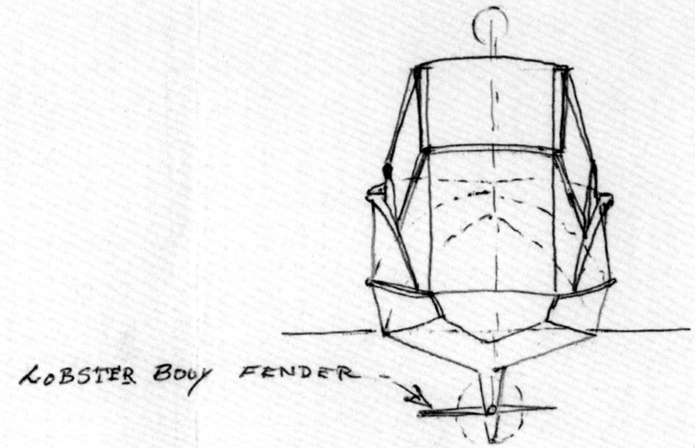

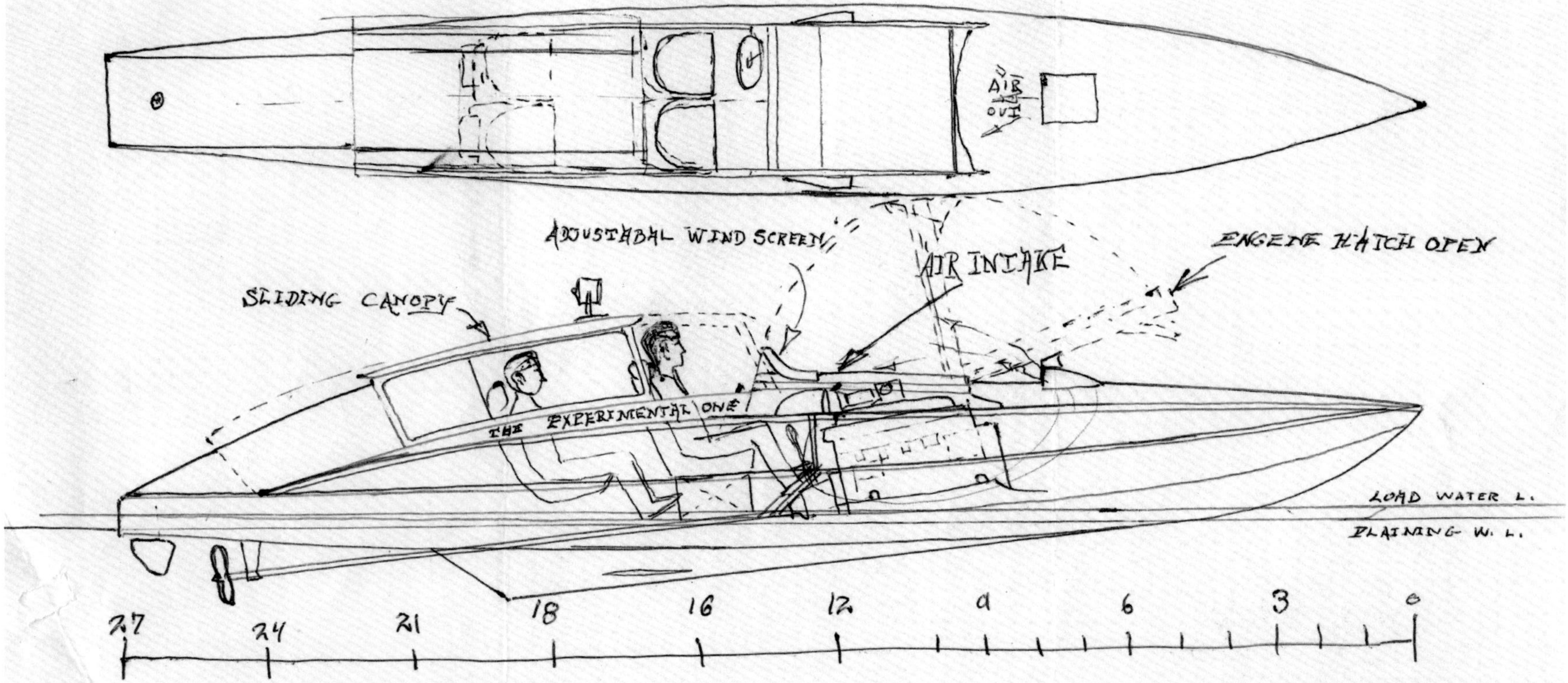

for yacht designing. In 1946, Francis determined to write his father's biography. He wanted to make a public record of Nathanael's attainments; he wanted to be the one to influence his father's reputation. Francis admired his father greatly; his biography would be an admiring account of Captain Nat's life and work. And writing it would finally release Francis from the anger and pain lingering from his banishment to The Farm. The publication of *Capt. Nat Herreshoff, The Wizard of Bristol: The Life and Achievements of Nathanael Greene Herreshoff, Together with an Account of Some of the Yachts He Designed* was Francis's catharsis.[66]

In 1944, Francis had written a biographical sketch of his father under the title, *Nathanael Greene Herreshoff 1848-1938: A life and appreciation of his work by his son L. Francis Herreshoff,* in conjunction with an exhibit on Nathanael's work at the Wadsworth Atheneum in Hartford, Connecticut. Two years later, with help from Nathanael's widow, Ann, he began to accumulate reference materials for a far longer work. In the summer of 1947, he had Mrs. Bolster drive him to Bristol to collect photographs, plans, and some of Nathanael's writings. His sister, Agnes, helped with her own photographs. A year later, he was ready to write.[67]

From the beginning, Francis intended the biography to be a book, but first he wrote it as a series of twenty-six articles for *The Rudder*, running from January 1949 through April 1951. During this period, his readers were treated not only to the story of the great N. G. Herreshoff, but also to the designs of the Meadow Lark and Sailski. When it came time to publish the book, in 1953, Boris decided it was not a project for the Rudder Publishing Company. He had experienced a high cost of production on *The Common Sense of Yacht*

LEFT: **Charles Nelson Stratton, of Rockport, Maine, sent this drawing to Francis in 1968. He found the Sailski's hulls so appealing that he took the asymmetry out of one, gave it a higher deck forward, a streamlined deck shelter, and an Econopower Lehman, six-cylinder, 100-horsepower motor, then named his four-passenger, high-speed launch *The Experimental One.* Francis thought the concept was "very ingenious," but warned that "Although a launch of this type will be very much self-righting while under way, still she will be very cranky when people move around in her when not under way."** (Mystic Seaport Museum, G. W. Blunt White Library, 138:6/3) ABOVE: **A sketch of Nathanael Greene Herreshoff, made from the most famous photograph of him. It was sent to Francis by the artist.** (© Mystic Seaport Museum, 1990.37.163)

ABOVE: **Francis made this drawing of the *Riviera,* being sailed by his father Nathanael and his uncle Lewis, as an illustration for his biography of his father. The two had built the 17-footer for an inland-waters cruise in Europe in 1874. Francis got to sail this boat as a youngster in Bristol, but with a much-cut-down rig compared to the original one he shows (see volume 1, page 35). The *Riviera* was destroyed in the 1938 hurricane.** (© Mystic Seaport Museum, Daniel S. Gregory Ships Plans Library, SP38.377.1) RIGHT: **Francis about to sign a copy of his biography of his father.** (Mystic Seaport Museum, 1999-8-216)

Design, with its many illustrations, and was alarmed by the great number of photographs of Herreshoff yachts that Francis had gathered for the biography. He arranged for publication by Sheridan House, a small firm in New York started in 1940.

Tom Davin was Francis's editor at Sheridan House, and the two worked smoothly, under Boris's watchful eye.[68]

Francis dedicated his book "To the Memory of my Father." As background, he wrote about his father's (and, or course, his own) ancestors. He didn't mention his great-grandfather Charles Frederick Herreshoff's suicide (see volume 1, page 11). And he ignored a serous falling-out between his father and his uncle John, two months before John's death in 1915 over whether or not to sign a contract with the Russian Navy to build torpedo boats. John wanted to go ahead with the business, but Nathanael exercised his veto power, upholding his pacifist views. Samuel Carter covered both episodes in the book that Francis hated, *The Boatbuilders of Bristol*.[69]

Francis's account of his father's early life made clear the genius of Capt. Nat. And his writing about Nathanael's home life at Love Rocks and his work habits took his readers behind the scenes at the Herreshoff Manufacturing Company and, in so doing, illuminated his own childhood. In reviewing his father's towering career, Francis chose dozens of his designs from hundreds, to illustrate and tell about, and explained his father's many innovations in the design and construction of yachts. His book is an outstanding reference on the prodigious output of the Herreshoff yard. A valuable appendix is an alphabetical list, with particulars, of every vessel launched, by name. And *Capt. Nat* gives the

reader insight to the personality of a man who, though famous, liked to stay out of the public eye. Francis did not delve into his father's descendants. He spoke not at all of his own work, and there was no mention of Mr. Sidney. These matters were outside the scope of his biography of his father, but Francis was certainly aware that the Herreshoff genius did not end with N. G. Herreshoff, any more than it had begun with him.

The *Rudder* articles and the book were well received, particularly by knowledgeable readers. One reviewer, Richard Philbrick, praised its content but not its writing. He wrote: "L. Francis Herreshoff is a far better yacht designer than he is writer. But he has made clear his father's heritage and his attainments, and Capt. Nat is such a fine subject and the life he led is so full of interest, readers will readily forgive shortcomings in writing style." Nevertheless, clarity in writing is high praise.[70]

Henry C. White, creator of dreamy pastels of his beloved Connecticut shore and an admiring customer of Nathanael's (moreover, the artist who had arranged the Herreshoff exhibit at the Wadsworth) wrote to Francis as soon as the last installment of "Capt. Nat" came out in *The Rudder*: "You were pre-eminently the one to write it. No one else could have done it nearly as well for you were equipped and qualified in every way. It is an invaluable work and will stand for all time as the supreme authority, the classic tribute to your Father's genius and to his memory."[71]

Malcolm MacNaught, Francis's mentor of long ago in the Herreshoff small-boat shop, wrote simply, "I think you have done a wonderful job." Francis replied: "I was very glad to get your letter, and it means a great deal to me that you liked the book for you are the only one of all the old timers left who remembers the old times. Tom Brightman [former foreman at the Herreshoff yard] also likes the book, and you might get Cora Hill [the English teacher of a young, dyslexic Francis] to read it over and see if she can correct the spelling. Maybe she knows how to spell tautog and aquiteague, but I could not find them in my dictionary."[72]

Writing a laudatory biography of Capt. Nat Herreshoff was Francis's way of charting a course to the freedom of forgiveness.

CHAPTER 23

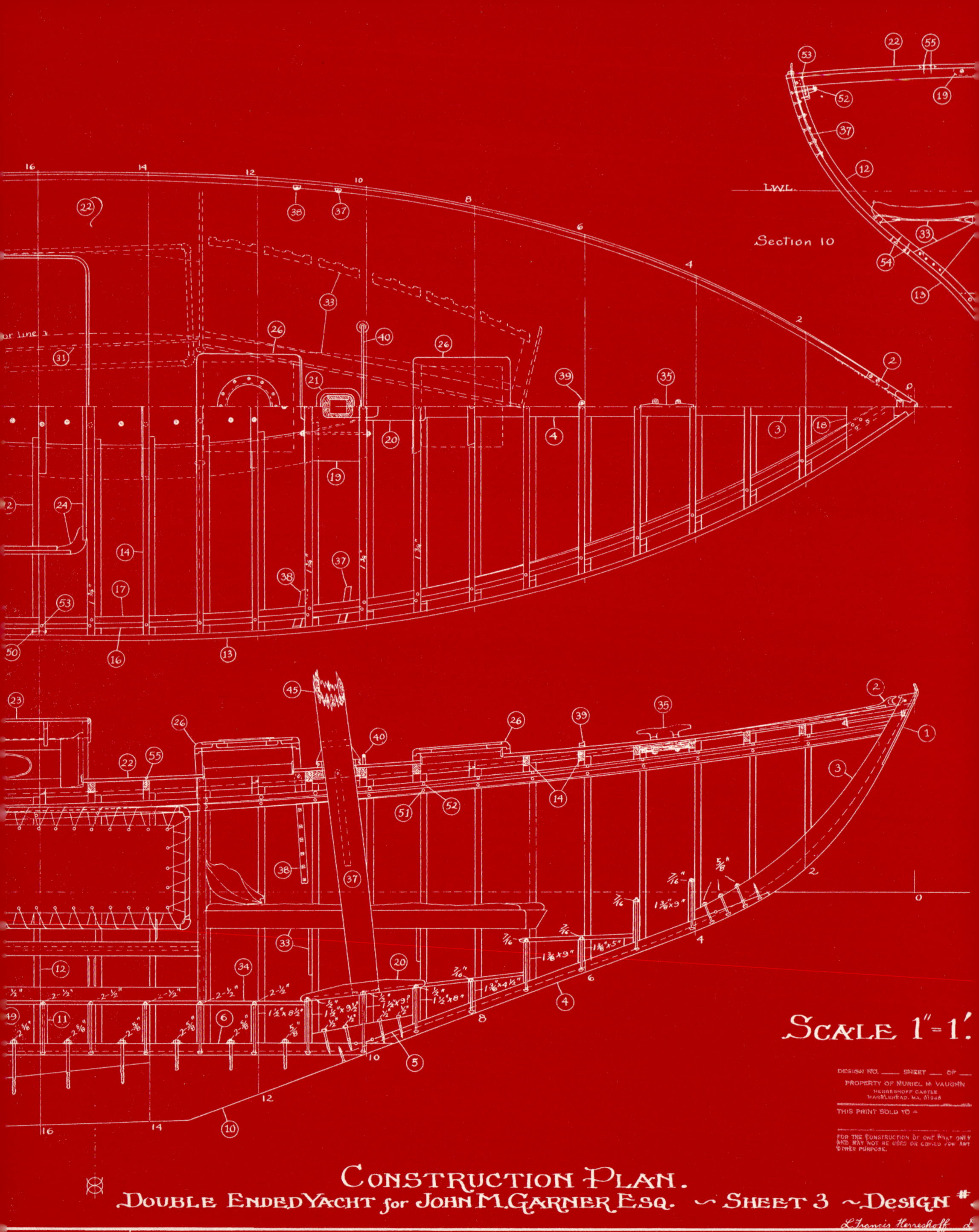

Construction Plan.

Double Ended Yacht for John M. Garner Esq. ~ Sheet 3 ~ Design #

L. Francis Herreshoff

THE COMPLEAT CRUISER SPAWNS THE ROZINANTE

"To a sailor, a romantic looking vessel is one that looks like a good sea boat, one which has a good sheer, and nicely proportioned ends, a vessel that he falls in love with at first sight, as we all did when we saw the *Rozinante*."

—GODDARD, IN THE COMPLEAT CRUISER, BY L. FRANCIS HERRESHOFF

L. Francis Herreshoff was not one of those sailors who scorns powerboats. His first cruising as a child had been in his father's steam and gasoline-driven yachts. As a yacht designer, he was just as fascinated by the design and performance of an engine as he was by the design of a sailing rig. He thought that the shape of a powerboat's hull was equally important to that of a sailing boat, and he believed that a properly designed motorboat could share the aesthetic qualities of, say, a sloop, if not, perhaps, a schooner. As early as 1943, Francis and Boris Lauer-Leonardi talked of his designing a power cruiser for a *Rudder* How-To-Build series.[1]

In "The Common Sense of Yacht Design," Francis had waxed eloquent in describing the bliss of coastal cruising in a fine launch "in which people could go places and come back again without nerve strain and discomfort, for the launch that can maintain a speed of fifteen miles an hour can cover a hundred and fifty miles of coast in ten hours and her crew can see a variety of beautiful sights." He believed: "The launch is usually much better than the sailboat for this purpose as with her shallow draft and ability to go up rivers against wind and tide she can visit the most picturesque places. Often, too, there is more opportunity to enjoy the view, since on the sailboat the sailing, so to say, will demand a certain amount of attention. As I write this," he continued, "I recall runs through Vineyard Sound as the afternoon fog was clearing away and the brown and green hills of Nashawena appeared off to leeward while on our after weather quarter the cliffs of Gay Head were pink in the afternoon sunlight, and the launch in the meantime was dancing over transparent green water. And runs along the Maine coast in a brisk northwester when the spray would fly outward and astern, when the islands appeared as clearcut as a cameo, and the distant pine clad hills were clothed in blue and green. These are the sort of days when the air seems charged with wellbeing and the drinker of this air is much happier than if he had had champagne. These are the days when the power boat is worth her cost."[2]

In 1950, Francis designed a 49-foot twin-screw motor launch, and Boris published her plans with Francis's commentary as "How To Build Barracuda." There were only four installments between March and July. Francis included two construction drawings with specifications, but there was no complete construction plan or cabin plan; his drawings for the Barracuda were incomplete, according to his standards. This design had an element of a crusade. Francis thought that the motorboats of the day, wide and flat, with big deckhouses, and gas-guzzling engines, were overly expensive and inefficient, and were uncomfortable in rough water to the point of being unseaworthy. The Barracuda was to be the antithesis of such craft. But the crusade showed no signs of gathering support. No one was tempted by Francis's lyrical description of sightseeing in a fast, able launch. By October, he was writing, "apparently some people dislike her enough to write in to the editor and say they had given up their subscription to the magazine because such a boat was being sponsored." Both Boris and Francis realized they were beating a dead horse, and Francis made no more drawings for No. 91. No Barracuda has ever carried a rapt crew along a pretty coast.[3]

Aside from Starling Burgess, Francis's best friends had been among his clients: Charlie Welch, Waldo Brown, and Billy Strawbridge. All five men were friends because they were deeply fascinated by the problems of yacht design. Waldo had inspired the design of his schooner, the *Joann,* and even helped Francis with her plans (see volume 1, pages 99-111), but Billy would collaborate fully with Francis in the design of the powerboat he finally decided on. He rejected the 36-footer for which Francis drew him lines in January 1950. Then he and Francis put their heads together and came up with a radical concept: go back to N. G. Herreshoff's tow-testing experiments that showed that the hull form for a powerboat with the least resistance was a narrow double-ender, and combine that conclusion with the modern, lightweight, efficient gasoline engine to create a fast launch that could cover the miles without burning a lot of gas.

Billy Strawbridge thought that this was a spicy project, so he named his long, skinny, fast boat the *Piquant*. Francis made some of the parts

L. Francis Herreshoff. (Courtesy *Providence Journal-Bulletin*)

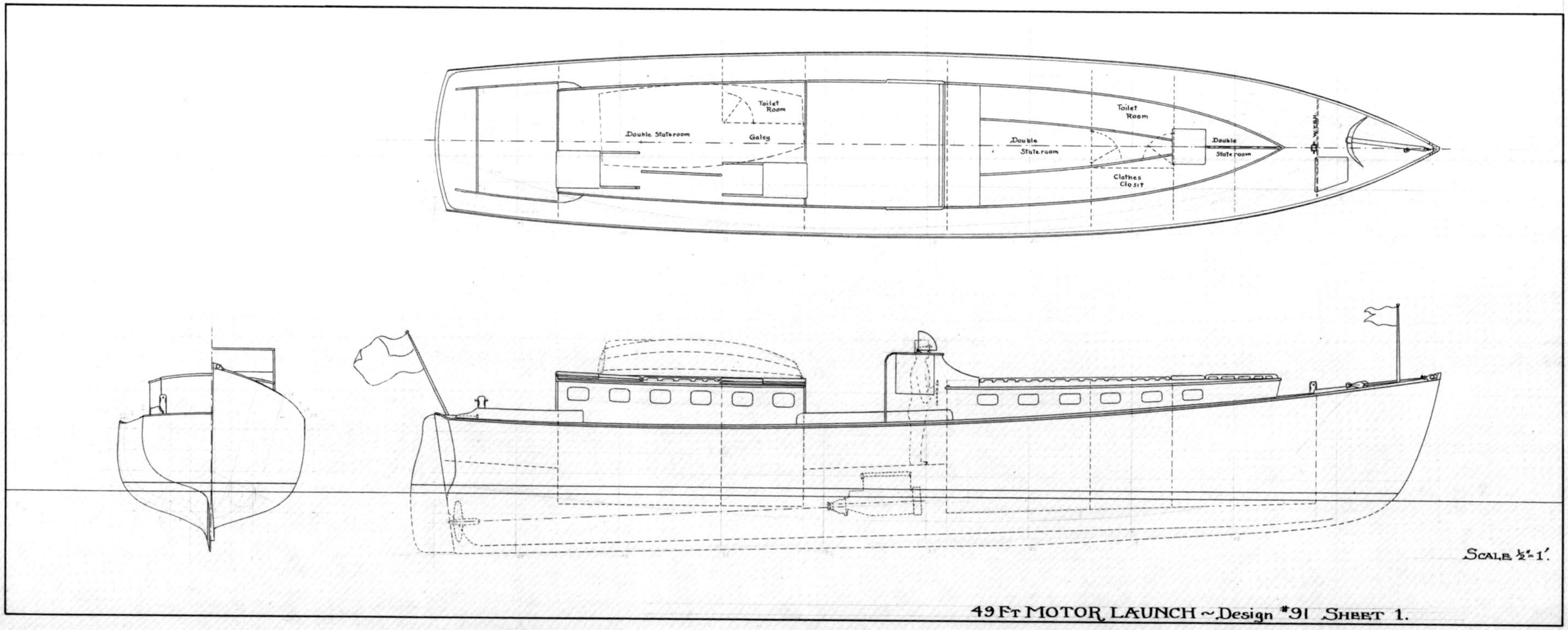

Francis thought that *The Rudder* should have a good cruising launch in its How-To-Build series, so in 1950 he designed the Barracuda, his No. 91. She is a long, lean, twin-screw boat with accommodations for six and an open steering station amidships. Forward are a small forepeak for stowage, which also gives waist-high support when handling the anchor; two double staterooms (the forward of which seems to be like a forecastle, entered primarily from the deck); and a toilet room. Aft are the galley, a second toilet room, and the main cabin, which can sleep two. There are deep cockpits amidships and in the stern, and the 'midships one has a windscreen around its forward end. She carries a 10-foot pram. The engines are LH-6 Lathrops, developing 60 horsepower each at 2,000 rpm. Francis thought she would make 15 knots opened up and 10 knots at 1,500 rpm. (© Mystic Seaport Museum, Daniel S. Gregory Ships Plans Library, SP38.88.2)

		49	45	40	35	30	25	20	15	10	5	0		
HEIGHTS	Deck at Side	3-7-1	3-4-6	3-3-0	3-2-5	3-3-4	3-5-7	3-9-0	4-1-4	4-7-0	5-2-0	5-11-0	Deck at Side	HEIGHTS
	Buttock 3'	+1-3-0	+0-5-4	-0-1-7	-0-6-6	-0-9-2	-0-9-6	-0-8-3	-0-1-0	3-0-4			Buttock 3'	
	" 2'	+0-6-4	-0-0-1	-0-6-4	-0-11-0	-1-1-7	-1-2-7	-1-2-5	-0-11-1	0-0-1	4-4-6		" 2'	
	" 1'	+0-2-0	-0-5-2	-1-0-1	-1-4-4	-1-6-0	-1-7-0	-1-6-2	-1-4-4	-0-11-6	0-9-7		" 1'	
	Rabbet		-2-6-0	-2-4-0	-2-2-0	-2-0-0	-1-10-0	-1-8-0	-1-6-0	-1-4-0	-0-11-0		Rabbet	
	Keel Bottom	-3-0-0	-2-10-6	-2-9-2	-2-7-6	-2-6-2	-2-4-4	-2-3-0	-1-11-4	-1-5-7	-1-2-0	5-11-0	Keel Bottom	
HALF BREADTHS	Deck at Side	3-4-2	3-9-0	4-1-3	4-3-6	4-5-1	4-6-0	4-4-6	4-1-4	3-6-4	2-4-0	0-1-4	Deck at Side	HALF BREADTHS
	W.L. +4'								4-1-2	3-3-5	1-10-4		W.L. +4'	
	" +3'	3-5-1	3-9-7	4-2-1	4-4-5	4-6-0	4-5-7	4-3-5	3-10-6	2-11-7	1-7-3		" +3'	
	" +2'	3-4-2	3-10-0	4-3-1	4-5-6	4-7-0	4-5-5	4-2-4	3-8-2	2-8-6	1-4-1		" +2'	
	" +1'	2-9-0	3-5-5	4-1-1	4-5-2	4-6-2	4-4-4	4-0-4	3-5-1	2-5-1	1-0-5		" +1'	
	L.W.L.	0-8-0	2-0-1	3-3-2	3-10-4	4-0-7	4-0-1	3-7-5	2-0-0	1-11-7	0-8-0		L.W.L.	
	W.L. -1'	0-2-0	0-5-2	1-0-2	1-9-4	2-4-0	2-7-5	2-5-6	1-10-6	1-0-0	0-2-0		W.L. -1'	
	Diagonal 1	0-5-6	0-11-4	1-5-0	1-9-0	1-11-0	2-0-1	2-0-0	1-9-6	1-4-4	0-5-4		Diagonal 1	
	" 2	1-6-0	2-3-0	2-10-5	3-4-4	3-7-5	3-8-4	3-6-1	3-0-2	2-3-0	1-0-0		" 2	
	" 3	2-11-5	3-70	4-2-0	4-6-1	4-7-4	4-6-1	4-2-0	3-6-6	2-7-4	1-3-6		" 3	

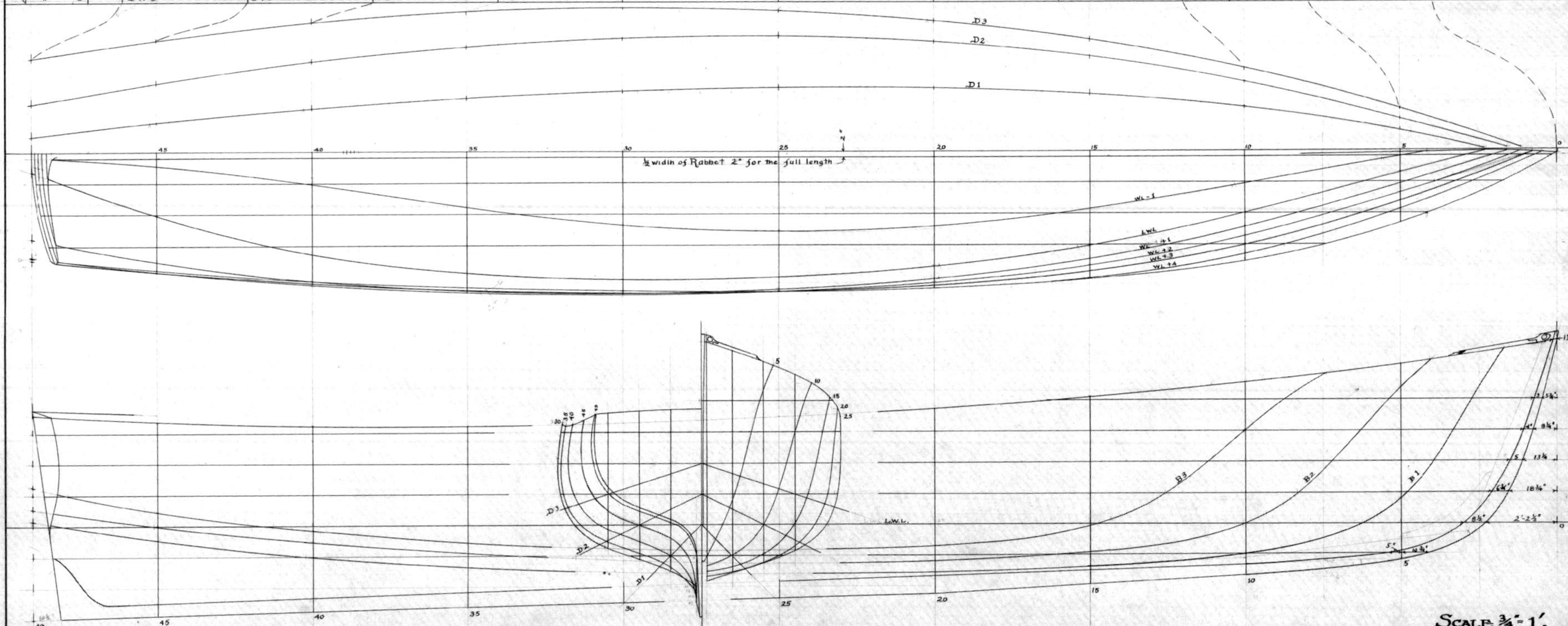

SCALE ¾" = 1'.

THE LINES of 49 Ft MOTOR LAUNCH Design 91 SHEET 2

for the *Piquant* himself. He fashioned a number of her metal fittings and wrote to Billy: "It is a fact that I worked a few hours a day for about three months on these parts. As I enjoyed the work I do not want to charge much for it." He asked and got $100 from Strawbridge. He also made the boat's rudder, as well as the cedar bucket, with a top "that I think will not offend the eyes of anyone." He and Strawbridge were so obsessed with eliminating weight from their light boat that Francis informed Billy that the bucket's top added a pound to its 3½ pounds. The *Piquant* cost $14,878.37 at Luders. Because of the collaborative design, Francis's commission was 5 percent, instead of 10: $743.91 (actually, a penny short).[4]

After testing her out in the summer of 1950, Francis was able to report in *The Rudder,* "*Piquant* was designed principally to be economical in fuel consumption, and after comparing notes with other launches we are under the impression that she is one of the most economical launches in the world." And Francis wrote to Billy, "I think you and I have produced something vastly better than the usual motor launch of today."[5]

It was not long before Lindsay Lord, and his protégé Philip Bolger, challenged this statement. Three months after Francis's report on the *Piquant* had appeared in *The Rudder*, they presented in the magazine a design for a 35-foot, planing powerboat with the same engines as in the *Piquant*, and claimed she would "equal or better" the *Piquant*'s speed and fuel economy. But this was theory, with no boat to back it up. It took Bolger twenty years, but he did make good on his claim with the design of the *Tiger Lily,* a planing boat that just did equal the *Piquant*'s speed and gas economy.[6]

George Swift of the Luders yard delivered the *Piquant* from Stamford to Marblehead. He described the trip as "one of the most pleasant and enlightening cruises I have made." Presumably, the chief enlightenment occurred when he arrived in Marblehead with enough gas so that he could have turned around and gone back to Stamford without refueling. Francis had his first chance to measure the boat's efficiency himself, when he took her on to Portland, Maine. She made the 84-mile run at 12.75 knots (1,600 rpm) on 17 gallons of gas, or nearly 5 miles per gallon, twice the mileage Francis was expecting.[7]

After his first season with the *Piquant*, enjoying Francis's idyll of watching Maine islands go by, Billy Strawbridge reported: "The boat was certainly most satisfactory and I think lived up to, or proved all our ideas to be correct. I had one opportunity to test her in a very bad short lumpy sea, and her motion was the best I have ever felt in any boat or ship."[8]

Billy Strawbridge happily used the *Piquant*, chiefly as a picnic boat, based in Northeast Harbor, Maine, for eight years. Then, in 1958, he and Francis made a trade: the *Piquant* went to Francis, and Billy got Francis's Mercedes Gull Wing coupe. Francis renamed his launch the *Freelance.* He kept her on a mooring off the Eastern Yacht Club. Francis was not a member; he had Phil Clark of the harbor's longtime ferry service, the Marblehead Transportation Company, run him out to his boat from Tucker's Wharf on Ferry Lane, not many steps from his Castle door. He had the launch hauled for winter storage and maintenance at the Graves yard. Francis was as fussy with his boat's engines as he was with those of his cars. He had

LEFT: **The Barracuda's lines and offsets. Francis shaped her hull with the two principal objectives of being able to drive into a head sea comfortably at speed and to steer well in a following sea. Her flare forward is moderate, so when she pitches she will not jump. Her long, flat run aft, with a deep skeg, keeps her stern from slewing too much in a quartering sea. She is 49 feet long, with a beam of 9 feet, and a draft of 3 feet.** (© Mystic Seaport Museum, Daniel S. Gregory Ships Plans Library, SP38.88.1)

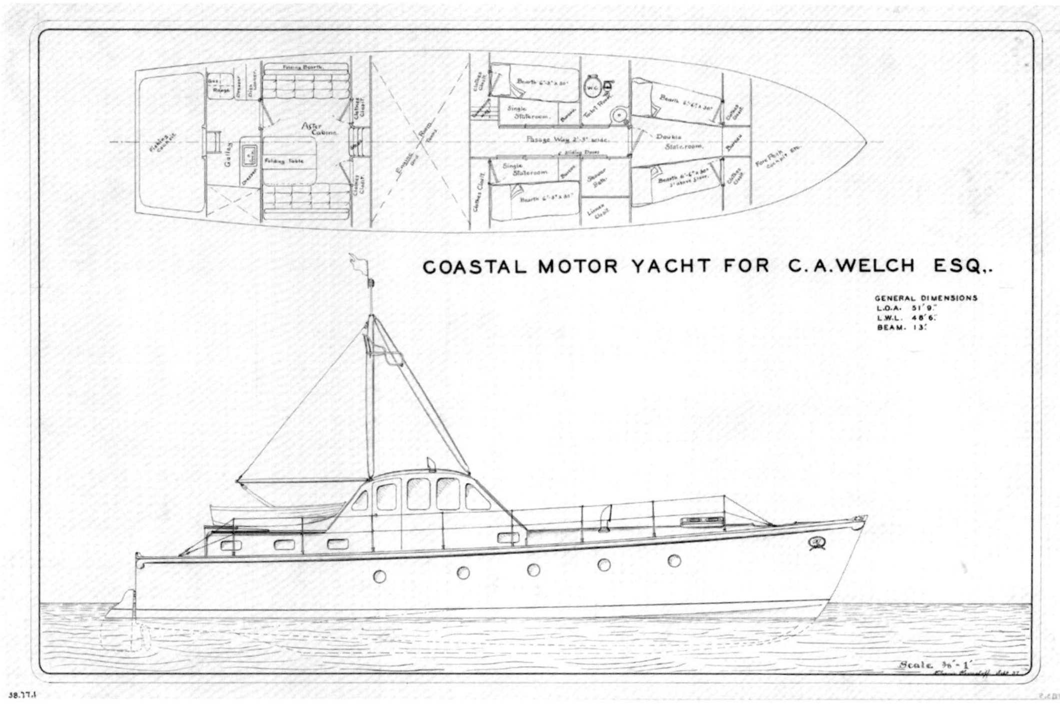

Graves take the engines out and repaint them. And, during his first summer with the boat, he ran her to Mystic, Connecticut, so the mechanics at the Lathrop Engine Company could rebuild their eight-year-old motors to perfection. On the return trip, it was extra rough on both sides of the Cape Cod Canal, and "we had to slow down quite a little because she would throw one or the other of her propellers out enough to make it necessary to slow the engines down."[9]

As we have seen, Francis had leased launches, one of them of his father's design, but the *Freelance* was his own boat, and she was the only sizeable craft of his own design that he ever had. He would

---

ABOVE: **The fast "Coastal Motor Yacht" that Francis designed for Charlie Welch was a little remindful of the Chrysler Airflow, with her stylish, curved wheelhouse. The Airflow was just ending three years of successful production under the direction of Francis's brother, Griswold. Francis had used streamlining back in 1930 on the *Whirlwind*'s deckhouse, but on this motorboat, as in the Airflow, the reduction of wind resistance would be more important because of greater speed. Welch's boat was to be a fast, planing boat with, for Francis, a rare vee-bottom. Note the tripod mast with a chair for the lookout. Charlie got his fishing cockpit in the stern, but he was not to enjoy it, for he decided not to build, and the design went no further than this preliminary plan. She would have been 51 feet, 9 inches long on deck; with a waterline length of 48 feet, 6 inches; a beam of 13 feet; and a draft of 3 feet. This plan, the last Francis drew for Charlie Welch, is dated September 1937. Soon afterward, Francis did enough work on a design for a 58-foot "Diesel Cruiser" for George Upton to give it the number 72, but that project also came to nothing.** (© Mystic Seaport Museum, Daniel S. Gregory Ships Plans Library, SP38.77.1 RIGHT: **Francis drew these lines of a 36-foot launch for Billy Strawbridge at the same time he was working up the design for the Barracuda. She is 34 feet long on the waterline; with a beam of only 6 feet, 4½ inches; and a draft of 2 feet, 6 inches. Knowing Billy, Francis did not bother to figure the offsets until he got a go-ahead. Sure enough, his friend changed his mind, and the design went no further.** (© Mystic Seaport Museum, Daniel S. Gregory Ships Plans Library, SP38.87.1)

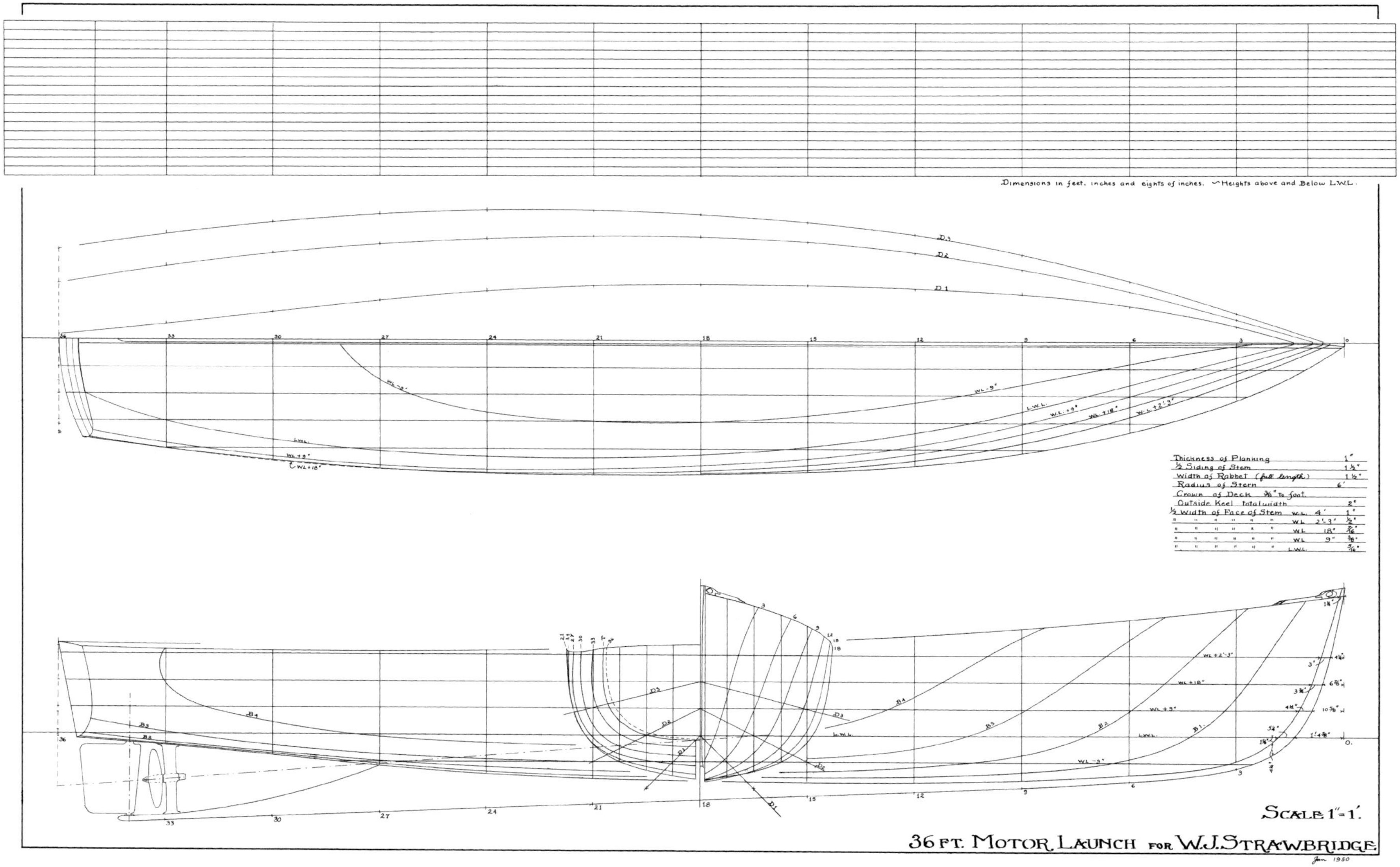
Dimensions in feet, inches and eights of inches. ~Heights above and Below L.W.L.
Thickness of Planking 1"
½ Siding of Stem 1½"
Width of Rabbet (full length) 1½"
Radius of Stern 6'
Crown of Deck ⅜" to foot.
Outside Keel total width 2"
½ Width of Face of Stem W.L. 4' 1"
" " " " " " W.L. 2'-3" ½"
" " " " " " W.L. 18" 7/16"
" " " " " " W.L. 9" ⅜"
" " " " " " L.W.L. 5/16"
Scale 1" = 1'.
36 FT. MOTOR LAUNCH FOR W.J. STRAWBRIDGE
Jan 1950

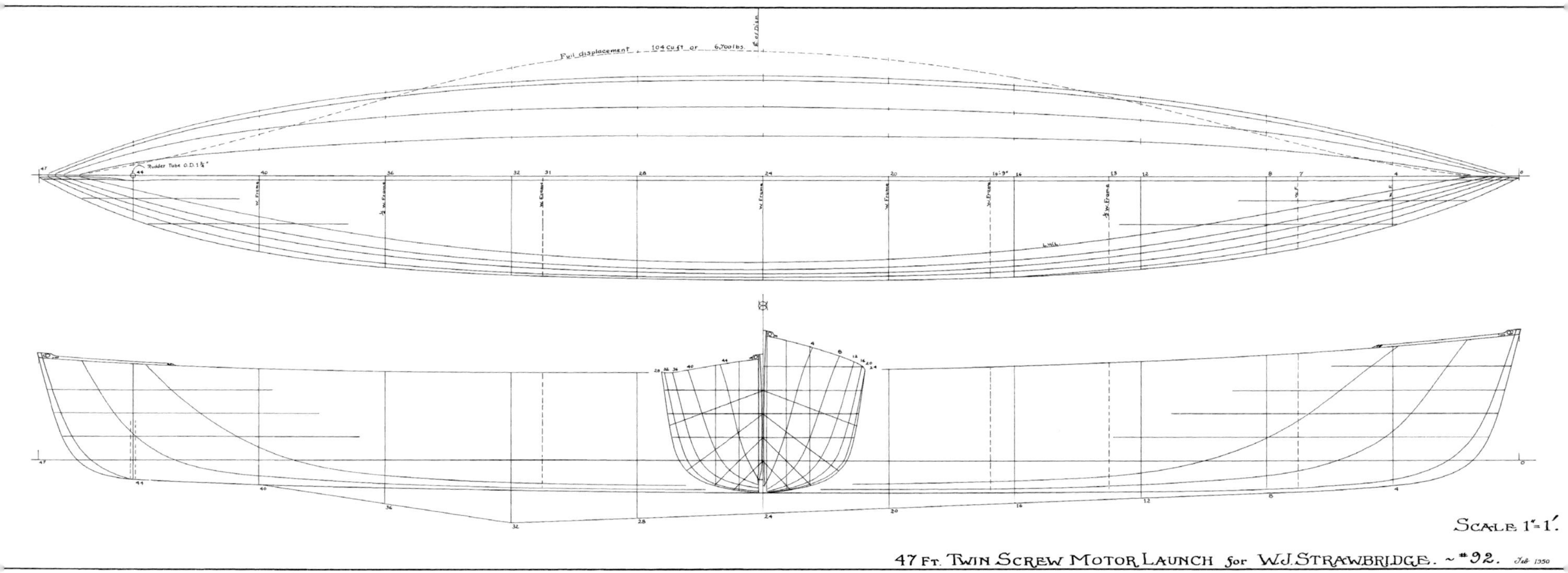

The lines of the *Piquant*, a 47-foot, twin-screw motor launch, Francis's design No. 92. This was another design for Billy Strawbridge, but this one would be built, because she was "Designed by Strawbridge working in collaboration with" L. Francis Herreshoff, a true fifty-fifty project. After much discussion, Strawbridge drew these lines, and Francis approved them, perhaps with minor modifications. Given that this was a joint project, Francis did not sign the drawing, instead merely dating it "Feb 1950." She is certainly long and narrow, and she was so lightly built that she really did float as high as the waterline shown. Her hull form was inspired by N. G. Herreshoff's fast steam launches of about 1880. Francis called her an enlarged, high-sided kayak. The *Piquant* has a beam of only 6 feet, 6 inches, a draft of only 2 feet, and a displacement of only 6,700 pounds. She is all length.

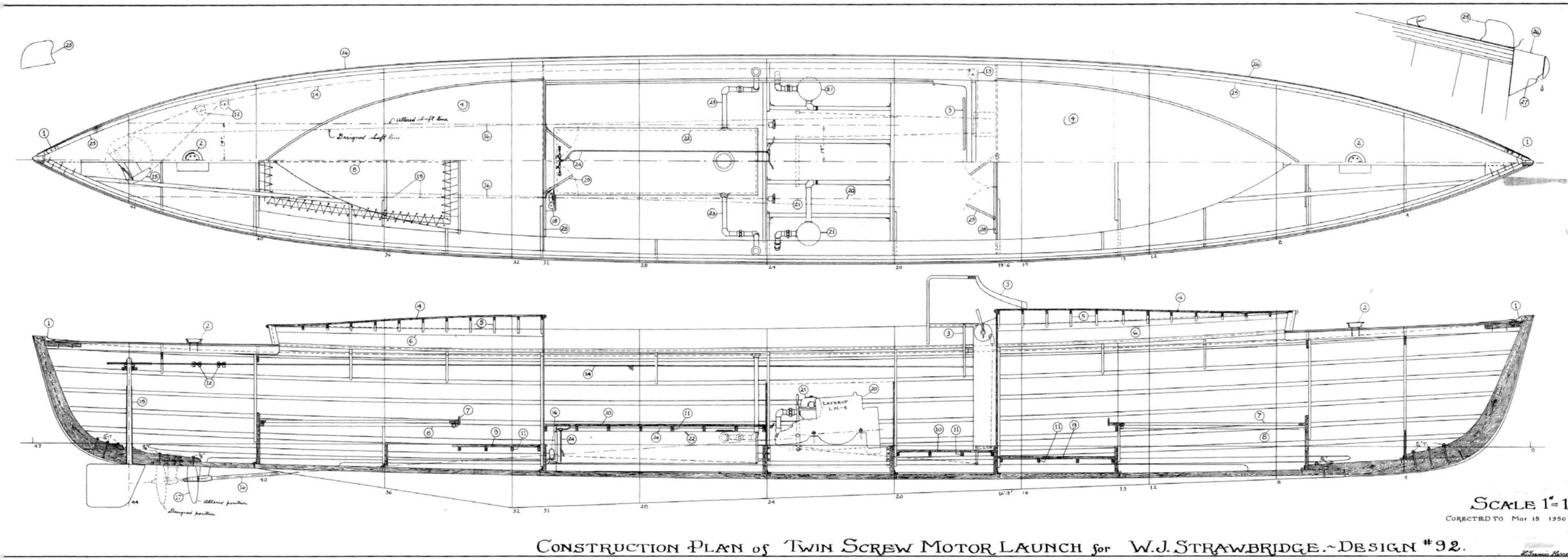

The *Piquant*'s construction and arrangement plan. Francis did sign this drawing, showing his longitudinal system for achieving a strong, light structure. The boat was built by the Luders Marine Construction Company at Stamford, Connecticut. Planking was double, the inner layer diagonal, the outer fore-and-aft, to a total thickness of ⅞ inch. She developed minor bulges in the planking, because, Francis thought, "Luders didn't taper all the planks." The engines were a pair of Lathrop LH-4s, developing 35 horsepower each at 2,000 rpm. She made 18 mph at 1,900 rpm, and 15 mph at 1,700. At the latter speed, she went 5 miles on a gallon of gas. She has a 100-gallon gas tank, so her range was 500 miles. Francis wrote that at that speed, "I looked at the propellers when in calm, clear water and could see that they were not cavitating at all." The drawing shows that the propellers were moved forward a bit from their designed position. Primarily a day-boat, the *Piquant* has a 14-foot cockpit, divided by the engine compartment, on which is a 6-foot-by-4-foot cushion. She does have Spartan accommodations for four. In the end of each cabin is a non-folding pipe berth the full width of the boat, with a "bundling" spar down the center under the canvas to keep two sleepers from rolling into each other. There is space for a small galley in the forward cabin; the aft cabin boasts a cedar bucket (not shown). Note the round bollards fore and aft, instead of cleats that might jam; these are perhaps the outcome of a few hours of yarning by the two friends. (© Mystic Seaport Museum, Daniel S. Gregory Ships Plans Library, SP38.89.2)

use the launch mostly for day trips, but, with her cabins, she was also capable of a cruise, and, with her speed, she could leave Marblehead in the morning and be in Portland or Mystic before dark. He was sixty-seven years old when he got the *Freelance*. His balance was becoming unreliable, so he never trusted himself to go out alone in her; he always had someone with him, either friends or Marblehead watermen like Bobby Russell or Rod Bowden. Russell recalled the boat gliding quietly through the water without rolling.[10]

Francis would keep the *Freelance* for four

ABOVE: **The two designers trying out their creation at Stamford. Billy Strawbridge is at the wheel; Francis is peering out from behind the windscreen. Judging by Strawbridge's private signal on the bow, she is making knots, although she is making very little fuss going through the water. Billy said the wind scoop didn't work very well, because the boat didn't go fast enough to make it effective. A. E. Luders Jr. wrote to Francis, "I think you have certainly produced the most level running boat at that speed [18 mph] that I have ever seen." Francis observed that, at 18 mph, her bow rose 5 inches and her stern settled only 2 inches. In this photograph, she looks to be making about 15 mph. Note the propeller guard, just below the rail at the stern, to keep the protruding blades from hitting a wharf when landing.** (SEAF Photo Service photo, courtesy *National Fisherman*, author's collection) RIGHT: **Francis at the wheel of the *Freelance*, as he renamed the *Piquant*, after he had traded his Mercedes Gull Wing to Billy Strawbridge for her. She is just idling along, otherwise he wouldn't be wearing his "*Freelance* hat." This photo was shot by Bobby Russell, a Marbleheader who often crewed for Francis.** (Mystic Seaport Museum, 1999-10-344)

years. He allowed that he was out in rough weather only twice. "She threw some spray in a good-sized sea and had to be slowed down some but this didn't happen very often, otherwise her motion was very pleasant and she steered without trying to yaw in a following sea." Francis concluded, "*Freelance* pleases me more and more the longer I use her."[11]

After the 1959 season, Francis reported to Billy Strawbridge: "I have made several nice runs in *Freelance* this summer with the rpm at 2,200 when she seemed to pass everything and I like her very much." He used the launch to watch races off Marblehead. And, as we have seen, he took the *Freelance* on a cruise to Buzzards Bay to watch the *Araminta* race in August 1960. On that occasion, in the Buzzards Bay chop, Allan Vaitses, the *Araminta*'s builder, found the *Freelance* to be a remarkably steady platform for photography. That summer, Francis told Billy, he had run the boat maybe 1,500 miles, the engines, of course, running fine. His report to Billy for 1961 included eight circumnavigations of Cape Ann. He'd go out around the Cape and come back through the Annisquam River, then, in Gloucester Harbor, ease round into Smith Cove to see if any interesting boats had come in, before heading back to Marblehead. Phil Bolger remembered: "I loved to see that boat. She made no fuss at all. He handled the *Freelance* very well, and it wasn't easy. She was a very slow-turning boat. Terry Kilborn went to take a look at her underway in a 36-foot sport fisherman I had designed for him. She had two 110-h.p. diesels. *Freelance* didn't seem to be moving at all, but he had to keep altering course and found himself in her wake."[12]

As we have seen, Francis took Hans Stinnes and his daughter Gretl to Newport in the *Freelance* to watch the 1962 America's Cup races. On a rough day, they had watched from the *Ticonderoga*, for Francis realized that the *Freelance* would be too uncomfortable. Gretl Stinnes agreed. She remembered that on the way to Newport, coming out of

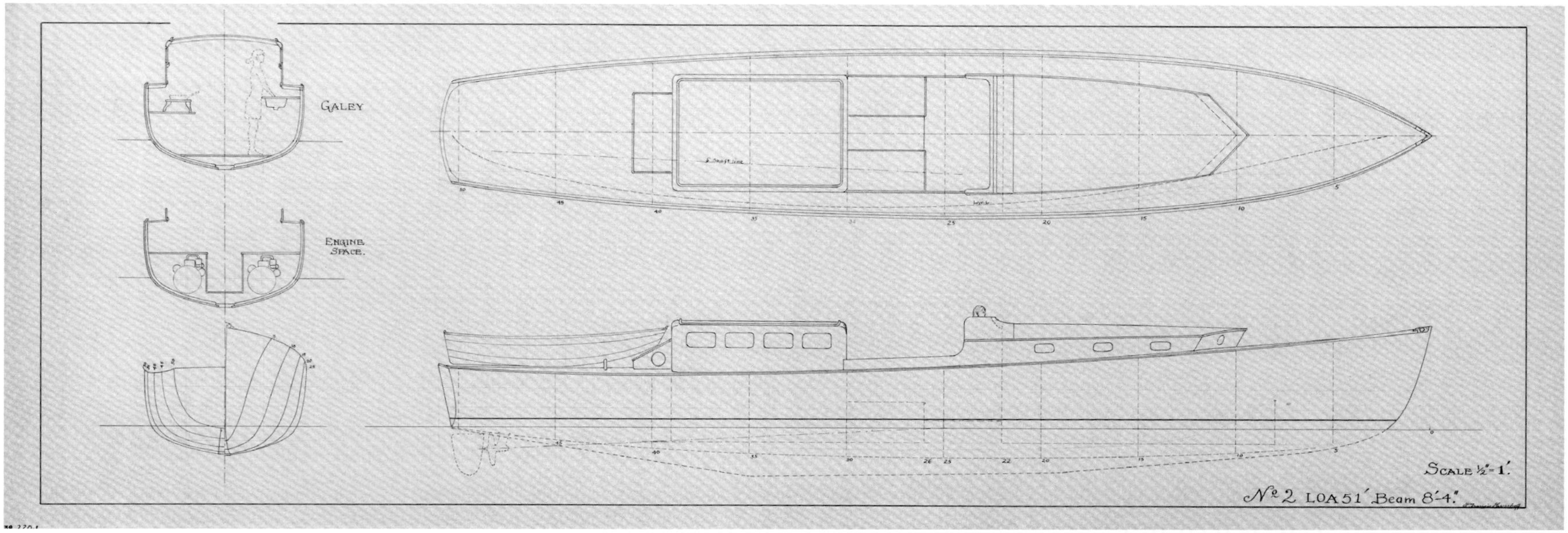

Galey
Engine Space.
Scale ½" = 1'
№ 2 LOA 51' Beam 8'-4"

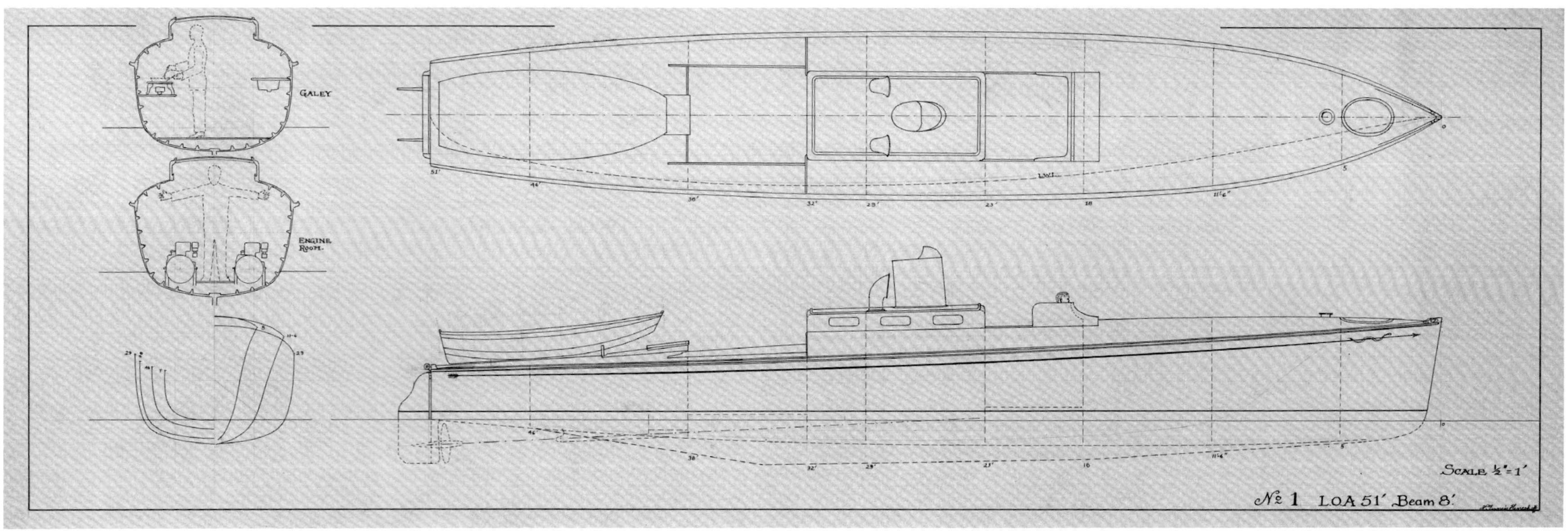

Galey
Engine Room.
Scale ½" = 1'
№ 1 LOA 51' Beam 8'

LEFT: After his experience with the *Freelance*, Francis drew up studies of two 51-foot, twin-engine launches that were less extreme than No. 92. He numbered them simply 1 and 2. He increased the beam of these boats to make them less cramped, but they were still long and narrow. They had transom sterns allowing for a pram to be carried. These boats have low displacement for their length, so they would be economical on fuel, though not so stingy as the *Piquant*. Francis thought they would be "smooth running in a choppy sea," more so than the *Piquant*. He envisioned longitudinal construction for No. 1, and possibly for No. 2 as well. No. 1 has an especially low stern for handling the pram. She has twin rudders and contra propellers. There is a crowned deck forward to gain headroom. To avoid having to walk on this deck, there is passage below, forward to the cockpit in the bow, for handling the anchor or bow line. Up forward there is a toilet and pipe berth; next aft is the main cabin, with two pipe berths; abaft the steering cockpit, under the house, is the engine room, with full headroom and a passage between the engines leading aft; the galley is in the after end of the house; there is a big aft cockpit; and an aft stateroom with a double berth and low headroom. No. 2 has a single rudder between her propellers. In the bow, there is a half collision bulkhead, rising to 18 inches above the waterline, allowing access to a forepeak. No. 2 has a toilet and pipe berth under the forward end of the trunk cabin; then, coming aft, a stateroom with two pipe berths; the steering cockpit with engine boxes and a passage between them. The galley and main cabin, with two pipe berths, are in the deckhouse. Francis shows the silhouette of a woman in one of his drawings, which is rare for him; but, predictably, he places her at the galley sink. There is a double berth under the low deck aft. Francis wrote: "It would be hard for me to guess which of the two launches #1 or #2 is the more desirable but a launch with an after cockpit has the advantage of allowing some of the passengers to be away from the helmsman, and it must be admitted some people's conversation is very tiring on a long run." Neither launch was desirable to a customer. These drawings remained studies. Below is a table that Francis drew up to compare the performance of Nos. 1 and 2 against that of the *Piquant*:

	PIQUANT #1	#2	(LATHROP 2# LH-4S)	(LATHROP LH MASTERS)
Horsepower	50	200	75	125
Displacement [lbs.]	6,700	9,000	10,000	10,000
Speed [mph]	15	20	13	17
Gallons per hour	3	12	4.5	7.5
Miles per gallon	5	1.7	2.9	2.3

the Cape Cod Canal into the steep chop of Buzzards Bay, the *Freelance* had "rolled and pitched every which way you could imagine." The motion of a boat in rough water (as we found with the Marco Polo) is in the stomach of the rollee; some find it exhilarating, others, sickening. Fortunately, Miss Stinnes was not quite seasick that day.[13]

When Francis brought the *Freelance* into Newport, he drove her through the anchored fleet wide open. Gretl Stinnes got the impression that the stunt was "to show today's stupid yachtsmen what a real boat should look like, not leaving any wake." Then he landed alongside the Australian challenger, the *Gretel*, and started to climb on board. "Sir, you can't do that." "Well, I'm Francis Herreshoff, and I would like to see the boat." "I'm terribly sorry, but you can't come aboard." Francis exited. Expecting any Australian sailor to know who he was, he had set himself up, and he felt insulted.[14]

The three lived on board the *Freelance* in Newport during the racing. "I had to do the cooking," Gretl recalled. "It was amusing. We would spend the evenings together in the after cabin which was not that roomy to begin with, and I remember its being a bit crowded especially when we could or would not eat outside. But I don't think it really bothered any of us." Gretl slept forward; her father and Francis bundled aft.[15]

The *Freelance* had her limitations. The return run to Marblehead from the Cup races had to be aborted at Onset at the head of a very rough Buzzards Bay. The Stinneses left, on schedule, but from Onset, not Marblehead; next day, Gretl had to find a hand and bring him down to help Francis get the boat home. Francis was upset that things had not gone smoothly for his guests. He seems to have been disappointed in his boat, probably unjustly. That day, at any rate, his launch could not take his passengers where they wanted to go. Within the month, he put the *Freelance* on the market, asking $12,000.[16]

She was sold to F. L. Higginson Jr. of North Hampton, New Hampshire, who donated her to Harvard for a crew launch. Yes, she was hard to turn in the confines of the Charles River, but so was an eight. Francis reported, "she has been liked very much because she makes practically no wave at speed around 12 mph."[17]

Eventually, the *Freelance* returned to yachting. She went through a major rebuild from 1979 to 1992, and there were major modifications, with much application of fiberglass and epoxy. Her twin Lathrops were replaced by a single Westerbeke diesel of the same total horsepower, with a centerline propeller and rudder, supported by a skeg. She grew a lead ballast keel and rolling chocks. There was temporary, later permanent, shelter over the steering station. The after part of the cockpit was enclosed under a trunk cabin to gain accommodations. Every conceivable comfort of home was crammed into her, much of it fed by a separate generating plant. The cedar bucket was ousted for an electric macerator toilet. True, there was a sensible heating stove, fed by wood. Fortunately, L. Francis Herreshoff did not live to see what had become of his nice boat. Lord only knows what he would have said had he cast his eagle eye upon her fake clipper bow![18]

Francis sold a few sets of seven drawings of the *Piquant*'s design at prices ranging from $60 to $85. In 1978, William Cooper built a boat to design No. 92. She was given a good-looking, permanent shelter over the steering station. She also has, for some reason, a mizzenmast with sail. Named the *Stiletto* after one of N. G. Herreshoff's fast steamers—a type that inspired the *Piquant*—she was donated to the Herreshoff Marine Museum in Bristol by Brian O'Neill, the real-estate developer.[19]

Like the Marco Polo, the *Piquant* is a remarkable design that fulfills her main objective to a very high degree. But no more sailors want a somewhat cramped, 47-foot motorboat than want a somewhat cramped, 55-foot ocean cruiser, even though both designs are hard to beat for motoring or ocean cruising. The *Piquant* type never became popular, but both her designers at least had the fun of running a boat that could just "pass everything" without seeming to try.

After Billy Strawbridge had enjoyed the *Piquant* for three seasons, he thought, why not have Francis design him a full-fledged cruising powerboat, a vessel that could accommodate several people for as long as they cared to stay afloat? There was enough discussion of this new boat so that Billy would later refer to her as the powerboat "that we designed," but the plans that ensued were entirely Francis's work. He gave the design No. 94. The size agreed upon for the yacht was a hull ten feet longer than the *Piquant* and a full six feet wider. But Billy couldn't make up his mind about just what accommodations he wanted in the bigger hull.[20]

In the spring of 1954, Francis was in correspondence with Walter F. Lathrop, who would supply the diesel engine for the boat: "The design for the motor boat to use a D-100 is progressing slowly [and had been for months] but there is no doubt she will be built. Some of the holdup has been that the owner cannot decide on the cabin plan." Rather than wait any longer, Francis sent the construction plan that he had completed to three builders for a cost estimate: Graves Boat Yard, in Marblehead; Luders Marine Construction Company, Stamford, Connecticut, and Abeking and Rasmussen, Lemwerder, Germany. He asked if they could bid on building the boat without interior arrangements, and include an estimate for the cabin, based on their experience with such vessels.[21]

Meanwhile, he wrote to Billy, "some sort of payment would be very much appreciated for I think I have done quite a lot of work—or at least put in a lot of time [on No. 94]."[22]

The Graves yard didn't care to bid without complete plans; Rasmussen estimated $32,000 without the cabin and thought the transatlantic shipping would cost $3,300; and Luders bid $49,088 without cabin, and came up, somehow, with $18,687 for the cabin, for a total cost of $67,775. When Francis relayed these results to Billy, he also complained: "From day to day I have expected you to come in to talk over the designs for in many cases I am stuck and do not know what to do until you approve of some of the arrangements. It is a little discouraging not knowing what to do as all the drawings I have made represent quite an effort." Two months later, Francis heard from Billy: "Don't do any more work on the plans." A month later, Billy cautioned Francis, "there is no rush on the plans as I would definitely not build for the present anyway, and we may have to revise to bring down the cost." Francis replied, "it would be advantageous for me to know whether to go ahead with this [No. 94] as I have other work in mind and have been putting it off from week to week."[23]

Francis realized by now that there would probably be no commission on No. 94 of 10 percent of the cost of building. Billy Strawbridge did pay him, at this point, $1,000 for his work on the twenty drawings. Billy knew that his own indecisiveness had been frustrating for his friend. Francis wrote, "thank you very much for the check which was very much needed because for almost a year I have not done any other work than on #94, and, although the work progressed very slowly, it was because I did not know what was wanted in many cases and had to hold up my work thinking you might be back at any time." Francis certainly never punched a time clock when at his drawing board or when doodling ideas for a boat, but his hourly wage for designing No. 94 was undoubtedly low. For sixteen other yachts that he had to mark "Not Built" on his plans list, his pay was nothing. L. Francis Herreshoff's designs that were not built were—literally—labors of love.[24]

Billy Strawbridge, with other pastimes than yachting, including a long trip to Scotland during the incubation of No. 94, had been put off by the

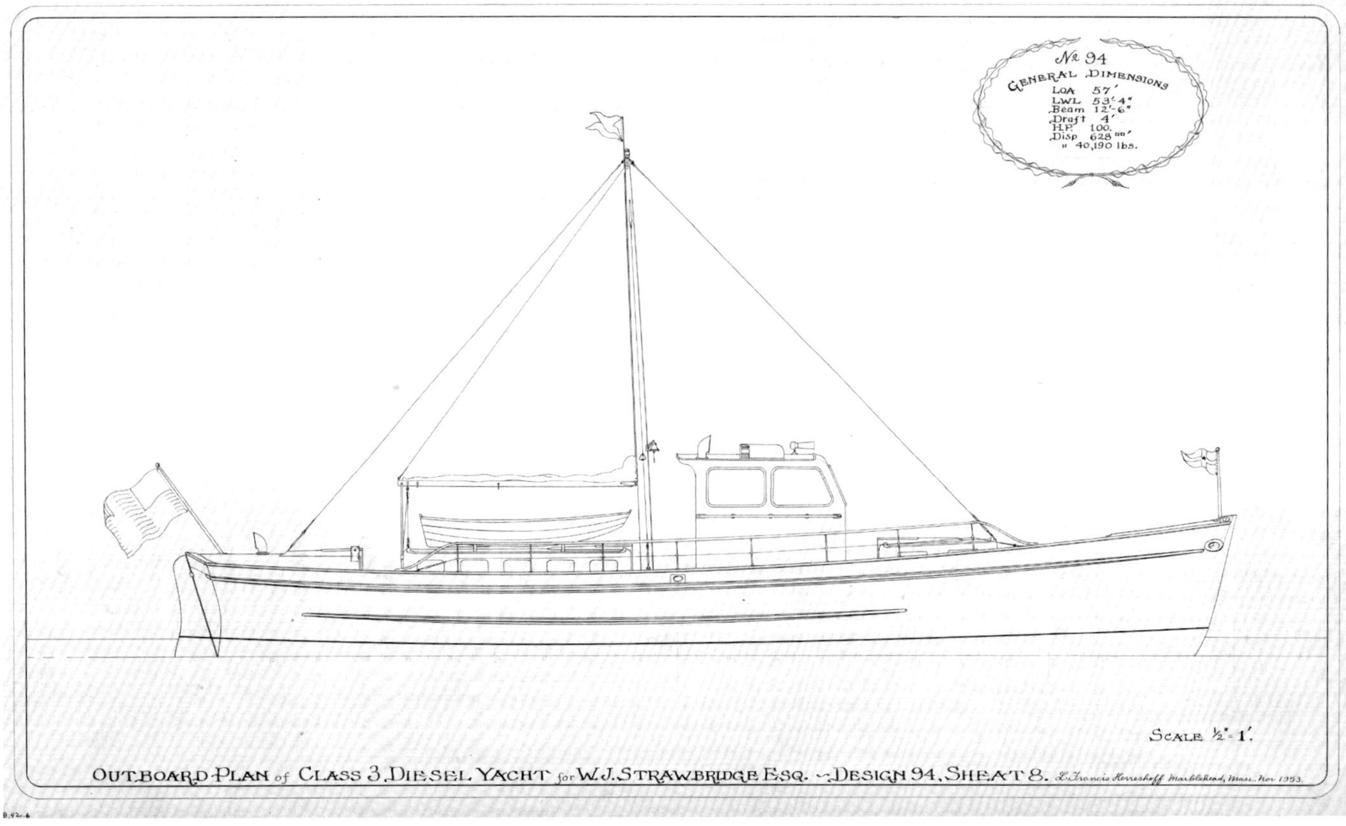

high cost of building a big motor cruiser, but he had also simply lost interest in the project. He didn't ask Francis to send him the plans of the boat until 1963, nine years later, when a trip on the Continent got him very excited about coastal and inland-water cruising in Europe. He wrote Francis a long letter glowing with the possibilities, and said he thought that the 57-foot powerboat "that we designed would be just about ideal." But this enthusiasm was not sufficiently enduring to build a boat. No. 94 is still a dream ship.[25]

As a part of Francis's crusade to save yachting through his writings for *The Rudder*, he devised "*The Rudder* Rating Rule for Small Racing Sailboats," which appeared in the July 1950 issue. The primary objective of the rule was to create open classes that would encourage the development of hull shapes and different rigs, so it was a continuation of his efforts with the Development Classes of 1928 and 1930 (see

The outboard profile of a 57-foot diesel yacht, Francis's design No. 94. She was for Billy Strawbridge. Francis worked on the design for upwards of a year in 1953-54, making twenty drawings, including construction details of many of her parts. There was no cabin plan, though, because Billy couldn't decide what he wanted. Then, when builders estimated the cost based on the incomplete plans, Billy shied away and the project died. She would have been a handsome vessel. She has a turtle-back stern, like Charlie Welch's *Walrus*, perhaps to be used, as on that boat, for a galley and wardroom. Her steadying sail would dampen rolling. Francis shows a Marco Polo dinghy atop the cabin house. (© Mystic Seaport Museum, Daniel S. Gregory Ships Plans Library, SP38.42.6)

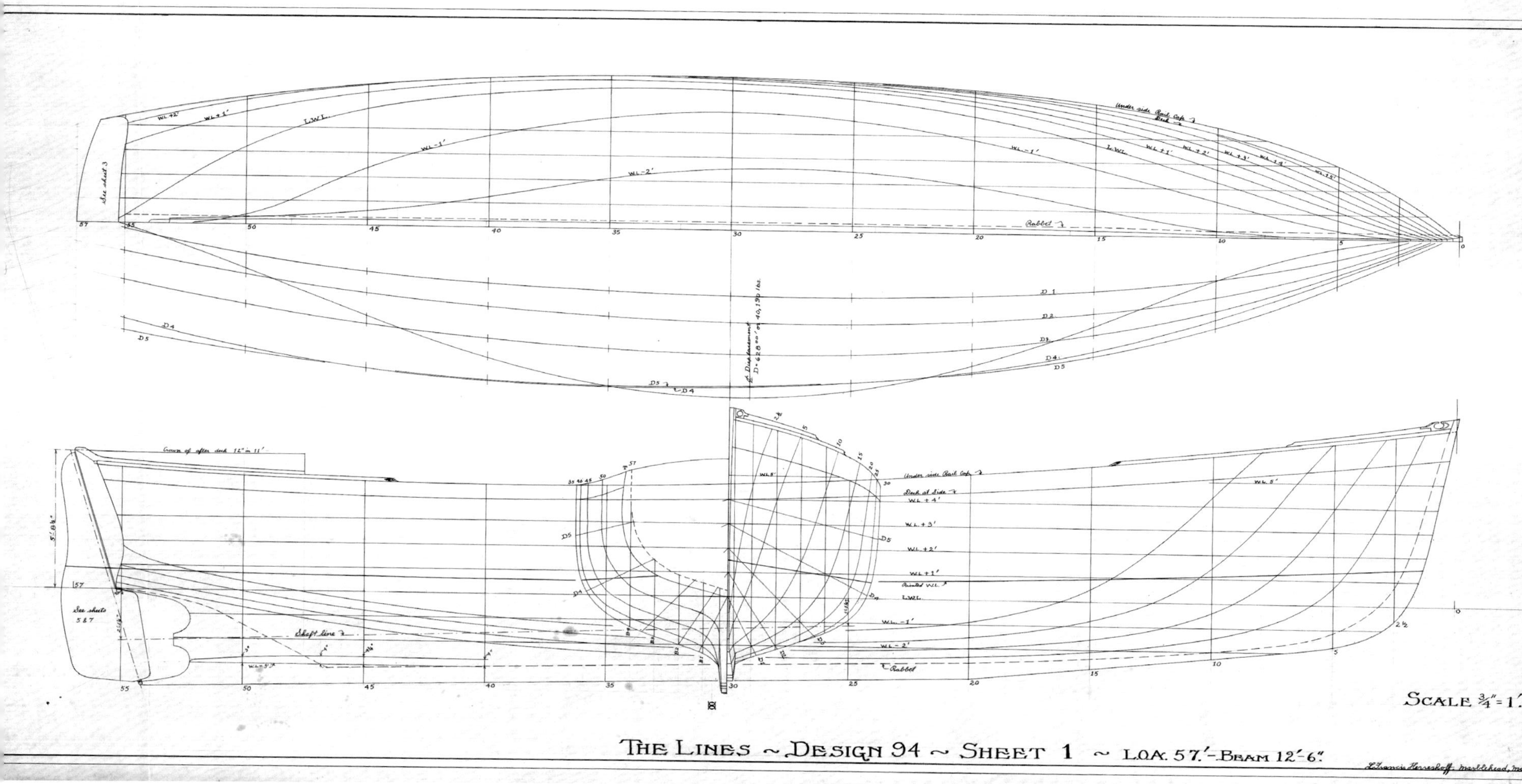

The lines of No. 94. She is a husky boat with a seaworthy model, yet is fine-lined enough to drive easily. Length on the waterline is 53 feet, 4 inches; beam, 12 feet, 6 inches; and draft, 4 feet. Francis figured her displacement at 40,190 pounds. He specified 3,100 pounds of lead, well aft on the outside keel. She was to have a 100-horsepower engine.

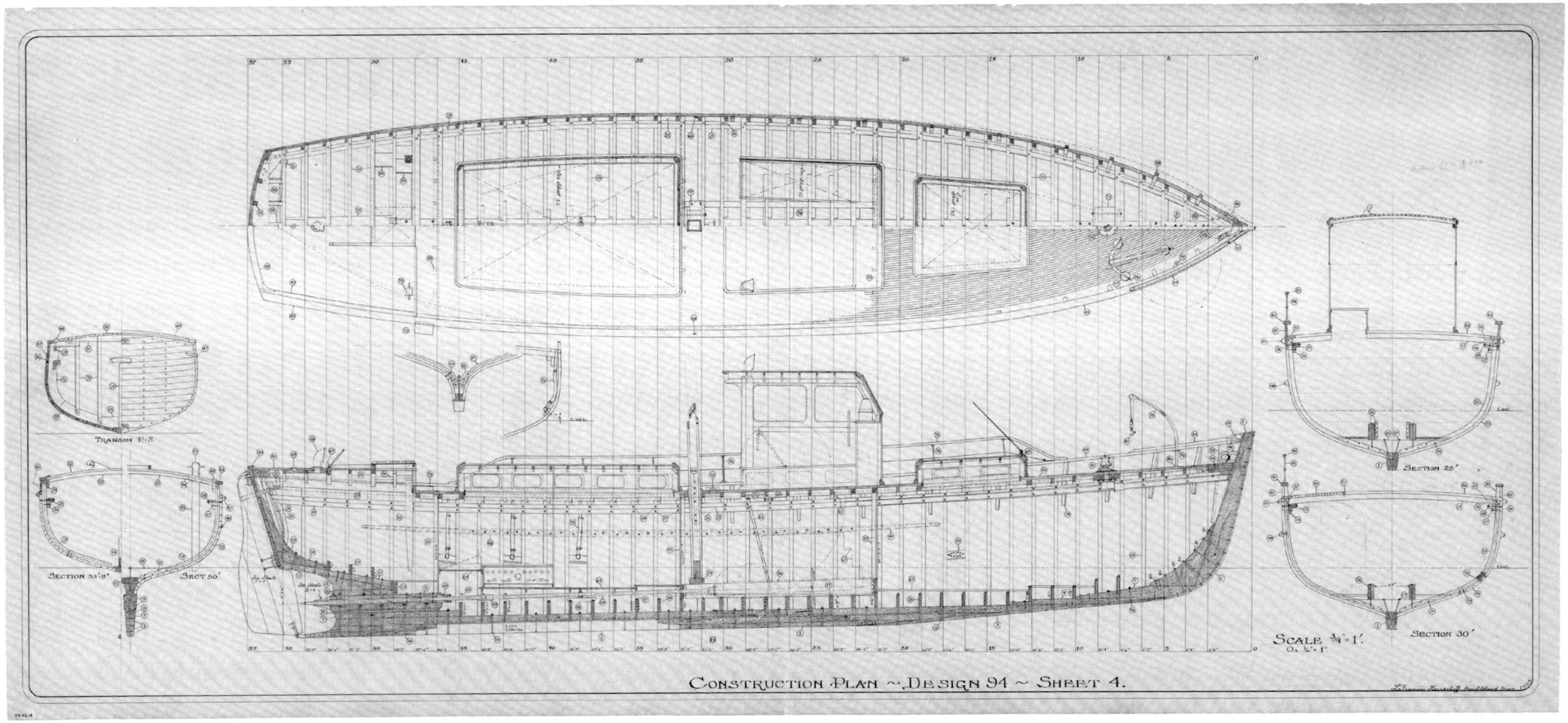

Many hours of Francis's expert, skilled work went into this construction plan for No. 94. The eighty-one numbered parts he shows took him twenty-two penciled pages to describe. This beautiful drawing represents an outstanding example of traditional plank-on-frame construction. Alas, it has never been used. (© Mystic Seaport Museum, Daniel S. Gregory Ships Plans Library, SP38.42.4)

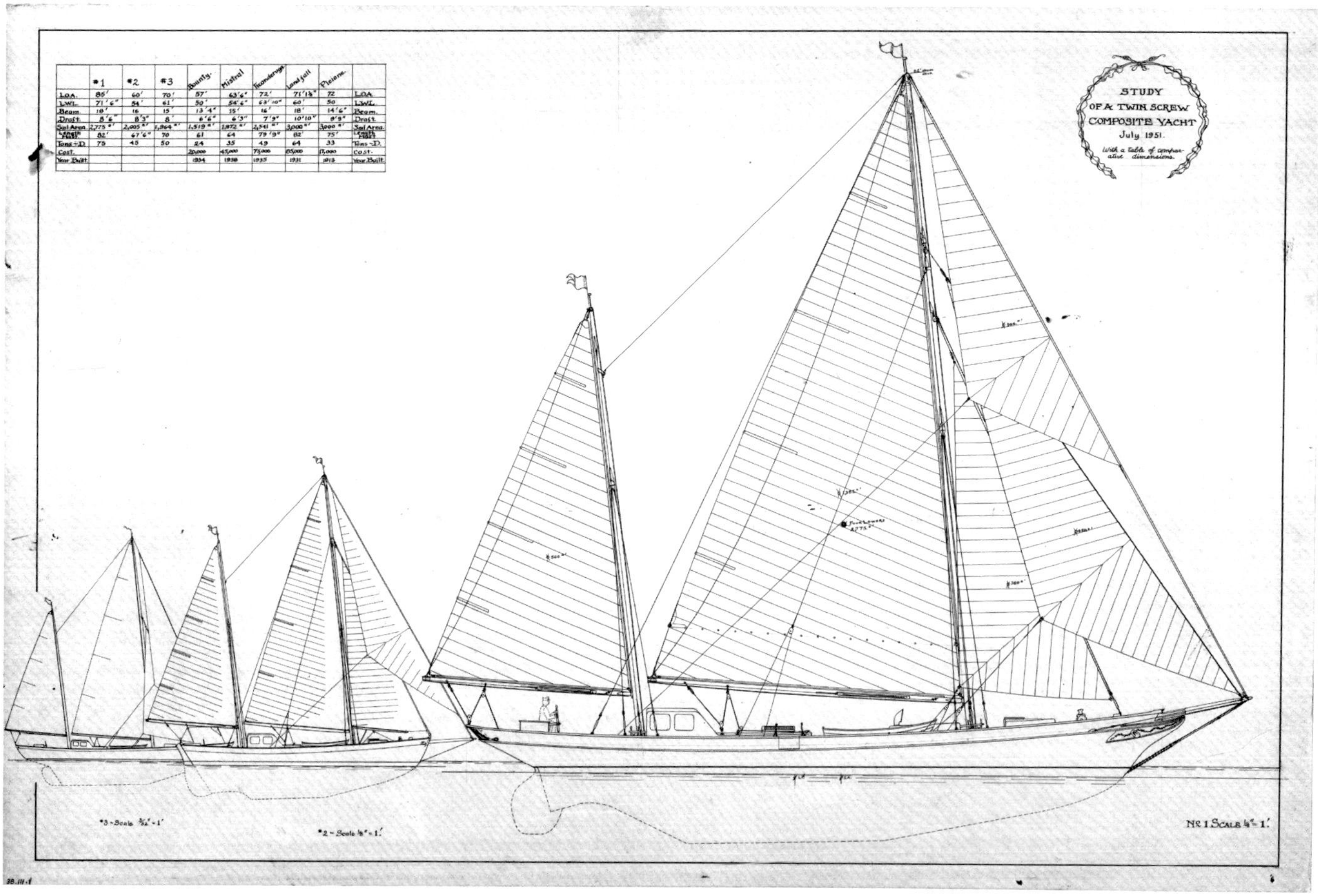

Francis drew this "Study of a Twin Screw Composite Yacht," actually three such vessels, to tempt Edward Dane, owner of the *Bounty*, into commissioning him to design a larger successor, as he had for Harry Noyes with the *Ticonderoga*. He made the drawing in July 1951; it was a rare case of his taking the initiative to try to get work. Francis numbered his proposed ketches 1, 2, and 3, from right to left. He wanted these yachts to have something of a big-ship feel: all have substantial bulwarks, which allow taller deck shelters than would otherwise look well. No. 1 is 85 feet long; No. 2, 60 feet; and No. 3, 70 feet. Francis wrote: "No. 1 is quite large and would have more than three times the usable room below deck than *Bounty*, but a smaller yacht of this model does not seem to appear well with high bulwarks, whereas a model like No. 2 seems to take high bulwarks without much detriment to looks. No. 2 is also a good all-around type: economical to build, a fine sea boat, and one that would rate low under the C.C.A. measurement rule [!]. No. 3 is a long, moderately narrow double ender that would drive easily under either sail or power." No. 1 is particularly interesting, combining Francis's clipper bow with the round stern of a North Sea pilot schooner, gracefully elongated. But none of the three appealed enough to Dane to warrant giving up his *Bounty*. "Study" was the operable word in the drawing's title. (© Mystic Seaport Museum, Daniel S. Gregory Ships Plans Library, SP38.111.1)

volume 1, pages 268 and 279). Francis apparently thought that if he put *The Rudder's* name on his rule, it would have a better chance of acceptance.[26]

The rule was comparatively simple, containing but twelve paragraphs. Francis proposed four classes, rating 10, 12½, 15, and 17½ feet. The rating equaled the square root of the sail area, plus 1. The sail area would be measured as the area of all sails used for sailing close-hauled (including that of a Genoa jib, if used), plus one-third of the area of any light sails used for reaching and running, such as a balloon jib or spinnaker. There was a penalty for excessively high, narrow sails (with a leach more than twice the width). Extremes in the hull were discouraged by penalties for exceeding the following proportions: beam less than 25 percent of length; freeboard less than 8 percent of length; and cube root of displacement in pounds less than 55 percent of square root of sail area in feet. Length was measured as length on deck plus length on the waterline divided by 2.

This proposal was a common-sense approach to the use of light sails for racing. Francis's rule attempted to level the playing field between those sailors who wanted the fun, excitement, challenge, and expense of setting light sails on the racecourse and those who preferred to see what they could do with just a generous working rig. As usual, however, the ability to set light sails whose area went unmeasured was too ingrained and too opportunistic to be resisted. The minimal response to *The Rudder* Rating Rule for Small Racing Sailboats could hardly be called a crusade.

The rule's death was not immediate, however. It was a topic of much discussion between Francis and Hans Stinnes when the two were together in 1962 on board the *Freelance,* resulting in a modified version that Francis wrote in 1964. The crusading small-boat racers adjusted the numbers in the rule, decreed a maximum ballast-displacement ratio of 55 percent, prevented a droopy boom from adding unmeasured sail area, and came up with a scantling rule that would prevent the use of heavy construction low in the boat as unmeasured inside ballast. But the most gallant blow struck by these knights in shining armor was: "The yacht must have a fair concave sheer between the farthest point forward to the farthest point aft." They would wipe out ugly, reverse-sheered boats if they could. But this version of the rule was not even published. Humpbacked boats survived.[27]

L. Francis Herreshoff and Frank C. Paine had been close friends in the 1920s when they both worked for Starling Burgess as yacht designers. After Starling broke up Burgess, Swasey and Paine in 1926, they drifted apart and had little contact for twenty years. But Georgina Paine Fisher Howland, married to the widower Llewellyn Howland, insisted that it was time her brother Frank resume his friendship with Francis Herreshoff. The resumption was easy, for although the two men approached yacht design in very different ways, both had an abiding interest in machine work on their lathes (see volume 1, page 155). These two designers of racing sailboats were fascinated by the design and making of engines.

Back in 1944, Francis had written, "there will undoubtedly be some mechanical improvements, like the arrangement of cylinders around the crankshaft, that will improve both the gasoline and heavy oil [diesel] engine equally." By 1950, Francis and Frank were combining efforts to try to improve the efficiency of the internal combustion engine in just that way, and in others. They came up with modifications to the diesel engine that effectively resulted in adding a cycle to the four-cycle engine. Later, they developed a way of converting the reciprocal motion of the pistons to the rotary motion of the drive shaft via oscillating disks. Both these changes to engine design, the inventors thought, would increase horsepower per pound of engine weight. The two would share the credit for these ideas; Francis made the drawings illustrating them, and Frank arranged for and participated in the building of prototype motors.[28]

Francis and Frank would meet in Frank's machine shop at his country place, "Greenways," in Wayland, a western suburb of Boston. In late 1950, Frank wrote to Francis: "With regard to the first sample engine which I am trying to built [this is one dyslexic writing to another; see volume 1, page 70], I have got two cylinders, the material for the crank shaft, valves, etc., and have had a couple of castings made for the crank case so that I am already to begin work. If you would like to I would certainly appreciate it if you would make up a drawing for the number two engine as I am sure you would be able to work it out much better and incorporate many more original ideas than would ever occur to me."[29]

Seven months later, Francis sent his drawing of the engine with the combination of opposed pistons and oscillating-disk crankshaft to Robert S. Sanborn, of Dike, Porter and Sanborn, patent attorneys in Boston. Sanborn's evaluation, citing five patents, was, "all of these patents seem to show the combination of an opposed piston arrangement in a 'wobble motor' and, therefore, your invention is broadly anticipated and unpatentable." Not discouraged, the inventors continued to try improvements to their motor. They replaced the oscillating disks with an eccentric cone arrangement and made three of the six cylinders into "compressors or scavengers to force the air or explosive mixture into the remaining three cylinders which act as explosion or driving cylinders." Sanborn thought that two or three features of this engine design might be patentable, but the inventors did not pursue the matter. The attorney wrote: "I might add that I am impressed by the marked simplicity of the over-all design of your engine as compared with the complicated and expensive designs shown in the enclosed patents."[30]

At the same time when these two inventive yacht designers were trying to patent improvements to the internal combustion engine, they were also trying to make it easier for skiers to climb hills and for sleepers to stay cool on hot, summer nights. But their "Hill-Climbing Attachment for Skis" had been anticipated by a 1927 patent, and their "Water-Cooled Mattress" was never made in the face of small air-conditioners coming on the market. Francis's questing mind was akin to those of his father, and of his uncles Francis and James (see volume 1, pages 13, 14).[31]

In the midst of all this creative energy, Frank Paine was diagnosed with intestinal cancer. Francis sent him a ball of well-tarred marline in the hospital "to smell once in awhile." Frank died the day after he received it, on October 28, 1952. Francis reported the sad news to his yacht-designer friend Nick Potter with, "Mr. Frank was a wonderful man and I will miss him very much." Frank's sister Georgina wrote, "Frank was shy all his life long, but it only made people love him better." And she wrote a memoir about her childhood that emphasized her love for her brother. Their mother had called these two later children her "afterthoughts," and Georgina Howland used that word for her title. Francis told her that *Afterthoughts* was the only book that he ever read right over again. Frank's death ended Francis's efforts to improve the design of the internal combustion engine, but those efforts had reunited the friends. Looking back on their interrupted years as cooperating machinists, Francis wrote to Frank's widow, Virginia, "I appreciate his many kindnesses to me." A last kindness was Frank's bequest of $1,000 to Francis.[32]

John M. Garber of Cincinnati followed the writings and designs of L. Francis Herreshoff in *The Rudder*. He wrote to Francis of his love of exotic woods and of their ready availability in his inland city. He dreamed of using them in a boat that he would ask Francis to design, a boat for family cruising on the coast of Maine. By June of 1951, Francis had made a preliminary drawing of a 30-

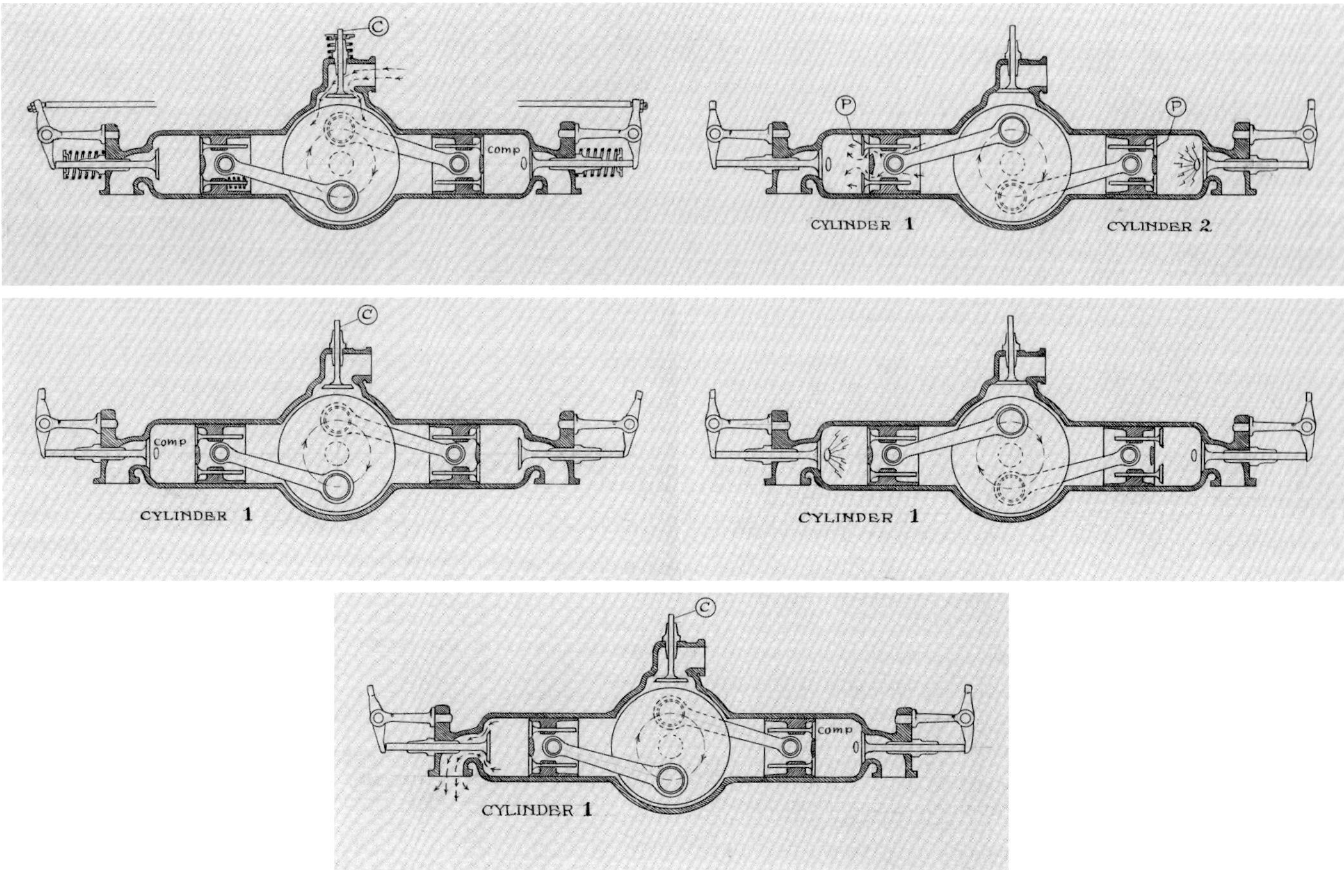

In the early 1950s, Francis and Frank Paine reconnected as inventors of improvements to the internal combustion engine. Here is Francis's drawing of a five-cycle, supercharged, opposed-piston engine, showing, from left to right and top to bottom, the functional strokes in one pair of cylinders. He wrote: "The five cycles or functionable strokes are as follows: 1. Pistons traveling outward thereby charging crankcase with mixture. 2. Pistons travelling inward forcing double charge in one cylinder or combustion space [supercharging by the action of the piston itself]. 3. Pistons travelling outward compressing charge in the cylinder that has closed valves. 4. Pistons travelling inward on power or explosion stroke. 5. Pistons travelling outward and exhausting burnt gasses in cylinder which fired on pervious stroke." Although the mechanical parts are in the same position in cycles 1 and 5, in cycle 5 the function of expelling exhaust gases is performed by the combustion-chamber side of the left-hand piston, so Francis considered this to be a separate cycle. He believed that this design simplified supercharging and cooling and would increase the horsepower in the engine without increasing its size and weight. Helen Bolster noted that she typed Francis's text accompanying this drawing at 10:50 a.m. on March 5, 1951, this to be the operative time of the invention in case it could be patented. (© Mystic Seaport Museum, Daniel S. Gregory Ships Plans Library, SP38.364.1)

foot double-ended sloop with an outboard rudder. Four months later, Garber made the pilgrimage to The Castle to discuss details of the design, by now No. 93. They talked of straightening the bow profile a little, increasing the rake of the sternpost, and shortening the waterline by three inches. Perhaps the dinghy-stowage space on deck should be bigger? Could the mast be taller to increase sail area? In the end, the latter was the only change Francis made to his preliminary drawing. In January 1952, Francis sent Garber a construction plan, with eight pages of specifications, typed single-spaced by Helen Bolster.[33]

John Garber and his wife, Amey, were architects. When he got the construction plan for his sloop, Garber wrote to Francis: "I can appreciate your thought and thoroughness. I have also enjoyed reading through the specifications. It is seldom that a designer will tell his reasons for doing thus and so. Most people who have a little knowledge like to keep it to themselves and make much mystery of the matter. I have noticed, however, that those with the *most* knowledge are likely to be willing to part with it, and to put it forth in simple language."[34]

More than a year went by, though, without Garber ordering his exotic wood. Yet he remained enthusiastic about No. 93. He wrote to Francis: "It looks to me like an ocean type boat, a Maine type boat, the kind of a boat we would love very much. It is a boat with delicacy of expression and considerable self confidence—quietly expressed. It is a

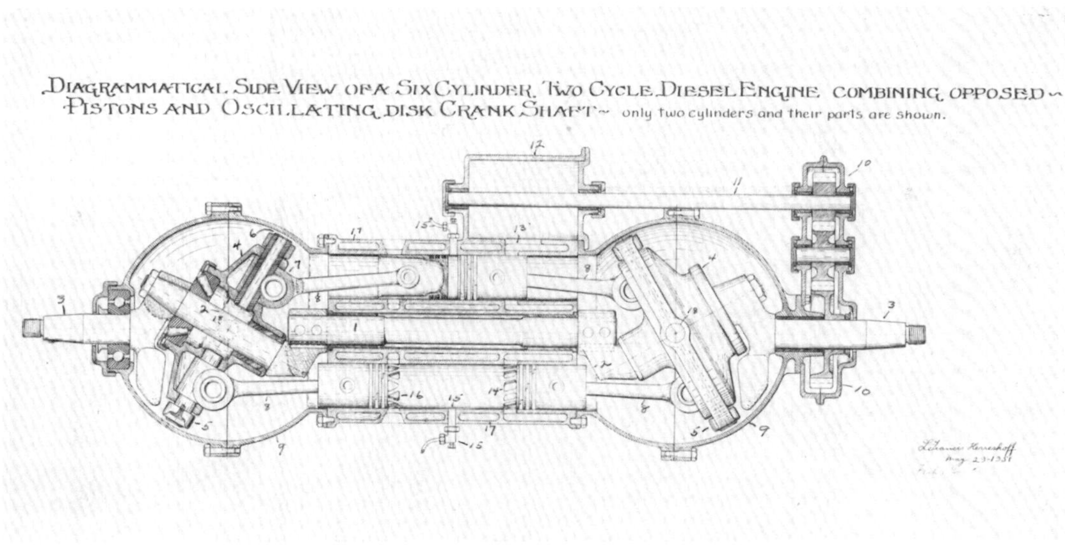

Francis and Frank both signed Francis's drawing of a further invention, showing a side view of two cylinders of their six-cylinder, opposed-piston diesel engine, with an oscillating-disk crankshaft. The crankshaft, extending, in effect, horizontally right through the center of the engine and available to take off power at either end, is rotated by the two oscillating disks in their large, globular housings. The disks make the connection between the center and ends of the crankshaft, converting the reciprocal motion of the pistons to rotary motion. In this drawing, the two pistons in the upper cylinder are shown moved together, and the two in the lower cylinder are apart. Francis believed that this engine would be light, compact, and perfectly balanced, with neither the complication of valves, nor the inefficiency of heat-absorbing cylinder heads. (© Mystic Seaport Museum, Daniel S. Gregory Ships Plans Library, SP38.359.1)

graceful, little boat. It is pretty. And it doesn't try to look like a larger boat—or an expensive boat—or a correct boat. It looks to me like a *boat* and I think that is the ultimate satisfaction."[35]

Garber was now thinking of getting cost estimates to build No. 93, and Francis offered to make detailed drawings of spars, mast fittings, and rudder details, as well as a rigging and block list, if Garber decided to go ahead. Garber didn't commit himself to building, but he did agree to pay $100 for each drawing as Francis completed them, echoing Edwin Hill's arrangement for the *Araminta*. Over the next three years, Francis made more drawings for No. 93 to a total of six, and wrote to Garber, "I never have made so many full size details for a boat that was not definitely to be built, or under construction." Finally, Garber did get cost estimates. In January 1956, both the Hodgdon and Hinckley yards in Maine said that No. 93 would cost about $13,500. Garber said he couldn't afford that much for his dream boat, that he had found a used Folkboat that he could afford, and wondered what Francis thought of that? Francis thought the Maine prices to be too high and suggested getting bids from the Quincy Adams yard and from Rasmussen in Germany. As to the Folkboat—a handsome, able, and popular 25-foot sloop with minimal cruising accommodations designed in Sweden in 1942 by Tord Sunden—Francis said he liked the design quite well. Garber sent in his final $100 check for Sheet 6 of No. 93, and that was that.[36]

Boris Lauer-Leonardi published the plans of No. 93 in the February 1956 issue of *The Rudder*. Francis penciled a two-paragraph description of the design for Mrs. Bolster to type up for Boris. He wrote, "this design is rather unique in having a space to carry a tender without obstructing the vision unreasonably." Helen Bolster, good grammarian that she was, knew that there are no degrees of uniqueness, so she exercised rare editing and changed "rather unique" to "a little unusual." Miss Cora Hill would have approved, and so did Francis, if he noticed.[37]

Over the next decade, Francis sold a few sets of plans for No. 93 at $55 per set. One customer, Bruce A. Tyson, of Devonport, Tasmania, wrote, in 1970, that he was slowly building the sloop. If she was launched, Francis didn't live to know it. But perhaps this "very able and seaworthy" vessel did grace waters Down Under.[38]

William A. Shirley was a merchant seaman on board a National Bulk Carrier tanker, the *Wagon Box*, delivering "product" all across the Pacific. On his time off, he liked to make some of the trips in his own boat, single-handed, and had built himself an H-28 for the purpose. Back on board ship, he would take out his set of H-28 plans and doodle on them, seeking to create a boat more suitable for his ocean passages. In 1956, Shirley wrote a four-page letter to the designer of the H-28: "I would like to commission you to Design a 30 foot double-ender for me along the following lines," and he enclosed his marked-up H-28 plans, with detailed comments on his proposed changes. "With the freeboard like in your design #93," he wrote. He kept the H-28's full deadwood. He also suggested keeping the H-28's ballast-displacement ratio of 31 percent, but, since he had written, "in drawing up the lines, please use your own discretion," Francis gave him 51 percent, for offshore work. With the letter, Shirley sent a check for $200 and said, "Please send a bill for the rest of your fee."[39]

Here was a customer who meant business. Francis was between major assignments from Boris, and he went right to work on what would become design No. 99. It seemed that the boat Shirley had in mind and on paper was essentially a ketch-rigged No. 93. Shirley claimed he only needed the answers to a few specific questions on construction, and would use the plans he already had for the H-28, *Didikai*, and Nereia, for guidance. Thus, there would be no need for Francis to make up a construction plan for No. 99. Able Seaman Shirley commissioned his design, paid for it, built his boat, named her after his current ship, the *Wagon Box,* and put to sea. His actions

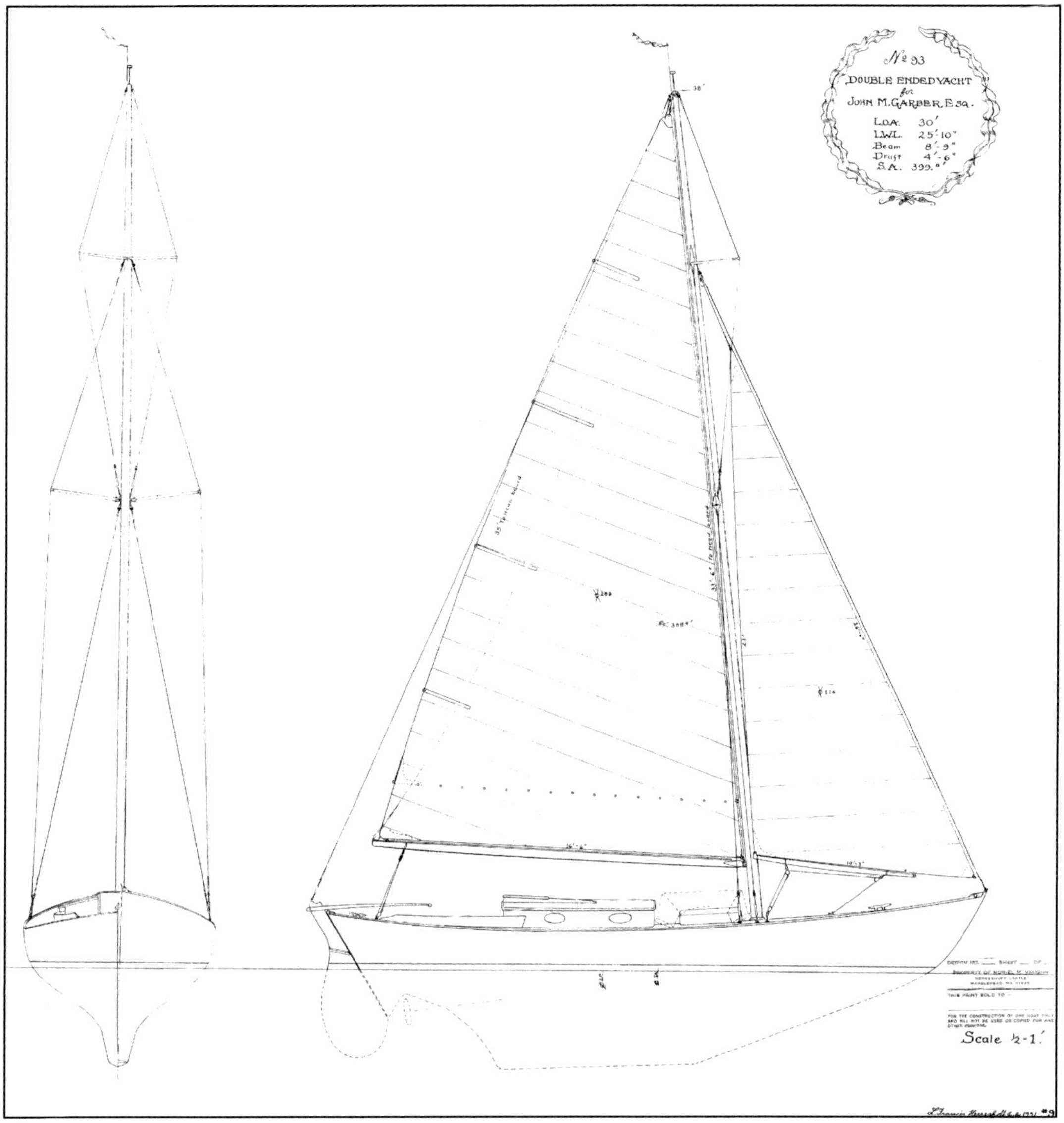

The outboard profile and sail plan of Francis's design No. 93 of 1951, a 30-foot, double-ended cruising sloop for John M. Garber, an architect in Cincinnati. Her well-raked rig is simple, with a self-tending, partial-club jib and no running backstays. Francis kept her cabin house short to allow space on deck to stow a pram athwartships. Sail area is 399 square feet, with 285 in the mainsail and 114 in the jib. Garber did not want to put in an engine at first, but wanted space for one later, under the cockpit, so Francis shows a propeller. (© Mystic Seaport Museum, Daniel S. Gregory Ships Plans Library, SP38.179.3)

Station Numbers	30	28	26	24	22	20	18	16	14	12	10	8	6	4	2	0
Height of Deck at Side	2-6-7	2-3-0	2-0-3	1-10-5	1-9-5	1-9-2	1-9-2	1-9-6	1-10-5	2-0-0	2-1-5	2-4-0	2-6-5	2-9-6	3-1-4	3-6-0
" " B #3				0-5-4	0-3-0	0-8-0	0-11-0	1-0-1	-0-11-4	-0-7-4	-0-1-3	0-9-7	2-1-7	3-9-4		
" " B #2			+0-5-2	0-3-7	0-10-3	1-3-0	1-6-2	-1-8-2	-1-7-7	-1-5-1	-1-0-3	-0-4-5	0-7-2	2-1-7	3-10-0	
" " B #1		+0-11-0	-0-2-6	-0-10-5	-1-5-2	-1-10-4	-2-2-5	-2-5-4	-2-6-3	-2-4-4	-1-11-0	-1-3-4	-0-6-2	0-6-3	2-4-3	4-8-3
" " Rabbet	+2-9-1	-0-3-4	-1-1-7	-1-10-4	-2-7-0	-2-11-2	-2-11-2	-2-11-2	-2-11-2	-2-11-2	-2-10-2	-2-1-4	-1-4-6	-0-7-2	0-7-7	3-7-7
" " Profile	2-6-7	0-10-4 ✓ 3-9-4	1-3-6	2-2-6	4-6-0	4-5-2	4-4-4	4-3-6	4-3-0	3-9-0	2-11-6	2-3-7	1-5-7	-0-8-7	0-5-0	3-6-0
Half Width of Deck	0-0-7	1-9-2	2-10-1	3-6-1	3-10-2	4-2-0	4-3-4	4-4-0	4-4-0	4-3-1	4-0-7	3-8-5	3-2-1	2-5-2	1-5-0	0-1-2
" " W.L. 2'		1-8-2	2-10-1							4-3-1	4-0-2	3-7-2	2-10-4	1-10-6	0-9-3	
" " W.L. 1'		1-0-7	2-6-2	3-4-0	3-10-0	4-1-4	4-3-4	4-4-2	4-3-3	4-1-0	3-8-3	3-1-2	2-3-1	1-3-3	0-3-5	
" " L.W.L.		0-3-3	1-4-4	2-6-0	3-3-2	3-8-5	3-11-3	4-0-2	3-10-0	3-7-0	3-1-0	2-4-4	1-5-5	0-7-2		
" " W.L.-1'			0-2-4	0-10-0	1-8-4	2-5-3	2-10-2	3-0-1	2-11-2	2-6-3	2-0-1	1-3-7	0-6-4			
" " W.L.-2'				0-1-4	0-6-2	0-10-6	1-2-6	1-5-4	1-6-0	1-3-6	0-11-0	0-3-4				
" " W.L.-3'					0-2-5	0-4-7	0-7-1	0-8-4	0-8-4	0-7-0						
" " W.L.-4'					0-1-4	0-4-1	0-6-1	0-6-6	0-5-3							
" " Rabbet	0-1-7	0-1-7	0-1-7	0-1-7	0-2-6	0-5-0	0-7-2	0-8-7	0-8-6	0-7-3	0-3-3	0-2-7	0-2-2	0-1-7	0-1-7	0-1-7
" " Profile	0-0-7	0-0-7	0-0-0	0-0-0	0-1-3	0-3-4	0-5-5	0-6-0	0-4-4	0-2-4	0-2-0	0-1-4	0-1-0	0-0-5	0-0-4	0-1-2
Diagonal #1		0-3-4	0-9-6	1-3-7	1-9-4	2-1-6	2-4-7	2-6-4	2-6-3	2-4-3	2-0-7	1-7-5	1-1-0	0-6-0		
" #2		0-9-5	1-8-6	2-4-5	2-11-2	3-3-4	3-6-2	3-7-4	3-6-5	3-3-4	2-11-3	2-5-3	1-9-3	1-0-7	0-3-3	
" #3		1-6-3	2-8-4	3-5-2	3-11-2	4-3-1	4-5-3	4-6-0	4-5-0	4-2-0	3-9-3	3-2-5	2-5-7	1-7-6	0-8-3	

Offsets in Feet, inches and eights of inches.
Hights above and below L.W.L.

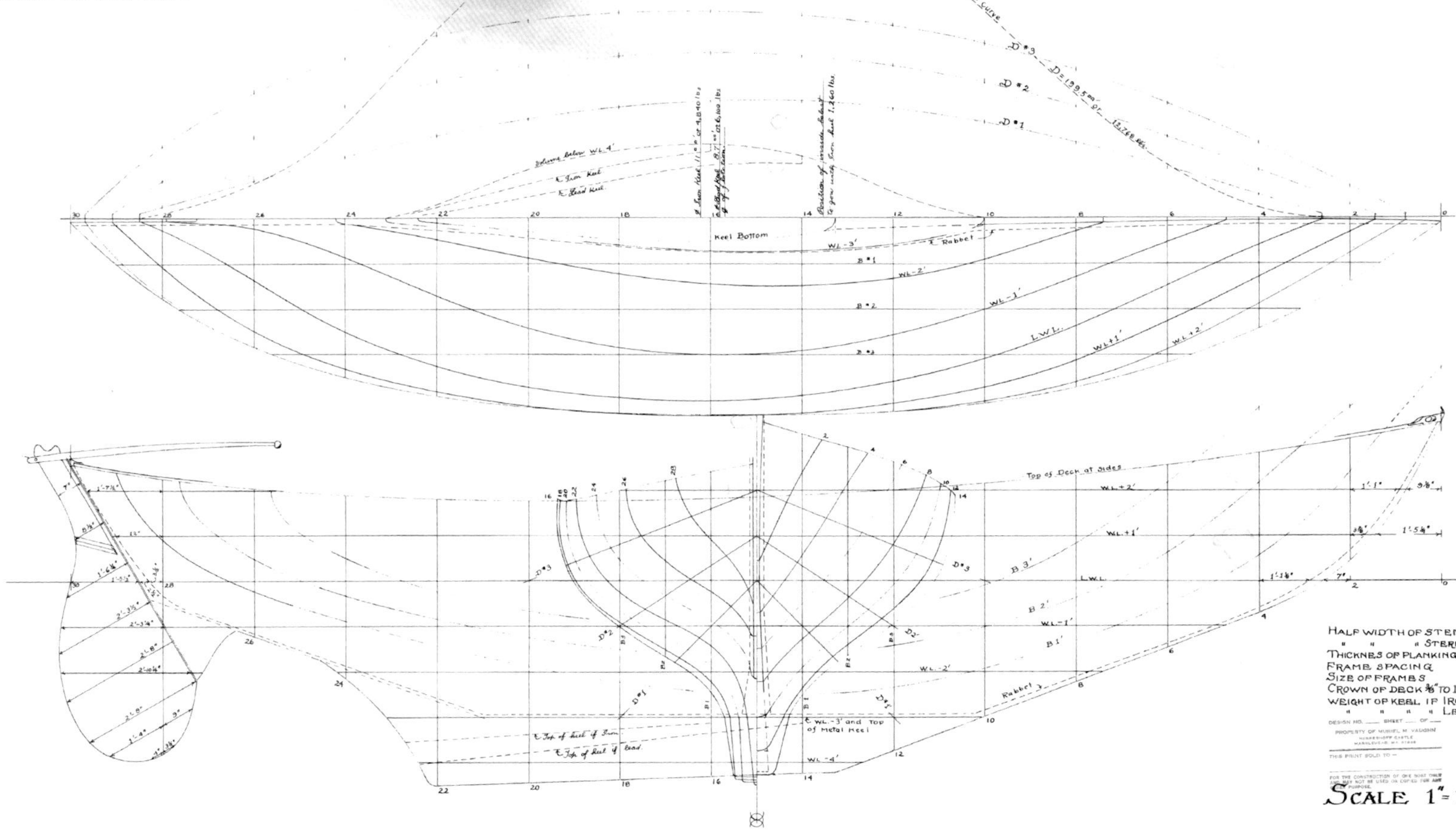

Half width of stem 1⅞"
" " " Stern post 1⅞"
Thicknes of planking 1⅛"
Frame spacing 12"
Size of frames 1⅜" x 1⅜"
Crown of deck ⅜" to 1' or 3⅜" in 9'
Weight of keel if Iron 4,840 lbs.
" " " " Lead 6,100 lbs.

Design No. ___ Sheet ___ of ___
Property of Muriel M. Vaughn
Herreshoff Castle
Marblehead, MA

This print sold to —

For the construction of one boat only and may not be used or copied for any other purpose.

Scale 1" = 1'.

The Lines of № 93 Double Ended Yacht for John M. Garber, Esq. ~ Sheet 2. #93

may have made up for at least a few of Francis's frustrating "not-built" designs—like No. 93.

And design No. 99 appealed to another big-ship mariner. On Maine's Penobscot Bay, William E. Abbott was a pilot for fifty-four years. He sailed his Wagon Box, built in 1978, in fifteen Retired Skippers races, a local event that he helped found.

Back in 1943, Boris Lauer-Leonardi began writing a non-technical book with the working title "*Introduction to Cruising.*" He wanted L. Francis Herreshoff to illustrate the book with fifty drawings, for which he would pay $3.00 each. Although Francis agreed to accommodate Boris, nothing came of the project. But a seed was planted for both men. Five years later, Boris suggested that Francis write articles for *The Rudder* that could become such a book. Francis thought that *The Amateur Seaman*, by H. S. "Skipper" Smith already filled that bill. But by 1952, after finishing the biography of his father, he was ready to write about "The Art, Practice and Enjoyment of Boating," which became the subtitle of his *The Compleat Cruiser.* Francis believed that "no better style for instructing (than carrying on a narrative) has been formulated since the famous writing of Honest Ike [Izaak Walton's *The Compleat Angler*] some 300 years ago."[40]

So Francis wrote his manual on how to cruise by inventing characters and boats for them to cruise in, and put them through a variety of weather along the part of the New England coast that he knew so well, between Gloucester, Massachusetts, and New London, Connecticut. By the time the book ended, his skippers and crews had gone through just about every cruising situation that the author himself had gone through. Francis's cruising experience was intense, if not broad, and his imagination easily filled in any gaps. Any sailor who was attracted and held by his quaint, low-keyed style of storytelling, in which his characters' main roles were either as teachers or students, could learn much about "the art, practice and enjoyment of boating." And Francis used "The Compleat Cruiser," which ran as thirty articles in *The Rudder* from March 1952 through August 1954, to continue his crusade to restore what he thought of as "decency" to boating. His teaching is effective because it is memorable, and it is memorable because of his strong opinions. He preaches decency—and simplicity. All through "The Compleat Cruiser," Francis shows that the simple way is the most effective and enjoyable way.

There is Coridon and his crewman, Briggs, in the 24-foot Cape Cod catboat *Piscator*. Coridon is "a middle-aged bachelor, always full of enthusiasm and knew all the secrets of doing things easily and quickly. He had, you might say, mastered the art of cruising simply, and of getting the most fun for the money that it was possible to do on the water." Briggs is a young racing sailor, new to cruising.

LEFT: **The lines and offsets of the Garber sloop. Francis wrote that he designed her to be "very able and seaworthy." Yet compared to his *Dulcinea* of twenty years earlier, a double-ended hull of about the same length, she has less freeboard and a foot more beam, so she would wet her deck in conditions when the *Dulcinea* would stay dry. No. 93 would be helped, however, by a higher ballast-to-displacement ratio than the *Dulcinea* (48 percent against 40 percent). And No. 93 would be handy to maneuver, with her cutaway deadwood and big outboard rudder. Garber intended the boat for the Maine coast, however, where that rudder might snag a lobster trap warp. No. 93 is 25 feet, 10 inches long on the waterline; with a beam of 8 feet, 9 inches; and a draft of 4 feet, 6 inches. Francis figured the displacement at 12,768 pounds.** (© Mystic Seaport Museum, Daniel S. Gregory Ships Plans Library, SP38.179.1)

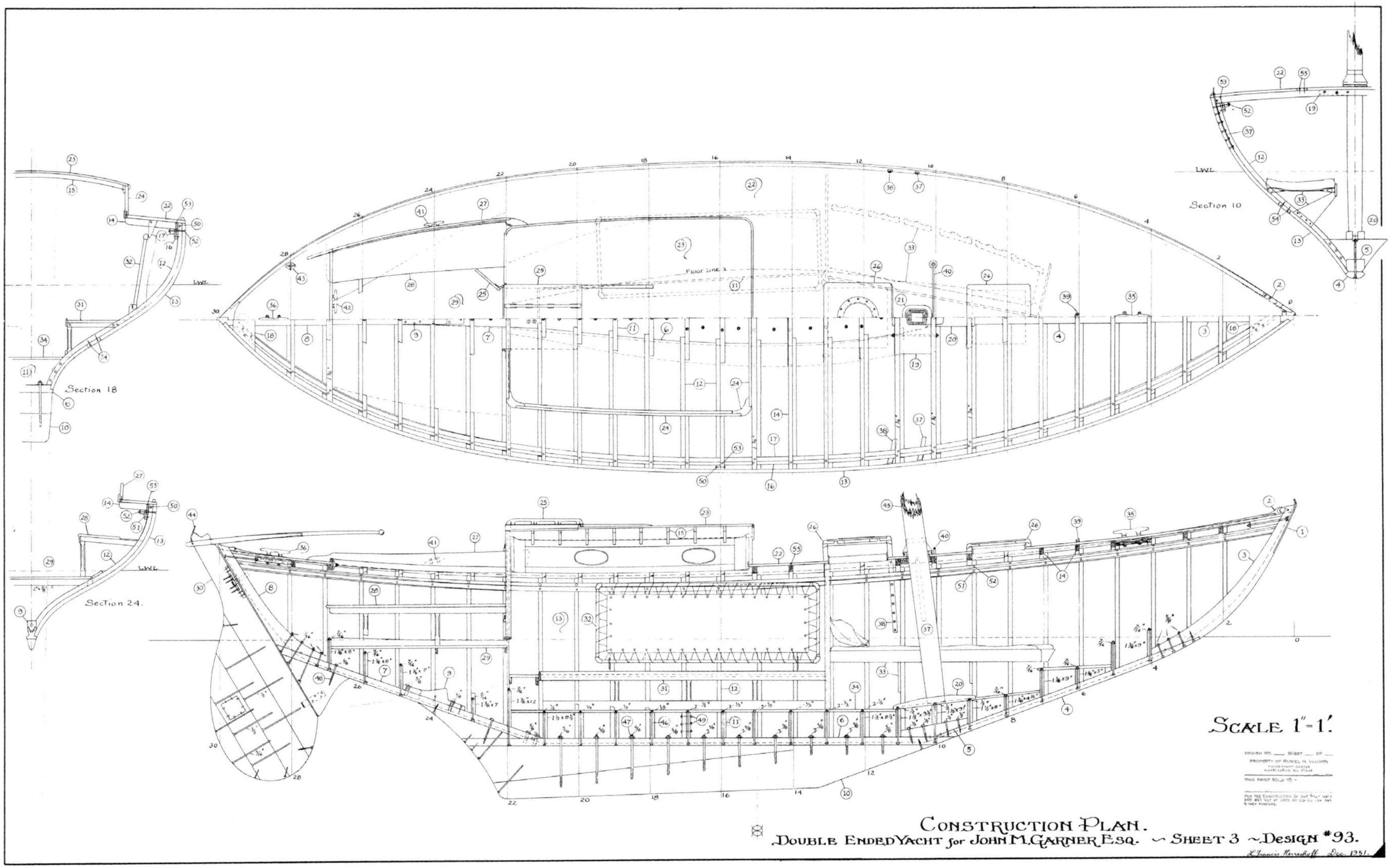
Section 18
Section 24.
Section 10
LWL.
Floor Line
Scale 1"=1'.
Construction Plan.
Double Ended Yacht for John M. Garner Esq. ~ Sheet 3 ~ Design #93.
L. Francis Herreshoff Dec. 1951.

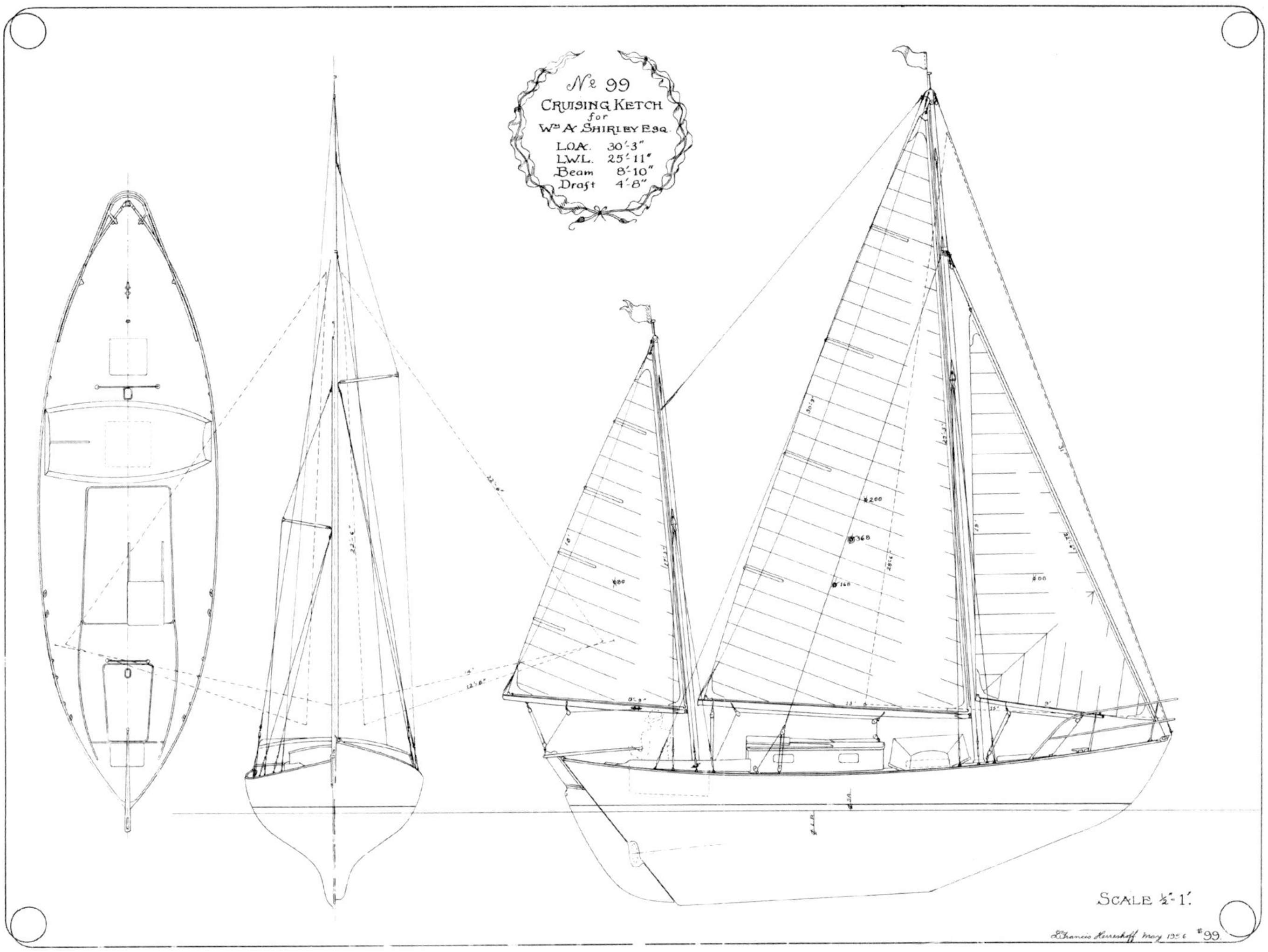

LEFT: **The construction plan of No. 93. She was to be a conventional plank-on-frame boat with a wood keelson. She has no bridge deck between cockpit and cabin, as has the *Dulcinea*, so shipping a sea in the cockpit would be a far more serious matter for No. 93. Garber's dream was to cruise with his wife and two children; the sloop is laid out with four berths. The galley space is aft under the house, where the headroom is six feet. Presumably, there would be a cedar bucket. On this drawing, Francis has misspelled the owner's name as "Garner."** (© Mystic Seaport Museum, Daniel S. Gregory Ships Plans Library, SP38.179.2 ABOVE: **Very similar to No. 93, but for her ketch rig, is No. 99, the *Wagon Box*, that Francis designed in 1956 for William A. Shirley, a man who earned his living at sea in order to pursue his avocation, which was putting to sea. She sports the only bow pulpit that L. Francis Herreshoff ever drew. Her cabin house is narrower than that of No. 93, and her cockpit, enclosing a bridge deck, has less volume. Sail area (about 10 percent less than No. 93) is 368 square feet, with 200 in the mainsail, 80 in the mizzen, and 88 in the jib. Francis shows a masthead balloon jib of 214 square feet for reaching, and twin spinnakers of 135 square feet each, for running. Boris published this drawing of No. 99 in the May 1957 issue of *The Rudder*. There was no headline; had he labeled her "Seagoing Ketch for a Single-Hander," she might have become popular.** (© Mystic Seaport Museum, Daniel S. Gregory Ships Plans Library, SP38.191.4)

		30	28	26	24	22	20	18	16	14	12	10	8	6	4	2	0	
	Station numbers	30	28	26	24	22	20	18	16	14	12	10	8	6	4	2	0	Station numbers
Heights	Top of Deck at Sides	2-7-0	2-3-1	2-0-3	1-10-4	1-9-4	1-9-0	1-9-0	1-9-5	1-10-4	1-11-7	2-1-4	2-3-6	2-6-3	2-9-4	3-1-2	3-5-5	Top of deck at sides
	Top of Lead				4-0-0	3-9-5	3-7-2	3-4-7	3-2-4	3-0-0	2-9-5	2-7-3	(2-4-7)					" " Lead
	Rabbet	2-4-3	-0-0-4	2-0-0	3-7-0	4-0-2	3-9-6	3-7-4	3-5-0	3-2-5	3-0-1	2-9-6	2-4-2	1-6-5	0-9-2	+0-6-4	3-7-4	Rabbet
	Profile	2-3-4	-0-3-0	2-9-6	4-8-0	4-6-6	4-5-2	4-4-0	4-2-5	4-1-2	4-0-0	3-2-6	2-5-4	1-8-1	0-10-6	+0-2-7	3-5-5	Profile
	Buttock 1	3-7-0	2-1-7	-0-9-1	1-1-4	1-8-1	2-1-0	2-4-3	2-7-0	2-7-1	2-5-1	2-0-3	1-5-4	0-8-3	+0-4-2	2-4-3	4-6-2	Buttock 1
	B 2		2-8-4	0-7-1	-0-4-2	0-11-0	1-4-0	1-7-4	1-8-7	1-8-4	1-6-1	1-1-3	+0-5-7	1-4-4	1-10-0	3-11-0		" 2
	B 3			2-9-0	0-6-4	-0-3-0	0-8-3	0-11-2	1-0-6	1-0-0	0-8-6	0-2-2	+0-7-0	1-10-1	3-7-0			" 3
Half Widths	Deck at side	0-4-1	1-10-0	2-9-7	3-6-0	3-11-4	4-2-7	4-4-4	4-5-2	4-5-3	4-4-3	4-2-1	3-10-1	3-4-0	2-7-0	1-6-1	0-1-0	Deck at side
	W.L. +2′		1-7-6	2-9-7							4-4-3	4-1-5	3-8-6	3-0-7	2-1-1	0-9-6		W.L. +2′
	W.L. +1′		0-10-2	2-4-0	3-3-1	3-9-6	4-1-4	4-4-0	4-4-6	4-3-6	4-1-7	3-9-4	3-3-0	2-5-6	1-5-3	0-4-2		W.L. +1′
	L.W.L.		0-2-3	1-3-6	2-5-4	3-3-0	3-8-4	3-11-0	4-0-0	3-10-7	3-7-6	3-2-0	2-6-0	1-8-0	0-9-0			L.W.L.
	W.L. -1′			0-5-0	1-1-2	1-10-4	2-6-4	2-11-2	3-0-7	3-9-0	2-8-1	2-1-6	1-5-6	0-8-4				W.L. -1′
	W.L. -2′			0-1-7	0-4-6	0-8-5	1-0-5	1-4-2	1-7-1	1-7-0	1-5-0	1-0-5	0-5-5					W.L. -2′
	W.L. -3′				0-2-2	0-4-0	0-5-7	0-7-6	0-8-7	0-8-6	0-7-0	0-2-7						W.L. -3′
	W.L. -4′				0-1-4	0-2-5	0-3-7	0-4-4	0-4-7	0-4-6								W.L. -4′
	Rabbet	0-1-7	0-1-7	0-1-7	0-1-7	0-2-5	0-4-1	0-5-5	0-6-7	0-7-3	0-7-0	0-4-1	0-1-7	0-1-7	0-1-7	0-1-7	0-1-7	Rabbet
	Face	0-1-0	0-1-0	0-1-0	0-1-1	0-1-5	0-2-2	0-3-0	0-3-4	0-3-0	0-1-4	0-1-2	0-0-7	0-0-6	0-0-5	0-0-4	0-1-0	Face

Dimensions in feet, inches, and eights of inches above and below the L.W.L. and out from center line
Planking thickness, between 1" and 1¼".
½ siding of Stem and Stern post 1⅞".

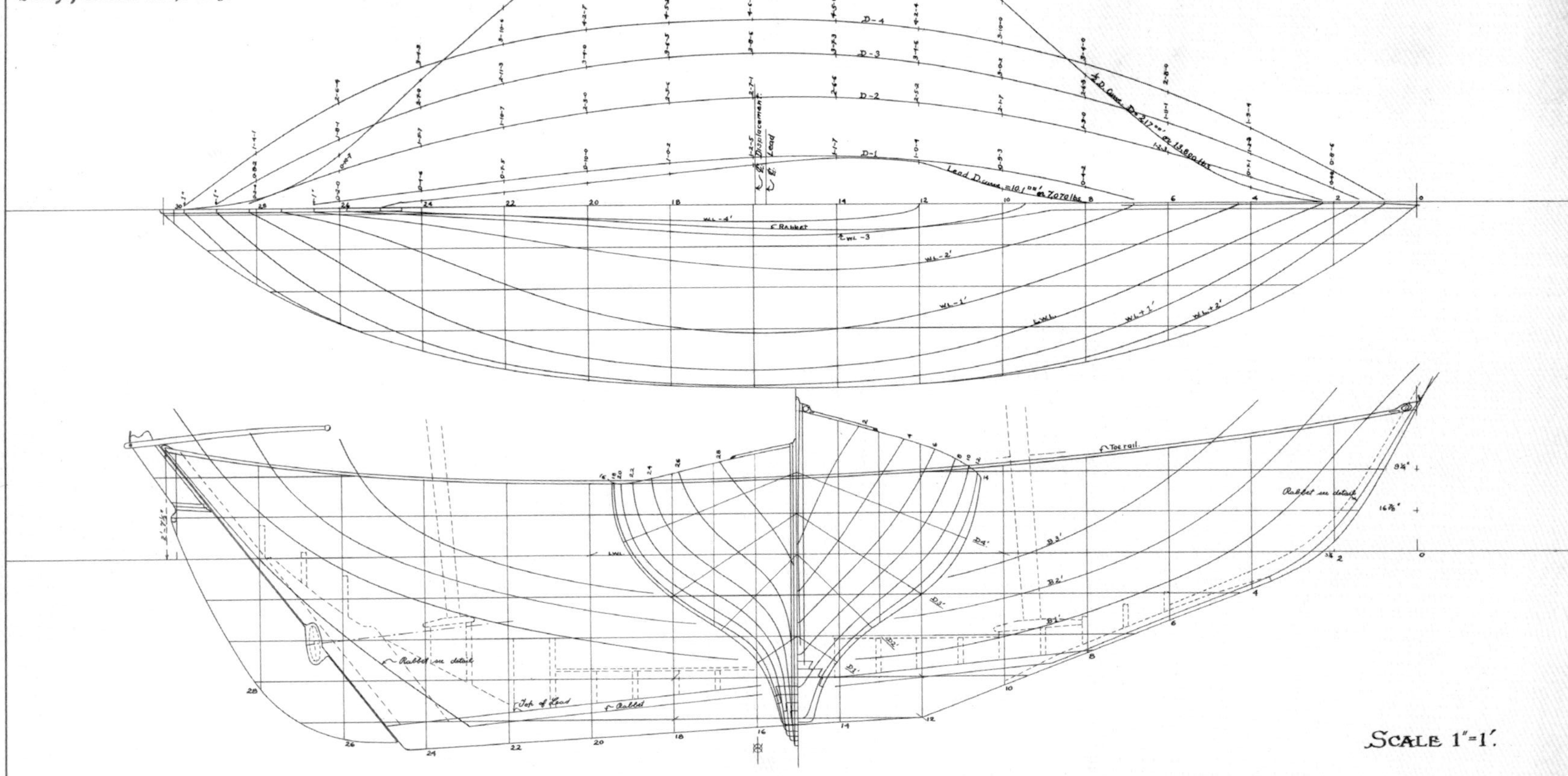

CRUISING KETCH for WM A. SHIRLEY ESQ. DESIGN No 99 ~ SHEET 2

L. Francis Herreshoff July 1950

38.191.2

Then there is Goddard and his daughter, Prim, in the 32-foot "roomy" cruising ketch *Viator*, apparently a bigger version of the H-28. Goddard is "a Boston lawyer," who, "although of moderate means, had for years made a hobby of cruising." His "nearly fifteen year old" daughter is his only crew, for his wife has turned to gardening. Prim is "far from being prim." Her father said, "I hardly knew what cruising was until I took the young one along, for she enjoyed all of it, fair weather and foul." The two boats cruise in company, and the combination of experienced skippers with crews just learning the game leads to plenty of instruction in each boat and as well as when all hands gather on board the *Viator*.[41]

These little vessels, both home-ported at Manchester, Massachusetts, close to Marblehead, proceed to Gloucester and Annisquam, the catboat skirting close round Cape Ann, the ketch motoring through the Blynman Canal and Annisquam River. They raft up in an anchorage that Goddard chooses for its view and enjoy his haddock chowder (the building of which Francis explains in detail), but it is not long after it has been consumed before Coridon launches into a diatribe against ocean racing. These characters in *The Compleat Cruiser* share autobiographical hallmarks with their creator: Coridon, the bachelor who is comfortable with the simple amenities of his catboat, has no use for ocean racing; Goddard, the romantic for whom scenery is vital, the expert cruiser who can explain the secrets of a chowder and of the wood fire that cooked it and who even served in the navy in World War I, as Francis had, particularly enjoys mentoring his daughter—who could be modeled on Kay Jones. That evening in Annisquam Harbor, before he turned in, Goddard stood admiring his view from the *Viator*'s companionway, "with his head above deck but his body not far from the stove," just as L. Francis Herreshoff had done on those nights offshore in the ketch *Stormy Petrel* (see volume 1, page 95).[42]

There is a close race back around Cape Ann to Manchester, followed by an invitation to dinner at the Goddard's home so that Goddard can show off his workshop, which turns out to be remarkably similar to that of L. Francis Herreshoff at The Castle, except that, instead of being in the third story, it was on the ground floor so that any small boats built there could be launched directly out its big doors at one end. And it appears that Goddard has a few tools that had once belonged to his father and that he advises washing one's hands before touching, which would have sounded familiar to any reader who knew Francis well. Goddard even says, "I am quite sure that lathe has given me more enjoyment than anything I ever had including my various boats and canoes."[43]

In the library, Goddard starts a discourse on cruising in small craft, particularly as practiced by John MacGregor and Nathaniel H. Bishop and described in their books about the voyages of the canoe *Rob Roy* and the sneakbox duck boat *Centennial Republic*. Later, on board the *Viator*, Goddard brings out plans of a beach cruiser for perusal, a boat inspired by Bishop's sneakbox and drawn by a "friend" (of course the author of *The Compleat Cruiser*). Francis later wrote: "The beach cruiser is a very interesting boat. I think her arrangement of using the sail for a tent and various

LEFT: **The lines and offsets of the *Wagon Box*. Her hull shape is very like that of No. 93, but her deadwood is not cut away, and her deep, narrow rudder is fully attached to it. She has a small propeller aperture on the centerline. No. 99 is 30 feet, 3 inches long on deck; 25 feet, 11 inches on the waterline; with a beam of 8 feet, 10 inches; and a draft of 4 feet, 8 inches. Displacement is 13,800 pounds with 7,070 pounds of lead, for a displacement-length ratio of 51 percent.** (© Mystic Seaport Museum, Daniel S. Gregory Ships Plans Library, SP38.191.2)

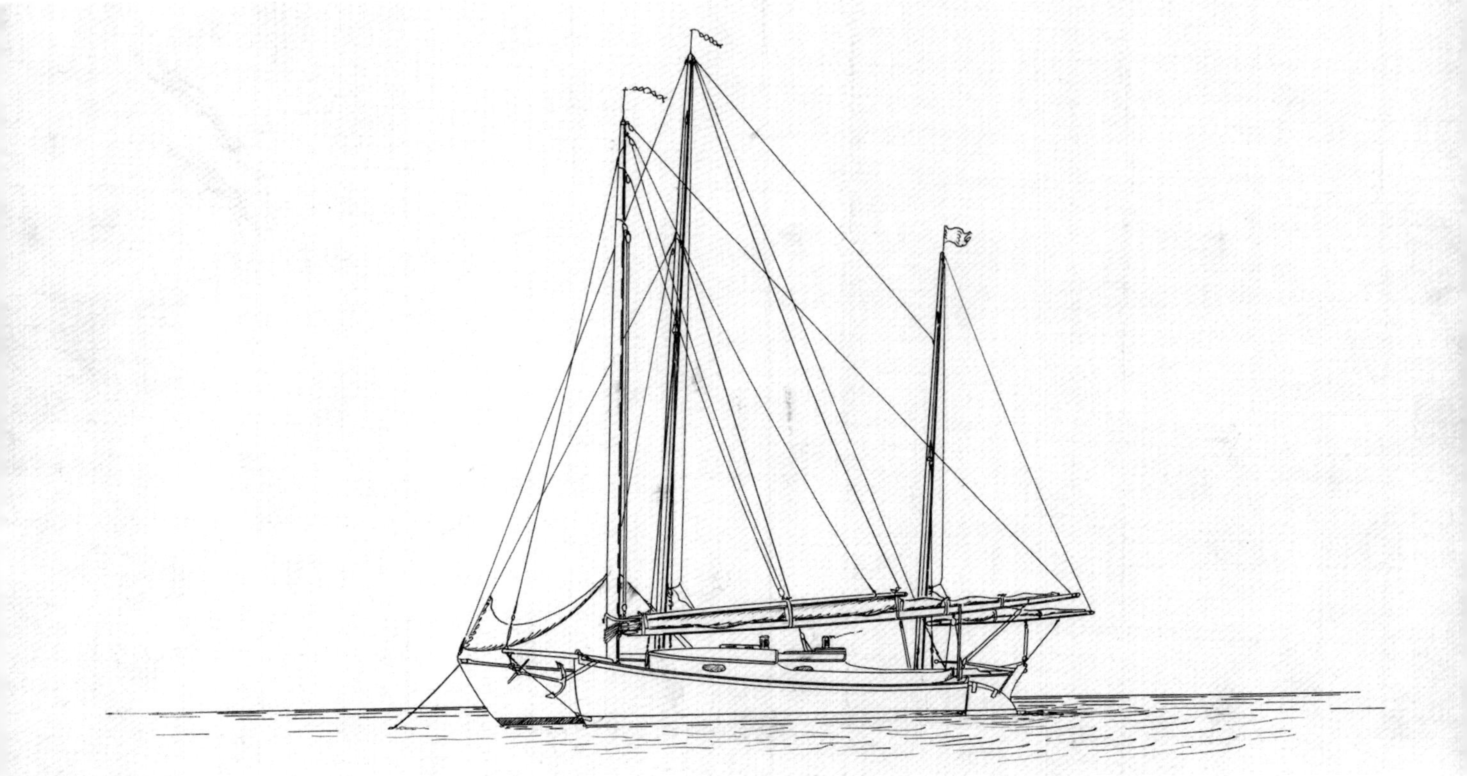

other things would make a boat capable of giving a remarkable amount of pleasure. If I were a little younger I should like to have one myself." In this case, we can take Francis's expressed desire to own one of designs at face value; the beach cruiser was L. Francis Herreshoff's kind of boat, totally simple and easy to use frequently. And we can take his comment as evidence that when he was no longer young enough to want to go beach cruising, he still made many a vicarious voyage in the little vessel.[44]

The *Viator* and the *Piscator* go off cruising in company and head south, across Massachusetts Bay to Scituate, where they see a skinny, 24-foot-waterline, double-ended ketch called the *Rozinante,* with a pram tender named the *Sancho Panza*. Her skipper, Weldon, invites the crews of the *Piscator* and *Viator* on board to look her over. Thus were readers of "The Compleat Cruiser" introduced, in the November 1952 issue of *The Rudder,* to what would become one of L. Francis Herreshoff's best-loved designs. Francis, himself, was intrigued enough by the fictional boat to draw her sail plan and lines for his articles. Weldon, too, has distinct traits of his creator, as does Don

ABOVE **Francis's drawing of the catboat *Piscator* rafted up to the ketch *Viator*, made as an illustration for *The Compleat Cruiser*.** (© Mystic Seaport Museum, Daniel S. Gregory Ships Plans Library, SP38.320.1) RIGHT: **Goddard, Miss Prim, and Briggs, yarning in the *Viator*'s cabin, one of Francis's drawings for *The Compleat Cruiser*.** (© Mystic Seaport Museum, Daniel S. Gregory Ships Plans Library, SP38.320.2)

Quixote himself, whose horse Rocinante (which in Spanish can mean being a workhorse, or in Cervantes's accounting, being "the foremost nag in all the world") inspired the name of Weldon's boat. Weldon is a fan of Don Quixote and his "remarkable adventures." Francis has Weldon say, "perhaps seven-eighths of the romance of these adventures took place in Quixote's mind, for he was a great reader of romance who rather looked down on the times in which he lived." This appraisal of Don Quixote certainly fits L. Francis Herreshoff. He would have been happier living a half-century earlier.[45]

Weldon designs "complicated electrical and mechanical devices" for a living, so he wants a cruising boat entirely free from such gadgets. He explains to his visitors on board the *Rozinante*, "after searching for a boat several years and finding nothing worth considering, I went to Old Fussbudget, the yacht designer." Thus does author Herreshoff introduce himself into his story. "I went to him because he was one of the few left who could design a boat which was a good sailor and still had romance in her looks." Francis has Goddard explain to Prim what is meant by a boat being romantic: "When a thing is out of the usual and pleasing to contemplate it is romantic. When an object is nicely proportioned and has retained some well-proven ancient quality, it is romantic looking. I suppose to a sailor a romantic looking vessel is one that looks like a good sea boat, one which has a good sheer, and nicely proportioned ends: in short, a vessel that he falls in love with at first sight, as we all did when we saw the *Rozinante*."[46]

The *Viator* and *Rozinante* cruise in company to Provincetown, where Weldon waxes poetic

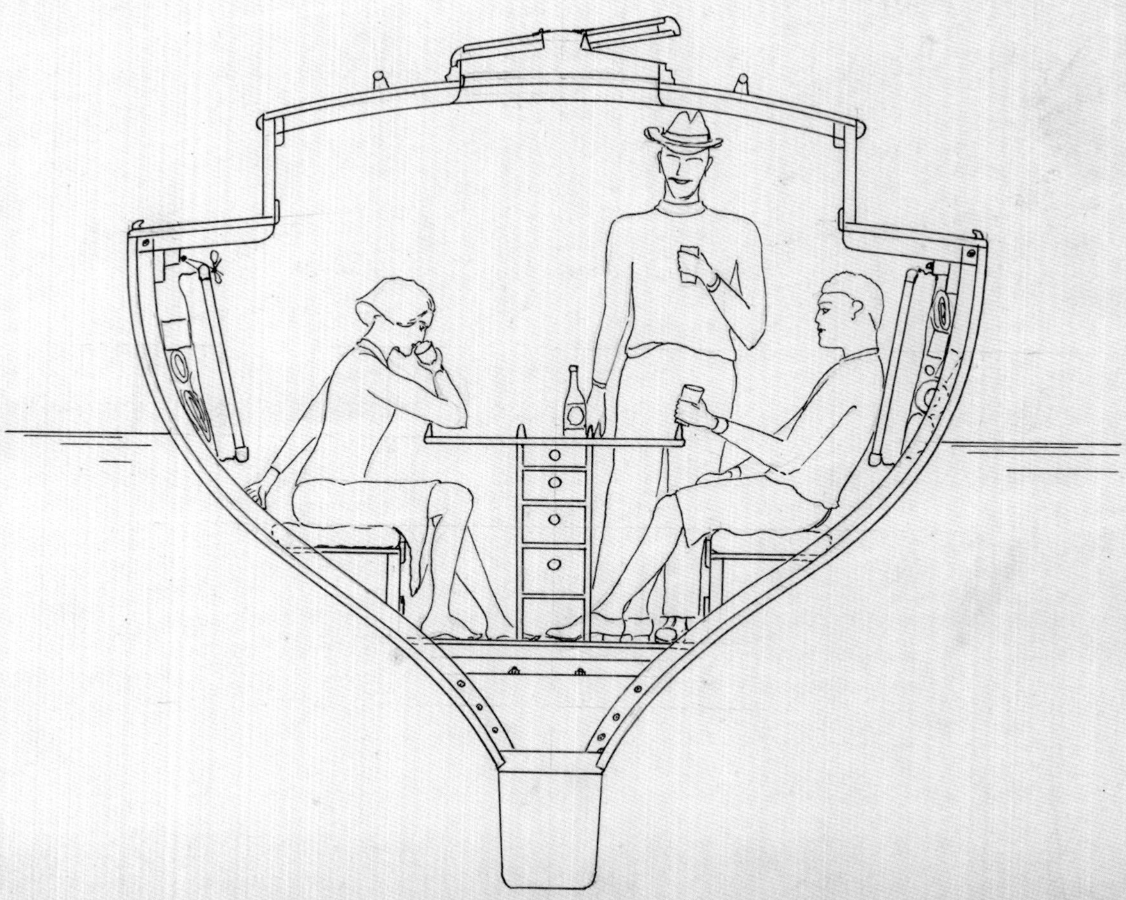

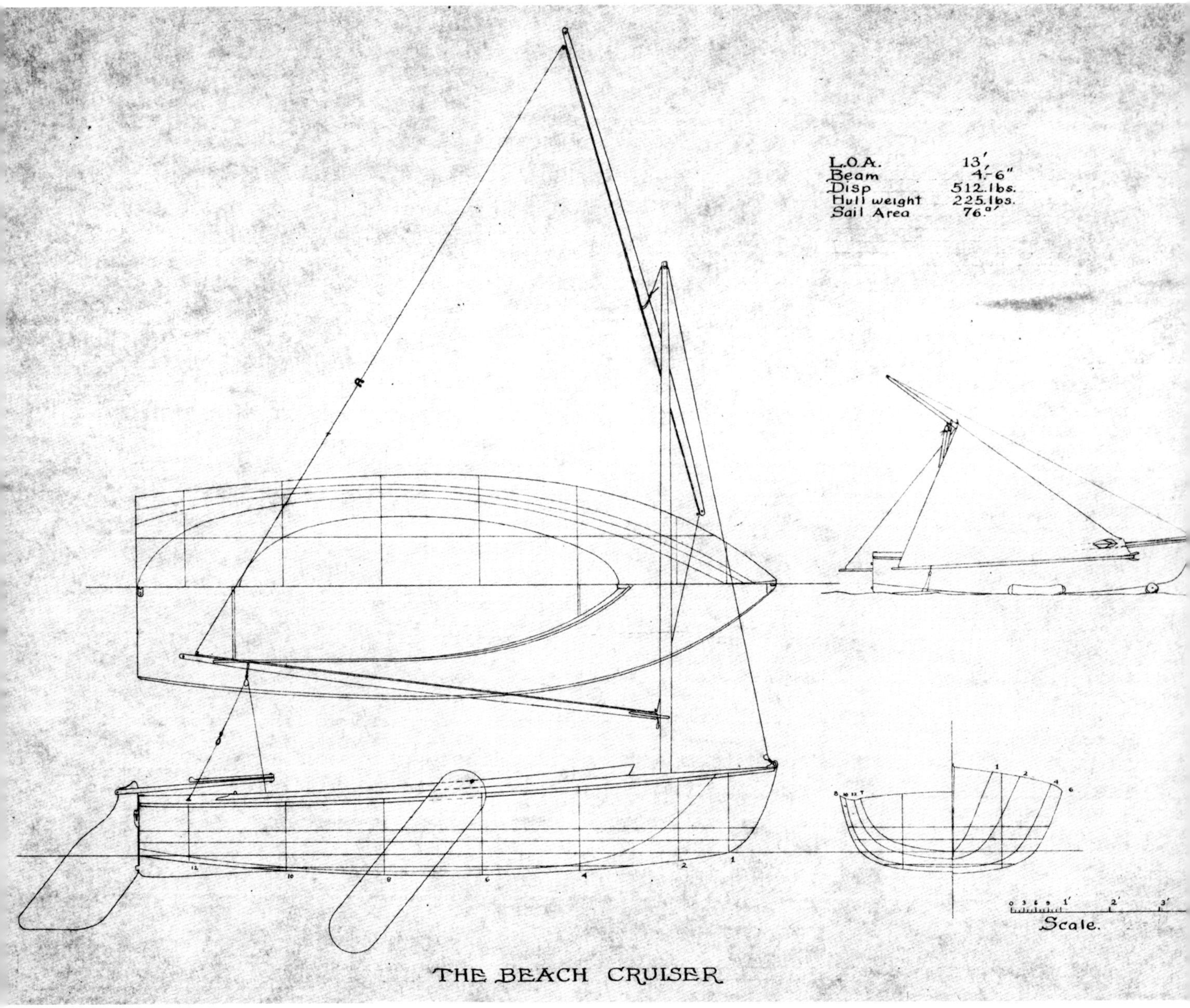

The plans of the beach cruiser that Francis designed as Goddard's "friend" in *The Compleat Cruiser*. She is 13 feet long on deck, with a beam of 4 feet, 6 inches. Sail area is 76 square feet. The boat would weigh about 225 pounds; at the 5-inch draft shown, she displaces 512 pounds and so is carrying some 287 pounds. For sailing in shallow water with leeboards raised, her rudder is taken in and she is steered with an oar in an oarlock on the stern. Her sail doubles as a tent, with the mast as ridgepole, held up by crossed 7-foot oars, as shown in the sketch at top right. Her crew could sleep on a 40-inch-wide air mattress, spread across her cockpit floor, since she had no centerboard trunk. The author of *The Compleat Cruiser* envisioned that she would be built like a canvas-covered canoe. Alternatively, he mentioned double-diagonal, thin planking covered with fiberglass [!]. Navigation on the beach would be accomplished by inflatable rollers. (© Mystic Seaport Museum, Daniel S. Gregory Ships Plans Library, SP38.164.2)

about walking the dunes in winter, just as Francis did when he lived there working for Starling Burgess (see volume 1, page 70). Then the two boats stage a 75-mile race to Nantucket, the *Viator* going through the Cape Cod Canal and Woods Hole, and the *Rozinante* going outside the Cape. In Nantucket Harbor, they spot a good-sized ketch, rigged with short gaffs like the *Rozinante*. She also has leeboards. This interesting craft is named the *Tranquilo*, and her owner, Brewster, invites the cruisers on board, giving Francis the chance to describe her. They learn that this fictional 46-footer, drawing but 2 feet, is designed by "old William Taffrail Garboard-Strake himself, who, as you know, can produce something a little out of the ordinary, for he does not belong to that fraternity whose members copy one another and are only in business for the almighty dollar." The *Tranquilo* will become the *Golden Ball*, another of Francis's important designs. Brewster, too, has a resemblance to Francis: his early cruising has been in his father's steam yacht, and his objective in having his shoal-draft ketch is to be able to anchor "where none of the noise-makers can come very close, and if it were not for the outboard motor boats we should be perfectly tranquil most of the time," just the kind of cruising Francis advocated.[47]

On the next leg of Francis's cruise, the *Tranquilo* joins the *Viator* and *Rozinante* for a run to Edgartown, on Martha's Vineyard. Until the wind comes up, the *Tranquilo* tows the *Rozinante*. All three boats go around outside Nantucket Island instead of through the Sound, "For there are few places pleasanter than the south side of Nantucket where you can skirt the shore very closely if you want to." At Edgartown, Weldon, who now has his nephews Jim and Dan on board, gives a fine lecture on "the early fishing boats of New England," illustrated by sketches on the *Rozinante*'s small, portable blackboard, used mostly for navigation notes. He expounds on and shows the New England fishing smack, the Maine pinky schooner, the Isles of Shoals boat, the Boston Harbor paddy boat, the Nomans Land boat, and the Woods Hole boat. Francis turned the cockpit of the *Rozinante* into a schoolroom, and, as he wrote the dialogue that ensued, he must have heard his father's voice telling him about these same local boats.[48]

The *Tranquilo* heads back to Nantucket, but the *Viator* and *Rozinante* continue to the westward together. They call at Cuttyhunk, that delightful little last of the Elizabeth Islands that separate Vineyard Sound from Buzzards Bay, where Weldon continues to enlighten his nephews by adding the West Island boat and the Newport Point boat to his curriculum of traditional craft, for the next day they will sail to Newport itself. Now the cruisers are entering the home waters of their author's youth, so Goddard gives his shipmates a full exposition on the history and culture of Newport. And it seems that Weldon also served in the navy in World War I (did Francis forget that he had already assigned that piece of his own history to Goddard?), so he sails the *Rozinante* around all the warships moored off the Torpedo Station, War College, and Training Station in order to give his excited nephews a good look at them.

For the two small ketches, there is a foggy run to Block Island, which gives Weldon the excuse to round out his collection of New England boats explained with the Block Island boat. Weldon tells Jim and Dan, "it is interesting that Captain Nat Herreshoff, the principal developer of the modern yacht, lived within a day's sail of Block Island and was a great admirer of the Block Island boats." In Block Island's New Harbor, or Great Salt Pond, the cruisers admire another unusual boat, the *Lampooner*, a 66-foot, double-ended power-boat with longitudinal construction. Her owner, Townsend, invites them on board. She is an enlarged *Piquant*, and, with her ability to travel comfortably at 20 knots in rough going, she is named to make fun of the "three-decks-and-no-bottom" motor cruisers that she would leave behind. Francis drew her profile and lines to illustrate his story, but,

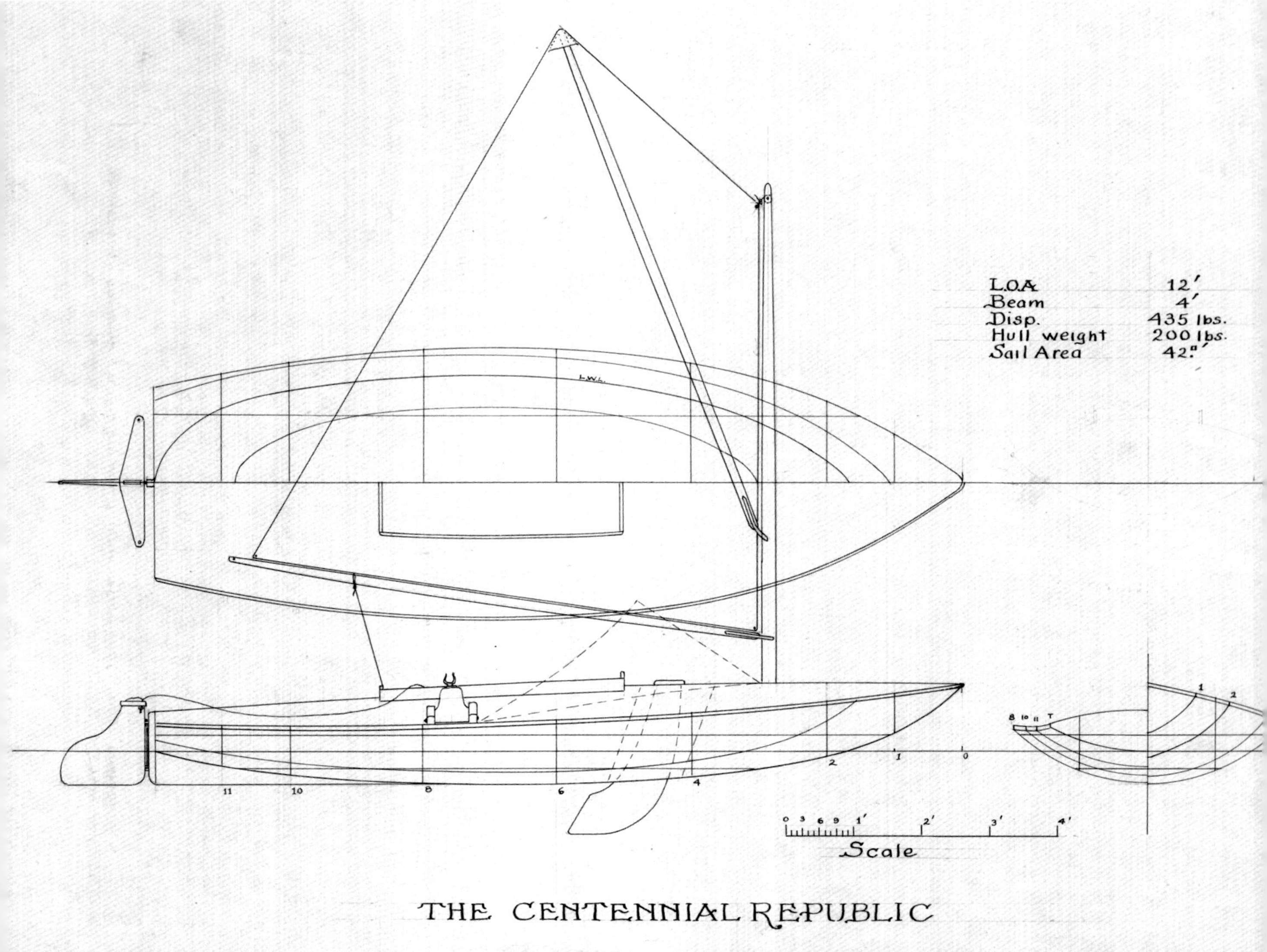

Francis's drawing of Nathaniel H. Bishop's *Centennial Republic* for the edification of the young sailors in *The Compleat Cruiser*. This boat, the heroine of Bishop's book *Four Months in a Sneak-Box*, would later be the inspiration for Francis's Madoc duck boat. Bishop's boat was 12 feet long with a beam of 4 feet. The hull weighed 200 pounds; at the waterline shown, she is displacing 435 pounds. Sail area is 42 square feet. Note the yoke steering, rather than a tiller. (© Mystic Seaport Museum, Daniel S. Gregory Ships Plans Library, SP38.261.1)

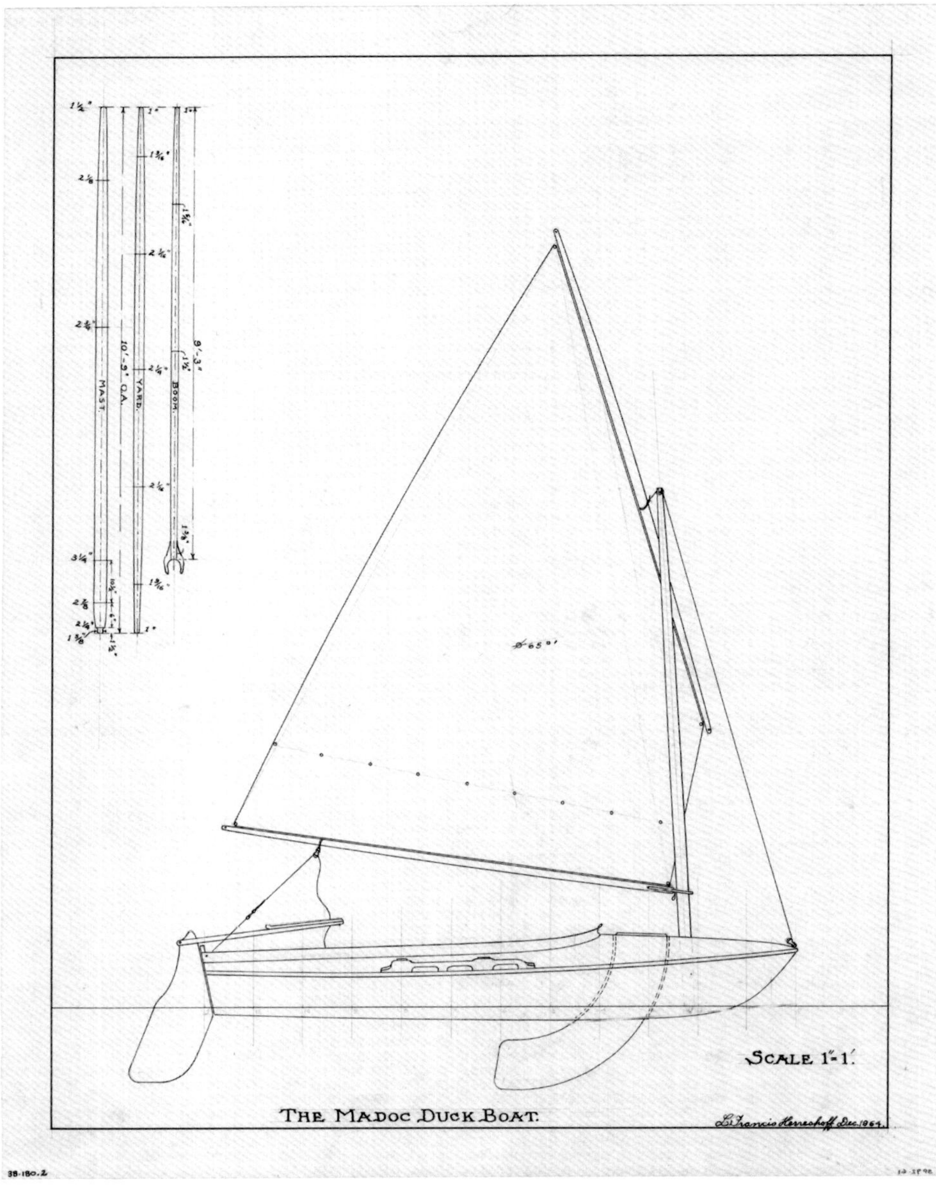

Francis was seventy-four years old when he drew this plan for the Madoc duck boat. He received congratulations from Allan R. Chadwick, who had built "hundreds of sneakboxes" in Barnegat, New Jersey, for being the first to improve on the "1837 Barnegat Bay Sneakbox." She may not have fooled any more ducks than a sneak-box, but she was certainly more of a sailing craft than her low, flat ancestors. And Francis designed her to take an outboard motor of up to 15 horsepower. He has accentuated the curved centerboard, which allows the trunk to be forward out of the way, while still placing the lateral resistance aft where it needs to be. Sail area is 65 square feet. There is a hiking stick on the tiller, and Francis shows two rowing positions. (© Mystic Seaport Museum, Daniel S. Gregory Ships Plans Library, SP38.180.2)

TABLE OF OFFSETS, *In feet, inches and eigths of inches, above and below L.W.L. and out from center line.*

	STATION NOS.	12′	10′	8′	6′	4′	2′	1′	6″	0
HEIGHTS	CENTER OF DECK	1-2-6	1-7-1	1-9-4	1-7-0	1-6-0	1-3-5	1-2-5	1-2-2	1-2-0
	SHEER LINE	0-9-0	0-8-4	0-8-4	0-9-0	0-10-0	0-11-4	1-0-6	1-1-2	1-2-0
	BUTTOCK 1	0-0-5	0-1-6	0-2-4	0-2-6	0-1-2	+0-5-2	0-11-5		
	PROFILE	0-1-4	0-2-2	0-3-0	0-3-2	0-3-2	- 0-2-2	+0-1-2	0-6-0	1-2-0
	DIAGONAL	1-11-4	2-2-3	2-3-2	2-2-6	2-0-0	1-6-0	1-0-6	0-9-6	
½ WIDTH	SHEER LINE	1-9-0	2-1-0	2-3-1	2-3-0	2-0-3	1-6-3	1-1-0	0-8-7	
	W.L. + 6″	1-8-0	2-0-3	2-2-5	2-2-0	1-9-6	1-0-4	0-5-5	0-0-0	
	W.L. + 3″	1-5-7	1-11-2	2-1-2	2-0-0	1-7-4	0-9-2	0-2-3		
	L.W.L.	1-1-5	1-7-7	1-9-7	1-8-3	1-3-1	0-5-5			

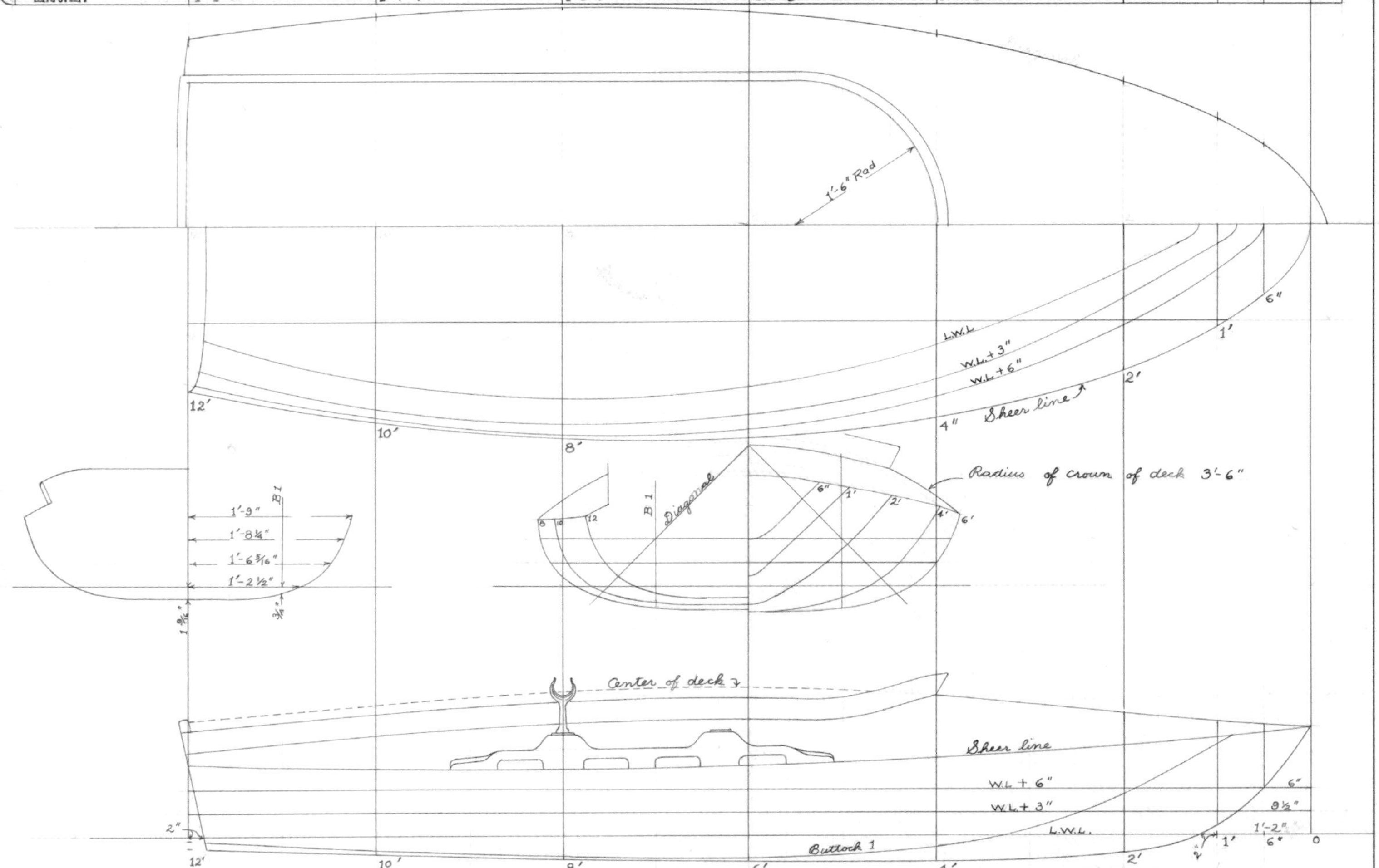

SCALE 1½″ = 1′
Or ⅛″ = 1″

12′ DUCK BOAT *For rowing, sailing and outboard motor.*

L. Francis Herreshoff Oct 1967

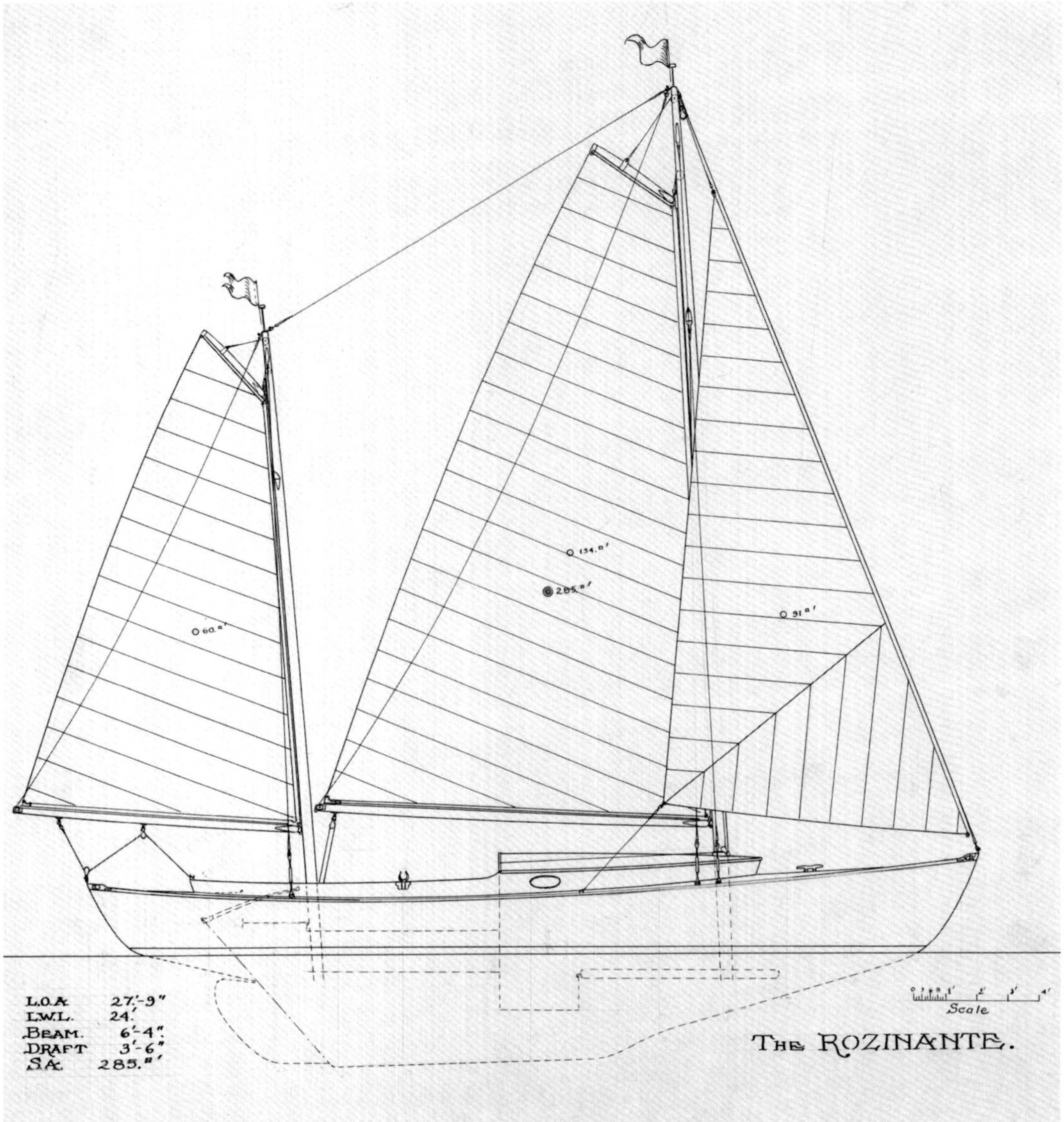

LEFT: **The lines and offsets of the Madoc duck boat. She is 12 feet long, with a beam of 4 feet, 6 inches, and a draft of 3 inches at the waterline shown. As built of fiberglass by Madoc, Incorporated, of Marblehead, she weighed 160 pounds and could carry 450 pounds at the 3-inch draft. Not many boats were built, for the Madoc plant burned in 1967, soon after production started.** (© Mystic Seaport Museum, Daniel S. Gregory Ships Plans Library, SP38.180.1) ABOVE: **The sail plan of Weldon's *Rozinante*.** (© Mystic Seaport Museum, Daniel S. Gregory Ships Plans Library, SP38.167.20)

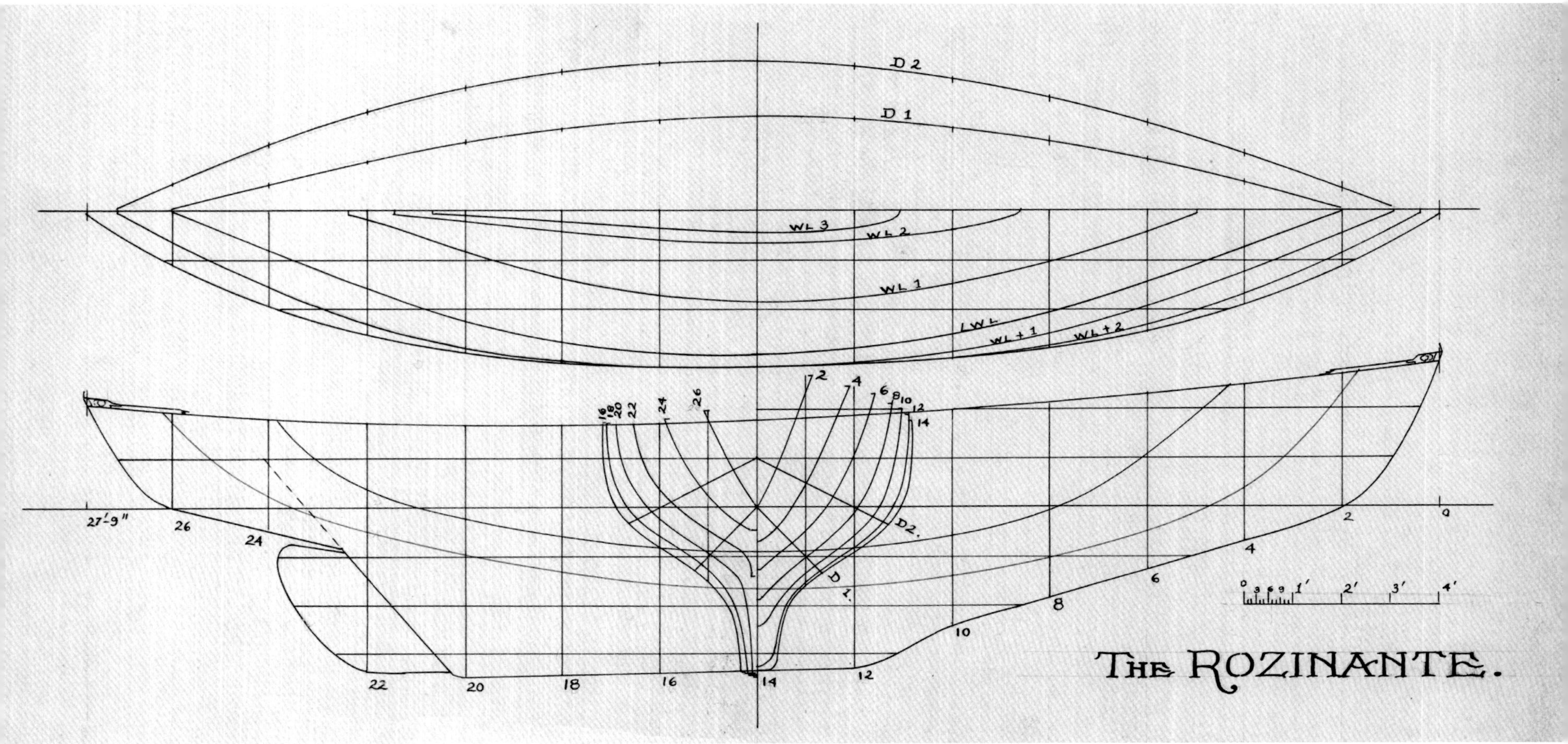

The *Rozinante*'s lines. (© Mystic Seaport Museum, Daniel S. Gregory Ships Plans Library, SP38.167.19)

unlike the *Rozinante* and *Tranquilo*, she aroused no clamor to complete her design.[49]

On the last leg of the cruise, a run to New London, the *Viator* takes the *Rozinante* in tow, for the wind is very light at first, and there are twenty-seven miles to go. But the afternoon sou'wester makes up as usual, the towline is let go, and each boat makes her own way into the Thames River to anchor, where Francis leaves them and their crews. "And thus ends this overly long story."[50]

At least, that is how the story ended when "The Compleat Cruiser" was published as a book in 1956 by Sheridan House in New York. In *The Rudder*, Francis brought Coridon and Briggs back as crew for the ketches for a race home. They have a memorable sail to Marion, in Buzzards Bay, and then, after the *Viator* tows the *Rozinante* through the Cape Cod Canal, another fine run north to Manchester. And on this last run, Francis reveals himself, through Weldon, at the tiller of the *Rozinante* on a fast broad reach: "Now, feeling the kick of the helm as the *Rozinante* rushed onward, his spirit seemed to leave his body and soar away in pleasant thoughts as the soul is said to do after death. Sometimes he recited poetry and at times he hummed a tune, but all in his mind, for never a sound was made. His body, left behind, steered by instinct since it and the *Rozinante* were old partners of the dance." Here is L. Francis Herreshoff's romantic imagination at work. This is why he had no need to put his yacht designs through sea trials.[51]

But readers of *The Compleat Cruiser* in book form missed this nugget. Sheridan House agreed that Francis's story was "overly long." They cut it by about a third. Francis apparently had no say in the matter; he was particularly disappointed because most of the passages between ports were lost, together with all the seamanship instruction along the way. Missing was the exciting tale of Goddard falling overboard in a squall and Prim maneuvering the *Viator* to recover him. And there was censorship of any paragraph that contained the word "rum." Even mention of the necessity (and method) of dealing with a greasy frying pan in the galley was deemed too indelicate and was deep-sixed. The Sheridan House editor wielded a hawser axe, not a red pencil.

But one valuable element was added to the book: "An Index of Boating Skills." For even after all the cuts, *The Compleat Cruiser* had plenty of lessons. To name just a few: Under "Anchors and Anchoring," there were instructions for anchoring on fouled ground, freeing a fouled anchor, handling stockless anchors, putting out a heavy anchor with a dinghy, securing the anchor on deck, and testing anchor holding power. The rest of the index included detailed discussions of binoculars; careening to clean the bottom; handling sails in a squall; kayak cruising; launching a dinghy from a beach in surf; lifesaving; open vs. self-bailing cockpits; operating a coal stove; picking up a towline; piloting; reefing and furling; relieving sunburn; righting a capsized dinghy in the water; steering without a rudder; stowing galley gear; towing a dinghy; weather lore; and, of course, the design and operation of the cedar bucket.

In *The Common Sense of Yacht Design*, L. Francis Herreshoff poured out his knowledge and experience of designing yachts; in *The Compleat Cruiser*, he poured out his knowledge and experience of using yachts. The two books, taken together, provide an outstanding course of instruction for sailors; they also tell us much about the proud, conservative, sensible, opinionated, and gentle ways of being of this marine genius.

As soon as the last installment of *The* "Compleat Cruiser" appeared in *The Rudder* in August 1954, John Ives Sewall of Buffalo wrote to Francis, "I am charmed and fascinated by the *Rozinante*." He wanted Francis to complete the design for him, but he cautioned Mr. Herreshoff that it would be five years before

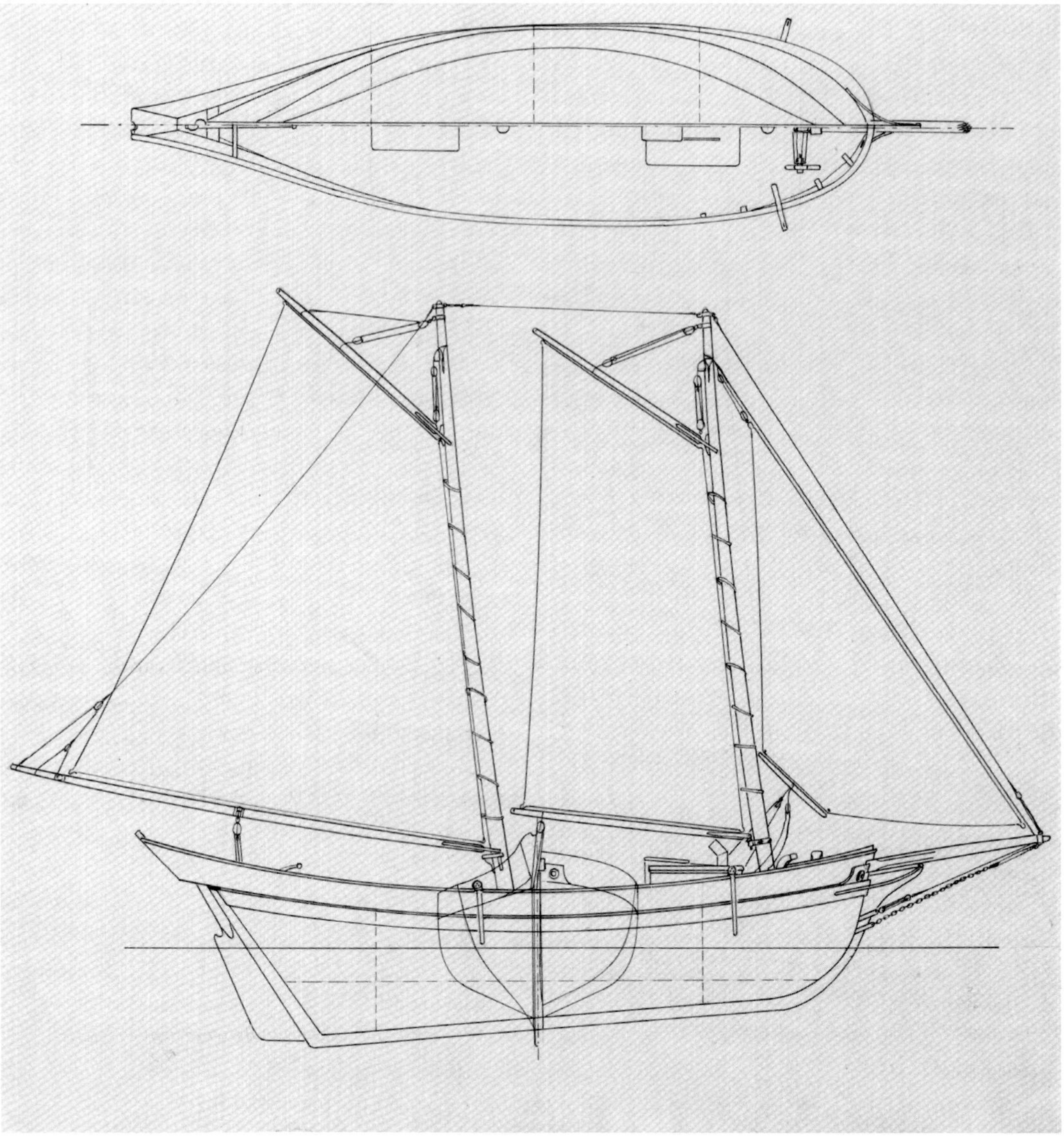

Weldon's blackboard sketch of a Maine pinky has been refined by *The Compleat Cruiser's* illustrator, L. Francis Herreshoff, who probably sailed many vicarious miles in the little vessel. (© Mystic Seaport Museum, Daniel S. Gregory Ships Plans Library, SP38.253.1)

he would be able to afford to have the boat built. Sewall summered on the coast of Maine, where he was a shipmate of Ed Hill in the *Araminta.* He asked if he might have Hill's arrangement of paying for the *Araminta*'s plans as they were gradually drawn, such payment to be deducted from the designer's commission when and if the boat came to be. Francis found common interests with Sewall in marine engines, cars, and guns, as well as in boat design; he agreed to the proposal and in seven months had finished a sail plan and lines drawing. Neither client nor designer was in a hurry. It was another two and a half years before Francis finished the last sheet of details on what had become his design No. 96. He was confident enough that the boat would be built that he had already made fittings for her and presented them to Sewall as a gift.[52]

But three months after receiving the last drawing needed, Sewall wrote to Francis, "it will still be several years before I can consider building." He paid Francis the last of the total of $500 for the plans of No. 96. John Ives Sewall never did build his Rozinante.[53]

But in 1970, Francis, at age eighty, did get to make more No. 96 hardware for a boat that was built. By then, as we shall soon see, he had designed an improved Rozinante, his design No. 98. Gene Akre, of Erie, Pennsylvania, like Sewall, wanted a Rozinante with an engine, so he chose the slightly fuller lines of No. 96 for his *Gjoa,* and installed a Yanmar 7.5-horsepower diesel. Akre embellished her spinnaker with a large Norwegian flag and enjoyed his boat for twenty-five years. Then his friend Dave Forsman took her over. Forsman wrote: "I find the boat to be the most enjoyable to sail of any boat that I have owned (twelve), or of any that I have sailed, and there have been many. Each time I go out I marvel at how easy the boat is to handle and sail."[54]

When Francis was dreaming up boats for *The Compleat Cruiser*, he wanted one of them to be the smallest and simplest craft he could imagine that would be fast and able, and provide cruising accommodations, however minimal. And, of course, she had to be good looking. What came to mind for him was the English canoe yawl, a boat developed toward the end of the nineteenth century for cruising in semi-protected waters along the coast, particularly in the large river estuaries. The decked sailing canoe was already the first true recreational sailboat in England. Enthusiastic skippers responded to the beckoning horizon. They started building canoes as big as a ship's yawl boat for cruising, and called them canoe yawls. It is also possible that the name came from the yawl rig of the first cruising canoes, though later versions had various rigs. Two English artists, George Holmes and Albert Strange, designed the best canoe yawls as the type reached its full flower between the world wars. But yacht designer L. Francis Herreshoff took the canoe yawl to a much higher level with the Rozinante. She is the prettiest canoe yawl, the fastest, and the most seaworthy for coastal cruising.[55]

Francis wrote:

> *I, myself, am old enough to remember when the canoe yawls were still in vogue, so I will tell you what some of their characteristics were and that will partly explain Rozinante. A canoe yawl should be light and rather narrow so that she may be easily propelled by rowing when necessary. It should be a good sea boat and be a fast sailer under a small sail plan. It should be comparatively shallow draft so that occasionally a person can land from one without a tender and, although Rozinante is quite a little deeper than is usual for a canoe yawl, (many of them had a center-*

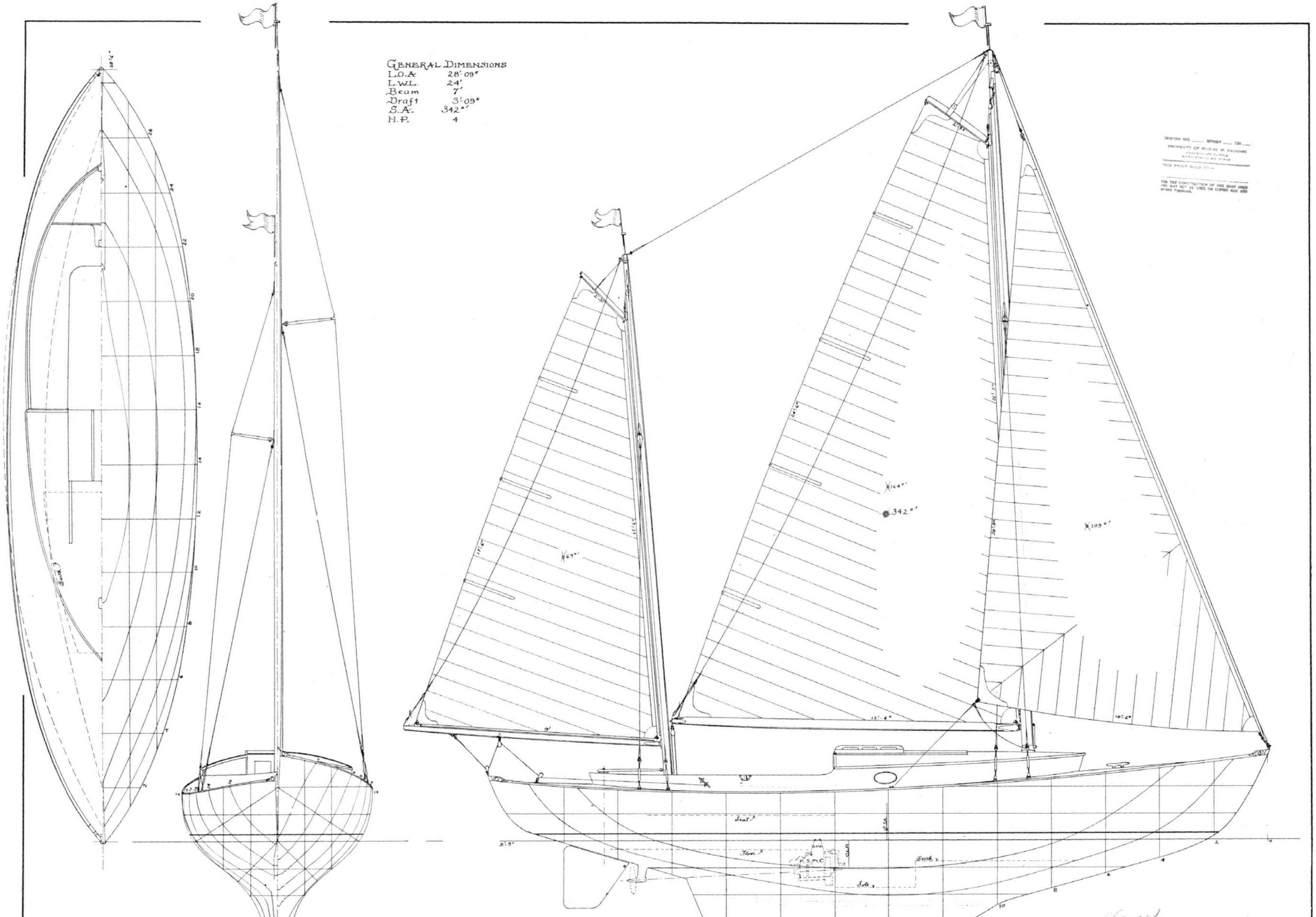

Auxiliary Canoe-Yawl for John Ives Sewall Esq. ~ Design #96 ~ Sheet 1 ~ Scale 3/4" = 1'

board that went through a shallow ballast keel) still I think there are many quiet places where Rozinante could be rowed close enough to shore so one could land over the bow in less than two feet of water.

A good canoe yawl should not have any combustible or noise makers on board so that one can really relax and commune with God and Mother Nature but still use his wits in the interesting game of getting the most out of tide and wind. A good canoe yawl will give more lasting pleasure for the dollar than any other vessel excepting a double paddle canoe, and while her first cost may be considerable these days, if she is treated sensibly she will not depreciate much in forty years, and her annual expense will be negligible. Best of all a canoe yawl can be about the safest vessel that can be had for, if the whaleboats used on whaling ships were the most seaworthy open boats ever known, Rozinante is a partly decked-over whaleboat with a ballast keel that will make her non-capsizable. She is rigged with a sail plan which can be decreased without perceptibly affecting her balance, and she can be made to lay to in a seaway under the mizzen alone. A boat of this type can be gotten under way or laid up for the night in a few minutes so that she is practical to use on summer evenings, often the pleasantest times of all for sailing, while evening sailing is generally out of the question with the more complicated or larger craft on account of the time factor.[56]

In *The Compleat Cruiser*, Francis had Weldon explain his reasons for not having a "combustible or noise-maker" on board his canoe yawl: "The cost of engine and installation; the cost of fuel and repairs; the drag of the propeller; the weight of the engine; the space required by the engine, tank and exhaust line; the smell and dirt; the compass deviation it causes." Then Weldon added, "But I dislike an engine most because it takes the romance out of sailing."[57]

Calvin T. Howell of Milwaukee saw the plans of No. 96 in the March 1956 *Rudder* and wrote to Francis asking him to design him a Rozinante, but closer to Weldon's boat in *The Compleat Cruiser* than was the 96. Francis suggested conventional construction and a Marconi rig. He also suggested that they work under the Ed Hill formula of paying

LEFT: **In 1955, Francis developed Weldon's *Rozinante* from *The Compleat Cruiser* into his design No. 96 for John Ives Sewall. The prospective owner wanted a small engine in the boat, and he insisted on a centerline propeller, which led Francis to cut away the deadwood and give her a freestanding rudder. The short gaffs allow altering the draft of the sails by adjusting the peak halyards. The center of effort of the sail plan remains the same for full sail, mainsail alone, or jib and mizzen, so Francis shows no reefs. But taking the slack out of a topping lift and easing a peak halyard is the equivalent of tying in a temporary reef. The only stay holding the mainmast aft is the spring stay to the mizzen masthead; on the wind, the mainmast depends on main and mizzen sheets for support; there was discussion of running main backstays for reaching and running. Francis thought that Weldon's *Rozinante* needed a little more sail area, so he increased her mast height a bit. Sail area is 342 square feet, with 164 in the mainsail, 69 in the mizzen, and 109 in the jib. Francis has given No. 96 a fuller midsection than that he showed for Weldon's *Rozinante* in order to gain the space necessary for Sewall's single-cylinder, 4-horsepower Stuart Turner P5MC. She is 28 feet, 9 inches long on deck; with a waterline length of 24 feet; a beam of 7 feet; and a draft of 3 feet, 9 inches. Displacement is 7,840 pounds, with 3,915 pounds of outside iron, for a ballast-displacement ratio of 50 percent. This drawing was published in the March 1956 issue of *The Rudder*.** (© Mystic Seaport Museum, Daniel S. Gregory Ships Plans Library, SP38.163.2)

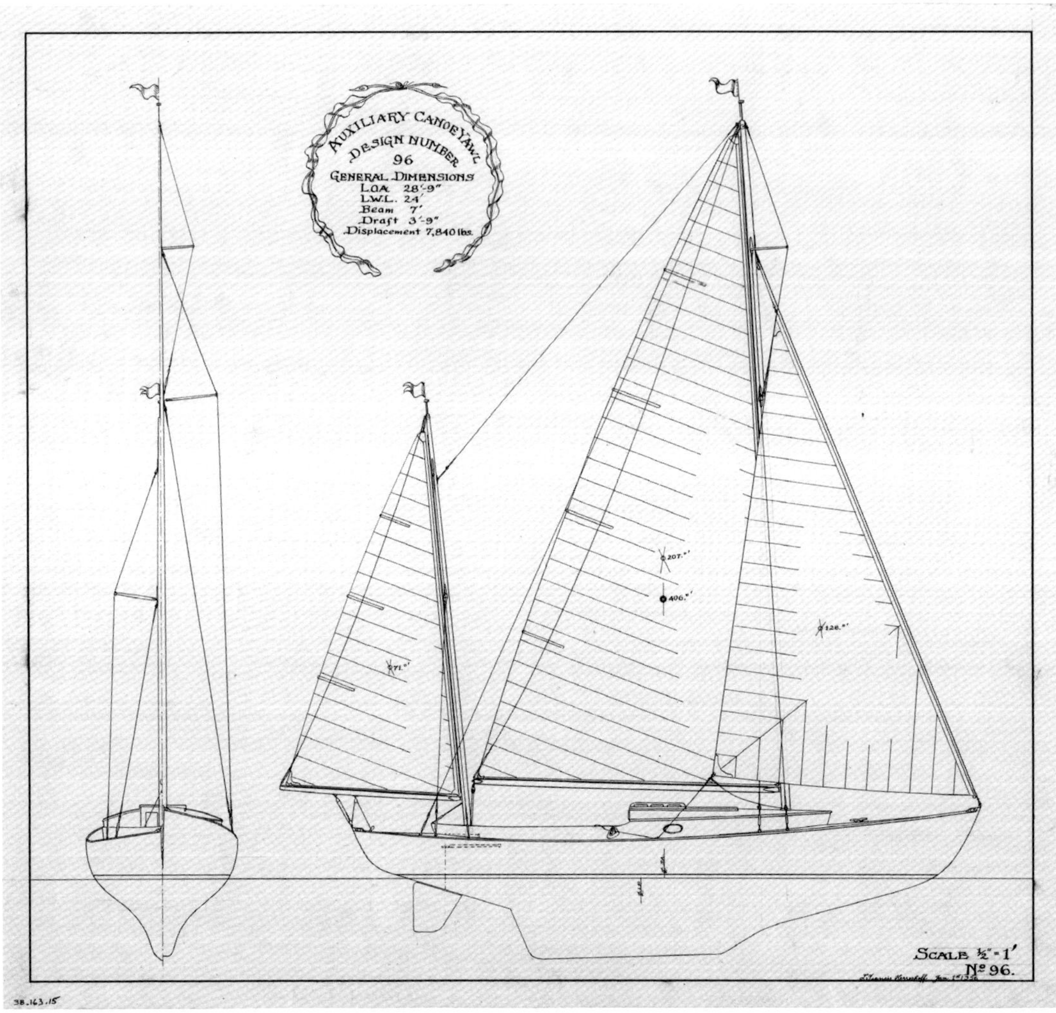

ABOVE: **Francis dated this revised sail plan for No. 96 on January 1, 1956. Sewall had baulked at the gaff rig without a main backstay, and he wanted still more sail area. So Francis gave him a standard Marconi rig of 406 square feet, with 207 in the mainsail, 71 in the mizzen, and 128 in the jib. He has moved the mizzenmast aft a little and then had to step it on deck so it wouldn't obstruct the tiller; he gives the mast the support of a short preventer to the after end of the coaming.** (© Mystic Seaport Museum, Daniel S. Gregory Ships Plans Library, SP38.163.15) RIGHT: **Francis suggested his longitudinal construction system for No. 96, with web frames of laminated wood, and double, diagonal planking—covered with fiberglass. He has cut away the depth of the web frame just abaft the mainmast, because of its interference with the forward berth. The watertight cockpit floor is just below the waterline, so it is not self-bailing; nor does the low sill protect the cabin from flooding in the event of a knockdown, but this boat is very stiff once heeled to rail-down. The headroom in the cuddy is 4 feet, 10 inches: actually 2 inches more than in the H-28.** (© Mystic Seaport Museum, Daniel S. Gregory Ships Plans Library, SP38.163.4)

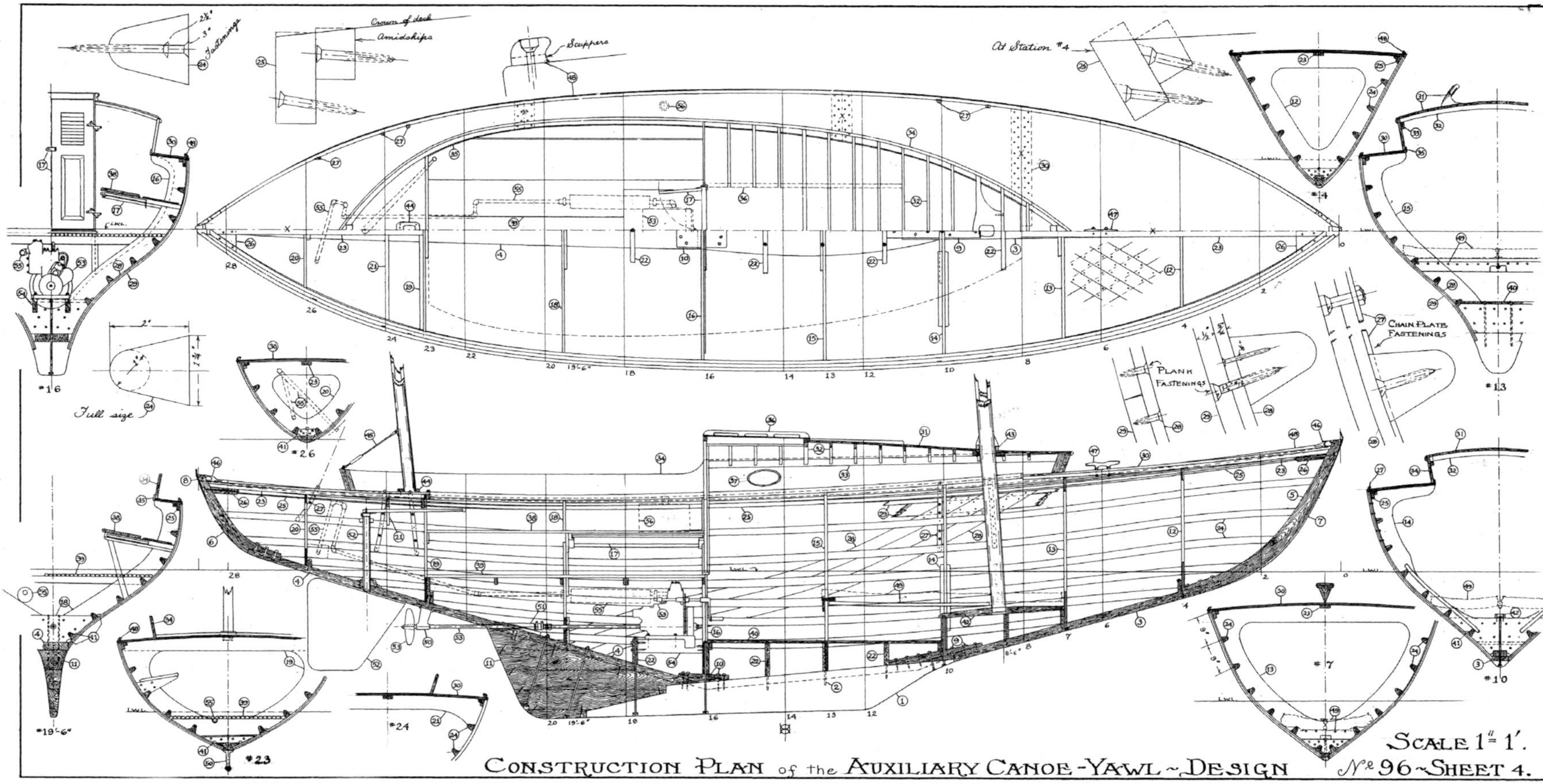
Crown of deck
Amidships
Fastenings
Scuppers
At Station #4
Plank Fastenings
Chain Plate Fastenings
Full size
#16
#26
#13
#10
#7
#19'-6"
#23
#24
Scale 1" = 1'.
Construction Plan of the Auxiliary Canoe-Yawl ~ Design
No. 96 ~ Sheet 4.

for plans as they were drawn. As he worked on Howell's design, which would be his No. 98, Francis also offered to fabricate the fittings for the boat and sell the lot to Howell for $100. Embarrassed that it took him over a year to complete the construction plan, he reduced even that low price.[58]

By the end of 1957, Howell had lofted the boat in his cellar, completed the forms for each station so frames could be shaped, and had started on templates for the backbone and deadwood. At that early stage, he decided to have a professional builder take over. But it would be another four years before the Livingston Boat Shop in Northport, Michigan, started on her; perhaps it took Howell that long to save up. The *Sprite,* as Howell called his Rozinante, was finally launched in the late summer of 1962.[59]

Meanwhile, Francis had gotten permission from Howell to have the plans of No. 98 published in *Yachting*. Associate Editor Ham de Fontaine gave "A Herreshoff-Designed Ketch-Rigged Canoe Yawl" a nice write-up in the July 1957 issue. Boris Lauer-Leonardi must have been neglecting his most important writer. Since the conclusion of "The Compleat Cruiser" in April 1954, Francis had written only three articles for *The Rudder*. The appearance of the Rozinante in *Yachting* apparently had the desired effect: by October 1957, Francis's byline was back in *The Rudder*, and he would soon start a major series for Boris on the history of yachting.[60]

When the drawings of Weldon's Rozinante had appeared in the November 1952 issue of *The Rudder,* as part of "The Compleat Cruiser," Robert S. Sanborn, the patent attorney Francis had dealt with about his and Frank Paine's ideas for improving the internal combustion engine, immediately wrote him suggesting that the boat would make a good subject for a *Rudder* How-To-Build series. Somehow, that excellent and perhaps obvious suggestion bore no fruit until May 1961, when Boris finally got around to running "How To Build Rozinante" as a special, sixteen-page supplement in the magazine, to be sold separately after publication for $1.00, and for which Francis was paid $500. The supplement included all of Francis's usual detailed plans for building hull, spars, and fittings, and making up the standing and running rigging, together with his instructions about the fashioning of fifty-nine elements singled out on the construction plan. And Francis wrote an idiosyncratic, whimsical explanation of his philosophy behind the design, a dissertation in which he got "a little excited" while exhorting on the value of simplicity when it came to cooking arrangements in the Rozinante. This writing was among the last he did for *The Rudder.*[61]

The Rozinante's construction plan included the outline of a sailor using the cedar bucket, a figure that became somewhat famous. Francis wrote three couplets about the bucket, unpublished until now:

> *The old open bucket with hoops made of brass*
> *Its corners well rounded and kind on the arse*
> *We can trust you to serve us in day time or night*
> *To bail out the bilge or a fire to fight*
> *We love your simplicity and the feel of the wood*
> *I would praise you more kindly if only I could* [62]

Francis wrote to Boris, "we can't hope that she will be as popular as the H-28, but she is a little boat that I should much rather have for myself." At age seventy, with a balance problem, Francis wasn't going to have another boat, and he never did sail in a Rozinante, except for thousands of miles in all conditions in his imagination, perhaps having more vicarious experience in this perfect small sailing boat than in any other of his designs. For Boris's part, the old enthusiasm for L. Francis Herreshoff material in his magazine was still there. He wrote: "Rozinante swept the yachting

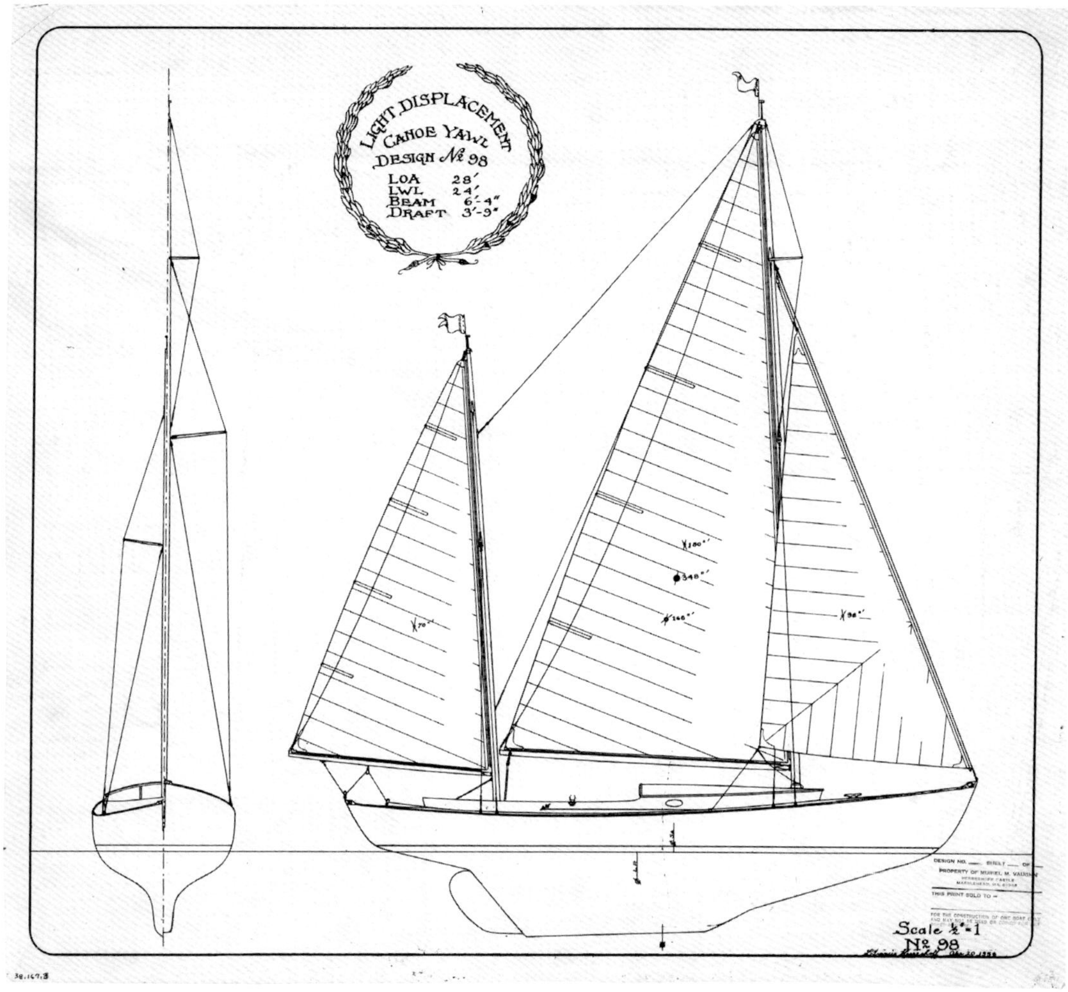

The outboard profile and sail plan of the second canoe-yawl Rozinante that Francis designed, this one in 1956 for Calvin T. Howell of Milwaukee. This was his design No. 98 that would become popular through a *Rudder* How-To-Build special supplement published in May 1961. Of the three Rozinantes—Weldon's in *The Compleat Cruiser*, Sewall's No. 96, and Howell's No. 98—the latter became the bona fide Rozinante. Howell wanted a pure sailing boat without an engine, so Francis was free to reverse the changes he had made to Weldon's fictional boat to accommodate an engine in No. 96. Back came the deadwood and deep rudder; the mizzenmast went forward where it belonged, but Francis has retained the short preventer to steady its lower part, even though the spar now has its own step across two floor timbers, instead of being stepped on deck as in No. 96. Howell also wanted a Marconi rig, and Francis gave the boat a permanent main backstay (coming to the mizzenmast) and his jumper stays. On this drawing, he shows a total sail area of 348 square feet, although the mainsail of 168 square feet, mizzen of 70, and jib of 98 add up to only 336 square feet. The Rozinante's rig is almost identical to that of the H-28 and *Quiet Tune*, with a slightly bigger jib and a slightly smaller mizzen. (© Mystic Seaport Museum, Daniel S. Gregory Ships Plans Library, SP38.167.3)

Notes

The ½ width of the Stem and Sternpost also Rabbet is 1¾" for the full length of these parts.

The Planking can be ¾" thick if firm wood and ⅞" if softer wood.

The Offsets are given in feet, inches, and eights of inches, from the center line and above and below the L.W.L.

STATION NUMBERS	28	26	24	22	20	18	16	14	12	10	8	6	4	2	0	
Height of Deck at side	2-1-0	1-10-5	1-8-7	1-7-6	1-7-0	1-6-6	1-7-0	1-8-0	1-9-3	1-10-5	2-0-5	2-2-7	2-5-5	2-8-5	3-0-0	Deck
" " Buttock #2				0-3-4	-0-3-4	0-8-0	0-10-4	0-11-2	0-10-7	0-7-0	0-0-1	+1-0-0				Buttock 2
" " " #1		1-6-3	0-1-1	-0-5-4	0-11-2	1-3-5	1-6-3	1-7-6	1-6-4	1-4-0	0-11-4	0-5-4	+0-5-7	-2-5-2		" 1
" " Rabbet	2-2-6	0-0-6	-0-5-0	0-10-5	0-4-1	1-9-4	2-3-0	2-3-4	2-3-4	2-3-4	1-10-3	1-3-1	0-8-2	+0-2-1	3-2-0	Rabbet
" " Profile	2-1-0	0-0-0	-0-5-4	1-5-2	3-9-0	3-8-2	3-7-4	3-6-6	3-6-0 / 3-5-4	2-6-2	1-10-7	1-3-7	0-9-0	0-0-0	3-0-0	Profile
" " Top of Lead					-3-3-0	3-1-0	2-11-0	3-4-0 / 2-3-0	2-4-0	2-4-0						Face
Half width at Deck	0-0-5	1-2-1	1-10-6	2-5-1	2-9-4	3-0-2	3-1-6	3-2-0	3-1-4	3-0-2	2-10-0	2-5-1	1-10-6	1-1-6	0-0-7	Deck
" " W.L. +2'												2-4-4	1-8-3	0-9-7		WL +2'
" " W.L. +1'		0-8-6	1-7-3	2-3-4	2-8-7	3-0-4	3-2-1	3-2-1	3-1-2	2-11-1	2-6-5	2-0-0	1-3-1	0-5-2		WL +1'
" " W.L. +6"		0-5-2	1-3-7	2-1-2	2-7-4	2-11-2	3-1-2	3-1-2	3-0-1	2-9-2	2-4-0	1-8-7	1-0-1	0-2-6		WL +6"
" " L.W.L.		0-0-3	0-10-7	1-8-7	2-4-1	2-8-4	2-10-7	2-11-1	2-9-5	2-6-1	2-0-2	1-4-6	0-8-4	0-0-3		L.W.L.
" " W.L. -6"				0-11-2	1-8-1	2-2-4	2-6-1	2-7-1	2-5-2	1-6-5	1-6-4	0-11-4	0-3-6			WL -6"
" " W.L. -1'				0-1-4	0-10-5	1-6-0	1-9-6	1-11-0	1-9-4	1-5-4	0-11-4	0-5-0				WL -1'
" " W.L. -2'				0-0-4	0-1-7	0-4-3	0-7-0	0-8-4	0-8-0	0-5-1						WL -2'
" " W.L. -3'					0-1-2	0-2-6	0-4-1	0-4-4	0-3-4							WL -3'
" " Rabbet	0-1-3	0-1-3	0-1-3	0-2-4	0-3-7	0-5-0	0-6-0	0-6-7	0-6-0	0-2-6						Rabbet
" " Face before [illegible]	0-0-6	0-0-3	0-0-6	0-0-3 / 0-0-6	0-0-6	0-2-2	0-3-5	0-3-5	round	round	round	round	0-0-5	0-0-3	0-0-7	Face
Diagonal #1			0-5-6	0-11-2	1-4-2	1-8-0	1-10-2	1-11-2	1-10-3	1-8-2	1-4-5	1-0-3	0-7-0			D #1
" #2		1-1-4	1-11-0	2-7-0	3-0-6	3-4-2	3-6-2	3-6-4	3-5-2	3-2-2	2-9-3	2-3-1	1-6-7	0-9-3		D #2

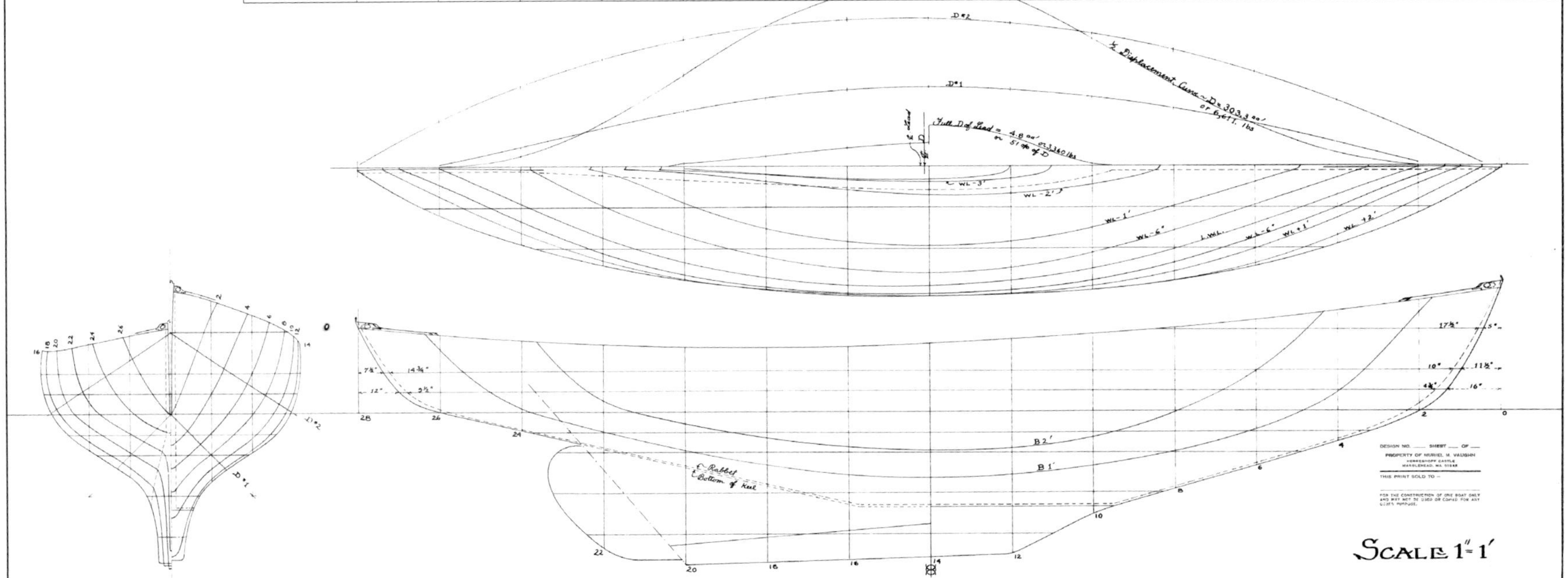

SCALE 1"=1'

LINES OF THE LIGHT DISPLACEMENT CANOE YAWL ~ DESIGN № 98 ~ SHEET 2

L.F. Herreshoff Oct 1956

circles. Plans are selling like mad." Yet Francis was right; although there must be a couple of hundred Rozinantes in the world, the canoe yawl did not achieve the numbers reached by the H-28, the quintessential small cruiser.[63]

Frederic Farnham, of Mattapoisett on Buzzards Bay, was intent on getting a Rozinante; so intent that he made a fine half-model of the design. But then came the chance to buy a Buzzards Bay 25-footer, one of N. G. Herreshoff's most beautiful one-design racers. When Farnham told Mr. Herreshoff of the switch, Francis hid his disappointment by telling him he was getting almost as good a boat as the Rozinante. Farnham gave his Rozinante model to Francis.[64]

Robert T. Todd, of London, Ontario, went straight to a professional builder for his Rozinante, the *Phalarope* in 1963. He got the lowest cost estimate from the Smith and Rhuland yard in Lunenburg, Nova Scotia, and went Down East to Bluenose country to meet the builders and inspect their facility. He liked what he found. "I am sure, Mr. Herreshoff," Todd reported, "that you would approve of these people. In many respects they appear old fashioned but they are well organized and seem to have a lot of highly skilled people and some of them quite old. In the yard they have great piles of timber including huge oak timbers that are nearly black from seasoning. They also—believe it or not—have large piles of grown crooks and knees. It is a real treat to sec some of these old boys climbing around—sighting along the grain and finally selecting the piece that is seemingly designed by nature for its specific place in a vessel. You will be interested to know that in Mr. Fred Rhuland's office is the most 'dog-eared' set of the 'Common Sense of Yacht Design' I've ever seen. When I commented on this, Mr. Rhuland said that they used it for reference all the time." Little wonder that Francis sent future inquirers about Rozinante builders to Smith and Rhuland.[65]

Todd sailed his *Phalarope* to her home port of Sarnia, Ontario, at the foot of Lake Huron, in stages during the summers of 1964 and 1965, via the St. Lawrence River and the Trent Severn Waterway. He described for Francis a 90-mile run in the open water of Lake Huron from Tobermory south to Kincardine:

> *Saturday morning dawned clear, with a gentle north-easterly—so out we went at 9:00 A. M. When we turned west to go out through the Cape Hurd Channel, we found that the large sea was still running and the wind too light to steady the sails. In spite of all, the Phalarope kept going and we rounded Cape Hurd at 12:00 noon. Running off before the seas was somewhat easier and we made much better progress. The wind steadily freshened during the afternoon and by 4:00 P.M. we were off Stokes Bay. Here we had to decide whether to go in for the night or sail all night. On such a beautiful, clear,*

LEFT: **The lines and offsets of the Rozinante. With no need for engine space, her sections are more cut away than those of No. 96; her lines are very close to what Francis drew merely to illustrate his instructional cruising yarn. A key to the Rozinante's beauty seems to be the exact profile of the double-ended stern; any slight variation by the builder has a striking effect on appearance. So it is surprising to notice that Francis tried more curve in the stern on 96 but then, for 98, returned to the original line he had struck for Weldon's boat. This artistic genius had no need to go back and try to improve his work. No. 98 is 28 feet long on deck; 24 feet on the waterline; with a beam of 6 feet, 4 inches; and a draft of 3 feet, 9 inches. Displacement is 6,611 pounds, with 3,360 pounds of lead ballast, for a ballast-displacement ratio of 51 percent.** (© Mystic Seaport Museum, Daniel S. Gregory Ships Plans Library, SP38.167.1)

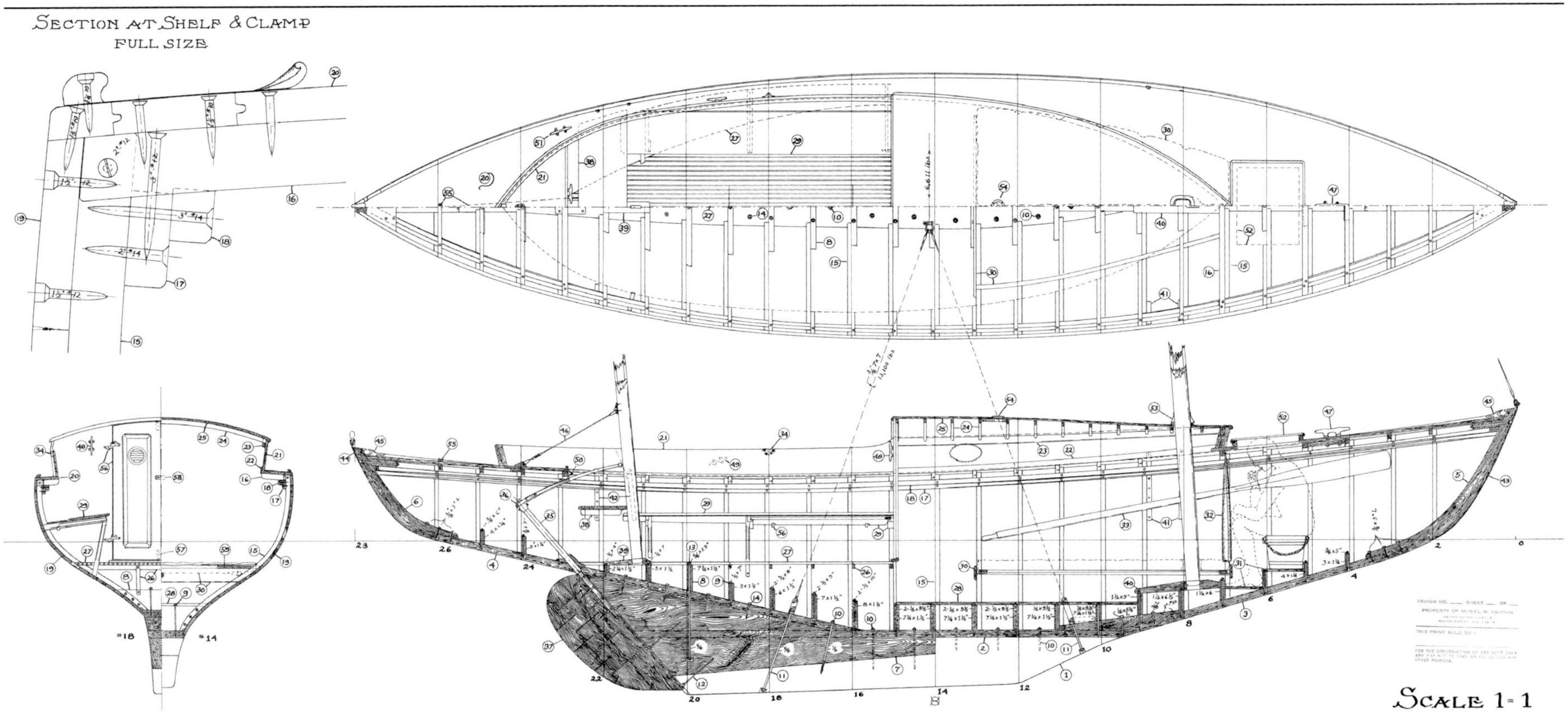

CONSTRUCTION PLAN OF THE LIGHT DISPLACEMENT CANOE YAWL ~ DESIGN № 98 ~ SHEET 3

crisp day, the decision was easy—carry on. Shortly, the wind, which, for a couple of hours, had been westerly, switched to the east and freshened some more and we really began to make knots. We were well out of sight of land when the sun went down in a glorious sunset. A half hour later the nearly full moon rose and made the tumbling seas (old sea NW—new sea E) a beautiful eerie silver. By now the Phalarope really had her shoulder into it and was moving nearly at her full speed. She is quite wonderful, you know, with a very easy motion, and was quite dry in spite of the tumbling seas. Occasionally, she would literally shoot over one of the pyramidal seas and land in the hollow beyond without any great shock, and with sheets of spray and foam going far outboard—lighted red and green by our running lights. At 3:00 A. M. Sunday, we were close off Kincardine, which we had decided was our destination—although we had estimated 6:00 A. M. as our arrival time. Finding our way into this little port was no picnic as the outer range light for the entrance channel was out. When we did find the entrance (which is very narrow) my crew was all set to climb the high pier walls and tow us in, as the wind was blowing straight out the channel. He was certainly startled when I told him we would tack in. I don't think he really believed it could be done—until we were safely in the basin and tied up. Of course, he didn't know the Phalarope's abilities as well as I do.

Todd's Rozinante made the trip at an average speed of a little over 6 knots.[66]

Todd also reported to Francis that with a dinghy lashed alongside, equipped with a 2-horsepower British Seagull outboard, the *Phalarope* covered 30 miles on 2 imperial gallons of gas. And that in a squall reported ashore to have blown 60 knots, he hove her to under jib and mizzen. At times, she buried the lee rail to the coaming, but she shipped no water. A 35-foot ketch nearby heeled to 35 degrees with bare poles.[67]

Smith and Rhuland built another half dozen Rozinantes after the *Phalarope.* One, at Francis's

LEFT: **The Rozinante's construction plan. Adhering to his principle of simplicity in a small cruising boat, Francis shows conventional plank-on-frame construction, rather than the longitudinal construction of No. 96. The wood keel is 14 inches wide by 2 inches thick, and 12 feet, 4 inches long, preferably of white oak, as are the stem, sternpost, floor timbers, frames, and deck beams. Frames are 1¼ inches square. Planking is ⅞-inch fine, rift-grain fir or soft pine, or ¾-inch Philippine mahogany. In the sectional drawing at the lower left, we can see that the cockpit coaming in the left half and the side of the cabin house in the right half both slant outboard at an angle of eight degrees. The open cockpit floor is made up of teak slats, 1-inch wide and ¾-inch thick, spaced ¼ inch apart. The thwart just abaft the mizzenmast is 2 inches higher than the cockpit seats and is removable. There is no hatchway at the after end of the cuddy; later Francis suggested lowering the cockpit floor just abaft the house by 15-18 inches to increase the ducking headroom and also give a nice place to stand while watching her go. Up forward, there is a small platform where Francis shows a cramped, pipe-smoking user of the cedar bucket, with the fore hatch shut on a rainy day, but one of his many arguments for the device was that it may be used at any convenient place in the boat. A full-width double berth takes up much of the cabin; at its after end is space for a simple galley on one side and for a canvas easy chair on the other. The full-size drawing in the upper left shows the construction of the shelf and clamp. One builder wanted to know why there was no rub rail on the outside of the planking. Francis said, "we don't bump into things."** (© Mystic Seaport Museum, Daniel S. Gregory Ships Plans Library, SP38.167.2)

suggestion, was for Ted Sprague, who sailed his *Arete* (the Greek term for moral virtue, or excellence) out of Rockport, Maine. Sprague wrote: "Throughout the process of selecting a design to carry the name of *Arete*, procurement of materials, fabrication of fittings and fitting-out, Mr. Herreshoff, always the gentleman, always ready in his words 'to lend a hand,' showed how closely he had come in his personal life to living the ideals that show so plainly in his many writings. From my initial contact with Mr. Herreshoff, he was always sensitive to my particular interests and needs. All suggested modifications and deviations from his published plans were carefully addressed, benefits and sacrifices and his own thoughts offered for consideration."[68]

Sprague's modifications were to split the main backstay and secure the legs of the bridle to chainplates in order to make the stay independent of the mizzenmast; to provide a companionway hatch into the cuddy; and to install galley furniture at the aft end of the cabin, instead of Weldon's easy chair and heating stove. Francis didn't object to any of this, but he thought the companionway hatch would cost $150, "and I would duck my head many times for that sum." Sprague wrote, "Mr. Herreshoff took a very liberal view of cabin arrangements; considering them entirely up to the individual as long as they did not compromise the performance, safety and maintainability of the craft." However, Francis's view of making more basic deviations from his design of the Rozinante was quite different: "My advice to you, Gentle Reader, is, if you want to make changes, by all means get a modern boat for your changes cannot make her any worse."[69]

Another Smith and Rhuland Rozinante had no immediate buyer and languished "way back in the corner of the boatbulding shed" until Niels W. Jannasch of nearby Seabright, Nova Scotia, spotted her, fell in love, bought her for $6,400, and sailed her 31 miles home at 7 knots. "Well, there she is now," he wrote to Francis, "on her mooring in our own little cove, painted a very dark green, with a white boot top and copper below, varnished coaming etc. and a light grey deck. The whole family is in love with her—my own feelings I won't even mention." Francis replied, "I want to thank you for your nice letter for this is the kind of thing that makes yacht designing a pleasure and affords me more satisfaction than winning a lot of races."[70]

Sam Morris was a Philadelphia lawyer and Billy Strawbridge's half-brother. He and Francis were on a first-name basis. Morris had his Rozinante, the *Eurynome* (a Titan goddess, an Oceanid), built by Allan Vaitses in Mattapoisett in 1966. Morris left the day she was launched, heading west down Buzzards Bay toward his home mooring at Avondale, Rhode Island, on the Pawcatuck River. "She sailed beautifully," he reported to Francis. "The helm was perfect, just enough to keep her eating out to weather, but you can steer her on the wind with a finger. At first there was about a rail down breeze, and she made a wave in that for almost her full waterline. Then we had a little more, enough to get the leeward turnbuckles wet, and she went even better. She knifed through the small amount of chop there was and threw relatively little spray. Later that evening, the breeze lightened up considerably, yet she seemed to sail just as well. I have never sailed as nice a boat." But then, disaster. Trying to work the *Eurynome* into the narrow entrance to the cove behind Salter's Point, between Padanaram and Westport, she "went aground on the rocks, and hit a very sharp pinnacle which punched a hole in her. She sank right there in about three or four minutes." The hull was barely submerged; no one was hurt; the boat was raised onto a barge from New Bedford next day; she was returned to the Vaitses yard and repaired. When the *Eurynome* reached home, Morris gave Francis the most rewarding possible appraisal: "The boat has drawn numerous favorable comments since coming to Avondale. One man called her 'the prettiest thing in the river,' with which I agree. Even your father's boats can't touch her looks."[71]

But Smith and Rhuland and Allan Vaitses were not the only pro builders turning out Rozinantes. In the Balearic Islands, Stanley Woodward Jr.'s Yacht and Boat Construction Company in Puerto Polensa was building boats to No. 98 that Francis judged, from photographs, "are very nicely built and very much like the drawings." Paul Luke's yard in East Boothbay, Maine, built a Rozinante in twenty-eight days—a foot a day. No vacation was allowed until the boat was done. A cardboard mock-up of a bulkhead goes up, off to lunch, come back, the wood bulkhead is in and painted! And, much later, Damien McLaughlin, in North Falmouth, Massachusetts, on Cape Cod, would turn out a Rozinante using the West System of epoxy and wood, and the Rockland Apprenticeshop would choose L. Francis Herreshoff's design No. 98 for a project to teach wooden boat construction. These Rozinantes would be offered for sale at $65,000 and $55,000 respectively.[72]

Arthur Brendze was a young man with severe, incurable boat disease who made the pilgrimage to The Castle and became a protégé and close friend to Skipper Herreshoff. Brendze's acquisition of a Rozinante that he sailed out of Marblehead Harbor rekindled Francis's fervor for No. 98. Francis was appalled that Brendze had paid more than $5,000 for his Rozinante. Near the end of his life, he urged his friend Lee Nielsen, who had established Lee's Boatshop in Rockland, Maine, to build Rozinantes, hopefully at a lower price than either Smith and Rhuland or Vaitses. Francis even contracted for his own Rozinante from Lee. At $8,420, she cost no less than a boat from Lunenburg (though far less than one from Mattapoisett), but Francis wanted to help Lee's Boatshop, and the agreement gave him a good excuse to have Brendze drive him to Maine to see how things were coming on his boat. Francis never intended to take delivery of her; he was sure that she would find another buyer quickly, which she did. Lee's Boatshop built about ten Rozinantes, several of which, according to the brokers selling them, are said to be "the one built for L. Francis Herreshoff himself."[73]

A good many Rozinantes could be advertised as having "fittings and hardware made by L. Francis Herreshoff himself." That is, Francis made the patterns, had the fittings cast by the Jefferson Bronze and Aluminum Company in nearby Salem, and then smoothed and polished them. He made "perhaps twenty sets." Francis charged $300 a set and thought he took in perhaps 25 cents an hour for his labor. He wrote: "They are light, well-designed, and beautifully made. Besides that, like most objects of honest craftsmanship, they are nice to look at, and I have some of them on my desk at this moment, where they afford my eyes a pleasant relief."[74]

It was inevitable that there would be fiberglass Rozinantes. Perhaps the best-known were those from the Cheoy Lee Shipyard in Hong Kong. In 1963, franchised dealers like Eastern Shore Yacht Sales, in Oxford, Maryland; Herbert Hayes Yacht Sales, in Greenwich, Connecticut, and Fort Lauderdale; and Roland Reed Associates ("Sole U. S. Representative"), in Alameda, California, were offering Cheoy Lee Rozinantes for less than $7,000, sails not included. The Kenner Boat Company in Knoxville, Arkansas, sold "kits," as well as finished boats; South Coast Seacraft, in Shreveport, Louisiana, sold bare hulls. Francis received no commission on sales of fiberglass Rozinantes. "I certainly don't recommend them," he wrote, "for plastic hulls are so heavy that the ballast has to be reduced so much that these boats can not carry their designed sail plans, and are slower than the boats built as designed." Monroe B. Hall, of Annapolis, Maryland, was perfectly happy with his Cheoy Lee Rozinante, taking her on many a quiet evening sail under just jib and mizzen, but it is not known whether he ever raced her against a wooden one.[75]

Art Brendze would talk over possible modifications to his Rozinante with Skipper Herreshoff at The Castle. Francis would unfurl his long

index finger to as straight as it would still go and say, "Don't you do it!" But he suggested one change himself. Realizing that Brendze often sailed single-handed, he thought a self-tending jib would be good. For a two-thirds-length club, he told Brendze to look in the northwest corner of the Tower room over the garage, where he would find the trunk of the 1929 Christmas tree, carefully saved for just such an emergency. Skipper doodled in the new, slightly smaller jib, with a traveler, on a sail plan—the sketch was frameable. Brendze loved the sail; it even tended to stay wung out on its own before the wind.[76]

On one overnight run Down East to Tenants Harbor, Maine, from Marblehead, Brendze found himself, during the long night watch, among a pod of whales. Luckily, he didn't bump into any. When he related the experience to Skipper, Francis said if it happened again, he should warn the leviathans of his presence by lifting a floorboard and tapping on a keel bolt with a penny. Common sense.[77]

Brendze often felt Skipper's presence on board his Rozinante. When the boat drew admiring attention, Brendze found it hard to say thank you, because he didn't really feel it was his boat. Skipper said, "Oh, you have my permission."[78]

Another inevitability was requests to L. Francis Herreshoff to design bigger Rozinantes with more cruising accommodations. Francis, himself, was tempted. On the back of one of the Sailski drawings, he penciled a preliminary outboard profile of a 35-foot Rozinante, with a waterline of 31 feet, a beam of 8 feet, and a draft of 4 feet, 6 inches. He drew similar plans of Rozinante boats (as he called them, pronouncing the name of Quixote's horse with his flat Rhode Island accent—ending in "ant," like the insect, not "ante") with lengths of 34, 36, and 40 feet. And there is even a 32-foot-6-inch fast Rozinante and a 35-foot, shoal Rozinante. Unfortunately, these drawings are not reproducible.[79]

George E. Stuart of Durban, South Africa, took matters into his own hands. He simply enlarged the lines of No. 98 to a length on deck of 35 feet, beam 8 feet, and a draft 5 feet, gave her a sloop rig, and built his *Carina*. She was first to finish in a number of races against bigger boats. Stuart wrote to Francis, "I could not have been more pleased with *Carina* and must thank you for designing such a perfect yacht."[80]

Phil Bolger said: "I get hypnotized like a bird with a snake every time I look at a Rozinante. Boy! How did he do it?" In a way, the Rozinante is an irony: as a very fine-lined boat, she leaves little record of her passage through the water; but as one of the great yacht designs, she has made an unforgettable impression on many sailors. L. Francis Herreshoff told Arthur Brendze, "I designed the Rozinante to be a gallant little yacht in which somebody could ride off on a wonderful adventure."[81]

A Rozinante on the wind, passing a Maine island. She is so fine-lined and slippery that her modest sail area is moving her fast, even in just a gentle breeze, as indicated by that gorgeous, long bow wave. (Author photo)

CHAPTER 24

DIMENTIONS OF DESIGN № 103

L.O.A.	39'-9"	FRAMES	1¾" x 1¾"
BEAM	9'-6"	PLANKING	1⅛"
DRAFT	3'	DECK	1¼" TEAK
DISPLACEMENT		DECK BEAMS	2" x 1½"

MOTOR ONE *Chrysler Imperial model M 45 with 3 to 1 reduction gear*
FRAME SPACE 1'
STEM AND KEEL SIDED 4"

Owner J. W. Strawbridge Esq.

OUTBOARD PLAN of № 103 ~ SHEET 1 Scale ½" = 1'.

COILING DOWN

"I no longer have the strong eyesight and the patience to make drawings that have a great deal of fine detail."

—L. FRANCIS HERRESHOFF, 1960

In the late 1950s, changes came about at the Rudder Publishing Company over which Boris Lauer-Leonardi, and certainly L. Francis Herreshoff, had no control. New people came into ownership and management positions who looked upon *The Rudder* more as a business proposition than as an educational—and even inspirational—medium for sailors. Editorial content shrank and seemed to be aimed at pleasing advertisers more than subscribers. The traditions of yachting that Francis had long complained were being neglected in the magazine seemed further and further away.

The magazine started making leeway in 1950, with the death of its longtime managing editor and president, Andrew Patterson. His obituary called him "an outstanding personality in the pleasure boat world for over half a century." Even though he had to keep a tight grip on the purse strings, Patterson had always encouraged Boris to make *The Rudder* the best magazine he could. *The Rudder* was printed by Thomson and Company, located at 9 Murray Street, near City Hall in Lower Manhattan, and the Thomson family had owned the magazine for many years. John Thomson succeeded Patterson as managing editor of *The Rudder.* His brother, James, was already production manager. The Thomson family had the magazine's best interests at heart, but they were not part of the pleasure-boat world. In any case, they sold Thomson and Company, together with *The Rudder,* in 1957. The new owner, John B. Watkins, set himself up as *The Rudder*'s publisher, but his real interest was in the printing business.[1]

Boris did not get along with Watkins. By May 1958 he was writing to Francis: "The pressure on me to cheapen the magazine became so great, that I had no choice but to leave." Boris Lauer-Leonardi's fifteen-year watch at the editorial helm of *The Rudder* ended, or rather was interrupted, for he would return.[2]

Before he left, Boris did one last favor for his readers: he arranged for the publication of another long series of articles—they would run to twenty-two—from L. Francis Herreshoff. Francis wrote his take on the history of yachting, starting with the Egyptian pleasure barges of 6,000 B.C.E. His story is both a valuable reference and a continuation of his crusade against what he

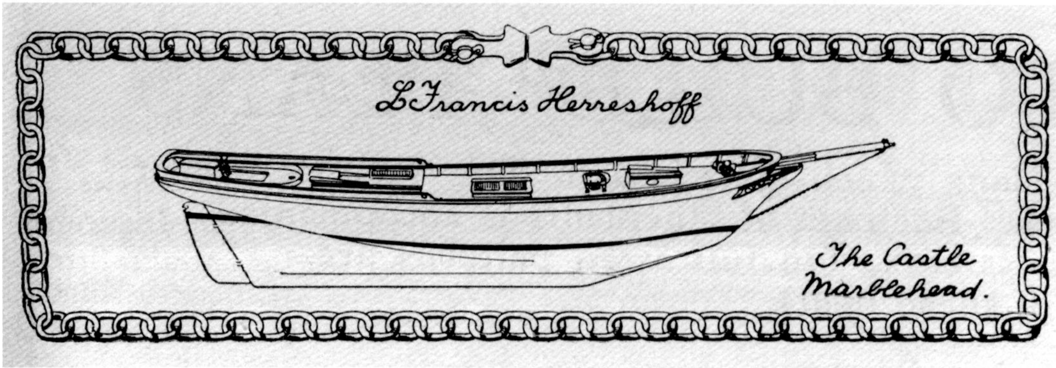

saw as the pollution of yachting. He hoped that by enlightening his readers on the traditions of the great sport, buttressed by stories and illustrations of beautiful yachts of the past, he could turn the tide against the likes of high, wide, ugly boats powered either by huge, unmeasured light sails or big, gas-guzzling motors, filled with every sort of unnecessary gadget, and advertised to the unwary in the profit-oriented boating magazines by scantily clad women. His series, which ran in *The Rudder* from April 1958 through June 1961, was called "An Introduction to Yachting." It is excellent, informal history, spiced with Francis's occasional opinionated diatribes. And the series gave its readers the opportunity to explore Francis's yachting library and his collection of yachting photographs through the publication of the 150 illustrations that he selected from The Castle's shelves and drawers. One reader wrote in: "Your April issue is priceless. It has been many months [four] since we heard from Mr. Herreshoff, but he sure came back with a big one [the first installment was fifteen pages, printed on heavy, creamy paper]. I am looking forward to the rest of the series and can hardly wait for May." Another wrote, "give me a little Herreshoff and I can survive pages of fiberglass tail fins."[3]

When he was halfway through the writing of "An Introduction to Yachting," in the March 1959 issue, Francis wrote to Boris, "I am endeavoring to get through this series as quickly as I can because I am certainly disgusted with it." With Boris gone

---

ABOVE: **Francis's calling-card advertisement ran in *The Rudder* from August 1948, when he retired the "Re-Tired" ad, through January 1962. His sketch of a *Tioga*-type yacht was not one of his designs, but simply a doodle that he hoped might entice a reader to beat a path to his door. Well, it may be that the ad suggested to Edwin Hill the possibility of an *Araminta*.** (*The Rudder* (August 1948): 81) RIGHT TOP: **Francis's design No. 95, made in 1955, was for this 15-foot double-paddle white-water canoe. The customer was named Keith Anderson. The little boat has considerable tumblehome amidships to keep her rail out of rough water. Beam is 28 inches. Her hull is nearly symmetrical, but she draws a little more water aft than forward. Francis shows a displacement curve at 260 pounds.** (© Mystic Seaport Museum, Daniel S. Gregory Ships Plans Library, SP38.201.2) RIGHT BOTTOM: **Francis designed another white-water canoe for Anderson in 1957, this one specifically for racing. Anderson paddled both his canoes on the Colorado River. This is design No. 101. She is 5 inches longer than No. 95, 4 inches narrower, and 10 pounds lighter. Francis hoped this hull would steer all right without a keel, which he eliminated to reduce wetted surface, but he showed a shallow keel in dotted lines, just in case.** (© Mystic Seaport Museum, Daniel S. Gregory Ships Plans Library, SP38.186.1)

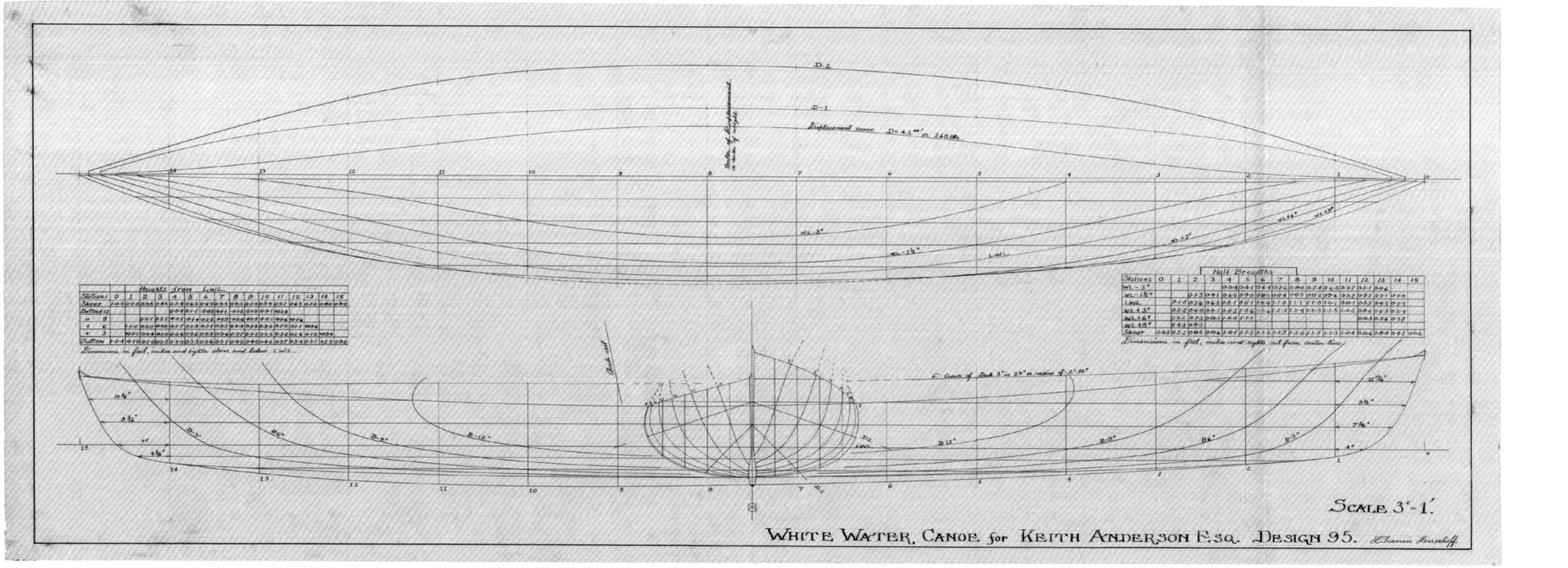
Scale 3" = 1'
White Water Canoe for Keith Anderson Esq. Design 95.

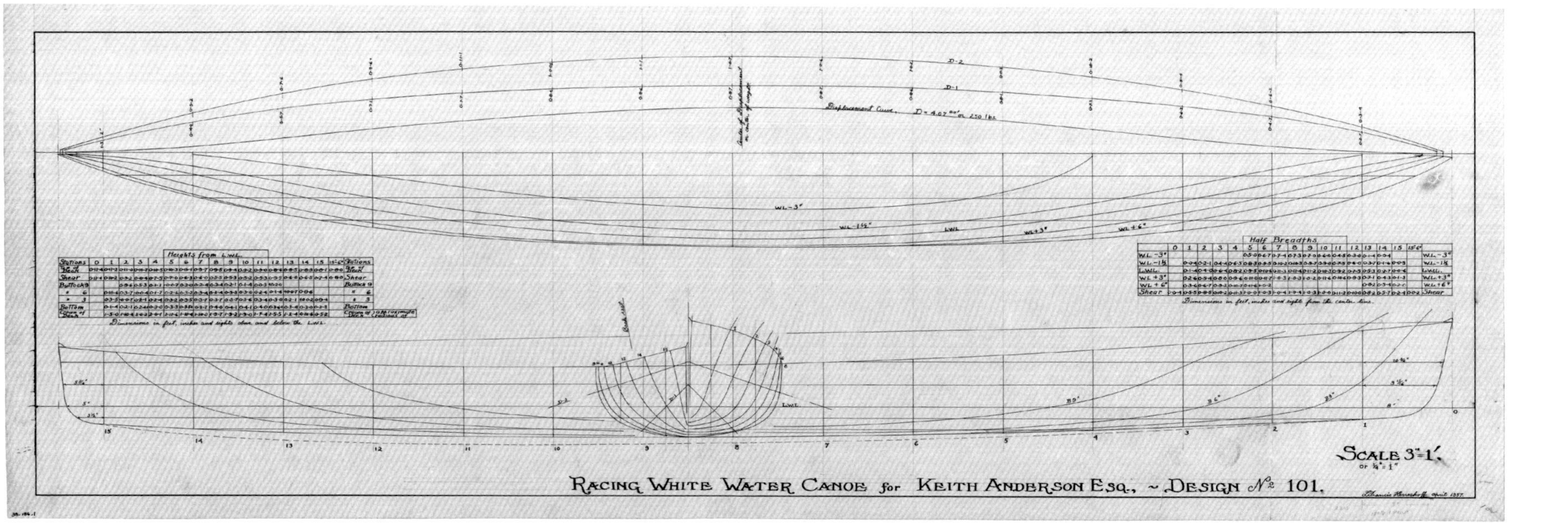
Scale 3" = 1'
Racing White Water Canoe for Keith Anderson Esq., ~ Design No. 101.

temporarily, there was no encouraging editor, telling him how much the readers liked his writing and forwarding fan mail. Instead, the new editor, Moulton H. "Monk" Farnham found it necessary, with a nod to his advertisers, to insert a preamble to Francis's fifth article in the series: "As firm believers in the tradition of free speech, we wish to point out that Mr. Herreshoff's opinions are his own, and do not necessarily represent those of the publication." (To be sure, Boris had done the same when Francis went after plywood and plastics.) Despite Boris's return to the editor's chair in April 1959, with yet another change in the ownership of *The Rudder*, Francis decided to halt "An Introduction to Yachting" somewhat prematurely, taking the story only to the year 1920. He wrote to Boris: "I am going to end this long series because I am sure that it is not at all popular and it is hard work for me to do." Francis was losing interest in the project, but he wanted to take his history of yachting at least up through the sea change of World War I. That took three more installments—and a whole year. It was his last major writing for *The Rudder.*[4]

But Boris was excited to be back. He wrote to Francis: "A powerful new group has purchased *The Rudder* and I have returned as editor. We will all make another heroic try (with your help)." Alas, the "powerful new group" was Fawcett Publications, purveyor of *True Confessions* and *Daring Detective,* and inventor of Captain Marvel. The fact that Fawcett's flagship magazine, *Mechanix Illustrated*, had catapulted Jack Hanna's Tahiti ketch to popularity back in 1935 cut more ice with Boris than it did with Francis. *The Rudder* moved uptown, from 9 Murray Street to 585 Lexington Avenue. Boris actually thought of purchasing the magazine himself. But he wrote to Francis, "I gave up the idea of buying *The Rudder*, mainly because the magazine has been so badly run down that it would take years to rehabilitate it." In January 1963, two *Rudder* contributors, Conrad Miller and Pete Smyth, persuaded the then publisher, Ellery Mann, that *The Rudder*'s problem was Boris. Mann fired Boris and made Miller editor. Boris's last issue was January 1963. Francis's status at the magazine diminished to nothing. The May 1965 issue of *The Rudder* contained Smyth's article, "75 Years of Yachting History As Seen Through The Pages of Rudder." There was no mention of any contribution to the story by Contributing Editor L. Francis Herreshoff.[5]

Francis would write just one more article for *The Rudder,* a piece on naphtha launches, published in the November 1965 issue. With Boris's encouragement and astute handling, he had been the magazine's star for more than twenty years, writing 234 articles and making designs for seven How-To-Build series boats. He had been listed on the masthead as Contributing Editor since the January 1947 issue, and—with a puzzling hiatus during much of the publication of "An Introduction to Yachting"—he would be so listed, in hopes of further contributions, to the end of his life. But the long, successful association of editor and designer-writer was over, to the great detriment of *The Rudder.* The magazine, despite being well-named, would soon be blown way off course.

An Introduction to Yachting was published as a book by Sheridan House in 1963. Francis's dedication was "To the Memory of my Father," repeating that of his biography of Nathanael. The list price was $15.00, but Rudder's agreement was now for "all rights," so the royalty went to Fawcett, not to Francis. His disappointment went beyond money. Francis wrote to William A. Robinson in Tahiti: "I have had less fan mail from this book than any of the others that I wrote before."[6]

We have seen how little L. Francis Herreshoff thought of the catboat in his derogation of the type to one of its champions, his sometime draftsman Fenwick Williams. Nathanael had designed cat yawls for cruising early in his career, and Francis reverted to that type in an attempt to design a small cruising boat that would retain the roominess, moderate draft, and simplicity of the catboat, while doing away with its disadvantages. He listed no fewer than ten drawbacks to the catboat, concentrating on the difficulties of making certain maneuvers with a single sail and on the twisting strains induced by a necessarily heavy mast (with no shrouds) right up in the bow. His design to minimize these problems, a cat yawl, No. 102, was published in *The Rudder* in November 1957.[7]

In the text accompanying the design, Francis began by objecting to new terminology: "First of all, as to the name of the rig: all vessels without head sails but having two masts with the after one the smaller are cat yawls. The term 'cat ketch' is incorrect and never used until recently." And he went on to explain how No. 102 would steer easily according to how the mizzen was trimmed; would lie-to nicely under just the mizzen; and had a relatively light mainmast, well stayed to her flaring bow.[8]

Francis hoped that the publication of the lines and sail plan of the cat yawl would generate letters asking him to complete the design with a construction plan. It was not to be. "Not one single person showed interest," Francis wrote. He was wrong. There would be no construction plan, but there would be a few boats built to No. 102. Franklin P. Blaisdell of Lynn, Massachusetts, went ahead and built a cat yawl to Francis's lines, making up his own construction details as he went. His *Dancing Feather* turned out beautifully, and gained a reputation for speed around Marblehead. And Francis did sell several sets of plans for No. 102 and answered the many questions of one amateur builder with scantlings for sixteen parts of the boat. The design accomplished its purpose: L. Francis Herreshoff tamed Fenwick Williams's catboat.[9]

In 1958, Francis designed one more boat for Billy Strawbridge. This would be his eighth design for his friend of the changeable mind and the fifth that would be built, the previous four being the 12-Metre *Mitena*, the *Persephone*, the Northeast Harbor One-Design, and the *Piquant*. This last one was his design No. 103, a 40-foot launch with a deck shelter that Billy could use as a picnic boat and "tender for small racing sailboats" at his summer place at Northeast Harbor, Maine. Billy would name her the *Melantho*, after Neptune's favorite nymph.[10]

Francis got building bids from Norman Hodgdon Jr. in Boothbay Harbor, Maine, and Harry Towne in Bristol, Rhode Island. Hodgdon estimated $16,000 if single-planked, $18,000 if double. He wrote Francis a long letter, saying he was so anxious to get the job that he would give up any profit and build on a basis of cost (labor at $2.00 per hour) plus overhead. Hodgdon wrote: "I have really enjoyed so much working with your plans that I am sure a job of this type would be very interesting. I sometimes wonder if the owners realize the thought and work that goes into the planning. I must also add that the thoroughness and fine work of your plans really has saved many hours in the construction and building. The old saying a job well planned is half done is fine and really a lot of Truth too." Despite all this, Billy Strawbridge chose Harry Towne, who estimated $20,000, with no mention of double planking. Towne would build the *Melantho* in one of the old construction sheds of the Herreshoff Manufacturing Company. Her cost would come in at $27,720, on which Billy paid Francis the usual 10 percent commission.[11]

Despite having to add substantial ballast and correct a steering problem, Billy wrote to Francis after running the *Melantho* for three summers: "She certainly has turned out to be a most satisfactory boat and very much admired. I know I

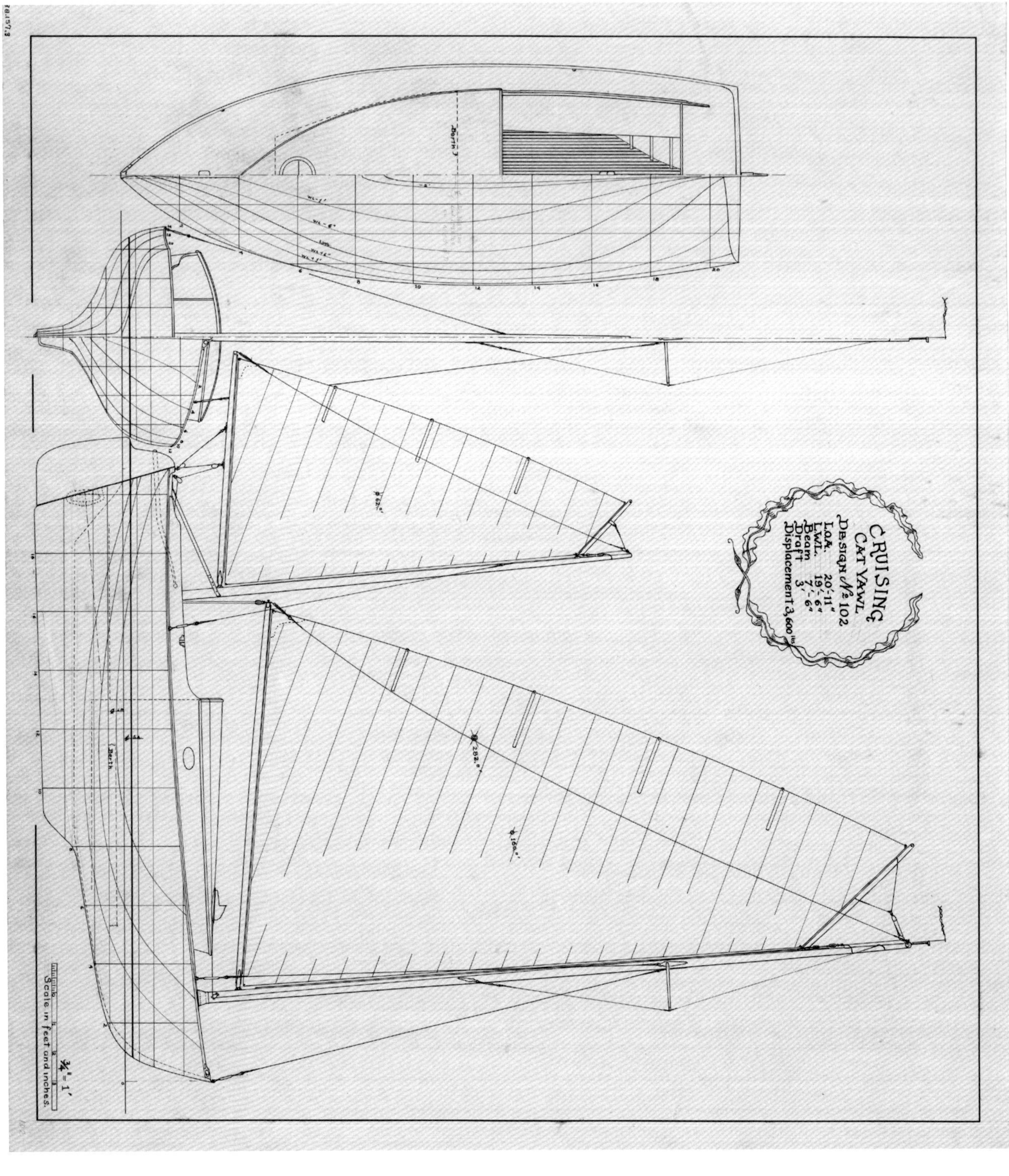
CRUISING
CAT YAWL
DESIGN No 102
L.O.A. 20'-11"
L.W.L. 19'-6"
Beam 7'-6"
Draft 3'
Displacement 3,600 lbs
Scale in feet and inches.
¾" = 1'

LEFT: Francis's design No. 102 was this handsome little cat yawl. She was an exercise in taming the catboat by dividing the rig so that the boat not only would be easier and safer to handle than a catboat, but also would be less prone to twisting at the bow. The gaff sails set on tracks, instead of using masthoops, to facilitate standing rigging (including a rare use of jumper stays with gaff rig), that allowed relatively light masts. Francis shows oarlock sockets on the coaming in solid lines, but a propeller in its aperture in dotted lines. The boat has a large, open cockpit and a wide double berth forward in the cuddy. She is 20 feet, 11 inches long on deck; 19 feet, 6 inches on the waterline; with a beam of 7 feet, 6 inches, and a draft of 3 feet. Displacement is 3,600 pounds, with 1,550 pounds of lead outside ballast, for a ballast-displacement ratio of 43 percent. Sail area is 283 square feet. (© Mystic Seaport Museum, Daniel S. Gregory Ships Plans Library, SP38.157.3) ABOVE: The *Dancing Feather* was built to design No. 102 by her owner, Franklin P. Blaisdell of Lynn, Massachusetts, who sailed her out of Beverly Cove, just north of Marblehead, past Salem. On this day in the spring of 1958, she has been brought out to be inspected under sail by her designer. The specific purpose was to detect improvements that could be made to her rig, but none was discerned. The photograph was made by Bobby Russell, crewing for Francis in his launch, the *Freelance.* (The short main gaff happens to be aligned with the masthead, making the sail look jibheaded). (Mystic Seaport Museum, 1999-10-345)

	50		45		40	35	30	25	22'-6"	20	17'-6"	15	10	5		0
Height Under side Rail Cap	3-6-0		3-2-3		3-0-2	2-11-4	3-0-0	3-1-3		3-4-0		3-7-4	3-11-7	4-5-1	5-0-0	Under side of Rail Cap
" of Deck at sides	3-2-0		2-10-1		2-7-3	2-6-0	2-5-6	2-6-5		2-8-6		3-0-0	3-3-5	3-8-4	4-2-3	Height of Deck at sides.
" " Buttock 4					0-10-4	+0-2-0	0-8-2	1-0-0		-0-8-0		1-3-1				" " Buttock 4
" " " 3			2-2-6		+0-7-3	0-7-0	1-6-4	1-10-2		1-8-2		-0-7-0	2-1-4			" " " 3
" " " 2	3-2-1		1-7-1		+0-1-3	1-3-3	2-2-7	2-10-5		2-5-7		-1-7-2	+0-1-7	4-2-4		" " " 2
" " " 1	2-10-4		+1-2-4		-0-4-4	2-3-2	3-2-4	3-11-0		3-8-2		2-8-0	-1-0-6	1-6-5		" " " 1
" " Rabbet	2-8-4		+0-10-6		-1-9-7	5-3-0	4-11-2	4-7-4		4-3-0		3-9-0	-1-10-5	+0-1-2	5-3-4	" " Rabbet
" " Profile	2-8-4		+0-10-6		3-0-0 and 5-6-7	5-10-5	5-10-6	5-8-7		5-9-0		3-11-0	2-0-7	-0-2-2	5-0-0	" " Profile
½ width Under side Rail Cap	2-5-0		3-4-0		4-1-0	4-7-4	4-11-5	5-0-0		4-10-5		4-4-7	3-6-0	2-1-2	0-1-0	½ Width at Under side Rail Cap
" at Deck			3-3-1		4-1-2	4-8-2	5-0-0	5-0-0		4-10-2		4-4-1	3-9-7	1-11-2		" " " Deck
" " WL+3	1-6-0		3-3-4		4-1-1			5-0-0		4-10-4		4-4-1	3-3-0	1-7-0		" " " WL+3
" " WL+2			2-9-0		4-0-5	4-8-6	5-0-3	5-0-0		4-9-6		4-2-3	2-11-2	1-2-3		" " " WL+2
" " WL+1			0-4-3		3-5-6	4-6-1	4-11-1	4-11-2		4-7-5		3-10-7	2-5-4	0-8-0		" " " WL+1
" " LWL					1-10-0	3-10-0	4-6-6	4-8-3		4-4-2		3-5-0	1-10-3	0-1-5		" " " LWL
" " WL -1					0-5-6	2-4-3	3-8-0	4-0-1		3-8-0		2-7-0	1-0-4			" " " WL -1
" " WL -2					0-2-4	1-1-6	2-3-3	2-9-5		2-7-2		1-6-5	0-1-4			" " " WL -2
" " WL -3					0-1-4	0-7-3	1-3-0	1-8-0		1-5-4		0-8-7				" " " WL -3
" " WL -4					0-1-0	0-4-2	0-6-7	0-11-0	0-11-4	0-10-0	0-7-0					" " " WL -4
" " WL -5					0-0-5	0-3-3	0-6-6	0-7-2	0-7-3	0-6-2						" " " WL -5
" " Rabbet		0-2-4	0-2-4	0-2-4	0-2-6	0-3-1	0-6-0	0-8-6		0-8-6		0-2-6	0-2-4	0-2-4	0-2-4	" " " Rabbet
" " Profile		0-0-6	0-1-5	0-2-0	0-0-4	0-3-0	0-5-5	0-6-0	0-6-0	5" rad.		rounding	rounding	0-0-5	0-1-0	" " " Profile
Diagonal 1					0-2-6	0-11-4	1-7-4	1-11-7		1-10-0		1-2-4	0-0-7 ?			Diagonal 1
" 2					1-0-0	2-3-0	3-0-4	3-4-1		3-2-4		2-6-3	1-5-4	0-1-6		" 2
" 3			0-2-0		2-1-0	3-5-2	4-2-6	4-5-5		4-3-0		3-4-5	2-1-4	0-7-3		" 3
" 4			1-11-0		3-8-2	4-7-2	5-0-2	5-1-0		4-3-0		4-0-4	2-8-7	1-1-1		" 4

Heights / ½ Widths / Diags

½ width of Stem 2½"
Thickness of Planking 1¼"

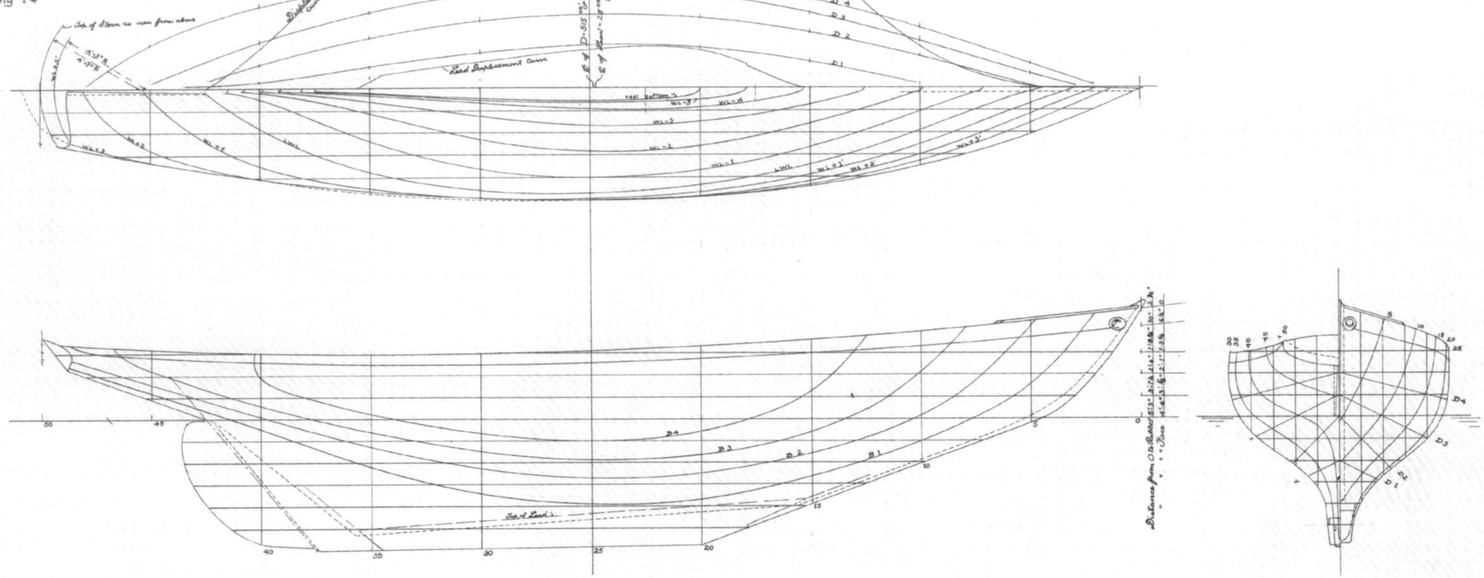

SCALE ½" = 1'

THE LINES OF A SAILING YACHT for NORMAN M. COUTY, ESQ. № 105.

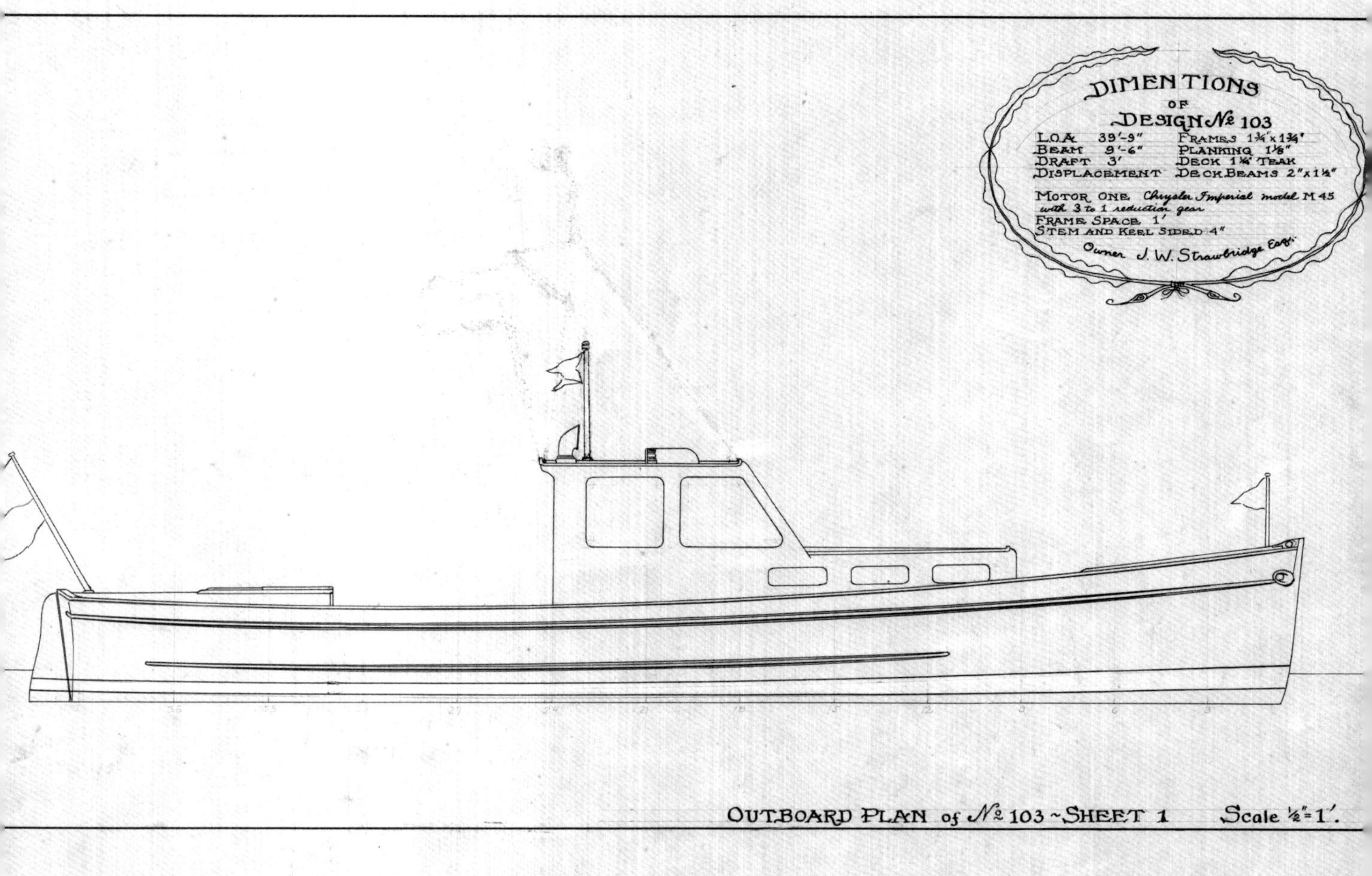

LEFT: **In November 1958, Francis inked this drawing of the lines and offsets of a 50-foot sloop for Norman M. Couty. The design, although given No. 105, proceeded no further. She is a narrower, shoaler version of the *Persephone,* the CCA yawl that Francis had drawn in 1936, and so would have been one of Francis's boats that could sail fast under a moderate rig. Waterline length is 37 feet, 6 inches; beam, 9 feet, 11 inches; and draft, 5 feet, 11 inches. Displacement is 32,960 pounds, with 17,500 pounds of lead outside ballast, for a ballast-displacement ratio of 53 percent.** (© Mystic Seaport Museum, Daniel S. Gregory Ships Plans Library, SP38.203.1) ABOVE: **The outboard profile of the *Melantho*, Francis's design No. 103, drawn in 1958 for Billy Strawbridge. She is a particularly clean-looking launch, with her nicely proportioned wheelhouse and unobtrusive aft cabin. Francis's dyslexia is evident in his misspelling of "Dimensions" and his juxtaposition of Billy's initials, but his artistry easily overpowers his spelling errors.** (© Mystic Seaport Museum, Daniel S. Gregory Ships Plans Library, SP38.120.13)

	Station	39'-9"	36'	33'	30'	27'	24'	21'	18'	15'	12'	9'	6'	3	0
Heights	Rail under side	3-3-0	3-0-7	3-0-0	2-11-6	3-0-1	3-0-5	3-1-6	3-3-3	3-5-4	3-8-1	3-11-2	4-2-7	4-7-2	5-0-0
	Deck at side	2-9-7	2-7-7	2-6-7	2-6-3	2-6-3	2-6-7	2-7-6	2-9-1	2-11-0	3-1-2	3-3-5	3-6-5	3-9-5	4-1-2
	Buttock 3'	1-5-0	0-4-0	-0-2-4	-0-6-2	-0-8-3	-0-9-5	-0-8-2	-0-7-7	-0-5-2	0-1-3	1-10-2	4-0-5		
	" 2'	0-10-3	-0-0-5	-0-7-0	-0-10-7	-1-1-5	-1-2-5	-1-2-5	-1-2-2	-1-1-1	-0-10-2	-0-3-5	1-7-1	4-7-2	
	" 1'	0-4-6	-0-5-3	-1-0-1	-1-4-3	-1-6-7	-1-7-6	-1-7-6	-1-7-3	-1-6-4	-0-5-3	-1-3-0	-0-8-5	1-11-2	
	Rabbet	-0-0-4	-1-4-0	-2-3-7	-2-2-7	-2-1-7	-2-1-0	-2-0-0	-1-10-7	-1-10-0	-1-9-0	-1-8-0	-1-6-5	-1-1-1	
	Keel bottom	-0-2-0 (-3-0-0)						Straight				-2-0-0	-1-9-0	-1-5-4	
½ widths	Rail at side	3-6-0	4-1-7	4-5-6	4-8-0	4-9-0	4-9-0	4-8-5	4-7-5	4-6-1	4-3-1	3-9-7	3-1-4	2-0-0	0-1-2
	Deck	3-5-6	4-1-5	4-5-4	4-7-6	4-8-6	4-8-6	4-8-2	4-7-0	4-4-5	4-0-4	3-6-5	2-8-3	1-7-0	
	W.L. 3'							4-8-3	4-7-0	4-4-6	4-0-1	3-4-6	2-5-7	1-3-7	
	W.L. 27"	3-5-0	4-1-2	4-5-2	4-7-4	4-8-4	4-8-4	4-7-6	4-5-7	4-2-7	3-8-5	3-1-3	2-2-3	1-1-0	
	W.L. 18	3-0-3	3-11-4	4-4-2	4-6-5	4-7-6	4-7-6	4-6-5	4-4-2	4-0-5	3-7-2	2-10-6	1-11-4	0-10-5	
	W.L. 9"	1-9-4	3-7-0	4-1-5	4-4-5	4-5-4	4-5-4	4-4-2	4-1-5	3-9-5	3-4-3	2-7-4	1-8-5	0-8-6	
	L.W.L.	0-3-4	2-2-0	3-4-5	3-10-3	4-0-0	4-0-0	3-11-3	3-9-0	3-4-7	2-11-0	2-2-7	1-5-1	0-6-5	
	W.L. -9"		0-6-5	1-7-3	2-6-0	2-11-2	3-1-2	3-1-2	2-11-0	2-7-7	2-2-5	1-8-0	0-11-7	0-3-7	
	W.L. -18"		0-2-4	0-5-4	0-9-4	1-1-4	1-3-4	1-4-6	1-3-6	1-1-1	0-10-6	0-6-6	0-2-7		
	Rabbet	0-2-0	0-2-6	0-2-0	0-2-0	0-2-0	0-2-0	0-2-0	0-2-0	0-2-0	0-2-0	0-2-0	0-2-0	0-2-0	
	Keel	0-1-6	0-1-4	0-2-0	0-2-0	0-2-0	0-2-0	0-2-0	0-2-0	0-2-0	0-2-0	0-2-0	0-1-3	0-0-6	
	Diagonal #1	3-9-4	4-5-6	4-10-5	5-1-1	5-2-3	5-2-3	5-0-7	4-10-4	4-7-1	4-1-7	3-5-5	2-7-3	1-6-1	
	" #2	3-2-1	4-1-5	4-7-5	4-11-0	5-0-2	5-0-2	4-11-2	4-9-3	4-5-6	4-0-6	3-4-5	2-5-4	1-4-0	
	" #3	1-6-1	2-4-4	2-11-0	3-3-0	3-5-4	3-6-5	3-7-0	3-5-7	3-4-4	3-1-5	2-8-6	2-0-5	1-0-4	
	" #4	0-2-5	0-11-2	1-4-6	1-8-1	1-10-3	1-10-7	1-11-3	1-11-1	1-10-2	1-9-1	1-7-1	1-3-2	0-8-1	

Offsets in feet, inches and eights of inches from centerline and above and below L.W.L.

½ Siding of Keel and Stem 2"
Frame space 12"
Planking thickness 1⅛"
Frames 1¾" x 1¾"
Crown of main deck ⅜" to 1' or 3¾" in 10'
Main deck 1¼ thick
Crown of after deck ¾" to 1' or 7½" in 10'
After deck ⅞" thick

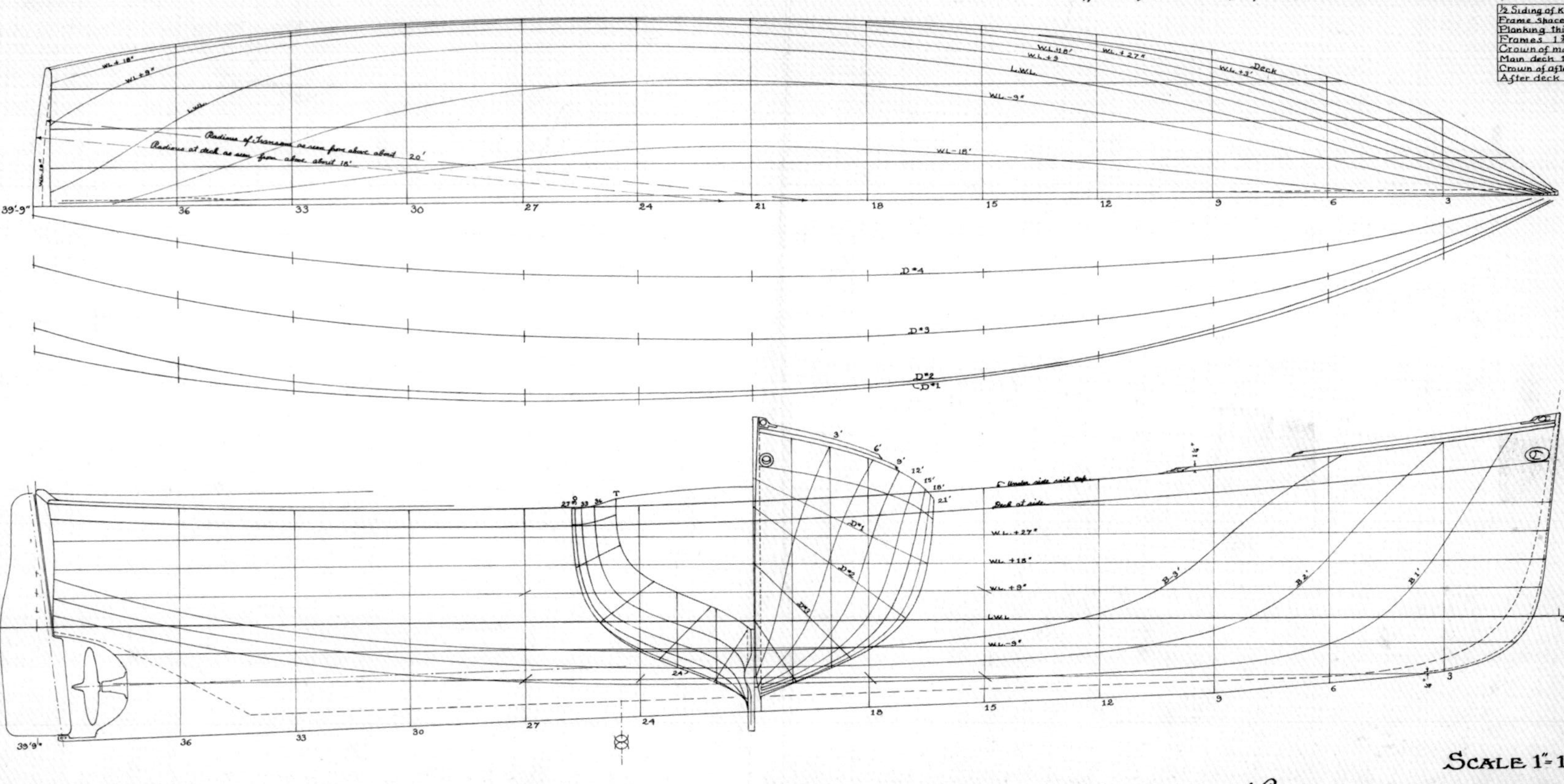

Distance from 0 to Stem band face	1-2-6	0-8-0	0-5-4	0-4-2	0-3-2	0-2-2	0-1-0	0-0-0
" " 0 " Wood face	1-4-4	0-9-3	0-6-2	0-4-6	0-3-5	0-2-4	0-1-1½	0-0-2
" " 0 " Rabbet line	2-2-6	1-5-0	1-0-0	0-8-6	0-6-6	0-5-2	0-3-2	0-1-5
Width of Stem band face	0-0-2	0-0-2	0-0-2+	0-0-3	0-0-4	0-0-5	0-1-0	0-1-3

SCALE 1" = 1'.

THE LINES OF DESIGN No. 103 ~ SHEET 2

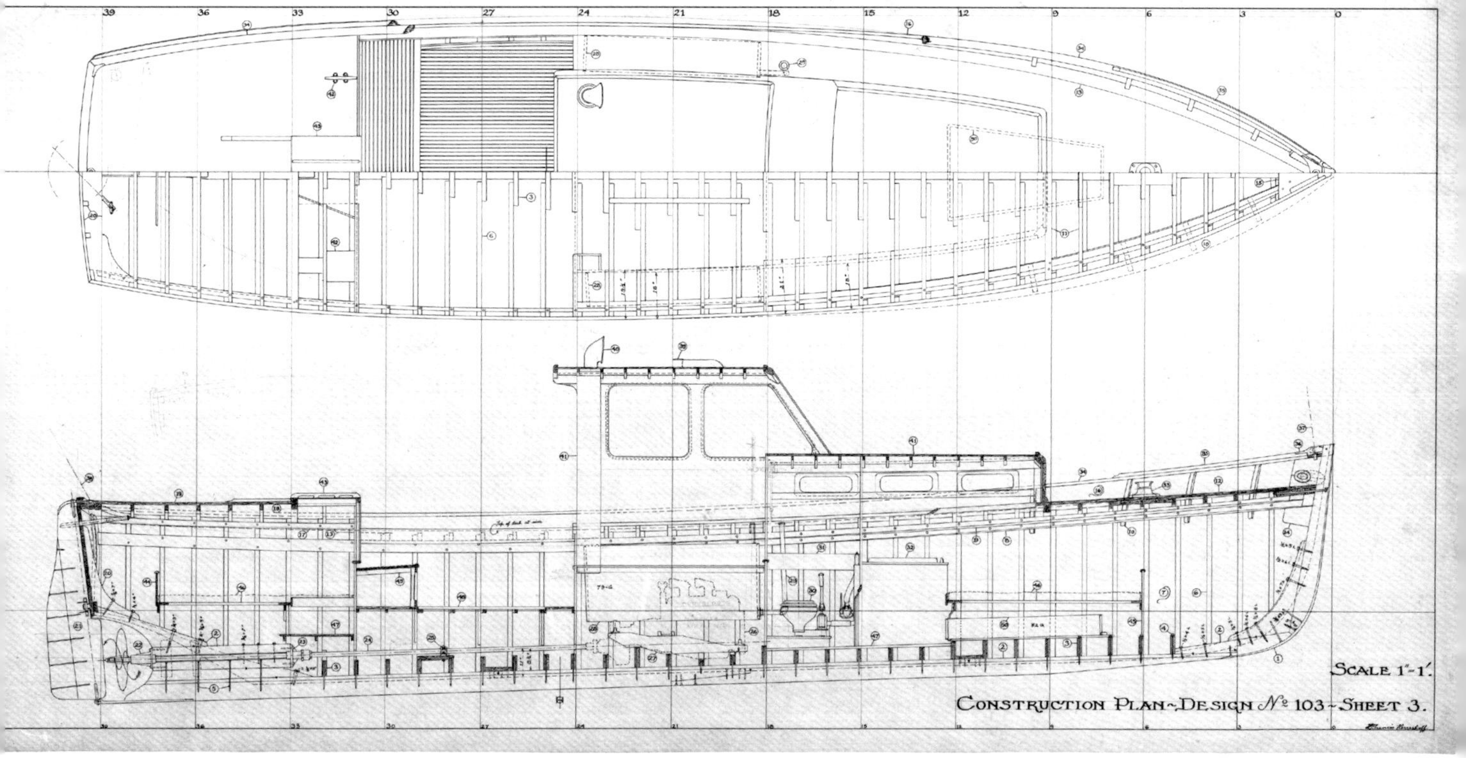

have had more use and more pleasure out of her than any boat I have ever had." That would include his previous launch, a 39-footer that Billy had had designed by Sparkman and Stephens and built by Henry B. Nevins at City Island in 1940. This boat, the *Escort*, had no deck shelter and was a much faster boat; powered with two big Gray Marine engines, and with small, exposed propellers and rudders, she could make 28½ miles per hour. Francis's irritation at Billy's contributions to the design of the *Melantho*—"bad changes in arrangements"—may have been exacerbated by

LEFT: **The *Melantho*'s lines and offsets. She has enough keel to reduce rolling, enough flare forward to reduce spray on deck, and enough radius to the wineglass transom to reduce clumsiness at the stern. Her rudder is slightly balanced, with a small area forward of its axis; she was fitted with Francis's contra-propeller. She had a mysterious steering problem: at speed (15 knots maximum, 12.5 knots cruising), her bow pulled to the left, requiring right rudder. Removal of the contra-propeller didn't help. The mystery deepens, because Francis indicated on his construction drawing a left-turning propeller, which would tend to walk her stern to the left, not her bow. Her length on deck is 39 feet, 9 inches; beam, 9 feet, 6 inches; and draft, 3 feet. Billy Strawbridge reported that it took a whopping 5,000 pounds of lead inside ballast to bring her down to her designed waterline.** (© Mystic Seaport Museum, Daniel S. Gregory Ships Plans Library, SP38.120.1) ABOVE: **The construction plan for the *Melantho*. There is a small sleeping cabin in the stern and a deep cockpit just abaft the wheelhouse. The engine shown is a Chrysler Imperial M 45. Planking thickness is 1⅛ inches, with frames 1¾ inches square on 12-inch centers.** (© Mystic Seaport Museum, Daniel S. Gregory Ships Plans Library, SP38.120.15)

the knowledge that Billy had gone to the abhorred company of Olin Stephens for the *Escort*. And Billy kept on trying to find the perfect launch. After Francis's death, he would return to Stephens for help in creating the *Truant,* a boat quite like the *Piquant*, except for a square stern.[12]

As for the *Melantho*, she ended up in the collection of the Herreshoff Marine Museum in Bristol, but, being in bad shape and not having been designed by N. G. Herreshoff, she was broken up as of September 1, 2008.[13]

As early as 1953, Francis contemplated making a complete How-To-Build design for *The Rudder* based on his drawings of the *Tranquillo* in *The Compleat Cruiser.* He had worked out the shallow-draft boat so carefully that only a few minor modifications were necessary when, in 1958, he got around to making full-size drawings for what would be his design No. 104. Francis completed his usual, detailed construction plan and wrote his usual detailed construction instructions, but, somehow, *The Rudder,* drifting in baffling airs, failed to publish his material for this design.[14]

The impetus for No. 104 came from Robert P. Gibbs, the Cataumet oil distributor who had been happily sailing his Meadow Lark, the *Loon,* on Buzzards Bay. Gibbs was thinking of moving to Florida's west coast and wanted a boat similar to the Meadow Lark, but big enough to take out parties. Gibbs was in no hurry, and there was no publishing schedule from *The Rudder*. Despite having a fine prototype in the *Tranquillo,* Francis took three years to complete the fourteen detailed drawings he made for No. 104.[15]

Francis was really happy with this design. He wrote: "With a boat of this draft you can get away from the obnoxious crowd that is swarming on the water most everywhere." If his crusade to reform yachting was failing, he would find a way for like-minded sailors to escape. He lamented, "if I could have afforded her when I was younger, I would have had a boat to this design." Well, probably not. In fact, Francis was loath to leave his Castle, with its lathes, long drawing board, hearth, fascinating collections, cars, dogs, roof-lookout, and stove-heated, cozy downstairs room. He really preferred to do his cruising in his imagination. Any time he wanted, he could go up to his hanging file of plans on the third floor, pull out a drawing of an exquisite yacht, select his bit of coastline and just the breeze and seaway that he wanted, and have himself a lovely sail.[16]

Gibbs named his large "Shallow Draft Cruising Yacht" the *Golden Ball*, and he hoisted a golden ball to the masthead as his owner-on-board signal. She was built by Barlow's Boat Yard at Pocasset, next to Cataumet near the head of Buzzards Bay. Bucky Barlow launched her in 1962.[17]

Francis wrote of the *Golden Ball*: "A shallow boat such as this should never be taken to sea except by an experienced crew, but don't let that

RIGHT, INSIDE FOLDOUT: **The lines and offsets of the *Golden Ball*. Francis claimed that on the bigger boat a round bottom would be cheaper to build than the sharper chine of the Meadow Lark. Her knuckle bow is less pronounced in profile than most of Francis's, and there is only a faint suggestion of hollow in the bow waterline. The large, flat, well-raked transom only faintly suggests a wineglass. Late in his career, L. Francis Herreshoff is making his trademark shapes extremely subtle. He was well pleased with the result. The *Golden Ball* is 46 feet, 6 inches long on deck; with a waterline length of 40 feet, 9 inches; a beam of 11 feet; and a draft of 2 feet. Displacement is 21,120 pounds, with 4,200 pounds of outside ballast, and 4,920 pounds of inside ballast, for a ballast-displacement ratio of 43 percent.** (© Mystic Seaport Museum, Daniel S. Gregory Ships Plans Library, SP38.165.4)

	Transom	44	40	36	32	28	24	20	16	12	8	4	
Deck at Side	3-2-4	3-1-0	2-10-4	2-9-2	2-8-7	2-9-4	2-11-1	3-1-6	3-5-0	3-8-4	4-1-1	4-6-2	Height of Deck at Side
Heights B-5				1-1-1	0-2-4	0-0-0	0-1-0	0-8-6	2-6-0				" " Buttock 5
Heights B-4		1-10-4	0-7-4	-0-2-1	-0-8-2	0-11-0	0-10-7	0-8-2	0-1-0	+1-6-6	4-5-6		" " " 4
Heights B-3	1-2-6	0-10-7	0-0-0	-0-8-1	-1-1-3	1-4-1	1-4-3	1-2-7	0-11-0	-0-1-4	+2-1-4		" " " 3
Heights B-2	0-8-4	0-5-3	-0-5-4	1-0-3	1-4-6	1-7-1	1-7-2	1-6-4	1-4-0	0-10-4	+0-4-5	3-8-0	" " " 2
Heights B-1	0-4-0	0-1-0	-0-10-0	-1-3-7	1-7-4	1-9-0	1-9-1	1-8-7	1-7-5	1-4-2	0-7-4	+1-5-4	" " " 1
Heights Rabbet	0-0-0	0-2-4	1-0-4	1-6-0	1-8-5	1-9-4	1-9-4	1-9-4	1-9-1	1-7-0	1-1-0	+0-2-2	" " Rabbet
Heights Keel Bottom		2-0-0	2-0-0	2-0-0	2-0-0	2-0-0	2-0-0	2-0-0	2-0-0	1-9-0	1-3-0	0-0-0	" " Keel Bottom
½ Width at Deck	3-11-0	4-3-0	4-9-4	5-2-0	5-4-5	5-6-0	5-6-0	5-4-6	5-1-7	4-8-1	3-9-7	2-5-0	½ Width at Deck
" " W.L.+4'											3-9-4	2-1-4	" " " W.L.+4
" " W.L.+3'									5-1-0	4-5-5	3-4-4	1-8-4	" " " W.L.+3
" " W.L.+2'	3-8-5	4-0-3	4-8-6	5-2-1	5-5-1	5-6-2	5-5-4	5-3-3	4-8-6	4-2-1	2-11-2	1-3-3	" " " W.L.+2
" " W.L.+1'	2-7-0	3-1-3	4-3-3	4-11-4	5-3-6	5-5-0	5-3-7	5-0-7	4-7-2	3-9-2	2-5-1	0-9-0	" " " W.L.+1
" " L.W.L.	0-2-0	0-9-4	3-0-0	4-2-2	4-9-6	5-0-0	4-11-3	4-8-0	4-1-2	3-1-3	1-8-0	0-0-7	" " " L.W.L.
" " W.L.-1'			0-5-0	2-0-5	3-3-1	3-9-4	3-10-0	3-6-2	2-10-2	1-9-3	0-4-6		" " " W.L.-1
" " Rabbet	0-2-0	0-2-1	0-2-7	0-4-1	0-5-5	0-7-0	0-7-6	0-7-3	0-6-0	0-4-2	0-2-5	0-2-2	" " " Rabbet
" " D-1		0-3-4	1-2-5	1-9-1	2-1-4	2-3-6	2-4-1	2-3-4	2-1-4	1-9-2	1-1-2		" " " Diagonal 1
" " D-2	1-3-4	1-7-4	2-9-2	3-6-4	4-0-7	4-4-0	4-4-3	4-2-1	3-9-2	3-0-5	1-11-6	0-7-4	" " " " 2
" " D-3	3-1-2	3-5-2	4-4-4	5-0-0	5-4-5	5-5-4	5-4-7	5-1-7	4-8-3	3-10-7	2-8-4	1-2-0	" " " " 3

Offsets in feet, inches, and eights of inches to the outside of planking.
Average thickness of planking 1½" garboard thicker, topsides thinner.
See details of Stem Stern Etc Sheet #3
Crown of main deck 4½" in 12'

Half width of the face of Stem at W.L. 5'-3" 1½"
" 5 1⅜"
" 4 1⅛"
" 3 1"
" 2 ⅞+"
" 1 ⅞"
" L.W.L. ⅞"

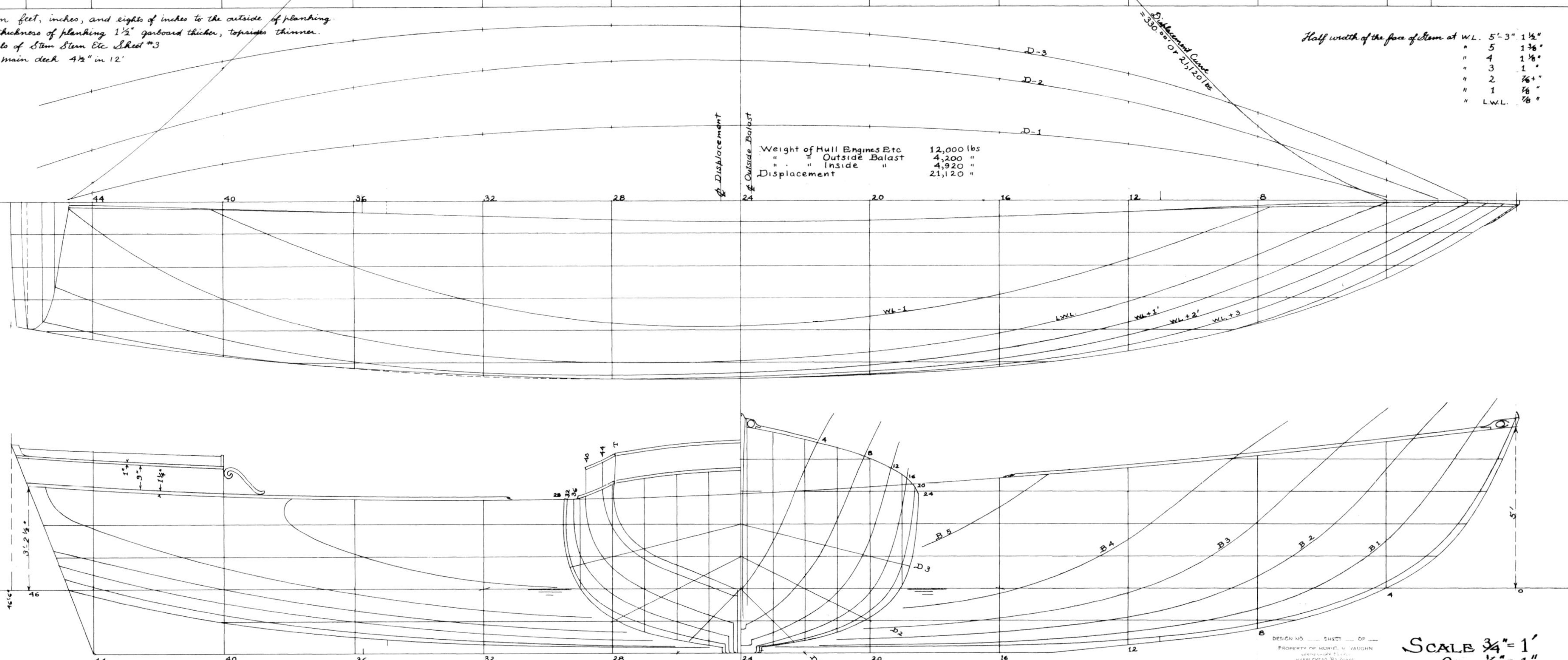

Scale ¾" = 1'
Or 1/16" = 1".

The Lines of No 104 ~ Sheet 2.

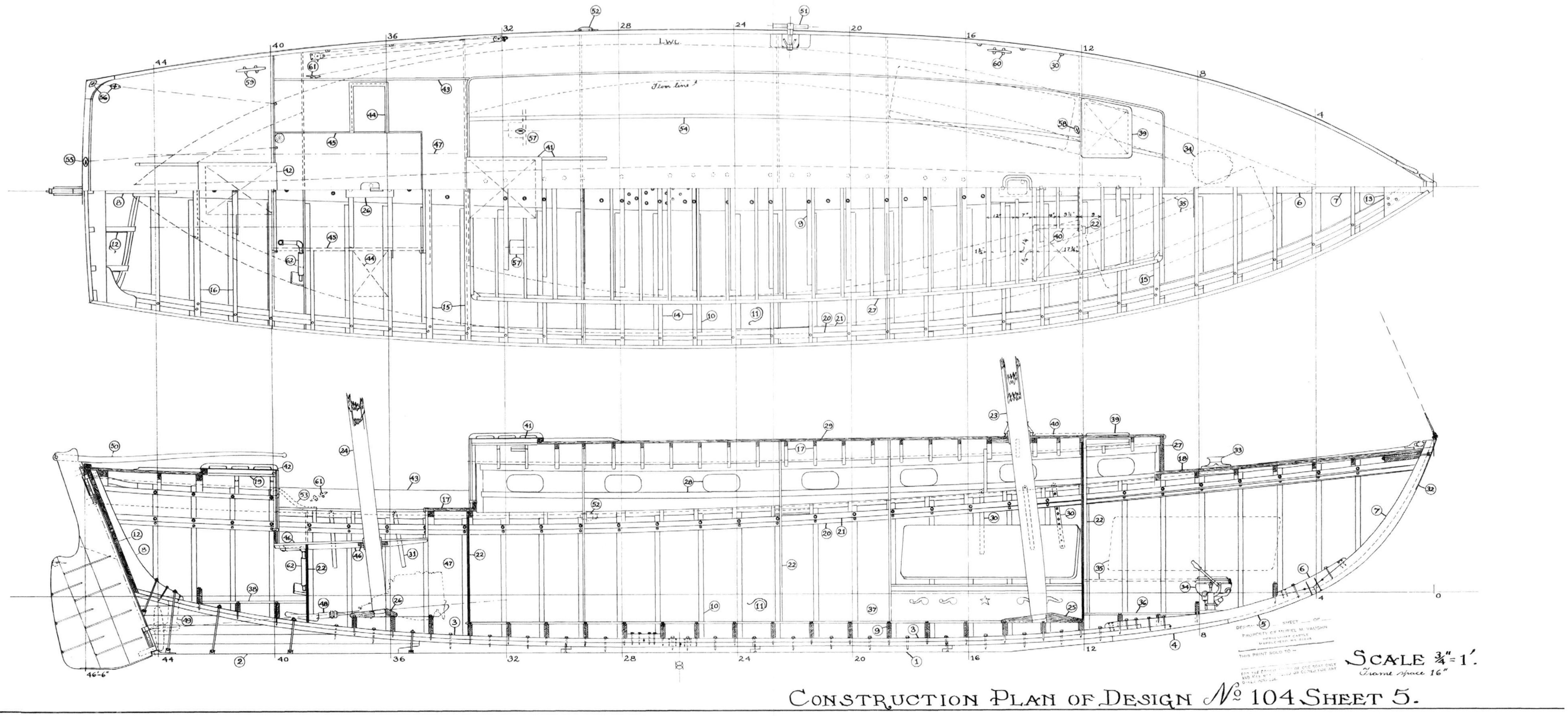

The *Golden Ball*'s construction plan. With leeboards raised in shallow water, the rudder might be the first thing to hit bottom, so Francis designed it to lift on its pintles to the depth of the hull if that happened. She was to have two 25-horsepower motors under the cockpit; there was a 50-gallon tank outboard of each, the port one for fuel, the starboard for water. In the bow, she has a separate fo'c's'le with its own hatch in the forward port corner of the cabin house and its own toilet. It sleeps one or two, depending on one's willingness to sleep in the pipe berth that folds down right on top of the toilet. Francis arranged the long cabin space in a conventional manner, with double stateroom forward; head compartment; saloon; and galley. Headroom throughout this part of the boat is 6 feet. Under the raised stern deck is another two-berth cabin, with sitting headroom. So, the *Golden Ball* could sleep seven or eight, and Francis believed that she had the most accommodations for cost of any boat he designed. He drew the wood keel in two layers and said the bent frames could also be made in two layers if desired; the bow frames, being straighter, would be sawn. Frames were to be 2 inches square on 16-inch centers. Floor timbers were 1½ inches thick by from 4 inches to 8½ inches deep. The clamp was to be 1½ inches by 4 inches; the shelf, 2¼ inches square. Planking was to average 1½ inches thick, from 1¾-inch garboards to 1¼-inch sheer strakes. This variation was to gain stability. (© Mystic Seaport Museum, Daniel S. Gregory Ships Plans Library, SP38.165.7)

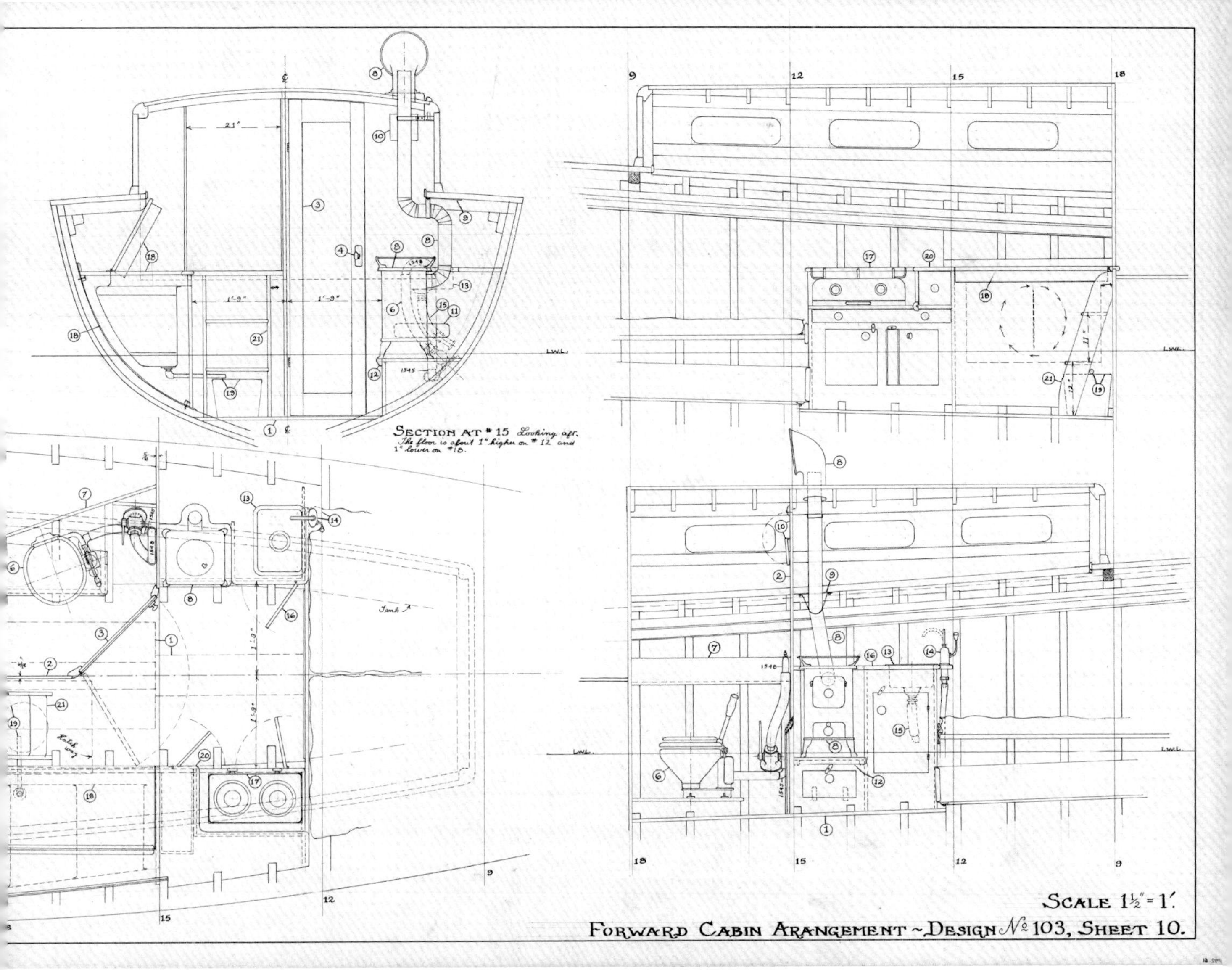

The *Melantho*'s forward cabin has full-width berths forward, with the galley and head compartment aft. The galley has a heating stove to port and a cooking stove to starboard. There is a big icebox next to the companionway (draining into a bucket rather than the bilge). All this was too much complexity for Francis. He wrote to Boris Lauer-Leonardi: "I should not like to have the drawings of Mr. Strawbridge's launch published for two good reasons. One reason is that she is almost all designed up to his ideas, most of which I do not approve; and in the second place the last part of the time he made some bad changes in arrangements and I should not like to have my name associated with the design." (© Mystic Seaport Museum, Daniel S. Gregory Ships Plans Library, SP38.120.12)

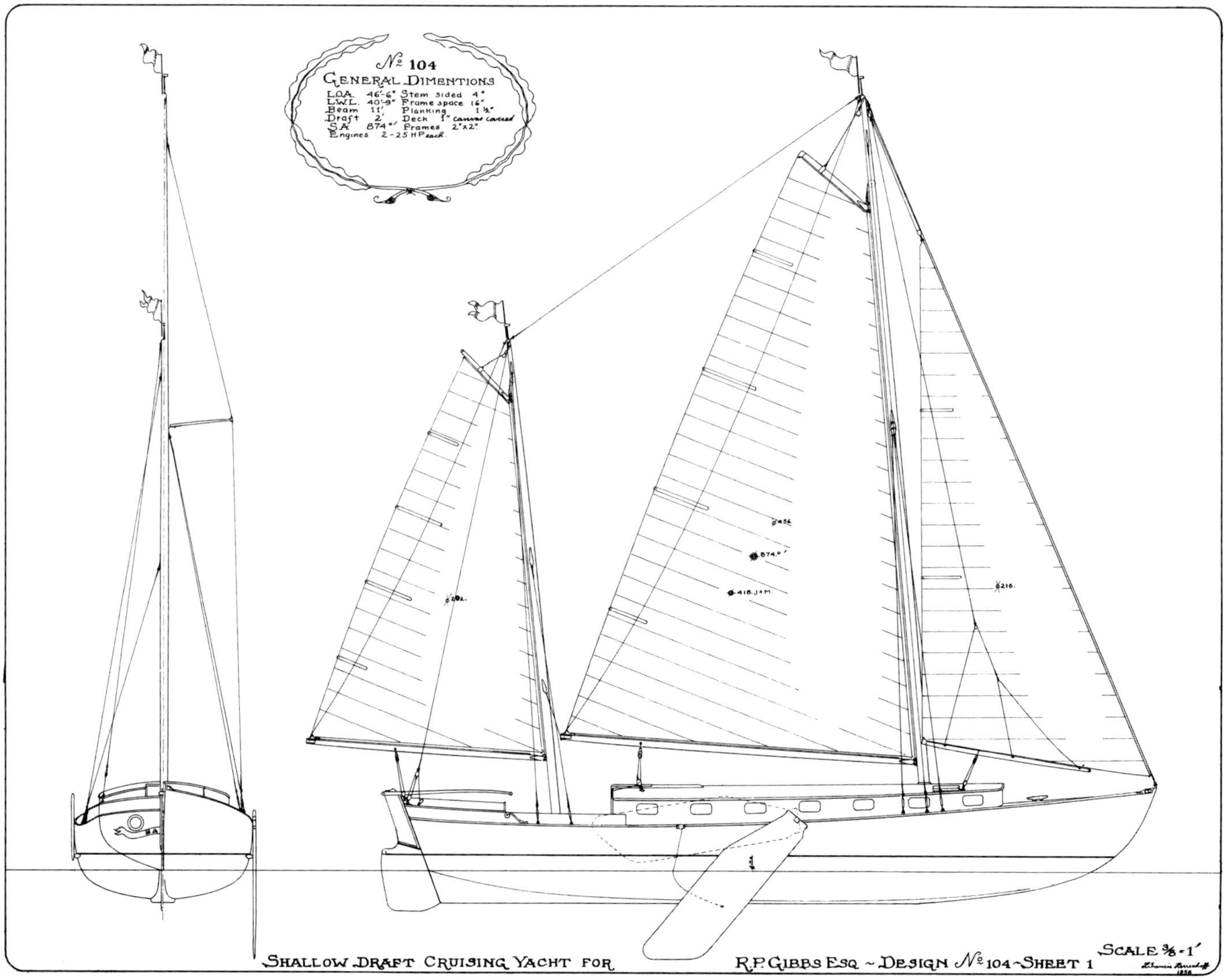

ABOVE: **Francis's design No. 104 of 1958 was for this "Shallow Draft Cruising Yacht" for Robert P. Gibbs, who loved his Meadow Lark, the *Loon,* and wanted a similar, but bigger, boat to take out parties. He would name the new boat the *Golden Ball.* Note that the partial jib club is long enough to fetch up against the mast when tacking; this was intentional; the sail would help the bow round until the breeze on the new tack lifted the club enough to release it. Francis recommended padding the after end of the club with rubber. Note also the running backstays on the mizzen for use reaching or running in a strong breeze. Sail area is 874 square feet, with 456 in the mainsail, 202 in the mizzen, and 216 in the jib. Finally, note that she has stern ports lighting the cabin under the after deck.** (© Mystic Seaport Museum, Daniel S. Gregory Ships Plans Library, SP38.165.1) RIGHT: **As on the Meadow Lark, Francis attached the *Golden Ball*'s leeboards so that they could not only be raised and lowered, but also could swing out away from the side of the boat. When a boat rolls toward a leeboard that is fixed to the side of the boat, the board acts like a canoe-paddler making a J-stroke, dragging the boat to leeward. This was avoided by letting the leeboard swing out. The arrangement also reduced the strain on the board when the boat rolled toward it; when the boat rolled back away from the board, it didn't bang, but came back gently.** (© Mystic Seaport Museum, Daniel S. Gregory Ships Plans Library, SP38.165.8)

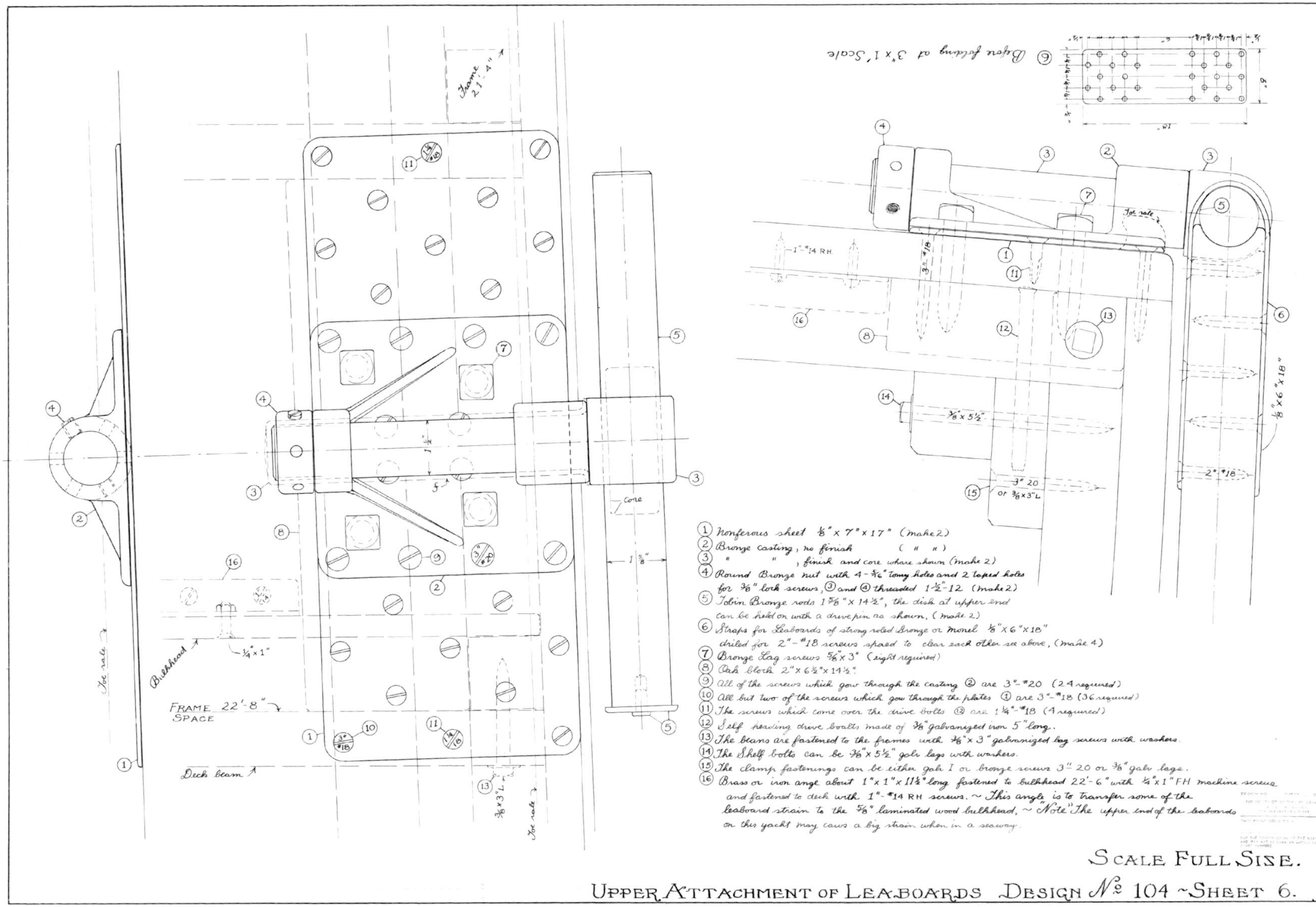

6 Before folding at 3" x 1' Scale
Frame 21'-4"
Frame 22'-8" Space
Bulkhead
Deck beam
Ice rale
1/4" x 1"
1"-#14 RH
3"-#18
3/8" x 5 1/2"
3" 20 or 3/8 x 3"L
2"-#18
1/8" x 6" x 18"
3/8 x 3"L
core
1 5/8"
1) Nonferous sheet 1/8" x 7" x 17" (make 2)
2) Bronze casting, no finish (" ")
3) " " , finish and core where shown (make 2)
4) Round Bronze nut with 4-5/16" tomy holes and 2 taped holes for 3/8" lock screws, 3 and 4 threaded 1 1/2"-12 (make 2)
5) Tobin Bronze rods 1 5/8" x 14 1/2", the disk at upper end can be held on with a drive pin as shown, (make 2)
6) Straps for Leaboards of strong roled Bronze or Monel 1/8" x 6" x 18" driled for 2"-#18 screws spaced to clear each other see above, (make 4)
7) Bronze Lag screws 5/8" x 3" (eight required)
8) Oak block 2" x 6 1/2" x 14 1/2".
9) All of the screws which gow through the casting 2 are 3"-#20 (24 requred)
10) All but two of the screws which gow through the plates 1 are 3"-#18 (36 requred)
11) The screws which come over the drive bolts 12 are 1 1/4"-#18 (4 requred)
12) Self heading drive boalts made of 3/8" galvanized iron 5" long.
13) The beans are fastened to the frames with 3/8" x 3" galvanized lag screws with washers.
14) The Shelf bolts can be 3/8" x 5 1/2" galv lags with washers.
15) The clamp fastenings can be either galv I or bronze screws 3" 20 or 3/8" galv lags.
16) Brass or iron angle about 1" x 1" x 11 1/2" long fastened to bulkhead 22'-6" with 1/4" x 1" FH machine screws and fastened to deck with 1"-#14 RH screws. ~ This angle is to transfer some of the leaboard strain to the 5/8" laminated wood bulkhead, ~ "Note" The upper end of the leaboards on this yacht may caus a big strain when in a seaway.
Scale Full Sise.
Upper Attachment of Leaboards Design No. 104 ~ Sheet 6.

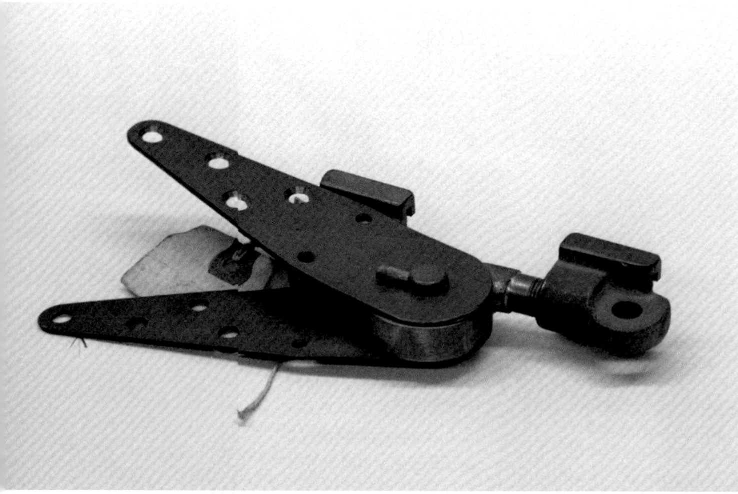

statement scare you. *Golden Ball* is as self-righting as Captain Slocum's *Spray* or Captain Voss's *Tilicum*." Gibbs was confident of his own experience, so he took his shallow boat offshore, even though it was winter. On November 29, he set off in the *Golden Ball* for his new home port of Port Richey, up the Gulf Coast from St. Petersburg. He arrived on January 4, 1963, after a cold trip that was not entirely free of difficulty. The first leg was a fast, 32-hour passage from Pocasset outside Block Island and Long Island to Atlantic City, New Jersey. Heading south on the Intracoastal Waterway, the port engine quit, costing a four-day wait for parts at Ocean City. A fixed low bridge forced him outside again, heading for Norfolk, but then "a full gale with rain and sleet" caused him to seek shelter at Cape May. After the storm, the *Golden Ball* made another fast, 29-hour run outside to Norfolk. Gibbs's only comment to Francis about taking his shoal-draft boat offshore in winter was: "The boat sails well, carries her sail beautifully, and does not leak." His only other problem with the boat was that the fastenings on the mizzen mast-track kept working loose, so that, on one occasion, he couldn't lower the sail until a navy crane at Norfolk gave him a lift aloft.[18]

At Norfolk, Gibbs's crew had to leave, and he proceeded through the Dismal Swamp Canal, across Albemarle Sound, and on to Morehead City single-handed. "During this passage," Gibbs reported to Francis: "The boat got loaded with ice. The spray froze from the stem to the stern about 4 inches thick on the house and flush out to the rail on each side. I spent the next day chopping ice." Gibbs continued south inside to Jacksonville, where a friend joined him for an outside passage to Fort Pierce. Then it was back inside and across the Okeechobee Waterway, which required taking the mainmast out at Stuart. He arrived at Port Richey after "not a very fast passage but a very cold one. After this voyage I can fully appreciate the warm Florida sunshine. I think the *Golden Ball* will be ideal in these waters."[19]

Gibbs's prediction proved true. His dock was only a half hour's run from the Gulf, and he had Tampa Bay at hand also. He took plenty of people out sailing, handling the boat by himself. "Most of my customers have never sailed before," he wrote to Francis. "Not all enjoy it but for the most part they are enthusiastic." One passenger, John Hart Knox, a seasoned sailor from Clearwater, was

ABOVE: **One of the gooseneck fittings that Francis made for a Golden Ball when he was in his seventies. Although his hands were too shaky for drafting, he could still do fine work in his machine shop on the top floor of The Castle.** (Mystic Seaport Museum, 1990.37.349) RIGHT: **Details of the *Golden Ball*'s cabin. The head compartment can be used the full width of the vessel, or as a separate washroom to starboard and toilet room to port. Campstools would be needed to sit at the starboard side of the cabin table. The galley has a cooking stove to port and a Concordia heating stove to starboard. There are two ice boxes, one either side of the companionway ladder. In all, Francis made fourteen drawings showing how to build the *Golden Ball*; he sold the set for $200.** (© Mystic Seaport Museum, Daniel S. Gregory Ships Plans Library, SP38.165.12

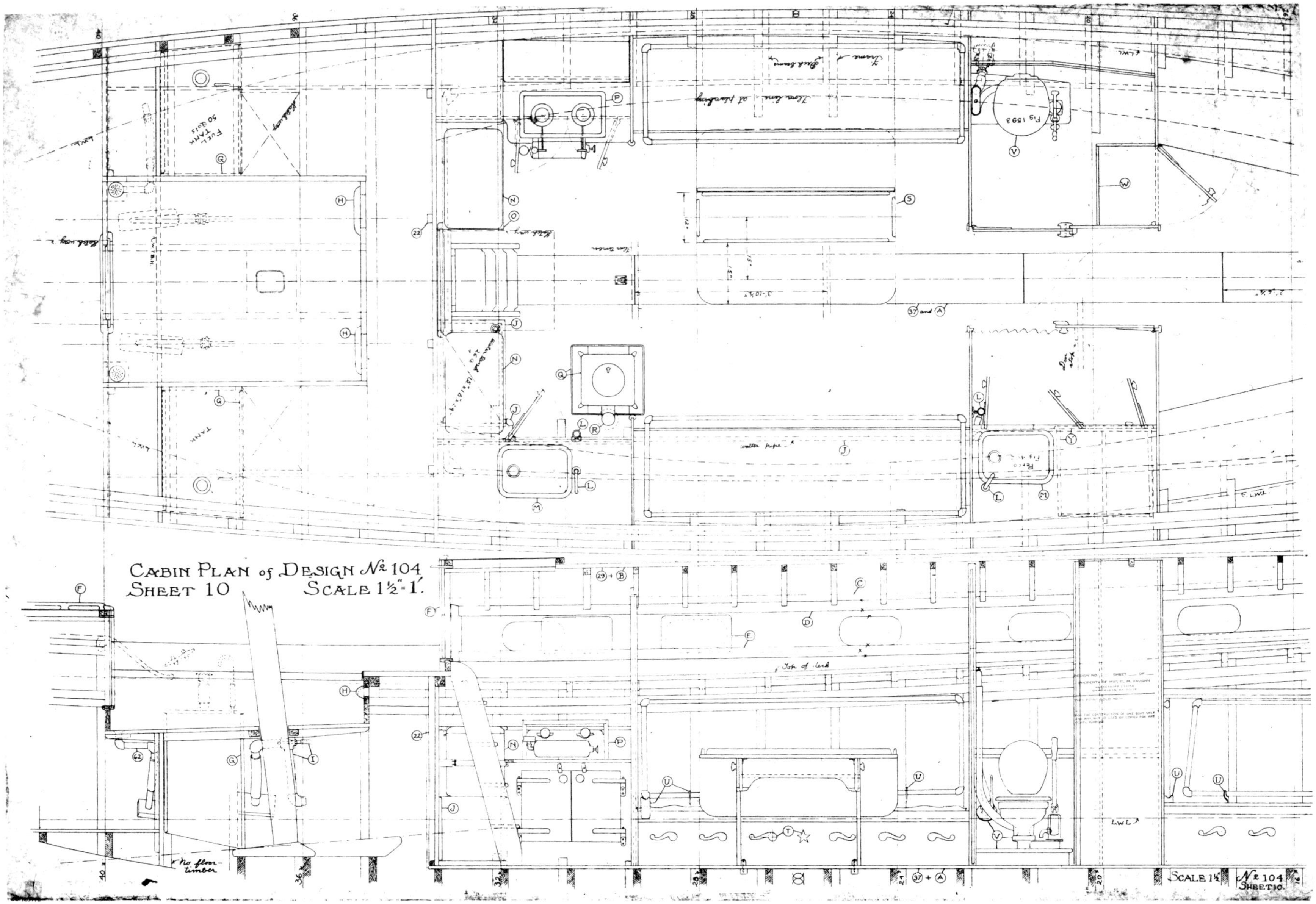

CABIN PLAN of DESIGN № 104
SHEET 10
SCALE 1½" = 1'
FUEL TANK 50 Gals
TANK
Fig 1593
water pipe
Top of deck
No floor timber
LWL
SCALE 1½"
№ 104
SHEET 10.

favorably impressed by Gibbs's operation with the *Golden Ball.* Despite familiarity with shoal-draft, centerboard boats—or perhaps because of that familiarity—he had misgivings about venturing out into the Gulf on a windy day in this strange leeboard craft. But, he wrote, "our sail not only eased my mind, it generated a genuine admiration for her excellent balance on the wind and her dryness despite a short, steep chop." And he marveled at Gibbs's ability to leave the tiller and steer the boat simply by shifting his weight about, on deck or even below![20]

Gibbs occasionally used the *Golden Ball* as a towboat, and he had a serious accident. As he reported to Francis: "While towing a floating dock from Port Richey to St. Petersburg Beach a draw bridge attended by an incompetent operator failed to open and the *Ball* struck the abutment breaking the stem band, and then went through the [closed] draw sideways with a fair current. The rig was subjected to tremendous strain and was not supported by the head stay, yet sustained very little damage. The insurance surveyor could not believe that there was not any hull damage. The chain plates did not move and their deck seal was not broken."[21]

Gibbs claimed "some rather good passages" in the *Golden Ball.* He made two runs at an average speed of 6.2 knots, one of 180 miles from Pass-a-Grille to Key West, and one of 160 miles from the Dry Tortugas to Sarasota. And on a 32-mile run from Venice to Pass-a-Grille, he averaged a solid 8 knots. This latter is only 1.25 times the square root of the *Ball's* waterline length. Surely this boat could be driven at 9½ knots for a watch under ideal conditions. Francis thought she would be very fast off the wind in a breeze. Bobby Gibbs had the reputation of being a big sail-carrier in the *Loon* on Buzzards Bay; perhaps he was learning caution as he experienced the vagaries of weather in the Gulf of Mexico. In any event, Gibbs sailed his *Golden Ball* for fun and profit for many years.[22]

A later owner, Michael Rew, who bought the *Golden Ball* in 1992 after she had been laid up for nearly a decade, corroborated both her balance and her speed. He wrote of her: "*Golden Ball* is a delight to sail. She self tends from a broad reach all the way to hard on the wind. I've sailed her full sail in 20 knots and she really moves, what a thrill." Rew lived on board and sailed in the Keys and Florida Bay, "for which the boat is perfectly suited."[23]

By 2003, the *Golden Ball* needed repairs. Maynard Bray wrote her up on his "Save a Classic"

Bobby Gibbs takes a party out into the Gulf of Mexico in the *Golden Ball.* (Clyde Eagleton photo, Mystic Seaport Museum, 1990.37.129)

page in *WoodenBoat.* Jaime Canfield, a real estate man in Bradenton, Florida, came to the rescue and arranged for much restoration, in which he participated himself. There was a plan for the boat to be used as a schoolship, but the associated school closed. Canfield did get to sail her some. He experienced the same mast-track problem that had bothered Gibbs, but on the mainmast, rather than the mizzen. He found the *Golden Ball*'s shoal draft to be as problematical as it was advantageous: with his boat drawing only two feet, he was altogether too bold about venturing into the shallows. By 2012, Canfield felt "overwhelmed" by the care and feeding of a 47-foot wooden boat that was feeling her fifty years. He donated the *Golden Ball* to the Apalachicola Maritime Museum, on Florida's panhandle coast, where she has her own shed and is being restored to go into the museum's sailing program alongside the *Heritage*, John Kendall's Mobjack.[24]

Francis wrote of the *Golden Ball*: "I think she is about the best design I have made. While I believe she will become popular in the future, she is so different from the usual boat of today that most people hesitate to build her." It was the second part of his prophecy that came true. Only a handful of No. 104s have been built. Francis knew of three that were launched in New England in the 1960s, and he enjoyed machining the mast hardware himself for the two owned by W. F. Wood, of Holliston, Massachusetts, and Robert E. Rohr, of Duxbury, Massachusetts. The shallow, tidal waters of Duxbury Bay certainly provided an ideal realm for a Golden Ball to show off the advantages of her two-foot draft.[25]

As we have seen, Allan Vaitses, in Mattapoisett, had become a great admirer of L. Francis Herreshoff and built fine boats to several of his designs. He wrote to Francis in 1960, "starting with your writings which inspired me to get out of the dark ages type of boat yard and start this business, you probably don't realize how responsible you are for any success that we may have." In 1966, he proposed to pay a 10 percent commission on any future boat he built to one of Francis's designs. Francis declined this generous offer with thanks, and asked only that he buy a new set of plans for each boat, because the building process would wear out the drawings. One of the boats that Vaitses wanted to build was a Golden Ball, but he didn't get the chance until after Francis died. He gave his version of No. 104 a fiberglass hull and tandem centerboards instead of leeboards. She was Allan Vaitses's last boat, built for the man to whom he sold his business. And this fine vessel was all the buyer ended up with, because, under his direction, the yard failed.[26]

And the Golden Ball design, published posthumously in Francis's book, *Sensible Cruising Designs,* continues to attract sailors. The Pease Boatworks and Marine Railway at Chatham, on the elbow of Cape Cod, launched a Golden Ball in 2016. Could it be that the Golden Ball "will become popular in the future"?[27]

Stanley Woodward, busy establishing the Mallorca Yacht and Boat Construction Association in Puerto Polensa, Balearic Isles, nonetheless dreamt of building a large cruising boat for his own use. In early 1960, he wrote to L. Francis Herreshoff: "I wish to inquire what you would charge for designing a sixty foot waterline cruising auxiliary sail boat somewhat between a vessel such as *Ticonderoga* and *Varua.* I have some very definite ideas about features and simplicity. I believe these will follow closely your reasoning and provide many pleasant hours for both of us. At the moment, I am not in the (money) to build, but I would like to start formulating some of my ideas with your experience on paper for the possible future plan."[28]

Woodward was a seasoned boat owner: at the time, he was maintaining and "improving" the *Belisarius,* the cruising yawl that had been

Nathanael's last design. Francis was approaching seventy, and he was not looking for major work, but he could not resist the opportunity Woodward presented. He replied, "if you let me know some of your general ideas I should be glad to make up a preliminary sail plan," and said that he would simply charge a fee for each drawing as the design proceeded: $100 each for a sail plan and lines, drawings he could still make himself, but $500 each for construction and cabin plans, for which "I should hire a draftsman to help me because I no longer have the strong eyesight and the patience to make drawings that have a great deal of fine detail."[29]

Woodward's general idea was a vessel in which he and his wife could live comfortably and which would be capable of occasional, long, fast, ocean passages. In several letters, he listed for Francis many particulars he wanted, including cabin features and arrangements. He told Francis that the ship he had in mind would be named the *Unicorn*, and Francis said, "I think you have selected a wonderful name, the best I have heard for some time."[30]

Francis went ahead with the preliminary sail plan, which also involved basic profile, plan, and sectional drawings of the hull. What he created for Woodward was a modified *Ticonderoga*, making the new hull slightly shorter, wider, and shoaler, with more freeboard, displacement, and ballast, and a little less sail area, converting the great day-sailer-turned-ocean-racer into more of a cruiser. Although he gave the *Unicorn* his usual ketch rig, he borrowed from the rig he had designed for the *Varua* by adding the ability to set square sails on the mainmast. The two yards to spread raffee, topsail, and course were to be rigged like that of the *Marco Polo*; they could be hoisted into place on their cranes or lowered to the deck, as needed. The cranes—short, horizontal bars to hold the yards to the mast—would keep the yards far enough forward of the mast so that the square sails could be set with the wind as far forward as abeam. Francis wrote of taking in the square sails: "In most cases you should bear right off before the wind and lower everything to the deck—sails, spars, and all, which of course will take several men to do this work at once. If you think I can design a square rigger to be handled by a small crew you are flattering me and making me out a smarter man than has been found in several thousand years."[31]

Francis was no ocean cruiser; nevertheless, he could let his imagination take him on board the evolving *Unicorn* to enjoy her shippiness. He liked her square rig, her "quite high" bulwarks, breaks in the deck, monkey rail, stern davits, and, of course, her clipper bow with its carved trailboards. He

---

RIGHT: **Francis's preliminary drawing of the *Unicorn*, his design No. 106 of 1960. He drew her for boatbuilder Stanley Woodward of Mallorca as a husky cruising version of the *Ticonderoga*. She has raised decks fore and aft, a trunk cabin forward, a sunken deckhouse, and a long monkey rail. Francis shows a pram on stern davits, a departure from his usual stowage of a boat on deck. Sail area is 2,417 square feet (124 square feet less than the *Ticonderoga*), with 1,092 in the roller-reefing mainsail, 462 in the mizzen, 360 in the forestaysail, and 503 in the jib. She is fitted with square rig that has almost as much area as her mainsail and mizzen: 688 square feet in the course, 430 in the topsail, and 308 in the raffee, for a total of 1,426 square feet. Notice the true cathead on the bow, a short, protruding arm to take the tack of the lower square sail when reaching; true because in traditional style Francis has drawn a cat's face on its outboard end. Francis arranged the accommodations in accordance with the owner's requirements. Entering the deckhouse, there would be a chartroom to port and a large washroom to starboard; then, still in the deckhouse, a stateroom to starboard and a large WC with sail storage opposite; then, going forward, the engine room to starboard and a generator room to port, with a passage between; and then the main cabin, galley, and fo'c's'le in the bow. Woodward would have his *Unicorn,* but she would not be built to this design, which remains a dream-ship.** (© Mystic Seaport Museum, Daniel S. Gregory Ships Plans Library, SP38.102.3)

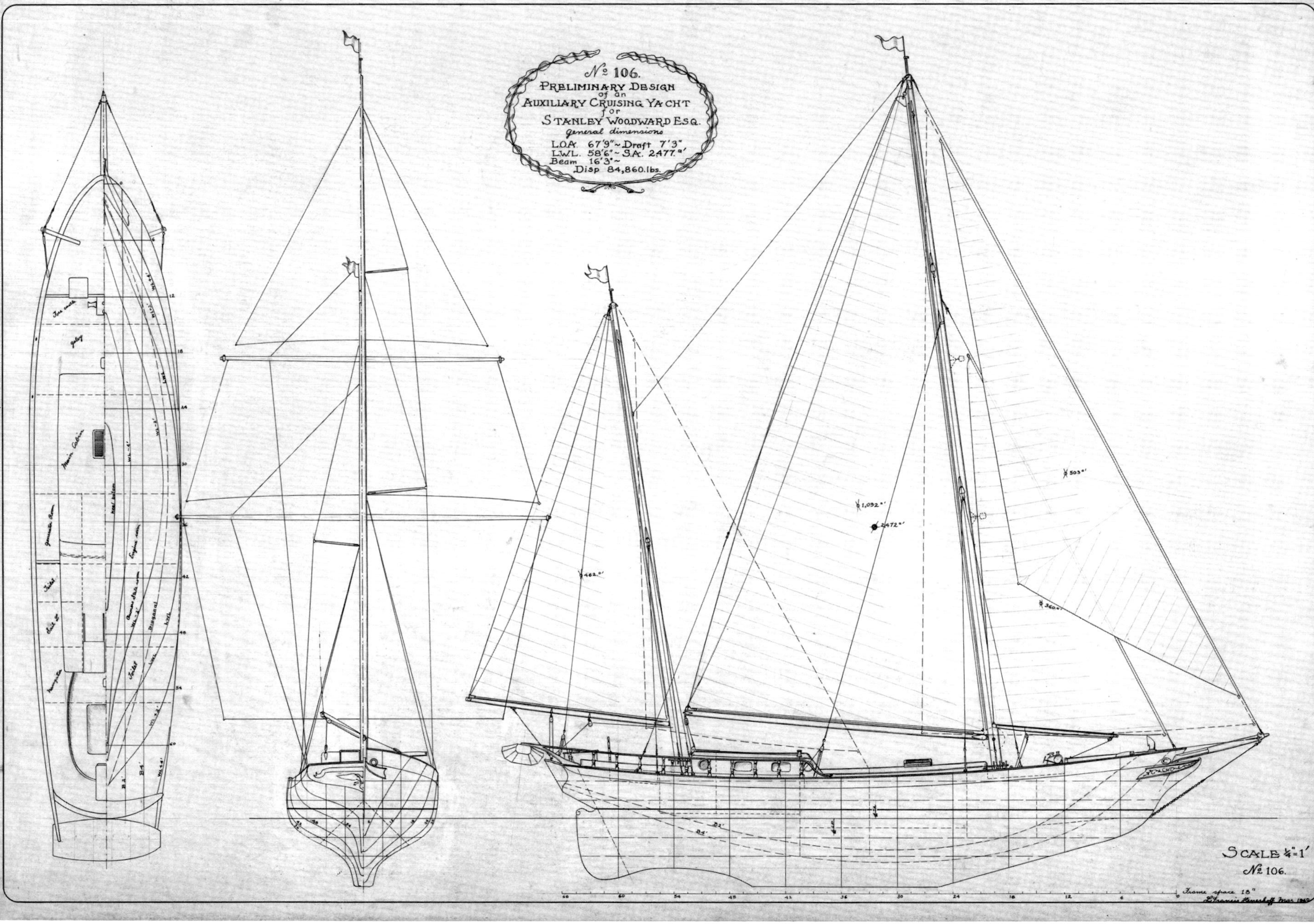
№ 106.
Preliminary Design of an Auxiliary Cruising Yacht for Stanley Woodward Esq.
general dimensions
L.O.A. 67'9" ~ Draft 7'3"
L.W.L. 58'6" ~ S.A. 2477.□'
Beam 16'3" ~
Disp 84,860. lbs.
Scale ¼" = 1'
№ 106.
Frame space 18"

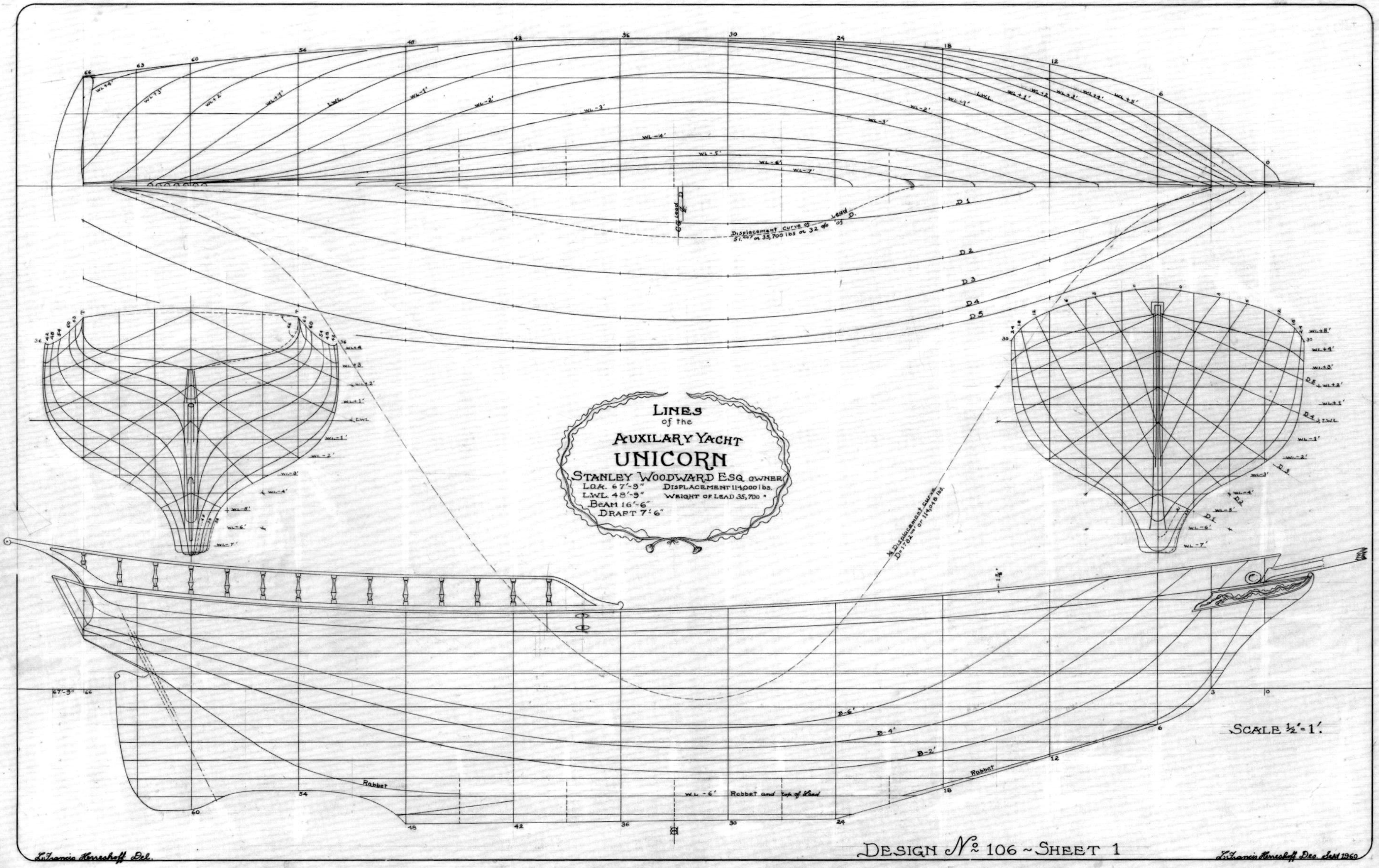
LINES
of the
AUXILARY YACHT
UNICORN
STANLEY WOODWARD ESQ OWNER
L.O.A. 67'-9"
DISPLACEMENT 114,000 lbs.
L.W.L. 48'-9"
WEIGHT OF LEAD 35,700 "
BEAM 16'-6"
DRAFT 7'-6"
Displacement Curve
D1
D2
D3
D4
D5
B-6'
B-4'
B-2'
Rabbet
Rabbet
Rabbet and top of Lead
SCALE ½" = 1'.
DESIGN No. 106 ~ SHEET 1
L. Francis Herreshoff Del.
L. Francis Herreshoff Des. Sept 1960

waxed enthusiastic to Woodward about having a netting under the bowsprit, stretched to the catheads, "where most everybody off duty lies in hot weather." Working out the details of the vessel did "provide many pleasant hours" for designer and client. But Woodward kept questioning this and that and wanted to keep adding to the design. Francis wrote him: "I hope you will go slow and not get too excited about this yacht for I believe the original sketch has the possibility of being the finest cruising boat that has ever been built. But in perfecting something of this kind we do not want to change too many things around. I am quite sure she would please a sailorman more than any boat that has ever been built."[32]

There is no reason to believe that Stanley Woodward was not pleased with the design of the *Unicorn*, yet she never would be built. In November 1960, he wrote to Francis: "I must ask you not to proceed further with any plans for *Unicorn* at the moment. I am not in a position at present to continue or encourage you to continue further design of *Unicorn*." He explained that all his money and energy were going into his boatbuilding business. "Please understand my choice," he asked. Francis replied, "Naturally I was very much disappointed that the work on *Unicorn* will be halted. Nevertheless I feel relieved of the amount of hard work of designing all this yacht single handed." Francis was feeling his three score years and ten. Eighteen months later, Woodward wrote that now he had the money to build himself a *Unicorn*, but that he thought he wanted her to be a Bounty with a wishbone ketch rig. Woodward would build more than one Bounty, but Francis was not involved with their details.[33]

Some of Francis's many aborted designs bore later fruit. He had long been intrigued with the concept of the shallow-draft cruiser, and he turned to that type for his final major design, his No. 107 of 1963. For her hull, he harkened back to his design No. 75 of 1938, one of the boats he drew for Billy Strawbridge that was never built. This was a 39-foot, 8-inch ketch with a shallow keel drawing 3 feet, 4 inches. No. 75 had a centerboard, but for No. 107 Francis used leeboards, as he had on the Meadow Lark and Golden Ball.[34]

When Robert T. Todd, owner of the Rozinante *Phalarope* on Lake Huron, visited Francis in Marblehead and saw the lines and sail plan of No. 107, he recognized it as the perfect boat to live aboard with his wife and for cruising in their retirement. That is, provided he could get Mr. Herreshoff to complete the design with a construction plan. But Francis told Todd that it was doubtful he could continue working on No. 107 because of his "shaky hands." Todd kept gently pressing the issue; finally, in 1969, Francis told him that he'd try to get someone to ink a

LEFT: **The lines of No. 106. Woodward wanted a lot of cabin space, so Francis gave the *Unicorn* higher freeboard than was customary for his clipper-bowed designs. He cut away the deadwood only moderately. She was 67 feet, 9 inches long on deck (4 feet, 2 inches less than the *Ticonderoga*); 58 feet, 9 inches on the waterline (5 feet, 1 inch less than *Ti*); with a beam of 16 feet, 6 inches (6 inches more than *Ti*); and a draft of 7 feet, 6 inches (3 inches less than *Ti*). Displacement was 114,048 pounds (5,760 pounds more than *Ti*). Ballast was to be 35,700 pounds, 31 percent of displacement (*Ti's* ballast-displacement ratio is 28 percent). With a little less length and sail area, and a little more displacement than the *Ticonderoga*, the *Unicorn* would not have been quite as fast, but she could have turned in quick passages. And had dolphins adorned the forward ends of her monkey rail, they would have been harder to drown than *Ti's*.** (© Mystic Seaport Museum, Daniel S. Gregory Ships Plans Library, SP38.102.1)

construction plan if he could draw one—maybe in two years' time, or, as he would have said, "some Tuesday next week." Even this tardy, hazy promise was good news to Todd. He wrote to Francis, "I think she will turn out to be another of your masterpieces of which you will be very proud." But Francis never did make a construction plan for No. 107, and Todd didn't get his retirement boat. Francis was winding down.[35]

It was the enthusiasm for L. Francis Herreshoff designs Down Under that saved design No. 107 from oblivion. Wayne Roberts in Waitara, on the west coast of New Zealand's North Island, saw her plans in *Sensible Cruising Designs,* and, despite the lack of construction detail, decided to build. He lofted the lines in 1978 and launched his *Tern* in 1981. With his family, Roberts cruised widely in the Pacific for the next seven years. Then Chris Powell bought the boat, and she continued to call at many a Pacific island and even win races. The *Tern* is now owned by the Robertses' son Jed, who was conceived on board. Other New Zealand boats have been inspired by No. 107, but were much modified.[36]

Chris Powell wrote, "I have loved owning *Tern,* have done two trips through the Pacific, circumnavigated New Zealand and won many yacht racing trophies in her, such as the Mahurangi Regatta and the Tall Ships Race in the Bay of Islands." He says she is particularly fast off the wind, and he reports that she only needs her leeboards when hard on the wind. Start the sheets a little, and the leeboard just slows her down, he says. He adds that with a leeboard down, she will hold her course as long as the breeze holds steady. On a trip back to New Zealand from Fiji, the *Tern* encountered a three-day whole gale of over 50 knots on the beam; Beaufort's scale describes the resulting sea as "very high waves with overhanging crests." The *Tern* reached along safely under just a storm jib, her shallow hull letting her give to the punches. Francis never knew of this great performance, but he may well have had similar, imaginary trysts with the sea in the 107.[37]

While Francis no longer felt physically able to continue his fine draftsmanship, he could still find much pleasure and an outlet for his creative energy at his lathes. At age eighty-one, he wrote to his friend, Bror Tamm, "the last few years have been about the happiest of my life and I enjoy my workshop particularly in the winter's bad weather."[38]

Francis's good customer and admirer, John Kendall, appreciated his talent for making beautiful objects in his workshop. It may well have been Kendall who started Francis on making brass saluting cannons back in the 1950s; at any rate, he was an early recipient of one. Even after glaucoma had impaired his eyesight, Francis could still make his perfect metal-to-metal fits using his extremely sensitive touch.[39]

RIGHT: **Francis's sail plan and general arrangement plan for a 38-foot leeboard ketch, his No. 107, drawn in 1963, his last major design, at age seventy-two. With a draft of 3 feet, she is a bit deeper than his previous leeboard ketches, the Meadow Lark and Golden Ball. Sail area is 602 square feet, with 314 in the mainsail, 152 in the mizzen, and 136 in the jib. There is an overlapping jib of 220 square feet. As on the *Dancing Feather,* Francis has combined his jumper stays on the mainmast with his short-gaff rig. Note the running backstays on the mizzen. He shows his favorite way of stowing a pram on deck, despite its obstruction to fore-and-aft travel. The cabin was to be conventionally arranged with a forward stateroom, head compartment, main cabin, and galley. Headroom in the cabin is 6 feet. The engine is just forward of the mizzenmast.** (© Mystic Seaport Museum, Daniel S. Gregory Ships Plans Library, SP38.166.2)

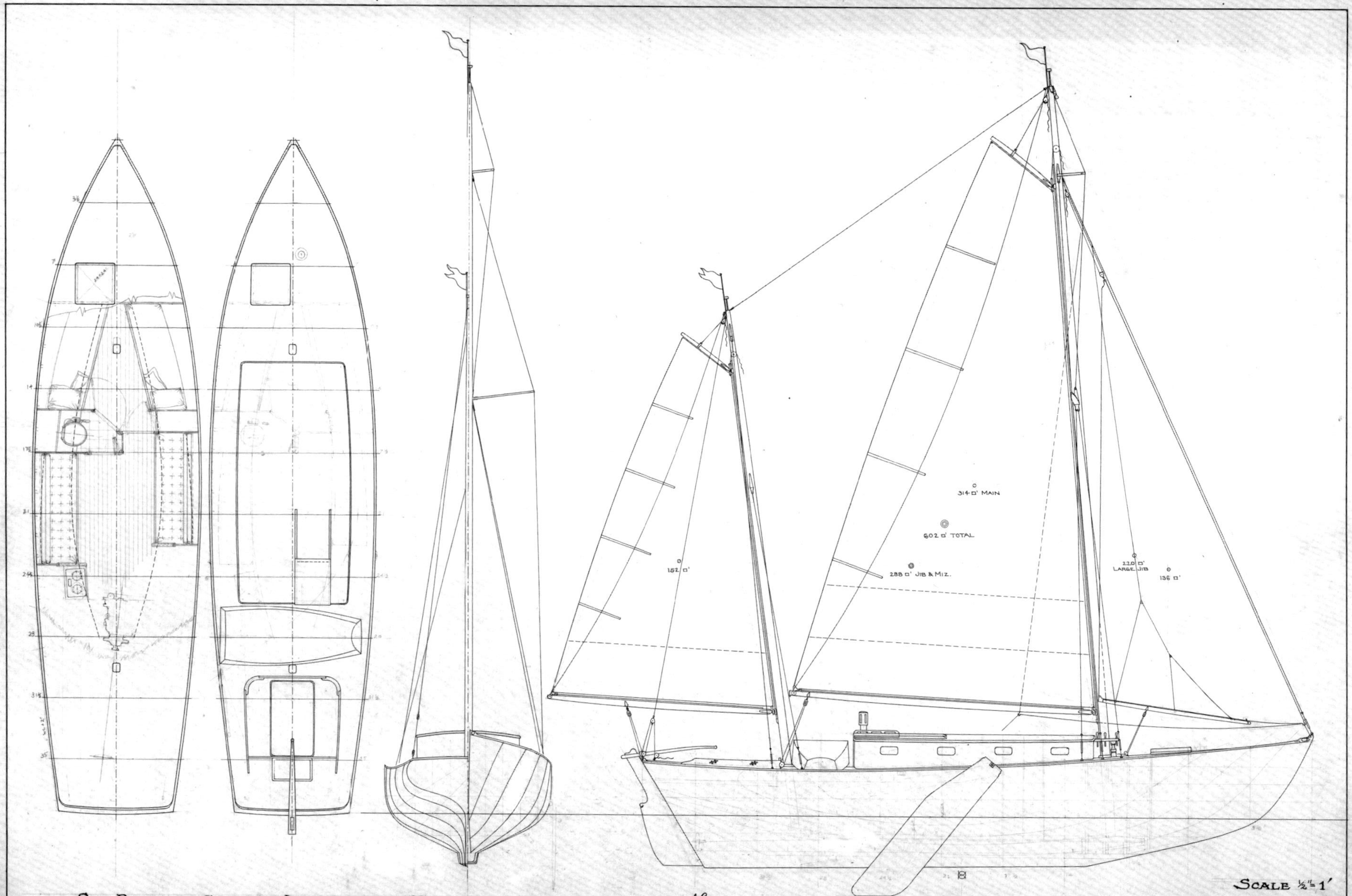

SAIL PLAN AND GENERAL ARRANGEMENT PLAN OF THE LEABOARD KETCH № 107. ~ L.O.A. 38'. L.W.L. 33'-3". BEAM 9'-6". DRAFT 3'.

HEIGHTS	38	35	31½	28	24½	21	17½	14	10½	7	3½	HEIGHTS
DECK AT SIDES	3-0-0	2-9-3	2-7-4	2-6-7	2-7-2	2-8-3	2-10-2	3-1-1	3-4-2	3-8-3	4-0-7	DECK AT SIDES
BUTOCK 4			1-2-5	0-4-0	-0-3-2	-0-6-0	-0-2-6	0-11-4	3-0-2	~		BUTTOCK 4
" 3	1-9-0	1-0-6	0-3-2	-0-10-2	-0-10-6	1-1-3	-1-0-6	-0-6-6	0-8-0	3-0-5		" 3
" 2	1-6-0	0-7-4	-0-2-5	-1-5-0	-1-4-2	1-7-3	-2-7-6	-1-4-2	-0-7-2	1-0-4	4-0-7	" 2
" 1	1-4-0	0-2-1	0-9-0		-1-10-2	2-1-0	-2-1-2	-1-11-4	-1-6-2	-0-6-6	2-0-0	" 1
RABBET		-0-7-0	The Rabbet is on sheet #3 ~ between stations 10½ and 31½						-2-2-1	-1-4-4	-0-0-5	RABBET
FACE		-2-1-6	2-11-4	2-11-0	2-10-4	2-10-0	2-9-4	2-9-0	2-2-7	1-5-5	-0-4-0	FACE
½ WIDTHS												½ WIDTHS
½ W AT DECK	3-3-0	3-7-7	4-0-6	4-4-4	4-7-4	4-9-0	4-8-7	4-6-5	4-1-4	3-3-4	2-0-0	½ WIDTH AT DECK
" " WL +3'								4-6-3	4-0-0	2-11-4	1-5-3	" " " WL+3'
" " WL +2'		3-8-5	4-1-4	4-5-4	4-8-1	4-9-0	4-8-0	4-4-0	3-7-4	2-5-6	1-0-0	" " " WL+2'
" " WL +1'		2-10-2	3-10-2	4-4-0	4-7-3	4-8-3	4-6-0	4-0-3	3-2-1	1-11-7	0-7-0	" " " WL+1'
" " L.W.L.		0-7-4	2-5-5	3-8-3	4-3-0	4-4-5	4-1-6	3-6-0	2-6-2	1-5-0	0-2-3	" " " LWL
" " WL -1'		0-1-2	0-7-2	1-8-0	2-9-3	3-2-4	3-1-2	2-6-0	1-7-1	0-6-4		" " " WL -1'
" " TOP LEAD		0-1-1	0-2-0	0-3-7	0-5-6	0-7-1	0-6-7	0-5-0				" " " TOP OF LEAD
" " FACE			0-1-4	0-3-0	0-4-6	0-6-0	0-5-6	0-3-3	0-1-1	0-0-7	0-0-5	" " " FACE
DIAGONAL 1		0-5-4	1-2-1	1-8-7	2-2-1	2-5-2	2-5-7	2-3-1	1-9-6	1-1-5	0-2-4	DIAGONAL #1
" 2		2-1-6	3-0-4	3-8-1	4-1-6	4-4-1	4-3-6	3-11-0	3-3-0	2-3-7	1-0-0	" #2
" 3		3-6-0	4-3-0	4-9-6	5-2-2	5-3-7	5-1-1	4-6-7	3-9-1	2-8-4	1-4-2	" #3

½ width of the face of Stem at waterline 4'-6" 1¼"
" 3' 7/8"
" 2' ¾"
" 1' 5/8"
" L.W.L. 5/8"

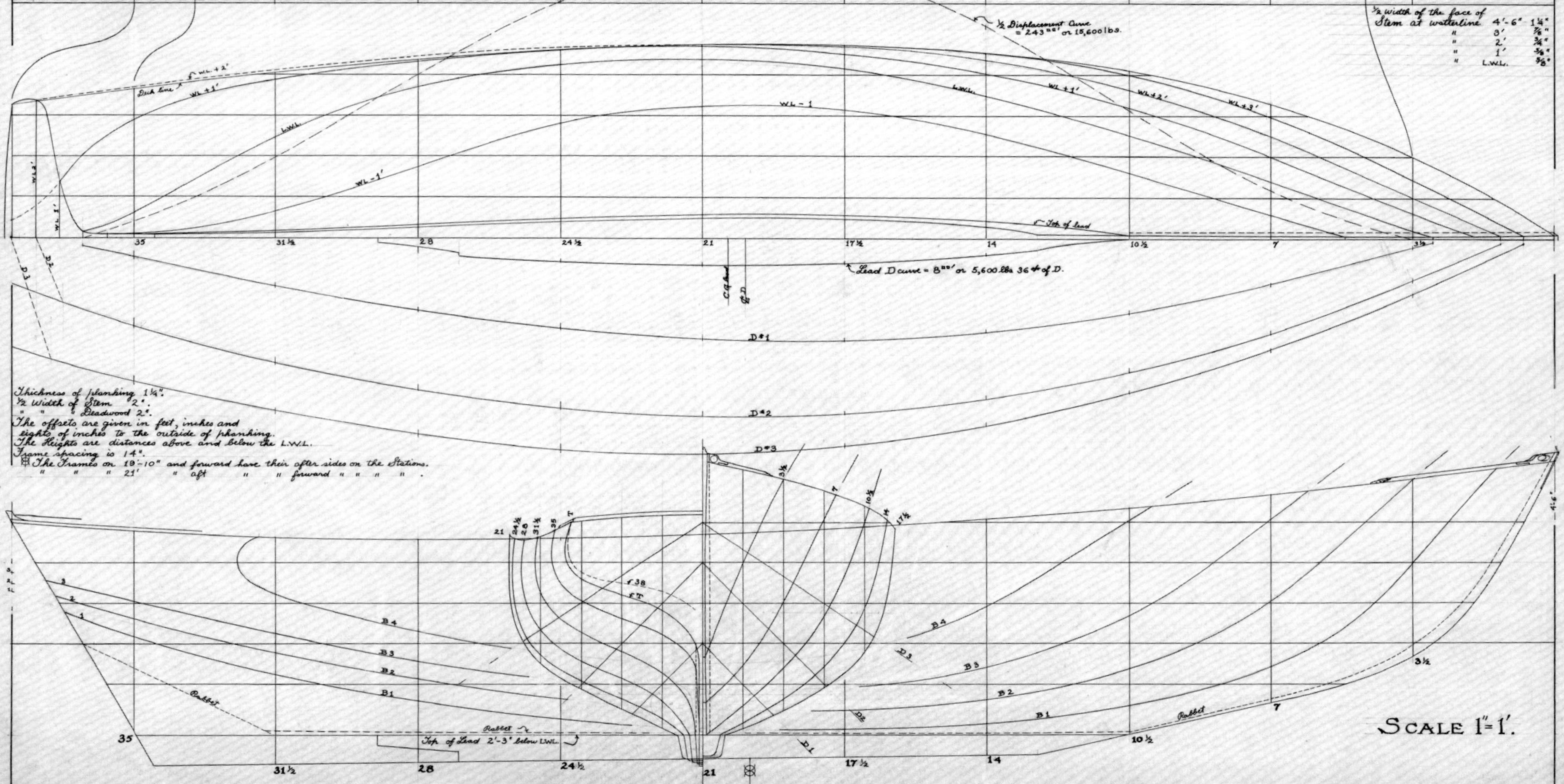

Thickness of planking 1¼".
½ Width of Stem 2".
" " " Deadwood 2".
The offsets are given in feet, inches and eights of inches to the outside of planking.
The Heights are distances above and below the L.W.L.
Frame spacing is 14".
⊠ The Frames on 19'-10" and forward have their after sides on the Stations.
" " " 21' " aft " " forward " " " ".

SCALE 1"=1'.

L.O.A. 38' ~ L.W.L. 33'-3" ~ Beam 9'-6" ~ Draft 3' ~ Displacement 15,600 lbs.

THE LINES OF № 107 SHEET 2.

LEFT: **The lines and offsets of No. 107. Waterline length is 33 feet, 3 inches; and beam is 9 feet, 6 inches. Displacement is 15,600 pounds, with 5,600 pounds of lead ballast, for a ballast-displacement ratio of 31 percent. Francis thought she would need 1,500 pounds of inside ballast to bring her down to the load waterline shown. He noted a few construction details on this drawing, including planking thickness of 1¼ inches and frame spacing of 14 inches. Her barely knuckled bow with its slightly hollow waterline is subtle, but still is in balance with the pronounced wineglass curves in the flat, raked transom. "Old Fussbudget," as L. Francis Herreshoff referred to himself in *The Compleat Cruiser*, produced, in these lines of his final sailing cruiser, a boat that may look ordinary at first glance, but that is, in fact, a fine example of his artistry.** (© Mystic Seaport Museum, Daniel S. Gregory Ships Plans Library, SP38.166.1) ABOVE: **The No. 107, *Tern*, hustling along on the wind with the aid of a big overlapping jib, but without the aid of her raised leeboard. Owner Chris Powell hated to drop a leeboard and slow her down, even a little; apparently her leeway was minimal, despite her shoal draft. Her wake certainly doesn't appear to be trailing to windward. Note the shadow on her mainsail of her short mizzen gaff.** (Steve Stone photo, courtesy Off Center Harbor)

ABOVE: **Parts laid out on a newspaper for a lot of ten of Francis's bronze saluting cannons. As the number of completed parts grew, they would be spread over all the tables in The Castle's great hall. The cannons were breechloaders firing a 10-gauge blank shell, and each was mounted on a four-wheel, mahogany carriage. The metal was "real gun metal which is a composition bronze and is about gold in color," Francis wrote. They came with a wooden mallet for firing; when Francis heard that some people accidentally hit the wooden elevating quoin when firing, he shifted to an elevating screw. When he started making the cannons in 1963, Francis charged $200 for one, but by 1969 he increased the price to $300, just to break even. He figured he made $1.00 per hour for his labor. He made three lots of ten and may have completed a fourth lot. When he was seventy-nine, his then secretary, Muriel Vaughn, wrote, "he is very well and works seven days a week in his workshop making model ship saluting cannons."** (Gilbert E. Friedberg photo, courtesy Paul Glynn, Mystic Seaport Museum, 1999-8-212) RIGHT: **Francis designed this anchor, apparently as late as 1970 (the date on the drawing, March 20, 1970, could have been added later) for improved holding power, chiefly through the stock, shaped in section like the blade of a bulldozer, and for easy stowage, since the stock can swing through 90 degrees and then slide down along the shank. Like a "patented" anchor, which it wasn't, it has plenty of surface area for its weight.** (© Mystic Seaport Museum, Daniel S. Gregory Ships Plans Library, SP38.435)

Predictably, Francis's cannon was historically correct. "I took quite a little trouble," he wrote, "to look up what the average French, English, Dutch and Colonial American cannons were like. So that this design is a good average of a ships cannon between 1700-1850 when they did not change much and when all the proportions were derived from the bore." And, of course, these carefully designed cannons were exquisitely made by L. Francis Herreshoff, even late in life. When R. H. Coleman, president of the Remington Arms Company of Bridgeport, Connecticut, received one as a gift from John M. Case, of the Cutts and Case boatyard in Oxford, Maryland, he wrote to Francis: "Just a note to tell you how delighted I am to have one of your model ships cannons. The workmanship over-all and the extremely fine tolerances are a tribute to a master builder. I think, as a firearms manufacturer, I am better qualified than some to express a valid opinion." Francis replied that "it really made me feel good that someone with your qualifications has liked the workmanship of the little ships cannon."[40]

Yachtsmen's wives lined up to order cannons from Francis as the perfect present for their husbands. Sally Chamberlin, in St. Croix, gave one to her husband, Tom, and wrote to Francis: "It is beautiful! He is so proud of it. Has shown it to all of his friends and kept it on a stand in the living-room where he can sit and admire it. It is one of the few gifts I've ever given him that I've felt complete satisfaction in and am so grateful to you for having

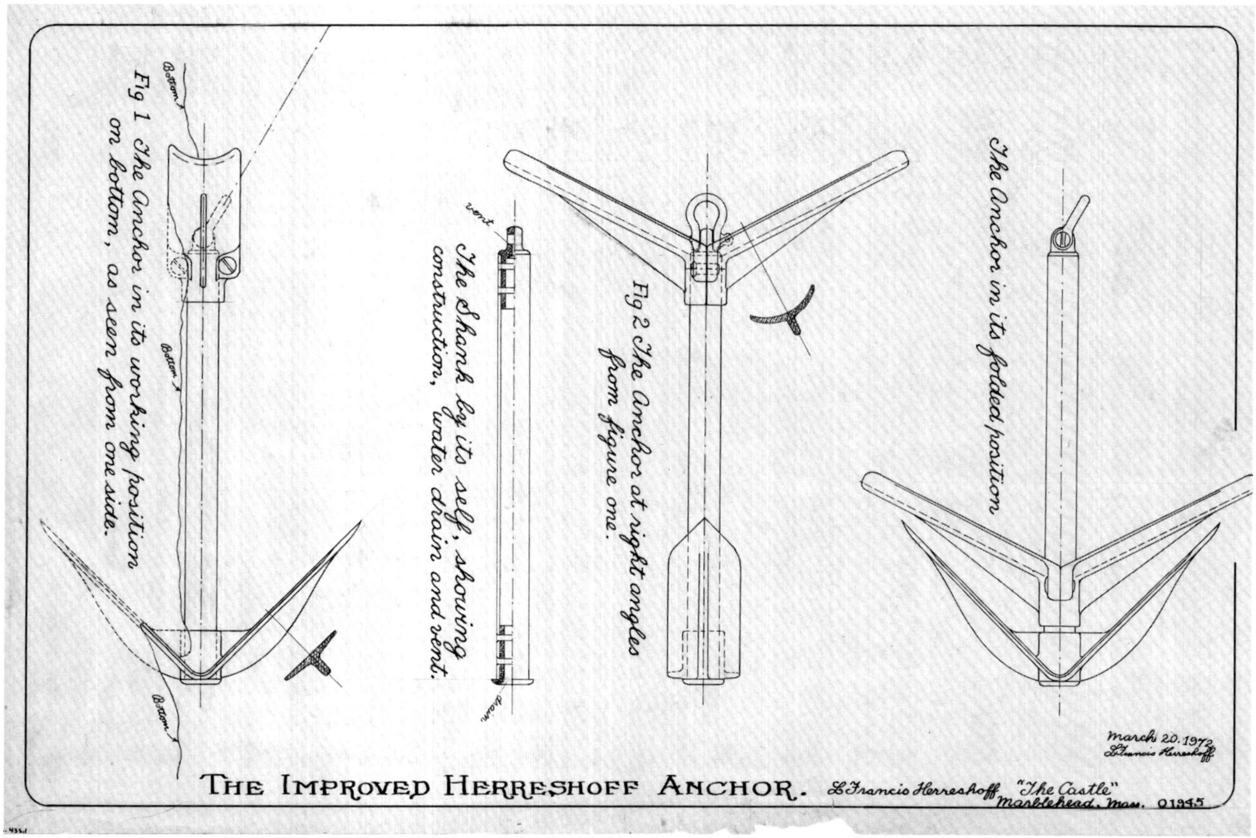

made it." The "little ships cannons" were a mark of the joy and pride that L. Francis Herreshoff took in working with his lathes and were a fitting culmination of a lifetime of superlative accomplishments in his workshop.[41]

By the time Boris Lauer-Leonardi left *The Rudder* in 1963, his wife Barbara had died and he had remarried. His second wife, Julie, had an independent income. Boris had moved from Port Washington to Lakeville, Connecticut, and had bought an apartment in New York. He also established a winter place in the Bahamas at Man-O-War Key, Abaco, from which vantage point, he would "fire away as yachts enter the harbor" with his Herreshoff-made brass cannon.[42]

Boris went to work for the Livingston Publishing Company at 521 Fifth Avenue. The firm had published Vincent Gilpin's *The Good Little Ship* in 1952, about Commodore Ralph Munroe's Presto-boat, shoal-draft cruisers. Francis had written the foreword to the book, which he used, in part, as a platform from which to fire another broadside at racing measurement rules, applauding Munroe for ignoring them. By 1966, Boris had established his own book firm, at first Leonardi Publishing Company, in the same building with Livingston, and soon changed to Poseidon Publishing Company, at 200 Park Avenue.

One of the titles that Boris brought out was *Yachts, Designs, and Much Miscellaneous Information*, with much of the miscellaneous information being in a chapter by Francis titled "The Answers to Some Interesting Nautical Questions." This was a piece that *The Rudder* had turned down; Boris paid Francis $250 for it. It covered "Light and Heavy Displacement; Shapes of Rudders; Keels; Bows, Stern, and Overhangs; The Advantages and Disadvantages of Different Rigs; The Pros and Cons of Gaff and Leg O' Mutton Sails and Some Discourses About Bowsprits." But this book that Boris published led to contention between writer and editor. It presented a variety of yacht designs, and Boris asked Francis to join in. Francis refused in no uncertain terms, and Boris was offended. He wrote to Francis, "in regard to your refusal to be represented in my forthcoming book of designs, this is, of course, your privilege, but I was somewhat annoyed by your statement that you do not wish to be in the company of such 'swill.'" Francis explained that his term "swill" applied to the designs, not the designers. He didn't want his boats associated with

ABOVE: **Helen Bolster in about 1960. The big lap dog is Sam, a Rhodesian Ridgeback that belonged to her daughter, Anne. Mrs. B was a dog person; Francis's poodles were her particular friends.** (Courtesy Anne Lawrence Bondy, author's collection)
RIGHT: **Margrete L. "Gretl" Stinnes in her mid-thirties at Newport, 1962.** (Hanns Stinnes photo, courtesy Margrete Stinnes, author's collection)

modern boats. Boris wrote back: "I understand your position, and I will consider the matter closed. You and I have been friends for a long time, and I was hurt. However, no harm done."[43]

Poseidon lasted only two years. Boris shut it down and retired in 1969. In 1971, Boris Lauer-Leonardi died at age sixty-five. More than Starling Burgess, under whom Francis had first designed a famous racing boat, more than his best customers and friends Charlie Welch, Waldo Brown, and Billy Strawbridge, Boris had brought Francis into the public eye and enhanced his reputation. When Francis had seen his "Common Sense of Yacht Design" articles gathered into two handsome volumes, he realized how much Boris had done for him. And Pete Smyth's lack of recognition notwithstanding, he also knew that his writings for Boris's *Rudder* had been vital to the magazine's success. Francis did get as much fan mail for his writing as for his designs. Yet all of this success was dampened by the apparent lack of effect of his campaign to reverse the trend of yachting away from the traditional and beautiful toward the modern and ugly—in both boats and behavior—and by the failure of most of the yachting public to appreciate his *Rudder* designs. The death of Boris Lauer-Leonardi, Francis's fellow crusader, added to a growing sadness and pessimism about his chosen profession.

Helen Bolster, who had been Francis's secretary since 1926, was diagnosed with cancer in 1960. Over the next few years, she would have to be "away," as Francis reported in tardy responses to correspondents, for a month or two at a time. He didn't send out his usual sixty or seventy Christmas cards in 1962, because he couldn't face addressing them himself. In March 1967, "Mrs. B" was forced by her illness to retire. She had been L. Francis Herreshoff's right-hand woman for forty-one years, tending to his every secretarial and administrative need—correcting his dyslexic spelling along the way.[44]

They had a formal relationship. In forty-one years, Francis never used Helen Bolster's first name. Yet, they could squabble. "Everybody always said they behaved like an old, married couple," Mrs. Bolster's daughter, Anne, remembered. Francis took his secretary's work for granted, although he did put nice inscriptions in the copies of his books that her gave her. But it was not until she was dying that he wrote to her, "I want you to know how much I appreciate your loyal and efficient help during the last 40 years and I want you to know that I realize I never could have put together 5 or 6 books without

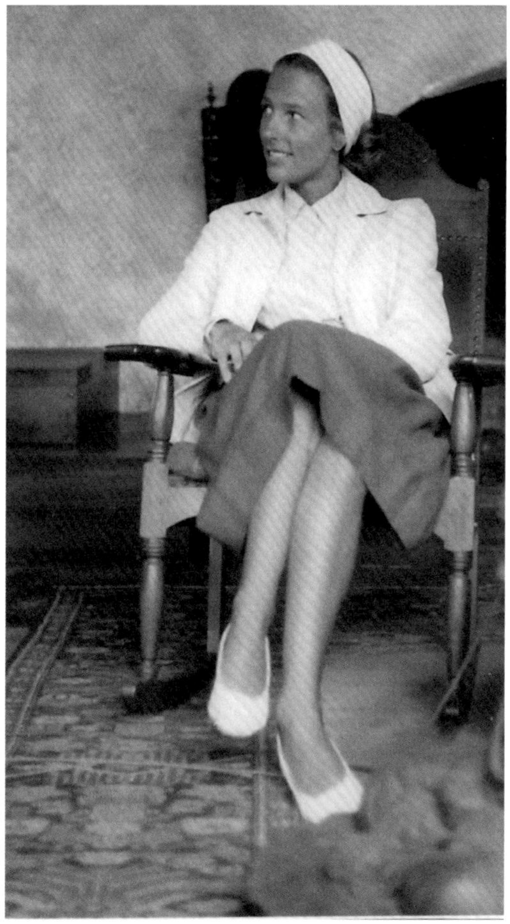

your help." He signed the carefully hand-written letter, "yours moast effectionately Francis."[45]

Francis tried to interest Margrete Stinnes in taking Helen Bolster's place. Hanns Stinnes, Francis's longtime friend from 30-Square-Metre boat days, traveled across the Atlantic from Germany whenever he could to witness American yacht racing and yarn with Francis. Gretl always accompanied her father on these visits to Marblehead. The Stinneses began a tradition of visiting Francis on November 11, his birthday, arriving on that day in 1965, his seventy-fifth, as a surprise. "I came into The Castle first," Gretl remembered, "then my father stood in the door. Francis was absolutely speechless. He said it was one of the best birthday gifts he ever had. We had a good visit with no one else there."[46]

Gretl Stinnes came to America on her own for six months in 1961, and by 1966 she had emigrated permanently and found work in New York. She would fly into Boston's Logan Airport, where Francis would pick her up. "He showed me around the whole area," she recalled, "Gloucester, Rockport, Ipswich, the beaches." They went together to the exhibit on the *Ticonderoga* at MIT, remembering their day on board her off Newport. Francis made exquisite objects for her: a tiny cupboard, "an absolutely beautiful little thing"; a miniature teak table like the one in the *Ticonderoga*'s main cabin; a teak lamp with several brass clamps to hold it to different table tops. "He was a very special man to me," Gretl said. "He sort of became a second father to me." Their difference in ages was forty years.[47]

Francis knew that Gretl would be a good secretary, and he enjoyed her company. "He planned to build a room over his garage so I would have a place to stay," Stinnes recalled. "But I couldn't tear myself away from New York City. It wasn't the kind of work I wanted." (She became senior analyst for debt administration for the Amerada Hess Corporation.) "My father would have been delighted if Francis and I had become a team. If I had become his secretary, he would have taught me all kinds of things, but I wasn't ready to do that. Francis was disappointed, but it didn't do any harm to our friendship."[48]

Muriel Vaughn was a part-time bookkeeper

RIGHT TOP: **Francis's drawing of the hand bilge pump he invented is dated February 1961. The pump is about 2 feet long and 2 inches in diameter. It is not double acting, but it will throw a stream of water that "is hard to believe," in Boris Lauer-Leonardi's words. It will also, according to Francis, "pass strings, matches, and various other kinds of dirt without clogging up." There was a long syringe attachment for pumping the lee bilge of a sailing dinghy from the weather rail. Francis patented the sliding seal and valve arrangement on the plunger, Patent No. 3,319,577, dated May 16, 1967. The patent was in Margrete Stinnes's name, as her father was to manufacture the pump, and she would be his US agent. Francis had two dozen of the pumps made of brass by the Whitehead Metal Products Company of Cambridge, Massachusetts, which he was to sell at $25, but the ones made in Germany were to be of plastic. As a business proposition, the project fizzled for lack of market, and Francis was disgusted. He wrote to Stinnes, "certainly I never should have attempted getting the patent or any other business arrangements for I do not understand business methods."** (© Mystic Seaport Museum, Daniel S. Gregory Ships Plans Library, SP38.343.1) BOTTOM: **In 1964, Francis devised this efficient plastic squirt gun for Hanns Stinnes to make in Germany. The gun was about 30 inches long, but Francis noted dimensions of its parts in metric measure for Stinnes's convenience. The purpose of the implement was to force gazo zalem into seams. It would also be used as an onboard fire extinguisher, drawing water from overboard; Francis planned to make an attachment that could hold "fire extinguishing liquid." John Kendall, devotee of Francis and owner of several boats built to his designs, obtained one of the guns for $20; other than that, the project went nowhere.** (© Mystic Seaport Museum, Daniel S. Gregory Ships Plans Library, SP38.344.1)

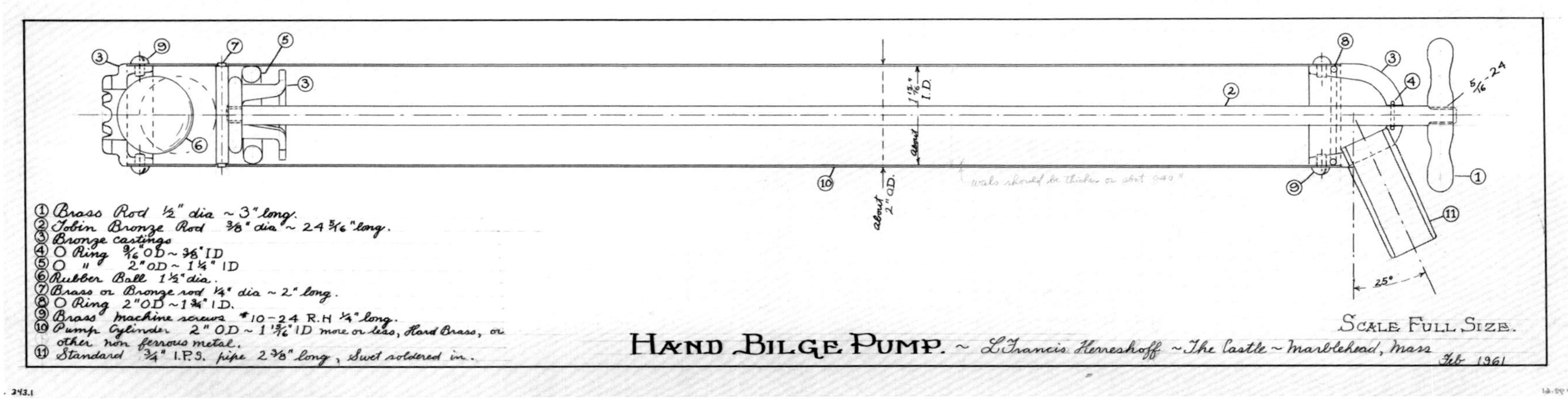

① Brass Rod ½" dia ~ 3" long.
② Tobin Bronze Rod ⅜" dia ~ 24 5/16" long.
③ Bronze castings
④ O Ring 9/16" OD ~ ⅜" ID
⑤ O " 2" OD ~ 1¼" ID
⑥ Rubber Ball 1½" dia.
⑦ Brass or Bronze rod ¼" dia ~ 2" long.
⑧ O Ring 2" OD ~ 1¾" I.D.
⑨ Brass machine screws #10-24 R.H ¼" long.
⑩ Pump Cylinder 2" OD ~ 1 13/16" ID more or less, Hard Brass, or other non ferrous metal.
⑪ Standard ¾" I.P.S. pipe 2⅜" long, Swet soldered in.
about 2" O.D.
about 1 13/16" I.D.
5/16-24
25°
SCALE FULL SIZE.
HAND BILGE PUMP. ~ L. Francis Herreshoff ~ The Castle ~ Marblehead, Mass
Feb 1961

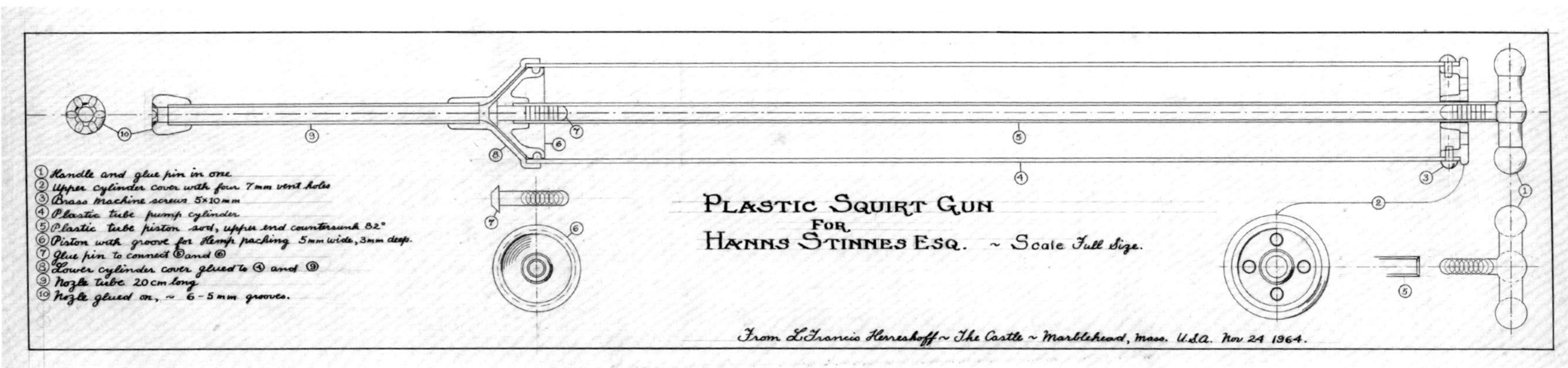

① Handle and glue pin in one
② Upper cylinder cover with four 7mm vent holes
③ Brass machine screws 5×10mm
④ Plastic tube pump cylinder
⑤ Plastic tube piston rod, upper end countersunk 82°
⑥ Piston with groove for Hemp packing 5mm wide, 3mm deep.
⑦ Glue pin to connect ⑤ and ⑥
⑧ Lower cylinder cover glued to ④ and ⑨
⑨ Nozle tube 20cm long
⑩ Nozle glued on, ~ 6-5mm grooves.
PLASTIC SQUIRT GUN
FOR
HANNS STINNES ESQ. ~ Scale Full Size.
From L. Francis Herreshoff ~ The Castle ~ Marblehead, Mass. U.S.A. Nov 24 1964.

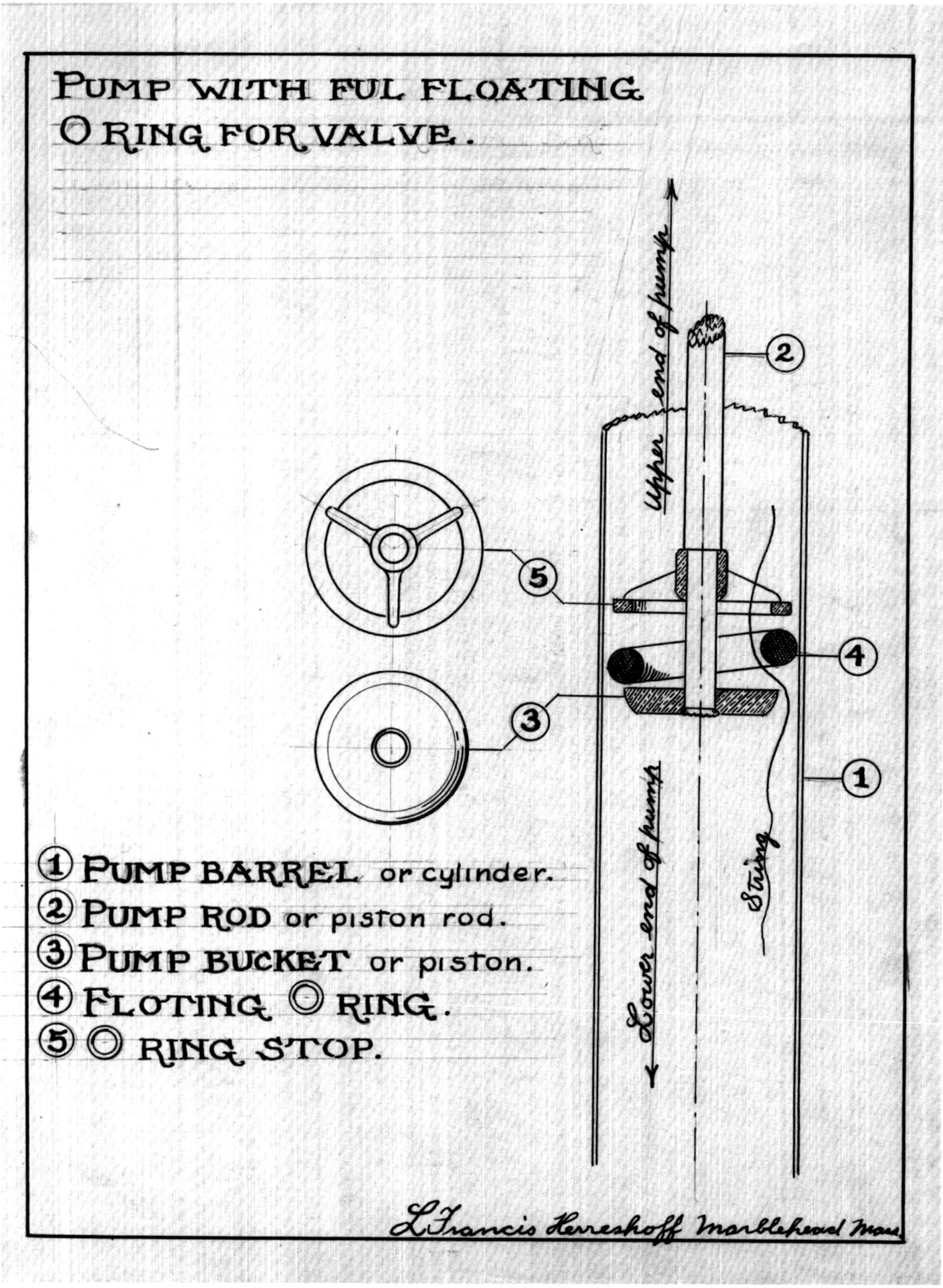
PUMP WITH FUL FLOATING
O RING FOR VALVE.
Upper end of pump
2
5
4
3
1
Lower end of pump
String
① PUMP BARREL or cylinder.
② PUMP ROD or piston rod.
③ PUMP BUCKET or piston.
④ FLOTING ◎ RING.
⑤ ◎ RING STOP.
L. Francis Herreshoff Marblehead Mass

at Eaton Apothecary, where her husband was the pharmacist and where Francis traded. She was part of the old-time Marblehead culture that by then included Francis, whose members stuck together as the town became more and more gentrified as its population tripled. When Vaughn saw that Francis was lost without Helen Bolster, she recognized an opportunity for herself, as well as a way to help one of Marblehead's great old characters. She offered her services as secretary and, in April 1967, Francis took her on. Part-time work for Francis became full-time and, when her husband died, Francis said to her, "Madam [he never used her first name, either], it would be easier if you moved in here." So Muriel would often sleep in The Castle's upstairs bedroom, for convenience, although she kept her half of a duplex, nearby at 53 Gregory Street.[49]

Francis's dealings with Muriel Vaughn were different from his relationship with Helen Bolster. Although twenty-five years Francis's junior, Muriel came on strong with Francis; way too strong for an employee. When Katherine Jones Vosburgh's daughter Dale would visit, Muriel would butt in with girl talk and local gossip, and Francis would snap: "Madam, why don't you go make some tea for us? I'm trying to talk to her about something." Muriel would back off, but she was "mouthy" all the same, Dale remembered. Yet Muriel Vaughn did bring a welcome liveliness into The Castle. How many people could put up with L. Francis Herreshoff, Dale wondered. "He was a bone-headed, stubborn, old coot, if you wanted to look at him not as a famous yacht designer." Muriel could be grating, and Francis would get mad at her, but somehow they managed to get along together. She could also be fun. And Muriel Vaughn cared deeply about L. Francis Herreshoff. "He was my man," she said.[50]

Dan Brayton, the Marblehead sailor who resurrected Francis's design No. 65, the double-ended cruising ketch, used to say that Muriel Vaughn was L. Francis Herreshoff's Dulcinea. While we have noted the resemblance between Francis and Don Quixote, it is more difficult to see the Muriel Vaughn-Dulcinea connection. We do know, however, that L. Francis Herreshoff had a prodigious imagination. His relationship with women had always been difficult, starting with the loss, at age fifteen, of the mother he adored. There had been the disastrous iceboat accident with Christine Howe. There was the devastation of his affair of the heart with Katherine Jones. There was the disappointment that Gretl Stinnes would not be his secretary. Muriel Vaughn was, at least, something of a companion to him. She told several of his devotees that he had once blurted out, "I've never fucked a woman!" While the supposed statement is undoubtedly true, it is hard to believe that L. Francis Herreshoff ever uttered such words or expressed in any way such a personal thought to anyone. Perhaps Muriel simply wanted to appear to be that person to whom he might so reveal himself. But in telling the story, Muriel Vaughn seems to be putting a great distance between herself and Dulcinea.[51]

In any event, Muriel was not the professional secretary that Helen Bolster had been. She took Francis's dictation in longhand, not shorthand. She was not good at details, and she was a poor organizer. But she did continue Helen Bolster's practice of copying Francis's answers to letters on the reverse, and she saved them all. She was the practical help he needed in his old age. She was his chauffeur. She put the finishing polish on his brass cannons. She was a fierce protector of his reputation. Muriel suffered from an addiction to alcohol

---

LEFT: **With this drawing, Francis showed how his floating O-ring could act as a seal for the bilge pump, but still pass a piece of string.** (© Mystic Seaport Museum, Daniel S. Gregory Ships Plans Library, SP38.350.1)

and could be histrionic when under the influence. Francis excused most of this behavior and avoided mentioning it.[52]

When Robert T. Todd visited The Castle to encourage Francis to complete the design of No. 107, he found Muriel Vaughn to be splendid. He wrote to Francis: "Mrs. Vaughn is certainly a wonderful addition to the Herreshoff household. Her cheerfulness, interest in your work, and knowledge of the household inventory is great—and certainly made a real contribution to our happy visit. We hope she stays around a long time." Others were less positive. It distressed Lee Nielsen to think that Muriel Vaughn was trying to boss Francis around. Anne Lawrence, Helen Bolster's daughter, had to argue her way past Muriel just to get to see Francis.[53]

After some three years of Muriel Vaughn's secretarial work, the great flow of letters from L. Francis Herreshoff trickled, and then stopped. But Muriel stayed on, and she answered inquiries herself with Francis's advice, and continued to serve Francis's practical needs. A year before he died, she wrote, "I do my best to help him in any way I can."[54]

One morning in mid-September 1972, Francis awoke with severe pain in his left hip. At the Mary A. Alley Hospital in Marblehead, it was found that the hip was fractured, caused by erosion of the bone by a tumor, perhaps originating in

Muriel D. Vaughn, Francis's secretary and helpmate in his final years. Some even thought she was his Dulcinea. (Courtesy Muriel Vaughn, author's collection)

the prostate gland. After ten days in the hospital, Francis was sent home. He was able to make his way around in The Castle with Muriel's help and the aid of a walker. But on the night of October 9, the pain suddenly worsened, and the next day he was taken to Massachusetts General Hospital in Boston. During surgery on the eleventh, the head and neck of the diseased femur were removed and replaced by a prosthesis. Over the next seven weeks in the hospital, Francis suffered a variety of complications. A swallowing dysfunction led to aspirational pneumonia, which ultimately caused pulmonary failure and cardio-respiratory arrest. L. Francis Herreshoff died on December 3, 1972.[55]

Halsey was the only family member who visited Francis in the hospital. Lee Nielsen came to see Francis. He was under a netting, breathing with difficulty, attempting, without success, to say something to his old friend. Lee leaned inside, trying to catch any words. Francis put his face right up to Lee's face, in the only gesture of affection Lee ever remembered getting from the stilted Francis. Paul Glynn, his car mechanic, paid Francis a visit the day he died. Arthur Brendze was a regular visitor, along with Muriel. Missing was Francis's good friend, Anne Lawrence, by then, Anne Bondy. Muriel hadn't told her predecessor's daughter that he was in the hospital. Anne learned of Francis's illness by reading his obituary. Dale Calloway lamented, "I never said goodbye to him—I thought he'd always be there. He was very, very good to me. I loved him."[56]

The *Boston Evening Globe* printed a long, accurate, sensitive obituary of Francis with photographs of both him and the *Ticonderoga*. The *New York Times* obituary was shorter, and its writer seemed to think that Francis had played an active role building boats at the Herreshoff yard, which he placed in Bristol, Connecticut. But the *Times* copy-desk man, in his headline, did bill Francis as "Dean of U. S. Yacht Designers."[57]

Muriel Vaughn's mother had made an arrangement with George E. McQuesten, for whom Francis had designed the first 30-Square-Metre boat (see volume 1, page 316) to look after him in his old age in return for an inheritance. (Despite McQuesten's considerable wealth, the inheritance could not have been large, judging by Muriel's straitened circumstances.) When Muriel had gone to work for Francis, she had a similar arrangement in mind.[58]

Anne Lawrence had understood from Francis back when she was sailing with him a lot that The Castle would be left to her (and that Francis's collection of marine prints and paintings would go to Billy Strawbridge). But, in 1950, Anne married Eugene Bondy, an outsider (meaning from outside Marblehead and even New England) and a Jew, and that did not sit well with Francis. "He didn't approve of my husband," Anne said. "He was still very friendly, always glad to see me, but it was very different." Anne learned, but not from Francis, that The Castle would not be hers after all.[59]

Francis's will of 1966 left everything to Margrete Stinnes. Gretl didn't take that act of generosity seriously; she somehow didn't expect to ever be mistress of a castle. In 1970, after more than three years of having Muriel Vaughn work for him, Francis altered his will to name her the sole beneficiary. Muriel inherited The Castle (valued at $48,000) and all its contents (valued at $25,000), together with Francis's modest income of $6,000 from his father's estate. She moved into The Castle permanently to look after things and continued to answer inquiries about his designs as best she could.[60]

Among the people who cared about L. Francis Herreshoff's yacht designs, there were many ideas about what should happen to his plans and collections. Dale Calloway believed that Francis, himself, thought that Muriel would somehow turn The Castle into a museum. In 1967, Charles R. Schultz, librarian at Mystic Seaport Museum, had written to Francis suggesting he might think about donating his plans and letters to the museum. Francis replied: "My will is already made, with

another disposition [to Margrete Stinnes] of my things." After Francis's death, John Kendall tried unsuccessfully to get control of his plans and letters in order to put them into the public domain.[61]

As for his family, Francis never thought of leaving anything to them. When his sister Agnes died in 1965, the family gathered to see who wanted what from her house. Francis just took an old cane, and it seemed to him that the rest of the family members were acting like vultures. He believed that neither his brother Sidney nor his nephew Halsey, both yacht designers, cared anything about his plans and even ridiculed his ideas—some people in a similar position, he said, leave everything to their cats. It's true that Sidney and Francis had gone their separate ways as yacht designers, and when Sidney established the Herreshoff Marine Museum in 1971, he had no thought to include his brother's work in its mission. The focus was on his father and the Herreshoff Manufacturing Company. Halsey couldn't understand why his uncle had left his estate to Muriel Vaughn. Sidney, Griswold, and Francis's nieces, Clara and Natalie, wondered at Francis's lack of good stewardship, when he let family heirlooms, especially the portraits of George and Martha Washington, pass into the hands of a stranger, and they tried, without success, to break his will. Only Clarence voiced no objection.[62]

Francis's will directed that his body be cremated "and the ashes thereof scattered on the waters in the proximity of Half Way Rock, located east of said town of Marblehead, and that there be no memorial marker or other gravestone erected to my memory." Muriel kept the urn in the downstairs room where Francis had lived, waiting for an opportunity to carry out his wish. The ideal chance came seven months later, when the *Ticonderoga* called at Marblehead. Muriel, with help from an old Marblehead friend, Donald R. "Fritz" Schaller, chartered the big ketch, and, with her owners, Ken and Fran Mackenzie, and a few close friends, went out on July 30, 1973, to carry out Francis's instruction. A tearful Muriel upended the urn from the *Ticonderoga*'s deck, and off the ashes went—floating in a neatly tied, plastic bag! In a sort of man-overboard drill, the *Ticonderoga* was maneuvered back alongside, holes were poked, the ashes were freed, and Francis was saved from making his final voyage in a plastic vessel. Another ceremony went more smoothly. Francis's neighbor, Suzy Coe, launched a small, model open-boat that Francis had carved for her from the Town Landing in Marblehead Harbor at sunset

L. Francis Herreshoff at the relaunching of the *Bounty* as the *Poquita*, at Lee's Boatshop in Rockland, Maine, September 1972, three months before his death. Looking at the most beautiful yacht in the world, Francis liked what he saw. (John Hammer photo, Rockland Courier-Gazette, courtesy O. Lie-Nielsen)

as a way to say goodbye. "He was special," she said. Perhaps Francis's spirit navigated this boat, more to his liking, out among the islands where he loved to paddle.[63]

Muriel Vaughn was distraught after Francis's death. Her drinking increased. She formed the habit of giving away things from The Castle, particularly during cocktail hour, to Herreshoff fans whom she deemed deserving. Fortunately, her gifts did not extend to inked yacht plans or letters. They did, however, include books, photographs, art objects, and, perhaps most distressing, penciled, preliminary drawings of yacht designs. Eventually, however, Muriel Vaughn did the right thing. At the skillful and patient urging of Mystic Seaport Museum staffers Barry Thomas and Maynard Bray, she donated all of L. Francis Herreshoff's plans and letters to Mystic Seaport Museum. Muriel retained the rights to build to the plans, and these passed to her daughter, Elizabeth, who has since ceded them to Mystic Seaport Museum.[64]

The Castle still huddles in the shelter of its Crocker Park ledge, perhaps reminding elderly Marbleheaders of its former eccentric inhabitant. The unusual stone structure has passed into other private hands. It would, of course, have made a wonderful museum.

L. Francis Herreshoff's life defined what it means to be an artist. He could imagine beautiful shapes and put them on paper in elegant mechanical drawings. His beautiful shapes, moreover, were practical; made into boats, they were seaworthy and fast. They could move through the water with minimal resistance, whether propelled by wind or motor. Francis's practical side came to the fore with his construction drawings. He knew just the best ways to build a boat, and he could draw every detail of those ways for a builder to follow. His extraordinary sense of proportion—necessary for an artist—allowed him to size the structural members of a boat without the need to use formulas.

Francis perfected the double-ender, in both racing and cruising boats. He loved the pointed stern as an artist and as a seaman. In the *Tioga*, he perfected the clipper bow and designed the most beautiful yacht in the world. In the *Ticonderoga*, he drew the handsomest yacht in the world and one of the most famous, thanks to her speed, as well as her beauty.

Sailors take for granted their generous headsail areas, a change in rig proportion that Francis recognized early in his career. His mast tang, never patented, is an invention that has been in common use for nearly a hundred years.

Francis's artistic talent extended to his writing. He could be poetic and whimsical, as well as technically accurate and argumentative.

He was a master craftsman, whether working in metal or wood. His artistry shows in every one of the thousands of lovely objects he fashioned.

With his beard, his beret, his poodles, and his sports cars tooling slowly along Marblehead's streets in high gear—not to mention his one-man, stone castle—L. Francis Herreshoff cut an eccentric figure. He was an outsider. As an adult, his only close relationship in his family was with his father, and that was fraught with difficulty. Francis did not make friends easily. The dozen close friends he had were those he could trust to support him.

Francis could be pessimistic, and he could play the role of victim, yet his bachelor's life was basically a happy one. Seldom a day went by when his advice wasn't sought by friend, acquaintance, or stranger. He surrounded himself with beauty, much of it of his own devising. Each day he could exercise his enormous artistic and engineering abilities and manual skill. Each day, he could teach in conversation and in writing. He must have looked forward to many a day with anticipation of good things to come, and he must have looked back on many a day with a sense of satisfaction.

Francis exceeded his great father's accomplishments at times with the high quality of his designs, though certainly not their quantity. His clipper-bowed yachts in particular, but also his H-28 and his Rozinante boat, came closer to perfection than Nathanael's designs for boats with similar purposes. Yet he lived in his father's shadow for his whole life, even after his father died.

Francis also labored in the shadow of his contemporaries. For every L. Francis Herreshoff boat, there were many John Alden boats, as well as Olin Stephens, Phil Rhodes, and Starling Burgess boats, with William Garden and even the young Phil Bolger catching up fast. With the exception of the H-28, Francis's exquisite designs gathered dust.

Although L. Francis Herreshoff left a reputation for beautiful, fast boats, he died believing that his work was misunderstood and unappreciated. In fact, his designs and writing were about to help fuel an unexpected revival of wooden boatbuilding and interest in classic boat design. He needs no "memorial marker or other gravestone." His yacht designs and books will do. And even this "overly long story," as I am sure he would call it, may serve his memory.

In many parts of the watery world, sailors are steering boats designed by L. Francis Herreshoff. Off Marblehead, a Rozinante boat runs for the harbor, wing-and-wing, using the last of a dying southeast breeze to get in before dark. As she takes a quick little roll, the sailor at her tiller gazes aft and smiles at her slim stern sliding along, leaving hardly a trace of its passage. In the Golden Gate, a 1,000-square-foot Restricted-Sail-Area cruiser, the *Harmony,* walks to windward footing 8.5 knots under just jib and mizzen, her 55-foot, double-ended hull remarkably steady and dry in the strong-breeze chop. Being an imaginary craft, she is on a vicarious voyage, merely out to meet the late afternoon fog blowing in from the Farallones. On a passage from Bermuda to Block Island, a Marco Polo heads for the Gulf Stream on an easy beam reach, her big diesel helping her four working sails to give her 8 knots and another 200-mile day. And here's the magnificent *Ticonderoga,* down for the Antigua Classic Yacht Regatta. She's the one with the gorgeous hull, spitting a trade-wind sea off her lee bow to send suds racing down her side just out of reach of the bronze dolphins. A Meadow Lark, running north on Currituck Sound in North Carolina, has the whole place to herself. She is making knots in the fresh, quartering breeze that has followed a serious rainsquall. Leeboards up, she has a myriad of choices for a berth for the night. Maybe, her skipper thinks, I'll just duck into Parker Creek at Waterlily and stick her nose in the marsh grass. And think of the H-28s out there! The *Snarke* herself is becalmed in the moonlight, her crew dreaming and asking each other, "What's it all mean?"

Chronology
Endnotes, Bibliography
Index

AN L. FRANCIS HERRESHOFF CHRONOLOGY, 1930–1972

1930
May 15: Francis is designing the *Dulcinea* (Design No. 55).

July: Francis designs a 10-foot pram for Charlie Welch.

July 25: Francis is designing an ocean racing ketch for Dudley Wolfe (Design No. 47), not built (Wolfe built the *Highland Light* instead, designed by Frank Paine).

September 30: Francis is designing the *Landfall*, 71-foot ketch (Design No. 49) for Paul Hammond for the 1931 Transatlantic Race.

October 12: Francis makes preliminary design for Special Inshore Patrol Boat (no design number), not built.

November 10: Francis is designing the *Hayseed*, 18-foot LWL Sonder boat type, (no design number), not built.

December: Francis designs an eight-oared shell for Chandler Hovey, design not finished, not built.

1931
Francis has appendix removed.

Francis makes preliminary design for a 130-foot, three-masted schooner, design not finished, not built.

Francis makes preliminary designs for a 30-foot Marconi yawl; a 30-foot sloop, a la Fisher's Island 31; and a 38-foot, hard-chine ketch. None built. Depression times are hard.

January 26: Francis is designing a 250-square-foot class for Corinthian Yacht Club, not built.

March 5: Francis draws lines for a model of the *Walrus*.

April 1: Francis designs an anchor windlass.

ca. April 1: Francis sells the *Visitor*.

April: Francis designs the releasing sheet winch.

April: Francis is designing the *Dulcinea* (Design No. 55)..

April 18: Francis designs the new lapping jib for the R-boat *Mary*, "From the Office of L. Francis Herreshoff."

May 26: Francis designs third new rig for the *Nor'easter IV*, an Alden Q-boat.

May 28: Francis makes preliminary design, "Study of a[n] Elongated Norwegian Pilot Boat."

May 29: Francis draws lines for the *Tioga* (Design No. 50), 57-foot ketch for Waldo H. Brown.

Summer: O. "Lee" Lie-Nielsen goes to work for Francis, mostly inspecting construction, and lives at 20 Lee Street.

June 25: Francis is designing the *Albatross* (Design No. 51), an 83-foot motor-sailer for Charlie Welch, not built.

July 4: Transatlantic Race starts. The *Landfall*, scratch boat, finishes second (to *Dorade*), comes in sixth of ten on corrected time.

August 15: Francis designs a new rig for the *Valiant*, a Crocker sloop built by Lawley's in 1927.

1932

January 2: First frostbite dinghy race held at Manhasset Bay, Port Washington, Long Island.

January 25: Francis is designing the *Ben-My-Chree* (Design No. 53).

Spring: The *Tioga* launched at the Britt Brothers yard in Lynn, Massachusetts.

May 2: Francis designs the fourth new rig for the *Nor'easter IV*, now *Taygeta.*

Summer: Norman Skene goes kayaking off Marblehead. Kayak found empty and adrift, Skene is presumed drowned.

September 17: Francis is designing the 30-Square-Metre one-design class for the Beverly Yacht Club.

September 17: Francis draws lines for the Beverly Yacht Club 30-Square-Metre class (Design No. 52).

October: Francis designs new rig for Willoughby Stuart's Bear Island Boat.

November 7: Francis is designing the *La Petite* (Design No. 54), frostbite dinghy.

Winter 1932-33: Francis makes forty kayak trips.

December 25: Francis goes for a sail in his dinghy, *La Petite.*

1933

March 17: Francis is designing a Class B dinghy *Whim* (Design No. 56).

June 19: Francis designs fifth new rig for the *Nor'easter IV*, now *Taygeta.*

July 10: Francis makes preliminary design for 57-foot version of the *Walrus* (not built).

August: Fenwick Williams is working for Francis as a draftsman. (Also designing on his own after leaving Murray Peterson.)

August 8: Francis is designing the dory-type double paddle canoe (Design No. 57), later to be a How-To-Build boat for *The Rudder,* September 1947.

ca. September 1: Katherine Jones is sent off to Italy.

November 14: Francis is designing the *Bounty*, 57-foot ketch (Design No. 58), for Edward B. Dane, a keel version of *Tioga.*

Winter 1933-34: Francis makes seventeen kayak trips.

1934

Francis, friendly with Uffa Fox, contributes to Fox's *Second Book*, published in 1935.

January 5: Francis designs tender for the *Bounty.*

February 4: Francis writes to his younger brother Clarence.

Early 1934: Lee-Nielsen moves out of 20 Lee Street.

March: Captain John Albert Chambers, USN (Ret.) rooms and boards with Francis at 20 Lee Street. Early in 1935 he will move out for a year, then moves back in until early 1943. He will handle what little brokerage business Francis does. The friendship lasts until Chambers's death in spring 1962.

Spring: William J. Strawbridge buys the *Istalena*. He will become a good friend to Francis, will have him design eight boats (three not built), from the 12-Metre *Mitena* of 1935, through the powerboat *Melantho* of 1958. The friendship will last until Francis's death in 1972.

June: Francis sends Nathanael a nice Father's Day note.

June 28: Francis is designing the *Gadget*, a launch for Charlie Welch (Design No. 59).

July: Francis makes preliminary design for a wide cutter for ocean racing.

September: Katherine Jones returns to Marblehead from Italy.

September: Francis makes preliminary sail plan for the *Tioga II*, 72-foot ketch (Design No. 66), for Harry Noyes. Francis makes acquaintance of Noyes. Relationship starts out friendly enough, but sours. Noyes owns Quincy Adams, the yard that builds *Tioga II*. Francis believes Noyes paid his design commission based on a deflated construction cost.

September 7: Francis is designing a 17-foot sailing canoe for the American Canoe Association (Design No. 60). (He will send plans to Clarence on January 3, 1935.)

September, October: Thomas B. F. Davis, owner of the Herreshoff schooner *Westward*, asks Nathanael for a design for a J-boat. Nathanael, age 86, writes Francis, saying he's too old, and offers to recommend Francis to Davis. Francis: No thanks.

November 24: Francis makes preliminary design for a 50-foot version of the *Stormy Petrel*.

Winter 1934-35: Nathanael stays in Bristol, rather than going to Florida.

Winter 1934-35: Francis makes eight kayak trips.

December: Francis makes preliminary design for an eight-oared shell.

December 3: Francis starts design for the *Mobjack*, a 45-foot ketch (Design No. 63).

Christmas: Francis goes to Bristol.

1935

January: Francis designs the *So And So*, 15-foot sailing dinghy, (Design No. 64), built by the Herreshoff Manufacturing Company and finished by himself, for his own use.

January: Francis designs racing kayak for Ludwig Hanson to build in Denmark.

January: Francis makes preliminary design for an 18-foot launch for Ludwig Hanson in Denmark (not built).

ca. January 20: Francis starts design for the *Mitena*, (Design No. 62) a 12-Metre boat for William J. Strawbridge.

May: Francis designs a 38-foot double-ended ketch for Larry Johnson (Design No. 65), not built (until Dan Brayton builds her, 1984-87, as the sloop, *Deva*).

ca. June 1: *Mitena* launched.

July: Fred Goeller is hired by Francis as a draftsman. Works on *Tioga II* plans.

August 31: Francis starts design for a 48-foot launch for Miss Louise N. Grace (Design No. 67), not finished or built.

September 10: Francis draws sail plan for *Tioga II*.

Winter 1935-36: K. Aage Nielsen works for Francis as draftsman.

Winter 1935-36: Francis employs "six or eight" draftsmen, but lets them all go in 1936. They include Samuel H. Brown Jr., K. Aage Nielsen, Fenwick Williams, and Fred Goeller.

1936

Francis has a nice Buick.

ca. May 1: Francis buys 25 Front Street and moves there from 20 Lee Street.

June 16: Francis is paid $833 for "adjusted service" in the US Navy during World War I.

August 10: The *Tioga II* (later renamed *Ticonderoga*) is launched at Quincy Adams yard, falling over on the ways. Repaired, she is re-launched the next day.

September: Francis designs a 51-foot Block Island boat for William J. Strawbridge (Design No. 68), not built.

November 7: Francis designs a pistol.

November: Francis designs the *Persephone*, a 55-foot yawl to the CCA ocean-racing rule for William J. Strawbridge (Design No. 69).

November: Francis designs the *Koala*, a small, keel version of the *Ben-My-Chree* (Design No. 70) for Willoughby Stuart (boat is for his 16-year-old son Harborne).

November: Francis designs a cat-ketch sail plan for a 14-foot Whitehall dinghy for Willoughby Stuart.

1937
Francis makes a preliminary design for a 58-foot motor-sailer for George Upton, not built.

February: Francis designs the *Hard Tack*, a keel modification of the *Prudence* for R. P. Jenks, (Design No. 71). This design will become "How To Build the H-23" in *The Rudder*, October 1945.

April: Francis's article on the Yankee One-Design class published in *The Rudder*.

September: Francis makes preliminary design for a 52-foot coastal power cruiser for Charlie Welch, not built.

November: Francis designs a double-paddle.

November: Francis designs the schooner *Mistral* (Design No. 73).

1938
March-April: Francis designs the *Diddikai*, a 38-foot double-ended ketch (Design No. 74), not built. Plans published in *The Rudder*, June 1942. Several built starting in 1946.

June 2: Nathanael dies at age 90.

Francis photographs Nathanael's model room, the only such record made.

July: Francis makes preliminary design for a shoal-draft ketch for William J. Strawbridge (Design No. 75), design not finished, not built.

August: Francis makes a preliminary design for a 39-foot cruising sloop, design not finished.

August: Francis makes a preliminary design for a 40-foot keel-and-centerboard sloop, design not finished.

September 21: Hurricane strikes New England.

1939
January 1: Francis designs new fore triangle for the *Nor'easter V* (Design No. 26), now *Spindle*.

February 23: William J. Strawbridge is designing his own version of the Development boat *Flutterby* (Design No. 48).

April 4: Francis's friend Waldo H. Brown, for whom he had designed the *Joann* and the *Tioga*, dies in a naval aviation accident at Quincy, Massachusetts.

Francis designs new yawl rig for the Bar Harbor 31 *Cricket*.

1940
February 15: Francis is designing the *Solitaire*, a 28-foot sloop (Design No. 76).

June: Francis designs the Northeast Harbor One-Design (Design No. 77). World War II stopped production after two boats built.

July: Francis makes preliminary design for a 145-foot "Submarine Destroyer" (Design No. 78), not built.

1941
Francis makes preliminary design for a 69-foot fishing vessel, lines only (Design No. 79), design not finished, not built.

May: Francis designs a new sail plan for Rolf Armstrong's sailing canoe, the "Damosel," presumably *Damsel*.

Summer: Francis meets Boris Lauer-Leonardi, who has a travel agency in Cambridge.

December 7: Pearl Harbor attack.

1942
May: Boris becomes associate editor of *The Rudder*. He has a limp, which keeps him out of the armed forces.

September: Plans of the H-23 (Design No. 71) published in *The Rudder*.

September: Boris becomes editor of *The Rudder* when William F. Crosby joins the war effort, working for the navy.

Fall: Francis designs the H-28 (Design No. 80) for Boris and *The Rudder*.

November: Francis designs a 49-foot ocean cruising ketch for William A. Robinson (Design No. 81), not built.

December: First How-to-Build article by Francis printed in *The Rudder*, the start of the H-28 series, which will run through December 1943.

Winter 1942-43: Francis sells the *So And So* to Rolf Armstrong.

1943

Francis befriends young near-by neighbor children Peter, Chris, and Suzy Coe. He makes them lots of beautiful things of wood, including, eventually, wedding presents.

April: Francis's first imaginative writing, "The Building of the Snarke," published in *The Rudder*.

ca. June 1: Al Chambers moves out of the studio at the rear of 25 Front Street, and Rolf Armstrong moves in. Armstrong will take room and board with Francis for the next several summers, having a room at The Castle starting in 1945. He makes a good living painting beautiful, mostly fanciful women, lives on Long Island (later in New York), likes sailing canoes, is very generous with Francis. The friendship will last until he moves to Hawaii in 1956 and dies in 1960.

June: First crusading article by Francis, "Lapping Jibs and Double Spinnakers," on the foolishness of unmeasured light sails, published in *The Rudder*.

June-September: Francis working leisurely on design for the *Quiet Tune* (Design No. 82), as Edwin Hill won't have her built until after the War.

September: Francis's "A Sail in the Alerion" published in *The Rudder*.

October: Francis's "A Midsummer Night's Sail" published in *The Rudder*.

October 17: Francis is working on sail plan for clipper-bowed sloop for Russell Genner (Design No. 83), design process continues beyond September 16, 1947, but not finished.

November: Francis's "Cutters, Laying To" etc., published in *The Rudder*.

November 16: Francis's poodle, Princess, had puppies. He keeps two: Aurora and Aphrodite.

1944

January: Francis's "Marine Pictures" published in *The Rudder*.

March: Plans for the Genner sloop (Design No. 83) published in *The Rudder*.

March: First installment of Francis's "The Common Sense of Yacht Design" published in *The Rudder*. The series will run through January 1948

Francis designs brigantine rig for William A. Robinson's *Varua* (designed by Starling Burgess, who is doing design work for the navy).

July, August: Francis's two-part series, "How To Build H-14," published in *The Rudder*.

Francis moves from 25 Front Street to The Castle sometime between September 21, 1944, and January 10, 1945.

October: Llewellyn Howland's first article published in *The Rudder*.

December: Francis's "A Scheme for Remembering the Storm Signals and a Short Discourse on Barometer Indications" published in *The Rudder*.

December 8: Francis sends card to *The Rudder* for an ad on designers' page. Ad appears in January 1945 and advertises Francis as Retired.

December: Francis sends his first article on the Marco Polo to *The Rudder*. Series will run through February 1947 (concurrently with "Common Sense").

1945
October: Francis's single article, "How To Build Prudence, H-23," published in *The Rudder.* Other writings, some including design work, are being published throughout 1945.

1946
Francis designs sixth new rig for the Q-boat *Nor'easter IV*, now *Taygeta*.

Francis has a Mercedes-Benz diesel.

February: Francis designs the Buzzard's Bay 14-footer (Design No. 86) for Llewellyn Howland.

July: Francis's first book, *The Writings of L. Francis Herreshoff*, published by Rudder Publishing.

September: Francis designs staysail schooner rig change for the *Pleione*, a New York 50.

September: Francis's poodle Princess dies.

December: Rudder Publishing brings out *The Common Sense of Yacht Design*, volume 1. It includes ten chapters that had been published in the magazine through February 1946.

December: Boris doubles Francis's rate of pay in *The Rudder* (from $15 per page to $30 per page).

December: Francis designs new rig for the *Santee*, Burgess, Swasey and Paine Design No. 269.

Francis earned $1,886 from *The Rudder in 1946.*

1947
January: Francis listed as Contributing Editor on *The Rudder* masthead.

March: First installment of Francis's "How to Build Nereia" published in *The Rudder.* The series will run through July 1948.

March 19: Starling Burgess dies.

May: Francis's obituary of Starling Burgess published in *The Rudder.*

September: Francis's "The Double-Paddle Canoe" published in *The Rudder.*

Francis earned $3,327.45 from *The Rudder* in 1947.

1948
February: Francis's "Paddles, Backrests" etc., published in *The Rudde*r.

March: Francis's "Naming the Yacht" published in *The Rudder.*

April: Francis's "The Dry Breakers" published in *The Rudder.*

May, June: Francis's "Capt. Charley Barr" published in *The Rudder.*

July: Francis's "Yachting in the 1900s" published in *The Rudder.*

August: Francis's "The Names of Some of the Yacht Sails" published in *The Rudder.*

August: First installment of Francis's "How to Build Meadow Lark" published in *The Rudder*. Series will run through March 1949.

August 31: *The Common Sense of Yacht Design*, volume 2, published by Rudder. Francis gets his author's copies.

September: Francis's "The Names of Some of the Rigging" published in *The Rudde*r.

November, December: Francis's "Some Hints on Model Making" published in *The Rudder.*

November 5: Francis begins to design the *Araminta* (Design No. 89), finishing in March 1949.

1949
January: First installment of Francis's "N. G. Herreshoff and Some of the Yachts he Designed" published in *The Rudder*. Series will run through April 1951.

May: First installment of Francis's "How to Build Sailski" published in *The Rudder*. Series will run through February 1950.

1950
January: Francis designs 36-foot powerboat for William J. Strawbridge, not built.

March: First installment of Francis's "How to Build Barracuda" published in *The Rudder*. Series will continue in April, May, and July 1950.

March: Francis designs the *Piquant* (Design No. 92) for William J. Strawbridge.

April: Francis designs another rig change for the *Pleione*.

July: Francis's "Rudder Rating Rule for Small Racing Sailboats" published in *The Rudder*.

1951

Francis makes drawing of three preliminary designs for cruising ketches, 60-85 feet, trying to sell Edward Dane on the idea. Francis wants to design one more big, important yacht. Dane doesn't bite.

March 1-November 14: Francis works with Frank Paine on the design of an oscillating-disk crankshaft.

June 22: Francis is designing a clipper-bowed sloop for John Garber (Design No. 93), not built. Design drags out to at least January 12, 1956.

July: Francis's article on the schooner yacht *America* published in *The Rudder*.

1952

March: First installment of Francis's "The Compleat Cruiser" published in *The Rudder*. Series will run through August 1954.

October 28: Frank Paine dies.

1953

November: Francis designs a 57-foot powerboat for William J. Strawbridge (Design No. 94), not built.

1954

Francis inherits money after Ann Roebuck Herreshoff dies.

Francis has a telephone, and a radio. He will never have a television.

Francis designs white-water kayak (Design No. 95).

April: Francis's design for the *Araminta* published in *The Rudder*.

December 4: Francis begins to design a canoe yawl based on the *Rozinante* of *The Compleat Cruiser* for John Sewall (Design No. 96). Design process will continue through March 21, 1955.

1955

Allan Vaitses, boatbuilder at Mattapoisett, Massachusetts, inspired by *The Common Sense of Yacht Design*, wants to build designs by Francis and makes the pilgrimage to The Castle. He will build many Meadow Larks, the *Dulcinea*, Rozinantes, a Nereia. The friendship lasts until Francis's death in 1972.

April: Francis's "The Theory of the Contrapropeller" published in *The Rudder*.

December 15: Francis is designing a 60-foot vedette boat (Design No. 97), not built.

1956

January 30: Francis begins to draw construction plan for the Rozinante (Design No. 98) for Calvin T. Howell. Design process continues through April 4, 1957.

February: Francis's "Trailboards and Figureheads" published in *The Rudder*.

April-May: Francis designs a whitewater canoe (Design No. 101).

April: Francis off masthead of *The Rudder* as Contributing Editor through May 1958.

May-July: Francis designs *Wagon Box* (Design No. 99), for W. H. Shirley.

July: Lee Nielsen makes a model of a car-top boat he hopes to market; Francis takes lines off model for him.

November: Francis's design for the cat yawl *Dancing Feather* (Design No. 102) published in *The Rudder*.

Late 1957: *The Rudder* changes ownership from the Thomson family to "one of the large New York publishing companies" (Fawcett). No mention of this in the magazine.

1958

April: First installment of Francis's "An Introduction to Yachting" published in *The Rudder*. Series will run through June 1961.

April 21-October 10: Francis designs the *Melantho* (Design No.103), a 40-foot powerboat for William J. Strawbridge.

May: Boris Lauer-Leonardi leaves *The Rudder*. His understudy, Ralph J. Ianuzzi, becomes editor.

ca. May 1: Francis trades his Mercedes 300SL to William J. Strawbridge in exchange for the *Piquant*, which he renames *Freelance*.

August: Moulton H. Farnham replaces Ianuzzi as editor of *The Rudder*.

October 6: Francis sends Calvin Howell fittings he's made for his Rozinante.

Francis designs the *Golden Ball* (Design No 104).

December 1: Francis finishes lines of the *Persephone* (not the ocean-racing yawl), not built.

1959

After trading the Mercedes to William J. Strawbridge, Francis's next car is an Aston-Martin.

April: Boris Lauer-Leonardi back as editor of *The Rudder*.

John Kendall buys the *Araminta*. A wealthy and able man, he becomes a devotee of Francis and will later get a Nereia, a Mobjack, and a Bounty.

December: Ellery W. Mann Jr. becomes publisher of *The Rudder* (he had been the magazine's treasurer).

1960

Francis gets $50 per page for text and illustrations in *The Rudder*.

February: *The Rudder* moves to 575 Lexington Avenue.

June 18-September 12: Francis designs the *Unicorn* (Design No. 106) for Stanley Woodward, not built.

October: Francis sells the Aston-Martin and gets a Lancia, which he will keep until his death.

1961

February: Francis designs a plastic bilge pump.

Margrete Stinnes, daughter of Hans, comes to the U. S. to live and work in New York. Francis treats her like a daughter when she visits. (He will later propose that she come to work as his assistant, living in a room he'll finish over the garage. She's tempted, but elects to stay with her work in New York.)

1962

January: Last appearance of Francis's designer's (retired) ad in *The Rudder*.

Spring: Al Chambers dies.

April: Francis makes a preliminary design for a 66-foot powerboat (Design No. 100), not built.

September: Francis, Hans Stinnes, and Margrete Stinnes cruise to Newport in the *Freelance* to see the America's Cup Races.

1963

February: Boris Lauer-Leonardi leaves the *The Rudder* for good. He is replaced by Conrad Miller, a contributing editor who wrote about engines.

July 17: Francis is designing a 38-foot, shoal-draft, leeboard ketch (Design No. 107), his last major design.

1964

Francis buys new a 1963 Ferrari, which he has at his death.

August 3-November 17: Francis makes up a table of vessels' fastest runs to show off the performances of the *Ticonderoga.*

November 24: Francis designs plastic squirt gun for shooting gazoozalum into crevices in wood. The plan for Hans Stinnes to manufacture them in Germany fizzles.

December: Francis designs 12-foot Madoc duck boat.

1965

Francis spends much time working on his lathes through the 1960s, making numerous small brass cannons.

October: Francis sells the *Freelance* (ex-*Piquant*). She becomes the Harvard crew-coaching launch.

November: Francis's "Naptha Launches" is published in *The Rudder*. It is his last article published.

December: Dan Brayton, a neighbor, makes the pilgrimage to The Castle and becomes a devotee of Francis. He will have a Design No. 65 built in 1987.

1966

June 26-October 10: Francis designs an "improved O-ring."

August 5: Francis makes will, leaving his estate to Margrete Stinnes.

1967

Annie Klein at Caravan Maritime Books reprints *The Common Sense of Yacht Design* in one volume. (John Gardner reviews it favorably in *National Fisherman*.)

Boris Lauer-Leonardi, at his Poseidon Press, publishes *Yachts, Designs, and Much Miscellaneous Information,* which includes Francis's "The Answers to Some Interesting Nautical Questions."

March: Helen Bolster retires as Francis's secretary, having worked for him for forty-one years.

April 3: Muriel Vaughn starts work for Francis as secretary.

April 3: Francis writes to *Rudder* editor Mark Penzer, "I think I can write something for *The Rudder* if we can think of an interesting subject," but nothing comes of this.

1968

Paul Glynn, an auto mechanic who takes care of Francis's cars, becomes a devotee and friend. He and Francis talk cars at The Castle. After Francis's death, he will buy his Ferrari.

Francis befriends Dale Vosburgh, Katherine Jones Vosburgh's daughter, and becomes a mentor for this craftswoman.

Arthur Brendze becomes a friend and confidant of Francis. During the last years of Francis's life, Brendze visits The Castle almost daily.

1970

Lee Nielsen builds three Rozinantes, one to Francis's order. This boat is bought by Rudy Talbot. Francis is just financing the boat; he wasn't going to take delivery.

The Boatbuilders of Bristol published. Francis makes violent marginal notes in the copy he's given.

June 30: Francis makes a new will, changing his beneficiary from Margrete Stinnes to Muriel Vaughn.

1971

Sidney and Rebecca Herreshoff found the Herreshoff Marine Museum in Bristol.

1972

September: Francis attends relaunching of the *Bounty* (now named *Poquita*) at Lee's Boatshop in Rockland Maine.

September: Francis enters hospital with broken hip.

October: Francis reenters hospital for hip replacement.

October 27: Uffa Fox dies.

December 3: Francis dies. He has prostate cancer, but cause of death is pneumonia.

1973

February: Francis's obituary published in *The Rudder.*

July 30: Francis's ashes scattered off Half Way Rock east of Marblehead by Muriel Vaughn from the *Ticonderoga*.

HERRESHOFF FAMILY TREE

Corporal Eschoff (dates unknown)
Married ca. 1760
Agnes Müller (-ca. 1768)

Karl Friederich Herreshoff (1763-1819)
(changed to Charles Frederick Herreshoff 1785)
Married 1801

Anna Francis (1802-1887) unmarried
Sarah (1803-1882) unmarried
John Brown (1805-1861) unmarried
Agnes (1807-1849) unmarried
Charles Frederick (1809-1888)
James Brown (1811-1812)

John Brown (1736-1803)
Married 1760
Sarah Smith (1738-1825)

James (1761-1834)
Benjamin (1763-1773)
Abigail (1764-1766)
Abigail (Abby) (1766-1821)
Sarah (Sally) (1773-1846)
Alice (1777-1823)

Married 1833
Julia Ann Lewis (1811-1901)

James Brown (1834-1930) **A**
Caroline Louisa (1837-1924) **B**
Charles Frederick (1839-1917) **C**
John Brown (1841-1915) **D**
Lewis (1844-1926) unmarried
Sally Brown (1845-1917) unmarried
Nathanael Greene (1848-1938) **E**
John Brown Francis (1850-1932) **F**
Julian Lewis (1854-1919) **G**

A
James Brown Herreshoff (1834-1930)
Married 1875
Jane Brown (1855-1924)

Jane (Jeannette) Brown (1876-1964)

James Brown (1878-1945)
Charles Frederick II (1880-1954)
William Stuart (1883-1969)
Anna Francis (1886-1978)

B
Caroline Louisa Herreshoff (1837-1924)
Married 1866
E. Stanton Chesebrough

Albert Stanton Chesebrough (1868-1916)

C

Charles Frederick Herreshoff (1839-1917)

Married (1) 1863
Mary Potter (1843-1866)
|
Julian Ann (1864-1942)

Married (2) 1868
Alice Almy (1838-1931)

D

John Brown Herreshoff (1841-1915)

Married (1) 1870
Sarah Lucas Kilton (1837-1906)
|
Katherine Kilton (1871-1954) H

Married (2) 1892
Eugenia Tams Tucker (1857-1940)

E

Nathanael Greene Herreshoff (1848-1938)

Married (1) 1883
Clara Ann DeWolf (1853-1905)
|
Agnes Müller (1884-1965)
Algernon Sidney DeWolf (1886-1977) I
Nathanael Greene Jr. (1888-1926) J
Alexander Griswold (1889-1986) K
Lewis Francis (1890-1972)
Clarence DeWolf (1895-1983) L

Married (2) 1915
Ann Roebuck (1873-1950)

F

John Brown Francis Herreshoff (1850-1932)

Married (1) 1876
Grace Eugenia Dyer (1851-1880)
|
Louise Chamberlin (1876-1967)

Married (2) 1882
Emilie Duval Lee (1863-1930)
|
Francis Lee (1883-1956)
Frederic (1888-1922)
Sarah Lothrop (1889-)

John Brown Francis Herreshoff (1850-1932)

Married (3) 1919
Carrie Ridley Enslow (ca. 1870-1924)

Married (4) 1925
Irma Grey Ridley (ca. 1873-1946)

G

Julian Lewis Herreshoff (1854-1919)
Married 1879
Ellen Frances Taft (1852-1922)
|
Grace (1881-1950)

H

Katherine Kilton Herreshoff (1871-1954)
Married 1896
Lewis Henry DeWolf (1855-1900)
|
Katherine Herreshoff DeWolf (Pendlebury) (1897-)
Louise Henry DeWolf (1898-1986)

I
Algernon Sidney DeWolf Herreshoff (1886-1977)
Married 1930
Rebecca Chase (1894-1991)
|
Nathanael Greene III (1931-)
Halsey Chase (1933-)

J
Nathanael Greene Herreshoff Jr. (1888-1926)
Married 1918
Helen Byron Warren (1895-1983)
|
Clara DeWolf (1920-1982)
Natalie Warren (1923-2002)

K
Alexander Griswold Herreshoff (1889-1986)
Married 1917
Henrietta Haines (1893-1990)

L
Clarence DeWolf Herreshoff (1895-1983)
Married ca. 1924, separated 1925, divorced 1931

(Source: Samuel Carter III, *The Boatbuilders of Bristol* (New York: Doubleday and Company, 1970), expanded in 1996 by Nathanael Greene Herreshoff III and Carleton Pinheiro, and updated in 2017 by Andrew W. German)

ENDNOTES

Abbreviations

Throughout the notes, L. Francis Herreshoff will be abbreviated as LFH, and his father Nathanael Greene Herreshoff will be abbreviated as NGH. LFH published "The Common Sense of Yacht Design" as a continuing series in *The Rudder* and as stand-alone volumes. Citations in the notes normally list the *Rudder* issue, with the corresponding volume listing in parenthesis.

The Daniel S. Gregory Ships Plans Library at Mystic Seaport Museum is abbreviated as DSGSPL.

The G. W. Blunt White Library at Mystic Seaport Museum is abbreviated as GWBWL.

Citations to box and folder locations in the L. Francis Herreshoff Collection, Collection 138 at the G. W. Blunt White Library are abbreviated as 138:box number/folder number.

The Herreshoff Marine Museum in Bristol, RI, is abbreviated as HMM.

Chapter 12

1. LFH to NGH, February 26, 1929, 138:17/5, GWBWL; see SP38.155.1, DSGSPL.
2. LFH to Paul Hammond, December 4, 1958, 138:4/9, GWBWL; *Yachting* (August 1929): 75; *The Rudder* (January 1928): 78, (March 1928): 68.
3. Uffa Fox, *Sailing, Seamanship, and Yacht Construction* (London: Peter Davies, 1934), 28.
4. Herbert L. Stone, *Yachting* (November 1931): 62.
5. LFH to Captain C. F. Cook, August 17, 1944, 138:2/6; LFH to Paul Hammond, November 2, 1964, 138:5/5, GWBWL.
6. Construction Record for LFH Designs, 138:15/40; Paul Hammond to LFH, October 14, 1959, 138:4/10, GWBWL.
7. *The Rudder* (October 1931): 76; LFH to Captain C. F. Cook, August 17, 1944, 138:2/6, GWBWL.
8. Susan Hammond to LFH, August 9, 1931, 138:1/2; LFH to NGH, January 22, 1931, 138:17/7; LFH to NGH, February 10, 1931, 138:17/7, GWBWL.
9. Lucia del Sol Knight and Daniel B. MacNaughton, *The Encyclopedia of Yacht Designers* (New York: W. W. Norton, 2006), 373; LFH to Edward Dane, May 23, 1951, 138:4/2, GWBWL.

10. Herbert L. Stone, *Yachting* (February 1931): 98.
11. LFH to NGH, July 20, 1931, 138:17/7, GWBWL.
12. Fox, *Sailing, Seamanship, and Yacht Construction*, 37; *Yachting* (July 1931): 16.
13. *The Rudder* (July 1931): 16, 68; *Yachting* (August 1931): 38, 83.
14. Fox, *Sailing, Seamanship, and Yacht Construction*, 43; Carl L. Weagant, "Across the Atlantic with the Racing Fleet," *Yachting* (September 1931): 37.
15. Weagant, "Across the Atlantic with the Racing Fleet," 38; *Yachting* (August 1931): 110.
16. Fox, *Sailing, Seamanship, and Yacht Construction*, 42.
17. Weagant, "Across the Atlantic with the Racing Fleet," 39. Weagant was navigator in the *Highland Light*.
18. Fox, *Sailing, Seamanship, and Yacht Construction*, 30, 44; Ben Ames, "Trans-Atlantic Aboard *Landfall*," *Yachting Monthly* (October 1931): 396. Ames was navigator in the *Landfall*.
19. Ames, "Trans-Atlantic Aboard *Landfall*," 398.
20. Ames, "Trans-Atlantic Aboard *Landfall*," 399; Fox, *Sailing, Seamanship, and Yacht Construction*, 27.
21. Weagant, "Across the Atlantic with the Racing Fleet," 85; Fox, *Sailing, Seamanship, and Yacht Construction*, 46.
22. Weagant, "Across the Atlantic with the Racing Fleet," 85; Fox, *Sailing, Seamanship, and Yacht Construction*, 46. The next year, in the 1932 Bermuda Race, the *Highland Light*, skippered by Frank Paine, set an elapsed-time record that stood for twenty-four years.
23. Fox, *Sailing, Seamanship, and Yacht Construction*, 42, 43; Ames, "Trans-Atlantic Aboard *Landfall*," 399.
24. LFH, "The Common Sense of Yacht Design," *The Rudder* (November 1946): 42-44. LFH wrote two years later that he thought ocean racing to be "a noble and manly sport," but that was an untypical, politically-correct sop in the midst of a harsh criticism of a rating rule that would send such an uncomfortable boat to sea as the light-displacement *Myth of Malham*, see LFH, *An L. Francis Herreshoff Reader* (Camden, ME: International Marine Publishing, 1978), 277.
25. *Yachting* (November 1931): cover; *Yachting* (September 1931): 78, 80.
26. LFH, "The Common Sense of Yacht Design," *The Rudder* (November 1946): 42-45; NGH to LFH, July 24, 1931, 138:17/7, GWBWL.
27. *The Rudder* (December 1942): 16; Christopher Paine, e-mail to author, October 5, 2015; Susan Hammond to LFH, August 9, 1931, 138:1/2, GWBWL; Susan Hammond, *Landfalls Remembered* (New York: A. S. Barnes, 1963).
28. Walter Paine, e-mail to author, December 4, 2012; Fred Leviseur to LFH, May 1945, 138:2/7; Construction Record for LFH Designs, 138:15/8, GWBWL. One night in a Paris restaurant, the author had the following conversation with a friend of a friend whose name he didn't catch. Him: "Well, and what are you up to?" Me: "Oh, I'm writing a book, for one thing." Him: "What about?" Me: "It's a biography of an American yacht designer." Him: "I don't know anything about boats. My grandfather had a boat, though, a big, beautiful sailboat. I think it had two masts. Maybe you know it?" Me: "I, I, there are a lot of boats with. . . ." Him: "The boat's name was *Landfall*." Me: "Oh my! Yes, maybe I do know that boat." It turned out that I was talking to the actor, Guillaume Gallienne, grandson of Georges; R. de Dampiere to LFH, May 7, 1965, 138:7/4, GWBWL.
29. Christopher Paine, e-mail to author, October 5, 2015.

Chapter 13

1. LFH to NGH, July 28, 1933, 138:17/9, GWBWL.
2. LFH to NGH, September 22, 1933, 138:17/9; NGH to LFH, April 28, 1936, 138:17/12; LFH to NGH, June 29, 1932, 138:17/8, GWBWL.
3. NGH to LFH, August 14, 1935, 138:17/11, GWBWL.
4. LFH to John Ives Sewall, August 16, 1954, 138:4/5, GWBWL; John Stephen Doherty, *A Ketch Called Tahiti* (Camden, ME: 1987, International Marine Publishing, 1987), 41; John G. Hanna, "The Watch Below," *The Rudder* (July 1942): 38.
5. *Yachting* (February 1932): 81.
6. LFH to Uffa Fox, January 14, 1935, 138:1/5, GWBWL.

7. LFH to Gary Mitchell, June 21, 1965, 138:5/6, GWBWL.
8. Howard W. Ahern to LFH, February 8, 1946, 138:2/9; LFH to Herman Gucinski, January 30, 1969, 138:6/4, GWBWL.
9. Allan H. Vaitses to LFH, December 3, 1957, 138:4/8, GWBWL.
10. Allan H. Vaitses to LFH, December 3, 1957, 138:4/8; LFH to Gary Mitchell, June 21, 1965, 138:5/6, GWBWL.
11. Allan H. Vaitses to LFH, January 6, 1957 [1958], 138:4/8, GWBWL.
12. Allan H. Vaitses to LFH, May 7, 1958. 138:4/9; LFH to Allan H. Vaitses, December 10, 1957, 138:4/8, GWBWL.
13. Philip C. Bolger, *Boats With an Open Mind* (Camden, ME: International Marine Publishing, 1994), 372.
14. Allan H. Vaitses to LFH, August 10, and October 9, 1958, 138:4/9, GWBWL.
15. LFH to Allan H. Vaitses, September 22, 1958, 138:4/9, GWBWL; *The Rudder* (February 1962): 4; see also Worksheet 38.92, DSGSPL.
16. Allan H. Vaitses to LFH, October 9, 1958, 138:4/9, GWBWL; Allan H. Vaitses to LFH, January 6, 1957 [1958], 138:4/8; LFH to M. Dale Troglin, February 11, 1965, 138:5/6; William D. Gluth to LFH, November 30, 1965, 138:5/7; Ernest M. Hardy to LFH, July 21, 1967, 138:6/1; David Pierce-Jones to LFH, 138:6/1, GWBWL.
17. Artisan Boatshop website, accessed October 13, 2015.
18. LFH to Harry E. Noyes and F. J. Leviseur, May 23, 1935, 138:1/5; LFH to J. H. Peacock, May 12, 1947, 138:3/2, GWBWL; Daniel Brayton, e-mail to author, April 1, 2014; website of the town of Essex, MA; Bolger, *Boats With An Open Mind*, 223.
20. Daniel Brayton Sr., interview with author, Marblehead, MA, November 28, 1999.
21. Dan Brayton Jr., "The Genesis of Deva," *WoodenBoat* 157 (November/December 2000): 88-93.
22. Brayton, "The Genesis of Deva," 88-93.
23. Daniel Brayton Sr., e-mail to author, April 1, 2014; see SP38.94.2, DSGSPL.
24. Daniel Brayton Sr., e-mail to author, April 1, 2014; Brayton, "The Genesis of Deva."
25. Daniel Brayton Sr., e-mail to author, April 1, 2014.
26. Arthur Brendze, interview with author on board the Concordia yawl *Portuna*, Bucks Harbor, ME, July 1, 1999.
27. Boris Lauer-Leonardi to LFH, May 13, 1942, 138:2/3, GWBWL; *The Rudder* (June 1942): 30, 31, 42.
28. LFH to W. G. A. Breave, October 12, 1942, 138:2/3, GWBWL.
29. LFH to Richard S. Flaherty, July 30 and August 7, 1945, 138:2/8, GWBWL.
30. Richard S. Flaherty to LFH, December 16, 1946, 138:3/1; Richard S. Flaherty to LFH, March 31, 1948, 138:3/4; Richard S. Flaherty to LFH, November 1, 1948, 138:3/5, GWBWL; builder plaque in the *Natoma*, reported by owners Christine and Jim Alkire, e-mail to author, December 2, 2017.
31. LFH to Richard S. Flaherty, April 5, 1948, 138:3/4, GWBWL.
32. Richard S. Flaherty to LFH, March 31, 1948, 138:3/4, GWBWL.
33. David Baker, "World Cruise for Diddikai," *The Rudder* (July 1957): 59; LFH to M. Pierre, April 8, 1965, 138:5/6, GWBWL.
34. Hermann Gucinski to LFH, January 12, 1969, 138:7/7, GWBWL; Baker, "World Cruise for Diddikai"; LFH to M. Pierre, April 8, 1965, 138:5/6; LFH to M. V. Glanville, March 28, 1968, 138:6/2, GWBWL.
35. Warren H. Miller Jr. to LFH, March 15, 1968, 138:6/2, GWBWL.
36. Warren H. Miller Jr. to LFH, March 21, 1968, 138:6/2, GWBWL. The author was privileged to have a fine sail in the *Moonspinner* in Florida's Indian River and can report that she is, of course, fast and responsive.
37. Parkins Marine drawing, September 2, 1986, author's collection.
38. LFH to Hermann Gucinski, October 7, 1968, 138:6/3; LFH to George Riley, June 21, 1965, 138:5/6, GWBWL. This is a remarkable comment in the light of LFH's design in 1944 of his ultimate ocean

cruiser, the 55-foot, three-masted lifeboat, the Marco Polo; LFH to William D. Gluth, November 18, 1965, 138:5/7, GWBWL.

39. Document, 138:1/1; LFH to NGH, February 10, 1931, 138:17/7, GWBWL.
40. Document, 138:16/9, GWBWL.
41. "A Proposed Restricted Sail Are Rule," *Yachting* (March 1931): 96, 97.
42. LFH to NGH, March 30, 1931, 138:17/7; NGH to LFH, March 26, 1931, 138:17/7, GWBWL.
43. LFH, "The Names of Some of the Rigging," *An L. Francis Herreshoff Reader* (Camden, ME: International Marine Publishing, 1978), 44. It is curious that Francis used these exact words in falsely accusing Manfred Curry of lack of sailing experience (volume 1, page 206).
44. O Lie-Nielsen was one, and realizing that I shared his high opinion of the ketch, he used to come in at the International Marine Publishing offices and try to sell me on the idea of having him build her for me. Lee had admired the design for years and was itching to see her take shape in his shop. I had to explain that for me she had to remain a lottery boat; M. Dale Troglin to LFH, October 18, 1964, 138:9/2, GWBWL.
45. Mrs. Charles D. Gowing (Stuart's daughter), interview with author, Cushing, ME, March 12, 1996.
46. Willoughby H. Stuart Jr. to LFH, June 23, 1937, 138:9/1, GWBWL.
47. William G. Harding, unpublished typescript, 1987, author's collection; A few sails with Bill Harding in both the *Ben* and in his own Stuart Knockabout, the *Buccaneer*, have shown that, no surprise, LFH's design No. 53 is a true thoroughbred. My wife, Kathleen, said, "Why do I enjoy this so much more than sailing on a bigger boat? It's an emotional thing. It just makes me feel good."
48. LFH to Norman H. Hodgdon Jr., April 14, 1955, 138:4/6, GWBWL.
49. LFH to Thomas Taylor, August 31, 1954, 138:4/6; LFH to Thomas Taylor, July 13, 1956, 138:4/7, GWBWL.
50. LFH to Willoughby H. Stuart Jr., June 29, 1957, 138:1/7; Willoughby H. Stuart Jr. to LFH, July 9, 1957, 138:9/1, GWBWL.
51. Willoughby H. Stuart Jr. to LFH, July 9 and August 1, 1937, 138:9/1, GWBWL.
52. LFH to Waldo H. Brown, October 16, 1936, 138:1/6, GWBWL; *The Rudder* (December 1936): 55.
53. See Dyer's letter in *The Rudder* (March 1934): 67.
54. Obituary of William H. Taylor, *New York Times*, January 8, 1966.
55. LFH to NGH, June 2, 1933, 138:17/9, GWBWL; There is a half-model of *La Petite* at Mystic Seaport Museum, accession number 1975.251.
56. NGH to LFH, June 27, 1932, 138:17/8, GWBWL.
57. "Along With the Frostbiters," *Yachting* (February 1933): 69.
58. LFH to Uffa Fox, November 28, 1934, 138:1/4, GWBWL.
59. LFH, *An L. Francis Herreshoff Reader*, 302-311; *The Rudder* (October 1943); LFH, *The Writings of L. Francis Herreshoff* (New York: The Rudder Publishing, 1946), 67-74.
60. LFH to NGH, February 21, 1933, 138:17/9; LFH to NGH, January 9, 1935, 138:17/11, GWBWL; "Along With the Frostbiters," 61.
61. The Cooley Gallery, website.
62. Henry Bill Selden to LFH, March 13, 1933, 138:9/1, GWBWL.
63. Henry Bill Selden to LFH, March 13, 1933, 138:9/1, GWBWL.
64. Henry Bill Selden to LFH, March 20, 1933, 138:9/1, GWBWL.
65. Henry Bill Selden to LFH, March 20 and April 10, 1933, 138:9/1, GWBWL.
66. Henry Bill Selden to LFH, May 22, 1933, 138:9/1, GWBWL.
67. Henry Bill Selden to LFH, May 22, 1933, 138:9/1, GWBWL.
68. Hazel Potter Selden to LFH, February 23, 1934, 138:9/1, GWBWL.
69. Henry Bill Selden to LFH, May 23, 1933, 138:9/1, GWBWL.
70. LFH to NGH, May 19, May 27 and June 2, 1933, 138:17/9, GWBWL.
71. LFH to NGH, July 28, 1933, 138:17/9, GWBWL.

72. LFH to NGH, September 3, 1935, 138:17/11, GWBWL.
73. LFH to NGH, August 13, 1936, 138:17/12, GWBWL; SP38.349.1, DSGSPL; Mystic Seaport Museum photograph, accession number 1990.37.121.
74. *Your New Boat* (New York: Yachting Publishing Corporation, 1946), 66; LFH to Boris Lauer-Leonardi, January 29, 1962, 138:5/3, GWBWL.
75. Anne Lawrence Bondy, interview with author, Mamaroneck, NY, June 26, 1998; LFH to Boris Lauer-Leonardi, August 13, 1945, 138:2/8, GWBWL.
76. Anne Lawrence Bondy, interview with author, previously cited.
77. LFH to John I. Sewall, November 5, 1953, 138:4/4, GWBWL; LFH, "The Double Paddle Canoe," *The Rudder* (September 1947): 34.
78. LFH to Carey C. Smith, January 3, 1948, 138:3/4, GWBWL; LFH, "The Double Paddle Canoe," 34.
79. LFH, Log of Canoe Cruises in 1930s, 138:16/2, GWBWL.
80. LFH, Log of Canoe Cruises in 1930s, 138:16/2, GWBWL.
81. LFH, "The Double Paddle Canoe," 33.
82. LFH to NGH, June 24, 1932, 138:17/8, GWBWL.
83. LFH to NGH, February 21, 1933, 138:17/9, GWBWL.
84. Anne Lawrence Bondy, interview with author, previously cited; LFH, Log of Canoe Cruises in 1930s, 138:16/2, GWBWL; O. Lie-Nielsen, interview with author, Rockland, ME, August 31, 1998.
85. Maynard Bray, Benjamin A. G. Fuller, and Peter T. Vermilya, *Mystic Seaport Museum Watercraft* (Mystic: Mystic Seaport Museum, 2001), 332, 333.
86. LFH to Agnes Herreshoff, June 6, 1947, 138:3/7; LFH to M. L. Kirkwood, March 21, 1968, 138:6/2, GWBWL.
87. LFH, *The Compleat Cruiser* (New York: Sheridan House, 1956), 62, 63; LFH, "The Common Sense of Yacht Design," *The Rudder* (February 1945): 35.
88. Quoted in Maynard Bray, "The Incredible Herreshoff Dugout," *WoodenBoat* 14 (January/February 1977): 56. 57.
89. Bray, "The Incredible Herreshoff Dugout," 56. 57; LFH, "The Double Paddle Canoe," 34.
90. LFH to Bror Tamm, December 2, 1971, 138:6/6, GWBWL; Bray, "The Incredible Herreshoff Dugout," 55; Graves Yacht Yards to LFH, May 23, 1966, 138:7/7, GWBWL.
91. LFH to W. Starling Burgess, December 8, 1936, 138:1/6, GWBWL.
92. Bill Peterson and Fred Bauer, "Fenwick Cushing Williams, Naval Architect: The Gentle Draftsman," *WoodenBoat* 151 (November/December 1999); Fenwick C. Williams, "L. Francis Herreshoff," *The Catboat Association Bulletin* (Spring 2007): 39, 40.
93. See advertisement in *Yachting* (January 1933): 15; Williams, "L. Francis Herreshoff," 39, 40; Philip C. Bolger to author, March 14, 1994; Dale Calloway, interview with author, East Lyme, CT, February 8, 1995.
94. Boris Lauer-Leonardi to LFH, no date (answered September 25, 1947), 138:3/3, GWBWL.
95. LFH, "The Double Paddle Canoe," 35; Boris Lauer-Leonardi to LFH, no date (answered February 2, 1948), 138:3/4, GWBWL.
96. LFH to H. J. Styer, September 10, 1969, 138:6/4, GWBWL; Letter in *The Rudder* (February 1956): 11; John J. Slager, "Double Paddle Canoe," *The Rudder* (October 1955): 29-31, 48; Letter in *The Rudder* (October 1962): 4; George B. Kelley to LFH, October 20, 1965, 138:5/7; LFH to George B. Kelley, October 25, 1965, 138:5/7, GWBWL.
97. Ludwig Hansen to LFH, August 13, 1935, 138:1/5, GWBWL.
98. Ludwig Hansen to LFH, August 13, 1935, 138:1/5; Ludwig Hansen to LFH, September 17, 1935, 138:1/5, GWBWL.
99. O. Lie-Nielsen, interview with author, previously cited.
100. Katherine Jones Vosburgh, interview with author, Newburyport, MA, May 2, 1999.
101. Interviews with Arthur Brendze previously cited.
102. Interview with Katherine Jones Vosburgh, previously cited.
103. LFH to John Ives Sewell, August 13 and 16, 1954, 138:4/5, GWBWL. Francis later donated the engine to the Hart Museum at the Massachusetts Institute

of Technology; Katherine Jones Vosburgh, interview with author, previously cited. On May 28, 1999, Katherine wrote me: "I thought it was important to tell you my part in Francis' life rather than have some people leaping to conclusions that would have been unjustified—I wanted to make it clear that he did not take advantage of me at a young age."

104. O. Lie-Nielsen, interview with author, previously cited.
105. LFH to James P. O'Hara, March 18, 1968, 138:6/2, GWBWL; LFH, "The Double Paddle Canoe," 35; Katherine Jones Vosburgh, interview with author, previously cited.
106. Katherine Jones Vosburgh, interview with author, previously cited.
107. Katherine Jones Vosburgh, interview with author, previously cited.
108. Katherine Jones Vosburgh, interview with author, previously cited.
109. Katherine Jones Vosburgh, interview with author, previously cited.
110. Katherine Jones Vosburgh, interview with author, previously cited.
111. Katherine Jones Vosburgh, interview with author, previously cited; see also, Arthur Brendze, interview with author, previously cited. Brendze was a longtime friend of Katherine Vosburgh.
112. Katherine Jones Vosburgh, interview with author, previously cited.

Chapter 14

1. SP38.34, DSGSPL.
2. William U. Swan, "Joshua Brown: 1828-1901," unpublished manuscript commissioned by Waldo H. Brown, 1937; Waldo Brown's son, John, has half models of both *Tioga*s; there is some resemblance, but LFH's *Tioga* is not a copy of Joshua Brown's *Tioga*; LFH, *An L. Francis Herreshoff Reader* (Camden, ME: International Marine Publishing, 1978), 192.
3. Paul Brown and O. Lie-Nielsen, interviews with author, previously cited.
4. Paul Brown interview with author, previously cited; John Brown, interview with author, January 8, 1997.
5. Paul Brown and John Brown, interviews with author, previously cited.
6. LFH, *An L. Francis Herreshoff Reader*, 3; LFH to Charles D. Childs, May 30, 1957, 138:4/8, GWBWL (LFH was buying a painting of her from the Childs Gallery).
7. LFH, "The Common Sense of Yacht Design," *The Rudder* (April 1944): 26.
8. Douglas Phillps-Birt, *An Eye For a Yacht* (London: Faber and Faber, 1955), 42.
9. LFH, marginal note in *An Eye For a Yacht*, 62; see also Tom Davin, "He Carries On the Great Herreshoff Tradition," *Boats* (September 1956): 52.
10. See LFH, "Trailboards and Figureheads," in *An L. Francis Herreshoff Reader*, 197, 198.
11. LFH, "The Common Sense of Yacht Design," *The Rudder* (January 1948): 47.
12. LFH, "The Common Sense of Yacht Design," *The Rudder* (January 1948): 47.
13. LFH to Philip C. Bolger, January 18, 1948, 138:3/4, GWBWL.
14. LFH to Francis A. Less'Ard, November 7, 1967, 138:6/1, GWBWL.
15. LFH to NGH, My 27, 1933, 138:17/9, GWBWL; Quoted by Davin in "He Carries on the Great Herreshoff Tradition," 52.
16. LFH to NGH, June 2, 1933, 138:17/9; NGH to LFH, December 7, 1928, 138:17/4, GWBWL.
17. LFH to J. R Dingle, June 30, 1944, 138:2/5, GWBWL.
18. LFH to O. Lie-Nielsen, January 10, 1966, 138:5/8; see also LFH to Gordon Thomson, January 8, 1969, 138:6/3, GWBWL; and LFH, *The Common Sense of Yacht Design*, vol. 1 (New York: The Rudder Publishing Company, 1947), 54; LFH to Ralph Wolbert, December 26, 1947, 138:3/3; LFH to B. U. McCime, November 17, 1944, 138:2/6, GWBWL; if you are having trouble following all this, you may, perhaps, take comfort from the fact that LFH himself got the propeller direction backwards

when he explained it in "The Common Sense of Yacht Design," *The Rudder* (October 1944): 29. He corrected this error when the "Common Sense" articles were later published in book form, vol. 1, 53.

19. John and Paul Brown, interviews with author, previously cited.
20. O. Lie-Nielsen, interview with author, previously cited.
21. O. Lie-Nielsen to his parents, June 16, 1931, translated from the Norwegian by Lie-Nielsen for the author.
22. O. Lie-Nielsen to his parents, June 16, 1931, translated from the Norwegian by Lie-Nielsen for the author.
23. O. Lie-Nielsen to his parents, June 16, 1931, translated from the Norwegian by Lie-Nielsen for the author; LFH to W. Wolf, October 30, 1967, 138:6/1, GWBWL.
24. LFH to unknown recipient, December 1971, 138:6/6, GWBWL.
25. O. Lie-Nielsen to Andy Britt, March 16, 1999, copied to author by Britt.
26. LFH, "The Common Sense of Yacht Design," *The Rudder* (April 1944): 23; Z. W. Hauk, *Schenley Yachting and Trophy Championship Book* (New York: Schenley Products Company, 1935), 23; see also *The Rudder* (October 1933): 47.
27. LFH to Francis Falzon, January, 5, 1969, 138:6/4, GWBWL.
28. Daniel E. Carter to LFH, August 25, 1968, 138:6/3, GWBWL.
29. Philip C. Bolger to author, March 14, 1998.
30. LFH to Richard C. Newick, May 2, 1968, 138:6/2, GWBWL.
31. SP38.230.1, DSGSPL.
32. LFH to William R. Chandler, March 10, 1964, 138:5/5, GWBWL.
33. LFH to NGH, May 4, 1934, 138:17/10, GWBWL; SP38.1.8, DSGSPL.
34. *Lynn Daily Item*, April 26, 1934; LFH to W. Wolf, October 30, 1967, 138:6/1; see also LFH to W. H. Kirby, October 21, 1969, 138:6/4, GWBWL.
35. LFH to Edward Dane, July 26, 1950, 138:4/1, GWBWL.
36. LFH to R. S. Wentworth, January 22, 1969, 138:6/4; NGH to LFH, June 21, 1934, 138:17/10, GWBWL.
37. LFH to Francis Falzon, December 30, 1968, 138:6/3, GWBWL.
38. LFH to William J. Strawbridge, February 4, 1952, 138:4/3, GWBWL; Robin Lloyd, "*Bounty*: A Boat with Many Lives," *Classic Boat* 301 (July 2013).
39. Stacy Lloyd to LFH, November 24, 1959, 138:4/10, GWBWL; Lloyd, "Twice the *Bounty*," *Classic Boat* 101 (November 1996): 29.
40. LFH to Stacy Lloyd, April 6, 1959, 138:4/10; Stacy Lloyd to LFH, September 5, 1965, 138:5/7, GWBWL.
41. Stacy Lloyd to LFH, June 3, 1964, 138:5/5, GWBWL; Lloyd, "Twice the *Bounty*," 26; LFH to Stacy Lloyd, June 9, 1964, 138:5/5, GWBWL.
42. I have not been able to discover which Alden schooner design the *Victoria* was. It is true that some Alden schooners, the *Malabar X*, for example, sailed very well indeed to windward, but most of them didn't. Francis's reference to "the Malabar" is general.
43. LFH to Stacy Lloyd, November 5, 1959, 138:4/10; William R. Chandler to LFH, no date, 138:5/6, GWBWL.
44. Lloyd, "Twice the *Bounty*," 29.
45. Stacy Lloyd to LFH, October 3, 1968, 138:8/3, GWBWL.
46. O. Lie-Nielsen, interview with author, previously cited; Muriel Vaughn, interview with author, Marblehead, MA, 1973.

47 Arthur Brendze, interview with author, previously cited.

48 Lloyd, "Twice the *Bounty*," 30; Lloyd, *Bounty*: A Boat with Many Lives."

49. Richard I. Robb to LFH, July 14, 1968, 138:8/9, GWBWL.
50. SP38.1.14, DSGSPL; John Barkhorn, "Charade—In the Herreshoff Tradition," *Sea and Pacific Motorboat* (January 1968): 154; William A. Robinson to LFH, May 5, 1969, 138:6/4, GWBWL.

Chapter 15

1. Bradley Noyes, interview with author, Key Largo, FL, February 17, 1998; John N. Brown, interview with author, previously cited.
2. LFH to NGH, July 16, 1935, 138:17/11, GWBWL; *Yachting* (September 1935): 89.
3. Bradley Noyes, interview with author, previously cited.
4. Jack A. Somer, *Ticonderoga: Tales of an Enchanted Yacht* (Mystic: Mystic Seaport Museum, 1997), 18. Thanks to Jack Somer's thoroughly researched (but not footnoted) biography of the *Ticonderoga* and her many owners, we have her complete story at hand; Bradley Noyes, interview with author, previously cited.
5. LFH to Harry E. Noyes, February 18, 1936, 138:1/6, GWBWL.
6. NGH to LFH, July 21, 1935, 138:17/11; LFH to NGH, July 31, 1935, 138: 17/11; LFH to NGH, September 7, 1934, 138:17/10, GWBWL.
7. Bradley Noyes, interview with author, previously cited; John Rousmaniere, review of *Classic Yachts* in *WoodenBoat* 207 (March/April 2009); see also Somer, *Ticonderoga*, 27.
8. LFH, "Description of Number 66," 138:15/13; LFH to David Cabot, April 15, 1948, 138:3/4, GWBWL.
9. Olin J. Stephens II, *All This and Sailing Too* (Mystic: Mystic Seaport Museum, 1999), 24, 269; LFH to Walter Hadley, October 31, 1966, 138:5/8, GWBWL.
10. Fred W. Goeller to LFH, June 30, 1935, and reply of July 8, 1935, 138:1/5, GWBWL; *The Rudder* (December 1923): 30, (January 1929): 28, (July 1929): 146; LFH, "The Common Sense of Yacht Design," *The Rudder* (April 1946): 44.
11. Lucia del Sol Knight and Daniel B. MacNaughton, *The Encyclopedia of Yacht Designers* (New York: W. W. Norton, 2006), 336, 338.
12. Bradley Noyes, interview with author, previously cited; LFH to Charles A. Harrison, April 19, 1945, 138:2/7, GWBWL.
13. Bradley Noyes, interview with author, previously cited; LFH to Ralph E. Richmond, June 30, 1936, 138:1/6, GWBWL; Somer, *Ticonderoga*, 17.
14. LFH to Harry E. Noyes, February 18, 1936, 138:1/6, GWBWL; Somer, *Ticonderoga*, 25; LFH to Willoughby H. Stuart, May 20, 1937, 138:1/7, GWBWL.
15. Edmund Cutts to Robert M. Steward, January 25, 1988, author's collection; see also LFH to NGH, May 8, 1936, 138:17/12; LFH to Harry E. Noyes, February 18, 1936, 138:1/6, GWBWL.
16. Bradley Noyes, interview with author, previously cited; LFH to Walter Hadley, October 31, 1966, and July 25, 1970, 138:5/8, 138:6/5, GWBWL; Robert J. Shekter, *Popular Boating* (September 1957): 71; see also Somer, *Ticonderoga*, 26; O. Lie-Nielsen, interview with author, previously cited.
17. LFH to Ratsey and Lapthorn, May 18, 1936, and George Ratsey's reply, May 19, 1936, 138:1/6, GWBWL; see also Somer, *Ticonderoga*, 25, 26; Arthur Brendze, interview with author, previously cited; *The Rudder* (August 1939): 20, (October 1939): 32, 56.
18. Bradley P. Noyes, "*Tioga*'s Launching," *Maine Boats and Harbors* (April/May 2000): 4; Art Hansen, *Photographic Memories of a T-Wharfer* (Boston: author, 1984); see also, Somer, *Ticonderoga*, 29-31; Joseph Garland, *The Eastern Yacht Club: A History from 1870-1985* (Camden, ME: Down East Books, 1989), 210.
19. LFH to NGH, August 13, 1936, 138:17/12, GWBWL.
20. LFH to NGH, August 24, 1936, 138:17/12; NGH to LFH, December 4, 1937, 138:17/13; LFH to NGH, December 7, 1937, 138:17/13, GWBWL.
21. Somer, *Ticonderoga*, vii.
22. Somer, *Ticonderoga*, 33.
23. Somer, *Ticonderoga*, 34.
24. *The Rudder* (April 1937): 11.
25. Somer, *Ticonderoga*, 37-39.
26. *The Rudder* (March 1940): 88; Somer, *Ticonderoga*, 40.
27. Bradley Noyes, interview with author, previously cited; Somer, *Ticonderoga*, 41.
28. Bradley Noyes, interview with author, previously cited.

29. See Dennis L. Noble, *The U. S. Coast Guard in World War II: The Beach Patrol and Corsair Fleet* (Washington, DC: Coast Guard Historian's Office, 1992); Somer, *Ticonderoga*, 47, 49; Mystic Seaport Museum, photograph, accession number 1990.37.291.
30. Somer, *Ticonderoga*, 54; Bradley Noyes, interview with author, previously cited.
31. Somer, *Ticonderoga*, 57-61.
32. Somer, *Ticonderoga*, 61-64; LFH to Boris Lauer-Leonardi, Februry 28, 1947, 138:3/1, GWBWL; George N. Holme, "Rough Passage," *The Rudder* (July 1947), 28; see also *The Rudder* (April 1947): 98; see Mystic Seaport Museum, photographs, accession numbers 1990.37.265 and 1990.37.267.
33. Somer, *Ticonderoga*, 64, 65, 66.
34. O. Lie-Nielsen, interview with author, previously cited; Somer, *Ticonderoga*, 69.
35. LFH to O. Lie-Nielsen, July 5, 1954, 138:4/5, GWBWL; see also Mystic Seaport Museum, photograph, accession number 1990.37.277; LFH to William A. Baker, October 7, 1965, and February 17, 1966, 138:5/7, 8; see also Ernest Dodge to LFH, April 5, 1966, 138:8/7, GWBWL.
36. *The Rudder* (March 1949): 53; see also, Somer, *Ticonderoga*, 67, 68; *The Rudder* (April 1949): 34.
37. Bradley Noyes, interview with author, previously cited. The author agrees with this opinion, having experienced that Len Hornick's *Mary Harrigan*, built to the design of the *Joann*, but with a centerboard added, sailed better beating to windward than Francis's own description of how the *Joann* performed; Maynard Bray, e-mail to author, February 14, 2005.
38. Kate Bertram, "Sir Thomas Lipton Cup Race," *The Rudder* (April 1950): 56; O. Lie-Nielsen to LFH, December 21, 1950, and reply, 138:4/1, GWBWL.
39. Somer, *Ticonderoga*, 73, 75, 78; O. Lie-Nielsen, interview with author, previously cited.
40. Somer, *Ticonderoga*, 80, 81.
41. Somer, *Ticonderoga*, 82, 83, 85; LFH, *Sensible Cruising Designs*, (Camden, ME: International Marine Publishing, 1973), 4; see also LFH to Halsey Herreshoff, May 28, 1970, 138:6/5, GWBWL.
42. Geoffrey G. Smith, *This Is the Story of* Ticonderoga *and Ocean Racing—1937-1952* (New York: The Rudder Publishing Company, 1958), as quoted in Somer, *Ticonderoga*, 87.
43. Somer, *Ticonderoga*, 87.
44. *The Rudder* (August 1954): 44.
45. Somer, *Ticonderoga*, 89-91.
46. Somer, *Ticonderoga*, 97, 98, 104, 105.
47. LFH to Dick Dawson, October 10, 1962, 138:5/3, GWBWL.
48. Margrete Stinnes, interview with author, Rockland, ME, August 31, 1998; Somer, *Ticonderoga*, 105, 106.
49. Somer, *Ticonderoga*, 116, 126.
50. Robert F. Johnson to LFH, no date, 138:5/8, GWBWL; Somer, *Ticonderoga*, 118.
51. Robert F. Johnson to LFH, no date, 138:5/8, GWBWL; Somer, *Ticonderoga*, 126.
52. Somer, *Ticonderoga*, 128.
53. *Yachting* (June 1965): 34; see also Somer, *Ticonderoga*, 129, 130.
54. Robert Johnson to LFH, July 16, 1965, 138:5/7, GWBWL.
55. Somer, *Ticonderoga*, 139-141; LFH to William J. Strawbridge, September 27, 1965, 138:5/7; LFH to Edwin M. Hill, September 2, 1965, 138:7/7; Robert Johnson to LFH, July 16, 1965, 138:5/7; Bolton C. Moise Jr. to LFH, July 15, 1965, 138:5/7, GWBWL.
56. Somer, *Ticonderoga*, 143.
57. Somer, *Ticonderoga*, 145, 146.
58. Robert Johnson to LFH, August 10, 1966, 138:5/8, GWBWL; Somer, *Ticonderoga*, 147.
59. Robert Johnson to LFH, August 10, 1966, 138:5/8, GWBWL; Somer, *Ticonderoga*, 147.
60. Somer, *Ticonderoga*, 149, 150, 151, 152, 153.
61. Somer, *Ticonderoga*, 155, 159, 160, 162.
62. Somer, *Ticonderoga*, 162, 163, 165-67.
63. Jay Greer, e-mail to author, April 7, 2005; Arthur Brendze, interview with author, previously cited; Somer, *Ticonderoga*, 170.
64. Somer, *Ticonderoga*, 176.
65. Somer, *Ticonderoga*, 177, 179, 180.
66. Somer, *Ticonderoga*, 185, 196.
67. Somer, *Ticonderoga*, 198, 201, 204.

68. Somer, *Ticonderoga*, 209, 211-15.
69. Somer, *Ticonderoga*, 223-46.
70. L. Scott Frantz, e-mail to author, August 6, 2015.
71. L. Scott Frantz, e-mail to author, August 6, 2015.
72. Mystic Seaport Museum, photograph, accession number 1990.37.1084.
73. Stanley Bishoprick, interview with author, October 2, 1996; see also "On the Waterfront," *WoodenBoat* 122 (January/February 1995): 21.
74. "On the Waterfront," 21.
75. Bruce King, interview with author, Newcastle, ME.
76. LFH to William A. Robinson, March 28, 1960, 138:5/1; LFH to Ronald D. Bretherton, October 20, 1967, 138:6/1; Vicomte R. de Dampierre to LFH, September 11, 1968, 138:6/3, GWBWL.
77. O. Lie-Nielsen, interview with author, previously cited; LFH to Critchell Rimington, April 19, 1946, 138:2/9, GWBWL.

Chapter 16

1. O. Lie-Nielsen and Anne Lawrence Bondy, interviews with author, previously cited; Suzy Coe Fernberger, interview with author, Marblehead, MA, September 25, 1999; John Albert Chambers to Alfred F. Loomis, ca. spring 1934, Edward Cutts to Robert M. Steward, January 25, 1988, author's collection.
2. Edo Potter, *The Last Farm on Chappaquiddick: Pimpneymouse Farm* (Edgartown, MA: Vineyard Stories, 2010), 168, 170; Llewellyn Howland III, unpublished manuscript, "Is Yacht Designing an Art or a Science?," 18; for more on the contra propeller, see volume 1, pages 182-83.
3. LFH, "General Description of No. 67," 138:15/14, GWBWL.
4. LFH to Louise N. Grace, November 20, 1935, and December 7, 1935, 138:1/5; A. S. Gomez to LFH, November 15, 1935, 138:1/5; C. W. Haffenreffer to LFH, December 2, 1935, 138:7/8; John R. Whiting to LFH, December 5, 1935, 138:1/5, GWBWL.
5. Agreement between LFH and George A. Brown, August 3, 1934, 138:1/4; LFH to George A. Gulliford, August 13, 1935, 138:1/5; LFH to A. Sidney deWolf Herreshoff, September 14, 1938, 138:1/8, GWBWL.
6. LFH to O. Lie-Nielsen, April 4, 1957, 138:4/8, GWBWL.
7. Maurice D. Wilt, "Canoeing Under Sail," in Edwin J. Shoettle, *Sailing Craft* (New York: MacMillan, 1943), 120, 130.
8. LFH to Daniel Zwart, January 8, 1948, 138:9/5, GWBWL; LFH, "The Common Sense of Yacht Design," *The Rudder* (December 1947): 28; LFH to Alan S. Harder, April 8, 1948, 138:3/4; LFH to NGH, September 7, 1934, 138:17/10, GWBWL.
9. LFH to Alan S. Harder, April 8, 1948, 138:3/4; LFH to NGH, April 26, 1935, 138:17/11, GWBWL.
10. LFH to Clarence Herreshoff, January 3, 1935, 138:1/5, GAWBL.
11. Allan H. Vaitses to LFH, January 30, 1957, 138:4/8, GWBWL.
12. LFH, "Mobjack, a Successful Cruising Ketch," *The Rudder* (March 1947): 48,49; LFH to Russell D. Bell, May 12, 1947, 138:3/2, GWBWL.
13. LFH to L. W. G. Werthheim-Aynes, February 3, 1970, 138:6/5; LFH to O. Lie-Nielsen, September 11, 1967, 138:6/1, GWBWL.
14. LFH to J. Thornton Mills, October 14, 1948, 138:3/5; LFH to Frederick E. Ellis, March 21, 1946, 138:2/9, GWBWL.
15. LFH, "Trailboards and Figureheads," in *An L. Francis Herreshoff Reader* (Camden, ME: International Marine Publishing, 1978), 198, 199.
16. LFH to Tweed Hunter, August 12, 1965, 138:5/7; LFH to Ratch Wallace, October 29, 1970, 138:6/5; F. Ch. Rimbaud to LFH, March 16, 1970, 138:8/9, GWBWL.
17. LFH to Paul Cravey, August 16, 1965, 138:5/7; LFH to Dr. William W. Sullivan, July 27, 1968, 138:6/3; LFH to Frank. C. Gonsalvies, September 19, 1970, 138:6/5, GWBWL; Frank C. Gonsalvies to author, no date (received May 15, 1995); LFH to Ralph Cannon, June 13, 1946, 138:2/9; LFH to Philip E. Hind, May 5, 1947, 138:3/2, GWBWL.
18. John P. Kendall to author, November 15, 2000.
19. LFH to Paul Cravey, August 16, 1965, 138:5/7, GWBWL.

20. SP38.80.1, DSGSPL.
21. Anne Lawrence Bondy, interview with author, previously cited; LFH to NGH, April 26, 1935, 138:17/11; NGH to LFH, July 14, July 21, September 8, 1935, 138:17/11; LFH to NGH, September 20, 1935, 138:17/11, GWBWL.
22. LFH to NGH, November 23, 1935, and November 20, 1936, 138:17/11, 12; LFH to NGH, December 22, 1936, and January 12, 1937, 138:17/12, 13, GWBWL.
23. Margrete Stinnes, interview with author, previously cited.
24. NGH to LFH, October 29, 1935, 138:17/11; LFH to NGH, November 5, 1935, 138:17/11, GWBWL.
25. LFH to NGH, December 28, 1936, January 12, January 24 and January 28, 1937, 138:17/13; LFH to W. Starling Burgess and Waldo H. Brown, January 5, 1937, 138:1/7, GWBWL.
26. LFH to NGH, April 23, 1937, 138:17/13, GWBWL.
27. *Yachting* (April 1935): 84.
28. *Yachting* (April 1935): 84.
29. LFH to NGH, January 9, 1935, 138:17/11; LFH to Uffa Fox, January 14, 1935, 138:1/5; LFH to NGH, February 23, 1934, 138:17/10, GWBWL; William J. Strawbridge III, interview with author, Easton, MD, April 19, 1996.
30. William J. Strawbridge III, interview with author, previously cited; William J. Strawbridge to LFH, no date, 138:9/1; LFH to William J. Strawbridge, August 26, 1936, 138:1/6, GWBWL.
31. NGH to LFH, February 4, and February 7, 1935, 138:17/11; LFH to NGH, February 8, 1935, 138:17/11, GWBWL.
32. Clinton H. Crane to LFH, April 15 and April 20, 1935, 138:1/5, GWBWL.
33. *Yachting* (April 1935): 106; LFH to John S. Heck, May 3, 1935, 138:1/5; LFH to NGH, November 24, 1936, 138:17/12, GWBWL; LFH, "The Common Sense of Yacht Design," *The Rudder* (January 1948): 46.
34. Contract, 138:15/11, GWBWL.
35. *Yachting* (July 1935): 96, 97; LFH to NGH, June 7, July 16, 1935, 138:17/11, GWBWL.
36. LFH to Uffa Fox, October 22, 1935, 138:1/5, GWBWL; *Yachting* (September 1935): 43.
37. Mystic Seaport Museum, photograph of document, accession number 1976.40; *Yachting* (October 1935): 37.
38. LFH to William J. Strawbridge, July 10, 1936, 138:1/6, GWBWL.
39. *The Rudder* (April 1937): 50.
40. LFH to William J. Strawbridge, August 31, 1937, 138:1/7, GWBWL.
41. LFH to Philip J. Roosevelt, December 3, 1935, 138:1/5, GWBWL.
42. LFH to NGH, May 1, and May 8, 1936, 138:17/12, GWBWL.
43. H. L. McCoy to LFH, April 26, 1935, 138:1/5; George B. Rawlings to LFH, August 6, 1936, 138:1/6; LFH to NGH, May 1, and May 8, 1936, 138:1/6, GWBWL.
44. LFH to NGH, May 8, 1936, 138:1/6, GWBWL.
45. NGH to LFH, May 12, 1936, 138:1/6; LFH to NGH, May 1, and May 8, 1936, 138:1/6, GWBWL.
46. LFH to NGH, May 8, 1936, 138:1/6, GWBWL; Anne Lawrence Bondy, interview with author, previously cited; Peter Coe, interview with author, Damariscotta, ME, January 22, 2000.
47. LFH to NGH, May 1, 1936, 138:1/6, GWBWL.
48. NGH to LFH, November 9, 1936, 138:17/12, GWBWL.
49. Bette Hunt, e-mail to author, February 19, 2005; Suzy Coe Fernberger, interview with author, previously cited.
50. Bobby Russell, interview with author, Marblehead, MA, September 26, 1999; LFH to George E. Ratsey, September 9, 1936, 138:1/6, GWBWL.
51. LFH, "The Dry Breakers," in *An L. Francis Herreshoff Reader*, 295.
52. NGH to LFH, January 14, February 6, 1938, 138:17/14; LFH to NGH, March 11, 1938, 138:17/14, GWBWL.
53. Bette Hunt, e-mail to author, February 19, 2005; Suzy Coe Fernberger, Peter Coe, and Anne Lawrence Bondy, interviews with author, previously cited; Edith Arnold Smith to LFH, September 8, 1944, 138:9/1, GWBWL.
54. LFH to NGH, September 9, 1936, 138:17/2 (misfiled because of error in date of letter as 1926); LFH to

Paule Loring, January 3, 1948, 138:3/4, GWBWL; LFH, *The Compleat Cruiser*, 336.
55. LFH to NGH, August 24, September 9, 1936, 138:17/12, 2, GWBWL.
56. NGH to LFH, September 5, 1936, 138:17/12, GWBWL.
57. LFH to NGH, September 9, 1936, 138:17/2 GWBWL.
58. LFH to William J. Strawbridge, August 26, 1936, 138:1/6; LFH to NGH, September 22, 1936, 138:17/12; NGH to LFH, (September 1936), 138:17/12, GWBWL.
59. William Strawbridge III, interview with author, previously cited; LFH to Midshipman Nolan R. Gibbons, November 3, 1944, 138:2/6, GWBWL.
60. NGH to LFH, November 9, 1936, 138:17/12, GWBWL.
61. LFH to NGH, April 23, 1937, 138:17/13, GWBWL.
62. LFH to William J. Strawbridge, December 10, September 17, 1936, December 22, 1936, 138:1/6, GWBWL.
63. "The Cruising Club Measurement Rule for Ocean Racing," *Yachting* (January 1934): 55.
64. "The Cruising Club Measurement Rule for Ocean Racing," 55.
65. Andrew Britt to author, November 20, 1998; "4 Hurt as Fire Sweeps Boats, Homes in Lynn," *Lynn Daily Item,* undated clipping; LFH to Brooks W. Hamilton, January 8, 1947, 138:3/1, GWBWL.
66. Britt Brothers to LFH, July 27, 1936, 138:1/6, GWBWL.
67. LFH to Britt Brothers, July 30, 1936, 138:1/6; LFH to William J. Strawbridge, December 10, 1936, January 5, March 12, 1937 138:1/6, 7; Britt Brothers to LFH, September 10, 1937, 138:1/7; Estimate from Ratsey and Lapthorn to LFH, March 29, 1937, 138:15/15; Ratsey and Lapthorn to LFH, June 17, August 23, 1937, 138:1/7; Ernest Ratsey to LFH, December 18, 1937, 138:1/7; LFH to NGH, April 23, 1937, 138:17/13, GWBWL.
68. LFH to NGH, July 19, 1937, 138:17/13, GWBWL.
69. Waldo H. Brown to LFH, July 30, 1937, 138:1/7; LFH to William J. Strawbridge, August 31, 1937, 138:1/7; NGH to LFH, September 15, 1937, 138:17/13, GWBWL; *The Rudder* (October 1937): 15.
70. William J. Strawbridge to LFH, October 20, (1937), 138:1/7; LFH to William J. Strawbridge, October 13, October 22, 1937, 138:1/7; LFH to W. Starling Burgess, July 27, 1937, 138:1/7, GWBWL.
71. Frederick S. Ford Jr. to LFH, July 31, 1947, 138:3/2, GWBWL; *The Rudder* (November 1947); Gordon M. Curtis Jr. to Andrew Britt, December 8, 1998, author's collection, courtesy Andrew Britt.
72. Gordon M. Curtis Jr. to Andrew Britt, December 8, 1998, author's collection, courtesy Andrew Britt.
73. Gordon M. Curtis Jr. to Andrew Britt, December 8, 1998, author's collection, courtesy Andrew Britt.
74. Gordon M. Curtis Jr. to Andrew Britt, December 8, 1998, author's collection, courtesy Andrew Britt; LFH to M. Dale Troglin, February 11, 1965, 138:5/6; LFH to David Pierce-Jones, June 9, 1969, 138:6/5, GWBWL.

Chapter 17

1. LFH to W. Starling Burgess, July 25, 1936, 138:1/6, GWBWL.
2. Marjorie Young Wolff, interview with author, Middletown, RI, February 15, 1999; W. Starling Burgess to LFH, July 27, 1936, 138:1/6, GWBWL.
3. W. Starling Burgess to LFH, July 27, 1936, 138:1/6, GWBWL.
4. Ann Burgess Hopps, interview with author, Camden, ME, October 29, 1998; Marjorie Young Wolff, interview with author, previously cited.
5. Marjorie Young Wolff, interview with author, previously cited.
6. Marjorie Young Wolff, interview with author, previously cited.
7. Olin J. Stephens II to author, March 15, 1997, author's collection.
8. Llewellyn Howland III, interview with author, Jamaica Plain, MA, March 11, 1997; Marjorie Young Wolff and Ann Burgess Hopps, interviews with author, previously cited.
9. LFH to Boris Lauer-Leonardi, April 11, 1949, 138:3/6, GWBWL.

10. Olin J. Stephens II to author, March 15, 1997, author's collection; LFH, "The Common Sense of Yacht Design," *The Rudder* (February 1947): 39; LFH to NGH, December 8, 1936, 138:17/12, GWBWL.
11. Olin J. Stephens II to author, March 15, 1997, author's collection.
12. W. Starling Burgess to LFH, November 11 and 30, 1936, 138:1/6; LFH to NGH, December 7, December 28, 1937, 138:17/13; LFH to W. Starling Burgess, December 24, 1937, 138:1/7, GWBWL; *The Rudder* (August 1937): 74; LFH, "The Common Sense of Yacht Design," *The Rudder* (May 1947): 38, 40; W. Starling Burgess to LFH, September 29, 1937, 138:1/7, GWBWL.
13. LFH, "The Common Sense of Yacht Design," *The Rudder* (May 1947): 40; LFH to NGH, December 7, 1937, 138:17/13, GWBWL.
14. LFH to W. Starling Burgess, January 5, 1937, 138:1/7, GWBWL.
15. Waldo H. Brown to Yacht Designers of New England, January 11, and January 21, 1937, 138:7/2, GWBWL.
16. Llewellyn Howland III, *No Ordinary Being* (Boston: David R. Godine, 2014), 335-38; *The Rudder* (February 1937): 59.
17. LFH to Waldo H. Brown, January 15, 1937, 138:1/7, GWBWL.
18. LFH to W. Starling Burgess, January 28, 1937, 138:1/7, GWBWL.
19. W. Starling Burgess to LFH, February 1, 1937, 138:1/7, GWBWL; Llewellyn Howland III, manuscript for *No Ordinary Being*, chapter 18, 45.
20. Howland, *No Ordinary Being*, 335-41; LFH to NGH, October 31, 1934, 138:17/10, GWBWL.
21. Waldo H. Brown to Yacht Designers of New England, February 17, 1937, 138:7/2, GWBWL; LFH, "Yankee One-Design Class Proposals," *The Rudder* (April 1937): 24.
22. W. Starling Burgess, "The Yankee One-Design Class," *Yachting* (April 1937): 62-65.
23. Burgess, "The Yankee One-Design Class," 62-65.
24. Burgess, "The Yankee One-Design Class," 62-65.
25. Waldo H. Brown, "Yankee Progress," *New England Yachtsman* (October 1937): 13, 14; LFH, "Yankee One-Design Class Proposals," 24, 25, 77.
26. W. Starling Burgess to Waldo H. Brown, June 1, 1937, copy in author's collection, courtesy Llewellyn Howland III; Howland, *No Ordinary Being*, 339.
27. Brown, "Yankee Progress," 10.
28. Brown, "Yankee Progress," 10.
29. John Brown, interview with author, previously cited.
30. Brown, "Yankee Progress," 12, 13.
31. LFH to William J. Strawbridge, October 13, 1937, 138:1/7, GWBWL; Howland, *No Ordinary Being*, 339; Brown, "Yankee Progress," 14.
32. Howland, *No Ordinary Being*, 341; Brown, "Yankee Progress," 14.

Chapter 18

1. LFH to William J. Strawbridge, October 22, 1937, 138:1/7, GWBWL.
2. NGH to LFH, January 14, 1938, 138:17/14; LFH to NGH, January 18, 1938, 138:17/14, GWBWL.
3. LFH to NGH, December 7, 1937, May 5, 1938, 138:17/13, 14, GWBWL; SP38.182.21, DSGSPL; LFH to Carl B. Cahill, June 15, 1970, 138:6/5, GWBWL.
4. LFH to NGH, May 5, 1938, 138:17/14, GWBWL; Nathanael G. Herreshoff III and Natalie Herreshoff, interviews with author, previously cited; LFH to NGH, January 28, 1935, 138:17/11; Ann Roebuck Herreshoff to LFH, December 12, 1937, and Francis's reply of December 17, 138:12/17, GWBWL; Anne Lawrence Bondy, Arthur Brendze, and O. Lie-Nielsen, interviews with author, previously cited.
5. LFH to Bror Tamm, April 4, 1960, 138:5/1, GWBWL; Halsey Herreshoff and Arthur Brensdze, interviews with author, previously cited.
6. LFH to NGH, January 18, 1938, 138:17/14, GWBWL.
7. LFH to NGH, January 18, 1938, 138:17/14, GWBWL.
8. LFH, *Capt. Nat Herreshoff, The Wizard of Bristol* (New York: Sheridan House, 1953), 321; LFH to H. S. Smith, April 2, 1951, 138:4/2, GWBWL.
9. Ann Roebuck Herreshoff to Clarence Herreshoff, June 13, 1940, HMM.
10. NGH to LFH, June 21, 1934, 138:17/10; LFH to NGH, November 16, 1934, 138:17/10, GWBWL.

11. Will of NGH, May 12, 1932, HMM; Probate Court of the Town of Bristol, "Estate of Nathanael Greene Herreshoff," August 16, 1938, HMM.
12. Probate Court of the Town of Bristol, "Estate of Nathanael Greene Herreshoff," August 16, 1938, HMM; Muriel Vaughn, petition to "The Probate Court in and for the County of Essex," March 6, 1973.
13. Lane Lambert, *Quincy Patriot Ledger,* April 5, 1939; Jim Ignasher, *New England Aviation History*, July 24, 2015; "Aviation Accidents: Massachusetts Military Aviation Accidents, Braintree, MA—April 4, 1939," New England Aviation website.
14. William F. Galvin, "Waldo Brown: The Man Behind the Wychmere Jetty Memorial," *Cape Cod Chronicle*, November 6, 2003; E. B. Mills, "Two Families: Two Truths," *Yankee* (February 1996): 58-64, 116-19.
15. John N. Brown, interview with author, previously cited.
16. LFH to Lcdr. D. M. Collins, October 1, 1940, 138:2/1, GWBWL.
17. LFH to Cyrus Hamlin, March 18, 1941, 138:2/2, GWBWL.
18. Lcdr. D. M. Collins to LFH, November 2, 1940, 138:2/1; LFH to Clay Prieto, September 21, 1944, 138:2/6, GWBWL.
19. John Ives Sewall to LFH, November 9, 1952, 138:4/3, GWBWL.
20. LFH to William J. Strawbridge, November 16, 1956, and September 16, 1957, 138:4/7, 8, GWBWL.
21. LFH, "Submarine Destroyer: Objects of the Design," July 1940, 138:15/19; LFH to W. J. A. Beare, October 12, 1942, 138:2/3, GWBWL.
22. Lcdr. D. M. Collins to LFH, November 2, 1940, 138:2/1; LFH to W. J. A Breare, October 12, 1942, 138:2/3; LFH to Lcdr D. M. Collins, November 8, 1940, 138:2/1, GWBWL; Francis's competitor, Sparkman & Stephens, submitted a winning design for an 81-foot PT boat to be built by Higgins Industries in 1938, as well as their Design 374 for a 110-foot wooden sub chaser in 1940, an amphibious Jeep, and the DUKW ("Duck") amphibious truck in 1942; see Robert J. Bulkley Jr., *At Close Quarters: PT Boats in the United States Navy* (Washington, DC: Naval History Division, 1962), part 2; William J. Veigele, *PC Patrol Craft of World War II: A History of the Ships and Their Crews* (Santa Barbara, CA: Astral Publishing, 1998), 28, 30, 56-57, 329-55. Of the 361 PCs, which were built at sixteen commercial and yacht yards around the country, Lawley's built 23 of them, including the class leader, PC-461, whose keel was laid in July 1941, with launch on December 23 and commissioning on March 19, 1942.
23. LFH, "Submarine Destroyer: Objects of the Design," July 1940, 138:15/19, GWBWL.
24. LFH, "Submarine Destroyer: Objects of the Design," July 1940, 138:15/19, GWBWL.
25. LFH to Lcdr. D. M. Collins, October 1, 1940, 138:2/1, GWBWL.
26. "Ned W. Glenn," West Point Memorials, website accessed April 15, 2017; Ned W. Glenn to LFH, November 10 and 30, 1955, 138:4/6, GWBWL.
27. Ned W. Glenn to LFH, November 10 and 30, 1955, 138:4/6, GWBWL.
28. LFH to Ned W. Glenn, December 8, 1955, 138:4/6, GWBWL.
29. Ned W. Glenn to LFH, March 30, 1956, 138:4/7; LFH to Ned W. Glenn, April 7, 1956, 138:4/7, GWBWL.
30. *The Rudder* (July 1931): 46.
31. Edmund A. Cutts to Robert Steward, January 25, 1988, author's collection; O. Lie-Nielsen and Anne Bondy, interviews with author, previously cited.
32. LFH to Paule Loring, January 3, 1948, 138:3/4, GWBWL; see also LFH, *An L. Francis Herreshoff Reader*, 165.
33. Boris Lauer-Leonardi to LFH, June 17, 1942, 138:8/11, GWBWL; "Small Cruising Sloop," *The Rudder* (September 1942): 32, 33; Russ Genner, "The Button," *The Rudder* (October 1942): 30, 41.
34. LFH to Jane Genner, October 9, 1943, 138:2/4, GWBWL.
35. Boris Lauer-Leonardi to LFH, September 5, 1945, 138:2/8, GWBWL.
36. LFH, "How to Build Prudence H 23," *The Rudder* (October 1945): 26-29, 70-72.
37. D. L. Pellett to LFH, May 8, 1946, 138:2/9, GWBWL.
38. LFH to W. A. Sargeaunt, October 16, 1942, 138:2/3,

GWBWL; Malcolm Seavey & Company advertisement, *The Rudder* (October 1945): 87; LFH to Gordon Stables Jr., October 30, 1967, 138:6/1, GWBWL.

39. SP38.197.1, DSGSPL.
40. Llewellyn Howland III, who helped with this information, credits Carola Paine with inspiring and mentoring his own maritime book business. See Carola Paine to LFH, September 5, 1944, 138:8/7, and LFH to Carola Paine, September 30, 1954, 138:4/5, GWBWL.
41. LFH to William B. Benzer, October 12, 1942, 138:4/5, GWBWL.
42. Craig R. Humphrey to LFH, February 19, 1969, 138:7/8, GWBWL.
43. Maureen Kane to author, January 12, 1995.
44. LFH to A. Lewis, March 1, 1965, 138:5/6; LFH to William A. Wilt, October 19, 1945, 138:2/8; John Atwood to LFH, February 20, 1965, 138:7/1, GWBWL.
45. LFH to Lyman Smith, December 10, 1937, 138:1/7, GWBWL.
46. Maynard Bray, e-mail to author, August 18, 2016.

Chapter 19

1. LFH, "H 28—Or the Building of the Snarke," *The Rudder* (April 1943): 37; LFH to William H. Calkins, September 2, 1947, 138:3/2, GWBWL.
2. Edmund A. Cutts to Robert Steward, January 14, 1988, author's collection. The writer can attest to this statement from personal experience. When I was starting up International Marine Publishing Company, Boris, whom I had never met, wrote that he was shutting down his Poseidon Publishing Company and was looking for a home for Robert Steward's book, *Boatbuilding Manual*. If I would publish the book and pay its author a royalty, he would give it to me, all ready to go in a new edition. *Boatbuilding Manual* was International Marine's all-time bestseller. And Bob Steward became such a good friend that he made for me a lovely half model of my old Buzzards Bay 25-footer, the *Aria*. *Boatbuilding Manual* happened to be one of the few books on the subject that Francis admired, see LFH to Peter H. Bury, December 17, 1965, 138:5/7, GWBWL.
3. LFH to Boris Lauer-Leonardi, May 11, 1948, 138:3/4; LFH to Boris Lauer-Leonardi, September 20, 1948, to which Helen Bolster added a postscript asking Boris to return the sticks because "soon he is going to be out of broom sticks, since witches went out of style some time ago," 138:3/5, GWBWL.
4. Boris Lauer-Leonardi to LFH, (ca. July 1, 1944), 138:8/11; LFH to Boris Lauer-Leonardi, July 7 and August 16, 1944, 138:2/6, GWBWL.
5. Boris Lauer-Leonardi to LFH, September 28, 1942, 138:8/11; LFH to Boris Lauer-Leonardi, November 10, 1942, 138:2/3, GWBWL.
6. LFH to Boris Lauer-Leonardi, June 15 and September 13, 1942, 138:2/3; Boris Lauer-Leonardi to LFH, September 1 and August 20, 1942, 138:8/11, GWBWL.
7. LFH, *The Common Sense of Yacht Design*, vol. 2 (New York: The Rudder Publishing Company, 1947), 61.
8. M. Dale Troglin to LFH, March 23, 1947, 138:3/1; LFH to Richard S. Bidleman, September 18, 1968, 138:6/3; LFH to Boris Lauer-Leonardi, May 17, 1943, 138:2/4, GWBWL.
9. LFH to Boris Lauer-Leonardi, March 5, 1943, 138:2/4; Boris Lauer-Leonardi to LFH, March 8, 1943, 138:2/4, GWBWL.
10. LFH to Boris Lauer-Leonardi, March 11 and March 10, 1943, 138:2/4, GWBWL.
11. LFH to Boris Lauer-Leonardi, January 31, 1943, 138:2/4; Boris Lauer-Leonardi to LFH, March 2and October 5, 1943, 138:2/4, GWBWL.
12. LFH, "How To Build H 28," *The Rudder* (March 1943): 41; LFH to F. Randolph Pearsall, February 4, 1947, 138:3/1, GWBWL.
13. LFH to author, January 26, 1948, 138:3/4, GWBWL.
14. Boris Lauer-Leonardi to LFH, early January 1943, 138:8/11; LFH to Boris Lauer-Leonardi, September 10, 1943, 138:2/4, GWBWL.
15. LFH to Boris Lauer-Leonardi, September 15 and April 24, 1943, 138:2/4, GWBWL; Marjorie Young Wolff, interview with author, previously cited.

16. LFH, "How to Build H 28," *The Rudder* (February 1943): 22; LFH to Boris Lauer-Leonardi, September 2, 1944, 138:2/6; LFH to Lewis K. Hughes, October 20, 1944, 138:2/6; LFH to Kenneth Abrahamsen, January 10, 1946, 138:2/9, GWBWL.
17. Boris Lauer-Leonardi to LFH, August 31, 1944, 138:2/6; LFH to Kenneth Abrahamsen, January 10, 1946, and January 22, 1946, 138:2/6; LFH to G. F. Hare, October 4, 1945, 138:2/8, GWBWL.
18. LFH to Leander Hamerla, January 25, 1943, 138:2/4; LFH to Howard Cagle, February 18, 1943, 138:2/4; Boris Lauer-Leonardi to LFH, March 2, September 10, 1943, and February 7, 1944, 138:2/4, 5; Boris Lauer-Leonardi to Lt. John C. Staniland, April 30, 1945, 138:2/7; *The Rudder*, royalty statement to LFH for April 1, 1946, through April 1, 1947, 138:8/11; LFH to Robert M. Ward, March 18, 1965, 138:5/6, GWBWL.
19. Boris Lauer-Leonardi to LFH, March 26, 1946, 138:2/9; LFH to Boris Lauer-Leonardi, April 2, 1946, 138:2/9; Boris Lauer-Leonardi to LFH, August 23, 1946, 138:2/10, GWBWL.
20. Boris Lauer-Leonardi to LFH, July 1, 1943, May 6 and June 13, 1946, 138:2/4, 9, GWBWL.
21. Boris Lauer-Leonardi to LFH, August 23, 1946, 138:2/10; Boris Lauer-Leonardi to LFH, May 12, 1947, 138:3/2, GWBWL. The writer has shared this experience in several ketches, including LFH designs. When lying to in a ketch, LFH recommended trimming the sail about for a close reach and leaving the tiller free. My experience when doing this is that the boat wanders a lot, first yawing to leeward, say, and gathering way, and then shooting up nearly head-to-wind, before falling off again; Boris Lauer-Leonardi to LFH, May 12, 1947, 138:3/2, GWBWL.
22. Boris Lauer-Leonardi to LFH, ca. May 30, 1947, 138:8/11, GWBWL.
23. Truscott Boat and Dock Company advertisement, *The Rudder* (November 1944): 9; Boris Lauer-Leonardi to LFH, September 24, 1945, 138:2/8; Charles Hakanson to LFH, February 13, 1946, 138:2/9, GWBWL.
24. Kendall S. Jones to LFH, December 28, 1946, 138:2/10; LFH to Kendall S. Jones, January 8, 1947, 138:3/1; copy of advertisement enclosed with Jones letter, 138:2/10, GWBWL.
25. H. W. Janson, letter, *The Rudder* (December 1956): 69.
26. LFH to Boris Lauer-Leonardi, February 16, 1944, 138:2/5, GWBWL.
27. Charles Hakanson to LFH, February 13, 1946, 138:2/9; LFH to Boris Lauer-Leonardi, February 26, 1946, 138:2/9, GWBWL.
28. Tom Davin, "He Carries On the Great Herreshoff Tradition," *Boats* (September 1956): 52.
29. J. R. Dingle to LFH, April 10, 1946, 138:2/9, GWBWL. Perhaps another argument for more tumblehome curvature in the transom?
30. J. R. Dingle to LFH, September 23, 1948, 138:3/5, GWBWL.
31. J. R. Dingle to LFH, September 23, 1948, 138:3/5, GWBWL.
32. "Club H 28 News," *The Rudder* (January 1948): 114.
33. H. V. Foxton, "H-28 Makes Rough Passage," *The Rudder* (June 1950): 2.
34. "Club H 28 News, *The Rudder* (November 1948): 69; Lt. Col. Robert R. Eaton to LFH, July 20, 1965, 138:7/5, GWBWL.
35. Ray Wilkinson, "Passage Home," *Yachting Monthly* (August 1965): 70-73, 97; Herman Gucinski to LFH, January 30, 1969, 138:6/4, GWBWL.
36. An article on this version of the H-28 in *Soundings* (October 1979), credited the design to Al Francis Herreshoff, which prompted me to address the editor as follows: "In your otherwise fine article about Al Francis Herreshoff's H-28, you spelled Al's father's name wrong. It's Nathanael, not Nathaniel. If you had known Al, you would know he is a stickler for spelling, so I think you owe it to Al's memory to correct the error in your next issue." Fortunately, this sarcastic message was ignored.
37. Brydon Galilee to author, author's collection; Jenny Green, "The H-28 Story," *Sea Spray* (August 1978).
38. W. M. Sutherland to LFH, July 24, 1968, 138:6/3, GWBWL.
39. LFH to Edwin M. Hill, January 25, 1943, 138:2/4;

LFH to Val D. Vernon, June 25, 1943, 138:2/4; LFH to John Ives Sewall, February 14, 1955, 138:4/6, GWBWL.

40. LFH to B. L. Makepeace, 1944, 138:2/4; LFH to Alfred Meyer, March 1 and April 2, 1946, 138:2/9; Roy H. Oakes to LFH, May 3, 1967, 138:6/1; LFH to Douglas J. Vincent Jr., February 1, 1968, 138:6/2, GWBWL.
41. Edwin Hill to LFH, October 14, 1961, 138:5/2, GWBWL; George M. Jenkins, interview with author, Wings Neck, Pocasset, MA, April 21, 1997.
42. LFH to V. L. Smith, July 31, 1968, 138:6/5, GWBWL.
43. Anne Lawrence Bondy, interview with author, previously cited; Charles G. Martignette and Louis K. Meisel, *The Great American Pin-Up* (New York: Tachen, 1996); Walter Reed, *The Illustrator in America, 1860-2000* (New York: New York Society of Illustrators, 2001), 164; Louis K. Meisel Gallery, 141 Prince Street, New York, NY; In 1999, his large oil paintings of Salome and Carmen were offered for sale at $185,000 each.
44. LFH, "The Common Sense of Yacht Design," *The Rudder* (December 1947): 26; Dale Calloway and Anne Lawrence Bondy, interviews with author, previously cited; Dale Calloway, e-mail to author, February 27, 2009.
45. Dale Calloway, e-mail to author, February 27, 2009; LFH to Boris Lauer-Leonardi, July 30, 1945, 138:2/8; Victor Tchetchet to LFH, November 1, 1950, and February 6, 1956, 138:9/2, 4/7; Robert S. Sanborn to LFH, November 4, 1950, 138:9/1, GWBWL.
46. *The Rudder* (September 1944): 60.
47. Boris Lauer Leonardi to LFH, ca. October 22, 1943, 138:2/4; LFH to Boris Lauer-Leonardi, October 26, 1943, 138:2/4; Boris Lauer-Leonardi to LFH, November 16, 1943, 138:2/4, GWBWL.
48. LFH to Boris Lauer-Leonardi, January 14, February 3, 1944, and February 13, 1944, 138:2/5, GWBWL.
49. Jane Genner to LFH, March 22, 1944, 138:2/5; LFH to Jane Genner, March 27, 1944, 138:2/5, GWBWL.
50. Boris Lauer-Leonardi to LFH, April 13, 1944, 138:2/5; Ensign J. Oakley to LFH, April 14, 1944, 138:2/5; LFH to Ensign J. Oakley, April 17, 1944, 138:2/5, GWBWL.
51. LFH, "How To Build H 14: Fourteen Foot Sailing Dinghy," *The Rudder* (July 1944): 20.
52. LFH, "How To Build H 14: Fourteen Foot Sailing Dinghy," 20.
53. Boris Lauer-Leaonardi to LFH, ca. August 1, 1944, 138:8/4; LFH to Boris Lauer-Leonardi, August 9, 1944, 138:2/6; LFH to Paul C. Johnson, October 28, 1948, 138:3/5; Lt. A. Christopher to LFH, January 27, 1945, 138:2/7, GWBWL.
54. Richard Henderson, *Philip L. Rhodes and his Yacht Designs* (Camden, ME: International Marine Publishing, 1981), 355; Snipe plans were published in *The Rudder* (July 1931): 46-48, plus foldout; Philip C. Bolger to LFH, July 23, 1963, 138:5/4; LFH to Philip C. Bolger, August 5, 1963, 138:5/4, GWBWL.
55. Boris Lauer-Leonardi to LFH, ca. October 10, 1942, and no date (ca. October 15, 1942), 138:8/11, GWBWL.
56. LFH to Boris Lauer-Leonardi, October 3, and November 10, 1942, 138:8/11; LFH to Boris Lauer-Leonardi, February 12, 1943, 138:2/4; Boris Lauer-Leonardi to LFH, November 15, 1943, 138:2/4, GWBWL.
57. LFH to George Cochrane, July 9, 1944, 138:2/6, GWBWL; LFH, "The Common Sense of Yacht Design," *The Rudder* (November 1945): 39; Dale Calloway, interview with author, previously cited; LFH, "The Common Sense of Yacht Design," *The Rudder* (November 1944): 33; Boris Lauer-Leonardi to LFH, May 3, 1946, 138:2/9; LFH to Boris Lauer-Leonardi, May 8, 1946, 138:2/9, GWBWL.
58. LFH, "The Common Sense of Yacht Design," *The Rudder* (January 1947): 36; LFH, "The Common Sense of Yacht Design," *The Rudder* (June 1945): 49.
59. LFH, "The Common Sense of Yacht Design," *The Rudder* (December 1946): 42.
60. LFH to Uffa Fox, January 14, 1935, 138:1/5, GWBWL.
61. LFH, "The Common Sense of Yacht Design," *The Rudder* (March 1944): 58; LFH, "The Common Sense of Yacht Design," *The Rudder* (June 1944): 31; LFH, "The Common Sense of Yacht Design," *The Rudder*

(September 1946): 41.

62. LFH to Boris Lauer-Leonardi, April 9, 1945, 138:2/7, GWBWL; C. Seaver Robinson, interview with author, Machiasport, ME, May 27, 1999. There are exceptions: when Francis wrote up the history of the 42-foot cutter *Shona* of 1884, designed by "G. L. Watson of Glasgow, Scotland, the greatest all-around yacht designer of all time," to be printed for Joseph V. Santry (the occasion was the installation of the famous boat's restored bow and stern in Santry's Red Gate Boathouse on Marblehead Neck), he began by writing out his text, but started dictating a third of the way through it, so that, when Helen Bolster typed the story out in italics, as usual, she worked first from Francis's handwritten text and then from her beautifully legible shorthand, LFH, *Shona*, 138:16/21, GWBWL.
63. LFH to Boris Lauer-Leonardi, May 7, 1945, 138:2/7, GWBWL.
64. LFH, "The Common Sense of Yacht Design," *The Rudder* (April 1945): 26; Bradley Noyes to Andrew Britt, August 9, 1999, author's collection; Russell Solwar to LFH, September 27, 1945, 138:2/8, GWBWL.
65. LFH, "The Common Sense of Yacht Design," *The Rudder* (April 1945): 24, 25; LFH, "The Common Sense of Yacht Design," *The Rudder* (June 1945): 49.
66. Boris Lauer-Leonardi, ca. February 15, 1945, 138:8/11, GWBWL; LFH, "The Common Sense of Yacht Design," *The Rudder* (November 1946): 43, 44; G. de Forest Larner to LFH, November 26, 1946, 138:2/10, GWBWL.
67. Boris Lauer-Leonardi to LFH, ca. September 20, 1946, 138:2/10, GWBWL.
68. LFH to Boris Lauer-Leonardi, September 27, 1946, 138:2/10, GWBWL.
69. Boris Lauer-Leonardi to LFH, ca. November 15, 1947, 138:2/10, GWBWL.
70. John G. Hanna, "The Watch Below," *The Rudder* (March 1943): 50; Boris Lauer-Leonardi to LFH, March 10, 1943, 138:2/4; Boris Lauer-Leonardi to LFH, November 28, 1945, 138:2/8, GWBWL.
71. Anne Lawrence Bondy, interview with author, previously cited; Boris Lauer-Leonardi to LFH, ca. July 1, 1948, 138:8/11, GWBWL; Anne Lawrence Bondy to author, April 3, 1997, author's collection; LFH to Boris Lauer-Leonardi, June 27 and July 3, 1946, 138:2/9, 10, GWBWL.
72. LFH, "The Common Sense of Yacht Design," *The Rudder* (January 1948): 47, 45, 46.
73. LFH, "The Common Sense of Yacht Design." *The Rudder* (April 1944): 27; LFH, "The Common Sense of Yacht Design," *The Rudder* (March 1947): 36-39.
74. Boris Lauer-Leonardi to LFH, February 9, 1944, 138:2/5; Boris Lauer-Leonardi to LFH, April 10, 1944, ca. May 1, 1944, late January 1946, 138:8/11; Boris Lauer-Leonardi to LFH, August 31, 1944, 138:2/6; Midshipman Nolan R. Gibbons to LFH, November 3, 1944, 138:2/6; Dick Shew to LFH, September 10, 1969, 138:6/4, GWBWL.
75. Siegried Hannah to LFH, February 17, 1947, 138:3/1; Boris Lauer-Leonardi to LFH, June 27, 1944, 138:2/5, GWBWL.
76. LFH to Boris Lauer-Leonardi, July 5, 1945, 138:2/8; Boris Lauer-Leonardi to LFH, August 17, 1943, 138:2/9; Boris Lauer-Leonardi to LFH, June 9, 1949, 138:3/6; Barbara Leonardi to LFH, August 18, 1945, 138:3/6, GWBWL.
77. LFH to Boris Lauer-Leonardi, November 20, 1947, 138:3/3, GWBWL.
78. Boris Lauer-Leonardi to LFH, October 1942, no date ca. December 3, 1946, ca. June 25, 1943, and April 1947, 138:8/11; Boris Lauer-Leonardi to LFH, April 13, 1948, 138:3/4; Boris Lauer-Leonardi to LFH, February 14, 1950, 138:4/1; LFH to Boris Lauer-Leonardi, July 9, 1945, 138:2/8, GWBWL.
79. Overton G. Ellis Jr. to LFH, July 26, 1945, 138:2/8; LFH to Lt. T. R. Mason, August 24, 1945, 138:2/8; LFH to C. R. Winfield, August 16, 1945, 138:2/8; E. K. Brown to LFH, January 27, 1945, 138:2/7; LFH to E. K. Brown, February 12, 1945, 138:2/7; LFH to Boris Lauer-Leonardi, August 13, 1945, 138:2/8, GWBWL.
80. Boris Lauer-Leonardi to LFH, January 10, 1944, 138:2/5; LFH to Boris Lauer-Leonardi, November 27, 1944, 138:2/6; Boris Lauer-Leonardi to LFH,

November 28, 1944, 138:2/6; LFH to Boris Lauer-Leonardi, February 26 and February 27, 1948, 138:3/4, GWBWL.

81. W. H. de Fontaine, "The Common Sense of Yacht Design, Volume II, by L. Francis Herreshoff," *Yachting* (November 1948): 139; LFH to Boris Lauer-Leonardi, November 12, 1948, 138:3/5, GWBWL.
82. *The Common Sense of Yacht Design* is crying out to be reprinted again.
83. John Gardner, *Building Classic Small Craft* (Camden, ME: International Marine Publishing, 1977), ix; John Gardner, "Herreshoff Reprint Makes Valuable Book Available Again," *National Fisherman* (January 1967): 19-C.
84. LFH to Boris Lauer-Leonardi, June 6, 1946, 138:2/9; LFH to Boris Lauer-Leonardi, August 31, 1948, 138:3/5, GWBWL.
85. Philip C. Bolger, interview with author, Gloucester, MA, April 22, 1995.
86. Boris Lauer-Leonardi to LFH, August 23, 1946, 138:2/10; LFH to Boris Lauer-Leonardi, February 2, 1948, 138:3/4; Frederic A. Fenger to LFH, July 31, 1945, 138:2/8, GWBWL. Later, Fenger would pay the dyslexic Francis an unusual compliment: "So far, you are the only one who has noticed that I spell my name with an 's' [Frits] after the Danish fashion," Frits Fenger to LFH, October 4, 1954, 138:4/5; Uffa Fox to LFH, May 30, 1956, 138:4/7; LFH to Boris Lauer-Leonardi, June 23, 1947, 138:3/2; LFH to Mrs. G. B. Achtmeyer, October 19, 1945, 138:2/8; Wallace S. MacClain to LFH, July 11, 1946, 138:3/4, GWBWL.

Chapter 20

1. *The Rudder* (November 1944): 37; LFH to Captain C. F. Cook, August 17, 1944, 138:2/6; LFH to Frederick E. Ellis, March 21, 1946, 138:2/9, GWBWL.
2. LFH, "The Common Sense of Yacht Design," *The Rudder* (September 1946): 44; *Boston Globe*, June 11, 1967.
3. *The Rudder* (January 1945): 67; Barry Thomas, interview with author, Mystic, CT, January 31, 1995.
4. LFH, "W. Starling Burgess," *An L. Francis Herreshoff Reader*, 267.
5. Priscilla Sawyer Lord and Virginia Clegg Gamage, *Marblehead: The Spirit of '76 Lives Here* (Philadelphia: Chilton, 1972), 245; Harry Wilkinson, "Memory Lane," *Marblehead Messenger*, July 7, 1976.
6. LFH to Boris Lauer-Leonardi, November 13 and December 26, 1945, 138:2/8; LFH to Boris Lauer-Leonardi, January 10, 1946, 138:2/9; LFH to Boris Lauer-Leonardi, July 3 and November 14, 1946, 138:2/10, GWBWL.
7. Arthur Brendze, interview with author, previously cited.
8. Jay Greer, e-mail to author, April 11, 2005; Lord and Gamage, *Marblehead*, 219, 245; Hunneman Company, real estate listing, no date (1996); Arthur Brendze, interview with author, previously cited.
9. LFH, "The Common Sense of Yacht Design," *The Rudder* (June 1947): 34; LFH to Frits Fenger, September 27, 1954, 138:4/5, GWBWL.
10. LFH to the Lynn Gas and Electric Company, January 10, 1955 (misdated 1954), 138:4/6; LFH to Allan Vaitses, October 17, 1955, 138:4/6, GWBWL; Peter Coe and Dale Calloway, interviews with author, previously cited; LFH, "The Dry Breakers," *An L. Francis Herreshoff Reader*, 299; Arthur Brendze, interview with author, previously cited; John Garber, "Double Ended Yacht for John M. Garber, Esq.," *Nautical Quarterly* 29 (Spring 1985): 92; John Kendall, interview with author, Marion, MA, February 14, 1996; Jay Greer, e-mail to author, April 10, 2005; C. Seaver Robinson, interview with author, previously cited; Paul Glynn, interview with author, Georgetown, MA, June 6, 1999.
11. LFH to Warren J. Thibodeau, August 8, 1946, 138:2/10, GWBWL; Suzy Coe Fernberger and Peter Coe, interviews with author, previously cited; Llewellyn Howland III, e-mail to author, October 31, 2015.
12. Lucille Bonner Hanscom, interview with author, Rockport, ME, March 17, 1999.
13. LFH to Agnes Herreshoff, July 17, 1947, 138:3/2; LFH to Sidney Herreshoff, August 13, 1947, 138:3/2;

LFH to Jack W. Swart, April 29, 1948, 138:3/4; LFH to Henry C. White, April 20, 1951, 138:4/2, GWBWL; Arthur Brendze, Margrete Stinnes, Halsey Herreshoff, and Nathanael G. Herreshoff III, interviews with author, previously cited; O. Lie-Nielsen to LFH, August 4, 1953, 138:4/4, GWBWL; Carleton Pinheiro, interview with author, Bristol, RI, February 12, 1996.

14. LFH to Virginia Paine, November 13, 1951, 138:4/2, GWBWL; Peter Coe, C. Seaver Robinson, and Anne Lawrence Bondy, interviews with author, previously cited.
15. Suzy Coe Fernberger, interview with author, previously cited; Llewellyn Howland, III, unpublished manuscript on LFH, 11; Jay Greer, interview with author, previously cited; Jay Greer, e-mail to author; Arthur Brendze, interview with author, previously cited.
16. Suzy Coe Fernberger and Arthur Brendze, interviews with author, previously cited; Llewellyn Howland III, unpublished manuscript on LFH, 10.
17. Natalie Herreshoff and Anne Lawrence Bondy, interviews with author, previously cited; LFH, "The Compleat Cruiser," *The Rudder* (September 1952): 29, and (October 1952): 48.
18. O. Lie-Nielsen, interview with author, previously cited; LFH to Boris Lauer-Leonardi, May 17, 1943, 138:2/4, GWBWL; Suzy Coe Fernberger, Anne Lawrence Bondy, Dale Calloway, C. Seaver Robinson, Katherine Jones Vosburgh, Arthur Brendze, and Paul Glynn, interviews with author, previously cited.
19. Anne Lawrence Bondy, Katherine Jones Vosburgh, Dale Calloway, Suzy Coe Fernberger, and Bobby Russell, interviews with author, previously cited.
20. Arthur Brendze, C. Seaver Robinson, and Paul Glynn, interviews with author, previously cited; Llewellyn Howland III, unpublished manuscript on LFH, 12, 13.
21. LFH to Stanley Stearns, February 3, 1968, 138:6/2, GWBWL.
22. C. Seaver Robinson and Margrete Stinnes, interviews with author, previously cited; Tasha Tudor to "Mr. Herring," (LFH), November 15, 1958, 138:4/9, GWBWL; Dale Calloway, Arthur Brendze, and John Kendall, interviews with author, previously cited; Victor Tchetchet to LFH, June 24, 1960, 138:5/1, GWBWL.
23. Dale Calloway, e-mail to author, March 24, 2017.
24. Katherine Vosburgh and Dale Calloway, interviews with author, previously cited; Dale Calloway, e-mail to author, March 24, 2017.
25. LFH, "Marine Pictures," *The Rudder* (January 1944).
26. LFH to Darmic Stillman, September 19, 1959, 138:4/9; LFH to Charles D. Childs, November 14, December 1, 1955, and July 18, 1956, 138:4/5, 6, GWBWL. Francis left the Washington portraits to his last secretary, Muriel Vaughn, who sold them to the museum in John Brown's house in Providence, where they remain (author's phone call with Kristin Hammersmith, John Brown House Museum, Providence, Rhode Island, January 31, 2017).
27. LFH to Mrs. Jacques N. Jacobsen, November 3, 1970, 138:6/5, GWBWL; in her acknowledgments, Jacobsen listed not only Francis, but also Sidney, Griswold, and Clarence (who perhaps had Cozzens art to lend her?); LFH to Bevil Warrington-Smyth, January 15, 1951, 138:4/2, GWBWL; LFH, "The Common Sense of Yacht Design," *The Rudder* (January 1948): 45.
28. LFH to Alfred M. Brooks, September 28, 1953, 138:4/4; LFH to J. M. Meertens, March 13, 1947, 138:3/1; LFH to C. L. Johnson, December 13, 1946, 138:2/10, GWBWL.
29. Llewellyn Howland III, unpublished manuscript on LFH, 19, 21; LFH to Charles D. Childs, Boston, May 30, 1957, 138:4/8, GWBWL.
30. Arthur Brendze, interview with author, previously cited.
31. Daniel Finamore, "The Yachting Photographs of Willard B. Jackson," Peabody Essex Museum, Traditional Fine Arts Organization website.
32. Francis's Jackson photo of the *Vesta* is Mystic Seaport Museum photograph, accession number 1990.37.999.
33. LFH to Eric Hofman, December 29, 1968, 138:6/3, GWBWL; Llewellyn Howland III, unpublished manuscript on LFH, 14.

34. LFH to Hugh Somerville, April 10, 1959, 138:4/10; LFH to Boris Lauer-Leonardi, June 24, 1944, 138:2/5; LFH to Boris Lauer Leonardi, December 3, 1946, 138:2/10, GWBWL.

35. LFH to NGH, January 28, 1938, 138:17/14, GWBWL; Paul Glynn, interview with author, previously cited; LFH to Walter Hadley, December 14, 1962, 138:5/3; Boris Lauer-Leonardi to LFH, December 14, 1959, and LFH's reply of December 21, 1959, 138:4/10; LFH to NGH, February 7, 1936, 138:17/12, GWBWL.

36. LFH to Chadwell O'Connor, July 17, 1947, 138:3/2; LFH to Walter Hadley, February 3, 1966, 138:5/8; LFH to Detroit Diesel Corporation, February 24, 1953, 138:4/4; LFH to Capt. L. S. McCready, August 22, 1968, 138:6/3, GWBWL; US Naval Institute membership certificate, November 17, 1927, HMM; notification of membership from US Naval Institute of December 16, 1947, 138:9/3; LFH to Dr. Harrison J. Hunt, December 22, 1947, 138:3/3, GWBWL.

37. LFH to Fernando de Avellar, June 30, 1947, 138:3/2, GWBWL. And so could the author, for LFH passed them on to the Nautical Society at Milton Academy, where I clipped out the good boats.

38. LFH to Albert B. Elliot, January 15, 1970, 138:6/5; Marguerite S. Crichton to LFH, May 23, 1956, 138:4/7, GWBWL.

39. Charles Lauriat to LFH, February 1936, 138:1/6, GWBWL; Llewellyn Howland III, unpublished manuscript on LFH, 23; copy of flyleaf of W. P. Stephens's *Traditions and Memories of American Yachting*, in the collection at Mystic Seaport Museum; later, Frank Paine's widow, Virginia, moved the book along to yachting historian Evers Burtner, who gave it to George Clapp in 1977.

40. LFH to John Ives Sewall, September 3, 1953, and Sewall's reply of November 1, 1953, 138:4/4, GWBWL.

41. Nathanael G. Herreshoff III and Margrete L. Stinnes, interviews with author, previously cited; LFH, "The Dry Breakers," in *An L. Francis Herreshoff Reader*, 300.

42. Anne Lawrence Bondy and Peter Coe, interviews with author, previously cited; LFH to Boris Lauer-Leonardi, with postscript by Helen Bolster, September 20, 1948, 138:3/5, GWBWL.

43. Llewellyn Howland III, unpublished manuscript on LFH, 15; Paul Glynn, Jay Greer, and Arthur Brendze, interviews with author, previously cited.

44. LFH, list of designs, 138:15/1, GWBWL; Paul Glynn, interview with author, previously cited; Llewellyn Howland III, unpublished manuscript on LFH, 16.

45. Jay Greer, interview with author, previously cited; LFH to Bror Tamm, December 4, 1958, 138:4/9, GWBWL.

46. LFH, *The Compleat Cruiser*, 63, 64; LFH to Preston Sturges, February 26, 1948, 138:3/4; LFH to NGH, January 14, 1930, 138:17/6, GWBWL.

47. George P. Swift to LFH, April 25, 1958, and LFH's reply of May 2, 1958, 138:4/9, GWBWL; Jay Greer and Paul Glynn, interviews with author, previously cited; LFH to Sidney Herreshoff, March 9, 1953, 138:4/4, GWBWL; "Notes on Rivett Company History," Rivett Lathe Company website.

48. LFH, "Notes on making Reversible Dynamometer Blades," July 17, 1952, 138:16/9, GWBWL; Christopher Coe to author, January 1995, author's collection; John Kendall and Arthur Brendze, interviews with author, previously cited; Peter Coe to author, previously cited.

49. Jay Greer, interview with author, previously cited; Tom Lie-Nielsen, interview with author, Warren, ME, March 13, 1996.

50. Arthur Brendze and John Kendall, interviews with author, previously cited; LFH, *The Compleat Cruiser*, 62.

51. NGH to LFH, March 30, 1938, 138:17/14, GWBWL; Peter Coe to author, previously cited; Anne Lawrence Bondy, interview with author, previously cited; Nannie Burgess to LFH, 1937, 138:1/7; LFH to Boris Lauer-Leonardi, September 2 and September 14, 1944, 138:2/6; LFH to Boris Lauer-Leonardi, May 12, 1943, and January 2, 1950, 138:2/4; Boris Lauer-Leonardi to LFH, November 3, 1950, 138:4/1, GWBWL.

52. Llewellyn Howland III, unpublished manuscript on

LFH, 16; Tudor to LFH, January 4, 1953, 138:4/4; LFH to Virginia Paine, October 23 and December 20, 1950, and December 2, 1954, 138:8/7; Tasha Tudor to LFH, January 15 and February 17, 1953, and September 10, 1955, 138:4/4, 6, GWBWL; Tasha Tudor and Richard Brown, *The Private World of Tasha Tudor* (Boston: Little, Brown, 1992), 119, 134.

53. O. Lie-Nielsen, interview with author, previously cited.
54. See also LFH, "The Common Sense of Yacht Design," *The Rudder* (February 1946): 33-36, for a complete description of drawing lines, using, for an example, the Marco Polo; LFH to Lt. Harold C. Hood, March 21, 1946, 138:2/9, GWBWL; LFH, "the Common Sense of Yacht Design, " *The Rudder* (April 1946): 44.
55. LFH to Clinton H. Crane, March 6, 1937, 138:1/7, GWBWL; LFH, "The Common Sense of Yacht Design," *The Rudder* (April 1946): 38-41; LFH to Boris Lauer-Leonardi, January 25, 1944, 138:2/5, GWBWL; LFH, "The Common Sense of Yacht Design," *The Rudder* (April 1946): 38, 39.
56. As Stephan Zweig said of Balzac's writing table.
57. C. Seaver Robinson and Suzy Coe Fernberger, interviews with author, previously cited; LFH to Dick Dawson, November 1, 1962, 138:5/3, GWBWL; Edmund A. Cutts to Robert Steward, January 25, 1988, author's collection.
58. LFH to NGH, January 28, 1935, 138:17/11, GWBWL; John Kendall, interview with author, previously cited; LFH to John Ives Sewall, November 30, 1953, 138:4/4; LFH to Commanding Officer, US Naval Experiment Station, New London, CT, October 26, 1918, 138:16/8, GWBWL.
59. LFH to Albert Austin November 19, 1945, 138:2/8; LFH to Austin S. Davenport, December 29, 1947, 138:3/3, GWBWL; Carleton Pinheiro, interview with author, previously cited; LFH to NGH, August 1, 1932, 138:17/8, GWBWL.
60. John Gardner, interview with author; LFH to Bror Tamm, June 28, 1967, 138:6/1, GWBWL.
61. Allan Vaitses to LFH, September 14, 1955, 138:4/6, GWBWL.
62. C. Seaver Robinson, interview with author, previously cited; LFH to Hans Stinnes, July 2, 1956, 138:4/7, GWBWL; Richard Allphin to author, ca. June 15, 1996, author's collection; LFH to William J. Strawbridge, October 10, 1958, 138:4/9, GWBWL.
63. LFH to Edwin Hill, October 30, 1958, 138: 4/9; LFH to Allen D. Slater, November 20, 1961, 138:5/2; LFH to William J. Strawbridge of January 11, 1962, 138:5/3, GWBWL.
64. Paul Glynn, interview with author, previously cited.
65. Paul Glynn, interview with author, previously cited.
66. Bette Hunt, e-mail to author, February 19, 2005.

Chapter 21

1. Robinson told the story of his circumnavigation in the *Svaap* in a series of articles that ran in *The Rudder* from March 1929 through July 1932. As the long series ended, the articles were published in book form by Harcourt, Brace and Company, New York, under the title, *10,000 Leagues Over the Sea* and, simultaneously in England, as *Deep Water and Shoal.* Robinson recounted the second voyage of the *Svaap* in his book, *Voyage to Galapagos* (New York: Harcourt, Brace and Company, 1936); Anthony J. Pagano to author, July 25, 1992, author's collection.
2. Robinson recorded the design, building, and several voyages of the *Varua* in his book, *To the Great Southern Sea* (London: Peter Davies, 1957), and also in *Return to the Sea* (Tuckahoe, NY: John de Graff, 1972).
3. On Robinson antagonizing Burgess's chief draftsman, see Timothy Mickleburgh, "*Varua*: Soul of the Southern Sea," *WoodenBoat* 65 (July/August 1985): 44-50.
4. Anne Lawrence Bondy, interview with author, previously cited; William A. Robinson to V. R. Bruce, March 24, 1944, author's collection; V. R. Bruce to LFH, March 27, 1944, 138:2/5; on LFH's friendship with Robinson, see LFH to Boris Lauer-Leonardi, March 14, 1944, 138:2/5, GWBWL; during his trip to Holland to learn the steel part of composite construction, Robinson bought a wonderful book in Dutch (*Schepen die Voorbijgaan*) about the many types of traditional craft in the

Netherlands. He later gave the book to Francis. After Francis's death, Muriel Vaughn passed it on to the author, who added it to the library on board his Dutch canal cruiser, the *Water Lily*.

5. LFH to Allan Vaitses, October 31, 1956, 138:4/7; LFH to K. W. Higgs, October 3, 1969, 138:6/4; LFH to Stanley Woodward, April 7, 1960, 138:5/1, GWBWL; William A. Robinson to author, March 7, 1977, author's collection; a detailed, illustrated description of the *Varua* may be found in the author's *More Good Boats* (Camden, ME: International Marine Publishing, 1979), 151-63.
6. William A. Robinson to V. R. Bruce, March 24, 1944, author's collection; LFH to Neal T. Walker, January 22, 1970, 138:6/5, GWBWL; these drawings are on the back of Francis's construction plan of design No. 81, SP38.184.10, DSGSPL.
7. LFH to Neal T. Walker, January 22, 1970, 138:6/5; LFH to Carl B. Cahill, June 10, 1970, 138:6/5, GWBWL.
8. LFH to Neal T. Walker, January 22, 1970, 138:6/5; LFH to Carl B. Cahill, May 17, 1969, 138:6/4, GWBWL.
9. LFH to Boris Lauer-Leonardi, November 5, 1943, 138:2/4, GWBWL.
10. LFH to Midshipman Nolan R. Gibbons, November 3, 1944, 138:2/6; LFH to John Ives Sewell, March 31, 1955, 138:4/6, GWBWL; Katherine Vosburgh and Philip C. Bolger, interviews with author, previously cited; LFH's charts in author's collection.
11. F-5 description, 138:16/22, GWBWL.
12. SP38.147.1, DSGSPL.
13. F-16 description, 138:16/18, GWBWL.
14. SP38.122.1, DSGSPL.
15. LFH to Uffa Fox, January 14, 1935, 138:1/5, GWBWL. Francis hoped his design F-16 would appear in Uffa Fox's *Second Book*, but it didn't.
16. NGH to LFH, May 2, 1926, 138:17/2, GWBWL.
17. V. R. Bruce to LFH, March 27, 1944, 138:2/5, GWBWL; see also John C. Voss, *The Venturesome Voyages of Captain Voss* (Boston: Charles E. Lauriat, 1927), and Tilikum*: Luxton's Pacific Crossing* (Sidney, British Columbia: Gray's Publishing, 1971).
18. LFH, "How to Build the Marco Polo H 55," *The Rudder* (January 1945): 54.
19. LFH, "Announcing the Marco Polo H 55," *The Rudder* (December 1944): 44.
20. John Ives Sewall to LFH, December 18, 1961, 138:5/2, GWBWL.
21. LFH, "How to Build the Marco Polo H 55," 54, 55.
22. Boris Lauer-Leonardi to LFH, December 19, 1944, 138:2/6, GWBWL.
23. Boris Lauer-Leonardi to LFH, December 28, 1944, 138:8/11; LFH to Boris Lauer-Leonardi, February 4, 1945, 138:2/7, GWBWL.
24. LFH to Vicompte R. de Dampierre, January 12, 1968, 138:6/2, GWBWL.
25. LFH, "How to Build the Marco Polo H 55, Part II, Lines," *The Rudder* (February 1945): 40.
26. LFH, "How to Build the Marco Polo H 55, Part IV, Power Plants," *The Rudder* (April 1945): 32.
27. LFH, "How to Build the Marco Polo H 55, Part IV, Power Plants," 34; LFH to Albert C. Cleveland, July 5, 1945, 138:2/8, GWBWL.
28. LFH, "How to Build the Marco Polo H 55," 54, 55; see also LFH to H. L. Forsyth, February 20, 1947, 138:3/1, GWBWL.
29. LFH to H. L. Forsyth, February 20, 1947, 138:3/1, GWBWL.
30. LFH, "How to Build the Marco Polo H 55, Part VII, Tanks," *The Rudder* (July 1945): 44.
31. *The Rudder* (August 1944): 29.
32. LFH, "How to Build the Marco Polo II 55, Part VI, Deck and Cabin Plan," *The Rudder* (June 1945): 28.
33. LFH, "How to Build the Marco Polo H 55, Part VI, Deck and Cabin Plan," 28.
34. LFH, "How to Build the Marco Polo, Part XI, Rudder and Steering Gear," *The Rudder* (November 1945): 52, 53, 82; "Part II, Lines," 40; Edmund A. Cutts, interview with author, Oxford, MD, April 19, 1996.
35. LFH, "How to Build the Marco Polo, Part XV, Dinghy," *The Rudder* (June 1946): 39, 40.
36. Calvin T. Howell to LFH, September 30, 1955, 138:4/6; LFH to Calvin T. Howell, October 6, 1955, 138:4/6; Calvin T. Howell to LFH, January 23, 1956, 138:4/7, GWBWL; Barry Thomas and John

P. Kendall, interviews with author, previously cited; Robert T. Todd to LFH, August 31, 1965, 138:5/7; Thomas A. Fletcher to LFH, October 20, 1968, 138:6/3, GWBWL; John Gardner, interview with author, previously cited. It is perhaps worth noting that Gardner, like that other great historian of vessels, Howard I. Chapelle, seldom went afloat.

37. LFH, "How to Build the Marco Polo, Part XXII, Squaresail Gear," *The Rudder* (February 1947): 45.
38. LFH, "How to Build the Marco Polo, Part IV, Power Plants," 32; LFH to Boyd Donaldson, May 21, 1945, 138:2/7, GWBWL.
39. LFH to Captain Robert P. Beebe, January 14, 1958, 138:4/9, GWBWL.
40. Richard Henderson, *Philip L. Rhodes and His Yacht Designs* (Camden, ME: International Marine Publishing, 1981), 150-57.
41. LFH, "How to Build the Marco Polo H 55," 45; "Part II, Lines," 40; LFH to Albert E. Peirce, January 27, 1945, 138:2/7; LFH to Boris Lauer-Leonardi, October 16, 1948, 138:3/5; LFH to Albert Samuel, July 30, 1945, 138:2/8, GWBWL.
42. Kenneth O'Meara, "Let's Get Together and Build the Marco Polo," *The Rudder* (September 1945): 24, 25, 69; "Builders Invited to Submit Bids on Marco Polo," *The Rudder* (December 1945): 101.
43. LFH to Boris Lauer-Leonardi, March 10, 1947, 138:3/1; Boris Lauer-Leonardi to LFH, April 10, 1947, 138:3/1; LFH to Boris Lauer-Leonardi, June 2, 1947, 138:3/2; Boris Lauer-Leonardi to LFH, June 14, 1946, 138:2/9; LFH to Charles F. Schoening, January 27, 1945, 138:2/7, GWBWL; a Marco Polo dinghy, built by Allan Vaitses in 1961, is in the Mystic Seaport Museum small craft collection, accession number 1991.91.
44. John E. Cherubini to LFH, November 24, 1947, 138:3/3, GWBWL; Cherubini, with his brother Frit and son Lee, would later design and build boats patterned after the *Tioga*.
45. Delavan P. Smith to LFH, January 4, 1955, 138:4/6, GWBWL.
46. Boris Lauer-Leonardi to LFH, July 19, 1949, 138:3/6; LFH to Delavan P. Smith, January 10, 1955, 138:4/6, GWBWL.
47. Delavan P. Smith, "Two Marco Polos Under Construction," *The Rudder* (December 1955): 55; LFH to Allan Vaitses, April 5, 1956, 138:4/7, GWBWL; Charles H. Doersam Jr., interview with author, on board the *Crusican*, Old Lyme, CT, July 31, 1996, and by telephone, March 22, 2000; J. R. Dingle to LFH, September 23, 1948, 138:3/5, GWBWL.
48. Robert P. Beebe, "Passage to the Bahamas," *The Rudder* (February 1958): 7, 8.
49. Beebe, "Passage to the Bahamas," 7, 8; Josiah T. Newcomb to LFH, July 28, 1956, 138:4/7, GWBWL.
50. Robert P. Beebe to LFH, April 17, 1946, 138:2/9, GWBWL.
51. Beebe, "Passage to the Bahamas," 6-11, 30-32.
52. LFH to Robert P. Beebe, January 14, 1958, 138:4/9, GWBWL.
53. Robert P. Beebe to LFH, January 20, 1958, and LFH's reply, January 23, 1958, 138:4/9, GWBWL.
54. Robert P. Beebe to Harmon Hunt, May 21, 1974, author's collection, courtesy Robert P. Beebe.
55. Robert P. Beebe to Harmon Hunt, May 21, 1974, author's collection, courtesy Robert P. Beebe; Robert P. Beebe to author, January 4, 1979, author's collection.
56. Richard Henry Dana, *Two Years Before the Mast* (1840; New York: Modern Library, 1936), 376.
57. Robert P. Beebe to LFH, January 20, 1958, 138:4/9; Pierre Deligant to LFH, August 11, 1964, 138:5/5, GWBWL.
58. LFH to Robert T. Todd, September 6, 1965, 138:5/7; LFH to Urban H. Wagner Jr., July 21, 1967, 138:6/1; see also LFH to Franz W. Gruber, December 29, 1968, 138:6/3, GWBWL.
59. LFH to G. E. Stuart, June 24, 1965, 138:5/6, GWBWL.
60. Charles Darcy, telephone interview with author, Centerville, MA, March 17, 2000.
61. Harmon Hunt to LFH, July 14, 1969, 138:6/4, GWBWL; Harmon Hunt, telephone interview with author, Island Falls, ME, January 2, 2001; Howard Boardman, telephone interview with author,

Charlestown, RI, January 2, 2001.

62. Steve Macek, interview with author, Woods Hole, MA.
63. LFH to Mrs. Josiah T. Newcomb, July 12, 1959, 138:4/10; LFH to William A. Grover, September 30, 1968, 138:6/3; Carl B. Cahill to LFH, October 28, 1970, 138:6/5, GWBWL.
64. LFH to Allan Vaitses, September 19, 1966, 138:5/8; LFH to William A. Grover, September 30, 1968, 138:6/3; LFH to Urban H. Wagner Jr., July 21, 1967, 138:6/1, GWBWL.
65. LFH to William A. Grover, September 30, 1968, 138:6/3; LFH to William J. Buff Jr., March 19, 1945, 138:2/7; B. Smith to LFH, January 10, 1946, 138:2/9; George A. Benny to LFH, May 15, 1947, 138:3/2; Franz M. Gruber to LFH, December 14, 1968, 138:6/3; Urban H. Wagner Jr. to LFH, March 17, 1969, 138:6/4; Bruce A. Tyson to LFH, February 17, 1965, 138:5/6, GWBWL.
66. Arthur Rowe and Steve Macek, interviews with author, previously cited.
67. LFH to Charles Evan King, December 6, 1948, 138:3/5; LFH to Robert Graham, June 30, 1968, 138:6/3, GWBWL; SP38.98.1, DSGSPL.
68. Nicholas Potter to LFH, July 25, 1966, and February 13, 1967, 138:5/8, 6/1, GWBWL.

Chapter 22

1. Boris Lauer-Leonardi to LFH, April 10, 1944, 138:8/11; LFH to Boris Lauer-Leonardi, April 22, 1944, 138:2/5; LFH to Boris Lauer-Leonardi, June 24, 1944; 138:2/5, GWBWL.
2. LFH to Boris Lauer-Leonardi, April 9, 1945, 138:2/7, GWBWL; Waldo Howland, *A Life in Boats: The Concordia Years* (Mystic: Mystic Seaport Museum, 1988), 44; LFH, *The Compleat Cruiser*, xi; Boris Lauer-Leonardi to LFH, December 19, 1944, 138:2/6, GWBWL.
3. Waldo Howland to author, December 7, 1976, author's collection; see also Waldo Howland, *A Life in Boats: The Concordia Years*, 44, 45.
4. LFH to Joseph Manton, January 15, 1946, 138:2/9, GWBWL.
5. SP38.20.11, DSGSPL.
6. LFH to Russell Genner, October 17, 1943, 138:2/4, GWBWL.
7. Russell Genner to LFH, October 30, 1943, and LFH's reply, November 5, 1943, 138:2/4; Russell Genner to LFH, November 8, 1943, 138:2/4, GWBWL.
8. LFH to Jane Genner, March 17, 1944, and Genner's reply, March 22, 1944, 138:2/5, GWBWL.
9. LFH to Eben C. Sprague, March 24, 1944, 138:2/5, GWBWL.
10. Boris Lauer-Leonardi to LFH, March 19, 1945, 138:2/7; Jane Genner to LFH, June 13, 1945, and LFH's reply, June 18, 1945, 138:2/7, GWBWL.
11. LFH to R. Keating, January 24, 1946, 138:2/9; Jane Genner to LFH, October 9, 1946, and LFH's reply, October 14, 1946, 138:2/10, GWBWL.
12. LFH to Russell Genner, September 16, 1947, 138:3/3, GWBWL.
13. LFH to Dr. H. V. Foxton, October 31, 1944, 138:2/6; LFH to Lt. Percy Brewer, June 14, 1945, 138:2/7; LFH to R. Wallace Ross, August 9, 1945, 138:2/8, GWBWL.
14. LFH, "How to Build Nereia," *The Rudder* (March 1947): 45.
15. LFH, "How to Build Nereia," 88.
16. LFH to James E. Moore, April 17, 1968, 138:6/2; LFH to Jean-Jacques Ferlard, June 24, 1965, 138:5/6; LFH to Denis Solomon, June 7, 1965, 138:5/6, GWBWL.
17. LFH to H. Wisenthal, October 10, 1946, 138:2/10, GWBWL.
18. LFH to J. R. Dingle, October 4, 1948, 138:3/5, GWBWL.
19. LFH to N. R. McDonald, October 7, 1947, 138:3/3, GWBWL.
20. LFH to N. R. McDonald, October 7, 1947, 138:3/3, GWBWL.
21. LFH, "How to Build Nereia," 19.
22. LFH, "How to Build Nereia," 19; James E. Moore to LFH, April 13, 1968, 138:6/2; Roger A. Kelsey to LFH, January 6, 1970, 138:6/5; Lt. Col. Ned W. Glenn to LFH, May 18 and May 30, 1956, 138:4/7, GWBWL.

23. J. R. Dingle to LFH, September 23, 1948, 138:3/5, GWBWL; advertisement, The *Rudder* (November 1954): 51; LFH to W. T. White, September 16, 1965, 138:5/7, GWBWL. The author and his wife, Kathleen Carney, also had the chance to examine the *Carastee* when she was for sale in 1989. It was a sad experience, for Dr. Simkin believed that his lovely boat was still just as he had built her, but she had been laid up for awhile, and ravages of rot were appearing.
24. Joyce McLoughlin, "Another Pygmalion and his Galatea," *The Rudder* (September 1960): 45, 46; A. W. McLoughlin, "*Galatea* Underway," The Mail Barrel, *The Rudder* (May 1961): 84; see Benjamin Mendlowitz's cover photo of the *Galatea*, *WoodenBoat* 56 (January/February 1984).
25. LFH to John Kendall, July 30, 1969, 138:6/4, GWBWL; John Kendall, interview with author, previously cited.
26. John Kendall, interview with author, previously cited; Allan Vaitses, interview with author, Mattapoisett, MA, April 23, 1995; John Kendall to LFH, May 13 and May 18, 1970, 138:6/5, GWBWL.
27. John Kendall, interview with author, previously cited.
28. Brian O'Donoghue to LFH, no date (answered by LFH July 23, 1969), copy furnished by O'Donoghue to author, June 2, 1973.
29. Advertisement in *Cruising World* (August 1987): 125; *Sailboat Buyer's Guide, 1994*, 171.
30. NGH to LFH, August 26, 1936, 138:17/12; LFH to Cdr. Robert P. Beebe, June 10, 1946, 138:2/9, GWBWL.
31. "Sully" to LFH, October 20, 1945, and LFH's reply, October 26, 1945, 138:2/8; Russell N. Dyer to LFH, January 5, 1946, and LFH's reply, January 22, 1946, 138:2/9, GWBWL.
32. Boris Lauer-Leonardi to LFH, March 18, 1948, 138:3/4; LFH to Vincent Gilpin, March 17, 1948, 138:3/4, GWBWL.
33. Boris Lauer-Leonardi to LFH, no date (answered April 12, 1948), 138:8/9, GWBWL.
34. LFH to Boris Lauer-Leonardi, April 12, 1948, 138:3/4, GWBWL.
35. See Ralph Munroe, *The Commodore's Story* (New York: Ives Washburn, 1930) and Howard I. Chapelle, *American Sailing Craft* (New York: Kennedy Brothers, 1936).
36. LFH, "How to Build Meadow Lark," *The Rudder* (August 1948): 35.
37. LFH to Walter M. Stites Jr., April 4, 1946, 138:2/9, GWBWL; LFH, "How To Build Meadow Lark," 35; LFH to Stanley Stearns, February 16, 1968, 138:6/2, GWBWL.
38. Philip C. Bolger, interview with author, previously cited; see Philip C. Bolger, *Small Boats* (Camden, ME: International Marine Publishing, 1973), *The Folding Schooner and Other Adventures in Boat Design* (Camden, ME: International Marine Publishing, 1976), *Thirty-Odd Boats* (Camden, ME: International Marine Publishing, 1982), and *Boats With an Open Mind* (Camden, ME, International Marine Publishing, 1994).
39. Allan H. Vaitses, "Hark the Lark," *The Rudder* (December 1961): 31; Robert T. Gibbs, "A Rudder Sharpie," *The Rudder* (October 1950): 10; LFH to Henry C. White, July 12 and July 24, 1951, 138:4/2, GWBWL.
40. LFH to Henry C. White, July 12, 1951, 138:4/2, GWBWL; *The Rudder* (May 1952): 4.
41. Allan H. Vaitses, "Hark the Lark," 30, 31, 74; the author got to enjoy 15-inch-draft voyaging, also, on a short cruise inside the elbow of Cape Cod in a Meadow Lark kindly loaned to him and one of his sons by Will Howard. We sailed out of Stage Harbor, and, when a northeaster breezed on, we anchored right up snug close to the beach in Pleasant Bay; LFH "Loon, a Meadow Lark," *The Rudder* (October 1959): 73; Lee Hill, *The Sharpie Sanderling* (Boston: Branden Press, 1971).
42. Allan H. Vaitses, interview with author, previously cited.
43. Allan H. Vaitses, interview with author, previously cited; LFH, "How To Build Meadow Lark," 33; Ian Scott, *Mudlark's Ghosts* (Dobb's Ferry, NY: Sheridan House, 2007), 107, 108.
44. Allan Vaitses to LFH, October 23, 1960, 138:5/1, GWBWL.

45. Allan H. Vaitses, interview with author, previously cited.
46. Allan H. Vaitses, interview with author, previously cited.
47. LFH to C. L. Johnson, November 15, 1944, 138:2/6; LFH to R. G. Haines, December 1, 1948, 138:3/5, GWBWL; Allan H. Vaitses, interview with author, previously cited.
48. Thomas A. Fletcher to LFH, April 24, 1965, 138:5/6, GWBWL.
49. LFH, "How to Build Meadow Lark," 56.
50. Edwin M. Hill letterhead, author's collection.
51. Edwin M. Hill to George Jenkins, March 5, 1973, author's collection.
52. Edwin M. Hill to LFH, October 28, 1958, 138:4/9, GWBWL; John Kendall, interview with author, previously cited.
53. LFH to Edwin M. Hill, August 17, 1960, 138:5/1, GWBWL; John Kendall, interview with author, previously cited.
54. John P. Kendall to LFH, July 24, 1968, 138:6/3, GWBWL; John Kendall, interview with author, previously cited.
55. LFH to Edwin M. Hill, March 25, 1968, 138:6/2; Allan H. Vaitses to LFH, August 13, 1970, 138:6/5, GWBWL.
56. LFH to NGH, May 2, 1929, 138:17/5, GWBWL; LFH, "The Common Sense of Yacht Design," *The Rudder* (August 1947): 37, 38.
57. LFH to Charles M. Saltsman, December 9, 1948, 138:3/5, GWBWL.
58. LFH to Herbert F. Brabner, April 3, 1967, 138:6/1; LFH to Francis E. Fredette, May 20, 1946, 138:2/9, GWBWL.
59. LFH to Boris Lauer-Leonardi, February 28, 1949, 138:3/6, GWBWL; LFH, "How To Build Sailski, A Sailing Machine," *The Rudder* (February 1950): 21; LFH to Raymond C. Ingersoll, February 23, 1969, 138:6/4, GWBWL.
60. LFH to Raymond C. Ingersoll, January 13, 1969, 138:6/4, GWBWL; LFH, "How To Build Sailski, A Sailing Machine," *The Rudder* (May 1949): 66.
61. William A. Berry Jr., "Scat Cat," *The Rudder* (February 1953): 24, 25, 70, 71.
62. Berry, "Scat Cat," 24, 25, 70, 71.
63. Berry, "Scat Cat," 24, 25, 70, 71.
64. Raymond C. Ingersoll to LFH, January 1 and January 15, 1969, 138:6/4, GWBWL; LFH to Raymond C. Ingersoll, January 13, 1969, 138:6/4, GWBWL.
65. LFH to Ann Roebuck Herreshoff, July 29, 1946, 138:2/10, GWBWL.
66. LFH to Agnes Herreshoff, June 6, 1947, 138:3/2; LFH to Boris Lauer-Leonardi, June 10, 1948, 138:3/5, GWBWL.
67. LFH to James S. Pitkin, January 19, 1948, 138:3/4; Boris Lauer-Leonardi to LFH, April 16, 1951, 138:8/11; LFH to H. S. Smith, April 2, 1951, 138:4/2, GWBWL.
68. Samuel Carter III, *The Boatbuilders of Bristol* (New York: Doubleday and Company, 1970), 160-162; see volume 1, page 410, endnote 4.
69. Richard Philbrick, "Herreshoff, Great Naval Architect," HMM files.
70. Henry C. White to LFH, April 16, 1951, 138:9/5, GWBWL.
71. Malcolm MacNaught to LFH, March 27, 1954, and LFH's reply, April 1, 1954, 138:4/5, GWBWL.

Chapter 23

1. LFH to Boris Lauer-Leonardi, June 25, 1943, 138:2/4, GWBWL.
2. LFH, "The Common Sense of Yacht Design," *The Rudder* (February 1947): 70.
3. LFH to John Ives Sewall, October 24, 1950, 138:4/1; LFH to Boris Lauer-Leonardi, July 21, 1950, 138:4/1, GWBWL.
4. LFH to Boris Lauer-Leonardi, July 21, 1950, 138:4/1; LFH to William J. Strawbridge, May 31, 1950, 138:4/1; William J. Strawbridge to LFH, September 12, [1951], 138:4/2, GWBWL.
5. LFH, "Piquant," *The Rudder* (February 1951): 14; LFH to William J. Strawbridge, August 4, 1950, 138:4/1, GWBWL.
6. P. C. Bolger and Lindsay Lord, "The Case for the Low Power Planing Boat," *The Rudder* (May 1951):

30, 61; Philip C. Bolger, *The Folding Schooner and Other Adventures in Boat Design* (Camden, ME: International Marine Publishing, 1977), 99.

7. George Swift to LFH, February 23, 1951, 138:4/2; LFH to A. E. Luders Jr., July 21, 1950, 138:4/1; LFH to Walter F. Lathrop, July 21, 1950, 138:4/1, GWBWL.
8. William J. Strawbridge to LFH, September 12, (1951), 138:4/1, GWBWL.
9. LFH to David N. Crofoot, November 21, 1950, 138:4/1; LFH to Allan Vaitses, May 12, 1958, 138:4/9, GWBWL; Robert Russell, interview with author, previously cited; LFH to E. Selman Graves Jr., October 20, 1958, February 6, 1959, and September 16, 1959, 138:4/9, 10; LFH to Robert Gibbs, July 17, 1959, 138:4/10; LFH to Samuel Morris, September 22, 1958, 138:4/9, GWBWL.
10. Philip C. Bolger, Robert Russell, and Anne Lawrence Bondy, interviews with author, previously cited.
11. LFH to James C. Fitzsimmons, September 21, 1967, 138:6/1; LFH to C. J. Frankham, April 24, 1971, 138:6/6; LFH to Edwin M. Hill, September 22, 1960, 138:5/1, GWBWL.
12. LFH to William J. Strawbridge, October 2, 1959, 138:4/10; LFH to Allan Vaitses, June 27, 1960, 138:5/1; LFH to Edwin M. Hill, August 17, 1960, 138:5/1; LFH to William J. Strawbridge, October 31, 1960, 138:5/1; LFH to William J. Strawbridge, January 11, 1962, 138:5/3, GWBWL; Philip C. Bolger, interview with author, previously cited.
13. Margrete Stinnes, interview with author, previously cited.
14. Margrete Stinnes, interview with author, previously cited.
15. Margrete Stinnes to author, August 31, 1995, author's collection.
16. Margrete Stinnes, interview with author, previously cited; LFH to Boris Lauer-Leonardi, September 7, 1962, 138:5/3, GWBWL.
17. LFH to Ernest Rolland, November 2, 1964, 138:5/5, GWBWL.
18. Brokerage listing by World Class Yacht Sales, New Port Richey, FL; personal inspection by author at Rockport, Maine, March 19, 1997.
19. Herreshoff Marine Museum, announcement of thirty-third annual meeting, May 8, 2004.
20. William J. Strawbridge to LFH, 1963, 138:9/1, GWBWL.
21. LFH to Walter F. Lathrop, April 26, 1954, 138:4/5; LFH to William J. Strawbridge, May 20, 1954, 138:4/5; LFH to Henry Rasmussen, June 3, 1954, 138:4/5, GWBWL.
22. LFH to William J. Strawbridge, June 10, 1954, 138:4/5, GWBWL.
23. LFH to William J. Strawbridge, July 22, 1954, 138:4/5; William J. Strawbridge to LFH, September 22 and October 20, 1954, 138:4/5; LFH to William J. Strawbridge, October 23, 1954, 138:4/5, GWBWL.
24. LFH to William J. Strawbridge, November 22, 1954, 138:4/5, GWBWL.
25. William J. Strawbridge to LFH, 1963, 138:9/1, GWBWL.
26. LFH, "The Rudder Rating Rule for Small Racing Sailboats," *The Rudder* (July 1950): 29-31.
27. LFH "A Rule for Measuring and Rating Sail Boats," unpublished manuscript, June 1964, 138:14/21, GWBWL.
28. LFH, "The Common Sense of Yacht Design," *The Rudder* (September 1944): 34.
29. Frank C. Paine to LFH, December 12, 1950, 138:4/1, GWBWL.
30. LFH to Robert S. Sanborn, July 2 and October 23, 1951, 138:4/2; Robert S. Sanborn to LFH, April 22, 1953, 138:4/4, GWBWL.
31. See SP38.478, DSGSPL; LFH to Frank C. Paine, August 13, 1951, 138:4/2, GWBWL.
32. Virginia Paine to LFH, late 1952, 138:8/7; LFH to Frank Paine, October 27, 1952, 138:8/7; LFH to Clinton H. Crane, November 28, 1952, 138:8/7; LFH to Nicholas Potter, late 1952, 138:8/7, GWBWL; Georgina Paine Howland to author, February 20, 1957, author's collection; LFH to Georgina Howland, 1955, 138:6/7; LFH to Virginia Paine, July 27, 1953, 138:4/4; Charles M. Ganson to LFH, July 20, 1953, 138:4/4, GWBWL.
33. John M. Garber to LFH, January 14, 1952, 138:4/3;

LFH to John M. Garber, June 22, 1951, 138:4/2; John M. Garber to LFH, October 25, 1951, 138:4/2; LFH, "Changes in #93," (written on the back of description of design No. 92), 138:15/27; LFH to John M. Garber, January 9, 1952, 138:4/3, GWBWL.

34. John M. Garber to LFH, January 14, 1952, 138:4/3, GWBWL.
35. John M. Garber to LFH, February 22, 1953, 138:4/4, GWBWL.
36. LFH to John M. Garber, March 3, 1953, 138:4/4; LFH to John M. Garber, December 1, 1955, 138:4/6; John M. Garber to LFH, January 24, 1956, 138:4/7; LFH to John M. Garber, January 30, 1956, 138:4/7, GWBWL.
37. LFH, description of Design No. 93, 138:15/28, GWBWL.
38. Bruce A. Tyson to LFH, November 16, 1970, 138:9/2, GWBWL.
39. William A. Shirley to LFH, April 3, 1956, 138:4/7, GWBWL.
40. Boris Lauer-Leonardi to LFH (answered October 26, 1943), 138:2/4; Boris Lauer-Leonardi, (answered April 22 1948), 138:3/4; LFH to Boris Lauer-Leonardi, April 22, 1948, 138:3/4, GWBWL; LFH, *The Compleat Cruiser*, ix.
41. LFH, *The Compleat Cruiser*, 6, 7.
42. LFH, *The Compleat Cruiser*, 36, 37.
43. LFH, *The Compleat Cruiser*, 63.
44. LFH, *The Compleat Cruiser*, 70-72, 85-92; LFH to Robert T. Todd, August 29, 1960, 138:5/1, GWBWL.
45. LFH, *The Compleat Cruiser*, 96; Miguel de Cervantes, *Don Quixote*, Edith Grossman, trans. (New York: HarperCollins, 2003), 22.
46. LFH, *The Compleat Cruiser*, 97, 98.
47. LFH, *The Compleat Cruiser*, 193, 194.
48. LFH, *The Compleat Cruiser*, 220, 264-276.
49. LFH, *The Compleat Cruiser*, 342, 351.
50. LFH, *The Compleat Cruiser*, 369.
51. John Ives Sewall to LFH, August 13, 1954, 138:4/5, GWBWL.
52. John Ives Sewall to LFH, August 13 and August 26, 1954, 138:4/5, GWBWL; LFH to John Ives Sewall, February 14, 1955 March 21, 1955, 138:4/5, 6; LFH to John Ives Sewall, September 16 and January 8, 1957, 138:4/8, GWBWL.
53. John Ives Sewall to LFH, December 2, 1957, and February 10, 1958, 138:4/8, 9; LFH to Leander Hamerla, September 19, 1968, 138:6/3, GWBWL.
54. Dave Forsman to author, November 11, 1995, author's collection.
55. See William P. Stephens, *Traditions and Memories of American Yachting* (Camden, ME: International Marine Publishing, 1981), 240, 241.
56. LFH, "How to Build Rozinante," *The Rudder* (May 1961): Special Supplement.
57. LFH, *The Compleat Cruiser*, 100. The author once observed a perfect example: On a run from Cuttyhunk to Newport, there was a long, noonday calm. We started the engine and overtook a single-hander in a Rozinante, waiting for the afternoon sou'wester. We offered him a tow, which he politely declined. We eventually had our little sail and anchored in Newport at the end of the afternoon. It was well after dark before we saw the dim running lights of the Rozinante, as she ghosted in on the last of the breeze. Her skipper had enjoyed a more romantic day than we had.
58. Calvin T. Howell to LFH, March 2, 1956, 138:4/7; LFH to Calvin T. Howell, March 6, 1956, January 6 and March 21, 1957, 138:4/7, 8, GWBWL.
59. Calvin T. Howell to LFH, December 4, 1957, 138:4/8; Robert T. Todd to LFH, July 17, 1963, 138:5/4, GWBWL.
60. LFH to Calvin T. Howell, April 4, 1957, 138:4/8, GWBWL; *Yachting* (July 1957): 81.
61. Robert S. Sanborn to LFH, November 13, 1952, 138:4/3, GWBWL.
62. SP38.184.12, DSGSPL. Since this is taken from LFH's penciled writing, I have corrected the spelling, as would Mrs. Bolster if she were typing it up for publication.
63. LFH to Boris Lauer-Leonardi, February 16, 1961, 138:5/2; Boris Lauer-Leonardi to LFH, January 25, 1962, 138:5/3, GWBWL.
64. Frederic Farnham to LFH, March 30, 1960, 138:5/1, GWBWL. The Buzzards Bay 25-footer was the *Aria*, which the author parted with after ten years of

bliss. This boat was given to the Herreshoff Marine Museum in Bristol by a later owner, Paul Bates of Noank, CT, where she remains, in pristine condition.

65. Robert T. Todd to LFH, October 6, 1963, 138:5/4, GWBWL.
66. Robert T. Todd to LFH, September 14, 1965, 138:5/7, GWBWL.
67. Robert T. Todd to LFH, November 6, 1970, 138:6/5, GWBWL.
68. LFH to Boris Lauer-Leonardi, February 24, 1966, 138:5/8, GWBWL; Ted Sprague to author, February 9, 1979, author's collection.
69. LFH, "How to Build Rozinante." As a different way to consider ducking into the cabin, consider Frank Lloyd Wright's use of a low ceiling at the entrance of a room to force one to stoop as a gesture of reverence upon passing into the space, see Sarah Susanka, with Kira Obolensky, *The Not So Big House* (Newtown, CT: Taunton Press, 1998), 16; Ted Sprague to author, February 9, 1979, author's collection. The author was so fortunate as to be able to sail the *Arete* for the summer that Ted Sprague had to be away from her. See my "Mr. Herreshoff's Wonderful Rozinante," *WoodenBoat* 26 (January/February 1979): 40-46; LFH, "How to Build Rozinante."
70. Niels W. Jannasch to LFH, June 10, 1967, 138:6/4, GWBWL.
71. Allan Vaitses to LFH, April 14, 1966, 138:5/8; Samuel W. Morris to LFH, June 8, June 23, and September 21, 1966, 138:5/8, GWBWL. "One man" was the author, but I have to admit that the call was made when the *Aria* was no longer on the Pawcatuck.
72. LFH to Boris Lauer-Leonardi, August 17, 1961, 138:5/2, GWBWL; see also "The Mail Barrel," *The Rudder* (December 1961): 4; Frank Luke, interview with author, Boothbay, ME, March 21, 1998.
73. LFH to O. Lie-Nielsen, August 14 and September 4, 1971, and January 27, 1972, 138:6/6; contract between LFH and O. Lie-Nielsen, September 14, 1971, 138:6/6, GWBWL; O. Lie-Nielsen, interview with author, previously cited; Arthur Brendze, interview with author, Sausalito, CA, April 27, 2007.
74. LFH to T. D. Hughston, April 8, 1965, 138:5/6; LFH to Ralph H. Minns, July 17, 1965, 138:5/7; LFH to Claude W. Wyant, December 28, 1967, 138:6/1; LFH to Boris Lauer-Leonardi, February 24, 1966, 138:5/8; LFH to Dick Dawson, April 9, 1962, 138:5/3; LFH to Robert K. Brandriff, May 4, 1968, 138:6/2, GWBWL.
75. Cheoy Lee Shipyard brochure, author's collection; *The Rudder* (June 1963): 96, 98, (July 1966): 64, (August 1963): 71; LFH to Victor Herr, June 29, 1969, 138:6/4; LFH to Geoffrey Rogers, September 22, 1967, 138:6/1, GWBWL.
76. Arthur Brendze, interview with author, previously cited.
77. Arthur Brendze, interview with author, previously cited.
78. Arthur Brendze, interview with author, previously cited.
79. After LFH's death, these pencil drawings were pressed into the questioning but unresisting hands of the author by Muriel Vaughn, LFH's last secretary. They will soon be found in the collection of Francis's plans, SP38, DSGSPL.
80. George E. Stuart to LFH, June 3, 1965, 138:5/6, GWBWL.
81. Philip C. Bolger and Arthur Brendze, interviews with author, previously cited.

Chapter 24

1. Andrew Patterson, *The Rudder* (September 1950).
2. Boris Lauer-Leonardi to LFH, May 1958, 138:6/7, GWBWL.
3. Maurice Dulmaye, *The Rudder* (May 1958): 75; Leroy Kramer Jr., "The Mail Barrel," *The Rudder* (February 1959): 4.
4. LFH to Boris Lauer-Leonardi, March 9, 1959, 138:4/10, GWBWL; *The Rudder* (August 1958): 28; LFH to Boris Lauer-Leonardi, June 13, 1960, 138:5/1, GWBWL.
5. Notecard from Boris Lauer-Leonardi to LFH, April 1959, 138:6/7; Boris Lauer-Leonardi to LFH, March 10, 1963, 138:8/3, GWBWL; Edmund Cutts, interview with author, previously cited; Edmund Cutts to Robert Steward, June 14, 1988, author's collection;

The Rudder (May 1965): 16.

6. Boris Lauer-Leonardi to LFH, January 18 and April 5, 1961, 138:5/2; LFH to Boris Lauer-Leonardi, April 13, 1961, 138:5/2; LFH to William A. Robinson, January 30, 1964, 138:5/5, GWBWL.
7. LFH, "Consider the Cat Yawl: Advantages and Disadvantages," *The Rudder* (November 1957): 30, 31.
8. LFH, "Consider the Cat Yawl: Advantages and Disadvantages," 30, 31.
9. LFH to The Reverend Stephen W. L. Gilbert, September 9, 1968, 138:6/3, GWBWL; Arthur Brendze, interview with author, previously cited. The author and his wife, Kathleen Carney, had the opportunity to experience the fine sailing qualities of the No. 102, *Sybil*, owned by David and Marcia Jewett, out of Rockland, ME, on June 5, 1990. We had a fluky northwester, from light to fresh, and she behaved beautifully in Penobscot Bay and the Mussel Ridge Channel, including a lively beat home; LFH to The Reverend Stephen W. L. Gilbert, September 19, 1968, 138:6/3, GWBWL.
10. LFH, "General Description of Design #103," 138:15a/6; LFH to Boris Lauer-Leonardi, June 17, 1965, 138:5/6, GWBWL.
11. Norman H. Hodgdon Jr. to LFH, October 24, 1958, 138:4/9; LFH to William J. Strawbridge, November 1, 1958, 138:4/9; LFH to Allan Vaitses, December 1, 1958, 138:4/9, GWBWL; Carlton Pinheiro, interview with author, previously cited; William J. Strawbridge to LFH, September 28, 1959, 138:4/10, GWBWL.
12. William J. Strawbridge to LFH, January 8, 1962, 138:5/3, GWBWL; "Sparkman and Stephens' Escort," *The Rudder* (December 1948): 54; William Strawbridge III, interview with author, previously cited.
13. Maynard Bray, e-mail to author, June 18, 2017.
14. LFH to Giles S. Gianelloni, September 14, 1953, 138:4/4, GWBWL; see LFH, *The Compleat Cruiser*, 191, 192, 225, 226.
15. LFH, "How to Build Golden Ball," *Sensible Cruising Designs* (Camden, ME: International Marine Publishing, 1974), 111; see also Robert P. Gibbs to LFH, April 29, 1958, 138:4/9; LFH to Robert T. Todd, January 8, 1969, 138:6/4, GWBWL.
16. LFH to Tweed Hunter, August 23, 1965, 138:5/7, GWBWL; LFH, "How to Build Golden Ball," *Sensible Cruising Designs*, 111.
17. Michael Rew to author, April 1995, author's collection.
18. LFH, "How to Build Golden Ball," *Sensible Cruising Designs*, 111; Robert P. Gibbs to LFH, January 18, 1963, 138:5/4, GWBWL.
19. Robert P. Gibbs to LFH, January 18, 1963, 138:5/4, GWBWL.
20. Robert P. Gibbs to LFH, December 19, 1965, 138:5/7, GWBWL; John Knox Hart to Samuel F. Manning, November 8, 1978, author's collection.
21. Robert P. Gibbs to LFH, February 1966, 138:6/7, GWBWL.
22. Robert P. Gibbs to LFH, February 1966, 138:6/7, GWBWL.
23. Michael Rew to author, May 1995, author's collection.
24. Maynard Bray, Robin Jettinghoff, and Patricia Lawn, "Where Are They Now?" *WoodenBoat* 228 (September/October 2012): 88; author's inspection, April 7, 2015; Jaime Canfield, telephone conversation with author, July 2, 2017.
25. LFH to C. J. Frankham, September 10, 1968, 138:6/3; LFH to Robert P. Gibbs, January 21, 1965, 138:5/6; LFH to Thomas A. Fletcher, May 3, 1965, 138:5/6; LFH to Tweed Hunter, August 23, 1965, 138:5/7; LFH to Allan Vaitses, September 19, 1966, 138:5/8, GWBWL.
26. Allan Vaitses to LFH, October 23, 1960, 138:5/1; LFH to Allan Vaitses, September 19, 1966, 138:5/8, GWBWL; Allan Vaitses, interview with author, previously cited. Kathleen and I fell in love with this boat, the *Shenandoah*, for sale in Fort Lauderdale in 1990, when we thought we wanted to emulate Bobby Gibbs and go into the charter business. But when we had her hauled out to look at the bottom, she revealed a mass of blisters.
27. *WoodenBoat* 249 (March/April 2016): 19.
28. Stanley Woodward to LFH, February 10, 1960,

138:5/1, GWBWL.

29. LFH to Stanley Woodward, February 18, 1960, 138:5/1, GWBWL.
30. Stanley Woodward to LFH, February 28 and April 12, 1960, 138:5/1; LFH to Stanley Woodward, April 7, 1960, 138:5/1, GWBWL.
31. LFH to Stanley Woodward, March 10 and April 7, 1960, 138:5/1, GWBWL.
32. LFH to Stanley Woodward, March 10 and April 7, 1960, 138:5/1, GWBWL.
33. Stanley Woodward to LFH, November 25, 1960, 138:5/1; LFH to Stanley Woodward, December 1, 1960, 138:5/1, GWBWL.
34. SP38.45.5, SP38.45.6, and SP38.46, DSGSPL.
35. Muriel Vaughn to William A. Baker, May 2, 1973, author's collection; LFH to Robert T. Todd, December 2, 1963, 138:5/4; Robert T. Todd to LFH, August 31, 1965, 138:5/7; LFH to Robert T. Todd, January 8, 1969, 138:6/4; Robert T. Todd to LFH, January 15, 1970, 138:6/5, GWBWL; as to LFH's "shaky hands," however, it can be noted that his distinctive, clear signature was still perfect three months before his death, LFH to O. Lie-Nielsen, August 27, 1972, 138:6/7, GWBWL.
36. Chris Powell, e-mails to author, July 14 and July 16, 2017.
37. Chris Powell, e-mails to author, July 14 and July 16, 2017.
38. LFH to Bror Tamm, December 2, 1971, 138:6/6, GWBWL.
39. LFH to Dean Doran, August 29, 1969, 138:6/4, GWBWL.
40. LFH to Dean Doran, August 29, 1969, 138:6/4; R. H. Coleman to LFH, June 8, 1970, 138:6/5; LFH to R. H. Coleman, June 15, 1970, 138:6/5, GWBWL.
41. LFH to Mrs. Tom Chamberlain, December 15, 1965, 138:5/7; Sally Chamberlin to LFH, January 11, 1966, 138:5/8, GWBWL.
42. Boris Lauer-Leonardi to LFH, (answered December 12,1962), 138:6/6; Boris Lauer-Leonardi to LFH, March 6 and February 29, 1964, 138:5/5, GWBWL.
43. Boris Lauer-Leonardi to LFH, October 18, 1966, 138:5/8, GWBWL. This material was later reprinted in *An L. Francis Herreshoff Reader*, Boris Lauer-Leonardi to LFH, March 15, 1966, 138:5/8; LFH to Boris Lauer-Leonardi, March 17, 1966, 138:5/8; Boris Lauer-Leonardi to LFH, March 21, 1966, 138:5/8, GWBWL.
44. LFH to Stanley Woodward, April 11, 1960, 138:5/1; LFH to John P. Kendall, May 19, 1960, 138:5/1; LFH to Boris Lauer-Leonardi, September 7, 1962, 138:5/3; LFH to Thomas Shipman, February 12, 1963, 138:5/4; LFH to Mr. and Mrs. Walter Hadley, April 3, 1967, 138:6/1, GWBWL.
45. Anne Lawrence Bondy, interview with author, previously cited; LFH to Helen Bolster, no date, 138:9/6, GWBWL.
46. Margrete Stinnes, interview with author, previously cited.
47. Margrete Stinnes, interview with author, previously cited.
48. Margrete Stinnes, interview with author, previously cited.
49. Anne Lawrence Bondy, Jay Greer, and Dale Calloway, interviews with author, previously cited.
50. Dale Calloway and Barry Thomas, interviews with author, previously cited; Muriel Vaughn, statement to author, 1973.
51. Dan Brayton and Arthur Brendze, interviews with author, previously cited; for example, Ben Fuller, curator of the Penobscot Marine Museum, sailmaker William Harding, or even the author.
52. Barry Thomas, John Kendall, Paul Glynn, and Arthur Brendze, interviews with author, previously cited.
53. Robert T. Todd to LFH, October 16, 1969, 138:9/2, GWBWL; O. Lie-Nielsen and Anne Lawrence Bondy, interviews with author, previously cited.
54. Muriel Vaughn to A. G. A. Correa, November 1, 1971, 138:6/6, GWBWL.
55. A doctor friend of the author obtained a copy of Francis's medical record from Massachusetts General Hospital. He wrote to me: "I'm not sure when one might consider what I'm doing a breach of confidentiality. I look at it as being in the interest of history."
56. O. Lie-Nielsen, Arthur Brendze, Paul Glynn, and Anne Lawrence Bondy, interviews with author,

previously cited.

57. *Boston Evening Globe*, December 4, 1972; *New York Times*, December 4, 1972.
58. Arthur Brendze, interview with author, previously cited.
59. Anne Lawrence Bondy, interview with author, previously cited.
60. Margrete Stinnes, interview with author, previously cited; Lewis Francis Herreshoff, will, August 5, 1966, Essex County (MA) Probate Court; Lewis Francis Herreshoff, will, June 30, 1970, same place.
61. Dale Jones Calloway and John Kendall, interviews with author, previously cited; Charles R. Schultz to LFH, June 28, 1967, and LFH's reply, June 30, 1967, 138:6/1, GWBWL.
62. Margrete Stinnes and Arthur Brendze, interviews with author, previously cited; David J. Palmer to John J. Costello, register Essex County Probate Court, January 3, 1973; Carleton Pinheiro, interview with author, previously cited.
63. Carleton Pinheiro, interview with author, previously cited; Jay Greer, e-mail to author, April 10, 2005. There are many sources for this story, for example, Peter Littlefield, memo to author, November 7, 2015, author's collection; Brooks Townes to author, December 24, 1994, author's collection; and Jack Somer, *Ticonderoga*, 171; Suzy Coe Fernberger, interview with author, previously cited.
64. Barry Thomas and Arthur Brendze, interviews with author, previously cited; as noted before, the author was the recipient of some of these pencil drawings, which have now been passed on to Mystic Seaport Museum; without this generous action, and the follow-up generosity of Muriel's daughter, Elizabeth Vaughn, this book could not have been contemplated.

BIBLIOGRAPHY

As with volume 1, the heart and soul of volume 2 are L. Francis Herreshoff's plans of his yacht designs, in Ships Plans Collection 38 in the Daniel S. Gregory Ships Plans Library at Mystic Seaport Museum, and his letters, in Manuscript Collection 138 in the G. W. Blunt White Library at Mystic Seaport Museum. These sources are closely followed by his published writings, which I urged you to read and re-read in the preface. These include the *Rudder* How-To-Build series articles referenced in the text. A new primary source for volume 2 is his unpublished notebook of logs of canoe cruises in the 1930s, Collection 138, box 16, folder 2. Many of the additional sources, published and unpublished, listed in the bibliography of volume 1 have been used also in volume 2. Below are listed new, secondary sources for volume 2.

Books

Alden, John (not the yacht designer). *American Steel Navy.* Annapolis, MD: US Naval Institute Press, 1972.

Bolger, Philip C. *Boats With an Open Mind.* Camden, ME: International Marine Publishing, 1994.

———. *Different Boats.* Camden, ME: International Marine Publishing, 1980.

———. *The Folding Schooner*. Camden, ME: International Marine Publishing, 1976.

———. *Small Boats.* Camden, ME: International Marine Publishing, 1973.

———. *Thirty-Odd Boats.* Camden, ME: International Marine Publishing, 1982.

Bray, Maynard, Benjamin A. G. Fuller, and Peter T. Vermilia. *Mystic Seaport Museum Watercraft,* Second Edition. Mystic: Mystic Seaport Museum, 2001.

———, and Tom Jackson. *Worthy of the Sea: K. Aage Nielsen and His Legacy of Yacht Design.* Gardiner, ME: Tilbury House, 2006.

Burnett, Constance Buel. *Let the Best Boat Win: The Study of America's Greatest Yacht Designers.* Boston: Houghton-Mifflin, 1957.

Cameron, Silver Donald. *Once Upon a Schooner: An Offshore Voyage in* Bluenose II. Halifax, NS: Formac Publishing, 1992.

Chamberlain, Samuel. *Old Marblehead: A Camera Impression.* New York: Hastings House, 1940.

Dana, Richard Henry. *Two Years Before the Mast.* 1840; New York: Modern Library, 1936.

Davin, Tom, ed. *The Rudder Treasury: A Companion for Lovers of Small Craft.* New York: Sheridan House, 1960.

Davis, Charles G. *Ships of the Past.* Salem, MA: Marine Research Society, 1929.

DeWolf, Katherine. *The Story of the America's Cup.* North Plymouth, MA: Plymouth Cordage, 1930.

Doherty, John Stephen. *A Ketch Called Tahiti: John G. Hanna and His Yacht Designs.* Camden, ME: International Marine Publishing, 1987.

Duncan, Roger. *Coastal Maine: A Maritime History.* New York: W. W. Norton, 1992.

Fox, Uffa. *Sailing, Seamanship, and Yacht Construction.* London: Peter Davies, 1934.

Gardner, John. *Building Classic Small Craft.* Camden, ME: International Marine Publishing, 1977.

Gillpin, Vincent. *The Good Little Ship.* New York: Livingston Publishing, 1952, 1961.

Hammond, Susan S. *Landfalls Remembered.* New York: A. S. Barnes, 1963.

Hansen, Art. *Photographic Memories of a T-Wharfer.* Boston: author, 1984.

Henderson, Richard. *Philip L. Rhodes and His Yacht Designs.* Camden, ME: International Marine Publishing, 1981.

Herreshoff, Jeanette B. *The Early Founding and Development of the Herreshoff Manufacturing Company.* Privately printed, 1949.

Hill, Lee. *The Sharpie* Sanderling. Boston: Branden Press, 1971.

Howe, George. *Mount Hope: A New England Chronicle.* New York: Viking, 1959.

Howe, Mark Antony DeWolf. *Bristol, R. I.: A Town Biography.* Cambridge, MA: Harvard University Press, 1930.

Howland, Llewellyn, III. *No Ordinary Being: W. Starling Burgess (1878-1947), A Biography.* Boston: David R. Godine, 2014.

Howland, Waldo. *A Life in Boats: The Concordia Years.* Mystic: Mystic Seaport Museum, 1988.

Jones, Gregory O. *Herreshoff Sailboats.* St. Paul, MN: MBI Publishing, 2004.

Knight, Lucia del Sol, and Daniel B. MacNaughton. *The Encyclopedia of Yacht Designers.* New York: W. W. Norton, 2006.

Lauer-Leonardi, Boris. *Soundings.* New York: Poseidon Publishing, 1966.

Leather, John. *The Big Class Racing Yachts.* London: Stanford Maritime Press, 1982.

Loomis, Alfred F. *Ocean Racing: The Great Blue Water Yacht Races.* New York: Yachting Publishing Corporation, 1935, 1946.

Martingette, Charles G., and Louis K. Meisel. *The Great American Pin-up.* New York: Tachen, 1996.

Munroe, Ralph M. *The Commodore's Story.* New York: Ives, Washburn, 1930.

Noble, Dennis L. *The U. S. Coast Guard in World War II: The Beach Patrol and Corsair Fleet.* Washington, DC: Coast Guard Historian's Office, 1992.

Phillips-Burt, Douglas. *An Eye For a Yacht.* London: Faber and Faber, 1955.

Poor, Charles Lane. *Men Against the Rule: A Century of Progress in Yacht Design.* New York: Derrydale, 1937.

Reed, Walter. *The Illustrator in America, 1860-2000.* New York: New York Society of Illustrators, 2001.

Robinson, Joseph S. *The Story of Marblehead.* Privately printed, 1936.

Robinson, William A. *Return to the Sea.* Tuckahoe, NY: John de Graff, 1972.

———. *10,000 Leagues Over the Sea.* New York: Harcourt, Brace, 1932.

———. *To the Great Southern Sea.* London: Peter Davies, 1957.

———. *Voyage to Galapagos.* New York: Harcourt, Brace, 1936.

Scott, Ian. *Mudlark's Ghosts.* Dobbs Ferry, NY: Sheridan House, 2007.

Skene, Norman L. *Elements of Yacht Design.* New York: Rudder Publishing Company, 1904.

Smith, Geoffrey G. *This is the Story of* Ticonderoga *and Ocean Racing, 1937-1952.* New York: Rudder Publishing Company, 1958.

Somer, Jack. *Ticonderoga: Tales of an Enchanted Yacht.* Mystic: Mystic Seaport Museum, 1997.

Stephens, William P. *Traditions and Memories of American Yachting,* Complete Edition. Camden, ME: International Marine Publishing, 1981.

Stone, Herbert L., and William H. Taylor. *The America's Cup Races.* New York: D. Van Nostrand, 1958.

Susanka, Sarah, and Kira Obulensky. *The Not So Big House.* Newtown, CT: Taunton Press, 1998.

Taylor, Roger C. *More Good Boats.* Camden, ME: International Marine Publishing, 1979.

Tudor, Tasha, and Richard Brown. *The Private World of Tasha Tudor.* Boston: Little, Brown, 1992.

Veigele, William J. *PC Patrol Craft of World War II: A History of the Ships and Their Crews.* Santa Barbara, CA: Astral Publishing, 1998.

Voss, John C., Eleanor Georgina, editor. *Tillicum: Luxton's Pacific Crossing.* Sidney, BC: Gray's Publishing, 1971.

Voss, John C. *The Venturesome Voyages of Captain Voss.* Boston: Charles E Lauriat, 1927.

Williams, Gurney, III. *Yachtsman's Choice: The Best of Rudder.* New York: David McKay, 1977.

Yachting Publishing Corporation. *Your New Boat.* New York: Yachting Publishing Corporation, 1946.

Articles

"Along With the Frostbiters." *Yachting,* February 1933.

Ames, Ben. "Trans-Atlantic Aboard *Landfall.*" *Yachting Monthly,* October 1931.

Baker, David. "World Cruiser for Diddikai." *The Rudder,* July 1957.

Barkhorn, John. "*Charade* in the Herreshoff Tradition." *Sea and Pacific Motorboat,* January 1968.

Beebe, Robert P. "Passage to the Bahamas." *The Rudder,* February 1958.

Berry, William A., Jr. "Scat Cat." *The Rudder,* February 1953.

Bertram, Kate. "Sir Thomas Lipton Cup Race." *The Rudder,* April 1950.

Bolger, Philip C. "The Case for the Low Power Planing Boat." *The Rudder,* May 1951.

Bray, Maynard. "The Incredible Herreshoff Dugout." *WoodenBoat* 14, January/February 1977.

Brayton, Dan, Jr. "The Genesis of Deva." *WoodenBoat* 157, November/December 2000.

Brown, Waldo H. "Yankee Progress." *New England Yachtsman,* October 1937.

Burgess, W. Starling. "The Yankee One-Design Class." *Yachting*, April 1937.

"The Cruising Club Measurement Rule for Ocean Racing." *Yachting,* January 1934.

Foxton, H. V. "H-28 Makes Rough Passage." *The Rudder*, June 1950.

Galvin, William. "Waldo Brown: The Man Behind the Wychmere Jetty Memorial." *Cape Cod Chronicle,* November 6, 2003.

Garber, John. "Double Ended Yacht for John M. Garber, Esq." *Nautical Quarterly* 29, Spring 1985.

Gardner, John. "Herreshoff Reprint Makes Valuable Book Available Again." *National Fisherman,* January 1967.

Genner, Russ. "The Button." *The Rudder*, October 1942.

Gibbs, Robert T. "A Rudder Sharpie." *The Rudder*, October 1950.

Green, Jenny. "The H-28 Story." *Sea Spray,* August 1978.

Hanna, John G. "The Watch Below." *The Rudder,* March 1943.

Herreshoff, L. Francis. "Consider the Cat Yawl: Advantages and Disadvantages." *The Rudder,* October 1957.

———. "The Double Paddle Canoe." *The Rudder,* September 1947.

———. "Loon, A Meadow Lark." *The Rudder*, October 1959.

———. "Marine Pictures." *The Rudder*, January 1944.

———. "Mobjack, A Successful Cruising Ketch." *The Rudder,* March 1947.

———. "Piquant." *The Rudder*, February 1951.

———. "A Proposed Restricted Sail Area Rule." *Yachting*, March 1931.

———. "The Rudder Rating Rule for Small Racing Sailboats." *The Rudder,* July 1950.

———. "Yankee One-Design Class Proposals." *The Rudder*, April 1937.

Holme, George N. "Rough Passage." *The Rudder,* July 1947.

Hoyt, C. Sherman. "Yachting in the Early 1900s." *Yachting*, February 1951.

Lloyd, Robin. "*Bounty*: A Boat with Many Lives." *Classic Boat*, July 2013. "

———. Twice the *Bounty*." *Classic Boat,* November 1996.

McLoughlin, Joyce. "Another Pygmalion and his Galatea." *The Rudder,* September 1960.

Mickleburgh, Timothy. "*Varua*: Soul of the Southern Sea." *WoodenBoat* 65, July/August 1985.

Mills, E. B. "Two Families: Two Truths." *Yankee*, February 1996.

Noyes, Bradley P. "*Tioga*'s Launching." *Maine Boats and Harbors*, April/May 2000.

O'Meara, Kenneth. "Let's Get Together and Build the Marco Polo." *The Rudder,* September 1945.

Owen, George. "Outstanding Types of New England Fishing Boats, Whalers, and Yachts." *Society of Naval Architects and Marine Engineers Journal: Historical Transactions, 1893-1943,* 1945.

Peterson, William, and Fred Bauer. "Fenwick Williams, Naval Architect: The Gentle Draftsman." *WoodenBoat* 151, November/December 1999.

Rousmaniere, John. Book review of *Classic Yachts. WoodenBoat* 207, March/April 2009.

Slager, John J. "Double Paddle Canoe." *The Rudder,* October 1955.

Smith, Delawan P. "Two Marco Polos Under Construction." *The Rudder*, December 1955.

Taylor, Roger C. "Mr. Herreshoff's Wonderful Rozinante." *WoodenBoat* 26, January/February 1979.

Vaitses, Allan H. "Hark the Lark." *The Rudder*, December 1961.

Weagant, Carl L. "Across the Atlantic With the Racing Fleet." *Yachting*, September 1931.

Wilkinson, Ray. "Passage Home." *Yachting Monthly,* August 1965.

Williams, Fenwick C. "L. Francis Herreshoff." *The Catboat Association Bulletin,* Spring 2007.

INDEX

Italic numerals indicate illustrations

H

I

J

K

N

O

P

Q

R

S

CHRONOLOGICAL INDEX
of L. Francis Herreshoff Designs

ROGER C. TAYLOR met L. Francis Herreshoff while a student at Milton Academy. He went on to study maritime history at Harvard, then served in the United States Navy as a deck officer in a destroyer and a diesel submarine. He was a leader at the U. S. Naval Institute in the 1960s and founder and leader of International Marine Publishing Company in the 1970s and '80s, where his publishing list included two books by Herreshoff. In "retirement," he has lived mostly afloat with his wife, Kathleen Carney, and he has worked his captain's license, adding to his life list of a couple of hundred boats sailed, including fourteen designed by L. Francis Herreshoff.

OTHER BOOKS BY ROGER C. TAYLOR

L. Francis Herreshoff: Yacht Designer (Volume 1, 2015)

Good Boats (1977)

More Good Boats (1979)

Still More Good Boats (1981)

The Elements of Seamanship (1982)

The Fourth Book of Boats (1984)

Thirty Classic Boat Designs: The Best of the Good Boats (1992)

Knowing the Ropes (1993)

The author checking notes for his book in the wheelhouse of the Dutch canal cruiser *Water Lily* somewhere in France. (Kathleen Carney photo)